Test Booklet No. **3947301**

Test Booklet Code **CH1**

MEDACE
NEET (UG)
SELF ASSESSMENT KIT

The Living World

Topics Covered

Characteristics of Living Beings, Diversity in Living World

Taxonomic Categories

Important Instructions

- This Booklet Contains – Two Topic Tests and One Test on Complete Chapter.
- Each question carries 4 marks.
- For each correct response, the candidate will get 4 marks. And for every incorrect response, 1 mark will be additionally deducted from total score.
- Use **Blue/Black** point pen only for filling the OMR.
- Rough work is to be done in the space provided for this purpose in the test booklet only.

Name of the Candidate (In Capitals) ________________

____

Candidate's Signature ________________

Invigilator's Signature ________________

Facsimile signature stamp of center superintendent________________

Do not open this booklet until you start attempting the test

Topical Follow Thru

Test 1

Syllabus
- What is Living?
- Biodiversity
- Need for Classification
- Taxonomy and Systematics
- Binomial Nomenclature

For deeper insight, **Scan the QR Code** 

Important Instructions

- The test is of 30 minutes duration and contains 25 Multiple Choice Questions (four options with a single correct answer).
- Choose the correct option and fill the OMR given on the last page of this test accordingly.
- At some instances, you may find more than 1 option to be correct. In such circumstances, you have to judge the most appropriate answer as per the conditions given in the question.

1. Which of the following is a defining characteristic of living organisms?
(a) Ability to produce sound
(b) Response to external stimuli
(c) Growth
(d) Reproduction

2. In *Amoeba*, reproduction is synonymous with
(a) digestion (b) growth
(c) locomotion (d) metabolism

3. Reproduction occurs in yeast and *Hydra* by which of the following methods?
(a) Conjugation (b) Sporulation
(c) Budding (d) Fragmentation

4. Process by which organisms are grouped into convenient category on the basis of some observable characters is called
(a) classification (b) nomenclature
(c) systematics (d) taxonomy

5. Which of the following is incorrect for reproduction?
(a) Unicellular organisms reproduce by cell division.
(b) Reproduction is characteristic of all living organisms.
(c) In unicellular organisms, reproduction and growth are linked together.
(d) Non-living objects are incapable of reproducing.

6. Select the incorrect statement with respect to growth.
(a) Increase in body mass is criterion for growth in non-living objects.
(b) Animals grow upto a certain age.
(c) Growth in plants is always definite.
(d) In living organisms, growth is from inside.

7. Find the incorrect match.
(a) Non-living objects — Irreversible growth
(b) Protonema of moss — Fragmentation
(c) Exclusive event in animals — Reproduction and growth
(d) Cellular organisation — Living things

8. In the context of test-tube, an isolated metabolic reaction outside the body of an organism can be categorised as
(a) living things
(b) non-living things
(c) neither living nor non-living
(d) occasionally living and occasionally non-living

9. Identify the correctly written scientific name of the mango, first described by Carolus Linnaeus.
(a) *Mangifera indica* Car Linn.
(b) *Mangifera indica* Linn.
(c) *Mangifera indica*
(d) *Mangifera Indica*

10. Given below are two statements.

Statement I The first word in a biological name represents the genus and the second word denotes specific epithet.

Statement II Both words, when handwritten, are generally kept in bold to indicate their Latin origin.

In the light of the above statement, choose the correct answer from the options given below.

(a) Statement I is incorrect, but statement II is correct.
(b) Both statement I and statement II are correct.
(c) Both statement I and statement II are incorrect.
(d) Statement I is correct, but statement II is incorrect.

11. Which of the following statement is incorrect?

(a) Carolus Linnaeus developed a system for naming of organisms.
(b) Binomial naming system is universally accepted.
(c) Scientific names are generally taken from Latin language.
(d) In the scientific name of lion, *leo* indicates its generic name.

12. Match List I with List II.

	List I		List II
A.	Biodiversity	1.	Correct description of an organism
B.	Nomenclature	2.	A system of providing a name with two components
C.	Identification	3.	The variety of living organisms
D.	Binomial nomenclature	4.	Naming of living organisms

Choose the correct answer from the options given below.

(a) A-3, B-4, C-1, D-2
(b) A-2, B-3, C-4, D-1
(c) A-4, B-1, C-2, D-3
(d) A-1, B-2, C-3, D-4

13. ICBN stands for

(a) Indian Congress of Biological Names
(b) International Congress of Biological Names
(c) Indian Code of Botanical Nomenclature
(d) International Code of Botanical Nomenclature

14. Given below are two statements; one is labelled as the Assertion (A) and the other is labelled as the Reason (R).

Assertion (A) Living beings exhibit metabolic processes.

Reason (R) Isolated metabolic reactions occurring *in vitro* are not considered as living reactions.

In the light of the above statements, choose the correct answer from the options given below.

(a) A is false, but R is true.
(b) Both A and R are true and R is the correct explanation of A.
(c) Both A and R are true, but R is not the correct explanation of A.
(d) A is true, but R is false.

15. Which of the following statement is correct?

(a) All living organisms detect changes in the surrounding.
(b) Self-consciousness is the characteristic feature of animals.
(c) Sensitivity is the ability to grow.
(d) Consciousness is not a feature of all living organism.

16. Given below are two statements; one is labelled as the Assertion (A) and the other is labelled as the Reason (R).

Assertion (A) Metabolism refers to the sum of chemical reactions that occur within living organisms.

Reason (R) Metabolic reactions occur simultaneously inside living organisms.

In the light of the above statements, choose the correct answer from the options given below.

(a) A is false, but R is true.
(b) Both A and R are true and R is the correct explanation of A.

(c) Both A and R are true, but R is not the correct explanation of A.
(d) A is true, but R is false.

17. Select the incorrect statement regarding the rule of priority in nomenclature.
(a) In autonyms, specific epithet and intraspecific epithet are identical
(b) Tautonyms are valid for plants, but not for zoological names
(c) In tautonyms, generic and specific epithet are identical
(d) In homonym, a name is spelled the same as another name, but belongs to a different taxon

18. Given below are two statements; one is labelled as the Assertion (A) and the other is labelled as the Reason (R).
Assertion (A) One of the defining property of living organisms is consciousness.
Reason (R) Human being is the only organism that has self-consciousness.
In the light of the above statements, choose the correct answer from the options given below.
(a) A is false, but R is true.
(b) Both A and R are true and R is the correct explanation of A.
(c) Both A and R are true, but R is not the correct explanation of A.
(d) A is true, but R is false.

19. In majority of higher animals and plants, reproduction and growth are
(a) mutually exclusive events
(b) synonymous event
(c) synonymous events during *in vitro* culture
(d) exclusive and synonymous based on different phases of growth and reproduction

20. Given below are two statements.
Statement I Living systems possess both anabolic and catabolic reactions.
Statement II All animals exhibit clear movements.
In the light of the above statements, choose the correct answer from the options given below.
(a) Statement I is incorrect, but statement II is correct.
(b) Both statement I and statement II are correct.
(c) Both statement I and statement II are incorrect.
(d) Statement I is correct, but statement II is incorrect.

21. Identify the exclusive characteristic of living beings from given characteristics.
(a) Isolated metabolic reactions occurring *in vitro*.
(b) Perception of an event happening in the environment and form its memory.
(c) Increase in mass from inside only
(d) Increase in mass by accumulation of materials both on surface as well as internally.

22. Given below are two statements.
Statement I A rolling ball of snow increasing in mass, volume and size is comparable to growth seen in the living organisms.
Statement II Whole moong dal is living, while broken moong dal is considered non-living.
In the light of the above statements, choose the correct answer from the options given below.
(a) Statement I is incorrect, but statement II is correct.
(b) Both statement I and statement II are correct.
(c) Both statement I and statement II are incorrect.
(d) Statement I is correct, but statement II is incorrect.

23. What can be understood by the statement 'Nothing lives forever, yet life continues'?
(a) Metabolism
(b) Embryogenesis
(c) Reproduction
(d) Replication

24. Select the correct statements.

I. Brain dead patient has no self-consciousness.

II. Flora refers to the total number of plants at a given time.

III. Both growth and development are continuous in all living beings.

IV. Fauna refers to the total number of animals at a given time.

Choose the correct answer from the options given below.

(a) I, II and III
(b) II, III and IV
(c) II and IV
(d) I, II and IV

25. Given below are two statements.

Statement I The properties of tissues are not the constituents of its cells.

Statement II *Amoeba* multiplying by mitotic cell division signifies growth, but not reproduction.

In the light of the above statements, choose the correct answer from the options given below.

(a) Statement I is incorrect, but statement II is correct.
(b) Both statement I and statement II are correct.
(c) Both statement I and statement II are incorrect.
(d) Statement I is correct, but statement II is incorrect.

Response Index

01	a	b	c	d	10	a	b	c	d	19	a	b	c	d
02	a	b	c	d	11	a	b	c	d	20	a	b	c	d
03	a	b	c	d	12	a	b	c	d	21	a	b	c	d
04	a	b	c	d	13	a	b	c	d	22	a	b	c	d
05	a	b	c	d	14	a	b	c	d	23	a	b	c	d
06	a	b	c	d	15	a	b	c	d	24	a	b	c	d
07	a	b	c	d	16	a	b	c	d	25	a	b	c	d
08	a	b	c	d	17	a	b	c	d					
09	a	b	c	d	18	a	b	c	d					

Performance Scanner

> 90% Excellent !	You have mastered these topics. The concepts of these topics are at your fingertips. Move on to the next test and maintain this momentum.
76-90% Very Good !	You have a good command over these topics. Revise these topics again after a few days and enhance your performance.
60-75% Good !	You have a wide scope to learn for these topics. Revise these topics again.
<60% Not Satisfactory!	You have a long way ahead of you to master these topics. Revise it thoroughly.

Test 2

Syllabus • Concept of Species • Taxonomical Hierarchy

For deeper insight, **Scan the QR Code**

Important Instructions

- The test is of 30 minutes duration and contains 25 Multiple Choice Questions (four options with a single correct answer).
- Choose the correct option and fill the OMR given on the last page of this test accordingly.
- At some instances, you may find more than 1 option to be correct. In such circumstances, you have to judge the most appropriate answer as per the conditions given in the question.

1. As we go from species to the kingdom in a taxonomic hierarchy, the number of common characteristics

(a) will decrease
(b) will increase
(c) remain the same
(d) may increase or decrease

2. Which of the following species is not included in the genus–*Solanum*?

(a) *nigrum* (b) *sativum*
(c) *tuberosum* (d) *melongena*

3. Which of the following best defines a taxon?

(a) A group of closely related organisms
(b) A group of individuals with fundamental similarities
(c) The highest rank of classification
(d) A unit of classification

4. Which among the following is the correct order of classification?

(a) Kingdom, Phylum, Genus, Division, Order, Class, Species, Family
(b) Phylum, Division, Class, Order, Genus, Species, Family, Kingdom
(c) Kingdom, Division, Class, Order, Family, Genus, Species
(d) Division, Genus, Family, Species, Class, Order, Kingdom, Phylum

5. The genera *Solanum*, *Petunia* and *Datura* are placed in the family–Solanaceae mainly on the basis of

I. vegetative characters
II. morphological characters
III. reproductive characters
IV. anatomical characters

Choose the correct answer from the options given below.

(a) I and III (b) II and IV
(c) I and IV (d) I, II and III

6. What does systematics primarily refer to?

(a) Understanding the diversity and relationships among different kinds of organisms
(b) Identifying and studying the organ systems of organisms
(c) Identifying and conserving organisms
(d) Studying the habitats of organisms and their classification

7. Leopard and big cats are put in the

(a) Genus—*Canis*
(b) Genus—*Panthera*
(c) Species—*panthera*
(d) Class—Carnivora

8. Two plants can be conclusively said, to belong to the same species, if they

(a) have more than 90% similar genes
(b) look similar and possess identical secondary metabolites
(c) have same number of chromosomes
(d) can reproduce freely with each other and form seeds

9. Which suffix is used in plant classification to indicate the taxonomic category 'family'?

(a) -ales (b) -onae
(c) -aceae (d) ae

10. Given below are two statements.

Statement I Taxonomical studies of all known organisms have led to the development of certain common categories such as kingdom, phylum, etc.

Statement II Potato and brinjal are two separate species belonging to same genus.
In the light of the above statements, choose the correct answer from the options given below.
(a) Statement I is incorrect, but statement II is correct.
(b) Both statement I and statement II are correct.
(c) Both statement I and statement II are incorrect.
(d) Statement I is correct, but statement II is incorrect.

11. If an organism shares the same class, but differs in family classification, it may belong to the same
(a) genus (b) species
(c) variety (d) order

12. Which of the following is correctly matched with its specific taxonomic category?
(a) Wheat - *poaceae*, the species
(b) Cat- Felidae, a family
(c) Humans - Primata, the family
(d) Housefly - Musca, an order

13. If two different genera are classified in the same taxonomic category, family, which of the following statement is correct about their classification?
(a) They belong to the same class, but different species
(b) They belong to the same phylum, but different classes
(c) They belong to different classes and orders
(d) They belong to different kingdoms and phyla

14. Which taxonomic category do mango and grass share?
(a) Order and family
(b) Only division
(c) Division, class and order
(d) Division and class

15. Given below are two statements, one is labelled as the Assertion (A) and the other is labelled as the Reason (R).
Assertion (A) Higher the category greater is the difficulty to determine the relationship to other taxa at the same level.
Reason (R) Lower the taxa, more are the characteristics that the members within the taxon share.
In the light of the above statements, choose the correct answer from the options given below.
(a) A is false, but R is true.
(b) Both A and R are true, and R is the correct explanation of A.
(c) Both A and R are true, but R is not the correct explanation of A.
(d) A is true, but R is false.

16. Choose the odd one out from the given options.
(a) Sapindales (b) Primata
(c) Insecta (d) Poales

17. The common characteristics between dog and cat will be maximum at the level of
(a) family (b) order
(c) genus (d) class

18. Which one of the following animal is correctly matched with its particular named taxonomic category?
(a) Tiger – *tigris*, the species
(b) Cuttle fish –Mollusca, a class
(c) Humans – Primata, the family
(d) Housefly – Musca, an order

19. Consider the following figures.

I.

II.

Choose the correct option showing the family of the first organism and order of the second organism.
(a) I- Felidae, II - Insecta
(b) I- Canidae, II - Diptera
(c) I-Felidae II - Diptera
(d) I-Canidae, II - Insecta

20. Consider the following statements.
I. Order-Primata comprising monkey, gorilla and gibbon is placed in class-Mammalia.
II. Class-Carnivora includes animals like tiger, cat, and elephant.
III. Species like *Panthera* involves different genera like *pardus*, *leo* and *tigris*.
IV. The taxonomic categories are completely same for plants and animals.

Choose the incorrect statements from the options given below.
(a) II, III and IV (b) I, II and III
(c) I, II, III and IV (d) III and IV

21. Given below are two statements.
Statement I The basics of taxonomy like identification, naming and classification of organisms are not universally evolved under international codes.
Statement II An organism represents a place in the system of classification.
In the light of the above statements, choose the correct answer from the options given below.
(a) Statement I is incorrect, but statement II is correct.
(b) Both statement I and statement II are correct.
(c) Both statement I and statement II are incorrect.
(d) Statement I is correct, but statement II is incorrect.

22. Given below are two statements.
Statement I Dogs, cats and elephants are all grouped under same taxa.
Statement II Dogs, mammals and animals represent taxa at same level.
In the light of the above statements, choose the correct answer from the options given below.
(a) Statement I is incorrect, but statement II is correct.
(b) Both statement I and statement II are correct.
(c) Both statement I and statement II are incorrect.
(d) Statement I is correct, but statement II is incorrect.

23. In wheat and *Brassica*, maximum similarity occurs at the level of
(a) family (b) class
(c) division (d) order

24. Which one of the following has least similar characters?
(a) Muscidae (b) Diptera
(c) Insecta (d) *Musca*

25. Given below is a hierarchical arrangement of taxonomic categories of wheat.

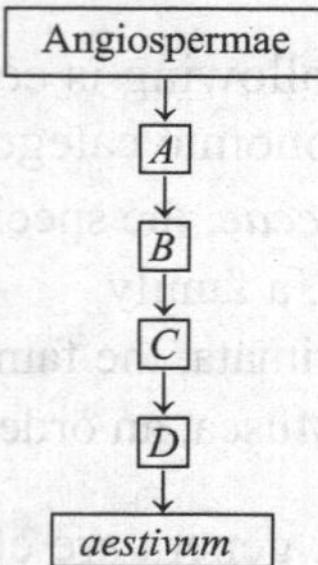

Choose the correct answer from the options given below.
(a) *A*- Dicotyledonae, *B*-Poaceae, *D*-*Triticum*
(b) *B*-Sapindales, *C*-Poaceae, *D*-*Triticum*
(c) *A*-Monocotyledonae, *B*-Poales, *D*-*Triticum*
(d) *A*-Monocotyledonae, *C*-Poaceae, *D*-Poaceae

Response Index

01	a	b	c	d	10	a	b	c	d	19	a	b	c	d
02	a	b	c	d	11	a	b	c	d	20	a	b	c	d
03	a	b	c	d	12	a	b	c	d	21	a	b	c	d
04	a	b	c	d	13	a	b	c	d	22	a	b	c	d
05	a	b	c	d	14	a	b	c	d	23	a	b	c	d
06	a	b	c	d	15	a	b	c	d	24	a	b	c	d
07	a	b	c	d	16	a	b	c	d	25	a	b	c	d
08	a	b	c	d	17	a	b	c	d					
09	a	b	c	d	18	a	b	c	d					

Performance Scanner

> 90% Excellent !	You have mastered these topics. The concepts of these topics are at your fingertips. Move on to the next test and maintain this momentum.
76-90% Very Good !	You have a good command over these topics. Revise these topics again after a few days and enhance your performance.
60-75% Good !	You have a wide scope to learn for these topics. Revise these topics again.
<60% Not Satisfactory!	You have a long way ahead of you to master these topics. Revise it thoroughly.

Chapter Break Thru

Syllabus	• What is Living? • Biodiversity • Need for Classification • Taxonomy and Systematics	• Binomial Nomenclature • Concept of Species • Taxonomical Hierarchy

Important Instructions

- The test is of 1 hour duration and contains 50 Multiple-Choice Questions (Four options with a single correct answer).
- Choose the correct option and fill the OMR given on the last page of this test accordingly.
- At some instances, you may find more than 1 option to be correct. In such circumstances, you have to judge the most appropriate answer as per the conditions given in the question.

1. The living organisms can be unexceptionally distinguished from the non-living things on the basis of their ability for

(a) responsive to touch
(b) metabolism
(c) growth and movement
(d) reproduction

2. The organism(s) that can be multiplied by fragmentation is/are

(a) bacteria (b) *Hydra*
(c) fungi (d) *Amoeba*

3. Which organisms exhibit reproduction that is synonymous with growth or cell division?

I. *Amoeba*
II. *Hydra*
III. Bacteria
IV. Mosses
V. Unicellular algae

Choose the correct option from the following.

(a) I, III and V
(b) I, II and IV
(c) I, IV and V
(d) I, II, III, IV and V

4. Which of the following statement about how organisms grow is not always true?

(a) Plants eventually stop growing through cell division.
(b) Non-living objects can increase in size by accumulating material.
(c) Multicellular organisms grow by dividing their cells.
(d) Counting cells can be used to track growth in single-celled organisms grown in a lab.

5. Who proposed the naming system which is widely used by biologists worldwide?

(a) Woese (b) Carolus Linnaeus
(c) Haeckel (d) Whittaker

6. Find the incorrect match.

(a) Taxon — Unit of classification
(b) Species — Most closely linked populations
(c) Classification — First step of taxonomy
(d) Binomial nomenclature — Genus and species

7. The number of similar characters of categories

(a) increase from species to kingdom
(b) decrease from kingdom to species
(c) decrease from lowest rank to highest rank
(d) increase from lowest rank to highest rank

8. Reptiles along with amphibians constitute the next higher category called phylum, which is based on common features like
(a) germ layers, coelom and level of organisation.
(b) habitat, reproduction and nutrition.
(c) notochord and dorsal hollow neural system.
(d) eukaryotes, germ layers and gill slits.

9. Which of the following statement is incorrect with respect to need for classification?
(a) All types of organisms do not occur in one locality.
(b) Without any system of classification organisms cannot be identified easily.
(c) The organisms of the past do not need to be classified.
(d) Classification helps in knowing the relationships amongst different groups of organisms.

10. Find the correct match.
(a) Animalia — Animals with maximum similarities
(b) Primata — Assemblage of related classes
(c) *sapiens* — Species of human beings
(d) *Panthera* — Specific epithet

11. Determination of correct place in a system of classification and finding out the correct name of the organism is called
(a) nomenclature (b) identification
(c) taxonomy (d) classification

12. Which of the following is the lowest taxonomic category that is characterised on the basis of both vegetative and reproductive features of plant species?

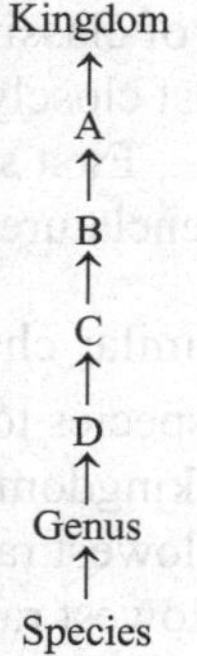

Choose the correct option from the following.
(a) A (b) B
(c) C (d) D

13. Identify the correct statement from the options given below.
(a) Cellular organisation of the body is the defining feature of non-living forms.
(b) Consciousness is a property shared by non-living organisms.
(c) A patient with a dead brain has no self-consciousness, yet is considered alive.
(d) Human beings are the only organisms aware of themselves, i.e. absolute consciousness.

14. Given below are few statements.
I. Common names can be misleading.
II. Vernacular names are easier to pronounce.
III. Vernacular names often have no scientific significance.

Choose the correct set of statements from following options.
(a) I and II (b) I, II and III
(c) Only II (d) Only III

15. Which one of the following statement is not included in universal rules of nomenclature?
(a) Generic names and specific epithet should be in Latin words.
(b) Generic name is immediately followed by name of taxonomists who described it firstly.
(c) Generic name must begin with capital letter.
(d) All letters of the specific name must be small.

16. Find the incorrect match.
(a) *Mangifera* — Genus
(b) *indica* — Specific epithet
(c) Genus (generic name) — Handwritten in Italics
(d) Binomial nomenclature — Carolus Linnaeus

17. Identify the correct statements.
I. In plants, classes with a few similar characteristics are grouped into a higher category called phylum.
II. The Convolvulaceae family is included in the Polymoniales order based on its vegetative characteristics.

III. A class consists of related orders.
IV. Sub-categories have been developed in the taxonomic hierarchy to ensure a more accurate and scientific placement of various taxa.

Choose the correct option from the following.
(a) III and IV
(b) II and III
(c) I, III and IV
(d) I, II, III and IV

18. Read the following statements w.r.t. taxonomic categories.
I. Classification is a single-step process.
II. Each category represents a rank and is known as taxon.
III. All organisms in both the Plantae and Animalia kingdoms, have species as an intermediate category.
IV. Genera are aggregates of closely related species.
V. Moving from species to kingdom, the number of common characters decreases.

Which of the following statements are correct?
(a) I, III and IV (b) II and V
(c) II, IV and V (d) III only

19. Given below are two statements; one is labelled as Assertion (A) and the other is labelled as Reason (R).
Assertion (A) Biological names are written in Italics.
Reason (R) Biological names are always derived from Latin.
In the light of the above statements, choose the correct answer from the options given below.
(a) A is false, but R is true.
(b) Both A and R are true and R is the correct explanation of A.
(c) Both A and R are true, but R is not the correct explanation of A.
(d) A is true, but R is false.

20. Given below are two statements.
Statement I For both plants and animals, scientific names are based on agreed criteria and principles provided in ICBN.
Statement II Local names of organisms varies from place to place.
In the light of the above statements, choose the correct answer from the options given below.
(a) Statement I is incorrect, but statement II is correct.
(b) Both statement I and statement II are correct.
(c) Both statement I and statement II are incorrect.
(d) Statement I is correct, but statement II is incorrect.

21. Match List I with List II.

	List I		List II
A.	Family	1.	Diptera
B.	Order	2.	Arthropoda
C.	Class	3.	Muscidae
D.	Phylum	4.	Insecta

Choose the correct answer from the options given below.

	A	B	C	D
(a)	4	2	1	3
(b)	3	1	4	2
(c)	3	2	4	1
(d)	4	3	1	2

22. Read the following statements.
I. Cats and lions belong to the family called Canidae.
II. Classes are group of related orders.
III. The similarities among the taxa increase as it becomes more inclusive.
IV. Presence or absence of notochord is one of the basis of classification in animal kingdom.
V. Characterisation, identification, classification and nomenclature are basic processes to systematics.

Which of the following statements are incorrect?
(a) II and IV (b) I, III and V
(c) IV and V (d) I and V

23. Given below are two statements; one is labelled as Assertion (A) and the other is labelled as Reason (R).
Assertion (A) There is a need to standardise the naming of living organisms.
Reason (R) Every organism has a unique ecological role and their standardised names should reflect this.

In the light of the above statements, choose the correct answer from the options given below.
(a) A is false, but R is true.
(b) Both A and R are true and R is the correct explanation of A.
(c) Both A and R are true, but R is not the correct explanation of A.
(d) A is true, but R is false.

24. Given below are two statements.

Statement I Category represents an abstract term connected to a ranking.

Statement II Species is a group of concrete biological objects.

In the light of the above statements, choose the correct answer from the options given below.
(a) Statement I is incorrect, but statement II is correct
(b) Both statement I and statement II are correct
(c) Both statement I and statement II are incorrect
(d) Statement I is correct, but statement II is incorrect

25. Match List I with List II.

List I	List II
A. Housefly	1. Potato, tomato and brinjal
B. Polymoniales	2. Group of orders
C. Class	3. *Musca domestica*
D. Same species	4. German shepherd, chihuahua and pug

Choose the correct answer from the options given below

	A	B	C	D
(a)	4	1	3	2
(b)	3	1	4	2
(c)	4	2	1	3
(d)	3	1	2	4

26. The formal starting date for purpose of priority in binomial nomenclature is 1st May, ... i.e., the year of the publication of *Species Plantarum* by ....
(a) 1883, Hooker
(b) 1953, Bentham
(c) 1753, Linnaeus
(d) 1783, de Candolle

27. Consider the following statements.

I. Photoperiod affects reproduction only in plants.
II. A brain-dead patient has no self-consciousness.
III. All organisms are linked to one another by the sharing of the common genetic material, but to varying degrees.
IV. Prokaryotes are not conscious of their surroundings.

Choose the incorrect statements out of the given options.
(a) II and III (b) I and IV
(c) I and III (d) II and IV

28. Given below are few statements.

I. Local names for one organism vary from place to place even within a country.
II. Nomenclature is possible only after the proper identification of organisms.
III. Binomial nomenclature system is being used by biologists all over the world.
IV. All the components of the binomial name are to be written in Italicised form, including author citation.

Choose the correct set of statements from the options given below.
(a) I, II and IV (b) I, III and IV
(c) I, II and III (d) II, III and IV

29. Identify the correct statements.

I. The tautonyms are not allowed in zoological nomenclature.
II. Use of underline, while printing, denotes the Latin origin of name.
III. Classification is based on some easily observable characters.
IV. ICZN stands for Indian Code of Zoological Nomenclature.

Choose the incorrect set of statements from the options given below.
(a) I, II and III (b) I, II and IV
(c) II and IV (d) I and II

30. Which of the following is written correctly according to the binomial nomenclature.
(a) *Panthera leo tigris*
(b) *Solanum lycopersicum*
(c) *Azadirachta Indica* Linn.
(d) *Homo Sapiens sapiens*

31. Growth is not considered a defining property of living organisms because

(a) non-living objects can also exhibit growth through the internal accumulation of material.

(b) living organisms always exhibit growth regardless of their metabolic state.

(c) Dead organisms do not show growth, but non-living objects can grow by internal processes.

(d) Both living and non-living objects can grow, but the process of growth differs between them.

32. Which of the following statement is incorrect regarding reproduction in organisms?

(a) In *Planaria*, a fragmented organism can regenerate lost parts to become a new organism.

(b) In fungi, asexual spores are produced in millions, facilitating easy multiplication.

(c) In unicellular organisms like *Amoeba*, growth and reproduction are distinct processes.

(d) In filamentous algae, fragmentation is a common mode of reproduction.

33. Which of the following practices does not confirm to the rules of binomial nomenclature?

(a) Writing the scientific name of mango as *Mangifera indica* in printed text.

(b) Underlining both components separately when writing the scientific name *Homo sapiens* by hand.

(c) Using Italics when printing the name *Panthera leo* to denote its Latin origin.

(d) Writing the scientific name *Escherichia Coli* with a capitalised starting letter of both genus name and specific epithet.

34. Given below are two statements.

Statement I The term taxa encompasses hierarchical levels in biological classification, ranging from broad categories like animals to specific ones like dogs.

Statement II The level of taxa is determined solely by the specific characteristics shared by organisms, without regard to their hierarchical relationships.

In the light of the above statements, choose the correct answer from the options given below.

(a) Statement I is incorrect, but statement II is correct

(b) Both statement I and statement II are correct

(c) Both statement I and statement II are incorrect

(d) Statement I is correct, but statement II is incorrect

35. Given below are two statements; one is labelled as Assertion (A) and the other is labelled as Reason (R).

Assertion (A) Systematics, derived from the Latin word '*systema*', refers to the systematic arrangement of organisms and includes the study of their relationships.

Reason (R) Linnaeus used "*Systema Naturae*" as the title of his publication to reflect his work on classifying organisms systematically.

In the light of the above statements, choose the correct answer from the options given below.

(a) A is false, but R is true

(b) Both A and R are true and R is the correct explanation of A

(c) Both A and R are true, but R is not the correct explanation of A

(d) A is true, but R is false

36. Read the following statements carefully.

I. Taxa include categories like species and families.

II. The taxonomic hierarchy does not represent evolutionary relationships.

III. Taxonomic categories are units of classification with specific ranks.

IV. Insects are classified by the number of legs only.

Choose the incorrect set of statements from the options given below.

(a) II and IV

(b) I and III

(c) III and IV

(d) I and II

37. Which of the following statement is incorrect about the organisms responses toward the environmental factors?

(a) Photoperiod affects reproduction in seasonal breeders, both plants and animals.

(b) All organisms, including prokaryotes, can sense and respond to environmental cues.

(c) The ability to handle chemicals entering the body is unique to complex eukaryotes.

(d) Environmental factors such as light, water and temperature influence the behaviour and physiology of organisms.

38. Which of the following organisation is responsible for the naming of cultivated plants?
(a) ICZN (b) ICBN
(c) ICNCP (d) ICVN

39. Which of the following is correctly matched without exception in regard to plant classification?
(a) Family– Poaceae – ae
(b) Division– Pteridophyta –phyta
(c) Class– Bryopsida – sida
(d) Genus – *Solanum* – *um*

40. Given below are two statements; one is labelled as Assertion (A) and the other is labelled as Reason (R).

Assertion (A) An order in taxonomy is a higher classification that groups together families sharing a number of common characteristics.

Reason (R) The plant family–Polymoniales is classified within the order–Convolvulaceae due to specific floral attributes.

In the light of the above statements, choose the correct answer from the options given below.
(a) A is false, but R is true
(b) Both A and R are true and R is the correct explanation of A
(c) Both A and R are true, but R is not the correct explanation of A
(d) A is true, but R is false

41. Which of the following statements are correct?
I. Primata (monkeys, gorillas, gibbons) is in class–Mammalia.
II. Carnivora (tigers, cats, dogs) is also in class–Mammalia.
III. Class–Mammalia belongs to the phylum–Chordata due to features like a notochord.
IV. In plants, classes are grouped into a higher category called order.
V. Orders like Primata and Carnivora are classified under Chordata due to reproductive traits.

Choose the correct set of statements.
(a) I, II and III (b) I, II and IV
(c) I, III and IV (d) II, III and V

42. Which of the following groups of taxa does not represent the same level of classification in taxonomy?
(a) Tiger, lion and leopard
(b) Potato, brinjal and tomato
(c) Wheat, rice and mango
(d) Wheat, monocots and angiosperms

43. Which of the following statement is correct?
(a) A species is considered a genetically open system.
(b) Tomato, dicots and plants represent same taxa at different hierarchical levels.
(c) The biological concept of species is based on reproductive isolation.
(d) A hybrid between a tiger and a lion is classified as a fertile true species.

44. Identify the group in which the taxa do not belong to the same taxonomic category.
(a) *Solanum*, *Panthera*, Felidae
(b) Canidae, Muscidae, Poaceae
(c) Mango, Wheat, Cat
(d) Monocotyledonae, Mammalia, Insecta

45. Fill in the blanks and choose the correct option.

	Category	Mango	Housefly	Cat
(i)	Class	*A*	Insecta	*D*
(ii)	Order	Sapindales	*C*	Carnivora
(iii)	Family	*B*	Muscidae	*E*

(a) *B*–Solanaceae, *C*–Primata, *D*–Mammalia
(b) *A*–Dicotyledonae, *C*–Musca, *E*–Canidae
(c) *A*–Dicotyledonae, *B*–Anacardiaceae, *C*–Diptera
(d) *A*–Monocotyledonae, *D*–Reptilia, *E*–Felidae

46. Two different genera are classified in the same taxonomic category 'family'. Which statement is correct about their classification?
(a) The same class, but different species
(b) A different class and different order
(c) The same phylum, but different class
(d) A different kingdom and different phylum

47. Which of the following statement correctly defines a homonym in taxonomy?

(a) The same name used for two different species
(b) Multiple names referring to a single taxon
(c) Repetition of the genus name in the species name
(d) An order name given in a language other than the official nomenclatural language

48. If two different genera are classified under the same taxonomic category (family), which of the following statement is correct about their classification?

(a) They belong to the same phylum but different classes
(b) They belong to the same class but different orders
(c) They belong to different kingdoms and different phyla
(d) They belong to different classes but the same order

49. Consider the following statements.

I. The groups represent category and the category further represents rank.
II. The order–Primata includes families like Felidae and Canidae.
III. The genera–*Solanum*, *Petunia* and *Datura* are all placed in the family–Solanaceae.
IV. The genus–*Panthera* includes species like lion, tiger and leopard, which differ from the genus–*Felis* that includes cats.
V. In the animal order–Hominidae, the families Felidae and Canidae are grouped together.

Which of the above statements are correct?

(a) I, II and V
(b) II, III and V
(c) I, III and IV
(d) I, IV and V

50. Read the statements given below and identify the incorrect statement.

(a) Scientific names are used all over the world
(b) Scientific names are often descriptive and tell us some important characters of an organism
(c) Scientific names indicate relationship between species
(d) Scientific names favour multiple naming for the same kind of an organism

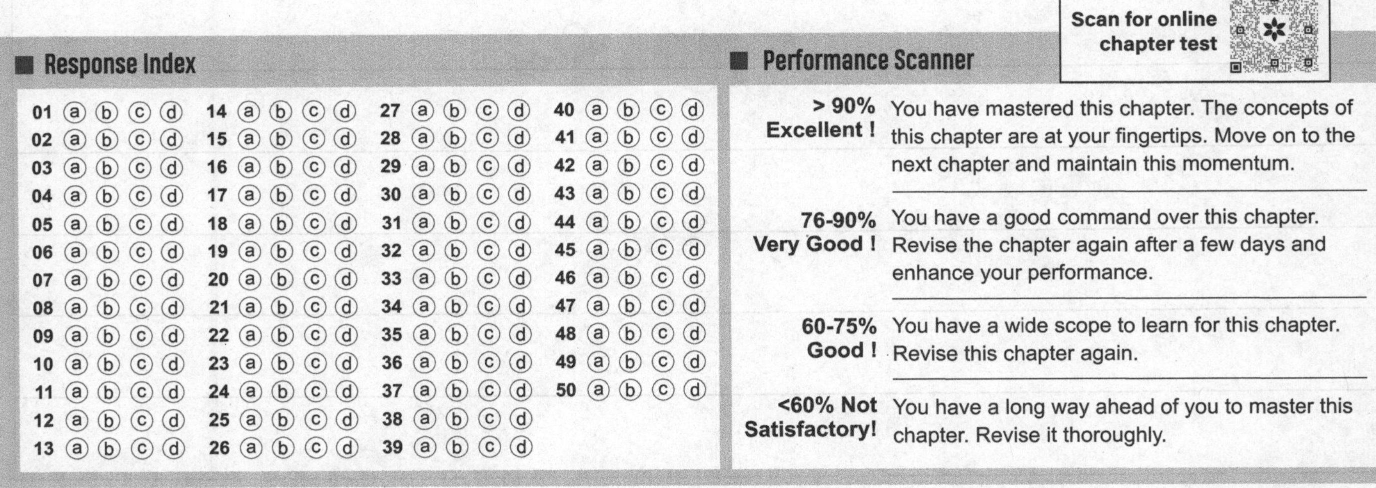

Space for Rough Work

Test Booklet No. **3947302**

Test Booklet Code **CH2**

MEDACE
NEET (UG)
SELF ASSESSMENT KIT

Biological Classification

Topics Covered

Classification of Organisms and Kingdom-Monera

Kingdom-Protista and Fungi

Acellular Organisms and Lichens

Important Instructions

- This Booklet Contains – Three Topic Tests and One Test on Complete Chapter.
- Each question carries 4 marks.
- For each correct response, the candidate will get 4 marks. And for every incorrect response, 1 mark will be additionally deducted from total score.
- Use **Blue/Black** point pen only for filling the OMR.
- Rough work is to be done in the space provided for this purpose in the test booklet only.

Name of the Candidate (In Capitals)

____

Candidate's Signature ____________

Invigilator's Signature ____________

Facsimile signature stamp of center superintendent____________

Do not open this booklet until you start attempting the test

Topical Follow Thru

Test 1

Syllabus
- Five Kingdom Classification
- Salient Features and Classification of Monera

For deeper insight, **Scan the QR Code**

Important Instructions
- The test is of 30 minutes duration and contains 15 Multiple Choice Questions (four options with a single correct answer).
- Choose the correct option and fill the OMR given on the last page of this test accordingly.
- At some instances, you may find more than 1 option to be correct. In such circumstances, you have to judge the most appropriate answer as per the conditions given in the question.

1. Aristotle was the earliest to attempt a more scientific basis for classification. Which of the following is/are the basis he used for classifying animals?
(a) Presence or absence of notochord
(b) Presence or absence of red blood
(c) Presence or absence of sexual characters
(d) Presence or absence of vasculature

2. Which statement accurately describes Archaea?
(a) Archaea share some novel features that are absent in other prokaryotes and eukaryotes.
(b) Archaea closely resemble eukaryotes in all respects.
(c) Archaea are fundamentally distinct from both prokaryotes and eukaryotes.
(d) Archaea are fundamentally distinct from prokaryotes.

3. Microscopic, single-celled eukaryotic organisms often pose a challenge for classification due to their simplicity. However, a key feature separates them from bacteria. Which of the following best describes this distinguishing characteristic?
(a) Presence of a rigid cell wall made of cellulose
(b) Possession of a true nucleus with a nuclear membrane
(c) Capability of movement using flagella or cilia
(d) Exclusive dependence on organic compounds for nutrition

4. In Whittaker's classification, how many of the following organisms are unicellular, photosynthetic autotrophs lacking membrane-bound organelles, sexually reproducing and have phycocyanin pigment?
Amoeba, *Spirogyra*, *Nostoc*, *Anabaena*, *Spirulina*, methanogens, mycoplasma, *Lactobacillus*, *Vibrio*, *Salmonella*.
(a) 4 (b) 3
(c) 5 (d) 6

5. In the classification system developed by Carolus Linnaeus, what characteristic was primarily used to group organisms?
(a) Eukaryotic and prokaryotic nature
(b) Presence or absence of cell wall
(c) Photosynthetic and non-photosynthetic nature
(d) Unicellularity and multicellularity

6. Which of the following is not a drawback of two kingdom classification?
(a) Bacteria and cyanobacteria were placed along with eukaryotes.
(b) Unicellular and multicellular organisms were placed together.
(c) *Chlamydomonas* and *Chlorella* were grouped under kingdom-Protista.
(d) *Chlamydomonas* and *Spirogyra* were placed together with algae.

7. Mycoplasma are organisms lacking cell wall. Which of these is not true for mycoplasma?
(a) They can survive without oxygen.
(b) They are pathogenic to plants and animals.
(c) They possess heterotrophic nutrition.
(d) Gram positive mycoplasma are smaller than the smallest bacteria.

8. Consider the following statement about bacteria and select the correct option.
(a) Bacteria exhibit simplicity in structure, but complexity in behaviour.
(b) Bacteria display complexity in structure, but simplicity in behaviour.
(c) Bacteria are characterised by simplicity in both structure and behaviour.
(d) Bacteria are characterised by complexity in both structure and behaviour.

9. Given below are few statements.
I. Archaebacteria possess peptidoglycan in their cell wall.
II. Eubacteria plays crucial role in decomposition.
III. Eubacteria can be either autotrophic or heterotrophic.
IV. Eubacteria can survive and tolerate extreme environment due to phospholipid membrane, unlike Archaebacteria.
V. Cyanobacteria can be unicellular (*Spirulina*), colonial (*Chlamydomonas*) or filamentous (*Nostoc*) algae.

Choose the correct set of statements from the options given below.
(a) I, III, IV and V (b) I, II and III
(c) II and III (d) I, II, III and IV

10. Given below are two statements.
Statement I Some bacteria are autotrophic.
Statement II The vast majority of bacteria depend on other organisms for food.
In the light of the above statements, choose the correct answer from the options given below.
(a) Statement I is incorrect, but statement II is correct.
(b) Both statement I and statement II are correct.
(c) Both statement I and statement II are incorrect.
(d) Statement I is correct, but statement II is incorrect.

11. In Whittaker's classification system, how many kingdoms strictly include organisms with only heterotrophic nutrition?
(a) One (b) Three
(c) Four (d) Two

12. Mycoplasma are pleomorphic due to
(a) their small size
(b) absence of cell wall
(c) presence of unique DNA material
(d) presence of soluble RNA and protein in their cytoplasm

13. Which scientist organised plants into the categories of trees, shrubs and herbs, and divided animals on the basis of presence and absence of red blood cells?
(a) RH Whittaker (b) Copeland
(c) Aristotle (d) Haeckel

14. Why do bacteria lack alternation of generations?
(a) Because there is neither syngamy nor reductional division
(b) Because they lack distinct chromosomes
(c) Because there is no conjugation
(d) Because there is no exchange of genetic material

15. Given below is a figure of an organism.

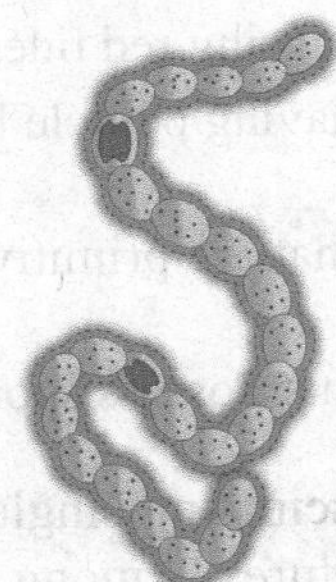

Choose the correct statement w.r.t. the given figure.
(a) The given figure represents an organism that is present in the gut of several ruminants.
(b) The given figure represents an organism with a specialised structure to fix atmospheric sulphur and nitrogen.
(c) The given figure represent an organism that often form blooms in polluted water bodies.
(d) The given figure is of an organism that is heterotrophic and play a major role in decomposition.

■ Response Index

01	ⓐ ⓑ ⓒ ⓓ	10	ⓐ ⓑ ⓒ ⓓ	19	ⓐ ⓑ ⓒ ⓓ
02	ⓐ ⓑ ⓒ ⓓ	11	ⓐ ⓑ ⓒ ⓓ	20	ⓐ ⓑ ⓒ ⓓ
03	ⓐ ⓑ ⓒ ⓓ	12	ⓐ ⓑ ⓒ ⓓ	21	ⓐ ⓑ ⓒ ⓓ
04	ⓐ ⓑ ⓒ ⓓ	13	ⓐ ⓑ ⓒ ⓓ	22	ⓐ ⓑ ⓒ ⓓ
05	ⓐ ⓑ ⓒ ⓓ	14	ⓐ ⓑ ⓒ ⓓ	23	ⓐ ⓑ ⓒ ⓓ
06	ⓐ ⓑ ⓒ ⓓ	15	ⓐ ⓑ ⓒ ⓓ	24	ⓐ ⓑ ⓒ ⓓ
07	ⓐ ⓑ ⓒ ⓓ	16	ⓐ ⓑ ⓒ ⓓ	25	ⓐ ⓑ ⓒ ⓓ
08	ⓐ ⓑ ⓒ ⓓ	17	ⓐ ⓑ ⓒ ⓓ		
09	ⓐ ⓑ ⓒ ⓓ	18	ⓐ ⓑ ⓒ ⓓ		

■ Performance Scanner

> 90% Excellent !	You have mastered these topics. The concepts of these topics are at your fingertips. Move on to the next topics and maintain this momentum.
76-90% Very Good !	You have a good command over these topics. Revise these topics again after a few days and enhance your performance.
60-75% Good !	You have a wide scope to learn for these topics. Revise these topics again.
<60% Not Satisfactory!	You have a long way ahead of you to master these topics. Revise it thoroughly.

Test 2

Syllabus

- Salient Features and Classification of Protista
- Salient Features and Classification of Fungi into Major Groups

For deeper insight, **Scan the QR Code**

Important Instructions

- The test is of 30 minutes duration and contains 15 Multiple Choice Questions (four options with a single correct answer).
- Choose the correct option and fill the OMR given on the last page of this test accordingly.
- At some instances, you may find more than 1 option to be correct. In such circumstances, you have to judge the most appropriate answer as per the conditions given in the question.

1. Which of the following possesses mixotrophic mode of nutrition?

(a) Organisms causing red tides
(b) Organisms having pellicle layer instead of cell wall
(c) Organisms that are primitive relative of animals
(d) Organisms that possess spores with true walls

2. Diatoms are fascinating single-celled organisms with unique features. Among the following statements, identify the one that seems least likely to be true about diatoms.

(a) Most diatom cells possess multiple flagella for movement.
(b) Their outer shell consists of two interlocking pieces.
(c) They are closely related to golden algae.
(d) Their cell walls might be strengthened with silica.

3. Identify the characteristic of the organism represented in the given figure.

(a) They release toxins.
(b) They can be used in filtration of oils and syrups.
(c) They contain pigments identical to those present in higher plants.
(d) Their spores are dispersed by air currents.

4. Red sea and red tides are caused by

(a) *Gonyaulax* and *Trichodesmium*, respectively
(b) *Trichodesmium* and *Gonyaulax*, respectively
(c) Diatoms and *Trichodesmium*, respectively
(d) Diatoms and *Gonyaulax*, respectively

5. Consider the following statements and identify the incorrect one regarding protozoans.
(a) *Entamoeba* has silica shell on their surface.
(b) *Entamoeba* is an example of ciliated protozoan.
(c) *Paramoecium* has gullet that opens to the outside of the cell surface.
(d) *Plasmodium* have an spore like stage in their cycle.

6. *Mucor*, *Rhizopus* and *Albugo* belong to which class of kingdom– Fungi?
(a) Ascomycetes (b) Phycomycetes
(c) Basidiomycetes (d) Deuteromycetes

7. Given below are two statements; one is labelled as the Assertion (A) and the other is labelled as the Reason (R).
Assertion (A) The discovery of sexual reproductive stages in some fungi, previously classified as Deuteromycetes has led to a reorganisation within fungal classification systems.
Reason (R) Fungal identification relies solely on the characteristics of the sexual reproductive stage.
In the light of the above statements, choose the correct answer from the options given below.
(a) A is false, but R is true
(b) Both A and R are true and R is the correct explanation of A
(c) Both A and R are true, but R is not the correct explanation of A
(d) A is true, but R is false

8. Which of the following is/are not included in the Basidiomycetes class of kingdom–Fungi?
(a) Smut (b) Morels
(c) Mushroom (d) Rust fungi

9. Choose the feature that is not associated with *Amoeba*.
(a) Presence of pseudopodia
(b) Presence of contractile vacuole
(c) Formation of fruiting body with weak-shelled spores
(d) Ingestion by phagocytosis

10. Which of the following feature is not true for dinoflagellates?
(a) Marine organisms
(b) Biflagellated
(c) Cell wall with stiff cellulosic plates
(d) Presence of protein rich pellicle

11. Given below are two statements.
Statement I Protozoans are believed to be primitive relatives of animals.
Statement II *Plasmodium* is categorised as a flagellated protozoan.
In the light of the above statements, choose the correct answer from the options given below.
(a) Statement I is incorrect, but statement II is correct
(b) Both statement I and statement II are correct
(c) Both statement I and statement II are incorrect
(d) Statement I is correct, but statement II is incorrect

12. Given below are two statements.
Statement I Fungal spores produced asexually exogenously at top or side of hyphae are called as zoospores.
Statement II The fusion of protoplasms between two motile or non-motile gametes are called plasmogamy.
In the light of the above statements, choose the correct answer from the options given below.
(a) Statement I is incorrect, but statement II is correct
(b) Both statement I and statement II are correct
(c) Both statement I and statement II are incorrect
(d) Statement I is correct, but statement II is incorrect

13. The motile and non-motile structures that help in asexual reproduction in members of Phycomycetes are, respectively
(a) zoospores and conidiophore
(b) ascospores and basidiospores
(c) aplanospores and zoospores
(d) zoospores and aplanospores

14. Identify the incorrect statement associated with Deuteromycetes.

(a) This class of fungi belongs to the artificial class of fungi.
(b) These fungi reproduce asexually only.
(c) Members of this group are mostly found in soil only.
(d) Mycelium in this fungi is septate and branched.

15. *Neurospora* is a ...*A*... fungi, whose thallus consists of ...*B*..., ...*C*... hyphae. Its mycelium is ...*D*..., but ...*E*... mycelium is also seen for a shorter duration. It is used as a model organism for genetics due to its simple genetics, wide availability, ...*F*... life cycle, easy growth.

(a) *A*- club, *B*- branched, *C*-septate, *D*-dikaryotic *E*- monokaryotic, *F*-haploid
(b) *A*-sac, *B*-branched, *C*- septate, *D*- monokaryotic, *E*-dikaryotic, *F*-haploid
(c) *A*- sac, *B*-branched, *C*-aseptate, *D*-dikaryotic, *E*-monokaryotic, *F*- diploid
(d) *A*- sac, *B*-branched, *C*-aseptate, *D*- monokaryotic, *E*-dikaryotic, *F*-haploid

Response Index

01	a	b	c	d	10	a	b	c	d	19	a	b	c	d
02	a	b	c	d	11	a	b	c	d	20	a	b	c	d
03	a	b	c	d	12	a	b	c	d	21	a	b	c	d
04	a	b	c	d	13	a	b	c	d	22	a	b	c	d
05	a	b	c	d	14	a	b	c	d	23	a	b	c	d
06	a	b	c	d	15	a	b	c	d	24	a	b	c	d
07	a	b	c	d	16	a	b	c	d	25	a	b	c	d
08	a	b	c	d	17	a	b	c	d					
09	a	b	c	d	18	a	b	c	d					

Performance Scanner

> 90% Excellent !	You have mastered these topics. The concepts of these topics are at your fingertips. Move on to the next topics and maintain this momentum.
76-90% Very Good !	You have a good command over these topics. Revise these topics again after a few days and enhance your performance.
60-75% Good !	You have a wide scope to learn for these topics. Revise these topics again.
<60% Not Satisfactory!	You have a long way ahead of you to master these topics. Revise it thoroughly.

Test 3

Syllabus
- Lichens
- Viruses and Viroids

For deeper insight, **Scan the QR Code**

Important Instructions

- The test is of 30 minutes duration and contains 15 Multiple Choice Questions (four options with a single correct answer).
- Choose the correct option and fill the OMR given on the last page of this test accordingly.
- At some instances, you may find more than 1 option to be correct. In such circumstances, you have to judge the most appropriate answer as per the conditions given in the question.

1. The most notable disease caused by organism '*A*' is BSE, commonly called the mad cow disease in cattle and its analogous variant '*B*' in human. Identify '*A*' and '*B*' from the given options.

(a) *A*-viroids , *B* - PSTV
(b) *A*-prions, *B*- CDJ
(c) *A*- prions, *B*- CJD
(d) *A*- viroids, *B*- PST

2. The capsomeres of bacteriophage consist of

(a) helical or polyhedral geometric form
(b) only capsomere
(c) spiral geometric form
(d) only *ds*RNA

3. Given below are few statements.

I. Viroids differ from viruses in having DNA molecule without a protein coat.

II. Scrapie disease is caused due to presence of abnormally folded protein molecules.
III. Lichens are also called as 'farmer of nature' due to their existence as pioneer species in succession.
IV. Bacteriophage is a helical shaped virus with *ds* DNA.
V. Viruses are very specific in terms of their host.

Choose the incorrect statements from the options given below.

(a) I, IV and V (b) I, II and IV
(c) I and IV (d) II, III and V

4. All viruses show the following common general characteristics, except the fact that
(a) their basic structure is simple with nucleic acid wrapped in a protein coat
(b) all viruses are enveloped particles
(c) they do not have a proper cellular organisation
(d) these are ultra-microscopic structures that can pass through bacterial filters easily

5. Which of the following component is present in viroids, but absent in prions?
(a) Abnormally folded glycoprotein
(b) Abnormally folded protein
(c) Free DNA molecule
(d) Free RNA molecule

6. Given below are two statements.

Statement I The viruses are non-cellular organisms that are characterised by having an inert crystalline structure outside the living cell.

Statement II A virus is a nucleoprotein and infectious genetic material (DNA or RNA) causing disease like mumps, smallpox, tuberculosis and herpes.

In the light of the above statements, choose the correct answer from the options given below.
(a) Statement I is incorrect but, statement II is correct.
(b) Both statement I and statement II are correct.
(c) Both statement I and statement II are incorrect.
(d) Statement I is correct, but statement II is incorrect.

7. Identify the incorrect statement w.r.t viroids.
(a) These are smallest known pathogens.
(b) These are capable of causing various plant diseases.
(c) These are small circular *ds*RNA molecules.
(d) The viroid molecule enters into the plant through a wound or an insect bite.

8. Match List I with List II.

List I	List II
A. TMV	1. Bovine spongiform encephalopathy
B. Herpes	2. Potato spindle tuber disease
C. Prions	3. Simplex virus
D. Viroids	4. Mosaic formation, yellowing of leaf

Choose the correct answer from the options given below.

	A	B	C	D		A	B	C	D
(a)	4	3	2	1	(b)	4	3	1	2
(c)	3	2	1	4	(d)	3	2	4	1

9. Which of the following statements is incorrect w.r.t. viruses?
(a) They are smaller than eubacteria.
(b) They are included in the classification given by R.H. Whittaker.
(c) They are an exception to the cell theory.
(d) Term 'virus' was coined by DJ Ivanowsky.

10. Consider the following statements and identify the correct option.
(a) TO Diener discovered lichen in 1935.
(b) WM Stanley showed that virus cannot be crystallised in 1935.
(c) TO Diener discovered infectious agent smaller than viruses in 1971.
(d) WM Stanley in 1971 recognised certain microbes as causative organism of mosaic disease in tobacco.

11. Given below are two statements.

Statement I Most of the plant viruses contain RNA as the genetic material.

Statement II Retroviruses are categorised under mild category of viruses.

In the light of the above statements, choose the correct answer from the options given below.

(a) Statement I is incorrect, but statement II is correct
(b) Both statement I and statement II are correct
(c) Both statement I and statement II are incorrect
(d) Statement I is correct, but statement II is incorrect

12. Viruses and viroids have everything in common, except

(a) acellularity
(b) presence of capsid and envelope
(c) reproduction inside the host
(d) infectious nature

13. Given below are two statements; one is labelled as Assertion (A) and the other is labelled as Reason (R).

Assertion (A) All viruses are classified based solely on the type of genetic material they contain (RNA or DNA).

Reason (R) No virus can possess both RNA and DNA as its genetic material.

In the light of the above statements, choose the correct answer from the options given below.

(a) A is false, but R is true
(b) Both A and R are true and R is the correct explanation of A
(c) Both A and R are true, but R is not the correct explanation of A
(d) A is true, but R is false

14. Prions are infectious agents responsible for certain neurological diseases. Unlike most infectious agents, they lack

(a) a capsid but can still infect host cells
(b) a cell wall but can replicate inside host cells
(c) Both a capsid and a cell wall, but require a specific receptor for infection
(d) genetic material (DNA or RNA), but can induce protein misfolding

15. Choose the incorrect statement w.r.t. lichens.

(a) They are pioneer species in xerarch succession.
(b) Lichens are indicators of SO_2.
(c) They are degraded due to air pollution due to the sensitivity of chlorophyll against the air pollution.
(d) Major part of lichen is constituted by phycobiont.

Response Index

01	a	b	c	d	10	a	b	c	d	19	a	b	c	d
02	a	b	c	d	11	a	b	c	d	20	a	b	c	d
03	a	b	c	d	12	a	b	c	d	21	a	b	c	d
04	a	b	c	d	13	a	b	c	d	22	a	b	c	d
05	a	b	c	d	14	a	b	c	d	23	a	b	c	d
06	a	b	c	d	15	a	b	c	d	24	a	b	c	d
07	a	b	c	d	16	a	b	c	d	25	a	b	c	d
08	a	b	c	d	17	a	b	c	d					
09	a	b	c	d	18	a	b	c	d					

Performance Scanner

> 90% Excellent !	You have mastered these topics. The concepts of these topics are at your fingertips. Move on to the next topics and maintain this momentum.
76-90% Very Good !	You have a good command over these topics. Revise these topics again after a few days and enhance your performance.
60-75% Good !	You have a wide scope to learn for these topics. Revise these topics again.
<60% Not Satisfactory!	You have a long way ahead of you to master these topics. Revise it thoroughly.

Chapter Break Thru

Syllabus	• Five Kingdom Classification • Salient Features and Classification of Monera, Protista and Fungi into Major Groups	• Lichens • Viruses and Viroids

Important Instructions

- The test is of 1 hour duration and contains 50 Multiple-Choice Questions (Four options with a single correct answer).
- Choose the correct option and fill the OMR given on the last page of this test accordingly.
- At some instances, you may find more than 1 option to be correct. In such circumstances, you have to judge the most appropriate answer as per the conditions given in the question.

1. The earlier classification system grouped bacteria, blue-green algae (BGA), fungi, mosses, and ferns under the category 'Plants' based on

(a) their mode of nutrition
(b) their body organisation and nuclear structure
(c) the nature of their cell wall
(d) the presence of a cell wall

2. Which of the following statement accurately distinguishes between fungi and green plants based on cell wall composition and nutritional mode?

(a) Both fungi and green plants have cellulosic walls, and fungi are heterotrophic.
(b) Both fungi and green plants have chitinous walls, and fungi are autotrophic.
(c) Fungi have chitinous walls and are heterotrophic, while green plants have cellulosic walls and are autotrophic.
(d) Fungi have cellulosic walls and are autotrophic, while green plants have chitinous walls and are heterotrophic.

3. Which of the following is the distinguishing feature between bacterium and cyanobacterium?

(a) The former is prokaryotic
(b) The latter reproduces by fission
(c) Both are devoid of proteins
(d) The latter lacks flagella

4. The hairy structure '*A*' present at the ends of the given figure are

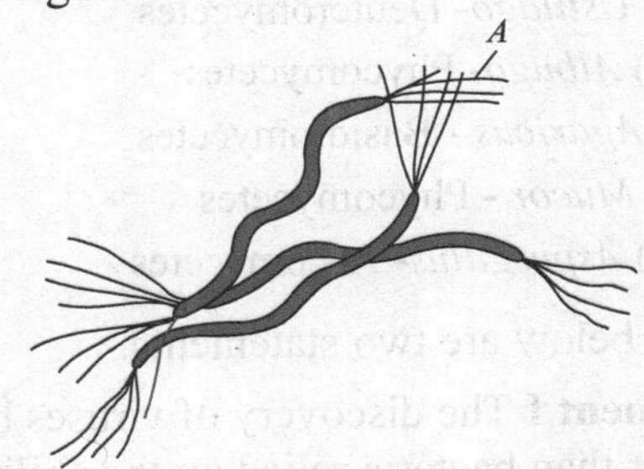

(a) cilia –involved in locomotion and sensory functions
(b) pili – facilitate DNA uptake and transfer
(c) flagellum – assists the movement of organisms
(d) hair – helps in movement and swapping of DNA

5. Identify the incorrect statement about euglenoids.
(a) Euglenoids are unicellular, flagellated protists.
(b) These are majorly found in stagnant water.
(c) Since, they are photosynthetic at certain point, they possess a well-developed cell wall.
(d) Euglenoid flagellates show creeping movement.

6. Three type of fungi are given below as (i), (ii) and (iii). Identify the correct matching pair along with their respective classes.

(i)

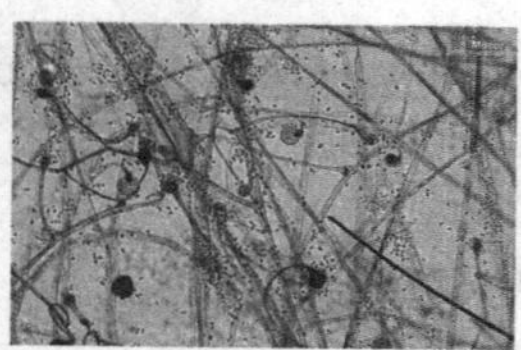
(ii)

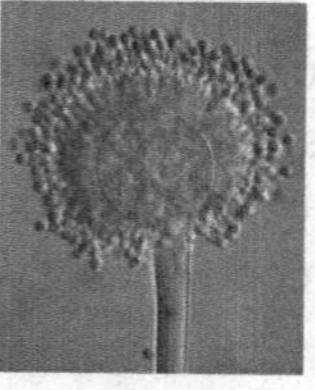
(iii)

(a) (i) *Mucor*- Phycomycetes
(ii) *Agaricus* - Ascomycetes
(iii) *Aspergillus* - Basidiomycetes
(b) (i) *Albugo*- Ascomycetes
(ii) *Neurospora*- Deuteromycetes
(iii) *Ustilago*-Basidiomycetes
(c) (i) *Agaricus*-Basidiomycetes
(ii) *Ustilago*- Deuteromycetes
(iii) *Albugo*- Phycomycetes
(d) (i) *Agaricus* - Basidiomycetes
(ii) *Mucor* - Phycomycetes
(iii) *Aspergillus*- Ascomycetes

7. Given below are two statements.
Statement I The discovery of viruses being smaller than bacteria relied on the ability of viruses to pass through filters that trapped bacteria.
Statement II MW Beijerinck's term "*Contagium vivum fluidum*" accurately describes viruses as living fluids.
In the light of the above statements, choose the correct answer from the options given below.
(a) Statement I is incorrect, but statement II is correct.
(b) Both statement I and statement II are correct.
(c) Both statement I and statement II are incorrect.
(d) Statement I is correct, but statement II is incorrect.

8. Match List I with List II.

	List I		List II
A.	Dinoflagellates	1.	Pellicle
B.	Diatoms	2.	*Plasmodium*
C.	Euglenoids	3.	Long and flat flagella
D.	Slime mould	4.	Hydrated silica

Choose the correct answer from the option given below.

	A	B	C	D
(a)	3	1	4	2
(b)	3	4	1	2
(c)	3	4	2	1
(d)	3	2	1	4

9. Which organisms exhibit characteristics of both plants and animals?
(a) *Amoeba*, *Paramoecium* and *Chlamydomonas*
(b) Slime moulds, *Euglena* and *Gonyaulax*
(c) *Euglena*, *Amoeba* and *Spirogyra*
(d) *Spirogyra*, *Paramoecium* and *Amoeba*

10. Which of the following statement about amoeboid protozoans is incorrect?
(a) *Entamoeba* exhibits holozoic nutrition.
(b) *Amoeba* uses pseudopodia for locomotion and capturing prey.
(c) They inhabit freshwater, seawater or moist soil.
(d) Marine forms are enclosed in shells made up of silica.

11. The body of the fungus is thalloid. This means that
(a) body bears leaf structures
(b) body is not differentiated into root, stem and leaf
(c) body contains organised mycelium
(d) hyphae contains apical growth

12. Read the following statements about eubacteria.
I. These can survive in any kind of environment.
II. These are generally enclosed in a porous but rigid cell wall.
III. All the form of bacteria reproduce by sexual means only.
IV. Cell wall of these bacteria have tiny pores to aid in movement of water and ions into the cell.
V. Genetic material floats freely in the cytoplasm.

Identify the correct set of statements from the options given below.
(a) I, II and V (b) II, IV and V
(c) I, II and IV (d) III and V

13. Match List I with List II.

	List I		List II
A.	Diatoms	1.	Red tides
B.	*Plasmodium*	2.	Pigments similar to plants
C.	*Gonyaulax*	3.	No fruiting bodies
D.	*Euglena*	4.	Wall embedded with silica

Choose the correct answer from the options given below.

	A	B	C	D
(a)	3	4	2	1
(b)	4	2	3	1
(c)	3	2	4	1
(d)	4	3	1	2

14. Given below are two statements; one is labelled as the Assertion (A) and the other is labelled as the Reason (R).

Assertion (A) *Euglena* exhibits movement and photosynthetic ability, resembling both animals and plants.

Reason (R) The two-kingdom system, which separates organisms into plants and animals, cannot accommodate *Euglena*.

In the light of the above statements, choose the correct answer from the options given below.
(a) A is false, but R is true
(b) Both A and R are true and R is the correct explanation of A
(c) Both A and R are true, but R is not the correct explanation of A
(d) A is true, but R is false

15. Membrane-bound organelles are absent in
(a) *Trypanosoma* (b) *Escherichia*
(c) *Saccharomyces* (d) *Paramoecium*

16. Crystallisation of viruses was first demonstrated by
(a) Ivanowsky (b) Diener
(c) Beijerinek (d) Stanley

17. Given below are two statements.

Statement I Chrysophytes include diatoms and golden algae, which are microscopic.

Statement II Most of the diatoms are photosynthetic and thus have autotrophic mode of nutrition.

In the light of the above statement, choose the correct answer from the options given below.
(a) Statement I is incorrect, but statement II is correct
(b) Both statement I and statement II are correct
(c) Both statement I and statement II are incorrect
(d) Statement I is correct, but statement II is incorrect

18. Read the following statements.
I. These are saprophytic decomposers.
II. The forms are mainly multicellular and rarely unicellular.
III. Both sexual and asexual spores are found.
IV. Some members are considered delicacies.
V. They grow on dung.

Which of the above class of fungi is being referred to here?
(a) Basidiomycetes
(b) Ascomycetes
(c) Phycomycetes
(d) Deuteromycetes

19. Which of the following properties is not associated with viruses?
(a) Viruses do not possess their own metabolic machinery.
(b) They can be pressurised as crystals outside the host cells.
(c) These do not undergo mutations as there are no acceptable change in their nucleic acid structure.
(d) They can easily pass through bacterial filters and are hence, ultramicroscopic.

20. Given below are two statements; one is labelled as Assertion (A) and the other is labelled as Reason (R).

Assertion (A) Diatomaceous earth is used for polishing and filtration due to its grittiness.

Reason (R) Diatoms have cell walls made of silica, which is indestructible.

In light of the above statements, choose the correct answer from the options given below.
(a) A is false, but R is true
(b) Both A and R are true and R is the correct explanation of A
(c) Both A and R are true, but R is not the correct explanation of A
(d) A is true, but R is false

21. Fungi like.......... are called smut fungi and cause serious diseases of ....
(a) *Agaricus*, barley
(b) *Ustilago*, wheat
(c) *Puccinia*, barley
(d) *Alternaria*, sugarcane

22. Match List I with List II.

	List I		List II
A.	Plant virus	1.	SARS
B.	Animal virus	2.	Smaller genome
C.	Viroid	3.	Fungi and algae
D.	Lichens	4.	TMV

Choose the correct answer from the options given below.

	A	B	C	D
(a)	3	2	4	1
(b)	4	2	3	1
(c)	4	1	2	3
(d)	3	1	2	4

23. Given below are two statements.
Statement I Yeasts include forms that are unicellular and are among the simplest of sac fungi.
Statement II Mycelium of yeast is well developed and branched.
In the light of the above statements, choose the correct answer from the options given below.
(a) Statement I is incorrect, but statement II is correct
(b) Both statement I and statement II are correct
(c) Both statement I and statement II are incorrect
(d) Statement I is correct, but statement II is incorrect

24. What kind of genetic material is present in the organism shown in the given figure?

(a) Double stranded RNA
(b) Single stranded RNA
(c) Single stranded DNA
(d) Double stranded DNA

25. Beijerinck's concluded that the cause of tobacco mosaic disease was not a filtrate toxin. Which of the following reason supports his conclusion?
(a) The infectious agent could be crystallised.
(b) The sap was infectious even though it was filtered to remove bacteria.
(c) The infectious agent reproduced and could be passed on from a plant infected with filtered sap.
(d) The infectious agent could not be cultivated on nutrient media.

26. Identify the set of fungi that does not have branched and septate mycelium.
(a) *Claviceps* and *Neurospora*
(b) *Puccinia* and *Ustilago*
(c) *Colletotrichum* and *Trichoderma*
(d) *Mucor* and *Rhizopus*

27. As per Whittaker's classification, an organism possessing eukaryotic cell structure, multicellular organisation, with a cell wall and nuclear membrane, showing heterotrophic nutrition can be placed under kingdom
(a) Monera
(b) Protista
(c) Plantae
(d) Fungi

28. Find the incorrect match with respect to bacteria.
(a) Nitrogen fixation – *Clostridium*
(b) Cyanobacteria – Fresh water forms
(c) Autotrophic bacteria – *Rhodospirillum*
(d) Mycoplasma – Pathogenic to fungi

29. The coenocytic condition in fungus can be best described by
(a) uninucleate hyphae without septum
(b) multinucleate hyphae without septum
(c) multicellular hyphae
(d) multiciliate hyphae

30. Find out the organism, which is scientifically named incorrectly or described incorrectly?
(a) *Plasmodium falciparum*–Protozoan pathogen causing the most serious type of malaria
(b) Diatoms–Very good pollution indicators
(c) *Trypanosoma gambiense*–The parasite of sleeping sickness
(d) *Noctiluca*–An autotrophic chrysophyte

31. Which of the following is a similarity between characteristics of Archaebacteria and Eubacteria?
(a) Both have well defined nucleus.
(b) Both have peptidoglycan in their cell walls.
(c) Both are found in extreme environmental conditions.
(d) Both have single-celled structure.

32. According to the five kingdom classification, which single kingdom contains a type of algae, disease causing parasite and planktons?
(a) Monera (b) Fungi
(c) Protista (d) Plantae

33. Identify a characteristic which is not unique to class–Basidiomycetes?
(a) Basidiospores are produced exogeneously.
(b) Edible morels and truffles belongs to this class.
(c) Smut of maize is a common fungal disease caused by *Ustilago*.
(d) Asexual reproduction by spores is absent.

34. Consider the following features.
I. Aquatic organism.
II. A cavity called gullet opens on the cell surface.
III. Numerous tiny outgrowths beat in coordinated patterns to facilitate movement.
IV. Gullet is used for ingestion of food particles.
Which of the following member of Protista is referred here?
(a) *Euglena* (b) *Plasmodium*
(c) *Paramoecium* (d) *Trypanosoma*

35. Which of the following is not a commonly known disease causing fungi?
(a) *Albugo* (b) *Puccinia*
(c) *Alternaria* (d) *Agaricus*

36. Which of the following statement accurately describes TO Diener's contribution to the discovery of viroids?
(a) TO Diener identified viroids as small, circular RNA molecules that cause plant diseases, lacking a protein coat and that are smaller than viruses.
(b) TO Diener discovered that viroids are small, circular DNA molecules responsible for certain plant infections.
(c) TO Diener's research led to the identification of viroids as large RNA viruses with a complex protein coat that infect plants and animals.
(d) TO Diener's work focused on characterising viroids as acellular cells that divide using host's machinery.

37. Given below are two statements.
Statement I In Protista, only heterotrophic mode of nutrition is present in organisms.
Statement II The kingdom–Fungi, according to Whittaker's classification, includes organisms that are mostly saprophytic in nature.
In the light of the above statements, choose the correct answer from the options given below.
(a) Statement I is incorrect, but statement II is correct.
(b) Both statement I and statement II are correct.
(c) Both statement I and statement II are incorrect.
(d) Statement I is correct, but statement II is incorrect.

38. Aristotle's classification system was primarily based on which of the given characteristics?
(a) Genetic similarities
(b) Morphological similarities
(c) Evolutionary relationships
(d) Behavioural traits

39. Identify the incorrect match.
(a) Conidia- exogenous spores
(b) Ascospores- endogenous spores
(c) Basidiospores- endogenous spores
(d) Zygospores- endogenous spores

40. Consider the following statements regarding acellular organisms.

I. They are inert outside living cell.
II. They replicate themselves within host machinery.
III. Genetic material comprises only double-stranded DNA.
IV. They cannot cross through bacterial filter paper.

Identify the correct answer from the options given below.
(a) I, II and IV
(b) I and II
(c) Only IV
(d) III and IV

41. Which of the following is a demerit according to two kingdom system of classification by Linnaeus?

I. Green algae and fungi were kept together under same group.
II. Eukaryotic *Amoeba* and prokaryotic bacteria were placed together.
III. Herbs, shrubs and trees were classified under same kingdom.
IV. Unicellular and multicellular organisms were placed together.

Identify the correct answer from the options given below.
(a) I, II and IV
(b) I and II
(c) Only IV
(d) II and IV

42. Identify the statement that accurately distinguishes the virus from the viroid in terms of their structural components.
(a) The virus has a protein coat, whereas the viroid lacks any protein coat and consists only of RNA.
(b) Both the virus and viroid have a protein coat, but the viroid's coat is smaller.
(c) The virus contains only RNA, whereas the viroid contains both RNA and a protein coat.
(d) The viroid has a lipid envelope, whereas the virus has only RNA without a protein coat.

43. Match List I with List II.

	List I		List II
A.	Potato spindle tuber disease	1.	*Albugo*
B.	Red rot of sugarcane	2.	*Xanthomonas*
C.	White rust on mustard	3.	Viroids
D.	Citrus canker	4.	*Colletotrichum*

Choose the correct answer from the options given below.

	A	B	C	D		A	B	C	D
(a)	3	4	1	2	(b)	4	1	3	2
(c)	4	3	1	2	(d)	2	1	2	4

44. Given below are two statements; one is labelled as Assertion (A) and the other is labelled as Reason (R).

Assertion (A) The five-kingdom classification system categorises living organisms into five distinct kingdoms based on their cellular organisation, mode of nutrition and other fundamental characteristics.

Reason (R) In this system, the kingdom-Monera includes prokaryotic organisms, while kingdom-Fungi consists of eukaryotic organisms that are primarily saprophytic.

In the light of the above statements, choose the correct answer from the options given below.
(a) A is false, but R is true
(b) Both A and R are true and R is the correct explanation of A
(c) Both A and R are true, but R is not the correct explanation of A
(d) A is true, but R is false

45. Which of the following statement correctly describes the flagellar structure in both dinoflagellates and *Euglena*?
(a) Dinoflagellates have two flagella arranged perpendicular to each other, while *Euglena* possesses a single, long flagellum extending from the anterior end.
(b) Dinoflagellates have a single, long flagellum used for feeding and *Euglena* have multiple short flagella distributed evenly over the cell surface for nutrient uptake.

(c) Dinoflagellates have two flagella of equal length and *Euglena* possesses a single short flagellum used exclusively for capturing prey.

(d) Dinoflagellates have 2 perpendicularly arranged flagella and *Euglena* possesses one long and another short flagella.

46. Consider the following characters.

I. Presence of membrane bound nucleus.

II. Autotrophic as well as heterotrophic mode of nutrition.

III. Single cell performs all metabolic functions.

IV. Cellular level of body organisation.

The characters not shared by Protista with other eukaryotes are

(a) I, II and IV (b) I and II

(c) III and IV (d) II and IV

47. Cellulose is a major component of cell wall in which of the following organisms?

(a) *Xanthomonas* (b) *Anabaena*

(c) Fern (d) *Saccharomyces*

48. Bacteria exhibit the most diverse metabolic diversity among living organisms primarily due to their ability to

(a) utilise various organic compounds as sources of energy

(b) perform only aerobic respiration

(c) use chlorophyll to synthesise their own food

(d) use sunlight for energy

49. Which of the following best describes the structural components of a typical bacteriophage?

(a) A bacteriophage consists of a lipid bilayer envelope, a helical RNA genome and spike proteins.

(b) A bacteriophage has a protein capsid, a tail sheath, tail fibers and a nucleic acid core that can either be DNA or RNA.

(c) A bacteriophage is composed of a rigid cell wall, a central nucleus and a surrounding lipid membrane.

(d) A bacteriophage is made up of a single-layer protein coat, a circular DNA genome and a lipid envelope.

50. Given below are two statements.

Statement I During the spore formation phase, slime moulds undergo a rapid, coordinated movement of individual cells to form a fruiting body, which can produce new spores for dispersal.

Statement II Dispersal of spores takes place with the help of water current.

In the light of the above statements, choose the correct answer from the options given below.

(a) Statement I is incorrect, but statement II is correct

(b) Both statement I and statement II are correct

(c) Both statement I and statement II are incorrect

(d) Statement I is correct, but statement II is incorrect

Scan for online chapter test

Response Index

01 ⓐ ⓑ ⓒ ⓓ	14 ⓐ ⓑ ⓒ ⓓ	27 ⓐ ⓑ ⓒ ⓓ	40 ⓐ ⓑ ⓒ ⓓ
02 ⓐ ⓑ ⓒ ⓓ	15 ⓐ ⓑ ⓒ ⓓ	28 ⓐ ⓑ ⓒ ⓓ	41 ⓐ ⓑ ⓒ ⓓ
03 ⓐ ⓑ ⓒ ⓓ	16 ⓐ ⓑ ⓒ ⓓ	29 ⓐ ⓑ ⓒ ⓓ	42 ⓐ ⓑ ⓒ ⓓ
04 ⓐ ⓑ ⓒ ⓓ	17 ⓐ ⓑ ⓒ ⓓ	30 ⓐ ⓑ ⓒ ⓓ	43 ⓐ ⓑ ⓒ ⓓ
05 ⓐ ⓑ ⓒ ⓓ	18 ⓐ ⓑ ⓒ ⓓ	31 ⓐ ⓑ ⓒ ⓓ	44 ⓐ ⓑ ⓒ ⓓ
06 ⓐ ⓑ ⓒ ⓓ	19 ⓐ ⓑ ⓒ ⓓ	32 ⓐ ⓑ ⓒ ⓓ	45 ⓐ ⓑ ⓒ ⓓ
07 ⓐ ⓑ ⓒ ⓓ	20 ⓐ ⓑ ⓒ ⓓ	33 ⓐ ⓑ ⓒ ⓓ	46 ⓐ ⓑ ⓒ ⓓ
08 ⓐ ⓑ ⓒ ⓓ	21 ⓐ ⓑ ⓒ ⓓ	34 ⓐ ⓑ ⓒ ⓓ	47 ⓐ ⓑ ⓒ ⓓ
09 ⓐ ⓑ ⓒ ⓓ	22 ⓐ ⓑ ⓒ ⓓ	35 ⓐ ⓑ ⓒ ⓓ	48 ⓐ ⓑ ⓒ ⓓ
10 ⓐ ⓑ ⓒ ⓓ	23 ⓐ ⓑ ⓒ ⓓ	36 ⓐ ⓑ ⓒ ⓓ	49 ⓐ ⓑ ⓒ ⓓ
11 ⓐ ⓑ ⓒ ⓓ	24 ⓐ ⓑ ⓒ ⓓ	37 ⓐ ⓑ ⓒ ⓓ	50 ⓐ ⓑ ⓒ ⓓ
12 ⓐ ⓑ ⓒ ⓓ	25 ⓐ ⓑ ⓒ ⓓ	38 ⓐ ⓑ ⓒ ⓓ	
13 ⓐ ⓑ ⓒ ⓓ	26 ⓐ ⓑ ⓒ ⓓ	39 ⓐ ⓑ ⓒ ⓓ	

Performance Scanner

> 90% Excellent !	You have mastered this chapter. The concepts of this chapter are at your fingertips. Move on to the next chapter and maintain this momentum.
76-90% Very Good !	You have a good command over this chapter. Revise the chapter again after a few days and enhance your performance.
60-75% Good !	You have a wide scope to learn for this chapter. Revise this chapter again.
<60% Not Satisfactory!	You have a long way ahead of you to master this chapter. Revise it thoroughly.

Space for Rough Work

Test Booklet No.	3947303
Test Booklet Code	CH3

MEDACE
NEET (UG)
SELF ASSESSMENT KIT

Plant Kingdom

Topics Covered

Systems of Classification and Algae

Bryophytes, Pteridophytes and Gymnosperms

Important Instructions

- This Booklet Contains – Two Topic Tests and One Test on Complete Chapter.
- Each question carries 4 marks.
- For each correct response, the candidate will get 4 marks. And for every incorrect response, 1 mark will be additionally deducted from total score.
- Use **Blue/Black** point pen only for filling the OMR.
- Rough work is to be done in the space provided for this purpose in the test booklet only.

Name of the Candidate (In Capitals) ______________________

____

Candidate's Signature ______________

Invigilator's Signature ______________

Facsimile signature stamp of center superintendent______________

Do not open this booklet until you start attempting the test

Topical Follow Thru

Test 1

Syllabus

- Biological Systems of Classification and Classification of Plants
- Salient Features of Algae

For deeper insight, **Scan the QR Code**

Important Instructions

- The test is of 30 minutes duration and contains 25 Multiple Choice Questions (four options with a single correct answer).
- Choose the correct option and fill the OMR given on the last page of this test accordingly.
- At some instances, you may find more than 1 option to be correct. In such circumstances, you have to judge the most appropriate answer as per the conditions given in the question.

1. Which of the following describes an artificial classification system?

(a) Primarily based on vegetative characteristics and the structure of the androecium
(b) Based on ultrastructural, anatomical and embryological features
(c) Based on both external and internal traits
(d) Based on chromosome count

2. Which of the following set does not contain examples of brown algae?

(a) *Laminaria*, *Sargassum*
(b) *Fucus*, *Ectocarpus*
(c) *Porphyra*, *Sargassum*
(d) *Dictyota*, *Ectocarpus*

3. The red thalli of most of the red algae is ………, showing more concentrations in ……… regions.

(a) multicellular, colder
(b) multicellular, warmer
(c) unicellular, moist
(d) unicellular, warmer

4. Which statement best describes the ecological significance of algae in aquatic ecosystems?

(a) Algae are primary producers that enhance dissolved oxygen levels through photosynthesis, supporting aquatic animal populations.
(b) Algae play a crucial role as consumers of organic matter, recycling nutrients within aquatic food webs.
(c) Algae contribute significantly to the oxygen content of aquatic environments by fixing nitrogen through photosynthesis.
(d) Algae regulate pH levels in aquatic habitats by secreting bicarbonates during metabolic processes.

5. Choose the pigment that is most likely to be present in the organism shown in following figure.

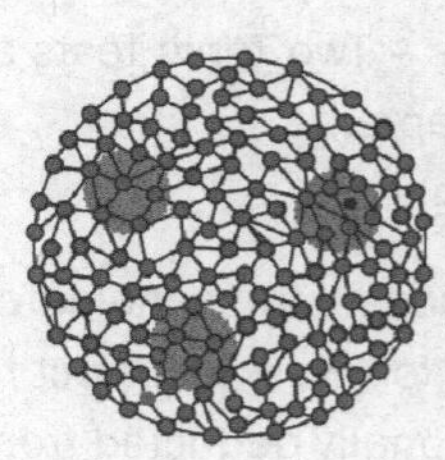

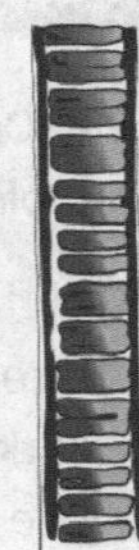

(a) Fucoxanthin
(b) Phycoerythrin
(c) Chlorophyll-*a* and *d*
(d) Chlorophyll-*a* and *b*

6. Which classification system was developed by George Bentham and Joseph Dalton Hooker?

(a) Artificial classification system
(b) Linnean system
(c) Natural classification system
(d) Phylogenetic classification

7. In which of the following algae is the food stored as floridean starch?

(a) *Polysiphonia* (b) *Ectocarpus*
(c) *Laminaria* (d) *Volvox*

8. In cytotaxonomy, which of the following is not studied for classification purposes?

(a) Chromosome number
(b) Chemical constituent of chromosome
(c) Chromosome size
(d) Meiosis and mitosis behaviour

9. Which of the following statement is not correct for sexual reproduction with respect to algae?

(a) Sex organs are unicellular or multicellular and are all fertile and generally non-jacketed.
(b) Embryonic stage is absent.
(c) There are only two types of gametes-isogamous and oogamous.
(d) Sporic or gametic or zygotic meiosis occurs in life cycle.

10. Engler and Prantl's system of classification focused on the

(a) evolutionary relationships between organisms
(b) ultrastructure of organisms
(c) overall similarities among organisms
(d) vegetative characters of organisms

11. Given below are two statements.

Statements I Pear-shaped gametes are found in *Dictyota*.

Statements II Luxuriant growth of algae in water reservoirs makes the water fit for drinking by addition of nutrients to it.

In the light of the above statements, choose the correct answer from the options given below.

(a) Statement I is incorrect, but statement II is correct.
(b) Both statement I and statement II are correct.
(c) Both statement I and statement II are incorrect.
(d) Statement I is correct, but statement II is incorrect.

12. Select the incorrect match.

(a) *Gelidium* – Red alga
(b) *Chlamydomonas* – Lateral flagella
(c) *Chlorella* – Unicellular alga
(d) *Laminaria* – Marine alga

13. Fusion between one large, non-motile female gamete and a smaller, motile male gamete is termed as ....

(a) isogamous
(b) anisogamous
(c) allogamous
(d) oogamous

14. Choose the correct statement related to algae.

(a) Most of the algae are freshwater and others are found in soil only.
(b) Some algae occur in association with fungi (lichen) and animals (e.g., on sloth bear).
(c) The plant body of algae lacks root, stem, leaf, but possesses gemma cups.
(d) *Volvox* and *Ulothrix* are filamentous and colonial forms of algae, respectively.

15. Given below are two statements; one is labelled as Assertion (A) and the other is labelled as Reason (R).

Assertion (A) Members of Phaeophyceae vary in colour from olive green to various shades of brown.

Reason (R) Members of Phaeophyceae possess chlorophyll-*a*, *c*, carotenoids and xanthophylls.

In the light of the above statements, choose the correct answer from the options given below.

(a) A is false, but R is true.
(b) Both A and R are true and R is the correct explanation of A.
(c) Both A and R are true, but R is not the correct explanation of A.
(d) A is true, but R is false.

16. Given below are few statements.

I. Absence of motile spores is seen in algae having red pigment in their body.
II. The plant body of brown algae possesses a leaf-like organ.
III. *Ectocarpus* is branched unlike kelps.
IV. Algae are primary producers of energy-rich compounds, which form the basis of the food cycles of all aquatic animals.

Choose the incorrect statement(s) from the options given below.

(a) I, II and IV (b) Only III
(c) I and II (d) I, II and III

17. The vegetative cells of brown algae possess a cellulosic wall usually covered on the outside by a gelatinous coating of ....

(a) pectin (b) lignin
(c) algin (d) carrageen

18. Given below are few statements.

I. Algae having red thalli possess complex body organisation.
II. The structure of floridean starch is very similar to amylose and glycogen in structure.
III. In Phaeophyceae, union of gametes takes place in the water.
IV. Green algae possess cell wall with inner pectose and outer cellulosic layer.

Choose the correct statements from the options given below.

(a) I, II and III (b) I, III and IV
(c) II, III and IV (d) I and III

19. Given below is a figure of an alga.

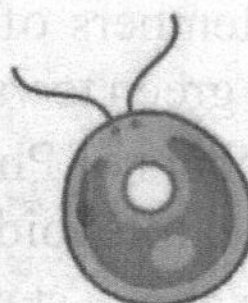

Choose the incorrect statement with respect to the given alga.

(a) It possesses asexual mode of reproduction.
(b) It is a unicellular form possessing a pyrenoid.
(c) Presence of chlorophyll-*a* is its distinguishing characteristic.
(d) It possesses pecto-cellulosic cell wall.

20. Consider the following statements with respect to algae.

I. Chlorophyll-*a* is found invariably in all the three main classes of algae.
II. *Spirulina* is a unicellular alga that is a good source of Single Cell Protein (SCP).
III. Fucoxanthin is a xanthophyll found in brown algae along with chlorophyll-*c* and carotenoids.
IV. In vegetative reproduction by fragmentation, each fragment develops into a filament.

Choose the correct statements out of the options given below.

(a) I, II and III (b) I, II and IV
(c) II, III and V (d) I and II

21. Which of the following statements is incorrect with respect to *A* and *B*?

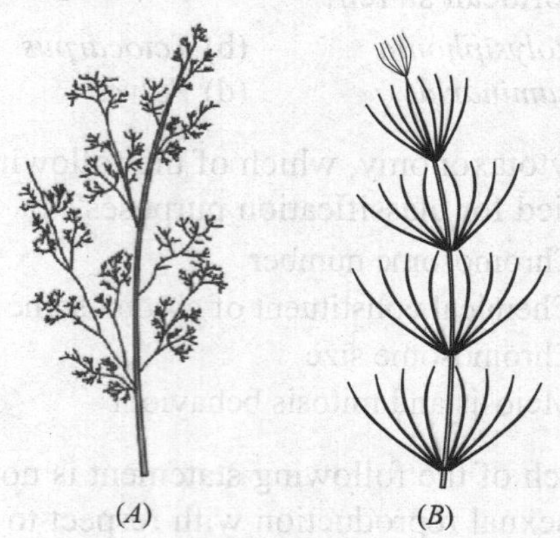

(a) *A* possesses *r*-phycoerythrin, while *B* possesses fucoxanthin.
(b) *A* possesses immotile spores, while *B* possesses motile spores.
(c) *A* possesses floridean starch as the stored food.
(d) *B* possesses cellulosic cell wall.

22. Male gametes are flagellated in

(a) *Volvox*, *Ectocarpus*
(b) *Sargassum*, *Polysiphonia*
(c) *Gracilaria*, *Gelidium*
(d) *Porphyra*, *Fucus*

23. *Spirogyra* filaments produce

(a) anisogametes (b) isogametes
(c) heterogametes (d) basidiogametes

24. Which one of the following statement is not true?

(a) *Chara* possesses nucule as the female reproductive structure.
(b) Bentham and Hooker's classification for flowering plants revolved only around the internal details.
(c) According to phylogenetic classification system, organisms belonging to the same taxa have a common ancestor.
(d) Algae is placed under thallophytes due to its thalloid body organisation.

25. Isogamous condition with flagellated gametes is found in

(a) *Chlamydomonas*
(b) *Spirogyra*
(c) *Eudorina*
(d) *Fucus*

■ Response Index

01	a	b	c	d	10	a	b	c	d	19	a	b	c	d
02	a	b	c	d	11	a	b	c	d	20	a	b	c	d
03	a	b	c	d	12	a	b	c	d	21	a	b	c	d
04	a	b	c	d	13	a	b	c	d	22	a	b	c	d
05	a	b	c	d	14	a	b	c	d	23	a	b	c	d
06	a	b	c	d	15	a	b	c	d	24	a	b	c	d
07	a	b	c	d	16	a	b	c	d	25	a	b	c	d
08	a	b	c	d	17	a	b	c	d					
09	a	b	c	d	18	a	b	c	d					

■ Performance Scanner

> 90% Excellent !	You have mastered these topics. The concepts of these topics are at your fingertips. Move on to the next topics and maintain this momentum.
76-90% Very Good !	You have a good command over these topics. Revise these topics again after a few days and enhance your performance.
60-75% Good !	You have a wide scope to learn for these topics. Revise these topics again.
<60% Not Satisfactory!	You have a long way ahead of you to master these topics. Revise it thoroughly.

Test 2

Syllabus
- Salient Features of Bryophytes
- Salient Features of Pteridophytes
- Salient Features of Gymnosperms

For deeper insight, **Scan the QR Code**

Important Instructions
- The test is of 30 minutes duration and contains 25 Multiple Choice Questions (four options with a single correct answer).
- Choose the correct option and fill the OMR given on the last page of this test accordingly.
- At some instances, you may find more than 1 option to be correct. In such circumstances, you have to judge the most appropriate answer as per the conditions given in the question.

1. A plant is employed by gardeners to keep seedlings and cut plants moist during transportation and propagation. Identify the plant.
(a) *Salvinia*
(b) *Polytrichum*
(c) *Marchantia*
(d) *Sphagnum*

2. Which of the following statement is not correct regarding protonema?
(a) It results from the germination of spores.
(b) It is a vegetative and transitory stage.
(c) It has non-green prostrate branches.
(d) It leads to the leafy stage.

3. Both male or female cones or strobili may be borne on the same tree such as
(a) *Cycas*
(b) *Dryopteris*
(c) *Pteris*
(d) *Pinus*

4. .... are green, multicellular, asexual buds which develop in small receptacles.
(a) Archegonium (b) Antheridium
(c) Gemmae (d) Rhizoids

5. Given below are few statements.
I. Gymnosperms do not possess an independent free-living male and female gametophytes.
II. Stems are branched in *Cedrus*, but unbranched in *Cycas*.
III. Gymnosperms have one of the tallest tree species.
IV. Prothallus is a free- living, mostly photosynthetic, leafy gametophyte found in pteridophytes.
V. In mosses, protonema stage bears the sex organs.
Choose the correct set of statements out of the given options.
(a) II, IV and V
(b) I, III, IV and V
(c) I, II, III, IV and V
(d) I, II and III

6. Which of the following statement correctly describes reproduction in pteridophytes?

(a) The gametophyte bears sporangia that are subtended by sporophylls.
(b) The sporophyte bears sporangia that are subtended by sporophylls.
(c) Sporophylls gets compacted to form strobili, as seen in ferns.
(d) Sporangia produce spores through mitosis in spore mother cells.

7. Identify the character that is not used as adaptation to land conditions by bryophytes.

(a) Rhizoids for absorption
(b) Chemotactic movement of sperms
(c) Jacketed reproductive structure
(d) Embryo formation

8. Which of the following term is correctly matched with its definition in *Pinus*?

(a) Monoecious - Male (microsporangiate) and female (megasporangiate) cones are produced on the same plant.
(b) Monoecious - Male and female sporophylls are borne on the same strobilus.
(c) Dioecious - Male and female cones are produced on different plants.
(d) Monoecious - Microsporangia and megasporangia develop on the same plant.

9. The dominant phase of bryophytes is

(a) free-living gametophyte
(b) free-living sporophyte
(c) gametophyte dependent on sporophyte
(d) sporophyte dependent on gametophyte

10. In gymnosperms, the ovule which develops within the ovary has massive parenchymatous body called

(a) integuments (b) nucellus
(c) endosperm (d) funicle

11. Which of the following is the heterosporous genera of pteridophytes?

(a) *Salvinia* (b) *Adiantum*
(c) *Equisetum* (d) *Psilotum*

12. The organism shown in the given figure shows the presence of

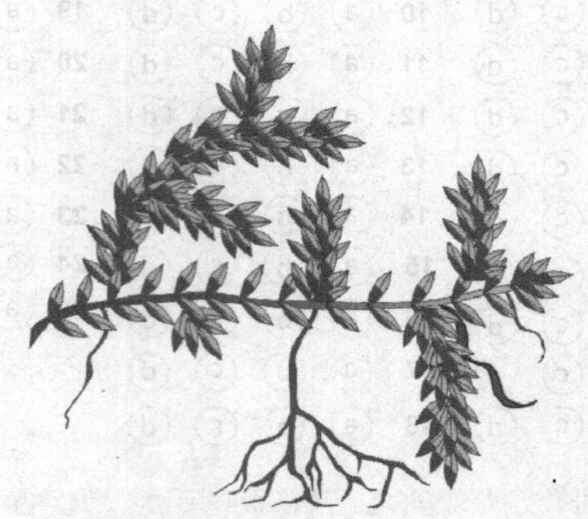

(a) macrophylls, protonema and homospory
(b) macrophylls, strobili and homospory.
(c) microphylls, protonema and heterospory
(d) microphylls, strobili and heterospory

13. Match List I with List II.

List I	List II
A. *Polytrichum*	1. Thalloid
B. *Marchantia*	2. Peat moss
C. *Sphagnum*	3. Protonema stage
D. *Selaginella*	4. Spike moss

Choose the correct answer from the options given below.

	A	B	C	D
(a)	2	1	3	4
(b)	1	3	2	4
(c)	1	2	3	4
(d)	3	1	2	4

14. Given below are two statements.

Statement I Pteriodophytes are avascular and seedless.

Statement II *Adiantum* is called walking fern.

In the light of the above statements, choose the correct answer from the options given below.

(a) Statement I is incorrect, but statement II is correct.
(b) Both statement I and statement II are correct.
(c) Both statement I and statement II are incorrect.
(d) Statement I is correct, but statement II is incorrect.

15. Given below are two statements; one is labelled as Assertion (A) and the other is labelled as Reason (R).

Assertion (A) In liverworts, both male and female sex organs can be found on the same thallus or on different thalli.

Reason (R) In liverworts, the zygote develops into a sporophyte, which is differentiated into foot, seta, and capsule.

In the light of the above statements, choose the correct answer from the options given below.
(a) A is false, but R is true.
(b) Both A and R are true and R is the correct explanation of A.
(c) Both A and R are true, but R is not the correct explanation of A.
(d) A is true, but R is false.

16. Given below are two statements.

Statement I Coralloid roots of *Cycas* are symbiotically associated with algae, whereas mycorrhizal roots of *Pinus* are symbiotically associated with fungi.

Statement II World's tallest tree, *Sequoia* belongs to gymnosperms.

In the light of the above statement, choose the correct answer from the options given below.
(a) Statement I is incorrect, but statement II is correct.
(b) Both statement I and statement II are correct.
(c) Both statement I and statement II are incorrect.
(d) Statement I is correct, but statement II is incorrect.

17. Given below are two statements; one is labelled as Assertion (A) and the other is labelled as Reason (R).

Assertion (A) *Gnetum* can be considered as the connecting link between gymnosperms and angiosperms.

Reason (R) *Gnetum* possesses vessel elements, double fertilisation mechanism along with presence of naked seeds.

In the light of the above statements, choose the correct answer from the options given below.
(a) A is false, but R is true.
(b) Both A and R are true and R is the correct explanation of A.
(c) Both A and R are true, but R is not the correct explanation of A.
(d) A is true, but R is false.

18. Fern prothallus develops from
(a) spores
(b) spore mother cells
(c) zygote
(d) rhizoids

19. Pteridophytes are different from bryophytes in having
(a) motile male gametes
(b) alternation of generation
(c) antheridia
(d) vascular tissue

20. Which of the following shows the heterospory and seed habit in the best way?
(a) *Equisetum* (b) *Selaginella*
(c) *Rhynia* (d) *Dryopteris*

21. Match List I with List II.

	List I		List II
A.	*Cycas revoluta*	1.	Chir pine
B.	*Pinus roxburghii*	2.	Chilgoza pine
C.	*Ginkgo biloba*	3.	Sago palm
D.	*Pinus gerardiana*	4.	Maiden hair tree

Choose the correct answer from the options given below.
(a) A-4, B-1, C-3, D-2
(b) A-3, B-1, C-4, D-2
(c) A-1, B-2, C-3, D-4
(d) A-3, B-2, C-4, D-1

22. Consider the following statements.

I. Mosses possess multicellular and branched rhizoids.
II. In bryophyte, sporophytic phase is not the dominant phase in life cycle.

III. Gemma cup is present in liverworts as green, asexual buds developed in small receptacle located on the thalli.

IV. Bryophytes possess free-living sporophyte.

Choose the correct set of statements out of the given options.
(a) I and IV
(b) I and III
(c) I, II and III
(d) II and IV

23. Pteridophytes comprise
(a) sporophyte of longer duration
(b) dominant phase of sporophyte which is parasitic on gametophyte
(c) dominant phase of gametophyte which is parasitic on sporophyte
(d) flask-shaped gametophytes

24. Given below is a figure of a bryophyte. Identify the incorrect description about sex organ produced by *X*.

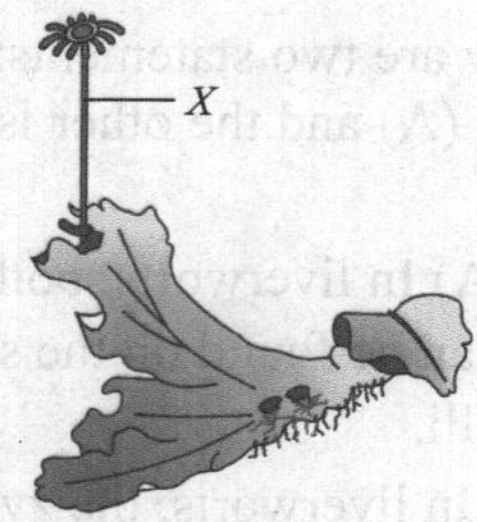

(a) Flask-shaped
(b) Multicellular
(c) Produces a single egg
(d) Produces biflagellated gamete

25. Given below are plants and their dominant phases of life cycle.

A. Bryophytes - Gametophyte
B. Gymnosperms - Sporophyte
C. Pteridophytes - Gametophyte

Choose the correct set of combinations.
(d) A and B (a) A, B and C
(b) A and C (c) B and C

■ Response Index

01	a	b	c	d	10	a	b	c	d	19	a	b	c	d
02	a	b	c	d	11	a	b	c	d	20	a	b	c	d
03	a	b	c	d	12	a	b	c	d	21	a	b	c	d
04	a	b	c	d	13	a	b	c	d	22	a	b	c	d
05	a	b	c	d	14	a	b	c	d	23	a	b	c	d
06	a	b	c	d	15	a	b	c	d	24	a	b	c	d
07	a	b	c	d	16	a	b	c	d	25	a	b	c	d
08	a	b	c	d	17	a	b	c	d					
09	a	b	c	d	18	a	b	c	d					

■ Performance Scanner

> 90% Excellent !	You have mastered these topics. The concepts of these topics are at your fingertips. Move on to the next topics and maintain this momentum.
76-90% Very Good !	You have a good command over these topics. Revise these topics again after a few days and enhance your performance.
60-75% Good !	You have a wide scope to learn for these topics. Revise these topics again.
<60% Not Satisfactory!	You have a long way ahead of you to master these topics. Revise it thoroughly.

Chapter Break Thru

Syllabus	• Systems of Classification and Classification of Plants	• Salient Features of Algae • Salient Features of Bryophytes	• Salient Features of Pteridophytes • Salient Features of Gymnosperms

Important Instructions

- The test is of 1 hour duration and contains 50 Multiple-Choice Questions (Four options with a single correct answer).
- Choose the correct option and fill the OMR given on the last page of this test accordingly.
- At some instances, you may find more than 1 option to be correct. In such circumstances, you have to judge the most appropriate answer as per the conditions given in the question.

1. Which of the following is the basis for the phylogenetic classification system?

(a) Morphological characteristics of different organisms
(b) Anatomical traits of different organisms
(c) Evolutionary relationships between different organisms
(d) Physiological features of different organisms

2. Find the correct match.

(a) *Dictyota* – Rhodophyceae
(b) *Sphagnum* – Club moss
(c) *Polytrichum* – Sporophytic plant body
(d) *Marchantia* – Gemma cups on dorsal surface

3. The reserve food of the given plants is

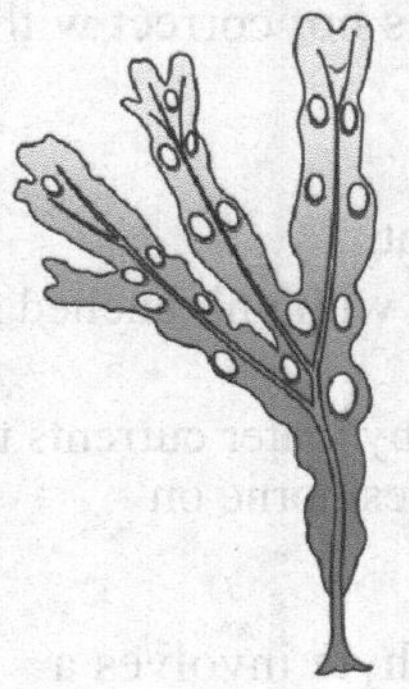
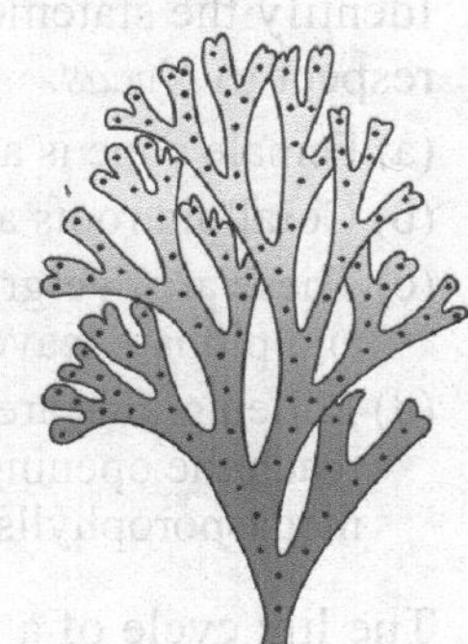

(a) starch and amylopectin
(b) laminarin and mannitol
(c) floridean starch
(d) amylopectin and fatty acids

4. Which of the following pair is incorrect?

(a) Numerical taxonomy - Number and code are assigned to all the characters and the data are then processed
(b) Chemotaxonomy - Based on phytochemistry
(c) Natural classification - Engler and Prantl
(d) Cytotaxonomy - Based on cytological information

5. *Spirogyra* is a free-floating green alga found in ponds, lakes, etc. Sexual reproduction in *Spirogyra* is an advanced feature as

(a) it has different sizes of motile sex organs
(b) it has same size of motile sex organs
(c) it has physiologically differentiated sex organs
(d) it has morphologically differentiated sex organs

6. Which of the following is not the characteristic of algae?

(a) They are eukaryotic, autotrophic, chlorophyllous and cryptogamic.
(b) They are aquatic organism.
(c) Reserve food is mainly starch.
(d) The vegetative reproduction takes place by budding.

7. Which of the following statement is correct regarding bryophytes?

(a) Meiosis occurs immediately after zygote formation.
(b) Water is required for transport of egg from archegonium to antheridium.

(c) Male sex organ is antheridium that produce tetra-flagellated antherozoids.
(d) Female sex organ is the archegonium which is flask-shaped and produces a single egg.

8. Given below is a diagram of a plant. Choose the incorrect statement with respect to it.

(a) It is a moss that provides peat that is used as fuel.
(b) Its predominant stage of life cycle is the sporophyte.
(c) It possesses the proper mechanism of spore dispersal.
(d) It has the ability to retain water.

9. Bryophytes undergo a fascinating life cycle. In the early stages of development, a spore germinates and gives rise to a unique structure. This structure plays a vital role in the bryophyte life cycle and is characterised by
(a) creeping growth pattern, green coloured due to chlorophyll, but lacking branches and exhibiting a thread-like form.
(b) lying flat on the ground, green coloured due to chlorophyll, with branching and a thread-like form.
(c) creeping growth pattern, green coloured due to chlorophyll, with frequent branching and a thread-like form.
(d) lying flat on the ground, lacking chlorophyll, with limited branching and a flattened shape.

10. How does vegetative reproduction occur in mosses?
(a) *Via* gemmae and tuber formation.
(b) Through gemmae and adventitious bud formation.
(c) By fragmentation and budding in the secondary protonema.
(d) By the formation of multiflagellated gametes.

11. Which of the following characteristic is correct with respect to the gametophyte in a heterosporous pteridophyte?
(a) It possesses structures analogous to roots and leaves.
(b) It exhibits vascular tissue.
(c) It is always dioecious.
(d) It may have both male and female reproductive structures on the same plant or separate male and female plants.

12. What is the primary difference between mosses and ferns?
(a) The life cycle of ferns possesses a predominant sporophyte, while the life cycle of a moss possesses a predominant gametophyte.
(b) In ferns, sporophylls form strobili carrying male or female structures, while the mosses possess a protonema stage bearing sex organs.
(c) In ferns, the gametophyte is represented by the prothallus, while the gametophytic phase in mosses comprises of protonemal stage only.
(d) Unlike mosses, in ferns, the male and the female gametophytes do not have an independent free-living existence.

13. Which of the following characteristic belongs exclusively to gymnosperms?
(a) Well-developed root system
(b) Presence of secondary growth
(c) Absence of xylem vessels and presence of albuminous cells
(d) Heterospory and absence of companion cells

14. Identify the statement that is not correct with respect to *Cycas*.
(a) Female cone is absent.
(b) Coralloid roots are present.
(c) These are evergreen trees with unbranched stems and pinnate leaves.
(d) Pollen grains are carried by water currents to reach the opening of ovules borne on megasporophylls.

15. The life cycle of a pteridophyte involves a short-lived, independent stage crucial for sexual reproduction. This stage, known as the prothallus, precedes the dominant sporophytic generation.

What is the primary function of prothallus in the pteridophytic life cycle?

(a) Production of specialised structures for sexual reproduction
(b) Formation of dormant spores with reduced metabolic activity
(c) Photosynthesis and anchoring for initial sporophyte development
(d) Nutrient exchange to facilitate the growth of the developing sporophyte

16. Coralloid roots associated with N_2-fixing cyanobacteria, are present in

(a) *Pinus* (b) *Cycas*
(c) *Wolffia* (d) *Ginkgo*

17. In which situation do gymnosperms fall regarding the enclosure of their ovules?

(a) Ovules are surrounded by an ovary wall, both during pre and post-fertilisation
(b) Ovules are exposed, with no ovary wall, both during pre and post-fertilisation
(c) Ovules are protected by an ovary wall before fertilisation, but not afterwards.
(d) Ovules are exposed before fertilisation, but enclosed by an ovary wall afterwards.

18. Despite belonging to different plant groups, *Funaria*, *Dryopteris*, and *Ginkgo* share a crucial feature in their life cycles. Which of the following best describes this commonality?

(a) Well-developed vascular tissues
(b) Independent sporophyte
(c) Presence of archegonia
(d) Independent gametophyte

19. Given below are few organisms.

Ulothrix, Ectocarpus, Dictyota, Polysiphonia, Sargassum, Porphyra, Gracilaria, Fucus

How many organisms among the given list possess complex post-fertilisation development.

(a) Three (b) Five
(c) Four (d) Six

20. Read the following statements and identify the correct set of statements.

I. Red algae is commonly called Rhodophyceae.
II. Red pigment, *r*-phycoerythrin is predominantly present in red-algae.
III. Majority of red algae are freshwater.
IV. In red algae, the food is stored in the form of complex proteins.
V. Red algae reproduce vegetatively by fragmentation.

Choose the correct answer from the option given below.

(a) I, III and V (b) II, III and IV
(c) I, II and V (d) III and II

21. Match the following algae with their respective economic uses.

	List I		List II
A.	Agar used in ice-creams and jelly preparations	1.	Single-cell protein, used as food supplements by space travellers
B.	Algin	2.	Red algae
C.	Carrageen	3.	Brown algae
D.	*Chlorella*	4.	*Gelidium, Gracilaria*

Choose the correct combination.

(a) A-1, B-2, C-3, D-4
(b) A-4, B-3, C-2, D-1
(c) A-2, B-1, C-3, D-4
(d) A-3, B-2, C-1, D-4

22. Given below is a figure of an organism belonging to kingdom-Plantae.

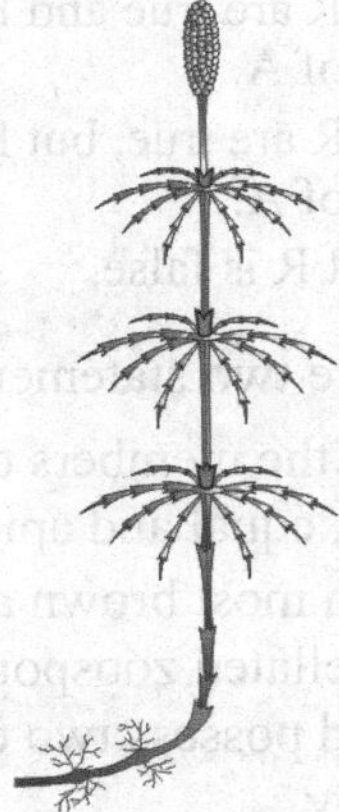

Choose the incorrect statement with respect to the given organism.

(a) Its sporophylls forms compact strobili.
(b) The gametophyte is represented by free-living prothallus.
(c) It belongs to class-Lycopsida.
(d) The main plant body belongs to *Equisetum*.

23. Given below are two statements.

Statement I The gametophytes of pteridophytes due to their efficient water transport mechanisms, can thrive in a wide range of habitats, from damp forests to dry grasslands.

Statement II The reliance on water for fertilisation in pteridophytes, due to the presence of flagellated sperm, restricts their ability to colonise diverse habitats.

In the light of the above statements, choose the correct answer from the options given below.

(a) Statement I is incorrect, but statement II is correct.
(b) Both statement I and statement II are correct.
(c) Both statement I and statement II are incorrect.
(d) Statement I is correct, but statement II is incorrect.

24. Given below are two statements; one is labelled as Assertion (A) and the other is labelled as Reason (R).

Assertion (A) Bryophytes are known as the amphibians of the plant kingdom.

Reason (R) Bryophytes typically inhabit swamps and transitional zones between water and land.

In the light of the above statements, choose the correct answer from the options given below.

(a) A is false, but R is true.
(b) Both A and R are true and R is the correct explanation of A.
(c) Both A and R are true, but R is not the correct explanation of A.
(d) A is true, but R is false.

25. Given below are two statements.

Statement I In the members of Chlorophyceae, the flagella are 2-8, equal and apical.

Statement II In most brown algae, reproduction involves biflagellated zoospores that are pear-shaped and possess two equal flagella attached apically.

In the light of the above statements, choose the correct answer from the options given below.

(a) Statement I is incorrect, but statement II is correct.
(b) Both statement I and statement II are correct.
(c) Both statement I and statement II are incorrect.
(d) Statement I is correct, but statement II is incorrect.

26. Consider the following statements. Identify the incorrect statement(s).

I. Pteridophytes are soil binders and are also used for medicinal purposes.
II. *Dryopteris* is commonly known as shield fern.
III. *Selaginella* is also used as resurrection plant.
IV. The heterospory originated due to reduction in the number of spores within sporangia.
V. The common name of *Selaginella* is spike moss.

Choose the correct answer from the options given below.

(a) I and II
(b) II only
(c) III and V
(d) IV only

27. Given below are two statements.

Statement I Bryophytes are characterised by the presence of an independent sporophyte and photosynthetic gametophyte.

Statement II The sex organs present in bryophytes are unicellular structures.

In the light of the above statements, choose the correct answer from the options given below.

(a) Statement I is incorrect, but statement II is correct.
(b) Both statement I and statement II are correct.
(c) Both statement I and statement II are incorrect.
(d) Statement I is correct, but statement II is incorrect.

28. Read the following statements and identify the correct set of statements.

I. Gymnosperms have an alternation of generations in their life cycle.
II. *Cycas* shows fern ancestry.
III. The microspores in gymnosperms develop into a male gametophytic generation which is highly enlarged.
IV. Each microsporophyll has one sporangium in the case of *Pinus*.
V. Gymnosperms are heterosporous, unlike bryophytes and some pteridophytes.

Choose the correct answer from the options given below.

(a) I, II and III
(b) I, II and IV
(c) II, III and V
(d) I, II and V

29. Given below are few figures of plant. Identify the correct matching pair along with their characters.

	(i)	(ii)
(A)	*Selaginella* - Macrophylls	*Sphagnum* - Homosporous
(B)	*Selaginella* - Microphylls	*Salvinia* - Homosporous
(C)	Fern - Macrophylls	*Salvinia* - Heterosporous
(D)	Fern - Microphylls	*Sphagnum* - Heterosporous

(a) A (b) B
(c) C (d) D

30. Given below are two statements; one is labelled as Assertion (A) and the other is labelled as Reason (R).

Assertion (A) *Cycas* is a living fossil.
Reason (R) *Cycas* has a long geographical record evidenced by its fossils, but still occurs in a limited area.

In the light of the above statements, choose the correct answer from the options given below.

(a) A is false, but R is true.
(b) Both A and R are true and R is the correct explanation of A.
(c) Both A and R are true, but R is not the correct explanation of A.
(d) A is true, but R is false.

31. Which of the following statement best explains that "the moss sporophyte has an elaborate mechanism of spore dispersal"?

(a) Moss sporophytes are capable of asexual reproduction
(b) The capsule structure is specialised to enhance spore release and dispersal
(c) The gametophyte assists in actively dispersing spores
(d) The seta and foot work together to eject spores forcibly from the gametophyte

32. If the prothallus in pteridophyte becomes dependent on the sporophyte for nutrition, how would this affect the life cycle of pteridophyte?

(a) The sporophyte would become dominant and eliminate the need for gametophytes.
(b) Gametophytes would remain free- living, but reproduce asexually.
(c) Pteridophytes would shift towards the seed habit, like in the case of gymnosperms.
(d) The need for water in reproduction would decrease, allowing greater geographic spread.

33. In mosses, the development of the leafy gametophyte from the secondary protonema is initiated by

(a) germination of the spore
(b) fertilisation between antheridium and archegonium
(c) development of lateral bud from the protonema
(d) the fragmentation of rhizoids

34. Given below are two statements; one is labelled as Assertion (A) and other is labelled as Reason (R).

Assertion (A) Phylogenetic classification systems are more accepted than artificial systems in modern taxonomy.
Reason (R) Phylogenetic classification system only works when the species have supporting fossil evidence.

In the light of the above statements, choose the correct answer from the options given below.

(a) A is false, but R is true.
(b) Both A and R are true and R is the correct explanation of A.
(c) Both A and R are true, but R is not the correct explanation of A.
(d) A is true, but R is false.

35. The flowchart of reproduction in bryophytes is given below.

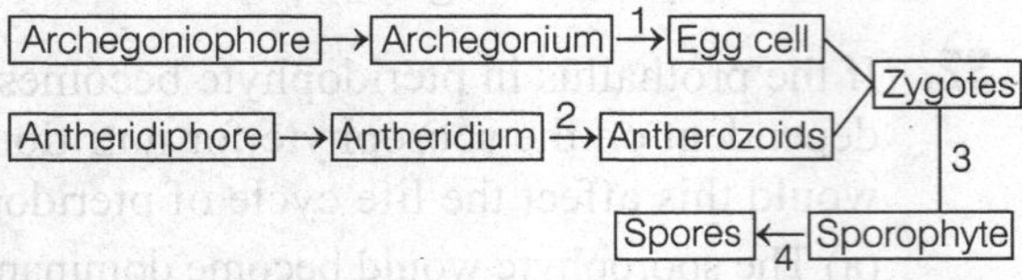

Choose the correct interpretation about the given flowchart.

(a) At stage 1, reduction division occurs which form haploid egg cell
(b) At stage 4, reduction division occurs which form haploid spores
(c) At stage 2, some of the antheridial cells undergoes meiosis to produce antherozoids
(d) Stages 3 and 4 represent meiosis-I and meiosis-II

36. Given below are two statements.

Statement I Algae play a crucial role in increasing the level of dissolved oxygen through photosynthesis.

Statement II At least a half of the total phosphorus fixation in aquatic medium is carried out by algae.

In the light of the above statements, choose the correct answer from the options given below.

(a) Statement I is incorrect, but statement II is correct.
(b) Both statement I and statement II are correct.
(c) Both statement I and statement II are incorrect.
(d) Statement I is correct, but statement II is incorrect.

37. Identify the incorrect statement regarding *Ectocarpus*.

(a) It has a rigid cell wall made of an inner layer of cellulose and an outer layer of pectose.
(b) It is a filamentous alga.
(c) Food is stored in the form of laminarin or mannitol
(d) Asexual reproduction takes place by biflagellated zoospores

38. Certain species of red algae are used in food products like ice-cream and jellies. How could the overharvesting of red algae for commercial purposes potentially affect marine ecosystems?

(a) It would have no significant effect as red algae are easily replenished due to higher reproductive rate
(b) It could disrupt marine food chains, affecting species that rely on red algae as a primary food source
(c) It would lead to an increase in marine biodiversity due to reduced competition from red algae
(d) Overharvesting would only affect the availability of human food products, not the marine environment.

39. Which of the following statement about gymnosperms is correct?

(a) The seeds of gymnosperms are enclosed by an ovary.
(b) They produce seeds that are exposed and not covered.
(c) All gymnosperms are herbaceous plants.
(d) They have fibrous root system like grasses.

40. What is the key difference between male and female reproductive structures in gymnosperms such as *Cycas*?

(a) Both male and female cones are found on the same plant
(b) Male cones are absent and reproduction is through spores only
(c) Male cones and megasporophylls are borne on different trees
(d) Female cones produce pollen grains and male cones bear ovules.

41. Given below are two statements.

Statement I In pteridophytes, the main plant body is a gametophyte, which is differentiated into true roots, stems and leaves.

Statement II In pteridophytes, the gametophytes bear male and female sex organs called antheridia and archegonia, respectively.

In the light of the above statements, choose the correct answer from the options given below.

(a) Statement I is incorrect, but statement II is correct.
(b) Both statement I and statement II are correct.
(c) Both statement I and statement II are incorrect.
(d) Statement I is correct, but statement II is incorrect.

42. Which of the following features belong to algae *Chara*?

I. Filamentous body
II. Pyrenoids
III. Pyriform gamete
IV. Secondary protonema
V. Floridean starch
VI. Fucoxanthin

Choose the correct answer from the options given below.

(a) I, II and IV (b) III, IV and V
(c) I, II, III and VI (d) IV, V and VI

43. Consider the following statements.

I. Bryophytes are well adapted to dry conditions.
II. Angiosperms produce seeds that are enclosed within fruits.
III. Pteridophytes do not produce seeds and reproduce *via* spores.
IV. Mosses and ferns are classified under gymnosperms.
V. Some algae occur in association with fungi and animals.

Choose the correct statements from the options given below.

(a) I, II and III (b) II, III and V
(c) II and V (d) II, III and IV

44. Which of the following statement is the correct interpretation of the presence of strobili in pteridophytes like *Selaginella* and *Equisetum*?

(a) Strobili help in the dispersal of seeds in diverse environment.
(b) They allow for the clustering of sporangia, increasing spore production.
(c) Strobili facilitate photosynthesis more efficiently than leaves.
(d) They provide protection to the developing seeds from herbivores.

45. In an experiment, if bryophytes were grown in an environment lacking water, but otherwise conducive for growth, what is the most likely impact on their reproductive cycle?

(a) The sporophytic generation would dominate over the gametophyte
(b) The gametophyte would develop, but fail to reproduce sexually
(c) The bryophytes would adapt by reproducing asexually
(d) The archegonia and antheridia would continue to function normally.

46. Which of the following characteristics of Phaeophyceae allows them to thrive in marine environments despite variable conditions such as strong currents and limited nutrients?

(a) The presence of fucoxanthin, a pigment that allows them to utilise light more efficiently
(b) The production of pyrenoids for food storage
(c) The presence of motile zoospores that disperse in ocean current
(d) Their ability to form holdfasts that anchor them to the ocean floor.

47. Identify the incorrect match pair from the following.

(a) *Cycas*- pinnate leaves persist for a few years
(b) Ovules- borne on megasporophyll
(c) *Equisetum*- Gametophyte as dominant phase
(d) *Pinus*- Roots possessing fungal association

48. Which of the following evolutionary trait in pteridophytes is considered a precursor to the seed habit seen in higher plants?

(a) The production of cones or strobili
(b) The formation of prothallus during the gametophyte phase
(c) Retention of female gametophytes on the parent sporophyte and embryonic development within them
(d) The use of water for fertilisation.

49. Identify the incorrect match.

(a) *Spirogyra* - Isogamy
(b) *Gelidium* - Anisogamy
(c) *Ulothrix* - Isogamy
(d) *Volvox* - Oogamy

50. Given below are two statements; one is labelled as Assertion (A) and other is labelled as Reason (R).

Assertion (A) Gymnosperms are heterosporous, producing two kinds of spores, i.e. microspores and megaspores.

Reason (R) Microspores develop into female gametophytes, while megaspores develop into male gametophytes.

In the light of above statements, choose the correct the correct answer from the options given below.

(a) A is false, but R is true.
(b) Both A and R are true and R is the correct explanation of A.
(c) Both A and R are true, but R is not the correct explanation of A.
(d) A is true, but R is false.

Scan for online chapter test

Response Index

01	ⓐ ⓑ ⓒ ⓓ	14	ⓐ ⓑ ⓒ ⓓ	27	ⓐ ⓑ ⓒ ⓓ	40	ⓐ ⓑ ⓒ ⓓ
02	ⓐ ⓑ ⓒ ⓓ	15	ⓐ ⓑ ⓒ ⓓ	28	ⓐ ⓑ ⓒ ⓓ	41	ⓐ ⓑ ⓒ ⓓ
03	ⓐ ⓑ ⓒ ⓓ	16	ⓐ ⓑ ⓒ ⓓ	29	ⓐ ⓑ ⓒ ⓓ	42	ⓐ ⓑ ⓒ ⓓ
04	ⓐ ⓑ ⓒ ⓓ	17	ⓐ ⓑ ⓒ ⓓ	30	ⓐ ⓑ ⓒ ⓓ	43	ⓐ ⓑ ⓒ ⓓ
05	ⓐ ⓑ ⓒ ⓓ	18	ⓐ ⓑ ⓒ ⓓ	31	ⓐ ⓑ ⓒ ⓓ	44	ⓐ ⓑ ⓒ ⓓ
06	ⓐ ⓑ ⓒ ⓓ	19	ⓐ ⓑ ⓒ ⓓ	32	ⓐ ⓑ ⓒ ⓓ	45	ⓐ ⓑ ⓒ ⓓ
07	ⓐ ⓑ ⓒ ⓓ	20	ⓐ ⓑ ⓒ ⓓ	33	ⓐ ⓑ ⓒ ⓓ	46	ⓐ ⓑ ⓒ ⓓ
08	ⓐ ⓑ ⓒ ⓓ	21	ⓐ ⓑ ⓒ ⓓ	34	ⓐ ⓑ ⓒ ⓓ	47	ⓐ ⓑ ⓒ ⓓ
09	ⓐ ⓑ ⓒ ⓓ	22	ⓐ ⓑ ⓒ ⓓ	35	ⓐ ⓑ ⓒ ⓓ	48	ⓐ ⓑ ⓒ ⓓ
10	ⓐ ⓑ ⓒ ⓓ	23	ⓐ ⓑ ⓒ ⓓ	36	ⓐ ⓑ ⓒ ⓓ	49	ⓐ ⓑ ⓒ ⓓ
11	ⓐ ⓑ ⓒ ⓓ	24	ⓐ ⓑ ⓒ ⓓ	37	ⓐ ⓑ ⓒ ⓓ	50	ⓐ ⓑ ⓒ ⓓ
12	ⓐ ⓑ ⓒ ⓓ	25	ⓐ ⓑ ⓒ ⓓ	38	ⓐ ⓑ ⓒ ⓓ		
13	ⓐ ⓑ ⓒ ⓓ	26	ⓐ ⓑ ⓒ ⓓ	39	ⓐ ⓑ ⓒ ⓓ		

Performance Scanner

>90% Excellent !	You have mastered this chapter. The concepts of this chapter are at your fingertips. Move on to the next chapter and maintain this momentum.
76-90% Very Good !	You have a good command over this chapter. Revise the chapter again after a few days and enhance your performance.
60-75% Good !	You have a wide scope to learn for this chapter. Revise this chapter again.
<60% Not Satisfactory!	You have a long way ahead of you to master this chapter. Revise it thoroughly.

Test Booklet No. 3947304

Test Booklet Code CH4

MEDACE
NEET (UG)
SELF ASSESSMENT KIT

Animal Kingdom

Topics Covered

Basis of Classification and Lower Invertebrates

Higher Invertebrates

Chordata

Important Instructions

- This Booklet Contains – Three Topic Tests and One Test on Complete Chapter.
- Each question carries 4 marks.
- For each correct response, the candidate will get 4 marks. And for every incorrect response, 1 mark will be additionally deducted from total score.
- Use **Blue/Black** point pen only for filling the OMR.
- Rough work is to be done in the space provided for this purpose in the test booklet only.

Name of the Candidate (In Capitals) ____________

____

____

Candidate's Signature ____________

Invigilator's Signature ____________

Facsimile signature stamp of center superintendent____________

Do not open this booklet until you start attempting the test

Topical Follow Thru

Test 1

Syllabus Salient Features and Classification of Animals upto Aschelminthes (Lower Invertebrates)

For deeper insight, **Scan the QR Code**

Important Instructions

- The test is of 30 minutes duration and contains 25 Multiple Choice Questions (four options with a single correct answer).
- Choose the correct option and fill the OMR given on the last page of this test accordingly.
- At some instances, you may find more than 1 option to be correct. In such circumstances, you have to judge the most appropriate answer as per the conditions given in the question.

1. The members of Ctenophora exhibit ______ fertilisation with ______ development.

(a) external, direct
(b) external, indirect
(c) internal, direct
(d) internal, indirect

2. During evolution, in which of the following groups does a true coelom first appear?

(a) Aschelminthes (b) Annelida
(c) Echinodermata (d) Platyhelminthes

3. Identify the phylum that exhibits metamerism, excluding Annelida and Arthropoda.

(a) Ctenophora (b) Chordata
(c) Mollusca (d) Echinodermata

4. Given below are two statements; one is labelled as Assertion (A) and the other is labelled as Reason (R).

Assertion (A) Nematodes and rotifers are acoelomate.

Reason (R) No internal body cavity (coelom) is formed in acoelomates.

In the light of the above statements, choose the correct answer from the options given below.

(a) A is false, but R is true
(b) Both A and R are true and R is the correct explanation of A
(c) Both A and R are true, but R is not the correct explanation of A
(d) A is true, but R is false

5. Select the incorrect combination.

(a) Closed circulatory system: Arteries, veins and capillaries present.
(b) Incomplete digestive system: Single opening system.
(c) Open circulatory system: Blood is circulated through tubes.
(d) Complete digestive system: Two openings, i.e. mouth and anus.

6. Consider the following characteristics to identify the phylum described by the statements.

(i) Exclusively marine, radially symmetrical, diploblastic organisms with tissue level of organization.
(ii) The body bears eight external rows of ciliated comb plates, which aids in locomotion.
(iii) Digestion is both extracellular and intracellular.
(iv) Reproduction occurs exclusively through sexual means.

Which phylum matches these descriptions?

(a) Platyhelminthes
(b) Arthropoda
(c) Mollusca
(d) Ctenophora

7. Identify the correct animals corresponding to each symmetry type shown in the figures.

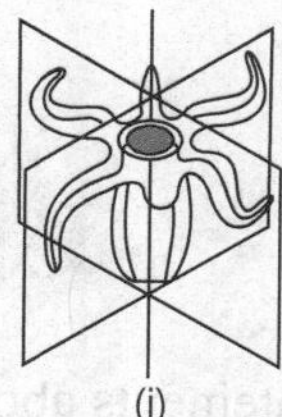
(i)

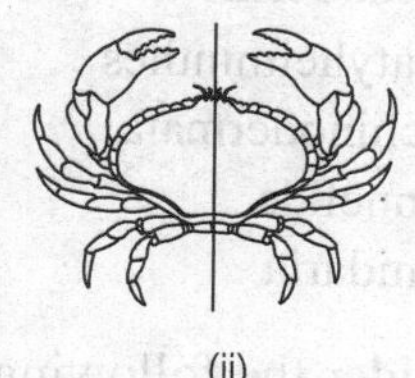
(ii)

(a) (i) *Echinus*, (ii) *Ctenoplana*
(b) (i) *Culex*, (ii) *Laccifer*
(c) (i) *Pleurobrachia*, (ii) *Nereis*
(d) (i) *Fasciola*, (ii) *Gorgonia*

8. Given below are the two statements regarding liver flukes.

Statement I There is an posterior triangular head with two lateral lobes.

Statement II Excretion occurs with the help of flame cells.

In the light of above statements, choose the correct answer from the options given below.

(a) Statement I is incorrect, but statement II is correct
(b) Both statement I and statement II are correct
(c) Both statement I and statement II are incorrect
(d) Statement I is correct, but statement II is incorrect

9. Identify the feature that is not a fundamental criteria for classifying animals.

(a) Cellular organisation pattern
(b) Number of germ layers
(c) Segmental repetition
(d) Water transport system pathway

10. Refer to the given diagrams, showing different coeloems and identify the phyla (*A*, *B* and *C*) in which these are likely to be found.

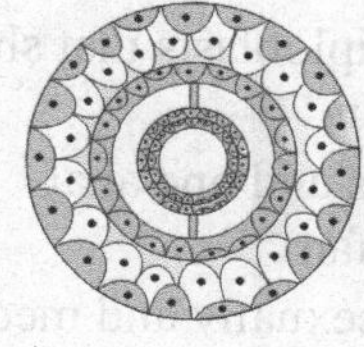
A

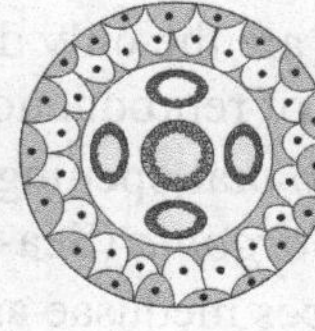
B

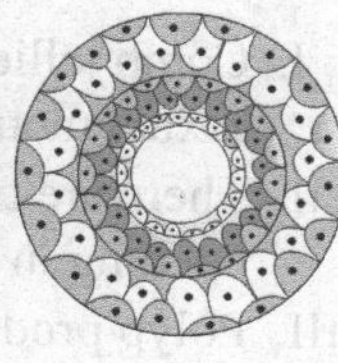
C

	A	B	C
(a)	Platyhelminthes	Aschelminthes	Annelida
(b)	Platyhelminthes	Annelida	Aschelminthes
(c)	Annelida	Platyhelminthes	Aschelminthes
(d)	Annelida	Aschelminthes	Platyhelminthes

11. Sponge skeleton is secreted by

(a) myocytes
(b) phagocytes
(c) scleroblasts
(d) chromocytes

12. ……… has excretory tube which removes body wastes from the body cavity through the excretory pore.

(a) Cnidaria
(b) Annelida
(c) Porifera
(d) Aschelminthes

13. Choose the incorrect statement for coelom.

(a) A large cavity with blood called haemocoel is found in Platyhelminthes.
(b) A coelom derived from blastocoel is known as pseudocoelom.
(c) Enterocoelom appeared first in the course of evolution in echinodermata.
(d) Schizocoelomates and enterocoelomates are true coelomates.

14. Sponges are multicellular organisms yet, they do not have respiratory organs. This is due to the reason that

I. the mode of respiration is anaerobic.
II. there is presence of highly porous body through which water flows.
III. there is a limited requirement of oxygen.
IV. the respiratory organs become non-functional in water.

Choose the correct answer from the options given below.

(a) I and II
(b) Only II
(c) Only IV
(d) III and IV

15. Identify the freshwater sponge among the following options.

(a) *Sycon*
(b) *Spongilla*
(c) *Euspongia*
(d) *Pennatula*

16. Following is the diagrammatic representation of the germinal layers in an organism.

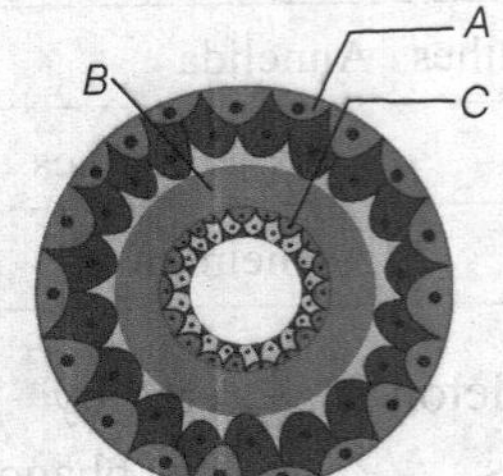

Which of the following is correct about the germinal layers?

(a) This type of organisation is observed in *Fasciola hepatica*.

(b) *B* forms different cell types in an organism.

(c) Cells in *A* and *C* do not have the ability to differentiate.

(d) A true germinal layer between *A* and *C* is present in chordates.

17. Given below are two statements.

Statement I Movement is restricted for the internal organs of acoelomates.

Statement II A coelom helps to reduce friction between different organs.

In the light of the above statements, choose the correct answer from the options given below.

(a) Statement I is incorrect, but statement II is correct

(b) Both statement I and statement II are correct

(c) Both statement I and statement II are incorrect

(d) Statement I is correct, but statement II is incorrect

18. A certain protein isolated from an organisms '*X*', when inserted into another organism makes the organism glow in dark. Which of the following could be that organisms?

I. *Aurelia* II. *Ctenoplana*

III. *Physalia* IV. *Euspongia*

Choose the correct answer from the options given below.

(a) I and II

(b) II only

(c) I only

(d) II and IV

19. Which of the following is the only radially symmetrical phylum that has a true coelom lined by mesoderm?

(a) Platyhelminthes

(b) Echinodermata

(c) Annelida

(d) Cnidaria

20. Consider the following statements about *Sycon*.

I. Choanocytes create the water flow to capture food.

II. Flagellar movement directs water into the spongocoel.

III. Osculum acts as a large ingestion pore.

IV. Absence of a proper supportive framework.

Choose the correct statements from the options given below.

(a) I only

(b) II and III

(c) I and II

(d) IV only

21. Given below are two statements; one is labelled as Assertion (A) and the other is labelled as Reason (R).

Assertion (A) A threatened cnidarian throws out thread like structures.

Reason (R) Cnidoblasts are used for anchorage to the substratum.

In the light of the above statement, choose the correct answer from the options given below.

(a) A is false, but R is true

(b) Both A and R are true and R is the correct explanation of A

(c) Both A and R are true, but R is not the correct explanation of A

(d) A is true, but R is false

22. Consider the following statements.

I. Comb jellies are the only diploblasts that show sexual mode of reproduction.

II. There are two oral openings and one anal opening in *Gorgonia* (Sea-fan).

III. Polyp produces medusae asexually and medusae produce polyps sexually.

IV. *Spongilla* and *Pleurobrachia* are both hermaphrodite invertebrates.

V. *Ancylostoma* have complete alimentary canal.

Choose the correct set of statements from the options given below.

(a) I, III and IV (b) III and V
(c) I and II (d) III, IV and V

23. Read the following statements and choose the incorrect statement regarding flatworms.

(a) The flat body is due to the absence of the body cavity
(b) Presence of a dorsally located mouth and ventral anus
(c) Respiration occurs by simple diffusion across the body
(d) Complex life cycle with one or more larval stages

24. Which of the following structure helps in ingesting the food due to a vigorous pumping action?

(a) Muscular pharynx in *Ancylostoma*
(b) Hypostome of *Adamsia*
(c) Osculum in sponges
(d) Oral tube in *Ascaris*

25. Following are the diagrammatic representation of two types of worms. Which of the following is/are the point(s) of difference between them?

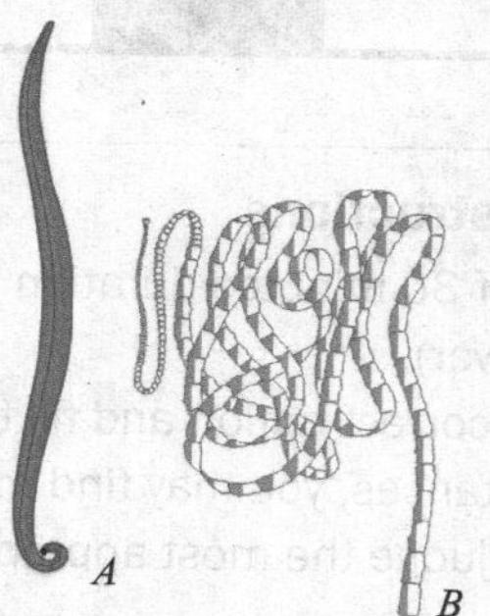

I. Mode of fertilisation
II. Sexual dimorphism
III. Feeding habit
IV. Body cavity or coelom

Choose the correct answer from the options given below.

(a) II only
(b) I and II
(c) II and III
(d) II and IV

Response Index

01	a	b	c	d	10	a	b	c	d	19	a	b	c	d
02	a	b	c	d	11	a	b	c	d	20	a	b	c	d
03	a	b	c	d	12	a	b	c	d	21	a	b	c	d
04	a	b	c	d	13	a	b	c	d	22	a	b	c	d
05	a	b	c	d	14	a	b	c	d	23	a	b	c	d
06	a	b	c	d	15	a	b	c	d	24	a	b	c	d
07	a	b	c	d	16	a	b	c	d	25	a	b	c	d
08	a	b	c	d	17	a	b	c	d					
09	a	b	c	d	18	a	b	c	d					

Performance Scanner

> 90% Excellent !	You have mastered these topics. The concepts of these topics are at your fingertips. Move on to the next topics and maintain this momentum.
76-90% Very Good !	You have a good command over these topics. Revise these topics again after a few days and enhance your performance.
60-75% Good !	You have a wide scope to learn for these topics. Revise these topics again.
<60% Not Satisfactory!	You have a long way ahead of you to master these topics. Revise it thoroughly.

Test 2

Syllabus

Salient Features and Classification of Animals upto Hemichordata (Higher Invertebrates)

For deeper insight, **Scan the QR Code**

Important Instructions

- The test is of 30 minutes duration and contains 15 Multiple Choice Questions (four options with a single correct answer).
- Choose the correct option and fill the OMR given on the last page of this test accordingly.
- At some instances, you may find more than 1 option to be correct. In such circumstances, you have to judge the most appropriate answer as per the conditions given in the question.

1. Some aquatic insects can rise from water surface and sink into water with proper coordination only due to the presence of

(a) statocysts (b) nematocysts
(c) antenna (d) compound eye

2. Among the given features, which of the following are common for leech, cockroach and scorpion?

(a) Antenna and monoecious
(b) Nephridia and dioecious
(c) Cephalisation and monoecious
(d) Ventral nerve cord and metameres

3. Read the following statement and choose the incorrect statement.

(a) A closed circulatory system is present in phylum-Annelida
(b) Excretion takes place through Malpighian tubules in annelids.
(c) Molluscs have organ system level of organisation
(d) Development is indirect in phylum-Echinodermata.

4. Which one of the following phyla is correctly matched with its two general characteristics?

(a) Hemichordata - Have organ level of organisation and development is indirect.
(b) Mollusca-Normally oviparous and development through a larva.
(c) Arthropoda- Body divided into head, thorax and abdomen; respiration by statocysts.
(d) Echinodermata- Radial symmetry and mostly internal fertilisation.

5. Identify the given animal and choose the correct statement with respect to the members of phylum it belong to.

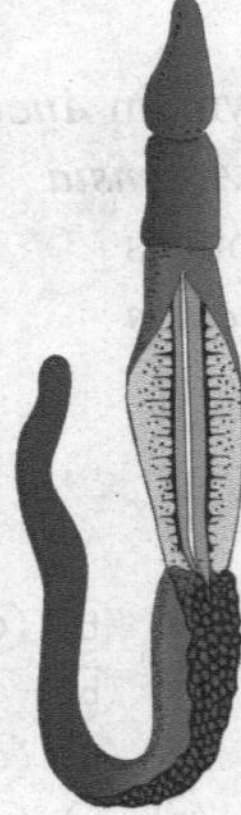

(a) They possess a file-like rasping organ called a radula within their mouth, used for feeding.
(b) They possess a primitive structure in the collar region known as the stomochord, which resembles the notochord.
(c) Their body is encased in a chitinous exoskeleton.
(d) The phylum includes *Antedon* and *Saccoglossus*.

6. All the given characteristics are true for the phylum-Mollusca, except

(a) it is the second largest animal phylum.
(b) the body surface is distinctly marked out into segments.
(c) its members are usually dioecious.
(d) the development is indirect.

7. Which of the following statement is correct regarding the following figure?

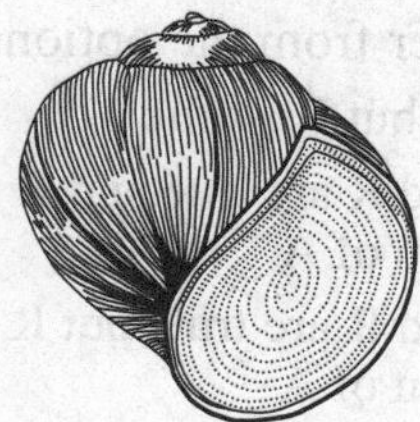

(a) They possesses feather-like gills which are present in the cavity and help in pulmonary activities.
(b) Their body is covered by a siliceous shell and is unsegmented.
(c) They possesses water-vascular system.
(d) They are dioecious and oviparous with direct development.

8. Which of the following statement is incorrect?
(a) Coelenterates and annelids have radial symmetry.
(b) Arthropods and molluscs exhibit organ level of organisation.
(c) Coelenterates are diploblastic animals.
(d) Arthropods and hemichordates have bilateral symmetry.

9. Given below are two statements.
Statement I The endoskeleton of echinoderms is made up of small calcareous elements, which are embedded in the dermis of wall.
Statement II Hemichordates have a rudimentary structure in the trunk region similar to notochord.
In the light of the above statements, choose the correct answer from the options given below.
(a) Statement I is incorrect, but statement II is correct
(b) Both statement I and statement II are correct
(c) Both statement I and statement II are incorrect
(d) Statement I is correct, but statement II is incorrect

10. Given below are some characteristics of the phylum to which *Saccoglossus* belongs.
I. Hermaphrodite, triploblastic.
II. Have probocsis gland for the removal of excreta.
III. Body surface is marked into metameres.
IV. Circulatory system is open type.
V. Worm- like marine animals.
Select the incorrect set of characters from the option given below.
(a) II, IV and V
(b) I, III and V
(c) III and V
(d) I and III

11. Which of the following are the points of similarities between the largest and second largest phylum of the animal kingdom?
I. Metamerism
II. Body plan
III. Coelom
IV. Sensory organ
Choose the correct answer from the options given below.
(a) III only
(b) II and III
(c) I and IV
(d) III and IV

12. Given below are two statements.
Statement I Radula in snails are used for rasping the food.
Statement II Radula contains calcareous teeth.
In the light of the above statements, choose the correct answer from the options given below.
(a) Statement I is incorrect, but statement II is correct
(b) Both statement I and statement II are correct
(c) Both statement I and statement II are incorrect
(d) Statement I is correct, but statement II is incorrect

13. Which of the following statement is correct about Star fishes?
(a) Water filter system is located on the ventral surface.
(b) Locomotion is conducted by muscular foot.
(c) Excretion is taken care of by the water vascular system.
(d) Fertilisation takes place within the mother's body.

14. Match List I with List II.

List I	List II
A. *Nereis*	1. Gills
B. *Culex*	2. Closed circulation
C. *Aplysia*	3. Metameres
D *Balanoglossus*	4. Feather-like gills

Choose the correct set of statement from the options given below

	A	B	C	D		A	B	C	D
(a)	2	3	4	1	(b)	2	3	1	4
(c)	2	4	3	1	(d)	2	1	3	4

15. Given below are two statements; one is labelled as Assertion (A) and the other is labelled as Reason (R).

Assertion (A) Hemichordates are no longer placed as a sub-phylum under chordates.

Reason (R) Stomochord is a rudimentary structure placed in the proboscis region.

In the light of the above statements, choose the correct answer from the options given below.

(a) A is false, but R is true
(b) Both A and R are true and R is the correct explanation of A
(c) Both A and R are true, but R is not the correct explanation of A
(d) A is true, but R is false

Response Index

01	a	b	c	d	10	a	b	c	d	19	a	b	c	d
02	a	b	c	d	11	a	b	c	d	20	a	b	c	d
03	a	b	c	d	12	a	b	c	d	21	a	b	c	d
04	a	b	c	d	13	a	b	c	d	22	a	b	c	d
05	a	b	c	d	14	a	b	c	d	23	a	b	c	d
06	a	b	c	d	15	a	b	c	d	24	a	b	c	d
07	a	b	c	d	16	a	b	c	d	25	a	b	c	d
08	a	b	c	d	17	a	b	c	d					
09	a	b	c	d	18	a	b	c	d					

Performance Scanner

> 90% Excellent !	You have mastered these topics. The concepts of these topics are at your fingertips. Move on to the next topics and maintain this momentum.
76-90% Very Good !	You have a good command over these topics. Revise these topics again after a few days and enhance your performance.
60-75% Good !	You have a wide scope to learn for these topics. Revise these topics again.
<60% Not Satisfactory!	You have a long way ahead of you to master these topics. Revise it thoroughly.

Test 3

Syllabus
- Salient Features and Classification of Chordata (upto Classes Level)

For deeper insight, **Scan the QR Code**

Important Instructions
- The test is of 30 minutes duration and contains 25 Multiple Choice Questions (four options with a single correct answer).
- Choose the correct option and fill the OMR given on the last page of this test accordingly.
- At some instances, you may find more than 1 option to be correct. In such circumstances, you have to judge the most appropriate answer as per the conditions given in the question.

1. Dry, cornified skin and epidermal scales are found in
(a) *Chelone* and *Testudo*
(b) *Hyla* and *Vipera*
(c) *Psittacula* and *Aptenodytes*
(d) *Macropus* and *Balaenoptera*

2. Which of the following is incorrect regarding protochordates?
(a) They include Urochordata and Cephalochordata
(b) They are exclusively marine
(c) Organisms like *Branchiostoma* possess notochord throughout their life
(d) They have a dorsal muscular heart

3. Few marine animals migrate to freshwater for spawning, these belong to
(a) Chondrichthyes
(b) Osteichthyes
(c) Cyclostomata
(d) Reptilia

4. Which of the following is not a characteristics of Aves?
(a) Presence of feathers, wings and beak
(b) Fully ossified endoskeleton with pneumatic bones
(c) Completely four-chambered heart
(d) Lack the capacity to regulate their body temperature

5. Given below are two statements; one is labelled as Assertion (A) and the other is labelled as Reason (R).

Assertion (A) Both *Pteropus* and *Balaenoptera* are classified as mammals.

Reason (R) Both *Pteropus* and *Balaenoptera* have four-chambered heart.

In the light of the above statements, choose the correct answer from the options given below.
(a) A is false, but R is true
(b) Both A and R are true and R is the correct explanation of A
(c) Both A and R are true, but R is not the correct explanation of A
(d) A is true, but R is false

6. Which of the following statement is incorrect about the occurrence of notochord?
(a) It is present only in larval tail of *Ascidian*.
(b) It is replaced by a vertebral column in adult form.
(c) It is absent throughout the life of humans from the very beginning.
(d) It is present throughout life in amphioxus.

7. Select the incorrect statement about amphibians?
(a) Body is divisible into head and trunk, while tail may be present in some
(b) Eyes have eyelids and tympanum represents the ear
(c) Oviparous animals with external fertilisation and indirect development
(d) Mode of locomotion is creeping or crawling

8. Given below are two statements regarding cartilaginous fishes.

Statement I Sexual dimorphism is absent.

Statement II The urinogenital and anal aperture is common.

In the light of the above statements, choose the correct answer from the options given below.
(a) Statement I is incorrect, but statement II is correct
(b) Both statement I and statement II are correct
(c) Both statement I and statement II are incorrect
(d) Statement I is correct, but statement II is incorrect

9. A fish 'X' have an elongated body bearing 6-15 pairs of gill slits. Its cranium and vertebral column are made up of cartilage. These fishes have closed type of circulation. The fish 'X' is
(a) *Pterophyllum*
(b) *Ichthyophis*
(c) *Myxine*
(d) *Clarias*

10. Identify the correct statement with respect to structures marked as *X* and *Y* in the diagram given below.

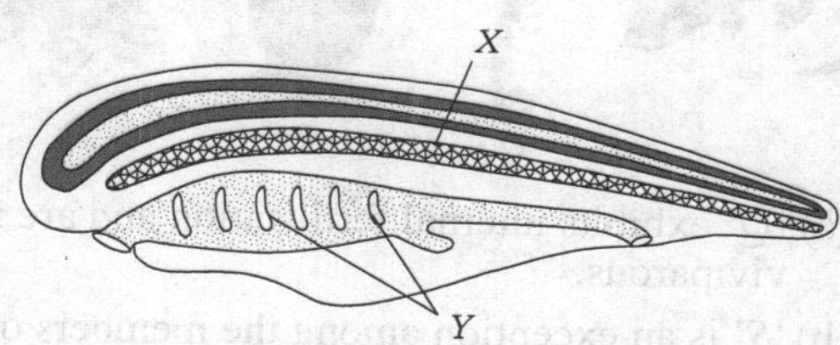

(a) Both *X* and *Y* are present throughout the life in Urochordate.
(b) Both *X* and *Y* take part in circulation of water for respiration.
(c) In vertebrates, *X* is replaced by a cartilaginous or bony vertebral column in adults and *Y* occurs only in embryonic stages in higher chordates.
(d) *X* may be present in few non-chordates, but *Y* is completely absent in them.

11. Match List I with List II.

	List I		List II
A.	*Torpedo*	1.	Poison sting
B.	*Scoliodon*	2.	Electric organs
C.	*Trygon*	3.	Dog fish
D.	*Pristis*	4.	Saw fish

Choose the correct answer from the options given below.

	A	B	C	D
(a)	2	1	4	3
(b)	2	3	1	4
(c)	1	4	2	3
(d)	1	3	2	4

12. Members of Chondrichthyes differ from members of Osteichthyes primarily in having

(a) monocondylic skull and well-developed nictitating membrane.

(b) placoid scales and gill slit without operculum

(c) paired and unpaired fins.

(d) mesonephric kidneys and two-chambered heart.

13. Identify the correct statement with respect to the animals given below.

(a) '*Q*' exhibits internal fertilisation and are mostly viviparous.

(b) '*S*' is an exception among the members of its class.

(c) '*P*' and '*R*' both belong to same class of super class–Tetrapoda.

(d) The bodies of *Q* and *R* are covered with dry and cornified skin.

14. Given below are two statements.

Statement I *Exocoetus* can stay at their current water depth without expending energy in swimming.

Statement II Some members of class–Reptilia shed their skin as it is an important process for their growth.

In light of the above statements, choose the correct answer from the options given below.

(a) Statement I is incorrect, but statement II is correct

(b) Both statement I and statement II are correct

(c) Both statement I and statement II are incorrect

(d) Statement I is correct, but statement II is incorrect

15. Which of the following are correct regarding Osteichthyes?

I. They include both marine and freshwater fishes with bony endoskeleton.

II. Air bladder is present.

III. They are also called cartilaginous fishes.

IV. They include sharks, rays and cat fishes.

Choose the correct answer from the options given below.

(a) I and II
(b) II, III and IV
(c) II and IV
(d) I and III

16. Which of the following do not have a cartilaginous vertebral column?

I. *Petromyzon*
II. *Ascidia*
III. *Branchiostoma*
IV. *Myxine*

Choose the correct answer from the options given below.

(a) I only
(b) I and IV
(c) II and III
(d) III only

17. Consider the following statements about amphioxus.

I. Larvae undergo metamorphosis to form adults.

II. Ciliary beating action is required to filter feed.

III. Circulation is of open type.

IV. Protonephridia are the excretory organs.

Choose the incorrect statement from the options given below.

(a) IV only
(b) I only
(c) IV only
(d) III only

18. Given below are two statements; one is labelled as Assertion (A) and the other is labelled as Reason (R).

Assertion (A) Lampreys have a sucking circular mouth without teeth.

Reason (R) Cyclostomes are ectoparasites on some fishes in the ocean.

In the light of the above statements, choose the correct answer from the options given below.

(a) A is false, but R is true

(b) Both A and R are true and R is the correct explanation of A

(c) Both A and R are true, but R is not the correct explanation of A

(d) A is true, but R is false

19. If claspers are incised out from the pelvic fins of male sharks, which of the following would be affected?

(a) Excretion (b) Respiration
(c) Fertilisation (d) Spermatogenesis

20. Following are certain characteristic features.

I. Persistent notochord
II. Presence of placoid scales
III. Absence of operculum
IV. Absence of buoyancy organ

Choose the group of organisms that represents all the characteristics.

(a) *Hippocampus, Trygon, Torpedo*
(b) *Betta, Pterophyllum, Rohu*
(c) *Exocoetus, Pristis, Trygon*
(d) *Pristis, Scoliodon, Torpedo*

21. Given below are two statements.

Statement I *Bufo* has a common passage for urine and sperms.

Statement II Moist skin facilitates gas exchange in tadpoles.

In the light of the above statements, choose the correct answer from the options given below.

(a) Statement I is incorrect, but statement II is correct
(b) Both statement I and statement II are correct
(c) Both statement I and statement II are incorrect
(d) Statement I is correct, but statement II is incorrect

22. Consider the following statements with respect to amphibians and reptiles.

I. Snake-like movement is observed in *Ichthyophis*.
II. Pinnae are absent in both *Hemidactylus* and *Hyla*.
III. Both amphibians and reptiles have the same mode of fertilisation.
IV. Two auricles and one ventricle gives rise to poikilothermy.

Choose the incorrect answer from the options given below.

(a) II only (b) II and III
(c) III only (d) I and IV

23. Given below are two statements; one is labelled as Assertion (A) and the other is labelled as Reason (R).

Assertion (A) Oil glands are epidermal glands located at the base of tail in Aves.

Reason (R) Oil is secreted all throughout the epidermal body surface of birds.

In the light of the above statements, choose the correct answer from the options given below.

(a) A is false, but R is true
(b) Both A and R are true and R is the correct explanation of A
(c) Both A and R are true, but R is not the correct explanation of A
(d) A is true, but R is false

24. Match List I with List II

	List I		List II
A.	*Aptenodytes*	1.	Scutes
B.	*Bangarus*	2.	Gizzard
C.	*Platypus*	3.	Cloaca
D.	*Rana*	4.	Oviparous

Choose the correct answer from the option given below.

	A	B	C	D
(a)	2	1	4	3
(b)	4	3	2	1
(c)	1	2	4	3
(d)	1	4	3	2

25. Given below are two statements.

Statement I Hair in mammals are an adaptation towards cold.

Statement II Air sacs increase energy load by unidirectional air flow in birds.

In the light of the above statements, choose the correct answer from the options given below.

(a) Statement I is incorrect, but statement II is correct
(b) Both statement I and statement II are correct
(c) Both statement I and statement II are incorrect
(d) Statement I is correct, but statement II is incorrect

■ **Response Index**

01	ⓐ	ⓑ	ⓒ	ⓓ	10	ⓐ	ⓑ	ⓒ	ⓓ	19	ⓐ	ⓑ	ⓒ	ⓓ
02	ⓐ	ⓑ	ⓒ	ⓓ	11	ⓐ	ⓑ	ⓒ	ⓓ	20	ⓐ	ⓑ	ⓒ	ⓓ
03	ⓐ	ⓑ	ⓒ	ⓓ	12	ⓐ	ⓑ	ⓒ	ⓓ	21	ⓐ	ⓑ	ⓒ	ⓓ
04	ⓐ	ⓑ	ⓒ	ⓓ	13	ⓐ	ⓑ	ⓒ	ⓓ	22	ⓐ	ⓑ	ⓒ	ⓓ
05	ⓐ	ⓑ	ⓒ	ⓓ	14	ⓐ	ⓑ	ⓒ	ⓓ	23	ⓐ	ⓑ	ⓒ	ⓓ
06	ⓐ	ⓑ	ⓒ	ⓓ	15	ⓐ	ⓑ	ⓒ	ⓓ	24	ⓐ	ⓑ	ⓒ	ⓓ
07	ⓐ	ⓑ	ⓒ	ⓓ	16	ⓐ	ⓑ	ⓒ	ⓓ	25	ⓐ	ⓑ	ⓒ	ⓓ
08	ⓐ	ⓑ	ⓒ	ⓓ	17	ⓐ	ⓑ	ⓒ	ⓓ					
09	ⓐ	ⓑ	ⓒ	ⓓ	18	ⓐ	ⓑ	ⓒ	ⓓ					

■ **Performance Scanner**

> 90% Excellent !	You have mastered these topics. The concepts of these topics are at your fingertips. Move on to the next topics and maintain this momentum.
76-90% Very Good !	You have a good command over these topics. Revise these topics again after a few days and enhance your performance.
60-75% Good !	You have a wide scope to learn for these topics. Revise these topics again.
<60% Not Satisfactory!	You have a long way ahead of you to master these topics. Revise it thoroughly.

Chapter Break Thru

Syllabus

- Salient Features and Classification of Animals-Non-chordates upto Phyla Level and Chordate upto Classes Level

Important Instructions

- The test is of 1 hour duration and contains 30 Multiple-Choice Questions (Four options with a single correct answer).
- Choose the correct option and fill the OMR given on the last page of this test accordingly.
- At some instances, you may find more than 1 option to be correct. In such circumstances, you have to judge the most appropriate answer as per the conditions given in the question.

1. A lizard-like member of Reptilia is sitting on a tree with its tail coiled around a twig. This animal could be

(a) *Chamaeleon* showing protective colouration.
(b) *Vipera* showing mimicry.
(c) Garden lizard (*Calotes*) showing camouflage.
(d) *Hemidactylus* showing sexual diamorphism.

2. Given below are two statements; one is labelled as Assertion (A) and the other is labelled as Reason (R).

Assertion (A) Annelids show metameric segmentation.

Reason (R) In annelids, external segmentation is absent, but an internal segmentation does occur.

In the light of the above statements, choose the correct answer from the options given below.

(a) A is false, but R is true.
(b) Both A and R are true and R is the correct explanation of A.
(c) Both A and R are ture, but R is not the correct explanation of A.
(d) A is true, but R is false.

3. Match List I with List II.

	List I		List II
A.	Malpighian tubules	1.	*Hirudinaria*
B.	Nephridia	2.	*Laccifer*
C.	Proboscis	3.	*Fasciola*
D	Flame cells	4.	*Balanoglossus*

Choose the correct answer from the options given below.

	A	B	C	D		A	B	C	D
(a)	1	2	4	3	(b)	2	1	3	4
(c)	2	1	4	3	(d)	1	2	3	4

4. Choose the correct option from the following with respect to the given diagrams.

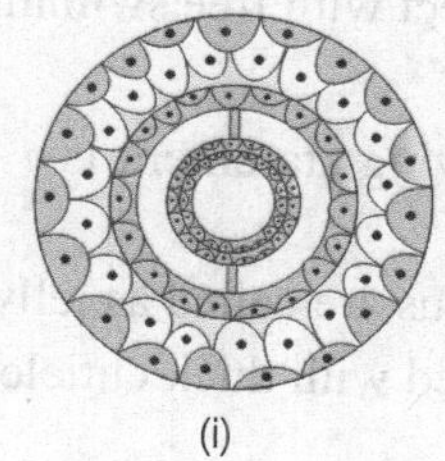
(i)

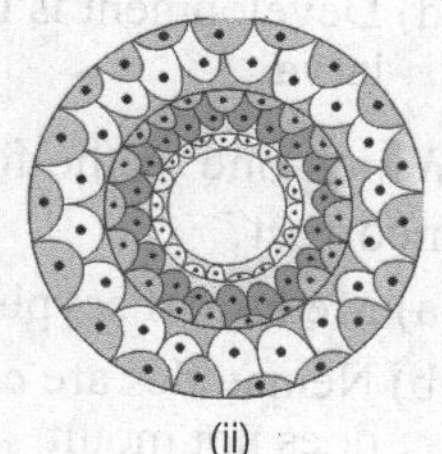
(ii)

(a) (i) *Sycon*, (ii) *Pennatula*
(b) (i) *Chaetopleura*, (ii) *Ophiura*
(c) (i) *Hirudinaria*, (ii) *Limulus*
(d) (i) *Loligo*, (ii) *Ctenoplana*

5. Which statement among the following is incorrect regarding the characteristics of different animal phyla?
(a) *Nereis* is monoecious, while *Pheretima* and *Hirudinaria* are dioecious.
(b) Coelenterates exhibit a relatively simple arrangement of cells.
(c) Simple and compound eyes are present in the phylum whose species comprising over two-thirds of all named species on earth, are primarily arthropods.
(d) Platyhelminthes have an incomplete digestive system.

6. Given below are two statements.
Statement I Some marine sponges have poisonous capsule which keep predators away from them.
Statement II Sponges have a special canal system in their body which facilitate the free water entry and exit.
In the light of above statements, choose the correct answer from the options given below.
(a) Statement I is incorrect, but statement II is correct.
(b) Both statement I and statement II are correct.
(c) Both statement I and statement II are incorrect.
(d) Statement I is correct, but statement II is incorrect.

7. Given below are two statements.
Statement I *Gorgonia* have a central gastrovascular cavity with mouth or hypostome.
Statement II Between hump and mantle, feather like gills are present in *Pinctada*.
In the light of above statements, choose the correct answer from the options given below.
(a) Statement I is incorrect, but statement II is correct
(b) Both statement I and statement II are correct
(c) Both statement I and statement II are incorrect
(d) Statement I is correct, but statement II is incorrect

8. Match List I with List II.

	List I	List II
A.	*Physalia*	1. Sea anemone
B.	*Adamsia*	2. Sea pen
C.	*Meandrina*	3. Brain coral
D.	*Pennatula*	4. Portuguese man-of-wear

Choose the correct answer from the options given below.

	A	B	C	D		A	B	C	D
(a)	1	4	3	2	(b)	4	2	1	3
(c)	4	1	3	2	(d)	1	2	3	4

9. In which pair of animal, mesoderm is present as scattered pouches in between the ectoderm and endoderm?
(a) *Taenia* and *Pleurobrachia*
(b) *Ancylostoma* and *Ascaris*
(c) *Nereis* and *Hirudinaria*
(d) *Chaetopleura* and *Dentalium*

10. Through which sequence does the water flow in Porifera?
(a) Spongocoel → Ostia → Osculum → Exterior
(b) Osculum → Ostia → Spongocoel → Exterior
(c) Osculum → Spongocoel → Ostia → Exterior
(d) Ostia → Spongocoel → Osculum → Exterior

11. Given below are the two statements.
Statement I Amphibia, Reptilia, Aves, Pisces, and Mammalia all grouped under Tetrapoda.
Statement II Aschelminthes are pseudocoelomates and include parasitic as well as non-parasitic round worms.

In the light of above statements, choose the correct answer from the options given below.
(a) Statement I is incorrect, but statement II is correct
(b) Both statement I and statement II are correct
(c) Both statement I and statement II are incorrect
(d) Statement I is correct, but statement II is incorrect

12. Identify the incorrect match from the following.
(a) Platyhelminthes - Triploblastic
(b) Molluscs - Radial symmetry in adults
(c) Coelenterates - Radial symmetry
(d) Ctenophores - Diploblastic

13. Which of the following echinoderm normally remains attached to substratum?
(a) *Echinus* (b) *Cucumaria*
(c) *Antedon* (d) *Ophiura*

14. Match List I with List II.

List I		List II	
A.	*Ascidia*	1.	Bilateral symmetry of larvae is lost to radial pentamerous symmetry.
B.	*Branchiostoma*	2.	Sac-like body and lack appendages.
C.	*Ophiura*	3.	Sexes are separate
D.	*Balanoglossus*	4.	Notochord extends from head to tail

Choose the correct answer from the options given below.

	A	B	C	D		A	B	C	D
(a)	2	4	1	3	(b)	3	2	4	1
(c)	1	3	2	4	(d)	1	2	3	4

15. Given below are two statements.
Statement I *Lancelets* are primitive vertebrates resembling fish, lacking jaws.
Statement II *Lancelets* possess a notochord, tubular nerve cord and pharyngeal gill slits throughout their entire life.
In the light of above statements, choose the correct answer from the options given below.
(a) Statement I is incorrect, but statement II is correct
(b) Both statement I and statement II are correct
(c) Both statement I and statement II are incorrect
(d) Statement I is in correct, but statement II is incorrect

16. Select the incorrect statement with respect to Echinodermata.
(a) These possess an endoskeleton of calcareous ossicles.
(b) Body is cylindrical comprising of proboscis, a collar and a long trunk.
(c) These do not possess excretory system.
(d) Development is indirect with free swimming larva.

17. Which one of the following statement is incorrect?
(a) Medusa of scyphozoans are called as jelly fishes.
(b) Nematodes are covered with thick cuticle that does not moult.
(c) Flat worm that have a digestive cavity, with an incomplete gut.
(d) Ctenophores are the largest animals that move with the help of cilia.

18. Given below are two statements; one is labelled as Assertion (A) and the other is labelled as Reason (R).
Assertion (A) The duck-billed *Platypus* and the spiny anteater are classified as mammals despite being egg-laying animals.
Reason (R) Both species possess seven cervical vertebrae and 12 pairs of cranial nerves.
In the light of the above statements, choose the correct answer from the options given below.
(a) A is false, but R is true
(b) Both A and R are true and R is the correct explanation of A
(c) Both A and R are true, but R is not the correct explanation of A
(d) A is true, but R is false

19. Given below are the two figures. Select the correct option with respect to these figures.

(a) (*Q*) produces (*P*) asexually and (*P*) forms (*Q*) sexually.
(b) (*P*) produces (*Q*) asexually and (*Q*) forms (*P*) sexually

(c) (*P*) and (*Q*) are false swimming forms.
(d) (*P*) and (*Q*) are sessile form.

20. What is not common between *Carcharodon* and *Exocoetus*?
(a) They are marine animals
(b) They are cold-blooded animals
(c) They have a two-chambered heart
(d) They have internal fertilisation.

21. Consider the following statements about Annelida.
I. Movement is associated with the longitudinal and circular muscles.
II. Parapodia are locomotory organs.
III. Nephridia help to maintain the ion balance of the body.
IV. All members are monoecious.
Choose the incorrect statement(s) from the options given below.
(a) Only II (b) I and IV
(c) Only IV (d) III and IV

22. Which of the following animal possesses hooks and suckers?

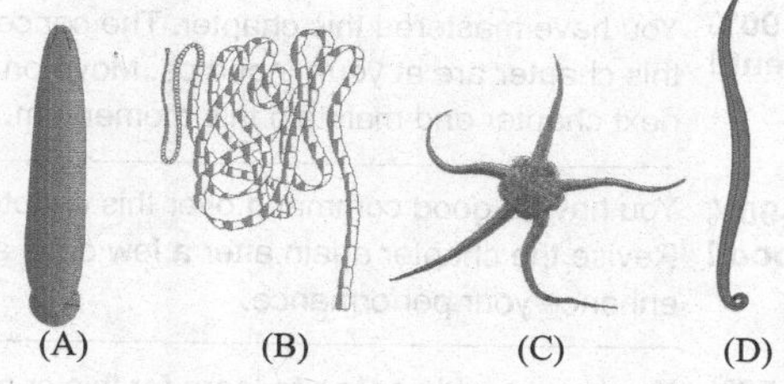

(a) A (b) B
(c) C (d) D

23. Presence of four pairs of gills and cycloid scales are seen in
(a) *Labeo* (b) *Myxine*
(c) *Carcharodon* (d) *Petromyzon*

24. How many of the examples mentioned below possess closed (C) and open (O) circulatory system.
Molluscas, Tunicates, Hemichordata, Annelids, Chordates, Arthropods.
(a) C – 2, O – 4
(b) C – 3, O – 3
(c) C – 4, O – 2
(d) C – 5, O – 1

25. Which characteristic does not apply to the following animal?

(a) Eyes lacking eyelids.
(b) Dioecious with external fertilisation, oviparous, and indirect development.
(c) Alimentary canal, urinary and reproductive tract open into a common chamber.
(d) Exchange of gases takes place through skin, gills and lungs.

26. Given below are two statements, one is labelled as Assertion (A) and the other is labelled as Reason (R).
Assertion (A) Arthropods locomotion is more rapid and efficient than other invertebrates.
Reason (R) In arthropods, exoskeleton is found that help in locomotion.
In the light of the above statements, choose the correct answer from the options given below.
(a) A is false, but R is true.
(b) Both A and R are true and R is the correct explanation of A.
(c) Both A and R are true, but R is not the correct explanation of A.
(d) A is true, but R is false.

27. Which of the following pair does not correctly match the genus name with its two defining characteristics and phylum?

	Genus name	Two characters	Phylum
A.	*Pila*	(i) Body segmented; Mouth with radula	Mollusca
B.	*Asterias*	(ii) Spiny skinned; Water vascular system	Echinodermata

C.	*Sycon*	(iii) Pore bearing; Canal system	Porifera
D.	*Periplaneta*	(iv) Jointed appendages; Chitinous exokeleton	Arthropoda

(a) A (b) B
(c) C (d) D

28. Given below are two statements.

Statement I Bioluminescence is present in *Ctenoplana* and *Pleurobrachia*.

Statement II *Bombyx* and *Limulus* have unsegmented body covered with a calcareous shell.

In the light of the above statements, choose the correct answer from the options given below.

(a) Statement I is incorrect, but statement II is correct.
(b) Both statement I and statement II are correct.
(c) Both statement I and statement II are incorrect.
(d) Statement I is correct, but statement II is incorrect.

29. Given below are two statements; one is labelled as Assertion (A) and other is labelled as Reason (R).

Assertion (A) Haemocoel in Arthropoda is not lined by the mesodermal epithelium.

Reason (R) Arthropods possess only true coelom.

In the light of the above statements, choose the correct answer from the options given below.

(a) A is false, but R is true.
(b) Both A and R are true and R is the correct explanation of A.
(c) Both A and R are true, but R is not the correct explanation of A.
(d) A is true, but R is false.

30. Identify the set of insects that includes beneficial species.

(a) *Laccifer*, *Bombyx* and *Apis*
(b) *Apis*, *Locusta* and *Limulus*
(c) *Aedes*, *Locusta* and *Bombyx*
(d) *Bombyx*, *Laccifer* and *Culex*

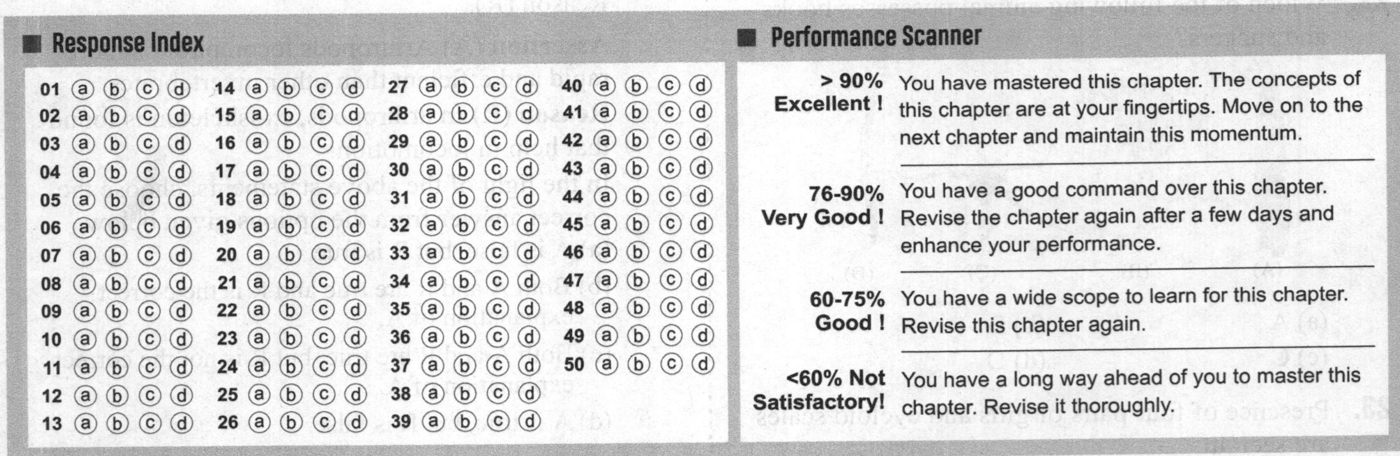

Scan for online chapter test

Scan for online unit test

Test Booklet No. 3947305

Test Booklet Code CH5

Morphology of Flowering Plants

Topics Covered

Morphology of Roots, Stems and Leaves

Flower, Fruits and Seeds

Angiospermic Families

Important Instructions

- This Booklet Contains – Three Topic Tests and One Test on Complete Chapter.
- Each question carries 4 marks.
- For each correct response, the candidate will get 4 marks. And for every incorrect response, 1 mark will be additionally deducted from total score.
- Use **Blue/Black** point pen only for filling the OMR.
- Rough work is to be done in the space provided for this purpose in the test booklet only.

Name of the Candidate (In Capitals) ________________

Candidate's Signature ____________

Invigilator's Signature ____________

Facsimile signature stamp of center superintendent ____________

Do not open this booklet until you start attempting the test

Topical Follow Thru

Test 1

Syllabus Morphology and Modifications of Different Parts of Flowering Plants (Roots, Stems and Leaves)

For deeper insight, **Scan the QR Code**

Important Instructions

- The test is of 30 minutes duration and contains 15 Multiple Choice Questions (four options with a single correct answer).
- Choose the correct option and fill the OMR given on the last page of this test accordingly.
- At some instances, you may find more than 1 option to be correct. In such circumstances, you have to judge the most appropriate answer as per the conditions given in the question.

1. How many of the given plants have the tap root system?

Wheat, Grass, Mustard, *Monstera*, Banyan, Pea

(a) One (b) Two
(c) Three (d) Four

2. Identify the region of the root tip from the given diagram which possesses small-sized cell, with thin walls and dense protoplasm.

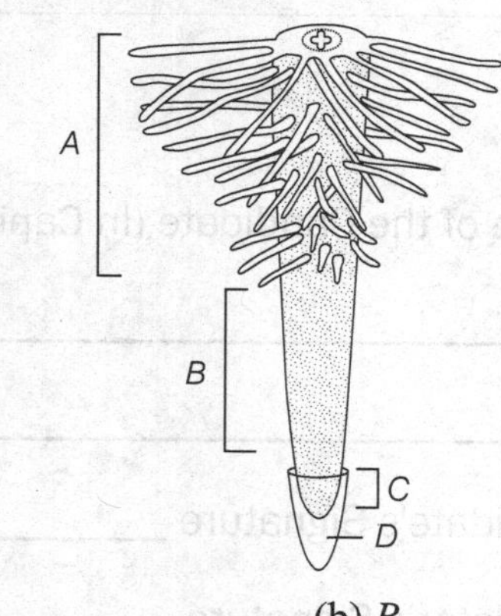

(a) *D* (b) *B*
(c) *A* (d) *C*

3. Which of the following is an aquatic plant in which stems are modified into a lateral branch with internodes and each node bears a rosette of leaves and tuft of roots?

(a) *Pistia* (b) *Aloe*
(c) *Agave* (d) *Colocacia*

4. Match List I with List II.

	List I		List II
A.	Neem	1.	Opposite phyllotaxy
B.	Mustard	2.	Pinnately compound leaf
C.	Guava	3.	Alternate phyllotaxy
D.	Silk cotton	4.	Palmately compound leaf

Choose the correct answer from the options given below.

	A	B	C	D		A	B	C	D
(a)	3	2	4	1	(b)	2	3	1	4
(c)	3	1	4	2	(d)	2	1	4	3

5. Given below are two statements; one is labelled as Assertion (A) and the other is labelled as Reason (R).

Assertion (A) Stems of *Opuntia* are modified into phylloclades.

Reason (R) Fleshy stems of *Opuntia* store water, so that the plants can grow even in dry soil.

In the light of the above statements, choose the correct answer from the options given below.

(a) A is false, but R is true
(b) Both A and R are true and R is the correct explanation of A
(c) Both A and R are true, but R is not the correct explanation of A
(d) A is true, but R is false

6. Choose the correct statements with respect to morphology of flowering plants.

I. Monocotyledonous plants typically have a tap root system with a dominant primary root.

II. In some dicotyledonous plants, adventitious roots arise from the base of the stem, forming a fibrous root system.

III. Adventitious roots can develop from various plant parts like stems, leaves, or even nodes.

IV. Wheat plants, with their fibrous root systems, are examples of dicotyledonous plants.

V. The banyan tree exhibits adventitious roots (aerial roots) that support its extensive canopy.

Choose the correct answer from the options given below.

(a) II, IV and V (b) III and V

(c) II, III and V (d) IV and V

7. Given below are two statements about stilt roots.

Statement I Maize and sugarcane have roots arising from the lower nodes of their stems, which contribute to the plant's stability.

Statement II These roots are the modifications of tap roots, extending deeper into the soil for better water and nutrient uptake.

In the light of the above statements, choose the correct answer from the options given below.

(a) Statement I is incorrect, but statement II is correct

(b) Both statement I and statement II are correct

(c) Both statement I and statement II are incorrect

(d) Statement I is correct, but statement II is incorrect

8. Match List I with List II.

	List I		List II
A.	*Pistia*	1.	Tendrils
B.	Cucumber	2.	Thorns
C.	*Citrus*	3.	Rhizome
D.	Ginger	4.	Offset

Choose the correct answer from the options given below.

	A	B	C	D
(a)	4	1	2	3
(b)	1	3	4	2
(c)	2	1	3	4
(d)	2	3	1	4

Direction For Q. no. 9-10

In each of the following question two statements are given; one is labelled as Assertion (A) and the other is labelled as Reason (R).

In the light of the given statements, choose the correct answer from the options given below.

(a) A is false, but R is true

(b) Both A and R are true and R is the correct explanation of A

(c) Both A and R are true, but R is not the correct explanation of A

(d) A is true, but R is false

9. **Assertion** (A) Removal of root cap will stop the growth of roots.

Reason (R) Root cap secretes substances that allow smooth penetration through soil.

10. **Assertion** (A) Water hyacinth can spread rapidly eliminating other species.

Reason (R) Water hyacinth bears a sub-aerial modification of stem.

11. Consider the following statements.

I. Runners are underground structures.

II. Both runners and stolons spread over a large area.

III. Stolons have photosynthetic activity.

IV. Stolons depends on mother plant for energy requirements.

Choose the correct answer from the options given below.

(a) I, III and IV (b) II and IV

(c) II and III (d) I and II

12. Which of the following region is responsible for the growth of the root in length?

(a) Region with active absorption of water and minerals

(b) Region proximal to the actively dividing region

(c) Region containing thin-walled cells with dense protoplasm

(d) Region bearing delicate, thread-like root hairs

13. Following is the figure of a particular type of leaf. Which of the following is correct with respect to the same?

(a) The common axis bearing leaflets is called the rachis.
(b) Incisions do not reach up to the midrib of lamina.
(c) This type of leaf is found in both neem and silk cotton.
(d) Axil of leaflets do not bear any bud.

Direction for Q.no. 14-15

In each of the following question two statements are given.

In the light of the given statements, choose the correct answer from the options given below.

(a) Statement I is incorrect, but statement II is correct
(b) Both statement I and statement II are correct
(c) Both statement I and statement II are incorrect
(d) Statement I is correct, but statement II is incorrect

14. **Statement I** Australian acacia lacks photosynthesis as leaves are inconspicuous.

Statement II Leaves can support other functions like support and defence in a plant.

15. **Statement I** Cutting down prop roots would not affect the plant since they are additional structures.

Statement II Prop roots are specialised adventitious roots that are present in many trees including banyan.

Response Index

01	a	b	c	d	10	a	b	c	d	19	a	b	c	d
02	a	b	c	d	11	a	b	c	d	20	a	b	c	d
03	a	b	c	d	12	a	b	c	d	21	a	b	c	d
04	a	b	c	d	13	a	b	c	d	22	a	b	c	d
05	a	b	c	d	14	a	b	c	d	23	a	b	c	d
06	a	b	c	d	15	a	b	c	d	24	a	b	c	d
07	a	b	c	d	16	a	b	c	d	25	a	b	c	d
08	a	b	c	d	17	a	b	c	d					
09	a	b	c	d	18	a	b	c	d					

Performance Scanner

> 90% Excellent !	You have mastered these topics. The concepts of these topics are at your fingertips. Move on to the next topics and maintain this momentum.
76-90% Very Good !	You have a good command over these topics. Revise these topics again after a few days and enhance your performance.
60-75% Good !	You have a wide scope to learn for these topics. Revise these topics again.
<60% Not Satisfactory!	You have a long way ahead of you to master these topics. Revise it thoroughly.

Test 2

Syllabus

- Inflorescence – Cymose and Racemose
- Flower, Fruit and Seed

For deeper insight, **Scan the QR Code**

Important Instructions

- The test is of 30 minutes duration and contains 25 Multiple Choice Questions (four options with a single correct answer).
- Choose the correct option and fill the OMR given on the last page of this test accordingly.
- At some instances, you may find more than 1 option to be correct. In such circumstances, you have to judge the most appropriate answer as per the conditions given in the question.

1. An example of zygomorphic flower with imbricate aestivation is

(a) mustard
(b) gulmohar
(c) *Hibiscus*
(d) banyan

2. In an inflorescence, where flowers develop sequentially from base to tip, which of the following best describes the position of the youngest floral bud?

(a) Proximal
(b) Distal
(c) Intercalary
(d) Anywhere on the axis

3. The aestivation in petals of bean and gulmohar can be shown respectively by.

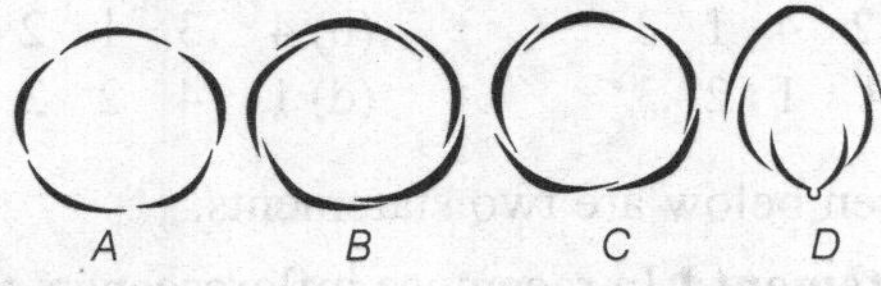

(a) *D* and *B* (b) *B* and *D*
(c) *C* and *D* (d) *D* and *C*

4. Which of the parts in the given section of fruit is edible?

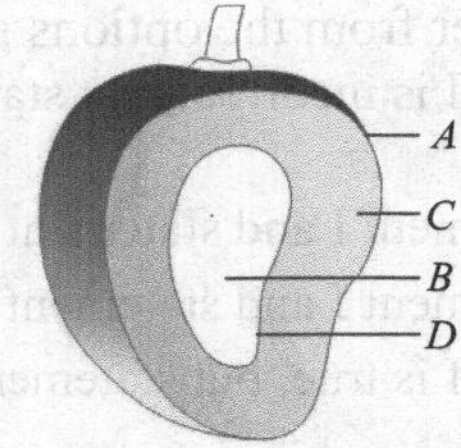

(a) *A*-Epicarp (b) *C*-Mesocarp
(c) *B*-Endocarp (d) *D*-Merocarp

5. Which of the following statements are correct?

I. In epipetalous condition, the cohesion occurs between sepals and the filament of the stamen.
II. In marginal placentation, the placenta forms a ridge along the ventral suture of the ovary.
III. Scutellum is a protective covering of plumule in grasses.
IV. In syncarpous conditions, carpels are fused.
V. Diadelphous condition is seen in pea.

Which of the following options is correct?
(a) II, III and IV
(b) I, II and IV
(c) II, III and V
(d) II, IV and V

Direction for Q.no. 6-7
In each of the following question two statements are given.
In the light of the given statements, choose the correct answer from the options given below.
(a) Statement I is incorrect, but statement II is correct
(b) Both statement I and statement II are correct
(c) Both statement I and statement II are incorrect
(d) Statement I is correct, but statement II is incorrect

6. **Statement I** In pea, the flowers can be divided into two equal halves in only one particular plane passing through the center.
Statement II Asymmetrical flowers are seen in mustard.

7. **Statement I** The margins are covered due to overlapping in valvate aestivation.
Statement II In mustard, the adjacent petals lie well apart from one another.

8. Given below are two statements; one is labelled as Assertion (A) and the other is labelled as Reason (R).
Assertion (A) Maize is an albuminous seed.
Reason (R) Endosperm is completely absorbed in maize seed by its growing embryo.
In the light of the above statements, choose the correct answer from the options given below.
(a) A is false, but R is true
(b) Both A and R are true and R is the correct explanation of A
(c) Both A and R are true, but R is not the correct explanation of A
(d) A is true, but R is false

9. Which of the following statement is correct?
(a) Floral axis continues to grow in cymose inflorescence.
(b) Flowers are borne laterally in cymose inflorescence.
(c) Young fruits are protected by flowers in cymose inflorescence.
(d) A shoot tip transforms into a flower and can be either solitary or a cyme.

10. Identify the correct statement regarding perigynous flowers.
(a) The thalamus is fused with the wall of the ovary.
(b) The gynoecium occupies the highest position.
(c) Parts of flowers except gynoecium are located on the rim of thalamus.
(d) The ovary is inferior and thalamus grows upward enclosing ovary.

11. Valvate type of aestivation of calyx is found in
I. Cotton II. *Calotropis*
III. *Cassia* IV. Lady's finger

Choose the correct option.

(a) I and IV (b) I and III
(c) II and IV (d) Only II

12. Which of the following placentation is found in *Argemone*?

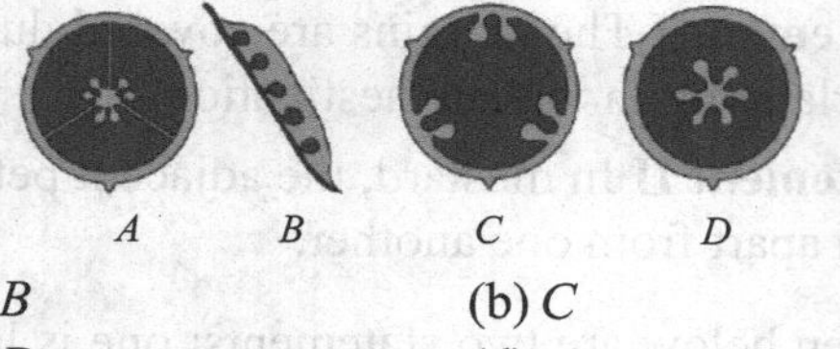

(a) *B* (b) *C*
(c) *D* (d) *A*

13. Given below are two statements.

Statement I Tegmen is thick, leathery and coloured.

Statement II Grain represents the fused pericarp and membranous testa.

In the light of the above statements, choose the correct answer from the options given below.

(a) Statement I is incorrect, but statement II is correct
(b) Both statement I and statement II are correct
(c) Both statement I and statement II are incorrect
(d) Statement I is correct, but statement II is incorrect

14. All statements are correct with reference to the given figure below, except

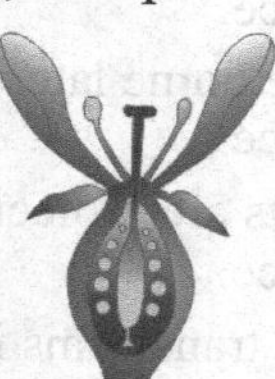

(a) the margin of thalamus grows upwards enclosing the ovary completely and getting fused with it
(b) ovary is said to be inferior
(c) the flower is said to be perigynous
(d) it is seen in the flowers of guava and cucumber

15. Match List I with List II.

	List I		List II
A.	*Hibiscus*	1.	Free central
B.	Pea	2.	Axile
C.	*Dianthus*	3.	Parietal
D.	*Brassica*	4.	Marginal

Choose the correct answer from the options given below.

	A	B	C	D		A	B	C	D
(a)	2	4	1	3	(b)	4	3	1	2
(c)	4	1	2	3	(d)	1	4	2	3

16. Given below are two statements.

Statement I In racemose inflorescence, the top flowers die faster than the bottom ones.

Statement II The terminal bud develops a terminal flower in racemose inflorescence.

In the light of the above statements, choose the correct answer from the options given below.

(a) Statement I is incorrect, but statement II is correct
(b) Both statement I and statement II are correct
(c) Both statement I and statement II are incorrrect
(d) Statement I is true, but statement II is incorrect

17. Consider the following statements.

I. *Hibiscus* is a complete flower.
II. Unisexual flowers can never be complete.
III. Essential whorls of a flower have supportive functions.
IV. Perianth is typical for flowers like lily.

Choose the incorrect statements from the following options.

(a) II and III (b) I only
(c) III only (d) I and IV

18. Which of the following is not a function of bracts?

(a) Provide protection to the inflorescence
(b) Perform photosynthesis
(c) Attract insects for pollination
(d) Support the primary foliage

19. Following is the image of the arrangement of the female whorl of flowers. Which of the pair given in the following options is correct?

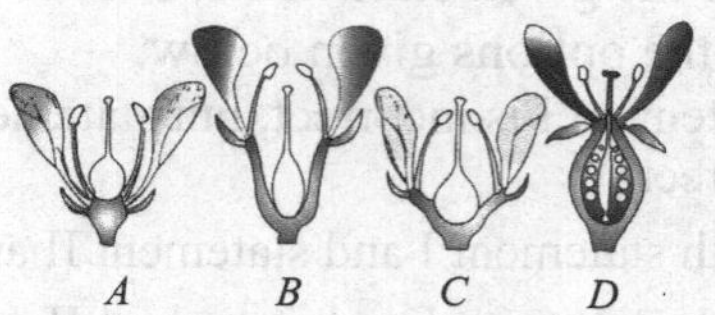

(a) *A* – Other whorls remain below the innermost whorl
(b) *B* – Ovary is at the centre, while stigma and style at the rim of base as in the ray florets of sunflower.

(c) *C* – Ovary is half inferior and observed in guava and cucumber

(d) *D* – Ovary is completely fused with sepals and is inferior

20. Which of the following are example of a gamosepalous flower having free petals?

(a) *Rosa* (b) *Hibiscus*

(c) *Datura* (d) *Camellia*

21. Match List I with List II.

	List I		List II
A.	Imbricate	1.	Non-overlapping sepals or petals
B.	Twisted	2.	Standard overlaps the two lateral petals
C.	Valvate	3.	Overlap at a single margin
D.	Vexillary	4.	Completely overlapped margins

Choose the correct answer from the options given below.

	A	B	C	D
(a)	4	3	1	2
(b)	1	3	4	2
(c)	4	2	1	3
(d)	1	4	2	3

Direction for Q. no. 22-23

In each of the following question two statements are given; one is labelled as Assertion (A) and the other is labelled as Reason (R).

In the light of the given statements, choose the correct answer from the options given below.

(a) A is false, but R is true

(b) Both A and R are true and R is the correct explanation of A

(c) Both A and R are true, but R is not the correct explanation of A

(d) A is true, but R is false

22. **Assertion** (A) The bisexual flowers with staminode can undergo only self-pollination.

Reason (R) *Hibiscus* flowers undergoes self-pollination.

23. **Assertion** (A) Pineapples are mostly propagated vegetatively.

Reason (R) Propagation through roots, stems or leaves occur asexually.

24. The number and arrangement of seeds in a fruit is dependent on which of the following feature of a plant?

(a) Inflorescence

(b) Aestivation

(c) Phyllotaxy

(d) Placentation

25. Consider the following statements.

I. Seeds absorb water and exchange gases through micropyle.

II. Seeds of beans, in the absence of endosperm, die at maturity.

III. In cereal grains, the pericarp remains fused with the seed coat.

IV. Radicle and plumule are enclosed within protective sheaths.

Choose the incorrect statement from the following options.

(a) II only (b) I only

(c) IV only (d) III only

Response Index

01	a	b	c	d	10	a	b	c	d	19	a	b	c	d
02	a	b	c	d	11	a	b	c	d	20	a	b	c	d
03	a	b	c	d	12	a	b	c	d	21	a	b	c	d
04	a	b	c	d	13	a	b	c	d	22	a	b	c	d
05	a	b	c	d	14	a	b	c	d	23	a	b	c	d
06	a	b	c	d	15	a	b	c	d	24	a	b	c	d
07	a	b	c	d	16	a	b	c	d	25	a	b	c	d
08	a	b	c	d	17	a	b	c	d					
09	a	b	c	d	18	a	b	c	d					

Performance Scanner

> 90% Excellent !	You have mastered these topics. The concepts of these topics are at your fingertips. Move on to the next topics and maintain this momentum.
76-90% Very Good !	You have a good command over these topics. Revise these topics again after a few days and enhance your performance.
60-75% Good !	You have a wide scope to learn for these topics. Revise these topics again.
<60% Not Satisfactory!	You have a long way ahead of you to master these topics. Revise it thoroughly.

Test 3

Syllabus
- Families (Malvaceae, Cruciferae, Gramineae, Leguminosae and Compositae)

For deeper insight, **Scan the QR Code**

Important Instructions

- The test is of 30 minutes duration and contains 15 Multiple Choice Questions (four options with a single correct answer).
- Choose the correct option and fill the OMR given on the last page of this test accordingly.
- At some instances, you may find more than 1 option to be correct. In such circumstances, you have to judge the most appropriate answer as per the conditions given in the question.

1. Which of the following is the correct floral formula of family-Fabaceae?

(a) $\% \ \text{⚥}\ K_{(5)}\widehat{C_{(5)}A_{(5)}}\ \underline{G}_{(2)}$

(b) $\oplus\ \text{⚥}\ K_{(5)}\widehat{C_{(5)}\ A_{3+3}}\ G_{(1)}$

(c) $\% \ \text{⚥}\ K_{(5)}\ C_{1+2+(2)}\ A_{(9)+1}\ \underline{G}_{1}$

(d) $\oplus\ \text{⚥}\ P_{3+3 \text{ or } (3+3)}\ A_{3+3}\ G_{(3)}$

2. Match List I with List II.

	List I		List II
A.	Lupin	1.	Fibres
B.	*Sesbania*	2.	Edible oil
C.	Sunhemp	3.	Fodder
D.	Soyabean	4.	Ornamentals

Choose the correct answer from the options given below.

	A	B	C	D
(a)	4	3	1	2
(b)	3	1	2	4
(c)	4	2	3	1
(d)	1	2	4	3

3. Plants with the given floral diagram

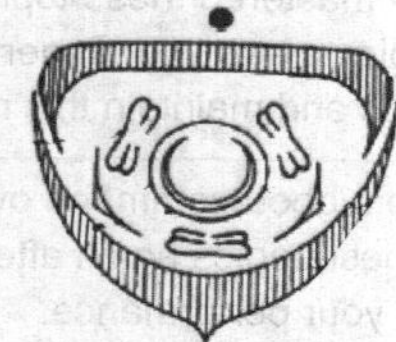

(a) provide medicine like mulaithi

(b) provide ornaments like jasmine

(c) provide cereals like rice

(d) provide fibres like cotton

4. The character of flower which is represented by floral formula, but not by floral diagram is

(a) placentation

(b) number of sepals and petals

(c) adhesion of stamen

(d) position of gynoecium

5. Consider the following plants. *Hibiscus*, *Brassica*, Sunhemp, Cotton, *Bambusa* and *Triticum*. Select the correct number of plant families to which they belong.

(a) 4 families (b) 6 families

(c) 2 families (d) 3 families

6. Select the correct match from the following.

(a) Siliqua – Lady's finger

(b) Capsule – Soybean

(c) Cypsela – *Chrysanthemum*

(d) Caryopsis – *Indigofera*

7. Identify the floral formula of disc florets of sunflower.

(a) $Br\ \oplus\ \text{⚥}\ K_{(Pappus)}\widehat{C_{5}\ A_{5}}\ \overline{G}_{(2)}$

(b) $Br\ \oplus\ \text{⚥}\ K_{5(Pappus)}C_{(5)}\ A_{(5)}\ G_{(2)}$

(c) $Br\ \oplus\ \text{⚥}\ K_{1(Pappus)}C_{5}\ A_{(0)}\ G_{(2)}$

(d) $Br\ \%\ \text{⚥}\ K_{(Pappus)}\widehat{C_{5}\ A_{(5)}}\ \underline{G}_{(2)}$

8. Which of the following is characteristic feature of Cruciferae?

(a) Sepals and petal free, cruciform calyx, didynamous androecium, monocarpellary, gynoecium, siliqua fruit

(b) Sepals and petals free, cruciform corolla, tetradynamous androecium, bicarpellary, siliqua fruit
(c) Actinomorphic flower (generally) hypogynous flower, superior ovary, parietal placentation, 10 stamens in two groups
(d) Ebracteate, actinomorphic (rarely) flower, cruciform aestivation, tetramerous flower, siliqua fruit

9. Consider the given floral diagram.

Which of the following floral formula correctly represents the given floral diagram?

(a) $Br \oplus ⚥ Epi_{3\text{-}9}\ K_{5 \text{ or } (5)}\ \overparen{C_5\ A_{(\infty)}}\ \underline{G}_{(2\text{-}\infty)}$
(b) $Br \oplus ⚥ Epi_{3\text{-}6}\ K_5\ C_5\ A_{(\infty)}\ \underline{G}_{(2\text{-}\infty)}$
(c) $Br \oplus ⚥ Epi_{2\text{-}8}\ K_{5 \text{ or } (5)}\ \overparen{C_5\ A_{\infty}}\ \underline{G}_{(2)}$
(d) $Br \oplus ⚥ Epi_{3\text{-}9}\ K_{5 \text{ or } (5)}\ \overparen{C\ A_{(\infty)}}\ \underline{G}_{(2\text{-}\infty)}$

10. A bisexual, bracteate, actinomorphic, complete, pentamerous, hypogynous flower might be found in the plant of
(a) cotton (b) mustard
(c) gram (d) sunflower

11. Which of the following is not related to family-Brassicaceae?
(a) Parietal placentation
(b) Variation in length of stamen
(c) Alternate phyllotaxy
(d) Perigynous flower

12. Consider the following features.
I. Flowers are zygomorphic and complete.
II. Flowers have cymose inflorescence.
III. Syncarpous with inferior ovary.
IV. Diadelphous with ten stamens

Which of the given floral features are correct about leguminosae family?
(a) I only (b) II and IV
(c) III only (d) I and IV

13. The partial floral formula of a flower is

$$K_{(5)}\,C_5\,A_{\infty}\,\underline{G}_{(5)}$$

Which of the following set of information is conveyed here?
(a) Gamosepalous, polypetalous, syncarpous and superior ovary
(b) Polysepalous, polypetalous, syncarpous and half-inferior ovary
(c) Gamosepalous, gamopetalous, polycarpous and superior ovary
(d) Gamosepalous, polypetalous, syncarpous and inferior ovary

14. Given below are two statements.
Statement I Perianth is present in family-Poaceae.
Statement II Perianth is a non-reproductive structure formed by fusion of sepals and petals.
In the light of the above statements, choose the correct answer from the options given below.
(a) Statement I is incorrect, but statement II is correct
(b) Both statement I and statement II are correct
(c) Both statement I and statement II are incorrrect
(d) Statement I is true, but statement II is incorrect

15. Following is the floral formula of a particular plant family. Which of the following group contains flowers belonging to this family denoted by the given floral formula?

$$Ebr \oplus ⚥\ K_{2+2}\ C_0\ A_{2+4}\ \underline{G}_{(2)}$$

(a) Sugarcane, Marigold, Radish, Mallow
(b) Mallow, Marigold, Turnip, Radish
(c) Turnip, Radish, Cabbage, Broccoli
(d) Broccoli, Tomato, Brinjal, Radish

■ **Response Index**

01	ⓐ	ⓑ	ⓒ	ⓓ	10	ⓐ	ⓑ	ⓒ	ⓓ	19	ⓐ	ⓑ	ⓒ	ⓓ
02	ⓐ	ⓑ	ⓒ	ⓓ	11	ⓐ	ⓑ	ⓒ	ⓓ	20	ⓐ	ⓑ	ⓒ	ⓓ
03	ⓐ	ⓑ	ⓒ	ⓓ	12	ⓐ	ⓑ	ⓒ	ⓓ	21	ⓐ	ⓑ	ⓒ	ⓓ
04	ⓐ	ⓑ	ⓒ	ⓓ	13	ⓐ	ⓑ	ⓒ	ⓓ	22	ⓐ	ⓑ	ⓒ	ⓓ
05	ⓐ	ⓑ	ⓒ	ⓓ	14	ⓐ	ⓑ	ⓒ	ⓓ	23	ⓐ	ⓑ	ⓒ	ⓓ
06	ⓐ	ⓑ	ⓒ	ⓓ	15	ⓐ	ⓑ	ⓒ	ⓓ	24	ⓐ	ⓑ	ⓒ	ⓓ
07	ⓐ	ⓑ	ⓒ	ⓓ	16	ⓐ	ⓑ	ⓒ	ⓓ	25	ⓐ	ⓑ	ⓒ	ⓓ
08	ⓐ	ⓑ	ⓒ	ⓓ	17	ⓐ	ⓑ	ⓒ	ⓓ					
09	ⓐ	ⓑ	ⓒ	ⓓ	18	ⓐ	ⓑ	ⓒ	ⓓ					

■ **Performance Scanner**

> 90% Excellent !	You have mastered these topics. The concepts of these topics are at your fingertips. Move on to the next topics and maintain this momentum.
76-90% Very Good !	You have a good command over these topics. Revise these topics again after a few days and enhance your performance.
60-75% Good !	You have a wide scope to learn for these topics. Revise these topics again.
<60% Not Satisfactory!	You have a long way ahead of you to master these topics. Revise it thoroughly.

Chapter Break Thru

Syllabus	• Morphology and Modifications of Different Parts of Flowering Plants (Roots, Stems and Leaves)	• Inflorescence – Cymose and Racemose • Flower, Fruit and Seed	• Families (Malvaceae, Leguminosae, Cruciferae, Compositae, Gramineae)

Important Instructions

- The test is of 1 hour duration and contains 50 Multiple-Choice Questions (Four options with a single correct answer).
- Choose the correct option and fill the OMR given on the last page of this test accordingly.
- At some instances, you may find more than 1 option to be correct. In such circumstances, you have to judge the most appropriate answer as per the conditions given in the question.

1. Which of the following option does not belong to monocot roots?

(a) Presence of fibrous root system
(b) Short-lived primary root
(c) Presence of secondary roots
(d) Origination of root from the base of the stem

2. Which part of the root is the most active in the absorption of water?

(a) Maturation zone (b) Root cap
(c) Meristematic zone (d) Zone of elongation

Direction for Q. no. 3-4

In each of the following question two statements are given.

In the light of the given statements, choose the correct answer from the options given below.

(a) Statement I is incorrect, but statement II is correct
(b) Both statement I and statement II are correct
(c) Both statement I and statement II are incorrect
(d) Statement I is correct, but statement II is incorrect

3. **Statement I** Flowers without a calyx have an epicalyx as a substitute structure.

Statement II A flower's floral appendages are classified as trimerous, tetramerous or pentamerous when they occur in multiples of 3, 4, or 5, respectively.

4. **Statement I** The plumule and radicle are enclosed in sheaths called coleorhiza and coleoptile, respectively.

Statement II Pericarp may be dry or fleshy.

5. The adventitious roots are present in

(a) grass, *Monstera* and banyan tree
(b) wheat, *Mangifera* and banyan tree
(c) wheat, *Monstera* and banyan tree
(d) grass, *Mangifera* and banyan tree

6. The stem develops from the plumule of a germinating seed and consists of nodes and internodes. Which of the following correctly describes the primary function of nodes on a stem?
(a) They are the portions between two internodes
(b) They bear branches and flowers, but not leaves
(c) They are the regions where leaves are borne
(d) They are the regions where buds are absent

7. Which of the following statement is incorrect about stem?
(a) Rhizome is an underground stem that grows horizontally.
(b) Stem of *Chrysanthemum* spread to new niches when older parts die off and new plants are formed.
(c) In pineapple, axillary branches arise from node of underground stem and become obliquely upward to serve as sucker.
(d) *Colocasia*, a corm, is the highly condensed form of stem.

8. Given below are two statements.
Statement I Stem tendrils of watermelon are slender and spirally coiled and help plants to climb.
Statement II Respiratory roots help in the exchange of gases by getting oxygen.
In the light of the above statements, choose the correct answer from the options given below.
(a) Statement I is incorrect, but statement II is correct
(b) Both statement I and statement II are correct
(c) Both statement I and statement II are incorrect
(d) Statement I is correct, but statement II is incorrect

9. The underground stems are found in
(a) potato, ginger, zaminkand, *Colocasia*
(b) potato, cucumber, zaminkand, *Colocasia*
(c) potato, *Citrus*, *Opuntia*, zaminkand
(d) ginger, turmeric, potato, *Opuntia*

10. Mustard plants differ from pea and China rose in its morphology in many ways. Pick out the option with characters specific to mustard and the ones that are not found in pea and China rose.
(a) Fused carpels, parietal placentation actinomorphic, false septum
(b) Syncarpous, marginal placentation, zygomorphic, perigynous flower
(c) Axile placentation, actinomorphic, valvate aestivation, apocarpous
(d) Parietal placentation, zygomorphic, imbricate aestivation, hypogynous flower

11. Given below are two statements.
Statement I In most dicot plants, the leaves have veins that run side by side within the leaf blade.
Statement II Veins in the leaves provide them the structure and serve as the pathways for water, nutrients and food.
In the light of the above statements, choose the correct answer from the options given below.
(a) Statement I is incorrect, but statement II is correct
(b) Both statement I and statement II are correct
(c) Both statement I and statement II are incorrect
(d) Statement I is correct, but statement II is incorrect

12. Fill in the blanks by choosing the correct option.
I. Leaf is connected to the stem by ...*A*... and often features two leaf-like structures known as ...*B*... .
II. ...*C*... provides the structural support to the leaf.

	A	*B*	*C*
(a)	petiole	hypanthodium	leaf base
(b)	leaf base	stipules	petiole
(c)	veins	petioles	axillary bud
(d)	veins	leaf base	bracts

13. Select the incorrectly matched pair.
(a) Pinnately compound leaves - *Alstonia*
(b) Palmately compound leaves - Silk cotton
(c) Alternate phyllotaxy - China rose
(d) Opposite phyllotaxy - Guava

14. Consider the following statements.
I. Opposite phyllotaxy is observed in *Calotropis*.
II. Veins provide rigidity to the leaf petiole.
III. Buds are present in the axil of leaflets of compound leaves.
IV. Pulvinus is present in some leguminous plants.
Choose the correct statements from the options given below.
(a) I and II
(b) I and IV
(c) II and III
(d) III and IV

15. Select the correct option with respect to the position of floral parts on the thalamus.
(a) Epigynous flower - Superior ovary - Cucumber
(b) Perigynous flower - Inferior ovary - Ray florets of sunflower
(c) Hypogynous flower - Superior ovary - China rose
(d) Hypogynous flower - Half inferior ovary - Rose

16. Given below are some statements. Identify the incorrect one(s).
I. In cymose inflorescence, the main axis terminates in a flower.
II. Leaf bears a bud in its axil.
III. In racemose inflorescence, the main axis does not terminate in a flower.
IV. Leaf takes its origin from root apical meristem.
Choose the correct option.
(a) Only IV (b) III and IV
(c) Only III (d) Only II

17. The figures given below show the position of floral parts on the thalamus. Match these columns.

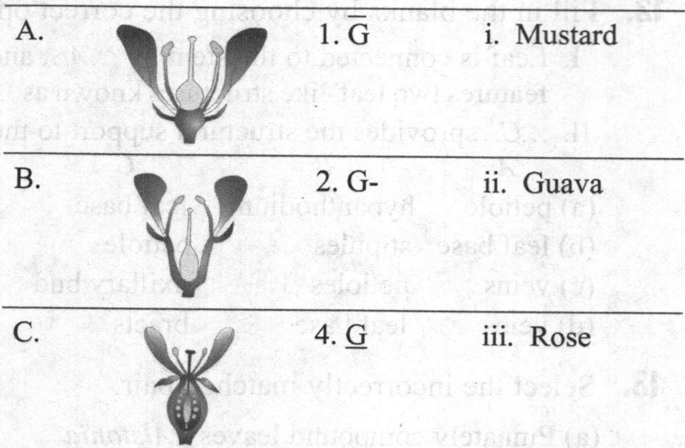

Choose the correct answer from the options given below.
(a) A-3-i, B-1-ii, C-2-iii
(b) A-2-ii, B-3-i, C-1-iii
(c) A-3-i, B-2-iii, C-1-ii
(d) A-1-iii, B-2-ii. C-3-i

18. Given below are two statements; one is labelled as Assertion (A) and the other is labelled as Reason (R).
Assertion (A) Petiole helps in cooling the leaf.
Reason (R) Short thick petiole allow the leaf to soak water during rainy days.
In the light of the above statements, choose the correct answer from the options given below.
(a) A is false, but R is true
(b) Both A and R are true and R is the correct explanation of A
(c) Both A and R are true, but R is not the correct explanation of A
(d) A is true, but R is false

19. Which of the following is correct for Vexillum?
(a) It is a standard petal of papilionaceous corolla
(b) It is a wing petal of papilionaceous corolla
(c) It is a standard petal of cruciferaceous corolla
(d) It is a wing petal of cruciferaceous corolla

20. Read the following statements.
I. *Salvia* and mustard have stamens with filaments of varying lengths.
II. In brinjal, the stamens are epiphyllous, while in lily, they are epipetalous.
III. Lemon grass, which is known for its culinary herbs for its citrus-like flavour, belongs to Gramineae family.
IV. China rose has polyadelphous stamens.
V. The pea plant exhibits both monoadelphous and diadelphous stamens.
How many of the above statements are incorrect?
(a) Two (b) Four (c) Five (d) Three

21. Given below are two statements.
Statement I Style is the receptive organ for pollen grain.
Statement II Style is located at the tip of the stigma.
In the light of the above statements, choose the correct answer from the options given below.
(a) Statement I is incorrect, but statement II is correct
(b) Both statement I and statement II are correct
(c) Both statement I and statement II are incorrect
(d) Statement I is correct, but statement II is incorrect

22. Match List I with List II.

	List I		List II
A.	Fleshy cylindrical stem	1.	*Opuntia*
B.	Flattened stem	2.	*Citrus*
C.	Stem thorns	3.	*Euphorbia*
D.	Stem tendrils	4.	Cucumber

Choose the correct answer from the following options.

	A	B	C	D		A	B	C	D
(a)	2	1	4	3	(b)	3	1	2	4
(c)	1	4	2	3	(d)	4	3	1	2

23. Identify the different types of roots shown in the diagram.

List I	List II	List III
A.	1. Constitutes primary root and its branches	i. Mustard
B.	2. Roots at base of stem	ii. *Monstera*
C.	3. Root from shoot	iii. Wheat

Match the three lists and choose the correct option.

(a) A-3-iii (b) A-2-i
(c) B-2-iii (d) C-1-ii

24. Given below are two statements.

Statement I Drupe is the fruit in both mango and coconut.

Statement II Mango and coconut develop from multicarpellary ovary.

In the light of the above statements, choose the correct answer from the options given below.

(a) Statement I is incorrect, but statement II is correct
(b) Both statement I and statement II are correct
(c) Both statement I and statement II are incorrect
(d) Statement I is correct, but statement II is incorrect

25. Match the given plants with their families.

	List I		List II
A.	Sweet pea	1.	Gramineae
B.	*Hibiscus*	2.	Compositae
C.	*Bambusa*	3.	Fabaceae
D.	*Helianthus*	4.	Malvaceae

Choose the correct answer from the following options.

	A	B	C	D
(a)	1	4	2	3
(b)	3	4	1	2
(c)	1	3	2	4
(d)	3	2	4	1

26. Plant *Indigofera* belongs to the family of which of the following floral diagram?

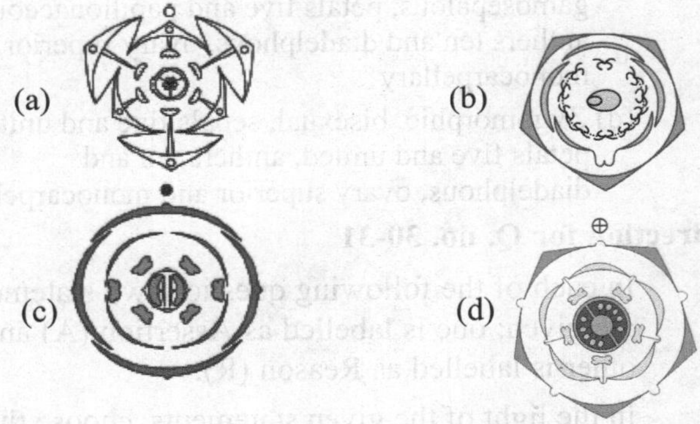

27. Given below are some statements.

I. Castor is a non-endospermic seed.
II. The flowers of chilli possesses zygomorphic symmetry, while that of *Cassia* shows actinomorphic symmetry.
III. Basal, alternate, linear, exstipulate leaves with parallel venation are found in the family-Malvaceae.
IV. Apocarpous gynoecium means that there are more than one carpel and they may be free or separate.

Which of the statement(s) are correct from following options?

(a) Only II
(b) Both III and IV
(c) Only I
(d) Both I and IV

28. Aleurone layer occurs in the peripheral region of *A* and is made up of *B*.
(a) *A* - Scutellum, *B* - Lipid
(b) *A* - Coleoptile, *B* - Protein
(c) *A* - Endosperm, *B* - Lipid
(d) *A*- Endosperm, *B* - Protein

29. Which one of the following is the correct explanation for the given floral formula?
% ⚥ $K_{(5)}\ C_{1+2+(2)}\ A_{(9)+1}\ \underline{G}_1$
(a) Zygomorphic, bisexual, sepals five and gamosepalous, petals five and papilionaceous, anthers ten and monoadelphous, ovary superior and monocarpellary
(b) Zygomorphic, unisexual, sepals five and gamosepalous, petals five and polypetalous, anthers nine united and one free, ovary superior and monocarpellary
(c) Zygomorphic, bisexual, sepals five and gamosepalous, petals five and papilionaceous, anthers ten and diadelphous, ovary superior and monocarpellary
(d) Zygomorphic, bisexual, sepals five and united, petals five and united, anthers ten and diadelphous, ovary superior and monocarpellary

Direction for Q. no. 30-31

In each of the following question two statements are given; one is labelled as Assertion (A) and the other is labelled as Reason (R).

In the light of the given statements, choose the correct answer from the options given below.
(a) A is false, but R is true
(b) Both A and R are true and R is the correct explanation of A
(c) Both A and R are true, but R is not the correct explanation of A
(d) A is true, but R is false

30. **Assertion** (A) Banana is a parthenocarpic fruit.
Reason (R) In banana, fruit is seedless and is formed directly from ovary without fertilisation.

31. **Assertion** (A) The fleshy stem of *Opuntia* perform photosynthesis.
Reason (R) Fleshy stem of *Opuntia* stores food.

32. Which of the following is correct about the root systems?
(a) Stilt roots of maize develop from the radicle.
(b) Potato is a modified root specialised for storage.
(c) *Asparagus* is a modified adventitious root.
(d) Banyan lacks roots developing from radicle.

33. Consider the following statements.
I. Axillary buds can have both supportive as well as protective functions.
II. Suckers often bear adventitious roots and shoots with leaves.
III. Ginger and turmeric develop from adventitious buds.
IV. Rhizomes store starch and proteins to surpass unfavourable conditions.

Choose the correct statements from the options given below.
(a) I, II and IV (b) III and IV
(c) II and III (d) I and II

34. Which of the following option contains all the correct characteristics of banana plants?
(a) Tap root, Parallel venation, Monocot
(b) Fibrous root, Parallel venation, Dicot
(c) Tap root, Reticulate venation, Dicot
(d) Fibrous root, Parallel venation, Monocot

35. Given below are two statements.
Statement I In opposite phyllotaxy, leaves attach to the stem in pairs.
Statement II Opposite phyllotaxy is usually seen in plants with short internodes.
In the light of the above statements, choose the correct answer from the options given below.
(a) Statement I is incorrect, but statement II is correct
(b) Both statement I and statement II are correct
(c) Both statement I and statement II are incorrect
(d) Statement I is correct, but statement II is incorrect

36. Which of the following statement is incorrect?
(a) Stem tendrils can develop from both apical and axillary buds.
(b) Leaf tendrils are modified leaves developing from nodes

(c) Leaves are usually arranged in basipetal succession.
(d) Several leaflets attach at the tip of petiole in silk cotton.

37. Which of the following flowers have their non-essential whorls and male whorl situated at the periphery of the cup-like receptacle?
(a) Plum, Rose, Peach
(b) Plum, Mustard, China rose
(c) Mustard, China rose, Brinjal
(d) Guava, Cucumber, Ray florets of sunflower

38. Which of the following statements is incorrect about lily?
(a) Calyx and corolla are undifferentiated
(b) They are polysepalous but gamopetalous
(c) They are characterised by the presence of tepals
(d) Stamens are attached to the perianth, hence epiphyllous

39. Following figures represents the different types of placentation.

P

Q

R

S

Which of the following belongs to the plant that shows the following characteristics
I. Variation in the length of filaments within a flower
II. Fused carpels
III. Hypogynous flower with superior ovary
(a) *P* (b) *Q*
(c) *R* (d) *S*

40. Which of the following part of almond is edible?
(a) Epicarp (b) Seed
(c) Mesocarp (d) Endocarp

41. Given below are two statements.
Statement I Aleurone layer is present external to the pericarp in monocots.
Statement II Aleurone layers offers protection to the developing embryo.
In the light of the above statements, choose the correct answer from the options given below.
(a) Statement I is incorrect, but statement II is correct
(b) Both statement I and statement II are correct
(c) Both statement I and statement II are incorrect
(d) Statement I is correct, but statement II is incorrect

42. Consider the following statements.
I. All dicot seeds are exalbuminous.
II. Testa protects the seed against dehydration.
III. Coleoptile helps in germination of the seedling.
IV. Cotyledons of endospermic seeds are fleshy.
Choose the incorrect statement from the options given below.
(a) II and III (b) I, III and IV
(c) I only (d) IV only

43. Consider the following description of a particular placentation.
I. Observed in multilocular ovaries.
II. Ovaries are partitioned into many chambers.
III. Ovules are arranged along the central axis of placenta.
Which of the following combinations of plants show the above placentation?
(a) China rose, Tomato, Lemon
(b) Mustard, *Argemone,* Pea
(c) *Dianthus*, Primrose, Lemon
(d) Sunflower, Marigold, Primrose

44. Following is the floral formula of a plant family. Which of the following can be concluded from the same?

$$\oplus ⚥ K_{(5)}\ \overset{\frown}{C_{(5)}\ A_5}\ \underline{G}_{(2)}$$

(a) Flowers are zygomorphic
(b) Five sepals, polysepalous
(c) Valvate aestivation
(d) Syncarpous with superior ovary

45. Following is the floral diagram of a plant family. Which of the following options contain all the plants belonging to the given family?

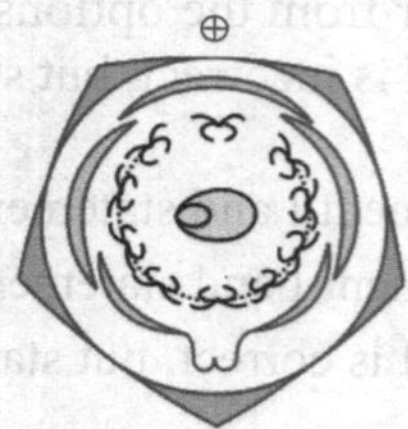

(a) Tobacco, *Atropa*, Ashwagandha
(b) *Asparagus, Colchicum, Gloriosa*
(c) *Aloe*, Tulip, *Atropa*
(d) *Sesbania, Trifolium, Indigofera*

46. Which of the following is the correct set of features for cabbage plants?
(a) Racemose, ebracteate, hypogynous, polysepalous, syncarpous, polypetalous
(b) Racemose, bracteate, perigynous, polysepalous, syncarpous, polypetalous
(c) Racemose, ebracteate, epigynous, polysepalous, syncarpous, polypetalous
(d) Racemose, ebracteate, hypogynous, gamosepalous, syncarpous, gamopetalous

47. Choose the family that is distinguished by the presence of bracteoles.
(a) Asteraceae (b) Malvaceae
(c) Poaceae (d) Fabaceae

48. Which of the following plants belonging to Poaceae family, can be used to derive an essential oil?
(a) Lemongrass
(b) Sunflower
(c) Groundnut
(d) Soyabean

49. If an angiospermic plant produces staminate, pis tillate and bisexual flowers on the same inflorescence, the condition would be termed as
(a) dioecious
(b) trioecious
(c) polygamous
(d) androgynoecious

50. Given below are two statements.
Statement I Sunflower seeds do not contain a triploid endosperm.
Statement II Fruits of *Helianthus* are called siliqua.
In the light of the above statements, choose the correct answer from the options given below.
(a) Statement I is incorrect, but statement II is correct
(b) Both statement I and statement II are correct
(c) Both statement I and statement II are incorrect
(d) Statement I is correct, but statement II is incorrect

Scan for online chapter test

■ **Response Index**

01	ⓐ ⓑ ⓒ ⓓ	14	ⓐ ⓑ ⓒ ⓓ	27	ⓐ ⓑ ⓒ ⓓ	40	ⓐ ⓑ ⓒ ⓓ
02	ⓐ ⓑ ⓒ ⓓ	15	ⓐ ⓑ ⓒ ⓓ	28	ⓐ ⓑ ⓒ ⓓ	41	ⓐ ⓑ ⓒ ⓓ
03	ⓐ ⓑ ⓒ ⓓ	16	ⓐ ⓑ ⓒ ⓓ	29	ⓐ ⓑ ⓒ ⓓ	42	ⓐ ⓑ ⓒ ⓓ
04	ⓐ ⓑ ⓒ ⓓ	17	ⓐ ⓑ ⓒ ⓓ	30	ⓐ ⓑ ⓒ ⓓ	43	ⓐ ⓑ ⓒ ⓓ
05	ⓐ ⓑ ⓒ ⓓ	18	ⓐ ⓑ ⓒ ⓓ	31	ⓐ ⓑ ⓒ ⓓ	44	ⓐ ⓑ ⓒ ⓓ
06	ⓐ ⓑ ⓒ ⓓ	19	ⓐ ⓑ ⓒ ⓓ	32	ⓐ ⓑ ⓒ ⓓ	45	ⓐ ⓑ ⓒ ⓓ
07	ⓐ ⓑ ⓒ ⓓ	20	ⓐ ⓑ ⓒ ⓓ	33	ⓐ ⓑ ⓒ ⓓ	46	ⓐ ⓑ ⓒ ⓓ
08	ⓐ ⓑ ⓒ ⓓ	21	ⓐ ⓑ ⓒ ⓓ	34	ⓐ ⓑ ⓒ ⓓ	47	ⓐ ⓑ ⓒ ⓓ
09	ⓐ ⓑ ⓒ ⓓ	22	ⓐ ⓑ ⓒ ⓓ	35	ⓐ ⓑ ⓒ ⓓ	48	ⓐ ⓑ ⓒ ⓓ
10	ⓐ ⓑ ⓒ ⓓ	23	ⓐ ⓑ ⓒ ⓓ	36	ⓐ ⓑ ⓒ ⓓ	49	ⓐ ⓑ ⓒ ⓓ
11	ⓐ ⓑ ⓒ ⓓ	24	ⓐ ⓑ ⓒ ⓓ	37	ⓐ ⓑ ⓒ ⓓ	50	ⓐ ⓑ ⓒ ⓓ
12	ⓐ ⓑ ⓒ ⓓ	25	ⓐ ⓑ ⓒ ⓓ	38	ⓐ ⓑ ⓒ ⓓ		
13	ⓐ ⓑ ⓒ ⓓ	26	ⓐ ⓑ ⓒ ⓓ	39	ⓐ ⓑ ⓒ ⓓ		

■ **Performance Scanner**

> 90% Excellent !	You have mastered this chapter. The concepts of this chapter are at your fingertips. Move on to the next chapter and maintain this momentum.
76-90% Very Good !	You have a good command over this chapter. Revise the chapter again after a few days and enhance your performance.
60-75% Good !	You have a wide scope to learn for this chapter. Revise this chapter again.
<60% Not Satisfactory!	You have a long way ahead of you to master this chapter. Revise it thoroughly.

Test Booklet No. **3947306**

Test Booklet Code **CH6**

MEDACE

NEET (UG)

SELF ASSESSMENT KIT

Anatomy of Flowering Plants

Topics Covered

Tissue and Tissue Systems

Anatomy of Dicotyledonous and Monocotyledonous Plants; Secondary Growth

Important Instructions

- This Booklet Contains – Two Topic Tests and One Test on Complete Chapter.
- Each question carries 4 marks.
- For each correct response, the candidate will get 4 marks. And for every incorrect response, 1 mark will be additionally deducted from total score.
- Use **Blue/Black** point pen only for filling the OMR.
- Rough work is to be done in the space provided for this purpose in the test booklet only.

Name of the Candidate (In Capitals) ____________________

____

Candidate's Signature ____________

Invigilator's Signature ____________

Facsimile signature stamp of center superintendent ____________

Do not open this booklet until you start attempting the test

Topical Follow Thru

Test 1

Syllabus • Plant Tissues

For deeper insight, **Scan the QR Code** 

Important Instructions

- The test is of 30 minutes duration and contains 25 Multiple Choice Questions (four options with a single correct answer).
- Choose the correct option and fill the OMR given on the last page of this test accordingly.
- At some instances, you may find more than 1 option to be correct. In such circumstances, you have to judge the most appropriate answer as per the conditions given in the question.

1. Cortex is the region present between the
(a) endodermis and vascular bundle
(b) pericycle and endodermis
(c) endodermis and pith
(d) epidermis and stele

2. Given below is a figure related to shoot apical meristem in plants. Identify the correct statements that relates to it.

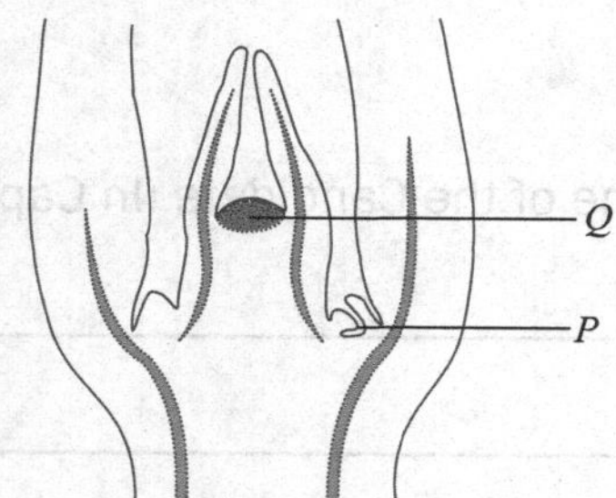

(a) *P* represents the apical bud found in the axils of leaves.
(b) *Q* represents the quiescent centre where cells are in the state of inactivity.
(c) *P* represents the axillary bud that is constituted by the cells of shoot apical meristem.
(d) *Q* represents the leaf primordium found in the shoot apical meristem.

3. Following are the types of plant tissue system, except
(a) epidermal tissue system
(b) fundamental tissue system
(c) conducting tissue system
(d) connective tissue system

4. Read the following statements regarding meristematic cells.
Statement I The cells are undifferentiated and undergo repeated division.
Statement II The cells are usually large and thick walled.
In the light of the above statements, choose the correct answer from the options given below.
(a) Satement I is incorrect, but statement II is correct
(b) Both statement I and statement II are correct.
(c) Both statement I and statement II are incorrect.
(d) Statement I is correct, but statement II is incorrect.

5. Given below are two statements; one is labelled as Assertion (A) and the other is labelled as Reason (R).

Assertion (A) Cuticle is waxy layer found outside the shoot epidermis, but is absent in root.
Reason (R) Cuticle prevents the loss of water.
In the light of the above statements, choose the correct answer from the options given below.
(a) A is false, but R is true.
(b) Both A and R are true and R is the correct explanation of A.
(c) Both A and R are true, but R is not the correct explanation of A.
(d) A is true, but R is false.

6. Following images illustrate the structure of stomata.

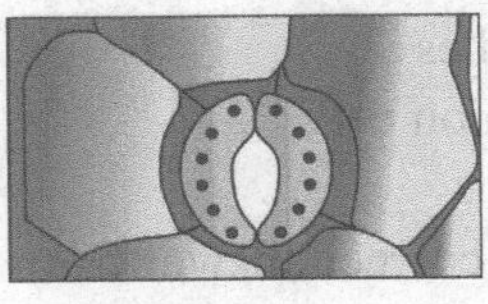

A

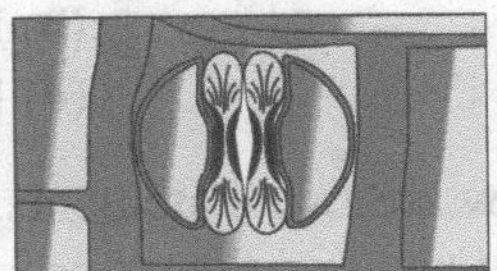

B

Choose the correct statement regarding the images.
(a) Image *A* belongs to monocot, whereas *B* to dicot plants
(b) Image *A* belongs to dicot, whereas *B* to monocot plants
(c) Both *A* and *B* belong to different families of dicot plants
(d) Both *A* and *B* belong to different families of monocot plants

7. Which of the following contributes to the formation of the primary plant body?
(a) Cork cambium
(b) Intercalary meristem
(c) Interfascicular cambium
(d) Intrafascicular cambium

8. Select the incorrect match.
(a) Parenchyma - Actively dividing cells
(b) Collenchyma - Mechanical support
(c) Sclerenchyma - Sclereids
(d) Meristem - Undifferentiated dividing cell

9. Which tissue consists of living cells with angular wall thickening that provides mechanical support?
(a) Epidermis (b) Collenchyma
(c) Sclerenchyma (d) Xylem

10. A conjoint and open vascular bundle will be seen in the transverse section of
(a) dicot root (b) monocot root
(c) monocot stem (d) dicot stem

11. Match the List I with List II.

	List I		List II
A.	Stomata	1.	Prevent loss of water
B.	Cuticle	2.	Modified epidermal cell surrounding stomata
C.	Guard cells	3.	Loss of water
D.	Subsidiary cells	4.	Regulate opening of stomata

Choose the correct answer from the options given below.

	A	B	C	D		A	B	C	D
(a)	3	1	4	2	(b)	4	1	3	2
(c)	3	4	2	1	(d)	3	4	1	2

12. Xylem vessels are generally absent in
(a) *Mangifera indica*
(b) *Triticum aestivum*
(c) *Pinus sylvestris*
(d) *Sorghum vulgare*

13. Which of the following are not the part of epidermal tissue system?
I. Stomata II. Root hair
III. Pith IV. Subsidiary cells
V. Trichome
Choose the correct option.
(a) II, III and V (b) II, III, IV and V
(c) Only III (d) Only V

14. In which of the following tissues can you generally find the bast fibres?
(a) Primary xylem
(b) Secondary xylem
(c) Secondary phloem
(d) Primary phloem

15. Which of the following statement is incorrect regarding tracheids?
(a) They are too efficient in conduction of sap.
(b) Pits are often bordered.
(c) Only pits occur and other thickenings are absent.
(d) They are found in all vascular plants.

16. Which of the following types of meristem contribute towards formation of branches in a plant?
(a) Apical (b) Lateral
(c) Intercalary (d) cambium

17. Which property of meristematic tissue is exploited in developing a disease free plant from a small portion of the diseased plant, using tissue culture techniques?
(a) Differentiation ability
(b) Cell division property
(c) Power of redifferentiation
(d) Regeneration power

18. Given below are two statements; one is labelled as Assertion (A) and the other is labelled as Reason (R).
Assertion (A) Petioles can resist strong winds and bend without breaking.
Reason (R) Petioles are made of parenchymatous tissue.
In the light of the above statements, choose the correct answer from the options given below.
(a) A is false, but R is true.
(b) Both A and R are true and R is the correct explanation of A
(c) Both A and R are true, but R is not the correct explanation of A
(d) A is true, but R is false

19. The pulp of mangoes and pears is composed of which of the following tissues, respectively?
(a) Parenchyma and collenchyma
(b) Collenchyma and parenchyma
(c) Parenchyma and sclerenchyma
(d) Collenchyma and sclerenchyma

20. Consider the following statements.
I. Protoxylem lies towards the pith in roots.
II. Companion cells control sieve tubes at maturity.
III. Exarch arrangement is a characteristic of roots.
IV. Water is conducted through tracheids, vessels and xylem parenchyma.
Choose the incorrect statement(s) from the following options.
(a) II only (b) I only
(c) IV only (d) III and IV

21. Which of the following cells are devoid of nucleus at maturity?
I. Xylem parenchyma
II. Sieve tubes
III. Companion cells
IV. Tracheids
Choose the correct answer from the options given below.
(a) II only (b) III and IV
(c) I, II and IV (d) II and IV

22. Given below are two statements; one is labelled as Assertion (A) and the other is labelled as Reason (R).
Assertion (A) Epidermal surface of roots lack cuticle.
Reason (R) Cuticle is a waxy layer that prevents water loss.
In the light of the above statement, choose the correct answer from the options given below.
(a) A is false, but R is true.
(b) Both A and R are true and R is the correct explanation of A.
(c) Both A and R are true, but R is not the correct explanation of A.
(d) A is true, but R is false.

23. What would be the possible effect, if chloroplasts are removed from the guard cells?
(a) Plant cannot synthesize food.
(b) Stomata would be unregulated.
(c) Plant cannot translocate food
(d) No upward conduction of water

24. Which property of dicot stems allow them to form wood and bark?

(a) Open vascular bundles
(b) Radial vascular bundles
(c) Conjoint vascular bundles
(d) Closed vascular bundles

25. Given below are two statements.

Statement I Epidermal projections in the stems are normally multicellular.

Statement II Ground tissues retain the ability of division.

In the light of the above statements, choose the correct answer from the options given below.

(a) Statement I is incorrect, but statement II is correct.
(b) Both statement I and statement II are correct.
(c) Both statement I and statement II are incorrect.
(d) Statement I is correct, but statement II is incorrect

Response Index

01	a	b	c	d	10	a	b	c	d	19	a	b	c	d
02	a	b	c	d	11	a	b	c	d	20	a	b	c	d
03	a	b	c	d	12	a	b	c	d	21	a	b	c	d
04	a	b	c	d	13	a	b	c	d	22	a	b	c	d
05	a	b	c	d	14	a	b	c	d	23	a	b	c	d
06	a	b	c	d	15	a	b	c	d	24	a	b	c	d
07	a	b	c	d	16	a	b	c	d	25	a	b	c	d
08	a	b	c	d	17	a	b	c	d					
09	a	b	c	d	18	a	b	c	d					

Performance Scanner

> 90% Excellent !	You have mastered these topics. The concepts of these topics are at your fingertips. Move on to the next topics and maintain this momentum.
76-90% Very Good !	You have a good command over these topics. Revise these topics again after a few days and enhance your performance.
60-75% Good !	You have a wide scope to learn for these topics. Revise these topics again.
<60% Not Satisfactory!	You have a long way ahead of you to master these topics. Revise it thoroughly.

Test 2

Syllabus
- Anatomy of Different Parts of Flowering Plants (Roots, Stems and Leaves)

For deeper insight, **Scan the QR Code**

Important Instructions

- The test is of 30 minutes duration and contains 25 Multiple Choice Questions (four options with a single correct answer).
- Choose the correct option and fill the OMR given on the last page of this test accordingly.
- At some instances, you may find more than 1 option to be correct. In such circumstances, you have to judge the most appropriate answer as per the conditions given in the question.

1. Which of the following is the correct sequence of the internal tissue organisation in dicot root?

(a) Epidermis $\rightarrow$ Endodermis $\rightarrow$ Cortex $\rightarrow$ Stele
(b) Epiblema $\rightarrow$ Endodermis $\rightarrow$ Cortex $\rightarrow$ Stele
(c) Epiblema $\rightarrow$ Cortex $\rightarrow$ Endodermis $\rightarrow$ Stele
(d) Epidermis $\rightarrow$ Cortex $\rightarrow$ Endodermis $\rightarrow$ Stele

2. Which of the following statement best defines secondary growth?

(a) It increases the length of the plant roots and shoots.
(b) It occurs only in herbaceous plants.
(c) It increases the girth or thickness of the plant roots and shoots.
(d) It is responsible for the formation of leaves and flowers.

3. Given below are two statements; one is labelled as Assertion (A) and the other is labelled as Reason (R).

Assertion (A) Lenticels are lens-shaped openings in the bark that permit the exchange of gases between the outer atmosphere and the internal tissues of the stem.

Reason (R) Lenticels are formed when the phellogen cuts off closely arranged parenchymatous cells on the outer side instead of cork cells.

In the light of the above statements, choose the correct answer from the options given below.

(a) A is false, but R is true.

(b) Both A and R are true and R is the correct explanation of A.

(c) Both A and R are true, but R is not the correct explanation of A.

(d) A is true, but R is false.

4. Which of the following statement is incorrect about dicot roots?

(a) Endodermis does not develop thickenings.

(b) Xylem vessels are polygonal in outline.

(c) Pericycle produces only lateral roots.

(d) Conjunctive tissue remains thin walled and parenchymatous.

5. Consider the following statements.

I. The pericycle gives rise to lateral roots consisting of parenchymatous cells.

II. Medullary rays are found in between the vascular bundle of monocot stem.

III. In a monocot stem, the hypodermis is collenchymatous.

IV. Bulliform cells can be found in isobilateral leaves.

V. Monocot roots show conjoint open arrangement of vascular bundles.

Choose the correct set of statements from the options given below.

(a) I and II (b) II and III

(c) I and IV (d) II and V

6. Which of the given characteristic differentiates a monocot root from a dicot root?

(a) Reduced endodermis

(b) Polyarch xylem

(c) Underdeveloped pith

(d) Primary growth

7. In dicot stem, secondary xylem and phloem are produced by

(a) phellogen (b) vascular cambium

(c) apical meristem (d) axillary meristem

8. In the given section of a plant organ, the vascular bundle is

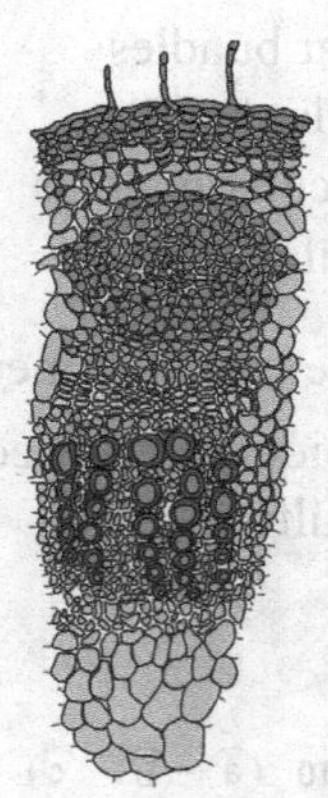

(a) radial (b) closed

(c) exarch (d) endarch

9. Given below are two statements; one is labelled as Assertion (A) and the other is labelled as Reason (R).

Assertion (A) The stem endodermis in dicot stem is called starch sheath.

Reason (R) In dicot stems, the endodermal cells develop additional thickenings with age.

In the light of the above statements, choose the correct answer from the options given below.

(a) A is false, but R is true.

(b) Both A and R are true and R is the correct explanation of A.

(c) Both A and R are true, but R is not the correct explanation of A.

(d) A is true, but R is false.

10. A person is looking at the T.S. of wheat root under a microscope. He observed all of the following, except

(a) large pith (b) interfascicular cambium

(c) casparian strips (d) polyarch xylem

11. A conjoint and open vascular bundle will be observed in the transverse section of

(a) monocot root (b) monocot stem

(c) dicot root (d) dicot stem

12. Select the incorrect match.

(a) Spring wood - Vessels with wider cavity

(b) Autumn wood - Large number of xylary elements

(c) Heart wood - Mechanical support

(d) Sap wood - Conduction of water and minerals

13. Given below are two statements about bark.

Statement I Bark includes all tissues exterior to the vascular cambium, encompassing periderm and secondary phloem.

Statement II Bark formed early in the season is called hard bark, while bark formed later is called soft bark.

In the light of the above statements, choose the correct answer from the options given below.

(a) Statement I is incorrect, but statement II is correct.
(b) Both statement I and statement II are correct.
(c) Both statement I and statement II are incorrect.
(d) Statement I is correct, but statement II is incorrect.

14. Which of the following statement is true about monocot leaf?

(a) Stomata are present only on the abaxial surface of the epidermis.
(b) Mesophyll is not differentiated into palisade and spongy parenchyma.
(c) It shows presence of reticulate leaf venation.
(d) It can be found in pulses.

15. Which of the following statements are correct?

I. All the structures surrounded by the endodermis (on the innerside) are constituents of the stele.
II. Bicollateral vascular bundles are always open.
III. Pericycle is absent in the stem of dicots.
IV. The cortex is the zone that lies between the endodermis and the pericycle.
V. The outer walls of guard cells are thin and the inner walls are highly thickened.

Choose the correct answer from the options given below.

(a) I, IV and V (b) I, II and V
(c) I and IV (d) II and IV

16. Given below are two statements.

Statement I Epiblema extends in roots to form unicellular root hairs.

Statement II Tissue found between vascular bundles are involved in food storage.

In the light of the above statements, choose the correct answer from the options given below.

(a) Statement I is incorrect, but statement II is correct.
(b) Both statement I and statement II are correct.
(c) Both statement I and statement II are incorrect.
(d) Statement I is correct, but statement II is incorrect.

17. Given below are two statements; one is labelled as Assertion (A) and the other is labelled as Reason (R).

Assertion (A) Water flows through plasmodesmata in the endodermis of roots.

Reason (R) Endodermis is the innermost layer of the cortex.

In the light of the above statements, choose the correct answer from the options given below.

(a) A is false, but R is true.
(b) Both A and R are true and R is the correct explanation of A
(c) Both A and R are true, but R is not the correct explanation of A
(d) A is true, but R is false

18. Following is the diagrammatic representation of a section of plant tissue. Which of the following is correct w.r.t. the same?

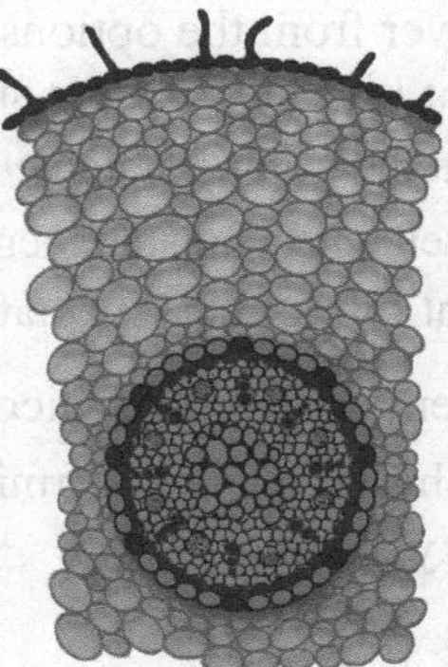

(a) Polyarch xylem bundles are observed
(b) Pith is inconspicuous
(c) Presence of secondary growth at maturity
(d) Vascular bundles are of open type

19. Identify the incorrect combination w.r.t. dicotyledonous stem.

(a) Hypodermis – Collenchyma
(b) Pericycle- Sclerenchyma
(c) Cortical layer – Parenchyma
(d) Medullary rays – Sclerenchyma

20. Following diagram shows a type of tissue in plants. Which of the following is incorrect?

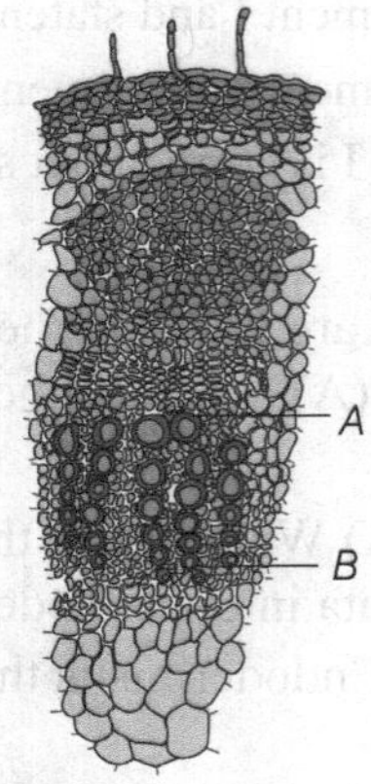

(a) *B* is the first formed xylem
(b) *A* is formed after primary xylem matures
(c) The given arrangement of xylem is exarch
(d) Characteristic ring arrangement is observed in this tissue

21. Given below are two statements.

Statement I Bundle sheath cells are characteristic of dicot leaves only.

Statement II Bundle sheath cells are mostly dead permanent cells.

In the light of the above statements, choose the correct answer from the options given below.

(a) Statement I is incorrect, but statement II is correct.
(b) Both statement I and statement II are correct.
(c) Both statement I and statement II are incorrect.
(d) Statement I is correct, but statement II is incorrect.

22. Monocot stem differs from dicot stem in having

I. Sclerenchymatous hypodermis
II. Exarch xylem
III. Closed vascular bundle
IV. Conjoint vascular bundle

Choose the correct answer from the options given below.

(a) II only (b) I and III
(c) IV only (d) I, III and IV

23. As humidity increases, cobalt chloride changes colour from sky blue to purple to pink. Which of the following plant surfaces would turn dry blue cobalt chloride paper pink faster?

(a) Adaxial surface of monocot leaves
(b) Abaxial surface of dicot leaves
(c) Abaxial surface of monocot leaves
(d) Adaxial surface of dicot leaves

24. Which of the following cell types are used as an adaptive strategy against abiotic stresses like water scarcity?

(a) Palisade mesophyll
(b) Spongy mesophyll
(c) Bulliform cells
(d) Bundle sheath cells

25. Consider the following statements.

I. Monocot or isobilateral leaves lack air cavities.
II. Venation is reticulate with vascular system in dicot leaves.
III. Half-moon shaped patches of sclerenchyma is unique to monocot stems.
IV. Endodermis of dicot stems store starch as reserved food in case of dicot stems.

Choose the incorrect statement(s) from the following options.

(a) II only (b) II and III
(c) I and IV (d) III only

Response Index

01	ⓐ	ⓑ	ⓒ	ⓓ	10	ⓐ	ⓑ	ⓒ	ⓓ	19	ⓐ	ⓑ	ⓒ	ⓓ
02	ⓐ	ⓑ	ⓒ	ⓓ	11	ⓐ	ⓑ	ⓒ	ⓓ	20	ⓐ	ⓑ	ⓒ	ⓓ
03	ⓐ	ⓑ	ⓒ	ⓓ	12	ⓐ	ⓑ	ⓒ	ⓓ	21	ⓐ	ⓑ	ⓒ	ⓓ
04	ⓐ	ⓑ	ⓒ	ⓓ	13	ⓐ	ⓑ	ⓒ	ⓓ	22	ⓐ	ⓑ	ⓒ	ⓓ
05	ⓐ	ⓑ	ⓒ	ⓓ	14	ⓐ	ⓑ	ⓒ	ⓓ	23	ⓐ	ⓑ	ⓒ	ⓓ
06	ⓐ	ⓑ	ⓒ	ⓓ	15	ⓐ	ⓑ	ⓒ	ⓓ	24	ⓐ	ⓑ	ⓒ	ⓓ
07	ⓐ	ⓑ	ⓒ	ⓓ	16	ⓐ	ⓑ	ⓒ	ⓓ	25	ⓐ	ⓑ	ⓒ	ⓓ
08	ⓐ	ⓑ	ⓒ	ⓓ	17	ⓐ	ⓑ	ⓒ	ⓓ					
09	ⓐ	ⓑ	ⓒ	ⓓ	18	ⓐ	ⓑ	ⓒ	ⓓ					

Performance Scanner

> 90% Excellent !	You have mastered these topics. The concepts of these topics are at your fingertips. Move on to the next topics and maintain this momentum.
76-90% Very Good !	You have a good command over these topics. Revise these topics again after a few days and enhance your performance.
60-75% Good !	You have a wide scope to learn for these topics. Revise these topics again.
<60% Not Satisfactory!	You have a long way ahead of you to master these topics. Revise it thoroughly.

Chapter Break Thru

Syllabus • Plant Tissues • Anatomy of Different Parts of Flowering Plants (Roots, Stems and Leaves)

Important Instructions

- The test is of 1 hour duration and contains 50 Multiple-Choice Questions (Four options with a single correct answer).
- Choose the correct option and fill the OMR given on the last page of this test accordingly.
- At some instances, you may find more than 1 option to be correct. In such circumstances, you have to judge the most appropriate answer as per the conditions given in the question.

1. Which of the following cells store food and water materials?

(a) Xylem fibres (b) Xylem parenchyma
(c) Tracheids (d) Sclereids

2. Which of the following statement is incorrect w.r.t. parenchyma?

(a) It forms the major part within organs.
(b) They contain tightly packed cells with no intercellular spaces.
(c) Secretory cells possess these type of cells.
(d) Phloem parenchyma has tapered cylindrical cells with dense cytoplasm and nucleus.

3. Phloem in gymnosperms is not composed of

(a) sieve tubes only
(b) companion cells only
(c) Both sieve tubes and companion cells
(d) albuminous cells and sieve cells

4. A characteristic "ring-arrangement" of vascular bundles can be easily seen in

(a) dicot root (b) monocot stem
(c) dicot stem (d) monocot leaf

5. The increase in length of petiole results from division of

(a) phellogen
(b) apical meristem
(c) lateral meristem
(d) intercalary meristem

6. Which plant tissue, when stained, showed the presence of hemicellulose and pectin in its cell walls?

(a) Xylem
(b) Collenchyma
(c) Meristem
(d) Sclerenchyma

7. Given below are few statements.

I. Apical meristem is found at the root and shoot apices of the plant.
II. Intercalary meristem is a secondary meristematic tissue.
III. Lateral meristem is found in the mature regions of the roots and shoots.
IV. Lateral meristematic tissue contributes in the secondary growth of the plant.

Read the statements regarding meristematic tissue and select the correct one(s).

(a) I only (b) II and III
(c) I, III and IV (d) I and III

8. Arrange the following tissues in order of their location from the periphery to centre in a dicotyledonous plant root.

I. Endodermis II. Metaxylem
III. Epidermal cell
IV. Phloem

Choose the correct option.

(a) IV, I, II, III (b) IV, II, III, I
(c) I, II, III, IV (d) III, I, IV, II

9. Given below are two statements.

Statement I The epidermal tissue system forms the outermost covering of the whole plant body and is devoid of stomata.

Statement II A layer of cuticle is present on the outside of epidermal cells.

In the light of the above statements, choose the correct answer from the options given below.

(a) Statement I is incorrect, but statement II is correct.
(b) Both statement I and statement II are correct.
(c) Both statement I and statement II are incorrect.
(d) Statement I is correct, but statement II is incorrect.

10. Complex tissues like xylem and phloem are composed of several sub elements. Which of the following is incorrect with respect to them?

(a) Gymnosperms generally lack vessels in their cells.
(b) Angiosperms possess albuminous cells.
(c) Phloem fibres possess thick cell wall
(d) Narrow sieve tubes are observed in the case of earlier formed phloem.

11. Which of the following statement is not correct for stomatal apparatus?

(a) Inner walls of guard cells are thick and elastic.
(b) Guard cells possess chloroplasts.
(c) Guard cells are surrounded by subsidiary cells.
(d) Stomata are involved in gaseous exchange.

12. Layers of thick walled parenchymatous cells present besides the endodermis are referred to as

(a) casparian strips
(b) pericycle
(c) conjunctive tissue
(d) stele

13. Which statement is correctly describing the following diagram?

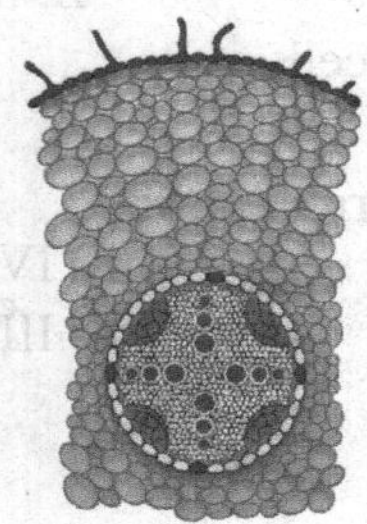

(a) It is a monocot root with the casparian strips found in the endodermis.
(b) It is a primary structure of the dicot root with endarch arrangement of xylem.
(c) It is a monocot root with an endarch arrangement of xylem.
(d) It is a primary structure of the dicot root with the casparian strips found in the endodermis.

14. Read the following statements.

I. The monocot stem has a collenchymatous hypodermis.
II. Mesophyll of isobilateral (monocot) leaves is undifferentiated.
III. Epidermis provide protection to the leaf interior.
IV. Spongy tissue or spongy parenchyma lies below the palisade parenchyma.
V. Xylem fibres primarily have a mechanical function.

Which of the following option is correct?

(a) I, III and IV are correct
(b) II, IV and V are correct
(c) II, III, IV and V are correct
(d) I, II, IV and V are correct

15. Given below are two statements.

Statement I Root hairs are unicellular, while stem hairs/trichomes are multicellular.

Statement II Trichomes may be branched or unbranched, soft or stiff, and prevent transpiration.

In the light of the above statements, choose the correct answer from the options given below.

(a) Statement I is incorrect, but statement II is correct.
(b) Both statement I and statement II are correct.
(c) Both statement I and statement II are incorrect.
(d) Statement I is correct, but statement II is incorrect.

16. Which statement is not correct regarding the endodermis of dicot root?

(a) It consists of barrel-shaped cell.
(b) No intercellular spaces are found in it.
(c) Deposition of lignin is found on the tangential wall of the epidermal cell.
(d) Endodermal cells are water impermeable in nature.

17. When observing a Transverse Section (TS) of a sunflower stem under the microscope, a student notices cells with angular thickenings. Where are these cells located?
(a) In the cortical region
(b) In the epidermis layer
(c) In the hypodermis layer
(d) In the endodermis layer

18. Select the incorrect statement w.r.t. epidermal tissue system.
(a) It forms the outermost covering of the plant body.
(b) Epidermal cells are parenchymatous cells that have a large amount of cytoplasm and a small vacuole.
(c) Stomata are absent in the epidermis of the root.
(d) Trichomes prevent water lose due to transpiration.

19. Which of the following is not a feature of bulliform cells?
(a) Found in grasses
(b) Modification of abaxial epidermal cells
(c) Large, empty, colourless cells
(d) Capable of absorbing water

20. Given below are two statements; one is labelled as Assertion (A) and the other is labelled as Reason (R).
Assertion (A) Dicot leaves are dorsiventral in nature.
Reason (R) The adaxial (upper surface) bears more stomata than the abaxial (lower surface) epidermis.
In the light of the above statements, choose the correct answer from the options given below.
(a) A is false, but R is true.
(b) Both A and R are true and R is the correct explanation of A.
(c) Both A and R are true, but R is not the correct explanation of A.
(d) A is true, but R is false.

21. TS of a particular leaf is given below.

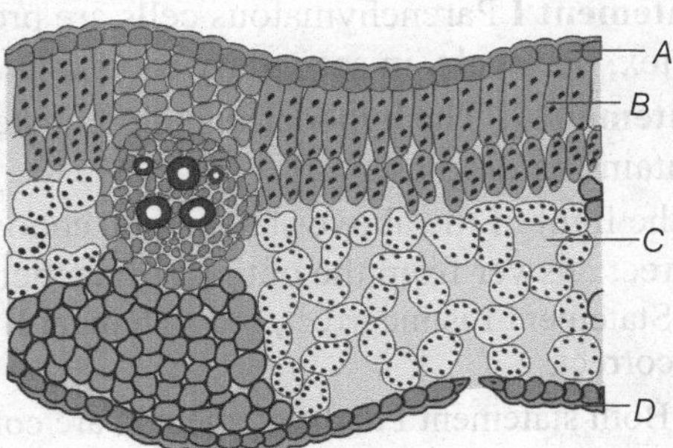

Choose the incorrect statement w.r.t. given figure.
(a) *B* represents abaxially placed palisade parenchyma made up of elongated cells.
(b) *C* represents loosely arranged spongy parenchyma which extends to the lower epidermis.
(c) *D* bears more number of stomata than *A*.
(d) *B* is attached to *A* in a vertical arrangement, and *A* may even lack stomata.

22. Why are apical and intercalary meristems called primary meristems?
(a) They are composed of various kinds of tissues.
(b) They contribute to the formation of the primary plant body and appear early in the plant's life.
(c) They occur in the mature regions of roots and shoots of many plants.
(d) They are involved in secondary growth.

23. Which of the following statements are true about heartwood?
I. It does not help in water conduction.
II. It is dark in colour, but is very soft.
III. It has tracheary elements which are filled with tannins, resins, etc.
IV. It is involved in conduction of water and minerals.

Choose the correct option.
(a) II, III and IV
(b) I and III
(c) I, II and III
(d) II and IV

24. Read the following two statements.

Statement I Parenchymatous cells are present in cortex, pericycle, in secondary roots only.

Statement II The hypodermis of dicot stem contains chloroplast.

In the light of the above statements, choose the correct answer from the options given below.

(a) Statement I is incorrect, but statement II is correct.

(b) Both statement I and statement II are correct.

(c) Both statement I and statement II are incorrect.

(d) Statement I is correct, but statement II is incorrect.

25. The condition where the first formed xylem element faces the periphery is called ...I... and it is seen in ...II... .

	I	II
(a)	exarch	roots
(b)	endarch	roots
(c)	exarch	stems
(d)	mexarch	roots

26. Given below are two statements; one is labelled as Assertion (A) and the other is labelled as Reason (R).

Assertion (A) Secondary growth is not found in the monocot stem.

Reason (R) Open vascular bundles occur in monocot stems.

In the light of the above statements, choose the correct answer from the options given below.

(a) A is false, but R is true.

(b) Both A and R are true and R is the correct explanation of A.

(c) Both A and R are true, but R is not the correct explanation of A.

(d) A is true, but R is false.

27. Consider the following statements.

Statement I In conjoint vascular bundle, the phloem is located on the outer side of xylem.

Statement II In conjoint vascular bundle, cambium is never found.

In the light of the above statements, choose the correct answer from the options given below.

(a) Statement I is incorrect, but statement II is correct.

(b) Both statement I and statement II are correct.

(c) Both statement I and statement II are incorrect.

(d) Statement I is correct, but statement II is incorrect.

28. Match List I with List II.

	List I		List II
A.	Cortex	1.	Transport of food and water
B.	Pericycle	2.	Stores excretory substances
C.	Pith	3.	Present between endodermis and stele
D.	Medullary rays	4.	Present between epidermis and pericycle

Choose the correct answer from the options given below.

	A	B	C	D
(a)	2	4	3	1
(b)	4	3	2	1
(c)	2	3	1	4
(d)	3	1	2	4

29. Which of the following statements are correct?

I. Stomata are composed of two bean-shaped epidermal cells called guard cells.

II. A mature sieve element possesses a cytoplasm with a large vacuole, but lacks a nucleus.

III. Pericycle gives rise to primary roots.

IV. All the elements of phloem are connected to each other through plasmodesmata.

V. Monocot roots do not undergo any secondary growth.

Choose the correct answer from the options given below.

(a) I, IV and V (b) I, II and V

(c) I and IV (d) II and IV

30. Select the incorrect match.

(a) Monocot stem - Secondary growth absent

(b) Dicot stem - Endodermis rich in starch sheath

(c) Monocot stem - Smaller peripheral vascular bundles

(d) Dicot stem - presence of bundle sheath along with vascular cambium

31. Which of the following feature of a mature sieve element makes its association with the companion cells compulsory?
(a) Presence of peripheral cytoplasm
(b) Absence of nucleus
(c) Absence of a prominent vacuole
(d) Perforated end walls

32. All of the following are components of stomatal apparatus, except
(a) guard cells (b) stomatal pore
(c) epidermal cells (d) subsidiary cells

33. Given below are two statements.
Statement I Intrafascicular cambium is ontogenetically a primary meristem.
Statement II Phellogen is a secondary meristem that causes secondary growth.
In the light of the above statements, choose the correct answer from the options given below.
(a) Statement I is incorrect, but statement II is correct.
(b) Both statement I and statement II are correct.
(c) Both statement I and statement II are incorrect.
(d) Statement I is correct, but statement II is incorrect.

34. A cell observed under a microscope appears elongated, with a narrow lumen, lacking a protoplast, devoid of nucleus and lignified. Which of the following simple tissue type is being examined?
(a) Sclerenchyma (b) Bast Fibres
(c) Xylem fibres (d) Vessels

35. Following image shows an arrangement pattern of vascular bundles. Which of the following is incorrect w.r.t the same?

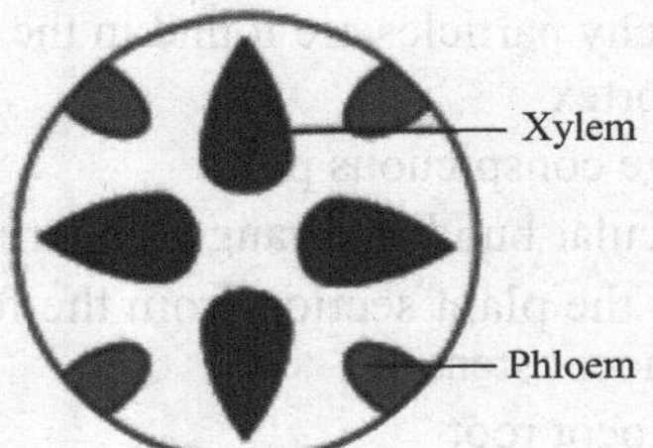

(a) This type of arrangement is prevalent in leaves and stems.
(b) In monocot roots, they cannot form secondary xylem and phloem.
(c) In dicot roots, a cambium develops between the vascular bundles.
(d) Phloem is normally located peripherally compared to the xylem.

36. Which of the following is not a function of the water impermeable suberin layer found in dicot roots?
(a) It forces substances to cross through the cytoplasm of the endodermal cells.
(b) It regulates the water flow between tissues and vascular bundles at the pith.
(c) It helps in loading of sugar into the sieve tubes of the phloem tissue.
(d) It prevents backflow of solutes and nutrients into the soil.

37. Consider the following statements with respect to pericycle in plant tissues.
I. It is the single layered structure which forms innermost to cortex.
II. It comprises of parenchymatous cells only.
III. It is present between the endodermis and vascular bundles.
IV. In monocots, it helps in development of lateral roots.
Choose the correct statement(s) from the options given below.
(a) III only (b) I and II
(c) IV only (d) I, II and IV

38. Which of the following materials present in phellem makes them impervious to gases and water?
(a) Lignin (b) Suberin
(c) Pectin (d) Cutin

39. A given tissue section has been sliced and stained appropriately prior to visualisation under a microscope. Which of the following feature confirms it to be a monocot root, and distinguishes it from a dicot root?
I. Presence of root hair
II. Absence of lateral roots
III. Polyarch xylem bundles
IV. Small pith
Choose the correct answer from the options given below.
(a) I and IV (b) II and III
(c) IV only (d) II only

40. Following is a tissue section as viewed under a microscope. Choose the correct combination for P and Q from the given options.

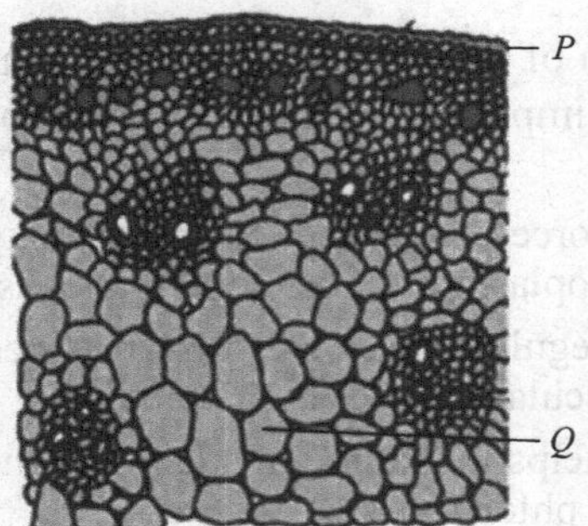

(a) P – Sclerenchyma; Q – Sclerenchyma
(b) P – Parenchyma; Q – Sclerenchyma
(c) P – Sclerenchyma; Q – Parenchyma
(d) P – Parenchyma; Q – Parenchyma

41. Conversion of the actively dividing cells found at the root and shoot tips into more complex tissues with function of specialisation is facilitated by the process of
(a) dedifferentiation (b) differentiation
(c) cell division (d) cell specialisation

42. Given below are two statements; one is labelled as Assertion (A) and the other is labelled as Reason (R).

Assertion (A) Jute fibres are naturally strong and used in making ropes and bags.

Reason (R) Sieve tubes form the jute fibres which are dead cells with lignified walls.

In the light of the above statement, choose the correct answer from the options given below.
(a) A is false, but R is true.
(b) Both A and R are true and R is the correct explanation of A.
(c) Both A and R are true, but R is not the correct explanation of A.
(d) A is true, but R is false.

43. Given below are two statements.

Statement I Protophloem appear before the appearance of metaphloem.

Statement II Early formed phloem has bigger sieve tubes than metaphloem.

In the light of the above statements, choose the correct answer from the options given below.
(a) Statement I is incorrect, but statement II is correct.
(b) Both statement I and statement II are correct.
(c) Both statement I and statement II are incorrect.
(d) Statement I is correct, but statement II is incorrect.

44. Which of the following is correct about the water conducting tissue in plants?
(a) Living cells of the tissue accumulate tannins.
(b) Fibres of the tissue are always aseptate.
(c) Vessels are the only water transporting element.
(d) Radial water conduction is supported by tracheids.

45. Match List I with List II.

List I	List II
A. Aerenchyma	1. Lignified cell wall
B. Collenchyma	2. Pectin deposition
C. Sclerenchyma	3. Plasmodesmatal connection
D. Phloem parenchyma	4. Buoyancy of water plants

Choose the correct answer from the options given below.
(a) A-4, B-2, C-1, D-3
(b) A-4, B-1, C-2, D-3
(c) A-4, B-1, C-3, D-2
(d) A-4, B-2, C-3, D-1

46. A certain plant section is observed under a microscope and reveals the following distinct features.
I. Cells below hypodermis are loosely packed.
II. Starchy particles are found in the innermost layer of cortex
III. Large conspicuous pith
IV. Vascular bundles arranged in a ring-like pattern

Identify the plant section from the features listed.
(a) Monocot stem
(b) Monocot root
(c) Dicot root
(d) Dicot stem

47. Which of the following is incorrect about medullary rays?

(a) They are parenchymatous cells found in dicot stems.

(b) They are also known as pith rays or vascular rays.

(c) They serve as a link between endodermis and cortex.

(d) They store food, tannins and help in transportation.

48. The following is the diagrammatic representation of a section of leaf. Which of the following cells labelled as P-S, shows the maximum chloroplast density?

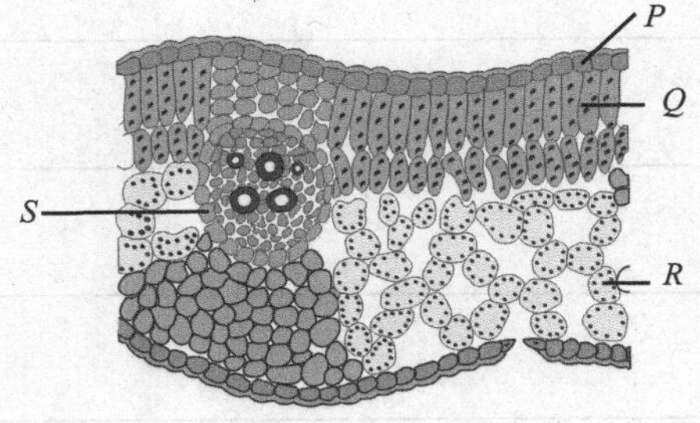

(a) *P* (b) *S*
(c) *Q* (d) *R*

49. A small section of a wilted grass leaf, shows the appearance of some colourless cells that have their cytoplasm withdrawn to a small region in the plasma membrane. Identify these cells from the following options.

(a) Bundle sheath cells
(b) Bulliform cells
(c) Xylem vessels
(d) Tracheary elements

50. Consider the following statements about monocot stems.

I. Vascular bundles are surrounded by parenchymatous bundle sheath.
II. Ground tissue is conspicuous and made of parenchyma.
III. Absence of cambium tissue between xylem and phloem.
IV. Phloem parenchyma is a living tissue that stores food.

Choose the incorrect statements and mark the correct option from the following.

(a) I and III
(b) I and IV
(c) II only
(d) II and IV

Scan for online chapter test

Response Index

01 ⓐ ⓑ ⓒ ⓓ	14 ⓐ ⓑ ⓒ ⓓ	27 ⓐ ⓑ ⓒ ⓓ	40 ⓐ ⓑ ⓒ ⓓ
02 ⓐ ⓑ ⓒ ⓓ	15 ⓐ ⓑ ⓒ ⓓ	28 ⓐ ⓑ ⓒ ⓓ	41 ⓐ ⓑ ⓒ ⓓ
03 ⓐ ⓑ ⓒ ⓓ	16 ⓐ ⓑ ⓒ ⓓ	29 ⓐ ⓑ ⓒ ⓓ	42 ⓐ ⓑ ⓒ ⓓ
04 ⓐ ⓑ ⓒ ⓓ	17 ⓐ ⓑ ⓒ ⓓ	30 ⓐ ⓑ ⓒ ⓓ	43 ⓐ ⓑ ⓒ ⓓ
05 ⓐ ⓑ ⓒ ⓓ	18 ⓐ ⓑ ⓒ ⓓ	31 ⓐ ⓑ ⓒ ⓓ	44 ⓐ ⓑ ⓒ ⓓ
06 ⓐ ⓑ ⓒ ⓓ	19 ⓐ ⓑ ⓒ ⓓ	32 ⓐ ⓑ ⓒ ⓓ	45 ⓐ ⓑ ⓒ ⓓ
07 ⓐ ⓑ ⓒ ⓓ	20 ⓐ ⓑ ⓒ ⓓ	33 ⓐ ⓑ ⓒ ⓓ	46 ⓐ ⓑ ⓒ ⓓ
08 ⓐ ⓑ ⓒ ⓓ	21 ⓐ ⓑ ⓒ ⓓ	34 ⓐ ⓑ ⓒ ⓓ	47 ⓐ ⓑ ⓒ ⓓ
09 ⓐ ⓑ ⓒ ⓓ	22 ⓐ ⓑ ⓒ ⓓ	35 ⓐ ⓑ ⓒ ⓓ	48 ⓐ ⓑ ⓒ ⓓ
10 ⓐ ⓑ ⓒ ⓓ	23 ⓐ ⓑ ⓒ ⓓ	36 ⓐ ⓑ ⓒ ⓓ	49 ⓐ ⓑ ⓒ ⓓ
11 ⓐ ⓑ ⓒ ⓓ	24 ⓐ ⓑ ⓒ ⓓ	37 ⓐ ⓑ ⓒ ⓓ	50 ⓐ ⓑ ⓒ ⓓ
12 ⓐ ⓑ ⓒ ⓓ	25 ⓐ ⓑ ⓒ ⓓ	38 ⓐ ⓑ ⓒ ⓓ	
13 ⓐ ⓑ ⓒ ⓓ	26 ⓐ ⓑ ⓒ ⓓ	39 ⓐ ⓑ ⓒ ⓓ	

Performance Scanner

> 90% Excellent !	You have mastered this chapter. The concepts of this chapter are at your fingertips. Move on to the next chapter and maintain this momentum.
76-90% Very Good !	You have a good command over this chapter. Revise the chapter again after a few days and enhance your performance.
60-75% Good !	You have a wide scope to learn for this chapter. Revise this chapter again.
<60% Not Satisfactory!	You have a long way ahead of you to master this chapter. Revise it thoroughly.

Space for Rough Work

Test Booklet No. 3947307

Test Booklet Code CH7

Structural Organisation in Animals

Topics Covered

Animal Tissues

Organ and Organ System; Morphology and Anatomy of Cockroach and Frog

Important Instructions

- This Booklet Contains – Two Topic Tests and One Test on Complete Chapter.
- Each question carries 4 marks.
- For each correct response, the candidate will get 4 marks. And for every incorrect response, 1 mark will be additionally deducted from total score.
- Use **Blue/Black** point pen only for filling the OMR.
- Rough work is to be done in the space provided for this purpose in the test booklet only.

Name of the Candidate (In Capitals) ____________________

____

____

Candidate's Signature ____________________

Invigilator's Signature ____________________

Facsimile signature stamp of center superintendent ____________________

Do not open this booklet until you start attempting the test

Topical Follow Thru

Test 1

Syllabus • Animal Tissues (Epithelium, Connective, Neural and Muscle Tissue)

For deeper insight, **Scan the QR Code** 

Important Instructions

- The test is of 30 minutes duration and contains 25 Multiple Choice Questions, (four options with a single correct answer).
- Choose the correct option and fill the OMR given on the last page of this test accordingly.
- At some instances, you may find more then 1 option may be correct. In such circumstances, you have to judge the most appropriate answer as per conditions given in the question.

1. Which type of epithelium is commonly found in ducts of glands and tubular parts of nephrons in kidneys?

(a) Columnar epithelium
(b) Cuboidal epithelium
(c) Squamous epithelium
(d) Glandular epithelium

2. Match List I with List II.

List I	List II
A. Squamous epithelium	1. Fallopian tube
B. Ciliated epithelium	2. Pharynx
C. Compound epithelium	3. Goblet cells
D. Glandular epithelium	4. Air sacs of lungs

Choose the correct answer from the options given below.

	A	B	C	D		A	B	C	D
(a)	4	1	2	3	(b)	4	2	3	1
(c)	1	4	3	2	(d)	4	3	2	1

3. Given below are two statements.

Statement I Tight junctions help to stop substances from leaking across a tissue.

Statement II Gap junctions facilitate the cells to communicate with each other.

In the light of the above statements, choose the correct answer from the options given below.

(a) Statement I is incorrect, but statement II is correct.
(b) Both statement I and statement II are correct.
(c) Both statement I and statement II are incorrect.
(d) Statement I is correct, but statement II is incorrect.

4. Consider the following statements.

I. Connective tissues are most abundant and widely distributed in the body of complex animals.
II. In all connective tissues except blood, the cells secrete fibres of structural proteins called collagen or elastin.
III. The fibres provide strength, elasticity and flexibility to the tissue.
IV. The cells of connective tissue also secrete modified proteins, which accumulate between cells and fibres and act as matrix.
V. Adipose tissue is a dense connective tissue.

Choose the correct set of statements from the options given below.

(a) I, II and V
(b) III, IV and V
(c) I, II and III
(d) II, III, IV and V

5. The cells which protect and support neurons are

(a) neurilemma
(b) neuroglial cells
(c) relay neuron
(d) Nissl's granules

6. Match List I with List II.

List I	List II
A. Tendons	1. Osteocytes
B. Ligament	2. Chondrocytes
C. Cartilage	3. Connects bones to bones
D. Bone	4. Connects muscles to bones

Choose the correct answer from the options given below.

	A	B	C	D		A	B	C	D
(a)	4	1	2	3	(b)	4	2	3	1
(c)	1	4	3	2	(d)	4	3	2	1

7. Given below are two statements regarding cardiac muscle tissue.

Statement I It is a contractile tissue present only in the heart.

Statement II The cells of this tissue do not show striations.

In the light of the above statements, choose the correct answer from the options given below.

(a) Statement I is incorrect, but statement II is correct
(b) Both statement I and statement II are correct
(c) Both statement I and statement II are incorrect
(d) Statement I is correct, but statement II is incorrect

8. Refer to the given figure of a connective tissue and choose the incorrect statement about it.

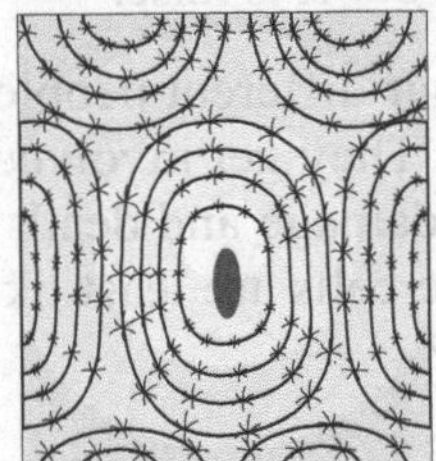

(a) It has hard and non-pliable ground substance, rich in proteins and collagen fibres.
(b) It is the main tissue that provides structural frame to the body.
(c) It supports and protects softer tissues and organs.
(d) Its cells are present in the spaces called lacunae.

9. Given below are two statements; one is labelled as Assertion (A) and other is labelled as Reason (R).

Assertion (A) Neurons are excitable cells.
Reason (R) Neurons stimulate electrical disturbance for signal transmission.

In the light of the above statements, choose the correct answer from the options given below.

(a) A is false, but R is true
(b) Both A and R are true and R is the correct explanation of A
(c) Both A and R are true, but R is not the correct explanation of A
(d) A is true, but R is false

10. Given below are two statements regarding adipose tissues.

Statement I These are dense connective tissue.

Statement II The cells of these tissues are specialised to store fats.

In the light of the above statements, choose the correct answer from the options given below.

(a) Statement I is incorrect, but statement II is correct
(b) Both statement I and statement II are correct
(c) Both statement I and statement II are incorrect
(d) Statement I is correct, but statement II is incorrect

11. Which of the following options is correct regarding white collagen fibres?

(a) They are generally longer.
(b) The fibres are branched.
(c) Gelatin is not produced on boiling.
(d) They provide strength and flexibility to the tissue.

12. Given below are two statements regarding striated muscle.

Statement I They get fatigued due to the production of lactic acid.

Statement II A myofibril is absent in these muscles.

In the light of the above statements, choose the correct answer from the options given below.

(a) Statement I is incorrect, but statement II is correct
(b) Both statement I and statement II are correct
(c) Both statement I and statement II are incorrect
(d) Statement I is correct, but statement II is incorrect

13. Given below are two statements; one is labelled as Assertion (A) and other is labelled as Reason (R).

Assertion (A) The presence of myelin sheath increases the velocity of conduction.
Reason (R) Myelin sheath reduces the energy expended in the process of conduction.

In the light of the above statements, choose the correct answer from the options given below.
(a) A is false, but R is true
(b) Both A and R are true and R is the correct explanation of A
(c) Both A and R are true, but R is not the correct explanation of A
(d) A is true, but R is false

14. Identify the figures and find out the correct labellings.

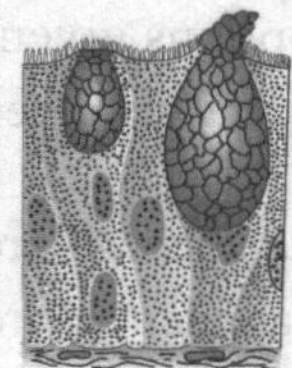
A

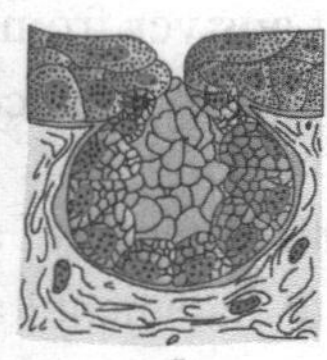
B

(a) *A*- Unicellular glandular epithelium like goblet cells of alimentary canal
B - Multicellular glandular epithelium like salivary gland
(b) *A* - Unicellular glandular epithelium like salivary gland
B - Multicellular glandular epithelium like goblet cells of alimentary canal
(c) *A* - Multicellular glandular epithelium like salivary gland
B - Unicellular glandular epithelium like goblet cells of alimentary canal
(d) *A* - Multicellular glandular epithelium like goblet cells of alimentary canal
B- Unicellular glandular epithelium like salivary gland

15. Which of the following statement is correct?
(a) Brown adipose tissue releases energy as ATP and functions as food reserve in most adult mammals.
(b) White adipose tissue acts as an insulator, thereby reducing heat loss from the body.
(c) Fibroblasts, upon activation, release granules containing serotonin and histamine.
(d) Collagen fibres are described as yellow, branched fibres that occur singly and are known for their stretchability.

16. Given below are two statements.
Statement I Saliva is secreted by an exocrine gland.
Statement II Areolar tissue is a type of connective tissue, where fibres and fibroblasts are compactly packed.
In the light of the above statements, choose the correct answer from the options given below.
(a) Statement I is incorrect, but statement II is correct
(b) Both statement I and statement II are correct
(c) Both statement I and statement II are incorrect
(d) Statement I is correct, but statement II is incorrect

17. Given below are two statements; one is labelled as Assertion (A) and other is labelled as Reason (R).
Assertion (A) Respiratory tract is made up of smooth muscles.
Reason (R) The functioning of smooth muscles is not directly controlled by us.
In the light of the above statements, choose the correct answer from the options given below.
(a) A is false, but R is true.
(b) Both A and R are true and R is the correct explanation of A.
(c) Both A and R are true, but R is not the correct explanation of A.
(d) A is true, but R is false.

18. There are four different people with healthy body functioning. They get involved in an accident resulting in damage and death of few cells. Which of the cells are least likely to be regenerated?
(a) Neurons
(b) Liver cells
(c) Malphigian layer of skin
(d) Osteocytes

19. In case the ligaments get cut or broken,
(a) there will be no movement of bones at joints
(b) bones will become fixed
(c) bones will become flexible
(d) there will be free movement of bones at joints

20. Which of the following is correct w.r.t. connective tissues?
(a) They are ectodermal in origin without intercellular spaces.
(b) They are mesodermal in origin with intercellular spaces.
(c) They are ectodermal in origin with intercellular spaces.
(d) They are mesodermal in origin without intercellular spaces.

21. Given below are figures showing different types of simple epithelium. Choose the type of epithelium, which is found in the inner surface of hollow organs like bronchiole.

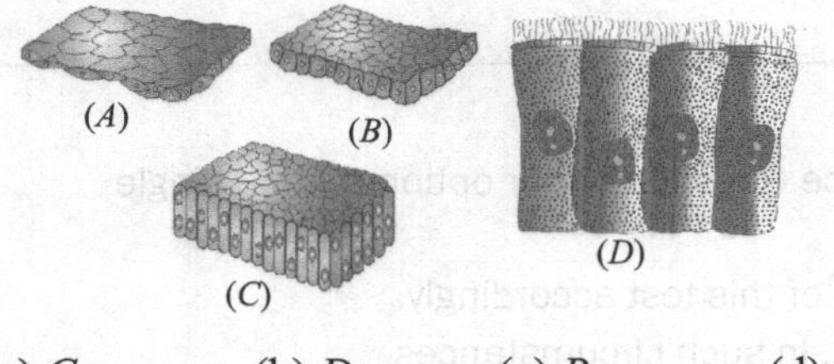

(a) *C* (b) *D* (c) *B* (d) *A*

22. Given below is a figure of a loose connective tissue. Choose the option that correctly marks the cells that produce and secrete fibres, and fibres of structural proteins that provide mechanical strength, respectively.

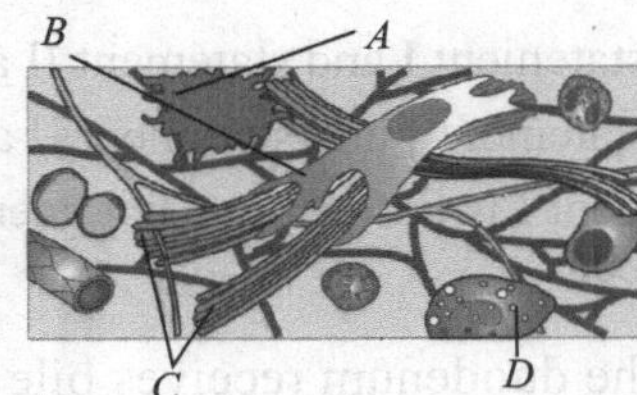

Choose the correct option.
(a) *B* and *C* (b) *A* and *C*
(c) *C* and *B* (d) *D* and *B*

23. Given below are two diagrams, A and B.

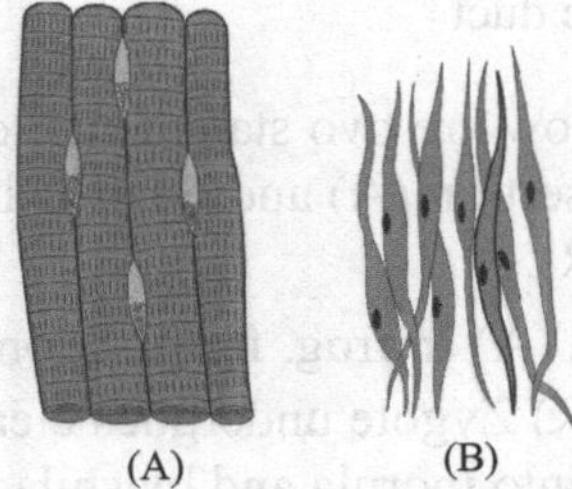

Choose the incorrect statement w.r.t. A and B.
(a) Both A and B are bundled together in a connective tissue sheath
(b) A is characterised by striations, while B do not show striation
(c) B is fusiform in its shape, while in A, muscle fibres are bundled together in a parallel fashion
(d) Both A and B are voluntary muscles

24. Consider the following statements.
I. Most of the cartilages in vertebrate embryos are replaced by bones in adults.
II. The nuclei of columnar epithelium are located at the base.
III. In all the connective tissues, the cells secrete modified polysaccharides, which acts as a matrix-after accumulating between cells and fibres.
IV. Cartilage is a specialised connective tissue.
Choose the correct set of statements out of the given options.
(a) I, II and IV (b) I, II, III and IV
(c) II, III and IV (d) I and IV

25. Given below are two statements.
Statement I Squamous epithelium lines the walls of blood vessels.
Statement II Tendons are examples of dense irregular connective tissue.
In the light of the above statements, choose the correct answer from the options given below.
(a) Statement I is incorrect, but statement II is correct
(b) Both statement I and statement II are correct
(c) Both statement I and statement II are incorrect
(d) Statement I is correct, but statement II is incorrect

Response Index

Performance Scanner

> 90% Excellent !	You have mastered these topics. The concepts of these topics are at your fingertips. Move on to the next topics and maintain this momentum.
76-90% Very Good !	You have a good command over these topics. Revise these topics again after a few days and enhance your performance.
60-75% Good !	You have a wide scope to learn for these topics. Revise these topics again.
<60% Not Satisfactory!	You have a long way ahead of you to master these topics. Revise it thoroughly.

Test 2

Syllabus

- Morphology, Anatomy and Function of Different System of Frog and Cockroach

For deeper insight, **Scan the QR Code**

Important Instructions

- The test is of 30 minutes duration and contains 25 Multiple Choice Questions (four options with a single correct answer).
- Choose the correct option and fill the OMR given on the last page of this test accordingly.
- At some instances, you may find more than 1 option to be correct. In such circumstances, you have to judge the most appropriate answer as per the conditions given in the question.

1. In cockroaches, the 10th segment bears a pair of jointed filamentous structures called

(a) gonapophysis
(b) anal cerci
(c) anal style
(d) caudal style

2. The correct sequence of the parts of foregut in cockroach is

(a) Mouth → Oesophagus → Pharynx → Crop → Gizzard
(b) Mouth → Crop → Pharynx → Oesophagus → Gizzard
(c) Mouth → Gizzard → Crop → Pharynx → Oesophagus
(d) Mouth → Pharynx → Oesophagus → Crop → Gizzard

3. Which of the following statement is incorrect about the respiratory system of cockroach?

(a) The trachea receives air through 10 pairs of spiracles.
(b) The spiracles always remain open.
(c) The opening of spiracles is regulated by sphincter.
(d) Tracheal tubes are further divided into tracheoles to carry oxygen to all part.

4. Given below are two statements regarding alimentary canal of cockroach.

Statement I Gizzard secretes digestive juice.

Statement II Gastric caeca helps in removal of excretory products from haemolymph.

In the light of the above statements, choose the correct answer from the options given below.

(a) Statement I is incorrect, but statement II is correct
(b) Both statement I and statement II are correct
(c) Both statement I and statement II are incorrect
(d) Statement I is correct, but statement II is incorrect

5. In frog, the duodenum receives bile from gall bladder and pancreatic juices from the pancreas through a

(a) common bile duct
(b) hepato-pancreatic duct
(c) cystic duct
(d) hepatic duct

6. Given below are two statements; one is labelled as the Assertion (A) and other is labelled as the Reason (R).

Assertion (A) In frog, fertilisation is external.

Reason (R) Zygote undergoes cleavage and develops into morula and blastula.

In the light of the above statements, choose the correct answer from the options given below.

(a) A is false, but R is true
(b) Both A and R are true and R is the correct explanation of A
(c) Both A and R are true, but R is not the correct explanation of A
(d) A is true, but R is false

7. Which of the following structure allow oxygen rich blood to enter the chambers of the cockroach heart?
(a) Spiracles
(b) Tracheoles
(c) Ostia
(d) Malpighian tubules

8. Read the following statements and find out the incorrect statement about frogs.
(a) Frog respire on land and in water by two different methods.
(b) Liver secretes bile that is stored in the gall bladder.
(c) Three chambered heart is situated in the upper part of body cavity.
(d) RBCs are enucleated and contain red coloured pigment called haemoglobin.

9. Match List I with List II with respect to cockroach.

List I	List II
A. Testes	1. 2th- 6th segments
B. Ovaries	2. 4th- 6th segments
C. Spermathecae	3. 6th- 7th segments
D. Mushroom gland	4. 6th- 9th segments

Choose the correct option given below.

	A	B	C	D
(a)	1	2	3	4
(b)	2	1	4	3
(c)	4	1	3	2
(d)	2	3	4	1

10. Consider the following statements.
I. Cockroaches are dioecious.
II. The external genitalia of cockroaches are represented by male gonapophysis or phallomere.
III. Each ovary of female cockroach is formed of a group of four ovarian tubules or ovarioles.
IV. Oviducts of each ovary of cockroach unite into a single median oviduct.
V. The fertilised eggs of cockroach are encased in capsules called spermatheca.

Identify the set of correct statements and choose the correct option.
(a) I, II, III and IV
(b) III, IV and V
(c) I, IV and V
(d) I, II and IV

11. Identify the set of incorrect statements about frog.
I. Male reproductive system consist of a pair of yellowish ovoid testes.
II. Vasa efferentia open into Bidder's canal.
III. Fertilisation is internal and takes place in water.
IV. Development does not involve any larval stage.
V. A mature female can lay 2500 to 3000 ova at a time.

Choose the correct answer out of the given options.
(a) I, II and III
(b) III and IV
(c) I, IV and V
(d) II, III and IV

12. Which of the following statement is incorrect?
(a) In cockroach the Malpighian tubules are present at the junction of midgut and hindgut.
(b) The internal organs of cockroach are present in a fluid filled cavity.
(c) In cockroach the glandular cells and ciliated cells of Malpighian tubule convert nitrogenous wastes into urea.
(d) In cockroach, absorption of digested food begins in mesenteron (midgut).

13. With the help of several ommatidia, a cockroach can receive several images of an object. This kind of vision is called
(a) nocturnal vision, being common during night
(b) mosaic vision, with more sensitivity, but less resolution
(c) mosaic vision with more resolution, but less sensitivity
(d) nocturnal vision with more sensitivity and more resolution

14. Given below are two statements.
Statement I In the heart of frogs the ventricles open into conus arteriosus.
Statement II Chordae tendinae in heart of frog is found in the wall of ventricle.
In the light of the above statements, choose the correct answer from the options given below.
(a) Statement I is incorrect, but statement II is correct
(b) Both statement I and statement II are correct
(c) Both statement I and statement II are incorrect
(d) Statement I is correct, but statement II is incorrect

15. Which of the following statements is incorrect about excretory system in frog?
(a) In male frog, each ureter contains a duct for transfer of sperms.
(b) Each kidney is composed of several structural and functional units called nephrons.
(c) In females, the ureters and oviduct open separately in the cloaca.
(d) Uric acid is formed from ammonia, which is released during deamination.

16. Given below are two statements; one is labelled as the Assertion (A) and other is labelled as the Reason (R).
Assertion (A) In frogs well developed hepatic portal system is observed.
Reason (R) It is a venous connection between liver and intestine.
In the light of the above statements, choose the correct answer from the options given below.
(a) A is false, but R is true
(b) Both A and R are true and R is the correct explanation of A
(c) Both A and R are true, but R is not the correct explanation of A
(d) A is true, but R is false

17. Identify the incorrect set of statements.
I. The head of cockroach lie posteriorly at right angles to the longitudinal body axis.
II. Head region of cockroach is formed by the fusion of fifth segment.
III. Posterior end of the cockroach head have biting and chewing type mouth parts.
IV. Prothorax act as a connecting bridge between head and thorax.
V. Labrum lies within the cavity enclosed by the mouth parts.
Choose the correct answer from the options given below.
(a) II, IV and V
(b) I, II, III
(c) III, IV and V
(d) I, II, III and V

18. Given below are two statements; one is labelled as the Assertion (A) and other is labelled as the Reason (R).
Assertion (A) Frogs are beneficial for mankind.
Reason (R) Frogs eat insects and protect crops.
In the light of the above statements, choose the correct answer from the options given below.
(a) A is false, but R is true
(b) Both A and R are true and R is the correct explanation of A
(c) Both A and R are true, but R is not the correct explanation of A
(d) A is true, but R is false

19. Given below are two statements about cockroaches
Statement I Malphigian tubules are lined by glandular and columnar cells.
Statement II The development observed in *P. americana* is paurometabolous.
In the light of the above statements, choose the correct answer from the options given below.
(a) Statement I is incorrect, but statement II is correct
(b) Both statement I and statement II are correct
(c) Both statement I and statement II are incorrect
(d) Statement I is correct, but statement II is incorrect

20. Some characteristics of cockroach are mentioned below. Identify which of these belong to male cockroach.
I. Accessory gland at 6th and 7th abdominal segment.
II. Reproductive organ on 2nd and 6th abdominal segment.
III. Pair of spermatheca at 6th segment.
IV. Presence of phallomere, a chitinous asymmetrical structure.
Choose the correct sets of characteristic from the options given below.
(a) I, III and IV
(b) I and IV
(c) II and III
(d) II, III and IV

21. A thin fold of membrane called mesorchium extends between
(a) two testes
(b) liver and kidneys
(c) kidneys and testes
(d) two kidneys

22. In frogs, eyes are located

(a) behind the external nostrils on each side of head
(b) in front of external nostrils on each side of head
(c) behind the external nostrils on one side of head
(d) in front of external nostrils on one side of head

23. In the given figure, which structure has an outer layer of thick circular muscles and thick inner cuticle?

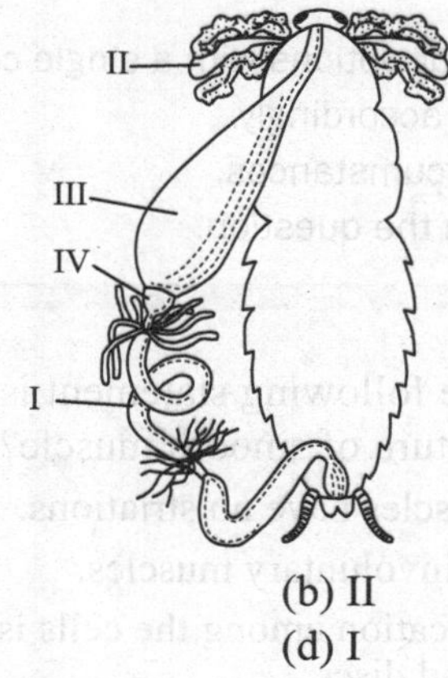

(a) III (b) II
(c) IV (d) I

24. Given below are two statements.

Statement I Bile juice secreted by gall bladder emulsifies fat, where as the pancreatic juice digest fats and carbohydrates.

Statement II The salivary glands are absent in frog, so digestion starts in stomach.

In the light of the above statements, choose the correct answer from the options given below.

(a) Statement I is incorrect, but statement II is correct
(b) Both statement I and statement II are correct
(c) Both statement I and statement II are incorrect
(d) Statement I is correct, but statement II is incorrect

25. Identify the incorrect statement w.r.t the following figure.

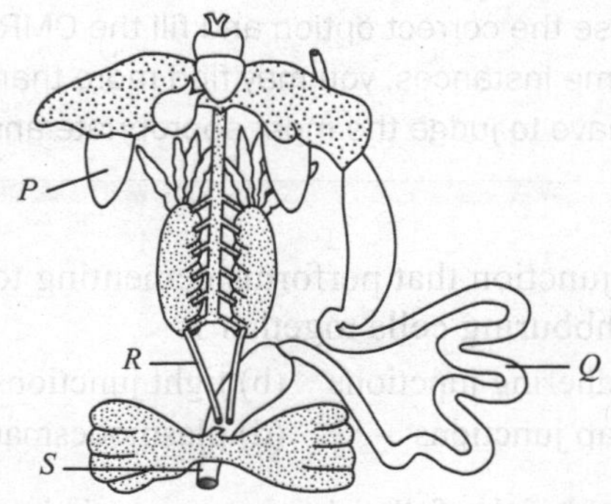

(a) '*P*' are sac-like structure present in the upper part of the thorax.
(b) '*Q*' is the site for complete digestion of food.
(c) '*R*' separately opens in '*S*' in male frogs.
(d) '*S*' is a small chamber used to pass sperms in males.

Response Index

01	a	b	c	d	10	a	b	c	d	19	a	b	c	d
02	a	b	c	d	11	a	b	c	d	20	a	b	c	d
03	a	b	c	d	12	a	b	c	d	21	a	b	c	d
04	a	b	c	d	13	a	b	c	d	22	a	b	c	d
05	a	b	c	d	14	a	b	c	d	23	a	b	c	d
06	a	b	c	d	15	a	b	c	d	24	a	b	c	d
07	a	b	c	d	16	a	b	c	d	25	a	b	c	d
08	a	b	c	d	17	a	b	c	d					
09	a	b	c	d	18	a	b	c	d					

Performance Scanner

> 90% Excellent !	You have mastered these topics. The concepts of these topics are at your fingertips. Move on to the next topics and maintain this momentum.
76-90% Very Good !	You have a good command over these topics. Revise these topics again after a few days and enhance your performance.
60-75% Good !	You have a wide scope to learn for these topics. Revise these topics again.
<60% Not Satisfactory!	You have a long way ahead of you to master these topics. Revise it thoroughly.

Chapter Break Thru

Syllabus
- Animal Tissues (Epithelium, Neural, Connective and Muscle Tissue)
- Morphology, Anatomy and Function of Different Systems of Frog and Cockroach

Important Instructions
- The test is of 1 hour duration and contains 50 Multiple-Choice Questions (Four options with a single correct answer).
- Choose the correct option and fill the OMR given on the last page of this test accordingly.
- At some instances, you may find more than 1 option to be correct. In such circumstances, you have to judge the most appropriate answer as per the conditions given in the question.

1. The junction that performs cementing to keep neighbouring cells together is
(a) adhering junctions (b) tight junctions
(c) gap junctions (d) plasmodesmata

2. Which of the following statement is incorrect about connective tissues?
(a) In all connective tissues except blood, the cells secrete fibres of structural proteins called collagen or elastin.
(b) The fibres provide strength, elasticity and flexibility to the tissue.
(c) Loose connective tissue has cells and fibres, loosely arranged in a semi-fluid ground substance.
(d) In the dense irregular connective tissues, the collagen fibres are present in rows between many parallel bundles of fibres.

3. Which type of simple epithelium found in wall of blood vessels and air sacs of lungs?
(a) Squamous epithelium
(b) Cuboidal epithelium
(c) Columnar epithelium
(d) Ciliated epithelium

4. Osteocytes are present in the ...I... and chondrocytes are present in ...II... .

	I	II
(a)	lacunae	cavities
(b)	cavities	lacunae
(c)	sinuses	hole
(d)	holes	lacunae

5. Which of the following statement is incorrect with respect to nature of smooth muscle?
(a) These muscles have no striations.
(b) They are involuntary muscles.
(c) Communication among the cells is performed by intercalated discs.
(d) These muscles are present in the wall of blood vessels.

6. Given below are two statements.
Statement I Fibrous cytoskeleton of microvilli helps in protection.
Statement II Cilia take part in creating currents for circulation of fluids.
In the light of the above statements, choose the correct answer from the options given below.
(a) Statement I is incorrect, but statement II is correct
(b) Both statement I and statement II are correct
(c) Both statement I and statement II are incorrect
(d) Statement I is correct, but statement II is incorrect

7. Match List I with List II.

	List I		List II
A.	Columnar epithelium	1.	Nephrons in kidney
B.	Pseudostratified columnar epithelium	2.	Mammary glands and salivary gland
C.	Cuboidal epithelium	3.	Lining of intestine and stomach
D.	Exocrine gland	4.	Trachea and large bronchi
		5.	Blood vessels

Choose the correct answer from the options given below.

	A	B	C	D
(a)	3	4	1	2
(b)	3	5	4	2
(c)	2	3	5	1
(d)	5	4	3	1

8. Read the following statements and choose the correct option.

I. Bones supports and protects softer tissues and organs.
II. Neuroglial cells protect and support the nephrons.
III. Bones are strong due to the presence of potassium salt and collagen fibres.
IV. Striated muscle fibres are bundle together in parallel fashion.
V. Biceps are involuntary and striated.

Choose the correct set of statements from the options given below.
(a) III and IV (b) I, II and IV
(c) II and IV (d) I and III

9. Consider the following statements.

Statement I Schwann cells are present where nerve is covered with myelin sheath.
Statement II When a neuron is suitably stimulated, an electrical disturbance is generated which swiftly travels along its plasma membrane.
In the light of the above statements, choose the correct answer from the options given below.
(a) Statement I is incorrect, but statement II is correct
(b) Both statement I and statement II are correct
(c) Both statement I and statement II are incorrect
(d) Statement I is correct, but statement II is incorrect

10. Given below are the types of tissues.

I. Epithelial tissues
II. Connective tissues
III. Muscular tissues
IV. Neural tissues

Which of the given tissues are constituent of human heart?
(a) I, II and III (b) II and III
(c) II, III and IV (d) I, II, III and IV

11. Consider the following statements.

I. The walls of blood vessels, stomach and intestine contain smooth muscle tissue.
II. Gap junctions communicate with each other by connecting nuclei of adjoining cells.
III. Desmosomes serve as the anchoring junctions between the cells.
IV. Cartilage is a non-vascular connective tissue having matrix of chondroitin.

Which of them are correct?
(a) I and II (b) I, III and IV
(c) II and III (d) III and IV

12. Find out the correct identification and description of the given structure.

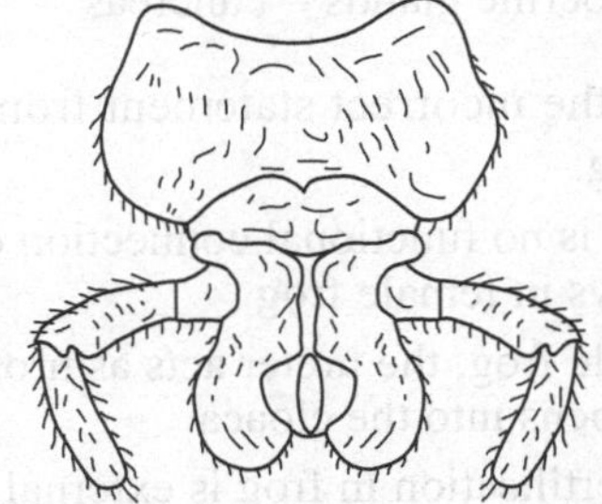

(a) Mandible–Mouth part having grinding and incising region
(b) Maxilla–Present beneath the mandible on either side of head capsule
(c) Labrum–Upper lip with sensory setae
(d) Labium– Lower lip with labial palps

13. Given below are two statements; one is labelled as Assertion (A) and other is labelled as Reason (R).

Assertion (A) Thick layers of muscles are present in the wall of alimentary canal.
Reason (R) These muscles help in the mixing of food materials with the enzymes coming from different glands in the alimentary canal.
In the light of the above statements, choose the correct answer from the options given below.
(a) A is false, but R is true
(b) Both A and R are true and R is the correct explanation of A
(c) Both A and R are true, but R is not the correct explanation of A
(d) A is true, but R is false

14. Which of the following statement is incorrect regarding frog?
(a) Renal portal vein in frog carries blood from lower part of the kidney
(b) Arterial system of frog begins with conus arteriosus or truncus
(c) External ears are absent and only tympanum can be seen
(d) The lymphatic system consists of lymph, lymph channels and lymph nodes.

15. Select the incorrect match pair.
(a) Apocrine glands – Mammary glands
(b) Holocrine glands – Sweat glands
(c) Exocrine glands – Salivary glands
(d) Heterocrine glands – Pancreas

16. Identify the incorrect statement from the following.
(a) There is no functional connection of ovaries with kidneys in female frog
(b) In male frog, the ureter acts as urogenital duct and opens into the cloaca
(c) The fertilisation in frog is external
(d) Development of frog is direct

17. Choose the correct statement regarding frog from the following.
(a) Frogs are harmful to mankind because they eat crops and damage the fields
(b) Frogs are ammonotelic animals
(c) Hindlimbs of frog ends in five digits and forelimbs ends in four digits
(d) Female frog contains sound producing vocal sacs which are absent in male frog

18. Following is the diagram of reproductive system of female cockroach with parts labelled *A, B, C* and *D*. Which of the following is incorrect identification with its features/functions?

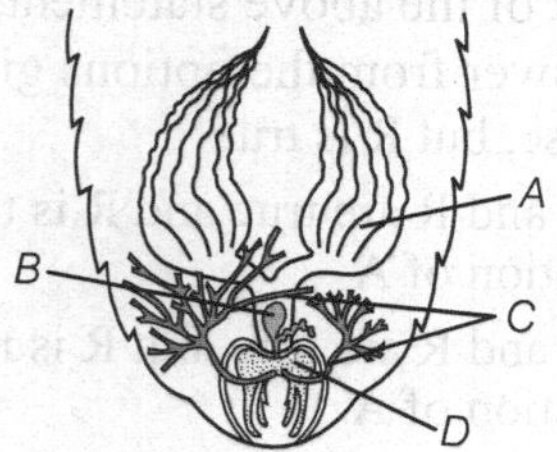

(a) *A*-Pair of ovaries lying laterally in 2nd-6th abdominal segments
(b) *B*-Pair of spermatheca in 6th segment
(c) *C*-Phallic gland which secretes ootheca
(d) *D*-Genital chamber which is a part of genital pouch in female

19. Match List I with List II.

List I	List II
A. Cloaca	1. Openings on the body surface through which air enters and exits, facilitating respiration.
B. Malpighian Tubules	2. Common chamber receiving waste, reproductive, and digestive materials before expulsion
C. Ventricle	3. Excretory organs that remove nitrogenous wastes from the blood
D. Spiracles	4. Pumps blood to both lungs and the rest of the body

Choose the correct answer from the options given below.

	A	B	C	D
(a)	4	1	2	3
(b)	4	2	3	1
(c)	2	3	4	1
(d)	4	3	2	1

20. Choose the correctly matched pair.
(a) Salivary cells – Stratified epithelium
(b) Proximal convoluted tubule – Brush bordered cuboidal epithelium
(c) Moist surface of buccal cavity – Keratinised squamous epithelium
(d) Intestinal glands – Endocrine glands

21. Read the following statements carefully.
I. Simple epithelium is composed of a single layer of cells and functions as a lining for body cavities, ducts and tubes.
II. Cuboidal epithelium is commonly found in ducts of glands and tubular parts of nephrons in kidneys.
III. The nuclei of columnar epithelial cells are located in the centre of the cell.

IV. The function of ciliated epithelium is to move particles or mucus in a specific direction over the epithelium.
V. Exocrine glands secrete hormones.

Choose the set of incorrect statements from the options given below.
(a) I, II and IV
(b) III and V
(c) IV and V
(d) II, IV and V

22. Which characteristics is incorrect about compound epithelium?
(a) It is found over surface subjected to wear and tear
(b) It provides little protection to underlying tissues
(c) It has little role in secretion, excretion and absorption
(d) Cells of only basal layer rest over basement membrane

23. Which one of the following is not a characteristic feature of frog?
(a) The skin is moist and slimy.
(b) The medulla oblongata exits through the foramen magnum and continues into the brain, which is enclosed in the vertebral column.
(c) During aestivation and hibernation, gaseous exchange takes place through skin.
(d) Skin, buccal cavity and lungs are the respiratory organs.

24. Given below are few statement regarding respiratory system of cockroach.
I. Consists of tracheae, tracheoles and spiracles.
II. Tracheal tubes carry oxygen from the air to all the parts.
III. Network of trachea opens through 12 pairs of spiracles.
IV. Exchange of gases takes place at the tracheoles by ventilation.

Choose the option containing correct statements.
(a) I, II and III (b) and II
(c) II and IV (d) I and III

25. Given below are two statements.
Statement I The striated skeletal muscle fibres are bundled together in a parallel fashion.
Statement II Smooth muscles are 'voluntary' as their functioning can be directly controlled.

In the light of the above statements, choose the correct answer from the options given below.
(a) Statement I is incorrect, but statement II is correct
(b) Both statement I and statement II are correct
(c) Both statement I and statement II are incorrect
(d) Statement I is correct, but statement II is incorrect

26. Choose the correct statement regarding figures *A* and *B* given below.

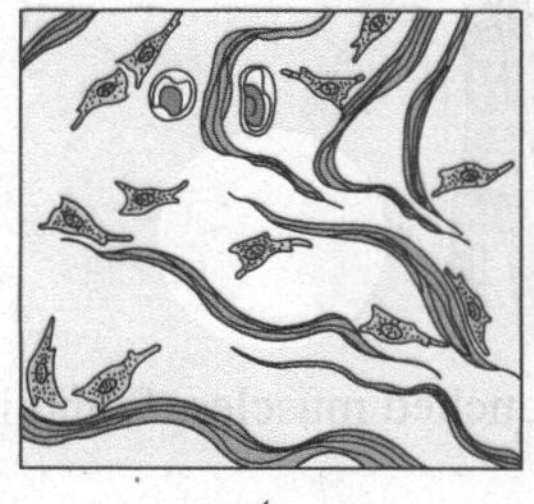
A

B

(a) *A* is dense regular connective tissue, whereas *B* is a tissue present in the skin.
(b) Both *A* and *B* are dense irregular connective tissues.
(c) *A* is present in skin, whereas tendons and ligaments are made of *B*.
(d) Both *A* and *B* are dense regular connective tissue.

27. Given below are two statements.
Statement I Bones support and protect softer tissues and organs.
Statement II The bone marrow in some bones is the site of production of stem cells.

In the light of the above statements, choose the correct answer from the options given below.
(a) Statement I is incorrect, but statement II is correct
(b) Both statement I and statement II are correct
(c) Both statement I and statement II are incorrect
(d) Statement I is correct, but statement II is incorrect

28. Given below are two statements; one is labelled as Assertion (A) and other is labelled as Reason (R).
Assertion (A) Neuroglia make up more than one half the volume of neural tissue in our body.
Reason (R) The neuroglial cells protect and support skeletal system.

In the light of the above statements, choose the correct answer from the options given below.
(a) A is false, but R is true
(b) Both A and R are true and R is the correct explanation of A
(c) Both A and R are true, but R is not the correct explanation of A
(d) A is true, but R is false

29. Identify the correct description about the given figure.

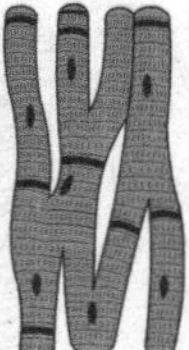

(a) Cardiac muscles, branched muscles, found in the walls of the heart.
(b) Smooth muscle, unbranched, found in blood vessels and intestine.
(c) Striated muscles, tapering at both ends, have communication junction at some fusion points.
(d) Skeletal muscles show striations and are closely attached with the bones.

30. In simple epithelium, the cells are
(a) continuously dividing to provide cells for forming an organ
(b) hardened to provide support to the organs
(c) loosely connected to one another to form an irregular layer
(d) cemented directly to one another to form a single layer

31. Given below are two statements; one is labelled as Assertion (A) and the other as Reason (R).
Assertion (A) Compound epithelium are composed of many cell layers.
Reason (R) Many cell layers protect against external environment.
In the light of the above statement, choose the correct answer from the options given below.
(a) A is false, but R is true.
(b) Both A and R are true and R is the correct explanation of A
(c) Both A and R are true, but R is not the correct explanation of A
(d) A is true, but R is false

32. Which of the following structures maintain the structural integrity of cells in a tissue?
(a) Plasmodesmata
(b) Intercellular spaces
(c) Adhering junctions
(d) Gap junctions

33. Which of the following tissue sections when added to water, would float on its surface?
(a) Adipose tissue (b) Areolar tissue
(c) Tendons (d) Ligaments

34. Given below are two statements.
Statement I The long bones interact with skeletal muscles in order to bring about movement.
Statement II Muscles of biceps are closely attached to skeleton bones.
In the light of the above statements, choose the correct answer from the options given below.
(a) Statement I is incorrect, but statement II is correct.
(b) Both statement I and statement II are correct.
(c) Both statement I and statement II are incorrect.
(d) Statement I is correct, but statement II is incorrect.

35. Which of the following structures provide mechanical and electrochemical connection between adjacent neighbouring cells in the auto-excitatory muscles?
(a) Actin
(b) Myosin
(c) Troponin
(d) Intercalated discs

36. Given below are two statements.
Statement I Absorption structure in frogs and mammals are different.
Statement II For absorbing nutrients from food, intestinal villi are present in frogs.
In the light of the above statements, choose the correct answer from the options given below.
(a) Statement I is incorrect, but statement II is correct.
(b) Both statement I and statement II are correct.
(c) Both statement I and statement II are incorrect.
(d) Statement I is correct, but statement II is incorrect.

37. Consider the following statements w.r.t cockroaches.

I. Cockroaches have closed type of circulatory system.
II. Trachea is subdivided into bronchioles.
III. Spiracles are present on the ventral side of the body.
IV. Opening of spiracles is regulated by sphincter muscles.

Choose the correct answer from the options given below.

(a) II and III (b) IV only
(c) III only (d) I and II

38. Given below are two statements; one is labelled as Assertion (A) and the other as Reason (R).

Assertion (A) Despite chopping off the head of a cockroach it will live for some days.

Reason (R) Ventral part of the body holds majority of the nervous system.

In the light of the above statements, choose the correct answer from the options given below.

(a) A is false, but R is true.
(b) Both A and R are true and R is the correct explanation of A
(c) Both A and R are true, but R is not the correct explanation of A
(d) A is true, but R is false

39. Which of the following statement is incorrect?

(a) A cockroach has no significant economic importance.
(b) Development of cockroach involves a nymphal stage.
(c) A cockroach moults about 13 times.
(d) Both nymph and adults have wings.

40. Which of the following structures are adaption of a frog for survival in water?

I. Nictitating membrane
II. Webbed feet
III. Copulatory pad
IV. Tympanum

Choose the correct answer from the options given below.

(a) I and III (b) II only
(c) I and II (d) II, III and IV

41. Which of the structures in a frog allows sexual dimorphism?

(a) Copulatory pads in females
(b) Vocal sacs in males
(c) Cloaca in males
(d) Sensory papillae in females

42. Which of the following tissue acts as a cushion to support internal organs?

(a) Adipose tissue
(b) Areolar tissue
(c) Ligament
(d) Cartilage

43. Which of the following structures provide energy to frogs during breeding season?

(a) Fat bodies (b) Cloaca
(c) Thyroxine (d) Urea

44. Given below is a diagrammatic representation of a tissue sample. Which of the following is correct about the same?

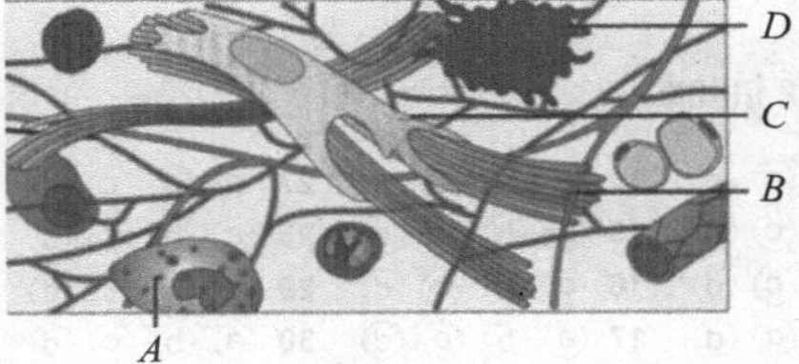

(a) Cell *A* are actively involved in allergic reactions.
(b) *B* provides elasticity to skin.
(c) *C* are components of extracellular matrix.
(d) *D* plays no role in immune system.

45. Given below are two statements.

Statement I Both skeletal and smooth muscles are uninucleated.

Statement II Muscles attached to bones usually exist in syncytium.

In the light of the above statements, choose the correct answer from the options given below

(a) Statement I is incorrect, but statement II is correct.
(b) Both statement I and statement II are correct.
(c) Both statement I and statement II are incorrect.
(d) Statement I is correct, but statement II is incorrect.

46. Which of the following is not a function of the neuroglial cells of the nervous system?
(a) Holds the neurons in place
(b) Proper functioning of synapses
(c) Impulse conduction
(d) Supply nutrients to the neurons

47. Which of the following structures in a cockroach helps them to detect vibrations in the air or on the ground?
(a) Antennae (b) Tegmina
(c) Anal cerci (d) Compound eyes

48. Given below are two statements; one is labelled as Assertion (A) and the other as Reason (R).
Assertion (A) Haemolymph in cockroaches are not involved in gas exchange.
Reason (R) Haemolymph does not contain any respiratory pigment.
In the light of the above statements, choose the correct answer from the options given below.
(a) A is false, but R is true.
(b) Both A and R are true and R is the correct explanation of A
(c) Both A and R are true, but R is not the correct explanation of A
(d) A is true, but R is false

49. Which part of the brain of a frog contain structures that regulate vision?
(a) Forebrain (b) Midbrain
(c) Hindbrain (d) Medulla

50. Which of the following statements is incorrect about the excretion of frogs and cockroaches?
(a) Cockroaches excrete more toxic nitrogenous waste than frogs.
(b) Malpighian tubules have the same function as frog kidneys.
(c) Spermatheca stores spermatozoa in female cockroaches.
(d) Bidder's canal in male frogs conduct sperms from testes

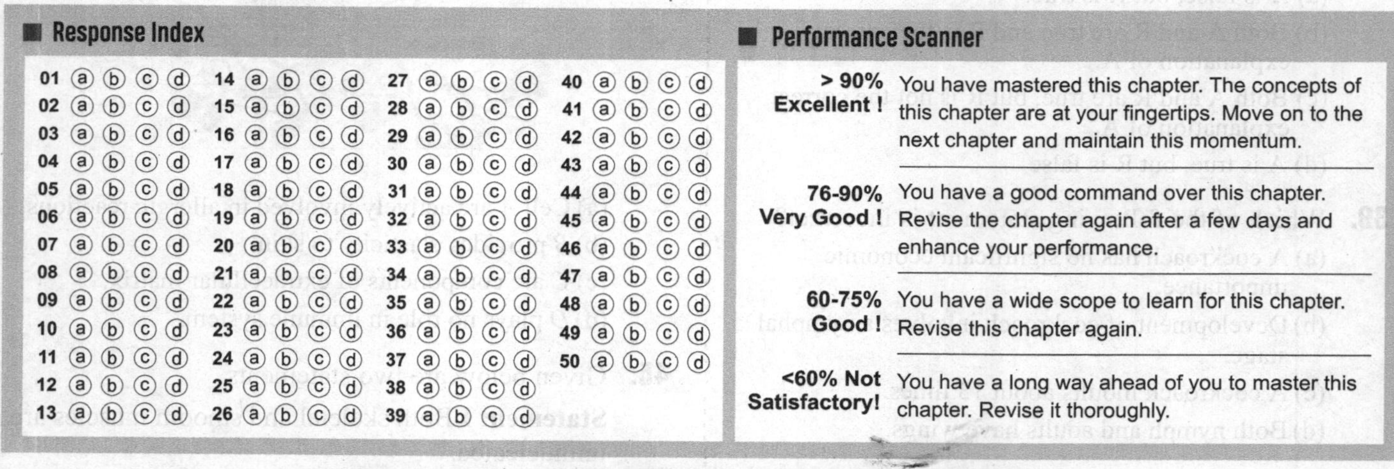

Scan for online chapter test

Scan for online unit test

Test Booklet No. 3947308

Test Booklet Code CH8

MEDACE
NEET (UG)
SELF ASSESSMENT KIT

Cell : The Unit Of Life

Topics Covered

- An Overview of Cell and Cell Theory
- Prokaryotic Cells
- Eukaryotic Cells

Important Instructions

- This Booklet Contains – Three Topic Tests and One Test on Complete Chapter.
- Each question carries 4 marks.
- For each correct response, the candidate will get 4 marks. And for every incorrect response, 1 mark will be additionally deducted from total score.
- Use **Blue/Black** point pen only for filling the OMR.
- Rough work is to be done in the space provided for this purpose in the test booklet only.

Name of the Candidate (In Capitals) ______________

____

Candidate's Signature ______________

Invigilator's Signature ______________

Facsimile signature stamp of center superintendent______________

Do not open this booklet until you start attempting the test

Topical Follow Thru

Test 1

Syllabus Cell Theory and Cell as the Basic Unit of Life

For deeper insight, **Scan the QR Code**

Important Instructions

- The test is of 30 minutes duration and contains 15 Multiple Choice Questions (four options with a single correct answer).
- Choose the correct option and fill the OMR given on the last page of this test accordingly.
- At some instances, you may find more than 1 option to be correct. In such circumstances, you have to judge the most appropriate answer as per the conditions given in the question.

1. Cells divide and new cells are formed from pre-existing cells, this theory was given by
(a) Theodore Schwann (b) Rudolf Virchow
(c) Matthias Schleiden (d) Nicolson

2. Select the incorrect match.
(a) RBCs - Round and biconcave
(b) WBCs - Elongated
(c) Mesophyll cells - Round and oval
(d) Columnar epithelial cells - Long and narrow

3. Which of the following cells are branched and narrow, respectively?
(a) WBCs and tracheid
(b) Nerve cell and columnar epithelial cells
(c) Mesophyll cells and tracheid
(d) Tracheid and RBCs

4. Which is correct about cell theory in view of current status of our knowledge about cell structure?
(a) It needs modification due to discovery of sub-cellular structures like chloroplasts and mitochondria
(b) Modified cell theory means that all living beings are composed of cells capable of reproducing
(c) Cell theory does not hold good because viruses do not have cellular organisation
(d) Cell theory means that all living objects consists of cells whether capable or not capable of reproducing

5. Different cells have different sizes. Arrange the following in an ascending order of their size.
I. Mycoplasma
II. Ostrich eggs
III. Human RBCs
IV. Bacteria
Choose the correct answer from the following.
(a) I, IV, III and II (b) I, II, III and IV
(c) II, I, III and IV (d) III, II, I and IV

6. Read the following statements.
Statement I Various chemical reactions occur in the cytoplasm to keep the cell in the living state.
Statement II Animal cell contain cytoplasm, which helps in cell division.
In the light of the above statements, choose the correct answer from the options given below.
(a) Statement I is incorrect, but statement II is correct
(b) Both statement I and statement II are correct
(c) Both statement I and statement II are incorrect
(d) Statement I is correct, but statement II is incorrect

7. Which scientist concluded that the presence of a cell wall is a unique characteristic of plant cells?
(a) Matthias Schleiden
(b) Antonie van Leeuwenhoek
(c) Theodore Schwann
(d) Rudolf Virchow

8. Given below are two statements; one is labelled as Assertion (A) and the other is labelled as Reason (R).

Assertion (A) Smaller cells are usually metabolically active cells.

Reason (R) In smaller cell nucleocytoplasmic ratio and surface volume ratio is higher.

In the light of the above statements, choose the correct answer from the options given below.

(a) A is false, but R is true
(b) Both A and R are true and R is the correct explanation of A
(c) Both A and R are true, but R is not the correct explanation of A
(d) A is true, but R is false

9. Which of the following statement is true about the structure of an onion cell as observed under a microscope?

(a) The cell wall is absent and only the plasma membrane is visible
(b) The cell wall is present as the outermost layer with the plasma membrane just inside it
(c) The cell membrane is the outermost layer with no cell wall
(d) The cell wall is present, but there is no visible plasma membrane

10. Which one of the following is incorrect about unicellular organisms?

(a) It is capable of independent existence
(b) Cell is structural and functional unit
(c) Anything less than a complete structure of a cell does not ensure independent living
(d) In unicellular organisms, tissues work in coordination to perform different functions

11. Read the following statements.

I. The prokaryotic cells lack membrane bound organelles.
II. The size of bacteria ranges from 5-10 μm.
III. Ribosomes are double membrane covered organelle.
IV. The cytoplasm is the main arena of cellular activities in both the plant and animal cells.
V. Animal cells contain centrosome, which helps in cell division.

Choose the correct set of statements from the options given below.

(a) I, III and V
(b) III, IV and V
(c) I, IV and V
(d) II, III and IV

12. A thin outer layer 'plasma membrane' was the finding of

(a) Robert Brown
(b) Theodore Schwann
(c) Antonie van Leeuwenhoek
(d) Nicolson and Singer

13. Select the incorrect statement.

(a) Leeuwenhoek first described a live cell
(b) Robert Hooke first saw a living cell
(c) Robert Brown discovered the nucleus
(d) Schwann proposed that bodies of animals and plants are composed of cells and products of cells

14. Which of the following organelles are specifically membrane-bound and found in eukaryotic cells but not in prokaryotic cells?

(a) Ribosomes and centrioles
(b) Mitochondria and endoplasmic reticulum
(c) Chromoplasts and rough ER
(d) Golgi complex and mesosome

15. Match List I with List II.

	List I		List II
A.	Schleiden and Schwann	1.	Nucleus
B.	Rudolf Virchow	2.	Cell
C.	Robert Brown	3.	Cell theory
D.	Robert Hooke	4.	*Omnis cellula-e-cellula*

Choose the correct answer from the options given below.

	A	B	C	D		A	B	C	D
(a)	2	1	3	4	(b)	3	4	1	2
(c)	3	1	4	2	(d)	1	3	4	2

Response Index

01	a	b	c	d	10	a	b	c	d	19	a	b	c	d
02	a	b	c	d	11	a	b	c	d	20	a	b	c	d
03	a	b	c	d	12	a	b	c	d	21	a	b	c	d
04	a	b	c	d	13	a	b	c	d	22	a	b	c	d
05	a	b	c	d	14	a	b	c	d	23	a	b	c	d
06	a	b	c	d	15	a	b	c	d	24	a	b	c	d
07	a	b	c	d	16	a	b	c	d	25	a	b	c	d
08	a	b	c	d	17	a	b	c	d					
09	a	b	c	d	18	a	b	c	d					

Performance Scanner

> 90% Excellent !	You have mastered these topics. The concepts of these topics are at your fingertips. Move on to the next topics and maintain this momentum.
76-90% Very Good !	You have a good command over these topics. Revise these topics again after a few days and enhance your performance.
60-75% Good !	You have a wide scope to learn for these topics. Revise these topics again.
<60% Not Satisfactory!	You have a long way ahead of you to master these topics. Revise it thoroughly.

Test 2

Syllabus
- Structures of Prokaryotic Cell

For deeper insight, **Scan the QR Code**

Important Instructions

- The test is of 30 minutes duration and contains 15 Multiple Choice Questions (four options with a single correct answer).
- Choose the correct option and fill the OMR given on the last page of this test accordingly.
- At some instances, you may find more than 1 option to be correct. In such circumstances, you have to judge the most appropriate answer as per the conditions given in the question.

1. How many of the following structures are present in bacteria?

Flagella, Cilia, Pili, Fimbriae

(a) 2 (b) 4
(c) 3 (d) 1

2. Mesosome have the following functions, except

(a) cell wall formation (b) DNA replication
(c) respiration (d) locomotion

3. Read the following statements.

Statement I Pili and fimbriae are surface structures of the bacteria that play important role in motility.

Statement II Pili are elongated tubular structure made of a special protein.

In the light of the above statements, choose the correct answer from the options given below.

(a) Statement I is incorrect, but statement II is correct
(b) Both statement I and statement II are correct
(c) Both statement I and statement II are incorrect
(d) Statement I is correct, but statement II is incorrect

4. Match List I with List II.

	List I		List II
A.	Bacillus	1.	Spiral
B.	Coccus	2.	Rod-like
C.	Vibrio	3.	Spherical
D.	Spirillum	4.	Comma-shaped

Choose the correct answer from the options given below.

	A	B	C	D		A	B	C	D
(a)	2	3	4	1	(b)	3	4	2	1
(c)	1	3	2	4	(d)	1	4	3	1

5. Ribosomes are .... in prokaryotic cells.

(a) 60S (b) 70S
(c) 80S (d) 90S

6. Identify the incorrect match pair from the following.
(a) Size of a typical eukaryotic cell – 10 - 20 μm
(b) Size of a typical bacteria – 1 - 2 μm
(c) Mesosome -Vesicles
(d) Mycoplasma - Cell wall

7. Read the following statements and select the incorrect one.
(a) Capsule allows the bacterium to hide from the host immune system.
(b) Slime layer is a loose sheath that protects the bacterium from the loss of water and nutrients.
(c) Mesosomes are formed by the invagination of cell membrane into the cytoplasm.
(d) Fimbriae are elongated tubular structure made of a special protein.

8. What is the function of plasmid DNA in prokaryotic cells?
(a) Regulation of cellular respiration
(b) Storage of genetic information for protein synthesis
(c) Confer unique phenotypic traits such as antibiotic resistance
(d) Production of ATP

9. Gas vacuoles are the characteristic of
(a) *Albugo* (b) Cyanobacteria
(c) *Spirogyra* (d) *Amoeba*

10. Read the following statements about glycocalyx.
Statement I This layer is composed of loose sheath known as capsule.
Statement II This layer protect the bacteria, since it is the outermost layer followed by cell wall.
In the light of the above statements, choose the correct answer from the options given below.
(a) Statement I is incorrect, but statement II is correct
(b) Both statement I and statement II are correct
(c) Both statement I and statement II are incorrect
(d) Statement I is correct, but statement II is incorrect

11. Which type of bacteria do not respond to Gram staining?
(a) *Streptococcus* (b) *Corynebacterium*
(c) *Pseudomonas* (d) *Streptomyces*

12. Which statement is incorrect about mesosomes?
(a) Mesosomes are the special membranous structure
(b) It is formed by extension of plasma membrane into the cell
(c) They help in cell wall formation, DNA replication, etc.
(d) Mesosome extensions are in the form of filament and hook

13. Which one of the following is not true about prokaryotic cells?
(a) Membrane bound organelles are absent
(b) Chlorophyll is not located in chloroplasts
(c) Only one chromosome is located in the nucleus
(d) Mesosome is the characteristic feature of prokaryotes

14. Which one of the following is not a cell inclusion body found in prokaryotic cells?
(a) Cyanophycean granule
(b) Glycogen granule
(c) Polysome
(d) Phosphate granule

15. Identify the correct sequence of layers in a typical prokaryotic cell envelope from the outside to the inside.
I. Cell wall
II. Glycocalyx
III. Plasma membrane
Choose the correct answer from the following
(a) II → I → III (b) I → II → III
(c) III → I → II (d) III → II → I

Response Index

01	a	b	c	d	10	a	b	c	d	19	a	b	c	d
02	a	b	c	d	11	a	b	c	d	20	a	b	c	d
03	a	b	c	d	12	a	b	c	d	21	a	b	c	d
04	a	b	c	d	13	a	b	c	d	22	a	b	c	d
05	a	b	c	d	14	a	b	c	d	23	a	b	c	d
06	a	b	c	d	15	a	b	c	d	24	a	b	c	d
07	a	b	c	d	16	a	b	c	d	25	a	b	c	d
08	a	b	c	d	17	a	b	c	d					
09	a	b	c	d	18	a	b	c	d					

Performance Scanner

> 90% Excellent !	You have mastered these topics. The concepts of these topics are at your fingertips. Move on to the next topics and maintain this momentum.
76-90% Very Good !	You have a good command over these topics. Revise these topics again after a few days and enhance your performance.
60-75% Good !	You have a wide scope to learn for these topics. Revise these topics again.
<60% Not Satisfactory!	You have a long way ahead of you to master these topics. Revise it thoroughly.

Test 3

Syllabus

- Structure of Eukaryotic Cell Plant Cell and Animal Cell Cell Envelope, Cell Membrane, Cell Wall, Cell Organelles-Structure and Function Endomembrane System-Endoplasmic Reticulum, Golgi Bodies, Lysosomes, Vacuoles, Mitochondria, Ribosomes, Plastids, Micro bodies, Cytoskeleton, Cilia, Flagella, Centrioles (ultra Structure and Function) Nucleus-Nuclear Membrane, Chromatin, Nucleolus.

For deeper insight, **Scan the QR Code**

Important Instructions

- The test is of 30 minutes duration and contains 25 Multiple Choice Questions (four options with a single correct answer).
- Choose the correct option and fill the OMR given on the last page of this test accordingly.
- At some instances, you may find more than 1 option to be correct. In such circumstances, you have to judge the most appropriate answer as per the conditions given in the question.

1. Cell wall consists of
(a) lignin, hemicellulose, protein and lipid
(b) hemicellulose, cellulose, tubulin and lignin
(c) lignin, hemicellulose, pectin and lipid
(d) lignin, hemicellulose, pectin and cellulose

2. Select the incorrect statement with respect to endoplasmic reticulum.
(a) Steroidal hormones are synthesised in SER
(b) RER is frequently observed in the cells actively involved in protein synthesis
(c) The ER is also included in the endomembrane system
(d) The endoplasmic reticulum often show ribosomes attached to their inner surface

3. Read the following statements about transitional vesicles.
Statement I These represent the zone of exclusion, a region of transition from ER and Golgi cisternae.
Statement II These are drop-like structure which are associated with the concave forming face of Golgi.
In the light of the above statements, choose the correct answer from the options given below.
(a) Statement I is incorrect, but statemen II is correct
(b) Both statement I and statement II are correct
(c) Both statement I and statement II are incorrect
(d) Statement I is correct, but statement II is incorrect

4. Which of the following statement is incorrect about lysosomes?
(a) Lysosomes enzymes can digest carbohydrate, proteins, lipids and nucleic acid
(b) Lysosomes have numerous hydrolytic enzymes
(c) Hydrolytic enzymes of lysosomes are active under acidic pH
(d) Lysosomes are formed by the process of packaging in the endoplasmic reticulum

5. Read the following statements regarding vacuoles.
Statement I Tonoplast facilitates the transport of a number of ions and other materials.
Statement II Most prokaryotes have a contractile vacuole.
In the light of the above statements, choose the correct answer from the options given below.
(a) Statement I is incorrect, but statemen II is correct
(b) Both statement I and statement II are correct
(c) Both statement I and statement II are incorrect
(d) Statement I is correct, but statement II is incorrect

6. Centrosome contains two centrioles which
(a) lie parallel to each other in which each centriole has cartwheel organisation
(b) are made up of eleven evenly spaced peripheral fibrils of tubulin
(c) help in organising the spindle fibres and astral rays during cell division
(d) contains hub that connects the tubules of peripheral doublets by radial spoke made up of protein

7. Which organelle is commonly found in animal cells, but absent in almost all plant cells?
(a) Mitochondria (b) Centrioles
(c) Plastids (d) Ribosomes

8. Given below are two statements; one is labelled as Assertion (A) and the other is labelled as Reason (R).
Assertion (A) Mitochondria is called the powerhouse of the cell.
Reason (R) Mitochondria produce cellular energy.
In the light of the above statements, choose the correct answer from the options given below.
(a) A is false, but R is true
(b) Both A and R are true and R is the correct explanation of A
(c) Both A and R are true, but R is not the correct explanation of A
(d) A is true, but R is false

9. What is the approximate percentage composition of proteins and lipids in the membrane of human erythrocytes?
(a) 52% proteins and 40% lipids
(b) 40% proteins and 52% lipids
(c) 40% proteins and 40% lipids
(d) 52% proteins and 52% lipids

10. Read the following statements regarding plastids.
Statement I Chloroplast synthesises food materials and no other products.
Statement II Chloroplast ribosomes are smaller than the cytoplasmic ribosomes.
In the light of the above statements, choose the correct answer from the options given below.
(a) Statement I is incorrect, but statement II is correct
(b) Both statement I and statement II are correct
(c) Both statement I and statement II are incorrect
(d) Statement I is correct, but statement II is incorrect

11. Which of the following statements are correct regarding the cytoskeleton?
I. It provides mechanical support.
II. It brings colloidal changes.
III. It is responsible for maintenance of shape of the cell cyclosis.
IV. It is involved in protein synthesis.
V. It helps in the absorption of carbon dioxide.
Choose the correct answer from the options given below.
(a) I, IV and V (b) I, II, III, IV and V
(c) I, II and III (d) I and III

12. Which type of molecules require a carrier protein to facilitate their transport across the membrane?
(a) Non-polar molecules
(b) Polar molecules
(c) Lipid-soluble molecules
(d) Gases like O_2 and CO_2

13. Given below are two statements; one is labelled as Assertion (A) and the other is labelled as Reason (R).

Assertion (A) Active transport of molecules of plasma membrane moves against their concentration gradient.

Reason (R) In active transport, molecules usually move from regions of low concentration to high concentration.

In the light of the above statements, choose the correct answer from the options given below.

(a) A is false, but R is true
(b) Both A and R are true and R is the correct explanation of A
(c) Both A and R are true, but R is not the correct explanation of A
(d) A is true, but R is false

14. Which of the following statement is correct w.r.t. mitochondria?

(a) The number of mitochondria per cell is variable depending on the physiological activity of the cells
(b) The number of mitochondria per cell is fixed and involved in the production of ATP
(c) These are double membrane bound with vesicular structure
(d) They contain several enzymes essential for the photosynthesis

15. Given below are two statements; one is labelled as Assertion (A) and the other is labelled as Reason (R).

Assertion (A) Ribosomes are first observed as a dense particle.

Reason (R) Ribosomes are made up of subunits.

In the light of the above statements, choose the correct answer from the options given below.

(a) A is false, but R is true
(b) Both A and R are true and R is the correct explanation of A
(c) Both A and R are true, but R is not the correct explanation of A
(d) A is true, but R is false

16. Centromere is

(a) enzyme containing membrane less structure
(b) membrane bound structure with hydrolytic enzymes
(c) primary constriction present on the chromosome
(d) non-staining secondary constriction

17. What is the significance of perinuclear space in nuclear envelope?

(a) Forms barrier (b) Protective layer
(c) Matrix (d) Contain chromosomes

18. Given below are two statements.

Statement I Depending on the ease of extraction membrane proteins can be classified as integral or peripheral.

Statement II Integral proteins lie on the surface of the membrane, while peripheral proteins are totally buried in the membrane.

In the light of the above statements, choose the correct answer from the options given below.

(a) Statement I is incorrect, but statement II is correct
(b) Both statement I and statement II are correct
(c) Both statement I and statement II are incorrect
(d) Statement I is correct, but statement II is incorrect

19. Consider the following statements and identify the correct one.

(a) Both chloroplast and mitochondria have an internal compartment, the thylakoid space bounded by the thylakoid membrane
(b) Both chloroplasts and mitochondria contain DNA
(c) The chloroplasts are generally smaller than mitochondria
(d) The inner membrane of the chloroplast is more permeable

20. The presence of .... allows eukaryotic cells to compartmentalise their cytoplasm into various organelles.

(a) ribosomes
(b) nuclear pores
(c) membrane bound organelles
(d) cytosol

21. Which of the following option is correct with respect to membrane of mitochondria?

(a) Outer membrane–Respiratory chain enzymes
(b) Outer membrane–Cristae
(c) Inner membrane–Matrix
(d) Inner membrane–Cristae

22. SER and RER can be distinguished with their presence in
(a) protein synthesising cells
(b) protein and lipid synthesising cells, respectively
(c) carbohydrates and fat synthesising cells, respectively
(d) lipid and protein synthesising cells, respectively

23. Given below are two statements; one is labelled as Assertion (A) and other is labelled as Reason (R).

Assertion (A) The mitochondria possess their own DNA and ribosomes.

Reason (R) Mitochondria can synthesise some of their own proteins and divide by fragmentation.

In the light of the above statements, choose the correct answer from the options given below.
(a) A is false, but R is true
(b) Both A and R are true and R is the correct explanation of A
(c) Both A and R are true, but R is not the correct explanation of A
(d) A is true, but R is false

24. Read the following statements.
I. ER, Golgi complex, lysosomes and vacuoles constitute an endomembrane system.
II. Golgi complex is responsible for packaging modifying the material and prepare it for secretion.
III. Golgi complex is a polymorphic organelle.
IV. Tonoplast is fully permeable as a result the concentration of ions is relatively low in the vacuole as compared to the cytoplasm.
V. The nuclear matrix contains nucleolus and chromatin.

Choose the correct answer from the options given below.
(a) III and IV (b) I, II III and IV
(c) I and IV (d) I, II and V

25. Read the following statements regarding cilia.
Statement I These are small structures, which cause movement of either cell or the surrounding fluid.
Statement II They posseses macrotubules running parallel to the long axis.

In the light of the above statements, choose the correct answer from the options given below.
(a) Statement I is incorrect, but statement II is correct
(b) Both statement I and statement II are correct
(c) Both statement I and statement II are incorrect
(d) Statement I is correct, but statement II is incorrect

Response Index

01	a	b	c	d	10	a	b	c	d	19	a	b	c	d
02	a	b	c	d	11	a	b	c	d	20	a	b	c	d
03	a	b	c	d	12	a	b	c	d	21	a	b	c	d
04	a	b	c	d	13	a	b	c	d	22	a	b	c	d
05	a	b	c	d	14	a	b	c	d	23	a	b	c	d
06	a	b	c	d	15	a	b	c	d	24	a	b	c	d
07	a	b	c	d	16	a	b	c	d	25	a	b	c	d
08	a	b	c	d	17	a	b	c	d					
09	a	b	c	d	18	a	b	c	d					

Performance Scanner

> 90% Excellent !	You have mastered these topics. The concepts of these topics are at your fingertips. Move on to the next topics and maintain this momentum.
76-90% Very Good !	You have a good command over these topics. Revise these topics again after a few days and enhance your performance.
60-75% Good !	You have a wide scope to learn for these topics. Revise these topics again.
<60% Not Satisfactory!	You have a long way ahead of you to master these topics. Revise it thoroughly.

Chapter Break Thru

Syllabus	• Cell Theory and Cell as the Basic Unit of Life. Structure of Prokaryotic and Eukaryotic Cell Plant Cell and Animal Cell Cell Envelope, Cell Membrane, Cell Wall Cell	• Organelles-Structure and Function • Endomembrane System-Endoplasmic Reticulum, Golgi Bodies, Lysosomes, Vacuoles, Mitochondria, Ribosomes, Plastids, Microbodies	Cytoskeleton, Cilia, Flagella, Centrioles (Ultra Structure and Function) Nucleus-Nuclear Membrane, Chromatin, Nucleolus.

Important Instructions

- The test is of 1 hour duration and contains 50 Multiple-Choice Questions (Four options with a single correct answer).
- Choose the correct option and fill the OMR given on the last page of this test accordingly.
- At some instances, you may find more than 1 option to be correct. In such circumstances, you have to judge the most appropriate answer as per the conditions given in the question.

1. A structure that connect the cytoplasm of neighbouring cells and another which holds or glues the different neighbouring cell together. These are
(a) cell wall and middle lamella, respectively
(b) plasmodesmata and middle lamella, respectively
(c) middle lamella and desmosomes, respectively
(d) middle lamella and plasmodesmata, respectively

2. Protein that are to be used outside the cell are synthesised
(a) on free ribosome
(b) in the mitochondria
(c) on the smooth endoplasmic reticulum
(d) on the rough endoplasmic reticulum

3. Identify the correct description about organelle '*X*' in the given figure.

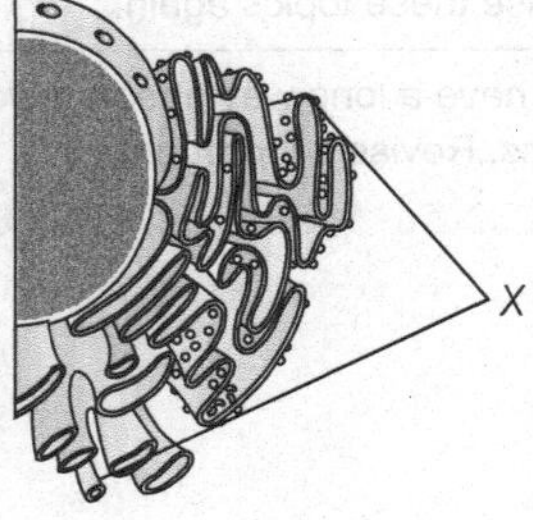

(a) The given organelle is not considered as the part of endomembrane system
(b) Golgi apparatus remain in close association to the given organelle
(c) It bear ribosome on their surface and synthesis lipid like steroidal hormones in animals cells
(d) These are network of tiny tubular structure, which form cluster in cytoplasm

4. Which one of the following is not a property of cell membrane?
(a) Proteins show flip-flop movement, but lipids cannot
(b) Polar molecules cannot pass through the non-polar lipids bilayer
(c) Ratio of protein and lipid varies considerably in different cell types
(d) Depending on the ease of extraction, proteins can be classified into two types

5. Which of the following category include the digestive enzyme present in the lysosomes for the digestion of macromolecule?
(a) Bile salt hydrolase
(b) Acid anhydrase
(c) Acid hydrolase
(d) Cholesterol anhydrase

6. The cell wall of a young plant cell, the primary wall is capable of growth, which gradually diminishes as the cell matures and the secondary wall is formed on the

(a) inner side of the cell (towards middle lamella)
(b) outer side of the cell (towards middle lamella)
(c) inner side of the cell (towards membrane)
(d) outer side of the cell (towards membrane)

7. A membranous structure formed by the extensions of plasma membrane into the cell and help in cell wall formation in prokaryotic cell is known as

(a) capsule
(b) slime layer
(c) mesosome
(d) lamellae

8. Match List I with List II.

	List I		List II
A.	Smooth ER	1.	Protein synthesis
B.	Mitochondria	2.	Synthesis of lipid
C.	Cristae	3.	Infoldings in mitochondria
D.	Rough ER	4.	Aerobic respiration

Choose the correct answer from the options given below.

A B C D
(a) 2 4 3 1
(b) 3 1 2 4
(c) 3 2 4 1
(d) 2 3 1 4

9. Which of the following statement is true for a secretory cell?

(a) Only SER is present
(b) Golgi apparatus is absent
(c) RER is easily observed in the cell
(d) Secretory granules are formed in nucleus

10. Identify the correct statements from the following.

I. Ribosomes are non-membrane bound organelles found in all cells, i.e., both eukaryotic as well as in prokaryotic cell
II. Schleiden and Schwann together formulated the cell theory and they explained the formation of new cells.
III. Rudolf Virchow first explained that cells divide and new cells are formed from pre-existing cells.
IV. Glycocalyx differs in composition and thickness among different bacteria.
V. The plasma membrane of prokaryotic cells are structurally different from eukaryotic cells.

Choose the correct answer from the options given below.

(a) II, III and V
(b) I, III and IV
(c) III and V
(d) III, IV and V

11. Which of the following statement is correct regarding acrocentric chromosome?

(a) It has centromeres at the middle, creating two equal arms
(b) It has one very short arm and one very long arm due to the centromere's location near the end
(c) It lacks a centromere, making it highly unstable during cell division
(d) It contains extra genetic material compared to other chromosomes

12. Match List I with List II.

	List I		List II
A.	Chromatin	1.	Basal body of cilia or flagella
B.	Cisternae	2.	Flat membranous sacs in stroma
C.	Thylakoids	3.	Condensed structure of DNA
D.	Centriole	4.	Disc-shaped sac in Golgi apparatus

Choose the correct answer from the options given below.

A B C D
(a) 3 4 2 1
(b) 2 1 4 3
(c) 1 3 2 4
(d) 1 2 3 4

13. Given below are two statements.

Statement I The cisternae in Golgi complex have *cis* face and *trans* face.

Statement II The *cis* face and *trans* face of Golgi complex are called forming face and maturing face, respectively.

In the light of the above statements, choose the correct answer from the options given below.

(a) Statement I is incorrect, but statement II is correct
(b) Both statement I and statement II are correct
(c) Both statement I and statement II are incorrect
(d) Statement I is correct, but statement II is incorrect

14. Which site is responsible for formation of glycoproteins and glycolipids?
(a) Plastid
(b) Chloroplast
(c) Golgi apparatus
(d) Mitochondria

15. Select the incorrect statement.
(a) Both chloroplasts and mitochondria contain DNA
(b) The chloroplasts are generally much larger than mitochondria
(c) Both chloroplasts and mitochondria contain an inner and an outer membrane
(d) Both chloroplasts and mitochondria have an internal compartment, the thylakoid

16. Match List I with List II.

List I	List II
A. Biconcave	1. Golgi apparatus
B. Glycocalyx	2. Water
C. Import and export	3. RBCs
D. Osmosis	4. Slime layer

Choose the correct answer from the options given below.

A B C D
(a) 4 2 1 3
(b) 3 4 1 2
(c) 1 4 3 2
(d) 4 2 1 3

17. Given below are two statements.

Statement I The axoneme's 9+0 structure facilitates the movement of cilia and flagella.
Statement II Both cilium and flagellum emerge from centriole like structure called the basal bodies.

In the light of the above statements, choose the correct answer from the options given below.
(a) Statement I is incorrect, but statement II is correct
(b) Both statement I and statement II are correct
(c) Both statement I and statement II are incorrect
(d) Statement I is correct, but statement II is incorrect

18. Select the correct statement.
(a) Fluid mosaic model of cell membrane was proposed by Danielli and Davson.
(b) Lipids and proteins are arranged in a bilayer.
(c) Proteins make up approximately 52% of the cell membrane.
(d) Na^+ and K^+ ions are transported against their concentration gradient across the cell membrane by passive transport.

19. Match List I with List II.

List I	List II
A. Acrocentric	1. Connects two neighbouring cells
B. Plasmodesmata	2. Centromere is terminal
C. Telocentric	3. Centromere is sub-terminal
D. Nuclear matrix	4. Nucleoplasm

Choose the correct answer from the options given below.

A B C D
(a) 3 4 1 2
(b) 3 1 2 4
(c) 4 3 2 1
(d) 3 4 2 1

20. Consider the following statements.
I. In human beings, the erythrocyte membrane has approximately 52% protein and 40% lipid.
II. In plant cells, a secondary cell wall is formed externally to the primary wall.
III. Golgi apparatus is an important site for the formation of starch and lipid.
IV. Plasmodesmata are living components in the dead cell wall and form a symplastic system between two cells.
V. Endoplasmic reticulum serves as an intracellular transport system.

Choose the option containing correct statements.
(a) I, II and III (b) I, IV and V
(c) III and IV (d) I and III

21. Which one of the following statement stands true for the finding of Schleiden?
(a) Animal tissues are made up of cells
(b) Cells have membranous covering
(c) Plant tissues consist of one or other types of cells
(d) Animal cells lack cell wall

22. The fluidity of membranes in a plant in cold weather may be maintained by
(a) increasing the number of phospholipids with unsaturated hydrocarbon tails
(b) increasing the proportion of integral proteins
(c) increasing concentration of cholesterol in membrane
(d) increasing the number of phospholipids with saturated hydrocarbon tail

23. Select the incorrect match.
(a) Smooth ER—Synthesis of lipids
(b) Cisternae—Flattened saccules
(c) Rough ER—Synthesis of glycogen
(d) Smooth vesicles—Secretory products

24. Read the following statements about cell wall.
Statement I The cell wall of young plant is the primary wall, which is capable of growth.
Statement II The secondary wall is formed after maturity of cell.
In the light of the above statements, choose the correct answer from the options given below.
(a) Statement I is incorrect, but statement II is correct
(b) Both statement I and statement II are correct
(c) Both statement I and statement II are incorrect
(d) Statement I is correct, but statement II is incorrect

25. During an experiment, a prokaryotic cell is observed to lack a cell wall. Which organism is most likely being observed?
(a) Cyanobacteria
(b) *Mycoplasma*
(c) *Spirillum*
(d) *Bacillus*

26. Read the following statements about rough endoplasmic reticulum.
Statement I RER are extensive and continuous with the outer membrane of the nucleus.
Statement II It is specialised to synthesise and transport lipids.
In the light of the above statements, choose the correct answer from the options given below.
(a) Statement I is incorrect, but statement II is correct
(b) Both statement I and statement II are correct
(c) Both statement I and statement II are incorrect
(d) Statement I is correct, but statement II is incorrect

27. What is a distinctive feature of certain chromosomes that have non-staining secondary constrictions?
(a) They contain no genetic material
(b) They are shorter chromosomes
(c) They do not have primary constriction on the side of disc-shaped structures called kinetochores
(d) They have a small fragment called the satellite

28. Given below are two statements; one is labelled as Assertion (A) and the other is labelled as Reason (R).
Assertion (A) The arrangement of axonemal microtubules is referred to as 9 + 2 array.
Reason (R) The peripheral doublets are also interconnected by linkers.
In the light of the above statements, choose the correct answer from the options given below.
(a) A is false, but R is true
(b) Both A and R are true and R is the correct explanation of A
(c) Both A and R are true, but R is not the correct explanation of A
(d) A is true, but R is false

29. If a prokaryotic cell is found to contain chromatophores, which of the following function are performed by these structures?
(a) Cellular respiration
(b) Photosynthesis
(c) Protein synthesis
(d) DNA synthesis

30. Match List I with List II.

List I	List II
A. Pili	1. Attachment to the surface
B. Fimbriae	2. Brings the two cells together
C. Flagella	3. DNA replication
D. Mesosome	4. Motility

Choose the correct answer from the options given below.

	A	B	C	D
(a)	2	1	4	3
(b)	1	2	4	3
(c)	1	2	3	4
(d)	3	2	1	4

31. Identify the correct statements from the following.

I. A typical eukaryotic cell consists of a cell membrane, nucleus and cytoplasm.

II. The endomembrane system includes ER, chloroplast, lysosomes, microbodies and vacuoles.

III. Centrosome and centriole form the basal body of cilia and flagella that facilitate locomotion.

IV. Nucleus contains nucleoli and chromatin network, that controls the activities of organelles and plays a major role in heredity.

V. Mitochondria help in oxidative phosphorylation and generation of adenosine triphosphate.

Choose the correct answer from the options given below.

(a) I, III, IV and V
(b) II, III and IV
(c) I, II and III
(d) II, III and V

32. Match List I with List II.

List I	List II
A. Sheath	1. 9 + 2 arrangement
B. Mitochondrial matrix	2. Extension of plasma membrane
C. Fibrils	3. Proteinaceous material
D. Double bridge	4. Colloidal complex

Choose the correct answer from the options given below.

	A	B	C	D
(a)	2	3	4	1
(b)	2	4	3	1
(c)	3	4	2	1
(d)	2	4	1	3

33. What is a unique feature of the genetic material of prokaryotic cells?

(a) It is enclosed within a nuclear membrane
(b) It is naked and not enclosed by nuclear membrane
(c) It is composed of RNA only
(d) It consists of multiple linear DNA

34. Select the correct match with respect to prokaryotes.

(a) Ribosomes - 80S
(b) Inclusion body - Phosphate granules
(c) Cell wall - Cellulose
(d) Plasmid - *ss* circular DNA

35. Study the diagram and select which of the following is correct regarding *X*.

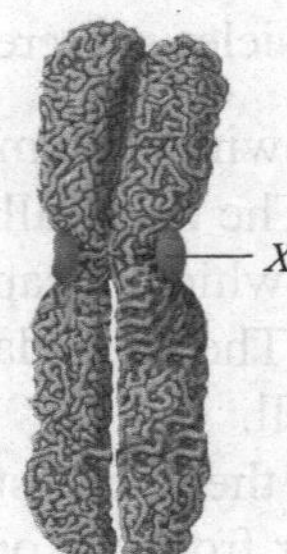

(a) Kinetochore–Site of spindle fibre attachment
(b) Centromere–Structure, which provides the shape of chromosome
(c) Primary constriction–A disc-shaped structure on chromosome.
(d) Secondary constriction–Non-staining part of chromosome at constant location.

36. Given below are two statements.

Statement I Chromosomes are only visible during cell division.

Statement II The centromere is the region of the cytoskeleton, where peripheral fibrils of tubulin protein are present.

In the light of the above statements, choose the correct answer from the options given below.
(a) Statement I is incorrect, but statement II is correct
(b) Both statement I and statement II are correct
(c) Both statement I and statement II are incorrect
(d) Statement I is correct, but statement II is incorrect

37. In a lipid bilayer, lipids are free to move but cannot leave the membrane.
This feature of plasma membrane was stated by
(a) Danielli and Davson
(b) Hilleir and Hoffman
(c) Robertson
(d) Singer and Nicolson

38. Given below are two statements regarding eukaryotic cell.
Statement I They contain mesosome that are infoldings of cell membrane.
Statement II The genetic material, DNA is not organised into distinct chromosomes.
In the light of the above statements, choose the correct answer from the options given below.
(a) Statement I is incorrect, but statement II is correct
(b) Both statement I and statement II are correct
(c) Both statement I and statement II are incorrect
(d) Statement I is correct, but statement II is incorrect

39. Which of the following statement regarding cilia is not correct?
(a) Cilia contain an outer ring of nine pairs of doublet microtubules surrounding two singlet microtubules
(b) The organised beating of cilia is controlled by fluxes of Ca^{2+} across the membrane
(c) Cilia are hair-like outgrowths of the cell membrane
(d) Axonemal microtubules is referred to as 9 +2 array.

40. Given below are two statements; one is labelled as Assertion (A) and the other is labelled as Reason (R).
Assertion (A) Polar molecules require a carrier protein to facilitate their transport across the membrane.
Reason (R) Polar molecules are hydrophobic in nature.
In the light of the above statements, choose the correct answer from the options given below.
(a) A is false, but R is true
(b) Both A and R are true and R is the correct explanation of A
(c) Both A and R are true, but R is not the correct explanation of A
(d) A is true, but R is false

41. Which of the following statement is correct in the context of cell movement through cilia and flagella?
(a) Cilia are responsible for the movement of the entire cell, while flagella move surrounding fluid
(b) Cilia move the surrounding fluid or the cell while, flagella are mainly for the movement of the cell itself
(c) Both cilia and flagella primarily move fluid around the cell
(d) Both cilia and flagella are stationary

42. In which type of cells are microbodies found?
(a) Only in plant cells
(b) Only in animal cells
(c) In both plant and animal cells
(d) In prokaryotic cells

43. Ribosomes in eukaryotic cells are divided into two subunits, i.e. ....
(a) 40S and 50S (b) 60S and 40S
(c) 60S and 30S (d) 50S and 30S

44. The outermost layer of cell envelope is called
(a) glycocalyx (b) glyoxysomes
(c) glycoprotein (d) plasma membrane

45. What are the disc shaped structures present on either side of the centromere called?
(a) Kinetochores (b) Telomeres
(c) Nucleosomes (d) Chromatids

46. Which statement is true about microbodies?
(a) They are unique to animal cells
(b) They contain genetic material for protein synthesis
(c) They are membrane- bound vesicles containing enzymes
(d) They are pigment containing organelles found in plant cells only

47. Which scientist first saw and described a live cell?
(a) Matthias Schleiden
(b) Antonie van Leeuwenhoek
(c) Robert Brown
(d) Theodre Schwann

48. Among multicelluar organisms, human red blood cells are about ……… in diameter.
(a) 3 μm (b) 0.1 μm
(c) 7 μm (d) 11 μm

49. The proteins that are responsible for the flow of materials and information into the cell are
(a) integral proteins
(b) carrier proteins
(c) membrane receptors
(d) mesosomes

50. Given below are two statement; one is labelled as Assertion (A) and the other one is labelled as Reason (R).

Assertion (A) Telocentric chromosomes have centromeres near the middle of the chromosomes

Reason (R) The telocentric chromosome has only one arm since the centromere is at the end

In the light of the above statements, choose the correct answer from the options given below.
(a) A is false, but R is true
(b) Both A and R are true and R is the correct explanation of A
(c) Both A and R are true, but R is not the correct explanation of A
(d) A is true, but R is false

Scan for online chapter test

Response Index

01	ⓐ ⓑ ⓒ ⓓ	14	ⓐ ⓑ ⓒ ⓓ	27	ⓐ ⓑ ⓒ ⓓ	40	ⓐ ⓑ ⓒ ⓓ
02	ⓐ ⓑ ⓒ ⓓ	15	ⓐ ⓑ ⓒ ⓓ	28	ⓐ ⓑ ⓒ ⓓ	41	ⓐ ⓑ ⓒ ⓓ
03	ⓐ ⓑ ⓒ ⓓ	16	ⓐ ⓑ ⓒ ⓓ	29	ⓐ ⓑ ⓒ ⓓ	42	ⓐ ⓑ ⓒ ⓓ
04	ⓐ ⓑ ⓒ ⓓ	17	ⓐ ⓑ ⓒ ⓓ	30	ⓐ ⓑ ⓒ ⓓ	43	ⓐ ⓑ ⓒ ⓓ
05	ⓐ ⓑ ⓒ ⓓ	18	ⓐ ⓑ ⓒ ⓓ	31	ⓐ ⓑ ⓒ ⓓ	44	ⓐ ⓑ ⓒ ⓓ
06	ⓐ ⓑ ⓒ ⓓ	19	ⓐ ⓑ ⓒ ⓓ	32	ⓐ ⓑ ⓒ ⓓ	45	ⓐ ⓑ ⓒ ⓓ
07	ⓐ ⓑ ⓒ ⓓ	20	ⓐ ⓑ ⓒ ⓓ	33	ⓐ ⓑ ⓒ ⓓ	46	ⓐ ⓑ ⓒ ⓓ
08	ⓐ ⓑ ⓒ ⓓ	21	ⓐ ⓑ ⓒ ⓓ	34	ⓐ ⓑ ⓒ ⓓ	47	ⓐ ⓑ ⓒ ⓓ
09	ⓐ ⓑ ⓒ ⓓ	22	ⓐ ⓑ ⓒ ⓓ	35	ⓐ ⓑ ⓒ ⓓ	48	ⓐ ⓑ ⓒ ⓓ
10	ⓐ ⓑ ⓒ ⓓ	23	ⓐ ⓑ ⓒ ⓓ	36	ⓐ ⓑ ⓒ ⓓ	49	ⓐ ⓑ ⓒ ⓓ
11	ⓐ ⓑ ⓒ ⓓ	24	ⓐ ⓑ ⓒ ⓓ	37	ⓐ ⓑ ⓒ ⓓ	50	ⓐ ⓑ ⓒ ⓓ
12	ⓐ ⓑ ⓒ ⓓ	25	ⓐ ⓑ ⓒ ⓓ	38	ⓐ ⓑ ⓒ ⓓ		
13	ⓐ ⓑ ⓒ ⓓ	26	ⓐ ⓑ ⓒ ⓓ	39	ⓐ ⓑ ⓒ ⓓ		

Performance Scanner

> 90% Excellent !	You have mastered this chapter. The concepts of this chapter are at your fingertips. Move on to the next chapter and maintain this momentum.
76-90% Very Good !	You have a good command over this chapter. Revise the chapter again after a few days and enhance your performance.
60-75% Good !	You have a wide scope to learn for this chapter. Revise this chapter again.
<60% Not Satisfactory!	You have a long way ahead of you to master this chapter. Revise it thoroughly.

Test Booklet No. **3947309**

Test Booklet Code **CH9**

MEDACE
NEET (UG)
SELF ASSESSMENT KIT

Biomolecules

Topics Covered

Chemical Composition of Cell and Metabolites

Carbohydrates, Proteins and Lipids

Nucleic Acids and Enzymes

Important Instructions

- This Booklet Contains – Three Topic Tests and One Test on Complete Chapter.
- Each question carries 4 marks.
- For each correct response, the candidate will get 4 marks. And for every incorrect response, 1 mark will be additionally deducted from total score.
- Use **Blue/Black** point pen only for filling the OMR.
- Rough work is to be done in the space provided for this purpose in the test booklet only.

Name of the Candidate (In Capitals) ____________

____

Candidate's Signature ____________

Invigilator's Signature ____________

Facsimile signature stamp of center superintendent____________

Do not open this booklet until you start attempting the test

Topical Follow Thru

Test 1

Syllabus
- Chemical Constituents of Living Cell
- Biomolecules

For deeper insight, **Scan the QR Code**

Important Instructions

- The test is of 30 minutes duration and contains 15 Multiple Choice Questions (four options with a single correct answer).
- Choose the correct option and fill the OMR given on the last page of this test accordingly.
- At some instances, you may find more than 1 option to be correct. In such circumstances, you have to judge the most appropriate answer as per the conditions given in the question.

1. Which of the following is not a true macromolecule?
(a) Proteins
(b) Nucleic acids
(c) Polysaccharides
(d) Lipids

2. Which of the following is the most abundant phospholipid in cell membrane?
(a) Cephalin
(b) Lecithin
(c) Phosphatidylserine
(d) Phosphatidyl inositol

3. Which of the following categories of macromolecules include representatives that frequently serve as energy storage molecules?
(a) Lipids and amino acids
(b) Proteins and nucleic acids
(c) Carbohydrates and proteins
(d) Lipids and carbohydrates

4. Consider the following statements and identify which one is incorrect about lipids?
(a) They are poorly soluble in water.
(b) A fatty acid has a hydroxyl group attached to an R group.
(c) They could be simple fatty acids.
(d) They are structural components of membranes.

5. Read the following statements.
I. Primary metabolites are formed by alteration of normal or primary metabolic pathways.
II. The macromolecules of cytoplasm and cell organelles appears in acid-soluble pellet.
III. The important ions found in ash are Na^+, K^+, Ca^{2+}, Mg^{2+} etc.
IV. Rubber, gums and cellulose are polymeric substances.
V. Monomers are simple small sized low molecular weight molecules.

Choose the correct set of statements from the options given below.
(a) II, III and IV
(b) III, IV and V
(c) I, III and V
(d) II, III and V

6. Select the incorrect match.
(a) Lectins – Concanavalin-A
(b) Drugs – Vinblastin
(c) Alkaloids – Curcumin
(d) Pigments – Anthocyanins

7. Which one of the following option consists of a pair of secondary metabolites?
(a) Antibiotics and cholesterol
(b) Cholesterol and lecithin
(c) Alkaloids and terpenoides
(d) Rubber and lecithin

8. Given below are two statements; one is labelled as Assertion (A) and other is labelled as Reason (R).

Assertion (A) Palmitic acid is an unsaturated fatty acid.

Reason (R) Unsaturated fatty acid carbon chains contain one or more double bonds with a terminal carboxylic group (—COOH).

In the light of the above statements, choose the correct answer from the options given below.

(a) A is false, but R is true
(b) Both A and R are true and R is the correct explanation of A
(c) Both A and R are true, but R is not the correct explanation of A
(d) A is true, but R is false

9. Which of the following are basic amino acids?

(a) Alanine, valine, glycine
(b) Tyrosine, tryptophan, phenylalanine
(c) Arginine, lysine, histidine
(d) Glutamate, aspartate

10. The cellular pool consists of

(a) Only inorganic molecules
(b) Only organic molecules
(c) Thousands of biomolecules
(d) Only crystalloids and colloids

11. Match List I with List II.

List I (Components of cell)	List II (% of the total cellular mass)
A. Proteins	1. 1
B. Lipids	2. 5−7
C. Ions	3. 2
D. Nucleic acids	4. 10-15

Choose the correct answer from the options given below.

	A	B	C	D		A	B	C	D
(a)	4	3	1	2	(b)	2	3	4	1
(c)	1	2	3	4	(d)	4	3	2	1

12. Following is the structure of an amino acid under a given condition of the medium. Which of the following represents the condition correctly?

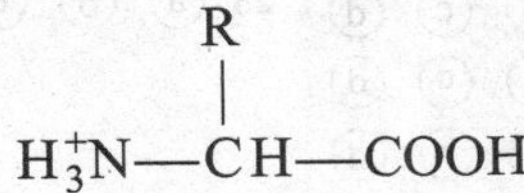

(a) Amino acids behave as acids
(b) Upon lowering the pH of media
(c) On adding NaOH to the media
(d) In strongly alkaline conditions

13. Select the incorrect statement.

(a) Cellular pool provides materials for the structure and functions of the cell.
(b) Acid soluble pool contains only the inorganic compounds.
(c) Some organic molecules occur in colloidal state
(d) Microbiomolecules found in the cellular pool have low molecular weights.

14. What happens to lipids when tissue is grounded and cell structures are disrupted?

(a) They dissolve in the acid-soluble pool
(b) They form vesicles that are water insoluble
(c) They remain as free small molecules
(d) They breakdown into small macromolecules

15. What is the typical molecular weight range for compounds found in the acid-soluble pool?

(a) 18 to 1800 Da
(b) 18 to 800 Da
(c) 10,000 to 1,00,000 Da
(d) Over 1,00,000 Da

Response Index

01	a	b	c	d	10	a	b	c	d	19	a	b	c	d
02	a	b	c	d	11	a	b	c	d	20	a	b	c	d
03	a	b	c	d	12	a	b	c	d	21	a	b	c	d
04	a	b	c	d	13	a	b	c	d	22	a	b	c	d
05	a	b	c	d	14	a	b	c	d	23	a	b	c	d
06	a	b	c	d	15	a	b	c	d	24	a	b	c	d
07	a	b	c	d	16	a	b	c	d	25	a	b	c	d
08	a	b	c	d	17	a	b	c	d					
09	a	b	c	d	18	a	b	c	d					

Performance Scanner

> 90% Excellent !	You have mastered these topics. The concepts of these topics are at your fingertips. Move on to the next topics and maintain this momentum.
76-90% Very Good !	You have a good command over these topics. Revise these topics again after a few days and enhance your performance.
60-75% Good !	You have a wide scope to learn for these topics. Revise these topics again.
<60% Not Satisfactory!	You have a long way ahead of you to master these topics. Revise it thoroughly.

Test 2

Syllabus Structure and Function of Proteins, Carbohydrates, Lipids

For deeper insight, **Scan the QR Code**

Important Instructions

- The test is of 30 minutes duration and contains 25 Multiple Choice Questions (four options with a single correct answer).
- Choose the correct option and fill the OMR given on the last page of this test accordingly.
- At some instances, you may find more than 1 option to be correct. In such circumstances, you have to judge the most appropriate answer as per the conditions given in the question.

1. The starch $-I_2$ complex give blue colour, because

(a) Starch forms helical tertiary structure
(b) Helical structure help in holding I_2 molecules
(c) Starch is a polysaccharide
(d) Starch is a homopolymeric compound

2. Which of the following is not a function of proteins?

(a) Transporting nutrients across cell membrane
(b) Fighting with infectious organisms
(c) Catalysing cellular reactions
(d) Storing genetic information

3. Which of the following functions would be halted if we remove the most abundant protein in the biosphere?

(a) Respiration
(b) Photosynthesis
(c) Support to ECM
(d) Elasticity of skin

4. Given below are two statements.

Statement I Polymer is formed by the process of polymerisation of repeating subunits.

Statement II All biomacromolecules are polymers.

In the light of the above statements, choose the correct answer from the options given below.

(a) Statement I is incorrect, but statement II is correct
(b) Both statement I and statement II are correct
(c) Both statement I and statement II are incorrect
(d) Statement I is correct, but statement II is incorrect

5. Consider the following statements and identify the correct statement(s).

I. Adult human haemoglobin is composed of a single polypeptide chain.
II. Haemoglobin consists of four subunits, two subunits of α type and two subunits of β types.

III. Haemoglobin is arranged in a linear string of β-sheets.
IV. Quaternary structure of protein affects the protein's function through specific arrangement of its subunits.

Choose the correct answer from the options given below.
(a) I and II
(b) II and III
(c) II and IV
(d) Only IV

6. Match List I with List II.

	List I		List II
A.	Modified sugar	1.	Glucosamine
B.	Protein secondary structure	2.	Most abundant enzyme
C.	Tertiary protein structure	3.	3-D view of protein
D.	RuBisCO	4.	β-pleated sheet

Choose the correct answer from the options given below.

	A	B	C	D
(a)	2	3	1	4
(b)	1	4	3	2
(c)	3	4	2	1
(d)	1	4	2	3

7. Given below are two statements.
Statement I Inulin is a polymer of lactose.
Statement II Paper made from cotton fibre is composed of starch.
In the light of the above statements, choose the correct answer from the options given below.
(a) Statement I is incorrect, but statement II is correct
(b) Both statement I and statement II are correct
(c) Both statement I and statement II are incorrect
(d) Statement I is correct, but statement II is incorrect

8. Identify the correct statements from the following.
I. All monosaccharides are reducing sugar.
II. Exoskeletons of arthropods have a complex polysaccharides called chitin.
III. Monosaccharide are insoluble in water.
IV. Cellulose is storehouse of energy in plants.
V. Glycogen shows reddish-brown colour in presence of iodine solution.

Choose the correct answer from the options given below.
(a) II, IV and V
(b) I, II and V
(c) I, III and V
(d) I, III and IV

9. Under fasting conditions, blood glucose level rises due to breakdown of glycogen by the hydrolysis of
(a) amide linkage
(b) ether bond
(c) glycosidic linkage
(d) phosphodiester bond

10. Which of the following statement is true about dietary proteins?
(a) They are not necessary as body produces all amino acids.
(b) They do not play any significant role in human health.
(c) They provide essential amino acids that body cannot synthesise.
(d) They are necessary only in patients affected with protein malnutrition.

11. Match List I with List II.

	List I		List II
A.	Essential fatty acid	1.	Cholesterol
B.	Steroid	2.	Stearic acid
C.	Saturated fatty acid	3.	Linolenic acid
D.	Phospholipid	4.	Lecithin

Choose the correct answer from the options given below.

	A	B	C	D
(a)	2	3	1	4
(b)	3	1	2	4
(c)	1	4	3	2
(d)	3	1	4	2

12. Repeating units of a polysaccharide are linked by
(a) amide bond
(b) ester bond
(c) glycosidic bond
(d) ether bond

13. Identify the given compound found in cell membrane and choose the correct answer from the options given below.

```
                    O
                    ‖
         CH2—O—C—R1
   O     |
   ‖     |
R2—C—O—CH          O
         |          ‖
         CH2—O—P—O—CH2—CH2
                   |          |
                   OH        N
                        CH3 / | \ CH3
                             CH3
```

(a) Cholesterol (b) Lecithin
(c) Alanine (d) Glycoprotein

14. Identify the incorrect statement regarding the structure of protein.
(a) In primary structure, left end is represented by the first amino acid.
(b) Tertiary structure is absolutely essential for many biological functions of the proteins.
(c) Only left hand helices are observed in proteins.
(d) The first amino acid is called as N-terminal amino acid.

15. Which of the following fatty acid has 20 carbon atoms (including carboxyl carbon) and 4 double bonds?
(a) Arachidonic acid
(b) Linolenic acid
(c) Palmitic acid
(d) Oleic acid

16. Given below are two statements; one is labelled as Assertion (A) and the other is labelled as Reason (R).
Assertion (A) Heat can degrade a protein, even at its primary structure.
Reason (R) Heating a protein breaks the H-bonds, which causes denaturation.
In the light of the above statements, choose the correct answer from the options given below.
(a) A is false, but R is true.
(b) Both A and R are true and R is the correct explanation of A
(c) Both A and R are true, but R is not the correct explanation of A
(d) A is true, but R is false

17. Given below are two statements.
Statement I Iodine solution is typically bluish-black in appearance.
Statement II Starch upon hydrolysis, gives a positive iodine test.
In the light of the above statements, choose the correct answer from the options given below.
(a) Statement I is incorrect, but statement II is correct
(b) Both statement I and statement II are correct
(c) Both statement I and statement II are incorrect
(d) Statement I is correct, but statement II is incorrect

18. Which of the following is correct about phospholipids in a membrane?
(a) Phospholipids have a non-polar head group.
(b) Phospholipid heads form the core of membrane.
(c) The R-groups of a phospholipid are hydrophilic.
(d) Ester bond links a glycerol to a phosphate molecule.

19. Consider the following statements.
I. Beta pleated sheets are stabilised by hydrogen bonds.
II. Covalent bonds are found only in the tertiary structure.
III. Structural identity of a protein governs its function.
IV. Quaternary structures lack disulphide bridges.
Choose the correct statement(s) from the options given below.
(a) I and II (b) I and III
(c) II and IV (d) III only

20. All of the following macromolecules are structurally homopolymers, except
(a) glycogen (b) starch
(c) heparin (d) chitin

21. Which of the following explains why unsaturated fats are liquid at room temperature?
(a) Higher melting point
(b) Compact structure
(c) Loosely packed hydrocarbons
(d) Longer fatty acid chains

22. Given below are two statements; one is labelled as Assertion (A) and the other is labelled as Reason (R).

Assertion (A) Polysaccharides like starch are known as non-reducing sugars.

Reason (R) Anomeric carbons in polysaccharides are linked by glycosidic bonds.

In the light of the above statements, choose the correct answer from the options given below.

(a) A is false, but R is true
(b) Both A and R are true and R is the correct explanation of A
(c) Both A and R are true, but R is not the correct explanation of A
(d) A is true, but R is false

23. Given below are two statements.

Statement I Cysteine is essential for the primary structure of proteins.

Statement II A dipeptide is stabilised by the formation of two peptide bonds.

In the light of the above statements, choose the correct answer from the options given below.

(a) Statement I is incorrect, but statement II is correct
(b) Both statement I and statement II are correct
(c) Both statement I and statement II are incorrect
(d) Statement I is correct, but statement II is incorrect

24. Following are the two types of organisation in a protein structure.

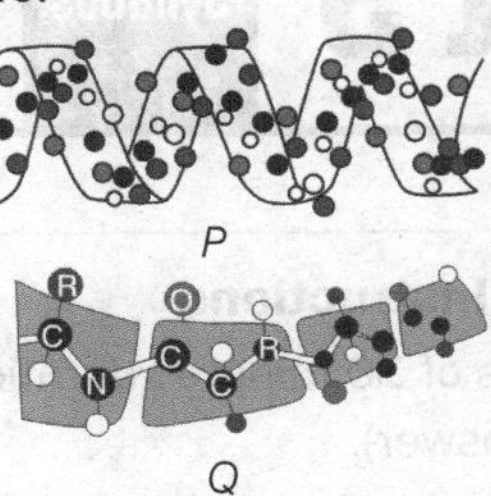

Which of the following bonding is found in P and Q?

(a) P – Covalent interaction; Q – Non-covalent interaction
(b) P – Hydrogen bond; Q – Non-covalent bond
(c) P – Disulphide bond; Q – Covalent bond
(d) P – Hydrogen bond; Q – Covalent bond

25. Match List I with List II.

List I	List II
A. Homopolysaccharide	1. Sucrose
B. Heteropolysaccharide	2. Protein
C. Non-reducing sugar	3. Glycogen
D. Heteropolymer	4. Peptidoglycan

Choose the correct answer from the options given below.

	A	B	C	D
(a)	1	3	4	2
(b)	2	3	1	4
(c)	3	2	1	4
(d)	3	4	1	2

Response Index

01	a	b	c	d	10	a	b	c	d	19	a	b	c	d
02	a	b	c	d	11	a	b	c	d	20	a	b	c	d
03	a	b	c	d	12	a	b	c	d	21	a	b	c	d
04	a	b	c	d	13	a	b	c	d	22	a	b	c	d
05	a	b	c	d	14	a	b	c	d	23	a	b	c	d
06	a	b	c	d	15	a	b	c	d	24	a	b	c	d
07	a	b	c	d	16	a	b	c	d	25	a	b	c	d
08	a	b	c	d	17	a	b	c	d					
09	a	b	c	d	18	a	b	c	d					

Performance Scanner

> 90% Excellent !	You have mastered these topics. The concepts of these topics are at your fingertips. Move on to the next topics and maintain this momentum.
76-90% Very Good !	You have a good command over these topics. Revise these topics again after a few days and enhance your performance.
60-75% Good !	You have a wide scope to learn for these topics. Revise these topics again.
<60% Not Satisfactory!	You have a long way ahead of you to master these topics. Revise it thoroughly.

Test 3

Syllabus

- Structure and Function of Nucleic Acids; Enzymes-Types, Properties, Enzyme Action, Classification and Nomenclature of Enzymes

For deeper insight, **Scan the QR Code**

Important Instructions

- The test is of 30 minutes duration and contains 15 Multiple Choice Questions (four options with a single correct answer).
- Choose the correct option and fill the OMR given on the last page of this test accordingly.
- At some instances, you may find more than 1 option to be correct. In such circumstances, you have to judge the most appropriate answer as per the conditions given in the question.

1. The enzyme which catalyses rearrangement of atomic groups, without changing the molecular weight or number of atoms present in compound is

(a) lyase (b) transferase
(c) isomerase (d) isozyme

2. The catabolic and anabolic pathways are often coupled in cell because

(a) the intermediates of a catabolic pathways are used in the anabolic pathways.
(b) the energy released from one pathway is used to drive the other.
(c) their enzymes are controlled by the same activators and inhibitors.
(d) both the pathways use the same energy.

3. An example of competitive inhibition of an enzyme is the inhibition of

(a) cytochrome oxidase by cyanide
(b) hexokinase by glucose-6-phosphate
(c) carbonic anhydrase by carbon dioxide
(d) succinic dehydrogenase by malonic acid

4. Given below are two statements.

Statement I Hydrolases remove water from compounds.

Statement II Condensation reactions are opposite of hydrolysis.

In the light of the above statements, choose the correct answer from the options given below.

(a) Statement I is incorrect, but statement II is correct
(b) Both statement I and statement II are correct
(c) Both statement I and statement II are incorrect
(d) Statement I is correct, but statement II is incorrect

5. Choose the type of enzyme involved in following reaction.

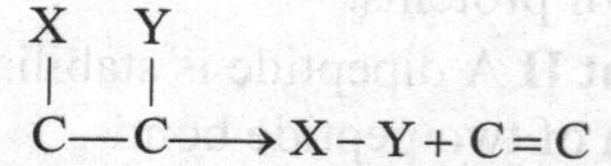

(a) Hydrolases (b) Lyases
(c) Isomerase (d) Transferase

6. Identify the correct graph displaying the effect of pH on the velocity of typical enzymatic reaction (V).

(a) 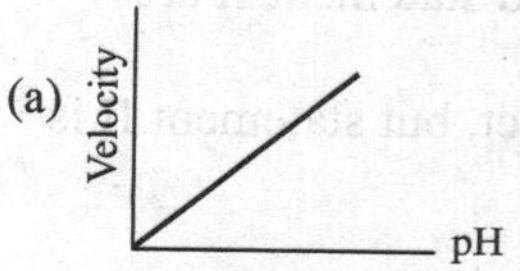

(b) 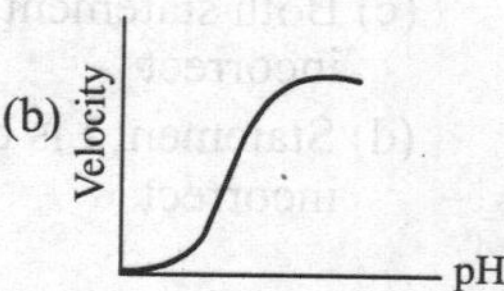

(c) 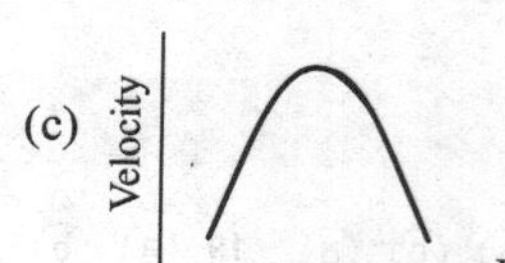

(b) 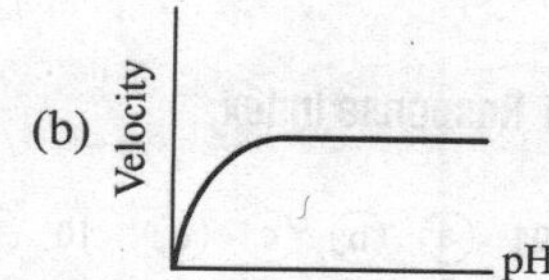

7. All of the following would inhibit the enzymatic activity of carboxypeptidase, except

(a) breaking of the side chain coordinate bonds
(b) removal of haem prosthetic group
(c) decreasing the optimal temperature by 20 %
(d) lowering the substrate concentration

8. Given below are two statements; one is labelled as Assertion (A) and the other is labelled as Reason (R).

Assertion (A) Change in pH above or below the optimum value reduces the rate of enzyme action.

Reason (R) Change in pH brings about change in degree of ionisation.

In the light of the above statements, choose the correct answer from the options given below.

(a) A is false, but R is true
(b) Both A and R are true and R is the correct explanation of A
(c) Both A and R are true, but R is not the correct explanation of A
(d) A is true, but R is false

9. The structure of substrate gets transformed into the structure of product through formation of

(a) catalysis
(b) transition state structure
(c) activation energy
(d) enzyme-product complex

10. Given below are two statements; one is labelled as Assertion (A) and the other is labelled as Reason (R).

Assertion (A) Coenzyme Nicotinamide Adenine Dinucleotide (NAD) and NADP contain a vitamin.

Reason (R) NAD acts as coenzyme for many oxidising enzymes.

In the light of the above statements, choose the correct answer from the options given below.

(a) A is false, but R is true
(b) Both A and R are true and R is the correct explanation of A
(c) Both A and R are true, but R is not the correct explanation of A
(d) A is true, but R is false

11. Which of the following can prevent inhibition of succinate dehydrogenase enzyme?

(a) Increasing the concentration of succinate
(b) Increasing the concentration of malonate
(c) Lowering the optimal temperature
(d) Increasing the pH of the reaction

12. Which of the following is a typical example of feedback inhibition?

(a) Sulpha drugs and folic acid synthesising bacteria
(b) Allosteric inhibition of hexokinase by glucose-6-phosphate
(c) Reaction between succinic dehydrogenase and succcinic acid
(d) Cyanide and cytochrome reaction

13. Read the following statements.

I. Ribozymes are the RNA enzymes.
II. Cofactor is the thermolabile non-protein part.
III. An enzyme has only one active site.
IV. Catalysts and enzymes do not change the reaction equilibria.
V. Isomerase bring about intramolecular rearrangement to form optical, geometrical or positional isomers.

Choose the correct answer from the options given below.

(a) I, IV and V
(b) II, III and IV
(c) I, II and V
(d) II, IV and V

14. Given below are two statements; one is labelled as Assertion (A) and the other is labelled as Reason (R).

Assertion (A) After reaching V_{max}, increase in substrate concentration increases the rate of reaction.

Reason (R) After saturation of substrate molecules, there are no free enzyme molecules to bind with additional substrate molecules.

In the light of the above statements, choose the correct answer from the options given below.

(a) A is false, but R is true
(b) Both A and R are true and R is the correct explanation of A
(c) Both A and R are true, but R is not the correct explanation of A.
(d) A is true, but R is false

15. Which of the following is not true about enzyme activity?

(a) Enzymes are considered as organic catalysts.
(b) Most enzymes work with a wide variety of substrates.
(c) Enzymes do not participate in the chemical reaction.
(d) Enzymes form transient compounds with their substrates.

Response Index

01	a	b	c	d	10	a	b	c	d	19	a	b	c	d
02	a	b	c	d	11	a	b	c	d	20	a	b	c	d
03	a	b	c	d	12	a	b	c	d	21	a	b	c	d
04	a	b	c	d	13	a	b	c	d	22	a	b	c	d
05	a	b	c	d	14	a	b	c	d	23	a	b	c	d
06	a	b	c	d	15	a	b	c	d	24	a	b	c	d
07	a	b	c	d	16	a	b	c	d	25	a	b	c	d
08	a	b	c	d	17	a	b	c	d					
09	a	b	c	d	18	a	b	c	d					

Performance Scanner

> 90% Excellent !	You have mastered these topics. The concepts of these topics are at your fingertips. Move on to the next topics and maintain this momentum.
76-90% Very Good !	You have a good command over these topics. Revise these topics again after a few days and enhance your performance.
60-75% Good !	You have a wide scope to learn for these topics. Revise these topics again.
<60% Not Satisfactory!	You have a long way ahead of you to master these topics. Revise it thoroughly.

Chapter Break Thru

Syllabus

- Chemical Constituents of Living Cells; Biomolecules-Structure and Function of Proteins, Carbohydrates, Lipids, Nucleic Acids; Enzymes-Types, Properties, Enzyme Action, Classification and Nomenclature of Enzymes

Important Instructions

- The test is of 1 hour duration and contains 30 Multiple-Choice Questions (Four options with a single correct answer).
- Choose the correct option and fill the OMR given on the last page of this test accordingly.
- At some instances, you may find more than 1 option to be correct. In such circumstances, you have to judge the most appropriate answer as per the conditions given in the question.

1. Names of some molecules are given below. Choose the correct answer from the options given below which categorises them correctly.

Guanylic acid, Cytidine, Adenosine, Adenine

	Nitrogenous base	Nucleoside	Nucleotide
A.	Adenine	Cytidine	Guanylic acid
B.	Adenine	Cytidine	Adenosine
C.	Cytidine	Adenosine	Guanylic acid
D.	Adenosine	Guanylic acid	Cytidine

(a) A (b) B
(c) C (d) D

2. Which of the following is correct for ribozymes?

(a) These are proteins that function as enzymes.
(b) These are carbohydrates that function as enzyme.
(c) These are nucleic acids that behave like enzymes.
(d) These are enzymes that behave like RNA.

3. Given below are two statements.

Statement I Lipids are classified under the macromolecular fraction despite having a molecular weight of less than 800 Dalton.

Statement II Lipids are small molecular weight compounds and arranged into structures like cell membrane and other membranes.

In the light of the above statements, choose the correct answer from the options given below.
(a) Statement I is incorrect, but statement II is correct.
(b) Both statement I and statement II are correct.
(c) Both statement I and statement II are incorrect.
(d) Statement I is correct, but statement II is incorrect.

4. Identify the correct statement w.r.t. compound given in the figure.

OH — P(=O)(OH) — OCH_2 — [ribose ring with OH, OH] — Adenine

(a) It is composed of a glycerol molecule bonded to three fatty acids.
(b) It is a long polymer chain that forms proteins.
(c) It forms long polymer chain that makes DNA.
(d) It consists of repeating unit of glucose.

5. Identify the incorrect statements from the following.

I. Amino acids are organic compounds containing an amino group and an acidic group substituents on the same carbon.
II. Amino acids are substituted methanes.
III. An amino acid has 3 substituent groups occupying the three valency positions of carbon.
IV. The chemical properties of amino acids are generally dependent on the carboxyl group only.
V. The physical properties of amino acids depend on the *R* group only.

Choose the correct answer from the options given below.
(a) III, IV and V
(b) I, II and III
(c) II and III
(d) I, III and V

6. Given below are two statements; one is labelled as Assertion (A) and other is labelled as Reason (R).

Assertion (A) Secondary metabolites play known roles in the normal physiological processes of host organisms.

Reason (R) Secondary metabolites such as alkaloids, flavonoids and essential oils are primarily involved in ecological interactions rather than basic metabolic functions.

In the light of the above statements, choose the correct answer from the options given below.
(a) A is false, but R is true
(b) Both A and R are true and R is the correct explanation of A
(c) Both A and R are true, but R is not the correct explanation of A
(d) A is true, but R is false

7. Match List I with List II.

	List I		List II
A.	Collagen	1.	Regulates glucose level
B.	Receptor	2.	Glucose transporter
C.	GLUT-4	3.	Sensory reception
D.	Insulin	4.	Intercellular ground substance

Choose the correct answer from the options given below.

	A	B	C	D
(a)	2	3	1	4
(b)	4	3	2	1
(c)	2	4	3	1
(d)	4	2	1	3

8. Which of the following statement about nucleotides is correct?
(a) These are the monomeric units, which act as basic building blocks of lipids.
(b) They are not involved in the synthesis of proteins.
(c) They form the structural units of nucleic acid like DNA and RNA.
(d) They do not participate in cellular signaling processes.

9. The primary structure of a protein refers to the
(a) 3-D arrangement of amino acids
(b) arrangement of protein subunits
(c) arrangement of helices and sheets
(d) 1-D sequence of amino acids in the proteins

10. If an enzyme extracted from a thermophilic organism is exposed to 90°C, which of the following scenario would correctly depict the above situation?

(a) The enzyme will denature immediately.
(b) The enzyme will work less efficiently than at lower temperature.
(c) The enzyme will be stable and retain their catalytic power.
(d) Their active site would change the configuration.

11. When the activation energy of the reaction is decreased, the rate of reaction

(a) remains unchanged
(b) decreases
(c) increases
(d) firstly increases then decreases

12. Match List I with List II.

List I	List II
A. Polysaccharide	1. Glucosamine
B. Polymeric substance	2. Gums
C. Toxin	3. Curcumin
D. Drug	4. Abrin

Choose the correct answer from the options given below.

	A	B	C	D
(a)	1	2	4	3
(b)	1	2	3	4
(c)	3	4	2	1
(d)	2	3	4	1

13. Identify the correct statement from the following.

(a) The macromolecules from cytoplasm and organelles become the acid insoluble fraction.
(b) The acid soluble pool predominantly consists of large polymeric substances like proteins and nucleic acids.
(c) The acid insoluble fraction is composed of molecules with molecular weights below 1000 Da.
(d) Biomicromolecules have molecular weights in the range of 10,000 Da and above.

14. Identify the incorrect match pair from the following.

(a) Acidic amino acid - Glutamic acid
(b) Basic amino acid- Lysine
(c) Neutral amino acid- Valine
(d) Aromatic amino acid- Glycine

15. Identify the correct statements from the following.

I. A physical change simply refers to a change in shape without breaking of bonds.
II. Hydrolysis of starch into glucose is an example of physical change.
III. Rate of physical or chemical process refers to the amount of product formed per unit time.
IV. Rates of physical and chemical processes are influenced by temperature among other factors.
V. Proteins are homopolymers made of amino acids.

Choose the correct answer from the options given below.

(a) I, II and III
(b) II, III and IV
(c) I, III and IV
(d) I, IV and V

16. Enzymes get denatured at temperatures typically above

(a) 20°C (b) 40°C
(c) 60°C (d) 100°C

17. Look at the following diagram, which depicts the energy diagram for a chemical reaction. Which point on the diagram represents the point at which the transition state exists?

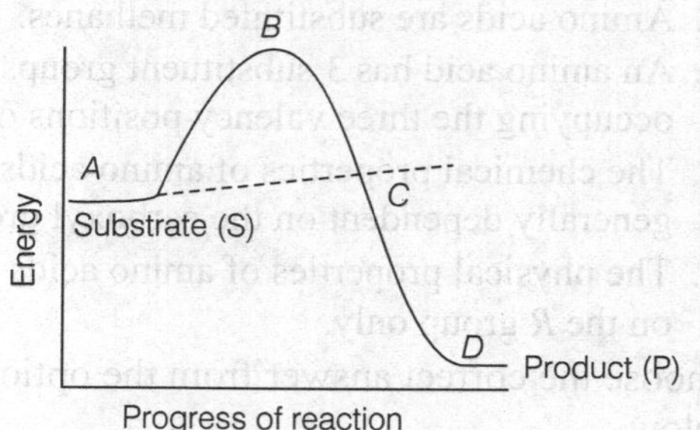

(a) *B* (b) *C*
(c) *D* (d) *A*

18. Given below are two statements; one is labelled as Assertion (A) and other is labelled as Reason (R).

Assertion (A) The remaining material after burning tissue is called ash, which contains inorganic elements.

Reason (R) Burning of tissue oxidises all carbon compounds to gaseous forms such as CO_2 and water vapour leaving behind inorganic elements.

In the light of the above statements, choose the correct answer from the options given below.
(a) A is false, but R is true
(b) Both A and R are true and R is the correct explanation of A
(c) Both A and R are true, but R is not the correct explanation of A
(d) A is true, but R is false

19. Identify the following steps of the enzyme catalytic cycle in the correct order.
I. Formation of the enzyme- product complex.
II. The substrate binds to the active site of the enzyme.
III. The enzyme releases the products and become ready for another catalytic cycle.
IV. The enzyme alters its shape to fit tightly around the substrate.
V. Formation of enzyme-substrate complex.
Choose the correct from the options given below.
(a) II, IV, V, I, III
(b) II, V, IV, I, III
(c) I, II, III, V, IV
(d) III, IV, V, I, II

20. Why fats having unsaturated fatty acids occur in liquid form even during winter?
(a) Melting point decreases as fats are tightly packed
(b) Melting point decreases with increase in number of double bonds
(c) Melting point increases with increase in number of double bonds
(d) Structure contains many hydrogen atoms

21. What is the function of metal ions as cofactors in enzyme?
(a) They serve as prosthetic groups
(b) They breakdown hydrogen bonds of products
(c) They are tightly bound to the apoenzyme
(d) They form coordination bonds with active site and substrate

22. Glycerol is a polyhydroxy alcohol. Which of the following is true about it?
(a) It is a dihydroxy propane.
(b) Esterification of glycerol and fatty acid forms proteins.
(c) It forms backbone of phospholipids.
(d) It is immiscible in water.

23. Given below are two statements.
Statement I Glycogen and starch serve as energy storage molecules in animals and plants, respectively.
Statement II Both glycogen and starch are polysaccharides that consist of glucose monomers.
In the light of the above statements, choose the correct answer from the options given below.
(a) Statement I is incorrect, but statement II is correct
(b) Both statement I and statement II are correct
(c) Both statement I and statement II are incorrect
(d) Statement I is correct, but statement II is incorrect

24. What is the purpose of grinding living tissue in trichloroacetic acid during chemical analysis?
(a) To dissolve inorganic compounds
(b) To isolate nucleic acids from the tissue
(c) To obtain an acid- soluble pool and an acid-insoluble fraction
(d) To extract lipids from the tissue

25. Identify the incorrect statement from the following.
I. Heterocyclic compounds in nucleic acids are the nitrogenous bases.
II. Paper made from plant pulp and cotton fibre is cellulosic.
III. Nucleic acids like DNA and RNA consist of nucleotides.
IV. Cellulose is a polymeric polysaccharide consisting of two types of monosaccharides.

Choose the correct answer from the options given below.

(a) IV only (b) I only
(c) III and IV (d) II and IV

26. Sulphonamides prevent microbial infection as they have a similar structure to PABA required for the synthesis of folic acids in microbes. In this type of inhibition, what type of change occurs in V_{max} and K_m?

(a) Decrease in both V_{max} and K_m
(b) Increase in both V_{max} and K_m
(c) V_{max} unchanged and increase in K_m
(d) K_m unchanged and V_{max} decreased

27. The β-pleated sheet in the secondary order of protein structure is formed due to

(a) the sequence of amino acids in the polypeptide
(b) the formation of peptide bonds between amino acids
(c) the coiling of the polypeptide chains bound by covalent bonds
(d) the linking of two regions of polypeptide chains (lying side by side) by hydrogen bonds

28. What is the common feature of enzymes like peroxidase and catalase with respect to their cofactor?

(a) Both of these utilise metal ions as cofactors and make coordination bonds with the substrate.
(b) Both of these have coenzymes that are tightly bound and catalyse the breakdown of glucose.
(c) Both of these have haem as the prosthetic group which is a part of the active site.
(d) Both of these are permanently attached to the enzyme's active site.

29. Consider the given graph representing effect of change in concentration of substrate on enzyme activity.

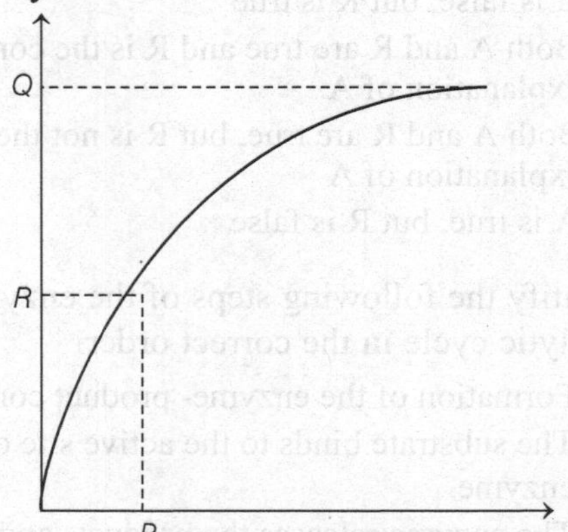

Identify *P*, *Q* and *R* from the following options.

	P	*Q*	*R*
A.	K_m	V_{max}	$\frac{V_{max}}{2}$
B.	V_{max}	Substrate	$\frac{V_{max}}{2}$
C.	K	V_{max}	limiting effect
D.	V_{max}	K_m	$\frac{V_{max}}{2}$

(a) A (b) B
(c) C (d) D

30. The active site of an enzyme is

(a) a region where proteins bind together
(b) a crevice or pocket where the substrate fits
(c) a region where product is formed
(d) a region where co-factors binds

Scan for online chapter test

Response Index

01 ⓐ ⓑ ⓒ ⓓ	14 ⓐ ⓑ ⓒ ⓓ	27 ⓐ ⓑ ⓒ ⓓ	40 ⓐ ⓑ ⓒ ⓓ
02 ⓐ ⓑ ⓒ ⓓ	15 ⓐ ⓑ ⓒ ⓓ	28 ⓐ ⓑ ⓒ ⓓ	41 ⓐ ⓑ ⓒ ⓓ
03 ⓐ ⓑ ⓒ ⓓ	16 ⓐ ⓑ ⓒ ⓓ	29 ⓐ ⓑ ⓒ ⓓ	42 ⓐ ⓑ ⓒ ⓓ
04 ⓐ ⓑ ⓒ ⓓ	17 ⓐ ⓑ ⓒ ⓓ	30 ⓐ ⓑ ⓒ ⓓ	43 ⓐ ⓑ ⓒ ⓓ
05 ⓐ ⓑ ⓒ ⓓ	18 ⓐ ⓑ ⓒ ⓓ	31 ⓐ ⓑ ⓒ ⓓ	44 ⓐ ⓑ ⓒ ⓓ
06 ⓐ ⓑ ⓒ ⓓ	19 ⓐ ⓑ ⓒ ⓓ	32 ⓐ ⓑ ⓒ ⓓ	45 ⓐ ⓑ ⓒ ⓓ
07 ⓐ ⓑ ⓒ ⓓ	20 ⓐ ⓑ ⓒ ⓓ	33 ⓐ ⓑ ⓒ ⓓ	46 ⓐ ⓑ ⓒ ⓓ
08 ⓐ ⓑ ⓒ ⓓ	21 ⓐ ⓑ ⓒ ⓓ	34 ⓐ ⓑ ⓒ ⓓ	47 ⓐ ⓑ ⓒ ⓓ
09 ⓐ ⓑ ⓒ ⓓ	22 ⓐ ⓑ ⓒ ⓓ	35 ⓐ ⓑ ⓒ ⓓ	48 ⓐ ⓑ ⓒ ⓓ
10 ⓐ ⓑ ⓒ ⓓ	23 ⓐ ⓑ ⓒ ⓓ	36 ⓐ ⓑ ⓒ ⓓ	49 ⓐ ⓑ ⓒ ⓓ
11 ⓐ ⓑ ⓒ ⓓ	24 ⓐ ⓑ ⓒ ⓓ	37 ⓐ ⓑ ⓒ ⓓ	50 ⓐ ⓑ ⓒ ⓓ
12 ⓐ ⓑ ⓒ ⓓ	25 ⓐ ⓑ ⓒ ⓓ	38 ⓐ ⓑ ⓒ ⓓ	
13 ⓐ ⓑ ⓒ ⓓ	26 ⓐ ⓑ ⓒ ⓓ	39 ⓐ ⓑ ⓒ ⓓ	

Performance Scanner

> 90% Excellent !	You have mastered this chapter. The concepts of this chapter are at your fingertips. Move on to the next chapter and maintain this momentum.
76-90% Very Good !	You have a good command over this chapter. Revise the chapter again after a few days and enhance your performance.
60-75% Good !	You have a wide scope to learn for this chapter. Revise this chapter again.
<60% Not Satisfactory!	You have a long way ahead of you to master this chapter. Revise it thoroughly.

Space for Rough Work

Space for Rough Work

arihant
SUCCESS AND NOTHING LESS

Test Booklet No. 3947310

Test Booklet Code CH10

Cell Cycle and Cell Division

Topics Covered

Cell Cycle and Mitosis

Meiosis

Important Instructions

- This Booklet Contains – Two Topic Tests and One Test on Complete Chapter.
- Each question carries 4 marks.
- For each correct response, the candidate will get 4 marks. And for every incorrect response, 1 mark will be additionally deducted from total score.
- Use **Blue/Black** point pen only for filling the OMR.
- Rough work is to be done in the space provided for this purpose in the test booklet only.

Name of the Candidate (In Capitals) ____________________

____

Candidate's Signature ____________

Invigilator's Signature ____________

Facsimile signature stamp of center superintendent ____________

Do not open this booklet until you start attempting the test

Topical Follow Thru

Test 1

Syllabus Cell Division : Cell Cycle, Mitosis and its Significance

For deeper insight, **Scan the QR Code**

Important Instructions

- The test is of 30 minutes duration and contains 25 Multiple Choice Questions (four options with a single correct answer).
- Choose the correct option and fill the OMR given on the last page of this test accordingly.
- At some instances, you may find more than 1 option to be correct. In such circumstances, you have to judge the most appropriate answer as per the conditions given in the question.

1. Interphase is the part of the cell cycle when
(a) mitosis proceeds
(b) a cell undergoes inactive state
(c) a cell grows and duplicates its DNA
(d) a germ cell forms its spindle apparatus

2. Select the incorrect match w.r.t. phases of the cell cycle.
(a) G_0-phase- Between M and S-phase
(b) G_1-phase- Preparatory phase for DNA replication
(c) G_2-phase- Preparatory phase for mitosis
(d) S-phase- Synthsis phase

3. Which one of the following statements is incorrect about interphase?
(a) It is called intermitosis because it occurs between two successive divisions
(b) It is called synthesis phase in which DNA molecules replicate
(c) It is called energy phase as it is metabolically quite active
(d) It is called preparatory phase as it prepares the cell to divides

4. Which statement about the G_1-phase is correct?
(a) Cell stops growing
(b) DNA in the cell does not replicate
(c) Cell is metabolically inactive
(d) It is not a phase of synthesis of macromolecules

5. Which of the following statement best defines the cell cycle?
(a) The process by which a cell replicates its DNA and divides into two
(b) The process by which a cell grows and performs its functions
(c) The sequence of events including growth, DNA replication, and cell division
(d) The period during which a cell remains inactive

6. Given below are two statements; one is labelled as Assertion (A) and the other is labelled as Reason (R).
Assertion (A) During G_1-phase, amount of DNA or chromatin remains same.
Reason (R) Cell size increase and nucleus also grows.

In the light of the above statements, choose the correct answer from the options given below.
(a) A is false, but R is true
(b) Both A and R are true and R is the correct explanation of A
(c) Both A and R are true, but R is not the correct explanation of A
(d) A is true, but R is false

7. Match List I with List II.

	List I		List II
A.	G_1-phase	1.	Cell grows
B.	S-phase	2.	DNA replication
C.	G_2-phase	3.	Cytoplasmic growth
D.	Metaphase in M-phase	4.	Alignment of chromosomes

Choose the correct answer from the options given below.

	A	B	C	D
(a)	3	2	1	4
(b)	3	4	1	2
(c)	4	1	2	3
(d)	1	2	3	4

8. Choose the odd one with respect to G_0-stage.
(a) Inactive stage
(b) Quiescent stage
(c) Cells no longer proliferate
(d) Cells remain metabolically inactive

9. Chromosomes are in their most extended form during
(a) G_1-phase (b) G_2-phase
(c) S-phase (d) M-phase

10. The following image illustrates various phases of the cell cycle designated as *A*, *B*, *C* and *D*. In which phase of the cell cycle proteins for the spindle fibers are formed?

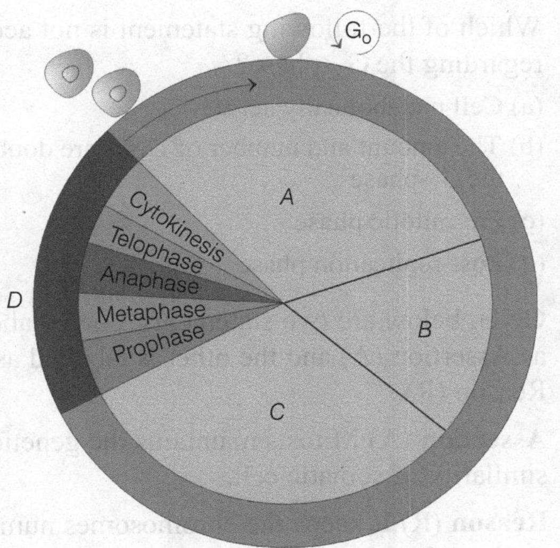

(a) *A* (b) *B*
(c) *C* (d) *D*

11. If a gamete of a diploid organism has 10 chromosomes then what will be the number of chromosomes in G_2-phase?
(a) 10 (b) 20
(c) 40 (d) 5

12. In the G_2-phase, a diploid cell contains the amount of DNA equal to
(a) hexaploid cell (b) tetraploid cell
(c) haploid cell (d) diploid cell

13. What characterises mitosis?
(a) Pairing of homologous chromosomes
(b) Division of the nucleus two times
(c) Reduction division
(d) Equal division

14. Condensation of chromosomes and appearance of astral rays occur during which phase?
(a) Prophase (b) Metaphase
(c) Anaphase (d) Telophase

15. Which of the following statement is not accurate regarding the G_2-phase?
(a) Cell metabolically active
(b) The amount and number of DNA are double the G_1-phase
(c) Pre-mitotic phase
(d) Post-replication phase

16. Given below are two statements; one is labelled as Assertion (A) and the other is labelled as Reason (R).

Assertion (A) Mitosis maintains the genetic similarity of somatic cell.

Reason (R) It keeps the chromosomes number constant in a species.

In the light of the above statements, choose the correct answer from the options given below.
(a) A is false, but R is true
(b) Both A and R are true and R is the correct explanation of A
(c) Both A and R are true, but R is not the correct explanation of A
(d) A is true, but R is false

17. Which statement about mitosis is correct?
(a) One round of DNA replication is followed by one round of separation
(b) One parent cell forms two daughter nuclei with half the amount of DNA
(c) Most animals produce gametes by mitotic division
(d) One parent cell forms two daughter nuclei with half the number of DNA

18. Given below are two statements regarding late prophase.
Statement I Golgi complex and endoplasmic reticulum become conspicuous.
Statement II Nuclear envelope breaks into small vessicles.
In the light of the above statements, choose the correct answer from the options given below.
(a) Statement I is incorrect, but statement II is correct
(b) Both statement I and statement II are correct
(c) Both statement I and statement II are incorrect
(d) Statement I is correct, but statement II is incorrect

19. What features in prokaryotes substitutes for the spindle action in eukaryotes?
(a) Looped DNA
(b) Centrioles with asters
(c) Fission instead of cytokinesis
(d) Elongation of plasma membrane

20. If a cell possesses twice as much DNA as in the functional cell, the cell
(a) is preparing to divide
(b) has completed division
(c) has ceased to function
(d) has reached end of its life span

21. What is correct about the stage of mitotic division represented by the following diagram?

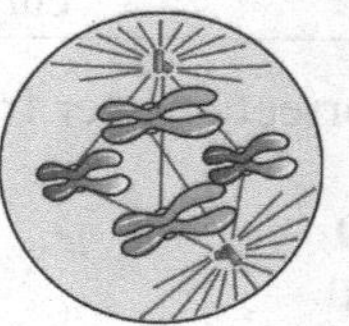

(a) This phase is the transition to metaphase from prophase
(b) Daughter chromosomes move to opposite poles
(c) Centrioles divide and move to opposite poles
(d) Crossing over has occurred between homologous chromosomes

22. Read the following statements and find out the incorrect statement.
(a) In an animal cell, cytokinesis is achieved by the appearance of a furrow in the plasma membrane
(b) Furrow formation starts in the center of cell and grows outward to meet the existing lateral walls
(c) Cell plate represents the middle lamella between the walls of two adjacent plant cells
(d) During cytokinesis, organelles like mitochondria and plastids get distributed between the two daughter cells

23. Select the incorrect match w.r.t. mitosis.
(a) Prophase - Movement of centriole towards opposite pole
(b) Metaphase - Study of chromosome structure
(c) Anaphase - Separation of homologous chromosomes
(d) Telophase - Last stage of karyokinesis

24. Starting of metaphase is marked by
(a) complete disintegration of nuclear membrane
(b) disappearance of ER, Golgi bodies, nucleolus and nuclear envelope
(c) initiation of condensation of chromosomal material
(d) chromosomes align at the equatorial plate

25. If a gamete of flowering plants contains 20 chromosomes then what will be the number of chromosomes in anaphase of mitosis?
(a) 40
(b) 80
(c) 20
(d) 60

Response Index

01	a	b	c	d	10	a	b	c	d	19	a	b	c	d
02	a	b	c	d	11	a	b	c	d	20	a	b	c	d
03	a	b	c	d	12	a	b	c	d	21	a	b	c	d
04	a	b	c	d	13	a	b	c	d	22	a	b	c	d
05	a	b	c	d	14	a	b	c	d	23	a	b	c	d
06	a	b	c	d	15	a	b	c	d	24	a	b	c	d
07	a	b	c	d	16	a	b	c	d	25	a	b	c	d
08	a	b	c	d	17	a	b	c	d					
09	a	b	c	d	18	a	b	c	d					

Performance Scanner

> 90% Excellent !	You have mastered these topics. The concepts of these topics are at your fingertips. Move on to the next topics and maintain this momentum.
76-90% Very Good !	You have a good command over these topics. Revise these topics again after a few days and enhance your performance.
60-75% Good !	You have a wide scope to learn for these topics. Revise these topics again.
<60% Not Satisfactory!	You have a long way ahead of you to master these topics. Revise it thoroughly.

Test 2

Syllabus • Meiosis and its Significance

For deeper insight, **Scan the QR Code**

Important Instructions

- The test is of 30 minutes duration and contains 25 Multiple Choice Questions (four options with a single correct answer).
- Choose the correct option and fill the OMR given on the last page of this test accordingly.
- At some instances, you may find more than 1 option to be correct. In such circumstances, you have to judge the most appropriate answer as per the conditions given in the question.

1. Which of the following event occurs exclusively during prophase-I of meiosis and not during mitosis?
(a) Chromosome condensation
(b) Synapsis and formation of tetrads
(c) Breakdown of the nuclear envelope
(d) Spindle fibre formation

2. The anaphase-II of meiosis-II begins with the simultaneous splitting of the centromere of each chromosome allowing them to move towards opposite poles of the cell by
(a) shortening of microtubules attached to kinetochores
(b) shortening of microtubules attached to centromere
(c) cytokinesis followed by karyokinesis
(d) karyokinesis followed by cytokinesis

3. The stage of meiotic prophase which shows terminalisation of chiasmata as its distinctive feature is
(a) leptotene (b) zygotene
(c) diakinesis (d) pachytene

4. Given below are two statements; one is labelled as Assertion (A) and the other is labelled as Reason (R).

Assertion (A) Same chromosome number is maintained from generation to generation through meiosis.

Reason (R) Nuclear division restores the original diploid chromosome number.

In the light of the above statements, choose the correct answer from the options given below.

(a) A is false, but R is true
(b) Both A and R are true and R is the correct explanation of A
(c) Both A and R are true, but R is not the correct explanation of A
(d) A is true, but R is false

5. Which one of the following statement is incorrect about meiosis?

(a) It involves two successive cell divisions
(b) Produces four haploid cells
(c) Does not involve DNA replication
(d) Helps in conservation of specific chromosome number from generation to generation

6. During which phase of meiosis does crossing over occur, and what is its significance?

(a) Prophase-I, genetic variation
(b) Metaphase-I, chromosome alignment
(c) Prophase-I, chromatid separation
(d) Telophase-I, nuclear reformation

7. Match List I with List II.

List I	List II
A. Zygotene	1. Terminalisation
B. Pachytene	2. Chiasmata
C. Diplotene	3. Crossing over
D. Diakinesis	4. Bivalent

Choose the correct answer from the options given below.

	A	B	C	D
(a)	4	3	2	1
(b)	1	2	4	3
(c)	2	4	3	1
(d)	4	2	3	1

8. Read the two statements regarding meiosis.

Statement I Meiosis occurs in bacteria and archaebacteria for the formation of gamete.

Statement II Onion root tip are specially used for the study of meiosis.

In the light of the above statements, choose the correct answer from the options given below.

(a) Statement I is incorrect, but statement II is correct
(b) Both statement I and statement II are correct
(c) Both statement I and statement II are incorrect
(d) Statement I is correct, but statement II is incorrect

9. Read the following statements.

I. The repulsive force between the homologous chromosomes decrease at metaphase-I.
II. Shorter chromosomes have more chiasmata than longer ones.
III. After anaphase-I, each pole has a haploid number of chromosomes.
IV. Chiasmata are mainly terminal during diakinesis.
V. Sometime cytokinesis is postponed till the end of second meiotic division.

Choose the correct answer from the options given below.

(a) I, III and IV
(b) III, IV and V
(c) I, II and III
(d) II, IV and V

10. Organisms that are exclusive for …*A*… reproduction undergo …*B*… at some stages of their life cycle.

(a) *A*-asexual, *B*-meiosis
(b) *A*-sexual, *B*-mitosis
(c) *A*-vegetative, *B*-meiosis
(d) *A*-sexual, *B*-meiosis

11. The homologous chromosomes segregate during

(a) mitosis
(b) meiosis-I
(c) meiosis-II
(d) fertilisation

12. Crossing over is

(a) the exchange of genetic material between non-homologous chromosomes
(b) the exchange of genetic material between sister chromatids
(c) the exchange of genetic material between homologous chromosomes
(d) the independent assortment of chromosomes

13. If $2n = 46$ the number of chromosome in anaphase-I will be

(a) 46 (b) 23
(c) 92 (d) 100

14. The following diagram depicts a phase of meiosis. Identify the phase and the primary event occurring in this phase.

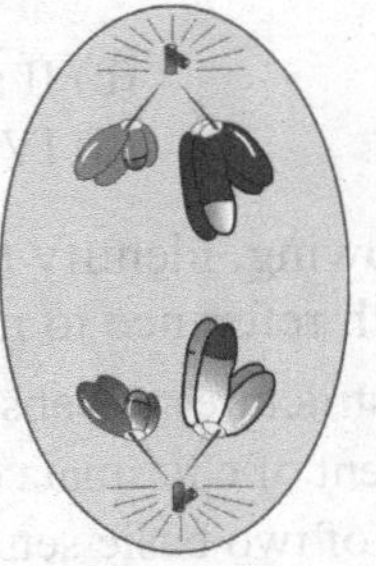

(a) Anaphase-I, separation of chromatids of chromosomes
(b) Anaphase-II, separation of chromatids of chromosomes
(c) Anaphase-I, separation of homologous chromosomes
(d) Anaphase-II, separation of homologous chromosomes

15. In meiosis, actual haploidy in terms of DNA comes in which phase

(a) interphase (b) anaphase-I
(c) anaphase-II (d) metaphase-I

16. Which statement best explains the evolutionary advantage of meiosis?

(a) Meiosis is necessary for sexual reproduction
(b) Genetic recombinations are possible from generation to generation
(c) Meiosis alternates with mitosis from generation to generation
(d) The same genetic system is passed on from generation to generation

17. Crossing over takes place between which chromatids and in which stage of the cell cycle?

(a) Non-sister chromatids of non-homologous chromosomes at zygotene stage of prophase-I
(b) Non-sister chromatids of homologous chromosomes at pachytene stage of prophase-I
(c) Non-sister chromatids of homologous chromosomes at zygotene stage of prophase-I
(d) Non-sister chromatids of non-homologous chromosomes at pachytene stage of prophase-I

18. Following is the diagrammatic representation of a definite stage of meiosis. Which of the following is incorrect about the same?

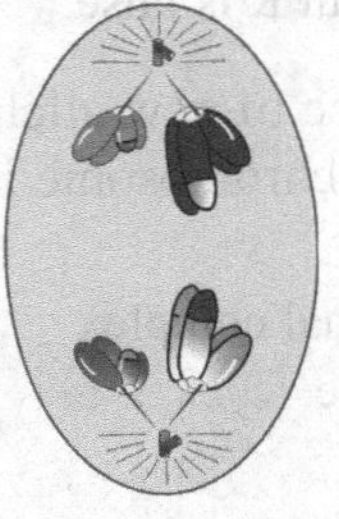

(a) Centromeres do not split
(b) Chromatids separate
(c) Microtubules contract
(d) Chromatids reach opposite poles

19. Given below are two statements.

Statement I Tetrads are most distinctly observed in the zygotene stage.

Statement II Chiasma terminalisation occurs in diakinesis stage.

In the light of the above statements, choose the correct answer from the options given below.

(a) Statement I is incorrect, but statement II is correct
(b) Both statement I and statement II are correct
(c) Both statement I and statement II are incorrect
(d) Statement I is correct, but statement II is incorrect

20. If the quantity of DNA is 8q during anaphase-I of meiosis-I, what will be the quantity during anaphase-II of meiosis-II?

(a) 4q (b) 16q
(c) 8q (d) 2q

21. Given below are two statements; one is labelled as Assertion (A) and the other is labelled as Reason (R).

Assertion (A) Crossing over between sister chromatids produce no variation.

Reason (R) Sister chromatids are formed by replicating the same chromosome.

In the light of the above statements, choose the correct answer from the options given below.

(a) A is false, but R is true
(b) Both A and R are true and R is the correct explanation of A
(c) Both A and R are true, but R is not the correct explanation of A
(d) A is true, but R is false

22. The appearance of new allelic combinations of a gene within a chromosome is made possible by

(a) nuclease
(b) synaptonemal complex
(c) recombinase
(d) tubulin

23. An abnormality in which of the following part of a chromosome will interfere with its segregation during the anaphase stage of cell division?

(a) Kinetochore (b) Centromere
(c) Chromatid (d) Telomere

24. Consider the following statements.

I. Telophase-II is the reverse of prophase-II.
II. DNA replication is restricted to the interkinesis stage.
III. Chromosomes start to condense before prophase-II.
IV. Cytokinesis always follows karyokinesis.

Choose the incorrect answer from the options given below.

(a) II only (b) II and III
(c) I and IV (d) IV only

25. From the following, identify the two correct statements with reference to meiosis.

I. Bead-like structures are absent on chromosomes.
II. Displacement of chiasmata occurs in diakinesis.
III. Separation of two basic sets of chromosomes.
IV. No division of centromere.

Choose the correct option.

(a) II and III (b) II and IV
(c) III and IV (d) I and III

Response Index

01	a	b	c	d	10	a	b	c	d	19	a	b	c	d
02	a	b	c	d	11	a	b	c	d	20	a	b	c	d
03	a	b	c	d	12	a	b	c	d	21	a	b	c	d
04	a	b	c	d	13	a	b	c	d	22	a	b	c	d
05	a	b	c	d	14	a	b	c	d	23	a	b	c	d
06	a	b	c	d	15	a	b	c	d	24	a	b	c	d
07	a	b	c	d	16	a	b	c	d	25	a	b	c	d
08	a	b	c	d	17	a	b	c	d					
09	a	b	c	d	18	a	b	c	d					

Performance Scanner

> 90% Excellent !	You have mastered these topics. The concepts of these topics are at your fingertips. Move on to the next topics and maintain this momentum.
76-90% Very Good !	You have a good command over these topics. Revise these topics again after a few days and enhance your performance.
60-75% Good !	You have a wide scope to learn for these topics. Revise these topics again.
<60% Not Satisfactory!	You have a long way ahead of you to master these topics. Revise it thoroughly.

Chapter Break Thru

Syllabus
- Cell Division : Cell Cycle, Mitosis, Meiosis and their Significance

Important Instructions
- The test is of 1 hour duration and contains 50 Multiple-Choice Questions (Four options with a single correct answer).
- Choose the correct option and fill the OMR given on the last page of this test accordingly.
- At some instances, you may find more than 1 option to be correct. In such circumstances, you have to judge the most appropriate answer as per the conditions given in the question.

1. Which of the following occurs during G_1-phase (Gap-1) of interphase ?
(a) Re-organisation of all cell components, takes place
(b) Cell is metabolically active, grows, but does not replicate its DNA
(c) Nuclear division takes place
(d) DNA synthesis or replication takes place

2. Choose the incorrect option with respect to mitosis.
(a) Growth (b) Cell repair
(c) Regeneration (d) Crossing over

3. The centriole undergoes duplication during which phase of cell cycle?
(a) S-phase (b) Prophase
(c) Metaphase (d) G_2-phase

4. Some dividing cells exit the cycle and enter an inactive stage called quiescent stage (G_0). This process occurs at the beginning of
(a) G_1-phase (b) S-phase
(c) G_2-phase (d) M-phase

5. Which statement accurately describes a stage of mitosis?
(a) Chromosomes move to the spindle equator and align along the equatorial plate in metaphase
(b) Chromatids separate but remain in the center of the cell in anaphase
(c) Chromatids start moving towards opposite poles in telophase
(d) Golgi complex and endoplasmic reticulum are still visible at the end of prophase

6. In humans, the number of tetrads formed during mitosis is
(a) 0 (b) 4
(c) 23 (d) 46

7. How many mitotic divisions are required for one cell to produce 256 cells?
(a) 14 (b) 16
(c) 8 (d) 128

8. The main protein of mitotic spindle is
(a) myosin (b) dynein
(c) tubulin (d) tropomyosin

9. At the equatorial plate during metaphase-I of meiosis, there are
(a) bivalents
(b) single chromosomes
(c) unpaired duplicated chromosomes
(d) always 23 chromosomes

10. Mitosis can be best studied in
(a) onion root tip
(b) young anther
(c) testis of grasshopper
(d) ovary of human female

11. What is the correct sequence of the number of DNA during G_1, G_2, metaphase, and anaphase in a diploid cell?

(a) $2n \rightarrow 2n \rightarrow 2n \rightarrow 4n$
(b) $n \rightarrow 2n \rightarrow 4n \rightarrow 8n$
(c) $2n \rightarrow 2n \rightarrow 2n \rightarrow 2n$
(d) $2n \rightarrow 2n \rightarrow 2n \rightarrow n$

12. At which stage of meiosis is the genetic constitution of gametes ultimately determined?

(a) Anaphase-I
(b) Metaphase-II
(c) Metaphase-I
(d) Anaphase-II

13. In which phase of meiosis can we find the bouquet stage?

(a) Zygotene (b) Pachytene
(c) Leptotene (d) Diakinesis

14. Which event or structure is not depicted in the following diagram?

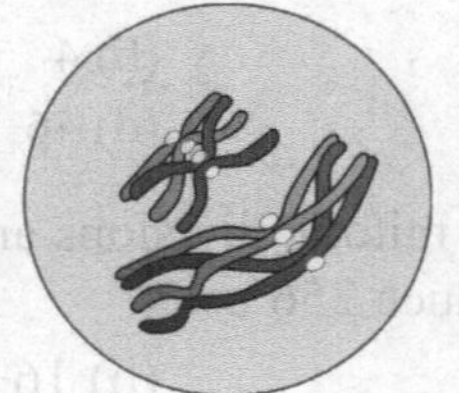

(a) Terminalisation
(b) Crossing over
(c) Chiasmata
(d) DNA replication

15. A bivalent during meiosis-I consists of

(a) four chromatids and two centromeres
(b) two chromatids and one centromere
(c) four chromatids and four centromeres
(d) two chromatids and two centromeres

16. In which of the following stage enzyme recombinase activated?

(a) Diplotene
(b) Pachytene
(c) Zygotene
(d) Diakinesis

17. What is the site on non-sister chromatids of homologous chromosomes where crossing over occurs called?

(a) Tetrad
(b) Synapse
(c) Chiasmata
(d) Recombination nodule

18. Which of the following statement about the recombinase enzyme during meiosis is correct?

(a) Recombinase enzyme is involved in the initial pairing of homologous chromosomes
(b) Recombinase enzyme exclusively facilitates the separation of sister chromatids
(c) Recombinase enzyme catalyses the exchange of genetic material between non-sister chromatids during crossing over
(d) Recombinase enzyme is responsible for the attachment of spindle fibers to centromeres

19. What is the main event depicted in the given diagram?

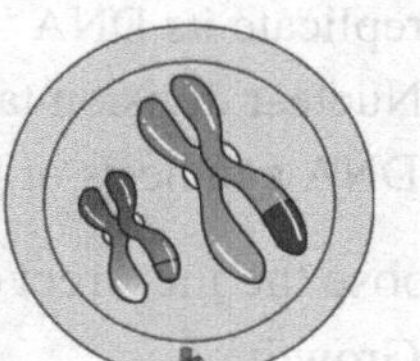

(a) Formation of bivalents during prophase-I
(b) Separation of homologous chromosomes during anaphase-I
(c) Crossing over between non-sister chromatids
(d) Formation of recombinant chromatids

20. What is interkinesis?

(a) A stage between karyokinesis and cytokinesis
(b) An interphase
(c) A stage between meiosis-I and meiosis-II
(d) A stage between two mitotic divisions

21. Which cellular structures consistently disappear during both mitosis and meiosis?

(a) Endoplasmic reticulum and plasma membrane
(b) Nucleolus and nuclear membrane
(c) Plastid and nuclear membrane
(d) Endoplasmic reticulum and mitochondria

22. Given below are two statements, one is labelled as Assertion (A) and other is labelled as Reason (R).

Assertion (A) Interphase is called the resting phase.

Reason (R) There is no apparent activity related to cell division.

In the light of the above statements, choose the correct answer from the options given below.

(a) A is false, but R is true
(b) Both A and R are true and R is the correct explanation of A
(c) Both A and R are true, but R is not the correct explanation of A
(d) A is true, but R is false

23. Match the List I with List II.

List I	List II
A. S-phase	1. Proteins are synthesised
B. G_2-phase	2. Inactive phase
C. G_0-stage	3. Cell is metabolically active
D. G_1-phase	4. DNA replication

Choose the correct answer from the options given below.

	A	B	C	D
(a)	3	2	1	4
(b)	4	2	3	1
(c)	4	1	2	3
(d)	2	4	3	1

24. If you are provided with onion root tips to count chromosomes, which stage is the most convenient to observe?

(a) Telophase (b) Metaphase
(c) Prophase (d) Anaphase

25. Which statement about cytokinesis is incorrect?

(a) Karyokinesis is followed by the separation of cytoplasm to complete the cell division
(b) In plant cells, cytokinesis is completed by the formation of a cell plate between two adjacent cells
(c) In an animal cell, cytokinesis is achieved by the formation of a furrow in the plasma membrane
(d) Syncytium is a multicellular condition that appears when karyokinesis is not followed by cytokinesis

26. Given below are two statements.

Statement I Growth in multicellular animals occurs due to mitosis only.

Statement II Mitosis is a mechanism for replacing old dead and worn out cells by new cells.

In the light of the above statements, choose the correct answer from the options given below.

(a) Statement I is incorrect, but statement II is correct
(b) Both statement I and statement II are correct
(c) Both statement I and statement II are incorrect
(d) Statement I is correct, but statement II is incorrect

27. Meiosis results in

I. production of gametes.
II. reduction in the number of chromosomes.
III. introduction of variation.
IV. regeneration.
V. vegetative reproduction.

Choose the correct answer from the options given below.

(a) I, II and IV (b) III and V
(c) I, II and III (d) IV and V

28. How do daughter cells formed after meiosis-I differ from the daughter cells formed after meiosis-II?

(a) Daughter cells after meiosis-I are haploid, while daughter cells after meiosis-II are diploid
(b) Daughter cells after meiosis-I contain homologous chromosomes, while daughter cells after meiosis-II contain sister chromatids
(c) Daughter cells after meiosis-I are diploid, while daughter cells after meiosis-II are haploid
(d) Daughter cells after meiosis-I contain sister chromatids, while daughter cells after meiosis-II contain homologous chromosomes

29. Meiosis involves pairing of

(a) non-homologous chromosomes and recombination between sister chromatids of homologous chromosomes
(b) homologous chromosomes and recombination between sister chromatids of homologous chromosomes
(c) homologous chromosomes and recombination between non-sister chromatids of homologous chromosomes
(d) non-homologous chromosomes and recombination between non-sister chromatids of homologous chromosomes

30. Choose the incorrect match pair.
(a) Chromatids — Centromere joins
(b) Sister chromatids — Non-homologous chromosomes
(c) Metaphase-I — Tetrad
(d) Meiosis — Four haploid daughter cells

31. Given below are two statements.
Statement I M-phase is the shortest phase of the cell cycle.
Statement II The cell enters a state of dormancy during interphase.
In the light of the above statements, choose the correct answer from the options given below.
(a) Statement I is incorrect, but statement II is correct
(b) Both statement I and statement II are correct
(c) Both statement I and statement II are incorrect
(d) Statement I is correct, but statement II is incorrect

32. Yeast cells take 90 minutes to divide into two daughter cells. How much time is taken to form 64 yeast cells?
(a) 360 minutes (b) 9 hrs
(c) 280 minutes (d) 6 hrs

33. Consider the following statements.
I. Cells in G_0 remain arrested permanently.
II. A DNA damage can prompt cells to exit cell cycle.
III. All somatic cells undergo equational division.
IV. DNA replication is dependent on cell division.
Choose the correct answer from the options given below.
(a) II and IV
(b) III only
(c) I and IV
(d) I only

34. Following is the diagrammatic representation of a particular stage in the cell cycle. Which of the following is correct about the same?

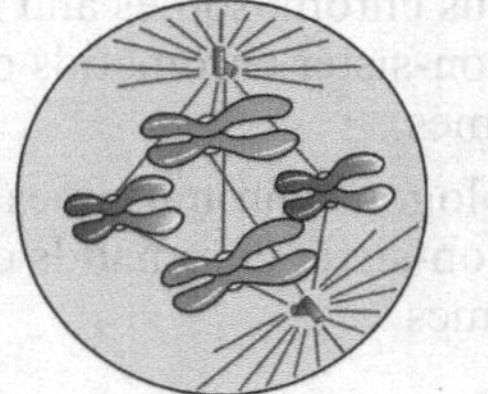

(a) It is the best studied phase of the cell cycle
(b) Chromosomes are arranged along the equator
(c) It is an intermediary stage between prophase and metaphase
(d) Spindle fibres contract to pull the chromatids

35. Given below are two statements; one is labelled as Assertion (A) and the other is labelled as Reason (R).
Assertion (A) Chromatid separation occurs in anaphase I.
Reason (R) Contraction of the spindle fibres pull the chromatids.
In the light of the above statement, choose the correct answer from the options given below.
(a) A is false, but R is true
(b) Both A and R are true and R is the correct explanation of A
(c) Both A and R are true, but R is not the correct explanation of A
(d) A is true, but R is false

36. Match List I with List II.

List I	List II
A. Late prophase	1. Chromosome condensation
B. Telophase	2. Centromere splits
C. Early prophase	3. Nuclear membrane disintegrates
D. Anaphase	4. Chromosome decondensation

Choose the correct answer from the options given below.

	A	B	C	D
(a)	3	4	1	2
(b)	3	2	4	1
(c)	2	4	1	3
(d)	4	3	2	1

37. Given below are two statements.
Statement I Karyokinesis and cytokinesis are independent events occurring simultaneously.
Statement II In liquid endosperm of coconut, cytokinesis is absent.
In the light of the above statements, choose the correct answer from the options given below.
(a) Statement I is incorrect, but statement II is correct
(b) Both statement I and statement II are correct
(c) Both statement I and statement II are incorrect
(d) Statement I is correct, but statement II is incorrect

38. A certain drug inhibits chiasma formation between homologous chromosomes. Which of the following would be the effect on the dividing cells?

(a) Failure of the segregation of homologues
(b) No variations which would slow down evolution
(c) Failure of plant cells to form middle lamella
(d) Polyploidy observed in a plant cell

39. A mutation in which of the protein scaffolds would prevent the process of crossing over during prophase-I of meiosis-I?

(a) Recombinase
(b) Tubulin
(c) Kinetin
(d) Synaptonemal Complex

40. Match List I with List II.

List I	List II
A. Zygotene	1. Enzyme active stage
B. Pachytene	2. Transition to metaphase
C. Diplotene	3. Short-lived stage
D. Diakinesis	4. Lasts for years in oocytes

Choose the correct answer from the options given below.

	A	B	C	D		A	B	C	D
(a)	1	4	3	2	(b)	2	1	4	3
(c)	3	1	4	2	(d)	1	2	3	4

41. Which of the following is not a characteristic of the stage being represented in the image?

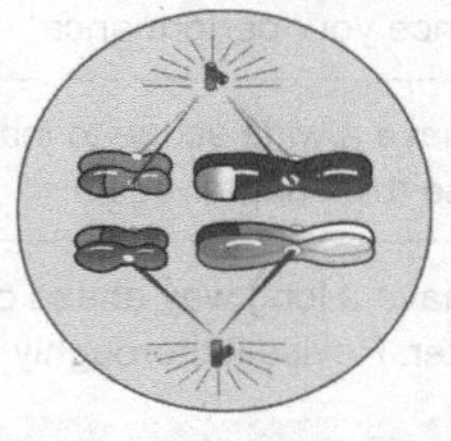

(a) Spindle fibres are attached to the kinetochore
(b) Nuclear envelope integrates completely
(c) Bivalents are arranged on the equatorial plate
(d) Centromere splits in the following stage

42. Given below are two statements; one is labelled as Assertion (A) and the other is labelled as Reason (R).

Assertion (A) Cell growth can disturb the nucleocytoplasmic ratio.

Reason (R) Ratio between nucleus and cytoplasm is maintained by mitosis.

In the light of the above statement, choose the correct answer from the options given below.

(a) A is false, but R is true
(b) Both A and R are true and R is the correct explanation of A
(c) Both A and R are true, but R is not the correct explanation of A
(d) A is true, but R is false

43. Which of the following events when passed, makes a cell commit to division?

(a) Translation of proteins
(b) Replication of DNA
(c) Synthesis of enzymes
(d) Operation of metabolic pathways

44. If anaphase-I of meiosis-I is deleted, what would be the effect on the daughter cells?

(a) Gain of chromosomes only
(b) Loss of chromosomes only
(c) Gain of chromosomes in some and loss in others
(d) Mutation in the genes present in chromosomes

45. Given below are two statements.

Statement I Bouquet formation is a characteristic of leptonema.

Statement II Telomeres of chromosomes contribute to the bouquet formation

In the light of the above statements, choose the correct answer from the options given below.

(a) Statement I is incorrect, but statement II is correct
(b) Both statement I and statement II are correct
(c) Both statement I and statement II are incorrect
(d) Statement I is correct, but statement II is incorrect

46. Which of the following is preceded by cytokinesis that results in formation of a tetrad of cells?
(a) Telophase-I (b) Telophase
(c) Interkinesis (d) Telophase-II

47. Which of the following best represents the phase that sandwiches between dyad and tetrad cell formation?
(a) Interphase (b) Early prophase
(c) Interkinesis (d) Late telophase

48. The exchange of genetic material, in the prophase-I of meiosis-I occurs between
(a) non-sister chromatids of homologous chromosomes
(b) sister chromatids of homologous chromosomes
(c) non-sister chromatids of non-homologous chromosomes
(d) sister chromatids of non-homologous chromosomes

49. Which of the following correctly represents the increasing order of the time taken by each phase of the cell cycle?
(a) G_1, S, G_2, M (b) M, G_2, S, G_1
(c) M, S, G_2, G_1 (d) G_1, S, M, G_2

50. Following is the diagrammatic representation of phases of cell cycle. Which of the following is not possible cause for the event being demonstrated by *A*?

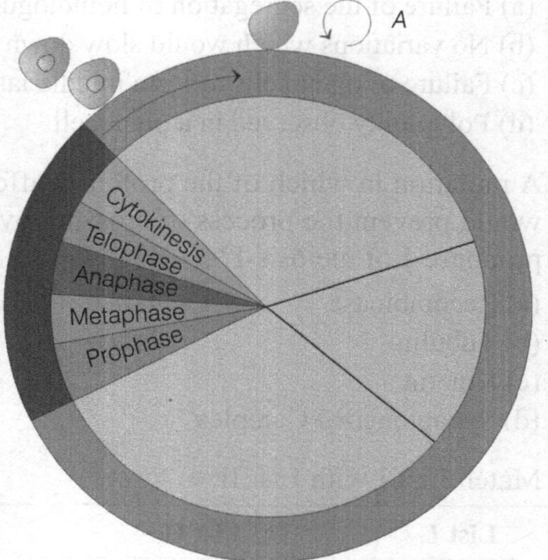

(a) Mutation in the genome
(b) Limiting nutrients
(c) Presence of growth factors
(d) Absence of cell signals

■ **Response Index**

01 ⓐ ⓑ ⓒ ⓓ	14 ⓐ ⓑ ⓒ ⓓ	27 ⓐ ⓑ ⓒ ⓓ	40 ⓐ ⓑ ⓒ ⓓ
02 ⓐ ⓑ ⓒ ⓓ	15 ⓐ ⓑ ⓒ ⓓ	28 ⓐ ⓑ ⓒ ⓓ	41 ⓐ ⓑ ⓒ ⓓ
03 ⓐ ⓑ ⓒ ⓓ	16 ⓐ ⓑ ⓒ ⓓ	29 ⓐ ⓑ ⓒ ⓓ	42 ⓐ ⓑ ⓒ ⓓ
04 ⓐ ⓑ ⓒ ⓓ	17 ⓐ ⓑ ⓒ ⓓ	30 ⓐ ⓑ ⓒ ⓓ	43 ⓐ ⓑ ⓒ ⓓ
05 ⓐ ⓑ ⓒ ⓓ	18 ⓐ ⓑ ⓒ ⓓ	31 ⓐ ⓑ ⓒ ⓓ	44 ⓐ ⓑ ⓒ ⓓ
06 ⓐ ⓑ ⓒ ⓓ	19 ⓐ ⓑ ⓒ ⓓ	32 ⓐ ⓑ ⓒ ⓓ	45 ⓐ ⓑ ⓒ ⓓ
07 ⓐ ⓑ ⓒ ⓓ	20 ⓐ ⓑ ⓒ ⓓ	33 ⓐ ⓑ ⓒ ⓓ	46 ⓐ ⓑ ⓒ ⓓ
08 ⓐ ⓑ ⓒ ⓓ	21 ⓐ ⓑ ⓒ ⓓ	34 ⓐ ⓑ ⓒ ⓓ	47 ⓐ ⓑ ⓒ ⓓ
09 ⓐ ⓑ ⓒ ⓓ	22 ⓐ ⓑ ⓒ ⓓ	35 ⓐ ⓑ ⓒ ⓓ	48 ⓐ ⓑ ⓒ ⓓ
10 ⓐ ⓑ ⓒ ⓓ	23 ⓐ ⓑ ⓒ ⓓ	36 ⓐ ⓑ ⓒ ⓓ	49 ⓐ ⓑ ⓒ ⓓ
11 ⓐ ⓑ ⓒ ⓓ	24 ⓐ ⓑ ⓒ ⓓ	37 ⓐ ⓑ ⓒ ⓓ	50 ⓐ ⓑ ⓒ ⓓ
12 ⓐ ⓑ ⓒ ⓓ	25 ⓐ ⓑ ⓒ ⓓ	38 ⓐ ⓑ ⓒ ⓓ	
13 ⓐ ⓑ ⓒ ⓓ	26 ⓐ ⓑ ⓒ ⓓ	39 ⓐ ⓑ ⓒ ⓓ	

■ **Performance Scanner**

> 90% Excellent !	You have mastered this chapter. The concepts of this chapter are at your fingertips. Move on to the next chapter and maintain this momentum.
76-90% Very Good !	You have a good command over this chapter. Revise the chapter again after a few days and enhance your performance.
60-75% Good !	You have a wide scope to learn for this chapter. Revise this chapter again.
<60% Not Satisfactory!	You have a long way ahead of you to master this chapter. Revise it thoroughly.

Scan for online chapter test

Scan for online unit test

Space for Rough Work

Space for Rough Work

Test Booklet No. 3947311

Test Booklet Code CH11

MEDACE
NEET (UG)
SELF ASSESSMENT KIT

Photosynthesis in Higher Plants

Topics Covered

Early Experiments, Site and Pigments Involved in Photosynthesis

Light Reaction and Dark Reaction : C_3 Cycle

C_4-pathway, Photorespiration and Factors Affecting Photosynthesis

Important Instructions

- This Booklet Contains – Three Topic Tests and One Test on Complete Chapter.
- Each question carries 4 marks.
- For each correct response, the candidate will get 4 marks. And for every incorrect response, 1 mark will be additionally deducted from total score.
- Use **Blue/Black** point pen only for filling the OMR.
- Rough work is to be done in the space provided for this purpose in the test booklet only.

Name of the Candidate (In Capitals) ____________

Candidate's Signature ____________

Invigilator's Signature ____________

Facsimile signature stamp of center superintendent ____________

Do not open this booklet until you start attempting the test

Topical Follow Thru

Test 1

Syllabus
- Photosynthesis as a Means of Autotrophic Nutrition
- Site of Photosynthesis takes Place
- Pigments Involved in Photosynthesis

For deeper insight, **Scan the QR Code**

Important Instructions
- The test is of 30 minutes duration and contains 15 Multiple Choice Questions (four options with a single correct answer).
- Choose the correct option and fill the OMR given on the last page of this test accordingly.
- At some instances, you may find more than 1 option to be correct. In such circumstances, you have to judge the most appropriate answer as per the conditions given in the question.

1. Which scientist correctly identified the photosynthetic product?
(a) Ingenhousz (b) Engelmann
(c) Priestley (d) Sachs

2. Which of the following statement is correct about photosynthesis?
(a) It is accompanied by loss of plant weight
(b) Raw materials are glucose and oxygen
(c) Products are carbon dioxide and water
(d) It is restricted to only plants and some lower organisms

3. Select the incorrect statements from the following.
I. Moll's half-leaf experiment tested for the presence of starch.
II. Jan Ingenhousz placed his experimental setup completely in the dark.
III. Jan Ingenhousz used xerophytic plant for his experiment.
IV. TW Engelmann prepared the first action spectrum of photosynthesis.
V. Cornelius van Niel demonstrated that photosynthesis is a light-dependent reaction.

Choose the correct answer from the options given below.
(a) II, III, IV and V
(b) I, IV and V
(c) II and III
(d) I, II and III

4. What does the given experiment demonstrate?

(a) Plants release carbon dioxide during photosynthesis.
(b) Plants require sunlight to survive.
(c) Plants produce oxygen during photosynthesis.
(d) Animals do not need oxygen to survive.

5. What would happen if in the classic split light experiment of Engelmann, the aerobic bacteria were replaced by anaerobic bacteria?
(a) Bacteria would accumulate in the blue and red light region.
(b) Bacteria would not grow at all in the suspension.
(c) Bacteria would flocculate in the region of absorption spectrum.
(d) Bacteria would flocculate in regions other than blue and red light.

6. Consider the following statements.
I. The first action spectrum of photosynthesis resembled the absorption spectrum of chlorophyll-*a* and *b*.
II. In green plants, CO_2 is the hydrogen donor and gives O_2.

III. Maximum absorption by chlorophyll-*a* is at the wavelength of blue and red regions.

IV. Chloroplasts align themselves perpendicular to the incident light when the light is of high intensity.

V. Accessory pigments like xanthophyll prevent photo-oxidation of chlorophyll-*a*.

Choose the correct set of statements from the options given below.

(a) I, II, III and V (b) I, II, III and IV
(c) I, III, IV and V (d) II, IV and V

7. Given below are two statements about the theory proposed by Jan Ingenhousz.

Statement I Sunlight is essential for purification of air fouled by burning candle.

Statement II Aquatic plants can release oxygen even in the absence of sunlight.

In the light of the above statements, choose the correct answer from the options given below.

(a) Statement I is incorrect, but statement II is correct.
(b) Both statement I and statement II are correct.
(c) Both statement I and statement II are incorrect.
(d) Statement I is correct, but statement II is incorrect.

8. '*X*' are yellowish to orange pigments which prevent photo-oxidation of chlorophyll pigments, whereas '*Y*' is bright or blue-green pigment and is the main photosynthetic pigment. Identify *X* and *Y*.

	X	*Y*
A.	Phycobilins	Chlorophyll-*a*
B.	Chlorophylls	Xanthophyll
C.	Carotenoids	Chlorophyll-*a*
D.	Chlorophylls	Carotenoid

(a) A (b) B
(c) C (d) D

9. Given below are two statements; one is labelled as Assertion (A) and the other is labelled as Reason (R).

Assertion (A) Reaction center is surrounded by a number of antenna molecules.

Reason (R) Reaction centers are pigment molecules that occur on the outer side of photosynthetic unit.

In the light of the above statements, choose the correct answer from the options given below.

(a) A is false, but R is true.
(b) Both A and R are true and R is the correct explanation of A.
(c) Both A and R are true, but R is not the correct explanation of A.
(d) A is true, but R is false.

10. When will the chloroplasts align their flat surfaces parallel to the walls of mesophyll cells?

(a) At high light intensity
(b) At low light intensity
(c) At moderate light intensity
(d) In the dark

11. Which of the following is the most abundant plant pigment in the world?

(a) Chlorophyll-*a*
(b) Chlorophyll-*b*
(c) Carotene
(d) Xanthophyll

12. Which of the following techniques uses polarity of mobile phase to move on a stationary phase and separate into its constituents?

(a) Paper chromatography
(b) Electrophoresis
(c) Spectroscopy
(d) Centrifugation

13. Select the incorrect match pair.

(a) Chlorophyll-*a* – Bluish-green
(b) Chlorophyll-*b* – Olive-green
(c) Bacteriochlorophyll – Green
(d) Xanthophylls – Orange

14. Action spectrum of photosynthesis indicates the

(a) light absorbed by each pigment
(b) rate of photosynthesis at each wavelength
(c) light absorbed by chlorophyll-*a*
(d) rate of photosynthesis in the blue region

15. The given graph shows the action spectrum of photosynthesis. This graph is drawn between the rate of photosynthesis and the wavelength of light. The rate of photosynthesis to prepare this action spectrum is measured by

(a) newly formed biomass
(b) released O_2
(c) consumed CO_2
(d) counting chloroplast in mesophyll cell

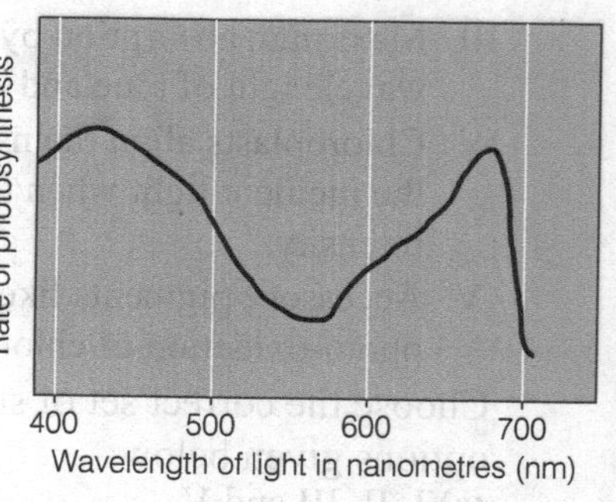

■ **Response Index**

01	a	b	c	d	10	a	b	c	d	19	a	b	c	d
02	a	b	c	d	11	a	b	c	d	20	a	b	c	d
03	a	b	c	d	12	a	b	c	d	21	a	b	c	d
04	a	b	c	d	13	a	b	c	d	22	a	b	c	d
05	a	b	c	d	14	a	b	c	d	23	a	b	c	d
06	a	b	c	d	15	a	b	c	d	24	a	b	c	d
07	a	b	c	d	16	a	b	c	d	25	a	b	c	d
08	a	b	c	d	17	a	b	c	d					
09	a	b	c	d	18	a	b	c	d					

■ **Performance Scanner**

> 90% Excellent !	You have mastered these topics. The concepts of these topics are at your fingertips. Move on to the next test and maintain this momentum.
76-90% Very Good !	You have a good command over these topics. Revise these topics again after a few days and enhance your performance.
60-75% Good !	You have a wide scope to learn for these topics. Revise these topics again.
<60% Not Satisfactory!	You have a long way ahead of you to master these topics. Revise it thoroughly.

Test 2

Syllabus

- Photochemical and Biosynthetic Phases of Photosynthesis
- Cyclic and Non-Cyclic Photophosphorylation
- Chemiosmotic Hypothesis and C_3-pathway

For deeper insight, Scan the QR Code

Important Instructions

- The test is of 30 minutes duration and contains 15 Multiple Choice Questions (four options with a single correct answer).
- Choose the correct option and fill the OMR given on the last page of this test accordingly.
- At some instances, you may find more than 1 option to be correct. In such circumstances, you have to judge the most appropriate answer as per the conditions given in the question.

1. Release of energy during ATP synthesis through chemiosmosis does not involve

(a) breakdown of electron gradient
(b) movement of protons across the membrane to the stroma
(c) reduction of $NADP^+$ to $NADPH_2$ on the stroma side of the membrane
(d) breakdown of proton gradient

2. Select the incorrect match w.r.t. photosystem.

(a) Reaction center - Chlorophyll-*a*
(b) Antenna molecule - Transfer solar energy to the reaction center
(c) Light-harvesting complex - Complex of protein and pigments
(d) Photosystem - Stroma of chloroplast

3. Given below are two statements.

Statement I Photolytic activity is linked to the reaction centre of PS-II through an electron carrier.

Statement II Photochemical phase cannot occur in complete darkness.

In the light of the above statements, choose the correct answer from the options given below.

(a) Statement I is incorrect, but statement II is correct.
(b) Both statement I and statement II are correct.
(c) Both statement I and statement II are incorrect.
(d) Statement I is correct, but statement II is incorrect.

4. The following diagram shows non-cyclic photophosphorylation, where electrons move from PS-II to PS-I and finally to $NADP^+$, which is then converted into NADPH. Where does this conversion occur?

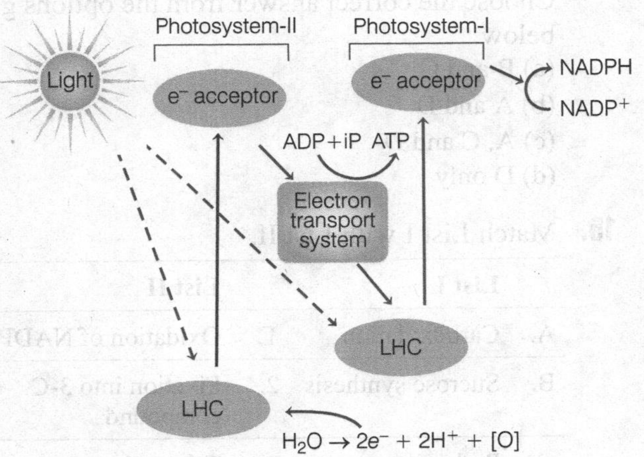

(a) Thylakoid lumen
(b) Cytoplasm
(c) Thylakoid membrane
(d) Stroma

5. Match List I with List II.

List I	List II
A. PS-II	1. Mobile electron carriers
B. Plastocyanin	2. Photolysis of water
C. Pheophytin	3. Synthesis of assimilatory power
D. Z-scheme	4. Resembles chlorophyll

Choose the correct answer from the options given below.

	A	B	C	D
(a)	2	4	3	1
(b)	2	1	4	3
(c)	3	1	2	4
(d)	1	2	4	3

6. The movement of electrons from PS-II to NADP is

I. first downhill, then uphill, followed by downhill and up movement.
II. first uphill, then downhill, followed by uphill and downhill movement.
III. from higher redox potential to lower.
IV. called the Z-scheme.
V. from PS-I to PS-II.

Choose the correct answer from the options given below.

(a) II and IV
(b) II, III and IV
(c) Only II
(d) I, III and V

7. Select the correct statements w.r.t. C_3 cycle.

I. C_3 cycle is discovered by Melvin Calvin.
II. It occurs in bundle sheath cells in C_3 plants.
III. The first stable product of the C_3 cycle is 3-phosphoglyceraldehyde.
IV. The acceptor molecule of CO_2 is a 2-carbon molecule.
V. All enzymes of the C_3 cycle are found in the stroma of the chloroplast.

Choose the correct answer from the options given below.

(a) I, II and V
(b) IV and V
(c) I and V
(d) III and IV

8. Which statement is incorrect regarding the enzyme responsible for the primary fixation of CO_2 in the C_3-pathway?

(a) It is the most abundant enzyme found in the world.
(b) It can interact with both CO_2 and O_2.
(c) It shows more affinity to O_2 than CO_2.
(d) The name of this enzyme is RuBisCO.

9. Given below are two statements.

Statement I Plastocyanin is the final e^- acceptor of PS-I.

Statement II Plastocyanin transfers e^- coming from cytochrome-b_6f to PS-I.

In the light of the above statements, choose the correct answer from the options given below.

(a) Statement I is incorrect, but statement II is correct.
(b) Both statement I and statement II are correct.
(c) Both statement I and statement II are incorrect.
(d) Statement I is correct, but statement II is incorrect.

10. Consider the following statements about cyclic phosphorylation.

I. Cyclic flow of electrons occurs at 680 nm light.
II. Only NADPH is produced but, not ATP.
III. Oxygen evolution does not occur.
IV. It is active in both grana and stromal lamellae.

Choose the correct answer from the options given below.

(a) II only (b) I only
(c) III only (d) IV only

11. Given below are two statements; one is labelled as Assertion (A) and the other is labelled as Reason (R).

Assertion (A) Plastoquinone reduction maintains the concentration gradient.

Reason (R) Plastoquinone is a mobile electron carrier between the photosystems.

In the light of the above statements, choose the correct answer from the options given below.

(a) A is false, but R is true.
(b) Both A and R are true and R is the correct explanation of A.
(c) Both A and R are true, but R is not the correct explanation of A.
(d) A is true, but R is false.

12. Following are the steps involved in chemiosmosis.

A. Facilitated diffusion across CF_0
B. Conformational change in CF_1
C. Reduction of $NADP^+$ to NADPH $+H^+$
D. Electron transfer by plastoquinone
E. Photolysis of water molecule

Choose the correct answer from the options given below.

(a) E-D-C-A-B (b) E-C-D-A-B
(c) E-C-D-B-A (d) E-D-C-B-A

13. How many ATP molecules would be needed to synthesise 6 glucose molecules by C_3 pathway?

(a) 6 ATP (b) 108 ATP
(c) 36 ATP (d) 3 ATP

14. In C_3 cycle, if 3-PGA is converted to Glyceraldehyde-3-Phosphate (G3P), then which of the following reactions will be involved?

A. Oxidation of NADPH
B. Reduction of $NADP^+$
C. Phosphorylation of 3PGA
D. ATP hydrolysis

Choose the correct answer from the options given below.

(a) B and C
(b) A and D
(c) A, C and D
(d) D only

15. Match List I with List II.

	List I		List II
A.	Carboxylation	1.	Oxidation of NADPH
B.	Sucrose synthesis	2.	Fixation into 3-C compound
C.	Reduction	3.	Triose phosphate as substrate
D.	Regeneration	4.	ATP hydrolysis

Choose the correct answer from the options given below.

	A	B	C	D
(a)	3	2	1	4
(b)	3	2	4	1
(c)	1	3	2	4
(d)	2	3	1	4

Response Index

01	a	b	c	d	10	a	b	c	d	19	a	b	c	d
02	a	b	c	d	11	a	b	c	d	20	a	b	c	d
03	a	b	c	d	12	a	b	c	d	21	a	b	c	d
04	a	b	c	d	13	a	b	c	d	22	a	b	c	d
05	a	b	c	d	14	a	b	c	d	23	a	b	c	d
06	a	b	c	d	15	a	b	c	d	24	a	b	c	d
07	a	b	c	d	16	a	b	c	d	25	a	b	c	d
08	a	b	c	d	17	a	b	c	d					
09	a	b	c	d	18	a	b	c	d					

Performance Scanner

> 90% Excellent !	You have mastered these topics. The concepts of these topics are at your fingertips. Move on to the next topics and maintain this momentum.
76-90% Very Good !	You have a good command over these topics. Revise these topics again after a few days and enhance your performance.
60-75% Good !	You have a wide scope to learn for these topics. Revise these topics again.
<60% Not Satisfactory!	You have a long way ahead of you to master these topics. Revise it thoroughly.

Test 3

Syllabus
- Photorespiration and C_4-pathway
- Factors Affecting Photosynthesis

For deeper insight, **Scan the QR Code**

Important Instructions
- The test is of 30 minutes duration and contains 15 Multiple Choice Questions (four options with a single correct answer).
- Choose the correct option and fill the OMR given on the last page of this test accordingly.
- At some instances, you may find more than 1 option to be correct. In such circumstances, you have to judge the most appropriate answer as per the conditions given in the question.

1. Photorespiration involves the synthesis of
(a) two molecules of one carbon compound
(b) one molecule of two carbon compound and one molecule of three carbon compound
(c) two molecules of three carbon compound
(d) one molecule of four carbon compound

2. Which of the following is incorrect about the primary CO_2 acceptor in C_4-pathway?
(a) It is a 3 carbon compound.
(b) It is present in mesophyll cells.
(c) Its regeneration step requires ATP.
(d) It is fixed into a 2 carbon compound.

3. Match List I with List II.

	List I		List II
A.	Oxaloacetic acid	1.	Highly productive crop
B.	Kranz anatomy	2.	First product of CO_2 fixation in sugarcane
C.	Mesophyll cells	3.	Bundle sheaths of large-sized chlorenchymatous cells
D.	C_4 group	4.	Reduced in C_4 plants

Choose the correct answer from the options given below.

	A	B	C	D		A	B	C	D
(a)	2	4	1	3	(b)	2	3	4	1
(c)	4	3	2	1	(d)	1	4	3	2

4. Given below are two statements about the Hatch-Slack cycle.

Statement I The bundle sheath cells are rich in an enzyme RuBisCO, but lack PEPcase.

Statement II C_4-photosynthesis overcomes the problem related to RuBisCO in C_3 plants.

In the light of the above statements, choose the correct answer from the options given below.

(a) Statement I is incorrect, but statement II is correct.
(b) Both statement I and statement II are correct.
(c) Both statement I and statement II are incorrect.
(d) Statement I is correct, but statement II is incorrect.

5. Following are the explanation of why photorespiration is wasteful process, except
(a) ATP is not synthesised
(b) NADPH is not synthesised
(c) Sugar is not synthesised
(d) Oxygen is not synthesised

6. Given below are two statements; one is labelled as Assertion (A) and the other is labelled as Reason (R).

Assertion (A) Productivity of C_3 plants is lesser than C_4 plants.

Reason (R) C_3 plants perform photorespiration in which O_2 is used and CO_2 is released under the influence of light.

In the light of the above statements, choose the correct answer from the options given below.
(a) A is false, but R is true.
(b) Both A and R are true and R is the correct explanation of A.
(c) Both A and R are true, but R is not the correct explanation of A.
(d) A is true, but R is false.

7. What would be the limiting factor for photosynthesis in cold and foggy areas?
(a) Light only
(b) Temperature only
(c) Light and temperature
(d) CO_2 concentration

8. At higher light intensities, the rate of photosynthesis decreases because of

I. other factors becoming limiting
II. photoxidation of chlorophyll
III. deactivation of antenna molecule
IV. destruction of carotenoids
V. saturation of photosystem

Choose the correct answer from the options given below.
(a) III and IV (b) I, II and V
(c) I and II (d) III and V

9. Following is the graph of effect of light intensity on the rate of photosynthesis.

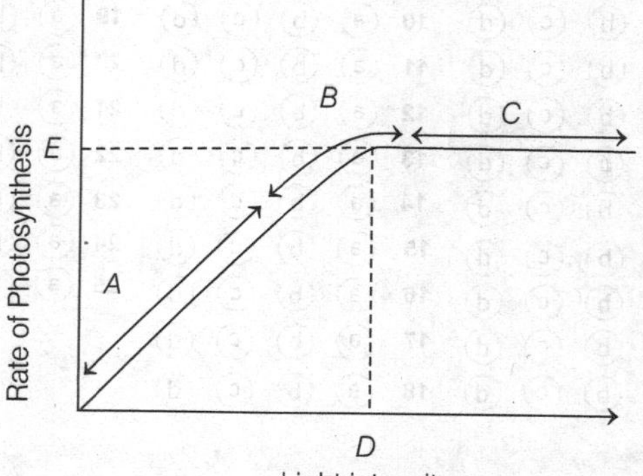

What does C represent in this graph?
(a) Saturation in light intensity
(b) Saturation in rate of photosynthesis
(c) Maximum value of light intensity
(d) The light intensity at which rate of photosynthesis become maximum

10. All of the following would be affected if plasmodesmata was absent between mesophyll cells and bundle sheath cells in C_4 plants, except
(a) biosynthesis of sugar
(b) regeneration of PEP
(c) synthesis of OAA
(d) transport of C_3 acid

11. Consider the following statements.

I. PEPCase is operational in bundle sheath cells.
II. Phosphoglycolate is formed in the mesophyll cell of C_4 plants.
III. RuBisCO is involved in sugar synthesis in C_4 plants.
IV. Atmospheric CO_2 is fixed in bundle sheath of C_4 plants.

Choose the correct statement from the options given below.
(a) II only (b) I only
(c) IV only (d) III only

12. Which of the following is not a direct effect of water stress on the photosynthetic rate?
(a) Decrease in $CO_2 : O_2$ levels
(b) Flaccidity of guard cells
(c) Incidence of light on lamina
(d) Chlorophyll synthesis

13. Given below are two statements; one is labelled as Assertion (A) and the other is labelled as Reason (R).

Assertion (A) Oxygenation by RuBisCO is inhibited in bundle sheath cells.

Reason (R) Decarboxylation of C_4 acid increases CO_2 concentration.

In the light of the above statements, choose the correct answer from the options given below.

(a) A is false, but R is true.

(b) Both A and R are true and R is the correct explanation of A.

(c) Both A and R are true, but R is not the correct explanation of A.

(d) A is true, but R is false.

14. Which of the following step is common to both 3PGA and 2-phosphoglycolate pathway?

(a) Evolution of CO_2

(b) Regeneration of RuBP

(c) Reduction of 3PGA

(d) Synthesis of glycine

15. Given below are two statements.

Statement I Very high CO_2 levels can decrease transpiration rate.

Statement II High CO_2 can promote damage to the plant cells due to toxicity.

In the light of the above statements, choose the correct answer from the options given below.

(a) Statement I is incorrect, but statement II is correct.

(b) Both statement I and statement II are correct.

(c) Both statement I and statement II are incorrect.

(d) Statement I is correct, but statement II is incorrect.

Response Index

01	a	b	c	d	10	a	b	c	d	19	a	b	c	d
02	a	b	c	d	11	a	b	c	d	20	a	b	c	d
03	a	b	c	d	12	a	b	c	d	21	a	b	c	d
04	a	b	c	d	13	a	b	c	d	22	a	b	c	d
05	a	b	c	d	14	a	b	c	d	23	a	b	c	d
06	a	b	c	d	15	a	b	c	d	24	a	b	c	d
07	a	b	c	d	16	a	b	c	d	25	a	b	c	d
08	a	b	c	d	17	a	b	c	d					
09	a	b	c	d	18	a	b	c	d					

Performance Scanner

> 90% Excellent !	You have mastered these topics. The concepts of these topics are at your fingertips. Move on to the next test and maintain this momentum.
76-90% Very Good !	You have a good command over these topics. Revise these topics again after a few days and enhance your performance.
60-75% Good !	You have a wide scope to learn for these topics. Revise these topics again.
<60% Not Satisfactory!	You have a long way ahead of you to master these topics. Revise it thoroughly.

Chapter Break Thru

Syllabus		
• Photosynthesis as a Means of Autotrophic Nutrition • Site of Photosynthesis • Pigments Involved in Photosynthesis	• Photochemical and Biosynthetic Phases of Photosynthesis • Cyclic and Non-Cyclic Photophosphorylation • Chemiosmotic Hypothesis and C_3 Pathway	• Photorespiraiton and C_4-pathway • Factors Affecting Photosynthesis

Important Instructions

- The test is of 1 hour duration and contains 50 Multiple-Choice Questions (Four options with a single correct answer).
- Choose the correct option and fill the OMR given on the last page of this test accordingly.
- At some instances, you may find more than 1 option to be correct. In such circumstances, you have to judge the most appropriate answer as per the conditions given in the question.

1. Accessory pigments absorb light and protect which of the following pigment from photo-oxidation?

(a) Chlorophyll-*b* (b) Xanthophyll
(c) Chlorophyll-*a* (d) Carotenoids

2. A scientist splits white light into its constituents using a prism and used it to illuminate a culture of *Cladophora* in a suspension of *Azotobacter*. Bacterial accumulation in specific regions represents

A. oxygen evolution
B. action spectrum of photosynthesis
C. carbon dioxide evolution
D. absorption spectrum of LHC

Choose the correct answer from the options given below.

(a) B and C (b) A and B
(c) A only (d) D only

3. Which of the following statement is incorrect about chlorophyll-*b*?

(a) It is an accessory photosynthetic pigment.
(b) It occurs in all oxygenic photoautotrophs.
(c) It transfers the light energy to chlorophyll-*a*.
(d) It shows maximum absorption in the blue-red region of the light spectrum.

4. Which of the following statement is incorrect about the absorption spectrum?

(a) It is a graph depicting the amount of wavelengths of light absorbed by a substance
(b) The height of the curve gives the amount of product or response at that wavelength
(c) A single exposure of the substance to full or white light depicts the absorption spectrum
(d) In the red region, height of the peak of chlorophyll-*a* is more than that of chlorophyll-*b*

5. PS-I and PS-II are found in

(a) grana of chloroplast
(b) stroma of chloroplast
(c) matrix of mitochondria
(d) inner membrane of mitochondria

6. Ferredoxin is a constituent of

(a) PS-I
(b) PS-II
(c) Hill reaction
(d) P_{680}

7. Cyclic photophosphorylation synthesises

(a) ATP and NADPH
(a) NADPH only
(c) ATP only
(d) Neither ATP nor NADPH

8. Select the incorrect match w.r.t. photosystem.
(a) Pheophytin - First electron acceptor
(b) Plastoquinone - Hydrogen carrier
(c) Plastocyanin - Membrane-bound electron carrier
(d) NADP reductase - Absent in stroma lamellae

9. Which of the following is functional in both cyclic and non-cyclic phosphorylation?
(a) Cytochrome-b_6f
(b) NADP reductase
(c) Plastoquinone
(d) Ferredoxin

10. During light reaction, plastoquinone facilitates the transfer of electrons from
(a) Cyt–b_6 f complex to PS-I
(b) PS-I to $NADP^+$
(c) PS-I to ATP synthase
(d) PS-II to cyt–b_6 f complex

11. Melvin Calvin used the radioactive ^{14}C in algal photosynthesis to study the sequence of dark reactions, which led to the discovery of the first CO_2 fixation product as
(a) 1, 3-bisphosphoglycerate
(b) PGA
(c) glyceraldehyde-3-phosphate
(d) phosphoglyceraldehyde

12. In the C_3-cycle, glycolytic reversal (reduction) reaction
(a) utilises one molecule of ATP for phosphorylation and one molecule of NADPH for reduction
(b) produces carbohydrate at the expense of ATP and NADPH
(c) forms two molecules of 3 PGA
(d) is similar to the glycolysis

13. How many ATP molecules are required to produce one molecule of triose phosphate in the Calvin cycle?
(a) 1 (b) 2
(c) 3 (d) 9

14. Which statement is true regarding the following diagram?

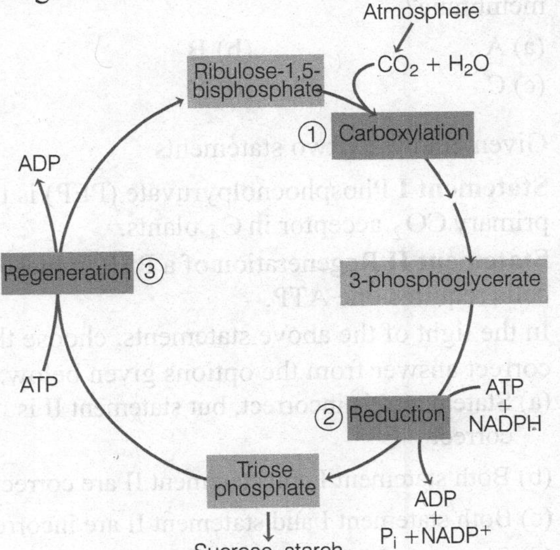

(a) This pathway was discovered by Hatch and Slack.
(b) This is the universal pathway for the production of glucose found in all photosynthetic plants.
(c) This pathway is restricted to C_3 plants.
(d) This pathway takes place in the mesophyll cell in all plants.

15. The following diagram illustrates the chemiosmotic hypothesis for the synthesis of ATP.

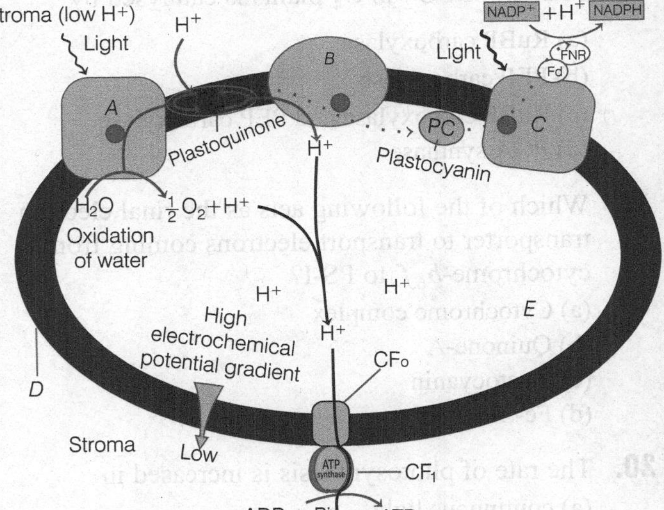

Which component creates the high electrochemical potential gradient across the membrane?

(a) A (b) B
(c) C (d) D

16. Given below are two statements.

Statement I Phosphoenolpyruvate (PEP) is the primary CO_2 acceptor in C_4 plants.

Statement II Regeneration of a PEP in mesophyll cells requires one ATP.

In the light of the above statements, choose the correct answer from the options given below.

(a) Statement I is incorrect, but statement II is correct
(b) Both statement I and statement II are correct
(c) Both statement I and statement II are incorrect
(d) Statement I is correct, but statement II is incorrect

17. How do C_4 plants differ from C_3 plants?

(a) Presence of Calvin cycle
(b) ATP used in glucose formation
(c) Presence of RuBisCO in bundle sheath cells
(d) NADPH used in glucose formation

18. The reaction that is responsible for the final fixation of CO_2 in C_4 plants is catalysed by

(a) RuBP carboxylase
(b) PEP carboxylase
(c) RuBP carboxylase and PEP carboxylase
(d) PGA synthase

19. Which of the following acts as the final electron transporter to transport electrons coming from cytochrome-b_6f to PS-I?

(a) Cytochrome complex
(b) Quinone-A
(c) Plastocyanin
(d) Fe-S centre

20. The rate of photosynthesis is increased in

(a) continuous light
(b) scattered light
(c) intermittent light
(d) parallel light

21. A deficiency of water decreases the rate of photosynthesis for the following reasons, except

(a) wilting of leaves
(b) water is the source of electrons in photosynthetic reactions
(c) turgidity of leaves
(d) closure of stomata

22. Find the incorrect match.

A.	Cornelius van Niel	—	Proved that O_2 evolved during light reaction comes from water, not from CO_2
B.	Engelmann	—	Used *Cladophora* to study action spectrum of photosynthetic pigments
C.	Joseph Priestley	—	Discovered oxygen
D.	Jan Ingenhousz	—	Used *Hydrilla* to show that in the presence of sunlight, green parts of the plants release oxygen

(a) A (b) B (c) C (d) D

23. Given below are two statements.

Statement I Joseph Priestley stated that plants obtain a portion of their nutrition from air.

Statement II Cornelius van Niel demonstrated that photosynthesis is essentially a light dependent reaction in which hydrogen from a suitable oxidisable compound reduces carbon dioxide to carbohydrate.

In the light of the above statements, choose the correct answer from the options given below.

(a) Statement I is incorrect, but statement II is correct.
(b) Both statement I and statement II are correct.
(c) Both statement I and statement II are incorrect.
(d) Statement I is correct, but statement II is incorrect.

24. Given below are two statements regarding non-cyclic photophosphorylation.

Statement I It involves two photosystems working in a series, first PS-II, then the PS-I.

Statement II The electrons from PS-II are passed on by an electron acceptor which passes them to an ETS consisting of ferredoxin.

In the light of the above statements, choose the correct answer from the options given below.

(a) Statement I is incorrect, but statement II is correct
(b) Both statement I and statement II are correct
(c) Both statement I and statement II are incorrect
(d) Statement I is correct, but statement II is incorrect

25. Which of the following statement about the ATP synthase enzyme in photosynthesis is incorrect?

(a) The catalytic part protrudes towards the stroma
(b) It synthesises ATP through photophosphorylation
(c) It is also known as CF_1-CF_0 particle
(d) It acts as a channel for protons to facilitate passive transport from the stroma to the thylakoid lumen

26. Given below are two statements; one is labelled as Assertion (A) and the other is labelled as Reason (R).

Assertion (A) According to chemiosmotic hypothesis, within the chloroplast, protons in the stroma decrease in number.

Reason (R) There is an accumulation of protons in the lumen.

In the light of the above statements, choose the correct answer from the options given below.

(a) A is false, but R is true.
(b) Both A and R are true and R is the correct explanation of A.
(c) Both A and R are true, but R is not the correct explanation of A.
(d) A is true, but R is false.

27. Match List I with List II.

List I	List II
A. Chlorophyll-*a*	1. Lacks RuBisCO in C_4 plants
B. C_3-pathway	2. Photo-conversion
C. C_4-pathway	3. PGA
D. Mesophyll cell	4. OAA

Choose the correct answer from the options given below.

	A	B	C	D		A	B	C	D
(a)	3	2	4	1	(b)	1	3	4	2
(c)	2	1	3	4	(d)	2	3	4	1

28. Given below are two statements; one is labelled as Assertion (A) and the other is labelled as Reason (R).

Assertion (A) Photorespiration may eventually reduce dry matter production and yield of the plant.

Reason (R) A large proportion of CO_2 assimilated by photosynthesis is lost through photorespiration.

In the light of the above statements, choose the correct answer from the options given below.

(a) A is false, but R is true
(b) Both A and R are true and R is the correct explanation of A
(c) Both A and R are true, but R is not the correct explanation of A
(d) A is true, but R is false

29. Mesophyll, during fixation of CO_2 in C_4 plants, is the site of production of

I. malic acid II. phosphoglyceric acid
III. glucose IV. aspartic acid
V. oxaloacetic acid

Choose the correct answer.

(a) II and III (b) I, IV and V
(c) II and V (d) I and III

30. Which of the following statement is not correct with reference to factors affecting the rate of photosynthesis?

(a) Light saturation for CO_2-fixation occurs at 10% of full sunlight
(b) Increasing atmospheric CO_2 concentration upto 0.05% can enhance CO_2-fixation rate
(c) C_3-plants respond to higher temperature with enhanced photosynthesis, while C_4- plants have much lower temperature optimum
(d) Tomato is a greenhouse crop, which can be grown in CO_2-enriched atmosphere for higher yield

31. Which of the following are the oxidised and reduced products in green and purple-sulphur bacteria?

(a) Oxidised product – SO_4^{2-}; Reduced product – $[CH_2O]$
(b) Oxidised product – O_2; Reduced product – $[CH_2O]$

(c) Oxidised product – $[CH_2O]$; Reduced product – $[S^{2-}]$

(d) Oxidised product – S^{2-}; Reduced product – $[CO_2]$

32. Following is the graphical representation of the action spectrum of photosynthesis. In an experiment, green alga in a suspension of aerobic bacteria, was illuminated with split white light. Which of the points in the graph represent the region of maximum and minimum bacterial density, respectively?

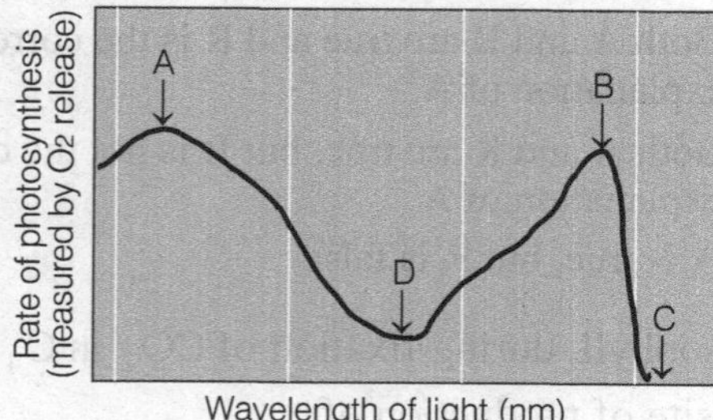

(a) A and D (b) B and D
(c) A and C (d) B and C

33. Given below are two statements; one is labelled as Assertion (A) and the other is labelled as Reason (R).

Assertion (A) Chloroplasts align at right angles to incident high intensity light.

Reason (R) Light incident on larger surface area, reduces photooxidative damage.

In the light of the above statements, choose the correct answer from the options given below.

(a) A is false, but R is true.
(b) Both A and R are true and R is the correct explanation of A.
(c) Both A and R are true, but R is not the correct explanation of A.
(d) A is true, but R is false.

34. Which of the following is incorrect about photochemical reactions taking place in chloroplast?

(a) The site of these reaction is the grana and the stromal lamellae.
(b) They do not require the functioning of any biological catalyst.
(c) Rate of formation of products determine the rate of sugar formation.
(d) Excitation of the reaction centres drive the synthesis of products.

35. Following is the graphical representation of the absorption spectrum of different pigments. Choose the correct combination from the following.

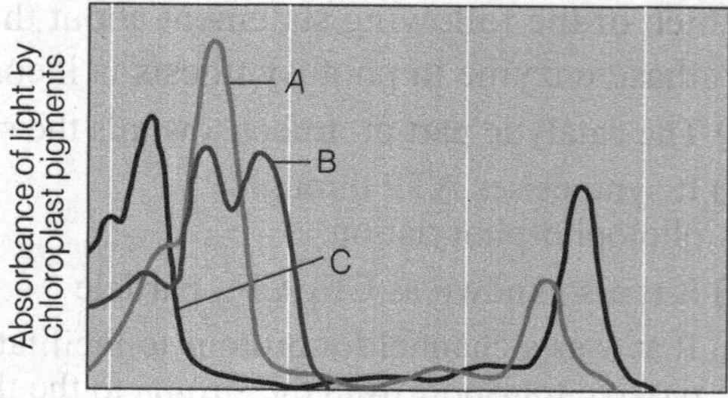

(a) *A* - Reaction centre; *B* - Imparts colour to fruits; *C* - Prevents photooxidation
(b) *A* - Reaction centre; *B* - Imparts colour to fruits; *C* - Transfers energy to reaction centre
(c) *A* - Transfers energy to reaction centre; B - Imparts colour to fruits; *C* - Prevents photooxidation
(d) *A* - Transfers energy to reaction centre; *B* - Imparts colour to fruits; *C* - Reaction centre

36. Consider the following statements.

I. Reaction centre is formed of all the pigments of LHC.
II. Chlorophyll-*a* has a fixed absorption maxima.
III. Pigment molecules of antennae are chemically proteins.
IV. Light of different wavelengths are absorbed by pigments.

Choose the correct set of statements from the options given below.

(a) II and III (b) IV only
(c) I and III (d) I, II and III

37. Which of the following is the probable outcome of absence of photolysis?

(a) Excitation of PS-II
(b) Stoppage of ATP synthesis
(c) Recirculation to PS-I
(d) Production of NADPH

38. Given below are two statements.

Statement I Plastocyanin is the final e^- acceptor in cyclic phosphorylation.

Statement II Cytochrome-b_6f is associated with both cyclic and non-cyclic e^- flow.

In the light of the above statements, choose the correct answer from the options given below.

(a) Statement I is incorrect, but statement II is correct
(b) Both statement I and statement II are correct
(c) Both statement I and statement II are incorrect
(d) Statement I is correct, but statement II is incorrect

39. Given below are two statements; one is labelled as Assertion (A) and the other is labelled as Reason (R).

Assertion (A) Cyclic electron flow cannot sustain photosynthesis.

Reason (R) Cyclic electron flow occurs under low CO_2 availability.

In the light of the above statements, choose the correct answer from the options given below.

(a) A is false, but R is true.
(b) Both A and R are true and R is the correct explanation of A.
(c) Both A and R are true, but R is not the correct explanation of A.
(d) A is true, but R is false.

40. What would be the effect of replacing the hydrogen carrier associated with PS-II with an electron carrier?

(a) No NADPH formation
(b) Electron transport would be halted
(c) Disturbance in the proton gradient
(d) Failure of excitation of PS-I

41. Match List I with List II.

List I	List II
A. NADP reductase	1. Involved in passive transport
B. Cytochrome-b_6f	2. Forms substrate of C_3 pathway
C. CF_0	3. Maintains acidic pH of thylakoid
D. Plastocyanin	4. Associated with divalent cation

Choose the correct answer from the options given below.

	A	B	C	D		A	B	C	D
(a)	3	2	1	4	(b)	2	3	1	4
(c)	3	2	4	1	(d)	2	3	4	1

42. Given below are two statements.

Statement I O_2 formed by water splitting accumulates in the thylakoid lumen.

Statement II Continuous supply of e^- to drive ATP synthesis comes from photolysis.

In the light of the above statements, choose the correct answer from the options given below.

(a) Statement I is incorrect, but statement II is correct
(b) Both statement I and statement II are correct
(c) Both statement I and statement II are incorrect
(d) Statement I is correct, but statement II is incorrect

43. In a closed system in a lab, C^{14} isotope was incorporated into CO_2. The radiolabelled CO_2 molecule was made available to a green alga in the closed system of the laboratory. Which of the molecules in the algae would show radioactivity?

(a) PGA (b) RuBP
(c) RuBisCO (d) PEP

44. Following are the statements related to dark reaction of photosynthesis.

I. C_3 is the primary biosynthetic pathway in all photosynthetic plants.
II. Oxaloacetic acid is a four carbon unstable intermediate in C_4 pathway.
III. 12 molecules of 3-phosphoglyceric acid makes 1 molecule of glucose.
IV. The reduction step of Calvin cycle involves two molecules of NADPH along with two molecules of ATP for phosphorylation and reduction per CO_2 molecules fixed, respectively.
V. At higher temperature, RuBisCO behaves as a carboxygenase.

Choose the correct statements from the options given below.

(a) II and III (b) I, III and IV
(c) III, IV and V (d) I and II

45. How many RuBP is/are regenerated per CO_2 molecule fixed through the Calvin cycle?

(a) One (b) Three
(c) Five (d) Six

46. Given below are two statements; one is labelled as Assertion (A) and the other is labelled as Reason (R).

Assertion (A) Peroxisomes play important role in C_3 plants.
Reason (R) In C_3 plants, glycolate shuttles to peroxisome.
In the light of the above statements, choose the correct answer from the options given below.
(a) A is false, but R is true.
(b) Both A and R are true and R is the correct explanation of A.
(c) Both A and R are true, but R is not the correct explanation of A.
(d) A is true, but R is false.

47. Which of the following steps is crucial for glucose production in C_4 plants?
(a) Transport of C_3 acid to mesophyll
(b) Conversion of C_3 acid to PEP
(c) Decarboxylation of C_4 acid
(d) Fixation of CO_2 to OAA

48. Which of the following is correct about photorespiration?
(a) It lowers the productivity in sugarcane and maize.
(b) At higher temperature, it is active in both C_3 and C_4 plants.
(c) Initial product is a two carbon compound.
(d) Lesser amount of CO_2 is fixed through this pathway.

49. Given below are two statements.
Statement I Light is a limiting factor for plants shadowed by canopy in forests.
Statement II Chloroplasts get fully saturated at 10% of available sunlight.
In the light of the above statements, choose the correct answer from the options given below.
(a) Statement I is incorrect, but statement II is correct
(b) Both statement I and statement II are correct
(c) Both statement I and statement II are incorrect
(d) Statement I is correct, but statement II is incorrect

50. Which of the following lowers productivity of rice plants at high temperature?
A. Photorespiration
B. Photooxidation
C. Enzyme denaturation
D. Enzyme inhibition
Choose the correct answer from the options given below.
(a) A and B
(b) B only
(c) A and C
(d) C and D

Response Index

01 ⓐ ⓑ ⓒ ⓓ	14 ⓐ ⓑ ⓒ ⓓ	27 ⓐ ⓑ ⓒ ⓓ	40 ⓐ ⓑ ⓒ ⓓ
02 ⓐ ⓑ ⓒ ⓓ	15 ⓐ ⓑ ⓒ ⓓ	28 ⓐ ⓑ ⓒ ⓓ	41 ⓐ ⓑ ⓒ ⓓ
03 ⓐ ⓑ ⓒ ⓓ	16 ⓐ ⓑ ⓒ ⓓ	29 ⓐ ⓑ ⓒ ⓓ	42 ⓐ ⓑ ⓒ ⓓ
04 ⓐ ⓑ ⓒ ⓓ	17 ⓐ ⓑ ⓒ ⓓ	30 ⓐ ⓑ ⓒ ⓓ	43 ⓐ ⓑ ⓒ ⓓ
05 ⓐ ⓑ ⓒ ⓓ	18 ⓐ ⓑ ⓒ ⓓ	31 ⓐ ⓑ ⓒ ⓓ	44 ⓐ ⓑ ⓒ ⓓ
06 ⓐ ⓑ ⓒ ⓓ	19 ⓐ ⓑ ⓒ ⓓ	32 ⓐ ⓑ ⓒ ⓓ	45 ⓐ ⓑ ⓒ ⓓ
07 ⓐ ⓑ ⓒ ⓓ	20 ⓐ ⓑ ⓒ ⓓ	33 ⓐ ⓑ ⓒ ⓓ	46 ⓐ ⓑ ⓒ ⓓ
08 ⓐ ⓑ ⓒ ⓓ	21 ⓐ ⓑ ⓒ ⓓ	34 ⓐ ⓑ ⓒ ⓓ	47 ⓐ ⓑ ⓒ ⓓ
09 ⓐ ⓑ ⓒ ⓓ	22 ⓐ ⓑ ⓒ ⓓ	35 ⓐ ⓑ ⓒ ⓓ	48 ⓐ ⓑ ⓒ ⓓ
10 ⓐ ⓑ ⓒ ⓓ	23 ⓐ ⓑ ⓒ ⓓ	36 ⓐ ⓑ ⓒ ⓓ	49 ⓐ ⓑ ⓒ ⓓ
11 ⓐ ⓑ ⓒ ⓓ	24 ⓐ ⓑ ⓒ ⓓ	37 ⓐ ⓑ ⓒ ⓓ	50 ⓐ ⓑ ⓒ ⓓ
12 ⓐ ⓑ ⓒ ⓓ	25 ⓐ ⓑ ⓒ ⓓ	38 ⓐ ⓑ ⓒ ⓓ	
13 ⓐ ⓑ ⓒ ⓓ	26 ⓐ ⓑ ⓒ ⓓ	39 ⓐ ⓑ ⓒ ⓓ	

Performance Scanner

Scan for online chapter test

> 90% Excellent !	You have mastered this chapter. The concepts of this chapter are at your fingertips. Move on to the next chapter and maintain this momentum.
76-90% Very Good !	You have a good command over this chapter. Revise the chapter again after a few days and enhance your performance.
60-75% Good !	You have a wide scope to learn for this chapter. Revise this chapter again.
<60% Not Satisfactory!	You have a long way ahead of you to master this chapter. Revise it thoroughly.

Test Booklet No. **3947312**

Test Booklet Code **CH12**

MEDACE
NEET (UG)
SELF ASSESSMENT KIT

Respiration in Plants

Topics Covered

Introduction to Respiration, Glycolysis and Fermentation

Aerobic Respiration and Respiratory Quotient

Important Instructions

- This Booklet Contains – Two Topic Tests and One Test on Complete Chapter.
- Each question carries 4 marks.
- For each correct response, the candidate will get 4 marks. And for every incorrect response, 1 mark will be additionally deducted from total score.
- Use **Blue/Black** point pen only for filling the OMR.
- Rough work is to be done in the space provided for this purpose in the test booklet only.

Name of the Candidate (In Capitals) __________

____

Candidate's Signature __________

Invigilator's Signature __________

Facsimile signature stamp of center superintendent __________

Do not open this booklet until you start attempting the test

Topical Follow Thru

Test 1

Syllabus
- Exchange of Gases
- Cellular Respiration-Glycolysis
- Fermentation (Anaerobic Respiration)

For deeper insight, **Scan the QR Code**

Important Instructions
- The test is of 30 minutes duration and contains 25 Multiple Choice Questions (four options with a single correct answer).
- Choose the correct option and fill the OMR given on the last page of this test accordingly.
- At some instances, you may find more than 1 option to be correct. In such circumstances, you have to judge the most appropriate answer as per the conditions given in the question.

1. What is the end product of cellular respiration where respiration takes place in the absence of oxygen?
(a) PEP
(b) PGAL
(c) Lactic acid
(d) Pyruvate

2. Which of the following functions as the primary respiratory substrate in the cellular respiration?
(a) Fat
(b) Carbohydrate
(c) Organic acid
(d) Protein

3. Given below are two statements regarding glycolysis.

Statement I One ATP is utilised during the conversion of PEP to pyruvic acid.
Statement II ATP is synthesised in the step of substrate level phosphorylation.
In the light of the above statements, choose the correct answer from the options given below.
(a) Statement I is incorrect, but statement II is correct.
(b) Both statement I and statement II are correct.
(c) Both statement I and statement II are incorrect.
(d) Statement I is correct, but statement II is incorrect.

4. How do facultative anaerobes differ from obligate anaerobes?
(a) Facultative anaerobes can survive only in the presence of oxygen, while obligate anaerobes can survive only in the absence of oxygen.
(b) Facultative anaerobes can switch between aerobic and anaerobic respiration, while obligate anaerobes can only perform anaerobic respiration.
(c) Facultative anaerobes cannot survive in the absence of oxygen, while obligate anaerobes can.
(d) Facultative anaerobes require oxygen for energy production, while obligate anaerobes do not.

5. Which of the following correctly denotes the net gain of ATP, when a molecule of glucose undergoes fermentation?
(a) 1 (b) 2
(c) 3 (d) 4

6. In fermentation, the total gain of NADH are
(a) two (b) zero
(c) one (d) four

7. Match List I with List II.

List I	List II
A. Hexokinase	1. Glucose 6-phosphate to fructose 6-phosphate
B. Mitochondria	2. Aerobic catabolism in prokaryotes
C. Cytoplasm	3. Aerobic catabolism in eukaryotes
D. Phosphogluco isomerase	4. Phosphorylation of glucose

Choose the correct answer from the options given below.

	A	B	C	D
(a)	4	1	2	3
(b)	4	3	2	1
(c)	2	3	1	4
(d)	2	4	3	1

8. Identify the reason why plants do not have a specialised respiratory organ.

(a) Plants do not require oxygen for respiration.
(b) Each plant cell is capable of exchanging gases independently.
(c) Plants rely solely on photosynthesis for their energy needs.
(d) Plants use their roots for the exchange of gases.

9. Given below are two statements; one is labelled as the Assertion (A) and the other is labelled as the Reason (R).

Assertion (A) The net ATP gain in the process of glycolysis is 2 ATP.
Reason (R) Two ATPs are utilised during the formation of glucose-6-phosphate and fructose-1,6-bisphosphate, whereas 4 ATPs are formed in glycolysis through substrate level phosphorylation.
In the light of the above statements, choose the correct answer from the options given below.

(a) A is false, but R is true.
(b) Both A and R are true and R is the correct explanation of A.
(c) Both A and R are true, but R is not the correct explanation of A.
(d) A is true, but R is false.

10. Read the following statements regarding glycolysis.

I. Glycolysis is the partial oxidation of glucose.
II. It is also called EMP pathway after the name of its discoverers, Embden, MacLeod and Pascal.
III. Glycolysis is referred to as universal pathway as it is found in all types of cells.
IV. It comprises10 enzyme regulated reactions.
V. The electrons released in glycolysis are carried by 2 molecules of NADPH.

Choose the incorrect answer from the options given below.

(a) II and V (b) I, II and V
(c) Only V (d) Only III

11. Which statement defines cellular respiration most appropriately?

(a) The process of exchange of oxygen and carbon dioxide with the help of stomata and lenticels.
(b) The process by which cells oxidise complex compounds, leading to the release of energy.
(c) The process by which cells synthesise proteins.
(d) The process by which cells transport oxygen throughout the body.

12. Which of the following condition is most suitable for incomplete oxidation of glucose in *Saccharomyces cerevisiae*?

(a) Presence of oxygen
(b) Absence of oxygen
(c) Sufficient oxygen
(d) Insufficient oxygen

13. Which enzyme catalyses the phosphorylation of glucose during glycolysis?

(a) Phosphorylase
(b) Hexokinase
(c) Phosphoglucomutase
(d) Phosphoglucoisomerase

14. Select the incorrect match.

	Types of respiration		Final electron carriers
A.	Alcoholic fermentation	–	Acetaldehyde
B.	Lactic acid fermentation	–	Pyruvate
C.	Anaerobic respiration	–	Water
D.	Aerobic respiration	–	Oxygen

(a) A (b) B
(c) C (d) D

15. Given below is a diagram related to fermentation.

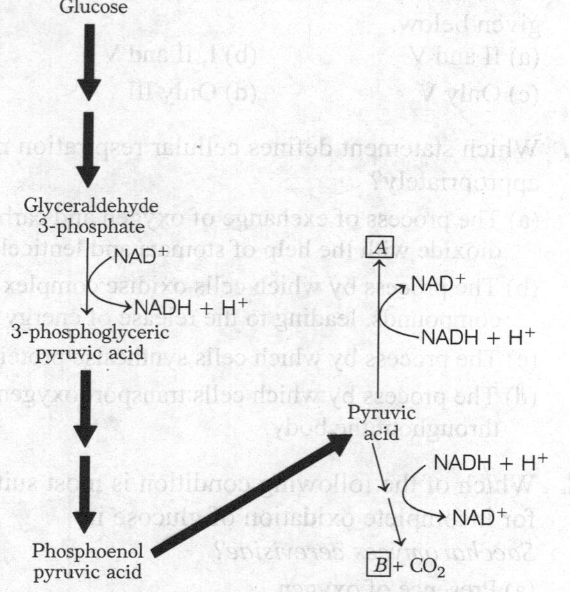

Choose the options with correct labelling of *A* and *B*.

(a) *A* – Ethanol, *B* – Lactic acid
(b) *A* – Lactic acid, *B* – Ethanol
(c) *A* – Lactic acid, *B* – Acetaldehyde
(d) *A* – Lactic acid, *B* – Acetyl Co- A

16. Identify the correct statement(s).

I. Fermentation is a better energy-yielding process than cellular respiration.
II. During fermentation, one $NADH + H^+$ is produced.
III. $NADH + H^+$ acts as a reducing agent in fermentation.
IV. Anaerobic respiration results in production of 4 ATP molecules.

Choose the correct answer from the options given below.

(a) III and IV
(b) I and III
(c) II and IV
(d) III only

17. Choose the option with correct sequence of substrates in glycolysis.

(a) G–6–P → DHAP → PGAL → BPGA → 2–PGA → 3–PGA → PEP
(b) G–6–P → DHAP → PGAL → BPGA → 3 –PGA → 2–PGA → PEP
(c) F–6–P → DHAP → BPGA → PGAL → PGA → PEP
(d) F–6–P → DHAP → PGAL → 2–PGA → 3–PGA → PEP

18. How can alcoholic beverages of alcohol content greater than 13% be obtained?

(a) Using more number of yeast cells.
(b) Using distillation process.
(c) Increasing the number of NAD^+.
(d) Using less number of yeast cells.

19. Given below are two statements.

Statement I All living organisms retain the enzymatic machinery to partially oxidise glucose without the help of oxygen.

Statement II Plants do not have any respiratory organs for gaseous exchange.

In the light of the above statements, choose the correct answer from the options given below.

(a) Statement I is incorrect, but statement II is correct.
(b) Both statement I and statement II are correct.
(c) Both statement I and statement II are incorrect.
(d) Statement I is correct, but statement II is incorrect.

20. Given below are two statements ; one is labelled as Assertion (A) and other is labelled as Reason (R).

Assertion (A) The maximum concentration of alcohol in naturally fermented beverages is upto 13%.

Reason (R) Yeasts poison themselves to death at an alcohol concentration more than 13%.

In the light of the above statements, choose the correct answer from the options given below.
(a) A is false, but R is true.
(b) Both A and R are true and R is the correct explanation of A.
(c) Both A and R are true, but R is not the correct explanation of A.
(d) A is true, but R is false.

21. In which of the following steps of glycolysis, removal of water from the substrate is observed?
(a) F-6-P → F-16-P
(b) Glucose → G-6-P
(c) 2-PGA → PEP
(d) PEP → Pyruvate

22. The useful purpose served by lactate fermentation is
(a) making lactose available for gluconeogenesis
(b) production of additional ATP in anaerobic conditions
(c) regeneration of NAD^+
(d) increased availability to oxygen for the skeletal muscle.

23. At which step, glycolysis reaches the break-even point, i.e. 2 molecules of ATP consumed and 2 new molecules synthesised?
(a) Conversion of BPGA to PG
(b) Splitting of F-6-P into two trioses
(c) Conversion of GADP to BPGA
(d) Conversion of DHAP to GADP

24. Identify the incorrect statements.
I. Two redox-equivalent are removed (in the form of two hydrogen atoms) from PGAL and transferred to a molecule of NADH.
II. In glycolysis, subsequent dehydrogenation and substrate level phosphorylation occurs in the formation of 9th and 10th products respectively.
III. The conversion of BPGA to PGA is an energy yielding processes.
IV. Fermentation can take place in all prokaryotes and all blue green algae.

Choose the correct answer from the options given below.
(a) I and II
(b) II and III
(c) III and IV
(d) I and IV

25. Given below are two statements.
Statement I In plants, glucose is derived from the end product of the photosynthesis.
Statement II During oxidation within a cell, all the energy contained in respiratory substrates is not released free into the cell.

In the light of the above statements, choose the correct answer from the options given below.
(a) Statement I is incorrect, but statement II is correct.
(b) Both statement I and statement II are correct.
(c) Both statement I and statement II are incorrect.
(d) Statement I is correct, but statement II is incorrect.

Response Index

01	a	b	c	d	10	a	b	c	d	19	a	b	c	d
02	a	b	c	d	11	a	b	c	d	20	a	b	c	d
03	a	b	c	d	12	a	b	c	d	21	a	b	c	d
04	a	b	c	d	13	a	b	c	d	22	a	b	c	d
05	a	b	c	d	14	a	b	c	d	23	a	b	c	d
06	a	b	c	d	15	a	b	c	d	24	a	b	c	d
07	a	b	c	d	16	a	b	c	d	25	a	b	c	d
08	a	b	c	d	17	a	b	c	d					
09	a	b	c	d	18	a	b	c	d					

Performance Scanner

> 90% Excellent !	You have mastered these topics. The concepts of these topics are at your fingertips. Move on to the next topics and maintain this momentum.
76-90% Very Good !	You have a good command over these topics. Revise these topics again after a few days and enhance your performance.
60-75% Good !	You have a wide scope to learn for these topics. Revise these topics again.
<60% Not Satisfactory!	You have a long way ahead of you to master these topics. Revise it thoroughly.

Test 2

Syllabus

- TCA Cycle and Electron Transport System (Aerobic)
- Energy Relations–Number of ATP Molecules Generated
- Amphibolic Pathways
- Respiratory Quotient

For deeper insight, **Scan the QR Code**

Important Instructions

- The test is of 30 minutes duration and contains 25 Multiple Choice Questions (four options with a single correct answer).
- Choose the correct option and fill the OMR given on the last page of this test accordingly.
- At some instances, you may find more than 1 option to be correct. In such circumstances, you have to judge the most appropriate answer as per the conditions given in the question.

1. Which of the following is not a fate of pyruvate?

(a) Reduced to form lactic acid in the deficiency of oxygen in the cytoplasm
(b) Oxidised to form acetyl Co-A
(c) Enters into the mitochondria
(d) Participates directly in the Krebs' cycle in the presence of oxygen

2. Within the mitochondrion, the proton gradient develops across the

(a) matrix
(b) inner membrane
(c) outer membrane
(d) intermembrane space

3. Which of the following statement is incorrect about Krebs' cycle?

(a) It requires a link reaction or gateway step.
(b) It is common step in both aerobic and anaerobic respiration.
(c) It is linked to electron transport chain.
(d) It generates 2 ATP molecules through substrate level phosphorylation.

4. Which process is responsible for converting NADH and $FADH_2$ back to NAD^+ and FAD?

(a) Electron transport chain
(b) Krebs' cycle
(c) Glycolysis
(d) Link reaction

5. Which of the following step does not occur in Krebs' cycle?

(a) Isocitrate $\rightarrow \alpha$-ketoglutarate
(b) Succinate $\rightarrow$ Fumarate
(c) Malate $\rightarrow$ Oxaloacetate
(d) 2-phosphoglycerate $\rightarrow$ Phosphoenolpyruvate

6. Given below are two statements regarding Krebs' cycle.

Statement I In link reaction, pyruvic acid, Co-A and NAD^+ are converted into acetyl Co-A + CO_2 and $NADH^+$ in the presence of enzyme succinate dehydrogenase.

Statement II In Krebs' cycle, total number of oxidative decarboxylation reactions are two.

In the light of the above statements, choose the correct answer from the options given below.

(a) Statement I is incorrect, but statement II is incorrect.
(b) Both statement I and statement II are correct.
(c) Both statement I and statement II are incorrect.
(d) Statement I is correct, but statement II is incorrect.

7. In given diagram, ...*A*... is condensed with acetyl Co-A to synthesise ...*B*... as a first product of the Krebs' cycle.

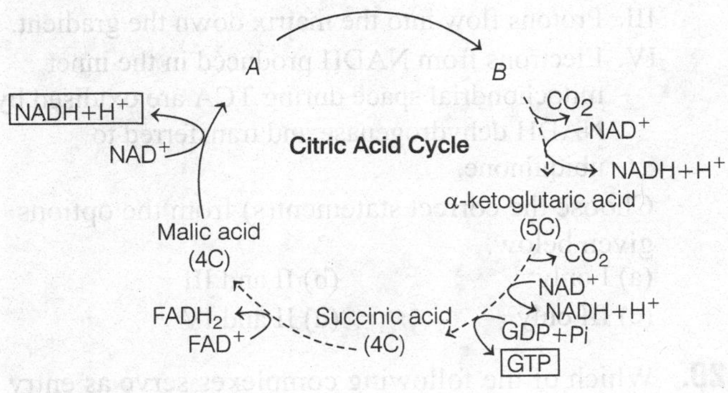

(a) *A* – Keto acid, *B* – Amino acid
(b) *A* – Dicarboxylic acid, *B* – Tricarboxylic acid
(c) *A* – Keto acid, *B* – Tricarboxylic acid
(d) *A* – Dicarboxylic acid, *B* – Keto acid

8. What is the ultimate electron acceptor of respiration in aerobic organisms?
(a) Pyruvate (b) Oxygen
(c) Hydrogen (d) Glucose

9. Given below are two statements; one is labelled as the Assertion (A) and the other is labelled as the Reason (R).
Assertion (A) Glycolysis is responsible for the production of 8 ATP in aerobic respiration.
Reason (R) Oxidation of one molecule of NADH gives rise to 3 molecules of ATP in ETC (Electron Transport Chain).
In the light of the above statements, choose the correct answer from the options given below.
(a) A is false, but R is true.
(b) Both A and R are true and R is the correct explanation of A.
(c) Both A and R are true, but R is not the correct explanation of A.
(d) A is true, but R is false.

10. How many ATPs are produced in electron transport chain?
(a) 20 (b) 34
(c) 30 (d) 28

11. RQ varies due to the presence of
(a) respiratory substrate only
(b) respiratory product and respiratory substrate
(c) temperature and respiratory product
(d) light, temperature and O_2

12. Match List I with List II.

	List I		List II
A.	Complex-I	1.	Succinate dehydrogenase
B.	Complex-II	2.	NADH dehydrogenase
C.	Complex-III	3.	Cytochrome-*c* oxidase
D.	Complex-IV	4.	Cytochrome-bc_1

Choose the correct codes from the options given below.

	A	B	C	D		A	B	C	D
(a)	3	2	4	1	(b)	2	1	4	3
(c)	2	1	3	4	(d)	4	2	1	3

13. Identify the correct statements.
I. If fatty acids were to be respired, they would first be degraded to acetyl CoA and enter the respiratory pathway.
II. Glycerol would enter the respiratory pathway after being converted to BPGA.
III. All carbohydrates enter the respiratory pathway directly.
IV. Respiratory pathway is better considered as an amphibolic pathway rather than as a catabolic one.
Choose the correct answer from the options given below.
(a) I, II, III and IV (b) I, III and IV
(c) II and IV (d) I and IV

14. Which statement best defines the Respiratory Quotient (RQ)?
(a) The ratio of oxygen consumed to carbon dioxide produced during respiration.
(b) The ratio of carbon dioxide produced to oxygen consumed during respiration.
(c) The ratio of ATP produced to glucose consumed during respiration.
(d) The ratio of glucose consumed to oxygen consumed during respiration.

15. Read the following statements.

I. Water formed during terminal oxidation is also called metabolic water.
II. Terminal oxidation occurs at the end of metabolic reaction of aerobic respiration.
III. Members of ETC take part only in the electron transport.
IV. The common quinone, ubiquinone are stable in cytoplasm matrix.
V. ATPase of elementary particles forms the complex.

Choose the correct answer from the options given below.

(a) I, II and III are correct
(b) II, III and V are correct
(c) I, II and IV are correct
(d) I, II and V are correct

16. How many molecules of CO_2 are released in the oxidative decarboxylation step of aerobic respiration, if three molecules of glucose is to be oxidised?

(a) 6 (b) 3 (c) 9 (d) 2

17. Following are the steps involved in aerobic respiration.

I. Substrate level phosphorylation
II. Transport of pyruvate into mitochondria
III. Condensation of acetyl CoA with OAA
IV. Hydration of fumarate
V. Isomerisation of citrate

Choose the correct order in which these steps occur from the options given below.

(a) II-III-V-I-IV (b) V-II-III-I-IV
(c) II-III-I-IV-V (d) V-III-I-II-IV

18. Given below are two statements.

Statement I 20 ATP molecules can be generated from one glucose in the TCA cycle alone.

Statement II One NADH molecule is oxidised to yield three ATP molecules in ETC.

In the light of the above statements, choose the correct answer from the options given below.

(a) Statement I is incorrect, but statement II is incorrect.
(b) Both statement I and statement II are correct.
(c) Both statement I and statement II are incorrect.
(d) Statement I is correct, but statement II is incorrect.

19. Consider the following statements.

I. $FADH_2$ is part of both glycolysis and TCA cycle.
II. F_0 has the catalytic site for ATP synthesis.
III. Protons flow into the matrix down the gradient.
IV. Electrons from NADH produced in the inner mitochondrial space during TCA are oxidised by NADH dehydrogenase and transferred to ubiquinone.

Choose the correct statement(s) from the options given below.

(a) I only (b) II and III
(c) III only (d) II and IV

20. Which of the following complexes serve as entry points of ETC?

I. NADH dehydrogenase
II. Complex-V
III. Complex-II
IV. Cytochrome-bc_1

Choose the correct answer from the options given below.

(a) I and IV (b) II and IV
(c) I and II (d) I and III

21. Given below are two statements; one is labelled as Assertion (A) and the other is labelled as Reason (R).

Assertion (A) Lysine and arginine can enter the respiratory pathway directly.

Reason (R) Molecules other than carbohydrates can act as respiratory substrates.

In the light of the above statements, choose the correct answer from the options given below.

(a) A is false, but R is true.
(b) Both A and R are true and R is the correct explanation of A
(c) Both A and R are true, but R is not the correct explanation of A
(d) A is true, but R is false

22. Consider the following steps of TCA cycle.

I. Decarboxylation of isocitrate
II. Hydration of fumarate
III. Conversion of succinate to fumarate
IV. Decarboxylation of α-ketoglutarate

Which of the following steps also finds application in ETC?

(a) III only (b) I and IV
(c) II, III and IV (d) I, III and IV

23. Which of the following best justifies why pure proteins and fats are not used as respiratory substrates?

(a) Due to their toxicity in cells.
(b) Due to their hydrophobicity
(c) Since their break down is time taking
(d) Instability of their structure.

24. A mutation in a particular gene makes defective non-functional proteases. If the carbohydrate falls short in a cell, which of the following respiratory substrates can be oxidised to derive energy?

I. Fats	II. Proteins
III. Glycerol	IV. Acetyl CoA

Choose the correct answer from the options given below.

(a) I and III	(b) I and II
(c) III and IV	(d) I, III and IV

25. Following is the diagrammatic representation of complex V of ETS. Which of the following statement is incorrect w.r.t the same?

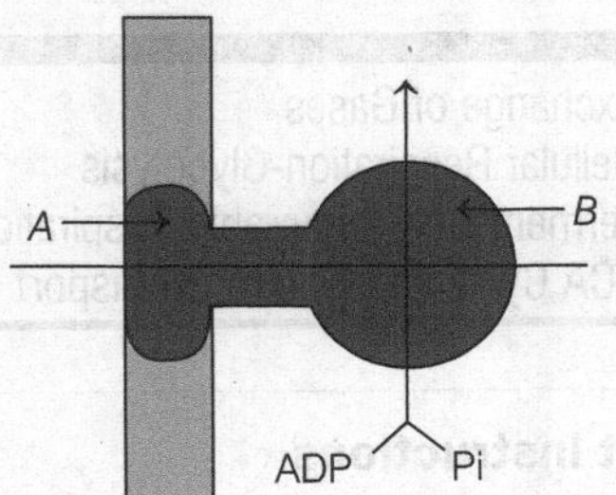

(a) *A* is the transmembrane protein part.
(b) *B* faces the matrix of mitochondria
(c) Protons are transported from inter-membrane space
(d) Protons flow through *A* against concentration gradient.

■ **Response Index**

01	a	b	c	d	10	a	b	c	d	19	a	b	c	d
02	a	b	c	d	11	a	b	c	d	20	a	b	c	d
03	a	b	c	d	12	a	b	c	d	21	a	b	c	d
04	a	b	c	d	13	a	b	c	d	22	a	b	c	d
05	a	b	c	d	14	a	b	c	d	23	a	b	c	d
06	a	b	c	d	15	a	b	c	d	24	a	b	c	d
07	a	b	c	d	16	a	b	c	d	25	a	b	c	d
08	a	b	c	d	17	a	b	c	d					
09	a	b	c	d	18	a	b	c	d					

■ **Performance Scanner**

> 90% Excellent !	You have mastered these topics. The concepts of these topics are at your fingertips. Move on to the next topics and maintain this momentum.
76-90% Very Good !	You have a good command over these topics. Revise these topics again after a few days and enhance your performance.
60-75% Good !	You have a wide scope to learn for these topics. Revise these topics again.
<60% Not Satisfactory!	You have a long way ahead of you to master these topics. Revise it thoroughly.

Chapter Break Thru

Syllabus

- Exchange of Gases
- Cellular Respiration-Glycolysis
- Fermentation (Anaerobic Respiration)
- TCA Cycle and Electron Transport System (Aerobic)
- Energy Relations–Number of ATP Molecules Generated
- Amphibolic Pathways
- Respiratory Quotient

Important Instructions

- The test is of 1 hour duration and contains 50 Multiple-Choice Questions (four options with a single correct answer).
- Choose the correct option and fill the OMR given on the last page of this test accordingly.
- At some instances, you may find more than 1 option to be correct. In such circumstances, you have to judge the most appropriate answer as per the conditions given in the question.

1. The first step of glycolysis is
(a) breakdown of glucose
(b) dehydration of glucose
(c) phosphorylation of glucose
(d) isomerisation of glucose

2. Which of the following statement is correct about anaerobic respiration?
(a) It occurs partly in cytoplasm and partly inside mitochondria.
(b) It occurs in majority of the organism.
(c) An electron transport chain or system is not required.
(d) Oxygen is the ultimate acceptor of electrons and protons.

3. Which of these processes occur in the cytosol?
I. Glycolysis
II. Citric acid cycle
III. Fermentation
IV. Electron transport system
Choose the correct answer.
(a) Only I (b) II and III
(c) I and III (d) Only IV

4. The common pathway in aerobic and anaerobic respiration is called
(a) Krebs' cycle
(b) tricarboxylic acid cycle
(c) EMP pathway
(d) Oxidative phosphorylation

5. Identify the incorrect statement considering glycolysis.
(a) Hexokinase transfers a phosphate group from ATP to glucose.
(b) Aldolase cleaves the fructose-1, 6-bisphosphate into two different 3-carbon sugars.
(c) The conversion between DHAP and G3P never reaches an equilibrium.
(d) During the conversion of 3-phosphoglycerate to 2-phosphoglycerate, 2 moles of ATP are released.

6. Pyruvic acid, the key product of glycolysis can have many metabolic fates. Under insufficient aerobic condition in muscles during rigorous exercise, it forms
(a) lactic acid (b) $CO_2 + H_2O$
(c) acetyl Co-A+ CO_2 (d) ethanol + CO_2

7. Which of the following intermediates undergoes splitting in glycolysis?
(a) Glucose-6-phosphate
(b) Glyceraldehyde-3-phosphate
(c) Fructose-1, 6-bisphosphate
(d) Dihydroxyacetone-3-phosphate

8. Select the correct match.

Respiratory substrates	**Respiratory quotients**
(a) Starch	- Less than one
(b) Protein	- More than one
(c) Palmitic acid	- One
(d) Tartaric acid	- More than one

9. Consider the following statements about Krebs' cycle.
I. It involves decarboxylation and oxidation of acetyl Co-A.
II. Pyruvate is directly converted to citrate in TCA cycle.
III. Energy stored in NADH + H^+ and $FADH_2$ are released in TCA cycle.
IV. Substrate level phsphorylation is observed at only two steps.
Choose the correct statement(s) from the options given below.
(a) I and II
(b) I only
(c) I, II and III
(d) I and II

10. The cytochromes are found in
(a) matrix of mitochondria
(b) cristae of mitochondria
(c) outer mitochondrial membrane
(d) entire inner mitochondrial membrane

11. Which of the following reaction does not take part in Krebs' cycle?
(a) Substrate level phosphorylation
(b) Acetylation
(c) Oxidative decarboxylation
(d) Oxidative phosphorylation

12. Malate is formed during which step in Krebs' cycle?
(a) Condensation (b) Isomerisation
(c) Hydration (d) Dehydrogenation

13. Identify *A*, *B* and *C*, respectively in given diagram.

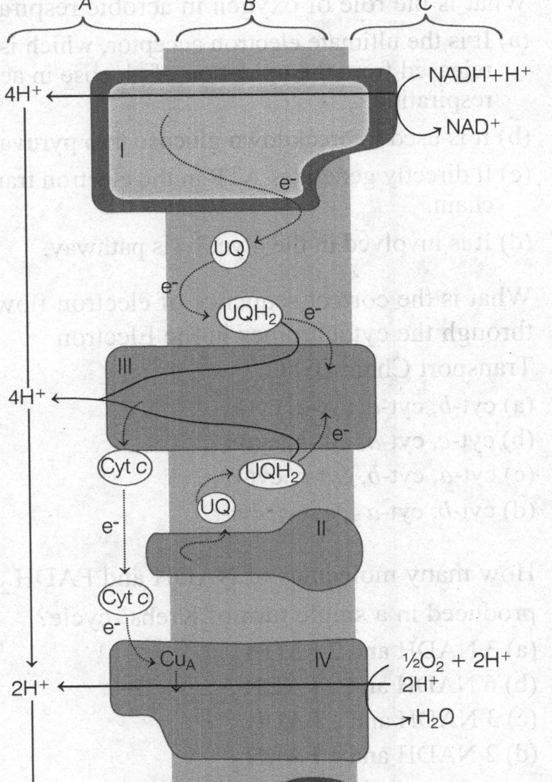

(a) Intermembrane space, inner mitochondrial membrane, matrix
(b) Matrix, inner mitochondrial membrane, intermembrane space
(c) Cytoplasm, inner mitochondrial membrane, matrix
(d) Cytoplasm, outer mitochondrial membrane, intermembrane space

14. Identify the enzyme that participates in both the TCA cycle and ETS.
(a) Pyruvate dehydrogenase
(b) NADH reductase
(c) Citrate synthase
(d) Succinate dehydrogenase

15. What is the role of oxygen in aerobic respiration?
(a) It is the ultimate electron acceptor, which is released from the oxidation of glucose in aerobic respiration.
(b) It is used to breakdown glucose into pyruvate.
(c) It directly generates ATP in the electron transport chain.
(d) It is involved in the glycolysis pathway.

16. What is the correct sequence of electron flow through the cytochromes in the Electron Transport Chain (ETC)?
(a) cyt-*b*, cyt-*c*, cyt-*a*, cyt-a_3
(b) cyt-*c*, cyt-*a*, cyt-*b*, cyt-a_3
(c) cyt-*a*, cyt-*b*, cyt-*c*, cyt-a_3
(d) cyt-*b*, cyt-a_3, cyt-*a*, cyt-*c*

17. How many molecules of NADH and $FADH_2$ are produced in a single turn of Krebs' cycle?
(a) 3 NADH and 2 $FADH_2$
(b) 6 NADH and 2 $FADH_2$
(c) 3 NADH and 1 $FADH_2$
(d) 2 NADH and 1 $FADH_2$

18. Which of the following monosaccharides readily enter the glycolytic pathway?
(a) Fructose and galactose
(b) Glucose and galactose
(c) Glucose and fructose
(d) Glucose, fructose and galactose

19. The biomolecule common to respiration-mediated breakdown of fats, carbohydrates and proteins is
(a) glucose-6-phosphate
(b) fructose1,6-bisphosphate
(c) pyruvic acid
(d) acetyl Co-A

20. Which of the following sequence is correct with respect to the RQ of various respiratory substrates?
(a) Fats > Proteins > Carbohydrates
(b) Carbohydrates > Proteins > Fats
(c) Carbohydrates > Fats > Proteins
(d) Proteins > Carbohydrates > Fats

21. Why do plants not have any transportation system to transport O_2 to the cells?
(a) Plants do not need oxygen for their cellular processes.
(b) Plants can transport oxygen through their vascular system.
(c) The distance that gases must diffuse even in large, bulky plants is not great.
(d) Oxygen is transported through the xylem in plants.

22. A pathway of cellular respiration having two phases occur in the cytosol of cells. The first phase is the investment phase and the second is the payoff phase. This pathway is known as
(a) glycolysis
(b) fermentation
(c) Krebs' cycle
(d) electron transport system

23. Given below are two statements; one is labelled as Assertion (A) and the other is labelled as Reason (R).

Assertion (A) When the electrons pass from one carrier to another *via* complex-I to IV in the ETS, they get coupled to complex-V for the production of ATP.

Reason (R) The number of ATP molecules synthesised depends on the nature of the electron donor.

In the light of the above statements, choose the correct answer from the options given below.
(a) A is false, but R is true.
(b) Both A and R are true and R is the correct explanation of A.

(c) Both A and R are true, but R is not the correct explanation of A.
(d) A is true, but R is false.

24. Given below are two statements.

Statement I In complex-II of electron transport chain, the electrons are picked up by ubiquinone to form ubiquinol.

Statement II Isocitrate is followed by two successive decarboxylation leading to the formation of succinyl Co-A and succinic acid.

In the light of the above statements, choose the correct answer from the options given below.
(a) Statement I is incorrect, but statement II is correct.
(b) Both statement I and statement II are correct.
(c) Both statement I and statement II are incorrect.
(d) Statement I is correct, but statement II is incorrect.

25. Which of the following statement is incorrect with respect to the electron transport system?
(a) Flavins are mobile electron carriers.
(b) Protons in the outer mitochondrial chamber creates a proton gradient across the inner mitochondrial membrane.
(c) Cytochrome–a_3 contains copper that helps to transfer electrons to oxygen.
(d) Oxygen acts as a terminal electron acceptor.

26. Select the incorrect match.

	Steps of respiration		Sites
A.	Glycolysis	–	Cytoplasm
B.	Oxidative decarboxylation of pyruvate	–	Cytoplasm
C.	TCA	–	Mitochondrial matrix
D.	ETC	–	Inner mitochondrial membrane

(a) A (b) B (c) C (d) D

27. Which of the following has the highest rate of respiration?
(a) Root tip (b) Germinating seed
(c) Growing shoot apex (d) Leaf bud

28. Match List I with List II.

	List I		List II
A.	Respirometer	1.	RQ is infinity
B.	Mixed diet	2.	RQ is about 0.85
C.	NADH	3.	Rate of respiration
D.	Fermentation	4.	Oxidative phosphorylation

Choose the correct answer from the options given below.

	A	B	C	D
(a)	1	2	4	3
(b)	3	1	2	4
(c)	3	2	4	1
(d)	4	3	2	1

29. Read the following statements.
I. The exchange of respiratory gases can be with liquid or gaseous environment.
II. Gaseous exchange occurs between cells and intercellular spaces in animals.
III. Trapping of energy in ATP makes any amount of energy available.
IV. Large amount of energy is produced in an anaerobic respiration.
V. Protein functions as respiratory substrates in protein rich seeds.

Choose the correct answer from the options given below.
(a) I, II and III are correct
(b) II, IV and V are correct
(c) I, III and V are correct
(d) II, III and IV are correct

30. Which of the following processes converts pyruvic acid (3C) to an acetyl group (2C)?
(a) Glycolysis
(b) Oxidation of pyruvic acid
(c) Krebs' citric acid cycle
(d) Electron transport

31. Following are certain altered conditions found in a hypothetical plant.
I. Compactly arranged parenchyma.
II. Absence of lenticels in woody stem.

Which of the following would be required under the above mentioned conditions in the hypothetical plant?
(a) Elaborate conducting system
(b) A committed respiratory organ
(c) Secretion of a waxy cuticle
(d) Stomatal opening in leaves.

32. Given below are two statements.
Statement I Facultative aerobes cannot survive in anoxic conditions.
Statement II The normal respiratory pathway for facultative aerobes require oxygen.
In the light of the above statements, choose the correct answer from the options given below.
(a) Statement I is incorrect, but statement II is correct
(b) Both statement I and statement II are correct
(c) Both statement I and statement II are incorrect
(d) Statement I is correct, but statement II is incorrect

33. How many of the following given molecules are isomers of one another?
I. DHAP and PGAL
II. Fructose and fructose-1, 6-bisphosphate
III. 3 PGA and 2PGA
IV. PEP and pyruvate
V. Glucose and galactose
Choose the correct answer from the options given below.
(a) 2 (b) 3
(c) 4 (d) 1

34. Which of the following steps of glycolysis can be regarded as the reverse of a phenomenon occurring during the conversion of fumarate to malate in TCA cycle?
(a) Conversion of PEP to pyruvate
(b) Splitting of Fructose-1, 6-bisphosphate
(c) Conversion of DHAP top PGAL
(d) Conversion of 2-PGA to PEP

35. How many molecules of ATP are involved in the energy yielding and energy expending steps of glycolysis, respectively per molecule of glucose?
(a) Two and four (b) Two and two
(c) Four and four (d) Four and two

36. In a cell, even if pyruvate is present in proper concentration, yet glycolysis precedes the anaerobic breakdown of pyruvate to lactate. Which of the following reasons explain the situation?
(a) Glycolysis generates ATP required by Lactate dehydrogenase.
(b) NADH generated by glycolysis is used to reduce pyruvate
(c) NADH produced in glycolysis accepts electrons from pyruvate.
(d) Glycolysis generates ATP needed to oxidise pyruvate.

37. How many molecules of glucose should be partially oxidised to release 8 molecules of ethanol?
(a) 8 (b) 2
(c) 4 (d) 6

38. Given below are two statements.
Statement I ATP hydrolysis powers GTP synthesis in TCA cycle.
Statement II Substrate level phosphorylation involves the direct formation of ATP or GTP by transferring a PO_4^{3-} group form a high energy compound to an ADP or GDP.
In the light of the above statements, choose the correct answer from the options given below.
(a) Statement I is incorrect, but statement II is correct.
(b) Both statement I and statement II are correct.
(c) Both statement I and statement II are incorrect.
(d) Statement I is correct, but statement II is incorrect.

39. How many turns of the citric acid cycle and how many molecules of glucose respectively, are required for generating 12 molecules of NADH?
(a) 4 and 2 (b) 12 and 4
(c) 4 and 8 (d) 2 and 4

40. Given below are two statements; one is labelled as Assertion (A) and the other is labelled as Reason (R).
Assertion (A) If succinate to fumarate conversion is halted, ETS is affected.
Reason (R) Succinate to fumarate conversion generates $NADH + H^+$.

In the light of the above statements, choose the correct answer from the options given below.
(a) A is false, but R is true
(b) Both A and R are true and R is the correct explanation of A
(c) Both A and R are true, but R is not the correct explanation of A
(d) A is true, but R is false

41. Consider the following statements.
I. FMNs are associated tightly with Complex I.
II. Fe-S clusters are associated with only complex II.
III. Ubiquinone is reduced by $FADH_2$ only.
IV. Cu ions act as cofactors for complex V.
Choose the correct statement(s) from the options given below.
(a) II and III (b) I only
(c) III and IV (d) I, II and IV

42. Which of the following conversions are catalysed by the transfer of electrons associated with complex II?
(a) Fe^{3+} to Fe^{2+} (b) Cu^{2+} to Cu^{+}
(c) Cu^{+} to Cu^{2+} (d) Fe^{2+} to Fe^{3+}

43. Given below are two statements; one is labelled as Assertion (A) and the other is labelled as Reason (R).
Assertion (A) Mitochondrial matrix has the lowest pH conditions.
Reason (R) Transport of electrons through ETS generates energy at each step.
In the light of the above statement, choose the correct answer from the options given below.
(a) A is false, but R is true
(b) Both A and R are true and R is the correct explanation of A
(c) Both A and R are true, but R is not the correct explanation of A
(d) A is true, but R is false

44. Given below are two statements.
Statement I Transport of protons from matrix to intermembrane space requires energy.
Statement II Flow of H^+ ions through F_0 channel of ATP synthase in ETS occurs passively.
In the light of the above statements, choose the correct answer from the options given below
(a) Statement I is incorrect, but statement II is correct.
(b) Both statement I and statement II are correct.
(c) Both statement I and statement II are incorrect.
(d) Statement I is correct, but statement II is incorrect.

45. How many molecules of ATP are generated by aerobic respiration in prokaryotes and eukaryotes, respectively?
(a) 36 and 38 (b) 36-38 and 38
(c) 36 and 36-38 (d) 38 and 36

46. Which of the following molecules is responsible for conversion of ubiquinol to ubiquinone?
(a) Complex II (b) Complex IV
(c) Complex III (d) Complex I

47. Given below are two statements; one is labelled as Assertion (A) and the other is labelled as Reason (R).
Assertion (A) NADH oxidation is rather slow in fermentation.
Reason (R) Electron acceptor of ETS is lacking in fermentation.
In the light of the above statements, choose the correct answer from the options given below.
(a) A is false, but R is true.
(b) Both A and R are true and R is the correct explanation of A
(c) Both A and R are true, but R is not the correct explanation of A
(d) A is true, but R is false

48. Following are the steps involved in oxidising proteins as a respiratory substrate.

I. Breakdown by proteases
II. Conversion into pyruvate
III. Deamination
IV. Condensation with OAA
V. Decarboxylation of pyruvate

Choose the correct order from the options given below.

(a) I-III-II-V-IV (b) I-II-III-V-IV
(c) I-III-V-II-IV (d) I-II-IV-V-III

49. Which of the following would have RQ more than 1?

I. Sucrose used as substrate
II. Palmitic acid is used as substrate
III. Arginine is catabolised
IV. Reduction of pyruvate to lactate

Choose the correct answer from the options given below.

(a) I and III (b) II only
(c) IV only (d) I, II and III

50. Given below are two statements.

Statement I Only NADH takes part in oxidative phosphorylation of ETS.

Statement II Catalytic site of ATP synthase faces the inner mitochondrial membrane.

In the light of the above statements, choose the correct answer from the options given below

(a) Statement I is incorrect, but statement II is correct.
(b) Both statement I and statement II are correct.
(c) Both statement I and statement II are incorrect.
(d) Statement I is correct, but statement II is incorrect.

■ **Response Index**

01	ⓐ ⓑ ⓒ ⓓ	14	ⓐ ⓑ ⓒ ⓓ	27	ⓐ ⓑ ⓒ ⓓ	40	ⓐ ⓑ ⓒ ⓓ
02	ⓐ ⓑ ⓒ ⓓ	15	ⓐ ⓑ ⓒ ⓓ	28	ⓐ ⓑ ⓒ ⓓ	41	ⓐ ⓑ ⓒ ⓓ
03	ⓐ ⓑ ⓒ ⓓ	16	ⓐ ⓑ ⓒ ⓓ	29	ⓐ ⓑ ⓒ ⓓ	42	ⓐ ⓑ ⓒ ⓓ
04	ⓐ ⓑ ⓒ ⓓ	17	ⓐ ⓑ ⓒ ⓓ	30	ⓐ ⓑ ⓒ ⓓ	43	ⓐ ⓑ ⓒ ⓓ
05	ⓐ ⓑ ⓒ ⓓ	18	ⓐ ⓑ ⓒ ⓓ	31	ⓐ ⓑ ⓒ ⓓ	44	ⓐ ⓑ ⓒ ⓓ
06	ⓐ ⓑ ⓒ ⓓ	19	ⓐ ⓑ ⓒ ⓓ	32	ⓐ ⓑ ⓒ ⓓ	45	ⓐ ⓑ ⓒ ⓓ
07	ⓐ ⓑ ⓒ ⓓ	20	ⓐ ⓑ ⓒ ⓓ	33	ⓐ ⓑ ⓒ ⓓ	46	ⓐ ⓑ ⓒ ⓓ
08	ⓐ ⓑ ⓒ ⓓ	21	ⓐ ⓑ ⓒ ⓓ	34	ⓐ ⓑ ⓒ ⓓ	47	ⓐ ⓑ ⓒ ⓓ
09	ⓐ ⓑ ⓒ ⓓ	22	ⓐ ⓑ ⓒ ⓓ	35	ⓐ ⓑ ⓒ ⓓ	48	ⓐ ⓑ ⓒ ⓓ
10	ⓐ ⓑ ⓒ ⓓ	23	ⓐ ⓑ ⓒ ⓓ	36	ⓐ ⓑ ⓒ ⓓ	49	ⓐ ⓑ ⓒ ⓓ
11	ⓐ ⓑ ⓒ ⓓ	24	ⓐ ⓑ ⓒ ⓓ	37	ⓐ ⓑ ⓒ ⓓ	50	ⓐ ⓑ ⓒ ⓓ
12	ⓐ ⓑ ⓒ ⓓ	25	ⓐ ⓑ ⓒ ⓓ	38	ⓐ ⓑ ⓒ ⓓ		
13	ⓐ ⓑ ⓒ ⓓ	26	ⓐ ⓑ ⓒ ⓓ	39	ⓐ ⓑ ⓒ ⓓ		

■ **Performance Scanner**

Scan for online chapter test

> 90% Excellent !	You have mastered this chapter. The concepts of this chapter are at your fingertips. Move on to the next chapter and maintain this momentum.
76-90% Very Good !	You have a good command over this chapter. Revise the chapter again after a few days and enhance your performance.
60-75% Good !	You have a wide scope to learn for this chapter. Revise this chapter again.
<60% Not Satisfactory!	You have a long way ahead of you to master this chapter. Revise it thoroughly.

MED ACE
NEET (UG)
SELF ASSESSMENT KIT

Test Booklet No. 3947313

Test Booklet Code CH13

Plant Growth and Development

Topics Covered

Growth and Development

Plant Growth Regulators

Important Instructions

- This Booklet Contains – Two Topic Tests and One Test on Complete Chapter.
- Each question carries 4 marks.
- For each correct response, the candidate will get 4 marks. And for every incorrect response, 1 mark will be additionally deducted from total score.
- Use **Blue/Black** point pen only for filling the OMR.
- Rough work is to be done in the space provided for this purpose in the test booklet only.

Name of the Candidate (In Capitals) ____________

Candidate's Signature ____________

Invigilator's Signature ____________

Facsimile signature stamp of center superintendent____________

Do not open this booklet until you start attempting the test

Topical Follow Thru

Test 1

Syllabus

- Seed Germination
- Phases of Plant Growth and Plant Growth Rate
- Conditions of Growth
- Differentiation, Dedifferentiation and Redifferentiation
- Sequence of Developmental Process in a Plant Cell

For deeper insight, **Scan the QR Code**

Important Instructions

- The test is of 30 minutes duration and contains 25 Multiple Choice Questions (four options with a single correct answer).
- Choose the correct option and fill the OMR given on the last page of this test accordingly.
- At some instances, you may find more than 1 option to be correct. In such circumstances, you have to judge the most appropriate answer as per the conditions given in the question.

1. Identify the group of plants that does not show plasticity.

(a) Cotton, coriander and larkspur
(b) Buttercup, cotton and coriander
(c) Buttercup, coriander and maize
(d) Cotton, larkspur and buttercup

2. Match List I with List II.

List I	List II
A. Arithmetic growth	1. Secondary phloem
B. Geometric growth	2. Root elongation
C. Dedifferentiation	3. Interfascicular cambium
D. Redifferentiation	4. Early embroyonic development

Choose the correct answer from the options given below.

	A	B	C	D		A	B	C	D
(a)	4	2	3	1	(b)	1	4	2	3
(c)	2	1	4	3	(d)	2	4	3	1

3. Read the following statements.

I. Auxanometer is used to measure increase in growth of plants.
II. Increased vacuolation, cell enlargement and new cell wall deposition are characteristics of the phase of elongation.
III. A sigmoid curve is typical for all cells.
IV. Phase of maturation is exhibited near the apex.
V. Plant growth is independent of temperature range.

Choose the incorrect statements from the options given below.

(a) I, II and III
(b) II and V
(c) IV and V
(d) III and IV

4. Which of the following statement is incorrect?

(a) Relative growth rate is expressed as growth per unit time per unit initial parameter.
(b) Absolute growth rate decreases with time.
(c) Arithmetic growth occurs when one of the daughter cells continues to divide.
(d) Geometric growth is gradual expansion in the early phase.

5. Given below are two statements about elongation phase.

Statement I Rate of respiration in cell is higher in elongation phase than that of cells in the formative phase.

Statement II In isodiametric cells, elongation may occur in all directions.

In the light of the above statements, choose the correct answer from the options given below.

(a) Statement I is incorrect, but statement II is correct.
(b) Both statement I and statement II are correct.
(c) Both statement I and statement II are incorrect.
(d) Statement I is correct, but statement II is incorrect.

6. Match List I with List II.

	List I		List II
A.	Meristematic phase	1.	Thickened wall
B.	Differentiation	2.	Intercellular spaces are absent
C.	Maturation phase	3.	Heterophylly
D.	Plasticity	4.	Tracheary elements

Choose the correct answer from the options given below.

	A	B	C	D
(a)	3	4	1	2
(b)	2	1	3	4
(c)	2	4	1	3
(d)	4	1	2	3

7. Given below are two statements.

Statement I Arithmetic growth occurs in microorganisms when they are provided with enough space and nutrition.

Statement II Geometric growth is rapid in the beginning and then declines slowly.

In the light of the above statements, choose the correct answer from the options given below.

(a) Statement I is incorrect, but statement II is correct.

(b) Both statement I and statement II are correct.

(c) Both statement I and statement II are incorrect.

(d) Statement I is correct, but statement II is incorrect.

8. Increased vacuolation and enlarged cells are present

(a) in root apex

(b) in shoot apex

(c) proximal to meristematic zone

(d) proximal to phase of elongation

9. The correct sequence of the developmental process in a plant cell is

(a) elongation, maturation, cell division, differentiation

(b) cell division, elongation, differentiation, maturation

(c) cell division, differentiation, maturation, elongation

(d) differentiation, cell division, maturation, elongation

10. Given below are two statements.

Statement I Growth is an irreversible permanent increase in size of an organ.

Statement II Growth is accompanied by metabolic processes that do not require energy.

In the light of the above statements, choose the correct answer from the options given below.

(a) Statement I is incorrect, but statement II is correct.

(b) Both statement I and statement II are correct.

(c) Both statement I and statement II are incorrect.

(d) Statement I is correct, but statement II is incorrect.

11. Among the following, which one is not the characteristic feature of continuously dividing cells present at the root apex?

(a) Dense cytoplasm

(b) Large conspicuous nucleus

(c) Secondary cell wall

(d) Abundant plasmodesmatal connections

12. Refer to the given figure related to plant growth and choose the incorrect statement about it.

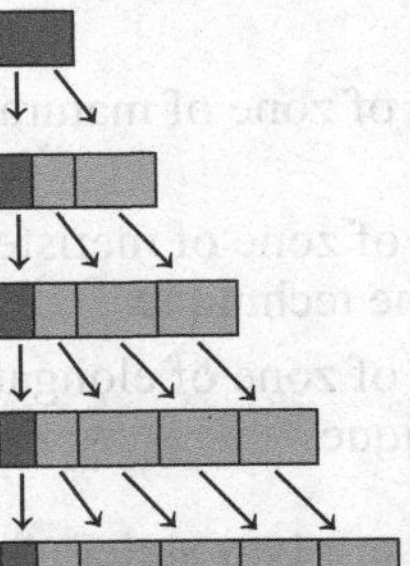

(a) Most daughter cells continue to divide while some get differentiated and mature.

(b) On plotting the length of the organ against time, a linear curve is obtained.

(c) Mathematically, it is expressed as $L_t = L_0 + rt$.

(d) Root elongation shows this type of growth.

13. Given below are two statements; one is labelled as Assertion (A) and other is labelled as Reason (R).

Assertion (A) A sigmoid curve is a characteristic of living organism growing in a natural environment.

Reason (R) A sigmoid curve is typical for all cells, tissues and organs of a plant.

In the light of the above statements, choose the correct answer from the options given below.
(a) A is false, but R is true.
(b) Both A and R are true and R is the correct explanation of A.
(c) Both A and R are true, but R is not the correct explanation of A.
(d) A is true, but R is false.

14. Observe the given figure carefully. What does it show?

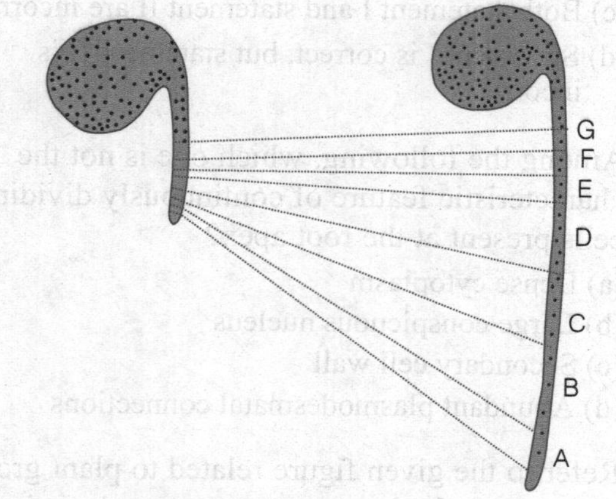

(a) Growth of the pollen tube in terms of surface area
(b) Detection of zone of maturation by parallel line technique
(c) Detection of zone of meristematic activity by the parallel line technique
(d) Detection of zone of elongation by the parallel line technique

15. Given below are two statements.
Statement I Development is considered as the sum of growth and differentiation.
Statement II Development in plants is solely under the control of intrinsic factors.
In the light of the above statements, choose the correct answer from the options given below.
(a) Statement I is incorrect, but statement II is correct.
(b) Both statement I and statement II are correct.
(c) Both statement I and statement II are incorrect.
(d) Statement I is correct, but statement II is incorrect.

16. A primary root grows from 6 cm to 20 cm in a week. Calculate the relative growth rate of the root over the period.
(a) 380%
(b) 233.33%
(c) 230%
(d) 130%

17. Given below are two statements.
Statement I The growth period is typically categorised in three phases, i.e., meristematic, elongation and maturation.
Statement II Growth is maximum in the phase of maturation.
In the light of the above statements, choose the correct answer from the options given below.
(a) Statement I is incorrect, but statement II is correct.
(b) Both statement I and statement II are correct.
(c) Both statement I and statement II are incorrect.
(d) Statement I is correct, but statement II is incorrect.

18. Given below is a figure representing a specific type of growth pattern.

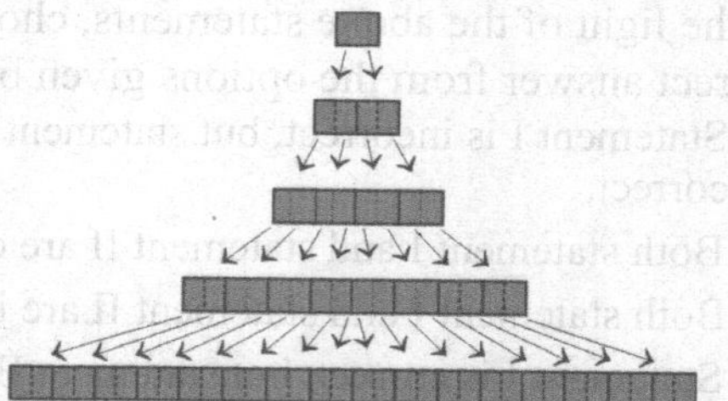

From the given mentioned statements, identify the incorrect statement.
(a) This type of growth is seen during the initial development of embryo from zygote.
(b) Such growth is rarely observed in natural environment.
(c) If we plot the parameter of this type of growth pattern, we get a typical S-curve.
(d) It cannot be exemplified by root elongation at a constant rate.

19. A leaf 'A' of $10\,cm^2$ grows $5\,cm^2$ in an hour, another leaf 'B' of $25\,cm^2$ grows $5\,cm^2$ in the same time.

The relative growth rates of leaf A and B, respectively, are
(a) 15% and 120% (b) 50% and 25%
(c) 50% and 20% (d) 15% and 20%

20. Consider the following statements.
I. When a cell loses the capacity to divide, it leads to differentiation.
II. Absolute growth rate remains constant throughout the life cycle of cell/tissue/ organ/organism.
III. Differentiation results in development of structures that is commensurate with the function the cells finally has to perform.
IV. The development in plant is rigid owing to its differentiation pattern.
Choose the incorrect statement(s) from the options given below.
(a) I, II and III (b) III only
(c) IV only (d) II, III and IV

21. In expression, $W_1 = W_0 e^{rt}$ of a special type of growth rate, W_1, r and e represent
(a) Initial size, growth rate, base of natural logarithms
(b) Initial size, time of growth, base of natural logarithms
(c) Final size, time of growth, natural increase
(d) Final size, growth rate, base of natural logarithms

22. What kind of a curve can you expect in a tree showing seasonal activities?
(a) Linear curve (b) Arithmetic curve
(c) Parabola curve (d) Sigmoid curve

23. Given below are few statements.
I. Stages during embryo development show early geometric growth phase and later arithmetic growth phase.
II. Growth in pollen tube is measured in terms of its surface area.
III. Turgidity of cells helps in extension growth.
IV. The cells of plant meristems possess the capacity to divide and self-perpetuate.
Choose the correct set of statements from the options given below.
(a) I, II and IV (b) I, III and IV
(c) II, III and IV (d) I and II

24. Match List I with List II.

	List I		List II
A.	Apical meristem	1.	Present at terminal position
B.	Intercalary meristem	2.	Secondary growth
C.	Lateral meristem	3.	Localised growth

Choose the correct answer from the options given below.

	A	B	C		A	B	C
(a)	1	2	3	(b)	3	1	2
(c)	3	2	1	(d)	1	3	2

25. Tumors and interfascicular cambium respectively are result of
(a) redifferentiation and dedifferentiation
(b) dedifferentiation and dedifferentiation
(c) differentiation and redifferentiation
(d) Senescence and plasmatic growth

Response Index

01 (a) (b) (c) (d) 10 (a) (b) (c) (d) 19 (a) (b) (c) (d)
02 (a) (b) (c) (d) 11 (a) (b) (c) (d) 20 (a) (b) (c) (d)
03 (a) (b) (c) (d) 12 (a) (b) (c) (d) 21 (a) (b) (c) (d)
04 (a) (b) (c) (d) 13 (a) (b) (c) (d) 22 (a) (b) (c) (d)
05 (a) (b) (c) (d) 14 (a) (b) (c) (d) 23 (a) (b) (c) (d)
06 (a) (b) (c) (d) 15 (a) (b) (c) (d) 24 (a) (b) (c) (d)
07 (a) (b) (c) (d) 16 (a) (b) (c) (d) 25 (a) (b) (c) (d)
08 (a) (b) (c) (d) 17 (a) (b) (c) (d)
09 (a) (b) (c) (d) 18 (a) (b) (c) (d)

Performance Scanner

> 90% Excellent !	You have mastered these topics. The concepts of these topics are at your fingertips. Move on to the next test and maintain this momentum.
76-90% Very Good !	You have a good command over these topics. Revise these topics again after a few days and enhance your performance.
60-75% Good !	You have a wide scope to learn for these topics. Revise these topics again.
<60% Not Satisfactory!	You have a long way ahead of you to master these topics. Revise it thoroughly.

Test 2

Syllabus Plant Growth Regulators (Auxins, Gibberellins, Cytokinins, Ethylene, Abscisic Acid)

For deeper insight, **Scan the QR Code**

Important Instructions

- The test is of 30 minutes duration and contains 25 Multiple Choice Questions (four options with a single correct answer).
- Choose the correct option and fill the OMR given on the last page of this test accordingly.
- At some instances, you may find more than 1 option to be correct. In such circumstances, you have to judge the most appropriate answer as per conditions given in the question.

1. The triple response shown by ethylene does not include

(a) swelling of nodes
(b) elongation of internodes of stem
(c) induction of horizontal growth of stem
(d) lateral growth of internodes of stem

2. Which of the following statement is incorrect about ethylene?

(a) It is produced in plants from amino acid methionine.
(b) Ethephon is used in its solid form.
(c) Maximum synthesis of ethylene occurs during ripening of fruits.
(d) Ethylene gas is released from it.

3. Given below are two statements; one is labelled as Assertion (A) and the other is labelled as Reason (R).

Assertion (A) Gibberellic acid can be used on fruits to make them last till the market period.
Reason (R) GA_1 and GA_2 are basic, while GA_3 is acidic in nature.

In the light of the above statements, choose the correct answer from the options given below.

(a) A is false, but R is true.
(b) Both A and R are true and R is the correct explanation of A.
(c) Both A and R are true, but R is not the correct explanation of A.
(d) A is true, but R is false.

4. Read the following statements carefully and choose the correct set of statements.

I. Cytokinins suppress the synthesis of chlorophyll.
II. Auxins control apical dominance.
III. Gibberellins promote shoot elongation.
IV. In response to water deficiency, plants release ABA to reduce transpirational loss of water.

(a) II and III
(b) II and IV
(c) I and III
(d) II, III and IV

5. Given below are two statements; one is labelled as Assertion (A) and the other is labelled as Reason (R).

Assertion (A) ABA is called the stress hormone.
Reason (R) ABA helps seeds to withstand desiccation and other factors unfavourable for growth.

In the light of the above statements, choose the correct answer from the options given below.

(a) A is false, but R is true.
(b) Both A and R are true and R is the correct explanation of A.
(c) Both A and R are true, but R is not the correct explanation of A.
(d) A is true, but R is false.

6. Given below are two statements regarding abscisic acid.

Statement I Under water stress conditions, ABA only inhibits the shoot growth.
Statement II In autumn and winter season, stoppage of cambial activity occurs due to ABA.

In the light of the above statements, choose the correct answer from the options given below.
(a) Statement I is incorrect, but statement II is correct.
(b) Both statement I and statement II are correct.
(c) Both statement I and statement II are incorrect.
(d) Statement I is correct, but statement II is incorrect.

7. Given below are two statements; one is labelled as Assertion (A) and the other is labelled as Reason (R).

Assertion (A) Spraying of ethephon on cucurbits results in increase in number of fruits.

Reason (R) Ethephon increases the number of male flowers and decreases the number of female flowers.

In the light of the above statements, choose the correct answer from the options given below.
(a) A is false, but R is true.
(b) Both A and R are true, and R is the correct explanation of A.
(c) Both A and R are true, but R is not the correct explanation of A.
(d) A is true, but R is false.

8. Match List I with List II.

	List I		List II
A.	Natural auxin	1.	Respiratory climactic
B.	Ethylene	2.	Malting process
C.	IBA	3.	Polar transport
D.	GA_3	4.	Horticulture

Choose the correct answer from the options given below.

	A	B	C	D
(a)	3	1	2	4
(b)	3	1	4	2
(c)	2	1	4	3
(d)	4	3	1	2

9. Read the two statements regarding ethylene.

Statement I Maximum ethylene is formed in ripening fruits and ageing tissues.

Statement II It inhibits root growth and root hair formation.

In the light of the above statements, choose the correct answer from the options given below.
(a) Statement I is incorrect, but statement II is correct.
(b) Both statement I and statement II are correct.
(c) Both statement I and statement II are incorrect.
(d) Statement I is correct, but statement II is incorrect.

10. Read the following statements about cytokinins.

Statement I They are synthesised in regions where cell elongation occurs.

Statement II They help to overcome apical dominance.

In the light of the above statements, choose the correct answer from the options given below.
(a) Statement I is incorrect, but statement II is correct.
(b) Both statement I and statement II are correct.
(c) Both statement I and statement II are incorrect.
(d) Statement I is correct, but statement II is incorrect.

11. Among these functions, which of the following is antagonistic to the function of ABA?
(a) Delay in cell division and cell elongation
(b) Inhibition of seed germination
(c) Enhancing senescence
(d) Promotion of flowering in long day plants

12. Select the incorrect match.
(a) Ethylene - Quickly ripens a fruit
(b) Cytokinin - Delays leaf senescence
(c) Gibberellin - Bolting of rosette plants
(d) Abscisic acid - Induces growth of axillary buds

13. Which of the following is incorrect about cytokinin?
(a) Kinetin is a synthetic form of cytokinin.
(b) Zeatin is natural cytokinin obtained from maize kernels.
(c) Kinetin is derivative of violaxanthin.
(d) It delays senescence.

14. Which of the following statement is incorrect about gibberellin?
(a) It influences the shape of certain fruits.
(b) It helps in breaking dormancy.

(c) It has no effect on the flowering of long day plants.
(d) It shows channel transport in different directions.

15. Given below are two statements; one is labelled as Assertion (A) and the other is labelled as Reason (R).
Assertion (A) The bud dormancy is regulated by a balance between gibberellins and ABA.
Reason (R) ABA inhibits seed dormancy and GA promotes seed germination.
In the light of the above statements, choose the correct answer from the options given below.
(a) A is false, but R is true.
(b) Both A and R are true and R is the correct explanation of A.
(c) Both A and R are true, but R is not the correct explanation of A.
(d) A is true, but R is false.

16. Choose the incorrect match pair from the following options.
(a) Richmond Lang effect-cytokinin
(b) Apical dominance–antagonistic action of auxin and cytokinin
(c) Sprouting of potato tubers-ethylene
(d) Apical hook formation in dicot seedlings-GA_3

17. Identify the incorrect statements.
I. TIBA is an important anti -auxin.
II. All the parts of plant show unlimited growth.
III. Synergistic action of hormones complements functioning of each other. So, there will be an enhanced effect of both the hormones.
IV. To increase sugar production in sugarcanes, they are sprayed with ethylene.
Choose the correct answer from the options given below.
(a) I, II and III (b) II and IV
(c) II and III (d) III and IV

18. What will be the most possible outcome if a person forgets to add cytokinins to the culture medium?
(a) There will be no differentiation of root and shoot.
(b) There will be no differentiation of shoot.
(c) There will be no callus formation.
(d) There will be no differentiation of root.

19. What would be expected if a rotten fruit gets mixed with unripe fruits?
(a) ABA released by rotten fruits will cause ripening of unripe fruits.
(b) Ethylene produced by rotten fruit will show climacteric phenomena and causes ripening of unripe fruits.
(c) ABA produced by rotten fruit will damage the unripe fruit completely.
(d) Ethylene produced by unripe fruit will repair the rotten fruit.

20. Given below are few statements.
I. Zeatin induces rooting in a twig.
II. Ethylene helps leaves to remain above water.
III. Flowering and fruit formation in walnut is accelerated by ethylene.
IV. Roles of hormones can be complementary or antagonistic.
V. IAA promotes the abscission of older mature leaves and fruits.
Choose the correct statements from the options given below.
(a) II, IV and V (b) I, II, IV and V
(c) I, III and IV (d) II and V

21. Match List I with List II.

	List I		List II
A.	Auxin	1.	Rice seedling
B.	Ethylene	2.	Inhibitors
C.	Gibberellins	3.	Ripened Oranges
D.	ABA	4.	Canary grass
E.	Cytokinins	5.	Yeast extract

Choose the correct answer from the options given below.

	A	B	C	D	E
(a)	5	4	1	2	3
(b)	4	3	1	2	5
(c)	1	2	3	4	5
(d)	5	3	2	1	4

22. Given below are two statements; one is labelled as Assertion (A) and the other is labelled as Reason (R).
Assertion (A) Correct concentration of auxin and cytokinin is required for organogenesis in a callus.

Reason (R) When the ratio of kinetin to auxin is greater, the shoot develops. When this ratio is low, roots develop.

In the light of the above statements, choose the correct answer from the options given below.

(a) A is false, but R is true.
(b) Both A and R are true and R is the correct explanation of A.
(c) Both A and R are true, but R is not the correct explanation of A.
(d) A is true, but R is false.

23. Given below are two statements.

Statement I Ethylene causes climacteric ripening of fruits.

Statement II Auxin can be bioassayed by α – amylase assay.

In the light of the above statements, choose the correct answer from the options given below.

(a) Statement I is incorrect, but statement II is correct.
(b) Both statement I and statement II are correct.
(c) Both statement I and statement II are incorrect.
(d) Statement I is correct, but statement II is incorrect.

24. Identify the PGA that are acidic in nature.

I. Auxin
II. Cytokinin
III. GA
IV. ABA

Choose the correct option.

(a) I and II (b) I, III and IV
(c) I, II and III (d) I, II, III and IV

25. It is often seen that fruits like apples are wrapped in a waxed paper. It is done so as to

(a) mark the fruit for tested quality.
(b) prevent ethylene production that in turns hastens the ripening process.
(c) prevent sunlight from changing its colour by degradation of pigments.
(d) prevent aerobic respiration by checking the oxygen entry.

Response Index

01	a	b	c	d	10	a	b	c	d	19	a	b	c	d
02	a	b	c	d	11	a	b	c	d	20	a	b	c	d
03	a	b	c	d	12	a	b	c	d	21	a	b	c	d
04	a	b	c	d	13	a	b	c	d	22	a	b	c	d
05	a	b	c	d	14	a	b	c	d	23	a	b	c	d
06	a	b	c	d	15	a	b	c	d	24	a	b	c	d
07	a	b	c	d	16	a	b	c	d	25	a	b	c	d
08	a	b	c	d	17	a	b	c	d					
09	a	b	c	d	18	a	b	c	d					

Performance Scanner

> 90% Excellent !	You have mastered these topics. The concepts of these topics are at your fingertips. Move on to the next test and maintain this momentum.
76-90% Very Good !	You have a good command over these topics. Revise these topics again after a few days and enhance your performance.
60-75% Good !	You have a wide scope to learn for these topics. Revise these topics again.
<60% Not Satisfactory!	You have a long way ahead of you to master these topics. Revise it thoroughly.

Chapter Break Thru

Syllabus

- Seed Germination
- Phases of Plant Growth and Plant Growth Rate, Conditions of Growth
- Differentiation, Dedifferentiation and Redifferentation
- Sequence of Developmental Process in a Plant Cell
- Plant Growth Regulators (Auxins, Cytokinins, Gibberellins,Ethylene and Abscisic Acid)

Important Instructions

- The test is of 1 hour duration and contains 30 Multiple-Choice Questions (Four options with a single correct answer).
- Choose the correct option and fill the OMR given on the last page of this test accordingly.
- At some instances, you may find more than 1 option to be correct. In such circumstances, you have to judge the most appropriate answer as per the conditions given in the question.

1. It takes very long time for pineapple plants to produce flowers. Which combination of hormones can be applied to artificially induce flowering in pineapple plants throughout the year to increase its yield?

(a) Gibberellin and abscisic acid
(b) Cytokinin and abscisic acid
(c) Auxin and ethylene
(d) Gibberellin and cytokinin

2. Choose the incorrect statement about open form of growth.

(a) In this growth, new cells are added to the plant body.
(b) Cells are added by the activity of meristematic cells.
(c) Meristematic cells are present at the apex of the root and shoot.
(d) The meristematic cells have a secondary or tertiary cell wall.

3. Match List I with List II.

	List I		List II
A.	Charles Darwin and Francis Darwin	1.	*Gibberella fujikuroi*
B.	E Kurosawa	2.	Cytokinin
C.	Miller *et. al.*	3.	Ethylene
D.	Cousins	4.	Auxin

Choose the correct answer from the options given below.

	A	B	C	D
(a)	3	2	4	1
(b)	4	1	2	3
(c)	3	4	1	2
(d)	2	1	4	3

4. Read the following statements.

Statement I Plants show determinate type of growth.

Statement II The ability of the plants to show unique growth pattern is due to the presence of meristems.

In the light of the above statements, choose the correct answer from the options given below.

(a) Statement I is incorrect, but statement II is correct.
(b) Both statement I and statement II are correct.
(c) Both statement I and statement II are incorrect.
(d) Statement I is correct, but statement II is incorrect.

5. Given below are two statements; one is labelled as Assertion (A) and the other is labelled as Reason (R).

Assertion (A) The lateral meristems, vascular cambium and cork-cambium that appear in plants are present from the beginning.

Reason (R) These are the meristems that cause the increase in the girth of the organs in which they are active.

In the light of the above statements, choose the correct answer from the options given below.

(a) A is false, but R is true.

(b) Both A and R are true and R is the correct explanation of A.

(c) Both A and R are true, but R is not the correct explanation of A.

(d) A is true, but R is false.

6. Read the following statements.

Statement I Natural cytokinins are synthesised in regions where rapid cell division occurs.

Statement II Natural cytokinin helps to produce new leaves and chloroplasts in leaves, etc.

In the light of the above statements, choose the correct answer from the options given below.

(a) Statement I is incorrect, but statement II is correct

(b) Both statement I and statement II are correct

(c) Both statement I and statement II are incorrect

(d) Statement I is correct, but statement II is incorrect

7. Given below are two statements; one is labelled as Assertion (A) and the other is labelled as Reason (R).

Assertion (A) In waterlogged conditions, plants show a fast and active growth rate.

Reason (R) Waterlogging inhibits roots growth and root activity.

In the light of the above statements, choose the correct answer from the options given below.

(a) A is false, but R is true.

(b) Both A and R are true and R is the correct explanation of A.

(c) Both A and R are true, but R is not the correct explanation of A.

(d) A is true, but R is false.

8. Exponential growth phase cannot be sustained for a long time due to

I. accumulation of nutrient agent.

II. limited space and nutrient.

III. unlimited space and nutrient.

Choose the correct option.

(a) I and III (b) Only II

(c) Only I (d) II and III

9. Read the following statements.

Statement I Growth is measured by a variety of parameters, some of which are-increase in fresh weight, dry weight, length, area, volume and cell number.

Statement II One single maize root apical meristem can give rise to more than 17,500 new cells per hour.

In the light of the above statements, choose the correct answer from the options given below.

(a) Statement I is incorrect, but statement II is correct.

(b) Both statement I and statement II are correct.

(c) Both statement I and statement II are incorrect.

(d) Statement I is correct, but statement II is incorrect.

10. Given below are few statements.

I. The chemical 'Dormin' was found chemically identical to abscisin II.

II. The log phase is represented by slower growth.

III. Exponential growth phase in arithmetic growth model is regarded as the 'grand phase of growth'.

IV. PGRs-Ethylene and ABA are exclusively considered as the plant growth inhibitors.

Choose the incorrect set of statements from the options given below.

(a) I and IV

(b) II and IV

(c) II, III and IV

(d) I, II and III

11. The phototropic curvature in the coleoptiles of canary grass in response to the unilateral illumination of light can possibly be the result of uneven distribution of

(a) Phytochrome (b) Kinetin

(c) IAA (d) Zeatin

12. Match List I with List II.

	List I		List II
A.	Meristematic zone	1.	Limited resources
B.	Elongation zone	2.	Primary cell wall
C.	Maturation zone	3.	Attain maximum size
D.	Geometrical growth	4.	Increased vacuolation

Choose the correct answer from the options given below.

	A	B	C	D
(a)	2	1	4	3
(b)	1	2	4	3
(c)	3	4	1	2
(d)	2	4	3	1

13. Dr. F Went observed that if coleoptile tips were removed and placed on agar for an hour, the agar would lead to a bending when placed on one side of freshly cut coleoptile part. What was the major finding of this experiment?

(a) It is the basis for quantitative determination of small amounts of growth-promoting substances.

(b) It made possible the isolation, purification and exact identification of auxin.

(c) It demonstrated the polar movement of auxins.

(d) It supported the hypothesis that IAA is auxin.

14. Refer to the given figure of leaves A and B and calculate their absolute growth for unit time period.

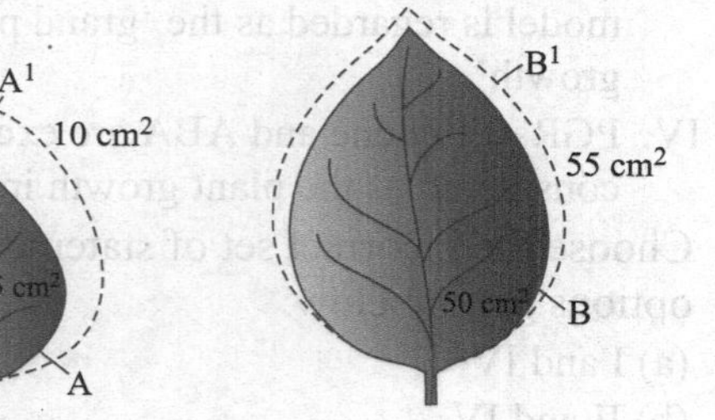

(a) 100% and 10%

(b) 5 cm^2 and 5 cm^2

(c) 10 cm^2 and 40 cm^2

(d) 10% and 100%

15. Read the following statements.

Statement I Water, oxygen and nutrients are very essential elements for growth.

Statement II The plant cells grow in size by cell enlargement.

In the light of the above statements, choose the correct answer from the options given below.

(a) Statement I is incorrect, but statement II is correct.

(b) Both statement I and statement II are correct

(c) Both statement I and statement II are incorrect

(d) Statement I is correct, but statement II is incorrect

16. Apical dominance in higher plants is due to

(a) balance between auxin and GA activity

(b) balance between auxin and cytokinin activity

(c) balance between cytokinin and GA activity

(d) balance between GA and ABA activity

17. Identify the option having correct set of examples of dedifferentiation.

(a) Cork cambium, formation of tracheary element

(b) Interfascicular cambium and cork cambium

(c) Shooting from callus, formation of tracheary element

(d) Cork cambium, rooting from callus

18. Consider the given statements.

I. Adventitious shoot formation is influenced by cytokinin's activity.

II. 2, 4–D is widely used to kill monocotyledonous weeds, but do not affect mature dicotyledonous plants.

III. Ethephon accelerates abscission in fruit of cherry.

IV. A life cycle of plant involves only one PGR at a specific time and event.

V. Vernalisation can be influenced by PGR like GA and temperature.

Choose the correct set of statements from the options given below.

(a) II, III, IV and V

(b) I, II, IV and V

(c) I, III and IV

(d) I, III and V

19. Refer to the given figure of leaves of a heterophyllous plant. This heterophylly is observed due to

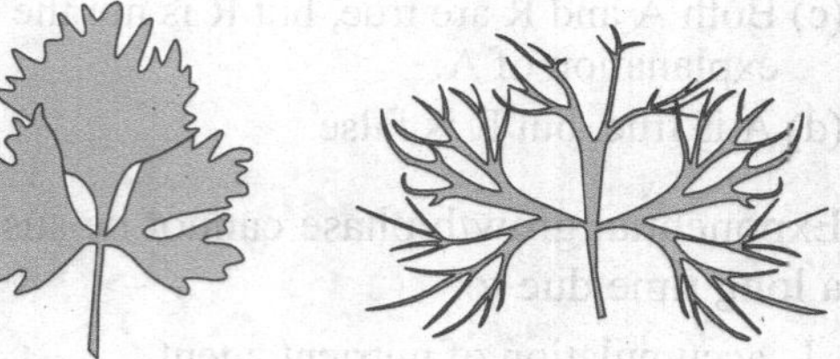

(a) stage of life cycle

(b) environmental conditions

(c) availability of water

(d) scarcity of nutrients

20. A student used coconut milk in his/her medium prepared for the tissue culture experiment. What can be the reason behind this?

(a) Coconut milk is a source of GA
(b) Coconut milk is a source of cytokinins
(c) Coconut milk provides alternate source of auxin
(d) Coconut milk contains ethylene

21. There are two hormones X and Y. X is involved in causing the increase in the length of grapes stalks, while Y is involved in the induction of flowering in mango. Identify X and Y.

(a) $X - GA_3, Y - ABA$
(b) $X - GA_3, Y - H_2C = CH_2$
(c) $X - H_2C = CH_2, Y - GA_3$
(d) $X - ABA, Y - H_2C = CH_2$

22. Which type of growth does a plant display?

(a) Open form of growth
(b) Closed form of growth
(c) Both open and closed forms of growth
(d) A fused form of growth.

23. Choose the incorrect pair from the following.

(a) Apical meristem- Increase in length
(b) Intercalary meristem- Elongation of internode
(c) Lateral meristem- Elongation of leaf
(d) Cork cambium- Secondary meristem

24. Read the following statements.

Statement I The period of growth is generally divided into three phases, namely, meristematic, elongation and maturation.

Statement II The constantly dividing cells, both at the root apex and the shoot apex, represent the maturation phase of growth.

In the light of the above statements, choose the correct answer from the options given below.

(a) Statement I is incorrect, but statement II is correct.
(b) Both statement I and statement II are correct.
(c) Both statement I and statement II are incorrect.
(d) Statement I is correct, but statement II is incorrect.

25. Given below are two statements; one is labelled as Assertion (A) and the other is labelled as Reason (R).

Assertion (A) Plants follow different pathways in response to environment or phases of life to form different kinds of structures.

Reason (R) Heterophylly in cotton and coriander are its example.

In the light of the above statements, choose the correct answer from the options given below.

(a) A is false, but R is true.
(b) Both A and R are true and R is the correct explanation of A.
(c) Both A and R are true, but R is not the correct explanation of A.
(d) A is true, but R is false.

26. Refer to the given graph and choose the incorrect statement about it.

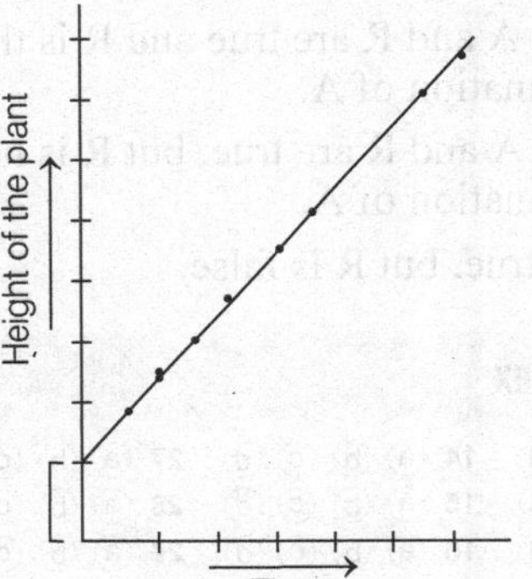

(a) It is showing constant linear growth.
(b) In this type of growth, only one daughter cell continues to divide, while the other differentiates and matures.
(c) Mathematically, it is expressed as $L_t = L_0 + rt$.
(d) It occurs when the resources are limited.

27. Match List I with List II.

	List I		List II
A.	2, 4-dichlorophenoxy acetic acid	1.	Regulates seed dormancy
B.	GA_3	2.	Synthetic auxin
C.	Ethephon	3.	Delay senescence
D.	ABA	4.	Source of ethylene

Choose the correct answer from the options given below.

	A	B	C	D
(a)	1	3	4	2
(b)	2	4	1	3
(c)	2	3	4	1
(d)	3	1	2	4

28. Given below are two statements; one is labelled as Assertion (A) and the other is labelled as Reason (R).

Assertion (A) To form a tracheary element, the cells would lose their protoplasm.

Reason (R) During differentiation, cells undergo few to major structural changes, both in their cell walls and protoplasm.

In the light of the above statements, choose the correct answer from the options given below.

(a) A is false, but R is true.

(b) Both A and R are true and R is the correct explanation of A.

(c) Both A and R are true, but R is not the correct explanation of A.

(d) A is true, but R is false.

29. Choose the incorrect statement about growth from the following options.

(a) The plant cells grow in size by cell enlargement which in turn requires water.

(b) Turgidity of cells helps in extension growth.

(c) Water also provides the medium for enzymatic activities needed for growth.

(d) Nitrogen helps in releasing metabolic energy essential for growth activities.

30. Given below are two statements.

Statement I ABA and GA are antagonistic to each other.

Statement II Ethylene and auxin have synergistic effect on flowering.

In the light of the above statements, choose the correct answer from the options given below.

(a) Statement I is incorrect, but statement II is correct.

(b) Both statement I and statement II are correct.

(c) Both statement I and statement II are incorrect.

(d) Statement I is correct, but statement II is incorrect.

Response Index

01 ⓐ ⓑ ⓒ ⓓ	14 ⓐ ⓑ ⓒ ⓓ	27 ⓐ ⓑ ⓒ ⓓ	40 ⓐ ⓑ ⓒ ⓓ
02 ⓐ ⓑ ⓒ ⓓ	15 ⓐ ⓑ ⓒ ⓓ	28 ⓐ ⓑ ⓒ ⓓ	41 ⓐ ⓑ ⓒ ⓓ
03 ⓐ ⓑ ⓒ ⓓ	16 ⓐ ⓑ ⓒ ⓓ	29 ⓐ ⓑ ⓒ ⓓ	42 ⓐ ⓑ ⓒ ⓓ
04 ⓐ ⓑ ⓒ ⓓ	17 ⓐ ⓑ ⓒ ⓓ	30 ⓐ ⓑ ⓒ ⓓ	43 ⓐ ⓑ ⓒ ⓓ
05 ⓐ ⓑ ⓒ ⓓ	18 ⓐ ⓑ ⓒ ⓓ	31 ⓐ ⓑ ⓒ ⓓ	44 ⓐ ⓑ ⓒ ⓓ
06 ⓐ ⓑ ⓒ ⓓ	19 ⓐ ⓑ ⓒ ⓓ	32 ⓐ ⓑ ⓒ ⓓ	45 ⓐ ⓑ ⓒ ⓓ
07 ⓐ ⓑ ⓒ ⓓ	20 ⓐ ⓑ ⓒ ⓓ	33 ⓐ ⓑ ⓒ ⓓ	46 ⓐ ⓑ ⓒ ⓓ
08 ⓐ ⓑ ⓒ ⓓ	21 ⓐ ⓑ ⓒ ⓓ	34 ⓐ ⓑ ⓒ ⓓ	47 ⓐ ⓑ ⓒ ⓓ
09 ⓐ ⓑ ⓒ ⓓ	22 ⓐ ⓑ ⓒ ⓓ	35 ⓐ ⓑ ⓒ ⓓ	48 ⓐ ⓑ ⓒ ⓓ
10 ⓐ ⓑ ⓒ ⓓ	23 ⓐ ⓑ ⓒ ⓓ	36 ⓐ ⓑ ⓒ ⓓ	49 ⓐ ⓑ ⓒ ⓓ
11 ⓐ ⓑ ⓒ ⓓ	24 ⓐ ⓑ ⓒ ⓓ	37 ⓐ ⓑ ⓒ ⓓ	50 ⓐ ⓑ ⓒ ⓓ
12 ⓐ ⓑ ⓒ ⓓ	25 ⓐ ⓑ ⓒ ⓓ	38 ⓐ ⓑ ⓒ ⓓ	
13 ⓐ ⓑ ⓒ ⓓ	26 ⓐ ⓑ ⓒ ⓓ	39 ⓐ ⓑ ⓒ ⓓ	

Performance Scanner

> 90% Excellent !	You have mastered this chapter. The concepts of this chapter are at your fingertips. Move on to the next chapter and maintain this momentum.
76-90% Very Good !	You have a good command over this chapter. Revise the chapter again after a few days and enhance your perfomance.
60-75% Good !	You have a wide scope to learn for this chapter. Revise this chapter again.
<60% Not Satisfactory!	You have a long way ahead of you to master this chapter. Revise it thoroughly.

Scan for online chapter test

Scan for online unit test

Space for Rough Work

Space for Rough Work

Test Booklet No. 3947314

Test Booklet Code CH14

MEDACE
NEET (UG)
SELF ASSESSMENT KIT

Breathing and Exchange of Gases

Topics Covered

Human Respiratory System and Mechanism of Breathing

Exchange and Transport of Gases Regulation of Respiration and Respiratory Disorder

Important Instructions

- This Booklet Contains – Two Topic Tests and One Test on Complete Chapter.
- Each question carries 4 marks.
- For each correct response, the candidate will get 4 marks. And for every incorrect response, 1 mark will be additionally deducted from total score.
- Use **Blue/Black** point pen only for filling the OMR.
- Rough work is to be done in the space provided for this purpose in the test booklet only.

Name of the Candidate (In Capitals) ____________

Candidate's Signature ____________

Invigilator's Signature ____________

Facsimile signature stamp of center superintendent ____________

Do not open this booklet until you start attempting the test

Topical Follow Thru

Test 1

Syllabus

- Respiratory Organs in Animals
- Respiratory System in Humans
- Mechanism of Breathing and its Regulation in Humans
- Respiratory Volume

For deeper insight, **Scan the QR Code**

Important Instructions

- The test is of 30 minutes duration and contains 25 Multiple Choice Questions (four options with a single correct answer).
- Choose the correct option and fill the OMR given on the last page of this test accordingly.
- At some instances, you may find more than 1 option to be correct. In such circumstances, you have to judge the most appropriate answer as per the conditions given in the question.

1. Trachea gets divided into a left and right primary bronchi at the level of

(a) third thoracic vertebra
(b) four thoracic vertebra
(c) fifth thoracic vertebra
(d) six thoracic vertebra

2. A person met with an accident. He died on the spot without any injury to brain, heart, stomach and kidney. Which of the following is the reason for his/her death?

(a) RBCs become coagulated
(b) Intestine got twisted
(c) Stomach stopped digestion
(d) Diaphragm got punctured

3. Arrange the following steps in the correct order of their occurrence during expiration.

I. Air expelled from lungs.
II. Volume of thorax decreases.
III. Pulmonary volume decreases
IV. Intrapulmonary pressure increases.
V. Relaxation of external intercostal muscles.
VI. Return of diaphragm and sternum to their normal position.

(a) V → IV → II → III → VI → I
(b) V → VI → II → III → IV → I
(c) IV → V → VI → III→ II → I
(d) IV → VI → V → II → III → I

4. Identify the correct and incorrect match about respiratory volume and capacities and mark the correct answer.

I. Inspiratory Capacity [IC] = Tidal Volume [TV] + Residual Volume [RV].
II. Vital Capacity [VC] = Tidal Volume [TV] + Inspiratory Reserve Volume [IRV] + Expiratory Reserve Volume [ERV].
III. Residual Volume [RV] = Vital Capacity [VC] – Inspiratory Reserve Volume [IRV].
IV. Tidal Volume [TV] = Inspiratory Capacity [IC] – Inspiratory Reserve Volume [IRV].

Choose the correct option.

(a) I, II and III incorrect, IV correct
(b) I and III incorrect, II and IV correct
(c) I, II and IV correct, III incorrect
(d) I, III, II and IV correct

5. Inspiration is initiated by the contraction of ...(i).... which increases the volume of thoracic chamber in the ...(ii)...

	(i)	(ii)
(A)	external inter - costal muscles	antero- posterior axis
(B)	internal inter- costal muscles	dorso-ventral axis
(C)	diaphragm	antero-posterior axis
(D)	diaphragm	dorso-ventral axis

(a) A (b) B (c) C (d) D

6. Given below are two statements.

Statement I Pharynx is protected by a small flap of tissue called the epiglottis.
Statement II At the end of each bronchiole, there are tiny air sac called alveoli.
In the light of the above statements, choose the correct answer from the options given below.

(a) Statement I is incorrect, but statement II is correct
(b) Both statement I and statement II are correct
(c) Both statement I and statement II are incorrect
(d) Statement I is correct, but statement II is incorrect

7. Which of the following structures are supported by incomplete cartilaginous rings to prevent collapsing in absence of air?

(a) Trachea, primary, secondary and tertiary bronchi and initial bronchioles
(b) Larynx, trachea, primary and secondary bronchiole
(c) Primary, secondary and tertiary bronchi
(d) Trachea, primary, secondary and tertiary bronchi and alveoli.

8. Breathing involved two stages- inspiration and expiration. Expiration occurs when

(a) diaphragm contracts and intercostal muscles relax
(b) diaphragm relaxes and intercostal muscles contracts
(c) Both diaphragm and intercostal muscles relax
(d) Both diaphragm and intercostal muscles contract

9. In which of the following set of animals, cutaneous respiration is the sole method of respiration?

(a) Earthworm and *nereis*
(b) Frog and earthworm
(c) Molluscs and fishes
(d) *Amoeba* and frog

10. Given below is the diagram of human respiratory system. Identify the labelled parts *A*, *B*, *C* and *D* and choose the incorrect option w.r.t. them.

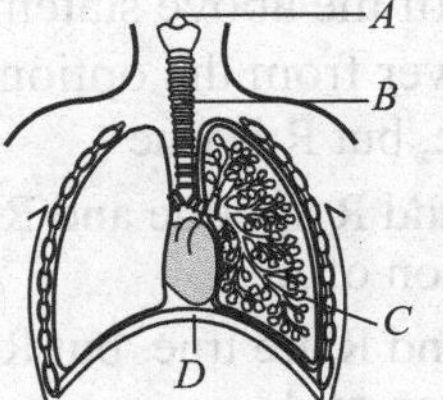

(a) *A*–A thin elastic cartilaginous flap that covers glottis.
(b) *B*–Cartilaginous box helps in sound production.
(c) *C*–Irregular walled and vascularised bag-like structure.
(d) *D*–Thoracic chamber formed by dome-shaped structure on lower side.

11. Match List I with List II.

	List I		List II
A.	Bronchial tree	1.	Passage for air from nasal cavity to larynx and for food from mouth cavity to oesophagus
B.	Larynx	2.	Conducts air from trachea to the alveoli and its mucus lining continues to filter air
C.	Trachea	3.	Passage way for air, prevents foreign objects from entering trachea and houses vocal cords
D.	Pharynx	4.	Flexible tube, which connects larynx with bronchial tree

Choose the correct answer from the options given below.

	A	B	C	D		A	B	C	D
(a)	1	2	3	4	(b)	2	3	4	1
(c)	4	3	2	1	(d)	3	2	1	4

12. Given below are two statements; one is labelled as Assertion (A) and the other is labelled as Reason (R).

Assertion (A) The strength of inspiration and expiration can be increased.

Reason (R) Diaphragm a specialised set of muscles-external and interna linter-coastal muscles between ribs help in expiration and inspiration.
In the light of the above statements, choose the correct answer from the options given below.
(a) A is false, but R is true
(b) Both A and R are true and R is the correct explanation of A
(c) Both A and R are true, but R is not the correct explanation of A
(d) A is true, but R is false

13. Which of the following statement is correct about nasal cavity ?
(a) The nasal cavity is a mucus-filled, hollow and small space that is present above the nose and in the middle of the face
(b) The cavities are produced by the union of the two nostrils, which is divided by the nasal septum
(c) The nasal cavity is found in the lower region of the pharynx
(d) It acts as a sensory organ that can recognise many different smells as the nasal cavity has an olfactory odour

14. Given below are two statements; one is labelled as Assertion (A) and the other is labelled as Reason (R).
Assertion (A) Terminal bronchioles are not lined by cartilaginous rings.
Reason (R) They prevent collapsing of bronchiole during expiration.
In the light of the above statements, choose the correct answer from the options given below.
(a) A is false, but R is true
(b) Both A and R are true and R is the correct explanation of A
(c) Both A and R are true, but R is not the correct explanation of A
(d) A is true, but R is false

15. Match List I with List II.

List I		List II
A. Tidal volume	1.	2500-3000 mL
B. Inspiratory reserve volume	2.	1000-1100 mL
C. Expiratory reserve volume	3.	1100-1200 mL
D. Residual volume	4.	500 mL

Choose the correct answer from the options given below.

	A	B	C	D		A	B	C	D
(a)	1	2	3	4	(b)	4	1	2	3
(c)	4	2	3	1	(d)	1	4	2	3

16. Match List I with List II.

List I		List II
A. Epiglottis	1.	Air sacs
B. Trachea	2.	Lid of larynx
C. Larynx	3.	Voice box
D. Alveoli	4.	Wind pipe

Choose the correct answer from the options given below.

	A	B	C	D		A	B	C	D
(a)	3	4	1	2	(b)	4	1	3	2
(c)	4	3	1	2	(d)	2	4	3	1

17. Which of the following do not belong to conducting part of respiratory system?
(a) External nostrils
(b) Terminal bronchiole
(c) Alveolar duct
(d) Secondary bronchi

18. Match List I with List II.

List I		List II
A. Posterior surface	1.	Ribs
B. Anterior surface	2.	Sternum
C. Ventral surface	3.	Vertebral column
D. Lateral surface	4.	Diaphragm

Choose the correct answer from the options given below.

	A	B	C	D		A	B	C	D
(a)	3	2	4	1	(b)	2	1	3	4
(c)	4	1	3	2	(d)	4	3	1	2

19. Arrange the following in the increasing order of their respiratory volume.
I. Expiratory capacity
II. Inspiratory capacity
III. Residual volume
IV. Tidal volume
Choose the correct answer from the options given below.
(a) IV I III II
(b) III IV I II
(c) IV III I II
(d) II I III IV

20. Which of the following pressures is always negative under normal conditions, ensuring that the lungs do not collapse?
(a) Intrapulmonary pressure
(b) Atmospheric pressure
(c) Intrapleural pressure
(d) Alveolar pressure

21. During normal inspiration, which of the following events does not occur?
(a) Intrapulmonary pressure becomes lower than atmospheric pressure, allowing air to flow into the lungs.
(b) The diaphragm contracts and flattens, increasing the vertical dimension of the thoracic cavity.
(c) The external intercostal muscles relax, causing the rib cage to move downward and inward, thereby increasing thoracic volume.
(d) Pleural pressure becomes more negative, causing the lungs to expand.

22. Given below are two statements, one is labelled as Assertion A and the other is labelled as Reason R.

Assertion (A) During deep inspiration, the volume of the thoracic cavity is increased due to contraction of both the diaphragm and external intercostal muscles.

Reason (R) The contraction of the external intercostal muscles lifts the rib cage upward and outward.

In the light of the above statements, choose the correct answer from the options given below
(a) A is false, but R is true.
(b) Both A and R are true, and the R is the correct explanation for the A.
(c) Both A and R are true, but the R is not the correct explanation for the A.
(d) A is true, but R is false.

23. Which of the following statement is incorrect regarding functioning of conducting part of respiratory system?
(a) It transport atmospheric air to alveoli.
(b) Brings air to constant body temperature.
(c) Diffusion site for oxygen and carbon dioxide.
(d) It clears respiratory tract from foreign particles.

24. Arrange the following respiratory structures in the increasing order of their complexity in organisms.

I. Gills II. Moist cuticle
III. Lungs IV. Tracheal tubes

Choose the correct answer from the options given below
(a) III→IV →I→II (b) IV→I→III→II
(c) IV→III→I→II (d) II→IV→I→III

25. Given below are two statements.

Statement I Lungs are anatomically located inside thorax such that change in volume of thoracic cavity is also observed in pulmonary cavity.

Statement II Pulmonary volume can be directly altered by changing rate of respiration.

In the light of the above statements, choose the correct answer from the options given below
(a) Statement I is incorrect, but statement II is correct
(b) Both statement I and statement II are correct.
(c) Both statement I and statement II are incorrect
(d) Statement I is correct, but statement II is incorrect

Response Index

01	a	b	c	d	10	a	b	c	d	19	a	b	c	d
02	a	b	c	d	11	a	b	c	d	20	a	b	c	d
03	a	b	c	d	12	a	b	c	d	21	a	b	c	d
04	a	b	c	d	13	a	b	c	d	22	a	b	c	d
05	a	b	c	d	14	a	b	c	d	23	a	b	c	d
06	a	b	c	d	15	a	b	c	d	24	a	b	c	d
07	a	b	c	d	16	a	b	c	d	25	a	b	c	d
08	a	b	c	d	17	a	b	c	d					
09	a	b	c	d	18	a	b	c	d					

Performance Scanner

> 90% Excellent !	You have mastered these topics. The concepts of these topics are at your fingertips. Move on to the next test and maintain this momentum.
76-90% Very Good !	You have a good command over these topics. Revise these topics again after a few days and enhance your performance.
60-75% Good !	You have a wide scope to learn for these topics. Revise these topics again.
<60% Not Satisfactory!	You have a long way ahead of you to master these topics. Revise it thoroughly.

Test 2

Syllabus
- Exchange of Gases
- Transport of Gases and Regulation of Respiration
- Disorders Related to Respiration (Asthma, Emphysema, Occupational Respiratory Disorders)

For deeper insight, **Scan the QR Code**

Important Instructions
- The test is of 30 minutes duration and contains 25 Multiple Choice Questions (four options with a single correct answer).
- Choose the correct option and fill the OMR given on the last page of this test accordingly.
- At some instances, you may find more than 1 option to be correct. In such circumstances, you have to judge the most appropriate answer as per the conditions given in the question.

1. Select which of the conditions are favourable for dissociation of oxygen from the oxyhaemoglobin?
(a) High pO_2 and high H^+ concentration
(b) Lower temperature and low pO_2
(c) High H^+ concentration and high temperature
(d) Low pO_2 and low pCO_2

2. Asthma is a chronic lungs disease characterised by
(a) running nose
(b) short breathing duration
(c) spasm in bronchial muscle
(d) chest pain

3. The partial pressure of O_2 is ...(i)... (higher/lesser) in systemic veins than in systemic arteries. The partial pressure of CO_2 is ....(ii)..... (higher/lesser) in tissues than in systemic arteries.

	(i)	(ii)
(a)	lesser	higher
(b)	higher	higher
(c)	lesser	lesser
(d)	higher	lesser

4. Given below are two statement; one is labelled as Assertion (A) and the other is labelled as Reason (R).

Assertion (A) In erythrocytes, the carbon dioxide combines with water and gets transported.

Reason (R) Carbonic anhydrase is present in the erythrocytes.

In the light of the above statements, choose the correct answer from the options given below.
(a) A is false, but R is true
(b) Both A and R are true and R is the correct explanation of A
(c) Both A and R are true, but R is not the correct explanation of A
(d) A is true, but R is false

5. Match List I with List II.

	List I		List II
A.	pCO_2 in oxygenated blood	1.	0.3 mm Hg
B.	pCO_2 in atmospheric air	2.	40 mm Hg
C.	pO_2 in oxygenated blood	3.	104 mm Hg
D.	pO_2 in alveoli	4.	95 mm Hg

Choose the correct answer from the options given below.

	A	B	C	D		A	B	C	D
(a)	1	2	3	4	(b)	2	1	4	3
(c)	2	3	4	1	(d)	3	4	1	2

6. If 100 mL of blood has 15 gm haemoglobin and 1 gm of haemoglobin carries about 1.34 mL of O_2. Then, 135 mL of same blood will carry how much oxygen?
(a) 24 mL
(b) 27 mL
(c) 26 mL
(d) 25 mL

7. A ...(i)... is situated adjacent to the ..(ii)..., which is highly sensitive to CO_2 and H^+ ion.

	(i)	(ii)
(a)	rhythm centre	chemosensitive area
(b)	pneumotoxic centre	medulla
(c)	rhythm centre	pons
(d)	chemosensitive area	rhythm centre

8. In the tissue, high concentration of CO_2

(a) increases the affinity of haemoglobin to both oxygen and hydrogen

(b) increases the affinity of haemoglobin to oxygen but decreases its affinity to hydrogen

(c) decreases the affinity of haemoglobin to oxygen but increases its affinity of hydrogen

(d) decreases the affinity of haemoglobin to both oxygen and hydrogen

9. Given below is the diagram of diffusion membrane. Observe it carefully and identify oxygen concentration in *A* and *B* by choosing the correct option.

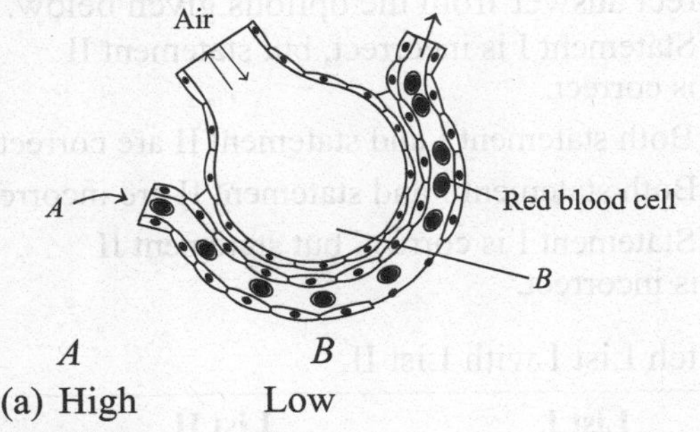

	A	*B*
(a)	High	Low
(b)	High	Low
(c)	Low	High
(d)	Low	High

10. Given below are two statements.

Statement I Every 100 mL of oxygenated blood can delivers around 20 mL of O_2 to the tissue under normal physiological conditions.

Statement II Every 100 mL of deoxygenated blood delivers approximately 4 mL of CO_2 to the alveoli.

In the light of the above statements, choose the correct answer from the options given below.

(a) Statement I is incorrect, but statement II is correct

(b) Both statement I and statement II are correct

(c) Both statement I and statement II are incorrect

(d) Statement I is correct, but statement II is incorrect

11. Consider the following statements.

I. The high solubility of CO_2 in blood facilitates its high rate of diffusion.

II. Approximately 8.9% of CO_2 is transported in dissolved state through plasma.

III. The carbon dioxide produced by the tissues, diffuses passively into the blood stream and passes into red blood corpuscles and react with water to form $H_2CO_3^-$.

IV. The oxyhaemoglobin (HbO_2) of the erythrocytes is basic.

V. The chloride ions diffuse from plasma into the erythrocytes to maintain ionic balance.

Choose the correct option.

(a) I, III and V are correct, II and IV are incorrect

(b) I, III and V are incorrect, II and IV are correct

(c) I, II and IV are correct, III and V are incorrect

(d) I, II and IV are incorrect, III and V are correct

12. Read following sentences carefully and select the incorrect one.

(a) During expiration pO_2 of expired air is more than alveolar air, but less than atmospheric air

(b) During expiration, pCO_2 of expired air is less than pCO_2 of alveolar air and more than pCO_2 of atmospheric air

(c) The partial pressure of O_2 and CO_2 in the systemic veins is same as that in pulmonary vein

(d) Sum of partial pressure of all gases at sea level is 760 mm Hg

13. Read the following statements about occupational respiratory disorder.

I. It is disfunction of a part of lung.

II. A part of lung is unable to perform exchange of gases.

III. There is proliferation of fibrous connective tissue.

IV. It is caused by chronic bronchitis.

V. There is spastic contraction of bronchiolar muscle during expiration.

Choose the correct set of statements from the options given below.

(a) II, III and V

(b) I, II and III

(c) I and IV

(d) III and IV

14. Basic rhythm of respiration is controlled by rhythmic center, another center in brain stem called pneumotaxic center, helps to co-ordinate the transition between inspiration and expiration.
In which region of brain stem this pneumotaxic center present?
(a) Medulla oblongata
(b) Pons
(c) Midbrain
(d) Cerebellum

15. Cigarette smoking is the usual cause of which of the following disease?
(a) Asthma (b) Asbestosis
(c) Emphysema (d) Tuberculosis

16. Consider the following statements.
I. In tissues high pO_2, low pCO_2 and lower temperature favour formation of oxyhaemoglobin.
II. At alveolar site, CO_2 diffuses into blood leading to the formation of water.
III. Surfactant produced by type-I alveolar cells reduces surface tension, preventing the alveoli from collapsing during exhalation.
IV. The partial pressure of oxygen in the alveoli is higher than that in the pulmonary capillaries, facilitating oxygen diffusion into the blood.
Choose the correct statement(s) from the options given below.
(a) I, II and IV (b) I and II
(c) III and IV (d) Only IV

17. How does carbon monoxide (CO) affect oxygen transport in the blood?
(a) It increases the release of oxygen from haemoglobin
(b) It decreases the binding of oxygen to haemoglobin
(c) It binds to haemoglobin more strongly than oxygen, reducing oxygen transport
(d) It does not affect oxygen transport

18. A patient's arterial blood gas analysis reveals a decreased pH, an increased partial pressure of carbon dioxide (pCO_2), and a slightly elevated body temperature.
Which of the following statement correctly explains the physiological implications of the observed shift in the oxygen-haemoglobin dissociation curve?
(a) The rightward shift indicates an increased affinity of haemoglobin for oxygen, enhancing oxygen loading in the lungs.
(b) The decreased pH, increased pCO_2 and elevated temperature contribute to the decreased affinity of haemoglobin for oxygen, facilitating oxygen release in the tissues.
(c) The rightward shift results in a decreased partial pressure of oxygen (pO_2) in the tissues, impairing oxygen delivery.
(d) A rightward shift in the curve is associated with a decreased carbon dioxide level, which increases haemoglobin's ability to release oxygen.

19. Given below are two statements.
Statement I Partial pressure of oxygen in systemic arteries is 95 mm Hg.
Statement II Systemic arteries carry oxygenated blood from left ventricle to other body tissues.
In the light of the above statements, choose the correct answer from the options given below.
(a) Statement I is incorrect, but statement II is correct.
(b) Both statement I and statement II are correct.
(c) Both statement I and statement II are incorrect.
(d) Statement I is correct, but statement II is incorrect.

20. Match List I with List II.

	List I		List II
A.	Chemosensitive area	1.	Reduce inspiration rate
B.	Pneumotaxic centre	2.	Hydrogen ions
C.	Rhythm center	3.	Controls respiratory rhythm
D.	Oxygen	4.	Insignificant role in regulation of respiratory rhythm

Choose the correct answer from the options given below.

	A	B	C	D		A	B	C	D
(a)	3	2	4	1	(b)	2	1	3	4
(c)	4	1	3	4	(d)	4	3	1	2

21. A 60-year-old man, presents to the emergency department with increasing shortness of breath and a chronic productive cough over the past 5 years. He has a history of heavy smoking.

Based on patients history and clinical presentation, which of the following diagnoses is most likely?

(a) Chronic bronchitis
(b) Emphysema
(c) Asthma
(d) Restrictive lung disease

22. Given below are two statements; one is labelled as Assertion A and the other is labelled as Reason R.

Assertion (A) Transport of CO_2 in blood is much greater than that of O_2

Reason (R) Rate of diffusion of gases depends upon thickness of membrane and solubility of gases.

In the light of the above statements, choose the correct answer from the options given below.

(a) A is false, but R is true.
(b) Both A and R are true and R is the correct explanation of A.
(c) Both A and R are true, but R is not the correct explanation of A.
(d) A is true, but R is false.

23. Which of the following statements is/are true regarding the chloride shift (Hamburger phenomenon) in red blood cells?

I. Chloride ions enter red blood cells in exchange for bicarbonate ions leaving the cells to maintain electrochemical balance.
II. The chloride shift primarily occurs in the lungs, where bicarbonate ions are converted to CO_2 for exhalation.
III. The chloride shift helps to stabilise the blood pH by directly influencing the concentration of hydrogen ions in the plasma.
IV. The chloride shift is more pronounced in tissues with low pCO levels compared to those with high pCO? levels.

Choose the correct answer from the options given below.

(a) I and IV
(b) I and II
(c) III and IV
(d) Only I

24. Which of the following best describes the role of haemoglobin in CO_2 transport?

(a) Haemoglobin binds CO_2 only in the lungs
(b) Haemoglobin primarily transports CO_2 as bicarbonate ions
(c) Haemoglobin binds CO_2 to form carbaminohemoglobin
(d) Haemoglobin does not participate in CO_2 transport

25. Given below are two statements.

Statement I The limit of exchange of gases between alveoli and pulmonary blood is called diffusing capacity.

Statement II Oxygen content of the blood after leaving lungs is greater than that of the blood entering the lungs.

In the light of the above statements, choose the correct answer from the options given below.

(a) Statement I is incorrect, but statement II is correct.
(b) Both statement I and statement II are correct.
(c) Both statement I and statement II are incorrect.
(d) Statement I is correct, but statement II is incorrect.

Response Index

01	a	b	c	d	10	a	b	c	d	19	a	b	c	d
02	a	b	c	d	11	a	b	c	d	20	a	b	c	d
03	a	b	c	d	12	a	b	c	d	21	a	b	c	d
04	a	b	c	d	13	a	b	c	d	22	a	b	c	d
05	a	b	c	d	14	a	b	c	d	23	a	b	c	d
06	a	b	c	d	15	a	b	c	d	24	a	b	c	d
07	a	b	c	d	16	a	b	c	d	25	a	b	c	d
08	a	b	c	d	17	a	b	c	d					
09	a	b	c	d	18	a	b	c	d					

Performance Scanner

> 90% Excellent !	You have mastered these topics. The concepts of these topics are at your fingertips. Move on to the next test and maintain this momentum.
76-90% Very Good !	You have a good command over these topics. Revise these topics again after a few days and enhance your performance.
60-75% Good !	You have a wide scope to learn for these topics. Revise these topics again.
<60% Not Satisfactory!	You have a long way ahead of you to master these topics. Revise it thoroughly.

Chapter Break Thru

Syllabus			
	• Respiratory Organs in Animals • Respiratory System in Humans • Mechanism of Breathing and its Regulation in Humans	• Respiratory Volume • Exchange of Gases • Transport of Gases and Regulation of Respiration	• Disorders Related to Respiration (Asthma, Emphysema, Occupational Respiratory Disorders)

Important Instructions

- The test is of 1 hour duration and contains 50 Multiple-Choice Questions (Four options with a single correct answer).
- Choose the correct option and fill the OMR given on the last page of this test accordingly.
- At some instances, you may find more than 1 option to be correct. In such circumstances, you have to judge the most appropriate answer as per the conditions given in the question.

1. Lungs do not collapse between breaths as some air always remains in the lungs which can never be expelled because
(a) pressure in the lungs is higher than the atmospheric pressure
(b) there is negative pressure in the lungs
(c) there is negative intrapleural pressure pulling at the lung walls
(d) pressure in the lungs is higher than the atmosheric pressure

2. Given below are two statements; one is labelled as Assertion (A) and the other is labelled as Reason (R).

Assertion (A) Vital capacity is higher in people living at high altitude.

Reason (R) It indicates the ability of a person to provide energy to the body for doing strenuous work.

In the light of the above statements, choose the correct answer from the options given below.
(a) A is false, but R is true
(b) Both A and R are true and R is the correct explanation of A
(c) Both A and R are true, but R is not the correct explanation of A
(d) A is true, but R is false

3. Lungs are covered by a double layered pleura with pleural fluild between them. This helps to
(a) reduce friction on the lung surface
(b) increase volume of the lungs
(c) reduce diffusion of O_2 in lungs
(d) transport atmospheric air to the lungs

4. Respiratory rhythm centre present in human beings regulate respiratory rhythm to suit the demands of body tissue. Name the neural region in which this respiratory rhythm centre is present.
(a) pons
(b) medulla oblongata
(c) lungs epithelium
(d) aortic arc

5. Given below are two statements.

Statement I The thoracic chamber is formed lateraly by the sternum.

Statement II The lungs are air tight chamber.

In the light of the above statements, choose the correct answer from the options given below.
(a) Statement I is incorrect, but statement II is correct
(b) Both statement I and statement II are correct
(c) Both statement I and statement II are incorrect
(d) Statement I is correct, but statement II is incorrect

6. Which of the following is entirely made up of cartilage?
(a) Nasal septum (b) Larynx
(c) Glottis (d) Trachea

7. The walls of trachea are non-collapsible due to the presence of
(a) complete rings of fibrous cartilage
(b) incomplete rings of hyaline cartilage
(c) incomplete rings of fibrous cartilage
(d) complete rings of hyaline cartilage

8. What will be amount of volume of air a person can expire by a forcible expiration if the tidal volume is 500 mL and expiratory capacity is 1500 mL?

(a) 500 mL (b) 1500 mL
(c) 1000 mL (d) 2000 mL

9. Given below are two statements.

Statement I Conducting part is the site of actual diffusion of O_2 and CO_2 between blood and atmosphere.

Statement II Any change in the volume of the thoracic cavity cannot bring changes in lung capacity.

In the light of the above statements, choose the correct answer from the options given below.

(a) Statement I is incorrect, but statement II is correct
(b) Both statement I and statement II are correct
(c) Both statement I and statement II are incorrect
(d) Statement I is correct, but statement II is incorrect

10. Inspiration can occur if the pressure within the lungs is….

(a) more than the atmospheric pressure
(b) less than the atmospheric pressure
(c) equal to the atmospheric pressure
(d) drastically more than the atmospheric pressure

11. Arrange the given steps in the correct order of their occurrence during the process of inspiration.

I. Volume of thorax increases in the dorso- ventral axis.
II. The contraction of external intercostal muscles raise the ribs and sternum.
III. Intrapulmonary pressure decreases.
IV. Air rushes into the lungs.
V. Diaphragm contraction.
VI. Volume of the thorax increases in the anterio-posterior axis.

(a) II → I → V → VI → III → IV
(b) V → I → II → VI → III → IV
(c) V → VI → II → I → III → IV
(d) II → VI → V → I → III → IV

12. Which of the following statement is incorrect regarding respiratory system?

(a) Each terminal bronchiole gives rise to a network of bronchus.
(b) The alveoli are highly vascularised.
(c) The lungs are covered by a double-layered membrane.
(d) The pleural fluid reduces friction on the hard surface.

13. Find incorrectly matched pair.

(a)	Inspiration	– Active process
(b)	Internal intercostal muscles	– Between the ribs
(c)	Expiration	– Diaphragm dome-shaped
(d)	Forceful expiration	– Passive process

14. Oxyhaemoglobin dissociates into oxygen and deoxyhaemoglobin when

(a) pO_2 is low in tissues
(b) pO_2 is high in tissues
(c) pO_2 is equal on both the inside and outside the tissue
(d) pO_2 is low in blood

15. Select the incorrect statement.

(a) Decrease in pO_2 promotes the amount of CO_2 transport.
(b) Oxyhaemoglobin acts as a strong alkali.
(c) The chloride content of RBC increase in deoxygenated blood.
(d) RBC contains high concentration of carbonic anhydrase.

16. Select the incorrectly matched pair with respect to pressure of oxygen.

(a) Atmospheric air	–	159 mm Hg
(b) Alveoli	–	104 mm Hg
(c) Deoxygenated blood	–	45 mm Hg
(d) Tissue	–	40 mm Hg

17. Consider the following statements regarding carbon dioxide transport.

I. About 7% of CO_2 is transported as dissolved in plasma, 23% as carbaminohaemoglobin and 70% as bicarbonates.

II. The CO_2 dissolved in plasma forms carbonic anhydrase.
III. The concentration of carbonic acid remains constant due to potassium.

Choose the correct statement from the options given below.
(a) Only II (b) Only III
(c) Only I (d) I, II and III

18. Neural center can regulate the breathing rate of human being. Name the region of brain which is responsible for shortening the duration of inspiration which leads to rapid inspiration.
(a) Apneustic center (b) Pneumotoxic center
(c) Midbrain (d) Cerebrum

19. Match List I with List II.

	List I		List II
A.	Total Lung capacity	1.	FRC+ TV+ IRV
B.	Expiratory capacity	2.	IRV+TV
C.	Inspiratory capacity	3.	ERV+TV
D.	Vital capacity	4.	ERV+TV+IRV

Choose the correct answer from the options given below.

	A	B	C	D
(a)	1	3	4	2
(b)	1	3	2	4
(c)	3	4	1	2
(d)	2	3	4	1

20. Blood analysis of a patient reveals an unusual high quantity of carboxyhaemoglobin content. Which of the following conclusions is most likely to be correct?
(a) The patient has been inhaling polluted air containing high content of carbon disulphide
(b) The patient has been inhaling polluted air containing high content of chloroform
(c) The patient has been inhaling polluted air containing high content of carbon dioxide
(d) The patient has been inhaling polluted air containing high content of carbon monoxide

21. What would happen, if partial pressure of CO_2 rises to 100 mm Hg?
I. The person would die due to oxygen deficiency.
II. The person would perform average respiration.
III. Haemoglobin would neither be able to load or unload oxygen.
IV. Haemoglobin would be able to load oxygen, but neither be able to load or unload carbon dioxide.

Choose the correct option.
(a) I and II (b) III and IV
(c) II and III (d) I and III

22. Match List I with List II.

	List I		List II
A.	Bohr's effect	1.	Hyperbolic curve
B.	Shift to right	2.	High H^+ ion concentration
C.	Shift to left	3.	Low H^+ ion concentration
D.	Myoglobin	4.	Dissociation of oxyhaemoglobin

Choose the correct answer from the options given below.

	A	B	C	D
(a)	4	2	3	1
(b)	4	3	2	1
(c)	1	4	3	2
(d)	3	2	4	1

23. Given below are two statements.
Statement I About 70% of CO_2 that enters RBCs changes into HCO_3^- for transport in plasma to the lungs where it reconvert into CO_2 for elimination.
Statement II About 40% of CO_2 that enters RBCs changes into carbamino-haemoglobin which releases O_2 in the lungs.
In the light of the above statements, choose the correct answer from the options given below.
(a) Statement I is incorrect, but statement II is correct
(b) Both statement I and statement II are correct
(c) Both statement I and statement II are incorrect
(d) Statement I is correct, but statement II is incorrect

24. Which of the following changes occur in diaphragm and intercostal muscles when expiration taken place?
(a) Internal intercostal muscles relax and diaphragm contracts
(b) External intercostal muscles contract and diaphragm relax
(c) Internal intercostal muscles contract and diaphragm relax
(d) External intercostal muscles and diaphragm contracts

25. The given figure in the diagrammatic representation of exchange of gases at the alveolus and the body tissues.

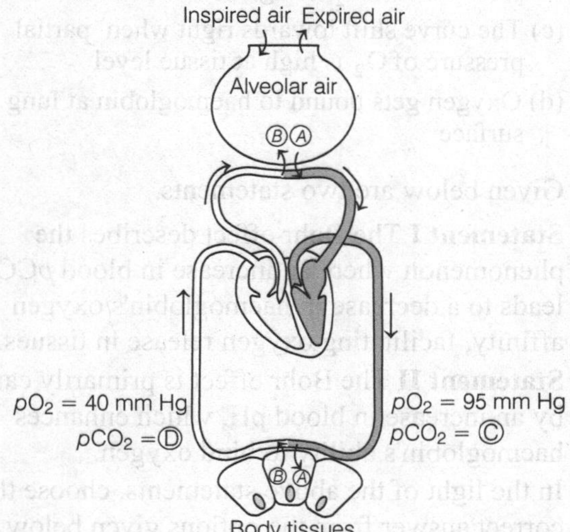

Identify *A*, *B*, *C* and *D* and choose the correct option.

	A	*B*	*C*	*D*
(a)	CO_2	O_2	40 mm Hg	45 mm Hg
(b)	O_2	CO_2	40 mm Hg	45 mm Hg
(c)	O_2	CO_2	45 mm Hg	40 mm Hg
(d)	CO_2	O_2	45 mm Hg	40 mm Hg

26. Which of the following statement is incorrect about steps of respiration ?

(a) Inhalation of oxygen rich atmospheric air and exhalation of CO_2 rich alveolar air.

(b) Diffusion of gases takes place across a vascular pleural membrane.

(c) Transport of gases by blood and diffusion of O_2 and CO_2 between blood and tissues.

(d) Utilisation of O_2 by cells to obtain energy and release of CO_2.

27. Read the following statements about respiration.

I. Oxyhaemoglobin dissociates near tissues due to decrease in acidity and increase pH.

II. Venous blood normally carries 14.4 mL of oxygen.

III. The amount of oxygen available during exercise is about 15mL/100 mL of blood.

IV. Venous blood carries 52 mL of CO_2 per 100 mL of blood.

V. Arterial blood does not carry carbon dioxide.

Choose the correct answer from the options given below.

(a) II, III and V (b) I, III and V
(c) I and IV (d) III and IV

28. A chronic disorder, emphysema can show symptom like

(a) pain in chest
(b) shortness of breath
(c) blocked airways
(d) cough

29. Match List I with List II.

List I	List II
A. Asthma	1. Occupational respiratory disorder
B. Silicosis	2. Abnormal distension of alveolar sac
C. Emphysema	3. Regular cough
D. Bronchitis	4. Inflammation of bronchi and bronchioles

Choose the correct answer from the options given below.

	A	B	C	D		A	B	C	D
(a)	1	3	4	2	(b)	3	4	1	2
(c)	4	1	2	3	(d)	3	4	2	1

30. Given below are two statements.

Statement I Long exposure to asbestos can give rise to inflammation of lungs leading to fibrosis.

Statement II Silicosis can be treated specifically.

In the light of the above statements, choose the correct answer from the options given below.

(a) Statement I is incorrect, but statement II is correct

(b) Both statement I and statement II are correct

(c) Both statement I and statement II are incorrect

(d) Statement I is correct, but statement II is incorrect

31. Consider the following statements and identify which of the following turns diaphragm into dome shaped structure

I. Relaxation of diaphragm.

II. Decrease in volume of thoracic cavity.

III. Contraction of diaphragm.

IV. Increase in volume of thoracic cavity.

Choose the correct answer from the options given below.

(a) I and IV (b) I and II
(c) III and IV (d) Only IV

32. Select the incorrect statement regarding respiratory capacities.
(a) Additional volume of air expire after forceful expiration in normal healthy human is 1000-1100 mL
(b) Volume of air remaining in lungs after forceful expiration is 1100-1200 mL
(c) ERV + RV together forms vital capacity.
(d) Total lung capacity is reprsented by sum of vital capacity + residual volume

33. Given below are two statements; one is labelled as Assertion (A) and the other is labelled as Reason (R).

Assertion (A) An increase in arterial pCO_2 rather than a decrease in arterial pO_2 is observed during strenuous activities.

Reason (R) The central chemoreceptors in the medulla oblongata are primarily sensitive to changes in pCO_2 and pH rather than changes in pO_2.

In the light of the above statements, choose the correct answer from the options given below.
(a) A is false, but R is true.
(b) Both A and R are true and R is the correct explanation A.
(c) Both A and R are true, but R is not the correct explanation of A.
(d) A is true, but R is false.

34. Which of the following volumes cannot be measured using a spirometer?
(a) Tidal Volume (TV)
(b) Inspiratory Reserve Volume (IRV)
(c) Residual Volume (RV)
(d) Expiratory Reserve Volume (ERV)

35. Consider the given graph and identify the incorrect statement.

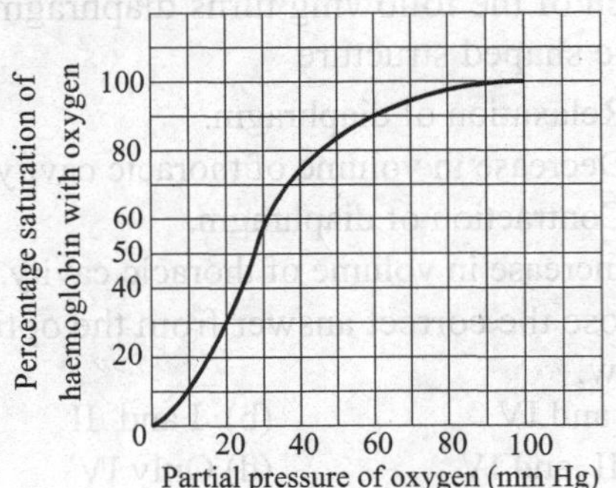

(a) The oxygen dissociation curve is sigmoidal in shape
(b) The curve shift towards right when partial pressure of CO_2 is high at tissue level
(c) The curve shift towards right when partial pressure of O_2 is high at tissue level
(d) Oxygen gets bound to haemoglobin at lung surface

36. Given below are two statements.

Statement I The Bohr effect describes the phenomenon where an increase in blood pCO_2 leads to a decrease in haemoglobin's oxygen affinity, facilitating oxygen release in tissues.

Statement II The Bohr effect is primarily caused by an increase in blood pH, which enhances haemoglobin's ability to bind oxygen.

In the light of the above statements, choose the correct answer from the options given below.
(a) Statement I is incorrect, but statement II is correct
(b) Both statement I and statement II are correct.
(c) Both statement I and statement II are incorrect
(d) Statement I is correct, but statement II is incorrect

37. Which of the following muscles are primarily responsible for increasing the volume of the thoracic cavity during inspiration?
(a) Internal intercostal muscles and abdominal muscles
(b) External intercostal muscles and diaphragm
(c) Diaphragm and internal oblique muscles
(d) External oblique muscles and abdominal muscle

38. Consider the following statements.
I. Tuberculosis (TB) primarily affects the upper lobes of the lungs and is caused by a bacterial infection with *Mycobacterium tuberculosis*.
II. Emphysema, a type of Chronic Obstructive Pulmonary Disease (COPD), primarily involves the destruction of alveolar walls and results in decreased lung elasticity.
III. Silicosis occurs due to excessive smoking.
IV. Asthma is characterised by chronic inflammation of the airways, leading to reversible airflow obstruction.

Choose the correct answer from the options given below.
(a) I, II and IV (b) I and II
(c) III and IV (d) Only IV

39. What is the primary function of the nasal cavity in the respiratory system?
(a) To humidify and filter air
(b) To exchange gases
(c) To produce sound
(d) To regulate airflow

40. Given below are two statements, one is labelled as Assertion (A) and the other is labelled as Reason (R).

Assertion (A) The oxygen-haemoglobin dissociation curve shifts to the left in response to increased body temperature.

Reason (R) A leftward shift in the oxygen-haemoglobin dissociation curve indicates increased haemoglobin affinity for oxygen, which facilitates oxygen release in the tissues.

In the light of the above statements, choose the correct answer from the options given below.
(a) A is false, but R is true.
(b) Both A and R are true and R is the correct explanation of A.
(c) Both A and R are true, but R is not the correct explanation of A.
(d) A is true, but R is false.

41. Which of the following accurately describes the Total Lung Capacity (TLC) and its components?
(a) TLC is the sum of tidal volume, inspiratory reserve volume, expiratory reserve volume, and residual volume.
(b) TLC is the sum of tidal volume and inspiratory reserve volume only.
(c) TLC is the difference between inspiratory capacity and expiratory reserve volume.
(d) TLC is the sum of vital capacity and residual volume, excluding tidal volume.

42. Consider the following statements.
I. Oxygen diffuses from the blood into the tissues where the partial pressure of oxygen is lower.
II. The diffusion of gases across the respiratory membrane is faster in areas with thicker membranes.
III. Carbon dioxide diffuses from the tissues into the blood where its partial pressure is low.
IV. The rate of diffusion of a CO_2 gas is 20-25 times greater than that of O_2 gas through a membrane.

Choose the correct answer from the options given below.
(a) I, III and IV (b) I and II
(c) III and IV (d) I only

43. Which of the following statements regarding the pleural membrane is/are correct?
I. The pleural cavity is the space between the parietal pleura and the visceral pleura that contains a small amount of serous fluid.
II. The parietal pleura adheres directly to the lung surface, while the visceral pleura lines the thoracic cavity.
III. During normal respiration, the pleural cavity pressure is always positive relative to atmospheric pressure to prevent lung collapse.
IV. The pleural fluid within the pleural cavity functions to reduce friction between the pleural layers during respiration.

Choose the correct answer from the options given below.
(a) II and III (b) I and II
(c) I and IV (d) Only IV

44. Given below are two statements.

Statement I The peripheral chemoreceptors are more sensitive to changes in arterial pO_2 than to pCO_2.

Statement II The central chemoreceptors in the medulla oblongata respond primarily to changes in arterial pCO_2 and pH.

In the light of the above statements, choose the correct answer from the options given below.
(a) Statement I is incorrect, but statement II is correct
(b) Both statement I and statement II are correct.
(c) Both statement I and statement II are incorrect.
(d) Statement I is correct, but statement II is incorrect.

45. Which of the following correctly describes the role of the diaphragm in breathing?
(a) The diaphragm relaxes and moves upward during inhalation.
(b) The diaphragm contracts and moves downward during inhalation.
(c) The diaphragm contracts and moves upward during exhalation.
(d) The diaphragm relaxes and moves downward during exhalation.

46. Given below are two statements; one is labelled as Assertion (A) and the other is labelled as Reason (R).

Assertion (A) Amphibians such as frog can respire through lungs as well as through moist skin.

Reason (R) Different groups of animals have different mechanism of breathing due to different habitats and level of organisation.

In the light of the above statements, choose the correct answer from the options given below.

(a) A is false, but R is true.
(b) Both A and R are true, and R is the correct explanation of A.
(c) Both A and R are true, but R is not the correct explanation of A.
(d) A is true, but R is false.

47. Arrange the following statements according to transportation of oxygen across blood.

I. Oxygen binds to haemoglobin in the pulmonary capillaries.
II. Oxygen diffuses from the alveoli into the pulmonary capillaries.
III. Oxygen is transported in the blood to systemic tissues.
IV. Oxygen dissociates from haemoglobin and diffuses into the tissues.
V. Oxygen-rich blood travels from the heart to the systemic circulation.

Choose the correct answer from the options given below.

(a) III → V → IV → I → II
(b) IV → I → III → II → V
(c) IV → III → V → I → II
(d) II → I → III → IV → V

48. Identify the incorrect match.

(a) Internal intercostal muscles - Muscles that aid in forced expiration
(b) External intercostal muscles - Muscles that aid in forced inspiration
(c) Epiglottis-Cartilaginous flap, covers glottis
(d) Diaphragm - Primary muscle involved in inspiration

49. Exchange of ions occur between RBCs and plasma at lung surface. Which of the following involves removal of CO_2 from blood?

(a) Efflux of bicarbonate ions from RBC
(b) Influx of chloride ions from RBC
(c) Influx of hydrogen ions from RBC
(d) Efflux of chloride ions from RBC

50. Given below are two statements.

Statement I Volume of air remaining in the lungs after forceful expiration is residual volume.

Statement II Total volume of air expired after normal expiration is expiratory capacity.

In the light of the above statements, choose the correct answer from the options given below.

(a) Statement I is incorrect, but Statement II is correct
(b) Both statement I and statement II are correct.
(c) Both statement I and statement II are incorrect
(d) Statement I is correct, but statement II is incorrect

Response Index

01 ⓐ ⓑ ⓒ ⓓ	14 ⓐ ⓑ ⓒ ⓓ	27 ⓐ ⓑ ⓒ ⓓ	40 ⓐ ⓑ ⓒ ⓓ
02 ⓐ ⓑ ⓒ ⓓ	15 ⓐ ⓑ ⓒ ⓓ	28 ⓐ ⓑ ⓒ ⓓ	41 ⓐ ⓑ ⓒ ⓓ
03 ⓐ ⓑ ⓒ ⓓ	16 ⓐ ⓑ ⓒ ⓓ	29 ⓐ ⓑ ⓒ ⓓ	42 ⓐ ⓑ ⓒ ⓓ
04 ⓐ ⓑ ⓒ ⓓ	17 ⓐ ⓑ ⓒ ⓓ	30 ⓐ ⓑ ⓒ ⓓ	43 ⓐ ⓑ ⓒ ⓓ
05 ⓐ ⓑ ⓒ ⓓ	18 ⓐ ⓑ ⓒ ⓓ	31 ⓐ ⓑ ⓒ ⓓ	44 ⓐ ⓑ ⓒ ⓓ
06 ⓐ ⓑ ⓒ ⓓ	19 ⓐ ⓑ ⓒ ⓓ	32 ⓐ ⓑ ⓒ ⓓ	45 ⓐ ⓑ ⓒ ⓓ
07 ⓐ ⓑ ⓒ ⓓ	20 ⓐ ⓑ ⓒ ⓓ	33 ⓐ ⓑ ⓒ ⓓ	46 ⓐ ⓑ ⓒ ⓓ
08 ⓐ ⓑ ⓒ ⓓ	21 ⓐ ⓑ ⓒ ⓓ	34 ⓐ ⓑ ⓒ ⓓ	47 ⓐ ⓑ ⓒ ⓓ
09 ⓐ ⓑ ⓒ ⓓ	22 ⓐ ⓑ ⓒ ⓓ	35 ⓐ ⓑ ⓒ ⓓ	48 ⓐ ⓑ ⓒ ⓓ
10 ⓐ ⓑ ⓒ ⓓ	23 ⓐ ⓑ ⓒ ⓓ	36 ⓐ ⓑ ⓒ ⓓ	49 ⓐ ⓑ ⓒ ⓓ
11 ⓐ ⓑ ⓒ ⓓ	24 ⓐ ⓑ ⓒ ⓓ	37 ⓐ ⓑ ⓒ ⓓ	50 ⓐ ⓑ ⓒ ⓓ
12 ⓐ ⓑ ⓒ ⓓ	25 ⓐ ⓑ ⓒ ⓓ	38 ⓐ ⓑ ⓒ ⓓ	
13 ⓐ ⓑ ⓒ ⓓ	26 ⓐ ⓑ ⓒ ⓓ	39 ⓐ ⓑ ⓒ ⓓ	

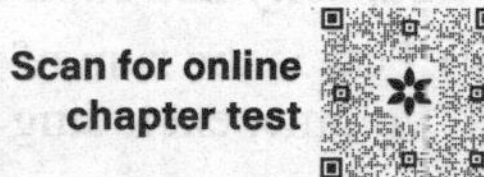

Performance Scanner

> 90% Excellent !	You have mastered this chapter. The concepts of this chapter are at your fingertips. Move on to the next chapter and maintain this momentum.
76-90% Very Good !	You have a good command over this chapter. Revise the chapter again after a few days and enhance your performance.
60-75% Good !	You have a wide scope to learn for this chapter. Revise this chapter again.
<60% Not Satisfactory!	You have a long way ahead of you to master this chapter. Revise it thoroughly.

MED+ACE
NEET (UG)
SELF ASSESSMENT KIT

Test Booklet No. 3947315

Test Booklet Code CH15

Body Fluids and Circulation

Topics Covered

Blood Grouping and Coagulation

Human Circulatory System

Important Instructions

- This Booklet Contains – Two Topic Tests and One Test on Complete Chapter.
- Each question carries 4 marks.
- For each correct response, the candidate will get 4 marks. And for every incorrect response, 1 mark will be additionally deducted from total score.
- Use **Blue/Black** point pen only for filling the OMR.
- Rough work is to be done in the space provided for this purpose in the test booklet only.

Name of the Candidate (In Capitals) ____________

Candidate's Signature ____________

Invigilator's Signature ____________

Facsimile signature stamp of center superintendent ____________

Do not open this booklet until you start attempting the test

Topical Follow Thru

Test 1

Syllabus
- Composition of Blood
- Blood Groups
- Coagulation of Blood
- Composition of Lymph and its Function

For deeper insight, **Scan the QR Code**

Important Instructions
- The test is of 30 minutes duration and contains 25 Multiple Choice Questions (four options with a single correct answer).
- Choose the correct option and fill the OMR given on the last page of this test accordingly.
- At some instances, you may find more than 1 option to be correct. In such circumstances, you have to judge the most appropriate answer as per the conditions given in the question.

1. A person with allergic reaction to peanuts, would show an increased percentage of which of the following leucocytes in blood?

(a) Neutrophils (b) Basophils
(c) Eosinophils (d) Monocytes

2. Given below are two statements; one is labelled as Assertion (A) and the other is labelled as Reason (R).

Assertion (A) A person with A^- blood cannot donate to a person with A^+ blood group.

Reason (R) Rh antigens stimulate the production of Rh antibodies in the blood.

In the light of the above statements, choose the correct answer from the options given below.

(a) A is false, but R is true
(b) Both A and R are true and R is the correct explanation of A
(c) Both A and R are true, but R is not the correct explanation of A
(d) A is true, but R is not true

3. Following are the statements about Rh blood group. Identify the set of correct statements.

I. Rh antibodies develop on the surface of RBCs in blood.
II. Rh^+ person can donate blood to Rh^- person only once.
III. Rh^+ mother can safely carry Rh^- child during pregnancy.
IV. Rh^+ mother is given anti-Rh antibody after first pregnancy.
V. Rh antibodies of the foetus react with Rh antigens of the mother.

Choose the most appropriate answer from the options given below.

(a) II and III only (b) I, II and III
(c) II, III and V (d) I, IV and V

4. Choose the incorrect statement about blood plasma from options given below.

(a) Trace amounts of minerals are present in blood plasma.
(b) A major component of blood plasma is just water.
(c) Coagulating factors are present in an active form in plasma.
(d) Albumins present in plasma maintain osmolarity of blood.

5. A person infected with dengue haemorrhagic fever has a high chance of internal bleeding, due to

(a) an increase in blood clotting factors
(b) a decrease in blood thrombocytes
(c) an increase in blood thrombocytes
(d) a decrease in blood clotting factors

6. Given below are two statements.

Statement I Bone marrow is regarded as the cemetery of RBCs.

Statement II Leucocytes live longer than erythrocytes of blood.

In the light of the above statements, choose the correct answer from the options given below.
(a) Statement I is incorrect, but statement II is correct
(b) Both statement I and statement II are correct
(c) Both statement I and statement II are incorrect
(d) Statement I is correct, but statement II is incorrect

7. Following are the stages involved in blood clotting.
A. Activation of prothrombin to thrombin.
B. Release of factors from injured site.
C. Conversion of fibrinogen to fibrin.
D. Formation of thrombokinase.
E. Formation of clot or coagulum.
Choose the correct sequence of blood clotting from the options given below.
(a) B-D-A-C-E (b) B-A-D-C-E
(c) B-A-C-D-E (d) B-D-C-A-E

8. Match List I with List II.

	List I		List II
A.	Neutrophils	1.	Phagocytosis
B.	Basophils	2.	2-3% of total WBC
C.	Eosinophils	3.	Heparin secretion
D.	Monocytes	4.	Most abundant WBC

Choose the correct answer from the options given below
(a) A-1, B-3, C-2, D-4
(b) A-1, B-2, C-4, D-3
(c) A-4, B-2, C-3, D-1
(d) A-4, B-3, C-2, D-1

9. Given below are two statements; one is labelled as Assertion (A) and the other is labelled as Reason (R).
Assertion (A) A person with calcium deficiency might develop clotting disorder.
Reason (R) Calcium ions are needed for the conversion of fibrin to fibrinogen.
In the light of the above statements, choose the correct answer from the options given below.
(a) A is false, but R is true
(b) Both A and R are true and R is the correct explanation of A
(c) Both A and R are true, but R is not the correct explanation of A
(d) A is true, but R is false

10. A person with B^- blood group can safely receive blood from which of the following blood groups?
(a) O^+ (b) AB^-
(c) O^- (d) B^+

11. Which of the following secretions of basophil is used in coating blood collecting vials, due to its anticoagulant property?
(a) Histamine
(b) Heparin
(c) Serotonin
(d) Immunoglobulin

12. Given below are two statements.
Statement I Exchange of gases between blood and cells occur through lymph.
Statement II Blood minus RBCs, platelets, certain proteins and salts is lymph.
In the light of the above statements, choose the correct answer from the options given below.
(a) Statement I is incorrect, but statement II is correct
(b) Both statement I and statement II are correct
(c) Both statement I and statement II are incorrect
(d) Statement I is correct, but statement II is incorrect

13. Under which of the following circumstances, an antigen-antibody reaction will not occur?
A person with
(a) type 'O' blood is given type 'A' blood
(b) type 'B' blood is given type 'AB' blood
(c) type 'A' blood is given type 'O' blood
(d) type 'A' blood is given type 'AB' blood

14. Which of the following is incorrect with respect to lymph?
(a) It is devoid of larger proteins found in plasma.
(b) It is brought back to circulation by veins.
(c) Basophils are abundant in lymphatic system.
(d) Absorption of fats occur *via* lymph in lacteals.

15. Read the following statements and select the correct ones.
I. Erythrocytes are nucleated and formed in the red bone marrow in the adult humans.
II. Lymphocytes are agranulocytes formed from megakaryocytes.
III. Blood platelets release thromboplastin.
IV. Blood group 'O' has no antibodies.
V. Serum cannot undergo clotting.
Choose the correct answer from the options given below.
(a) I and II (b) III, IV and V
(c) III and V (d) Only IV

16. Match List I with List II.

List I	List II
A. Clotting factors	1. Maintains osmolarity
B. Solutes	2. Inactive form in plasma
C. Fibrinogen	3. Involved in defence
D. Globulins	4. Soluble form

Choose the correct answer from the options given below.
(a) A-2, B-4, C-1, D-3
(b) A-3, B-4, C-1, D-2
(c) A-3, B-1, C-4, D-2
(d) A-2, B-1, C-4, D-3

17. A woman with 7 gms haemoglobin per 100 mL blood gets easily tired by daily routine work. This could be due to
(a) decreased amount of RBCs
(b) lesser oxygen reaching tissues
(c) abnormally high WBC count
(d) increase in the number of platelets

18. Given below are two statements; one is labelled as Assertion (A) and the other is labelled as Reason (R).
Assertion (A) Ant bites often cause swelling and itching of the skin.
Reason (R) Histamines released by eosinophils are associated with inflammation.
In the light of the above statements, choose the correct answer from the options given below.
(a) A is false, but R is true.
(b) Both A and R are true and R is the correct explanation of A.
(c) Both A and R are true, but R is not the correct explanation of A.
(d) A is true, but R is false.

19. A person infected with a deadly virus can be treated by injecting which of the following fluids from the body of a person who has recently recovered from the same disease?
(a) Serum (b) Plasma
(c) Lymph (d) Interstitial fluid

20. Which of the following statement is incorrect about blood plasma?
(a) Antibodies are lacking in serum.
(b) Plasma and serum both contains hormones.
(c) Serum on standing would not clot.
(d) Fibrinogens are absent in serum.

21. Match List I with List II.

List I	List II
A. A^-	1. Anti A, anti B
B. AB^+	2. Antigen A, anti B
C. O^-	3. Antigen A, antigen B, Rh antigen
D. O^+	4. Anti A, anti B, Rh antigen

Choose the correct answer from the options given below
(a) A-2, B-3, C-1, D-4
(b) A-2, B-3, C-4, D-1
(c) A-3, B-2, C-4, D-1
(d) A-3, B-2, C-1, D-4

22. The condition of erythroblastosis foetalis cannot be avoided when

(a) Rh^+ mother is pregnant with Rh^+ child for the first time.

(b) Rh^- mother is pregnant with Rh^+ child for the first time.

(c) Rh^+ mother is pregnant with Rh^- child for second time.

(d) Rh^- mother is pregnant with Rh^+ child for second time.

23. Given below are two statements.

Statement I Plasma plays a vital role in initiating coagulation.

Statement II Platelet transfusion is often required to treat clotting disorders.

In the light of the above statements, choose the correct answer from the options given below.

(a) Statement I is incorrect, but statement II is correct

(b) Both statement I and statement II are correct

(c) Both statement I and statement II are incorrect

(d) Statement I is correct, but statement II is incorrect

24. Following are the steps involved in blood coagulation.

I. Formation of thromboplastin
II. Release of platelet factors
III. Activation of thrombin
IV. Formation of fibrin threads

Which of the following steps are directly dependent on calcium ions?

(a) I and III (b) I, III and IV
(c) III and IV (d) IV only

25. What would be the effect, if interstitial fluid is not drained by the lymphatic system?

(a) Immunity would be compromised

(b) Rise in the osmotic pressure of blood.

(c) Inflammation of the tissue

(d) Fat malabsorption

Response Index

01	a	b	c	d	10	a	b	c	d	19	a	b	c	d
02	a	b	c	d	11	a	b	c	d	20	a	b	c	d
03	a	b	c	d	12	a	b	c	d	21	a	b	c	d
04	a	b	c	d	13	a	b	c	d	22	a	b	c	d
05	a	b	c	d	14	a	b	c	d	23	a	b	c	d
06	a	b	c	d	15	a	b	c	d	24	a	b	c	d
07	a	b	c	d	16	a	b	c	d	25	a	b	c	d
08	a	b	c	d	17	a	b	c	d					
09	a	b	c	d	18	a	b	c	d					

Performance Scanner

> 90% Excellent !	You have mastered these topics. The concepts of these topics are at your fingertips. Move on to the next test and maintain this momentum.
76-90% Very Good !	You have a good command over these topics. Revise these topics again after a few days and enhance your performance.
60-75% Good !	You have a wide scope to learn for these topics. Revise these topics again.
<60% Not Satisfactory!	You have a long way ahead of you to master these topics. Revise it thoroughly.

Test 2

Syllabus

- Human Circulatory System- Structure of Human Heart and Blood Vessel
- Cardiac Cycle
- Cardiac Output
- Electrocardiography (ECG)
- Double Circulation
- Regulation of Cardiac Activity
- Disorders of Circulatory System- Hypertension, Coronary Artery Disease, Angina Pectoris, Heart Failure

For deeper insight, **Scan the QR Code**

Important Instructions

- The test is of 30 minutes duration and contains 25 Multiple Choice Questions (four options with a single correct answer).
- Choose the correct option and fill the OMR given on the last page of this test accordingly.
- At some instances, you may find more than 1 option to be correct. In such circumstances, you have to judge the most appropriate answer as per the conditions given in the question.

1. Which layer of an artery makes a direct contact with blood?

(a) Tunica adventitia (b) Tunica intima
(c) Tunica externa (d) Tunica media

2. Given below are two statements; one is labelled as Assertion (A) and the other is labelled as Reason (R).

Assertion (A) A person with less than 45 beats/minute requires a pacemaker implantation.
Reason (R) SAN is located in the right upper region of the right atrium of the heart.
In the light of the above statements, choose the correct answer from the options given below.

(a) A is false, but R is true.
(b) Both A and R are true and R is the correct explanation of A.
(c) Both A and R are true, but R is not the correct explanation of A.
(d) A is true, but R is false.

3. The following diagram represents the circulation of blood between body and heart.

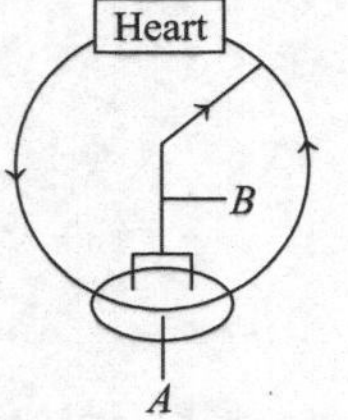

Choose the correct statement with regards to the structures labelled as *A* and *B* from the given options.

(a) *A* collects tissue fluid from the interstitial spaces
(b) *B* is formed by union of arteries and veins
(c) *A* drains blood int the veins
(d) *B* drains blood into the arteries

4. The following are the statements about blood circulation in frogs.

I. Oxygenation of blood occurs in the lungs and skin.
II. Left and right atrium receives oxygenated blood.
III. A single ventricle pumps out mixed blood.
IV. Circulation of frogs is more efficient than birds.
V. Double circulation in frogs is incomplete.

Choose the set of correct statements from the options given below.

(a) II and III (b) I, III and V
(c) II, III and V (d) I, IV and V

5. Given below are two statements.

Statement I Damage to the interventricular septum can lower oxygen levels in blood cells.
Statement II Partition between the right and left ventricles prevents mixing of blood.
In the light of the above statements, choose the correct answer from the options given below.

(a) Statement I is incorrect, but statement II is correct.
(b) Both statement I and statement II are correct
(c) Both statement I and statement II are incorrect
(d) Statement I is correct, but statement II is incorrect

6. Match List I with List II.

List I		List II	
A.	Earthworm	1.	Body cavities or sinuses
B.	Snail	2.	Closed network of blood vessels
C.	Crocodile	3.	Four-chambered heart
D.	Frog	4.	Three-chambered heart

Choose the correct answer from the options given below.

(a) A-1, B-3, C-2, D-4
(b) A-1, B-2, C-3, D-4
(c) A-2, B-1, C-3, D-4
(d) A-2, B-1, C-4, D-3

7. Which of the following are the strongest blood vessels with thicker and muscular walls?

(a) Carotid arteries (b) Vena cava
(c) Coronary vein (d) Hepatic portal vein

8. Following are the components of the impulse conducting system of the heart.

A. Purkinje fibres B. Sino atrial node
C. AV node D. AV bundle
E. Bundle of His

Choose the correct sequence of impulse conduction through the heart.

(a) B-C-D-E-A (b) B-D-C-E-A
(c) B-D-C-A-E (d) B-C-D-A-E

9. By what percentage the heart rate of a person increases during exercise, if the cardiac output increases to 5880 mL and each ventricle pump out 70 mL of blood, while the resting heart rate is 70 beats/minute?

(a) 25% (b) 20 %
(c) 50% (d) 0%

10. Given below are two statements.

Statement I Systolic pressure is the force inside the arteries when the heart contracts and pumps blood through the body.

Statement II The diastolic blood pressure is measured when the heart is at rest, i.e. in between the heartbeats.

In the light of the above statements, choose the correct answer from the options given below.

(a) Statement I is incorrect, but statement II is correct
(b) Both statement I and statement II are correct
(c) Both statement I and statement II are incorrect
(d) Statement I is correct, but statement II is incorrect

11. Which of the following does not carry deoxygenated blood?

(a) Pulmonary artery (b) Superior vena cava
(c) Inferior vena cava (d) Aortic arch

12. The following diagram represents the flow of blood through important organs. Identify the blood vessel that connects intestine to structure *P*.

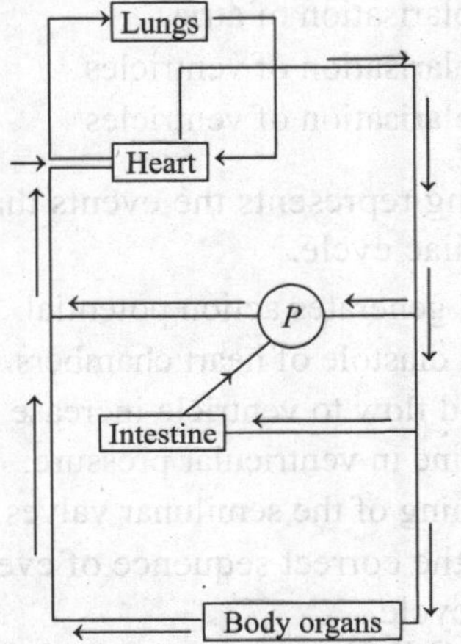

(a) Hepatic artery (b) Mesenteric artery
(c) Mesenteric vein (d) Hepatic portal vein

13. The following diagram represents double circulation in humans.

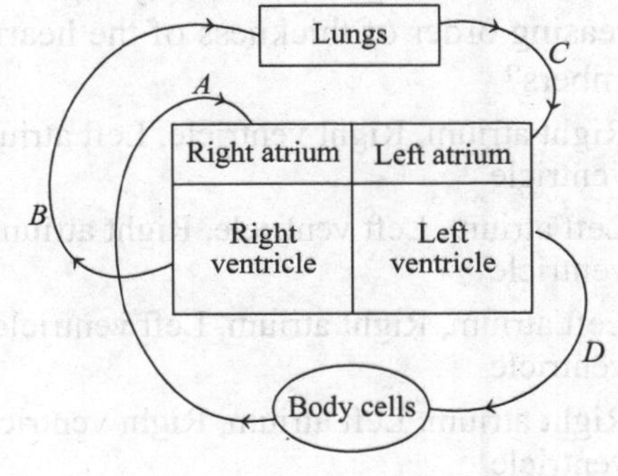

Which of the following blood vessels carry oxygenated blood?
(a) A and C (b) C and D
(c) B and C (d) A and D

14. Which of the following will not occur during ventricular systole?
(a) Opening of the semilunar valves
(b) Closure of atrio-ventricular valves
(c) Generation of heart sound 'dub'
(d) Increase in ventricular pressure

15. ECG depicts the depolarisation and repolarisation processes during the cardiac cycle. In the ECG of a normal healthy individual, which one of the following waves is not represented?
(a) Depolarisation of atria
(b) Repolarisation of atria
(c) Depolarisation of ventricles
(d) Repolarisation of ventricles

16. Following represents the events that occur during one cardiac cycle.
A. SAN generates action potential.
B. Joint diastole of heart chambers.
C. Blood flow to ventricle increase by 30%.
D. Decline in ventricular pressure.
E. Opening of the semilunar valves.
Choose the correct sequence of events during each cardiac cycle.
(a) B-A-C-D-E
(b) B-A-C-E-D
(c) A-B-C-E-D
(d) A-B-D-E-C

17. Which of the following correctly represents the increasing order of thickness of the heart chambers?
(a) Right atrium, Right ventricle, Left atrium, Left ventricle
(b) Left atrium, Left ventricle, Right atrium, Right ventricle
(c) Left atrium, Right atrium, Left ventricle, Right ventricle
(d) Right atrium, Left atrium, Right ventricle, Left ventricle

18. The following are the statements about the ECG of a normal person.
I. An abnormal P-wave could indicate problems in the SAN.
II. Contraction of the ventricles start shortly after R wave of QRS.
III. Counting the number of P waves can give the heart rate.
IV. T-wave represents the repolarisation of the ventricles.
V. At the end of T-wave, the contraction of the heart ends.
Choose the correct set of statements from the options given below.
(a) II and III (b) I, III and V
(c) II, III and V (d) I, IV and V

19. Which of the following part of heart is responsible for the higher efficiency of blood circulation observed in warm blooded organisms like mammals?
(a) Chordae tendinae
(b) Semilunar valves
(c) Septa
(d) Atrioventricular valves

20. A person suddenly attacked by a group of street dogs, experiences an elevated heart rate due to
(a) stimulation of adrenal medullary hormones and sympathetic branch of ANS
(b) stimulation of adrenal cortical hormones and sympathetic branch of ANS
(c) stimulation of adrenal cortical hormone and parasympathetic branch of ANS
(d) stimulation of adrenal medullary hormone and parasympathetic branch of ANS

21. Match List I with List II.

List I	List II
A. Bundle of His	1. Located close to AV septum
B. AV node	2. Divides into right and left bundles
C. Purkinje fibres	3. Ventricular contraction
D. SAN	4. Initiation of action potential

Choose the correct answer from the options given below.
(a) A-1, B-3, C-2, D-4
(b) A-1, B-2, C-3, D-4
(c) A-2, B-1, C-4, D-3
(d) A-2, B-1, C-3, D-4

22. A person with an injury in the medulla of his brain shows abnormality in all of the following, except
(a) strength of ventricular contraction
(b) Initiation of action potential
(c) Volume of blood pumped by ventricles/minute
(d) Speed of conduction of action potential

23. Which of the following is not correct about a person with acute chest pain radiating to his shoulders and jaw?
(a) Narrowed lumen of the arteries
(b) Deposition of calcium in the arteries
(c) Has regular oil and fat rich diet
(d) Heart suddenly stopped beating

24. Given below are two statements; one is labelled as Assertion (A) and the other is labelled as Reason (R).

Assertion (A) A person with hypertension may be prescribed with medications for kidney damage as well .

Reason (R) A persistent systolic pressure of 140 mm of Hg and diastolic pressure above 90 mm of Hg confirms hypertension.

In the light of the above statements, choose the correct answer from the options given below.
(a) A is false, but R is true
(b) Both A and R are true and R is the correct explanation of A
(c) Both A and R are true, but R is not the correct explanation of A
(d) A is true, but R is false

25. Which of the following statement is not correct about atherosclerosis?
(a) It occurs when enough blood does not reach the heart
(b) It primarily affects the blood vessels that supply blood to the heart
(c) The arteries get hardened because of the deposition of plaque
(d) Plaque is generally made up of fat cholesterol, calcium, etc.

Response Index

01	a b c d		10	a b c d		19	a b c d
02	a b c d		11	a b c d		20	a b c d
03	a b c d		12	a b c d		21	a b c d
04	a b c d		13	a b c d		22	a b c d
05	a b c d		14	a b c d		23	a b c d
06	a b c d		15	a b c d		24	a b c d
07	a b c d		16	a b c d		25	a b c d
08	a b c d		17	a b c d			
09	a b c d		18	a b c d			

Performance Scanner

> 90% Excellent !	You have mastered these topics. The concepts of these topics are at your fingertips. Move on to the next test and maintain this momentum.
76-90% Very Good !	You have a good command over these topics. Revise these topics again after a few days and enhance your performance.
60-75% Good !	You have a wide scope to learn for these topics. Revise these topics again.
<60% Not Satisfactory!	You have a long way ahead of you to master these topics. Revise it thoroughly.

Chapter Break Thru

Syllabus

- Composition of Blood
- Blood Groups
- Coagulation of Blood
- Composition of Lymph and its Function
- Human Circulatory System-Structure of Human Heart and Blood Vessels
- Cardiac Cycle
- Electrocardiography (ECG)
- Double Circulation
- Regulation of Cardiac Activity
- Disorders of Circulatory System-Hypertension, Coronary Artery Disease, Angina Pectoris, Heart Failure

Important Instructions

- The test is of 1 hour duration and contains 50 Multiple-Choice Questions (Four options with a single correct answer).
- Choose the correct option and fill the OMR given on the last page of this test accordingly.
- At some instances, you may find more than 1 option to be correct. In such circumstances, you have to judge the most appropriate answer as per the conditions given in the question.

1. Which of the following are the precursors of platelets?
(a) Leucocytes
(b) Thrombocytes
(c) Megakaryocytes
(d) Erythrocytes

2. Given below are two statements; one is labelled as Assertion (A) and the other is labelled as Reason (R).
Assertion (A) Individuals with O positive blood group can donate blood to any one without compatibility test.
Reason (R) Individuals with O positive blood group do not contain any blood group antigens on their RBCs.
In the light of the above statements, choose the correct answer from the options given below.
(a) A is false, but R is true
(b) Both A and R are true and R is the correct explanation of A
(c) Both A and R are true, but R is not the correct explanation of A
(d) A is true, but R is false

3. Following are few components of the blood.
A. Haemoglobin
B. Minerals and proteins
C. Glucose
D. Clotting factors
E. Water
Choose the components that make up the serum .
(a) A, B and C
(b) B, C and E
(c) B, C and D
(d) A, C and E

4. A person suffering from an inflammatory reaction shows elevated levels of a particular WBCs. Which of the following is not a property of such WBCs?
(a) They are the least abundant leukocytes in blood
(b) They have a lifespan comparable to RBCs
(c) They have many granules in their cytoplasm
(d) They secrete histamine, serotonin, heparin, etc.

5. Which of the valves are involved in regulating flow of only oxygenated blood?
(a) Tricuspid and bicuspid valves
(b) Tricuspid and aortic semilunar valve
(c) Bicuspid and pulmonary semilunar valve
(d) Bicuspid and aortic semilunar valve

6. The diagram given below represents the circulation of blood in a certain organism.

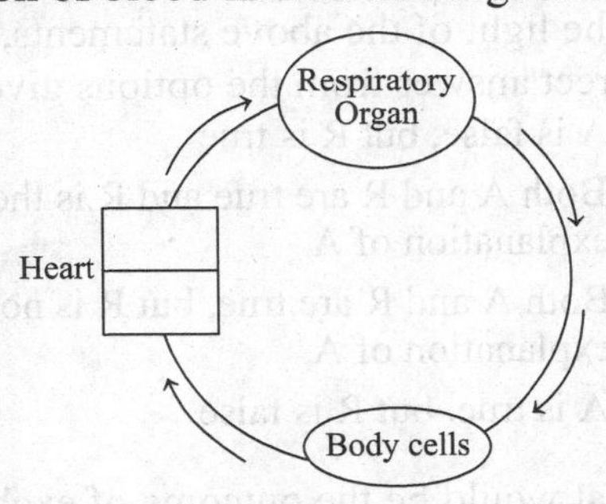

Which of the following correctly represents the type of circulation as shown in the image?
(a) Mixed double circuit
(b) Incomplete double circuit
(c) Single circuit
(d) Complete double circuit

7. Given below are two statements.
Statement I A fall in ventricular pressure forces open the semilunar valves.
Statement II SAN should initiate a new action potential for every cardiac cycle to begin.
In the light of the above statements, choose the correct answer from the options given below.
(a) Statement I is incorrect, but statement II is correct
(b) Both statement I and statement II are correct
(c) Both statement I and statement II are incorrect
(d) Statement I is correct, but statement II is incorrect

8. Inability of the AV valves to open at the end of ventricular diastole, would cause all of the following except
(a) blood cannot drain into ventricles
(b) SAN cannot generate action potential
(c) stroke volume would be altered
(d) cardiac output will be affected

9. Consider the following statements.
A. The S-wave of QRS complex is small negative wave.
B. The P-wave represents the end of cardiac cycle.
C. T-wave represents the excited state of atria.
D. QRS represents ventricular repolarisation.

Choose the correct answer from the options given below.
(a) B only
(b) A only
(c) C only
(d) D only

10. Which of the following cannot cause an increase in cardiac output?
(a) Sympathetic nerves of ANS
(b) Exhausting physical exercise
(c) Hormones of adrenal medulla
(d) Parasympathetic nerves of ANS

11. The diagram below represents the conducting pathway of the heart. Which of the following increases the blood flow to the ventricles by 30%?

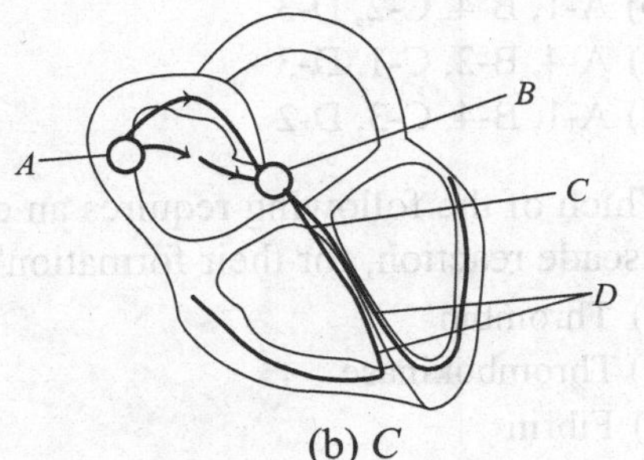

(a) *D*
(b) *C*
(c) *B*
(d) *A*

12. Which of the following is not a constituent of a coagulum or clot?
(a) Fibrinogen
(b) Thrombocytes
(c) Fibrins
(d) Erythrocytes

13. Given below are two statements.
Statement I Lymph has the same protein and mineral constituents like the plasma.
Statement II Lymphatic fluid runs separately without mixing with the main circulation.
In the light of the above statements, choose the correct answer from the options given below.
(a) Statement I is incorrect, but statement II is correct
(b) Both statement I and statement II are correct
(c) Both statement I and statement II are incorrect
(d) Statement I is correct, but statement II is incorrect

14. Match List I with List II.

List I	List II
A. B^-	1. Can receive from all Rh^- blood groups
B. AB^-	2. Can receive blood from Rh^+ once
C. Rh^-	3. Can donate to all blood types
D. O^-	4. Can receive blood from B^- and O^-

Choose the correct answer from the options given below.
(a) A-4, B-1, C-2, D-3
(b) A-1, B-4, C-2, D-3
(c) A-4, B-2, C-1, D-3
(d) A-1, B-4, C-3, D-2

15. Which of the following requires an enzyme cascade reaction, for their formation?
(a) Thrombin
(b) Thrombokinase
(c) Fibrin
(d) Prothrombin

16. Which of the following is incorrect with respect to circulation in insects?
(a) Blood pumped by heart flows through lacunae
(b) Blood is directly pumped into body sinuses
(c) Flow of blood can be regulated precisely
(d) Blood transports nutrients and gases in the body

17. The heart rate of a person increases by 20 % and the cardiac output becomes 6000 mL during physical exercise. Considering the resting heart beat to be 70 beats/minute, what will be the strokes volume during exercise?
(a) 70 mL (b) 71 mL
(c) 80 mL (d) 81 mL

18. Given below are two statements; one is labelled as Assertion (A) and the other is labelled as Reason (R).
Assertion (A) It is advisable to avoid regular junk food particularly for middle aged people.
Reason (R) Calcium deposits can cause atherosclerosis, increasing chances of heart attack.
In the light of the above statements, choose the correct answer from the options given below.
(a) A is false, but R is true
(b) Both A and R are true and R is the correct explanation of A
(c) Both A and R are true, but R is not the correct explanation of A
(d) A is true, but R is false

19. What would be the outcome of exchanging the walls of right and left ventricles?
(a) Blood would flow with lots of jerks in the pulmonary artery.
(b) The walls of the right ventricle would collapse and rupture.
(c) The walls of the left ventricle would be susceptible to damage.
(d) Blood flow through aorta will be under less pressure.

20. If human blood is centrifuged, which of the following components would be present in the top most separated layer?
A. RBCs
B. Mineral salts
C. Clotting factors
D. Amino acids
E. WBCs
Choose the correct answer from the options given below.
(a) B and C (b) A, C and D
(c) B, D and E (d) B, C and D

21. Which one of the following statement is correct with respect to the principle of safe blood transfusion?
(a) The donor's red blood corpuscles should not contain antibodies against the recipient's serum.
(b) The recipient's serum should not contain antigens against the donor's antibodies.
(c) The recipient's serum should not contain the antibodies against the red blood corpuscles of the donor.
(d) The recipient's red blood corpuscles should not contain antibodies against the donor's antigen.

22. Which of the following is wrongly represented in the blood profile of a person who took antibiotics against bacterial infections, only to develop allergies against the antibiotics?
(a) Neutrophil - 75%
(b) Monocytes- 12%
(c) Eosinophil - 2%
(d) Lymphocytes- 30%

23. The following are the statements about blood circulation in mammals.
I. Blood passes through the heart twice in warm blooded animals.
II. The pulmonary circuit deals only with oxygenated blood.
III. Blood flow into the pulmonary artery is not valve-regulated.
IV. Pulmonary veins carry oxygenated blood towards the heart.
V. Systemic circuit allows gas exchange between body and cells.
Choose the correct statements from the options given below
(a) II and III (b) I, III and V
(c) II, III and V (d) I, IV and V

24. In the diagram given below, choose the combination that represents the largest artery and vein, respectively.

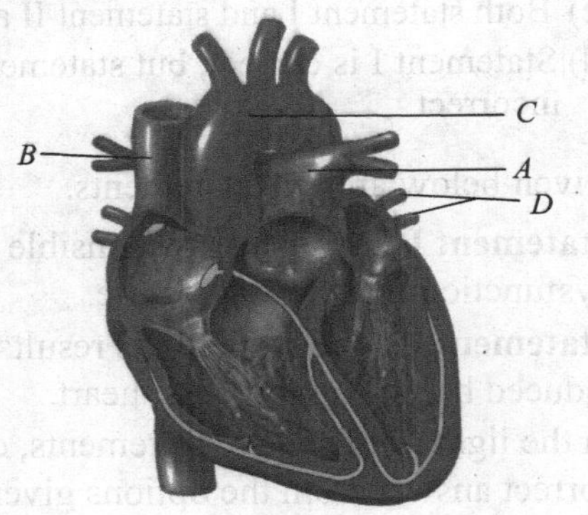

(a) *A* and *D* (b) *B* and *C*
(c) *C* and *B* (d) *D* and *A*

25. Following are the events of systemic circulation of the double circuit.
A. Left ventricle contracts
B. Blood flows through arteries
C. Blood collected by veins
D. Gas exchange at capillaries
E. Blood drained by vena cava
Choose the correct sequence of events during the systemic circulation of blood.
(a) A-B-D-C-E (b) A-C-D-B-E
(c) A-E-D-C-B (d) A-D-B-C-E

26. A person with lung congestion and no other respiratory symptoms could be experiencing
(a) atherosclerosis (b) heart failure
(c) cardiac arrest (d) heart attack

27. Given below are two statements; one is labelled as Assertion (A) and the other is labelled as Reason (R).
Assertion (A) In contrast to veins, blood flow through the arteries occurs with jerks.
Reason (R) Veins are provided with valves and have a thinner tunica media.
In the light of the above statements, choose the correct answer from the options given below.
(a) A is false, but R is true
(b) Both A and R are true and R is the correct explanation of A
(c) Both A and R are true, but R is not the correct explanation of A
(d) A is true, but R is false

28. In which of the following way can parasympathetic branch of the autonomic nervous system reduce the heart rate of a person?
(a) Delay the initiation of action potential
(b) Delay the conduction of action potential
(c) Increase the blood volume pumped by ventricles
(d) Increase the blood volume drained by vena cava

29. All of the following represents positive wave of an ECG, except
(a) P-wave (b) R-wave
(c) Q-wave (d) T-wave

30. Which of the following represents the electrically silent phase between two cardiac cycles?
(a) T-P segment
(b) P-P segment
(c) S-T segment
(d) T-T segment

31. Maximum amount of oxygen is lost from blood in
(a) arteries
(b) capillaries surrounding the alveoli
(c) left auricle of heart
(d) capillaries surrounding the tissue

32. Match List I with List II.

List I		List II	
A.	B-lymphocytes	1.	Most abundant immune cell
B.	Platelets	2.	Immunity
C.	RBCs	3.	Cell fragments
D.	Neutrophil	4.	Most abundant in blood

Choose the correct answer from the options given below.
(a) A-2, B-3, C- 1, D-4
(b) A-2, B-3, C- 4, D-1
(c) A-1, B-3, C-4, D-2
(d) A-1, B-3, C-2, D-4

33. A mother is administered with anti-Rh antibodies in her second pregnancy, since she bears the risk of losing her child due to
(a) hepatitis and leukemia
(b) hemorrhage and kidney failure
(c) jaundice and anaemia
(d) blood clot and atherosclerosis

34. Which of the following granulocytes are involved in the inactivation of antigen-antibody complexes and inflammatory substances?
(a) Neutrophils
(b) Monocytes
(c) Eosinophils
(d) Lymphocytes

35. Which of the following would not be found in the site of an ant bite on a person's hand?
(a) Histamine
(b) Fibrin
(c) Heparin
(d) Basophil

36. Given below are two statements; one is labelled as Assertion (A) and the other is labelled as Reason (R).

Assertion (A) Progressive viral infections are often treated by plasma of people recovered from such infections.

Reason (R) Plasma is the liquid portion of the blood without formed elements and contain several factors.

In the light of the above statements, choose the correct answer from the options given below.
(a) A is false, but R is true
(b) Both A and R are true and R is the correct explanation of A
(c) Both A and R are true, but R is not the correct explanation of A
(d) A is true, but R is false

37. Given below are two statements.

Statement I A person with B^- blood group cannot donate blood to B^+ individual.

Statement II Blood transfusion requires matching of Rh factors as well.

In the light of the above statements, choose the correct answer from the options given below.
(a) Statement I is incorrect, but statement II is correct
(b) Both statement I and statement II are correct
(c) Both statement I and statement II are incorrect
(d) Statement I is correct, but statement II is incorrect

38. Given below are two statements.

Statement I The factors responsible for CAD is dysfunctioning of left ventricle.

Statement II Angina pectoris results from reduced blood supply to the heart.

In the light of the above statements, choose the correct answer from the options given below.
(a) Statement I is incorrect, but statement II is correct
(b) Both statement I and statement II are correct
(c) Both statement I and statement II are incorrect
(d) Statement I is correct, but statement II is incorrect

39. Given below are two statements.

Statement I Contraction of the arteries is facilitated by the tunica intima layer.

Statement II Squamous endothelium resists the force of blood in the arteries.

In the light of the above statements, choose the correct answer from the options given below.

(a) Statement I is incorrect, but statement II is correct
(b) Both statement I and statement II are correct
(c) Both statement I and statement II are incorrect
(d) Statement I is correct, but statement II is incorrect

40. The pressure with which we feel the artery hitting our finger when we measure pulse is

(a) the sum of systolic blood pressure and diastolic blood pressure
(b) the product of systolic blood pressure and diastolic blood pressure
(c) the difference in systolic blood pressure and diastolic blood pressure
(d) the mean of systolic blood pressure and diastolic blood pressure

41. Match List I with List II.

List I	List II
A. Albumin	1. Clotting factor
B. Adrenaline	2. Cardiac output
C. Calcium	3. Osmoregulation
D. Globulin	4. Defence

Choose the correct answer from the options given below.

(a) A-3, B-2, C-1, D-4
(b) A-4, B-2, C-1, D-3
(c) A-4, B-2, C-3, D-4
(d) A-3, B-2, C-4, D-1

42. Match List I with List II.

List I	List II
A. P-wave	1. End of excitation of Purkinje fibres
B. QRS complex	2. Action potential at SA node
C. T-wave	3. One complete pulse
D. P-R interval	4. Time delay in AV node

Choose the correct answer from the options given below.

	A	B	C	D
(a)	1	4	2	3
(b)	2	3	1	4
(c)	1	2	4	3
(d)	2	4	1	3

43. If the number of QRS complexes appear to be 2100 in half an hour time interval in an ECG, then what will be the heart rate of that person?

(a) 72-80 beats/minute
(b) 70 beats/minute
(c) 80 beats/minute
(d) 75 beats/minute

44. Consider the following statements.

I. Drying of the pericardial fluid can damage heart membranes.
II. Absence of septum can cause back flow of blood.
III. Ventricles have a thicker wall than the atria.
IV. Mixing of blood is prevented by valves.
V. SAN generates 70-75 impulses per minute.

Choose the correct set of statements from the options given below.

(a) I, II and IV
(b) I, II and V
(c) I, III and V
(d) II and V

45. Which of the following is incorrect about circulation in reptiles?

(a) Most reptiles have a three-chambered heart.
(b) Efficiency of oxygen delivery to cells is poor.
(c) Atria pumps mixed blood to ventricles.
(d) Right atrium receives deoxygenated blood.

46. Given below are two statements.

Statement I A wound or injury can stimulate the release of platelet factors.

Statement II A mutated gene for thrombokinase can cause a person to bleed out.

In the light of the above statements, choose the correct answer from the options given below.

(a) Statement I is incorrect, but statement II is correct
(b) Both statement I and statement II are correct
(c) Both statement I and statement II are incorrect
(d) Statement I is correct, but statement II is incorrect

47. Given below are two statements; one is labelled as Assertion (A) and the other is labelled as Reason (R).

Assertion (A) Often lymph nodes in armpits are swollen in case of infections.

Reason (R) Neutrophils can phagocytose foreign pathogens in case of infections.

In the light of the above statements, choose the correct answer from the options given below.

(a) A is false, but R is true
(b) Both A and R are true and R is the correct explanation of A
(c) Both A and R are true, but R is not the correct explanation of A
(d) A is true, but R is false

48. Which of the following does not make up the walls of a vein?

(a) Endothelium (b) Stratified epithelium
(c) Elastic fibres (d) Collagen fibres

49. Which of the following is not correct about the sound 'lub' produced by the heart?

(a) Doctors use them to check heart conditions
(b) It is produced during ventricular systole
(c) A fall in ventricular pressure produces them
(d) Closure of the AV valves create the high pitch

50. Given below are two statements.

Statement I Fear is often triggered by the parasympathetic branch of the ANS.

Statement II Return of the body to normal state from excited one occurs *via* ANS.

In the light of the above statements, choose the correct answer from the options given below.

(a) Statement I is incorrect, but statement II is correct
(b) Both statement I and statement II are correct
(c) Both statement I and statement II are incorrect
(d) Statement I is correct, but statement II is incorrect

Response Index

01 ⓐ ⓑ ⓒ ⓓ	14 ⓐ ⓑ ⓒ ⓓ	27 ⓐ ⓑ ⓒ ⓓ	40 ⓐ ⓑ ⓒ ⓓ
02 ⓐ ⓑ ⓒ ⓓ	15 ⓐ ⓑ ⓒ ⓓ	28 ⓐ ⓑ ⓒ ⓓ	41 ⓐ ⓑ ⓒ ⓓ
03 ⓐ ⓑ ⓒ ⓓ	16 ⓐ ⓑ ⓒ ⓓ	29 ⓐ ⓑ ⓒ ⓓ	42 ⓐ ⓑ ⓒ ⓓ
04 ⓐ ⓑ ⓒ ⓓ	17 ⓐ ⓑ ⓒ ⓓ	30 ⓐ ⓑ ⓒ ⓓ	43 ⓐ ⓑ ⓒ ⓓ
05 ⓐ ⓑ ⓒ ⓓ	18 ⓐ ⓑ ⓒ ⓓ	31 ⓐ ⓑ ⓒ ⓓ	44 ⓐ ⓑ ⓒ ⓓ
06 ⓐ ⓑ ⓒ ⓓ	19 ⓐ ⓑ ⓒ ⓓ	32 ⓐ ⓑ ⓒ ⓓ	45 ⓐ ⓑ ⓒ ⓓ
07 ⓐ ⓑ ⓒ ⓓ	20 ⓐ ⓑ ⓒ ⓓ	33 ⓐ ⓑ ⓒ ⓓ	46 ⓐ ⓑ ⓒ ⓓ
08 ⓐ ⓑ ⓒ ⓓ	21 ⓐ ⓑ ⓒ ⓓ	34 ⓐ ⓑ ⓒ ⓓ	47 ⓐ ⓑ ⓒ ⓓ
09 ⓐ ⓑ ⓒ ⓓ	22 ⓐ ⓑ ⓒ ⓓ	35 ⓐ ⓑ ⓒ ⓓ	48 ⓐ ⓑ ⓒ ⓓ
10 ⓐ ⓑ ⓒ ⓓ	23 ⓐ ⓑ ⓒ ⓓ	36 ⓐ ⓑ ⓒ ⓓ	49 ⓐ ⓑ ⓒ ⓓ
11 ⓐ ⓑ ⓒ ⓓ	24 ⓐ ⓑ ⓒ ⓓ	37 ⓐ ⓑ ⓒ ⓓ	50 ⓐ ⓑ ⓒ ⓓ
12 ⓐ ⓑ ⓒ ⓓ	25 ⓐ ⓑ ⓒ ⓓ	38 ⓐ ⓑ ⓒ ⓓ	
13 ⓐ ⓑ ⓒ ⓓ	26 ⓐ ⓑ ⓒ ⓓ	39 ⓐ ⓑ ⓒ ⓓ	

Performance Scanner

Scan for online chapter test

> 90% Excellent !	You have mastered this chapter. The concepts of this chapter are at your fingertips. Move on to the next chapter and maintain this momentum.
76-90% Very Good !	You have a good command over this chapter. Revise the chapter again after a few days and enhance your performance.
60-75% Good !	You have a wide scope to learn for this chapter. Revise this chapter again.
<60% Not Satisfactory!	You have a long way ahead of you to master this chapter. Revise it thoroughly.

MED+ACE

NEET (UG)

SELF ASSESSMENT KIT

Test Booklet No. 3947316

Test Booklet Code CH16

Excretory Products and their Elimination

Topics Covered

Excretion in Animals and Human Excretory System

Mechanism and Regulation of Excretion

Important Instructions

- This Booklet Contains – Two Topic Tests and One Test on Complete Chapter.
- Each question carries 4 marks.
- For each correct response, the candidate will get 4 marks. And for every incorrect response, 1 mark will be additionally deducted from total score.
- Use **Blue/Black** point pen only for filling the OMR.
- Rough work is to be done in the space provided for this purpose in the test booklet only.

Name of the Candidate (In Capitals)

____

____

Candidate's Signature __________

Invigilator's Signature __________

Facsimile signature stamp of center superintendent__________

Do not open this booklet until you start attempting the test

Topical Follow Thru

Test 1

Syllabus

- Modes of Excretion –Ammonotelism, Ureotelism, Uricotelism
- Human Excretory System–Structure and Function
- Urine Formation

For deeper insight, **Scan the QR Code**

Important Instructions

- The test is of 30 minutes duration and contains 15 Multiple Choice Questions (four options with a single correct answer).
- Choose the correct option and fill the OMR given on the last page of booklet accordingly.
- At some instances, you may find more then 1 option may be correct in such circumstances, you have to judge the most appropriate answer as per the conditions given in the question.

1. Which of the following excretory products, if not removed immediately can bring about death of the organism due to their high toxicity?

(a) Urea and uric acid
(b) Uric acid and ammonia
(c) Uric acid
(d) Ammonia

2. Given below are two statements.

Statement I Hilum is present towards the centre of the inner concave surface of the kidney.

Statement II Cortex extends deeper into the calyces to form renal columns.

In the light of the above statements, choose the correct answer from the options given below.

(a) Statement I is incorrect, but statement II is correct
(b) Both statement I and statement II are correct
(c) Both statement I and statement II are incorrect
(d) Statement I is correct, but statement II is incorrect

3. Following shows the blood flow into the nephrons.

A. Vasa recta
B. Afferent arteriole
C. Peritubular capillaries
D. Glomerulus
E. Efferent arteriole

Choose the correct sequence of flow of blood into the nephrons, from the following.

(a) B-D-E-A-C
(b) B-D-E-C-A
(c) B-D-C-A-E
(d) B-D-A-C-E

4. Given below are two statements; one is labelled as Assertion (A) and the other is labelled as Reason (R).

Assertion (A) Majority of nephrons are confined to the cortical spaces of the kidneys.

Reason (R) Henle's loop is the only part that can extend to the medulla part of kidneys.

In the light of the above statements, choose the correct answer from the options given below.

(a) A is false, but R is true
(b) Both A and R are true and R is the correct explanation of A
(c) Both A and R are true, but R is not the correct explanation of A
(d) A is true, but R is false

5. Given below are two statements; one is labelled as Assertion (A) and the other is labelled as Reason (R).

Assertion (A) Reabsorption of most molecules in the renal tubules require energy.

Reason (R) Almost 90% of the glomerular filtrate is reabsorbed in the renal tubules.

In the light of the above statements, choose the correct answer from the options given below.
(a) A is false, but R is true
(b) Both A and R are true and R is the correct explanation of A
(c) Both A and R are true, but R is not the correct explanation of A
(d) A is true, but R is false

6. Given below is a diagramatic representation of nephron. Identify the labelled part 'X' and choose the correct statement w.r.t. it.

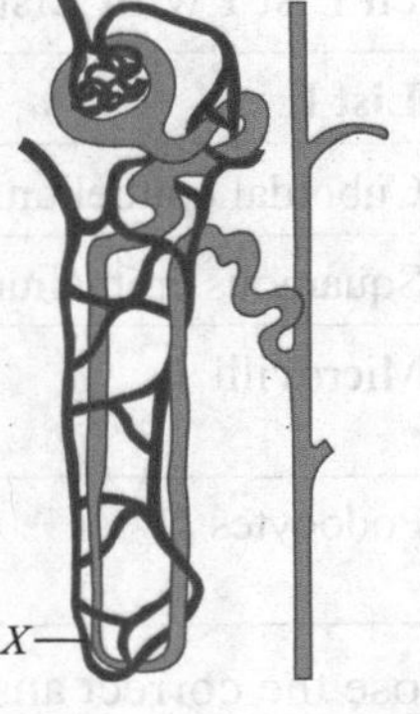

(a) 'X' arises from afferent arteriole rather than efferent arteriole.
(b) The descending limb of 'X' plays an important role in returning NaCl to the interstitium.
(c) 'X' carries deoxygenated blood rich in urea.
(d) 'X' is absent or highly reduced in cortical nephron.

7. Given below are two statements.
Statement I Afferent arteriole forms numerous peritubular capillaries in the medullary region around loop of Henle.
Statement II Blood from the vasa recta is released into the renal venule from where it escapes into renal vein.
In the light of the above statements, choose the correct answer from the options given below.
(a) Statement I is incorrect, but statement II is correct
(b) Both statement I and statement II are correct
(c) Both statement I and statement II are incorrect
(d) Statement I is correct, but statement II is incorrect

8. A person with acidification of blood, can possibly have defect in which of the following steps of urine formation?
(a) Reabsorption of glucose by the renal tubules
(b) Secretion of water by the distal convoluted tubules
(c) Secretion of K^+ and NH_3 by the Henle's loop
(d) Secretion of H^+ by the DCT and collecting duct

9. Match List I with List II.

List I	List II
A. PCT	1. Reabsorption of HCO_3^-
B. Henle's loop	2. Concentration of urine
C. Collecting duct	3. Reabsorption of 70-80% electrolytes
D. DCT	4. Minimum reabsorption

Choose the correct answer from the options given below.
(a) A-3, B-4, C-2, D-1
(b) A-1, B-4, C-2, D-3
(c) A-3, B-2, C-4, D-1
(d) A-1, B-2, C-4, D-3

10. Given below are two statements.
Statement I JGA apparatus is present at the junction of DCT and afferent arteriole.
Statement II JGA releases renin in response to rise in glomerular filteration rate.
In the light of the above statements, choose the correct answer from the options given below.
(a) Statement I is incorrect, but statement II is correct
(b) Both statement I and statement II are correct
(c) Both statement I and statement II are incorrect
(d) Statement I is correct, but statement II is incorrect

11. Following is the diagram of a longitudinal section of a kidney.

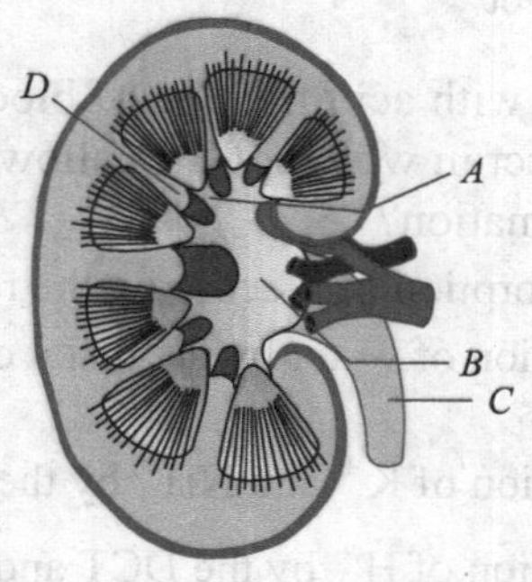

Which of the following labelled part serves as the site where several collecting ducts of nephrons open?

(a) *C* (b) *D*
(c) *B* (d) *A*

12. Following represents a schematic of urine flow through the renal tubules of a nephron.

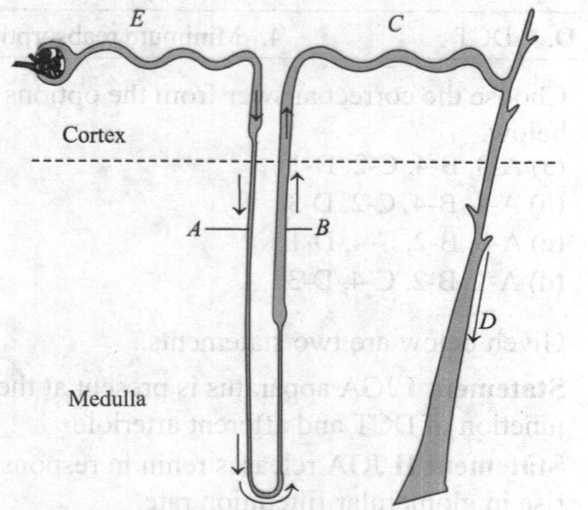

Choose the incorrect option from the following w.r.t. it.

(a) The filtrate flowing through *A* is hypertonic
(b) The filtrate flowing through *D* is hypotonic
(c) The filtrate flowing through *C* is hypotonic
(d) The filtrate flowing through *B* is hypotonic

13. Given below are two statements; one is labelled as Assertion A and the other is labelled as Reason R.

Assertion (A) The loop of Henle in the nephron is essential for the concentration of urine.

Reason (R) The descending limb of the loop of Henle is impermeable to water, but permeable to salts.

In the light of the above statements, choose the correct answer from the options given below.

(a) A is false, but R is true
(b) Both A and R are true and the R is the correct explanation of A
(c) Both A and R are true, but the R is not the correct explanation of A
(d) A is true, but R is false

14. Match List I with List II.

	List I		List II
A.	Cuboidal epithelium	1.	PCT
B.	Squamous epithelium	2.	Bowman's capsule
C.	Microvilli	3.	Thin segment of descending
D.	Podocytes	4.	Thick segment of descending limb

Choose the correct answer from the options given below.

	A	B	C	D
(a)	3	4	1	2
(b)	4	1	3	2
(c)	4	3	1	2
(d)	2	4	3	1

15. Consider the following statements related to excretion of urine in humans.

I. A person with GFR 125mL/min is likely to suffer from extreme dehydration.
II. Tubular epithelium does not require energy for reabsorption of materials.
III. Substances like glucose, amino acids, Na^+, etc., in the filtrate are reabsorbed by active mechanism.
IV. About 1100-1200 mL of blood is filtered by kidney per minute.
V. Ions added to the filtrate in the renal tubules maintain the pH of blood.

Choose the correct set of statements from the options given below.

(a) I, IV and V (b) II, III and IV
(c) I, II and III (d) III, IV and V

Response Index

01	a	b	c	d	10	a	b	c	d	19	a	b	c	d
02	a	b	c	d	11	a	b	c	d	20	a	b	c	d
03	a	b	c	d	12	a	b	c	d	21	a	b	c	d
04	a	b	c	d	13	a	b	c	d	22	a	b	c	d
05	a	b	c	d	14	a	b	c	d	23	a	b	c	d
06	a	b	c	d	15	a	b	c	d	24	a	b	c	d
07	a	b	c	d	16	a	b	c	d	25	a	b	c	d
08	a	b	c	d	17	a	b	c	d					
09	a	b	c	d	18	a	b	c	d					

Performance Scanner

> 90% Excellent !	You have mastered these topics. The concepts of these topics are at your fingertips. Move on to the next test and maintain this momentum.
76-90% Very Good !	You have a good command over these topics. Revise these topics again after a few days and enhance your performance.
60-75% Good !	You have a wide scope to learn for these topics. Revise these topics again.
<60% Not Satisfactory!	You have a long way ahead of you to master these topics. Revise it thoroughly.

Test 2

Syllabus

- Osmoregulation
- Regulation of Kidney Function - Renin - Angiotensin, Atrial Natriuretic Factor, ADH and Diabetes Insipidus
- Role of Other Organs in Excretion
- Disorders : Uremia, Renal Failure, Renal Calculi, Nephritis
- Dialysis and Artificial Kidney

For deeper insight, **Scan the QR Code**

Important Instructions

- The test is of 30 minutes duration and contains 25 Multiple Choice Questions (four options with a single correct answer).
- Choose the correct option and fill the OMR given on the last page of this test accordingly.
- At some instances, you may find more than 1 option to be correct. In such circumstances, you have to judge the most appropriate answer as per the conditions given in the question.

1. Which of the following is responsible for producing four times concentrated urine by the collecting ducts, in comparison to the initial filtrate formed by the glomerulus?

(a) Hypertonicity of medullary interstitium

(b) Hypotonicity of medullary interstitium

(c) Hypotonicity of collecting ducts

(d) Hypertonicity of cortical interstitium

2. Following are the steps involved in countering diuresis in a person.

A. Release of vasopressin by the posterior pituitary.

B. Activation of the osmoreceptors of the body.

C. Stimulation of the hypothalamus of the brain.

D. Decreased urine output by the kidneys.

E. Reabsorption of water from the kidney tubules.

Choose the correct order to deal with diuresis by the body.

(a) B-C-A-E-D (b) B-A-C-E-D

(c) C-B-A-E-D (d) C-B-E-A-D

3. Following is the diagram of a segment involved in concentrating the urine in the nephrons.

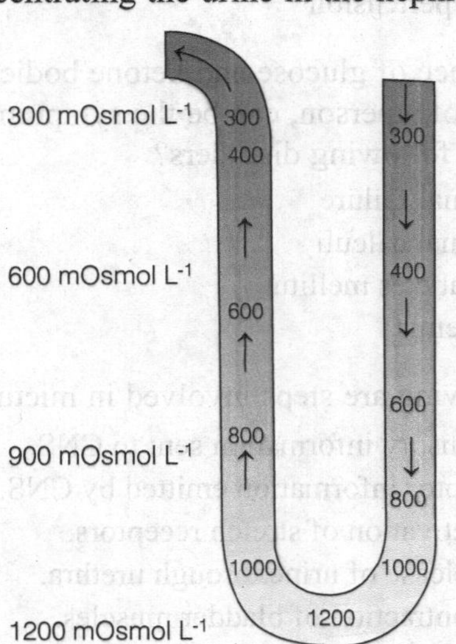

Which of the following causes an increase in osmolarity as observed in the diagram?

(a) Sodium chloride only
(b) Sodium chloride and urea
(c) Sodium chloride and ammonia
(d) Urea and ammonia

4. Given below are two statements; one is labelled as Assertion (A) and the other is labelled as Reason (R).
Assertion (A) Vasa recta located close to the Henle's loop, can disturb osmotic gradient.
Reason (R) Blood flow in the two limbs of vasa recta are opposite, forming counter current.
In the light of the above statements, choose the correct answer from the options given below.
(a) A is false, but R is true
(b) Both A and R are true and R is the correct explanation of A
(c) Both A and R are true, but R is not the correct explanation of A
(d) A is true, but R is false

5. The following schematic represents regulation of kidney functions. Which of the following condition, activates this pathway?

Heart ⟶ ANF < (Renin, Vasopressin) ⟶ NaCl and water reabsorption decreased

(a) Hypotension
(b) Diuresis
(c) Hypoglycemia
(d) Hypertension

6. Presence of glucose and ketone bodies in the urine of a person, can be the symptoms of which of the following disorders?
(a) Renal failure
(b) Renal calculi
(c) Diabetes mellitus
(d) Uremia

7. Following are steps involved in micturition reflex.
A. Sensory information sent to CNS.
B. Motor information emitted by CNS.
C. Activation of stretch receptors.
D. Release of urine through urethra.
E. Contraction of bladder muscles.
Choose the correct order of the steps involved in micturition, from the following options.
(a) C-A-E-B-D (b) C-A-B-E-D
(c) A-B-C-E-D (d) A-C-B-E-D

8. Given below are two statements.
Statement I A fall in glomerular blood pressure is dealt by stimulation of JG cells of the nephrons.
Statement II Stimulation of JG cells causes hyposecretion of aldosterone from the cortex.
In the light of the above statements, choose the correct answer from the options given below.
(a) Statement I is incorrect, but statement II is correct
(b) Both statement I and statement II are correct
(c) Both statement I and statement II are incorrect
(d) Statement I is correct, but statement II is incorrect

9. Which of the following statement about excretory organs is not correct?
(a) Oily coating of the skin is due to the deposition of sterols and waxes.
(b) Nitrogenous wastes are eliminated only through kidneys and sweat.
(c) Evaporation of water in sweat, regulates the body temperature.
(d) Yellowish colour of fecal wastes is due to bilirubin and biliverdin.

10. Which of the following statement is incorrect for the formation of concentrated urine?
(a) Active transport of sodium and chloride ions out of the ascending limb
(b) Increased levels of ADH hormone by posterior pituitary acting on collecting duct
(c) Decreased levels of ADH hormone by posterior pituitary acting on collecting duct
(d) Exchange of substances with interstitial fluid by vasa recta

11. Which of the following is correct about dialysing fluid?
(a) Osmotic pressure is greater than blood
(b) It is isotonic with respect to blood
(c) Osmotic pressure is lower than blood
(d) It is hypotonic with respect to blood

12. Match List I with List II.

	List I		List II
A.	Uremia	1.	Diabetes
B.	Ketonuria	2.	Caused by infection
C.	Glomerulonephritis	3.	Kidney failure
D.	Calculi	4.	Crystallised salts

Choose the correct answer from the following options.

(a) A-3, B-1, C-2, D-4
(b) A-2, B-3, C-1, D-4
(c) A-3, B-1, C-4, D-2
(d) A-2, B-3, C-4, D-1

13. Following are the statements with respect to the procedure followed in patients with uremia.

I. Blood drained from the artery of the patient is fed to the dialysing unit.
II. Cellophane membrane is a vital component of the dialysing unit, to enable filtration.
III. After filtration, blood is treated with heparin before release into the body.
IV. Filtered and cleared blood is pumped back to the body through a vein.
V. Nitrogenous wastes move through the membrane by the process of osmosis.

Choose the correct set of statements from the options given below.

(a) II and III (b) I, III and V
(c) I, II and IV (d) I, II and V

14. All of the following exerts similar effect on GFR except

(a) ANF (b) ADH
(c) aldosterone (d) angiotensin-II

15. Following diagram shows a segment of the nephrons.

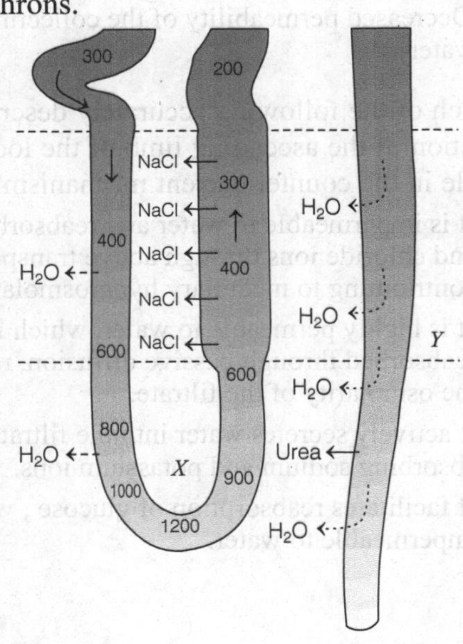

Which of the following processes allow the movement of water from segment *Y*, into the space outside?

(a) Simple diffusion
(b) Osmosis
(c) Active transport
(d) Facilitated diffusion

16. Given below are two statements.

Statement I Blood flow in the vasa recta runs parallel, but in the opposite direction to the flow of filtrate in the loop of Henle.

Statement II ADH secretion enhances the reabsorption of water in the ascending limb of the loop of Henle.

In the light of the above statements, choose the correct answer from the options given below

(a) Statement I is incorrect, but statement II is correct
(b) Both statement I and statement II are correct
(c) Both statement I and statement II are incorrect
(d) Statement I is correct, but statement II is incorrect

17. Given below are two statements.

Statement I A counter current flow is formed between ascending and descending limb of loop of Henle.

Statement II The flow of filtrate in both the limbs is in same direction which produces concentrated urine in mammals.

In the light of the above statements, choose the correct answer from the options given below.

(a) Statement I is incorrect, but statement II is correct
(b) Both statement I and statement II are correct
(c) Both statement I and statement II are incorrect
(d) Statement I is correct, but statement II is incorrect

18. The semi-permeable membrane plays an essential role in haemodialysis. Which of the following best describes its function?

(a) It allows large molecules such as proteins to pass through while blocking smaller molecules.
(b) It selectively allows waste products and excess electrolytes to pass through while retaining blood cells and proteins.

(c) It prevents the exchange of ions between the blood and filtrate.
(d) It enhances the production of new blood cells during dialysis.

19. Which of the following statement is incorrect about the micturition reflex?

(a) Voluntary signal for micturition are generated by CNS.
(b) Contraction of the external urethral sphincter leads to the release of urine.
(c) The transitional epithelium with stretch receptors is found in the bladder wall.
(d) The act of micturition involves both voluntary and involuntary muscles.

20. Which of the following best describes the effect of diabetes mellitus on the renal system of humans?

(a) Increased glucose reabsorption in PCT leads to decreased osmolarity of urine
(b) Elevated blood glucose levels causes glucosuria and osmotic diuresis
(c) It causes increased reabsorption of urea
(d) It results in decreased glomerular filteration rate

21. Match List I with List II.

	List I		List II
A.	Aldosterone	1.	Prevent diuresis
B.	ADH	2.	Glycosuria
C.	ANF	3.	Vasodilation
D.	Insulin	4.	Sodium reabsorption

Choose the correct answer from the options given below.

	A	B	C	D		A	B	C	D
(a)	3	4	1	2	(b)	4	1	3	2
(c)	4	3	1	2	(d)	2	4	3	1

22. Given below are two statements; one is labelled as Assertion (A) and the other is labelled as Reason (R).

Assertion (A) The kidneys are the only organs responsible for excreting all metabolic wastes from the body.

Reason (R) Sebum is a protective oily covering on body produced by sebaceous glands which contain sterols, hydrocarbon and wax.

In the light of the above statements, choose the correct answer from the options given below.

(a) A is false, but R is true
(b) Both A and R are true and the R is the correct explanation of A
(c) Both A and R are true, but the R is not the correct explanation of A
(d) A is true, but R is false

23. Which of the following statement is incorrect about urine?

(a) Urine analysis helps in clinical diagnosis of kidney.
(b) 25-30 gm of urea is excreted out per day.
(c) pH of urine is slightly alkaline.
(d) A neural mechanism is involved behind release of urine from bladder.

24. Which of the following is a direct effect of Atrial Natriuretic Factor (ANF) on the kidneys?

(a) Increased secretion of renin from the juxtaglomerular cells
(b) Constriction of afferent arterioles to reduce Glomerular Filtration Rate (GFR)
(c) Increased Glomerular Filtration Rate (GFR) and inhibition of sodium reabsorption in the collecting ducts
(d) Decreased permeability of the collecting ducts to water

25. Which of the following accurately describes the function of the ascending limb of the loop of Henle in the counter current mechanism?

(a) It is impermeable to water and reabsorbs sodium and chloride ions through active transport, contributing to medullary hyperosmolarity.
(b) It is highly permeable to water, which is reabsorbed through passive diffusion, reducing the osmolarity of the filtrate.
(c) It actively secretes water into the filtrate while absorbing sodium and potassium ions.
(d) It facilitates reabsorption of glucose , while being impermeable to water.

Response Index

01	a	b	c	d	10	a	b	c	d	19	a	b	c	d
02	a	b	c	d	11	a	b	c	d	20	a	b	c	d
03	a	b	c	d	12	a	b	c	d	21	a	b	c	d
04	a	b	c	d	13	a	b	c	d	22	a	b	c	d
05	a	b	c	d	14	a	b	c	d	23	a	b	c	d
06	a	b	c	d	15	a	b	c	d	24	a	b	c	d
07	a	b	c	d	16	a	b	c	d	25	a	b	c	d
08	a	b	c	d	17	a	b	c	d					
09	a	b	c	d	18	a	b	c	d					

Performance Scanner

> 90% Excellent !	You have mastered these topics. The concepts of these topics are at your fingertips. Move on to the next test and maintain this momentum.
76-90% Very Good !	You have a good command over these topics. Revise these topics again after a few days and enhance your performance.
60-75% Good !	You have a wide scope to learn for these topics. Revise these topics again.
<60% Not Satisfactory!	You have a long way ahead of you to master these topics. Revise it thoroughly.

Chapter Break Thru

Syllabus

- Mode of Excretion-Ammonotelism, Ureotelism and Uricotelism.
- Human Excretory System-Structure and Function
- Urine Formation
- Osmoregulation
- Regulation of Kidney Function - Renin - angiotensin, Atrial Natriuretic Factor, ADH and Diabetes Insipidus
- Role of Other Organs in Excretion
- Disorders : Uremia, Renal Failure, Renal Calculi, Nephritis
- Dialysis and Artificial Kidney

Important Instructions

- The test is of 1 hour duration and contains 50 Multiple-Choice Questions (Four options with a single correct answer).
- Choose the correct option and fill the OMR given on the last page of this test accordingly.
- At some instances, you may find more than 1 option to be correct. In such circumstances, you have to judge the most appropriate answer as per the conditions given in the question.

1. Consider the diagrammatic representation of the human excretory system. Which of the following hormone is secreted by the structure labelled as *X*?

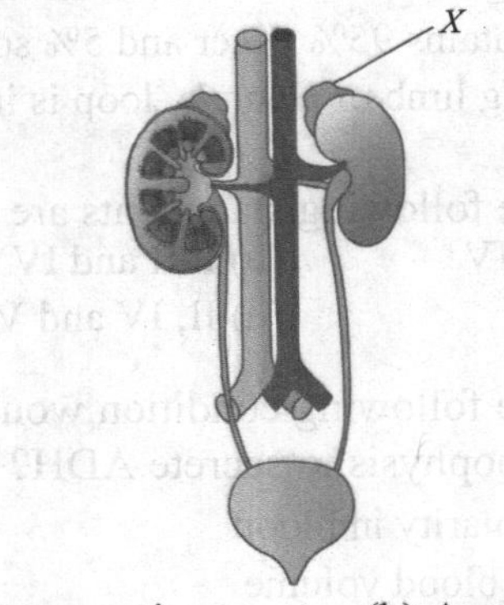

(a) Vasopressin (b) Angiotensin-II
(c) Aldosterone (d) Renin

2. Following are the steps involved in protein metabolism.

A. Formation of urea in liver.
B. Blood filtered in the nephrons.
C. Proteins broken down to ammonia.
D. Blood containing nitrogenous waste.
E. Purified blood drained into vena cava.

Choose the correct sequence from the following.

(a) C-A-D-B-E (b) A-C-D-B-E
(c) C-A-B-D-E (d) A-C-B-D-E

3. Presence of glucose in urine coupled with very small volumes of concentrated urine, is indicative of

(a) kidney stones and diabetes mellitus
(b) nephritis
(c) diabetes mellitus and nephritis
(d) renal calculi

4. Which of the following statement about excretion is not correct?
(a) Not all of the urea produced is excreted out by the body.
(b) Uric acid removal creates a water stress in the body of birds.
(c) Ammonia removal depends on its concentration gradient.
(d) Ammonia to urea conversion occurs in the liver.

5. Given below are two statements; one is labelled as Assertion (A) and the other is labelled as Reason (R).
Assertion (A) The afferent arteriole has a smaller diameter than the efferent arteriole.
Reason (R) The decreased diameter causes blood to flow with pressure in the glomerulus.
In the light of the above statements, choose the correct answer from the options given below.
(a) A is false, but R is true
(b) Both A and R are true and R is the correct explanation of A
(c) Both A and R are true, but R is not the correct explanation of A
(d) A is true, but R is false

6. If structural analysis of a section of kidney tissue shows the presence of well-defined vasa recta, which of the following is not correct about the tissue sample?
(a) The PCT and DCT are confined to the cortex of the kidneys.
(b) A fine branch of peritubular capillary runs parallel to Henle's loop.
(c) Loop of Henle runs deeper into the medullary space of the kidneys.
(d) The nephrons visible under the tissue section are cortical nephrons.

7. Given below are few statements.
I. Blood from the glomerulus is carried away by an efferent arteriole.
II. Conditional reabsorption of Na^+ and water takes place in the PCT.
III. Mammals have the ability to produce a concentrated urine due to presence of Henle's loop and vasa recta.
IV. On average, around 1 to 1.5 L of urea is excreted out of the human body.
V. Glycosuria can indicate diabetes mellitus.
Choose the correct set of statements out of the given options.
(a) I, II and V (b) II, III and IV
(c) I, III and V (d) I, II and IV

8. Given below are two statements.
Statement I If blood becomes too much alkaline, PCT secretes H^+ into the filtrate.
Statement II The pH of the blood is maintained only by the PCT and DCT of the nephrons.
In the light of the above statements, choose the correct answer from the options given below.
(a) Statement I is incorrect, but statement II is correct
(b) Both statement I and statement II are correct
(c) Both statement I and statement II are incorrect
(d) Statement I is correct, but statement II is incorrect

9. What would happen if urea is not returned to the medullary interstitium by the collecting duct?
(a) Sodium chloride cannot be returned to the medullary interstitium.
(b) The ascending limb of Henle's loop will fail to dilute the filtrate.
(c) Urine in the collecting tubules will fail to get concentrated.
(d) Osmolarity in the deeper parts of the medulla would increase.

10. Read the following statements.
I. Descending limb of loop of Henle makes filtrate hypertonic.
II. PCT reabsorbs whole glucose.
III. Collecting tubule is also called diluting segment.
IV. Urine contains 95% water and 5% solutes.
V. Ascending limb of Henle's loop is impermeable to salts.
Which of the following statements are correct?
(a) I, III and IV (b) I, II and IV
(c) I and IV (d) II, IV and V

11. Which of the following condition would stimulate the neurohypophysis to secrete ADH?
(a) Low osmolarity in blood
(b) Increased blood volume
(c) High GFR
(d) Low blood pressure

12. Following are the statements related to expulsion of urine from the body.

I. Micturition reflex is an involuntary signal of the central nervous system.
II. Receptors in the bladder are the first to receive micturition signal.
III. Motor neurons transmit information from the CNS to the bladder.
IV. Simultaneous contraction of urinary bladder and sphincter is involved.
V. After micturition, smooth muscles of the bladder relaxes.

Choose the correct answer from the given options.
(a) II and III
(b) I, III and IV
(c) II, III and V
(d) I, II and IV

13. Which of the following is an abnormal composition of glomerular filtrate?
(a) Water, salts, vitamins and ions
(b) Ions, water, glucose and ammonia
(c) Water, salts, ammonia and proteins
(d) Water, glucose, urea and ammonia

14. Which of the following resulted in clumping of blood after pumping it into the dialysing unit?
(a) The dialysing membrane was punctured.
(b) Dialysing fluid used was hypertonic.
(c) Blood was not treated with heparin.
(d) Filtered blood was not treated with anti-heparin.

15. Given below are two statements; one is labelled as Assertion (A) and the other is labelled as Reason (R).

Assertion (A) Complete absence of sweating can be toxic to the body cells.
Reason (R) Sweating provides a cooling effect, and brings temperature to normal.
In the light of the above statements, choose the correct answer from the options given below.
(a) A is false, but R is true
(b) Both A and R are true and R is the correct explanation of A
(c) Both A and R are true, but R is not the correct explanation of A
(d) A is true, but R is false

16. Following is the diagram of the filtration unit of the nephrons.

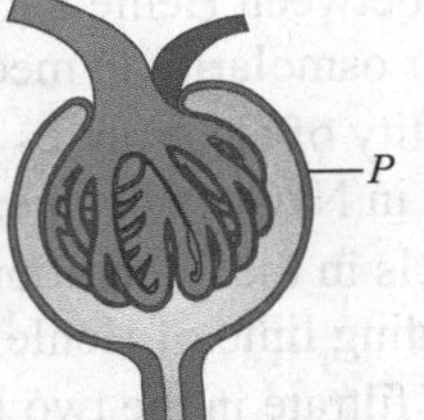

Which of the following are parts of the structure labelled as *P*, that are involved in filtration of blood?
(a) Podocytes only
(b) Endothelium only
(c) Podocytes and slit pores
(d) Endothelium and basement membrane

17. What would be the outcome of interchanging the permeability of water and electrolytes in the ascending limb of Henle's loop?
(a) Filtrate would be diluted in the ascending limb
(b) Filtrate would be hypotonic in collecting tubules
(c) A highly concentrated urine would be formed
(d) A very dilute filtrate would flow in the DCT

18. Given below are two statements; one is labelled as Assertion (A) and the other is labelled as Reason (R).

Assertion (A) A person with diabetes insipidus feels externely thirsty.
Reason (R) A person with diabetes insipidus suffers from excess secretion of vasopressin.
In the light of the above statements, choose the correct answer from the options given below.
(a) A is false, but R is true
(b) Both A and R are true and R is the correct explanation of A
(c) Both A and R are true, but R is not the correct explanation of A
(d) A is true, but R is false

19. Reabsorption in DCT depends upon
(a) adrenaline and vasopressin
(b) aldosterone and vasopressin
(c) cortisol, NaCl and urea concentration
(d) aldosterone, potassium and sodium ions concentration

20. Following are the statements related to concentration of urine.

I. Distance between Henle's loop and vasa recta is crucial for osmolarity in medulla.
II. Permeability of electrolytes in the ascending limb help in NaCl exchange.
III. NaCl levels in the interstitium is maintained by the ascending limb of Henle's loop.
IV. If flow of filtrate in the two limbs is in the same direction, the osmolarity is disturbed.
V. Interstitial gradient is established solely by urea flowing into the interstitium.

Choose the correct set of statements from the options given below.
(a) II and III (b) I, II and IV
(c) I, III and V (d) II, III and IV

21. Swelling of legs and feet in a person, can be related to fluid retention caused by
(a) uremia
(b) glomerulonephritis
(c) kidney stones
(d) renal calculi

22. Given below are two statements.

Statement I Low blood pressure, due to extreme dehydration stimulates adrenal cortex.

Statement II An increase in blood volume causes an increase in the osmolarity of blood.

In the light of the above statements, choose the correct answer from the options given below.
(a) Statement I is incorrect, but statement II is correct
(b) Both statement I and statement II are correct
(c) Both statement I and statement II are incorrect
(d) Statement I is correct, but statement II is incorrect

23. Match List I with List II.

	List I		List II
A.	*Amphioxus*	1.	Nephridia
B.	Earthworm	2.	Malpighian tubules
C.	Grasshopper	3.	Protonephridia
D.	Prawns	4.	Green glands

Choose the correct answer from the options given below.
(a) A-1, B-3, C-2, D-4
(b) A-3, B-1, C-2, D-4
(c) A-1, B-3, C-4, D-2
(d) A-3, B-1, C-4, D-2

24. Following diagram represents the functional unit of kidneys.

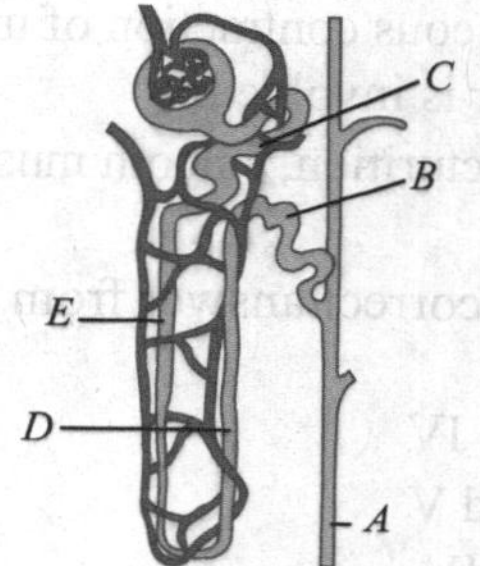

Which of the following labelled structures show the region of maximum and minimum reabsorption, respectively?
(a) *A* and *C* (b) *B* and *E*
(c) *A* and *D* (d) *C* and *D*

25. Given below are two statements; one is labelled as the Assertion (A) and the other is labelled as the Reason (R).

Assertion (A) The excreta of land snails are mostly in the form of pellet.

Reason (R) Terrestrial animals like land snails excrete lesser toxic forms of nitrogenous wastes.

In the light of the above statements, choose the correct answer from the options given below.
(a) A is false, but R is true
(b) Both A and R are true and R is the correct explanation of A
(c) Both A and R are true, but R is not the correct explanation of A
(d) A is true, but R is false

26. Which of the following consists of only substances that are transported without the expenditure of ATP?
(a) Na^+, NH_3, urea
(b) Urea, Na^+, water
(c) Urea, NH_3, water
(d) Amino acids, glucose, Na^+

27. Given below are two statements.

Statement I If blood becomes too alkaline, HCO_3^- reabsorption is increased in the DCT.

Statement II Reabsorption of bicarbonate ions helps in maintaining the pH of blood.

In the light of the above statements, choose the correct answer from the options given below.

(a) Statement I is incorrect, but statement II is correct.

(b) Both statement I and statement II are correct.

(c) Both statement I and statement II are incorrect.

(d) Statement I is correct, but statement II is incorrect.

28. Following are the steps involved in the mechanism which is counter-checked by the ANF mechanism.

A. Angiotensin-II stimulates the release of aldosterone.

B. A fall in Glomerular Filtration Rate (GFR).

C. Secretion of JG cells convert angiotensinogen.

D. Angiotensin-I is converted to angiotensin–II.

E. Reabsorption of Na^+ and water from the DCT.

Choose the correct order from the options given below.

(a) B-C-D-A-E (b) E-C-D-A-B
(c) B-D-C-A-E (d) E-D-C-A-B

29. Which of the following excretory organ maintains the level of amino acids in the blood?

(a) Skin (b) Lungs
(c) Liver (d) Kidneys

30. Presence of which hormone can prevent the reabsorption of sodium and water by the distal parts of the renal tubules?

(a) Aldosterone (b) Renin
(c) ADH (d) ANF

31. Consider the following statements about the arterioles and identify the correct statement.

(a) Both afferent and efferent arterioles are involved in filtering blood at the glomerulus but have no role in regulating blood pressure.

(b) The afferent arteriole carries blood away from the glomerulus, while the efferent arteriole supplies blood to the glomerulus.

(c) The efferent arteriole diameter is more than the afferent arteriole which carries blood away from the glomerulus.

(d) The afferent arteriole supplies blood to the glomerulus and is involved in regulating glomerular filtration rate (GFR), while the efferent arteriole carries blood away from the glomerulus.

32. The filtration barrier in the glomerulus selectively allows the passage of certain molecules. Which of the following molecules would normally be filtered out of the blood but retained in the bloodstream?

(a) Glucose
(b) Urea
(c) Albumin
(d) Sodium ions

33. Given below are two statements.

Statement I Ammonotelism is a process where ammonia, a toxic by product of protein metabolism, is excreted directly into the environment.

Statement II Ammonotelism is commonly observed in terrestrial animals because ammonia is less toxic and requires less water for excretion.

In the light of the above statements, choose the correct answer from the options given below.

(a) Statement I is incorrect, but statement II is correct

(b) Both statement I and statement II are correct.

(c) Both statement I and statement II are incorrect

(d) Statement I is correct, but statement II is incorrect

34. Which of the following condition would most likely result in an increased Glomerular Filtration Rate (GFR)?

(a) Increased colloid osmotic pressure in the blood

(b) Decreased hydrostatic pressure in the glomerulus

(c) Increased blood pressure in the glomerular capillaries

(d) Increased reabsorption of sodium and water in the proximal tubule

35. Match List I with List II.

List I		List II	
A.	Minute U shaped vessel	1.	Renal vein
B.	Carry oxygenate blood	2.	Glomerulus
C.	Carry deoxygenate blood	3.	Vasa recta
D.	Tuft of capillaries	4.	Renal artery

Choose the correct answer from the options given below.

	A	B	C	D		A	B	C	D
(a)	3	4	1	2	(b)	4	1	3	2
(c)	4	3	1	2	(d)	2	4	3	1

36. Majority of the excretory organs play important role in maintaining ionic balance or osmoregulation along with excreting harmful by-products. Which of the following is not primarily involved in osmoregulation?
(a) Malphigian tubule
(b) Protonephridia
(c) Antennal glands
(d) Aquatic gills

37. Which of the following statement accurately describes the composition and function of the Malpighian body?
(a) The Malpighian body consists of the Bowman's capsule and the glomerulus, and it is responsible for the secretion of urine.
(b) The Malpighian body includes the Bowman's capsule, glomerulus, and the proximal convoluted tubule, and it functions mainly in the reabsorption of glucose.
(c) The Malpighian body comprises the Bowman's capsule and the glomerulus, and it plays a crucial role in the filtration of blood to form filtrate.
(d) The Malpighian body includes the glomerulus and the loop of Henle, and it is involved in the concentration of urine.

38. Consider the following statements about glomerular filtration.
I. It is the first step in urine formation which involves filtration of blood.
II. GFR of healthy individual is 125ml/day.
III. Reabsorption of water occurs passively.
IV. 1/5th of the blood pumped out by each ventricle is filtered by kidney per minute.

Choose the correct set of statements from the options given below.
(a) I and IV (b) II only
(c) III and IV (d) I and II

39. How does the structure of the glomerular capillaries facilitate the process of filtration?
(a) The capillaries have thick, impermeable walls that allow selective filtration of only small molecules.
(b) The capillaries are lined with a single layer of flat epithelial cells that prevent large molecules from passing.
(c) The capillaries have numerous small pores and are surrounded by a filtration membrane that permits the passage of water and solutes but restricts larger molecules.
(d) The capillaries are surrounded by a thick layer of smooth muscle that controls the filtration rate.

40. Given below are two statements.
Statement I During tubular secretion, substances such as drugs, toxins, and metabolic waste products are secreted from the blood into the nephron's tubules, ensuring their excretion from the body in the urine.
Statement II Tubular reabsorption helps in maintenance of acid-base balance of body by secreting H^+ ions.
In the light of the above statements, choose the correct answer from the options given below.
(a) Statement I is incorrect, but statement II is correct
(b) Both statement I and statement II are correct.
(c) Both statement I and statement II are incorrect
(d) Statement I is correct, but statement II is incorrect

41. Arrange the following structures observed within longitudinal section of kidney from outer to innermost surface.
A. Renal cortex
B. Medullary pyramids
C. Renal columns of Bertini
D. Renal calyces
E. Collecting duct
Choose the correct answer from the options given below.
(a) D-A-C-B-E (b) B-A-C-D-E
(c) A-C-B-E-D (d) A-C-B-D-E

42. Renin is released by JG cells when a fall in GFR is observed. Which of the following is not a function of renin?
(a) Stimulates reabsorption of sodium ions from DCT
(b) Stimulates secretion of aldosterone from adrenal cortex
(c) Stimulates formation of angiotensin II in liver
(d) Prevents loss of electrolytes from urine

43. Match List I with List II.

	List I		List II
A.	Length of kidney	1.	2-3 cm
B.	Width of kidney	2.	120-170 gm
C.	Thickness of kidney	3.	10-12 cm
D.	Average weight	4.	5-7 cm

Choose the correct answer from the options given below.

	A	B	C	D
(a)	3	4	1	2
(b)	4	1	3	2
(c)	4	3	1	2
(d)	2	4	3	1

44. Consider the following statements about JGA .
I. The JGA is involved in the regulation of blood pressure by secreting renin.
II. It is a highly sensitive apparatus formed by cellular modifications.
III. The juxtaglomerular cells are located in the distal convoluted tubule and efferent arteriole and regulate the filtration rate based on sodium chloride concentration.
IV. The JGA is responsible for detecting changes in blood pressure and adjusting the release of antidiuretic hormone (ADH).

Choose the correct answer from the options given below.
(a) I, III and IV (b) I and II
(c) III and IV (d) I and IV

45. Given below are two statements; one is labelled as Assertion (A) and the other is labelled as Reason (R).

Assertion (A) The proximal convoluted tubule (PCT) is primarily responsible for the reabsorption of water, ions, and nutrients from the filtrate.

Reason (R) The PCT is lined with microvilli that increase its surface area, enhancing the reabsorption efficiency of these substances.

In the light of the above statements, choose the correct answer from the options given below.
(a) A is false, but R is true
(b) Both A and R are true and R is the correct explanation of A
(c) Both A and R are true, but of R is not the correct explanation of A
(d) A is true, but R is false

46. Given below are two statements.

Statement I Renal calculi, commonly known as kidney stones, are formed from the crystallisation of substances like calcium, oxalate, and uric acid within the renal pelvis or ureters.

Statement II Glomerulonephritis is an inflammatory condition of the glomeruli, the filtering units of the kidneys, which can result from autoimmune diseases.

In the light of the above statements, choose the correct answer from the options given below.
(a) Statement I is incorrect, but statement II is correct
(b) Both statement I and statement II are correct.
(c) Both statement I and statement II are incorrect
(d) Statement I is correct, but statement II is incorrect

47. Given below are two statements; one is labelled as Assertion (A) and the other is labelled as Reason (R).

Assertion (A) Tubular secretion helps in the removal of excess hydrogen ions and drugs from the blood into the tubular fluid.

Reason (R) Tubular secretion occurs primarily in the distal convoluted tubule and the collecting duct, where substances are actively transported from the blood into the tubular fluid.

In the light of the above statements, choose the correct answer from the options given below.
(a) A is false, but R is true
(b) Both A and R are true and R is the correct explanation A
(c) Both A and R are true, but R is not the correct explanation A
(d) A is true, but R is false

48. Which of the following do not constitute part of renal cortex?
(a) Malpighian corpuscle
(b) Duct of Bertini
(c) Proximal convoluted tubule
(d) Distal convoluted tubule

49. What is the main role of antidiuretic hormone (ADH) in the functioning of kidney?
(a) To increase the excretion of potassium ions
(b) To decrease the permeability of the collecting ducts to water
(c) To increase the permeability of the collecting ducts to water
(d) To stimulate the release of renin from the juxtaglomerular cells

50. What is the primary function of the long loops of Henle found in juxtamedullary nephrons?
(a) To reabsorb glucose and amino acids
(b) To create a hyperosmotic medullary environment essential for water reabsorption
(c) To filter large molecules and proteins from the blood
(d) To secrete excess electrolytes and urea into the urine

Scan for online chapter test

Response Index

01 ⓐ ⓑ ⓒ ⓓ	14 ⓐ ⓑ ⓒ ⓓ	27 ⓐ ⓑ ⓒ ⓓ	40 ⓐ ⓑ ⓒ ⓓ
02 ⓐ ⓑ ⓒ ⓓ	15 ⓐ ⓑ ⓒ ⓓ	28 ⓐ ⓑ ⓒ ⓓ	41 ⓐ ⓑ ⓒ ⓓ
03 ⓐ ⓑ ⓒ ⓓ	16 ⓐ ⓑ ⓒ ⓓ	29 ⓐ ⓑ ⓒ ⓓ	42 ⓐ ⓑ ⓒ ⓓ
04 ⓐ ⓑ ⓒ ⓓ	17 ⓐ ⓑ ⓒ ⓓ	30 ⓐ ⓑ ⓒ ⓓ	43 ⓐ ⓑ ⓒ ⓓ
05 ⓐ ⓑ ⓒ ⓓ	18 ⓐ ⓑ ⓒ ⓓ	31 ⓐ ⓑ ⓒ ⓓ	44 ⓐ ⓑ ⓒ ⓓ
06 ⓐ ⓑ ⓒ ⓓ	19 ⓐ ⓑ ⓒ ⓓ	32 ⓐ ⓑ ⓒ ⓓ	45 ⓐ ⓑ ⓒ ⓓ
07 ⓐ ⓑ ⓒ ⓓ	20 ⓐ ⓑ ⓒ ⓓ	33 ⓐ ⓑ ⓒ ⓓ	46 ⓐ ⓑ ⓒ ⓓ
08 ⓐ ⓑ ⓒ ⓓ	21 ⓐ ⓑ ⓒ ⓓ	34 ⓐ ⓑ ⓒ ⓓ	47 ⓐ ⓑ ⓒ ⓓ
09 ⓐ ⓑ ⓒ ⓓ	22 ⓐ ⓑ ⓒ ⓓ	35 ⓐ ⓑ ⓒ ⓓ	48 ⓐ ⓑ ⓒ ⓓ
10 ⓐ ⓑ ⓒ ⓓ	23 ⓐ ⓑ ⓒ ⓓ	36 ⓐ ⓑ ⓒ ⓓ	49 ⓐ ⓑ ⓒ ⓓ
11 ⓐ ⓑ ⓒ ⓓ	24 ⓐ ⓑ ⓒ ⓓ	37 ⓐ ⓑ ⓒ ⓓ	50 ⓐ ⓑ ⓒ ⓓ
12 ⓐ ⓑ ⓒ ⓓ	25 ⓐ ⓑ ⓒ ⓓ	38 ⓐ ⓑ ⓒ ⓓ	
13 ⓐ ⓑ ⓒ ⓓ	26 ⓐ ⓑ ⓒ ⓓ	39 ⓐ ⓑ ⓒ ⓓ	

Performance Scanner

> 90% Excellent !	You have mastered this chapter. The concepts of this chapter are at your fingertips. Move on to the next chapter and maintain this momentum.
76-90% Very Good !	You have a good command over this chapter. Revise the chapter again after a few days and enhance your performance.
60-75% Good !	You have a wide scope to learn for this chapter. Revise this chapter again.
<60% Not Satisfactory!	You have a long way ahead of you to master this chapter. Revise it thoroughly.

Test Booklet No. 3947317

Test Booklet Code CH17

MEDACE
NEET (UG)
SELF ASSESSMENT KIT

Locomotion and Movement

Topics Covered

Types of Movement and Muscle

Human Skeletal System; Joints and Disorders of Muscular and Skeletal System

Important Instructions

- This Booklet Contains – Two Topic Tests and One Test on Complete Chapter.
- Each question carries 4 marks.
- For each correct response, the candidate will get 4 marks. And for every incorrect response, 1 mark will be additionally deducted from total score.
- Use **Blue/Black** point pen only for filling the OMR.
- Rough work is to be done in the space provided for this purpose in the test booklet only.

Name of the Candidate (In Capitals) ____________

____

Candidate's Signature ____________

Invigilator's Signature ____________

Facsimile signature stamp of center superintendent____________

Do not open this booklet until you start attempting the test

Topical Follow Thru

Test 1

Syllabus

- Types of Movement - Ciliary, Flagellar, Muscular
- Skeletal Muscle-Contractile Protein and Muscle Contraction

For deeper insight, **Scan the QR Code**

Important Instructions

- The test is of 30 minutes duration and contains 15 Multiple Choice Questions (four options with a single correct answer).
- Choose the correct option and fill the OMR given on the last page of this test accordingly.
- At some instances, you may find more than 1 option to be correct. In such circumstances, you have to judge the most appropriate answer as per the conditions given in the question.

1. Which of the following represents only monomers?
(a) F-actin and G-actin
(b) G-actin and meromyosin
(c) Meromyosin and myosin
(d) Myosin and tropomyosin

2. Where would the calcium concentration be highest, in the presence of acetylcholine in the neuromuscular junction?
(a) Sarcolemma
(b) Sarcoplasmic reticulum
(c) Sarcoplasm
(d) Sarcomere

3. Following is an image of the functional unit of muscle contraction. Identify the structure labelled as X and choose the option that correctly represents the change in X during contraction phase.

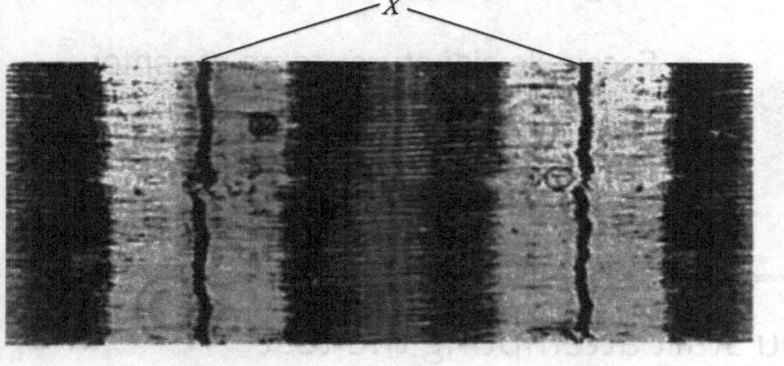

(a) Moves outwards
(b) Elongate
(c) No change
(d) Moves inward

4. Given below are two statements; one is labelled as Assertion (A) and other is labelled as Reason (R).

Assertion (A) Troponin is essential for maintaining the relaxed state of muscles.

Reason (R) Troponin is distributed at regular intervals on the two filaments of tropomyosin.

In the light of the above statements, choose the correct answer from the options given below.
(a) A is false, but R is true
(b) Both A and R are true and R is the correct explanation of A
(c) Both A and R are true, but R is not the correct explanation of A
(d) A is true, but R is false

5. Match List I with List II.

List I	List II
A. Tentacles	1. Spermatozoa
B. Cilia	2. Microfilaments
C. Protoplasmic streaming	3. Fallopian tube
D. Flagella	4. *Hydra*

Choose the correct answer from the options given below.
(a) A-4, B-3, C-2, D-1
(b) A-4, B-1, C-2, D-3
(c) A-4, B-3, C-1, D-2
(d) A-4, B-1, C-3, D-2

6. Consider the following statements and identify incorrect regarding muscle contraction.
(a) Neuromuscular junction is the junction between the nerve fibre and muscle fibre
(b) The impulses reaches the terminal ends of axons of neuromuscular junction
(c) Sarcolemma releases Ca^{2+} ions into the sarcoplasm, upon receiving the action potential
(d) Acetylcholine travels through synaptic cleft and action potential is generated within the sarcolemma

7. Given below are two statements; one is labelled as Assertion (A) and other is labelled as Reason (R).

Assertion (A) Bending down to pick up something cannot be regarded as locomotion.

Reason (R) Locomotion involves a change in position brought about by locomotory organs.

In the light of the above statements, choose the correct answer from the options given below.
(a) A is false, but R is true
(b) Both A and R are true and R is the correct explanation of A
(c) Both A and R are true, but R is not the correct explanation of A
(d) A is true, but R is false

8. Given below is a diagrammatic representation of cross section of a muscle. Degradation of which of the following component can cause the structure *A* to fall apart?

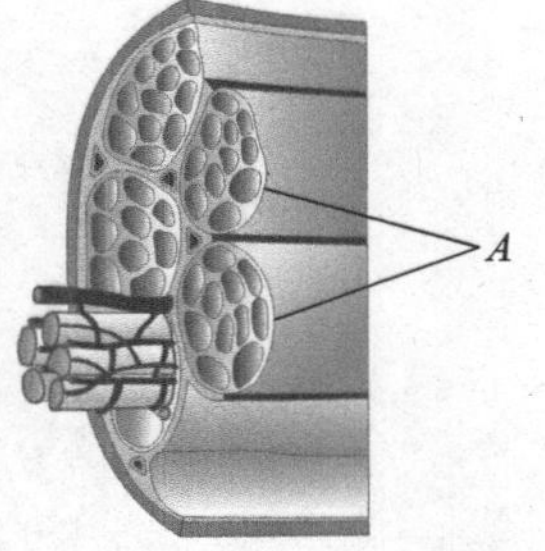

(a) Collagen (b) Myosin
(c) Actin (d) Troponin

9. The image given below represents a phenomenon in the muscle fibres. Which of the following does not occur during this stage?

(a) Shortening or contraction of the sarcomere
(b) Reduction in the length of isotropic bands
(c) Elongation of the anisotropic or A-bands
(d) H-zone gets completely overlapped by I-bands

10. Among the following, which one is not true for red fibres?
(a) Muscles contain a red coloured oxygen storing pigment
(b) Muscle contain plenty of mitochondria
(c) It is also known as aerobic muscles
(d) Number of sarcoplasmic reticulum is high

11. Match List I with List II.

	List I		List II
A.	M-line	1.	Unaltered in contraction
B.	H-zone	2.	Centre of sarcomere
C.	Z-line	3.	Vanishes during contraction
D.	A-band	4.	Boundaries of sarcomere

Choose the correct answer from the options given below
(a) A-2, B-3, C-4, D-1 (b) A-4, B-3, C-2, D-1
(c) A-4, B-1, C-2, D-3 (d) A-2, B-1, C-4, D-3

12. All of the following occurs, if a neural signal fails to release acetylcholine at the motor-end plate, except
(a) troponin keeps the binding site on actin masked
(b) ATP does not hydrolyse into ADP and Pi
(c) influx of calcium ions into the sarcoplasm
(d) impulses do not run through the sarcolemma

13. H-zone of the muscle fibres contain
(a) Z-line
(b) thick and thin filaments
(c) thin filaments only
(d) thick filaments only

14. White muscle fibres contain more sarcoplasmic reticulum because
(a) they help in high energy activities for short duration
(b) their contraction phase is long and they get tired easily
(c) their sarcoplasm is rich in glycogen
(d) they have a slower contraction rate

15. Consider the following statements.
I. Sarcoplasmic reticulum is higher in aerobic muscles.
II. Muscle with abundant myoglobin has less mitochondria.
III. Lactic acid accumulation is faster in red muscle fibres.
IV. White fibres show a fast rate of contraction.
Choose the correct statement(s) from the options given below.
(a) II and IV
(b) Only I
(c) II and III
(d) Only IV

Response Index

01	a b c d	10	a b c d	19	a b c d
02	a b c d	11	a b c d	20	a b c d
03	a b c d	12	a b c d	21	a b c d
04	a b c d	13	a b c d	22	a b c d
05	a b c d	14	a b c d	23	a b c d
06	a b c d	15	a b c d	24	a b c d
07	a b c d	16	a b c d	25	a b c d
08	a b c d	17	a b c d		
09	a b c d	18	a b c d		

Performance Scanner

> 90% Excellent !	You have mastered these topics. The concepts of these topics are at your fingertips. Move on to the next test and maintain this momentum.
76-90% Very Good !	You have a good command over these topics. Revise these topics again after a few days and enhance your performance.
60-75% Good !	You have a wide scope to learn for these topics. Revise these topics again.
<60% Not Satisfactory!	You have a long way ahead of you to master these topics. Revise it thoroughly.

Test 2

Syllabus
- Skeletal System and its Functions, Joints
- Disorders of Muscular and Skeletal System-Myasthenia Gravis, Tetany, Muscular Dystrophy, Arthritis, Osteoporosis and Gout.

For deeper insight, **Scan the QR Code**

Important Instructions

- The test is of 30 minutes duration and contains 25 Multiple Choice Questions (four options with a single correct answer).
- Choose the correct option and fill the OMR given on the last page of this test accordingly.
- At some instances, you may find more than 1 option to be correct. In such circumstances, you have to judge the most appropriate answer as per the conditions given in the question.

1. In which of the following disorder, a low protein diet is advisable?
(a) Arthritis
(b) Gout
(c) Osteoporosis
(d) Muscular dystrophy

2. The wrist movement when someone is waving, is shown by
(a) gliding joint (b) saddle joint
(c) hinge joint (d) pivot joint

3. Given below are two statements.
Statement I The hyoid bone of the axial skeleton helps in swallowing food.
Statement II A U-shaped skull bone is present at the base of buccal cavity.
In the light of the above statements, choose the correct answer from the options given below.
(a) Statement I is incorrect, but statement II is correct
(b) Both statement I and statement II are correct
(c) Both statement I and statement II are incorrect
(d) Statement I is correct, but statement II is incorrect

4. Given below are two statements; one is labelled as Assertion (A) and other is labelled as Reason (R).
Assertion (A) The intervertebral disc separates adjacent vertebra in the vertebral column.
Reason (R) The discs in the vertebral column are fibrocartilages that allow limited mobility.
In the light of the above statements, choose the correct answer from the options given below.
(a) A is false, but R is true
(b) Both A and R are true and R is the correct explanation of A
(c) Both A and R are true, but R is not the correct explanation of A
(d) A is true, but R is false

5. Which of the following can be moved while we speak?
(a) Maxilla (b) Zygomatic
(c) Hyoid (d) Mandible

6. In the case of shoulder dislocation, humerus dislocated from
(a) acromion (b) glenoid
(c) acetabulum (d) coxal

7. Given below are two statements; one is labelled as Assertion (A) and other is labelled as Reason (R).
Assertion (A) In women bones become increasingly fragile with age.
Reason (R) Loss of ovarian functions is observed in females, with age.
In the light of the above statements, choose the correct answer from the options given below.
(a) A is false, but R is true
(b) Both A and R are true and R is the correct explanation of A
(c) Both A and R are true, but R is not the correct explanation of A
(d) A is true, but R is false

8. Following are the statements related to joints in a human body.

I. Saddle joint is present between the metacarpal of thumb and carpals.

II. At the sutures of the cranium, bones are attached together by loose cartilages.

III. Cartilaginous joints do not allow any movement, to maintain the integrity of back bone.

IV. Synovial fluid lubricates the articulating bone surfaces and prevents friction.

V. The considerable movement between atlas and axis is due to synovial joint.

Choose the correct sets of statements from the options given below.

(a) I and III
(b) II, IV and V
(c) I, IV and V
(d) I, II and III

9. Given below are two statements.

Statement I The ankle joint in the leg is made up of three bones.

Statement II The ankle joint is a type of pivot synovial joint.

In the light of the above statements, choose the correct answer from the options given below.

(a) Statement I is incorrect, but statement II is correct
(b) Both statement I and statement II are correct
(c) Both statement I and statement II are incorrect
(d) Statement I is correct, but statement II is incorrect

10. Among the following, identify the odd statement regarding pelvic girdle.

(a) It transfers the weight of the body to the legs.
(b) Support vertebral column.
(c) It provides articulation to the arm bones.
(d) It support and project the abdominal viscera.

11. Given below is the diagram of the human backbone. Which of the following forms the articulating surface for the ribs?

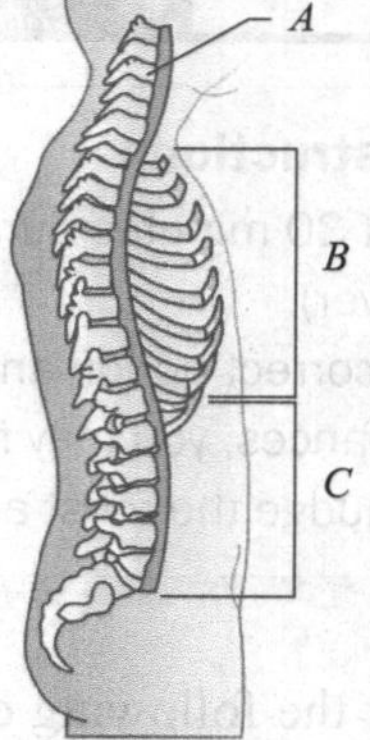

(a) *A* and *B*
(b) Only *B*
(c) Only *A*
(d) *A* and *C*

12. Match List I with List II.

	List I		List II
A.	Patella	1.	Fibrous cartilage
B.	Radius	2.	Palm
C.	Metacarpals	3.	Knee cap
D.	Pubic symphysis	4.	Arm bone

Choose the correct answer from the options given below.

(a) A-3, B-4, C-2, D-1
(b) A-3, B-2, C-4, D-1
(c) A-3, B-1, C-2, D-4
(d) A-3, B-1, C-4,D-2

13. Consider the following statements.

I. Each rib is a flat bone that connects ventrally to the vertebral column.

II. True ribs articulate with both the vertebral column and the sternum.

III. Hyaline cartilage supports 11th and 12th rib to the sternum ventrally.

IV. Floating ribs are connected ventrally and do not connect dorsally at all.

Choose the correct statement(s) from the options given below.

(a) Only II (b) I and IV
(c) I and III (d) Only IV

14. Following images represent the two girdles of human body.

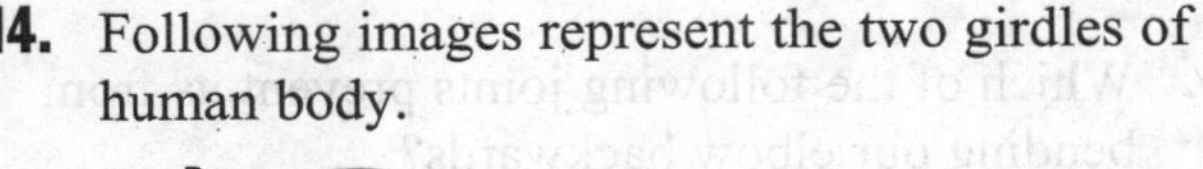

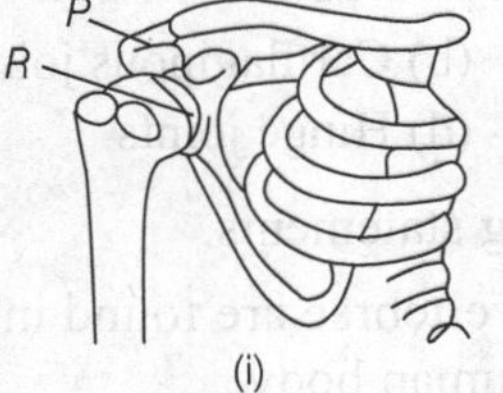

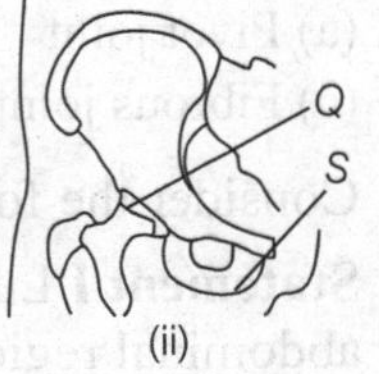

Choose the correct answer from the options given below.

(a) (i)-Pectoral girdle, *P* - Acromion, *R* - Glenoid
(ii)-Pelvic girdle, *Q* - Acetabulum, *S* - Ischium
(b) (i)-Pectoral girdle, *P* - Acromion, *R* - Glenoid
(ii)-Pelvic girdle, *Q*-Acetabulum, *S* - Ilium
(c) (i)-Pectoral girdle, *P* - Acromion, *R* - Acetabulum
(ii)-Pelvic girdle, *Q*- Glenoid, *S* - Ischium
(d) (i)-Pectoral girdle, *P* - Acromion, *R*- Acetabulum,
(ii)-Pelvic girdle, *Q* - Glenoid *S*-Ilium

15. Which of the following is not correct about rotational movement of the head?

(a) The side ways rotation is allowed by the pivot joint
(b) Synovial fluid lubricates the articulating bones of the joint
(c) Cartilaginous joint between atlas and axis allows rotation
(d) Atlas, the first vertebra articulates with the dicondylic skull

16. '*X*' provides a cushioning effect on bones present at the joints. Which of the following is an exclusive component of the matrix of *X*?

(a) Calcium phosphate (b) Chondroitin salts
(c) Calcium chloride (d) Collagen

17. Which of the following skull bones support the eyes and the structure that are involved in tear production?

(a) Zygomatic bone
(b) Sphenoid bone
(c) Maxilla
(d) Lacrimal

18. Given below are two statements; one is labelled as Assertion (A) and the other is labelled Reason (R).

Assertion (A) Fracture to the occipital condyle can cause immobilisation of head.

Reason (R) Human skull is dicondylic due to the presence of two occipital condyles .

In the light of the above statements, choose the correct answer from the options given below.

(a) A is false, but R is true
(b) Both A and R are true and R is the correct explanation of A
(c) Both A and R are true, but R is not the correct explanation of A
(d) A is true, but R is false

19. Given below are two statements.

Statement I Each vertebra is a solid structure present in the back bone.

Statement II Axis articulates directly with the occipital condyle of the skull.

In the light of the above statements, choose the correct answer from the options given below:

(a) Statement I is incorrect, but statement II is correct
(b) Both statement I and statement II are correct
(c) Both statement I and statement II are incorrect
(d) Statement I is correct, but statement II is incorrect

20. Ventral articulation of which of the following ribs would be affected if hyaline cartilage was damaged?

(a) True ribs only
(b) 8th, 9th and 10th pairs of ribs
(c) First 10 pairs of ribs
(d) False and floating ribs

21. Given below is the diagrammatic representation of a part of the appendicular skeleton. Which of the following joints allow the maximum flexibility and movement?

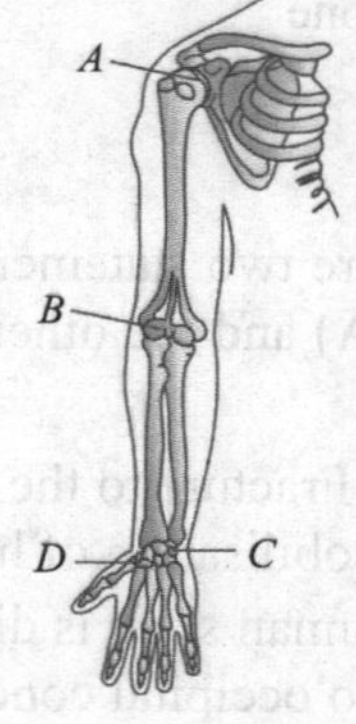

(a) A (b) D
(c) B (d) C

22. Given below are two statements.

Statement I Ischium is one of the hip bone that forms the pelvic girdle.

Statement II A coxal bone is a fused structure in the pelvic girdle.

In the light of the above statements, choose the correct answer from the options given below.

(a) Statement I is incorrect, but statement II is correct
(b) Both statement I and statement II are correct
(c) Both statement I and statement II are incorrect
(d) Statement I is correct, but statement II is incorrect

23. Which of the following disorder of the skeletomuscular system, can be transmitted by a person to his children?

(a) Myasthenia gravis
(b) Muscular dystrophy
(c) Osteoporosis
(d) Gout

24. Which of the following joints prevent us from bending our elbow backwards?

(a) Pivot joint (b) Cartilaginous joints
(c) Fibrous joints (d) Hinge joints

25. Consider the following statements.

Statement I Lumbar vertebrae are found in abdominal region in human body.

Statement II Lumbar vertebrae lack foramen in the transverse process.

In the light of the above statements, choose the correct answer from the options given below.

(a) Statement I is incorrect, but statement II is correct
(b) Both statement I and statement II are correct
(c) Both statement I and statement II are incorrect
(d) Statement I is correct, but statement II is incorrect

Response Index

01	a	b	c	d	10	a	b	c	d	19	a	b	c	d
02	a	b	c	d	11	a	b	c	d	20	a	b	c	d
03	a	b	c	d	12	a	b	c	d	21	a	b	c	d
04	a	b	c	d	13	a	b	c	d	22	a	b	c	d
05	a	b	c	d	14	a	b	c	d	23	a	b	c	d
06	a	b	c	d	15	a	b	c	d	24	a	b	c	d
07	a	b	c	d	16	a	b	c	d	25	a	b	c	d
08	a	b	c	d	17	a	b	c	d					
09	a	b	c	d	18	a	b	c	d					

Performance Scanner

> 90% Excellent !	You have mastered these topics. The concepts of these topics are at your fingertips. Move on to the next test and maintain this momentum.
76-90% Very Good !	You have a good command over these topics. Revise these topics again after a few days and enhance your performance.
60-75% Good !	You have a wide scope to learn for these topics. Revise these topics again.
<60% Not Satisfactory!	You have a long way ahead of you to master these topics. Revise it thoroughly.

Chapter Break Thru

Syllabus

- Types of Movement-Ciliary, Flagellar, Muscular; Skeletal Muscle-Contractile Proteins and Muscle Contraction;
- Skeletal System and its Function
- Joints;
- Disorders of Muscular and Skeletal System-Myasthenia Gravis, Tetany, Muscular Dystrophy, Arthritis, Osteoporososis and Gout.

Important Instructions

- The test is of 1 hour duration and contains 50 Multiple-Choice Questions (Four options with a single correct answer).
- Choose the correct option and fill the OMR given on the last page of this test accordingly.
- At some instances, you may find more than 1 option to be correct. In such circumstances, you have to judge the most appropriate answer as per the conditions given in the question.

1. Following is the diagrammatic representation of changes associated with myofibrils.

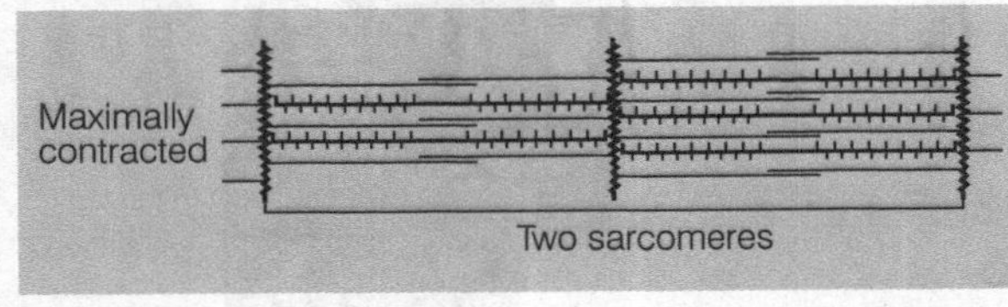

Which of the following is correct about the given representation?

(a) The change is associated with an increase in Ca2+ level in sarcoplasmic reticulum.

(b) Energy is driven by ATP hydrolysis by the globular proteins of the actin filaments.

(c) Inward movement of the Z lines causes shortening and contraction of the sarcomere.

(d) The H-zone which makes up the central portion of the thin filaments is overlapped.

2. Given below are two statements; one is labelled as Assertion (A) and other is labelled as Reason (R).

Assertion (A) The red fibres contain more mitochondria than white fibres.

Reason (R) Red muscle fibres respire aerobically to meet their energy needs.

In the light of the above statements, choose the correct answer from the options given below.

(a) A is false, but R is true

(b) Both A and R are true and R is the correct explanation of A

(c) Both A and R are true, but R is not the correct explanation of A

(d) A is true, but R is false

3. Uncontrolled muscular contraction is caused due to

(a) genetic disorder (b) autoimmune disease

(c) low Ca^{2+} in plasma (d) high uric acid

4. Given below are two statements.

Statement I Bending of elbow is not a free circular movement.

Statement II Bones at the elbow joint are easily eroded by friction.

In the light of the above statements, choose the correct answer from the options given below.

(a) Statement I is incorrect, but statement II is correct

(b) Both statement I and statement II are correct

(c) Both statement I and statement II are incorrect

(d) Statement I is correct, but statement II is incorrect

5. Following is the diagrammatic representation of the thin filaments of myofibrils. Which of the following maintains relaxed state of the muscle fibres?

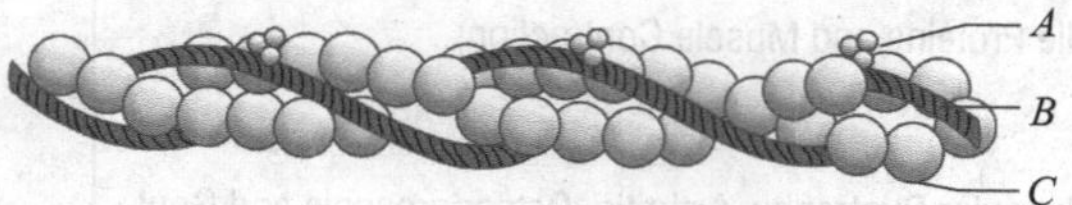

(a) *A* and *C* (b) *B* only
(c) *A* only (d) *A* and *B*

6. All of the following are included in the cross arm except
(a) tail (b) head
(c) short arm (d) ATP site

7. Following are the steps involved in initiation of contraction.
A. ATP hydrolyses to form cross bridge.
B. Increase in Ca^{2+} in the sarcoplasm.
C. Release of acetylcholine.
D. Impulse conduction at the motor unit.
E. Action potential at sarcolemma.
Choose the correct order from the options given below.
(a) D-C-E-B-A (b) C-D-E-B-A
(c) D-E-C-B-A (d) C-E-D-B-A

8. Up and down movement of the foot at the ankle is supported by
(a) gliding joint (b) hinge joint
(c) pivot joint (d) saddle joint

9. Which of the following joints allow movement in many direction?
(a) Saddle joint and gliding joint
(b) Ball and socket joint and saddle joint
(c) Pivot joint and hinge joint
(d) Ball and socket joint and hinge joint

10. Match List I with List II.

List I	List II
A. Maxilla	1. Fixed skull bone
B. Temporal	2. Supports the tongue
C. Hyoid	3. Smallest bone
D. Stapes	4. Supports the ear

Choose the correct answer from the options given below.
(a) A-1, B-3, C-2, D-4
(b) A-1, B-4, C-2, D-3
(c) A-2, B-4, C-1, D-3
(d) A-2, B-3, C-4, D-1

11. Which of the following pair is correct?
(a) Diaphragm – Visceral muscle
(b) Stomach wall – Striated muscle
(c) Uterus – Visceral muscle
(d) Urinary bladder – Striated muscle

12. Following is the diagrammatic representation of the cross-sectional view of a muscle. Identify the structure labelled as *A* and choose the incorrect statement regarding it from the options given below.

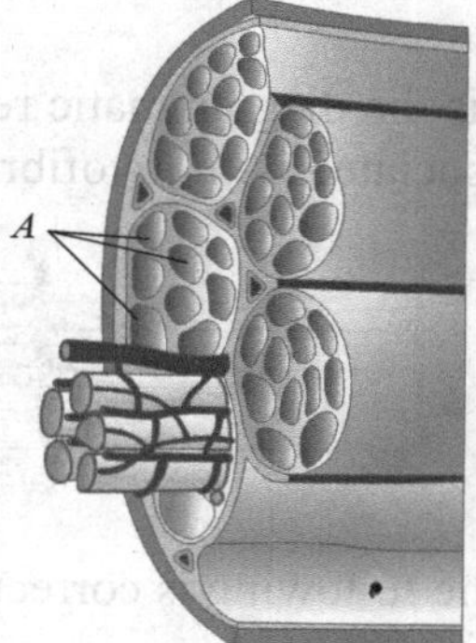

(a) Its membrane is permeable to certain molecules.
(b) The cytoplasm contains one distinct prominent nucleus.
(c) The ER acts as a reservoir of calcium ions.
(d) Filamentous proteins are arranged in the cytoplasm.

13. Consider the following statements regarding thin and thick filaments.
I. Elasticity of M-line facilitates its movement during contraction.
II. Alternate arrangement of A and I-bands account for the striations.
III. Changes in the A-band increase or decrease the length of sarcomere.
IV. H-zone completely disappears when the fibres are under relaxation.

Choose the correct statement from the options given below.

(a) II only (b) I only
(c) IV only (d) III only

14. Given below are two statements.

Statement I The elbow joint is formed from three bones.

Statement II Articulating surface in an elbow encloses a cavity.

In the light of the above statements, choose the correct answer from the options given below.

(a) Statement I is incorrect, but statement II is correct
(b) Both statement I and statement II are correct
(c) Both statement I and statement II are incorrect
(d) Statement I is correct, but statement II is incorrect

15. Given below diagram represents interaction between the thin and thick filaments. Which of the following does not lead to the event represented in the diagram?

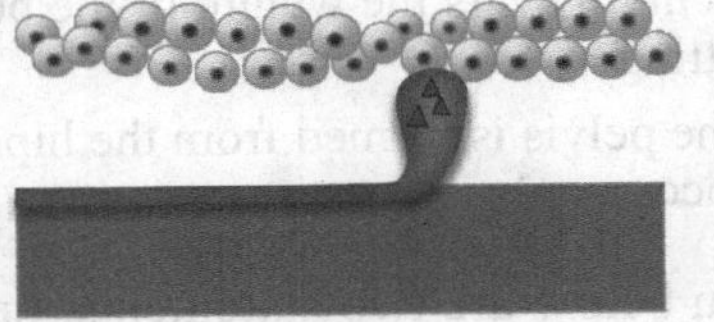

(a) Hydrolysis of ATP to form ADP and Pi
(b) Efflux of Ca^{2+} from sarcoplasmic reticulum
(c) Masking of active sites on actin
(d) Action potential spreading through sarcolemma

16. Which of the following has the highest mitochondrial density?

(a) Nerve cell
(b) Cardiac muscle
(c) Skin cell
(d) Adipocytes

17. Given below are two statements; one is labelled as Assertion (A) and other is labelled as Reason (R).

Assertion (A) Muscle contraction force increases with rise in strength of stimulus in case of involuntary muscles.

Reason (R) Increase in strength of stimulus increases the contraction of individual muscle fibre in voluntary muscle.

In the light of the above statements, choose the correct answer from the options given below.

(a) A is false, but R is true
(b) Both A and R are true and R is the correct explanation of A
(c) Both A and R are true, but R is not the correct explanation of A
(d) A is true, but R is false

18. The number of bones present in a skeleton that runs along the middle longitudinal axis of the body is

(a) 87 (b) 90
(c) 80 (d) 78

19. Two forms of actin protein present in thin filaments are

(a) monomeric G-actin and monomeric F-actin
(b) monomeric G-actin and polymeric F-actin
(c) polymeric G-actin and monomeric F-actin
(d) polymeric G-actin and polymeric F-actin

20. The number of bones that make up the rib cage is

(a) 37 (b) 24 (c) 25 (d) 21

21. All of the structures are formed from fusion of bones, except

(a) coxal (b) sternum
(c) sacrum (d) coccyx

22. Given below are two statements.

Statement I The vertebral column bears the weight of the skull.

Statement II Axis provides the articulating surface for the occipital condyles.

In the light of the above statements, choose the correct answer from the options given below.

(a) Statement I is incorrect, but statement II is correct
(b) Both statement I and statement II are correct
(c) Both statement I and statement II are incorrect
(d) Statement I is correct, but statement II is incorrect

23. Match List I with List II.

	List I	List II
A.	Cervical vertebrae	1. 8
B.	True ribs	2. 7
C.	Palm	3. 14
D.	Wrist	4. 5

Choose the correct answer from the options given below.
(a) A-2, B-3, C-4, D-1
(b) A-2, B-3, C-1, D-4
(c) A-4, B-3, C-2, D-1
(d) A-4, B-2, C-3, D-1

24. Following are the statements related to muscles in human body.

I. Leg muscles attached to tibia exist in syncytium.
II. Muscles of the bladder contain multiple nuclei.
III. Muscle in visceral organs have spindle shape.
IV. Muscle of the heart show a branching pattern.
V. All visceral muscles have branched appearance.

Choose the correct set of statements from the options given below.
(a) II and III (b) I, III and IV
(c) II, IV and V (d) I, II and IV

25. Given below are two statements.
Statement I Vestigial tail bone in humans is formed by fusion of four or five coccygeal bone.
Statement II Coccyx located adjacent to lumbar vertebrae, forms the last part of backbone.
In the light of the above statements, choose the correct answer from the options given below.
(a) Statement I is incorrect, but statement II is correct
(b) Both statement I and statement II are correct
(c) Both statement I and statement II are incorrect
(d) Statement I is correct, but statement II is incorrect

26. Match List I with List II.

List I	List II
A. Tetany	1. Attack by immune system
B. Osteoporosis	2. Inheritable
C. Myasthenia gravis	3. Common in women
D. Muscular dystrophy	4. Uncontrolled twitching

Choose the correct answer from the options given below.
(a) A-4, B-3, C-2, D-1 (b) A-4, B-2, C-1, D-3
(c) A-4, B-3, C-1, D-2 (d) A-4, B-2, C-3, D-1

27. Given below are two statements; one is labelled as Assertion (A) and other is labelled as Reason (R).
Assertion (A) Ca^{2+} regulates the breakage of cross bridge during relaxation.
Reason (R) Fall in Ca^{2+} levels in sarcoplasm, causes masking of myosin binding sites on actin.
In the light of the above statements, choose the correct answer from the options given below.
(a) A is false, but R is true
(b) Both A and R are true and R is the correct explanation of A
(c) Both A and R are true, but R is not the correct explanation of A
(d) A is true, but R is false

28. Which of the following is not correct about the pelvic girdle?
(a) Two halves of pelvic girdle is joined by a connective tissue.
(b) Acetabulum articulates with the longest bone in human body.
(c) Ischium bears the weight of the body while sitting.
(d) The pelvis is formed from the hip bone and the coccyx only.

29. Given below are two statements; one is labelled as Assertion (A) and the other is labelled as Reason (R).
Assertion (A) Some WBCs of the blood have no definite shape and move like an *Amoeba*.
Reason (R) WBCs play a major role in the defence of the body against invading germs.
In the light of the above statements, choose the correct answer from the options given below.
(a) A is false, but R is true
(b) Both A and R are true and R is the correct explanation of A
(c) Both A and R are true, but R is not the correct explanation of A
(d) A is true, but R is false

30. Given below is the diagrammatic representation of the thin and thick filaments under certain condition of the muscle. Which of the following is correct from the options given below?

(a) The appearance of *A* confirms contraction phase of muscles.
(b) During this phase, the distance between two successive *X* shortens.
(c) *B* is pulled outward to its normal position during the phase shown.
(d) *C* is pulled inward and its length decreases during the phase shown.

31. Given below are two statements.

Statement I All involuntary actions of human body are mediated by non-striated muscles only.

Statement II Most voluntary movements are facilitated by muscles with stripped appearance.

In the light of the above statements, choose the correct answer from the options given below.

(a) Statement I is incorrect, but statement II is correct
(b) Both statement I and statement II are correct
(c) Both statement I and statement II are incorrect
(d) Statement I is correct but statement II is incorrect

32. Given below are two statements; one is labelled as Assertion (A) and the other is labelled as Reason (R).

Assertion (A) A bands do not change their length during contraction.

Reason (R) The length of A band is the same as the myosin filament.

In the light of the above statements, choose the correct options given below.

(a) A is false, but R is true.
(b) Both A and R are true and R is the correct explanation of A
(c) Both A and R are true, but R is not the correct explanation of A
(d) A is true, but R is false

33. Match List I with List II.

List I	List II
A. Troponin	1. Cross arm
B. HMM	2. Monomeric protein
C. Globular head	3. Calcium binding site
D. G-actin	4. ATP binding site

Choose the correct answer from the options given below.

(a) A-3, B-1, C-4, D-2
(b) A-3, B-4, C-1, D-2
(c) A-2, B-1, C-4, D-3
(d) A-2, B-4, C-1, D-3

34. Given below are two statements.

Statement I Fascicles maintain the structural integrity of fascia.

Statement II Actin and myosin provide the striations to skeletal muscles.

In the light to the above statements, choose the correct answer from the options given below.

(a) Statement I is incorrect, but statement II is correct
(b) Both statement I and statement II are correct
(c) Both statement I and statement II are incorrect
(d) Statement I is correct, but statement II is incorrect

35. Formation of cross bridge is associated with

(a) ADP and *Pi* bound to HMM
(b) ATP bound to HMM
(c) ADP and *Pi* released from HMM
(d) ATP released from HMM

36. Following are the steps involved in relaxation of muscle fibres.

I. Breaking of cross-bridge at the actin-myosin site.
II. Binding of ATP by the globular myosin head.
III. Calcium ions pumped into sarcoplasmic reticulum.
IV. The sarcomere regains its original length.
V. Z-lines return to their original position

Choose the correct order from the options given below.

(a) II-I-III-IV-V
(b) II-I-III-V-IV
(c) III-II-I-V-IV
(d) III-I-II-IV-V

37. Muscle fibres relax and return to normal position when the troponin masks
(a) actin binding site (b) myosin binding site
(c) ATP binding site (d) calcium binding site

38. Consider the following functions mediated by muscles.
I. Flow of blood through arteries
II. Passage of urine through the urethra
III. Tongue involved in speaking
IV. Breathing in air by contracting diaphragm
Choose the function that involves unstriated muscles.
(a) I and IV (b) I and II
(c) I only (d) II and III

39. Which of the following would happen if the ATPase activity of HMM is impaired?
(a) Muscle fibres would be arrested in contraction phase
(b) Muscles would not be able to initiate contraction
(c) Cross bridge formed will not be able to break
(d) I-bands would be strained due to prolonged contraction

40. Given below are two statements; one is labelled as Assertion (A) and the other is labelled as Reason (R).
Assertion (A) A chemical inhibitor of muscle contraction should bind to HMM.
Reason (R) Globular head of heavy meromyosin is an active ATPase enzyme.
In the light of the above statements, choose the correct answer from the options given below.
(a) A is false, but R is true
(b) Both A and R are true and R is the correct explanation of A
(c) Both A and R are true, but R is not the correct explanation of A
(d) A is true, but R is false

41. Match the List I with List II.

	List I		List II
A.	Zygomatic bone	1.	Possess foramen magnum
B.	Parietal bone	2.	Inferior portion of nasal septum.
C.	Vomer	3.	Prominence of cheek
D.	Occipital bone	4.	Roof of cranial cavity

Choose the correct option from the options given below.

	A	B	C	D
(a)	2	4	3	1
(b)	4	2	1	3
(c)	3	1	4	2
(d)	3	4	2	1

42. Which of the following is incorrect with respect to ciliary movement?
(a) Cilia of choanocyte cells maintain a regular current of water through the canal system
(b) It occurs in internal tubular organs of higher animals
(c) It helps in removing waste substances inhaled along with air
(d) It facilitate the passage of ova through the female reproductive tract

43. The human ribs are termed as bicephalic because
(a) they have two articulations surfaces on their ventral end
(b) they have two articulations surfaces on their dorsal end
(c) they have two articulations surfaces on their ventral end and two on the dorsal end
(d) they have two articulations surfaces on their ventral end and one on the dorsal end

44. Given below are the two statements; one is labelled as Assertion (A) and the other is labelled as Reason (R).
Assertion (A) Muscle twitch is related with tetanus.
Reason (R) Tetanus is caused by many nerve impulse at a time.
In the light of the above statements, choose the correct answer from the options given below.
(a) A is false, but R is true
(b) Both A and R are true and R is the correct explanation of A
(c) Both A and R are true, but R is not the correct explanation of A
(d) A is true, but R is false

45. Sliding filament theory can be best explained as
(a) when myofilaments slide pass each other actin filaments shorten while myosin filament do not shorten
(b) actin and myosin filaments shorten and slide pass each other

(c) actin and myosin filaments do not shorten, but rather slide pass each other
(d) when myofilament slide pass each other myosin filament shorten while actin filaments do not shorten

46. In old age, stiffness of joints is due to the
(a) hardening of bones
(b) inefficiency of muscles
(c) decrease in synovial fluid
(d) enlargement of bones

47. Given below are two statements.
Statement I Gout is an inherited disorder of purine metabolism.
Statement II Muscular dystrophy disorder is characterised by damage and progressive skeletal muscle weakness overtime.
In the light of the above statements, choose the correct answer from the options given below.
(a) Statement I is incorrect, but statement II is correct
(b) Both statement I and statement II are correct
(c) Both statement I and statement II are incorrect
(d) Statement I is correct, but statement II is incorrect

48. Which of the following statement about human vertebral column is false?
(a) It is placed dorsally
(b) It consists of 26 vertebrae
(c) It extends from the base of skull and constituents the main framework of the trunk
(d) Neural canal in vertebra is the passage for spinal cord

49. Consider the following statements.
I. Sternum takes part in the formation of the protective thoracic basket.
II. The vertebrochondral ribs protect the heart and lungs from harm.
III. Scapula is a long, narrow S-shaped bone that forms the posterior part of shoulder girdle.
IV. Axis supports the head and it consist of a complete ring of bone.
V. Thoracic vertebrae are the largest and strongest vertebrae of human body.
Choose the incorrect set of statements from the options given below.
(a) II, III and IV
(b) I and II
(c) III, IV and V
(d) I and III

50. Consider the following diagram and identify the incorrect statement regarding labelled part.

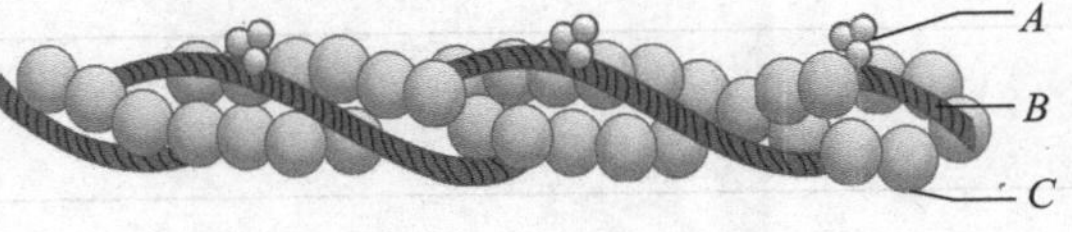

(a) A is a complex of three polypeptides, i.e., trimeric protein
(b) B prevents the contraction of muscle fibres, exposure of myosin binding site of actin.
(c) G-actin polymerises to the fibrous form 'C' in the presence of Mg^{2+}.
(d) A is responsible for keeping C in place when muscle is relaxed.

Scan for online chapter test

Response Index

01 ⓐ ⓑ ⓒ ⓓ	14 ⓐ ⓑ ⓒ ⓓ	27 ⓐ ⓑ ⓒ ⓓ	40 ⓐ ⓑ ⓒ ⓓ
02 ⓐ ⓑ ⓒ ⓓ	15 ⓐ ⓑ ⓒ ⓓ	28 ⓐ ⓑ ⓒ ⓓ	41 ⓐ ⓑ ⓒ ⓓ
03 ⓐ ⓑ ⓒ ⓓ	16 ⓐ ⓑ ⓒ ⓓ	29 ⓐ ⓑ ⓒ ⓓ	42 ⓐ ⓑ ⓒ ⓓ
04 ⓐ ⓑ ⓒ ⓓ	17 ⓐ ⓑ ⓒ ⓓ	30 ⓐ ⓑ ⓒ ⓓ	43 ⓐ ⓑ ⓒ ⓓ
05 ⓐ ⓑ ⓒ ⓓ	18 ⓐ ⓑ ⓒ ⓓ	31 ⓐ ⓑ ⓒ ⓓ	44 ⓐ ⓑ ⓒ ⓓ
06 ⓐ ⓑ ⓒ ⓓ	19 ⓐ ⓑ ⓒ ⓓ	32 ⓐ ⓑ ⓒ ⓓ	45 ⓐ ⓑ ⓒ ⓓ
07 ⓐ ⓑ ⓒ ⓓ	20 ⓐ ⓑ ⓒ ⓓ	33 ⓐ ⓑ ⓒ ⓓ	46 ⓐ ⓑ ⓒ ⓓ
08 ⓐ ⓑ ⓒ ⓓ	21 ⓐ ⓑ ⓒ ⓓ	34 ⓐ ⓑ ⓒ ⓓ	47 ⓐ ⓑ ⓒ ⓓ
09 ⓐ ⓑ ⓒ ⓓ	22 ⓐ ⓑ ⓒ ⓓ	35 ⓐ ⓑ ⓒ ⓓ	48 ⓐ ⓑ ⓒ ⓓ
10 ⓐ ⓑ ⓒ ⓓ	23 ⓐ ⓑ ⓒ ⓓ	36 ⓐ ⓑ ⓒ ⓓ	49 ⓐ ⓑ ⓒ ⓓ
11 ⓐ ⓑ ⓒ ⓓ	24 ⓐ ⓑ ⓒ ⓓ	37 ⓐ ⓑ ⓒ ⓓ	50 ⓐ ⓑ ⓒ ⓓ
12 ⓐ ⓑ ⓒ ⓓ	25 ⓐ ⓑ ⓒ ⓓ	38 ⓐ ⓑ ⓒ ⓓ	
13 ⓐ ⓑ ⓒ ⓓ	26 ⓐ ⓑ ⓒ ⓓ	39 ⓐ ⓑ ⓒ ⓓ	

Performance Scanner

> 90% Excellent !	You have mastered this chapter. The concepts of this chapter are at your fingertips. Move on to the next chapter and maintain this momentum.
76-90% Very Good !	You have a good command over this chapter. Revise the chapter again after a few days and enhance your performance.
60-75% Good !	You have a wide scope to learn for this chapter. Revise this chapter again.
<60% Not Satisfactory!	You have a long way ahead of you to master this chapter. Revise it thoroughly.

Space for Rough Work

MEDACE
NEET (UG)
SELF ASSESSMENT KIT

Test Booklet No. 3947318

Test Booklet Code CH18

Neural Control and Coordination

Topics Covered

Human Nervous System and Neurons

Central Nervous System

Important Instructions

- This Booklet Contains – Two Topic Tests and One Test on Complete Chapter.
- Each question carries 4 marks.
- For each correct response, the candidate will get 4 marks. And for every incorrect response, 1 mark will be additionally deducted from total score.
- Use **Blue/Black** point pen only for filling the OMR.
- Rough work is to be done in the space provided for this purpose in the test booklet only.

Name of the Candidate (In Capitals) ____________________

____

Candidate's Signature ____________________

Invigilator's Signature ____________________

Facsimile signature stamp of center superintendent ____________________

Do not open this booklet until you start attempting the test

Topical Follow Thru

Test 1

Syllabus

- Neuron and Nerves
- Generation and Conduction of Nerve Impulse
- Peripheral Nervous System
- Visceral Nervous System

For deeper insight, **Scan the QR Code**

Important Instructions

- The test is of 30 minutes duration and contains 25 Multiple Choice Questions (four options with a single correct answer).
- Choose the correct option and fill the OMR given on the last page of this test accordingly.
- At some instances, you may find more than 1 option to be correct. In such circumstances, you have to judge the most appropriate answer as per the conditions given in the question.

1. Which animal lacks a brain, but possesses nerve cells?

(a) *Pheretima*
(b) *Hydra*
(c) *Scypha*
(d) *Periplanata americana*

2. Suppose the terminal ends of axon are in contact with the dendrites of four adjacent neurons, the nerve impulse of the axon will

(a) travel in all the four neurons.
(b) get distributed in the four neurons resulting in a weak impulse.
(c) travel only in one neuron which is in closest contact and with the same intensity.
(d) travel in none of the neurons because the impulse travels from the dendrites of one neuron into the axon of another neuron.

3. Which of the following statements are correct regarding a myelinated nerve fibre?

I. It is found in cranial and spinal nerves.
II. It possesses a myelin sheath that is produced by Schwann cells in CNS.
III. It allows slow conduction of nerve impulses.
IV. It has nodes of Ranvier.

Choose the correct option from the following.

(a) I and IV
(b) II and III
(c) I, II and IV
(d) I, III and IV

4. Match the following descriptions (A-C) to the associated structure labelled as (1-8) in the given figure of neuron.

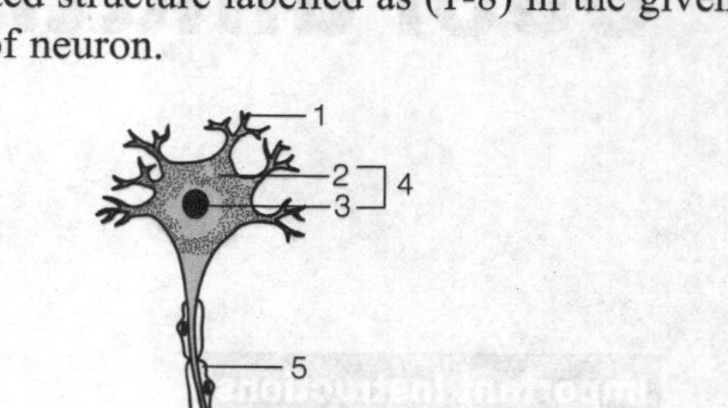

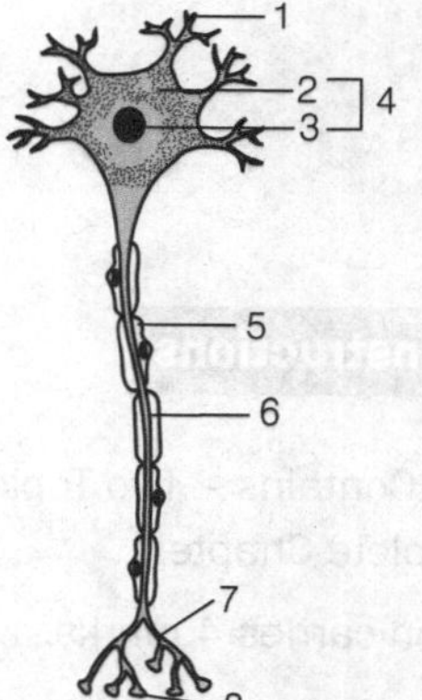

A. Structure is responsible for maintaining the metabolic and synthetic activities of neuron that are necessary for its survival and function.
B. Structure receives nerve impulses and passes them towards the cell body.
C. Structure contains vesicles of neurotransmitters.

Choose the correct option from the following.

(a) A-5, B-4 and C-8
(b) A-4, B-1 and C-8
(c) A-8, B-6 and C-1
(d) A-4, B-8 and C-6

5. Given below are two statements.

Statement I The sodium-potassium pump is essential for maintaining the resting membrane potential of neurons by actively transporting ions against their concentration gradients.

Statement II The endocrine system regulates physiological processes through neurotransmitters that modulate synaptic transmission between neurons.

In the light of the above statements, choose the correct answer from the options given below.

(a) Statement I is incorrect, but statement II is correct
(b) Both statement I and statement II are correct
(c) Both statement I and statement II are incorrect
(d) Statement I is correct, but statement II is incorrect

6. Which of the following statement is correct about dendrites?

(a) They are single cytoplasmic process.
(b) They transmit impulse from synapse to cell body.
(c) They are surrounded by neurilemma.
(d) They are called efferent processes.

7. Sensory information received by the body ultimately influences the brain's actions. Which type of neural pathway acts as the initial bridge for this information flow?

(a) Motor (b) Afferent
(c) Efferent (d) Mixed

8. The sequence of events in a nerve conduction is

(a) threshold → depolarisation → repolarisation → hyperpolarisation
(b) resting potential → repolarisation → depolarisation
(c) repolarisation → threshold → depolarisation → hyperpolarisation
(d) hyperpolarisation → repolarisation → depolarisation

9. The sodium-potassium pump actively transports ions to maintain an electrochemical gradient across the membrane. This gradient is crucial for nerve impulse transmission. Which statement accurately reflects the net effect of the pump on sodium (Na^+) and potassium (K^+) concentration?

(a) Decreased concentration of Na^+ outside the cell and increased concentration of K^+ inside the cell.
(b) Increased concentration of Na^+ outside the cell and decreased concentration of K^+ inside the cell.
(c) Increased concentration of Na^+ outside the cell and concentration of K^+ inside the cell.
(d) Decreased concentration of Na^+ inside the cell and decreased concentration of K^+ outside the cell.

10. Given below are two statements; one is labelled as Assertion (A) and other is labelled as Reason (R).

Assertion (A) Tiny packages called synaptic vesicles dot the pre-synaptic neuron. Their contents play a crucial role in neuronal communication.

Reason (R) A specialised gap separates neurons, but these vesicles bridge the gap with a chemical exchange.

In the light of above statements, choose the correct answer from the options given below.

(a) A is false, but R is true
(b) Both A and R are true and R is the correct explanation of A
(c) Both A and R are true, but R is not the correct explanation of A
(d) A is true, but R is false

11. Which of the following ions are necessary for nerve conduction?

(a) Calcium, sodium and potassium ions
(b) Calcium and magnesium ions
(c) Magnesium and potassium ions
(d) Sodium, potassium and magnesium ions

12. Which of the following best describes the structure of a bipolar neuron?

(a) Multiple dendrites and multiple axons
(b) One dendrite and multiple axons
(c) Multiple dendrites and one axon
(d) One dendrite and one axon

13. Select the correct match.

(a) Resting membrane potential – + 60 V
(b) Depolarisation– Opening of K^+ gated channels
(c) Repolarisation– Opening of Na^+ gated channels
(d) Sodium-potassium pump– Pump $3Na^+$ outside and $2K^+$ inside the axoplasm

14. Which of the following correctly describes a synaptic cleft?

(a) The space within the pre-synaptic neuron where neurotransmitters are synthesised.

(b) The space within the post-synaptic neuron where neurotransmitters are received.

(c) The space surrounding the synaptic vesicles inside the pre-synaptic neuron.

(d) The space separating the pre-synaptic and post-synaptic neurons where neurotransmitter communication occurs.

15. Which of the following statement is incorrect about the neural system?

(a) It provides an organised network of point-to-point connections for quick coordination.

(b) The coordination involves both electrical and chemical signals.

(c) It is the complex network of nerves and cells that carry massages.

(d) The coordination is fast and long-lived.

16. The sensory neuron enters the spinal cord through

(a) the dorsal root of the spinal nerve

(b) the ventral root of the spinal nerve

(c) Either dorsal or ventral root depending on the point of origin

(d) Both dorsal and ventral roots of the spinal nerves

17. Unmyelinated nerves fibres are

(a) myelin sheaths that are not enclosed by Schwann cells.

(b) surrounded by a Schwann cell that does not form a myelin sheath.

(c) myelin sheath formed by oligodendrocytes, not Schwann cells.

(d) not found in the autonomous or somatic nervous systems.

18. Which of the following statement is incorrect with respect to electrical synapse?

(a) Impulse conduction is faster.

(b) The neurotransmitter released from the pre-synaptic membrane binds to receptors on post-synaptic membrane.

(c) Transmission of an impulse is very similar to impulse conduction along a single axon.

(d) The impulse can flow directly from one neuron to other.

19. Which of the following statement about parasympathetic neurons is true?

(a) The nerve fibres are contained in spinal nerves.

(b) They synapse in terminal ganglia, either next to or within the organs innervated.

(c) They originate in thoracic and lumbar regions of the spinal cord.

(d) Post-ganglionic fibres are usually longer than those of sympathetic neurons.

20. When the neuron is not conducting any impulse, i.e. resting, the axonal membrane

(a) is comparatively more permeable to sodium ions and nearly impermeable to potassium ions.

(b) is freely permeable to sodium ions and potassium ions.

(c) is impermeable to sodium ions and potassium ions.

(d) is comparatively more permeable to potassium ions and nearly impermeable to sodium ions.

21. Which of the following statements are correct about resting state?

I. Neuron is not conducting any impulse.

II. Plasma membrane is electrically positive outside and negative inside.

III. The nerve fibre is stimulated and conducts mechanical or electrical impulse.

IV. Plasma membrane is negative outside and positive inside.

Choose the correct option.

(a) III and IV (b) I and IV

(c) II and III (d) I and II

22. In a resting fibre, the concentration of potassium ions is

(a) higher in the extracellular space than axoplasm

(b) higher in the axoplasm than extracellular space.

(c) Both ECF and axoplasm, have equal concentration

(d) first higher in ECF than in axoplasm

23. Given below are two statements; one is labelled as Assertion (A) and other is labelled as Reason (R).

Assertion (A) Neuroglial cells are known as the packing cells of brain.

Reason (R) A type of neuroglial cells forms the myelin sheath around axon.

In the light of the above statements, choose the correct answer from the options given below.

(a) A is false, but R is true
(b) Both A and R are true and R is the correct explanation of A
(c) Both A and R are true, but R is not the correct explanation of A
(d) A is true, but R is false

24. Given below are two statements.

Statement I Neural system is better organised in insects due to the presence of brain, ganglia and neural tissue.

Statement II Neural organisation is very simple in lower invertebrates.

In the light of the above statements, choose the correct answer from the options given below.

(a) Statement I is incorrect, but statement II is correct
(b) Both statement I and statement II are correct
(c) Both statement I and statement II are incorrect
(d) Statement I is correct, but statement II is incorrect.

25. Unidirectional transmission of a nerve impulse through nerve fibre is due to the fact that

(a) nerve fibre is covered by myelin sheath
(b) sodium pump starts operating only at the cyton and then continues into the nerve fibre
(c) neurotransmitters are released by dendrites and not by axon endings.
(d) neurotransmiters are released by the axon endings and not by dendrites.

Response Index

01	a	b	c	d	10	a	b	c	d	19	a	b	c	d
02	a	b	c	d	11	a	b	c	d	20	a	b	c	d
03	a	b	c	d	12	a	b	c	d	21	a	b	c	d
04	a	b	c	d	13	a	b	c	d	22	a	b	c	d
05	a	b	c	d	14	a	b	c	d	23	a	b	c	d
06	a	b	c	d	15	a	b	c	d	24	a	b	c	d
07	a	b	c	d	16	a	b	c	d	25	a	b	c	d
08	a	b	c	d	17	a	b	c	d					
09	a	b	c	d	18	a	b	c	d					

Performance Scanner

> 90% Excellent !	You have mastered these topics. The concepts of these topics are at your fingertips. Move on to the next test and maintain this momentum.
76-90% Very Good !	You have a good command over these topics. Revise these topics again after a few days and enhance your performance.
60-75% Good !	You have a wide scope to learn for these topics. Revise these topics again.
<60% Not Satisfactory!	You have a long way ahead of you to master these topics. Revise it thoroughly.

Test 2

Syllabus • Central Nervous System

For deeper insight, **Scan the QR Code**

Important Instructions

- The test is of 30 minutes duration and contains 15 Multiple Choice Questions (four options with a single correct answer).
- Choose the correct option and fill the OMR given on the last page of this test accordingly.
- At some instances, you may find more than 1 option to be correct. In such circumstances, you have to judge the most appropriate answer as per the conditions given in the question.

1. Which part of the brain serves as the main control center for the autonomic nervous system?

(a) Cerebellum (b) Pons
(c) Hypothalamus (d) Spinal cord

2. Consider the following statements and identify the incorrect one.

(a) Thalamus regulates body temperature, hunger and water balance
(b) Nerve leading to central nervous system are called afferent neurons
(c) The cerebellum is concerned with coordination and muscular movement
(d) Medulla oblongata of brain controls involuntary breathing

3. Match List I with List II.

	List I		List II
A.	Dura mater	1.	Between dura and arachnoid mater
B.	Arachnoid mater	2.	Thick, tough layer closest to the skull
C.	Pia mater	3.	Follows brain contours closely, rich in blood vessels
D.	Subdural space	4.	Delicate, web-like layer with projections

Choose the correct option.

	A	B	C	D
(a)	2	3	1	4
(b)	2	3	4	1
(c)	1	2	3	4
(d)	2	4	3	1

4. Which one of the following is not a lobe of cerebral hemisphere?

(a) Parietal lobe
(b) Occipital lobe
(c) Temporal lobe
(d) Olfactory lobe

5. Which of the following statement about the visceral neural system is correct?

(a) It is the site of information processing and control.
(b) The impulse travels from CNS to visceral and from visceral to CNS.
(c) It mainly involves the cerebrum.
(d) It controls the voluntary movement of involuntary organs.

6. Which of the following statement is incorrect?

(a) Brain maintains balance of both static and dynamic activities.
(b) Temperature regulation of body is called thermoregulation.
(c) 24-hour rhythm of body is called circadian rhythm.
(d) Ductless glands are not under the control of brain.

7. Given below are two statements.

Statement I The limbic system is responsible for olfaction, autonomic response, regulations of sexual behaviour and motivation.

Statement II Fibre tracts present in pons are responsible for inter-connecting different region of brain.

In the light of the above statements, choose the correct answer from the options given below.
(a) Statement I is incorrect, but statement II is correct
(b) Both statement I and statement II are correct
(c) Both statement I and statement II are incorrect
(d) Statement I is correct, but statement II is incorrect

8. Which of the following region of the brain is incorrectly paired with its function?
(a) Corpus callosum – Communication between the left and right cerebral cortices
(b) Cerebrum – Calculation and contemplation
(c) Medulla oblongata – Homeostatic control
(d) Cerebellum – Respiratory rate

9. Forebrain in early developmental stage is called
(a) prosencephalon (b) diencephalon
(c) telencephalon (d) rhombencephalon

10. Which of the following has most of the cerebrospinal fluid at any instant?
(a) Dural sinuses (b) Pia mater
(c) Subarachnoid space (d) Epidural space

11. Which of the following function(s) is/are not associated with the brain stem?
I. Regulation of heart rate and blood pressure.
II. Control of basic life functions such as breathing and consciousness.
III. Coordination of voluntary movements and fine motor skills.
IV. Relay of sensory information from the body to the thalamus.
Choose the correct option.
(a) I and II (b) I and III
(c) III only (d) IV only

12. Read the following statements and identify the incorrect statements.
I. The ventral portion of the midbrain consists mainly of four round swellings called corpora quadrigemina.
II. Midbrain, pons and medulla form the brain stem.
III. Corpora quadrigemina acts as the centre for audio and vision.
IV. The cerebellum wraps around a structure called thalamus.
Choose the correct option.
(a) II and III (b) I and II
(c) I and IV (d) II and IV

13. Which of the following function is performed by the part labelled as *C* in the given diagram?

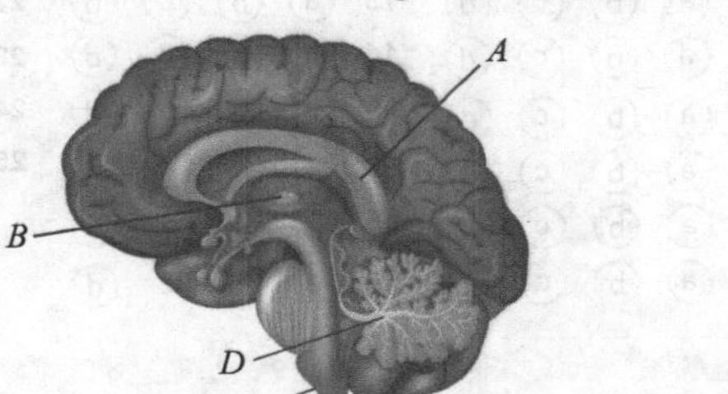

(a) Emotional regulation
(b) Regulation of gastric juices
(c) Learning and memory
(d) Maintenance of posture

14. Given below are two statements.
Statement I Spinal cord has a central canal filled with cerebrospinal fluid.
Statement II Gray matter surrounds the white matter in the spinal cord.
In the light of the above statements, choose the correct answer from the options given below.
(a) Statement I is incorrect, but statement II is correct.
(b) Both statement I and statement II are correct.
(c) Both statement I and statement II are incorrect
(d) Statement I is correct, but statement II is incorrect.

15. Given below are two statements; one is labelled as Assertion (A) and other is labelled as Reason (R).
Assertion (A) The cerebral cortex is referred to as the white matter of the brain and appears whitish.
Reason (R) The cerebral cortex contains high concentration of neuron cell bodies in it.
In the light of above statements, choose the correct answer from the options given below.
(a) A is false, but R is true
(b) Both A and R are true and R is the correct explanation of A.
(c) Both A and R are true, but R is not the correct explanation of A.
(d) A is true, but R is false.

Response Index

01	a	b	c	d	10	a	b	c	d	19	a	b	c	d
02	a	b	c	d	11	a	b	c	d	20	a	b	c	d
03	a	b	c	d	12	a	b	c	d	21	a	b	c	d
04	a	b	c	d	13	a	b	c	d	22	a	b	c	d
05	a	b	c	d	14	a	b	c	d	23	a	b	c	d
06	a	b	c	d	15	a	b	c	d	24	a	b	c	d
07	a	b	c	d	16	a	b	c	d	25	a	b	c	d
08	a	b	c	d	17	a	b	c	d					
09	a	b	c	d	18	a	b	c	d					

Performance Scanner

> 90% Excellent !	You have mastered these topics. The concepts of these topics are at your fingertips. Move on to the next test and maintain this momentum.
76-90% Very Good !	You have a good command over these topics. Revise these topics again after a few days and enhance your performance.
60-75% Good !	You have a wide scope to learn for these topics. Revise these topics again.
<60% Not Satisfactory!	You have a long way ahead of you to master these topics. Revise it thoroughly.

Chapter Break Thru

Syllabus

- Neuron and Nerves
- Nervous System in Humans
- Central Nervous System
- Peripheral Nervous System
- Visceral Nervous System
- Generation and Conduction of Nerve Impulse

Important Instructions

- The test is of 1 hour duration and contains 50 Multiple-Choice Questions (Four options with a single correct answer).
- Choose the correct option and fill the OMR given on the last page of this test accordingly.
- At some instances, you may find more than 1 option to be correct. In such circumstances, you have to judge the most appropriate answer as per the conditions given in the question.

1. Interneurons are located in the
(a) sensory receptors
(b) spinal cord
(c) efferent pathway
(d) effector

2. Which of the following function as a kind of index for recall of an event with its associated memory. It also converts information from short term to long term memory, essential in learning?
(a) Amygdala
(b) Hippocampus
(c) Septum
(d) Thalamus

3. The occurrence of resting potential takes place because
(a) mitochondrial energy production decreases.
(b) neurotransmitter substances are depleted by action potentials.
(c) ion concentration gradients exist across the cell membrane.
(d) action potentials initiate axoplasmic transport towards the cell body.

4. Electrical transmission is possible when
(a) it is mediated by neurotransmitters.
(b) it is carried out through chemical-gated channels.
(c) pre and post-synaptic membranes are in direct contact with each other.
(d) it occurs through synaptic gap.

5. Among the given combination of neuron types and their respective locations, identify the correct ones.

(i) Unipolar neuron – Embryonic stage
(ii) Bipolar neuron – Cornea of the eyes
(iii) Multipolar neuron – Cerebral cortex

Choose the correct option.

(a) (i) and (ii)
(b) (ii) and (iii)
(c) (i) and (iii)
(d) (i), (ii) and (iii)

6. The system that transmits impulse from the CNS to the involuntary organs and smooth muscles of the body is

(a) sympathetic neural system
(b) parasympathetic neural system
(c) somatic neural system
(d) autonomic neural system

7. If a patient exhibits symptoms such as tremors, halting speech and an irregular gait, it suggests trauma to which part of the brain?

(a) Cerebrum (b) Pons
(c) Cerebellum (d) Thalamus

8. Which of the following statement is incorrect about the cerebrum?

(a) It is a part of forebrain.
(b) It consists of two cerebellar hemisphere and vermis.
(c) Cerebral cortex forms the grey matter of the cerebrum.
(d) It is mainly concerned with intelligence and memories.

9. What will happen when Ca^{2+} channels are blocked using suitable blockers?

(a) Neurotransmitter will be released since Ca^{2+} has no significance in impulse conduction.
(b) Neurotransmitter will be released, but Na^+ channel in post-synaptic neuron will not open
(c) Neither neurotransmitter will be released, nor Na^+ channel in post-synaptic neuron will open up.
(d) Excess of Ca^{2+} will be released in the intracellular fluid.

10. Given below is the diagram of an axon terminal and synapse with labelled parts (1-7). Which of these parts are essential components of the synapse structure?

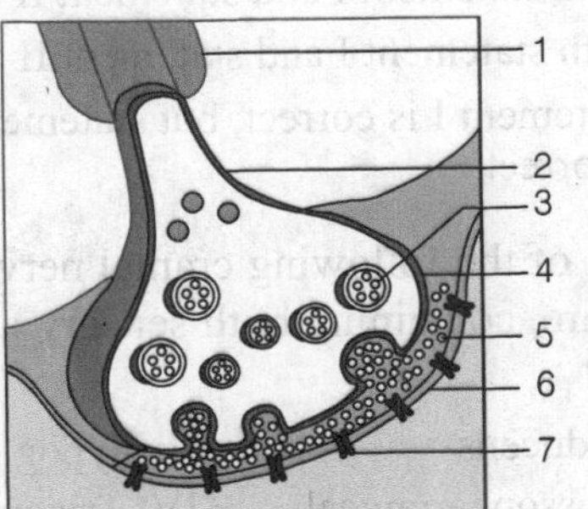

(a) 1, 2, 3 (b) 3, 4, 5
(c) 4, 5, 6 (d) 5, 6, 7

11. An action potential in a nerve fibre is generated when the electrical charges inside and outside the axon membrane are flipped. This occurs because

(a) more potassium ions move into the axon compared to sodium ions moving out
(b) more sodium ions move into the axon compared to potassium ions moving out
(c) all potassium ions exit the axon
(d) all sodium ions enter the axon

12. The given diagram is of human brain.

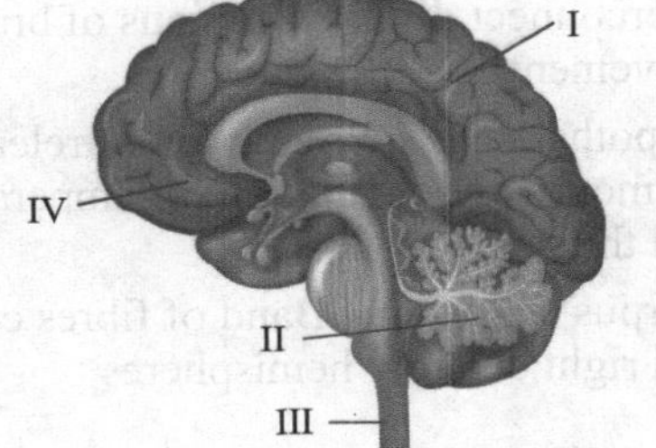

Identify the label showing the part that controls intelligence and memory.

(a) I (b) II
(c) III (d) IV

13. Given below are two statements.

Statement I Corpora quadrigemina acts as the centre for audio and vision.

Statement II The corpora quadrigemina is located in the mesencephalon.

In the light of the above statements, choose the correct answer from the options given below.
(a) Statement I is incorrect, but statement II is correct
(b) Both statement I and statement II are correct
(c) Both statement I and statement II are incorrect
(d) Statement I is correct, but statement II is incorrect

14. Which of the following cranial nerves are mixed in nature, containing both sensory and motor fibres?

I. Abducens II. Hypoglossal
III. Glossopharyngeal IV. Trigeminal

Choose the correct option.
(a) I and III (b) II and IV
(c) III and IV (d) II and III

15. The diencephalon is composed of three major parts of the brain. They are
(a) thalamus, hippocampus, epithalamus
(b) epithalamus, thalamus, hypothalamus
(c) hypothalamus, hippocampus, epithalamus
(d) thalamus, hypothalamus, hippocampus

16. Select the incorrect pair.
(a) Medulla oblongata – Controls respiration and cardiovascular reflexes
(b) Limbic system – Consists of fibrous tract that interconnect different regions of brain control movement
(c) Hypothalamus – Production of releasing hormones and regulation of temperature, hunger and thirst
(d) Corpus callosum – Band of fibres connecting left and right cerebral hemispheres

17. Axon ending releases from its synaptic vesicles, a neuro–transmitter substance known as
(a) acetylcholine
(b) acetylcholinesterase
(c) inositol-3 phosphate
(d) diacylglycerol

18. When P refers to dendrite, Q refers to axon, R refers to synapse and S refers to cell body. Which of the following options would correctly represent the sequence of structures present between a receptor and an effector?
(a) P – S – Q – R – Q – S – P
(b) Q – P – S – R – Q – P – S
(c) P – S – Q – R – P – S – Q
(d) P – Q – R – S – P – Q – S

19. Which of the following statement(s) is/are correct?

I. Motor neurons convey information away from CNS to the periphery.
II. Only two neurotransmitter substances are found in the nervous system, i.e. dopamine and acetylcholine.
III. Somatic motor nerves innervate skeletal muscles, while autonomic nerves innervate smooth muscle, cardiac muscle and glands.

Choose the correct codes from the options given below.
(a) I and II (b) II and III
(c) Only III (d) I and III

20. Which of the following term is incorrectly matched with its feature?
(a) Efferent neurons – Transmit signals from CNS to effectors.
(b) Axon terminal – Contains neurotransmitter containing vesicles.
(c) Limbic system – Involved in the regulation of sexual behavior, emotional reactions, and motivation, along with the hypothalamus.
(d) Association areas – Located in the cerebellum and responsible for functions such as intersensory associations, memory and communication.

21. Read the following statements.

I. The afferent nerve fibres transmit sensory impulses from tissue to CNS.
II. Efferent nerve fibres transmit motor impulses from tissue to CNS.
III. Skeletal muscles are supplied with somatic nerve fibres.
IV. Sympathetic and parasympathetic nervous system control voluntary actions.
V. The bundle of nerve fibres within the CNS are called tracts.

Choose the correct statements from the options given below.
(a) II and IV
(b) II, III and V
(c) I and IV
(d) I, III and V

22. Given below are two statements; one is labelled as Assertion (A) and the other is labelled as Reason (R).
Assertion (A) In the myelinated nerve fibres, the nerve impulses do not travel as a continuous wave of depolarisation.
Reason (R) Myelinated nerve fibres have node of Ranvier.
In the light of the above statements, choose the correct answer from the options given below.
(a) A is false, but R is true
(b) Both A and R are true and R is the correct explanation of A
(c) Both A and R are true, but R is not the correct explanation of A
(d) A is true, but R is false

23. Given below are two statements; one is labelled as Assertion (A) and the other is labelled as Reason (R).
Assertion (A) Fully formed nerve never divides and remains in interphase throughout life.
Reason (R) They do not have centrosome.
In the light of the above statements, choose the correct answer from the options given below.
(a) A is false, but R is true
(b) Both A and R are true and R is the correct explanation of A
(c) Both A and R are true, but R is not the correct explanation of A
(d) A is true, but R is false

24. Given below are two statements.
Statement I The thalamus coordinates reflex actions like vomiting, coughing and sneezing.
Statement II The medulla oblongata integrates various involuntary functions of the body.
In the light of the above statements, choose the correct answer from the options given below.
(a) Statement I is incorrect, but statement II is correct
(b) Both statement I and statement II are correct
(c) Both statement I and statement II are incorrect
(d) Statement I is correct, but statement II is incorrect

25. Match List I with List II.

List I	List II
A. Purkinje cells	1. Cyton
B. Nissl's granules	2. Cytoplasm
C. Perikaryon	3. Endoplasmic reticulum
D. Neuroplasm	4. Flask-shaped soma

Choose the correct answer from the options given below.

	A	B	C	D
(a)	3	4	2	1
(b)	3	4	1	2
(c)	4	3	1	2
(d)	2	3	4	1

26. Match the List I with List II.

List I	List II
A. Amygdala	1. Relay centre
B. Hippocampus	2. Almond shaped structure in limbic system
C. Thalamus	3. Memory formation and consolidation
D. Epithalamus	4. Pineal body

Choose the correct answer from the options given below.

	A	B	C	D
(a)	4	1	2	3
(b)	2	3	1	4
(c)	2	4	1	3
(d)	1	4	3	2

27. Pons Varolii of the brain stem does not have
(a) cardiac control centre
(b) rythm center
(c) fibres of cerebellar peduncle
(d) nuclei where some cranial nerves originate

28. Given below are two statements; one is labelled as Assertion (A) and the other is labelled as Reason (R).

Assertion (A) The neural organisation in vertebrates is more complex compared to invertebrates.

Reason (R) In insects, the ganglion functions as the brain.

In the light of the above statements, choose the correct answer from the options given below.

(a) A is false, but R is true
(b) Both A and R are true and R is the correct explanation of A
(c) Both A and R are true, but R is not the correct explanation of A
(d) A is true, but R is false

29. Match the List I with List II.

List I	List II
A. Frontal lobe	1. Responsible for understanding, spoken or written language
B. Occipital lobe	2. Contain primary visual cortex
C. Parietal lobe	3. Considered as centre of creativity and reasoning
D. Temporal lobe	4. Contain somatic sensory areas

Choose the correct option from the following.

(a) A-1, B-4, C-2, D-3
(b) A-3, B-2, C-4, D-1
(c) A-3, B-1, C-4, D-2
(d) A-2, B-1, C-4, D-3

30. Consider the following statements about the hypothalamus and the limbic system.

I. The hypothalamus contains centers that control body temperature, hunger and thirst.
II. The limbic system consists of the inner parts of the cerebral hemispheres and associated structures like the amygdala and hippocampus.
III. The hypothalamus, along with the limbic lobe/system, regulates sexual behaviour, emotional reactions, and motivation.
IV. The hypothalamus contains several groups of neurosecretory cells that produce hypothalamic hormones.
V. The hypothalamus is located at the base of the thalamus.

How many of the above statements are correct?

(a) Two (b) Three
(c) Four (d) Five

31. Given below are two statements; one is labelled as Assertion (A) and the other is labelled as Reason (R).

Assertion (A) The imbalance in concentration of sodium and potassium ions and proteins generates the resting potential.

Reason (R) To maintain unequal distribution of sodium and potassium, neurons use electrical energy.

In the light of the above statements, choose the correct answer from the options given below.

(a) A is false, but R is true
(b) Both A and R are true and R is the correct explanation of A
(c) Both A and R are true, but R is not the correct explanation of A
(d) A is true, but R is false.

32. Damage or injury in Broca's area may result, except

(a) aphasia
(b) anosmia
(c) affected readability and understanding
(d) auditory verbel disorder

33. Identify which one is matched correctly in the given comparison table.

	Name of organs	Sympathetic ANS	Parasympathetic ANS
(a)	Urinary bladder	Constrict	Relax
(b)	Pupil	Constrict	Dilate
(c)	Salivary gland	Stimulate secretion	Inhibit secretion
(d)	Renin	Increase	Decrease

34. Given below are two statements.

Statement I Motor functions senses certain changes both within body and outside body.

Statement II Sensory functions respond to stimuli by initiating muscular contractions or glandular secretions.

In the light of the above statements, choose the correct answer from the options given below.

(a) Statement I is incorrect, but statement II is correct
(b) Both statement I and statement II are correct
(c) Both statement I and statement II are incorrect
(d) Statement I is correct, but statement II is incorrect

35. Identify the incorrect statement from the following.

(a) Synapse is the area of functional contact between one neuron and another for the purpose of transferring information.
(b) Synapse is usually found between the fine terminal branches of the axon of one neuron and the dendrites or cell body of another.
(c) Bulbous expansion of dendrite known as pre-synaptic knob contains synaptic vesicles.
(d) The membrane of the synaptic knob nearest to the synapse is thickened and is called post-synaptic membrane.

36. Among the following which statement is correct regarding nervous system in animals?

(a) In Arthropoda, nerves are of mixed type and CNS is made up of nerve ring and ventral nerve cord.
(b) Echinodermates has simple and primitive type of nervous system found in the form of a nerve net.
(c) Nervous system of coelenterates marks the beginning of a centralised nervous system encountered in higher animals.
(d) In nematodes, nervous system is of primitive type resembling that of coelenterates with both dorsal and ventral nerve cord.

37. Consider the following diagram and identify which is known as the second largest portion of the brain.

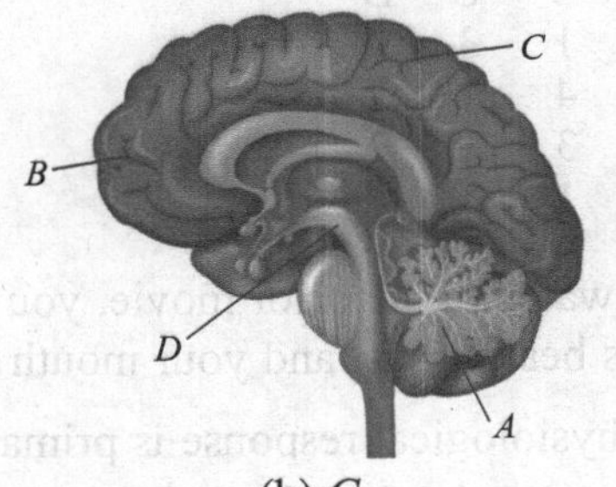

(a) *D* (b) *C*
(c) *B* (d) *A*

38. Given below are two statements.

Statement I Excitability is the ability of the nerve cells and fibres to enter into an active state in response to stimulus.

Statement II Nerve impulse is a wave of polarisation moving upward an axon.

In the light of the above statements, choose the correct answer from the options given below.

(a) Statement I is incorrect, but statement II is correct
(b) Both statement I and statement II are correct
(c) Both statement I and statement II are incorrect
(d) Statement I is correct, but statement is correct.

39. Nissl's granules are present in the ...I... and are made up of ...II... .

	I	II
(a)	neuron	DNA
(b)	mast cells	RNA
(c)	nephron	DNA
(d)	neuron	RNA

40. Match the List I with List II.

List I		List II	
A.	Gray matter	1.	Medullated nerve fibres
B.	Thoracic nerves	2.	8 pairs
C.	White matter	3.	12 pairs
D.	Cervical nerves	4.	Non-myelinated nerve fibres

Choose the correct option from the options given below.

	A	B	C	D
(a)	2	1	3	4
(b)	3	4	1	2
(c)	4	3	1	2
(d)	2	1	3	4

41. When watching a horror movie, you notice your heart is beating fast and your mouth is dry.

This physiological response is primarily due to

(a) Increased activity of sympathetic nervous system.

(b) Decreased activity of the sympathetic nervous system.

(c) Decreased activity of the parasympathetic nervous system.

(d) Increased activity of parasympathetic nervous system.

42. Match the List I with List II.

List I	List II
A. Cerebrum	1. Maintains body posture
B. Cerebellum	2. Seat of intelligence
C. Hypothalamus	3. Controls vision and hearing
D. Midbrain	4. Controls the pituitary

Choose the correct option from the options given below.

	A	B	C	D
(a)	4	2	3	1
(b)	4	3	2	1
(c)	2	1	4	3
(d)	2	1	3	4

43. Among the following, which are the three initial development regions of the brain?

(a) Telencephalon, prosencephalon, rhombencephalon

(b) Prosencephalon, mesencephalon, rhombencephalon

(c) Metencephalon, myelencephalon, prosencephalon

(d) Prosencephalon, diencephalon, mesencephalon

44. Given below are the two statements; one is labelled as Assertion (A) and the other is labelled as Reason (R).

Assertion (A) Motor nerve fibres that supply striped muscle and parasympathetic nerve fibres which innervate smooth muscle are cholinergic.

Reason (R) On stimulation, they secrete acetylcholine from their ends into the synaptic cleft.

In the light of the above statements, choose the correct answer from the options given below.

(a) A is false, but R is true

(b) Both A and R are true and R is the correct explanation of A

(c) Both A and R are true, but R is not the correct explanation of A

(d) A is true, but R is false

45. The two main neurotransmitters in vertebrate's nervous system are

(a) adrenaline and glycine

(b) acetylcholine and nor-adrenaline

(c) dopamine and epinephrine

(d) oxytocin and cholecystokinin

46. Which of the following statement is correct for 'nodes of Ranvier' of nerve?

(a) Axolemma is discontinuous

(b) Myelin sheath is discontinuous

(c) Both neurilemma and myelin sheath are discontinuous

(d) Covered by myelin sheath

47. Nerve gas affects neuromuscular activity by

(a) blocking the acetylcholine receptor sites

(b) inhibiting the release of acetylcholine

(c) inhibiting acetylcholinesterase

(d) enchancing the release of acetylcholine

48. Which one of the following statement is correct regarding spinal cord?
(a) It is composed of outer grey matter and inner white matter
(b) It is composed of outer white matter and inner grey matter
(c) It is composed of outer grey matter and inner colourless matter
(d) It is composed of grey matter only

49. Maintenance of the ionic gradients across the resting membrane is accomplished by
(a) active transport of ions
(b) passive transport of ions
(c) active transport of proteins
(d) passive transport of proteins

50. Following are the correct statements about efferent neurons, except
(a) they conduct impulse from CNS to the effectors.
(b) the axon terminals come in contact with motor end plate to form neuromuscular junction.
(c) they are motor in nature.
(d) their dendrites are modified to form receptors.

Scan for online chapter test

Response Index

01 ⓐ ⓑ ⓒ ⓓ	14 ⓐ ⓑ ⓒ ⓓ	27 ⓐ ⓑ ⓒ ⓓ	40 ⓐ ⓑ ⓒ ⓓ
02 ⓐ ⓑ ⓒ ⓓ	15 ⓐ ⓑ ⓒ ⓓ	28 ⓐ ⓑ ⓒ ⓓ	41 ⓐ ⓑ ⓒ ⓓ
03 ⓐ ⓑ ⓒ ⓓ	16 ⓐ ⓑ ⓒ ⓓ	29 ⓐ ⓑ ⓒ ⓓ	42 ⓐ ⓑ ⓒ ⓓ
04 ⓐ ⓑ ⓒ ⓓ	17 ⓐ ⓑ ⓒ ⓓ	30 ⓐ ⓑ ⓒ ⓓ	43 ⓐ ⓑ ⓒ ⓓ
05 ⓐ ⓑ ⓒ ⓓ	18 ⓐ ⓑ ⓒ ⓓ	31 ⓐ ⓑ ⓒ ⓓ	44 ⓐ ⓑ ⓒ ⓓ
06 ⓐ ⓑ ⓒ ⓓ	19 ⓐ ⓑ ⓒ ⓓ	32 ⓐ ⓑ ⓒ ⓓ	45 ⓐ ⓑ ⓒ ⓓ
07 ⓐ ⓑ ⓒ ⓓ	20 ⓐ ⓑ ⓒ ⓓ	33 ⓐ ⓑ ⓒ ⓓ	46 ⓐ ⓑ ⓒ ⓓ
08 ⓐ ⓑ ⓒ ⓓ	21 ⓐ ⓑ ⓒ ⓓ	34 ⓐ ⓑ ⓒ ⓓ	47 ⓐ ⓑ ⓒ ⓓ
09 ⓐ ⓑ ⓒ ⓓ	22 ⓐ ⓑ ⓒ ⓓ	35 ⓐ ⓑ ⓒ ⓓ	48 ⓐ ⓑ ⓒ ⓓ
10 ⓐ ⓑ ⓒ ⓓ	23 ⓐ ⓑ ⓒ ⓓ	36 ⓐ ⓑ ⓒ ⓓ	49 ⓐ ⓑ ⓒ ⓓ
11 ⓐ ⓑ ⓒ ⓓ	24 ⓐ ⓑ ⓒ ⓓ	37 ⓐ ⓑ ⓒ ⓓ	50 ⓐ ⓑ ⓒ ⓓ
12 ⓐ ⓑ ⓒ ⓓ	25 ⓐ ⓑ ⓒ ⓓ	38 ⓐ ⓑ ⓒ ⓓ	
13 ⓐ ⓑ ⓒ ⓓ	26 ⓐ ⓑ ⓒ ⓓ	39 ⓐ ⓑ ⓒ ⓓ	

Performance Scanner

> 90% Excellent !	You have mastered this chapter. The concepts of this chapter are at your fingertips. Move on to the next chapter and maintain this momentum.
76-90% Very Good !	You have a good command over this chapter. Revise the chapter again after a few days and enhance your performance.
60-75% Good !	You have a wide scope to learn for this chapter. Revise this chapter again.
<60% Not Satisfactory!	You have a long way ahead of you to master this chapter. Revise it thoroughly.

Space for Rough Work

Test Booklet No. **3947319**

Test Booklet Code **CH19**

MEDACE
NEET (UG)
SELF ASSESSMENT KIT

Chemical Coordination and Integration

Topics Covered

Endocrine Glands and Hormones-I

Endocrine Glands and Hormones-II, Non-endocrine Glands and Hormones

Important Instructions

- This Booklet Contains – Two Topic Tests and One Test on Complete Chapter.
- Each question carries 4 marks.
- For each correct response, the candidate will get 4 marks. And for every incorrect response, 1 mark will be additionally deducted from total score.
- Use **Blue/Black** point pen only for filling the OMR.
- Rough work is to be done in the space provided for this purpose in the test booklet only.

Name of the Candidate (In Capitals) ____________

Candidate's Signature ____________

Invigilator's Signature ____________

Facsimile signature stamp of center superintendent ____________

Do not open this booklet until you start attempting the test

Topical Follow Thru

Test 1

Syllabus

- Endocrine Glands and Hormones
- Human Endocrine System
- The Hypothalamus
- The Pituitary Gland
- The Pineal Gland
- Thyroid Gland
- Parathyroid Gland
- Hypo and Hyper activity and related disorders

For deeper insight, **Scan the QR Code** 

Important Instructions

- The test is of 30 minutes duration and contains 15 Multiple Choice Questions (four options with a single correct answer).
- Choose the correct option and fill the OMR given on the last page of this test accordingly.
- At some instances, you may find more than 1 option to be correct. In such circumstances, you have to judge the most appropriate answer as per the conditions given in the question.

1. Which of the following hormones do not require portal circulation to reach the pituitary?
(a) Releasing hormones
(b) Inhibiting hormones
(c) Somatostatin
(d) Gonadotrophins

2. Given below are two statements; one is labelled as Assertion (A) and the other is labelled as Reason (R).

Assertion (A) The anterior pituitary is stimulated under extreme dehydration.
Reason (R) Anterior pituitary is under the influence of hypothalamic hormones.
In the light of the above statements, choose the correct answer from the options given below.
(a) A is false, but R is true
(b) Both A and R are true and R is the correct explanation of A
(c) Both A and R are true, but R is not the correct explanation of A
(d) A is true, but R is false

3. Given below are two statements; one is labelled as Assertion (A) and the other is labelled as Reason (R).

Assertion (A) Increased blood calcium levels stimulate thyroid glands.
Reason (R) Thyroxine increases calcium absorption by bones.
In the light of the above statements, choose the correct answer from the options given below.
(a) A is false, but R is true
(b) Both A and R are true and R is the correct explanation of A
(c) Both A and R are true, but R is not the correct explanation of A
(d) A is true, but R is false

4. Which of the following statement is incorrect about hypothalamus?
(a) Endocrine function of hypothalamus is carried out by the nuclei.
(b) Pars distalis is the site of action of hypothalamic releasing hormones.
(c) Inhibiting hormones are transported axonally to the pars nervosa.
(d) Apart from endocrine function, hypothalamus controls body temperature.

5. Which of the following could cause the development of disproportionate facial structure at later stages of life in a person?
(a) Hyposecretion of anterior pituitary
(b) Tumour in the adenohypophysis
(c) Hypersecretion of GnRH
(d) Hypersecretion of somatostatin

6. By which of the following ways is it possible to increase Ca^{2+} concentration of blood?

I. Hypersecretion of thyrocalcitonin
II. Ca^{2+} reabsorption by renal tubules
III. Hyposecretion of parathyroid hormone
IV. Demineralisation of bones

Choose the correct answer from the options given below.

(a) I and II
(b) II and IV
(c) II and III
(d) IV only

7. Given below are two statements.

Statement I Both humoral and cell-mediated immunity depend on a peptide hormone.

Statement II Antibody production is related to cell-mediated immunity provided by T-cells.

In the light of the above statements, choose the correct answer from the options given below.

(a) Statement I is incorrect, but statement II is correct.
(b) Both statement I and statement II are correct
(c) Both statement I and statement II are incorrect
(d) Statement I is correct, but statement II is incorrect

8. Following are the statements related to the hormones of the master gland of the body.

I. Acromegaly is an abnormality in adults with hypersecretion of GH.
II. Oxytocin secretion occurs only during child birth process.
III. Pars intermedia of neurohypophysis, governs skin pigmentation.
IV. ACTH promotes secretion of glucocorticoids from cortex only.
V. Androgen secretion is essential in men during puberty.

Choose the correct set of statements from the options given below.

(a) II and III (b) I, IV and V
(c) I, II and III (d) III, IV and V

9. Following are the symptoms observed in an adult woman.

A. Reduced metabolism
B. Obesity
C. Irregular menstruation

Based on the above symptoms which of the following conditions is she suffering from?

(a) Hypothyroidism
(b) Hyperthyroidism
(c) Exopthalmic goitre
(d) Cretinism

10. Match List I with List II.

	List I		List II
A.	Melatonin	1.	Post pregnancy
B.	Oxytocin	2.	Body temperature
C.	Thyroxine	3.	Onset of puberty
D.	FSH	4.	Erythropoiesis

Choose the correct answer from the options given below.

(a) A-4, B-3, C-2, D-1
(b) A-2, B-3, C-4, D-1
(c) A-4, B-1, C-2, D-3
(d) A-2, B-1, C-4, D-3

11. Prolactin in mammals is secreted by

(a) pars nervosa or neurohypohysis
(b) pars intermedia part of adenohypophysis
(c) pars distalis part of adenohypophysis
(d) placenta and foetus

12. Given below are few statements.

I. ADH mainly acts on loop of Henle.
II. Sertoli cells are regulated by LH.
III. Melatonin is responsible for regulating skin pigmentation.
IV. Parathyroid glands can be seen clearly in the dorsal side of trachea.

Choose the incorrect set of statements.

(a) I, II and IV (b) I, II and III
(c) I and II (d) II and III

13. Match List I with List II.

List I (Hormones)		List II (Target glands or organs)	
A.	Hypothalmic hormone	1.	Pituitary gland
B.	TSH	2.	Adrenal gland
C.	ACTH	3.	Testis and ovary
D.	FSH	4.	Skin
E.	MSH	5.	Thyroid gland

Choose the correct answer from the options given below.

	A	B	C	D	E
(a)	1	3	5	2	4
(b)	2	4	3	5	1
(c)	1	5	2	3	4
(d)	2	1	5	4	3

14. Given below are two statements.

Statement I Fall in bone Ca^{2+} levels will stimulate parathyroid gland to release parathyroid hormone.

Statement II Thymus is a lobular structure located between lungs behind sternum on the dorsal side of the immune system.

In the light of the above statements, choose the correct answer from the options given below.

(a) Statement I is incorrect, but statement II is correct.
(b) Both statement I and statement II are correct
(c) Both statement I and statement II are incorrect
(d) Statement I is correct, but statement II is incorrect

15. Given below is a figure showing different endocrine glands in a human body.

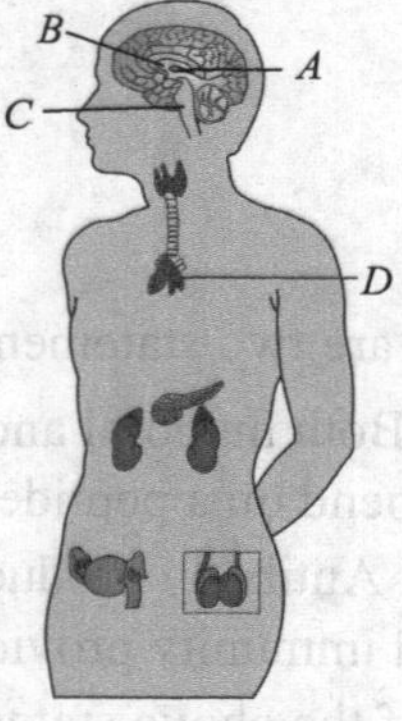

Which of the following option is correct w.r.t. the given figure?

(a) Hormones released from *B* go to *A via* portal connection or axonally
(b) Both *A* and *D* are involved in defence mechanism
(c) Some hormones that are released by A are stored in *C*
(d) *D* secretes a steroid hormone called thymosin

Response Index

01 ⓐ ⓑ ⓒ ⓓ 10 ⓐ ⓑ ⓒ ⓓ 19 ⓐ ⓑ ⓒ ⓓ
02 ⓐ ⓑ ⓒ ⓓ 11 ⓐ ⓑ ⓒ ⓓ 20 ⓐ ⓑ ⓒ ⓓ
03 ⓐ ⓑ ⓒ ⓓ 12 ⓐ ⓑ ⓒ ⓓ 21 ⓐ ⓑ ⓒ ⓓ
04 ⓐ ⓑ ⓒ ⓓ 13 ⓐ ⓑ ⓒ ⓓ 22 ⓐ ⓑ ⓒ ⓓ
05 ⓐ ⓑ ⓒ ⓓ 14 ⓐ ⓑ ⓒ ⓓ 23 ⓐ ⓑ ⓒ ⓓ
06 ⓐ ⓑ ⓒ ⓓ 15 ⓐ ⓑ ⓒ ⓓ 24 ⓐ ⓑ ⓒ ⓓ
07 ⓐ ⓑ ⓒ ⓓ 16 ⓐ ⓑ ⓒ ⓓ 25 ⓐ ⓑ ⓒ ⓓ
08 ⓐ ⓑ ⓒ ⓓ 17 ⓐ ⓑ ⓒ ⓓ
09 ⓐ ⓑ ⓒ ⓓ 18 ⓐ ⓑ ⓒ ⓓ

Performance Scanner

> 90% Excellent !	You have mastered these topics. The concepts of these topics are at your fingertips. Move on to the next test and maintain this momentum.
76-90% Very Good !	You have a good command over these topics. Revise these topics again after a few days and enhance your performance.
60-75% Good !	You have a wide scope to learn for these topics. Revise these topics again.
<60% Not Satisfactory!	You have a long way ahead of you to master these topics. Revise it thoroughly.

Test 2

Syllabus

- Adrenal Gland
- Pancreas
- Gonads
- Hypo and Hyper Activity and Related Disorders
- Mechanism of Hormone Action
- Role of Hormone as Messengers and Regulators

For deeper insight, Scan the QR Code 

Important Instructions

- The test is of 30 minutes duration and contains 25 Multiple Choice Questions(four options with a single correct answer).
- Choose the correct option and fill the OMR given on the last page of this test accordingly.
- At some instances, you may find more than 1 option to be correct. In such circumstances, you have to judge the most appropriate answer as per the conditions given in the question.

1. Which of the following is incorrect from the options given below?

(a) Glucagon – glycogenolysis, hyperglycemia
(b) Insulin – glycogenesis, hypoglycemia
(c) Glucagon – gluconeogenesis, hyperglycemia
(d) Insulin – gluconeogenesis, hypoglycemia

2. Consider the following statements related to male sex hormones.

I. Chemical nature of most sex hormones is steroids.
II. Steroid hormones interact mostly with membrane receptors.
III. Secretion of androgens require stimulation by pars distalis.
IV. Anabolic effects of androgens maintains metabolism.
V. Secretions of seminiferous tubules regulates body hair growth.

Choose the correct set of statements from the options given below.

(a) II and V
(b) I, III and IV
(c) I, II and V
(c) II, III and IV

3. Given below are two statements; one is labelled as Assertion (A) and the other is labelled as Reason (R).

Assertion (A) Secretin secretion is essential for exocrine function of pancreas.

Reason (R) Secretin increases the pH which is essential for digestion.

In the light of the above statements, choose the correct answer from the options given below.

(a) A is false, but R is true
(b) Both A and R are true and R is the correct explanation of A
(c) Both A and R are true, but R is not the correct explanation of A
(d) A is true, but R is false

4. Following are the steps involved in mode of action of T_3 and T_4 hormones.

A. T_3 and T_4 crosses the cell membrane
B. Interaction with genome
C. Secretion of T_4 and T_4
D. Secretion of TSH
E. Interaction with nuclear receptor

Choose the correct order from the options given below.

(a) D-C-A-E-B
(b) C-D-A-E-B
(c) D-C-E-A-B
(d) C-D-E-A-B

5. Given below are two statements.

Statement I Endocrine secretions of the GI tract are peptide in their chemical nature.

Statement II CCK plays an important role in digestion of fats in the intestine.

In the light of the above statements, choose the correct answer from the options given below.

(a) Statement I is incorrect, but statement II is correct.
(b) Both statement I and statement II are correct
(c) Both statement I and statement II are incorrect
(d) Statement I is correct, but statement II is incorrect

6. Which of the following hormones have the same effect on blood glucose?

I. Epinephrine and insulin
II. Cortisol and insulin
III. Epinephrine and glucagon
IV. Epinephrine and cortisol

Choose the correct answer from the options given below.

(a) I and III
(b) II and IV
(c) III and IV
(d) IV only

7. Given below are two statements; one is labelled as Assertion (A) and the other is labelled as Reason (R).

Assertion (A) Adrenaline is administered to a patient after organ transplantation.

Reason (R) Organ transplantation can often cause hyperactivity of immune system.

In the light of the above statements, choose the correct answer from the options given below.

(a) A is false, but R is true
(b) Both A and R are true and R is the correct explanation of A
(c) Both A and R are true, but R is not the correct explanation of A
(d) A is true, but R is false

8. Given below are two statements.

Statement I Progesterone has the same effect on mammary glands as prolactin.

Statement II Progesterone is the primary hormone stimulating secondary sexual features in females.

In the light of the above statements, choose the correct answer from the options given below.

(a) Statement I is incorrect, but statement II is correct.
(b) Both statement I and statement II are correct
(c) Both statement I and statement II are incorrect
(d) Statement I is correct, but statement II is incorrect

9. Which of the following is incorrect about FSH action on target cells?

(a) FSH does not cross the phospholipid bilayer.
(b) Cyclic AMP causes extracellular signal transduction
(c) Hormone-receptor complex remains on membrane
(d) Biochemical response depends on the quantity of hormone

10. Which of the following does not happen after consumption of a sugary snack?

(a) Uptake of glucose by hepatocytes and adipocytes
(b) Stimulation of β-cells of pancreas
(c) Glycogenesis in liver and muscles
(d) Gluconeogenesis in liver

11. Given below are two statements; one is labelled as Assertion (A) and the other is labelled as Reason (R).

Assertion (A) Complete protein digestion in intestine, requires gastrin at the first step.

Reason (R) Gastrin is a peptide hormone, which is secreted by the gastrointestinal tract.

In the light of the above statements, choose the correct answer from the options given below.

(a) A is false, but R is true
(b) Both A and R are true and R is the correct explanation of A
(c) Both A and R are true, but R is not the correct explanation of A
(d) A is true, but R is false

12. Match List I with List II.

	List I		List II
A.	Corpus luteum	1.	Oestrogen
B.	Aldosterone	2.	Progesterone
C.	Ovarian follicle	3.	Increases blood pressure
D.	ANF	4.	Decreases blood pressure

Choose the correct answer from the options given below.

	A	B	C	D
(a)	1	4	2	3
(b)	2	3	1	4
(c)	1	3	2	4
(d)	2	4	1	3

13. Which of the following gland is not involved in regulation of electrolyte balance of the body?

(a) Adrenal cortex
(b) Pituitary
(c) Thyroid
(d) Adrenal medulla

14. On which of the following grounds, are pituitary hormones and sex hormones completely different?
I. Interaction with receptors
II. Chemical nature
III. Effect on body
IV. Transportation
Choose the correct answer from the following options.
(a) I and II (b) III only
(c) III and IV (d) II only

15. Given below are two statements.
Statement I Insulin acts on the cells of liver and adipose tissue.
Statement II Insulin is capable of maintaining glucose homeostasis in blood by itself.
In the light of the above statements, choose the correct answer from the options given below.
(a) Statement I is incorrect, but statement II is correct.
(b) Both statement I and statement II are correct
(c) Both statement I and statement II are incorrect
(d) Statement I is correct, but statement II is incorrect

16. Given below are two statements; one is labelled as Assertion (A) and the other is labelled as Reason (R).
Assertion (A) Insulin resistance results in a disease called diabetes mellitus.
Reason (R) Insulin dependent diabetes mellitus is caused due to failure of α-cells to produce adequate amount of insulin.
In the light of the above statements, choose the correct answer from the options given below.
(a) A is false, but R is true
(b) Both A and R are true and R is the correct explanation of A
(c) Both A and R are true, but R is not the correct explanation of A
(d) A is true, but R is false

17. A female hormone that is involved in the maintenance of pregnancy, mammary gland development and lactation is
(a) prolactin (b) progesterone
(c) oestrogen (d) oxytocin

18. Which other hormones are released during stress, besides epinephrine and nor-epinephrine?
(a) PTH, vasopressin, glucagon and thyroxine
(b) Cortisol, vasopressin, insulin and PTH
(c) Cortisol, aldosterone, vasopressin and glucagon
(d) Thyroxine, cortisol, aldosterone and vasopressin

19. Given below are two statements; one is labelled as Assertion (A) and the other is labelled as Reason (R).
Assertion (A) Some hormones like FSH need secondary messengers.
Reason (R) Peptide hormone cannot cross cell membrane.
In the light of the above statements, choose the correct answer from the options given below.
(a) A is false, but R is true
(b) Both A and R are true and R is the correct explanation of A
(c) Both A and R are true, but R is not the correct explanation of A
(d) A is true, but R is false

20. Consider the following figure showing the mechanism of hormone action.

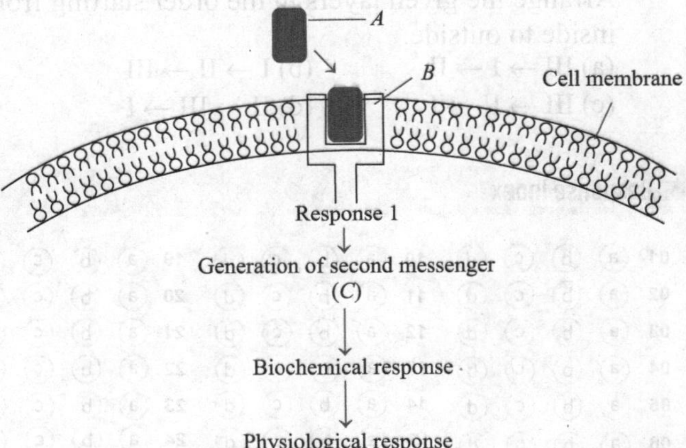

Choose the correct option in the given figure.
(a) *A*-Glucagon, *B*-Membrane-bound receptor, *C*-ATP
(b) *A*-Estradiol, *B*-Intracellular receptor, *C*-Ca^{2+}
(c) *A*-Insulin, *B*-Intracellular receptor, *C*-cAMP
(d) *A*-Prolactin, *B*-Membrane-bound receptor, *C*-IP_3

21. Identify the option, which correctly matches the gland with its hormone and its function in the following manner.

Gland > Hormone > Function

(a) Adrenal > Glucocorticoids > Glycogenesis, Lipolysis and Proteolysis

(b) Pancreas > Glucagon > Hypoglycemic hormone

(c) Cholecystokinin > GI tract > Stimulation of gall bladder and pancreas for secretion of pancreatic enzymes and intestinal juice

(d) Juxtaglomerular cell of kidney > Erythropoietin > Erythropoiesis

22. Mark the incorrect function of insulin.

(a) It increases the oxidation of glucose in the cells

(b) It increases the permeability of cell membrane to glucose

(c) It increases the conversion of glycogen to glucose

(d) It initiates the formation of hepatic glycogen from excess of glucose

23. Given below are the layers of adernal cortex.

I. Zona glomerulosa

II. Zona reticularis

III. Zona fasciculata

Arrange the given layers in the order starting from inside to outside.

(a) III $\rightarrow$ I $\rightarrow$ II (b) I $\rightarrow$ II $\rightarrow$ III

(c) III $\rightarrow$ II $\rightarrow$ I (d) II $\rightarrow$ III $\rightarrow$ I

24. Given below are two statements.

Statement I Inositol triphosphate (IP_3) is capable of driving a cascade of biochemical reactions and physiological changes in the target cell.

Statement II Several non-endocrine tissues secrete hormones called growth factors essential for normal growth of tissues and their repairing.

In the light of the above statements, choose the correct answer from the options given below.

(a) Statement I is incorrect, but statement II is correct.

(b) Both statement I and statement II are correct

(c) Both statement I and statement II are incorrect

(d) Statement I is correct, but statement II is incorrect

25. A person's heartbeat increases at the time of interview. Which one of the following is likely to happen in his neuro-hormonal control system?

(a) His parasympathetic nervous system is activated releasing epinephrine and nor-epinephrine from adrenal cortex

(b) His sympathetic nervous system is activated leading to release of epinephrine and nor-epinephrine from adrenal cortex

(c) His sympathetic nervous system is activated leading to release of adrenaline and nor-adrenaline from adrenal medulla

(d) His hypothalamus activates the parasympathetic division of brain to transmit neurotransmitter

Response Index

01	ⓐ ⓑ ⓒ ⓓ		10	ⓐ ⓑ ⓒ ⓓ		19	ⓐ ⓑ ⓒ ⓓ						
02	ⓐ ⓑ ⓒ ⓓ		11	ⓐ ⓑ ⓒ ⓓ		20	ⓐ ⓑ ⓒ ⓓ						
03	ⓐ ⓑ ⓒ ⓓ		12	ⓐ ⓑ ⓒ ⓓ		21	ⓐ ⓑ ⓒ ⓓ						
04	ⓐ ⓑ ⓒ ⓓ		13	ⓐ ⓑ ⓒ ⓓ		22	ⓐ ⓑ ⓒ ⓓ						
05	ⓐ ⓑ ⓒ ⓓ		14	ⓐ ⓑ ⓒ ⓓ		23	ⓐ ⓑ ⓒ ⓓ						
06	ⓐ ⓑ ⓒ ⓓ		15	ⓐ ⓑ ⓒ ⓓ		24	ⓐ ⓑ ⓒ ⓓ						
07	ⓐ ⓑ ⓒ ⓓ		16	ⓐ ⓑ ⓒ ⓓ		25	ⓐ ⓑ ⓒ ⓓ						
08	ⓐ ⓑ ⓒ ⓓ		17	ⓐ ⓑ ⓒ ⓓ									
09	ⓐ ⓑ ⓒ ⓓ		18	ⓐ ⓑ ⓒ ⓓ									

Performance Scanner

> 90% Excellent !	You have mastered these topics. The concepts of these topics are at your fingertips. Move on to the next test and maintain this momentum.
76-90% Very Good !	You have a good command over these topics. Revise these topics again after a few days and enhance your performance.
60-75% Good !	You have a wide scope to learn for these topics. Revise these topics again.
<60% Not Satisfactory!	You have a long way ahead of you to master these topics. Revise it thoroughly.

Chapter Break Thru

Syllabus			
	• Endocrine Glands and Hormones • Human Endocrine System • Hypothalamus • Pituitary Gland • Pineal Gland	• Thyroid Gland • Parathyroid Gland • Adrenal Gland • Pancreas • Gonads	• Mechanism of Hormone Action • Role of Hormone as Messengous and regulators • Hypo and Hyperactivity and Related Disorders

Important Instructions

- The test is of 1 hour duration and contains 50 Multiple-Choice Questions (Four options with a single correct answer).
- Choose the correct option and fill the OMR given on the last page of this test accordingly.
- At some instances, you may find more than 1 option to be correct. In such circumstances, you have to judge the most appropriate answer as per the conditions given in the question.

1. Following are the steps involved in the development process in males.

A. Stimulation of the interstitial cells
B. Development of vas deferens
C. Production of GnRH
D. Secretion of LH
E. Stimulation of pars distalis

Choose the correct order from the options given below.

(a) C-E-D-A-B
(b) C-D-E-A-B
(c) C-D-E-B-A
(d) C-E-A-D-B

2. Following is the diagrammatic representation of two endocrine glands. Which of the following is correct about the labelled parts?

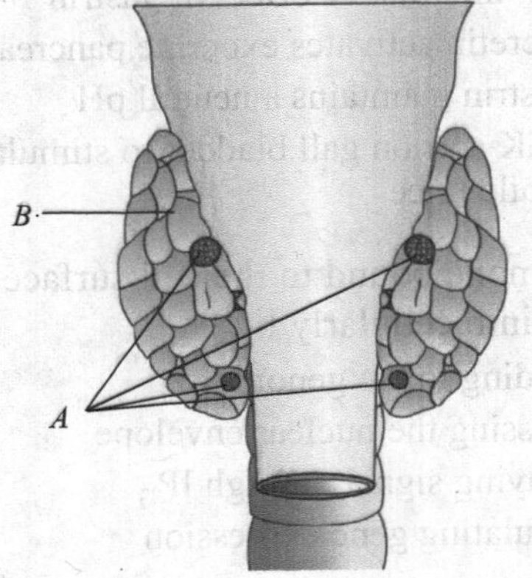

(a) *A* and *B* produce antagonistic effect on blood Ca^{2+}
(b) Stromal cells of *B* secrete two hormones-T_3 and T_4
(c) Hormone secreted by *A* is hypocalcemic
(d) Hormone secreted by *B* is hypercalcemic

3. Given below are two statements; one is labelled as Assertion (A) and the other is labelled as Reason (R).

Assertion (A) We mostly turn off lights before sleeping.

Reason (R) Melatonin production decreases in darkness.

In the light of the above statements, choose the correct answer from the options given below.

(a) A is false, but R is true
(b) Both A and R are true and R is the correct explanation of A
(c) Both A and R are true, but R is not the correct explanation of A
(d) A is true, but R is false

4. Match List I with List II.

List I	List II
A. Addison's disease	1. Diuresis
B. Cretinism	2. Low energy
C. Grave's disease	3. Mental retardation
D. Diabetes insipidus	4. Protruding eyes

Choose the correct answer from the following options.
(a) A-2, B-4, C-3, D-1
(b) A-2, B-3, C-4, D-1
(c) A-3, B-2, C-4, D-1
(d) A-3, B-4, C-2, D-1

5. Consider the following statements.
I. Hormones from the hypothalmic nuclei are transported by axons to pars distalis.
II. Hypothalamus, located at the base of forebrain, regulates temperature.
III. Somatostatin works synergistic to growth hormone on body.
IV. Hypothalmic hormones have a stimulating effect on all endocrine glands.
Choose the correct statement from the options given below.
(a) Only II (b) Only I
(c) Only IV (d) Only III

6. Given below are two statements.
Statement I Weak immune system can be associated with decreased activity of thymus.
Statement II Thymosin causes differentiation of T-cells that promote humoral immunity.
In the light of the above statements, choose the correct answer from the options given below.
(a) Statement I is incorrect, but statement II is correct.
(b) Both statement I and statement II are correct
(c) Both statement I and statement II are incorrect
(d) Statement I is correct, but statement II is incorrect

7. Which of the following condition can make bones fragile and prone to fracture?
(a) Increase in thyrocalcitonin in blood
(b) Decrease in bone demineralisation
(c) Increased secretion of parathyroid
(d) Increase in Ca^{2+} absorption by bones

8. Following are the statements associated with the adrenal glands.
I. Zona reticularis is the innermost region of adrenal gland.
II. Middle layer of outer adrenal zone is zona fasciculata.
III. Adrenaline and cortisol have same effect on blood glucose.
IV. Secretions of the adrenal glands are only peptide in nature.
V. Aldosterone has similar effect as vasopressin on the kidneys.
Choose the correct answer from the options given below.
(a) II and III (b) I, III and V
(c) II, III and V (d) I, IV and V

9. Which of the following stimulates erythropoiesis?
A. Thyroid glands
B. Juxtaglomerular apparatus
C. Parathyroid glands
D. Adrenal cortex
Choose the correct answer from the options given below?
(a) C and D (b) A and C
(c) A, B and D (d) B and D

10. Given below are two statements.
Statement I Oxytocin secretion and uterine contraction stimulate one another.
Statement II Oxytocin is produced by the posterior lobe of pituitary gland.
In the light of the above statements, choose the correct answer from the options given below.
(a) Statement I is incorrect, but statement II is correct.
(b) Both statement I and statement II are correct
(c) Both statement I and statement II are incorrect
(d) Statement I is correct, but statement II is incorrect

11. Choose the incorrect statement out of the given options.
(a) GIP inhibits the effect of gastrin
(b) Secretin activates exocrine pancreas
(c) Gastrin maintains a neutral pH
(d) CCK acts on gall bladder to stimulate secretion of bile juice

12. A hormone bound to the cell surface can exert its effect intracellularly by
(a) binding to the genome
(b) crossing the nuclear envelope
(c) relaying signal through IP_3
(d) regulating gene expression

13. Match List I with List II.

List I	List II
A. T_3 hormone	1. Amino acid
B. Cortisol	2. Iodothyronine
C. Adrenaline	3. Steroid
D. ANF	4. Peptide

Choose the correct match from the options given below.
(a) A-4, B-3, C- 1, D-2
(b) A-2, B-1, C- 3, D-4
(c) A-4, B-1, C- 3, D-2
(d) A-2, B-3, C- 1, D-4

14. Which of the following correctly matches the female hormone and the time of their maximum production?
(a) Oestrogen - Pregnancy
(b) Progesterone - Child birth
(c) Prolactin - Post pregnancy
(d) Oxytocin - Puberty

15. Given below are two statements; one is labelled as Assertion (A) and the other is labelled as Reason (R).

Assertion (A) Under fasting conditions, the pancreatic β-cells are stimulated.
Reason (R) Insulin causes glycogenesis in liver, opposing the effect of glucagon.
In the light of the above statements, choose the correct answer from the options given below.
(a) A is false, but R is true
(b) Both A and R are true and R is the correct explanation of A
(c) Both A and R are true, but R is not the correct explanation of A
(d) A is true, but R is false

16. Given below are two statements; one is labelled as Assertion (A) and the other as Reason (R).

Assertion (A) Pregnant women are advised to consume iodised salt.
Reason (R) Iodine is important for regulating metabolism of the body.

In the light of the above statements, choose the correct answer from the options given below.
(a) A is false, but R is true
(b) Both A and R are true and R is the correct explanation of A
(c) Both A and R are true, but R is not the correct explanation of A
(d) A is true, but R is false

17. Which of the following statement is correct about the anti-diuretic hormone?
(a) Hyposecretion can cause frequent urination.
(b) Hypersecretion can cause increased thirst.
(c) Hypersecretion can cause formation of ketone bodies.
(d) Hyposecretion can cause increase in blood pressure.

18. Given below are two statements.
Statement I CCK is produced by the intestine and acts on the liver.
Statement II CCK causes contraction of the gall bladder to release bile.
In the light of the above statements, choose the correct answer from the options given below.
(a) Statement I is incorrect, but statement II is correct.
(b) Both statement I and statement II are correct
(c) Both statement I and statement II are incorrect
(d) Statement I is correct, but statement II is incorrect

19. Consider the following statements about the endocrine glands situated at top of the kidneys.
I. Androgens secreted by adrenal and testes follows two separate routes.
II. Piloerection in response to fear is triggered by the adrenal cortex.
III. Glucocorticoids are effective to reduce the effects of inflammation.
IV. Increased energy during emergency, is due to the glycogenolysis.
Choose the incorrect statement from the options given below.
(a) Only II
(b) Only I
(c) Only IV
(d) Only III

20. An adult person does not experience further increase in height even after hypersecretion of growth hormone. What could be the possible reason behind this?

(a) Bones becomes insensitive to growth hormone in adults

(b) The epiphyseal plate becomes active after adolescence

(c) The epiphyseal plate ossifies and closes after adolescence

(d) The growth hormone becomes non-functional in adults.

21. Given below are two statements; one is labelled as Assertion (A) and the other is labelled as Reason (R).

Assertion (A) Development of ulcers in stomach is related to hypersecretion of gastrin.

Reason (R) Gastrin stimulates the secretion of pepsinogen for protein digestion.

In the light of the above statements, choose the correct answer from the options given below.

(a) A is false, but R is true

(b) Both A and R are true and R is the correct explanation of A

(c) Both A and R are true, but R is not the correct explanation of A

(d) A is true, but R is false

22. Consider the following statements

I. Growth in a person is completely controlled by pituitary.

II. Acromegaly and gigantism produce same effect on a person.

III. Dwarfism and somatostatin produces opposite effect on body.

IV. Growth is regulated by the activity of adenohypophysis.

Choose the correct statement from the options given below.

(a) II only (b) I only

(c) IV only (d) III only

23. Following are the steps involved in sperm production in a man.

A. Secretion of gonadotropins

B. Secretion of GnRH

C. Production of male gamete

D. Release into portal blood

E. Stimulation of Leydig cells

Choose the correct order from the options given below.

(a) A-D-B-E-C (b) B-D-A-E-C

(c) A-E-B-D-C (d) B-A-D-E-C

24. Match List I with List II.

List I	List II
A. Melatonin	1. Deep voice
B. Androgens	2. High pitch
C. Oestrogen	3. Immunity
D. MSH	4. Pigmentation

Choose the correct match from the options given below.

(a) A-3, B-1, C-2, D-4

(b) A-3, B-2, C-1, D-4

(c) A-4, B-2, C-1, D-3

(d) A-4, B-1, C-2, D-3

25. Given below are two statements; one is labelled as Assertion (A) and the other is labelled as Reason (R).

Assertion (A) Patients with osteoporosis are often given calcitonin.

Reason (R) Thyrocalcitonin causes increased absorption of Ca^{2+} by bones.

In the light of the above statements, choose the correct answer from the options given below.

(a) A is false, but R is true

(b) Both A and R are true and R is the correct explanation of A

(c) Both A and R are true, but R is not the correct explanation of A

(d) A is true, but R is false

26. Consider the following given processes.

A. Lipolysis

B. Gluconeogenesis

C. Glycogenesis

D. Glycogenolysis

Which of the following would be triggered under fasting?

(a) B and C (b) C and D

(c) A, B and D (d) D only

27. Which of the following causes hypersecretion of thyroxine from the thyroid gland?
(a) Over stimulation of posterior pituitary
(b) Hypersecretion of TSH
(c) Low iodine levels in diet
(d) High sodium levels in diet

28. Given below are two statements.
Statement I Thymus and pineal glands have one similar effect on the body.
Statement II Thymus and pineal glands secretion protect the body from invading pathogens.
In the light of the above statements, choose the correct answer from the options given below.
(a) Statement I is incorrect, but statement II is correct.
(b) Both statement I and statement II are correct
(c) Both statement I and statement II are incorrect
(d) Statement I is correct, but statement II is incorrect

29. Consider the following statements.
I. Hormones which do not enter a cell, interact with cell surface.
II. Follicle stimulating hormone interacts with nuclear envelope.
III. Androgens use cyclic AMP of calcium ions for signal transmission.
IV. Hormones with membrane-bound receptors are chemically steroids.
Choose the correct statement from the options given below.
(a) Only II (b) Only I
(c) Only IV (d) Only III

30. Given below are two statements; one is labelled as Assertion (A) and the other is labelled as Reason (R).
Assertion (A) Patients on insulin therapy, should never skip meals.
Reason (R) Insulin counters the effect of glucagon in the body.
In the light of the above statements, choose the correct answer from the options given below.
(a) A is false, but R is true
(b) Both A and R are true and R is the correct explanation of A
(c) Both A and R are true, but R is not the correct explanation of A
(d) A is true, but R is false

31. Given below are two statements; one is labelled as Assertion (A) and the other is labelled as Reason (R).
Assertion (A) Adrenal gland is known as 4-S glands.
Reason (R) Adrenal gland is capable of controlling sugar metabolism, salt retention, sex hormone secretion and is source of energy.
In the light of the above statements, choose the correct answer from the options given below.
(a) A is false, but R is true
(b) Both A and R are true and R is the correct explanation of A
(c) Both A and R are true, but R is not the correct explanation of A
(d) A is true, but R is false

32. Which of the following statement is incorrect w.r.t. the mechanism of hormone action?
(a) Polypeptide hormones interact with membrane-bound receptors
(b) Secondary messengers are involved in the case of iodothyronines
(c) Hormone-receptor complex interact with genome in case of cortisol to bring out a final physiological response
(d) Each receptor is specific to one hormone only

33. Given below are two statements; one is labelled as Assertion (A) and the other is labelled as Reason (R).
Assertion (A) Pancreas is a composite gland.
Reason (R) Pancreas contains glucagon and insulin, that are of peptide nature.
In the light of the above statements, choose the correct answer from the options given below.
(a) A is false, but R is true
(b) Both A and R are true and R is the correct explanation of A
(c) Both A and R are true, but R is not the correct explanation of A
(d) A is true, but R is false

34. Consider the following statements.

I. Addison's disease is caused due to hypersecretion of hormones from adrenal cortex.
II. Fight and flight reactions cause activation of adrenal medulla.
III. Diabetes insipidus exhibits frequent urination as a symptom.
IV. PTH and TCT are antagonistic in their working.

Choose the correct statements out of the given options.

(a) I, II, III and IV (b) II, III and IV
(c) II and IV (d) I and III

35. Given below is an incomplete table about certain hormones, their source glands and one major effect of each on the body in humans.

Identify the correct options for four blanks *A*, *B*, *C* and *D*.

Source glands	Hormones	Functions
A	LH	Androgen synthesis and secretion
β-cells of islets of Langerhans	*B*	Decrease blood sugar level
C	*D*	Stimulates synthesis and secretion of glucocorticoids

(a) *A*-Pars distalis, *B*-Insulin, *C*-Pars distalis, *D*-ACTH
(b) *A*-Neurohypophysis, *B*-Glucagon, *C*-Pars distalis, *D*-ACTH
(c) *A*-Pars nervosa, *B*-Glucagon, *C*-Pars nervosa, *D*-MSH
(d) *A*-Adenohypophysis, *B*-Insulin, *C*-Pars intermedia, *D*-Glucagon

36. An increase in the bleeding time and delay in the blood coagulation was observed in a person. What could be the possible hormonal deficiency in that person?

(a) Nor-adrenaline
(b) Thyroxine
(c) Adrenaline
(d) PTH

37. A girl got into an accident. She suffered injury to adrenal cortex. Which of the following is not affected in the given scenario?

(a) Secretion of aldosterone
(b) Secretion of adrenaline
(c) Secretion of cortisol
(d) Secretion of mineralocorticoids

38. The hormone, whose absence causes the disease diabetes mellitus is secreted by

(a) pituitary gland (b) adrenal gland
(c) islets of Langerhans (d) exocrine pancreas

39. Which organ is responsible for the production of erythropoietin?

(a) Bone marrow (b) Spleen
(c) Kidney (d) Megakaryocytes

40. Growth hormone work properly in the

(a) presence of adrenaline
(b) absence of adrenaline
(c) presence of thyroxine
(d) absence of thyroxine

41. Match List I with List II.

List I (Layers)	List II (Hormones)
A. Zona glomerulosa	1. Glucocorticoids
B. Zona fasciculata	2. Mineralocorticoids
C. Zona reticularis	3. Androgens

Choose the correct answer from the options given below.

(a) I-B, II-C, III-A (b) I-B, II-A, III-C
(c) I-A, II-B, III-C (d) I-C, II-B, III-A

42. Given below are few statements.

I. ADH is released in the kidney to conserve water (lost in excess through urine).
II. Thyroid cancer may suggest a diseased condition called hyperthyroidism in human body.
III. Diurnal rhythm in humans is maintained by pineal gland.
IV. Both follicular and stromal cells, of thyroid gland are responsible for synthesis of T_4 and T_3.

Choose the correct set of statements from the options given below.
(a) I, III and IV
(b) II and III
(c) II, III and IV
(d) II and IV

43. Given below are two statements.

Statement I The hormone important in the glucose metabolism is produced by thyroid gland.
Statement II The neuroendocrine control centre of vertebrates consists of hypothalamus and pineal gland.
In the light of the above statements, choose the correct answer from the options given below.
(a) Statement I is incorrect, but statement II is correct.
(b) Both statement I and statement II are correct
(c) Both statement I and statement II are incorrect
(d) Statement I is correct, but statement II is incorrect

44. Choose the correct match out of the following options.
(a) TCT-hyperglycemic hormone
(b) PTH-hypercalcemic hormone
(c) Glucagon-hypoglycemic hormone
(d) Insulin-hyperglycemic hormone

45. Consider the following figure and identify the incorrect statement w.r.t. it.

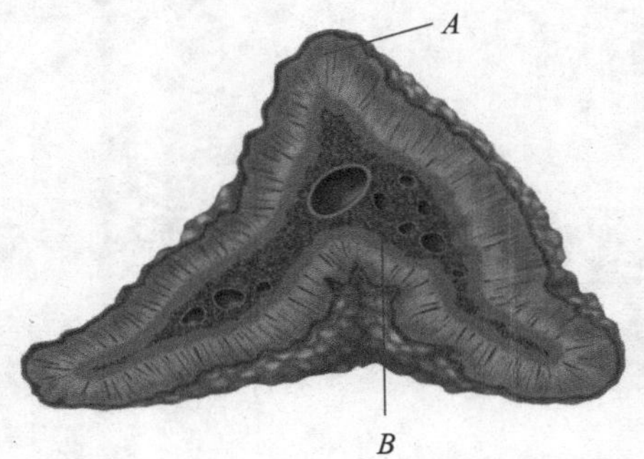

(a) Underproduction of hormones released by *A* will alter carbohydrate metabolism.
(b) Underproduction of hormones released by *B* will alter the breakdown of glycogen into glucose in the blood.
(c) Na^+, K^+ and PO_4^{3-} concentration in the renal tubule is controlled by the hormone released by *B*.
(d) The rate of respiration and the strength of heart contraction is increased by hormone released by *B*.

46. Given below are two statements.
Statement I Blood calcium level can be increased by the administration of PTH along with TCT.
Statement II Oxytocin is called the birth hormone as well as the love hormone.
In the light of the above statements, choose the correct answer from the options given below.
(a) Statement I is incorrect, but statement II is correct.
(b) Both statement I and statement II are correct
(c) Both statement I and statement II are incorrect
(d) Statement I is correct, but statement II is incorrect

47. Given below are two statements; one is labelled as Assertion (A) and the other is labelled as Reason (R).
Assertion (A) Heart releases a hormone called ANF that reduces blood pressure.
Reason (R) When blood pressure is increased, ANF is secreted, which causes constriction of the blood vessels.
In the light of the above statements, choose the correct answer from the options given below.
(a) A is false, but R is true
(b) Both A and R are true and R is the correct explanation of A
(c) Both A and R are true, but R is not the correct explanation of A
(d) A is true, but R is false

48. There was a quiz, where Ram was asked about two hormones based on their characteristics. First hormone influences male libido, while second hormone influences female libido. Identify their names, respectively.
(a) Androgen, progesterone
(b) Testosterone, progesterone
(c) Androgen, prolactin
(d) Testosterone, oestrogen

49. Given below are two statements.

Statement I Oestrogen is synthesised and secreted mainly by the stromal tissues of ovary.

Statement II Excess secretion of growth hormone in adults, especially in middle age, may lead to premature death, if unchecked.

In the light of the above statements, choose the correct answer from the options given below.

(a) Statement I is incorrect, but statement II is correct.
(b) Both statement I and statement II are correct
(c) Both statement I and statement II are incorrect
(d) Statement I is correct, but statement II is incorrect

50. The intense contraction in uterine wall during parturition is under the control is

(a) pars distalis
(b) pars intermedia
(c) pars nervosa
(d) ovaries

Response Index

01 (a) (b) (c) (d)	14 (a) (b) (c) (d)	27 (a) (b) (c) (d)	40 (a) (b) (c) (d)
02 (a) (b) (c) (d)	15 (a) (b) (c) (d)	28 (a) (b) (c) (d)	41 (a) (b) (c) (d)
03 (a) (b) (c) (d)	16 (a) (b) (c) (d)	29 (a) (b) (c) (d)	42 (a) (b) (c) (d)
04 (a) (b) (c) (d)	17 (a) (b) (c) (d)	30 (a) (b) (c) (d)	43 (a) (b) (c) (d)
05 (a) (b) (c) (d)	18 (a) (b) (c) (d)	31 (a) (b) (c) (d)	44 (a) (b) (c) (d)
06 (a) (b) (c) (d)	19 (a) (b) (c) (d)	32 (a) (b) (c) (d)	45 (a) (b) (c) (d)
07 (a) (b) (c) (d)	20 (a) (b) (c) (d)	33 (a) (b) (c) (d)	46 (a) (b) (c) (d)
08 (a) (b) (c) (d)	21 (a) (b) (c) (d)	34 (a) (b) (c) (d)	47 (a) (b) (c) (d)
09 (a) (b) (c) (d)	22 (a) (b) (c) (d)	35 (a) (b) (c) (d)	48 (a) (b) (c) (d)
10 (a) (b) (c) (d)	23 (a) (b) (c) (d)	36 (a) (b) (c) (d)	49 (a) (b) (c) (d)
11 (a) (b) (c) (d)	24 (a) (b) (c) (d)	37 (a) (b) (c) (d)	50 (a) (b) (c) (d)
12 (a) (b) (c) (d)	25 (a) (b) (c) (d)	38 (a) (b) (c) (d)	
13 (a) (b) (c) (d)	26 (a) (b) (c) (d)	39 (a) (b) (c) (d)	

Performance Scanner

> 90% Excellent !	You have mastered this chapter. The concepts of this chapter are at your fingertips. Move on to the next chapter and maintain this momentum.
76-90% Very Good !	You have a good command over this chapter. Revise the chapter again after a few days and enhance your performance.
60-75% Good !	You have a wide scope to learn for this chapter. Revise this chapter again.
<60% Not Satisfactory!	You have a long way ahead of you to master this chapter. Revise it thoroughly.

Scan for online chapter test

Scan for online unit test

Test Booklet No. **3947320**

Test Booklet Code **SPT1**

Syllabus Part Thru 1

(Half Syllabus Test)

Chapters Covered

- The Living World
- Biological Classification
- Plant Kingdom
- Animal Kingdom
- Morphology of Flowering Plants
- Anatomy of Flowering Plants
- Structural Organisation in Animals
- Cell : The Unit of Life
- Biomolecules
- Cell Cycle and Cell Division

Important Instructions

- The test is of **1 hours 30 minutes** duration and the Test Booklet contains **90** multiple-choice questions (four options with a single correct answer) from biology.
- Candidates are advised to read all questions before they start attempting the question paper.
- Each questions carries 4 marks. For each correct response, the candidate will get 4 marks. For each incorrect response, one marks will be deducted from the total scores.
- In the event of candidate marking more than one option one mark will be deducted. The maximum marks are 180.
- Use **Blue/Black Point Pen only** for writing particular on this page/ marking response on Answer Sheet.

Name of the Candidate (In Capitals) ____________________

____

Candidate's Signature ____________

Invigilator's Signature ____________

Facsimile signature stamp of center superintendent____________

Do not open this booklet until you start attempting the test

Biology

1. Gemmae are reproductive structures commonly found in liverworts. Which of the following statements accurately describes the location and function of gemmae on the thallus?
(a) Gemmae are found on the dorsal surface of the thallus, where they function as structures for sexual reproduction by producing gametes.
(b) Gemmae are located in specialised cup-shaped structures on the dorsal surface of the thallus, aiding in asexual reproduction by detaching and germinating into new thalli.
(c) Gemmae are situated on the ventral surface of the thallus and are primarily involved in the uptake of nutrients from the soil.
(d) Gemmae are located at the margins of the thallus and are responsible for photosynthesis and gas exchange in the liverworts.

2. Which of the following accurately describes the structure and function of the nerve cord in cockroaches?
(a) A single nerve running along the dorsal side of the body, coordinating sensory inputs.
(b) A paired nerve structure running along the ventral side of the body, controlling movements.
(c) A network of nerves in the head, controlling the movement of wings and legs.
(d) A network of nerves in the thorax, responsible for sensory and motor functions.

3. Given below are two statements.
Statement I Plant family-Solanaceae, comprises of different genera such as *Solanum*, *Petunia* and *Datura*.
Statement II *Triticum aestivum* belongs to order-Sapindales and class-Dicotyledonae.
In the light of the above statements, choose the correct answer from the options given below.
(a) Statement I is incorrect, but statement II is correct
(b) Both statement I and statement II are correct
(c) Both statement I and statement II are incorrect
(d) Statement I is correct, but statement II is incorrect

4. Match List I with List II.

List I	List II
A. Amoeboid protozoan	1. Spore-like stage
B. Ciliated protozoan	2. Silica shells
C. Sporozoans	3. Sleeping sickness
D. Flagellated protozoan	4. Cavity (gullet)

Choose the correct answer from the options given below.

	A	B	C	D		A	B	C	D
(a)	2	4	1	3	(b)	2	4	3	1
(c)	3	2	1	4	(d)	1	3	4	2

5. Given below are two statements; one is labelled as Assertion (A) and the other is labelled as Reason (R).
Assertion (A) Glandular epithelium has a limited role in secretion and absorption.
Reason (R) Glandular epithelium is mainly of two types, i.e., unicellular and multicellular.
In the light of the above statements, choose the correct answer from the options given below.
(a) A is false, but R is true
(b) Both A and R are true and R is the correct explanation of A
(c) Both A and R are true, but R is not the correct explanation of A
(d) A is true, but R is false

6. Read the following statements and choose the correct set of statements.
I. Root hairs are present below the region of meristematic activity.
II. The root is covered at the apex by a thimble-like structure called the root cap.
III. Fibrous root system is seen in mustard plant.
IV. Roots become modified to perform functions other than absorption and conduction of water.
V. The region of elongation undergoes rapid elongation and enlargement.

Choose the correct answer from the options given below.

(a) I and V (b) II, III and IV

(c) IV and V (d) II, IV and V

7. Match List I with List II.

List I		List II
A. Porifera	1.	Hypostome
B. Cnidaria	2.	Spicules
C. Ctenophora	3.	Hooks and suckers
D. Platyhelminthes	4.	Indirect development

Choose the correct answer from the options given below.

	A	B	C	D		A	B	C	D
(a)	2	1	4	3	(b)	3	4	2	1
(c)	1	3	4	2	(d)	1	4	2	3

8. Given below are two statements.

Statement I The body of cnidarian bears eight external rows of ciliated comb plates.

Statement II Bioluminescence property is well marked in cnidarians.

In the light of the above statements, choose the correct answer from the options given below.

(a) Statement I is incorrect, but statement II is correct

(b) Both statement I and statement II are correct

(c) Both statement I and statement II are incorrect

(d) Statement I is correct, but statement II is incorrect

9. The features of tracheids include

I. elongated or tube like cells.

II. thin walled and large cavity.

III. dead without protoplasm.

Choose the correct answer from the options given below.

(a) I only (b) I and III (c) II only (d) II and III

10. Choose the correct pathway through which water is transported out of the body of sponges.

(a) Spongocoel → Ostia → Osculum

(b) Ostia → Spongocoel → Osculum

(c) Osculum → Spongocoel → Ostia

(d) Osculum → Ostia → Spongocoel

11. Which one the following statements is incorrect?

(a) Xylem functions as a conducting tissue for water and minerals from roots to stem.

(b) The radial conduction of water takes place by the collenchymatous cells.

(c) Tracheids and vessels are the main water transporting elements.

(d) The presence of vessels is a characteristic feature of angiosperms.

12. Which of the following best describes the inner membrane of the mitochondria?

(a) It is smooth and permeable to most ions and molecules.

(b) It is folded into structures known as cristae to increase surface area for ATP production.

(c) It contains porins that allow the passage of large molecules and proteins.

(d) It is the site of anaerobic respiration.

13. Match List I with List II.

List I		List II
A. Pili	1.	Oil and fats
B. Fimbriae	2.	Carbohydrates
C. Amyloplast	3.	Special protein
D. Elaioplast	4.	Bristle-like fibres

Choose the correct answer from the options given below.

	A	B	C	D		A	B	C	D
(a)	2	3	4	1	(b)	3	4	2	1
(c)	1	4	3	2	(d)	2	4	1	3

14. The give graph shows the enzymatic activity w.r.t. one of the three parameters such as pH, temperature or substrate concentration.

What do the *X* and *Y* axes represent?

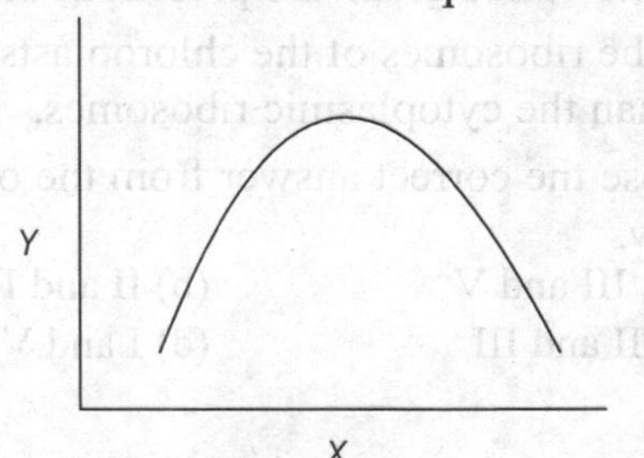

	X	Y
(a)	Enzyme activity	Temperature
(b)	Substrate concentration	Enzyme activity
(c)	Temperature	Enzyme activity
(d)	Enzyme activity	pH

15. Given below are two statements.

Statement I Cellulose is a heteropolymer that forms an important component of plant cell.

Statement II Inulin is a polymer of glucose.

In the light of the above statements, choose the correct answer from the options given below.

(a) Statement I is incorrect, but statement II is correct.
(b) Both statement I and statement II are correct.
(c) Both statement I and statement II are incorrect.
(d) Statement I is correct, but statement II is incorrect.

16. The homologous chromosomes separate, while sister chromatids remain associated at their centromere. This all indicates which stage of meiosis?

(a) Metaphase-I (b) Prophase-I
(c) Anaphase-I (d) Anaphase-II

17. Read the following statements and choose the correct set of statements.

I. The prokaryotic ribosomes are 80S, while the eukaryotic ribosomes are 70S.
II. Ribosomes are granular structures composed of ribonucleic acid and proteins.
III. Cilia are small structures which cause movement.
IV. A number of organised flattened membranous sacs called grana are present in the stroma.
V. The ribosomes of the chloroplasts are smaller than the cytoplasmic ribosomes.

Choose the correct answer from the options given below.

(a) II, III and V (b) II and IV
(c) I, II and III (d) I and V

18. Which of the following statement correctly describes the classes of fungi along with related species?

(a) Ascomycetes include mushrooms and puffballs.
(b) Basidiomycetes include yeasts and morels.
(c) Zygomycetes include bread molds like *Rhizopus*.
(d) Deuteromycetes include fungi like *Penicillium* and *Aspergillus*.

19. Listed below are few secondary metabolites. The polymeric substances include

I. Morphine II. Vinblastin
III. Rubber IV. Cellulose
V. Abrin

Choose the correct answer from the options given below.

(a) I only (b) II and III
(c) V only (d) III and IV

20. Given below are two statements; one is labelled as Assertion (A) and the other is labelled as Reason (R).

Assertion (A) Diatoms have left behind large amount of cell wall deposits in their habitat.

Reason (R) The walls of diatoms are made up of cellulose only.

In the light of the above statements, choose the correct answer from the options given below.

(a) A is false, but R is true
(b) Both A and R are true and R is the correct explanation of A
(c) Both A and R are true, but R is not the correct explanation of A
(d) A is true, but R is false

21. Read the following statements and choose the correct set of statements.

I. The male sex organ of bryophyte is called archegonium.
II. The female sex organ of bryophyte produce biflagellated antherozoids.
III. Asexual reproduction in liverworts takes place by fragmentation of thalli.
IV. Common example of mosses are *Funaria, Polytrichum* and *Sphagnum*.

Choose the correct answer from the options given below.

(a) I, II and IV (b) III and IV
(c) I and III (d) II, III and IV

22. Given below are two statements.

Statement I Palmitic acid has 20 carbons including carboxyl carbon.

Statement II Arachidonic acid has 15 carbon atoms only.

In the light of the above statements, choose the correct answer from the options given below.

(a) Statement I is incorrect, but statement II is correct
(b) Both statement I and statement II are correct
(c) Both statement I and statement II are incorrect
(d) Statement I is correct, but statement II is incorrect

23. Match List I with List II w.r.t. male cockroach.

List I	List II
A. Mushroom-shaped gland	1. Phallomere
B. Testes	2. 6th-7th abdominal segments
C. External genitalia	3. 4th-6th abdominal segments
D. Bundles of sperms	4. Spermatophores

Choose the correct answer from the options given below.

	A	B	C	D		A	B	C	D
(a)	2	3	4	1	(b)	1	3	4	2
(c)	3	2	4	1	(d)	2	3	1	4

24. Which of the following statement accurately describes a fruit and example of the Cruciferae family?

(a) Plants in this family produce fruits known as capsules and include species like radish.
(b) Thie family is characterised by its members producing fruits called legumes and includes crops such as beans and peas.
(c) This family is characterised by fruit called siliqua or silicula and includes plant like *Iberis*.
(d) This family includes plants that produce fruits called achenes and features ornamental plants such as sunflowers.

25. Given below are two statements.

Statement I In exarch, the protoxylem lies towards the centre and the metaxylem lies towards the periphery of the organ.

Statement II In endarch, the protoxylem lies towards periphery and metaxylem lies towards the centre.

In the light of the above statements, choose the correct answer from the options given below.

(a) Statement I is incorrect, but statement II is correct
(b) Both statement I and statement II are correct
(c) Both statement I and statement II are incorrect
(d) Statement I is correct, but statement II is incorrect

26. Match the List I with List II.

List I	List II
A. *Pinus*	1. Dioecious
B. *Cycas*	2. Monoecious
C. *Salvinia*	3. Heterosporous
D. *Equisetum*	4. Homosporous

Choose the correct answer from the options given below.

	A	B	C	D		A	B	C	D
(a)	1	2	4	3	(b)	1	2	3	4
(c)	2	1	3	4	(d)	2	1	4	3

27. Given below are two statements; one is labelled as Assertion (A) and the other is labelled Reason (R).

Assertion (A) Generally, all enzymes are proteins except ribozyme, but *vice-versa* is not true.

Reason (R) Enzymes are biocatalysts and have stable configuration with an active site.

In the light of the above statements, choose the correct answer from the options given below.

(a) A is false, but R is true.
(b) Both A and R are true and R is the correct explanation of A.
(c) Both A and R are true, but R is not the correct explanation of A.
(d) A is true, but R is false.

28. Which one of the following statement is incorrect?

(a) The nuclear membrane and nucleolus reappear in telophase-I.

(b) The stage between the two mitotic divisions is called interkinesis.

(c) Interkinesis is generally short-lived.

(d) Interkinesis is followed by prophase-II.

29. Which one of the following statements is incorrect ?

(a) *Solanum* includes species like *nigrum* and *melongena*.

(b) *Petunia*, *Datura* and *Felis* are placed in the family-Solanaceae.

(c) The system of providing a name with two components is called binomial nomenclature.

(d) Taxa can indicate categories at different levels.

30. Match List I with List II.

List I		List II
A. Hominidae	1.	Housefly
B. Muscidae	2.	Mango
C. Anacardiaceae	3.	Wheat
D. Poaceae	4.	Man

Choose the correct answer from the options given below.

	A	B	C	D		A	B	C	D
(a)	2	1	4	3	(b)	4	1	2	3
(c)	1	3	2	4	(d)	2	3	4	1

31. Match the List I with List II.

List I		List II
A. Aschelminthes	1.	Metameres
B. Annelida	2.	Sensory tentacles
C. Arthropoda	3.	Malpighian tubules
D. Mollusca	4.	Muscular pharynx

Choose the correct answer from the options given below.

	A	B	C	D
(a)	2	3	1	4
(b)	4	1	3	2
(c)	2	1	3	4
(d)	1	3	4	2

32. Martinus Beijerinck made a significant contribution to virology with his discovery. Which of the following statements accurately describes his discovery?

(a) Beijerinck was the first to identify the role of bacteria in plant diseases and develop vaccines against bacterial infections.

(b) Beijerinck discovered that viruses could be transmitted through contaminated soil and that they are different from bacteria because they require living cells to reproduce.

(c) Beijerinck demonstrated that viruses were composed of nucleic acids and proteins, and he was the first to visualise them using electron microscopy.

(d) Beijerinck identified and named the first virus as "tobacco mosaic virus" and proposed that it was caused by a "contagious living fluid."

33. Given below are two statements; one is labelled as Assertion (A) and the other is labelled as Reason (R).

Assertion (A) G_2-phase is also called as equational division.

Reason (R) In equational division, the number of chromosomes in the parent and progeny cells is the same.

In the light of the above statements, choose the correct from the options given below.

(a) A is false, but R is true.

(b) Both A and R are true and R is the correct explanation of A.

(c) Both A and R are true, but R is not the correct explanation of A.

(d) A is true, but R is false.

34. Match List I and List II.

List I		List II
A. Cuticle	1.	Present in monocot root
B. Polyarch bundles	2.	Absent in dicot root
C. Mesophyll	3.	Lacks nucleus
D. Sieve tube	4.	Palisade cells

Choose the correct answer from the options given below.

	A	B	C	D		A	B	C	D
(a)	2	1	4	3	(b)	2	4	1	3
(c)	2	1	3	4	(d)	1	2	3	4

35. Given below are two statements; one is labelled as Assertion (A) and the other is labelled as Reason (R).

Assertion (A) *Pleurobrachia* is dimorphic in nature and belongs to phylum-Cnidaria.

Reason (R) Cnidarians show polyp and medusa forms.

In the light of the above statements, choose the correct answer from the options given below.

(a) A is false, but R is true.
(b) Both A and R are true and R is the correct explanation of A.
(c) Both A and R are true, but R is not the correct explanation of A.
(d) A is true, but R is false.

36. Which of the following structure in cardiac muscles tissue allows for synchronised contraction of cells?

(a) Tight junctions (b) Desmosomes
(c) Intercalated discs (d) Gap junctions

37. Given below are two statements; one is labelled as Assertion (A) and the other is labelled as Reason (R).

Assertion (A) Slime moulds exhibit a unique life cycle that includes both a mobile, *Amoeba*-like phase and a stationary, spore-producing phase.

Reason (R) Slime moulds can form a multicellular structure called a plasmodium during their life cycle, which allows them to move and feed in a manner similar to *Amoeba* before forming sporangia to produce spores.

In the light of the above statements, choose the correct answer from the options given below.

(a) A is false, but R is true.
(b) Both A and R are true and the R is the correct explanation of A.
(c) Both A and R are true, but the R is not the correct explanation of A.
(d) A is true, but R is false.

38. Roots having fungal association are found in ...... and roots associated with N_2-fixing cyanobacteria are found in ....

(a) *Cycas, Pinus* (b) *Pinus, Cycas*
(c) *Pteris, Salvinia* (d) Pteris, Cedrus

39. Select the incorrect match.

(a) Axoneme- Radially arranged doublet
(b) Centriole- Amorphous pericentriolar material
(c) Hub- Lipid based central part of centriole
(d) Basal body- Origin of cilia and flagella

40. Given below are two statements.

Statement I The hindbrain of frog is characterised by a pair of optic lobes and unpaired diencephalon.

Statement II Midbrain of frog consists of cerebellum and medulla oblongata.

In the light of the above statements, choose the correct answer from the options given below.

(a) Statement I is incorrect, but statement II is correct
(b) Both statement I and statement II are correct
(c) Both statement I and statement II are incorrect
(d) Statement I is correct, but statement II is incorrect

41. Given below are two statements; one is labelled as Assertion (A) and the other is labelled as Reason (R).

Assertion (A) The leaves in gymnosperms are well adapted to withstand extremes of temperature, humidity and wind.

Reason (R) Gymnosperms produce haploid microspores and megaspores.

In the light of the above statements, choose the correct answer from the options given below.

(a) A is false, but R is true.
(b) Both A and R are true and R is the correct explanation of A.
(c) Both A and R are true, but R is not the correct explanation of A.
(d) A is true, but R is false.

42. Which of the following statement is correct regarding Bentham and Hooker's system of classification?

(a) Their classification is based solely on morphological characteristics without considering evolutionary relationships.
(b) Their classification considers assigning numbers and codes to each observable character.
(c) Their classification separated closely related species.
(d) Their classification includes both external and internal features.

43. Match List I with List II.

List I	List II
A. Vacuole	1. Pigments
B. Lysosomes	2. Tonoplast
C. Golgi apparatus	3. Hydrolytic enzymes
D. Plastids	4. Glycoproteins

Choose the correct answer from the options given below.

	A	B	C	D
(a)	1	3	4	2
(b)	2	3	4	1
(c)	2	4	1	3
(d)	3	4	1	2

44. Given below are few characteristics.

I. Food is stored in the form of starch.

II. Cell wall is made up of cellulose.

III. Found in freshwater and salt water.

The above characteristics belong to

(a) Chlorophyceae
(b) Phaeophyceae
(c) Liverworts
(d) Mosses

45. Which anatomical feature is more commonly pronounced in male frogs during the breeding season compared to females?

(a) Size of the eyes
(b) Size and prominence of the tympanum
(c) Size and development of the vocal sacs
(d) Number of fingers and toes

46. Observe the floral diagram given below.

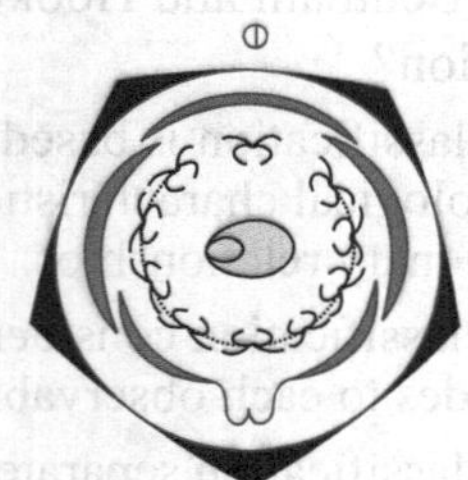

Members of which of the following classes can accurately represent the given diagram?

(a) Cruciferae (b) Leguminosae
(c) Malvaceae (d) Gramineae

47. Centrosome and centrioles are related to each other as

(a) centriole consists of two structures of centrosome
(b) centrosomes are located inside centriole
(c) centrosome contains two centrioles
(d) centriole is the outer lining of centrosome

48. Based on number of amino and carboxyl groups, there are basic and acidic amino acids such as

(a) lysine and valine, respectively
(b) lysine and glutamic acid, respectively
(c) tryptophan and tyrosine, respectively
(d) valine and phenylalanine, respectively

49. Which of the following structures is accurately described as originating from the protoderm rather than the secondary meristems or other tissues?

(a) Pith (b) Cork cambium
(c) Periderm (d) Epidermis

50. Given below are two statements.

Statement I Collagen is the most abundant protein in the whole of the biosphere.

Statement II RuBisCO is the most abundant protein in the animal world.

In the light of the above statements, choose the correct answer from the options given below.

(a) Statement I is incorrect, but statement II is correct
(b) Both statement I and statement II are correct
(c) Both statement I and statement II are incorrect
(d) Statement I is correct, but statement II is incorrect

51. Which of the following statement correctly describes a structural feature of a dicot seed and accurately reflects its role within the seed?

(a) The cotyledons in a dicot seed are primarily responsible for nutrient storage during seed germination.
(b) The endosperm in a dicot seed provides nutrients directly to the developed embryo.
(c) The micropyle in a dicot seed is a small opening through which carbon dioxide enter during seed germination.
(d) The seed coat of a dicot seed functions mainly in producing proteinceous layer.

52. Given below are two statements.

Statement I In castor, the endosperm is not present in mature seeds.

Statement II The cotyledons are often fleshy and full of reserve food materials.

In the light of the above statements, choose the correct answer from the options given below.

(a) Statement I is incorrect, but statement II is correct
(b) Both statement I and statement II are correct
(c) Both statement I and statement II are incorrect
(d) Statement I is correct, but statement II is incorrect

53. Consider the following characteristics.

I. V_{max} is lowered
II. Inhibition is irreversible
III. K_m increases

How many of these relate to non-competitive inhibition?

(a) 0 (b) 1
(c) 2 (d) 3

54. The parenchyma that is made up of elongated cells and are arranged vertically and parallel to each other is called

(a) spongy parenchyma
(b) palisade parenchyma
(c) vascular parenchyma
(d) cortical parenchyma

55. Observe the following diagram.

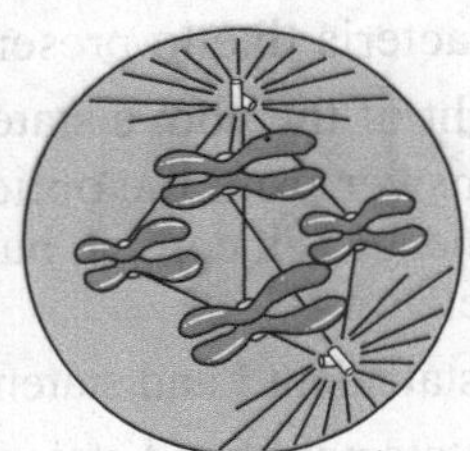

The above diagram indicates which stage of cell cycle?

(a) Late prophase
(b) Early prophase
(c) Transition to metaphase
(d) Metaphase

56. In a mature dicot stem, which of the following statements accurately describes the relationship between the vascular bundles and the types of tissues involved?

(a) The vascular bundles in a dicot stem are arranged in a scattered pattern throughout the ground tissue, with each bundle consisting of xylem and phloem tissues enclosed by a bundle sheath.
(b) In a dicot stem, the vascular bundles are arranged in a single circular layer in the cortex, with xylem located towards the outside and phloem towards the inside.
(c) The vascular bundles in a dicot stem are arranged in a ring in the ground tissue, with xylem towards the centre and phloem towards the periphery, separated by a cambium layer.
(d) In a dicot stem, vascular bundles are arranged in a continuous ring in the center of the stem, surrounded by a large amount of ground tissue, and there is no cambium present.

57. Observe the following diagram.

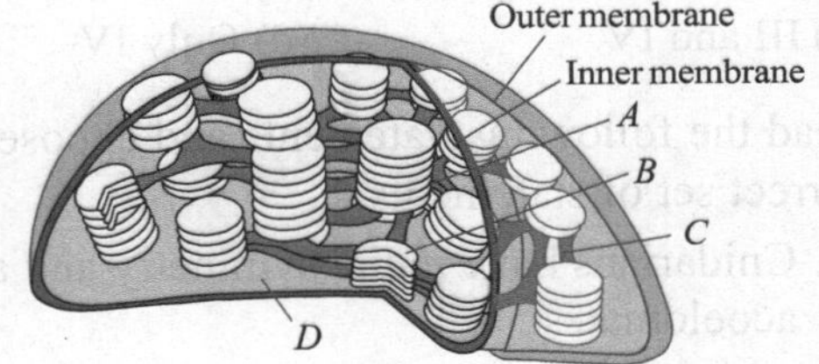

Which part of the given cell organelle contains enzyme required for the synthesis of carbohydrates and proteins?

(a) *A* (b) *B*
(c) *C* (d) *D*

58. Arrange the following steps in the correct sequence for the packing and transport of a protein from its synthesis to its final destination within the cell.

I. Transport vesicle fuses with the Golgi apparatus.
II. Protein synthesis occurs in the rough Endoplasmic Reticulum (ER).
III. Protein is modified and packaged in the Golgi apparatus.
IV. Protein is delivered to the plasma membrane or secretory granules.
V. Transport vesicle buds off from the rough ER.

Choose the correct option.
(a) II → V→ I → III → IV
(b) II → I→ V → III → IV
(c) V → II→ I → III → IV
(d) II → V→ III → I → IV

59. Consider the following statements.

I. The G_2-phase is characterised by the synthesis of proteins necessary for mitosis and the final preparation for cell division.
II. The M-phase (mitosis) involves the division of the nucleus and the cytoplasm, resulting in two daughter cells.
III. Telophase of mitosis results in formation of 4 genetically different daughter cells.
IV. The cell cycle is controlled by checkpoints that ensure proper progression through each phase,.

Choose the correct answer from the options given below.
(a) I, II and IV (b) I and II
(c) III and IV (d) Only IV

60. Read the following statements and choose the correct set of statements.

I. Cnidarians have radial symmetry and are acoelomates.
II. The body cavity which is lined by mesoderm is called coelom.
III. Platyhelminthes have radial symmetry.
IV. Poriferans are pseudocoelomates.
V. Annelids and molluscs possess true coelom.

Choose the correct answer from the options given below.
(a) I and II (b) I, II and V
(c) II and V (d) II, III and IV

61. Read the following statements and choose the correct set of statements.

I. Phloem fibres are made up of parenchymatous cells.
II. Phloem parenchyma is made up of elongated tapering cylindrical cells.
III. Companion cells are specialised parenchymatous cells.
IV. The first formed primary phloem is called metaphloem.
V. The functions of sieve tubes are controlled by the nucleus of companion cells.

Choose the correct answer from the options given below.
(a) I and III (b) II and IV
(c) II, III and V (d) I, II and IV

62. Which one of the following statement regarding prokaryotic cells is incorrect?
(a) They are smaller and multiply more rapidly.
(b) All prokaryotes lack cell wall.
(c) There is no well-defined nucleus.
(d) The fluid matrix filling the cell is the cytoplasm.

63. Which of the following statement accurately reflects a difference in the gill structure between cartilaginous and bony fish?
(a) Cartilaginous fishes have gill slits without an operculum, while bony fish have gill covers (operculum) that protect the gill slits.
(b) Cartilaginous fishes have an operculum that covers their gill slits, whereas bony fish lack this feature and have exposed gill slits.
(c) Both cartilaginous and bony fishes have gill slits covered by a single operculum.
(d) Cartilaginous fishes have multiple gill slits, but no operculum, while bony fishes have a single gill slit covered by an operculum.

64. Given below are two statements.

Statement I Plasmid is extra chromosomal DNA found in bacteria, which is associated with transformation of bacteria with foreign DNA.

Statement II Extensive compartmentalisation is seen in bacteria due to presence of plasmid.

In the light of the above statements, choose the correct answer from the options given below.
(a) Statement I is incorrect, but statement II is correct.
(b) Both statement I and statement II are correct.
(c) Both statement I and statement II are incorrect.
(d) Statement I is correct, but statement II is incorrect.

65. Which one of the following statement regarding nucleic acids is incorrect?
(a) A nucleotide has two chemically distinct components.
(b) Sugar found in polynucleotides is either ribose or deoxyribose.

(c) The skeletal heterocyclic ring is purine or pyrimidine.
(d) Nucleotide is the building block of nucleic acids.

66. Tight junctions perform functions like
(a) helping to stop substance from leaking
(b) perform cementing to keep cells together
(c) facilitating the cells to communicate with each other
(d) helping to cover the surface

67. Which of the following shows the correct sequence of events occurring during meiosis?
I. Formation of a recombination nodule.
II. Alignment of univalents at the equator.
III. Reduction in the number of chromosomes.
IV. Terminalisation of chiasmata.
Choose the correct answer from the options given below.
(a) I → IV → III → II
(b) I → II → IV → III
(c) II → IV → III → I
(d) III → I → IV → II

68. Given below are two statements: one is labelled as Assertion (A) and the other is labelled as Reason (R).
Assertion (A) Loose connective tissue is characterised by a relatively high proportion of ground substance and fewer fibres compared to dense connective tissue.
Reason (R) Dense connective tissue primarily functions in providing structural support and cushioning to organs, whereas loose connective tissue is more specialised for strength and rigidity due to its high fibre content.
Choose the correct answer from the options given below.
(a) A is false, but R is true.
(b) Both A and R are true and R is the correct explanation of A.
(c) Both A and R are true, but R is not the correct explanation of A.
(d) A is true, but R is false.

69. Match List I with List II.

List I		List II
A. Reptilia	1.	*Hyla*
B. Aves	2.	*Macropus*
C. Mammalia	3.	*Calotes*
D. Amphibia	4.	*Corvus*

Choose the correct answer from the options given below.

	A	B	C	D		A	B	C	D
(a)	2	3	4	1	(b)	3	4	1	2
(c)	2	4	3	1	(d)	3	4	2	1

70. Given below are two statements.
Statement I In animal cells, cytokinesis is achieved through the formation of a cell plate that eventually separates the two daughter cells.
Statement II During cytokinesis in plant cells, vesicles from the Golgi apparatus fuse at the centre of the cell to form the cell plate, which gradually develops into a new cell wall.
In the light of the above statements, choose the correct answer from the options given below.
(a) Statement I is incorrect, but statement II is correct.
(b) Both statement I and statement II are correct.
(c) Both statement I and statement II are incorrect.
(d) Statement I is correct, but statement II is incorrect.

71. Match List I with List II.

List I		List II
A. Perigynous flower	1.	Mustard
B. Hypogynous flower	2.	*Datura*
C. Actinomorphic flower	3.	Gulmohar
D. Zygomorphic flower	4.	Plum

Choose the correct answer from the options given below.

	A	B	C	D		A	B	C	D
(a)	1	4	2	3	(b)	4	1	2	3
(c)	1	4	3	2	(d)	4	1	3	2

72. Match List I with List II.

List I		List II
A. Metacentric chromosome	1.	Centromere close to the end
B. Acrocentric chromosomes	2.	Middle centromere
C. Telocentric chromosomes	3.	Terminal centromere
D. Sub-metacentric chromosomes	4.	Chromosomes slightly away from middle

Choose the correct answer from the options given below.

	A	B	C	D		A	B	C	D
(a)	2	1	3	4	(b)	1	2	4	3
(c)	4	1	3	2	(d)	2	3	1	4

73. Given below are two statements; one is labelled as Assertion (A) and the other is labelled as Reason (R).

Assertion (A) Presence of only motile gametes is characteristic of kingdom-Fungi and fusion of their protoplasm is called plasmogamy.

Reason (R) The sexual reproduction in fungi often involves the formation of specialised structures such as asci or basidia, which are crucial for the development and dispersal of the sexual spores.

(a) A is false, but R is true.
(b) Both A and R are true, and the R is the correct explanation of A.
(c) Both A and R are true, but the R is not the correct explanation of A.
(d) A is true, but R is false.

74. The cytoskeleton consists of

I. microtubules
II. microfilaments
III. hub
IV. spoke

Choose the correct answer from the options given below.

(a) I and III (b) I and II
(c) III and IV (d) II and IV

75. Given below are two statements; one is labelled as Assertion (A) and the other is labelled as Reason (R).

Assertion (A) Nephridia are excretory organs found in various invertebrates, including annelids and some arthropods.

Reason (R) Nephridia function by filtering body fluids to remove nitrogenous wastes and help maintain osmotic balance, and their structure varies depending on the organism's habitat.

In the light of the above statements, choose the correct answer from the options given below.

(a) A is false, but R is true.
(b) Both A and R are true and R is the correct explanation of A.
(c) Both A and R are true, but R is not the correct explanation of A.
(d) A is true, but R is false.

76. The red algae usually reproduce vegetatively by …….and brown algae reproduce asexually by……respectively.

(a) biflagellated zoospores, fragmentation
(b) flagellated zoospores, anisogamy
(c) fragmentation, biflagellated zoospores
(d) non-motile spores, isogamy

77. Read the following statements and choose the correct set of statements.

I. Most fungi are heterotrophic and are called saprophytes.
II. In some fungi, the fusion of two haploid cells immediately results in diploid cells.
III. *Mucor* and *Rhizopus* belong to Ascomycetes.
IV. Reproduction in class-Phycomycetes takes place by zoospores or by aplanospores.
V. Rusts and smuts are parasites that belong to class-Deuteromycetes.

Choose the correct answer from the options given below.

(a) I, II and IV
(b) II and III
(c) I, II and V
(d) III and V

78. Consider the representation of an organelle and identify the correct statement related to it.

(a) The double membraned structure consists of cristae present in between the outer and the inner membrane.
(b) Knob-like structures visible over cristae, are oxysomes and are involved in ATP release.
(c) Enzymes responsible for Krebs' cycle are found in cristae, while those involved in ETS are found in matrix.
(d) This organelle can be easily found in cells and tissues that are not metabolically active.

79. Read the following statements and choose the incorrect set of statements.

I. *Petromyzon* belongs to class- Cyclostomata.
II. Notochord is persistent throughout life in Chondrichthyes.
III. *Pristis* and *Trygon* belong to class- Osteichthyes.
IV. Air bladder is absent in Osteichthyes.
V. Sexes are separate in Chondrichthyes and Osteichthyes.

Choose the correct answer from the options given below.

(a) I and II (b) III and IV
(c) IV and V (d) III and V

80. Given below are two statements.

Statement I In gymnosperms, the male and female gametophytes do not have an independent free living existence.

Statement II In pteridophytes, the main plant body is a sporophyte that has two life cycle.

In the light of the above statements, choose the correct answer from the options given below.

(a) Statement I is incorrect, but statement II is correct
(b) Both statement I and statement II are correct
(c) Both statement I and statement II are incorrect
(d) Statement I is correct, but statement II is incorrect

81. Read the following statements and choose the incorrect set of statements.

I. Frogs have 15 pairs of cranial nerves and 10 pairs of spinal nerves, arising from spinal cord.
II. Frogs have underdeveloped reproductive system.
III. Frogs have different types of sense organs.
IV. Fertilisation is external in frogs.
V. Frogs maintain ecological balance.

Choose the correct answer from the options given below.

(a) I and II
(b) III and IV
(c) I and V
(d) II and IV

82. Which of the following statement is correct regarding an evolutionary adaptation in the heart structure among the chordates?

(a) The heart of cartilaginous fish, such as sharks, has single atrium and single ventricle, which is efficient in separating oxygenated and deoxygenated blood.
(b) In amphibians, the heart has three chambers and provides partial separation of oxygenated and deoxygenated blood through a partially divided ventricle.
(c) In reptiles, including crocodiles, the heart has a complete four-chambered structure with two atria and two ventricles, preventing any mixing of oxygenated and deoxygenated blood.
(d) In birds, the heart's adaptation includes a three-chambered structure with two ventricles that separates oxygenated and deoxygenated blood.

83. Which one of the following statement is incorrect?

(a) Skeletal muscle tissue is closely attached to skeletal bones.
(b) The bone cells are present in the spaces called lacunae.
(c) Blood is the main circulating fluid.
(d) Tendon attaches one bone to another.

84. Given below are few floral characters.

I. Inflorescence is a spike raceme.
II. Calyx is absent in flowers.
III. Flowers or florets are usually small.
IV. Corolla is absent.

These characters indicate which family?

(a) Malvaceae
(b) Leguminosae
(c) Gramineae
(d) Cruciferae

85. Choose the incorrect statement from the options given below.

(a) Mammalia have milk producing mammary glands.
(b) Air sacs of Aves are connected to lungs for respiration.
(c) Reptilia are viviparous animals.
(d) Body of amphibia is divisible into head and trunk.

86. Given below are two statements.

Statement I Mesosome is formed by the extension of plasma membrane into cell.

Statement II The extensions of plasma membranes are in the form of tubules, fibrils and pili.

In the light of the above statements, choose the correct answer from the options given below.

(a) Statement I is incorrect, but statement II is correct
(b) Both statement I and statement II are correct
(c) Both statement I and statement II are incorrect
(d) Statement I is correct, but statement II is incorrect

87. Match List I with List II.

List I		List II
A. Phycomycetes	1.	Bracket fungi
B. Ascomycetes	2.	Conidia
C. Basidiomycetes	3.	Obligate parasites
D. Deuteromycetes	4.	Coprophilous

Choose the correct answer from the options given below.

	A	B	C	D
(a)	3	4	1	2
(b)	2	3	4	1
(c)	2	3	1	4
(d)	1	4	2	3

88. Which of the following statement is true for the role of the enzyme recombinase during meiosis?

(a) Recombinase catalyses formation of synapsis.
(b) Recombinase facilitates the exchange of genetic material between homologous chromosomes by catalysing the formation of chiasmata.
(c) Recombinase is responsible for the separation of sister chromatids during anaphase of mitosis.
(d) Recombinase assists in condensation of chromosomes.

89. Given below are two statements.

Statement I The transition state of a reaction is the high-energy, stable intermediate that forms during the process of breaking and forming bonds, and is stabilised by the enzyme to lower the activation energy.

Statement II Activation energy is the energy required by the reactants to reach the transition state in a chemical reaction.

In the light of the above statements, choose the correct answer from the options given below.

(a) Statement I is incorrect, but statement II is correct.
(b) Both statement I and statement II are correct.
(c) Both statement I and statement II are incorrect.
(d) Statement I is correct, but statement II is incorrect.

90. Read the following statements and choose the correct set of statements.

I. When stamens are attached to the petals, they are epiphyllous.

II. Epipetalous condition is seen in flowers of lily.

III. When more than one carpel is present are free, they are called apocarpous.

IV. Syncarpous refers to condition when carpels are free.

V. Monoadelphous stamens are seen in china rose.

Choose the correct answer from the options given below.

(a) I, II and IV
(b) III, IV and V
(c) I and IV
(d) III and V

Response Index

01 ⓐ ⓑ ⓒ ⓓ	26 ⓐ ⓑ ⓒ ⓓ	51 ⓐ ⓑ ⓒ ⓓ	76 ⓐ ⓑ ⓒ ⓓ
02 ⓐ ⓑ ⓒ ⓓ	27 ⓐ ⓑ ⓒ ⓓ	52 ⓐ ⓑ ⓒ ⓓ	77 ⓐ ⓑ ⓒ ⓓ
03 ⓐ ⓑ ⓒ ⓓ	28 ⓐ ⓑ ⓒ ⓓ	53 ⓐ ⓑ ⓒ ⓓ	78 ⓐ ⓑ ⓒ ⓓ
04 ⓐ ⓑ ⓒ ⓓ	29 ⓐ ⓑ ⓒ ⓓ	54 ⓐ ⓑ ⓒ ⓓ	79 ⓐ ⓑ ⓒ ⓓ
05 ⓐ ⓑ ⓒ ⓓ	30 ⓐ ⓑ ⓒ ⓓ	55 ⓐ ⓑ ⓒ ⓓ	80 ⓐ ⓑ ⓒ ⓓ
06 ⓐ ⓑ ⓒ ⓓ	31 ⓐ ⓑ ⓒ ⓓ	56 ⓐ ⓑ ⓒ ⓓ	81 ⓐ ⓑ ⓒ ⓓ
07 ⓐ ⓑ ⓒ ⓓ	32 ⓐ ⓑ ⓒ ⓓ	57 ⓐ ⓑ ⓒ ⓓ	82 ⓐ ⓑ ⓒ ⓓ
08 ⓐ ⓑ ⓒ ⓓ	33 ⓐ ⓑ ⓒ ⓓ	58 ⓐ ⓑ ⓒ ⓓ	83 ⓐ ⓑ ⓒ ⓓ
09 ⓐ ⓑ ⓒ ⓓ	34 ⓐ ⓑ ⓒ ⓓ	59 ⓐ ⓑ ⓒ ⓓ	84 ⓐ ⓑ ⓒ ⓓ
10 ⓐ ⓑ ⓒ ⓓ	35 ⓐ ⓑ ⓒ ⓓ	60 ⓐ ⓑ ⓒ ⓓ	85 ⓐ ⓑ ⓒ ⓓ
11 ⓐ ⓑ ⓒ ⓓ	36 ⓐ ⓑ ⓒ ⓓ	61 ⓐ ⓑ ⓒ ⓓ	86 ⓐ ⓑ ⓒ ⓓ
12 ⓐ ⓑ ⓒ ⓓ	37 ⓐ ⓑ ⓒ ⓓ	62 ⓐ ⓑ ⓒ ⓓ	87 ⓐ ⓑ ⓒ ⓓ
13 ⓐ ⓑ ⓒ ⓓ	38 ⓐ ⓑ ⓒ ⓓ	63 ⓐ ⓑ ⓒ ⓓ	88 ⓐ ⓑ ⓒ ⓓ
14 ⓐ ⓑ ⓒ ⓓ	39 ⓐ ⓑ ⓒ ⓓ	64 ⓐ ⓑ ⓒ ⓓ	89 ⓐ ⓑ ⓒ ⓓ
15 ⓐ ⓑ ⓒ ⓓ	40 ⓐ ⓑ ⓒ ⓓ	65 ⓐ ⓑ ⓒ ⓓ	90 ⓐ ⓑ ⓒ ⓓ
16 ⓐ ⓑ ⓒ ⓓ	41 ⓐ ⓑ ⓒ ⓓ	66 ⓐ ⓑ ⓒ ⓓ	
17 ⓐ ⓑ ⓒ ⓓ	42 ⓐ ⓑ ⓒ ⓓ	67 ⓐ ⓑ ⓒ ⓓ	
18 ⓐ ⓑ ⓒ ⓓ	43 ⓐ ⓑ ⓒ ⓓ	68 ⓐ ⓑ ⓒ ⓓ	
19 ⓐ ⓑ ⓒ ⓓ	44 ⓐ ⓑ ⓒ ⓓ	69 ⓐ ⓑ ⓒ ⓓ	
20 ⓐ ⓑ ⓒ ⓓ	45 ⓐ ⓑ ⓒ ⓓ	70 ⓐ ⓑ ⓒ ⓓ	
21 ⓐ ⓑ ⓒ ⓓ	46 ⓐ ⓑ ⓒ ⓓ	71 ⓐ ⓑ ⓒ ⓓ	
22 ⓐ ⓑ ⓒ ⓓ	47 ⓐ ⓑ ⓒ ⓓ	72 ⓐ ⓑ ⓒ ⓓ	
23 ⓐ ⓑ ⓒ ⓓ	48 ⓐ ⓑ ⓒ ⓓ	73 ⓐ ⓑ ⓒ ⓓ	
24 ⓐ ⓑ ⓒ ⓓ	49 ⓐ ⓑ ⓒ ⓓ	74 ⓐ ⓑ ⓒ ⓓ	
25 ⓐ ⓑ ⓒ ⓓ	50 ⓐ ⓑ ⓒ ⓓ	75 ⓐ ⓑ ⓒ ⓓ	

Performance Scanner

> 90% Excellent !	You have mastered the first half of NEET syllabus (11th). The concepts of this syllabus are on your fingertips. Maintain this momentum.
76-90% Very Good !	You have a good command over the first half of NEET syllabus (11th). Revise it again after a few days and enhance your performance.
60-75% Good !	You have a wide scope to learn for the first half of NEET syllabus (11th). Revise it again.
<60% Not Satisfactory!	You have a long way ahead of you to master the first half of NEET syllabus (11th). Revise it thoroughly.

Scan for online part test

Space for Rough Work

MEDACE NEET (UG)

SELF ASSESSMENT KIT

Test Booklet No. 3947321

Test Booklet Code SPT2

Syllabus Part Thru 2

(Half Syllabus Test)

Important Instructions

- The test is of **1 hours 30 minutes** duration and the Test Booklet contains **90** multiple-choice questions (four options with a single correct answer) from biology.
- Candidates are advised to read all questions before they start attempting the question paper.
- Each questions carries 4 marks. For each correct response, the candidate will get 4 marks. For each incorrect response, one marks will be deducted from the total scores.
- In the event of candidate marking more than one option one mark will be deducted. The maximum marks are 180.
- Use **Blue/Black Point Pen only** for writing particular on this page/ marking response on Answer Sheet.

Chapters Covered

- Photosynthesis in Higher Plants
- Respiration in Plants
- Plant Growth and Development
- Breathing and Exchange of Gases
- Body Fluids and Circulation
- Excretory Products and their Elimination
- Locomotion and Movement
- Neural Control and Coordination
- Chemical Coordination and Integration

Name of the Candidate (In Capitals) ____________________

____

Candidate's Signature ____________

Invigilator's Signature ____________

Facsimile signature stamp of center superintendent____________

Do not open this booklet until you start attempting the test

Biology

1. Identify the effect that is not induced by kinetin.
   (a) It promotes cell elongation at root and shoot apices.
   (b) Together with GA, it delays senescence.
   (c) It inhibits the effect of auxin on apical buds.
   (d) It promote photosynthesis in leaves indirectly.

2. Following are the steps involved in complete oxidation of pyruvate in mitochondrial matrix.
   A. Decarboxylation to form 5-C compound.
   B. Substrate level phosphorylation.
   C. Reduction of FAD^+ to $FADH_2$.
   D. Condensation of 4-C and 2-C compound.
   E. Final reduction of NAD^+ to $NADH + H^+$.
   Choose the correct order from the options given below.
   (a) D-A-C-B-E
   (b) D-A-B-C-E
   (c) D-A-B-E-C
   (d) D-A-E-C-B

3. Which of the following statement is incorrect?
   (a) The T-wave corresponds to the closure of semilunar valves.
   (b) P-Q gap denotes conduction of impulses to the ventricles.
   (c) S is the first negative deflection recorded in an ECG.
   (d) T-P gap denotes end of one and beginning of another cycle.

4. The second heart sound is associated with
   (a) joint diastole
   (b) ventricular systole
   (c) atrial systole
   (d) ventricular diastole

5. Given below is the diagrammatic representation of hormone action at the target site. Which of the following does not take place in this pathway?

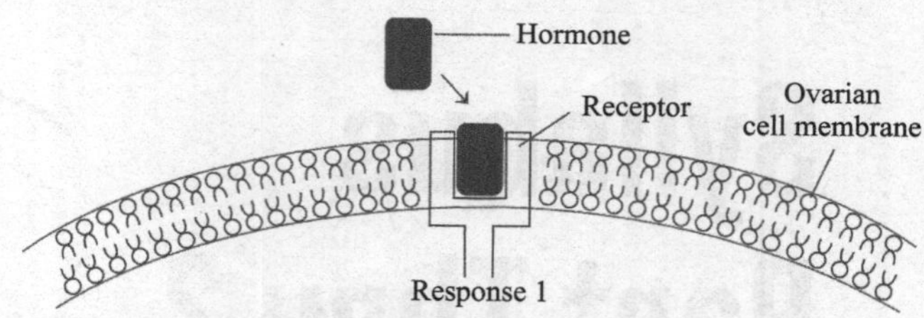

   (a) Relay of signal by IP_3 or Ca^{2+}
   (b) Binding of FSH to its receptor
   (c) Hormone crosses the cell membrane
   (d) Regulation of metabolism

6. Which of the following are not products of redifferentiation?
   I. Secondary phloem
   II. Secondary xylem
   III. Cork cambium
   IV. Interfascicular cambium
   Choose the correct answer from the options given below.
   (a) I and II (b) II and III
   (c) Only IV (d) III and IV

7. Following is the graphical representation of how size of a plant varies with time. Which of the following is correct for the given labels?

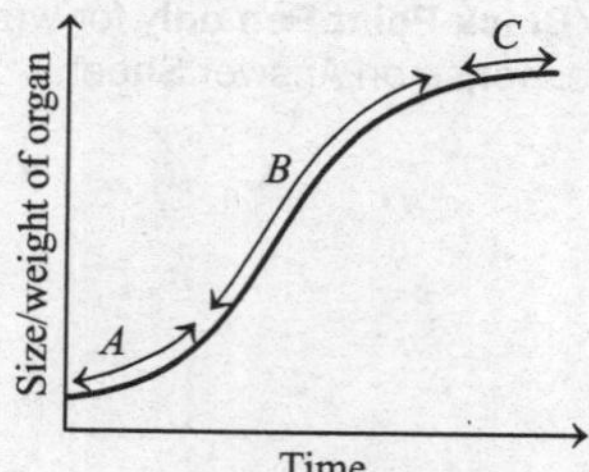

(a) *A* – Cell acclimatisation; *B* – Both the daughter cells divide; *C* – Cells are metabolically inactive

(b) *A* – Cell acclimatisation; *B* – Both the daughter cells differentiate; *C* – Cells are metabolically inactive

(c) *A* – Cell acclimatisation; *B* – Both daughter cells divide; *C* – Cells are metabolically active

(d) *A* – Cell acclimatisation; *B* – One cell differentiate; *C* – Cells are metabolically inactive

8. Which of the following will be found in the blood of a person with a viral infection?

(a) Abnormally high macrophages

(b) Abnormally high platelets

(c) Abnormally low eosinophils

(d) Abnormally low lymphocytes

9. Following are the steps which occur after an injury or a wound.

A. Activation of enzyme cascade.

B. Release of platelet factors.

C. Formation of enzyme complex.

D. Formation of insoluble threads.

E. Activation of thrombin by Ca^{2+}.

Choose the correct order from the options given below.

(a) B-A-C-E-D

(b) B-C-A-E-D

(c) A-B-E-C-D

(d) A-B-C-E-D

10. Given below are two statements.

Statement I CO_2 saturation is reached at higher concentrations in C_4 plants.

Statement II C_4 plants show increased biosynthesis at higher temperatures.

In the light of the above statements, choose the correct answer from the options given below.

(a) Statement I is incorrect, but statement II is correct.

(b) Both statement I and statement II are correct.

(c) Both statement I and statement II are incorrect.

(d) Statement I is correct, but statement II is incorrect.

11. Given below are two statements; one is labelled as Assertion (A) and the other is labelled as Reason (R).

Assertion (A) Photo-oxidative damage to chlorophyll-*a* is prevented by accessory pigments.

Reason (R) Accessory pigments radiate the excess light energy to the surrounding.

In the light of the above statements, choose the correct answer from the options given below.

(a) A is false, but R is true

(b) Both A and R are true and R is the correct explanation of A

(c) Both A and R are true, but R is not the correct explanation of A

(d) A is true, but R is false

12. Filtrate is isotonic with respect to blood plasma in

(a) PCT and DCT

(b) PCT only

(c) Henle's loop only

(d) Henle's loop and DCT

13. Increased blood calcium levels can be countered by which of the following ways?

A. Hypersecretion of parathyroid gland

B. Hypersecretion of thyrocalcitonin

C. Reabsorption of Ca^{2+} by renal tubules

D. Increased absorption of Ca^{2+} from intestine

Choose the correct answer from the options given below.

(a) B only (b) A only

(c) D only (d) C only

14. Following are the steps involved in oxidative phosphorylation in inner mitochondrial membrane.

A. Transfer of electrons by mobile e^- carrier.

B. Oxidation by NADH dehydrogenase

C. Oxidation of ubiquinol

D. Reduction of final electron acceptor

E. Reduction by $FADH_2$

Choose the correct order from the options given below.

(a) B-E-C-A-D (b) B-C-E-A-D

(c) B-E-A-C-D (d) B-C-A-E-D

15. Given below are two statements.

Statement I Photosystem not coupled with water splitting, triggers cyclic flow of electrons.

Statement II In non-cyclic electron flow, the product of light reaction is only ATP.

In the light of the above statements, choose the correct answer from the options given below.

(a) Statement I is incorrect, but statement II is correct.
(b) Both statement I and statement II are correct.
(c) Both statement I and statement II are incorrect.
(d) Statement I is correct, but statement II is incorrect.

16. Following are the steps operating in maize to prevent photorespiration.

A. Decarboxylation of C_4 acid in bundle sheath cells.
B. Fixation by C_3 cycle in bundle sheath cell.
C. Action of PEP carboxylase in mesophyll.
D. Transport of C_4 acid into bundle sheath cells.
E. Transport of C_3 acid into mesophyll cells.

Choose the correct order from the options given below.

(a) C-D-A-B-E (b) C-D-B-A-E
(c) C-D-A-E-B (d) C-D-E-B-A

17. Given below is the diagram of the functional unit of kidneys. Which of the following is correct from the options given below?

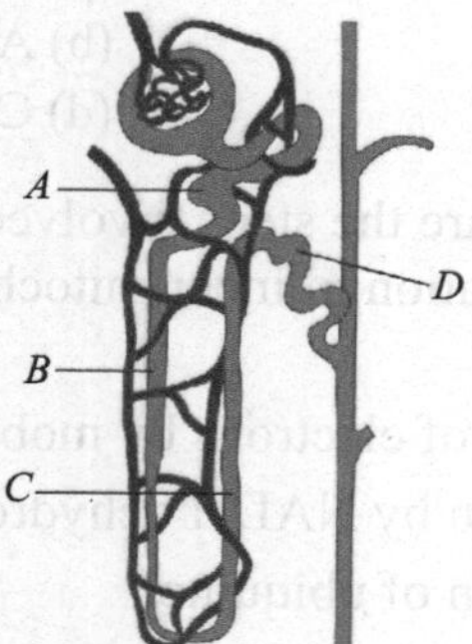

(a) Fluid in *A* is hypotonic with respect to blood.
(b) Fluid in *B* is hypotonic with respect to blood.
(c) Fluid in *C* is hypertonic with respect to blood.
(d) Fluid in *D* is hypotonic with respect to blood.

18. Given below are two statements.

Statement I Oestrogen and oxytocin are involved in milk secretion by the mammary cells.

Statement II Oestrogen and progesterone also regulate development of mammary glands.

In the light of the above statements, choose the correct answer from the options given below.

(a) Statement I is incorrect, but statement II is correct.
(b) Both statement I and statement II are correct.
(c) Both statement I and statement II are incorrect.
(d) Statement I is correct, but statement II is incorrect.

19. Following are the statements related to the lower limbs of the human body.

I. Two coxal bones of the pelvic girdle bear three fused bones.
II. The pelvic girdle bears the weight of the body while sitting.
III. Shoulder blade is a ventrally located bone of the pectoral girdle.
IV. Collar bone of the neck articulates with acromion of scapula.
V. Glenoid cavity articulates with the longest bone of the body.

Choose the correct answer from the options given below.

(a) II and III (b) I, II and IV
(c) II, III and V (d) I, III and V

20. Match List I with List II.

List I		List II
A. Rotifers	1.	Nephridia
B. Leech	2.	Protonephridia
C. Cockroaches	3.	Green glands
D. Prawns	4.	Malpighian tubules

Choose the correct answer from the options given below.

(a) A-1, B-2, C-4, D-3
(b) A-2, B-1, C-4, D-3
(c) A-2, B-1, C-3, D-4
(d) A-1, B-2, C-3, D-4

21. Following are the statements related to partial oxidation of glucose in plants.

I. Sucrose is the first molecule to enter the glycolytic pathway.

II. Glycolysis is the anaerobic breakdown of glucose into pyruvate.

III. In one round of glycolysis, 2 ATP molecules are formed.

IV. Glucose-6-phosphate and fructose-6-phosphate are isomers.

V. One of the glycolytic steps involves oxidation of NAD^+.

Choose the correct statements from the options given below.
(a) II and IV
(b) I, II and IV
(c) II, III and V
(d) I, III and V

22. Given below are two statements; one is labelled as Assertion (A) and the other is labelled as Reason (R).

Assertion (A) Phototropic bending of coleoptile shoot is promoted by auxin.

Reason (R) Auxin accumulates on the illuminated side and promotes cell elongation.

In the light of the above statements, choose the correct answer from the options given below.
(a) A is false, but R is true
(b) Both A and R are true and R is the correct explanation of A
(c) Both A and R are true, but R is not the correct explanation of A
(d) A is true, but R is false

23. Given below are two statements.

Statement I Heterophylly at different growth phase is observed in leaves of coriander.

Statement II Heterophylly is a defensive strategy used by plants to survive predators.

In the light of the above statements, choose the correct answer from the options given below.
(a) Statement I is incorrect, but statement II is correct.
(b) Both statement I and statement II are correct.
(c) Both statement I and statement II are incorrect.
(d) Statement I is correct, but statement II is incorrect.

24. Match List I with List II.

List I	List II
A. Steroids	1. Glycogenesis
B. Hypoglycemia	2. Suppress inflammation
C. Cortisol	3. Spermatogenesis
D. FSH	4. Secondary sexual features

Choose the correct answer from the options given below.
(a) A-4, B-1, C-3, D-2
(b) A-4, B-1, C-2, D-3
(c) A-3, B-1, C-4, D-2
(d) A-3, B-1, C-2, D-4

25. If an athelete's tidal volume is 500 mL and expiratory reserve volume is 1000 mL, what is his expiratory capacity, given that the residual volume is 1200 mL.
(a) 1700 mL
(b) 1500 mL
(c) 2200 mL
(d) 2700 mL

26. Following are the steps involved in flow of blood from the kidneys to the heart.

A. Flow of blood through the efferent arterioles.
B. Flow of blood into the renal venules.
C. Flow of blood into the renal veins.
D. Flow of blood through the vasa recta.
E. Flow of blood through peritubular capillaries.

Choose the correct order from the options given below.
(a) A-E-D-B-C
(b) A-D-E-B-C
(c) A-E-D-C-B
(d) A-D-E-C-B

27. Given below are two statements; one is labelled as Assertion (A) and the other is labelled as Reason (R).

Assertion (A) Pure proteins as respiratory substrates are never preferred over carbohydrates.

Reason (R) Pure proteins or fats cannot be broken down into simpler molecules.

In the light of the above statements, choose the correct answer from the options given below.
(a) A is false, but R is true.
(b) Both A and R are true and R is the correct explanation of A
(c) Both A and R are true, but R is not the correct explanation of A
(d) A is true, but R is false

28. How many rounds of Calvin cycle and how many ATP and NADPH would be required to produce 3 glucose molecules?

(a) 6 cycles, 18 ATP and 12 NADPH
(b) 3 cycles, 9 ATP and 6 NADPH
(c) 18 cycles, 54 ATP and 36 NADPH
(d) 9 cycles, 27 ATP and 18 NADPH

29. Which of the following pair contains the H^+ acceptor and final electron acceptor of PS-II respectively?

(a) Phaeophytin and plastocyanin
(b) Plastoquinone and plastocyanin
(c) Plastocyanin and phaeophytin
(d) Plastocyanin and plastoquinone

30. Following are the statements related to glucose breakdown in cytoplasm.

I. Lactic acid formation in muscles is independent of pyruvate.
II. Fructose 1,6-bisphosphate generates two isomeric forms.
III. Reduced NAD^+ is oxidised during ethanol production.
IV. 1 glucose molecules ferments to alcohol, to produce 4 ATP.
V. 2-phosphoglycerate to PEP is a condensation reaction.

Choose the correct answer from the options given below.

(a) II and III (b) I, IV and V
(c) II, III and V (d) I, II and V

31. Match List I with List II.

List I	List II
A. Muscular dystrophy	1. High protein diet
B. Tetany	2. Age related
C. Osteoporosis	3. Low plasma calcium
D. Gout	4. Genetic

Choose the correct answer from the options given below.

(a) A-4, B-3, C-2, D-1
(b) A-2, B-3, C-4, D-1
(c) A-4, B-2, C-3, D-1
(d) A-2, B-3, C-1, D-4

32. Following is the diagram of a synapse. Identify the type of synapse and the parts labelled *P*, *Q*, *R* and *S*.

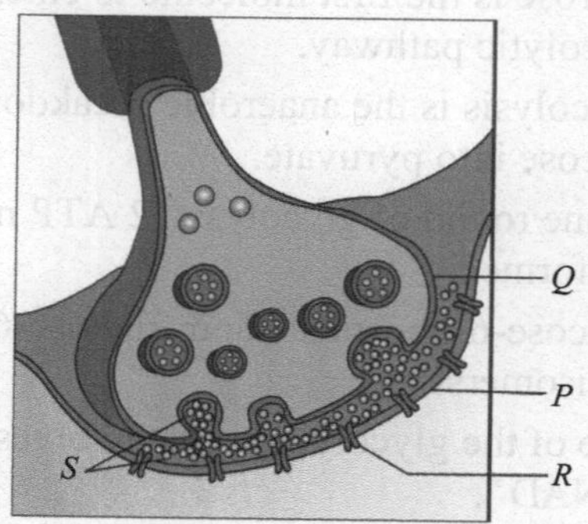

Choose the correct option.

(a) Chemical synapse; *P*–Post-synaptic membrane; *Q*–Pre-synaptic membrane; *R*–Receptor; *S*–Acetylcholine
(b) Electrical synapse; *P*–Pre-synaptic membrane; *Q*–Post-synaptic membrane; *R*–Receptor; *S*–Neurotransmitter
(c) Electrical synapse; *P*–Post synaptic membrane; *Q*–Pre-synaptic membrane; *R*–Receptor; *S*–Acetylcholine
(d) Chemical synapse; *P*–Pre-synaptic membrane; *Q*–Post-synaptic membrane; *R*–Receptor; *S*–Neurotransmitter

33. Give below is the diagrammatic representation of impulse conduction across axonal membrane.

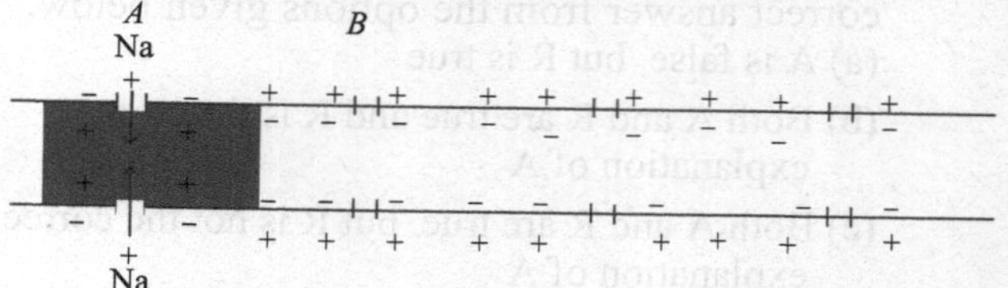

Which of the following is correct about points *A* and *B* marked in the diagram?

I. Resting potential is disturbed at point *A*.
II. Potential at point *B* is maintained by efflux of two Na^+ ions.
III. Depolarisation travels from point *B* to point *A*.
IV. Efflux of K^+ ions return the potential at *A* to normal.

Choose the correct statement(s) from the options given below.

(a) I and IV (b) I and III
(c) II and III (c) Only I

34. Given below are two statements; one is labelled as Assertion (A) and the other is labelled as Reason (R).

Assertion (A) Oxidative decarboxylation of pyruvate cannot proceed without NAD^+.

Reason (R) NAD^+ acts as the electron acceptor during decarboxylation of pyruvate into acetyl Co-A.

In the light of the above statements, choose the correct answer from the options given below.

(a) A is false, but R is true.

(b) Both A and R are true and R is the correct explanation of A.

(c) Both A and R are true, but R is not the correct explanation of A.

(d) A is true, but R is false.

35. Match List I with List II.

List I	List II
A. Ubiquinol	1. Copper centres
B. Cytochrome- *c* oxidase	2. Complex-III
C. Complex-V	3. Oxidation of succinate
D. Cytochrome-bc_1	4. Integral membrane protein

Choose the correct answer from the options given below.

(a) A-3, B-2, C-4, D-1

(b) A-3, B-1, C-4, D-2

(c) A-3, B-2, C-1, D-4

(d) A-3, B-1, C-2, D-4

36. Choose the correct option that shows the outcome of using anaerobic bacteria in Engelmann's experiment.

(a) Splitting of monochromatic light into a spectrum would be hindered.

(b) Anaerobic bacteria would flocculate at the wavelength of 450-700 nm.

(c) Action spectrum would be different from the region of bacterial accumulation.

(d) Regions of high bacterial density coincided with absorption spectrum of chlorophyll.

37. Choose the correct statement about anoxygenic photosynthesis.

(a) Light energy cannot be converted to chemical energy.

(b) Energy in the form of ATP cannot be produced.

(c) H_2S is the reducing agent, which oxidises to sulphur.

(d) It is common in most eukaryotic systems.

38. Match List I with List II.

List I	List II
A. Pons	1. Connects brain with spinal cord
B. Brain stem	2. Controls cardiovascular reflexes
C. Medulla	3. Interconnects all brain parts
D. Cerebellum	4. Controls body coordination

Choose the correct answer from the options given below.

(a) A -3, B-1, C-2, D-4

(b) A-2, B- 1, C-3, D-4

(c) A-2, B-3, C- 1, D-4

(d) A-3, B- 2, C-1, D-4

39. Given below are two statements; one is labelled as Assertion (A) and the other is labelled as Reason (R).

Assertion (A) K^+ permeability is crucial for re-excitation of axon at the end of a stimulus.

Reason (R) Resting potential of the axon is maintained by the sodium-potassium pump .

In the light of the above statements, choose the correct answer from the options given below.

(a) A is false, but R is true

(b) Both A and R are true and R is the correct explanation of A

(c) Both A and R are true, but R is not the correct explanation of A

(d) A is true, but R is false

40. Following are the steps involved in the endocrine regulation of ovulation.

A. Release of ovum from the ovary.

B. Hypothalamus releases GnRH.

C. Pars distalis secretes gonadotrophins.

D. GnRH is released into portal circulation.

E. Stimulation of ovaries by pituitary.

Choose the correct order from the options given below.

(a) C-B-D-E-A (b) B-D-C-E-A

(c) B-D-E-C-A (d) C-B-E-D-A

41. Which of the following condition will cause electrons to flow in a cyclic manner during photochemical phase?

(a) Reaction takes place in stromal lamellae
(b) Reduction of $NADP^+$ occurs
(c) Photolysis of water supplies electrons
(d) 680 nm light excites the photosystem

42. Given below are two statements.

Statement I One turn of the Krebs' cycle produces 28 molecules of ATP.

Statement II One turn of Krebs' cycle produces 6 molecules of NADH.

In the light of the above statements, choose the correct answer from the options given below.

(a) Statement I is incorrect, but statement II is correct.
(b) Both statement I and statement II are correct.
(c) Both statement I and statement II are incorrect.
(d) Statement I is correct, but statement II is incorrect.

43. The following are the few steps involved in partial glucose oxidation in cytoplasm.

A. Glucose ⟶ Glucose-6-phosphate
B. Fructose-6-phosphate ⟶ Fructose-1,6-bisphosphate
C. 1,3-bisphosphoglycerate ⟶ 3-phosphoglycerate
D. 2-phosphoenol pyruvate ⟶ pyruvic acid

Which of the following are the energy yielding steps?

(a) C and D
(b) A and C
(c) B and C
(d) A and B

44. Consider the following statements about forebrain.

I. Minor part of cerebral cortex is associated with complex functions like memory.
II. Myelinated neurons of the cortex gives the characteristic opaque coloration.
III. Cerebrum contains centres which have neural as well as endocrine functions.
IV. Motivation drive in a person is controlled by the part around which cerebrum wraps.

Choose the correct statement(s) from the options given below.

(a) II and IV
(b) I only
(c) IV and III
(d) III only

45. Given below are two statements.

Statement I Proton gradient works opposite in photophosphorylation and chemiosmosis.

Statement II In chemiosmosis, 2 protons are displaced for every ATP produced.

In the light of the above statements, choose the correct answer from the options given below.

(a) Statement I is incorrect, but statement II is correct.
(b) Both statement I and statement II are correct.
(c) Both statement I and statement II are incorrect.
(d) Statement I is correct, but statement II is incorrect.

46. Which of the following is not observed in tissues?

(a) Formation of bicarbonate ions
(b) High partial pressure of CO_2
(c) Dissociation of carbaminohaemoglobin
(d) Dissociation of oxyhaemoglobin

47. Given below are two statements; one is labelled as Assertion (A) and the other is labelled as Reason (R).

Assertion (A) Watching a movie can often spark an array of emotions in a person.

Reason (R) Midbrain controls the emotional behaviour of a person under different situations.

In the light of the above statements, choose the correct answer from the options given below.

(a) A is false, but R is true.
(b) Both A and R are true and R is the correct explanation of A
(c) Both A and R are true, but R is not the correct explanation of A
(d) A is true, but R is false

48. Consider the following conditions.

A. High O_2 in bundle sheath cells
B. High temperature
C. 3-C primary acceptor
D. Fixation in mesophyll
E. 5-C first stable product

Which of the following conditions operate in C_4 plants?

(a) B and C
(b) A, D and E
(c) B, C and D
(d) A, C and E

49. The following are the statements related to regulation of heart.

I. Initiation and maintenance of impulses is done by the nodal tissue.

II. Damage to medulla can affect the blood pressure in a person.

III. Sympathetic branch can decrease the cardiac output during emergency.

IV. Adrenaline exerts the same effect on heart as parasympathetic branch.

V. ANS can alter the heart rate by increasing the force of ventricular contraction.

Choose the correct statements from the options given below.

(a) I, II and V
(b) II and III
(c) I, III and IV
(d) II, IV and V

50. Following are the steps involved in regulating respiration in response to suffocation.

A. Contraction of diaphragm.

B. Acidosis and increased CO_2 in blood.

C. Increased rate of inspiration.

D. Activation of chemosensitive area.

E. Activation of rhythm centre.

Choose the correct order from the options given below.

(a) B-D-E-A-C
(b) B-E-D-A-C
(c) B-D-E-C-A
(d) B-E-D-C-A

51. Given below are two statements; one is labelled as Assertion (A) and the other is labelled as Reason (R).

Assertion (A) The PS-II reaction centre receives a continuous supply of electrons.

Reason (R) Continuous splitting of water molecules maintains a steady supply of electrons.

In the light of the above statements, choose the correct answer from the options given below.

(a) A is false, but R is true.
(b) Both A and R are true and R is the correct explanation of A.
(c) Both A and R are true, but R is not the correct explanation of A
(d) A is true, but R is false

52. Which of the following does not occur during conversion of succinyl Co-A to succinic acid in the TCA cycle?

(a) Conversion of GDP to GTP
(b) Conversion of ADP to ATP
(c) Substrate level phosphorylation
(d) Conversion of ATP to ADP

53. Given below are two statements; one is labelled as Assertion (A) and the other is labelled as Reason (R).

Assertion (A) S-shaped curve is more realistic for an organism in real world.

Reason (R) Limited nutrients, resources and competition affects growth rate.

In the light of the above statements, choose the correct answer from the options given below.

(a) A is false, but R is true
(b) Both A and R are true and R is the correct explanation of A
(c) Both A and R are true, but R is not the correct explanation of A
(d) A is true, but R is false

54. Given below are two statements; one is labelled as Assertion (A) and the other is labelled as Reason (R).

Assertion (A) Pulmonary semilunar valves withstand the highest pressure out of all valves.

Reason (R) Blood pumped by the right ventricle creates pressure on the pulmonary arteries.

In the light of the above statements, choose the correct answer from the options given below.

(a) A is false, but R is true.
(b) Both A and R are true and R is the correct explanation of A
(c) Both A and R are true, but R is not the correct explanation of A
(d) A is true, but R is false

55. Given below are two statements.

Statement I SAN is responsible for initiation and conduction of action potential.

Statement II At the end of every cardiac cycle, the action potential declines.

In the light of the above statements, choose the correct answer from the options given below.

(a) Statement I is incorrect, but statement II is correct.
(b) Both statement I and statement II are correct.
(c) Both statement I and statement II are incorrect.
(d) Statement I is correct, but statement II is incorrect.

56. Which of the following is correct about the neurons of the somatic nervous system?

(a) The Schwann cells secrete myelin sheath around the axons.

(b) Nodes of Ranvier are absent in neurons of the somatic branch.

(c) Conduction of nerve impulses are faster compared to spinal nerves.

(d) Most internal organs are mostly innervated by such neurons.

57. Following are the steps involved in expulsion of air from the lungs.

A. Development of positive pressure in the lungs.
B. Return of sternum to original position.
C. Relaxation of external intercostal muscles.
D. Decrease in dorso-ventral thoracic volume.
E. Expiration of oxygen deficient air

Choose the correct order from the options given below.

(a) C-B-D-A-E
(b) B-C-D-A-E
(c) B-C-A-D-E
(d) C-B-A-D-E

58. Following diagram represents interaction between the thin and thick filaments.

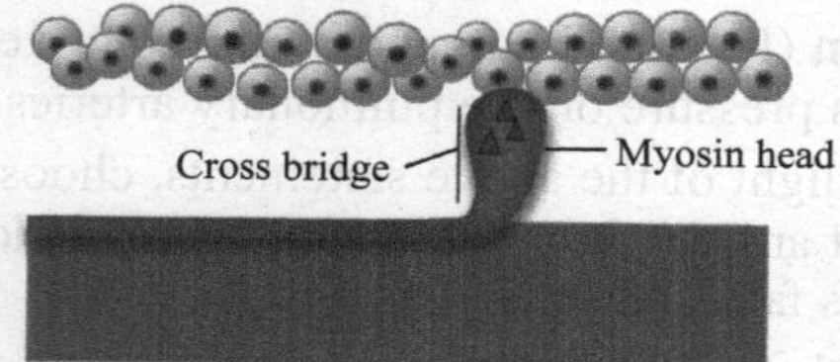

Which of the following is correct about the given image?

(a) Calcium ions are bound to tropomyosin on actin filaments.

(b) Energy is derived from the activity of light meromyosin.

(c) H-zone completely disappears due to contraction of I-bands.

(d) Interaction between the filaments is independent of Ca^{2+} ions.

59. Given below are two statements.

Statement I ATP is the phosphate donor of glucose in the first step of glycolysis.

Statement II Breaking of high energy bonds in ATP liberates inorganic phosphate.

In the light of the above statements, choose the correct answer from the options given below.

(a) Statement I is incorrect, but statement II is correct.
(b) Both statement I and statement II are correct.
(c) Both statement I and statement II are incorrect.
(d) Statement I is correct, but statement II is incorrect.

60. Choose the condition in which light behaves as a limiting factor.

(a) Plants growing in desert
(b) Trees emerging from canopy
(c) Plants growing in forest core
(d) Plants climbing on top of trees

61. Given below are two statements.

Statement I Aerobic and anaerobic pathways of respiration occurs sequentially.

Statement II Functioning of cells require direct use of energy from oxidation of substrates.

In the light of the above statements, choose the correct answer from the options given below.

(a) Statement I is incorrect, but statement II is correct.
(b) Both statement I and statement II are correct.
(c) Both statement I and statement II are incorrect.
(d) Statement I is correct, but statement II is incorrect.

62. Which of the following is incorrect about the pathway operating in inner mitochondrial membrane?

(a) Oxidation of reducing equivalents is coupled to ATP synthesis.

(b) Role of terminal hydrogen acceptor is limited to final stages.

(c) Cytochrome-*c* shuffles electrons between complex III and IV.

(d) Oxidation of $FADH_2$ generates ubiquinone from ubiquinol.

63. Following is the diagram of gas exchange occurring at different sites in the human body.

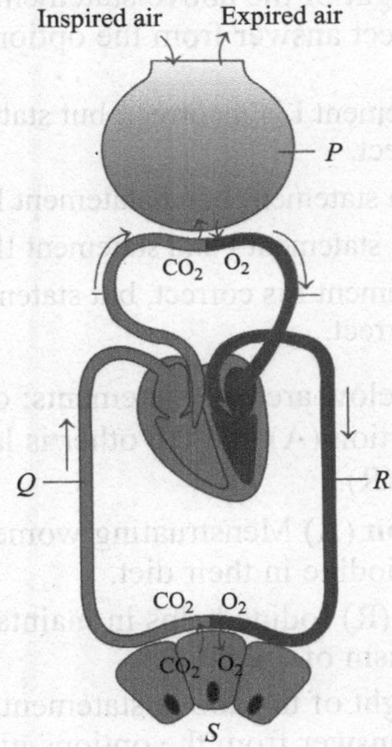

Which of the following is correct from the options given below? (values given in mmHg)

(a) $P : pO_2–104; Q : pCO_2–45; R : pCO_2 – 40; S : pO_2 – 40$

(b) $P : pO_2 – 104; Q : pO_2 – 45; R : pCO_2 – 40; S : pCO_2 – 40$

(c) $P : pO_2–104; Q : pCO_2 – 45; R : pO_2– 40; S : pO_2 – 40$

(d) $P : pO_2–104; Q : pCO_2–45; R : pCO_2 – 40; S : pCO_2 – 40$

64. Given below are two statements; one is labelled as Assertion (A) and the other is labelled as Reason (R).

Assertion (A) CO_2 diffuses at a much faster rate than O_2 through the diffusion membrane.

Reason (R) The thickness of diffusion membrane is less than one millimetre.

In the light of the above statements, choose the correct answer from the options given below.

(a) A is false, but R is true.

(b) Both A and R are true and R is the correct explanation of A

(c) Both A and R are true, but R is not the correct explanation of A

(d) A is true, but R is false

65. Given below are two statements.

Statement I Cartilaginous joint is present between atlas and axis.

Statement II Cartilaginous joints do not permit any movement.

In the light of the above statements, choose the correct answer from the options given below.

(a) Statement I is incorrect, but statement II is correct.

(b) Both statement I and statement II are correct.

(c) Both statement I and statement II are incorrect.

(d) Statement I is correct, but statement II is incorrect.

66. Match List I with List II.

List I		List II
A. Inspiratory reserve volume	1.	Sum of ERV, TV and IRV
B. Functional residual capacity	2.	Sum of TV and IRV
C. Vital capacity	3.	Sum of ERV and RV
D. Inspiratory capacity	4.	2500-3000 mL

Choose the correct answer from the options given below.

(a) A-1, B-3, C-4, D-2

(b) A-4, B-3, C-1, D-2

(c) A-1, B-2, C-4, D-3

(d) A-4, B-2, C-1, D-3

67 Following are the statements related to endocrine glands and their secretions.

I. Piloerection while watching a horror movie is induced by adrenal cortex.

II. During fasting, liver cells undergo glycogenesis, to maintain blood glucose.

III. Recovery from pathogenic infections is slowed down as people age.

IV. Exopthalmic goitre and simple goitre are opposite conditions of T_4.

V. Low energy can be associated with slowed down adrenal glands.

Choose the correct statements from the options given below.

(a) II and III

(b) I, II and IV

(c) III, IV and V

(d) I, III and V

68. Choose the incorrect statement related to phytohormones.
(a) Auxin and cytokinin are synergistic in their effect on cell growth.
(b) Gibberellins and ethylene promote synergistic effect on senescence.
(c) Seed dormancy promoted by ABA is important for seed germination.
(d) Ethylene is the major phytohormone used in agriculture.

69. The following flow chart represents two pathways operating on the product of glycolysis. Which of the following is correct about the pathway?

Lactic acid $\xleftarrow{(i)}$ Pyruvic acid $\xrightarrow{(ii)} \longrightarrow$ Ethanol + CO_2

(a) (i) NADH + H^+ is oxidised; (ii) NADH + H^+ is oxidised
(b) (i) NADH + H^+ is reduced; (ii) NAD^+ is oxidised
(c) (i) NADH + H^+ is oxidised; (ii) NAD^+ is reduced
(d) (i) NADH + H^+ is reduced; (ii) NADH + H^+ is reduced

70. Identify the correct statement.
(a) C_3 cycle is the primary pathway for sugar synthesis in C_4 plants.
(b) In C_4 plants, biosynthesis occurs in mesophyll cells.
(c) RuBisCO behaves as oxygenase in bundle sheath cells.
(d) Phosphoglycolate is formed in the mesophyll cells of C_4 plants.

71. Given below are two statements; one is labelled as Assertion (A) and the other is labelled as Reason (R).

Assertion (A) If blood becomes too alkaline, PCT increases the secretion of Cl^- ions.

Reason (R) Both PCT and DCT are involved in regulating the pH and ionic balance of blood.

In the light of the above statements, choose the correct answer from the options given below.
(a) A is false, but R is true
(b) Both A and R are true and R is the correct explanation of A
(c) Both A and R are true, but R is not the correct explanation of A
(d) A is true, but R is false

72. Given below are two statements.

Statement I Masking of myosin binding site depends on Ca^{2+} levels.

Statement II HMM contains only the globular head of meromyosin.

In the light of the above statements, choose the correct answer from the options given below.
(a) Statement I is incorrect, but statement II is correct.
(b) Both statement I and statement II are correct.
(c) Both statement I and statement II are incorrect.
(d) Statement I is correct, but statement II is incorrect.

73. Given below are two statements; one is labelled as Assertion (A) and the other is labelled as Reason (R).

Assertion (A) Menstruating women should include iodine in their diet.

Reason (R) Iodine helps in maintaining basal metabolism of the body.

In the light of the above statements, choose the correct answer from the options given below.
(a) A is false, but R is true.
(b) Both A and R are true and R is the correct explanation of A
(c) Both A and R are true, but R is not the correct explanation of A
(d) A is true, but R is false

74. Following are the steps involved in transmission of an inhibitory signal across neurons.
A. Influx of Na^+ ions and reversal of polarity.
B. Binding of neurotransmitter to receptors.
C. Fusion of synaptic vesicles with plasmalemma.
D. Conduction of action potential across axon terminal.
E. Opening of ion channels in post-synaptic membrane.

Choose the correct order from the options given below.
(a) D-A-C-B-E
(b) A-D-B-C-E
(c) D-A-B-C-E
(d) A-D-C-B-E

75. Following is the graphical representation of a type of growth pattern in plants.

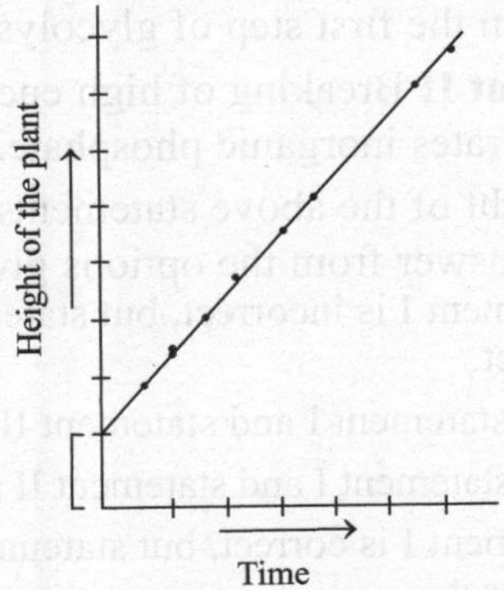

Which of the following is correct from the options given below?

(a) Both the daughter cells formed undergo mitotic division.

(b) Daughter cells are formed by reductional division.

(c) One of the daughter cell, formed by meiosis, differentiates.

(d) One of the daughter cell, formed by mitosis, divides.

76. Given below are two statements; one is labelled as Assertion (A) and the other is labelled as Reason (R).

Assertion (A) C_4 plants show greater biomass productivity than C_3 plants.

Reason (R) O_2 competes with CO_2 for the same binding site on RuBisCO.

In the light of the above statements, choose the correct answer from the options given below.

(a) A is false, but R is true.

(b) Both A and R are true and R is the correct explanation of A

(c) Both A and R are true, but R is not the correct explanation of A

(d) A is true, but R is false

77. Conversion of a plant tissue into undifferentiated mass of cells called callus, in tissue culture, is an example of

(a) differentiation and dedifferentiation

(b) dedifferentiation and redifferentiation

(c) redifferentiation only

(d) dedifferentiation only

78. Which of the following hormones can be given to patients after organ transplantation?

(a) Adrenaline (b) Cortisol

(c) Insulin (d) Thymosin

79. Following graph measures oxygen binding as a function of partial pressure of oxygen.

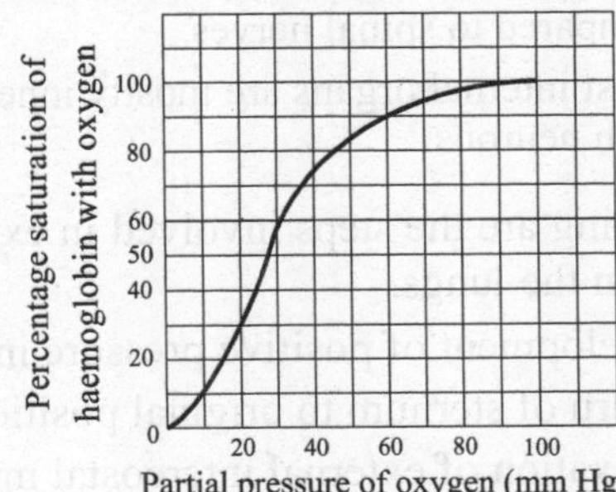

Which of the below given conditions would cause the curve to shift right?

(a) Acidosis of blood (b) Low temperature

(c) High pO_2 (d) Low pCO_2

80. Given below are two statements; one is labelled as Assertion (A) and the other is labelled as Reason (R).

Assertion (A) Permeability of ascending limb of Henle's loop is crucial for concentration of urine.

Reason (R) Ascending limb of Henle is permeable to water and impermeable to electrolytes.

In the light of the above statements, choose the correct answer from the options given below.

(a) A is false, but R is true.

(b) Both A and R are true and R is the correct explanation of A

(c) Both A and R are true, but R is not the correct explanation of A

(d) A is true, but R is false

81. The given diagram shows the thin and thick filaments of a muscle fibre. Which of the following is correct from the options given below?

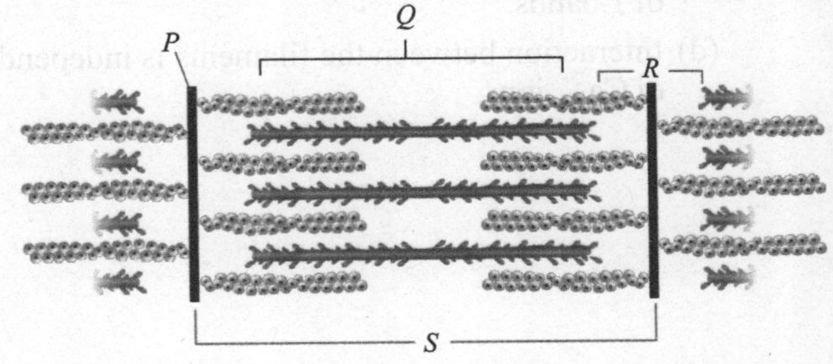

56. Which of the following is correct about the neurons of the somatic nervous system?

(a) The Schwann cells secrete myelin sheath around the axons.

(b) Nodes of Ranvier are absent in neurons of the somatic branch.

(c) Conduction of nerve impulses are faster compared to spinal nerves.

(d) Most internal organs are mostly innervated by such neurons.

57. Following are the steps involved in expulsion of air from the lungs.

A. Development of positive pressure in the lungs.
B. Return of sternum to original position.
C. Relaxation of external intercostal muscles.
D. Decrease in dorso-ventral thoracic volume.
E. Expiration of oxygen deficient air

Choose the correct order from the options given below.

(a) C-B-D-A-E
(b) B-C-D-A-E
(c) B-C-A-D-E
(d) C-B-A-D-E

58. Following diagram represents interaction between the thin and thick filaments.

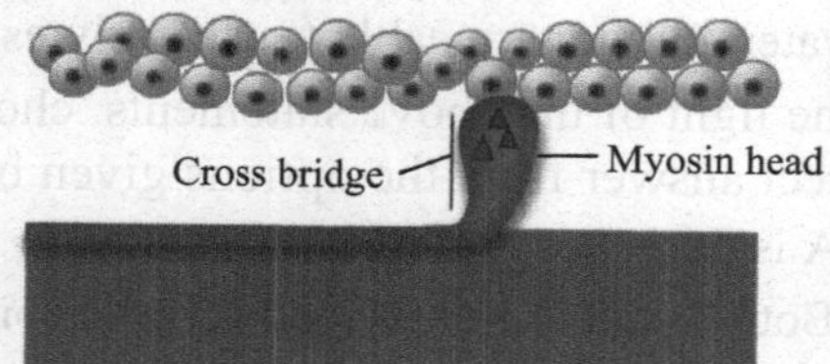

Which of the following is correct about the given image?

(a) Calcium ions are bound to tropomyosin on actin filaments.

(b) Energy is derived from the activity of light meromyosin.

(c) H-zone completely disappears due to contraction of I-bands.

(d) Interaction between the filaments is independent of Ca^{2+} ions.

59. Given below are two statements.

Statement I ATP is the phosphate donor of glucose in the first step of glycolysis.

Statement II Breaking of high energy bonds in ATP liberates inorganic phosphate.

In the light of the above statements, choose the correct answer from the options given below.

(a) Statement I is incorrect, but statement II is correct.

(b) Both statement I and statement II are correct.

(c) Both statement I and statement II are incorrect.

(d) Statement I is correct, but statement II is incorrect.

60. Choose the condition in which light behaves as a limiting factor.

(a) Plants growing in desert
(b) Trees emerging from canopy
(c) Plants growing in forest core
(d) Plants climbing on top of trees

61. Given below are two statements.

Statement I Aerobic and anaerobic pathways of respiration occurs sequentially.

Statement II Functioning of cells require direct use of energy from oxidation of substrates.

In the light of the above statements, choose the correct answer from the options given below.

(a) Statement I is incorrect, but statement II is correct.

(b) Both statement I and statement II are correct.

(c) Both statement I and statement II are incorrect.

(d) Statement I is correct, but statement II is incorrect.

62. Which of the following is incorrect about the pathway operating in inner mitochondrial membrane?

(a) Oxidation of reducing equivalents is coupled to ATP synthesis.

(b) Role of terminal hydrogen acceptor is limited to final stages.

(c) Cytochrome-*c* shuffles electrons between complex III and IV.

(d) Oxidation of $FADH_2$ generates ubiquinone from ubiquinol.

63. Following is the diagram of gas exchange occurring at different sites in the human body.

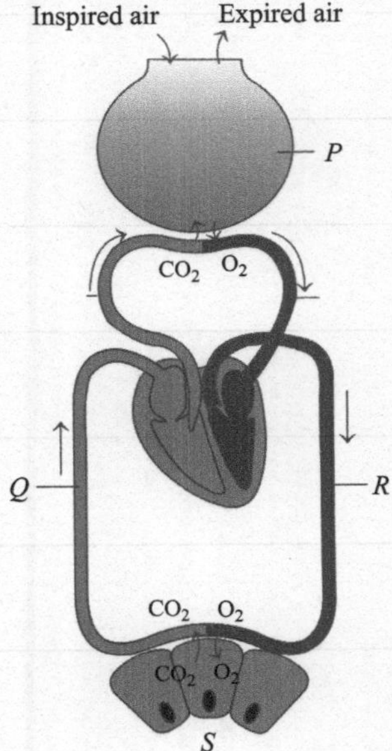

Which of the following is correct from the options given below? (values given in mmHg)

(a) $P : pO_2$–104; $Q : pCO_2$–45; $R : pCO_2 - 40$; $S : pO_2 - 40$

(b) $P : pO_2 - 104$; $Q : pO_2 - 45$; $R : pCO_2 - 40$; $S : pCO_2 - 40$

(c) $P : pO_2$–104; $Q : pCO_2 - 45$; $R : pO_2$– 40; $S : pO_2 - 40$

(d) $P : pO_2$–104; $Q : pCO_2$–45; $R : pCO_2 - 40$; $S : pCO_2 - 40$

64. Given below are two statements; one is labelled as Assertion (A) and the other is labelled as Reason (R).

Assertion (A) CO_2 diffuses at a much faster rate than O_2 through the diffusion membrane.

Reason (R) The thickness of diffusion membrane is less than one millimetre.

In the light of the above statements, choose the correct answer from the options given below.

(a) A is false, but R is true.

(b) Both A and R are true and R is the correct explanation of A

(c) Both A and R are true, but R is not the correct explanation of A

(d) A is true, but R is false

65. Given below are two statements.

Statement I Cartilaginous joint is present between atlas and axis.

Statement II Cartilaginous joints do not permit any movement.

In the light of the above statements, choose the correct answer from the options given below.

(a) Statement I is incorrect, but statement II is correct.

(b) Both statement I and statement II are correct.

(c) Both statement I and statement II are incorrect.

(d) Statement I is correct, but statement II is incorrect.

66. Match List I with List II.

List I		List II
A. Inspiratory reserve volume	1.	Sum of ERV, TV and IRV
B. Functional residual capacity	2.	Sum of TV and IRV
C. Vital capacity	3.	Sum of ERV and RV
D. Inspiratory capacity	4.	2500-3000 mL

Choose the correct answer from the options given below.

(a) A-1, B-3, C-4, D-2

(b) A-4, B-3, C-1, D-2

(c) A-1, B-2, C-4, D-3

(d) A-4, B-2, C-1, D-3

67 Following are the statements related to endocrine glands and their secretions.

I. Piloerection while watching a horror movie is induced by adrenal cortex.

II. During fasting, liver cells undergo glycogenesis, to maintain blood glucose.

III. Recovery from pathogenic infections is slowed down as people age.

IV. Exopthalmic goitre and simple goitre are opposite conditions of T_4.

V. Low energy can be associated with slowed down adrenal glands.

Choose the correct statements from the options given below.

(a) II and III

(b) I, II and IV

(c) III, IV and V

(d) I, III and V

Space for Rough Work

Test Booklet No. **3947322**

Test Booklet Code **NSS1**

MEDACE

NEET (UG)

SELF ASSESSMENT KIT

NEET Stepping Stones 1

(Complete Syllabus Test 11th)

Name of the Candidate (In Capitals)

____

____

____

Candidate's Signature ____________

Invigilator's Signature ____________

Facsimile signature stamp of center superintendent____________

Important Instructions

- The test is of **1 hours 30 minutes** duration and the Test Booklet contains **90** multiple-choice questions (four options with a single correct answer) from biology.
- Candidates are advised to read all questions before they start attempting the question paper.
- Each questions carries 4 marks. For each correct response, the candidate will get 4 marks. For each incorrect response, one marks will be deducted from the total scores.
- In the event of candidate marking more than one option one mark will be deducted. The maximum marks are 180.
- Use **Blue/Black Point Pen only** for writing particular on this page/ marking response on Answer Sheet.

Do not open this booklet until you start attempting the test

Biology

1. Which of the following pairs belong to the same genus?
(a) Potato and cucumber
(b) Potato and brinjal
(c) Wheat and brinjal
(d) Wheat and rice

2. Match List I with List II.

List I	List II
A. Causative agent of bovine spongiform encephalopathy	1. Viroids
B. Double-stranded DNA viruses	2. Lichen
C. Symbiotic association between algae and fungi	3. Prions
D. Causative agent of potato spindle tuber disease	4. Bacteriophages

Choose the correct answer from the options given below.
(a) A-1, B-3, C-2, D-4
(b) A-2, B-1, C-3, D-4
(c) A-2, B-3, C-1, D-4
(d) A-3, B-4, C-2, D-1

3. Given below are two statements.

Statement I Methanogens are found in the guts of ruminant animals and help to produce methane.

Statement II Methanogens have a similar cell wall structure as found in other bacteria.

In the light of the above statements, choose the correct answer from the options given below.
(a) Statement I is incorrect, but statement II is correct
(b) Both statement I and statement II are correct
(c) Both statement I and statement II are incorrect
(d) Statement I is correct, but statement II is incorrect

4. Identify the correct description about the given figure:

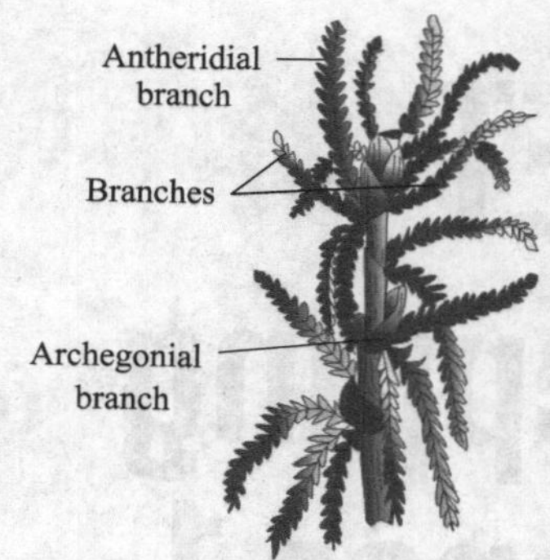

(a) It provides peat that has long been used as fuel.
(b) It produces large amounts of hydrocolloids which are used commercially.
(c) It is used to grow microbes and in preparations of ice-creams and jellies.
(d) It is rich in proteins and is used as a food supplement by space travellers.

5. Match List I with List II.

List I	List II
A. Sponges, coelenterates, flatworms	1. Network of tracheal tubes
B. Earthworms	2. Moist cuticle
C. Insects	3. Simple diffusion over the entire body surface
D. Aquatic arthropods and molluscs	4. Employ gills for aquatic respiration

Choose the correct answer from the options given below.
(a) A-2, B-3, C-4, D-1
(b) A-4, B-1, C-2, D-3
(c) A-3, B-2, C-1, D-4
(d) A-3, B-4, C-1, D-2

6. Match List I with List II.

List I	List II
A. Afferent nerve fibres	1. Division of the PNS
B. Efferent nerve fibres	2. Transmit regulatory impulses from the CNS
C. Autonomic nervous system	3. Transmit impulses to the CNS
D. Myelinated nerve fibres	4. Enveloped by Schwann cells

Choose the correct answer from the options given below.
(a) A-2, B-3, C-4, D-1
(b) A-4, B-1, C-2, D-3
(c) A-3, B-2, C-1, D-4
(d) A-3, B-4, C-1, D-2

7. Dinoflagellates are primarily
(a) freshwater and saprophytic
(b) marine and photosynthetic
(c) terrestrial and photosynthetic
(d) freshwater and photosynthetic

8. Which characteristic is unique to brown algae (Phaeophyceae)?
(a) Vegetative cells with rigid cell walls made of cellulose.
(b) Asexual reproduction by biflagellate zoospores.
(c) Presence of holdfast, stipe and frond in the plant body.
(d) Sexual reproduction that is exclusively isogamous.

9. Which characteristic defines animals as coelomates, pseudocoelomates and acoelomates respectively?
(a) Presence of a mesoderm-lined body cavity, presence of mesodermal pouches and complete absence of a body cavity
(b) Presence of a body cavity lined by endoderm, presence of a body cavity lined by mesoderm and absence of a body cavity
(c) Absence of a body cavity, presence of a body cavity lined by mesoderm, and presence of a body cavity lined by endoderm
(d) Absence of a body cavity, presence of endodermal pouches and absence of mesoderm lining the body cavity

10. Which fungi are known for producing their asexual spores called conidiophores exogenously on special mycelium?
(a) Phycomycetes
(b) Ascomycetes
(c) Basidiomycetes
(d) Deuteromycetes

11. Given below are two statements.

Statement I Podocytes in the glomerulus create large spaces to allow proteins and blood cells to pass through.

Statement II Glomerular filtration occurs at a rate of 1100-1200 mL per minute, which constitute roughly 1/6th of the blood pumped out by each ventricle of the heart.

In the light of the above statements, choose the correct answer from the options given below
(a) Statement I is incorrect, but statement II is correct
(b) Both statement I and statement II are correct
(c) Both statement I and statement II are incorrect
(d) Statement I is correct, but statement II is incorrect

12. The *cis* and *trans* faces of the Golgi apparatus are
(a) similar but not interconnected
(b) similar and interconnected
(c) entirely different but interconnected
(d) entirely different and not interconnected

13. Match List I with List II.

List I	List II
A. Pyruvic acid	1. Three-carbon product of glycolysis
B. NADH + H^+	2. Co-enzyme involved in redox reactions during glycolysis
C. Alcoholic fermentation	3. Conversion of pyruvic acid to ethanol and CO_2
D. Krebs' cycle	4. Complete oxidation of pyruvate

Choose the correct answer from the options given below.
(a) A-3, B-4, C-1, D-2
(b) A-4, B-1, C-2, D-3
(c) A-1, B-2, C-3, D-4
(d) A-2, B-3, C-4, D-1

14. Match List I with List II.

	List I	List II
A.	Region of elongation	1. Protection of tender root apex
B.	Root cap	2. Conducts water, minerals, and photosynthates
C.	Stem	3. Main site of photosynthesis
D.	Leaf lamina	4. Responsible for growth in root length

Choose the correct answer from the options given below.

(a) A-2, B-3, C-4, D-1
(b) A-3, B-4, C-1, D-2
(c) A-4, B-1, C-2, D-3
(d) A-1, B-2, C-3, D-4

15. Three different animals are given as *A*, *B* and *C*. Identify the correct match pair along with their phylum.

A B C

(a) *A– Adamsia* - Ctenophora, *B–Spongilla*- Coelenterata, *C–Pila*- Echinodermata
(b) *A–Physalia* - Mollusca, *B–Sycon*- Porifera, *C–Pila*- Echinodermata
(c) *A–Meandrina*-Echinodermata, *B–Spongilla*- Coelenterata, *C–Pila*-Porifera
(d) *A–Aurelia*-Coelenterata, *B–Euspongia*-Porifera, *C–Pila*-Mollusca

16. The hypothalamus is part of which region of the brain?

(a) Midbrain, hindbrain
(b) Hindbrain, spinal cord
(c) Forebrain, diencephalon
(d) Spinal cord, brainstem

17. Given below are two statements:

Statement I Parenchyma cells are usually present in the cortex, pericycle, pith, and medullary rays.

Statement II Unlike monocotyledonous stems, in dicotyledonous stems, cambium is not found between the phloem and xylem.

In the light of the above statements, choose the correct answer from the options given below.

(a) Statement I is incorrect, but statement II is correct.
(b) Both statement I and statement II are correct
(c) Both statement I and statement II are incorrect
(d) Statement I is correct, but statement II is incorrect

18. Match List I with List II.

	List I	List II
A.	Blood group A	1. Contain antigen B
B.	Blood group AB	2. Contain no antigen
C.	Blood group O	3. Contain antigens A and B
D.	Blood group B	4. Contain antigen A

Choose the correct answer from the options given below

(a) A-3, B-4, C-1, D-2
(b) A-4, B-3, C-2, D-1
(c) A-1, B-2, C-3, D-4
(d) A-2, B-1, C-3, D-4

19. Venation plays a crucial role in supporting the leaf structure and facilitates the transport of water, minerals, and photosynthetic products throughout the plant. The correct description of the leaf venation is

(a) monocotyledonous plants typically exhibit reticulate venation
(b) veins in leaves of dicotyledonous plants run parallel to each other
(c) venation refers to the arrangement of lamina, petiole, and leaf base
(d) reticulate venation is characterised by the formation of network by veinlets

20. Which term accurately describes the arrangement of vascular bundles in stem of *Triticum aestivum*?

(a) Radial, closed and collateral
(b) Conjoint, closed and collateral
(c) Endarch, open and collateral
(d) Apical, open and concentric

21. Identify the hormones that do not fall under the category of peptide, polypeptide or protein hormones.

(a) Insulin, glucagon
(b) Pituitary hormones, hypothalamic hormones
(c) Cortisol, testosterone
(d) Glucagon, pituitary hormones

22. Which type of aestivation is characteristic of pea and bean flowers, respectively?
(a) Valvate, vexillary
(b) Vexillary, twisted
(c) Imbricate, twisted
(d) Vexillary, vexillary

23. In the given figure, which component is responsible for the secondary growth in plants? Also mention the type of given vascular bundle.

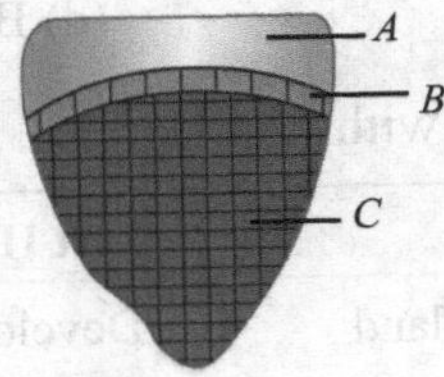

(a) *A* only; conjoint open
(b) *B* only; conjoint open
(c) *C* only; conjoint closed
(d) *A* and *C* only; radial closed

24. Given below are two statements; one is labelled as Assertion (A) and the other is labelled as Reason (R)

Assertion (A) Osteichthyes have a streamlined body with cycloid or ctenoid scales.

Reason (R) They possess two-chambered heart with one auricle and one ventricle.

In the light of the above statements, choose the correct answer from the options given below.
(a) A is false, but R is true
(b) Both A and R are true and R is the correct explanation of A
(c) Both A and R are true, but R is not the correct explanation of A
(d) A is true, but R is false

25. The Purkinje fibres in the heart
(a) generate action potentials and are located in the atria
(b) conduct action potentials and are located in the atria
(c) generate action potentials and are located in the ventricles
(d) conduct action potentials and are located in the ventricles

26. Identify the type of phyllotaxy based on the position of leaves in the given figures (*A*) and (*B*).

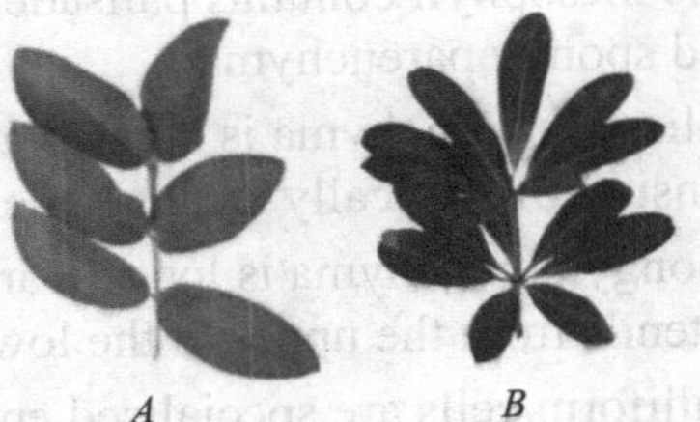

(a) *A*-Alternate, *B*-Opposite
(b) *A*-Opposite, *B*-Whorled
(c) *A*-Whorled, *B*-Alternate
(d) *A*-Alternate, *B*-Whorled

27. Match List I with List II.

List I	List II
A. Aschelminthes	1. Calcium carbonate shell, muscular foot, and radula
B. Annelida	2. Metamerically segmented with closed circulatory system and parapodia
C. Arthropoda	3. Chitinous exoskeleton, jointed appendages, and open circulatory system
D. Mollusca	4. Round body with complete alimentary canal and pseudocoelomate structure

Choose the correct answer from the options given below.
(a) A-2, B-4, C-1, D-3
(b) A-4, B-3, C-2, D-1
(c) A-4, B-2, C-3, D-1
(d) A-2, B-1, C-4, D-3

28. The floral characteristic that defines a flower's actinomorphic nature is
(a) presence of bracts at the base of the pedicel
(b) floral appendages in multiples of 3, 4, or 5
(c) ability to be divided into two equal radial halves in any plane
(d) ability to be divided into two similar halves only in one particular vertical plane

29. In a dorsiventral (dicotyledonous) leaf, which statement(s) about the mesophyll is/are correct?

I. The mesophyll contains palisade parenchyma and spongy parenchyma.

II. Palisade parenchyma is located adaxially and consists of vertically arranged cells.

III. Spongy parenchyma is loosely arranged and extends from the upper to the lower epidermis.

IV. Bulliform cells are specialised epidermal cells found in the mesophyll of dicot leaves.

V. The mesophyll lacks chloroplasts and is involved primarily in structural support.

Choose the correct answer from the options given below.

(a) I, II and III (b) II, III and IV
(c) I, III and IV (d) II, III and V

30. In the given figure, which component is seven in number in almost all mammals including human beings?

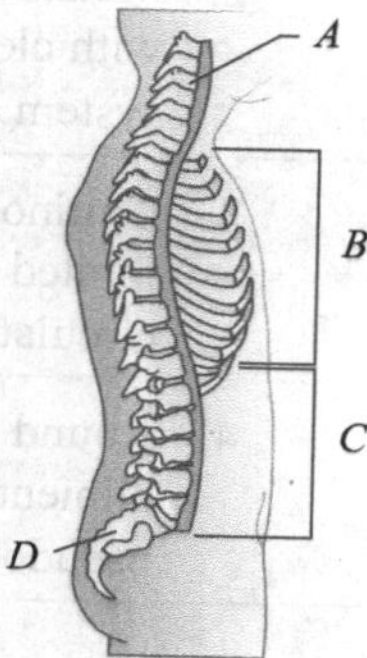

(a) *A* (b) *B*
(c) *C* (d) *D*

31. Given below are two statements.

Statement I The calyx may exhibit gamosepalous or polysepalous conditions depending on whether sepals are united or free.

Statement II Corolla can have various shapes such as tubular, bell-shaped, funnel-shaped, or wheel-shaped.

Choose the correct answer from the options given below.

(a) Statement I is incorrect but statement II is correct.

(b) Both statement I and statement II are correct.

(c) Both statement I and statement II are incorrect.

(d) Statement I is correct, but statement II is incorrect.

32. Which among the following phylum exhibits a canal system, choanocytes for feeding, and reproduction through both asexual fragmentation and sexual formation of gametes?

A. Porifera B. Cnidaria C. Echinodermata
D. Ctenophora E. Platyhelminthes

Choose the most appropriate answer from the options given below

(a) C and B (b) D and E
(c) A only (d) B only

33. Match List I with List II.

List I	List II
A. Thyroid gland	1. Development of immune system.
B. Thymus	2. Production of oestrogen and progesterone.
C. Adrenal medulla	3. Regulation of blood calcium levels.
D. Ovary	4. Secretion of catecholamines.

Choose the correct answer from the options given below.

(a) A-1, B-3, C-2, D-4
(b) A-3, B-4, C-2, D-1
(c) A-2, B-3, C-1, D-4
(d) A-3, B-1, C-4, D-2

34. In temperate region plants, the wood with fewer xylary elements and narrow vessels, is termed as

(a) spring wood (b) autumn wood
(c) sap wood (d) heart wood

35. In marginal placentation, the placenta forms a ridge along the

(a) ventral suture of the ovary
(b) anterior suture of the ovary
(c) posterior suture of the ovary
(d) dorsal suture of the ovary

36. Among the following characteristics of phylum-Platyhelminthes, which one is true?

(a) They exhibit radial symmetry.
(b) They have a closed circulatory system.
(c) They lack specialised cells for osmoregulation.
(d) They include endoparasites with hooks and suckers.

37. Match List I with List II.

List I	List II
A. Epiblema	1. Layer of thick-walled parenchymatous cells
B. Endodermis	2. Outermost layer of the root that bears root hairs
C. Pericycle	3. Innermost layer with casparian strips
D. Pith	4. Central region of parenchymatous cells in the root

Choose the correct answer from the options given below.
(a) A-3, B-4, C-2, D-1
(b) A-1, B-2, C-3, D-4
(c) A-3, B-2, C-4, D-1
(d) A-2, B-3, C-1, D-4

38. If the external inter-costal muscles were paralysed and unable to function properly, then
(a) inspiration would be unaffected, but expiration would become laboured
(b) both inspiration and expiration would be impaired due to the inability to change thoracic volume
(c) inspiration would become impossible, leading to immediate respiratory arrest
(d) expiration would occur normally, but inspiration would require conscious effort

39. Match List I with List II.

List I	List II
A. Pressure gradient	1. Difference in gas pressure that drives movement across systems.
B. Diffusion membrane	2. Layers that allow gases to exchange between air and blood.
C. Partial pressure	3. Tiny air sacs in the lungs.
D. Alveoli	4. Pressure exerted by a gas, driving movement during exchange.

Choose the correct answer from the options given below
(a) A-2, B-3, C-4, D-1
(b) A-3, B-4, C-1, D-2
(c) A-4, B-1, C-2, D-3
(d) A-1, B-2, C-4, D-3

40. The floral formula of ashwagandha is

$$\oplus ⚥ K_{(5)} \overset{\frown}{C_{(5)} A_5} G_{(2)}$$

In this formula, $C_{(5)}$ represents
(a) five united petals
(b) calyx with five united sepals
(c) bicarpellary gynoecium obligately placed
(d) solitary inflorescence

41. Given below are two statements.

Statement I TCA cycle occurs in the mitochondrial matrix, generating NADH, FAD H_2 and ATP.

Statement II The electron transport system (ETS) occurs in the inner mitochondrial membrane, producing ATP through oxidative phosphorylation.

In the light of the above statements, choose the correct answer from the options given below:
(a) Statement I is incorrect, but statement II is correct.
(b) Both statement I and statement II are correct.
(c) Both statement I and statement II are incorrect.
(d) Statement I is correct, but statement II is incorrect.

42. Match List I with List II.

List I	List II
A. Skeletal muscle	1. Striated in appearance, involuntary.
B. Visceral muscle	2. Contain actin and myosin filaments.
C. Cardiac muscle	3. Striated appearance, voluntary.
D. Myofibrils	4. Involuntary and smooth in appearance.

Choose the correct answer from the options given below.
(a) A-2, B-3, C-4, D-1
(b) A-3, B-4, C-1, D-2
(c) A-4, B-1, C-2, D-3
(d) A-1, B-2, C-4, D-3

43. Match List I with List II.

List I	List II
A. Plasticity	1. Ability of plants to adapt their growth based on environmental conditions
B. Heterophylly	2. Small molecules influencing plant growth and development
C. Plant growth regulators	3. Variation in leaf shape within a plant species due to different environments
D. Apical dominance	4. Inhibition of growth of lateral buds

Choose the correct answer from the options given below.
(a) A-3, B-2, C-1, D-4
(b) A-4, B-3, C-2, D-1
(c) A-3, B-2, C-4, D-1
(d) A-1, B-3, C-2, D-4

44. Given below are two statements; one is labelled as Assertion (A) and the other is labelled as Reason (R).

Assertion (A) Neurons are excitable cells.

Reason (R) The neuron's membrane in polarised state possess differential permeability to ions such as K^+ and Na^+, maintained by the sodium-potassium pump.

In the light of the above statements, choose the correct answer from the options given below
(a) A is false, but R is true
(b) Both A and R are true and R is the correct explanation of A
(c) Both A and R are true, but R is not the correct explanation of A
(d) A is true, but R is false

45. What is the function of the corpora quadrigemina in the midbrain?
(a) Coordination of motor movements
(b) Regulation of body temperature
(c) Processing visual and auditory information
(d) Control of cardiovascular reflexes

46. Identify the correct options for *A*, *B* and *C*, respectively with respect to the Calvin cycle.

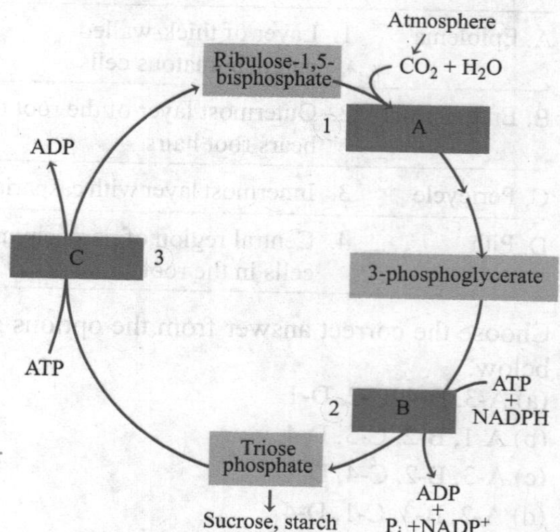

(a) Carboxylation, reduction, regeneration
(b) Reduction, carboxylation, regeneration
(c) Carboxylation, regeneration, reduction
(d) Regeneration, reduction, carboxylation

47. Epithelial tissue or epithelium is the covering tissue in our body. This tissue possesses all these characteristics, except
(a) does not have a free surface
(b) provides a covering for some part of the body
(c) cells are compactly packed
(d) derived from ectoderm, mesoderm and endoderm

48. Given below are two statements; one is labelled as Assertion (A) and the other is labelled as Reason (R).

Assertion (A) The primary method for analysing the chemical composition of living tissue is by grinding it in trichloroacetic acid.

Reason (R) Trichloroacetic acid helps in separating organic compounds into the acid-soluble pool and acid-insoluble fraction.

In the light of the above statements, choose the correct answer from the options given below.
(a) A is false, but R is true
(b) Both A and R are true and R is the correct explanation of A
(c) Both A and R are true, but R is not the correct explanation of A
(d) A is true, but R is false

49. What are the functions of gibberellins (GAs) in plants?

(a) Promote internode elongation before flowering and delay senescence in fruits.
(b) Inhibit bolting in beet and enhance the shape of fruits like apples.
(c) Stimulate early seed production in juvenile conifers and promote senescence.
(d) Enhance root growth and suppress stem elongation.

50. Why does the skin of a frog need to be kept moist?

(a) To prevent dehydration and facilitate gaseous exchange
(b) To maintain a slippery texture for efficient movement
(c) To protect against predators by emitting toxins
(d) To enhance camouflage by changing colouration

51. Given below are two statements.

Statement I Chromosomes align at the equatorial plane of the cell during metaphase.

Statement II The nuclear envelope disintegrates completely during metaphase.

In the light of the above statements, choose the most appropriate answer from the options given below.

(a) Statement I is incorrect, but statement II is correct
(b) Both statement I and statement II are correct
(c) Both statement I and statement II are incorrect
(d) Statement I is correct, but statement II is incorrect

52. Match List I with List II.

	List I		List II
A.	Differentiation	1.	Abnormal cell growth
B.	Dedifferentiation	2.	Divided cells mature into specific types.
C.	Redifferentiation	3.	Cells regain the ability to divide.
D.	Tumour	4.	Cells mature to perform specific functions.

Choose the correct answer from the options given below.

(a) A-3, B-4, C-1, D-2
(b) A-4, B-3, C-2, D-1
(c) A-1, B-2, C-3, D-4
(d) A-4, B-2, C-3, D-1

53. Which of these options represents the zwitter-ionic form?

(a) $H_3\overset{+}{N}-\underset{}{\overset{R}{\overset{|}{C}H}}-COOH$

(b) $H_3\overset{+}{N}-\overset{R}{\overset{|}{C}H}-COO^-$

(c) $H_2N-\overset{R}{\overset{|}{C}H}-COO^-$

(d) $H_2N-\overset{R}{\overset{|}{C}H}-NH_2$

54. Inclusion bodies are found in bacteria as particles of aggregated protein. The characteristics and functions of inclusion bodies in prokaryotic cells are

(a) gas vacuoles-involved in protein synthesis
(b) phosphate granules-bound by a membrane system
(c) glycogen granules-lie free in the cytoplasm
(d) cyanophycean granules - assist in motility

55. Which of the following correctly describes a characteristic of C_4 plants compared to C_3plants?

I. C_4 plants have a special type of leaf anatomy called Kranz anatomy.
II. C_4 plants are adapted to lower temperatures.
III. C_4 plants exhibit high rates of photorespiration.
IV. C_4 plants have lesser productivity of biomass.

Choose the correct answer from the options given below.

(a) I and II
(b) I and III
(c) II and IV
(d) I Only

56. Given below are two statements; one is labelled as Assertion (A) and the other is labelled as Reason (R).

Assertion (A) Cellulose is a homopolymer.

Reason (R) Cellulose is a polymer of fructose.

In the light of the above statements, choose the correct answer from the options given below
(a) A is false, but R is true
(b) Both A and R are true and R is the correct explanation of A
(c) Both A and R are true, but R is not the correct explanation of A
(d) A is true, but R is false

57. At the end of cell division, the process of cytokinesis differs between animal and plant cells primarily because
(a) animal cells form a furrow in the plasma membrane, while plant cells form a cell plate
(b) animal cells synthesise a new cell wall, while plant cells undergo plasma membrane constriction
(c) animal cells divide by forming a cell plate, while plant cells divide through plasma membrane ingression
(d) animal cells have rigid cell walls that prevent cytokinesis, while plant cells rely on furrow formation

58. The following diagram shows the different phases of the cell cycle. Find the appropriate description of steps labelled as *A*- *E*.

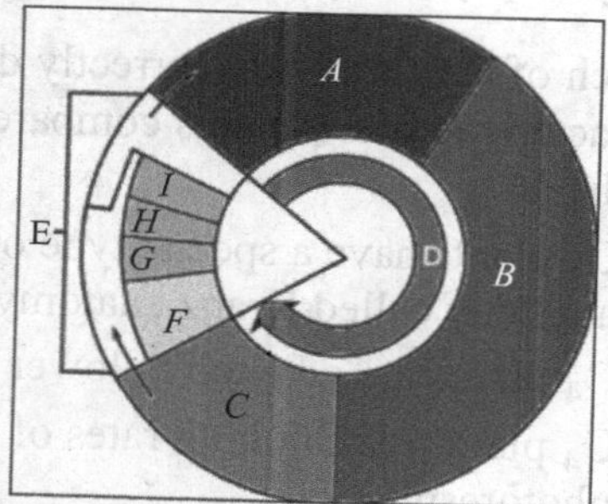

(a) The phase *E* is called the resting phase of the cell cycle.
(b) In the 24-hour average duration of the cell cycle of a human cell, phase *D* lasts for only about an hour.
(c) During phase *B*, DNA replication begins in the nucleus, and the centriole duplicates in the cytoplasm.
(d) Phase *A* is characterised by the metabolically inactive cell and restriction of growth.

59. Consider the following statements about the respiratory pathway.
I. The respiratory pathway exclusively involves the breakdown of substrates to generate energy.
II. Fatty acids must be converted to acetyl Co-A before entering the respiratory pathway.
III. Respiratory intermediates are utilised in both breakdown (catabolism) and synthesis (anabolism) processes.
IV. The respiratory pathway is exclusively a catabolic pathway.

Choose the correct answer from the options given below.
(a) I and II (b) II and III
(c) III and IV (d) I and III

60. The arrangement of phospholipids in a bilayer is critical for the function of the plasma membrane because it
(a) allows for the formation of integral and peripheral proteins.
(b) enables selective permeability by protecting hydrophobic tails from the aqueous environment
(c) ensures that the membrane remains rigid and impermeable
(d) permits the membrane to carry out passive transport exclusively

61. Given below are two statements.
Statement I Brush-bordered cuboidal epithelium is found in proximal convoluted tubule.
Statement II The columnar epithelium is composed of multiple layers of short and non-nucleated cells.
In the light of the above statements, choose the correct answer from the options given below.
(a) Statement I is incorrect, but statement II is correct
(b) Both statement I and statement II are correct
(c) Both statement I and statement II are incorrect
(d) Statement I is correct, but statement II is incorrect

62. Which of the following statement about the light reactions (photochemical phase) of photosynthesis is incorrect?
(a) Photosystem II (PS-II) absorbs light at 680 nm.
(b) Photosystem I (PS-I) absorbs light at 700 nm.
(c) The reaction centre, chlorophyll-*a* in PS-I is called P680.
(d) ATP and NADPH are formed as high-energy chemical intermediates.

63. Read the following statements about the frog's reproductive system and select the correct set of statements.
I. Male frogs have paired testis situated near the kidneys.
II. Female frogs have a pair of ovaries located near the kidneys.
III. The female frog lays 2500 to 3000 eggs at a time.
IV. Fertilisation in frogs is external and occurs in water.
V. Frogs undergo direct development.
Choose the correct answer from the options given below.
(a) I, II, III and IV (b) I, III, IV and V
(c) II, III, IV and V (d) I, II, IV and V

64. Match List I with List II.

List I	List II
A. Interphase	1. Period of cell growth and preparation for mitosis
B. S-phase	2. Majority of the cell cycle duration
C. G_2-phase	3. Phase when DNA replication occurs
D. G_0-phase	4. Metabolically active, but non-dividing stage

Choose the correct answer from the options given below:
(a) A-2, B-3, C-1, D-4
(b) A-3, B-1, C-4, D-2
(c) A-4, B-2, C-3, D-1
(d) A-1, B-3, C-2, D-4

65. Match List I with List II.

List I	List II
A. Vinblastin	1. Toxin
B. Morphine	2. Lectin
C. Ricin	3. Alkaloid
D. Concanavalin-A	4. Drug

Choose the correct answer from the options given below.
(a) A-3, B-4, C-1, D-2
(b) A-4, B-3, C-1, D-2
(c) A-2, B-4, C-1, D-3
(d) A-3, B-2, C-4, D-1

66. The animal tissue that performs the function of forming a diffusion boundary is
(a) columnar epithelium
(b) squamous epithelium
(c) cuboidal epithelium
(d) ciliated epithelium

67. The characteristic that distinguishes enzymes from inorganic catalysts is
(a) enzymes function best at high temperatures
(b) enzymes are composed of nucleic acids
(c) enzymes catalyse reactions by lowering the activation energy
(d) enzymes are unaffected by pH changes

68. Match List I with List II.

List I	List II
A. Chlorophyll-*a*	1. Bright or blue-green
B. Chlorophyll-*b*	2. Yellow to yellow-orange
C. Xanthophylls	3. Yellow-green
D. Carotenoids	4. Yellow

Choose the correct answer from the options given below.
(a) A-2, B-3, C-1, D-4
(b) A-4, B-2, C-1, D-3
(c) A-1, B-3, C-4, D-2
(d) A-3, B-2, C-4, D-1

69. The following are the statements about lipids.

I. Lipids are generally water-insoluble.

II. Oils have very high melting point.

III. Phospholipids contain phosphorus and are found in cell membrane.

IV. Arachidonic acid is an example of a fatty acid with 20 carbon atoms.

V. Saturated fatty acids contain only one double bond between carbon atoms.

Choose the correct statements from the options given below.

(a) I and II
(b) I, III and IV
(c) I, II and V
(d) I, III, IV and V

70. Recognise the following flow chart and find the correct option regarding taxonomic hierarchy.

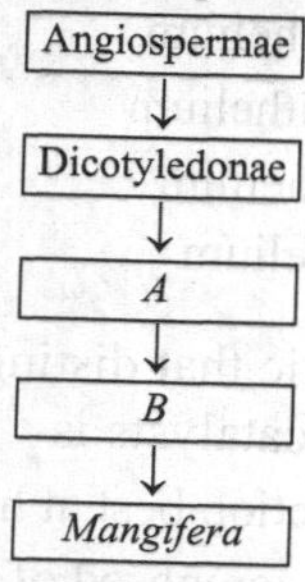

(a) *A*-Sapindales, *B*-Diptera
(b) *A*-Anacardiaceae, *B*-Poaceae
(c) *A*-Sapindales, *B*-Anacardiaceae
(d) *A*-Anacardiaceae, *B*-Sapindales

71. Which of the following statements about the bones of the appendicular skeleton is correct?

I. The bones of the hand (forelimb) include the humerus, tibia, fibula, carpals, metacarpals and phalanges

II. The bones of the leg (hindlimb) include the femur, tibia, fibula, tarsals, metatarsals, and phalanges.

III. The pectoral girdle is formed of the clavicle and scapula, with the glenoid cavity articulating with the head of the humerus.

IV. The pelvic girdle consists of two coxal bones formed by the fusion of the ilium, ischium and pubis with the acetabulum articulating with the femur.

Choose the correct statements from the options given below.

(a) I, II and III
(b) I, III and IV
(c) II, III and IV
(d) I, II, III and IV

72. Match List I with List II.

List I	List II
A. RuBisCO	1. Helical secondary structure
B. Cellulose	2. Apoenzyme
C. Starch	3. Most abundant protein in the whole of the biosphere
D. Prosthetic group	4. Polymeric polysaccharide

Choose the correct answer from the options given below

(a) A-3, B-4, C-1, D-2
(b) A-2, B-4, C-1, D-3
(c) A-2, B-1, C-4, D-3
(d) A-3, B-1, C-2, D-4

73. Consider the following pathway and find the correct terms for *A*, *B* and *C*.

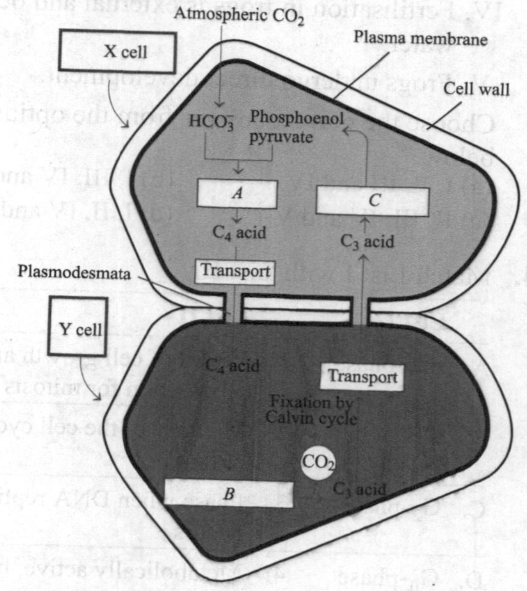

(a) *A*-Carboxylation, *B*-Regeneration, *C*-Transport
(b) *A*-Fixation, *B*-Decarboxylation, *C*- Regeneration
(c) *A*-Fixation, *B*-Carboxylation, *C*- Decarboxylation
(d) *A*-Regeneration, *B*-Fixation, *C*- Decarboxylation

74. Which of the following statements are correct regarding cyanobacteria?

I. They are photosynthetic autotrophs.

II. They can fix atmospheric nitrogen.

III. They are also known as blue-green algae.
IV. They lack a rigid cell wall.
V. They often form blooms in polluted water bodies.

Choose the correct answer from the options given below.
(a) I, II, III and V (b) I, II and IV
(c) II, IV and V (d) I, III and V

75. Given below are two statements.

Statement I Myasthenia gravis is an autoimmune disorder that affects the neuromuscular junction.

Statement II Tetany is characterised by rapid spasms in muscles due to low calcium levels in the body fluids.

In the light of the above statements, choose the correct answer from the options given below
(a) Statement I is incorrect, but statement II is correct
(b) Both statement I and statement II are correct
(c) Both statement I and statement II are incorrect
(d) Statement I is correct, but statement II is incorrect

76. Which of the following statement is not correct about proteins and polysaccharides?
(a) Proteins are composed of linear chains of amino acids linked by peptide bonds
(b) Collagen, as the most abundant protein in animals, primarily functions as an energy storage molecule
(c) Polysaccharides like cellulose consist of long chains of glucose monomers and provide structural support in plant cell walls
(d) Starch is a polysaccharide used by plants to store energy and is made up of glucose units

77. Consider the following statements regarding amino acids.
I. Amino acids are organic compounds containing amino and carboxylic acid groups.
II. There are only twenty types of amino acids found in proteins.
III. Glycine is an amino acid in which the R group is a hydrogen atom.
IV. Tryptophan is an example of basic amino acid.

Choose the correct statement(s) from the options given below
(a) Only I (b) I and II
(c) I, II and III (d) I, II, III and IV

78. Match List I with List II.

List I	List II
A. *Salvinia*	1. Giant redwood
B. Carrageen	2. Heterosporous
C. *Cycas*	3. Coralloid roots
D. Sequoia	4. Red algae

Choose the correct answer from the options given below.
(a) A-3, B-1, C-4, D-2 (b) A-2, B-4, C-3, D-1
(c) A-1, B-3, C-2, D-4 (d) A-4, B-3, C-1, D-2

79. Match List I with List II.

List I	List II
A. Glycocalyx	1. Helps in attachment to surfaces and host tissue.
B. Flagella	2. Composed of a special protein, elongated tubular structures.
C. Pili	3. Composed of a loose sheath or a thick capsule.
D. Fimbriae	4. Surface structures involved in motility.

Choose the correct answer from the options given below
(a) A-3, B-4, C-2, D-1 (b) A-1, B-2, C-3, D-4
(c) A-3, B-2, C-4, D-1 (d) A-2, B-3, C-1, D-4

80. Match List I with List II.

List I	List II
A. Proximal convoluted tubule	1. Reabsorption of water and urea.
B. Henle's loop	2. Conditional reabsorption of Na^+ and water, maintenance of pH and sodium-potassium balance.
C. Distal convoluted tubule	3. Reabsorption of essential nutrients and electrolytes.
D. Collecting duct	4. Maintenance of high osmolarity of medullary fluid.

Choose the correct answer from the options given below
(a) A-3, B-4, C-2, D-1 (b) A-1, B-2, C-3, D-4
(c) A-3, B-2, C-4, D-1 (d) A-2, B-3, C-1, D-4

81. Which statement correctly describes an important aspect of cell theory?

(a) Cells are the fundamental units of structure and function in all living organisms

(b) Some bacteria, WBCs and xylem parenchyma hold an exception towards cell theory

(c) Rudolf Virchow proposed that cells arise from non-living material

(d) Matthias Schleiden discovered bacteria using an electron microscope

82. Match List I with List II.

List I	List II
A. Glomerulus	1. Tuft of capillaries formed by the afferent arteriole
B. Bowman's capsule	2. Tough outer layer of the kidney
C. Distal convoluted tubule	3. Double-walled cup-like structure enclosing the glomerulus
D. Renal capsule	4. Highly coiled tubular region following the proximal convoluted tubule

Choose the correct answer from the options given below.

(a) A-2, B-3, C-1, D-4
(b) A-4, B-2, C-1, D-3
(c) A-1, B-3, C-4, D-2
(d) A-3, B-2, C-4, D-1

83. Which of the following does not explain the role of chemosynthetic autotrophic bacteria in nature?

(a) Oxidation of inorganic substances
(b) ATP production
(c) Decomposition of organic matter
(d) Recycling of nutrients

84. Match List I with List II.

List I	List II
A. Fibrinogen	1. Granulocytes that secrete histamine and heparin.
B. Globulins	2. Involved in defense mechanisms of the body.
C. Albumins	3. Blood component needed for clotting.
D. Basophils	4. Help in osmotic balance in blood

Choose the correct answer from the options given below.

(a) A-3, B-4, C-2, D-1
(b) A-1, B-2, C-3, D-4
(c) A-3, B-2, C-4, D-1
(d) A-2, B-3, C-1, D-4

85. Which feature is unique to prokaryotic cells compared to eukaryotic cells?

I. Presence of inclusion bodies as well as mesosome

II. Presence of a well-defined nucleus.

III. Presence of plasmids in addition to genomic DNA.

IV. Presence of a nuclear membrane.

Choose the correct answer.

(a) I and II
(b) II and IV
(c) I and III
(d) II and III

86. Which of the following statement is incorrect about myoglobin?

(a) Red color O_2 storing pigment
(b) Present in high amount in muscles
(c) Contains less number of mitochondria
(d) Depends on aerobic process for energy

87. Given below are two statements.

Statement I In gymnosperms, the seeds that develop post-fertilisation are not covered, and remain naked.

Statement II In gymnosperms, the male and female gametophytes have an independent free-living existence.

In the light of the above statements, choose the correct answer from the options given below.

(a) Statement I is incorrect, but statement II is correct
(b) Both statement I and statement II are correct
(c) Both statement I and statement II are incorrect
(d) Statement I is correct, but statement II is incorrect

88. Match List I with List II.

List I	List II
A. Endoplasmic Reticulum	1. Membrane-bound; stores water and waste
B. Golgi Apparatus	2. Modifies and packages proteins and lipids; has *cis* and *trans* faces
C. Lysosomes	3. Network of tubules; protein and lipid synthesis
D. Vacuoles	4. Vesicles with enzymes; digests macromolecules

Choose the correct answer from the options given below

(a) A-3, B-4, C-2, D-1

(b) A-1, B-2, C-3, D-4

(c) A-3, B-2, C-4, D-1

(d) A-2, B-3, C-1, D-4

89. Match List I with List II.

List I	List II
A. Oxaloacetic Acid (OAA)	1. Another name for the C_4 pathway
B. Bundle sheath cells	2. Large cells around the vascular bundles in C_4 plants
C. Phosphoenol pyruvate	3. The first CO_2 fixation product in C_4 plants
D. Hatch and Slack pathway	4. The main CO_2 acceptor in the mesophyll cells of C_4 plants

Choose the correct answer from the options given below.

(a) A-2, B-3, C-1, D-4

(b) A-4, B-2, C-1, D-3

(c) A-1, B-3, C-4, D-2

(d) A-3, B-2, C-4, D-1

90. Identify the correct description about the given figure.

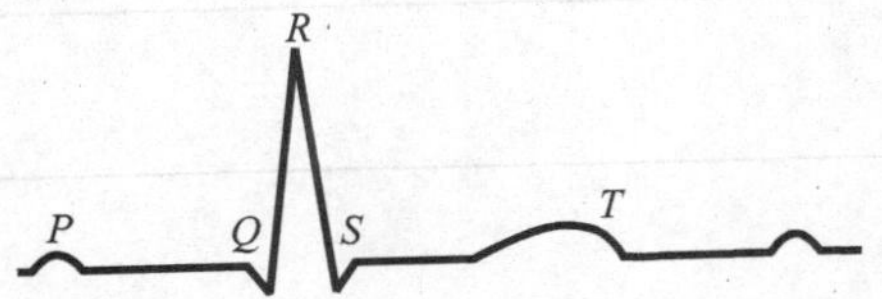

(a) The P-wave represents the depolarisation of the ventricles

(b) The QRS complex represents the repolarisation of the ventricles

(c) The T-wave represents the depolarisation of the atria

(d) The QRS complex represents the depolarisation of the ventricles

Response Index

01	ⓐ ⓑ ⓒ ⓓ	26	ⓐ ⓑ ⓒ ⓓ	51	ⓐ ⓑ ⓒ ⓓ	76	ⓐ ⓑ ⓒ ⓓ
02	ⓐ ⓑ ⓒ ⓓ	27	ⓐ ⓑ ⓒ ⓓ	52	ⓐ ⓑ ⓒ ⓓ	77	ⓐ ⓑ ⓒ ⓓ
03	ⓐ ⓑ ⓒ ⓓ	28	ⓐ ⓑ ⓒ ⓓ	53	ⓐ ⓑ ⓒ ⓓ	78	ⓐ ⓑ ⓒ ⓓ
04	ⓐ ⓑ ⓒ ⓓ	29	ⓐ ⓑ ⓒ ⓓ	54	ⓐ ⓑ ⓒ ⓓ	79	ⓐ ⓑ ⓒ ⓓ
05	ⓐ ⓑ ⓒ ⓓ	30	ⓐ ⓑ ⓒ ⓓ	55	ⓐ ⓑ ⓒ ⓓ	80	ⓐ ⓑ ⓒ ⓓ
06	ⓐ ⓑ ⓒ ⓓ	31	ⓐ ⓑ ⓒ ⓓ	56	ⓐ ⓑ ⓒ ⓓ	81	ⓐ ⓑ ⓒ ⓓ
07	ⓐ ⓑ ⓒ ⓓ	32	ⓐ ⓑ ⓒ ⓓ	57	ⓐ ⓑ ⓒ ⓓ	82	ⓐ ⓑ ⓒ ⓓ
08	ⓐ ⓑ ⓒ ⓓ	33	ⓐ ⓑ ⓒ ⓓ	58	ⓐ ⓑ ⓒ ⓓ	83	ⓐ ⓑ ⓒ ⓓ
09	ⓐ ⓑ ⓒ ⓓ	34	ⓐ ⓑ ⓒ ⓓ	59	ⓐ ⓑ ⓒ ⓓ	84	ⓐ ⓑ ⓒ ⓓ
10	ⓐ ⓑ ⓒ ⓓ	35	ⓐ ⓑ ⓒ ⓓ	60	ⓐ ⓑ ⓒ ⓓ	85	ⓐ ⓑ ⓒ ⓓ
11	ⓐ ⓑ ⓒ ⓓ	36	ⓐ ⓑ ⓒ ⓓ	61	ⓐ ⓑ ⓒ ⓓ	86	ⓐ ⓑ ⓒ ⓓ
12	ⓐ ⓑ ⓒ ⓓ	37	ⓐ ⓑ ⓒ ⓓ	62	ⓐ ⓑ ⓒ ⓓ	87	ⓐ ⓑ ⓒ ⓓ
13	ⓐ ⓑ ⓒ ⓓ	38	ⓐ ⓑ ⓒ ⓓ	63	ⓐ ⓑ ⓒ ⓓ	88	ⓐ ⓑ ⓒ ⓓ
14	ⓐ ⓑ ⓒ ⓓ	39	ⓐ ⓑ ⓒ ⓓ	64	ⓐ ⓑ ⓒ ⓓ	89	ⓐ ⓑ ⓒ ⓓ
15	ⓐ ⓑ ⓒ ⓓ	40	ⓐ ⓑ ⓒ ⓓ	65	ⓐ ⓑ ⓒ ⓓ	90	ⓐ ⓑ ⓒ ⓓ
16	ⓐ ⓑ ⓒ ⓓ	41	ⓐ ⓑ ⓒ ⓓ	66	ⓐ ⓑ ⓒ ⓓ		
17	ⓐ ⓑ ⓒ ⓓ	42	ⓐ ⓑ ⓒ ⓓ	67	ⓐ ⓑ ⓒ ⓓ		
18	ⓐ ⓑ ⓒ ⓓ	43	ⓐ ⓑ ⓒ ⓓ	68	ⓐ ⓑ ⓒ ⓓ		
19	ⓐ ⓑ ⓒ ⓓ	44	ⓐ ⓑ ⓒ ⓓ	69	ⓐ ⓑ ⓒ ⓓ		
20	ⓐ ⓑ ⓒ ⓓ	45	ⓐ ⓑ ⓒ ⓓ	70	ⓐ ⓑ ⓒ ⓓ		
21	ⓐ ⓑ ⓒ ⓓ	46	ⓐ ⓑ ⓒ ⓓ	71	ⓐ ⓑ ⓒ ⓓ		
22	ⓐ ⓑ ⓒ ⓓ	47	ⓐ ⓑ ⓒ ⓓ	72	ⓐ ⓑ ⓒ ⓓ		
23	ⓐ ⓑ ⓒ ⓓ	48	ⓐ ⓑ ⓒ ⓓ	73	ⓐ ⓑ ⓒ ⓓ		
24	ⓐ ⓑ ⓒ ⓓ	49	ⓐ ⓑ ⓒ ⓓ	74	ⓐ ⓑ ⓒ ⓓ		
25	ⓐ ⓑ ⓒ ⓓ	50	ⓐ ⓑ ⓒ ⓓ	75	ⓐ ⓑ ⓒ ⓓ		

Performance Scanner

> 90% Excellent !	You have mastered the NEET syllabus (11th). The concepts of this entire syllabus are at your fingertips. Maintain this momentum.
76-90% Very Good !	You have a good command over the entire NEET syllabus (11th). Revise it again after a few days to enhance your performance.
60-75% Good !	You have a wide scope to learn for the entire NEET syllabus (11th). Revise it again.
<60% Not Satisfactory!	You have a long way ahead of you to master the NEET syllabus (11th). Revise it thoroughly.

Space for Rough Work

Test Booklet No. **3947323**

Test Booklet Code **NSS2**

NEET Stepping Stones 2

(Complete Syllabus Test 11th)

Name of the Candidate (In Capitals)

____

____

____

Candidate's Signature ______________

Invigilator's Signature ______________

Facsimile signature stamp of center superintendent________________

Important Instructions

- The test is of **1 hours 30 minutes** duration and the Test Booklet contains **90** multiple-choice questions (four options with a single correct answer) from biology.
- Candidates are advised to read all questions before they start attempting the question paper.
- Each questions carries 4 marks. For each correct response, the candidate will get 4 marks. For each incorrect response, one marks will be deducted from the total scores.
- In the event of candidate marking more than one option one mark will be deducted. The maximum marks are 180.
- Use **Blue/Black Point Pen only** for writing particular on this page/ marking response on Answer Sheet.

Do not open this booklet until you start attempting the test

Biology

1. Stem of grasses and related plants is elongated by the activity of
(a) lateral meristem
(b) apical meristem
(c) both apical and lateral meristem
(d) intercalary meristem

2. Which of the following are not the effects of parathyroid hormone?
I. Stimulates the process of bone resorption
II. Decreases Ca^{2+} level in blood
III. Reabsorption of Ca^{2+} by renal tubules
IV. Decreases the absorption of Ca^{2+} from digested food
V. Increases metabolism of carbohydrates
Choose the correct answer from the options given below
(a) I and III (b) II, IV and V
(c) I and V (d) II and III

3. Given below are two statements.
Statement I Slime moulds are saprophytic protists.
Statement II Under favourable conditions, slime mold forms an aggregation called plasmodium.
In the light of the above statements, choose the correct answer from the options given below.
(a) Statement I is incorrect, but statement II is correct
(b) Both statement I and statement II are correct
(c) Both statement I and statement II are incorrect
(d) Statement I is correct, but statement II is incorrect

4. In most situations, abscisic acid acts as the
(a) agonist to auxin
(b) antagonist to gibberellins
(c) antagonist to auxin
(d) agonist to gibberellins

5. Match List I with List II.

List I	List II
A. P-wave	1. Important determinant of cardiac output
B. QRS complex	2. Represents returns of ventricles from excited to normal state
C. T-wave	3. Initiates ventricular contraction
D. Stroke volume	4. leads to contraction of atria

Choose the correct answer from the options given below
(a) A-4, B-2, C-3, D-1
(b) A-4, B-3, C-2, D-1
(c) A-1, B-3, C-4, D-2
(d) A-3, B-2, C-4, D-1

6. The quiescent centre in root meristem serves as a
(a) site for storage of food, which is utilised during maturation.
(b) reservoir for growth and development
(c) reservoir for replenishment of damaged cells of the meristem
(d) region for absorption of water

7. Which of the following are involved in the production of curd from milk?
(a) Chemosynthetic autotrophic bacteria
(b) Heterotrophic bacteria
(c) Photosynthetic autotrophic bacteria
(d) Saprophytic bacteria

8. Match List I with List II.

List I	List II
A. Erythrocytes	1. Resist infections
B. Eosinophils	2. Gas transport
C. Thrombocytes	3. Contraction of heart muscle
D. Systole	4. Coagulation

Choose the correct answer from the options given below

(a) A-2, B-3, C-4, D-1 (b) A-2, B-1, C-3, D-4
(c) A-1, B-2, C-4, D-3 (d) A-2, B-1, C-4, D-3

9. Given below are two statements.

Statement I Veins provide rigidity to the leaf blade and act as the channel of transport for water, minerals.

Statement II Leaves of most of the dicotyledonous plants bear veins that run parallel to each other within a lamina.

In the light of the above statements, choose the correct answer from the options given below.

(a) Statement I is incorrect, but statement II is correct
(b) Both statements I and II are correct
(c) Both statements I and II are incorrect
(d) Statement I is correct, but statement II is incorrect

10. After grinding a living tissue in trichloroacetic acid, two types of fractions are obtained on staining, i.e. acid soluble and acid insoluble fraction. The acid insoluble fraction does not contain

(a) nucleic acids
(b) polysaccharides
(c) lipids
(d) flavonoids and alkaloids

11. Given below are two statements; one is labelled as Assertion (A) and the other is labelled as Reason (R).

Assertion (A) Cyclostomes are marine, but spawn in freshwater.

Reason (R) Freshwater reduces the risk of predations for jawless fishes.

In the light of the above statements, choose the correct answer from the options given below.

(a) A is false, but R is true.
(b) Both A and R are true and R is the correct explanation of A.
(c) Both A and R are true, but R is not the correct explanation of A.
(d) A is true, but R is false.

12. Read the following statements and choose the set of correct statements.

I. The sclereids are spherical, oval or cylindrical, highly thickened dead cells with very narrow cavities called lumen.

II. The companion cells are specialised parenchymatous cells, which are closely associated with phloem parenchyma to control their activity.

III. The outer walls of guard cells are thin and the inner walls are highly thickened.

IV. Collenchyma are generally isodiametric, spherical, oval, round, polygonal or elongated in shape.

V. The parenchymatous cells, which lie between the xylem and the phloem are called conjunctive tissue.

Choose the correct answer from the options given below

(a) I, III and IV
(b) I, III and V
(c) Only II
(d) I, II, III and IV

13. Match the List I with List II.

	List I		List II
A.	*Meandrina*	1.	Blood sucking leach
B.	*Wuchereria*	2.	Sea cucumber
C.	*Cucumaria*	3.	Brain coral
D.	*Hirudinaria*	4.	Filarial worm

Choose the correct answer from the options given below.

(a) A-3, B-4, C-1, D-2
(b) A-3, B-2, C-4, D-1
(c) A-3, B-4, C-2, D-1
(d) A-4, B-3, C-1, D-2

14. The number of mitochondria increase in cells of

(a) dormant seeds
(b) germinating seeds
(c) dry seeds
(d) dead seeds

15. Match List I with List II.

	List I		List II
A.	Psilopsida	1.	*Selaginella*
B.	Lycopsida	2.	*Psilotum*
C.	Sphenopsida	3.	*Adiantum*
D.	Pteropsida	4.	*Equisetum*

Choose the correct answer from the options given below.

(a) A-1, B-3, C-2, D-4
(b) A-2, B-4, C-1, D-3
(c) A-2, B-1, C-4, D-3
(d) A-2, B-1, C-3, D-4

16. Identify the given tissue and its function from the options given below.

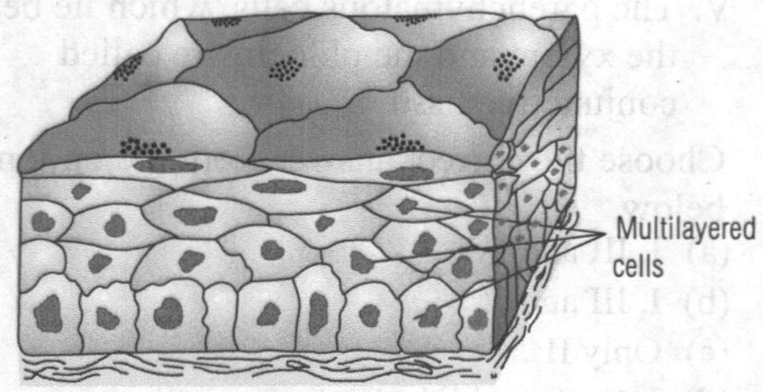

(a) Compound epithelium provides protection against chemical and mechanical stresses
(b) Squamous epithelium found in the walls of blood vessels.
(c) Cuboidal epithelium, helps in secretion and absorption
(d) Columnar epithelium found in lining of stomach

17. Identify the correctly matched pair.

(a) Cork cambium - phellem
(b) Cork - phellogen
(c) Secondary cortex - phelloderm
(d) Spring wood - late wood

18. Which of the following combination is necessary for chemiosmosis to occur?

(a) Membrane, proton pump, proton gradient, NADPH synthas
(b) Proton pump, electron gradient, ADP synthase
(c) Proton pump, electron gradient, NADP synthase
(d) Membrane, proton pump, proton gradient, ATP synthase

19. Match List I with List II.

	List I		List II
A.	*Sycon*	1.	Water vascular system with radial symmetry
B.	*Asterias*	2.	Exoskeleton made up of cuticle
C.	*Pleurobrachia*	3.	Body with pores and canals in walls
D.	*Bombyx*	4.	Comb plates for locomotion

Choose the correct answer from the options given below

(a) A-3, B-2, C-1, D-4
(b) A-4, B-3, C-2, D-1
(c) A-3, B-2, C-4, D-1
(d) A-3, B-1, C-4, D-2

20. Given below are two statements.

Statement I The G_1-phase of the cell cycle is a check point, where cell assesses its readiness to divide.

Statement II The cell cycle consists of interphase and mitotic phase.

In the light of the above statements, choose the correct answer from the options given below.

(a) Statement I is incorrect, but statement II is correct
(b) Both statement I and statement II are correct
(c) Both statement I and statement II are incorrect
(d) Statement I is correct, but statement II is incorrect

21. Which of the following statement is incorrect?

(a) Quaternary structure refers to the spatial relations between individual polypeptide chains in a multichained protein.
(b) The tertiary structure is absolutely necessary for many biological activities of protein.
(c) Biologists describe the protein structures at three levels only.
(d) Protein structure is correlated with protein function.

22. Match List I with List II.

	List I		List II
A.	Oxaloacetic acid	1.	6C compound
B.	Phosphoglyceraldehyde	2.	5C compound
C.	Isocitrate	3.	4C compound
D.	α – ketoglutarate	4.	3C compound

Choose the correct answer from the options given below.

(a) A-4, B-3, C-1, D-2
(b) A-3, B-4, C-1, D-2
(c) A-3, B-4, C-2, D-1
(d) A-4, B-2, C-1, D-3

23. Given below are two statements.

Statement I In frog, the undigested solid waste is passed out through the cloaca.

Statement II In male frogs, the ureter and oviduct open separately in the cloaca.

In the light of the above statements, choose the correct answer from the options given below.

(a) Statement I is incorrect, but statement II is correct
(b) Both statement I and statement II are correct
(c) Both statement I and statement II are incorrect
(d) Statement I is correct, but statement II is incorrect

24. Given below are two statements; one is labelled as Assertion (A) and the other is labelled as Reason (R).

Assertion (A) The heterocyclic compound in nucleic acid are the nitrogenous bases.

Reason (R) Uracil, cytosine and thymine have 9 membered ring structure, while adenine and guanine have 6 membered ring structure.

In the light of the above statements, choose the correct answer from the options given below.

(a) A is false, but R is true
(b) Both A and R are true and R is the correct explanation of A
(c) Both A and R are true, but R is not the correct explanation of A
(d) A is true, but R is false

25. Given below are two statements.

Statement I Monocytes destroy the foreign organisms from entering the body.

Statement II Atrio-ventricular node is located on the lower left corner of the left atrium.

In the light of the above statements, choose the correct answer from the options given below.

(a) Statement I is incorrect, but statement II is correct
(b) Both statement I and statement II are correct
(c) Both statement I and statement II are incorrect
(d) Statement I is correct, but statement II is incorrect

26. Give below are two statements.

Statement I Phosphoenolpyruvate serves as the primary CO_2 acceptor in C_4 plants and is located in the mesophyll cells.

Statement II Mesophyll cell of C_4 plants do not contain the RuBisCO enzyme.

In the light of the above statements, choose the correct answer from the options given below.

(a) Statement I is incorrect, but statement II is correct
(b) Both statement I and statement II are correct
(c) Both statement I and statement II are incorrect
(d) Statement I is correct, but statement II is incorrect

27. Given below are two statements.

Statement I Cnidarians exhibit two basic body forms called polyp and medusa.

Statement II Polyp is a free-swimming form and medusa is sessile.

In the light of the above statements, choose the correct answer from the options given below.

(a) Statement I is incorrect, but statement II is correct
(b) Both statement I and statement II are correct
(c) Both statement I and statement II are incorrect
(d) Statement I is correct, but statement II is incorrect

28. The membrane bound enzyme of Krebs' cycle is
(a) aconitase
(b) pyruvic decarboxylase
(c) succinic dehydrogenase
(d) fumarase

29. Ultra-filtration occurs mainly due to
(a) osmotic concentration in collecting duct
(b) circulating blood in the body
(c) glomerular capillary blood pressure
(d) secretion of nitrogenous waste in the liver

30. Match List I with List II.

	List I		List II
A.	Pasteur	1.	*Contagium vivum fluidum*
B.	Stanley	2.	Crystallisation of virus
C.	Beijerinck	3.	Proposed the term 'virus'

Choose the correct answer from the options given below.
(a) A-3, B-2, C-1 (b) A-2, B-3, C-1
(c) A-3, B-1, C-2 (d) A-1, B-3, C-2

31. Given below are two statements.
Statement I Thymosins play a major role in the differentiation of lymphocytes providing cell mediated immunity.
Statement II Thymus is a lobular structure located on the ventral side of the heart.
In the light of the above statements, choose the correct answer from the options given below.
(a) Statement I is incorrect, but statement II is correct
(b) Both statement I and statement II are correct
(c) Both statement I and statement II are incorrect
(d) Statement I is correct, but statement II is incorrect

32. '*X*' is tract of nerve fibres that connects both the left and right cerebral hemispheres. Identify 'X'
(a) Cerebral cortex
(b) Cerebellum
(c) Corpus callosum
(d) Thalamus

33. Which of the following statement is incorrect ?
(a) Parthenocarpy can be induced by application of IAA in a paste form to the stigma of a flower or by spraying the flowers with a dilute solution of IAA.
(b) In maize, application of NAA during the period of inflorescence differentiation can induce formation of hermaphrodite or female flowers in a male inflorescence.
(c) Abscisic acid promotes cold hardiness and inhibits the growth of pathogens.
(d) In low concentration, abscisic acid simulates root initiation and growth of lateral roots and root hair.

34. Match List I with List II.

	List I		List II
A.	Osteoporosis	1.	Weakening and paralysis of skeletal muscle
B.	Muscular dystrophy	2.	Caused due to accumulation of uric acid crystals
C.	Gout	3.	Age related disorder caused due to decreased level of estrogen
D.	Myasthenia gravis	4.	Progressive degeneration of skeletal muscle

Choose the correct answer from the options given below.
(a) A-3, B-4, C-2, D-1 (b) A-3, B-2, C-4, D-1
(c) A-2, B-3, C-1, D-4 (d) A-4, B-2, C-1, D-3

35. Which of the following is not correctly matched?
(a) Adenine derivative- Kinetin
(b) Carotenoid derivative- Abscisic acid
(c) Terpenes - IAA
(d) Indole compound - IBA

36. Select the correct sequence of taxonomic hierarchy in ascending order.
(a) *Solanum* → *melongena* → Tracheophyta → Solanales
(b) *Mangifera* → Sapindales → Dicotyledonae → Angiospermae
(c) Angiospermae → Monocotyledons → Poales → *Triticum*
(d) Sapindales → Anacardiaceae → Dicotyledonae → Angiospermae

37. Which of the following structure is similar to the notochord in phylum-Hemichordata?

(a) Proboscis (b) Collar
(c) Trunk (d) Stomochord

38. Match List I with List II.

List I	List II
A. Tight junctions	1. Performs cementing to keep neighbouring cells together
B. Adhering junctions	2. Facilitate cells to communicate with each other
C. Gap junctions	3. Helps to stop leakage of substances

Choose the correct answer from the options given below

(a) A-1, B-2, C-3
(b) A-2, B-1, C-3
(c) A-3, B-1, C-2
(d) A-3, B-2, C-1

39. Plant growth is unique because plants retain the capacity for unlimited growth throughout their life. The elongation phase of growth is characterised by

(a) increased vacuolation, cell enlargement and new cell wall deposition.
(b) decreased vacuolation, cell enlargement and cell wall deposition.
(c) low protoplasm content, complete absence of vacuolation and conspicuous nuclei.
(d) cell maturation, conspicuous nuclei and new cell wall deposition.

40. Given below are two statements; one is labelled as Assertion (A) other one is labelled as Reason (R).

Assertion (A) Haemoglobin can not get saturated with oxygen more than 97% .

Reason (R) With a rise in O_2, affinity between O_2 and haemoglobin also increases.

In the light of the above statements, choose the correct answer from the options given below.

(a) A is false, but R is true
(b) Both A and R are true and R is the correct explanation of A
(c) Both A and R are true, but R is not the correct explanation of A
(d) A is true, but R is false

41. Match List I with List II.

List I	List II
A. Metacentric chromosome	1. Centromere situated close to the end forming one extremely short and one very long arms
B. Acrocentric chromosome	2 Centromere in the middle forming two equal arms of chromosomes
C. Sub-metacentric chromosome	3. Chromosome with a terminal centromere
D. Telocentric chromosome	4. Centromere slightly away from the middle forming one shorter arm and one longer arm

Choose the correct answer from the options given below

(a) A-2, B-1, C-4, D-3
(b) A-1, B-3, C-2, D-4
(c) A-2, B-3, C-4, D-1
(d) A-1, B-2, C-3, D-4

42. Gamosepalous calyx, imbricate aestivation and zygomorphic flowers are found in which of the following families of plants?

(a) Cruciferae (b) Compositae
(c) Leguminosae (d) Malvaceae

43. Radial symmetry is observed in which of the following phylum?

I. Platyhelminthes
II. Coelenterates
III. Annelids
IV. Echinodermata
V. Aschelminthes

Choose the correct answer from the options given below.
(a) II and IV
(b) I, II and IV
(c) Only IV
(d) II, III and IV

44. Match List I with List II.

	List I		List II
A.	Rudolf Virchow	1.	Discovered nucleus
B.	Schwann	2.	*Omnis cellula-e- cellula*
C.	Antonie van Leeuwenhoek	3.	Animals composed of cells
D.	Robert Brown	4.	Described a live cell

Choose the correct answer from the options given below.
(a) A-2, B-1, C-3, D-4
(b) A-2, B-3, C-4, D-1
(c) A-1, B-2, C-3, D-4
(d) A-2, B-3, C-1, D-4

45. Select the incorrectly matched pair.
(a) Collagen- Intercellular ground substance
(b) Trypsin- An essential enzyme
(c) GLUT-4- Sensory receptors for smell, taste, etc
(d) Antibody- Fights infectious agents

46. Match List I with List II.

	List I		List II
A.	Cymose	1.	Unbranched, elongated and with sessile flowers
B.	Umbel	2.	Flat-topped cluster of stalked flowers
C.	Spike	3.	Arrangement of flowers in basipetal succession
D.	Racemose	4.	Arrangement of flowers in acropetal succession

Choose the correct answer from the options given below.
(a) A-3, B-2, C-1, D-4
(b) A-2, B-1, C-3, D-4
(c) A-3, B-2, C-4, D- 1
(d) A-4, B-1, C-3, D-2

47. Given below are two statements.
Statement I Interkinesis is generally short lived and followed by prophase-II.
Statement II Crossing over is enzyme mediated process and the enzyme involved is called thrombokinase.
In the light of the above statements, choose the correct answer from the options given below
(a) Statement I is incorrect, but statement II is correct
(b) Both statement I and statement II are correct.
(c) Both statement I and statement II are incorrect
(d) Statement I is correct, but statement II is incorrect

48. Given below are two statements.
Statement I NADP is a universal hydrogen acceptor produced only during aerobic respiration and works as coenzyme in ATP generation through ETS.
Statement II Energy released from biological oxidation is used in the formation of high energy phosphate bond of ATP, NAD and FAD.
In the light of the above statements, choose the correct answer from the options given below.
(a) Statement I is incorrect, but statement II is correct
(b) Both statement I and statement II are correct
(c) Both statement I and statement II are incorrect
(d) Statement I is correct, but statement II is incorrect

49. Identify the incorrectly matched pair.
(a) Pars nervosa- vasopressin
(b) Pars intermedia- melanocyte stimulating hormone
(c) Pars distalis - oxytocin
(d) Pars distalis- prolactin

50. Match List I with List II.

	List I		List II
A.	Cerebellum	1.	Regulation of body temperature, hunger and thirst.
B.	Hypothalamus	2.	Coordination of voluntary movements and balance.
C.	Medulla oblongata	3.	Control of involuntary functions like breathing and heartbeat.

Choose the correct answer from the options given below.

(a) A-2, B-3, C-1 (b) A-2, B-1, C-3
(c) A-1, B-2, C-3 (d) A-3, B-1, C-2

51. Given below are two statements; one is labelled as Assertion (A) and other is labelled as Reason (R).

Assertion (A) Elevated blood flow in the heart can trigger the release of atrial natriuretic factor.

Reason (R) Atrial natriuretic factor mechanism acts as a check on the renin- angiotensin mechanism.

In the light of the above statements, choose the correct answer from the options given below.

(a) A is false, but R is true
(b) Both A and R are true and R is the correct explanation of A
(c) Both A and R are true, but R is not the correct explanation of A
(d) A is true, but R is false

52. Identify the incorrect match pair.

(a) Staminode - sterile stamen
(b) Epiphyllous - flowers of lily
(c) Polyadelphous - multiple bundle of stamens
(d) Epipetalous - stamens are attached to perianth

53. Given below are two statements.

Statement I *Calotropis* shows valvate aestivation as one margin of the appendage overlaps the next one.

Statement II Beans shows papilionaceous or vexillary aestivation.

In the light of the above statements, choose the correct answer from the options given below.

(a) Statement I is incorrect, but statement II is correct
(b) Both statement I and statement II are correct
(c) Both statement I and statement II are incorrect
(d) Statement I is correct, but statement II is incorrect

54. During the process of meiosis, the specific event that signifies the transition from diakinesis indicating that the cell is ready to proceed with chromosomal alignment is

(a) complete separation of chromatid.
(b) assembly of the meiotic spindle at poles.
(c) disappearance of the nucleolus and nuclear envelop.
(d) alignment of haploid chromatids on the equatorial plate.

55. Given below are two statements.

Statement I During the phase of synthesis, of DNA the amount of DNA per cell doubles.

Statement II In humans, the cell division lasts for about three hours.

In the light of the above statements, choose the correct answer from the options given below.

(a) Statement I is incorrect, but statement II is correct
(b) Both statement I and statement II are correct
(c) Both statement I and statement II are incorrect
(d) Statement I is correct, but statement II is incorrect

56. Match List I with List II.

	List I		List II
A.	Urea	1.	Reabsorbed in the proximal convoluted tubule and loop of Henle
B.	Uric acid	2.	Excreted by mammals, most amphibians and sharks
C.	Ammonia	3.	Excreted by reptiles, birds and insects
D.	Water	4.	Excreted by aquatic fishes and aquatic insects.

Choose the correct answer from the options given below.

(a) A-2, B-4, C-3, D-1
(b) A-1, B-2, C-3, D-4
(c) A-2, B-3, C-4, D-1
(d) A-2, B-4, C-1, D-3

57. Which one of the following are the examples of de-differentiation?

(a) Procambium and vascular cambium
(b) Cork cambium and interfascicular cambium
(c) Cork cambium and vascular cambium
(d) Pro cambium and cork cambium

58. Which is the 1st carbon dioxide acceptor in C_4 plants?
(a) Phosphoenolpyruvate
(b) Ribulose 1,5-diphosphate
(c) Oxaloacetic acid
(d) Phosphoglyceric acid

59. Given below are two statements.
Statement I Impulse transmission across a chemical synapse is faster than electrical synapses.
Statement II Chemical synapse involves neurotransmitter.
In the light of the above statements, choose the correct answer from the options given below.
(a) Statement I is incorrect, but statement II is correct
(b) Both statement I and statement II are correct
(c) Both statement I and statement II are incorrect
(d) Statement I is correct, but statement II is incorrect

60. Which of the following statement is correct?
(a) Protonema of moss is sporophytic, whereas prothallus of fern is gametophytic.
(b) Protonema of moss and prothallus of *Dryopteris* are gametophytic.
(c) Plant body of moss is gametophytic and plant body of *Dryopteris* is both gametophytic and sporophytic.
(d) Moss protonema is sporophytic and *Pteris* prothallus is gametophytic, but plant body is sporophytic in *Pteris* and gametophytic in *Funaria*.

61. Which of the following statement regarding coenzymes and prosthetic groups of enzymes is not true?
(a) Both are required for enzyme action
(b) Both can be separated from enzyme by dialysis
(c) Both are organic compounds
(d) Both are not polypeptides

62. The figure represents the different structure of proteins. Identify *A*, *B* and *C*.

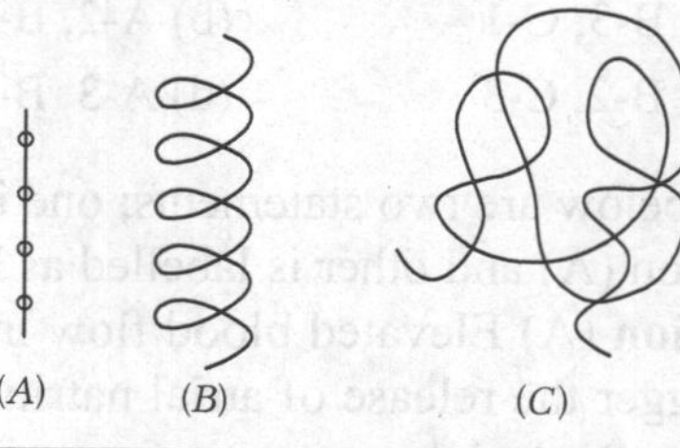

	A	*B*	*C*
(a)	1° structure	2° structure	3° structure
(b)	3° structure	2° structure	1° structure
(c)	2° structure	1° structure	3° structure
(d)	1° structure	3° structure	2° structure

63. Which of the following structure in *Periplaneta americana* helps in the removal of excretory products from the haemolymph?
(a) Gizzard
(b) Nephridia
(c) Malpighian tubules
(d) Gastric caecae

64. Which of the following function of the skeleton system is not related to locomotion?
(a) Production of red blood cells
(b) Providing attachment points for muscles
(c) Protection of internal organs
(d) Storage of minerals like calcium and phosphorus

65. Match List I with List II.

List I	List II
A. *Chlorella*	1. Inner layer made up of cellulose and outer layer of pectose.
B. *Ulothrix*	2. Food is stored in the form of mannitol.
C. *Polysiphonia*	3. Food is stored in the form of floridean starch.
D. *Fucus*	4. Used as a food supplement by space travellers.

Choose the correct answer from the options given below

(a) A-4, B-2, C-3, D-1
(b) A-4, B-1, C-3, D-2
(c) A-3, B-1, C-2, D-4
(d) A-2, B-3, C-1, D-4

66. Refer to the given figure and answer the following question.

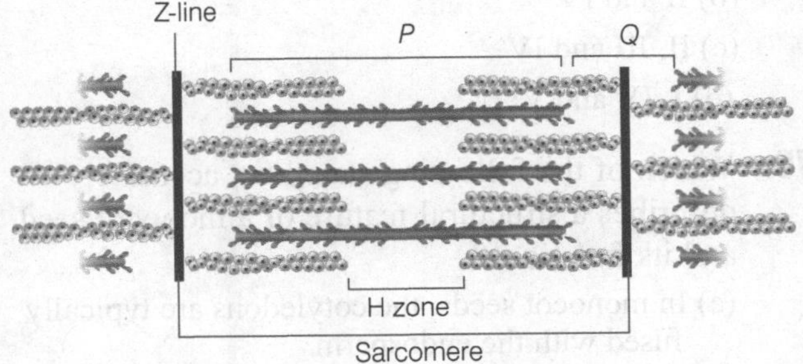

Which of the following is the incorrect distinctive feature of *P* and *Q*?

(a) *P* has wide zone and *Q* has thin Z-line.
(b) *P* gives light appearance and *Q* gives dark appearance.
(c) *P* contains myosin filaments and *Q* contains actin filaments.
(d) *P* remains unchanged during muscle contraction and *Q* shortens during muscle contraction.

67. Match List I with List II.

	List I		List II
A.	Chloroplast	1.	Store carbohydrates
B.	Amyloplasts	2.	Na^+/K^+ pump
C.	Active transport	3.	Store fats
D.	Elaioplasts	4.	*ds* circular DNA

Choose the correct answer from the options given below.

(a) A-4, B-1, C-2, D-3
(b) A-2, B-1, C-4, D-3
(c) A-3, B-2, C-1, D-4
(d) A-4, B-2, C-3, D-1

68. Given below are few statements.

I. Water reabsorption occurs actively in the first segments of the nephron.
II. Henle's loop aids in maintaining the pH and ionic balance of the body fluid by selective secretion of H^+, K^+ ions, ammonia and HCO_3^- into the filtrate.
III. Extension of collecting duct is from cortex of the kidney to the inner parts of the medulla.
IV. Increasing osmolarity towards the inner medullary interstitium forms a gradient, which is mainly caused by NaCl and Urea.
V. Descending portion of vasa recta returns NaCl to the interstitium.

Choose the correct statements from the options given below.

(a) III, IV and V
(b) I, II and III
(c) I, IV and V
(d) I, III and IV

69. Apples are generally wrapped in waxed paper to

(a) prevent sunlight for changing its colour
(b) prevent aerobic respiration by checking the entry of oxygen
(c) prevent ethylene formation that hastens ripening
(d) make the apples look attractive

70. Match List I with List II.

	List I		List II
A.	Volume of air remaining in the lungs even after forcible expiration	1.	500 mL
B.	Additional volume of air a person can inspire	2.	1100 mL to 1200 mL
C.	Additional volume of air a person can expire	3.	2500 mL to 3000 mL
D.	Volume of air inspired or expired during normal respiration	4.	1000 mL to 1100 mL

Choose the correct answer from the options given below.

(a) A-2, B-3, C-4, D-1
(b) A-2, B-3, C-1, D-4
(c) A-1, B-3, C-4, D-2
(d) A-1, B-2, C-3, D-4

71. A respiratory centre situated adjacent to rhythm centre and highly sensitive to hydrogen ions is

(a) pneumotaxic centre
(b) chemosensitive area
(c) receptor associated with carotid artery
(d) dorsal group of neurons

72. *Selaginella* and *Salvinia* are considered representing a significant step towards evolution of seed habit because

(a) female gametophyte is free and gets dispersed like seeds.
(b) female gametophyte lacks archegonia.
(c) magaspores possess endosperm and embryo is surrounded by seed coat.
(d) embryo develops in female gametophyte, which is retained on parent sporophyte.

73. Match List I with List II.

	List I		List II
A.	Thyroid gland	1.	Calcium ions
B.	Goitre	2.	T-lymphocytes
C.	Thymosin	3.	Stromal tissues
D.	PTH	4.	Iodine

Choose the correct answer from the options given below

(a) A-4, B-1, C-2, D-3
(b) A-3, B-4, C-2, D-1
(c) A-2, B-3, C-1, D-4
(d) A-2, B-1, C-4, D-3

74. Choose the incorrect statements.

I. Skull, vertebral column, sternum and ribs constitute the axial skeleton.
II. A pair of hyoid bone is present at the base of buccal cavity.
III. Sternum, a flat bone is present on the ventral midline of thorax.
IV. Clavicle articulates with the head of humerus to form shoulder joint.
V. Pelvic girdle consists of two coxal bones.

Choose the correct answer from the options given below.

(a) I, II and III
(b) II and IV
(c) II, III and IV
(d) I, IV and V

75. Which of the following statement accurately describes a structural feature of a monocot seed and its functions?

(a) In monocot seeds, the cotyledons are typically fused with the endosperm.
(b) The monocot seeds has a double cotyledon that is often referred to as the scutellum.
(c) Monocot seeds contain a large, central endosperm that serves as the primary nutrient source for the developing embryo.
(d) Micropyle is a prominent region that is found in seed.

76. Match List I with List II.

	List I		List II
A.	Collateral vascular bundle	1.	Found in monocot stems with phloem located both on the inside and outside of xylem
B.	Bicollateral vascular bundle	2.	Found in dicot stems with phloem located outside the xylem
C.	Radial vascular bundle	3.	Found in roots with xylem and phloem arranged alternately around the central core

Choose the correct answer from the options given below.

(a) A-3, B-1, C-2
(b) A-1, B-3, C-2
(c) A-2, B-3, C-1
(d) A-2, B-1, C-3

77. Which of the following statement correctly describes the events occurring during telophase-I of meiosis?

(a) During telophase-I, sister chromatids are separated into two daughter cells.

(b) Telophase-I involves the separation of homologous chromosomes into two daughter cells.

(c) In telophase-I, the spindle fibres disassemble and the chromosomes are replicated to form two identical sets within each cell.

(d) Telophase-I is characterised by the alignment of chromosomes along the equatorial plane, where homologous chromosomes prepare for separation in the subsequent division.

78. Which of the following statement is incorrect about vascular system of cockroach?

(a) Haemolymph contain haemocytes.
(b) Heart is located along mid-ventral line.
(c) Blood vessels are poorly developed.
(d) Body cavity is called haemocoel.

79. Which of the following statement regarding cyclic flow of electron during light reactions is false?

(a) This process takes place in the stromal lamellae
(b) ATP synthesis takes place
(c) NADPH $+H^+$ is synthesised
(d) It takes place only when light of wavelength beyond 680 nm is available for excitation

80. Choose the enzyme involved in the following reaction.

$S-G+S'\rightarrow S+S'-G$

(a) Oxidoreductase (b) Hydrolase
(c) Transferase (d) Lyase

81. Read the following statements and identify the incorrect statement with respect to the diagram given below.

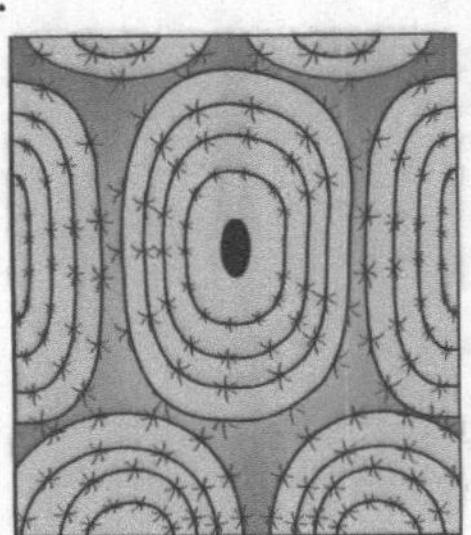

(a) It provides structural framework to the body.
(b) It supports and protects softer tissues and organs.
(c) It is rich in calcium salts and collagen fibres.
(d) It has soft and pliable ground substance.

82. Choose the correct statement w.r.t. bones.

(a) Acetabulum is the cavity present between the fusion point of these bones, i.e. ilium, ischium and pubis.
(b) The shank region consists of tarsals and metatarsals.
(c) Phalanges constitute 18 bones in a hindlimb.
(d) Patella is the largest bone among ethmoid bones.

83. Match List I with List II.

	List I		List II
A.	Lectins	1	Diterpenes
B.	Terpenoides	2.	Vinblastin
C.	Drugs	3.	Concanavalin-A
D.	Toxins	4.	Ricin

Choose the correct answer from the options given below.

(a) A-2, B-1, C-4; D-3
(b) A-3, B-2, C-1, D-4
(c) A-3, B-1, C-2, D-4
(d) A-4, B-1, C-2, D-3

84. Given description refers to a plant organ.

I. 2-4 xylem and phloem.
II. Endodermis with passage cell.
III. Unicellular (epidermal elongations)
IV. Cambium rings developed between xylem and phloem.
V. Radial vascular bundle.
VI. Pith is small and inconspicuous.

Choose the correct tissue from the options given below.

(a) Monocot root
(b) Monocot stem
(c) Dicot root
(d) Dicot stem

85. Choose the incorrectly matched pair of given animals and its respiratory structure.

(a)	Prawn	Gills
(b)	Earthworm	Skin
(c)	Scorpion	Trachea
(d)	Spiders	Book lungs

86. Which of the following traits is not a characteristic of echinoderms?

I. They have a complete digestive system with two separate openings.

II. They possess a complex haemal and perihaemal system for circulation.

III. Removal of nitrogenous waste takes place through cloacal aperture.

IV. Sense organs are poorly developed.

Choose the correct answer from the options given below.

(a) I and II (b) II and III

(c) Only III (d) I and IV

87. Given below are two statements; one is labelled as Assertion (A) and other one is labelled as Reason (R).

Assertion (A) The conversion of glyceraldehyde- 3 phosphate into 1,3-bisphosphoglycerate is an oxidation reaction.

Reason (R) The reaction in which 1, 3-bisphosphoglycerate is formed from glyceraldehyde-3 phosphate utilises NAD^+.

In the light of the above statements, choose the correct answer from the options given below

(a) A is false, but R is true

(b) Both A and R are true R is the correct explanation of A

(c) Both A and R are true, but R is not the correct explanation of A

(d) A is true, but R is false

88. What would be the heart rate of a person if the cardiac output is 4L, blood volume in the verticle at the end of diastole is 100 mL and at the end of ventricular systole is 50 mL?

(a) 100 beats per minute

(b) 72 beats per minute

(c) 80 beats per minute

(d) 50 beats per minute

89. An enzyme increases the rate of a reaction by

(a) supplying the energy required to start the reaction.

(b) increasing the rate of random collisions of molecules.

(c) removing the product of the reaction, so allowing it to continue.

(d) bringing the reacting molecules into precise orientation with each other.

90. To which of the following, a specialised muscle bundle connecting the atrial and ventricular chambers of the heart passes stimulus of contraction?

(a) AV node (b) SA node

(c) Purkinje fibre (d) Atrium

Response Index

01 ⓐ ⓑ ⓒ ⓓ	26 ⓐ ⓑ ⓒ ⓓ	51 ⓐ ⓑ ⓒ ⓓ	76 ⓐ ⓑ ⓒ ⓓ
02 ⓐ ⓑ ⓒ ⓓ	27 ⓐ ⓑ ⓒ ⓓ	52 ⓐ ⓑ ⓒ ⓓ	77 ⓐ ⓑ ⓒ ⓓ
03 ⓐ ⓑ ⓒ ⓓ	28 ⓐ ⓑ ⓒ ⓓ	53 ⓐ ⓑ ⓒ ⓓ	78 ⓐ ⓑ ⓒ ⓓ
04 ⓐ ⓑ ⓒ ⓓ	29 ⓐ ⓑ ⓒ ⓓ	54 ⓐ ⓑ ⓒ ⓓ	79 ⓐ ⓑ ⓒ ⓓ
05 ⓐ ⓑ ⓒ ⓓ	30 ⓐ ⓑ ⓒ ⓓ	55 ⓐ ⓑ ⓒ ⓓ	80 ⓐ ⓑ ⓒ ⓓ
06 ⓐ ⓑ ⓒ ⓓ	31 ⓐ ⓑ ⓒ ⓓ	56 ⓐ ⓑ ⓒ ⓓ	81 ⓐ ⓑ ⓒ ⓓ
07 ⓐ ⓑ ⓒ ⓓ	32 ⓐ ⓑ ⓒ ⓓ	57 ⓐ ⓑ ⓒ ⓓ	82 ⓐ ⓑ ⓒ ⓓ
08 ⓐ ⓑ ⓒ ⓓ	33 ⓐ ⓑ ⓒ ⓓ	58 ⓐ ⓑ ⓒ ⓓ	83 ⓐ ⓑ ⓒ ⓓ
09 ⓐ ⓑ ⓒ ⓓ	34 ⓐ ⓑ ⓒ ⓓ	59 ⓐ ⓑ ⓒ ⓓ	84 ⓐ ⓑ ⓒ ⓓ
10 ⓐ ⓑ ⓒ ⓓ	35 ⓐ ⓑ ⓒ ⓓ	60 ⓐ ⓑ ⓒ ⓓ	85 ⓐ ⓑ ⓒ ⓓ
11 ⓐ ⓑ ⓒ ⓓ	36 ⓐ ⓑ ⓒ ⓓ	61 ⓐ ⓑ ⓒ ⓓ	86 ⓐ ⓑ ⓒ ⓓ
12 ⓐ ⓑ ⓒ ⓓ	37 ⓐ ⓑ ⓒ ⓓ	62 ⓐ ⓑ ⓒ ⓓ	87 ⓐ ⓑ ⓒ ⓓ
13 ⓐ ⓑ ⓒ ⓓ	38 ⓐ ⓑ ⓒ ⓓ	63 ⓐ ⓑ ⓒ ⓓ	88 ⓐ ⓑ ⓒ ⓓ
14 ⓐ ⓑ ⓒ ⓓ	39 ⓐ ⓑ ⓒ ⓓ	64 ⓐ ⓑ ⓒ ⓓ	89 ⓐ ⓑ ⓒ ⓓ
15 ⓐ ⓑ ⓒ ⓓ	40 ⓐ ⓑ ⓒ ⓓ	65 ⓐ ⓑ ⓒ ⓓ	90 ⓐ ⓑ ⓒ ⓓ
16 ⓐ ⓑ ⓒ ⓓ	41 ⓐ ⓑ ⓒ ⓓ	66 ⓐ ⓑ ⓒ ⓓ	
17 ⓐ ⓑ ⓒ ⓓ	42 ⓐ ⓑ ⓒ ⓓ	67 ⓐ ⓑ ⓒ ⓓ	
18 ⓐ ⓑ ⓒ ⓓ	43 ⓐ ⓑ ⓒ ⓓ	68 ⓐ ⓑ ⓒ ⓓ	
19 ⓐ ⓑ ⓒ ⓓ	44 ⓐ ⓑ ⓒ ⓓ	69 ⓐ ⓑ ⓒ ⓓ	
20 ⓐ ⓑ ⓒ ⓓ	45 ⓐ ⓑ ⓒ ⓓ	70 ⓐ ⓑ ⓒ ⓓ	
21 ⓐ ⓑ ⓒ ⓓ	46 ⓐ ⓑ ⓒ ⓓ	71 ⓐ ⓑ ⓒ ⓓ	
22 ⓐ ⓑ ⓒ ⓓ	47 ⓐ ⓑ ⓒ ⓓ	72 ⓐ ⓑ ⓒ ⓓ	
23 ⓐ ⓑ ⓒ ⓓ	48 ⓐ ⓑ ⓒ ⓓ	73 ⓐ ⓑ ⓒ ⓓ	
24 ⓐ ⓑ ⓒ ⓓ	49 ⓐ ⓑ ⓒ ⓓ	74 ⓐ ⓑ ⓒ ⓓ	
25 ⓐ ⓑ ⓒ ⓓ	50 ⓐ ⓑ ⓒ ⓓ	75 ⓐ ⓑ ⓒ ⓓ	

Performance Scanner

> 90% Excellent !	You have mastered the NEET syllabus (11th). The concepts of this entire syllabus are at your fingertips. Maintain this momentum.
76-90% Very Good !	You have a good command over the entire NEET syllabus (11th). Revise it again after a few days to enhance your performance.
60-75% Good !	You have a wide scope to learn for the entire NEET syllabus (11th). Revise it again.
<60% Not Satisfactory!	You have a long way ahead of you to master the NEET syllabus (11th). Revise it thoroughly.

Space for Rough Work

Test Booklet No. **3947324**

Test Booklet Code **NSS3**

NEET Stepping Stones 3

(Complete Syllabus Test 11th)

Name of the Candidate (In Capitals)

____

____

____

Candidate's Signature ______________

Invigilator's Signature ______________

Facsimile signature stamp of center superintendent______________

Important Instructions

- The test is of **1 hours 30 minutes** duration and the Test Booklet contains **90** multiple-choice questions (four options with a single correct answer) from biology.
- Candidates are advised to read all questions before they start attempting the question paper.
- Each questions carries 4 marks. For each correct response, the candidate will get 4 marks. For each incorrect response, one marks will be deducted from the total scores.
- In the event of candidate marking more than one option one mark will be deducted. The maximum marks are 180.
- Use **Blue/Black Point Pen only** for writing particular on this page/ marking response on Answer Sheet.

Do not open this booklet until you start attempting the test

Biology

1. In which of the following phase of meiosis, sister chromatids move towards the opposite poles?
   (a) Anaphase-I
   (b) Anaphase-II
   (c) Metaphase-I
   (d) Metaphase-II

2. In which of the following plants, the primary root is short-lived and is replaced by a large number of roots?
   (a) *Solanum tuberosum*
   (b) Mustard
   (c) Banyan
   (d) *Triticum aestivum*

3. Given below are two statements.
   Statement I The chemical and physical properties of amino acids are essentially of the amino, carboxyl and hydrogen groups.
   Statement II Gingelly oil have high melting point.
   In the light of the above statements, choose the correct answer from the options given below.
   (a) Statement I is incorrect, but statement II is correct
   (b) Both statement I and statement II are correct
   (c) Both statement I and statement II are incorrect
   (d) Statement I is correct, but statement II is incorrect

4. Read the following statements carefully.
   I. The word 'systematics' is derived from the Latin word '*Systema*'.
   II. Linnaeus used *Systema Naturae* as the title of his publication.
   III. Biological names are generally in Greek and written in italics.
   IV. The number of species that are known and described range between 1.6-1.9 million.
   V. The scientific names ensure that each organism has only one name.

   Choose the incorrect set of statements from the options given below.
   (a) II, III, and IV
   (b) II, IV and V
   (c) I and III
   (d) III and IV

5. Match List I with List II.

List I	List II
A. Pharynx	1. Irregular-walled and vascularised.
B. Vocal cord	2. At the level of 5th thoracic vertebrae.
C. Alveoli	3. Common passage of air and food.
D. Primary bronchi	4. Cartilaginous box.

   Choose the correct answer from the options given below
   (a) A-2, B-3, C-4, D-1 (b) A-1, B-2, C-4, D-3
   (c) A-1, B-3, C-4, D-2 (d) A-3, B-4, C-1, D-2

6. Universally evolved under international codes, identification, naming and classification of organisms are basics of which of the following?
   (a) Taxonomy (b) Nomenclature
   (c) Biodiversity (d) Taxon

7. Given below are two statements.
   Statement I The M-phase starts with karyokinesis and usually ends with cytokinesis.
   Statement II In animal cells, during the S-phase, both DNA replication and the centriole duplication begins in the nucleus.
   In the light of the above statements, choose the correct answer from the options given below.
   (a) Statement I is incorrect, but statement II is correct
   (b) Both statement I and statement II are correct
   (c) Both statement I and statement II are incorrect
   (d) Statement I is correct, but statement II is incorrect

8. Consider the following statements.

I. A bud is present in the axils of petioles in simple leaves as well as in the axils of leaflet in compound leaves.

II. Pinnately compound leaves are present in neem.

III. Parallel venation is the characteristic of most monocotyledonous plants.

IV. Leaf is a lateral outgrowth of stem developed endogeneously at the node.

V. The presence of nodes and internodes are the morphological features of stem and leaves.

Choose the correct set of statements from the options given below.

(a) I, II and III (b) III, IV and V
(c) II and III (d) I, IV and V

9. Match List I with List II.

List I	List II
A. Albumins	1. Histamine, heparin
B. Erythrocytes	2. Osmotic balance
C. Basophils	3. Associated with allergy
D. Eosinophils	4. Most abundant cells in blood

Choose the correct answer from the options given below.

(a) A-3, B-1, C-4, D-2
(b) A-2, B-4, C-1, D-3
(c) A-3, B-2, C-4, D-1
(d) A-2, B-4, C-3, D-1

10. Given below are two statements.

Statement I Various chemical reactions occur in cytoplasm to keep the cell in the 'living state'.

Statement II Plant cells contain non-membrane bound organelle called centrosome.

In the light of the above statements, choose one correct answer from the options given below.

(a) Statement I is incorrect, but statement II is correct
(b) Both statement I and statement II are correct
(c) Both statement I and statement II are incorrect
(d) Statement I is correct, but statement II is incorrect

11. The hypothalamic hormones that reach the pituitary gland through a portal circulatory system and regulate the functions of the anterior pituitary are

(a) GnRH and growth hormone
(b) Somatostatin and adrenocorticotropic hormone
(c) Oxytocin and ADH
(d) GnRH and somatostatins

12. Which of the following structure is known to help attach the bacteria to rocks in streams and also to the host tissues?

(a) Pili (b) Capsule
(c) Fimbriae (d) Flagellum

13. Match List I with List II.

List I	List II
A. *Sycon*	1. External skeleton of shell usually present.
B. *Ctenoplana*	2. Worm-like with proboscis, collar and trunk.
C. *Saccoglossus*	3. Comb plates for locomotion.
D. *Dentalium*	4. Body with pores and canals in walls.

Choose the correct answer from the options given below.

(a) A-4, B-3, C-2, D-1 (b) A-3, B-1, C-2, D-4
(c) A-4, B-3, C-1, D-2 (d) A-2, B-1, C-4, D-3

14. Identify the part of the algal photosynthetic organ.

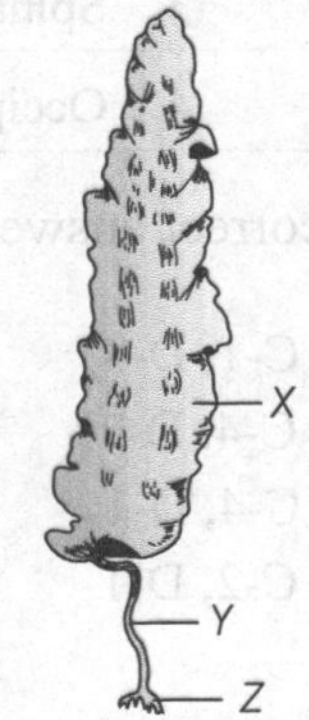

(a) *X* and *Y* (b) Only *Y*
(c) Only *X* (d) *X* and *Z*

15. During which of the following stage, the axonal membrane is comparatively more permeable to potassium ions (K^+) and nearly impermeable to sodium ions (Na^+)?

(a) Action potential
(b) Resting potential
(c) Repolarisation
(d) Depolarisation

16. Match List I with List II.

List I	List II
A. Proton gradient	1. PEP
B. Light reaction	2. Calvin cycle
C. Dark reaction	3. Synthesis of hydrogen and oxygen
D. C_4 plants	4. ATP synthesis in PS-II

Choose the correct answer from the options given below.

(a) A-4, B-2, C-1, D-3
(b) A-4, B-3, C-2, D-1
(c) A-3, B-4, C-2, D-1
(d) A-2, B-3, C-1, D-4

17. Match List I with List II.

List I	List II
A. Ribs	1. Acromion process
B. Neural canal	2. Thin flat bone connected dorsally to the vertebral column.
C. Atlas	3. Spinal cord
D. Scapula	4. Occipital condyles

Choose the correct answer from the options given below.

(a) A-2, B-3, C-1, D-4
(b) A-2, B-1, C-4, D-3
(c) A-2, B-3, C-4, D-1
(d) A-3, B-4, C-2, D-1

18. Identify the part of the seed from the given figure through which seeds are attached to the fruit.

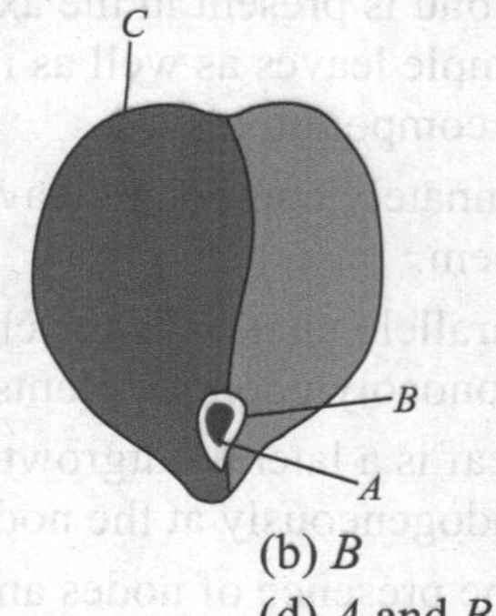

(a) *A*
(b) *B*
(c) *C*
(d) *A* and *B*

19. Which of the following are regarded as characteristic features of family–Leguminosae?

I. Mostly trees
II. Parallel venation
III. Bisexual, zygomorphic
IV. Diadelphous
V. Imbricate aestivation

Choose the correct option.

(a) I, II and III
(b) III, IV and V
(c) I, III and V
(d) III and V

20. Match List I with List II.

List I	List II
A. Leaves	1. Leguminous plants
B. Node	2. Middle prominent vein
C. Pulvinus	3. Shoot apical meristems
D. Midrib	4. The region of the stem where leaves are born

Choose the correct answer from the options below.

(a) A-2, B-3, C-4 D-1
(b) A-3, B-4, C-1, D-2
(c) A-3, B-1, C-2, D-4
(d) A-1, B-4, C-3, D-2

21. The end product formed in a light-dependent cyclic process in C_3 plant, which needs O_2 and doesn't produce energy, rather consumes energy is
(a) glucose
(b) phosphoenol pyruvate
(c) ribulose bisphosphate
(d) phosphoglycolate

22. All the elements present in a sample of earth's crust are also present in a sample of living tissue. Which of the following elements are present in earth's crust in abundance compared to that of living tissue?
(a) Na, N and Ca (b) C, H and O
(c) Si, Ca and Na (d) H, C and S

23. What divides the luminal and extra luminal compartments?
(a) mitochondria
(b) endoplasmic reticulum
(c) cytoskeleton
(d) ribosomes

24. Given below are two statements; one is labelled as Assertion (A) and the other is labelled as Reason (R).
Assertion (A) When glomerular filtration rate reduces, ANF is released by atrial wall.
Reason (R) ANF is a vasodilator.
In the light of the above statements, choose the correct answer from the options given below.
(a) A is false, but R is true
(b) Both A and R are true and R is the correct explanation of A
(c) Both A and R are true, but R is not the correct explanation of A
(d) A is true, but R is false

25. In floral diagram, the position of the mother axis with respect to the flower is represented by
(a) a line drawn above the symbols of the floral parts
(b) a dot on the top of the floral diagram
(c) enclosing the figure within bracket
(d) a line drawn below the symbols of the floral parts

26. Match List I with List II.

List I	List II
A. Melatonin	1. Sleep-wake cycle
B. Acromegaly	2. Reduces loss of water
C. ADH	3. Pars distalis
D. ACTH	4. Severe disfigurement

Choose the correct answer from the options given below.
(a) A-2, B-1, C-4, D-3
(b) A-2, B-1, C-3, D-4
(c) A-2, B-3, C-4, D-1
(d) A-1, B-4, C-2, D-3

27. Match List I with List II.

List I	List II
A. Prophase	1. Appearance of Golgi complex
B. Telophase	2. Division of centromere
C. Anaphase	3. Replication of DNA
D. S-phase	4. Disintegration of nuclear membrane

Choose the correct answer from the options given below.
(a) A-3, B-1, C-4, D-2
(b) A-1, B-3, C-4, D-2
(c) A-1, B-2, C-4, D-3
(d) A-4, B-1, C-2, D-3

28. Following are the types of leucocytes in the blood.
I. eosinophils
II. monocytes
III. neutrophils
IV. basophils
V. lymphocytes
Choose the correct sequence of leucocytes according to their abundance in increasing order.
(a) I-II-III-IV-V (b) IV-I-II-V-III
(c) II-III-IV-I-V (d) V-III-IV-II-I

29. Match List I with List II.

List I	List II
A. Sarcomere	1. Light band
B. Actin filament	2. Contractile unit
C. Red muscle	3. Anaerobic respiration
D. White muscle	4. Myoglobin

Choose the correct answer from the options given below.
(a) A-3, B-4, C-2, D-1
(b) A-2, B-1, C-4, D-3
(c) A-2, B-3, C-4, D-1
(d) A-2, B-4, C-1, D-3

30. Which of the following is a characteristic of the organism that forms red tides?
(a) Forms diatomaceous earth
(b) Lives as predators
(c) Chief producer of ocean
(d) Kills marine animals such as fishes by toxin

31. Given below are two statements, one is labelled as Assertion (A) and the other is labelled as Reason (R).

Assertion (A) Potato and brinjal belong to the genus-*Solanum.*

Reason (R) They are two different species.

In the light of the above statements, choose the correct answer from the options given below.
(a) A is false, but R is true
(b) Both A and R are true and R is the correct explanation of A
(c) Both A and R are true, but R is not the correct explanation of A
(d) A is true, but R is false

32. Given below are two statements.

Statement I The cerebellum wraps around a structure called thalamus, which is a major coordinating centre for sensory and motor signaling.

Statement II The ventral portion of the midbrain consists mainly of four round swellings (lobes) called corpora quadrigemina.

In the light of the above statements, choose the correct answer from the options given below.
(a) Statement I is incorrect, but statement II is correct
(b) Both statement I and statement II are correct
(c) Both statement I and statement II are incorrect
(d) Statement I is correct, but statement II is incorrect

33. Match List I with List II.

List I	List II
A. Polysome	1. Purple and green photosynthetic bacteria.
B. Gas vacuoles	2. Extensions of plasma membrane.
C. Mesosome	3. Loose glycocalyx sheath.
D. Slime layer	4. Several ribosomes may attach to a single *m*RNA.

Choose the correct answer from the options given below.
(a) A-3, B-4, C-1, D-2
(b) A-4, B-1, C-3, D-2
(c) A-4, B-1, C-2, D-3
(d) A-2, B-3, C-4, D-1

34. In which of the following category of taxonomic hierarchy, the similar characters are least in number (among the four options)?
(a) Order
(b) Genus
(c) Family
(d) Class

35. Match List I with List II.

List I	List II
A. *Puccinia*	1. Absorb soluble organic matter from dead substrates.
B. Saprophytes	2. Aplanospores (non-motile).
C. Phycomycetes	3. Rusts and smuts
D. Basidiomycetes	4. Wheat rust

Choose the correct answer from the options given below.
(a) A-4, B-1, C-3, D-3
(b) A-2, B-4, C-3, D-1
(c) A-3, B-4, C-2, D-1
(d) A-1, B-3, C-4, D-2

36. Match List I with List II with respect to the reproductive system of frog.

List I	List II
A. Testes	1. Mesorchium
B. Vasa efferentia	2. Urinogenital tract
C. Cloaca	3. Bidder's canal
D. Ovaries	4. 2500-3000 eggs

Choose the correct answer from the options given below.
(a) A-1, B-3, C-2, D-4
(b) A-2, B-1, C-4, D-3
(c) A-1, B-3, C-4, D-2
(d) A-1, B-2, C-3, D-4

37. The sudden elongation of the internode just before flowering in rosette plants is called
(a) differentiation (b) bolting
(c) dedifferentiation (d) vernalisation

38. Which of the following statement is incorrect?
(a) Mitosis usually results in the production of diploid daughter cells with identical genetic complement.
(b) Cell growth results in equalising the ratio between the nucleus and the cytoplasm.
(c) The cells of the upper layer of the epidermis, cells of the lining of the gut and blood cells are being constantly replaced.
(d) Mitotic divisions in the meristematic tissues result in a continuous growth of plants throughout their life.

39. Given below are two statements.
Statement I The petioles of Australian *Acacia* modify in order to synthesis food for the plant.
Statement II The long, thin, flexible stipules allow leaf blades to flutter in wind.
In the light of the above statements, choose one correct answer from the options given below.
(a) Statement I is incorrect, but statement II is correct
(b) Both statement I and statement II are correct
(c) Both statement I and statement II are incorrect
(d) Statement I is correct, but statement II is incorrect

40. In mustard and *Argemone*,
(a) the placenta forms a ridge along the ventral suture of the ovary and the ovules are borne on this ridge forming two rows.
(b) ovary is one-chambered, but it becomes two-chambered due to the formation of the false septum.
(c) ovary is two-chambered, but it becomes four-chambered due to the formation of the false septum.
(d) the placenta develops at the base of ovary and a single ovule is attached to it.

41. During a cardiac cycle, each ventricle pumps out approximately 80 mL of blood and heart rate is 70 beats per minute. What would be cardiac output of the person?
(a) 5600 mL (b) 4800 mL
(c) 6000 mL (d) 4200 mL

42. Identify the set of correct statements.
I. In cell membrane, the major lipids are phospholipids that are arranged in a bilayer.
II. The lipids are arranged within the membrane with the polar head towards the outer sides and the hydrophobic tails towards the inner part.
III. In plasma membrane, the polar tail of saturated hydrocarbon is protected from the aqueous environment.
IV. Phospholipid membranes also contain cholesterol.
V. In human beings, the membrane of the erythrocyte has approximately 40 per cent protein and 52 per cent lipids.

Choose the correct answer from the options given below.
(a) I, II and V (b) II, III and V
(c) I, II and IV (d) II, III and IV

43. Match List I with List II.

List I	List II
A. Nephridia	1. Rotifers
B. Antennal glands	2. Annelids
C. Malpighian tubules	3. Crustaceans
D. Protonephridia	4. Insects

Choose the correct answer from the options given below.
(a) A-2, B-3, C-4, D-1
(b) A-1, B-3, C-4, D-2
(c) A-3, B-4, C-2, D-1
(d) A-1, B-2, C-4, D-3

44. Algal cell wall is made up of
(a) cellulose, hemicellulose, pectins and proteins
(b) cellulose, galactans, mannans and calcium carbonate
(c) cellulose, galactans and mannans
(d) cellulose and peptidoglycan

45. Match List I with List II.

List I	List II
A. Carbaminohaemoglobin	1. Less H^+ ion concentration
B. Pneumotaxic center	2. High temperature
C. Chemosensitive areas	3. Pons
D. Oxyhaemoglobin	4. Respiratory rhythm centre

Choose the correct answer from the options given below.
(a) A-3, B-4, C-2, D-1
(b) A-1, B-3, C-4, D-2
(c) A-2, B-3, C-4, D-1
(d) A-2, B-1, C-3, D-4

46. In which of the following labelled part, the collecting ducts converge and open?

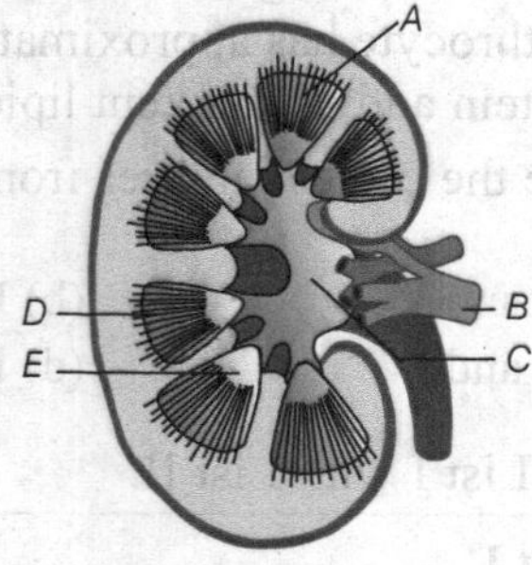

(a) *A* (b) *B*
(c) *E* (d) *C*

47. Match List I with List II.

List I	List II
A. Passive transport	1. Energy dependent transport.
B. Osmosis	2. Fluid mosaic model.
C. Active transport	3. Movement of water.
D. Singer and Nicolson	4. Without any requirement of energy.

Choose the correct answer from the options given below.
(a) A-2, B-3, C-1, D-4
(b) A-3, B-2, C-1, D-4
(c) A-4, B-3, C-1, D-2
(d) A-1, B-3, C-4, D-2

48. The role-played by luteinizing hormones in males and females, respectively is
(a) secretion of androgens from Leydig cells and ovulation
(b) secretion of testosterone from Sertoli cells and ovulation
(c) spermatogenesis and oogenesis
(d) secretion of testosterone and follicular growth

49. Match List I with List II.

List I	List II
A. Scutellum	1. Castor seed
B. Endosperm	2. Coconut
C. Fibrous mesocarp	3. Lily flowers
D. Epiphyllous	4. Cotyledon of monocots

Choose the correct answer from the options given below.
(a) A-4, B-2, C-1, D-3
(b) A-3, B-4, C-1, D-2
(c) A-4, B-3, C-1, D-2
(d) A-4, B-1, C-2, D-3

50. Read the following statements carefully.

I. In *Salpa*, notochord is replaced by bony vertebral column.

II. In *Pristis*, air bladder is present which regulates buoyancy.

III. Amphibians are oviparous and have indirect development.

IV. In snakes and lizards, tympanum represents the ear.

V. In birds, forelimbs are modified into wings.

Choose the correct set of statements from the options given below.

(a) III, IV and V
(b) I and III
(c) I, II and III
(d) II, IV and V

51. Match List I with List II.

List I	List II
A. Association areas	1. Interconnect different regions of the brain.
B. Limbic system	2. Memory and communication.
C. Pons	3. Regulation of sexual behavior.
D. Brain stem	4. The brain and spinal cord.

Choose the correct answer from the options given below.

(a) A-3, B-2, C-4, D-1
(b) A-2, B-3, C-1, D-4
(c) A-2, B-4, C-3, D-1
(d) A-1, B-3, C-4, D-2

52. In which of the following ways, metaphase-I differs from metaphase-II?

(a) Sister chromatids are separated.
(b) Homologous chromosomes line at the equatorial plate.
(c) Spindle fibres are attached to the kinetochores.
(d) Nucleolus and nuclear membrane disappear.

53. Match List I with List II.

List I	List II
A. RQ of carbohydrate	1. 0.7
B. RQ of lipid	2. 0.9
C. RQ of protein	3. 4.0
D. RQ of organic acid	4. 1.0

Choose the correct answer from the options given below.

(a) A-4, B-1, C-2, D-3
(b) A-2, B-1, C-3, D-4
(c) A-2, B-4, C-1, D-3
(d) A-2, B-4, C-3, D-1

54. Which of the following enzymes catalyse condensation of two molecules to form a new molecule?

(a) Ligases
(b) Lyases
(c) Isomerases
(d) Transferases

55. Match List I with List II.

List I	List II
A. PCT	1. Sodium-potassium balance in blood.
B. Henle's loop	2. Role in the maintenance of high osmolarity of medullary interstitial fluid.
C. DCT	3. Reabsorption of large amount of water to produce urine.
D. Collecting duct	4. Simple cuboidal brush border epithelium.

Choose the correct answer from the options given below.

(a) A-2, B-3, C-4, D-1
(b) A-4, B-2, C-1, D-3
(c) A-3, B-4, C-2, D-1
(d) A-2, B-1, C-4, D-3

56. The central portion of dicot stem is occupied by
(a) sclerenchymatous cells with large intercellular space
(b) sclerenchymatous cells without intercellular space
(c) parenchymatous cells with large intercellular space
(d) parenchymatous cells without intercellular space

57. Match List I with List II.

List I	List II
A. Multipolar neurons	1. Myelinated nerve fibres
B. Nodes of Ranvier	2. Cerebral cortex
C. Visceral nervous system	3. Gaps between two adjacent myelin sheaths
D. Schwann cells	4. Peripheral nervous system

Choose the correct answer from the options given below.
(a) A-1, B-3, C-4, D-2
(b) A-3, B-2, C-5, D-1
(c) A-2, B-3, C-4, D-1
(d) A-1, B-2, C-4, D-3

58. These are regarded as characteristic features of mitochondria
I. diameter of 1.0-4.1 μm
II. single circular DNA
III. 80S ribosomes
IV. divide by fission
V. cristae towards the matrix
Choose the correct features of mitochondria from the options given below.
(a) II, III, and IV
(b) I, IV and V
(c) II, III and V
(d) II, IV and V

59. Given below are two statements.
Statement I P-wave represents the electrical excitation of the atria, which leads to the contraction of one of the atria.
Statement II The end of the T-wave marks the end of diastole.
In the light of the above statements, choose the correct answer from the options given below.
(a) Statement I is incorrect, but statement II is correct
(b) Both statement I and statement II are correct
(c) Both statement I and statement II are incorrect
(d) Statement I is correct, but statement II is incorrect

60. In adult women, irregular menstrual cycle can be due to
(a) hyperthyroidism
(b) hypothyroidism
(c) hypoparathyroidism
(d) hyperparathyroidism

61. Match List I wtih List II.

List I	List II
A. Zeatin	1. Closure of stomata
B. Ethylene	2. Cytokinin-like activities
C. ABA	3. Dicotyledonous weeds
D. 2, 4-D	4. Enhances the respiration

Choose the correct answer from the options given below.
(a) A-2, B-4, C-3, D-1
(b) A-2, B-3, C-1, D-4
(c) A-3, B-4, C-1, D-2
(d) A-2, B-4, C-1, D-3

62. Given below are two statements.
Statement I Phloem fibres are generally absent in the primary phloem, but are found in the secondary phloem.
Statement II Phloem fibres are much elongated, branched and have needle-like apices.
In the light of the above statements, choose the correct answer from the options given below.
(a) Statement I is incorrect, but statement II is correct
(b) Both statement I and statement II are correct
(c) Both statement I and statement II are incorrect
(d) Statement I is correct, but statement II is incorrect

63. A person with trace amounts of glucose and significant amounts of ketone bodies in the urine, should consume

(a) low iodine based diet
(b) high salt based diet
(c) low carbohydrate based diet
(d) a proper balanced diet

64. Match List I with List II.

List I	List II
A. Lecithin	1. Nucleoside
B. Adenosine	2. Heteropolysaccharide
C. Peptidoglycan	3. Non-equilibrium steady state
D. Living state	4. Component of plasma membrane

Choose the correct answer from the options given below.

(a) A-4, B-1, C-2, D-3
(b) A-1, B-2, C-4, D-3
(c) A-3, B-1, C-4, D-2
(d) A-1, B-4, C-2, D-3

65. Match List I with List II.

List I	List II
A. Hexokinase	1. Cytochrome *c*
B. ETS	2. Phosphorylation of glucose
C. ATP + H_2O	3. Inner mitochondrial membrane
D. Electron acceptor	4. Oxidative phosphorylation

Choose the correct answer from the options given below.

(a) A-4, B-3, C-1, D-2
(b) A-2, B-3, C-1, D-4
(c) A-2, B-3, C-4, D-1
(d) A-2, B-4, C-1, D-3

66. Which of the following are the features of dorsiventral leaves?

I. More stomata on abaxial epidermis
II. Parallelly arranged spongy parenchyma
III. Vascular bundles equal in size
IV. Bulliform cells
V. Bundle sheath

Choose the correct answer from the options given below.

(a) IV and V
(b) I, II and III
(c) II, III and IV
(d) I and V

67. Match List I with List II.

List I	List II
A. *Ichthyophis*	1. Garden lizard
B. *Calotes*	2. Limbless amphibia
C. *Aptenodytes*	3. Blue whale
D. *Balaenoptera*	4. Penguin

Choose the correct answer from the options given below.

(a) A-2, B-4, C-3, D-1
(b) A-2, B-4, C-1, D-3
(c) A-1, B-2, C-4, D-3
(d) A-2, B-1, C-4, D-3

68. Archaebacteria survive in the gut of several ruminant animals such as cows and buffaloes because

(a) they are most primitive
(b) they have 70S ribosome
(c) their DNA is circular
(d) they have a different cell wall structure

69. Given below are two statements.

Statement I The function of our visceral organs is controlled by sympathetic and somatic neural system.

Statement II The axons transmit nerve impulses towards the cell body to a synapse or to a neuro-muscular junction.

In the light of the above statements, choose the correct answer from the options given below.

(a) Statement I is incorrect, but statement II is correct
(b) Both statement I and statement II are correct
(c) Both statement I and statement II are incorrect
(d) Statement I is correct, but statement II is incorrect

70. Match List I with List II.

List I	List II
A. Cambium	1. Phloem located on the outer side of xylem
B. Conjoint vascular bundles	2. Unicellular root hair
C. Epiblema	3. Conjunctive tissue
D. Parenchymatous cells	4 Secondary xylem and secondary phloem

Choose the correct answer from the options given below.

(a) A-4, B-1, C-2, D-3
(b) A-3, B-2, C-1, D-4
(c) A-2, B-1, C-4, D-3
(d) A-1, B-3, C-4, D-2

71. Consider the following statements.

I. In the five kingdom classification of Whittaker, there is a mention of lichens.
II. Virus means venom or poisonous fluid.
III. MW Beijerinck (1892) recognised certain microbes as causal organism of the mosaic disease of tobacco.
IV. Dmitri Ivanowsky (1898) demonstrated that the extract of the infected plants of tobacco could cause infection in healthy plants.
V. WM Stanley (1935) showed that viruses could be crystallised and crystals consist largely of proteins.

Choose the correct set of statements from the options given below.

(a) I, III, and IV
(b) II, IV and V
(c) II, III and V
(d) II and V

72. In which of the following pairs of plants, the male and the female gametophytes do not have an independent free-living existence?

(a) *Cycas* and *Pinus*
(b) *Selaginella* and *Lycopodium*
(c) *Funaria* and *Polytrichum*
(d) *Laminaria* and *Sargassum*

73. Match List I with List II.

List I	List II
A. Thymosins	1. Adrenaline and noradrenaline
B. Adrenal medulla	2. Regulate balance of electrolytes and water
C. Insulin	3. Cell-mediated immunity
D. Mineralo-corticoids	4 Hepatocytes and adipocytes

Choose the correct answer from the options given below

(a) A-3, B-1, C-4, D-2
(b) A-2, B-4, C-1, D-3
(c) A-3, B-2, C-1, D-4
(d) A-4, B-1, C-2, D-3

74. Which of the following pair of flowers can be divided into two equal radial halves in any radial plane passing through the center?

(a) Pea and gulmoher
(b) Bean and *Cassia*
(c) Mustard and *Datura*
(d) *Canna* and chilli

75. Which of the following describes the given graph correctly?

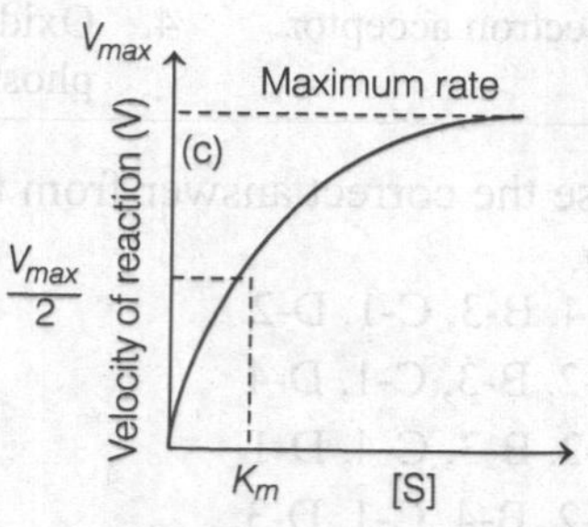

(a) K_m is the concentration of substrate at which rate of reaction is half of the maximum value.
(b) The rate of enzymatic activity is independent of substrate concentration.

(c) K_m is the substrate concentration without enzyme.
(d) Reactions between enzymes and substrates are non-specific.

76. Given below are two statements.

Statement I The root hairs are multicellular elongations of the epidermal cells and help to absorb water and minerals from the soil.

Statement II The trichomes in the shoot system are usually multicellular.

In the light of the above statements, choose the correct answer from the options given below.
(a) Statement I is incorrect, but statement II is correct
(b) Both statement I and statement II are correct
(c) Both statement I and statement II are incorrect
(d) Statement I is correct, but statement II is incorrect

77. Match List I with List II.

List I	List II
A. Uremia	1. Process of removal of urea from blood
B. Hemodialysis	2. Kidney failure
C. Renal calculi	3. Inflammation of glomeruli
D. Glomerulonephritis	4. Insoluble mass of crystallised salts

Choose the correct answer from the options given below.
(a) A-2, B-1, C-4, D-3
(b) A-1, B-4, C-2, D-3
(c) A-3, B-2, C-4, D-1
(d) A-1, B-2, C-4, D-3

78. Identify the set of correct statements.

I. Joseph Priestley, in 1770, performed a series of experiments that revealed the essential role of air in the growth of *Cladophora*.
II. Jan Ingenhousz showed that in the presence of sunlight, it is only the green part of the plants that could release oxygen.
III. TW Engelmann experimented on green plants.
IV. Cornelius van Niel demonstrated in purple and green bacteria that during photosynthesis, hydrogen released from a suitable oxidisable compound reduces carbon dioxide to carbohydrates.
V. Part of the spectrum used in photosynthesis has a wavelength between 300-760 nm.

Choose the correct answer from the options given below.
(a) II, III, and IV
(b) II and IV
(c) II, IV and V
(d) I, II, III and V

79. Identify the biomolecule given in the figure.

$$H_2N-\underset{\underset{CH_2OH}{|}}{\overset{\overset{COOH}{|}}{C}}-H$$

(a) Acidic amino acid
(b) Basic amino acid
(c) Neutral amino acid
(d) Aromatic amino acid

80. Given below are two statements; one is labelled as Assertion (A) and the other is labelled as Reason (R).

Assertion (A) Spraying juvenile conifers with GAs hastens the maturity period.

Reason (R) Gibberellins are the PGRs that can delay senescence.

In the light of the above statements, choose the correct answer from the options given below.
(a) A is false, but R is true
(b) Both A and R are true and R is the correct explanation of A
(c) Both A and R are true, but R is not the correct explanation of A
(d) A is true, but R is false

81. Following are intermediates formed during glycolysis.

I. Glyceraldehyde-3-phosphate
II. Fructose-1, 6-bisphosphate
III. 1, 3-bisphosphoglyceric acid
IV. 2-phosphoglycerate
V. Glucose-6-phosphate

Choose the option showing correct sequence of their formation.
(a) I, III, IV, V, II
(b) V, III, II, I, IV
(c) V, II, I, III, IV
(d) I, II, V, IV, III

82. Regarding events of M-phase, select the correct sequential step.

I. Chromosomes are moved to spindle equator and get aligned along metaphase plate through spindle fibres to both the poles.

II. Nucleolus, Golgi complex and ER reform.

III. Chromatids move to opposite poles.

IV. Centrosome which had undergone duplication during interphase, begins to move towards opposite poles of the cell.

Choose the correct answer from the options given below.

(a) IV, III, II, I
(b) I, IV, III, II
(c) I, IV, II, III
(d) IV, I, III, II

83. To avoid erythroblastosis foetalis, anti-Rh antibodies are administered immediately

(a) to the Rh^+ve mother after the delivery of the first child
(b) to the Rh-ve mother after the delivery of the first child
(c) to the Rh-ve mother after the delivery of the second child
(d) to the Rh-ve mother before the delivery of the first child

84. Study the following flow chart and fill up the blank by selecting the correct option.

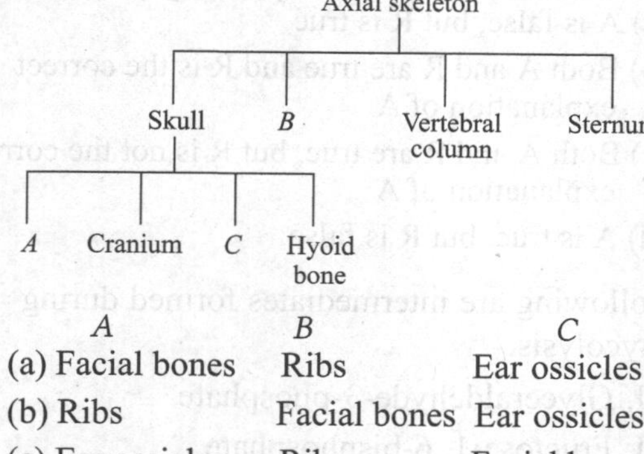

	A	B	C
(a)	Facial bones	Ribs	Ear ossicles
(b)	Ribs	Facial bones	Ear ossicles
(c)	Ear ossicles	Ribs	Facial bones
(d)	Limb bones	Ribs	Girdle bones

85. Consider the following statements.

I. The steroid responsible for balance of water and electrolytes in our body is aldosterone.

II. Thymosin is responsible for raising the blood calcium level.

III. In the mechanism of action of a protein hormone, one of the most common secondary messenger is cyclic AMP.

IV. Leydig cells produce a group of hormones called gonadotropins.

V. Corpus luteum secretes pregnancy supporting hormone.

Choose the correct answer from the options given below.

(a) I, III and V
(b) III and V
(c) I, II and IV
(d) III, IV and V

86. Match List I with List II.

List I	List II
A. Ball and socket joint	1. Between atlas and axis.
B. Hinge joint	2. Between humerus and pectoral girdle.
C. Saddle joint	3. Knee joint.
D. Pivot joint	4 Between carpal and metacarpal of thumb.

Choose the correct answer from the options given below.

(a) A-2, B-4, C-3, D-1
(b) A-2, B-3, C-4, D-1
(c) A-4, B-3, C-2, D-1
(d) A-3, B-4, C-1, D-2

87. Which of the following labelled parts in the given diagram binds with calcium as it has more affinity for the same?

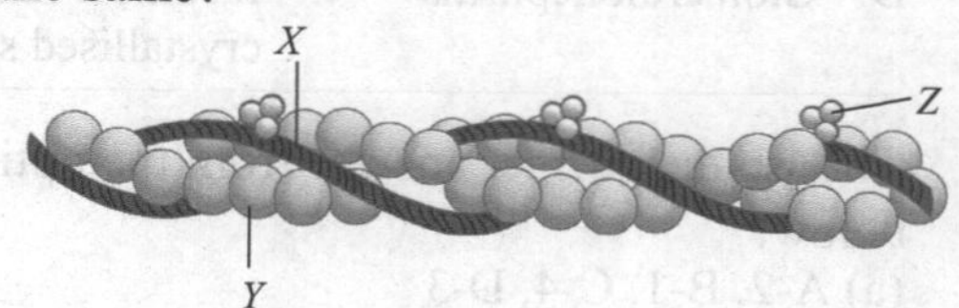

(a) X
(b) Y
(c) Z
(d) X and Z

88. Match List I with List II.

List I	List II
A. Myasthenia gravis	1. Accumulation of uric acid crystals.
B. Muscular dystrophy	2. Wild contractions in muscle.
C. Gout	3. Weakening and paralysis of skeletal muscle.
D. Tetany	4. Progressive degeneration of skeletal muscle.

Choose the correct answer from the options given below.

(a) A-3, B-4, C-1, D-2 (b) A-3, B-1, C-4, D-2
(c) A-2, B-3, C-1, D-4 (d) A-1, B-2, C-3, D-4

89. Consider the following statements.

I. Platyhelminthes have organ system level of organisation.
II. Poriferans have tissue level of organisation.
III. Adult echinoderms have organ level of organisation.
IV. Arthropods have organ system level of organisation.

Choose the correct statement from the options given below.

(a) II only (b) I only
(c) IV only (d) III only

90. Match List I with List II.

	List I		List II
A.	Leptotene	1.	Separation of homologous chromosomes.
B.	Zygotene	2.	Compaction of chromosomes.
C.	Pachytene	3.	Synaptonemal complex.
D.	Diakinesis	4.	Recombination nodules.

Choose the correct answer from the given below.

(a) A-1, B-4, C-3, D-2
(b) A-3, B-1, C-4, D-2
(c) A-2, B-3, C-4, D-1
(d) A-3, B-1, C-2, D-4

Response Index

01	ⓐ ⓑ ⓒ ⓓ	26	ⓐ ⓑ ⓒ ⓓ	51	ⓐ ⓑ ⓒ ⓓ	76	ⓐ ⓑ ⓒ ⓓ
02	ⓐ ⓑ ⓒ ⓓ	27	ⓐ ⓑ ⓒ ⓓ	52	ⓐ ⓑ ⓒ ⓓ	77	ⓐ ⓑ ⓒ ⓓ
03	ⓐ ⓑ ⓒ ⓓ	28	ⓐ ⓑ ⓒ ⓓ	53	ⓐ ⓑ ⓒ ⓓ	78	ⓐ ⓑ ⓒ ⓓ
04	ⓐ ⓑ ⓒ ⓓ	29	ⓐ ⓑ ⓒ ⓓ	54	ⓐ ⓑ ⓒ ⓓ	79	ⓐ ⓑ ⓒ ⓓ
05	ⓐ ⓑ ⓒ ⓓ	30	ⓐ ⓑ ⓒ ⓓ	55	ⓐ ⓑ ⓒ ⓓ	80	ⓐ ⓑ ⓒ ⓓ
06	ⓐ ⓑ ⓒ ⓓ	31	ⓐ ⓑ ⓒ ⓓ	56	ⓐ ⓑ ⓒ ⓓ	81	ⓐ ⓑ ⓒ ⓓ
07	ⓐ ⓑ ⓒ ⓓ	32	ⓐ ⓑ ⓒ ⓓ	57	ⓐ ⓑ ⓒ ⓓ	82	ⓐ ⓑ ⓒ ⓓ
08	ⓐ ⓑ ⓒ ⓓ	33	ⓐ ⓑ ⓒ ⓓ	58	ⓐ ⓑ ⓒ ⓓ	83	ⓐ ⓑ ⓒ ⓓ
09	ⓐ ⓑ ⓒ ⓓ	34	ⓐ ⓑ ⓒ ⓓ	59	ⓐ ⓑ ⓒ ⓓ	84	ⓐ ⓑ ⓒ ⓓ
10	ⓐ ⓑ ⓒ ⓓ	35	ⓐ ⓑ ⓒ ⓓ	60	ⓐ ⓑ ⓒ ⓓ	85	ⓐ ⓑ ⓒ ⓓ
11	ⓐ ⓑ ⓒ ⓓ	36	ⓐ ⓑ ⓒ ⓓ	61	ⓐ ⓑ ⓒ ⓓ	86	ⓐ ⓑ ⓒ ⓓ
12	ⓐ ⓑ ⓒ ⓓ	37	ⓐ ⓑ ⓒ ⓓ	62	ⓐ ⓑ ⓒ ⓓ	87	ⓐ ⓑ ⓒ ⓓ
13	ⓐ ⓑ ⓒ ⓓ	38	ⓐ ⓑ ⓒ ⓓ	63	ⓐ ⓑ ⓒ ⓓ	88	ⓐ ⓑ ⓒ ⓓ
14	ⓐ ⓑ ⓒ ⓓ	39	ⓐ ⓑ ⓒ ⓓ	64	ⓐ ⓑ ⓒ ⓓ	89	ⓐ ⓑ ⓒ ⓓ
15	ⓐ ⓑ ⓒ ⓓ	40	ⓐ ⓑ ⓒ ⓓ	65	ⓐ ⓑ ⓒ ⓓ	90	ⓐ ⓑ ⓒ ⓓ
16	ⓐ ⓑ ⓒ ⓓ	41	ⓐ ⓑ ⓒ ⓓ	66	ⓐ ⓑ ⓒ ⓓ		
17	ⓐ ⓑ ⓒ ⓓ	42	ⓐ ⓑ ⓒ ⓓ	67	ⓐ ⓑ ⓒ ⓓ		
18	ⓐ ⓑ ⓒ ⓓ	43	ⓐ ⓑ ⓒ ⓓ	68	ⓐ ⓑ ⓒ ⓓ		
19	ⓐ ⓑ ⓒ ⓓ	44	ⓐ ⓑ ⓒ ⓓ	69	ⓐ ⓑ ⓒ ⓓ		
20	ⓐ ⓑ ⓒ ⓓ	45	ⓐ ⓑ ⓒ ⓓ	70	ⓐ ⓑ ⓒ ⓓ		
21	ⓐ ⓑ ⓒ ⓓ	46	ⓐ ⓑ ⓒ ⓓ	71	ⓐ ⓑ ⓒ ⓓ		
22	ⓐ ⓑ ⓒ ⓓ	47	ⓐ ⓑ ⓒ ⓓ	72	ⓐ ⓑ ⓒ ⓓ		
23	ⓐ ⓑ ⓒ ⓓ	48	ⓐ ⓑ ⓒ ⓓ	73	ⓐ ⓑ ⓒ ⓓ		
24	ⓐ ⓑ ⓒ ⓓ	49	ⓐ ⓑ ⓒ ⓓ	74	ⓐ ⓑ ⓒ ⓓ		
25	ⓐ ⓑ ⓒ ⓓ	50	ⓐ ⓑ ⓒ ⓓ	75	ⓐ ⓑ ⓒ ⓓ		

Performance Scanner

> 90% Excellent !	You have mastered the NEET syllabus (11th). The concepts of this entire syllabus are at your fingertips. Maintain this momentum.
76-90% Very Good !	You have a good command over the entire NEET syllabus (11th). Revise it again after a few days to enhance your performance.
60-75% Good !	You have a wide scope to learn for the entire NEET syllabus (11th). Revise it again.
<60% Not Satisfactory!	You have a long way ahead of you to master the NEET syllabus (11th). Revise it thoroughly.

Space for Rough Work

Test Booklet No. 3947325

Test Booklet Code NSS4

MEDACE

NEET (UG)

SELF ASSESSMENT KIT

NEET Stepping Stones 4

(Complete Syllabus Test 11th)

Name of the Candidate (In Capitals)

____

____

____

Candidate's Signature ____________

Invigilator's Signature ____________

Facsimile signature stamp of center superintendent____________

Important Instructions

- The test is of **1 hours 30 minutes** duration and the Test Booklet contains **90** multiple-choice questions (four options with a single correct answer) from biology.
- Candidates are advised to read all questions before they start attempting the question paper.
- Each questions carries 4 marks. For each correct response, the candidate will get 4 marks. For each incorrect response, one marks will be deducted from the total scores.
- In the event of candidate marking more than one option one mark will be deducted. The maximum marks are 180.
- Use **Blue/Black Point Pen only** for writing particular on this page/ marking response on Answer Sheet.

Do not open this booklet until you start attempting the test

Biology

1. What is identical between euglenoids and higher plants?
(a) Cell structure
(b) Mode of reproduction
(c) Type of pigments
(d) Habitat

2. Which statement about the respiratory system is incorrect?
(a) The epiglottis covers the glottis during swallowing to prevent food from entering the larynx
(b) The trachea divides into right and left primary bronchi at the level of the 5th thoracic vertebra
(c) Alveoli are irregular-walled structures that participate in the exchange of gases between blood and atmospheric air
(d) Each bronchus and bronchiole is supported by complete cartilaginous rings

3. Which one of the following can explain the characteristic features of meiosis?
I. It involves two sequential cycles of nuclear and cell division but only a single cycle of DNA replication.
II. Meiosis-I is initiated after the parental chromosomes have replicated to produce identical sister chromatids during the G_2 phase.
III. Meiosis ensures the production of the diploid phase in the life cycle of sexually reproducing organisms.
IV. Meiosis involves the pairing of homologous chromosomes and recombination between sister chromatids.
V. Four haploid cells are formed at the end of meiosis-II.

Choose the correct answer from the options given below.
(a) I and V
(b) II and III
(c) I and IV
(d) III and V

4. Identify the correct description about the given figure.

(a) The centromeres remain intact whereas the chromatids separate.
(b) Chromatids move to the equatorial plate.
(c) The centromeres remain directed towards the poles.
(d) The arms of the chromosome lead the movement towards the poles.

5. Given below are two statements.
Statement I Alveoli are the primary sites of exchange of gases in the human respiratory system.
Statement II Oxygen (O_2) and carbon dioxide (CO_2) are exchanged in alveoli by active transport.
In the light of the above statements, choose the correct answer from the options given below
(a) Statement I is incorrect, but statement II is correct
(b) Both statement I and statement II are correct
(c) Both statement I and statement II are incorrect
(d) Statement I is correct, but statement II is incorrect

6. Match List I with List II.

	List I		List II
A.	Ribosomes	1.	Found in photosynthetic bacteria for buoyancy control
B.	Polysomes	2.	Reserve materials stored in the cytoplasm
C.	Inclusion bodies	3.	Site of protein synthesis
D.	Gas vacuoles	4.	Chains of ribosomes attached to *m*RNA

Choose the correct answer from the options given below.

	A	B	C	D		A	B	C	D
(a)	1	3	2	4	(b)	2	1	3	4
(c)	4	3	1	2	(d)	3	4	2	1

7. Given below are two statements.

Statement I Cyanobacteria are photosynthetic autotrophs with chlorophyll-*a* as photosynthetic pigment.

Statement II Cyanobacteria cannot fix atmospheric nitrogen.

In the light of the above statements, choose the correct answer from the options given below.

(a) Statement I is incorrect, but statement II is correct
(b) Both statement I and statement II are correct
(c) Both statement I and statement II are incorrect
(d) Statement I is correct, but statement II is incorrect

8. In the given figure, which component has connection to a flat bone with the help of hyaline cartilage?

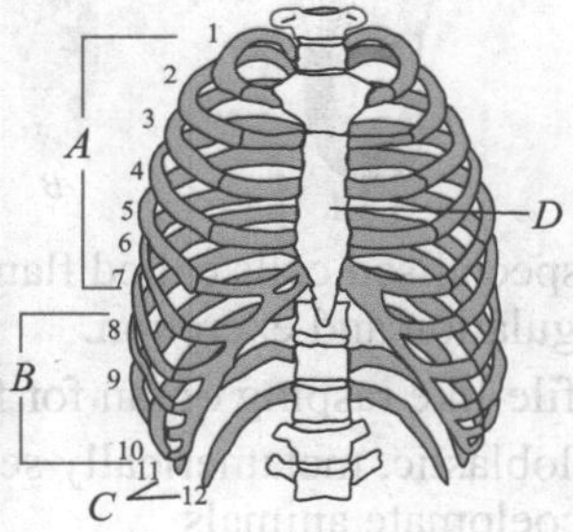

(a) *A* (b) *B*
(c) *C* (d) *D*

9. Which of the following statements are true about the reproduction of bacteria?

I. Bacteria mainly reproduce by fission.
II. Under unfavourable conditions, bacteria produce spores.
III. Bacteria reproduce sexually by meiosis.
IV. Bacteria sometimes reproduce by a primitive type of DNA transfer.
V. Bacteria reproduce only asexually.

Choose the correct answer from the options given below.

(a) I, II and IV (b) II, III and V
(c) I, IV and V (d) II, III and IV

10. Given below are two statements; one is labelled as Assertion (A) and the other is labelled as Reason (R).

Assertion (A) The autonomic neural system is classified into sympathetic and parasympathetic neural systems.

Reason (R) The autonomic neural system transmits impulses from the CNS to the involuntary organs and smooth muscles of the body.

In the light of the above statements, choose the correct answer from the options given below.

(a) A is false, but R is true
(b) Both A and R are true and R is the correct explanation of A
(c) Both A and R are true, but R is not the correct explanation of A
(d) A is true, but R is false

11. Given below are two statements.

Statement I Centrioles in a centrosomes lie perpendicular to each other.

Statement II Almost all plant cells lack centrioles which are present in animal cells.

In the light of the above statements, choose the correct answer from the options given below.

(a) Statement I is incorrect, but statement II is correct
(b) Both statement I and statement II are correct
(c) Both statement I and statement II are incorrect
(d) Statement I is correct, but statement II is incorrect

12. Given below are two statements.

Statement I Photosynthesis occurs only in the green leaves of plants.

Statement II The light reactions of photosynthesis take place in the grana, while the dark reactions occur in the stroma of the chloroplasts.

In the light of the above statements, choose the correct answer from the options given below.

(a) Statement I is incorrect, but statement II is correct
(b) Both statement I and statement II are correct
(c) Both statement I and statement II are incorrect
(d) Statement I is correct, but statement II is incorrect

13. Arrange the steps of respiration in humans in the correct sequence.

A. Breathing or pulmonary ventilation

B. Diffusion of gases (O_2 and CO_2) across alveolar membrane

C. Transport of gases by the blood

D. Diffusion of O_2 and CO_2 between blood and tissues

E. Utilisation of O_2 by the cells for catabolic reactions and release of CO_2

Choose the correct sequence from the options given below.

(a) A-B-C-D-E

(b) B-A-C-D-E

(c) A-B-D-C-E

(d) A-B-C-E-D

14. Given below are two statements.

Statement I The chemical nature of hormones is always proteinaceous.

Statement II Hormones are non-nutrient chemicals that act as intercellular messengers and are produced in trace amounts.

In the light of the above statements, choose the correct answer from the options given below.

(a) Statement I is incorrect, but statement II is correct.

(b) Both statement I and statement II are correct.

(c) Both statement I and statement II are incorrect.

(d) Statement I is correct, but statement II is incorrect.

15. Which features best describes integral membrane proteins?

(A) Partially buried, hydrophobic

(B) Surface-bound, hydrophilic

(C) Fully buried, hydrophilic

(D) Partially exposed, hydrophobic

Choose the correct answer from the options given below.

(a) A and B (b) B and C

(c) A and D (d) C and D

16. Given below are two statements; one is labelled as Assertion (A) and the other is labelled as Reason (R).

Assertion (A) Bacterial cell envelope consists of glycocalyx, cell wall and plasma membrane.

Reason (R) Glycocalyx occurs as a loose sheath in the slime layer.

In the light of the above statements, choose the correct answer from the options given below

(a) A is false, but R is true

(b) Both A and R are true and R is the correct explanation of A

(c) Both A and R are true, but R is not the correct explanation of A

(d) A is true, but R is false

17. Identify the correct description about *A* and *B* below.

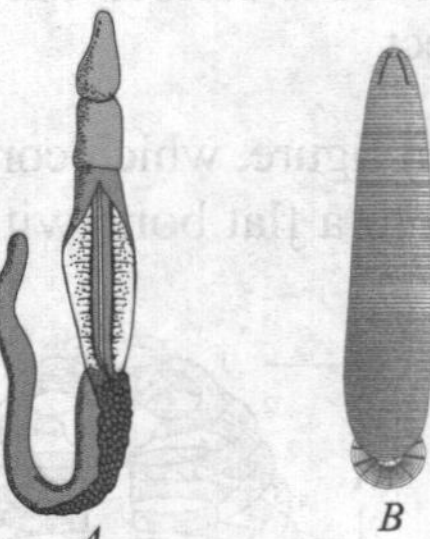

(a) *B* have specialised cells called flame cells for osmoregulation and excretion.

(b) *A* have file-like rasping organ for feeding

(c) *B* is triploblastic, metamerically segmented and pseudocoelomate animals

(d) *A* have organ-system level of organisation

18. Which of the following is likely to be affected if mesosomes are absent or removed from a prokaryotic cell?

A. Protein synthesis

B. DNA to RNA formation

C. Cellular respiration

D. Cell reproduction

Choose the correct answer from the options given below.

(a) C only (b) D only

(c) B only (d) A only

19. Match List I with List II.

	List I		List II
A.	Dendrites	1.	Gaps between adjacent myelin sheaths
B.	Synaptic knob	2.	Contains synaptic vesicles with neurotransmitters
C.	Nodes of Ranvier	3.	Transmit impulses towards the cell body
D.	Schwann cells	4.	Form the myelin sheath around myelinated axons

Choose the correct answer from the options given below.
(a) A-2, B-1, C-3, D-4
(b) A-3, B-2, C-1, D-4
(c) A-4, B-1, C-2, D-3
(d) A-1, B-3, C-4, D-2

20. Given below are two statements; one is labelled as Assertion (A) and the other is labelled as Reason (R).
Assertion (A) Cellulose is a homopolymer made up of glucose.
Reason (R) Starch forms helical secondary structures that can hold I_2 molecules, giving a blue colour.
In the light of the above statements, choose the correct answer from the options given below
(a) A is false, but R is true
(b) Both A and R are correct and R is the correct explanation of A
(c) Both A and R are correct, but R is not the true explanation of A
(d) A is true, but R is false

21. Which of the following statement about cell membrane is true?
(a) The cell membrane is mainly composed of carbohydrates and proteins.
(b) Phospholipids in the membrane are arranged with their polar heads facing inward.
(c) Cholesterol is absent in cell membranes.
(d) Integral proteins are embedded partially or completely within the membrane.

22. Read the following statements and choose the set of correct statements regarding the phylogenetic classification system.
I. It is based on evolutionary relationships between various organisms.
II. It assumes that organisms belonging to the same taxa have a common ancestor.
III. Numerical Taxonomy which considers chromosome number and structure, is used to resolve classification confusion.
IV. It uses information from many sources to resolve classification difficulties.
V. Fossil evidence is always available to support phylogenetic classification.

Choose the correct answer from the options given below.
(a) I, II and IV
(b) I, III and V
(c) II, IV and V
(d) I, II, III and IV

23. Match List I with List II.

	List I		List II
A.	*Volvox*	1.	Used as a food supplement by space travellers
B.	*Ulothrix*	2.	Produces hydrocolloids called algin
C.	*Fucus*	3.	Filamentous form with isogamous reproduction
D.	*Chlorella*	4.	Oogamous reproduction

Choose the correct answer from the options given below.

	A	B	C	D
(a)	4	3	2	1
(b)	2	1	3	4
(c)	3	2	4	1
(d)	1	4	2	3

24. What distinguishes the genus-*Felis* from the genus-*Panthera* within the family-Felidae?
(a) *Felis* includes lions and tigers, while *Panthera* includes cats
(b) *Felis* includes cats, while *Panthera* includes lions, tigers, and leopards
(c) *Felis* includes dogs, while *Panthera* includes cats
(d) *Felis* includes dogs, while *Panthera* includes tigers.

25. Match List I with List II.

	List I	List II
A.	Joseph Priestley	1. Oxygen evolution is highest in blue and red-light regions
B.	Jan Ingenhousz	2. Sunlight is essential for the purification of air by plants
C.	Julius von Sachs	3. Plants restore the air component that breathing animals and burning candles remove
D.	TW Engelmann	4. Glucose is produced and stored as starch in green parts of plants.

Choose the correct answer from the options given below.

	A	B	C	D		A	B	C	D
(a)	4	3	2	1	(b)	2	1	3	4
(c)	3	2	4	1	(d)	1	4	2	3

26. Match List I with List II.

	List I	List II
A.	Pineal Gland	1. Maintains circadian rhythm
B.	Thyroid Gland	2. Immunity
C.	Parathyroid Gland	3. Decrease blood Ca^{2+}
D.	Thymus	4. Increase blood Ca^{2+}

Choose the correct answer from the options given below.

(a) A-2, B-1, C-3, D-4
(b) A-3, B-2, C-1, D-4
(c) A-4, B-1, C-2, D-3
(d) A-1, B-3, C-4, D-2

27. Given below are two statements.

Statement I The process of naming living organisms using a two-component system is called binomial nomenclature.

Statement II The specific epithet in a scientific name starts with a capital letter.

In the light of the above statements, choose the correct answer from the options given below.

(a) Statement I is incorrect, but statement II is correct
(b) Both statement I and statement II are correct
(c) Both statement I and statement II are incorrect
(d) Statement I is correct, but statement II is incorrect

28. Given below are two statements.

Statement I In gymnosperms, the seeds that develop post-fertilisation are not covered, i.e., they are naked.

Statement II In gymnosperms, the male and female gametophytes have an independent free-living existence.

In the light of the above statements, choose the correct answer from the options given below.

(a) Statement I is incorrect, but statement II is correct
(b) Both statement I and statement II are correct
(c) Both statement I and statement II are incorrect
(d) Statement I is correct, but statement II is incorrect

29. Choose the incorrect statement out of the following options.

(a) Each actin filament is made of two filamentous (F) actins helically wound to each other.
(b) Tropomyosin is distributed at regular intervals on the actin filaments.
(c) Troponin masks the active binding sites for myosin on the actin filaments in the resting state.
(d) Each myosin filament is made of polymerised monomeric proteins called meromyosins.

30. Identify the correct description w.r.t. *Agaricus*.

(a) The vegetative reproduction commonly occurs by fragmentation.
(b) The mycelium is aseptate and coenocytic.
(c) Asexual reproduction takes place by zoospores (motile) or by aplanospores (non-motile).
(d) Sexual spores are called ascospores which are produced endogenously in sac-like asci.

31. In which of the following plants, roots originate from parts of the plant other than, the radicle?
(a) Mustard
(b) Wheat
(c) Grass and *Monstera*
(d) Mustard and wheat

32. Which of the following organelles would be densely packed in the hepatocytes of an alcoholic person?
(a) Golgi apparatus
(b) Lysosomes
(c) Smooth Endoplasmic Reticulum (SER)
(d) Rough Endoplasmic Reticulum (RER)

33. If mitosis fails to occur in the human body, which of the following consequences is most likely to happen?
(a) The production of gametes will be impaired
(b) The cells of the upper layer of the epidermis will be constantly replaced
(c) Growth of multicellular organisms will remain unaffected
(d) Cell repair and replacement in tissues will be disrupted

34. Match List I with List II.

List I	List II
A. Cnidaria	1. Bioluminescence, *Pleurobrachia*
B. Ctenophora	2. Radial symmetry, *Physalia*
C. Platyhelminthes	3. Flatworms, *Planaria*
D. Aschelminthes	4. Pseudocoelomate, *Ascaris*

Choose the correct answer from the options given below.
(a) A-2, B-1, C-3, D-4
(b) A-3, B-2, C-1, D-4
(c) A-4, B-1, C-2, D-3
(d) A-1, B-3, C-4, D-2

35. Arrange the following animals in the correct sequence based on their classification from the most primitive to the most advanced.
A. *Exocoetus* (Flying fish)
B. *Corvus* (Crow)
C. *Chelone* (Turtle)
D. *Bufo* (Toad)
Choose the correct sequence.
(a) C-D-A-B (b) A-C-D-B
(c) C-A-D-B (d) A-D-C-B

36. Which statement accurately describes the relationship between chlorophyll-*a* absorption spectrum and photosynthesis action spectrum?
(a) They show complete overlapping across all wavelengths
(b) They overlap primarily in the blue and red regions of the spectrum
(c) There is no overlaping between the absorption spectrum and the action spectrum
(d) Chlorophyll *a* absorbs light only in the green wavelengths, which coincides with peak photosynthesis

37. During the cell cycle, the characteristic of metaphase is
(a) chromosomes condense and become invisible under the microscope
(b) spindle fibres attach to the kinetochores of chromosomes
(c) chromosomes move to opposite poles of the cell
(d) chromosomes are dispersed throughout the cytoplasm

38. Given below are two statements; one is labelled as Assertion (A) and the other is labelled as Reason (R).

Assertion (A) Bracteate and ebracteate are terms used to describe flowers based on the presence or absence of bracts.

Reason (R) Bracteate flowers have reduced leaf-like structures at the base of the pedicel, while ebracteate flowers lack these structures.

In the light of the above statements, choose the correct answer from the options given below
(a) A is false, but R is true
(b) Both A and R are true and R is the correct explanation of A.
(c) Both A and R are true, but R is not the correct explanation of A.
(d) A is true, but R is false

39. Epithelial tissues are characterised by
(a) being non-cellular and devoid of intercellular substances.
(b) having multiple free surfaces facing body fluids or the outside environment.
(c) being structurally and functionally isolated from neighbouring cells.
(d) possessing one free surface facing either a body fluid or the outside environment, with cells connected at junctions.

40. In photosynthesis, which process directly requires products that are generated by light reactions?
(a) Functioning of grana (b) RNA synthesis
(c) Carbon fixation (d) Glucose absorption

41. Match List I with List II.

List I	List II
A. Leaf base	1. Expanded into a sheath in monocotyledons
B. Petiole	2. Attaches the leaf blade to the stem
C. Pulvinus	3. Swollen structure at the base of the leaf petiole
D. Stipules	4. Small lateral leaf-like structures at the base of the leaf

Choose the correct answer from the options given below.
(a) A - 2, B - 1, C - 4, D - 3
(b) A - 4, B - 3, C - 1, D - 2
(c) A - 3, B - 2, C - 1, D - 4
(d) A - 1, B - 2, C - 3, D - 4

42. Identify the features that characterise the gastrovascular cavity of *Meandrina*.
(a) Single opening, extracellular and intracellular digestion
(b) Multiple openings, collar cells for digestion
(c) Highly compartmentalised, direct absorption through body wall
(d) Enclosed cavity with separate openings, Intercellular digestion

43. Read the following statements regarding floral morphology.
I. The stamen consists of a filament and an anther with bilobed chambers called pollen-sacs.
II. Epipetalous stamens are attached to the perianth as in the flowers of lily.
III. Monocarpellary gynoecium is observed in pea flowers.
IV. Syncarpous ovaries have fused carpels, as seen in mustard and tomato.
V. Parietal placentation occurs when ovules develop on the inner wall of the ovary.

Choose the correct set of statements from the options given below.
(a) I, II, III and IV
(b) I, II, III and V
(c) I, III, IV and V
(d) II, III, IV and V

44. There are two hormones *A* and *B*. *A* controls the metabolism of carbohydrates, proteins and fat along with maintenance of water and electrolyte balance. *B* induces ovulation of fully mature follicles and maintains the corpus luteum in female. Identify *A* and *B*.
(a) *A*-PTH, *B*-LH
(b) *A*-Thyroxine, *B*-LH
(c) *A*-Thymosin, *B*-FSH
(d) *A*-Adrenal, *B*-FSH

45. Identify the correct features for the cells shown in figures A and B.

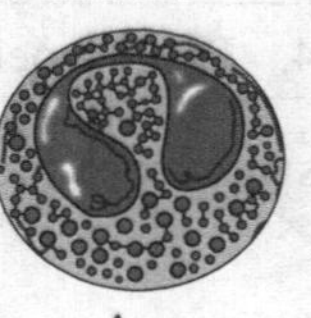
A

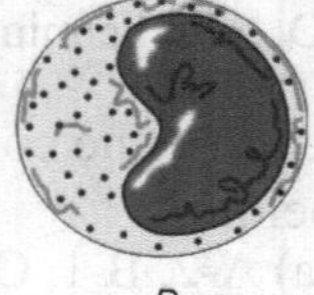
B

(a) *A*- resist infections, *B*- destroy foreign organisms
(b) *A*- most abundant cells, *B*- least abundant cells
(c) *A*- agranulocyte, *B*- granulocyte
(d) *A*- secretes histamine, *B*- secretes serotonin

46. Which of the following statement correctly describes the racemose type of inflorescence?

(a) The main axis terminates in a flower, restricting further growth.

(b) Flowers are borne laterally in an acropetal succession along the main axis.

(c) Floral appendages replace leaves at successive nodes.

(d) Flowers are arranged basipetally on the floral axis.

47. Given below are two statements.

Statement I Roundworms have a complete alimentary canal with a muscular pharynx.

Statement II Roundworms exhibit radial symmetry and lack a defined body cavity.

In the light of the above statements, choose the correct answer from the options given below

(a) Statement I is incorrect, but statement II is correct

(b) Both statement I and statement II are correct

(c) Both statement I and statement II are incorrect

(d) Statement I is correct, but statement II is incorrect

48. Following are the statements about primary and secondary metabolites.

I. Primary metabolites include compounds like amino acids and sugars.

II. Secondary metabolites include compounds like alkaloids and flavonoids.

III. Primary metabolites have identifiable functions in normal physiological processes.

IV. Secondary metabolites are not useful to human welfare.

V. Secondary metabolites can have ecological importance.

Choose the correct set of statements from the options given below.

(a) I, II, III and V

(b) I, III and IV

(c) II, III, IV and V

(d) I, II and III

49. Read the following statements about the members of echinodermata.

I. An endoskeleton consisting of calcareous ossicles is present.

II. Adults exhibit radial symmetry, while larvae are bilaterally symmetrical.

III. Water vascular system is present for locomotion, food capture and respiration.

IV. Circulatory system is of closed type with a heart for pumping blood.

V. Excretory system consists of specialised organs known as Malpighian tubules.

Choose the correct set of statements from the options given below.

(a) I, II and III

(b) I, III and IV

(c) I, II, III and IV

(d) I, III and V

50. Which of the following statements about connective tissues are correct?

I. Connective tissues are named for their function of linking and supporting other tissues and organs in the body.

II. All connective tissues, including blood, secrete fibres of structural proteins called collagen or elastin.

III. Connective tissues range from soft connective tissues to specialised types such as cartilage, bone, adipose, and blood.

IV. The fibres in connective tissues provide strength, elasticity, and flexibility.

V. Connective tissues are classified into loose connective tissue, dense connective tissue, and specialised connective tissue.

Choose the correct answer from the options given below.

(a) I, III, IV and V

(b) I, II, III and IV

(c) II, III, IV and V

(d) I, II, III and V

51. A structure emerging as a unicellular or multicellular outgrowth and is secretory in nature in certain plants, forms a part of
(a) cortex
(b) epidermis
(c) pericycle
(d) pith

52. Identify the plants in which the gynoecium is situated in the centre and other parts of the flower are located on the rim of the thalamus almost at the same level.
(a) Sunflower, guava, cucumber
(b) Plum, rose, peach
(c) Mustard, China rose, brinjal
(d) Sunflower, peach, China rose

53. Given below are two statements; one is labelled as Assertion (A) and the other is labelled as Reason (R).

Assertion (A) The brain of a frog is divided into forebrain, midbrain and hindbrain.

Reason (R) The hindbrain of a frog consists of the cerebellum and medulla oblongata.

In the light of the above statements, choose the correct answer from the options given below
(a) A is false, but R is true
(b) Both A and R are true and R is the correct explanation of A
(c) Both A and R are true, but R is not the correct explanation of A
(d) A is true, but R is false

54. Match List I with List II.

List I	List II
A. Palmitic acid	1. 20 carbon atoms
B. Arachidonic acid	2. Trihydroxy propane
C. Glycerol	3. 16 carbon atoms
D. Lecithin	4. Found in cell membrane

Choose the correct answer from the options given below.
(a) A-2, B-1, C-3, D-4
(b) A-3, B-1, C-2, D-4
(c) A-4, B-1, C-2, D-3
(d) A-1, B-3, C-4 D-2

55. Regarding the stages of prophase-I in meiosis, select the correct sequential order.

I. Chromosomes are visible under the light microscope.
II. Chromosomes start pairing and form a synaptonemal complex.
III. Synaptonemal complex dissolves and chiasmata form.
IV. Recombination nodules appear and crossing over occurs.
V. Chromosomes fully condense and meiotic spindle assembles.

Choose the correct answer from the options given below.
(a) II, I, III, IV, V
(b) V, IV, III, II, I
(c) I, II, III, IV, V
(d) I, II, IV, III, V

56. Which statement about ethylene's role in plant physiology is not correct?
(a) Promotes senescence and abscission of leaves and flowers
(b) Enhances the root growth and formation of root hairs
(c) Initiates germination in peanut seeds and sprouting of potato tubers
(d) Inhibits fruit ripening and reduces the respiratory rate

57. Identify the correct statement about erythrocytes (red blood cells).
(a) These are nucleated when mature in most mammals.
(b) They have a biconcave shape due to the presence of haemoglobin.
(c) They are devoid of respiratory pigment.
(d) Erythrocytes are produced in the spleen.

58. Which statement accurately describes the difference between vascular bundles in dicotyledonous and monocotyledonous plants?
(a) Dicotyledonous vascular bundles contain cambium and can produce secondary tissues, whereas monocotyledonous vascular bundles lack cambium and cannot produce secondary tissues.
(b) Dicotyledonous vascular bundles lack cambium and are therefore unable to produce secondary tissues, whereas monocotyledonous vascular bundles contain cambium and can produce secondary tissues.

(c) Both dicotyledonous and monocotyledonous vascular bundles lack cambium and are therefore unable to produce secondary tissues.
(d) Dicotyledonous and monocotyledonous vascular bundles both contain cambium and can produce secondary tissues.

59. Match List I with List II.

List I		List II	
A.	Kidney	1.	Funnel-shaped space
B.	Renal pelvis	2.	Surrounded by tough outer capsule
C.	Nephron	3.	Functional unit
D.	Glomerulus	4.	Tuft of capillaries

Choose the correct answer from the options given below.
(a) A-2, B-1, C-3, D-4
(b) A-3, B-2, C-1, D-4
(c) A-4, B-1, C-2, D-3
(d) A-1, B-3, C-4 D-2

60. Given below are two statements; one is labelled as Assertion (A) and the other is labelled as Reason (R).

Assertion (A) Lipids are included in the acid insoluble fraction of cellular components.

Reason (R) Lipids, despite having molecular weights not exceeding 800 Da, form vesicles that are not water soluble, when cell membranes are disrupted.

In the light of the above statements, choose the correct answer from the options given below.
(a) A is false, but R is true
(b) Both A and R are true, and R is the correct explanation of A
(c) Both A and R are true, but R is not the correct explanation of A
(d) A is true, but R is false

61. Which of the following is true regarding the structure of the dicot root?

I. The outermost layer is the endodermis.
II. Cortex consists of thin-walled parenchyma cells.
III. Endodermal cells lack deposition of suberin.
IV. Pericycle is involved in the initiation of lateral roots and vascular cambium.
V. Pith is the largest component of the root stele.

Choose the correct answer from the options given below.
(a) I and II (b) II and IV
(c) III and V (d) I and IV

62. In a plant where sucrose cannot be converted into glucose and fructose, and glucose and fructose cannot be phosphorylated, which enzymes are likely to be absent or non-functioning?
(a) Sucrase, glucokinase
(b) Invertase, hexokinase
(c) Phosphoglucomutase, phosphofructokinase
(d) ATP synthase, pyruvate kinase

63. Regarding the classification of amino acids based on the nature of the R group, select the correct statements.

I. Glycine has a hydrogen as its R group.
II. Alanine has a methyl group as its R group.
III. Serine has a hydroxy methyl group as its R group.
IV. Lysine is an aromatic amino acid.
V. Glutamic acid is a basic amino acid.

Choose the correct answer from the options given below.
(a) I, II and IV (b) II, III and V
(c) I, III and V (d) I, II and III

64. Match List I with List II.

List I		List II	
A.	Malic Acid	1.	Initial CO_2 acceptor in mesophyll cells, forming oxaloacetic acid
B.	PEP Carboxylase	2.	4-carbon compound formed in mesophyll cells and transported to bundle sheath cells
C.	Phosphoenol pyruvate	3.	Enzyme that fixes CO_2 to phosphoenolpyruvate (PEP) in mesophyll cells
D.	RuBisCO	4.	Enzyme found in bundle sheath cells that catalyses the Calvin cycle

Choose the correct answer from the options given below.
(a) A-2, B-3, C-1, D-4 (b) A-1, B-2 C-4, D-4
(c) A-2, B-1, C-4, D-3 (d) A-4, B-3, C-2, D-1

65. Given below are two statements.

Statement I The DCT selectively reabsorbs Na^+ and water, it is involved in maintaining pH and sodium-potassium balance in blood.

Statement II The ascending limb of the Loop of Henle actively transports water, but is impermeable to electrolytes, leading to dilution of the filtrate.

In the light of the above statements, choose the correct answer from the options given below

(a) Statement I is incorrect, but statement II is correct
(b) Both Statement I and statement II are correct
(c) Both statement I and statement II are incorrect
(d) Statement I is correct, but statement II is incorrect

66. In the given figure, which of the following part serve as the site of enzyme catalysed reaction involved in starch synthesis in plants?

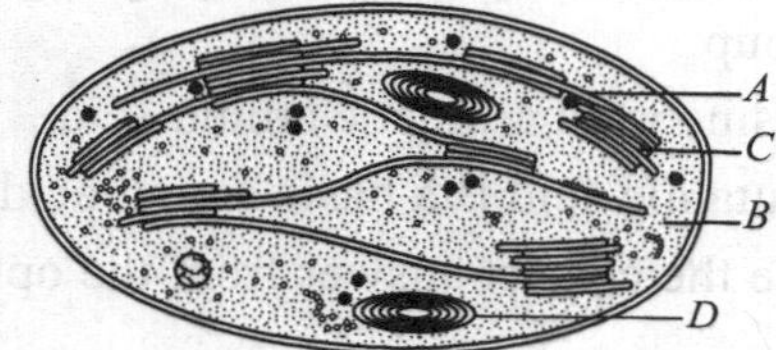

(a) *B* (b) *A*
(c) *D* (d) *C*

67. Read the following statements and choose the set of correct statements regarding blood groups and Rh grouping.

I. ABO grouping is based on the presence or absence of antigens A and B on red blood cells (RBCs).
II. Blood group AB individuals can donate blood to any other blood group.
III. Rh antigen is found on the surface of RBCs of approximately 80% of humans.
IV. Rh-ve mothers can form antibodies against Rh antigen if exposed to Rh+ve blood during pregnancy.
V. Erythroblastosis foetalis can occur due to Rh incompatibility between Rh-ve mothers and Rh+ve foetus.

Choose the correct answer from the options given below.

(a) I and II (b) I, III and IV
(c) I, III, IV and V (d) I, II, III, IV and V

68. Which statement regarding enzyme inhibition by competitive inhibitors is correct?

(a) Competitive inhibitors bind irreversibly to the enzyme's active site
(b) Competitive inhibitors increase enzyme activity by enhancing substrate binding
(c) Competitive inhibitors structurally resemble the enzyme's substrate
(d) Competitive inhibitors do not affect enzyme activity in any way

69. Given below are two statements.

Statement I The monocot stem has a sclerenchymatous hypodermis and a large number of scattered vascular bundles.

Statement II In the vascular bundles of monocot stem, phloem parenchyma is absent, and water-containing cavities are present.

In the light of the above statements, choose the correct answer from the options given below.

(a) Statement I is incorrect, but statement II is correct
(b) Both statement I and statement II are correct
(c) Both statement I and statement II are incorrect
(d) Statement I is correct, but statement II is incorrect

70. Given below are two statements; one is labelled as the Assertion (A) and the other is labelled as the Reason (R).

Assertion (A) Plant growth is unique due to the presence of meristems that allows for unlimited growth throughout their life.

Reason (R) Meristems contain cells capable of perpetual division, contributing to the continuous addition of new cells to the plant body.

In the light of the above statements, choose the correct answer from the options given below

(a) A is false, but R is true
(b) Both A and R are true and R is the correct explanation of A

(c) Both A and R are false, but R is not the correct explanation of A
(d) A is true, but R is false.

71. Which of the following enzymes convert a soluble plasma protein into an insoluble one that traps the RBCs in a clot?
(a) Thrombin (b) Thrombokinase
(c) Prothrombin (d) Fibrinogen

72. Consider the following statements regarding the digestive system of frogs.
I. The alimentary canal in frogs is relatively short due to their carnivorous diet.
II. The oesophagus opens into the stomach, which continues as the intestine, rectum and cloaca.
III. Pancreatic juice in frogs contains digestive enzymes that primarily digest fats.
IV. Villi and microvilli in the intestine of frogs aid in the absorption of digested food.

Choose the correct answer from the options given below.
(a) I and II
(b) II and III
(c) I, II and IV
(d) I, III and IV

73. Which statement accurately describes the relationship between Respiratory Quotient (RQ) values and respiratory substrates?
(a) RQ values can vary significantly depending on the organism's metabolic state and the type of substrate being oxidised.
(b) The RQ for proteins is consistently higher than carbohydrates due to their complex structure.
(c) Using a single respiratory substrate results in an RQ of exactly 1, regardless of the type of substrate.
(d) Fats, when used as a respiratory substrate, consistently yield an RQ of 2 due to their high energy content.

74. The phase of growth characterised by increased vacuolation, cell enlargement and deposition of new cell walls is
(a) meristematic (b) elongation
(c) maturation (d) differentiation

75. Two types of blood vessels are shown as *A* and *B* in the picture given below. Identify the correct matching pair of their name and characteristics in the human body.

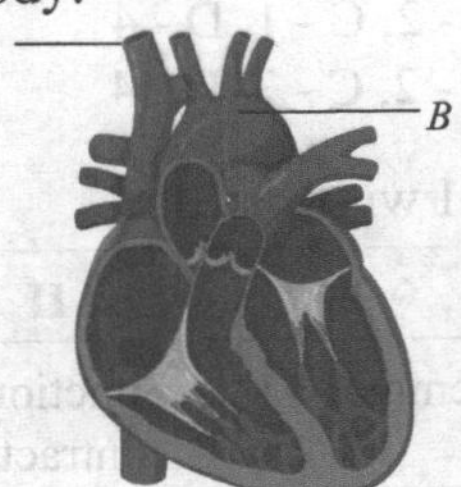

(a) *A*- empties blood into the right atrium; *B*- carries blood to tissues
(b) *A*- carries blood to tissues; *B*- emptied into the right atrium
(c) *A*-carries blood to lungs; *B*-carries blood to tissues
(d) *A*- carries blood to tissues; *B*-carries blood to lungs

76. Which excretory structure is primarily concerned with ionic and fluid volume regulation in Platyhelminthes and some annelids?
(a) Protonephridia
(b) Nephridia
(c) Malpighian tubules
(d) Antennal glands

77. Match List I with List II.

List I	List II
A. Epidermis	1. Contains chloroplasts and carries out photosynthesis, made up of elongated cells arranged vertically
B. Mesophyll	2. Tissue between upper and lower epidermis, includes spongy parenchyma with large air cavities
C. Palisade parenchyma	3. Covers both upper and lower leaf surfaces, bears more stomata on the lower surface
D. Vascular tissue	4. Includes vascular bundles visible in veins and midrib, surrounded by thick-walled bundle sheath cells

Choose the correct answer from the options given below.
(a) A - 2, B - 1, C - 4, D - 3
(b) A - 4, B - 3, C - 1, D - 2
(c) A - 3, B - 2, C - 1, D - 4
(d) A - 1, B - 2, C - 3, D - 4

78. Match List I withList II.

	List I		List II
A.	Sarcolemma	1.	Functional unit of muscle contraction
B.	Sarcomere	2.	Elastic fibre bisecting the I-band
C.	Z-line	3.	Storehouse of calcium ions in muscle fibres
D.	Sarcoplasmic reticulum	4.	Plasma membrane of a muscle fibre

Choose the correct answer from the options given below.
(a) A-2, B-1, C-3, D-4
(b) A-3, B-2, C-1, D-4
(c) A-4, B-1, C-2, D-3
(d) A-1, B-3, C-4, D-2

79. Given below are two statements; one is labelled as the Assertion (A) and the other is labelled as the Reason (R).

Assertion (A) Stomata are structures present in the epidermis of leaves that regulate transpiration and gaseous exchange.

Reason (R) Subsidiary cells are specialised cells within the stomatal aperture that regulate its opening and closing.

In the light of the above statements, choose the correct answer from the options given below.
(a) A is false, but R is true
(b) Both A and R are true and R is the correct explanation of A
(c) Both A and R are true, but R is not the correct explanation of A
(d) A is true, but R is false

80. Which part of the bacterial flagellum is actually involed in locomotion?
(a) Filament
(b) Hook
(c) Basal body
(d) Membranous extensions

81. Identify the correct description of the plant shown in the figure given below.

(a) Bryophyte- *Selaginella*
(b) Algae- *Porphyra*
(c) Pteridophyte- *Salvinia*
(d) Gymnosperm- *Equisetum*

82. Which of the following are characteristics of *Mycoplasma*?
A. Lack cell wall
B. Ability to survive without oxygen
C. Largest known living cells
D. Pathogenic to animals and plants
E. Mostly autotrophic

Choose the correct answer from the options given below.
(a) A, B and D
(b) A, B and C
(c) A, C and E
(d) B, D and E

83. Given below are two statements.

Statement I The remaining material after drying a living tissue sample is called wet weight.

Statement II The remaining material after fully burning a dried tissue sample is called ash.

In the light of the above statements, choose the correct answer from the options given below
(a) Statement I is incorrect, but statement II is correct
(b) Both statement I and statement II are correct
(c) Both statement I and statement II are incorrect
(d) Statement I is correct, but statement II is incorrect

84. Match List I with List II.

List I	List II
A. Valvate	1. Sepals or petals touch each other at the margin without overlapping.
B. Twisted	2. One margin of the appendage overlaps the next one in a spiral manner.
C. Imbricate	3. Sepals or petals overlap each other, not in any specific direction.
D. Vexillary	4. Largest petal overlaps the lateral petals, which in turn overlap the two smallest anterior petals

Choose the correct answer from the options given below.
(a) A-2, B-3, C-1, D-4
(b) A-1, B-2, C-3, D-4
(c) A-2, B-1, C-4, D-3
(d) A-4, B-3, C-2, D-1

85. The following diagram is showing an axon terminal and synapse. Identify the function of part labelled as *X*.

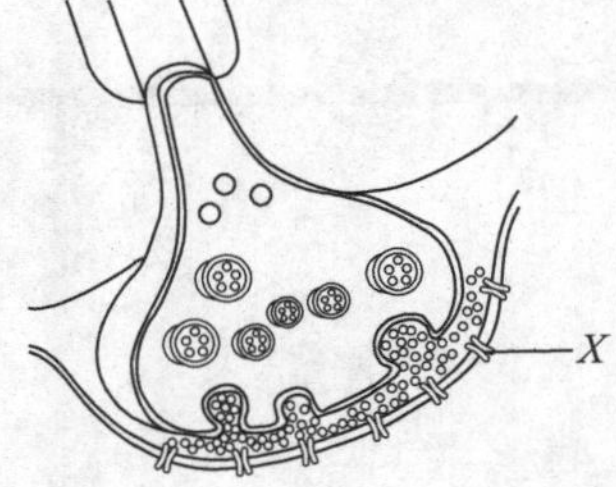

(a) Upon binding with a chemical, it helps to propagate the action potential in subsequent neuron
(b) It is responsible for release of chemicals called neurotransmitters that are involved in the transmission of impulses at these synapses
(c) It stimulates the movement of the synaptic vesicles towards the membrane where they fuse with the plasma membrane
(d) It helps in the development of inhibitory potential at the synapse

86. Given below are two statements.

Statement I In both lactic acid and alcohol fermentation, less than seven percent of the energy in glucose is released and not all of it is trapped as high-energy bonds of ATP.

Statement II Fermentation is not the default pathway of respiration in facultative anaerobes.

In the light of the above statements, choose the correct answer from the options given below.
(a) Statement I is incorrect, but statement II is correct
(b) Both statement I and statement II are correct
(c) Both statement I and statement II are incorrect
(d) Statement I is correct, but statement II is incorrect

87. Which of the following statement is incorrect?
(a) Proteins are homopolymers consisting of a single type of amino acid
(b) Collagen is the most abundant protein in the animal world
(c) Essential amino acids must be obtained through our diet
(d) Proteins can function as enzymes, hormones, and transporters

88. Which of the following are characteristics of skeletal muscles?
A. Involuntary control
B. Striated appearance
C. Exist in syncitium
D. Branched

Choose the correct answer from the options given below.
(a) A and D
(b) B and C
(c) C and D
(d) A and B

89. Which term best describes the tissue in a dicotyledonous stem that is characterised by semi-lunar patches of sclerenchyma above the phloem and radially placed parenchymatous cells between vascular bundles?

(a) Pericycle (b) Medullary rays
(c) Protoxylem (d) Pith

90. Choose the correct description about the structure labelled as *X* in the picture given below.

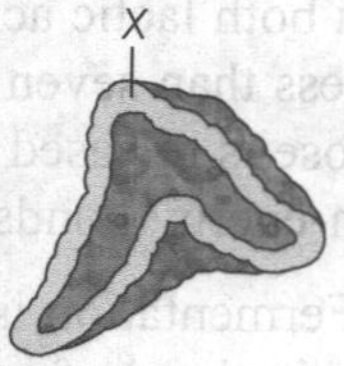

(a) Underproduction of hormones by *X* alters carbohydrate metabolism causing acute weakness and fatigue
(b) X secretes hormones called as catecholamines
(c) *X* secretes a peptide hormone that plays an important role in maintaining the normal blood glucose levels
(d) Peptide hormone secreted by *X* regulate the development, maturation and functions of the female accessory sex organs

■ Response Index

01 ⓐ ⓑ ⓒ ⓓ	26 ⓐ ⓑ ⓒ ⓓ	51 ⓐ ⓑ ⓒ ⓓ	76 ⓐ ⓑ ⓒ ⓓ
02 ⓐ ⓑ ⓒ ⓓ	27 ⓐ ⓑ ⓒ ⓓ	52 ⓐ ⓑ ⓒ ⓓ	77 ⓐ ⓑ ⓒ ⓓ
03 ⓐ ⓑ ⓒ ⓓ	28 ⓐ ⓑ ⓒ ⓓ	53 ⓐ ⓑ ⓒ ⓓ	78 ⓐ ⓑ ⓒ ⓓ
04 ⓐ ⓑ ⓒ ⓓ	29 ⓐ ⓑ ⓒ ⓓ	54 ⓐ ⓑ ⓒ ⓓ	79 ⓐ ⓑ ⓒ ⓓ
05 ⓐ ⓑ ⓒ ⓓ	30 ⓐ ⓑ ⓒ ⓓ	55 ⓐ ⓑ ⓒ ⓓ	80 ⓐ ⓑ ⓒ ⓓ
06 ⓐ ⓑ ⓒ ⓓ	31 ⓐ ⓑ ⓒ ⓓ	56 ⓐ ⓑ ⓒ ⓓ	81 ⓐ ⓑ ⓒ ⓓ
07 ⓐ ⓑ ⓒ ⓓ	32 ⓐ ⓑ ⓒ ⓓ	57 ⓐ ⓑ ⓒ ⓓ	82 ⓐ ⓑ ⓒ ⓓ
08 ⓐ ⓑ ⓒ ⓓ	33 ⓐ ⓑ ⓒ ⓓ	58 ⓐ ⓑ ⓒ ⓓ	83 ⓐ ⓑ ⓒ ⓓ
09 ⓐ ⓑ ⓒ ⓓ	34 ⓐ ⓑ ⓒ ⓓ	59 ⓐ ⓑ ⓒ ⓓ	84 ⓐ ⓑ ⓒ ⓓ
10 ⓐ ⓑ ⓒ ⓓ	35 ⓐ ⓑ ⓒ ⓓ	60 ⓐ ⓑ ⓒ ⓓ	85 ⓐ ⓑ ⓒ ⓓ
11 ⓐ ⓑ ⓒ ⓓ	36 ⓐ ⓑ ⓒ ⓓ	61 ⓐ ⓑ ⓒ ⓓ	86 ⓐ ⓑ ⓒ ⓓ
12 ⓐ ⓑ ⓒ ⓓ	37 ⓐ ⓑ ⓒ ⓓ	62 ⓐ ⓑ ⓒ ⓓ	87 ⓐ ⓑ ⓒ ⓓ
13 ⓐ ⓑ ⓒ ⓓ	38 ⓐ ⓑ ⓒ ⓓ	63 ⓐ ⓑ ⓒ ⓓ	88 ⓐ ⓑ ⓒ ⓓ
14 ⓐ ⓑ ⓒ ⓓ	39 ⓐ ⓑ ⓒ ⓓ	64 ⓐ ⓑ ⓒ ⓓ	89 ⓐ ⓑ ⓒ ⓓ
15 ⓐ ⓑ ⓒ ⓓ	40 ⓐ ⓑ ⓒ ⓓ	65 ⓐ ⓑ ⓒ ⓓ	90 ⓐ ⓑ ⓒ ⓓ
16 ⓐ ⓑ ⓒ ⓓ	41 ⓐ ⓑ ⓒ ⓓ	66 ⓐ ⓑ ⓒ ⓓ	
17 ⓐ ⓑ ⓒ ⓓ	42 ⓐ ⓑ ⓒ ⓓ	67 ⓐ ⓑ ⓒ ⓓ	
18 ⓐ ⓑ ⓒ ⓓ	43 ⓐ ⓑ ⓒ ⓓ	68 ⓐ ⓑ ⓒ ⓓ	
19 ⓐ ⓑ ⓒ ⓓ	44 ⓐ ⓑ ⓒ ⓓ	69 ⓐ ⓑ ⓒ ⓓ	
20 ⓐ ⓑ ⓒ ⓓ	45 ⓐ ⓑ ⓒ ⓓ	70 ⓐ ⓑ ⓒ ⓓ	
21 ⓐ ⓑ ⓒ ⓓ	46 ⓐ ⓑ ⓒ ⓓ	71 ⓐ ⓑ ⓒ ⓓ	
22 ⓐ ⓑ ⓒ ⓓ	47 ⓐ ⓑ ⓒ ⓓ	72 ⓐ ⓑ ⓒ ⓓ	
23 ⓐ ⓑ ⓒ ⓓ	48 ⓐ ⓑ ⓒ ⓓ	73 ⓐ ⓑ ⓒ ⓓ	
24 ⓐ ⓑ ⓒ ⓓ	49 ⓐ ⓑ ⓒ ⓓ	74 ⓐ ⓑ ⓒ ⓓ	
25 ⓐ ⓑ ⓒ ⓓ	50 ⓐ ⓑ ⓒ ⓓ	75 ⓐ ⓑ ⓒ ⓓ	

■ Performance Scanner

> 90% Excellent !	You have mastered the NEET syllabus (11th). The concepts of this entire syllabus are at your fingertips. Maintain this momentum.
76-90% Very Good !	You have a good command over the entire NEET syllabus (11th). Revise it again after a few days to enhance your performance.
60-75% Good !	You have a wide scope to learn for the entire NEET syllabus (11th). Revise it again.
<60% Not Satisfactory!	You have a long way ahead of you to master the NEET syllabus (11th). Revise it thoroughly.

Test Booklet No.	3947326

Test Booklet Code	NSS5

NEET Stepping Stones 5

(Complete Syllabus Test 11th)

Name of the Candidate (In Capitals)

____

____

____

Candidate's Signature ______________

Invigilator's Signature ______________

Facsimile signature stamp of center superintendent______________

Important Instructions

- The test is of **1 hours 30 minutes** duration and the Test Booklet contains **90** multiple-choice questions (four options with a single correct answer) from biology.
- Candidates are advised to read all questions before they start attempting the question paper.
- Each questions carries 4 marks. For each correct response, the candidate will get 4 marks. For each incorrect response, one marks will be deducted from the total scores.
- In the event of candidate marking more than one option one mark will be deducted. The maximum marks are 180.
- Use **Blue/Black Point Pen only** for writing particular on this page/ marking response on Answer Sheet.

Do not open this booklet until you start attempting the test

Biology

1. Stem tendrils are slender and spirally coiled structures that develop from axillary buds. These are found in

(a) cucumber, pumpkin, watermelon
(b) peas, *Bougainvillea*, tomatoes
(c) cucumber, cactus, grapevine
(d) *Citrus*, *Opuntia*, cucumber

2. Match List I with List II.

	List I		List II
A.	ETS	1.	Mitochondrial matrix
B.	Glycolysis	2.	Oxidative phosphorylation
C.	Alcoholic fermentation	3.	Oxidation of glucose into pyruvate
D.	TCA	4.	Microorganism

Choose the correct answer from the the options given below.

(a) A-2, B-3, C-1, D-4
(b) A-3, B-4, C-1, D-2
(c) A-3, B-1, C-1, D-4
(d) A-2, B-3, C-4, D-1

3. Underfunction of which of the following hormones results in a diminished ability of the kidney to conserve water, leading to water loss and dehydration?

(a) Aldosterone
(b) Vasopressin
(c) Corticosteroids
(d) Insulin

4. Cr-Jacob Disease (CJD) in humans is caused by an analogous variant of

(a) prions of bovine spongiform encephalopathy
(b) viroids causing potato spindle tuber disease
(c) virus causing TMV
(d) virus causing mumps

5. Given below are two statements.

Statement I Yeast can progress through the cell cycle in only about 95 minutes.

Statement II In the 24 hour average duration of cell cycle of a human cell, the cell division phase lasts for only about half an hour.

In the light of the above statements, choose the correct answer from the options given below.

(a) Statement I is incorrect, but statement II is correct.
(b) Both statement I and statement II are correct.
(c) Both statement I and statement II are incorrect.
(d) Statement I is correct, but statement II is incorrect.

6. The sporophylls are distinct and compact in

(a) *Selaginella* and *Equisetum*
(b) *Funaria* and *Selaginella*
(c) *Psilotum* and *Selaginella*
(d) *Lycopodium* and *Psilotum*

7. Match the List I with List II.

	List I		List II
A.	Single circulation	1.	Blood passes through large vessels into open spaces.
B.	Incomplete double circulation	2.	Blood is always circulated through a closed network of blood vessels.
C.	Open circulatory system	3.	Heart pumps out deoxygenated blood.
D.	Closed circulatory system	4.	Single ventricle pumps out mixed blood.

Choose the correct answer from the options given below.

(a) A-2, B-1, C-3, D-4
(b) A-3, B-4, C-1, D-2
(c) A-2, B-3, C-4, D-1
(d) A-3, B-1, C-2, D-4

8. Identify the set of correct statements.

I. ICBN stands for International for Botanical Nomenclature.

II. Systematics takes into account evolutionary relationships between organisms.

III. Plant families Convolvulaceae and Solanaceae are included in the order-Sapindales, mainly based on the floral characters.

IV. Higher the category, the greater the difficulty in determining the relationship to other taxa at the same level.

V. All the categories constitute a taxonomic hierarchy.

Choose the correct answer from the options given below.

(a) I, II and III (b) III, IV and V
(c) II and III (d) II, IV and V

9. Ammonia produced by metabolism is converted into urea in the 'X' of ureotelic animals and released into the 'Y', which is filtered and excreted out by the kidneys. Identify 'X' and 'Y', respectively.

(a) Liver and blood (b) Kidney and lymph
(c) Intestine and blood (d) Heart and blood

10. Match List I with List II.

	List I		List II
A.	*Colletotrichum* and *Trichoderma*	1.	The parasitic fungi on mustard
B.	*Ustilago* and *Puccinia*	2.	Imperfect fungi
C.	*Aspergillus* and *Neurospora*	3.	Sex organs are absent
D.	*Albugo*	4.	Sac fungi

Choose the correct answer from the the options given below.

(a) A-3, B-2, C-4, D-1
(b) A-1, B-4, C-3, D-2
(c) A-2, B-3, C-4, D-1
(d) A-3, B-1, C-4, D-2

11. Read the following statements.

I. Mycoplasmas are only 0.5 micrometre in size.

II. Bacteria are 0.1 - 0.8 micrometer in size.

III. The largest isolated single cell is the egg of an ostrich.

IV. Human red blood cells are about 7.0 micrometre in diameter.

V. All cells have similar shape and perform similar type of functions.

Choose the correct statements from the options given below.

(a) III and IV (b) I, III and IV
(c) II, IV and V (d) I, II and V

12. The efferent arteriole emerging from the glomerulus forms a fine capillary network around the renal tubule called

(a) renal vein
(b) peritubular capillaries
(c) vasa recta
(d) afferent arteriole

13. Given below are two statements.

Statement I In *Rhizopus*, many roots, come out of the ground and grow vertically upward to get oxygen for respiration.

Statement II The cells present in region of elongation are very small, thin walled with dense protoplasm.

In the light of the above statements, choose the correct answer from the options given below.

(a) Statement I is incorrect, but statement II is correct.
(b) Both statement I and statement II are correct.
(c) Both statement I and statement II are incorrect.
(d) Statement I is correct, but statement II is incorrect.

14. Match the List I with List II.

	List I		List II
A.	Atrio-ventricular septum	1.	Separates right and left ventricles.
B.	Interatrial septum	2.	A double-walled membranous bag.
C.	Interventricular septum	3.	Separates right and left atria.
D.	Pericardium	4.	Tricuspid and bicuspid valves.

Choose the correct answer from the options given below.

(a) A-1, B-2, C-3, D-4 (b) A-4, B-3, C-1, D-2
(c) A-2, B-1, C-4, D-3 (d) A-1, B-3, C-2, D-4

15. Which of the following labelled part of the given diagram is capable of forming branch or a flower?

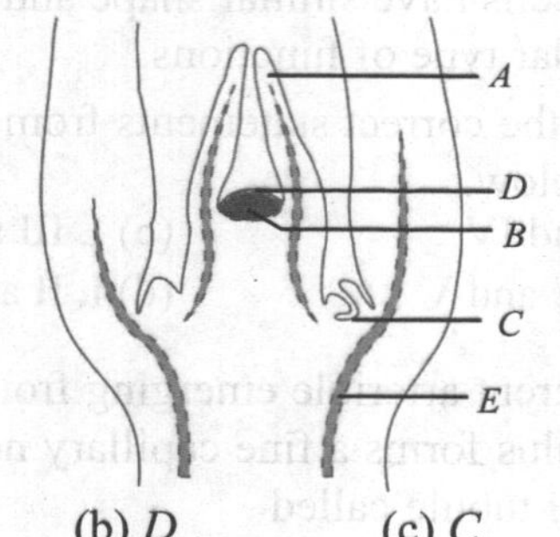

(a) *A* (b) *D* (c) *C* (d) *E*

16. Given below are two statements.

Statement I Enzymes generally function in a wide range of temperature and pH.

Statement II A general rule of thumb is that rate of reaction doubles or decreases by half for every 10°C change in temperature, either up or down.

In the light of the above statements, choose the correct answer from the options given below.

(a) Statement I is incorrect, but statement II is correct.
(b) Both statement I and statement II are correct.
(c) Both statement I and statement II are incorrect.
(d) Statement I is correct, but statement II is incorrect.

17. Match List I with List II.

	List I		List II
A.	Trypsin	1.	Zwitter ionic form
B.	Alkaloids	2.	Monoterpenes
C.	$H_3^+N—\underset{\mid}{\overset{R}{CH}}—COO^-$	3.	Codeine
D.	Lipids	4.	Concanavalin-A
E.	Terpenoids	5	Enzyme
		6.	2% of total cellular mass
		7.	Hormone

Choose the correct answer from the options given below.

	A	B	C	D	E
(a)	2	6	1	5	3
(b)	5	3	1	6	2
(c)	2	1	6	3	7
(d)	4	6	5	2	3

18. How many ATP and NADPH molecules will be required to make half of a molecule of glucose through the Calvin pathway?

(a) 18 and 12, respectively
(b) 9 and 6, respectively
(c) 6 and 3, respectively
(d) 12 and 6, respectively

19. Match List I with List II.

List I	List II
A. Cranial meninges	1. Covering of brain
B. Arachnoid	2. Inner layer
C. Dura mater	3. Middle layer
D. Pia mater	4. Outer layer

Choose the correct answer from the options given below.

	A	B	C	D		A	B	C	D
(a)	1	3	4	2	(b)	4	3	2	1
(c)	3	4	2	1	(d)	1	2	3	4

20. Following are the steps of the TCA cycle.

I. The oxidative decarboxylation of α-ketoglutarate (5C) produces succinyl Co-A (4C).
II. The succinyl Co-A converts to succinate.
III. The acetyl Co-A condenses with oxaloacetate (4C) to form citrate (6C).
IV. The oxidative decarboxylation of isocitrate to α-ketoglutarate (5C).
V. The dehydrogenation of malate forming oxaloacetate (4C).

Choose the correct sequence of reactions from the given options.

(a) I, III, IV, V, II
(b) V, III, II, I, VI
(c) III, IV, I, II, V
(d) I, II, V, IV, III

21. Match the List I with List II.

List I	List II
A. Primary structure	1. Haemoglobin
B. Glucosamine	2. Homopolymer
C. Quaternary structure	3. The positional information of an amino acid in a protein
D. Cellulose	4. Amino sugar

Choose the correct answer from the options given below.
(a) A-3, B-4, C-1, D-2
(b) A-2, B-4, C-1, D-3
(c) A-1, B-3, C-4, D-2
(d) A-2, B-1, C-3, D-4

22. The three core molecules present in photosystem are
(a) chlorophyll, electron acceptor and electron donor
(b) chloroplast, cytoplasm and mitochondria
(c) photosystem-I and photosystem-II
(d) stromal lamella, grana, starch granules

23. Regarding catalytic cycle of an enzyme action, select the correct sequential steps.
I. The binding of the substrate induces the enzyme to alter its shape, fitting more tightly around the substrate.
II. The enzyme releases the products of the reaction and the free enzyme is ready to bind to another molecule of the substrate and run through the catalytic cycle once again.
III. The substrate binds to the active site of the enzyme, fitting into the active site.
IV. The active site of the enzyme, now in close proximity of the substrate breaks the chemical bonds of the substrate and the new enzyme-product complex is formed.

Choose the correct answer from the options given below.
(a) I → III → IV → II
(b) IV → II → I → III
(c) III → I → IV → II
(d) II → IV → III → I

24. Given below are two statements, one is labelled as Assertion (A) and the other is labelled as Reason (R).
Assertion (A) Plants retain the capacity for unlimited growth throughout their life.
Reason (R) Temporary plant tissues are replaced by permanent tissues.
In the light of the above statements, choose the correct answer from the options given below.
(a) A is false, but R is true.
(b) Both A and R are true and R is the correct explanation of A.
(c) Both A and R are true, but R is not the correct explanation of A.
(d) A is true, but R is false.

25. Which of the following is correct about the given graph?

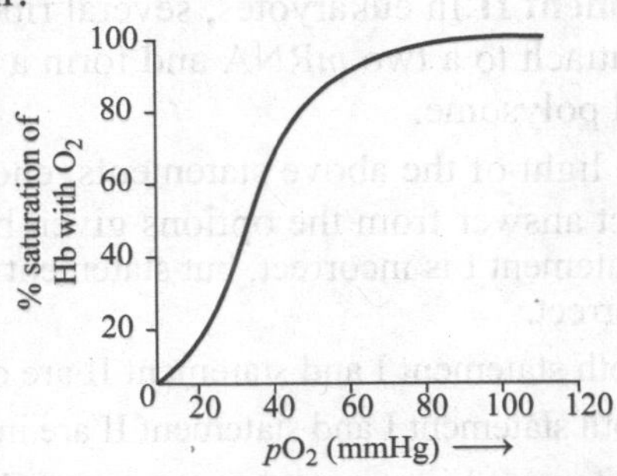

(a) The sigmoid curve moves to the left when H^+ ions concentration is more.
(b) The curve represents affinity of haemoglobin for CO_2.
(c) It represents, that every 100 ml of oxygenated blood can deliver around 5 ml of O_2 to the tissue.
(d) It is useful in studying the effect of factors like pCO_2, H^+ concentration, etc. on binding of O_2 with haemoglobin.

26. Match List I with List II.

	List I		List II
A.	Casparian strips	1.	Dicotyledonous stem
B.	Polyarch xylem bundle	2.	Monocotyledonous stem
C.	Conjoint, open vascular bundle	3.	Monocotyledonous root
D.	Sclerenchymatous hypodermis	4.	Dicotyledonous root

Choose the correct answer from the the options given below.
(a) A-4, B-3, C-1, D-2
(b) A-2, B-3, C-1, D-4
(c) A-1, B-4, C-3, D-2
(d) A-3, B-2, C-4, D-1

27. Which of the following synthetic hormones is widely used as herbicides to kill only dicotyledonous weeds?
(a) NAA (b) 2, 4-D
(c) IAA (d) IBA

28. Given below are two statements.

Statement I The organisation of prokaryotic cells is fundamentally similar, even though prokaryotes exhibit a wide variety of shapes and functions.

Statement II In eukaryotes, several ribosomes may attach to a two *m*RNA and form a chain called polysome.

In the light of the above statements, choose the correct answer from the options given below.

(a) Statement I is incorrect, but statement II is correct.

(b) Both statement I and statement II are correct.

(c) Both statement I and statement II are incorrect.

(d) Statement I is correct, but statement II is incorrect.

29. Following are the steps involved in ovulation in females.

A. Secretion of releasing hormone

B. Secretion of FSH and LH secretion

C. Stimulation of pars distalis

D. Rupture of follicle by LH

E. Development of follicles

Choose the correct order from the options given below.

(a) A-C-B-E-D

(b) C-A-E-B-D

(c) A-C-E-B-D

(d) A-C-B-E-D

30. Given below are two statements, one is labelled as Assertion (A) and the other is labelled as Reason (R).

Assertion (A) Large amount of water could be reabsorbed from collecting duct to produce concentrated urine.

Reason (R) Conditional reabsorption of sodium ions and water takes place in collecting duct.

In the light of the above statements, choose the correct answer from the options given below.

(a) A is false, but R is true.

(b) Both A and R are true and R is the correct explanation of A.

(c) Both A and R are true, but R is not the correct explanation of A.

(d) A is true, but R is false.

31. Match List I with List II.

	List I		List II
A.	C_3-pathway	1.	Photosystem-I
B.	C_4-pathway	2.	RuBP
C.	Non-cyclic photo phosphorylation	3.	Oxalic acid
D.	Cyclic photo phosphorylation	4.	Oxygen

Choose the correct answer from the the options given below.

(a) A-1, B-3, C-4, D-2

(b) A-1, B-3, C-2, D-4

(c) A-2, B-4, C-1, D-3

(d) A-2, B-3, C-4, D-1

32. Identify the correct features of xylem from the following.

I. Made up of tracheids, vessels, xylem fibres and xylem parenchyma.

II. Vessels and tracheids are main transporting material.

III. Protoxylem and the metaxylem are two types of secondary xylem.

IV. In stems, there is endarch organisation with metaxylem towards the centre.

V. In roots, there is exarch organisation.

Choose the correct answer from the options given below.

(a) I, II and V

(b) I, II, III and IV

(c) III, IV and V

(d) I, II, III, IV and V

33. Neural signal from the pons

(a) can reduce the duration of inspiration to alter the respiratory rate.

(b) can reduce the duration of expiration to alter the respiratory rate.

(c) increase the tidal volume to regulate respiratory rate.

(d) can increase the duration of inspiration to alter respiratory rate.

34. Which of the following statement is incorrect?

(a) Adenine and guanine are substituted purines.

(b) Biologically active protein has quaternary structure.

(c) Competitive inhibitors show close structural similarity to the substrate of enzyme.
(d) Rate of a physical or chemical process refers to the amount of product formed per unit time.

35. Match the List I with List II.

	List I		List II
A.	Metacentric chromosome	1.	One extremely short and one very long arm
B.	Sub-metacentric chromosome	2.	Two equal arms of the chromosome
C.	Telocentric chromosome	3.	One shorter arm and one longer arm
D.	Acrocentric chromosome	4.	Terminal centromere

Choose the correct answer from the options given below.
(a) A-2, B-4, C-3, D-1
(b) A-3, B-2, C-4, D-1
(c) A-2, B-3, C-4, D-1
(d) A-4, B-1, C-3, D-2

36. Given below are two statements.
Statement I ATP formation directly through the oxidation of substrate with ETS is called oxidative phosphorylation.
Statement II Glucose and fructose are phosphorylated to give rise to glucose 1,6-phosphate by the activity of hexokinase.
In the light of the above statements, choose the correct answer from the options given below.
(a) Statement I is incorrect, but statement II is correct.
(b) Both statement I and statement II are correct.
(c) Both statement I and statement II are incorrect.
(d) Statement I is correct, but statement II is incorrect.

37. Match List I with List II.

	List I		List II
A.	Whorled phyllotaxy	1.	*Hibiscus*
B.	Pinnately compound leaves	2.	*Alstonia*
C.	Palmately compound leaves	3.	Leaflets are present on a common axis.
D.	Alternate phyllotaxy	4.	Leaflets are attached to a common point.

Choose the correct answer from the the options given below.
(a) A-2, B-1, C-4, D-3
(b) A-2, B-3, C-4, D-1
(c) A-2, B-4, C-1, D-3
(d) A-1, B-3, C-4, D-2

38. Read the following statements and choose the correct set of statements.
I. A fatty acid has a carboxyl group attached to an *R* group.
II. Palmitic acid has 16 carbons excluding carboxyl carbon.
III. Arachidonic acid has 20 carbon atoms including the carboxyl carbon.
IV. Fatty acids could be saturated (without double bond) or unsaturated (with one or more C=C double bonds).
V. Simple lipid, glycerol is tetrahydroxy propane.

Choose the correct answer from the options given below.
(a) I, III and IV
(b) III, IV and V
(c) II, IV and V
(d) I, III, IV and V

39. Identify the animal (X) and name the phylum to which it belongs (Y)

(a) X- *Hemidactylus*, Y- Vertebrata
(b) X- *Salamandra*, Y- Chordata
(c) X- *Crocodilus*, Y- Vertebrata
(d) X- *Salamandra*, Y- Vertebrata

40. In which of the following phase of meiosis, the four chromatids of each bivalent chromosomes becomes distinct and clearly appears as tetrads?
(a) Prophase-II; pachytene
(b) Prophase-I; pachytene
(c) Prophase-I; leptotene
(d) Prophase-II; zygotene

41. Match List I with List II.

List I	List II
A. Auxins	1. Induces immediate stomatal closure in leaves
B. Ethylene	2. Induce rooting in a twig
C. Cytokinins	3. Ripens the fruit
D. Abscisic acid	4 Induce growth of axillary buds

Choose the correct answer from the options given below.

(a) A-2, B-1, C-4, D-3
(b) A-2, B-3, C-4, D-1
(c) A-2, B-3, C-1, D-4
(d) A-1, B-3, C-4, D-2

42. Which of the following contractile protein contains an active site for ATPase that allows for the binding of actin?

(a) Myosin (b) Actin
(c) Tubulin (d) Tropomyosin

43. Match List I with List II.

List I	List II
A. Lysosomes	1. Stores oils and fats
B. Golgi apparatus	2. Hydrolytic enzymes
C. Centriole	3. Glycoproteins and glycolipids
D. Elaioplast	4. Cartwheel organisation

Choose the correct answer from the options given below.

(a) A-3, B-1, C-4, D-2
(b) A-1, B-3, C-4, D-2
(c) A-2, B-3, C-4, D-1
(d) A-1, B-2, C-4, D-3

44. Given below are two statements.

Statement I In catalase and oxidase enzymes haem is the prosthetic group and loosely attached to the apoenzyme.

Statement II Zinc is a co-factor for the proteolytic enzyme carboxypeptidase.

In the light of the above statements, choose the correct answer from the options given below.

(a) Statement I is incorrect, but statement II is correct.
(b) Both statement I and statement II are correct.
(c) Both statement I and statement II are incorrect.
(d) Statement I is correct, but statement II is incorrect.

45. Match the List I with List II.

List I	List II
A. Smooth endoplasmic reticulum	1. Packing of biomolecules
B. Phospholipids	2. Hydrolytic enzymes
C. Lysosome	3. Limited permeability of plasma membrane
D. Golgi bodies	4. Steroid synthesis

Choose the correct answer from the options given below.

(a) A-1, B-4, C-3, D-2
(b) A-3, B-4, C-1, D-2
(c) A-4, B-3, C-2, D-1
(d) A-4, B-1, C-3, D-2

46. The beginning of diplotene is recognised by

(a) the terminalisation of chiasmata
(b) the dissolution of the synaptonemal complex
(c) the formation of the synaptonemal complex
(d) the appearance of recombination nodules

47. In which of the chordates subphylum, notochord is present only in larval stage?

(a) Cephalochordates
(b) Cyclostomes
(c) Tunicates
(d) Hemichordates

48. Which of the following secondary metabolites are used as drugs?

(a) Concanavalin-A, valine
(b) Vinblastin, curcumin
(c) Monoterpenes, diterpenes
(d) Morphine, codeine

49. Given below are two statements, one is labelled as Assertion (A) and the other is labelled as Reason (R).

Assertion (A) At the tissue site, partial pressure of CO_2 is high.

Reason (B) CO_2 diffuses into blood and forms HCO_3^- and H^+.

In the light of the above statements, choose the correct answer from the options given below.
(a) A is false, but R is true.
(b) Both A and R are true and R is the correct explanation of A.
(c) Both A and R are true, but R is not the correct explanation of A.
(d) A is true, but R is false.

50. Some features of cell organelle *X* are given below.

I. Found in all plants and euglenoids
II. Stores nutrients
III. Double membrane bound

Identify the cell organelle '*X*'.
(a) Sphaerosome (b) Mitochondria
(c) Leucoplast (d) SER

51. Which of the following hormones regulates the secretion of the pituitary hormone which induces ovulation of fully matured Graafian follicles and maintains the corpus luteum?
(a) Luteinizing hormone
(b) Follicle stimulating hormone
(c) Gonadotropin releasing hormone
(d) Gonadotropins

52. What is the role of water in photosynthesis?
(a) It acts as a solvent for nutrients
(b) It provides the electrons needed for the light reactions
(c) It absorbs light energy
(d) It is a product of photosynthesis

53. Read the following statements and choose the correct set of statements.

I. A nerve impulse is transmitted from one neuron to another through junctions called synapse.
II. A synapse is formed by the membranes of a pre-synaptic neuron and a post-synaptic neuron.
III. At chemical synapses, the membranes of pre and post-synaptic neurons are in very close proximity.
IV. Impulse transmission across an electrical synapse is always faster than that across a chemical synapse.
V. Electrical synapses are absent in our system.

Choose the correct answer from the options given below.
(a) I, II and IV
(b) II, IV and V
(c) II, III and V
(d) I, II, IV and V

54. Increased vacuolation, cell enlargement and new cell wall deposition are the characteristics of the cells in
(a) phase of maturation
(b) phase of elongation
(c) meristematic phase
(d) formative phase

55. Match the List I with List II.

	List I		List II
A.	NADP reductase	1.	Inorganic substances
B.	PAR	2.	Light harvesting system
C.	Antennae	3.	Thylakoid of the chloroplast
D.	Chemosynthetic bacteria	4.	400 - 700 nm

Choose the correct answer from the options given below.
(a) A-3, B-4, C-2, D-1
(b) A-2, B-1, C-4, D-3
(c) A-1, B-3, C-4, D-2
(d) A-4, B-2, C-1, D-3

56. In which of the following set of animals, the digestive tract has additional chambers, the crop and gizzard?
(a) *Corvus, Columba* and *Psittacula*
(b) *Macropus, Pteropus* and *Camelus*
(c) *Chelone,* Testudo and *Chameleon*
(d) *Hippocampus, Labeo* and *Clarias*

57. Given below are two statements.

Statement I The P-wave represents the electrical excitation of the atria, which leads to the relaxation of both the atria.

Statement II The QRS complex represents the depolarisation of the ventricles, which initiates the ventricular repolarisation.

In the light of the above statements, choose the correct answer from the options given below.

(a) Statement I is incorrect, but statement II is correct.
(b) Both statement I and statement II are correct.
(c) Both statement I and statement II are incorrect.
(d) Statement I is correct, but statement II is incorrect.

58. Which of the following options correctly identifies *X, Y* and *Z* in the given diagram?

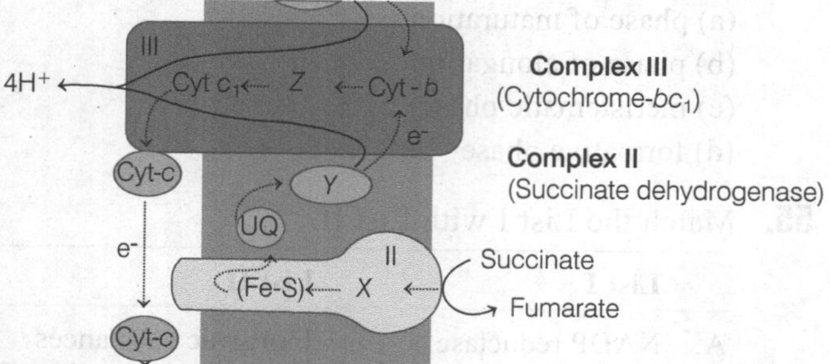

(a) *X*-Fe, *Y*-Cyt-*a*, *Z*-Fe-S
(b) *X*-UQ, *Y*-FMN, *Z*-FAD
(c) *X*-FAD, *Y*-UQ, *Z*-Fe-S
(d) *X*-FAD, *Y*-UQH_2, *Z*-Fe-S

59. Match the List I with List II.

	List I		List II
A.	Asthma	1.	Protective masks
B.	Emphysema	2.	Inflammation of bronchi and bronchioles
C.	Lung fibrosis	3.	Respiratory surface is decreased
D.	Occupational respiratory disorders	4.	Pulmonary damage

Choose the correct answer from the options given below.

(a) A-2, B-4, C-3, D-1
(b) A-1, B-4, C-3, D-2
(c) A-4, B-3, C-2, D-1
(d) A-2, B-3, C-4, D-1

60. Read the following statements and choose the correct set of statements.

I. Collagen is the most abundant protein in the animal world.
II. Ribulose Bisphosphate Carboxylase-Oxygenase (RuBisCO) is the most abundant protein in the whole of the biosphere.
III. Ribozymes are proteins with catalytic power.
IV. Proteinaceous enzymes exhibit substrate specificity and require optimum temperature and pH for maximal activity.
V. Enzymes lower the activation energy of reactions and greatly reduce the rate of the reactions.

Choose the correct answer from the options given below.

(a) I, II and IV
(b) II, IV and V
(c) III, IV and V
(d) I, II, and V

61. Which of the following is the main characteristics of the figure shown below?

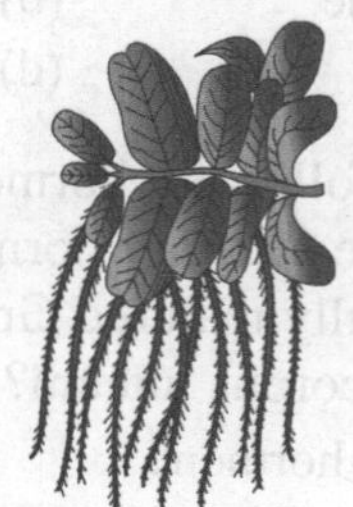

(a) Main plant body is haploid
(b) Sexual reproduction is oogamous
(c) Vegetative reproduction by budding
(d) Produces two kind of spores

62. Match the List I with List II.

	List I		List II
A.	Vena cava	1.	Between right atrium and right ventricle
B.	Aorta	2.	Drains oxygenated blood into left atrium
C.	Tricuspid valves	3.	Drains deoxygenated blood into right atrium
D.	Pulmonary veins	4.	Arises from left ventricle

Choose the correct answer from the options given below.

(a) A-3, B-4, C-1, D-2
(b) A-1, B-2, C-3, D-4
(c) A-4, B-2, C-3, D-1
(d) A-2, B-3, C-4, D-1

63. Match the List I with List II.

List I	List II
A. *Gracilaria* and *Gelidium*	1. Protonema and leafy stage
B. *Marchantia*	2. Ribbon-shaped chloroplast
C. *Spirogyra*	3. Rhodophyceae
D. *Funaria* and *Polytrichum*	4. Thalloid body

Choose the correct answer from the options given below.
(a) A-2, B-4, C-3, D-1
(b) A-3, B-4, C-2, D-1
(c) A-1, B-2, C-4, D-3
(d) A-1, B-2, C-3, D-4

64. In which of the following phase of mitosis, chromosomes lose their individuality?
(a) Prophase (b) Metaphase
(c) Anaphase (d) Telophase

65. Match the List I with List II.

List I	List II
A. PCT	1. Glomerular filtration
B. Columns of Bertini	2. Maintenance of high osmolarity in medulla.
C. Bowman's capsule	3. Maintains the pH and ionic balance of the body fluids.
D. Henle's loop	4. The cortex extending between medullary pyramid.

Choose the correct answer from the options given below.
(a) A-2, B-4, C-1, D-3
(b) A-3, B-4, C-1, D-2
(c) A-1, B-3, C-2, D-4
(d) A-1, B-3, C-4, D-2

66. Read the following statements and choose the set of correct statements.
I. Meiosis occurs in both haploid and diploid cells.
II. Meiosis-I is called the reduction division since it reduces the chromosome number by half, while making the gametes.
III. Meiosis-II has a long prophase, which is divided further into five phases.
IV. In metaphase-II, the bivalents arrange on the equatorial plate.
V. In anaphase-I, homologous chromosomes separate, while sister chromatids remain associated at their centromeres.

Choose the correct answer from the options given below.
(a) I, II, III and V (b) II and V
(c) III, IV and V (d) II, IV and V

67. Given below are two statements.
Statement I The neural system coordinates and integrates functions as well as metabolic and homeostatic activities of all the organs.
Statement II The nerve impulse is conducted along the neurilemma in the form of a wave of depolarisation and repolarisation.
In the light of the above statements, choose the correct answer from the options given below.
(a) Statement I is incorrect, but statement II is correct.
(b) Both statement I and statement II are correct.
(c) Both statement I and statement II are incorrect.
(d) Statement I is correct, but statement II is incorrect.

68. Which of the following protists, during unfavorable conditions, differentiates and forms fruiting bodies bearing spores at their tips?
(a) Dinoflagellates (b) Diatoms
(c) Slime moulds (d) Protozoans

69. Match the List I with List II.

List I	List II
A. Bivalents	1. Zygotene
B. Crossing over	2. Homologous chromosomes
C. Synaptonemal complex	3. Recombinase enzyme
D. Chiasmata	4. Sites of crossovers

Choose the correct answer from the options given below.
(a) A-2, B-3, C-1, D-4
(b) A-2, B-4, C-3, D-1
(c) A-2, B-1, C-4, D-3
(d) A-1, B-4, C-2, D-3

70. Which of the statement is correct about blood group?

(a) Persons with 'AB' group can donate blood to persons with AB as well as the other groups of blood.

(b) Erythroblastosis foetalis can be avoided by administering anti-Rh antibodies to the mother immediately after the delivery of the first child.

(c) Person with blood group A^- can receive blood from O^+ donor.

(d) Nearly 60% humans are Rh+.

71. Given below are two statements.

Statement I The LHC are made up of hundreds of pigment molecules bound to proteins.

Statement II The photosynthesis takes place only in the blue and red regions of the spectrum.

In the light of the above statements, choose the correct answer from the options given below.

(a) Statement I is incorrect, but statement II is correct.

(b) Both statement I and statement II are correct.

(c) Both statement I and statement II are incorrect.

(d) Statement I is correct, but statement II is incorrect.

72. Given below are two statements.

Statement I Partial pressure of CO_2 in oxygenated blood is 45 mm Hg.

Statement II 15-20 percent of carbon dioxide is carried by haemoglobin as carbamino-haemoglobin.

In the light of the above statements, choose the correct answer from the options given below.

(a) Statement I is incorrect, but statement II is correct.

(b) Both statement I and statement II are correct.

(c) Both statement I and statement II are incorrect.

(d) Statement I is correct, but statement II is incorrect.

73. Which of the following conversions involve NADH synthesis during glycolysis?

(a) Fructose 6-P → Fructose-1, 6-bisphosphate

(b) 2-phosphoglycerate → 2-phosphoenol pyruvate

(c) 1, 3-bisphosphoglyceric acid → 3-phosphoglyceric acid

(d) Glyceraldehyde 3- phosphate → 1, 3-bisphosphoglyceric acid

74. Match the List I with List II.

	List I		List II
A.	NADP	1.	Removal of groups from substrates
B.	Ligases	2.	Vitamin niacin
C.	Malonate	3.	Catalyse linking together of two compounds.
D.	Lyases	4.	Succinic dehydrogenase

Choose the correct answer from the options given below.

(a) A-2, B-1, C-4, D-3
(b) A-2, B-3, C-4, D-1
(c) A-1, B-3, C-4, D-2
(d) A-1, B-2, C-4, D-3

75. Which of the following statement is correct?

(a) Cartilaginous joint is present in the flat bone of skull.

(b) Gliding joint is present between atlas and axis.

(c) Synovial joints allow considerable movements and play a significant role in locomotion.

(d) The synovial joint between the adjacent vertebrae in the vertebral column permits limited movements.

76. Match the List I with List II.

	List I		List II
A.	Algin	1.	Brown algae
B.	Carrageenan	2.	Protein rich
C.	*Chlorella*	3.	Red algae
D.	*Porphyra*	4.	Marine algae

Choose the correct answer from the options given below.

(a) A-1, B-2, C-3, D-4
(b) A-4, B-4, C-2, D-1
(c) A-2, B-1, C-4, D-3
(d) A-1, B-3, C-2, D-4

77. Read the following statements considering gymnosperms and choose the set of correct statements.

I. The giant redwood tree *Sequoia* is one of the tallest tree species.

II. In *Cycas*, roots have fungal association in the form of mycorrhiza.

III. The male and the female gametophytes have an independent free-living existence.

IV. The pollen grain is released from the microsporangium.

V. The ovules are borne on megasporophylls, which may be clustered to form the female cones.

Choose the correct answer from the options given below.

(a) I, III and IV (b) II, IV and V
(c) I, IV and V (d) II, III, IV and V

78. Match the List I with List II.

List I	List II
A. Antidiuretic Hormone (ADH)	1. Decreases blood pressure
B. JGA cells	2. Vasoconstrictor
C. ANF	3. Prevent diuresis
D. Angiotensin-II	4. Renin

Choose the correct answer from the options given below.

(a) A-3, B-4, C-1, D-2 (b) A-2, B-4, C-1, D-3
(c) A-4, B-1, C-2, D-3 (d) A-1, B-3, C-4, D-2

79. Given below are two statements.

Statement I Fibrins are formed by the conversion of inactive fibrinogens in the plasma by the enzyme thrombin.

Statement II Clot is formed by a series of linked enzymatic reactions involving a number of factors present in the platelets in an inactive state.

In the light of the above statements, choose the correct answer from the options given below.

(a) Statement I is incorrect, but statement II is correct.
(b) Both statement I and statement II are correct.
(c) Both statement I and statement II are incorrect.
(d) Statement I is correct, but statement II is incorrect.

80. Match the List I with List II.

List I	List II
A. Monera	1. Cellular organisation
B. Plantae	2. Chitinous cell wall
C. Fungi	3. Non-cellulosic cell wall
D. Protista	4. Cellulosic cell wall

Choose the correct answer from the options given below.

(a) A-2, B-1, C-3, D-4
(b) A-3, B-4, C-2, D-1
(c) A-1, B-2, C-4, D-3
(d) A-4, B-3, C-2, D-1

81. Which of the following statements is incorrect?

(a) Parenchyma forms the major components within plant organs.
(b) Collenchyma provides mechanical support to the growing parts of the plant.
(c) Sclereids are present in the pulps of guava and pears.
(d) Angiosperms lack vessels in their xylem.

82. Match the List I with List II.

List I	List II
A. *Ichthyophis*	1. Epidermal scales or scutes.
B. *Calotes*	2. Viviparous and development is direct.
C. *Balaenoptera*	3. Endoskeleton is fully ossified.
D. *Aptenodytes*	4. External fertilisation

Choose the correct answer from the options given below.

(a) A-1, B-4, C-3, D-2 (b) A-1, B-3, C-4, D-2
(c) A-4, B-3, C-2, D-1 (d) A-4, B-1, C-2, D-3

83. Match the List I with List II.

List I	List II
A. Antonie van Leeuwenhoek	1. *Omnis cellula-e-cellula*
B. Robert Brown	2. A live cell
C. Singer and Nicolson	3. Nucleus
D. Rudolf Virchow	4. Fluid mosaic model

Choose the correct answer from the options given below.

(a) A-1, B-2, C-3, D-4
(b) A-3, B-2, C-4, D-1
(c) A-2, B-3, C-4, D-1
(d) A-4, B-3, C-2, D-1

84. Which of the following are hormonal disorders due to overproduction or under secretion of thyroid hormones?

I. Gigantism
II. Addison's disease
III. Exopthalmic goiter
IV. Diabetes
V. Cretinism
VI. Myxedema

Choose the correct answer from the options given below.

(a) III, IV and VI (b) I, II and IV
(c) I, II and V (d) III, V and VI

85. Which of the following molecules formed during TCA cycle have four carbon atoms?

(a) Citric acid, malic acid and succinic acid
(b) Succinic acid, malic acid and oxaloacetic acid
(c) α-ketoglutaric acid, malic acid and succinic acid
(d) Acetyl Co-A, malic acid and succinic acid

86. Match the List I with List II.

List I		List II
A. Schwann cells	1.	One axon and one dendrite.
B. Nissl's granules	2.	Forms myelin sheath around the axon
C. Nodes of Ranvier	3.	Gaps between two adjacent myelin sheaths.
D. Bipolar neurons	4.	Present in cyton and dendrites.

Choose the correct answer from the options given below.

(a) A-4, B-1, C-3, D-2
(b) A-1, B-4, C-3, D-2
(c) A-2, B-4, C-3, D-1
(d) A-2, B-1, C-4, D-3

87. Number of carbons in the primary CO_2-fixation product in C_3 and C_4 plants are

(a) 4 and 5, respectively
(b) 3 and 5, respectively
(c) 3 and 4, respectively
(d) 5 and 4, respectively

88. Identify the correct statements w.r.t. frog.

I. The alimentary canal is short because frogs are carnivores.
II. During aestivation and hibernation, gaseous exchange takes place through skin.
III. A triangular structure called conus arteriosus joins the right atrium. It receives blood. through the major veins called vena cava.
IV. The excretory system consists of a pair of kidneys, ureters, cloaca and urinary bladder.

Choose the correct answer from the options given below.

(a) II and III (b) I and II
(c) I, II and IV (d) III and IV

89. Choose the correct statement regarding hemichordates from the options given below.

(a) Their body is segmented.
(b) They have notochord in the collar region.
(c) Fertilisation is internal.
(d) Development is indirect.

90. Match the List I with List II.

List I		List II
A. Ciliary movement	1.	Cytoskeletal elements
B. Flagellar movement	2.	Peristalsis
C. Amoeboid movement	3.	Internal tubular organs
D. Muscular movement	4.	Spermatozoa

Choose the correct answer from the options given below.

(a) A-3, B-4, C-2, D-1
(b) A-4, B-1, C-3, D-2
(c) A-1, B-3, C-2, D-4
(d) A-3, B-4, C-1, D-2

Response Index

01 ⓐ ⓑ ⓒ ⓓ	26 ⓐ ⓑ ⓒ ⓓ	51 ⓐ ⓑ ⓒ ⓓ	76 ⓐ ⓑ ⓒ ⓓ
02 ⓐ ⓑ ⓒ ⓓ	27 ⓐ ⓑ ⓒ ⓓ	52 ⓐ ⓑ ⓒ ⓓ	77 ⓐ ⓑ ⓒ ⓓ
03 ⓐ ⓑ ⓒ ⓓ	28 ⓐ ⓑ ⓒ ⓓ	53 ⓐ ⓑ ⓒ ⓓ	78 ⓐ ⓑ ⓒ ⓓ
04 ⓐ ⓑ ⓒ ⓓ	29 ⓐ ⓑ ⓒ ⓓ	54 ⓐ ⓑ ⓒ ⓓ	79 ⓐ ⓑ ⓒ ⓓ
05 ⓐ ⓑ ⓒ ⓓ	30 ⓐ ⓑ ⓒ ⓓ	55 ⓐ ⓑ ⓒ ⓓ	80 ⓐ ⓑ ⓒ ⓓ
06 ⓐ ⓑ ⓒ ⓓ	31 ⓐ ⓑ ⓒ ⓓ	56 ⓐ ⓑ ⓒ ⓓ	81 ⓐ ⓑ ⓒ ⓓ
07 ⓐ ⓑ ⓒ ⓓ	32 ⓐ ⓑ ⓒ ⓓ	57 ⓐ ⓑ ⓒ ⓓ	82 ⓐ ⓑ ⓒ ⓓ
08 ⓐ ⓑ ⓒ ⓓ	33 ⓐ ⓑ ⓒ ⓓ	58 ⓐ ⓑ ⓒ ⓓ	83 ⓐ ⓑ ⓒ ⓓ
09 ⓐ ⓑ ⓒ ⓓ	34 ⓐ ⓑ ⓒ ⓓ	59 ⓐ ⓑ ⓒ ⓓ	84 ⓐ ⓑ ⓒ ⓓ
10 ⓐ ⓑ ⓒ ⓓ	35 ⓐ ⓑ ⓒ ⓓ	60 ⓐ ⓑ ⓒ ⓓ	85 ⓐ ⓑ ⓒ ⓓ
11 ⓐ ⓑ ⓒ ⓓ	36 ⓐ ⓑ ⓒ ⓓ	61 ⓐ ⓑ ⓒ ⓓ	86 ⓐ ⓑ ⓒ ⓓ
12 ⓐ ⓑ ⓒ ⓓ	37 ⓐ ⓑ ⓒ ⓓ	62 ⓐ ⓑ ⓒ ⓓ	87 ⓐ ⓑ ⓒ ⓓ
13 ⓐ ⓑ ⓒ ⓓ	38 ⓐ ⓑ ⓒ ⓓ	63 ⓐ ⓑ ⓒ ⓓ	88 ⓐ ⓑ ⓒ ⓓ
14 ⓐ ⓑ ⓒ ⓓ	39 ⓐ ⓑ ⓒ ⓓ	64 ⓐ ⓑ ⓒ ⓓ	89 ⓐ ⓑ ⓒ ⓓ
15 ⓐ ⓑ ⓒ ⓓ	40 ⓐ ⓑ ⓒ ⓓ	65 ⓐ ⓑ ⓒ ⓓ	90 ⓐ ⓑ ⓒ ⓓ
16 ⓐ ⓑ ⓒ ⓓ	41 ⓐ ⓑ ⓒ ⓓ	66 ⓐ ⓑ ⓒ ⓓ	
17 ⓐ ⓑ ⓒ ⓓ	42 ⓐ ⓑ ⓒ ⓓ	67 ⓐ ⓑ ⓒ ⓓ	
18 ⓐ ⓑ ⓒ ⓓ	43 ⓐ ⓑ ⓒ ⓓ	68 ⓐ ⓑ ⓒ ⓓ	
19 ⓐ ⓑ ⓒ ⓓ	44 ⓐ ⓑ ⓒ ⓓ	69 ⓐ ⓑ ⓒ ⓓ	
20 ⓐ ⓑ ⓒ ⓓ	45 ⓐ ⓑ ⓒ ⓓ	70 ⓐ ⓑ ⓒ ⓓ	
21 ⓐ ⓑ ⓒ ⓓ	46 ⓐ ⓑ ⓒ ⓓ	71 ⓐ ⓑ ⓒ ⓓ	
22 ⓐ ⓑ ⓒ ⓓ	47 ⓐ ⓑ ⓒ ⓓ	72 ⓐ ⓑ ⓒ ⓓ	
23 ⓐ ⓑ ⓒ ⓓ	48 ⓐ ⓑ ⓒ ⓓ	73 ⓐ ⓑ ⓒ ⓓ	
24 ⓐ ⓑ ⓒ ⓓ	49 ⓐ ⓑ ⓒ ⓓ	74 ⓐ ⓑ ⓒ ⓓ	
25 ⓐ ⓑ ⓒ ⓓ	50 ⓐ ⓑ ⓒ ⓓ	75 ⓐ ⓑ ⓒ ⓓ	

Performance Scanner

> 90% Excellent !	You have mastered the NEET syllabus (11th). The concepts of this entire syllabus are at your fingertips. Maintain this momentum.
76-90% Very Good !	You have a good command over the entire NEET syllabus (11th). Revise it again after a few days to enhance your performance.
60-75% Good !	You have a wide scope to learn for the entire NEET syllabus (11th). Revise it again.
<60% Not Satisfactory!	You have a long way ahead of you to master the NEET syllabus (11th). Revise it thoroughly.

Space for Rough Work

MED+ACE

NEET (UG)

SELF ASSESSMENT KIT

Exactly as per the Latest pattern of NTA

BIOLOGY – XIth

Hints, Explanations & Mind Maps Booklet

Authors

Rakhi Bisht, Kashvi & Anita

ARIHANT PRAKASHAN (SERIES), MEERUT

卐 **Administrative & Production Offices**

Regd. Office

'Ramchhaya' 4577/15, Agarwal Road, Darya Ganj, New Delhi -110002
Tele: 011- 47630600, 43518550

卐 **Head Office**

Kalindi, TP Nagar, Meerut (UP) - 250002
Tel: 0121-7156203, 7156204

卐 **Sales & Support Offices**

Agra, Ahmedabad, Bengaluru, Bareilly, Chennai, Delhi, Guwahati, Hyderabad, Jaipur, Jhansi, Kolkata, Lucknow, Nagpur & Pune.

卐 **PRICE** ₹ 1200.00

卐 **PO No :** TXT-59-T063619-03-25

Published by Arihant Publications (India) Ltd.

For further information about the books published by Arihant, log on to www.arihantbooks.com or e-mail at info@arihantbooks.com

BIOLOGY-XIth

CONTENT LIST

MED+ACE

NEET (UG)

SELF ASSESSMENT KIT

HINTS & EXPLANATIONS

Ch-1 The Living World

Topical Follow Thru

Test 1

1. (*b*) Response to external stimuli is a fundamental characteristic of living organisms. All living organisms respond to the changes in their environment, which is crucial for their survival and adaptation.

2. (*b*) *Amoeba* reproduces asexually through a process called binary fission. In *Amoeba*, reproduction is synonymous with growth because both involve an increase in number of cells.

3. (*c*) Budding is the primary method of asexual reproduction in both yeast and *Hydra*. In this process, a new organism grows out of the body of the parent organism. In yeast, a small bud forms on the parent cell and eventually separates to become a new individual.
In *Hydra*, a small bud develops into a new *Hydra*, which then detaches from the parent.

4. (*a*) Classification is the process of arranging organisms into groups based on their shared characteristics or traits. It involves categorising entities into hierarchial levels according to their similarities and differences.

5. (*b*) The incorrect statement for reproduction can be corrected as
Reproduction is a common characteristic of living organisms, but there are some exceptions. For example, the mule is a living organism, but is sterile and cannot reproduce, infertile human couple and worker bees also do not reproduce, but are living organisms. Thus, reproduction cannot be a characteristic of living organisms.

6. (*c*) The incorrect statement with respect to growth can be corrected as
Plant growth is usually indeterminate, i.e. plants can continue to grow throughout their life. Unlike most animals, they do not have a fixed size and can keep growing as long as environmental conditions are favourable. For example, trees can continue to grow in height and girth over many years.

7. (*a*) In non-living objects growth is due to the accumulation of matter on the surface, not an internal process like growth in living organisms, thus it is reversible.

8. (*c*) In a test-tube, an isolated metabolic reaction is not considered living because it lacks the essential characteristics of living organisms, such as organisation, growth, reproduction, and response to stimuli. On the other hand, it is not purely non-living either, as it involves biochemical processes typical of living systems. Therefore, it falls into the category of neither living nor non-living.

9. (*b*) The properly formatted and correctly written scientific name of the mango, is *Mangifera indica* Linn. *Mangifera* is the genus name and its first letter is capitalised, while *indica* is the specific epithet and it begins with small letter. Both are italicised when printed and underlined when handwritten.
Linn. abbreviation refers to Linnaeus, indicating that the species was first described and classified by Carolus Linnaeus.

10. (*d*) Statement I is correct, but statement II is incorrect. The incorrect statement can be corrected as
Traditionally, when both genus and species names are handwritten, they are separately underlined or printed in Italics to indicate their Latin origin and to differentiate them from normal text.

11. (*d*) The incorrect statement can be corrected as
In the scientific name of the lion (*Panthera leo*), '*Panthera*' is the generic name and *'leo'* is the specific epithet.

12. (*a*) The correct match is A-3, B-4, C-1, D-2.
Biodiversity refers to the variety of living organisms in a particular habitat or on earth as a whole.
Nomenclature refers to the process or system of naming things, particularly in biology, it involves the naming of living organisms.
Identification involves the process of recognising or describing an organism based on its characteristics or traits.
Binomial nomenclature refers to the formal system of naming living organisms using two names, i.e. a generic name (genus) and a specific epithet (species name).

13. (*d*) ICBN stands for International Code of Botanical Nomenclature.
This code establishes a set of internationally agreed-upon rules and recommendations for naming plants, fungi and algae. It ensures that each taxonomic group within these categories has a single, accepted scientific name that is recognised worldwide.

14. (*d*) A is true, but R is false. R can be corrected as
Isolated metabolic reactions can be conducted in a test tube using enzymes and molecules extracted from living organisms. These reactions can demonstrate some of the chemical processes that occur within living cells. These can be considered as the living reactions, but are not the indicative of living beings.

15. (*a*) The correct statement can be explained as
Sensitivity is the ability to detect changes in the surrounding environment. It is a characteristic feature of living organisms. It allows organisms to respond to stimuli such as light, temperature,

touch and chemicals. This responsiveness is essential for survival and adaptation in varying environments.

Other incorrect statements can be corrected as

Self-consciousness is the characteristic feature of human beings. Consciousness is an important feature of living organism.

16. (*c*) Both A and R are true, but R is not the correct explanation of A.

All living organisms are made of chemicals. These chemicals, small and big, belonging to various classes, sizes, functions, etc. are constantly being made and changed into some other biomolecules. These conversions are chemical reactions or metabolic reactions.

17. (*b*) The incorrect statement can be corrected as

Tautonyms are the names with same generic and specific epithets. These are not valid for plants, though these are commonly used for zoological names, i.e. *Rattus rattus*.

Rest statements are correct regarding the rule of priority in nomenclature.

18. (*c*) Both A and R are true, but R is not the correct explanation of A.

All living organisms from prokaryotes to most complex eukaryotes have an inherent ability to sense their surroundings or environment and respond these environmental stimuli. This is called consciousness.

19. (*a*) In majority of the higher organisms (plants and animals), reproduction and growth are mutually exclusive events as increase in the body size of living beings do not alter the rate of reproduction or *vice-versa*.

20. (*d*) Statement I is correct, but statement II is incorrect. The incorrect statement can be corrected as

Some sessile animals like sponges and some coelenterates do not show clear movements.

21. (*b*) All living organism can sense or perceive an event happening in the environment and form its memory. This character, called consciousness, is an exclusive characteristic of living beings.

22. (*a*) Statement I is incorrect, but statement II is correct. The incorrect statement can be corrected as

A rolling ball of snow increasing in mass, volume and size is not comparable to growth seen in the living organism because this, growth is a result of accumulation from external surface (accretion) on the ball of snow and not from inside, like a living cell. Other statement can be explained as

The whole moong dal is considered living, while broken is considered non-living due to the difference in their ability to respire and germinate.

23. (*c*) Reproduction is not essential for the survival of individuals. However, it is essential and required for the survival of population because it helps to compensate the loss of life, i.e. death.

So, the statement 'Nothing lives forever yet life continues' is best understood by the process of reproduction.

24. (*d*) Statements I, II and IV are correct. Statement III is incorrect and can be corrected as

Growth is not continuous in all living organisms, e.g. in plants, it is continuous, but in animals, it is definite. Development can be considered as a continuous process.

25. (*d*) Statement I is correct, but statement II is incorrect. The incorrect statement can be corrected as

Amoeba multiplying by mitotic cell division signifies growth as well as reproduction.

Test 2

1. (*a*) Species are defined by a specific set of characteristics shared among individuals that can interbreed and produce fertile offspring. Kingdom is the highest taxonomic rank, encompassing diverse groups of organisms that share very few common characteristics compared to species.

Therefore, as we move up from species to kingdom, the number of common characteristics generally decreases because taxa at higher levels include more diverse organisms with varying characteristics.

2. (*b*) *Solanum sativum* is not a recognised species. The other species, namely, *nigrum*, *tuberosum* and *melongena* are commonly known as black nightshade, tomato and eggplant, respectively.

3. (*d*) A taxon refers to any group or rank used in biological classification, ranging from the most specific (species) to more inclusive groups (genus, family, order, etc.). Each taxon represents a category or unit used to organise and classify organisms based on shared characteristics and evolutionary relationships.

4. (*c*) The correct order of classification is : Kingdom, Division, Class, Order, Family, Genus, Species.

Kingdom: The highest taxonomic rank, grouping organisms based on broad similarities.

Division/Phylum: This rank, represents the major groups within kingdoms. Division is used for plants, while phylum is used for animals.

Class: Within a phylum/division, organisms are further grouped into classes based on similar characteristics.

Order: Subdivision of a class, grouping related families.

Family: Grouping of similar genera.

Genus: A group of closely related species.

Species: The most specific level, representing individual types of organisms.

5. (*a*) Families are characterised on the basis of both vegetative and reproductive features. Thus, genera *Solanum*, *Petunia* and *Datura* are placed in the family–Solanaceae mainly on the basis of vegetative and reproductive characters.

6. (*a*) Systematics focuses on the study of the diversity of life (biodiversity) and the evolutionary relationships among different organisms. It involves classification (taxonomy) and phylogenetics to categorise and understand the evolutionary history of species.

7. (*b*) Leopard and big cats are put in the genus–*Panthera*. Genus is an assembly of a set of similar species that are involved in common ancestory and consists of common characters known as correlated characters. Other options can be corrected as

Canis is the genus for dog, wolves, etc. Carnivora is an order, not a class.

8. (*d*) Two plants can be conclusively said, to belong to the same species if they can reproduce freely with each other and form seeds. Species are those group of organisms which are capable of interbreeding among themselves and can exchange the genes. They are closely related.

9. (*c*) Suffix -aceae is used to indicate the family level in plant taxonomy (e.g., Rosaceae, Fabaceae).

10. (*b*) Both statement I and statement II are correct.

Taxonomical studies of all known organisms have led to the development of certain common categories like kingdom, phylum, class, order, family, genus and species. Potato and brinjal are two different species, which belong to the genus–*Solanum*.

11. (*d*) If organisms are in the same class but not in the same family, they could potentially belong to the same order. Orders group together families that share broader similarities, but are less closely related than families.

12. (*b*) The correct match is Cat-Felidae, a family. All the other matches are discussed below

Wheat : It belongs to Poaceae family.

Cats : They belong to the family–Felidae, which includes all true cats like domestic cats, lions, tigers, etc.

Humans: They belong to the family–Hominidae within the order Primata.

Housefly: It belongs to the order Diptera, and its scientific name is *Musca domestica*.

13. (*a*) Genera within the same family can share the same class (at a higher taxonomic level) but consist of different species (at a lower taxonomic level). Genera within the same family can belong to the same class because the classification hierarchy places class above family. Classes may contain multiple families, each representing distinct but related groups of genera.

Genera in the same family can have different species because genera are more narrowly defined than families, encompassing species that share more specific characteristics.

14. (*b*) Both mango and grass belong to the same division–Angiospermae. Their classes are Dicotyledonae and Monocotyledonae, respectively.

15. (*c*) Both A and R are true, but R is not the correct explanation of A.

It is more difficult to determine the relationships between organisms at higher taxonomic categories because the categories are broader and there is more diversity.

16. (*c*) The odd one out from the given options is Insecta. As it represent a class, while the other represents order.

17. (*b*) The lowest common taxonomical category between dog and cat is order-Carnivora. Thus, they show maximum similarity at the level of order.

18. (*a*) Option (a) is correctly matched with its particular named taxonomic category as *tigris* is the species of tiger.

Other incorrectly matched pairs can be corrected as

Mollusca is a phylum, Primata is an order and *Musca* is a genus.

19. (*b*) Organism I is dog, which belongs to family-Canidae and organism II is housefly, which belongs to order-Diptera.

20. (*a*) Statements II, III and IV are incorrect. These can be corrected as

Carnivora represents an order containing tiger and cat. Elephant is not placed under order-Carnivora.

Genus like *Panthera* involves different species like *P. pardus* (leopard), *P. tigris* (tiger) and *P. leo* (lion).

The taxonomic categories are same for plants and animals except for one, i.e. Phylum/Division, where the former is used for animals and latter is used for plants.

21. (*a*) Statement I is incorrect, but statement II is correct. The incorrect statement can be corrected as

The basics of taxonomy like identification, naming and classification of organisms are universally evolved under international codes.

22. (*d*) Statement I is correct, but statement II is incorrect. The incorrect statement can be corrected as

Dog is a species which belongs to class-Mammalia of kingdom-Animalia. Therefore, animals, mammals and dogs represent taxa at different levels.

23. (*c*) The lowest common taxonomic categories between wheat (*Triticum aestivum*) and *Brassica* is division-Angiospermae. Thus, they show maximum similarity at the level of division only.

24. (*c*) *Musca* represents genus, Muscidae represents family, Diptera represents order and Insecta represents class.

As we go from lowest taxon to highest taxon, number of common characteristics increases. Thus, genus, i.e. *Musca* possesses the most similar characters, while the class-Insecta will possess the least similar characters.

25. (*c*) The correct hierarchical arrangement of taxonomic categories of wheat is

Division – Angiospermae

Class – Monocotyledonae (A)

Order – Poales (B)

Family – Poaceae (C)

Genus – *Triticum* (D)

Species – *aestivum*.

Chapter Break Thru

1. (*b*) Metabolism is the sum of all chemical reactions occurring within a living organism. It is a defining characteristic of living organisms that does not occur in non-living things. It includes processes such as anabolism and catabolism, which are essential for maintaining life.
2. (*c*) Many fungi, such as moulds, can reproduce by fragmentation. Hyphae, the filamentous structures of fungi, can break off and form new fungal colonies.
3. (*a*) The organisms in which growth and reproduction are synonymous to each other are *Amoeba*, bacteria and unicellular algae.
Bacteria reproduce by binary fission, where one cell divides into two, leading to both growth and reproduction.
Unicellular algae reproduce by binary fission or similar processes where cell division leads directly to reproduction.
Amoeba reproduces by binary fission, where one cell divides into two, leading to both growth and reproduction.
4. (*c*) Incorrect statement can be corrected as
While cell division is a fundamental process in growth, especially during early development and tissue renewal in multicellular organisms. Growth in multicellular organisms also involves cell enlargement (hypertrophy) and differentiation, not just cell division.
5. (*b*) Carolus Linnaeus, a Swedish botanist and zoologist, is credited with developing the binomial nomenclature system in the 18th century. This system provides a formalised way of naming organisms using two Latinised names: the genus (generic name) and the species (specific epithet). Linnaeus system revolutionised taxonomy and classification and it remains the standard naming convention used by biologists worldwide.
6. (*c*) The incorrect match pair can be corrected as
The steps in taxonomy involve characterisation (describing features), identification (determining the identity of an organism), and then classification (arranging organisms into groups based on similarities). Thus, classification is not the initial step in the process.
7. (*c*) In taxonomy, as we move from lower taxonomic ranks (like species) to higher ranks (like kingdom), the number of common characteristics generally decreases.
At the species level, organisms within a species share a large number of specific characteristics.
As we move up the taxonomic hierarchy to higher ranks such as genus, family, order, class, phylum, and kingdom, the groups become more inclusive, encompassing organisms with increasingly diverse traits.
8. (*c*) Both reptiles and amphibians share some key features. Such as notochord and dorsal hollow neural system and thus are placed together in phylum–Chordata.
9. (*c*) The incorrect statement can be corrected as
Classification is relevant and necessary for understanding all organisms, including those from the past.
10. (*c*) The correct match pair is *sapiens* —Species of human beings.
Other incorrect match pairs can be corrected as
Animalia refers to the kingdom, which includes all animals. However, it does not imply that animals within this kingdom have the maximum similarities. The similarities decrease as you move to higher taxonomic levels like kingdom to lower levels of species.
Primata is an order, not an assemblage of related classes, Primates include humans, apes, monkeys and others.
Panthera is a genus name, not a specific epithet. The genus–*Panthera* includes big cats like lions (*Panthera leo*), tigers (*Panthera tigris*) and leopards (*Panthera pardus*).
11. (*b*) Identification is the specific process of determining the exact taxonomic category to which an organism belongs. It involves comparing the characteristics of an unknown organism to those of known organisms to place it in the correct taxonomic category. This also includes finding the correct scientific name for the organism.
12. (*d*) Among all the taxonomic categories, Family (*D*) is the lower category that is characterised on the basis of both vegetative and reproductive features of plant species.
13. (*c*) A patient who has experienced brain death has lost all self-consciousness and awareness, yet his body can still be kept alive through artificial means such as life support. In such cases, the patient's organs can still function even though brain activity has ceased.
Other incorrect statements can be corrected as
• Cellular organisation of the body is the defining feature of all living forms.
• Consciousness is a defining characteristic of living organisms.
• Human beings are the only organisms that are aware of themselves, i.e. self-consciousness.
14. (*b*) Statements I, II and III are correct.
Common names can indeed be misleading because they vary regionally and may apply to different species.
Vernacular names are generally easier to pronounce than the scientific names, which are often in Latin.
Vernacular names can lack scientific significance as they are not standardised and may not convey accurate information about the organism.
15. (*b*) The incorrect statement can be corrected as
The name of the taxonomist who first described the species can be included immediately after specific epithet and is often done so in citations, it is not a requirement in the formal scientific name. The formal scientific name consists of

only the genus and species names (and sometimes the subspecies or variety).

16. (*c*) The incorrect matched pair can be corrected as
Both the generic name and the specific epithet are separately underlined when handwritten and are printed in Italics.

17. (*a*) Statements III and IV are correct. Other incorrect statements can be corrected as
In plants, classes with a few similar characteristics are grouped into a higher category called division, not phylum. The Convolvulaceae family is included in the Polymoniales order based on its floral structures, not vegetative structures.

18. (*c*) Statements II, IV and V are correct. Other statements are incorrect and can be corrected as
Classification is a multi-step process involving the identification, description and arrangement of organisms into hierarchial taxonomic categories based on their shared characteristics.
Species is not an intermediate category, but rather the fundamental category in the taxonomic hierarchy.

19. (*d*) A is true, but R is false. R can be corrected as
Biological names are primarily derived from Latin, although some may be Latinised versions of words from other languages, e.g. *Azadirachta indica, Saraca asoca*.

20. (*a*) Statement I is incorrect, but statement II is correct. Incorrect statement can be corrected as
While scientific names for plants are indeed governed by the International Code of Botanical Nomenclature, animals follow the rules set by the International Code of Zoological Nomenclature (ICZN), not the ICBN (International Code of Botanical Nomenclature).

21. (*b*) The correct match is A-3, B-1, C-4, D-2.
Muscidae is a family within the order–Diptera.
Diptera is an order within the class–Insecta.
Insecta is a class within the phylum–Arthropoda.
Arthropoda is a phylum within the kingdom–Animalia.

22. (*b*) Statements II and IV are correct, while statements I, III and V are incorrect. These can be corrected as
Cats (domestic cats and big cats like lions) belong to the family–Felidae, not Canidae. This family also includes dogs, wolves and foxes.
As we move to more inclusive taxonomic categories (from species to kingdom), the similarities among the organisms decrease because these categories group a broader range of organisms.
Characterisation, identification, classification and nomenclature are basic processes to taxonomy.

23. (*d*) A is true, but R is false.
R can be corrected as
Every organism indeed has a unique ecological role, the primary purpose of standardising scientific names is to provide a universal, unambiguous system for identifying organisms, not necessarily to reflect their ecological roles.

24. (*d*) Statement I is correct, but statement II is incorrect.
Statement II can be corrected as
A species is not just a collection of objects. Its a population of organisms that can interbreed and produce fertile offspring. While individual organisms within a species are concrete biological objects, the concept of 'species' itself is a category within the taxonomic ranking system.

25. (*d*) The correct match is A-3, B-1, C-2, D-4.
Scientific name of housefly is *Musca domestica*.
Polymoniales is an order comprising members of Solanaceae like potato (*Solanum tuberosum*), tomato (*Solanum lycopersicum*) and brinjal (*Solanum melongena*).
Class is a category including groups of related orders. Potato, tomato and brinjal belong to the same class, which is Magnoliopsida (or dicotyledons).
German shepherd, chihuahua and pug are different breeds, but belong to the same species, *Canis lupus familiaris*.

26. (*c*) Valid publication of binomial nomenclature is usually considered beginning in 1st May 1753, the date of publication of *Species Plantarum* vol. I by Linnaeus.

27. (*b*) Statements I and IV are incorrect and can be corrected as
Photoperiod affects reproduction in seasonal breeders, both plants and animals.
All organisms, from prokaryotes to the most complex eukaryotes can sense and respond to environmental cues.

28. (*c*) Statements I, II and III are correct. Statement IV can be corrected as
The author citation in the binomial nomenclature is not Italicised. It is written in following manner
Mangifera indica Linn.

29. (*b*) Statements I, II and IV are incorrect and can be corrected as
The tautonyms are allowed in zoological nomenclature, but not in botanical nomenclature.
Underline is only used, while the scientific name is handwritten to denote the Latin origin of name. While printing, Italicised words are used for the same.
ICZN stands for International Code of Zoological Nomenclature.

30. (*b*) The correctly written binomial name is *Solanum lycopersicum*, i.e. used for tomato. Other options can be corrected as
Panthera leo scientific name of (Lion). *Azadirachta indica* scientific name of neem plant. *Homo sapiens sapiens* scientific name of modern human.

31. (*d*) Growth occurs in both living and non-living things, but through different mechanisms
Living organisms grow internally due to the metabolic activities.

Non-living objects grow externally by accumulating material.
Since, both can grow, but in different ways, growth alone is not a defining feature of life.

32. (*c*) The incorrect statement regarding reproduction in organism can be corrected as
In unicellular organisms like *Amoeba*, growth (increase in number of cells) is synonymous with reproduction.

33. (*d*) The starting letter of specific epithet *Coli* should not be capitalised. It should be written as '*coli*' because according to the universal rules of nomenclature specific epithet should start with small letter. All other options correctly follow the binomial nomenclature rules.

34. (*d*) Statement I is correct, but statement II is incorrect. The incorrect statement can be corrected as
The classification of taxa involves not only specific characteristics shared by organisms, but also their hierarchical relationships.
Taxonomic ranks (like species, genus, family, etc.) are structured in a hierarchy that reflects evolutionary relationships and levels of classification. For instance, dogs are classified under mammals, which in turn are classified under animals. Thus, the classification is based on both shared characteristics and their position in the broader hierarchical context.

35. (*c*) Both A and R are true, but R is not the correct explanation of A.
Systematics is the study of the systematic arrangement of organisms and their relationships. Linnaeus used *Systema Naturae* as the title for his publication, it reflects Linnaeus's work in taxonomy, which is a part of systematics.

36. (*a*) Statements I and III are correct, while II and IV are incorrect. These can be corrected as
The taxonomic hierarchy does reflect evolutionary relationships.
While having three pairs of legs is one of the key feature of insects, their classification also considers various other characteristics such as body structure, wing presence and type, antennae structure and reproductive features.

37. (*c*) The incorrect statement can be corrected as
The ability to handle chemicals is not unique to complex eukaryotes; even prokaryotes and simpler organisms have mechanisms to manage chemicals entering their bodies. The rest other options accurately describe the responses of organisms to environmental factors.

38. (*c*) The International Code of Nomenclature for Cultivated Plants (ICNCP) is responsible for the naming of cultivated plants.

39. (*a*) The correct match pair can be explained as
All plant families end with suffix-ae.
Other options, show exceptions like division possesses suffix phyta or spermae, class might end with nae or opsida and genus has no definite suffix at all.

40. (*d*) A is true, but R is false. R can be corrected as
Plant families like Convolvulaceae and Solanaceae are included in the order–Polymoniales.

41. (*a*) Statements I, II and III are correct and statements IV and V are incorrect. These can be corrected as
In plants, classes are grouped into a higher category called division.
Primata and Carnivora are classified in Chordata based on structural features, not reproductive traits.

42. (*d*) Wheat is a species, while monocots and angiosperms represent higher taxonomic levels (class and phylum, respectively). Thus, they do not represent the same level of classification.

43. (*c*) The incorrect statements can be corrected as
A species is not considered a genetically open system; it is generally considered a closed system with limited genetic exchange.
Tomato (a species), dicots (a class), and plants (a kingdom) represent different levels of taxonomic hierarchy, but not the same rank.
Hybrids like tigons and ligers (tiger-lion hybrids) are not considered true species as they are typically infertile and do not form stable populations in the wild.

44. (*a*) *Solanum* and *Panthera* are genera, while Felidae is a family, making this group a mix of different taxonomic levels.

45. (*c*) Mango belongs to class–Dicotyledonae (A) and family–Anacardiaceae (B), while housefly belongs to order–Diptera (C).

46. (*a*) In taxonomic categories, family is placed between class and species. Family can accommodate different genera, but species are different, e.g. dog, jackal, wolf belong to same genera–*Canis*, but species are different. But they belong to same class. More similar characteristics of order are grouped in same class.

47. (*a*) In taxonomy, a homonym refers to an identical name used for two different species. This can lead to confusion and is usually resolved by revising the nomenclature to ensure unique names for each taxon.

48. (*a*) Genera classified under the same family are generally within the same order and phylum, but they may belong to different classes within that phylum. This means, they share a broader taxonomic category, but differ in more specific levels like class.

49. (*c*) Statements I, III and IV are correct and statements II and V are incorrect. These can be corrected as
The order–Primata includes monkeys, gorillas and gibbons, not families like Felidae and Canidae. The families Felidae and Canidae belong to the order–Carnivora. Hominidae represents family and not order.

50. (*d*) The incorrect statement can be corrected as
The scientific names ensure that each organism has only one name. They also ensure that such a name has not been used for any other known organism.
Rest all other statements are correct.

Ch-2 Biological Classification

Topical Follow Thru

Test 1

1. (*b*) Aristotle was the earliest to attempt a more scientific basis for classification. He used simple morphological characters to classify plants into trees, shrubs and herbs. He also divided animals into two groups, those that had red blood (enaima) and those that did not (anaima).

2. (*a*) Archaea are a distinct domain of life, separated from both prokaryotes (bacteria) and eukaryotes (plants, animals, fungi, and protists). They possess unique molecular and biochemical characteristics that set them apart. While Archaea share some basic cellular features with other organisms (such as DNA replication and protein synthesis mechanisms), they also exhibit unique traits such as different membrane lipids and unusual metabolic pathways.

3. (*b*) Microscopic, single-celled eukaryotic organisms, such as protists, pose a challenge for classification due to their diversity and simplicity. Unlike bacteria, which are prokaryotic and lack a true nucleus with a nuclear membrane, protists are eukaryotic organisms that possess a true nucleus enclosed within a nuclear membrane. This characteristic distinguishes them from bacteria and is fundamental in their classification as eukaryotes.

4. (*b*) In Whittaker's classification (5- kingdom classification), the given characteristics, i.e. unicellularity, photosynthetic or autotrophic nature, lack of membrane bound organelles and sexual reproduction along with the presence of chlorophyll-*a*, phycoerythrin, phycocyanin, etc. corresponds to cyanobacteria of Eubacteria, e.g. *Nostoc*, *Anabaena* and *Spirulina*. Other organisms belong to different categories.

5. (*b*) Linnaeus relied on observable physical characteristics to group organisms. One such characteristic was the presence or absence of a cell wall, which is a visible structural difference. This distinction helped him categorise plants (having cell walls) and animals (lacking cell walls) into separate kingdoms.

6. (*c*) Statement (c) is not a drawback of two-kingdom classification system, Algae, such as *Chlamydomonas* and *Chlorella*, grouped under kingdom-Protista is the drawback of five-kingdom classification and not two kingdom classification.

7. (*d*) Mycoplasma are indeed the smallest living cells. They are pathogenic to both plants and animals and possess heterotrophic nutrition. Mycoplasma do not have a cell wall and therefore, they do not retain the Gram stain. So, they cannot be classified as Gram-positive or Gram-negative. Furthermore, Gram-positive bacteria typically have a thicker peptidoglycan layer and are not generally smaller than mycoplasma.

8. (*a*) Bacteria are unicellular organisms with relatively simple structures compared to multicellular organisms. However, they exhibit complex behaviours such as chemotaxis (movement towards or away from chemicals), biofilm formation, quorum sensing (communication between bacterial cells) and various mechanisms for nutrient acquisition and defence.

9. (*c*) Statements II and III are correct. The incorrect statements can be corrected as

- Archaebacteria possess pseudo-peptidoglycan in their cell wall.
- Archaebacteria possess the ability to withstand extreme environment due to their cell wall structure, that is different from eubacteria and plants.
- Cyanobacteria can be unicellular (*Spirulina*), colonial (*Nostoc*) and filamentous (*Anabaena*) algae. *Chlamydomonas* is a single-celled green alga.

10. (*b*) Both statement I and statement II are correct.

Some bacteria are indeed autotrophic, meaning they can produce their own food through processes like photosynthesis or chemosynthesis. Examples include cyanobacteria (photosynthetic) and certain chemosynthetic bacteria. But, the vast majority of bacteria are heterotrophic, and they rely on other organisms or organic compounds for their food.

11. (*d*) There are two kingdoms in Whittaker's classification system that strictly include organisms with only heterotrophic nutrition: kingdom Fungi and kingdom-Animalia. Fungi are strictly heterotrophic organisms that obtain nutrients through absorption of organic matter. Whereas, animals are also strictly heterotrophic, obtaining nutrients by consuming other organisms or organic matter.

12. (*b*) Mycoplasma are pleomorphic due to the absence of cell wall and thus, they are able to alter their shape or size in response to environmental conditions.

13. (*c*) Aristotle was the first scientist responsible for the biological classification. He is renowned for his contributions to biology, where he systematically grouped plants according to their physical characteristics (trees, shrubs, and herbs) and separated animals based on the presence or absence of red blood cells.

14. (*a*) Alternation of generation refers to a life cycle characteristic, where there are distinct haploid and diploid phases in an organism's life cycle, typically involving meiosis and fertilisation (syngamy). In bacteria, reproduction typically involves asexual processes such as binary fission, where the genetic material replicates and divides into two daughter cells without the formation of haploid and diploid phases or the alternation between them. Bacteria do not undergo meiosis (reduction division) to form haploid cells, nor do they undergo syngamy (fertilisation) to produce a diploid state.

15. (*c*) The given figure represents a filamentous blue-green alga (cyanobacteria), *Nostoc* that often forms blooms in polluted water bodies. It is a filamentous alga. This organism possesses specialised cells called heterocysts that are involved in atmospheric nitrogen fixation.

Test 2

1. (*b*) Mixotrophic mode of nutrition (i.e., autotrophic + heterotrophic) is found in the euglenoids, belonging to kingdom-Protista. Euglenoids are freshwater organisms found in stagnant water. Instead of a cell wall, they have a proteinaceous pellicle layer, which makes their body flexible. They have pigments that are identical to those present in higher plants, e.g. *Euglena*.

2. (*a*) Diatoms are predominantly non-motile or have limited motility. Diatoms typically do not possess flagella for movement. Instead, they move passively in water using mucilage pads or by gliding along surfaces.

3. (*a*) The given figure is that of dinoflagellates. They release toxins in large quantities that can potentially lead to the mortality of other marine animals, including fish.

4. (*b*) Red sea is caused by *Trichodesmium erythraeum*, a blue-green alga. This is due to presence of colour phycoerythrin.

Red tide is caused by *Gonyaulax* sp., a dinoflagellate. This is due to their red colour and the toxin caused by such large number as a result of rapid multiplication.

5. (*b*) The incorrect statement can be corrected as

Paramoecium is an example of ciliated protozoans. These are aquatic actively moving organism. They have a cavity (gullet) that opens to the outside of the cell surface. The coordinated movement of rows of cilia causes the water laden with food to be steered into the gullet.

6. (*b*) *Mucor*, *Rhizopus* and *Albugo* are all examples of fungi that belong to the class-Phycomycetes. This class is characterised by its aseptate and coenocytic hyphae, which supports efficient nutrient transport and multinucleate growth. It also exhibits sexual reproduction through the formation of zygospores, although asexual reproduction is more common in many species.

7. (*d*) A is true, but R is false. R can be corrected as

The sexual reproductive stage is important in the fungal classification, the fungal identification, but classification also considers other characteristics such as morphology, genetic data, and asexual reproductive structures.

8. (*b*) Morels belong to the class-Ascomycetes, not Basidiomycetes. They are known for their distinctive honeycomb-like appearance and are known as edible fungi.

9. (*c*) *Amoeba* does not possess feature given in option (c).

In *Amoeba*, under unfavourable condition, the plasmodium forms fruiting bodies with spores at their tip. These spores are true-walled and are resistant to adverse condition.

10. (*d*) The incorrect feature (d) w.r.t. dinoflagellates can be explained as

The presence of a protein-rich pellicle is characteristic of euglenoids, not dinoflagellates. Dinoflagellates have cellulosic plates, not a pellicle.

11. (*d*) Statement I is correct, but statement II is incorrect. The incorrect staement can be corrected as

Plasmodium, the parasite responsible for malaria, is not a flagellated protozoan. It belongs to the sporozoans. They are characterised by having complex organelles at their apical end, and it primarily moves through gliding motility. It does not have flagella.

12. (*a*) Statement I is incorrect, but statement II is correct. Statement I can be corrected as

Zoospores are types of spores that are typically formed within specialised structures such as zoosporangia or sporangia (endogenously), not at the top or side of hyphae.

13. (*d*) Phycomycetes, a group of lower fungi including aquatic fungi like water molds, reproduce asexually through spores, which can be motile or non-motile.

Zoospores are motile asexual spores with flagella, characteristic of many aquatic fungi in Phycomycetes, allowing them to swim to new locations.

Aplanospores are non-motile asexual spores without flagella, produced by some fungi in Phycomycetes, and dispersed by water currents to new locations for germination.

14. (*c*) Deuteromycetes are not restricted only to soil; they can inhabit a variety of environments beyond soil, including plant surfaces and decaying organic matter.

15. (*b*) *Neurospora* is a sac (*A*) fungi (Ascomycetes) whose thallus consists of branched (*B*), septate (*C*) hyphae. Its mycelium is monokaryotic (*D*), but dikaryotic (*E*) mycelium is also found for a short period. It is used as a model a organism for genetics due to its simple genetics, wide availability, haploid (*F*) life cycle and easy growth.

Test 3

1. (*c*) Prions are infectious agents consisting of abnormally folded protein, the most notable disease caused by prions are Bovine Spongi-form Encephalopathy (BSE) commonly called mad cow disease in cattle and its analogous variant Cr-Jacob Disease (CJD) in humans.

2. (*a*) The capsomeres of bacteriophages consist of protein subunits arranged in helical or polyhedral geometric forms. These structures form the capsid, which protects the viral genetic material and aids in infecting host cells.

3. (*c*) Statements I and IV are incorrect. These can be corrected as
- Viroids differ from viruses in having RNA molecule without a protein coat.
- Bacteriophage is a complex icosahedral shaped virus with *ds*DNA. One example of helical shaped viruses are TMVs.

4. (*b*) Viruses may or may not be enveloped. In enveloped viruses, a lipid bilayer membrane is present, e.g. HIV. In non-enveloped or naked viruses, a lipid bilayer membrane is absent, e.g. adenoviruses.

5. (*d*) Viroid is an infectious agent that is smaller than viruses. It was found to be free RNA. The RNA of the viroids is of low molecular weight.
Prions are infectious agents consisting of abnormally folded protein. The agent was similar in size to viruses.

6. (*d*) Statement I is correct, but statement II is incorrect. The incorrect statement can be corrected as
A virus is a nucleoprotein and infectious genetic material (DNA or RNA) causing diseases like mumps, smallpox, and herpes. Tuberculosis is caused due to a bacterium *Mycobacterium tuberculosis*.

7. (*c*) Incorrect statement can be corrected as
Viroids are actually small circular RNA molecules, not *ds*RNA (double-stranded RNA). They are known for being the smallest known pathogens capable of causing various plant diseases. Viroids do not encode proteins and rely on host cell machinery for replication. They enter plants through wounds or mechanical damage, not typically through insect bites.

8. (*b*) The correct match is A-4, B-3, C-1, D-2.
TMV (Tobacco Mosaic Virus) infects tobacco plants and other members of the nightshade family, causing characteristic mosaic patterns of discoloration on the leaves.
Herpes simplex virus causes infections characterised by painful sores or blisters on the skin and mucous membranes.
Prions are smaller in size to viruses and are responsible for causing Bovine Spongiform Encephalopathy (BSE), commonly called mad cow disease in cattle.
Viroids are infectious agents smaller than viruses and lack protein coat. They cause potato spindle tuber disease in potato plant.

9. (*b*) Statement (b) is incorrect w.r.t. viruses and can be corrected as
Viruses are not included in the five kingdom classification given by RH Whittaker along with other acellular organisms like viroids and prions.

10. (*c*) Viroids were discovered by TO Diener in 1971. Unlike typical viruses, viroids are small, circular RNA molecules that do not encode proteins but are capable of causing various plant diseases. Their discovery marked a significant advancement in understanding infectious agents that differ from conventional viruses due to their unique genetic and structural characteristics.

11. (*d*) Statement I is correct, but statement II is incorrect. Statement II can be corrected as
Retroviruses are not categorised as "mild" viruses. These are a family of enveloped RNA viruses that use reverse transcriptase to convert their RNA genome into DNA upon infection of a host cell. They include significant human pathogens such as HIV (Human Immunodeficiency Virus).

12. (*b*) The main difference between viruses and viroids is that viruses have a capsid (protein coat) and may have an envelope, whereas viroids lack both a capsid and an envelope. Viroids consist only of a short strand of RNA and do not have any protein component.

13. (*a*) A is false, but R is true. A can be corrected as
Viruses are classified based on multiple criteria, including their genetic material (RNA or DNA), structure, replication cycle, host range and other characteristics.
Therefore, genetic material type alone does not determine virus classification.

14. (*d*) Prions are unique infectious agents primarily composed of misfolded proteins. Unlike viruses, bacteria, and other pathogens, prions do not contain genetic material such as DNA or RNA. Instead, they induce abnormal folding of normal cellular prion proteins, leading to the formation of aggregates that disrupt normal cellular functions. Prions can replicate by converting normal proteins into the abnormal prion form, perpetuating their infectious nature without the need for typical genetic material like DNA or RNA.

15. (*d*) Statement (d) is incorrect w.r.t. lichens. Major part of lichen is constituted by mycobiont (fungal part), while phycobiont (algal component) constitutes only 5% part of lichen body.

Chapter Break Thru

1. (*d*) In the earlier systems of classification, organisms such as bacteria, blue-green algae (BGA), fungi, mosses, and ferns were grouped together under plants primarily because they all have cell walls. This classification did not consider significant differences in cellular structure, modes of reproduction or other fundamental biological characteristics. The presence of a cell wall was a common feature that these diverse groups shared, leading to their classification under a single kingdom despite their differences.

2. (*c*) Fungi have chitinous walls, providing structural support and protection. Their mode of nutrition is heterotrophic, i.e. they absorb nutrients by breaking down organic matter with enzymes.

While green plants have cellulosic walls giving rigidity and strength to maintain shape and resist osmotic pressure. Their mode of nutrition is autotrophic and produce food through photosynthesis using light, carbon dioxide and water.

3. (*d*) While many bacteria have flagella and use them for movement, cyanobacteria typically do not have flagella. Cyanobacteria often move by gliding or by buoyancy regulation using gas vesicles.

Other options can be explained as

- Both bacteria and cyanobacteria are prokaryotic. Prokaryotes are organisms, whose cells lack a well-defined nucleus and other membrane-bound organelles.
- Both bacteria and cyanobacteria can reproduce by binary fission.
- Both bacteria and cyanobacteria contain proteins. Proteins are essential macromolecules involved in various cellular functions, including enzymes, structural components, and transport molecules.

4. (*c*) '*A*' represents flagellum. It is hair-like structure present at the ends of many bacteria, and it plays a crucial role in bacterial motility.

5. (*c*) Although euglenoids are photosynthetic, they do not have a well-developed cell wall. Instead, they have a flexible protein-rich layer called a pellicle that allows them to change shape.

6. (*d*) The fungi (i), (ii) and (iii) are *Agaricus*, *Mucor* and *Aspergillus*, respectively. They belong to different classes of kingdom fungi. *Agaricus* belong the Basidomycetes. *Mucor* belong to Phycomycetes and *Aspergillus* belong the Ascomycetes.

7. (*d*) Statement I is correct, but statement II is incorrect. The incorrect statement can be corrected as

While MW Beijerinck did describe viruses as "*Contagium vivum fluidum*" (which translates to "contagious living fluid"), the term reflects the idea that viruses could cause disease and being infectious agents they are not literally fluids. Viruses are not fluids; they are particles that can exist in a fluid state but are actually composed of protein and nucleic acid.

8. (*b*) The correct match is A-3, B-4, C-1, D-2.

Dinoflagellates have one long flagellum and the ribbon-like flat flagella.

Diatoms contain a unique glass like wall made of hydrated silica embedded in an organic matrix.

Euglenoids are devoid of cell wall. They have a protein rich layer under the plasma membrane called pellicle (also called as periplast, which makes their body flexible.

Slime moulds can generally be divided into 2 main groups-plasmodial slime mould and cellular slime mould. Under favourable conditions, they form plasmodium which may grow and spread over several feet.

9. (*b*) The combination of slime moulds, *Euglena* and *Gonyaulax* best fits the criteria of organisms showing characteristics of both plants and animals. These can be explained as

Euglena is a well-known example of an organism that exhibits both plant-like and animal-like characteristics. It has chloroplasts and performs photosynthesis like plants, but it can also move using a flagellum and ingest food like animals, when light is not available.

Slime moulds can behave like amoeboid protozoans (animal-like), moving and ingesting food, and like fungi (plant-like), producing spores.

Gonyaulax is a dinoflagellate that is marine and photosynthetic with cellulosic cell wall (plant-like). It also possesses flagella for movements (like animals).

10. (*a*) Incorrect statement (a) w.r.t. amoeboid protozoans can be corrected as

Entamoeba, a genus of amoeboid protozoans, primarily exhibits phagocytosis as its nutritional mode, where it engulfs particles of food rather than consuming entire organisms (holozoic nutrition).

11. (*b*) Fungi, unlike plants, do not have true roots, stems or leaves. Instead, they consist of a thallus, which is an undifferentiated body plan that typically includes a network of hyphae (mycelium) forming a mass or structure without specialised tissues for these plant-like organs.

12. (*b*) Statements II, IV and V are correct, while statements I and III are incorrect. The incorrect statements can be corrected as

Eubacteria (true bacteria) exhibit a vast diversity in their environmental tolerance, but they cannot survive in all environments. Some thrive in extreme conditions (extremophiles), while others have specific requirements.

While some Eubacteria can undergo conjugation (a form of sexual reproduction), asexual reproduction by binary fission is far more common.

13. (*d*) The correct match is A-4, B-3, C-1, D-2.

Diatoms are characterised by their cell walls embedded with silica.

Plasmodium is known for causing malaria and does not form fruiting bodies.

Gonyaulax is a dinoflagellate known for causing red tides.

Euglena has pigments similar to those found in plants, allowing it to perform photosynthesis.

14. (*c*) Both A and R are true, but R is not the correct explanation of A.

Euglena is an unicellular organism that exhibits both plant-like and animal-like characteristics. It can move using its flagellum and photosynthesise. *Euglena*'s characteristics overlap with both kingdoms (i.e. plant and animal) making it difficult to fit into either category. Moreover, the two-kingdom system is outdated and does not account for other organism.

15. (*b*) Membrane-bound organelles are absent in prokaryotic cell. In the given organisms, *Escherichia* is the only prokaryote, thus it lacks membrane–bound organelles like ER, mitochondria, etc. *Trypanosoma* and *Paramoecium* are protists, while *Saccharomyces* is a unicellular fungus. They are eukaryotic and possess such organelles along with a well-defined nucleus.

16. (*d*) WM Stanley showed that viruses could be crystallised and the crystals consisted of proteins.

17. (*b*) Both statement I and statement II are correct.

Chrysophytes are a group that includes diatoms and golden algae (also known as golden-brown algae) and they are indeed microscopic.

Most diatoms are photosynthetic and have an autotrophic mode of nutrition, meaning they produce their own food through photosynthesis.

18. (*b*) Members belonging to the class-Ascomycetes are predominantly multicellular and occasionally unicellular. They are saprophytic decomposers and can grow on dung (coprophilous). Ascomycetes reproduce through both sexual (ascospores) and asexual (conidia) spores. Many members of this class, such as morels and truffles, are edible and highly prized as delicacies.

19. (*c*) Incorrect statement w.r.t. viruses can be corrected as

Viruses may undergo mutations as they can make changes in their nucleic acid structure. This continuous change is a result of genetic selection and adapting mechanism for viruses. Mutation occurs, when an error is incorporated in the viral genome.

20. (*c*) Both A and R are true, but R is not the correct explanation of A.

Diatomaceous earth, composed of fossilised remains of diatoms (which have silica cell walls), is used in various industrial applications such as polishing agents and filtration due to its abrasive and porous nature.

21. (*b*) Smut fungi belong to the genus *Ustilago*. They are plant pathogens that infect various grass species, including wheat. These fungi cause diseases known as smuts, which manifest as dark, powdery masses of spores replacing normal plant tissues, such as kernels of wheat.

22. (*c*) The correct match is A-4, B-1, C-2, D-3

Plant viruses, e.g. TMV (Tobacco Mosaic Virus), affect various plants.

Animal viruses like SARS, affect humans in a negative way.

Viroids are smaller circular single - stranded RNA molecules. They have a smaller genome size.

Lichens are symbiotic association between algae and fungi.

23. (*d*) Statement I is correct, but statement II is incorrect. Incorrect statement can be corrected as

Yeasts do not typically form well-developed mycelium. Instead, they exist as individual cells or may form pseudohyphae (chains of cells), but they do not produce true branched mycelium like other filamentous fungi.

Yeasts are a group of fungi that typically exist as unicellular organisms.

They belong to the phylum-Ascomycota (sac fungi), and their simplicity as unicellular organisms is well recognised.

24. (*b*) The given diagram is of Tobacco Mosaic Virus (TMV). It causes disease in tobacco plant.

TMV has single-stranded RNA.

25. (*b*) MW Beijerinck concluded that the cause of tobacco mosaic disease was not a filtrate toxin because the sap was infectious even though it was filtered to remove becteria.

26. (*d*) *Mucor* and *Rhizopus* are common examples of Phycomycetes.

Members of phycomycetes are found in aquatic habitats and on decaying wood in moist and damp places or as obligate parasite on plants. The mycelium is aseptate and coenocytic.

27. (*d*) As per Whittaker classification, given characters belong to kingdom-Fungi. Whittaker classified organisms into following five kingdoms.

Monera	Enveloped or naked prokaryotes.
Protista	Simple, unicellular eukaryotes.
Fungi	Multicellular, chitinous cell wall, eukaryotes with heterotrophic nutrition.
Plantae	Multicellular, cellulosic cell wall, eukaryotes with autotrophic nutrition.
Animalia	Multicellular, eukaryotes with heterotrophic nutrition, cell wall absent.

28. (*d*) Mycoplasma are monerans, which cause diseases in various plants and animals but are not typically associated with pathogenicity in fungi.

29. (*b*) Continued nuclear division in fungus makes the hyphae multinucleate. If the whole mycelium is without septum, the condition is called coenocytic.

30. (*d*) Incorrect match pair can be corrected as

Noctiluca is a heterotrophic dinoflagellate.

Rest other options are correctly scientific named, but incorrectly described.

31. (*d*) Both Archaebacteria and Eubacteria are single-celled organisms. However, Archaebacteria and Eubacteria differ in other characteristics such as the structure of their cell walls and the environments they inhabit. Archaebacteria do not have peptidoglycan in their cell walls, and they often live in extreme environments, while Eubacteria have peptidoglycan and can be found in a wider range of habitats.

32. (*c*) The kingdom–Protista includes a diverse group of organisms that are primarily unicellular. This kingdom encompasses various types of algae (such as diatoms), some disease-causing parasites (like *Plasmodium*, which causes malaria), and planktonic organisms (including various protozoans and golden algae).

33. (*b*) Edible morels and truffles are not unique to Basidiomycetes. These are edible sac fungi that belongs to the class–Ascomycetes.

34. (*c*) *Paramoecium* is a ciliated protozoan that moves actively due to presence of tiny microscopic outgrowth called cilia that beat in coordinated patterns for movement. The gullet is used by *Paramoecium* for the ingestion of food particles.

35. (*d*) *Agaricus* is primarily known for its edible species, such as *Agaricus bisporus*, the common button mushroom.
Agaricus species are cultivated for human consumption and are not associated with plant or human diseases.

36. (*a*) TO Diener is credited with discovering viroids, which are small, circular RNA molecules that can cause plant diseases. Unlike viruses, viroids do not have a protein coat and are much smaller, consisting only of RNA. This discovery was significant because it revealed a new category of infectious agents distinct from conventional viruses.

37. (*a*) Statement I is incorrect, but statement II is correct. The incorrect statement can be corrected as
The kingdom-Protista includes a variety of organisms with different modes of nutrition. For example, some protists, such as *Euglena*, can perform photosynthesis and are autotrophic, while others are heterotrophic.

38. (*b*) Aristotle's classification system focused on morphological similarities—the physical characteristics and structures of organisms. He classified animals based on their observable features, such as the presence or absence of certain body parts (e.g., whether they had blood, their habitat and their mode of reproduction).

39. (*c*) Basidiospores are exogenous spores produced externally on basidia in Basidiomycetes class of fungi (such as mushrooms). Basidia are arranged in fruiting bodies called basidiocarp.

40. (*b*) Statements I and II are correct w.r.t. acellular organisms. Statements III and IV can be corrected as
The genetic material of acellular organisms (viruses) can be either DNA or RNA, and it can be single-stranded or double-stranded. Virus affecting plants generally have single-stranded RNA, while virus affecting bacteria have double-stranded DNA. They are smaller than bacteria and can cross filter paper easily.

41. (*a*) Herbs, shrubs and trees are classified under the same kingdom (Plantae). This classification is based on their common characteristics and is not classified under two kingdom system of classification.

42. (*a*) Viruses have a protein coat known as a capsid, which encloses their genetic material. Viroids, on the other hand, are much simpler. They consist solely of a small, circular RNA molecule without a protein coat.

43. (*a*) The correct match is A-3, B-4, C-1, D-2.
Potato spindle tuber disease is caused by viroids, which is an infectious agent smaller than viruses.
Red rot of sugarcane is caused by *Colletotrichum*, which belongs to Deuteromycetes.
White rust on mustard is a parasitic infection of a fungus, *Albugo* belonging to Phycomycetes.
Citrus canker is a bacterial disease in which lesions are observed on leaves, fruits and stems of citrus plants. It is caused by the bacterium *Xanthomonas*.

44. (*b*) Both A and R are true, and the R is the correct explanation of A.
The five-kingdom classification system is a method of organising all living organisms into five broad categories or kingdoms. This system helps scientists understand and study the diversity of life by grouping organisms that share similar characteristics.
Kingdom-Monera includes prokaryotic organisms like bacteria and cyanobacteria.
Kingdom-Fungi consists of eukaryotic organisms that are primarily saprophytic, meaning they obtain nutrients by decomposing organic matter.

45. (*d*) Dinoflagellates protists typically have two flagella. One flagellum is located in a transverse groove around the middle of the cell (the "equatorial" flagellum) and the other is in a longitudinal groove that extends along the length of the cell, while *Euglena* possesses long flagellum extending from the anterior end of the cell.
This flagellum is used for locomotion. *Euglena* also have a shorter flagella.

46. (*c*) Protists are often unicellular, meaning that a single cell performs all metabolic functions. This is specific to Protista and does not apply to multicellular eukaryotes (such as plants, animals, and fungi), where different cells perform specialised functions. Protists have cellular body organisation.

47. (*c*) Ferns belong to kingdom-Plantae, and their cell walls contain cellulose, which provides structural support, while cell wall of fungi (*Saccharomyces*) contain polysaccharides and chitin.
The cell walls of cyanobacteria and bacteria (*Anabaena* and *Xanthomonas*) are made up of peptidoglycan.

48. (*a*) Bacteria are highly versatile in their metabolic processes. They can utilise a wide range of organic and inorganic compounds for energy. This ability allows them to thrive in diverse environments and contributes to their metabolic diversity.

49. (*b*) Bacteriophages typically have a protein capsid that encases their nucleic acid, a tail sheath and tail fibers used for attachment and injection of the genetic material into the host cell, and the core nucleic acid, which can either be DNA or RNA.

50. (*d*) Statement I is correct, but statement II is incorrect. The incorrect statement can be corrected as

The dispersal of slime mould spores is generally not facilitated by water currents. Instead, spores are typically dispersed by air currents or by mechanical means.

Ch-3 Plant Kingdom

Topical Follow Thru

Test-1

1. (*a*) An artificial classification system categorises organisms based on easily observable characteristics (gross superficial morphological characters) without considering their evolutionary relationships. These characteristics can be vegetative (related to plant structures like leaves and stems) or reproductive (related to flower parts like the androecium, which contains stamens).

2. (*c*) *Porphyra* is a type of red alga, not brown alga, while *Sargassum* is a brown alga. *Porphyra* belongs to the class-Rhodophyceae and is commonly known as nori, used in sushi. Other mentioned algae are examples of brown algae.

3. (*b*) Red algae, members of Rhodophyceae, commonly have multicellular thalli (body structure) and are typically found in warmer regions. These algae thrive in marine environments with moderate to warmer temperatures.

4. (*a*) Option (a) is the correct ecological significance of algae in aquatic ecosystems. Algae are primary producers that perform photosynthesis, which increases dissolved oxygen levels in aquatic environments. This supports the survival and growth of aquatic animals, making algae critical in aquatic food cycles.

5. (*d*) The figure represents the members of Chlorophyceae (*Volvox* and *Ulothrix*, respectively). Members of class Chlorophyceae, commonly known as green algae, are photosynthetic organisms that contain chlorophyll pigments in their chloroplasts. The primary pigments involved in photosynthesis in Chlorophyceae are chlorophyll-*a* and chlorophyll-*b* and they work synergistically to facilitate photosynthesis, contributing to their ecological success as primary producers in many ecosystems.

6. (*c*) The classification system developed by George Bentham and Joseph Dalton Hooker is referred to as the natural classification system. This system categorises plants based on a comprehensive set of morphological and structural characteristics, aiming to reflect the natural relationships among different species.

7. (*a*) Floridean starch is a type of storage carbohydrate that is characteristic of red algae (Rhodophyceae). *Polysiphonia* is a genus of red algae storing their food as floridean starch.

8. (*b*) Option (b) refers to the biochemical makeup of chromosomes, such as DNA, proteins and other molecular components. While it is important in molecular biology and genetics, this specific aspect is not the primary focus of cytotaxonomy, which deals more with structural and behavioural characteristics.

9. (*c*) Algae can also produce anisogamous gametes along with isogamous and oogamous gametes. In anisogamy, the gametes differ in size and possibly in other characteristics, but not to the extent seen in oogamous reproduction.

10. (*a*) Engler and Prantl's system primarily focused on evolutionary relationships, seeking to group plants based on their descent from common ancestors. This approach helps in understanding the diversification of plant species over time.

11. (*d*) Statement I is correct, but statement II is incorrect. The incorrect statement can be corrected as

Luxuriant growth of algae, especially in water reservoirs, can lead to water quality issues rather than improving it. Algal blooms can release toxins and organic matter into the water, causing taste and odour problems, and in some cases, toxins harmful to human health. Therefore, algal growth typically does not make water fit for drinking. Instead, it makes it unfit.

12. (*b*) *Chlamydomonas* is a unicellular green alga. It possesses cellulosic cell wall, starch as stored food, 2-8, equal, apical flagella and contains chlorophyll-*a* and *b*.

13. (*d*) Oogamous reproduction involves the fusion of a larger, non-motile egg (female gamete) with a smaller, motile sperm (male gamete). This type of reproduction is common in many multicellular organisms, including higher plants and most animals. The other types can be discussed as

Isogamous reproduction refers to the fusion of gametes that are similar in size and morphology, typically in unicellular organisms or some lower multicellular algae.

Anisogamous reproduction refers to the fusion of gametes that differ in size and often in other characteristics.

Allogamous reproduction refers to the fertilisation involving gametes from different individuals.

14. (*b*) Option (b) correctly emphasises the diverse ecological roles of algae in forming symbiotic associations. Algae collaborate with fungi to form lichens, showcasing their adaptability and ecological importance in various habitats. Algae can occasionally form associations with certain animals (such as sloth bear), demonstrating their versatility in ecological interactions.

15. (*b*) Both A and R are true and R is the correct explanation of A.
Members of the class Phaeophyceae, commonly known as brown algae, vary in color from olive green to various shades of brown.
Phaeophyceae possess a combination of pigments: chlorophyll-*a*, *c*, carotenoids and xanthophylls.
While chlorophyll-*a* contributes to the green colour, the presence of brown pigments called fucoxanthin (a type of xanthophyll) in Phaeophyceae masks some of the green colour. The amount of fucoxanthin relative to chlorophyll determines the final color variation seen in brown algae, ranging from olive green (more chlorophyll) to deeper brown (more fucoxanthin).

16. (*b*) Statement III is incorrect and can be corrected as
Ectocarpus is a simple branched, filamentous form, while kelps are profusely branched form.

17. (*c*) In Phaeophyceae, the vegetative cells have a cellulosic wall usually covered on the outside by a gelatinous coating of algin.

18. (*d*) Statements I and III are correct. Statements II and IV are incorrect and can be corrected as
The structure of floridean starch is very similar to amylopectin and glycogen.
Green algae possess cell wall with inner cellulosic and outer pectose layer.

19. (*c*) The given figure belongs to *Chlamydomonas* (a green alga).
Presence of chlorophyll- *b* is the characteristic feature of Chlorophyceae. Chlorophyll- *a* is found in all the three main classes of algae.

20. (*a*) Statements I, II, and III are correct. Statement IV is incorrect and can be corrected as
In vegetative reproduction by fragmentation, each fragment develops into a thallus.

21. (*a*) The figures A and B represent *Polysiphonia* and *Chara*, respectively.
Polysiphonia possesses *r*-phycoerythrin, while *Chara* possesses chlorophyll-*a* and *b*.
Fucoxanthin is present in brown algae, like *Ectocarpus*, *Fucus*, *Sargassum* and *Laminaria* etc.

22. (*a*) Male gametes are flagellated in class-Chlorophyceae (*Volvox*) and Phaeophyceae (*Ectocarpus, Fucus*).
Members of Rhodophyceae (*Sargassum, Polysiphonia, Gracilaria, Gelidium*) possess non-motile gametes.

23. (*b*) *Spirogyra* filaments show isogamy where the gametes are non-flagellated, but similar in size (isogametes).

24. (*b*) George Bentham and Joseph Dalton Hooker gave the natural classification system for flowering plant, which includes not only the external features, but also the internal features, like ultra structure, anatomy, embryology and phytochemistry.

25. (*a*) Sexual reproduction in *Chlamydomonas* may be isogamous, where the gametes are flagellated (motile) and similar in size. It also shows anisogamy and oogamy.

Test 2

1. (*d*) *Sphagnum* (peat moss) is highly valued by gardeners and horticulturists for its ability to retain water and provide a moist environment for plants. Its unique structure allows it to absorb and hold large amount of water, which it releases slowly, helping to keep seedlings and cut plants hydrated during transportation and propagation.

2. (*c*) The protonema typically consists of green, filamentous structures that perform photosynthesis. These structures are usually prostrate (growing along the ground), but they are green due to the presence of chlorophyll.

3. (*d*) *Pinus* (pines) is monoecious gymnosperm, meaning that individual plant bears both male and female cones. This allows a single tree to produce both pollen (in male cones) and ovules (in female cones), facilitating reproduction.

4. (*c*) Gemmae are specialised structures for asexual reproduction found in liverworts, such as *Marchantia*. These are small, green, multicellular buds that develop in cup-like receptacles known as gemma cups. When dispersed, usually by water, they can grow into new plants, allowing the organism to reproduce asexually and spread rapidly.

5. (*d*) Statements I, II and III are correct. Statements IV and V are incorrect and can be corrected as
Prothallus is a free-living, mostly photosynthetic, thalloid gametophyte found in pteridophytes.
In mosses, the leafy stage, not the protonema, bears the sex organs.

6. (*b*) In pteridophytes, the sporophytic generation is dominant and it bears sporangia. These sporangia are often subtended by specialised leaves called sporophylls.

7. (*b*) The "chemotactic movement of sperms" is an adaptation found in aquatic environments and moist conditions rather than a direct adaptation to land conditions.
Although, bryophytes do require water for sperm movement, this characteristic is more associated with their ancestors of aquatic origins.

8. (*a*) In monoecious plants, like *Pinus*, both male and female reproductive structures are found on the same plant. Male cones produce pollen, while female cones produce ovules. This ensures that a single tree can produce both types of cones for reproduction.

9. (*a*) In bryophytes, the gametophytic phase is the dominant, photosynthetic, and free-living part of the life cycle. It is the main stage that one would observe in the habitat where bryophytes grow. The sporophytic phase, which develops after fertilisation, is attached to and nutritionally dependent on the gametophyte.
The sporophyte's primary role is to produce and release spores, which will germinate to form new gametophytes.

10. (*b*) The nucellus is the massive parenchymatous tissue within the ovule in the gymnosperms. It provides nourishment to the developing embryo sac.

11. (*a*) Heterospory is seen in certain genera of pteridophytes such as *Salvinia*, *Selaginella*, and *Marsilea*. These genera produce two distinct types of spores: microspores (which develop into male gametophytes) and megaspores (which develop into female gametophytes). This adaptation is considered a significant evolutionary step towards the development of seeds.

12. (*d*) The given diagram is of *Selaginella*, a pteridophyte.
Selaginella has microphylls (small leaves with a single vein), strobili (cone-like structures where spores are produced), and it also exhibits heterospory (i.e., it produces both microspores and megaspores).

13. (*d*) The correct match is A-3, B-1, C-2, D-4.
Polytrichum is a genus of moss known for having a well-developed protonema stage.
Marchantia is a type of liverwort, which has a thalloid body form.
Sphagnum is commonly known as peat moss because it grows in acidic marshes (bogs) and helps in peat formation.
Selaginella is known as spike moss, which is a type of club moss, belonging to Pteridophyta.

14. (*a*) Statement I is incorrect, but statement II is correct. Statement I can be corrected as
Pteridophytes are vascular plants, meaning they have vascular tissues (xylem and phloem) for the transport of water and nutrients. However, they are indeed seedless, reproducing *via* spores.

15. (*c*) Both A and R are true, but R is not the correct explanation of A.
In liverworts, the male and female sex organs (antheridia and archegonia) can either be present on the same thallus (monoecious) or on different thalli (dioecious).

16. (*b*) Both statement I and statement II are correct.
Coralloid roots of *Cycas* are symbiotically associated with algae, whereas mycorrhizal roots of *Pinus* are symbiotically associated with fungi.
World's tallest tree, *Sequoia* (giant red wood), a gymnosperm, is about 125 m in height, 30 m in girth, about 4,000 years old and found in Red wood park of California.

17. (*b*) Both A and R are true and R is the correct explanation of A.
Gnetum acts as a connecting link between gymnosperms and angiosperms as it exhibits some characteristics of gymnosperms and some of angiosperms.
It possesses features like vessel elements and double fertilisation that are found in angiosperms, while also retaining some gymnospermic traits like naked seeds.

18. (*a*) The prothallus is developed from a spore. It is usually the gametophytic stage in the life cycle.
It develops from the germinating spore. It is short-lived and inconspicuous heart-shaped structure with number of rhizoids, growing underneath the sex organs, archegonium and antheridium.

19. (*d*) Pteridophytes possess vascular tissues like xylem and phloem, while bryophytes lack them.
Bryophytes possess similar structures called leptoids and hydroids.

20. (*b*) Heterospory and seed habit is best shown in the *Selaginella* plant. Most of the pteridophytes, i.e., *Equisetum*, *Lycopodium*, *Psilotum*, *Dryopteris* are homosporous, i.e., only one type of spores are formed in them. Heterospory is found in *Selaginella, Salvinia* and *Marsilea*.
Rhynia is a pteridophyte which is now extinct and only found as a fossil.

21. (*b*) The correct match is A-3, B-1, C-4, D-2.
Cycas revoluta is called as sago palm.
Pinus roxburghii is known as chir pine.
Ginkgo biloba is called maiden hair tree.
Pinus gerardiana is called as chilgoza pine.

22. (*c*) Statements I, II and III are correct. Statement IV is incorrect and can be corrected as
Bryophytes do not possess a free-living sporophyte. Instead, it is attached to the photosynthetic gametophyte and derives nutrition from it.

23. (*a*) Pteridophytes possess sporophyte as its main plant body, which is differentiated into true root, stem and leaves and is well-vascularised. The sporophytes also bear sporangia that are subtended by leaf-like appendages called sporophylls. They possess free-living gametophytes and sporophytes.

24. (*d*) The given diagram shows female thallus of *Marchantia*.
Label '*X*' represents archegoniophore that bears female reproductive organ which is flask-shaped, multicellular and produces a single egg.
Production of biflagelleted antherozoids is done by antheridia found on antheridiophore (male thallus).

25. (*a*) Bryophytes have gametophyte as the dominant phase of their life cycle. Gymnosperms and pteridophytes have sporophytic phase as the dominant phase of life cycle.

Chapter Break Thru

1. (*c*) Phylogenetic classification uses data from various sources, including genetic information, fossil records, and molecular data, to determine how organisms have evolved over time and how they are related to one another. This approach results in a tree-like diagram called a phylogenetic tree or cladogram, which illustrates the evolutionary pathways and connections between species.

2. (*d*) *Marchantia* is a liverwort that reproduces asexually through structures called gemma cups present on the dorsal surface of thallus, which contain gemmae for vegetative propagation.
The other incorrect matches can be corrected as
Dictyota is a genus of brown algae (class-Phaeophyceae), not red algae (class-Rhodophyceae).
Sphagnum is a genus of moss, not club mosses. Club mosses belong to the pteridophytes and related genera, not *Sphagnum*.
Polytrichum is a genus of mosses. Mosses like *Polytrichum* have a dominant gametophytic plant body.

3. (*b*) The given figure is that of *Fucus* and *Dictyota*, respectively. They belong to class-Phaeophyceae (Brown algae) which store their reserve food, primarily in the form of laminarin, a polysaccharide and mannitol, a sugar alcohol. These compounds serve as energy reserves for brown algae.

4. (*c*) The incorrect pairing can be corrected as
The natural classification system, groups organisms based on a variety of characteristics, including morphological, anatomical, and reproductive traits, aiming to reflect their natural relationships and common ancestry. The natural classification system was developed later by scientists such as George Bentham and Joseph Dalton Hooker. Engler and Prantl gave phylogenetic classification system.

5. (*c*) In *Spirogyra*, the gametes involved in sexual reproduction are not morphologically differentiated (they look the same), but they are physiologically differentiated.
During conjugation, the contents of one cell (male gamete) move through the conjugation tube to fuse with the contents of the other cell (female gamete) in the adjacent filament.
This physiological differentiation is seen because one gamete is considered more active in moving toward the other, indicating a degree of specialisation.

6. (*d*) Vegetative reproduction in algae typically occurs through various methods such as fragmentation, spore formation and sometimes by specialised structures like zoospores or akinetes. Budding is not a common method of vegetative reproduction in algae, it is a characteristic of certain fungi and some protozoans.

7. (*d*) The incorrect statements can be corrected as
In bryophytes, meiosis occurs after the zygote develops into a sporophyte, not immediately after zygote formation.
In bryophytes, water is not required for the transport of the egg. Instead, water is necessary for the transport of sperm (antherozoids) from the antheridium to the archegonium for fertilisation.
The male sex organ, antheridium, produces flagellated antherozoids (sperm cells), but typically with two flagella, not four.

8. (*b*) *Sphagnum* (peat moss) possesses gametophyte as predominant stage of life cycle which consists of two stages: protonema and leafy stage.

9. (*c*) The protonema stage in bryophytes is the first stage in the development of the gametophyte. It arises from a spore and is characterised by a creeping growth pattern, is green due to chlorophyll and is frequently branched and filamentous (thread-like). This structure plays a crucial role in the bryophyte's life cycle by giving rise to the leafy gametophyte. This stage maximizes the surface area for photosynthesis and nutrient absorption, which is essential for the growth and development of the bryophyte.

10. (*c*) In mosses, vegetative reproduction often occurs through fragmentation, where parts of the moss break off and grow into new plants. Additionally, the secondary protonema, which is a thread-like structure that develops from the spore, can produce buds that develop into new gametophytic plants.

11. (*c*) In heterosporous species of pteridophytes, prothallus is always dioecious. Microspores on germination gives rise to male prothalli and megaspores to the female prothalli.

12. (*a*) Option (a) is correct with respect to correct difference between mosses and ferns. The life cycle of ferns possesses a predominant sporophyte, while the life cycle of a moss possesses a predominant gametophyte.
Other incorrect statements can be corrected as
In ferns , sporophylls form strobili carrying male or female structures, while the mosses possess a leafy stage bearing sex organs.
In ferns, the gametophyte is represented by prothallus, while the gametophyte in mosses is represented by two stages : protonema and leafy stage.
The male and female gametophytes in mosses and ferns possess an independent free- living existence.

13. (*c*) Gymnosperms lack xylem vessels and companion cells, which distinguishes them from angiosperms. Gymnosperms have tracheids for water transport and sieve cells (albuminous cells) for nutrient transport, while angiosperms have vessels in their xylem and companion cells associated with their sieve tube elements in the phloem.

14. (*d*) In *Cycas*, pollen grains are released from the microsporangium. They are carried by air currents and come in contact of the ovules borne on megasporophylls.

15. (*a*) The prothallus bears the reproductive organs, the antheridia (male) and archegonia (female), which produce gametes for sexual reproduction. This function is essential for the continuation of the life cycle of a pteridophyte.

16. (*b*) *Cycas* species have coralloid roots, which are specialised roots that form a symbiotic relationship with nitrogen-fixing cyanobacteria, specifically of the genus–*Anabaena*. These roots help in nitrogen fixation, which benefits the plant in nutrient- deficient soils.

17. (*b*) Gymnosperms, such as pines, have ovules that are exposed on cone or scales. This means the ovules are not enclosed by any ovary wall at any point, neither before nor after fertilisation. In contrast, angiosperms have ovules that are enclosed within an ovary wall that develops into fruit after fertilisation.

18. (*c*) The presence of archegonia is a crucial feature shared by *Funaria* (a bryophyte), *Dryopteris* (a pteridophyte), and *Ginkgo* (a gymnosperm). Archegonia are the female reproductive organs present on the gametophytic generation of these plants.

19. (*a*) Among the given list, *Polysiphonia, Porphyra* and *Gracilaria* belong to the Rhodophyceae (red algae). Red algae possess oogamous sexual reproduction followed by complex post- fertilisation development. *Ulothrix* is a green alga, while *Dictyota, Ectocarpus, Fucus* and *Sargassum* are brown algae.

20. (*c*) Statements I, II and V are correct. Statements III and IV are incorrect and can be corrected as

The majority of red algae are actually marine, not freshwater. Red algae are well adapted to marine environments and are found predominantly in saltwater habitats rather than freshwater habitats.

Red algae do not store food in the form of complex proteins. Instead, red algae store food reserves, primarily in the form of floridean starch, which is a unique type of storage carbohydrate found in these algae.

21. (*b*) The correct match is A-4, B-3, C-2, D-1.

Agar is derived from red algae, specifically from genera such as *Gelidium* and *Gracilaria.*

Algin is derived from brown algae and is used as a thickening agent in foods and other products.

Carrageen (carrageenan) is derived from red algae and is used as a gelling, thickening, and stabilising agent in various food products.

Chlorella is a type of green alga used as a single-cell protein and is a nutritional supplement, particularly noted for its use as food in space travel.

22. (*c*) The given figure belongs to *Equisetum.*

The incorrect statement can be corrected as

Equisetum belongs to class-Sphenopsida.

23. (*a*) Statement I is incorrect, but statement II is correct. Incorrect statement can be corrected as

The gametophytes of pteridophytes are non-vascular, meaning they lack the efficient water transport mechanisms seen in vascular plants. As a result, they generally require moist environments to survive and do not thrive in dry habitats like grasslands.

24. (*b*) Both A and R are true and R is the correct explanation of A.

Bryophytes are often referred to as the amphibians of the plant kingdom because like amphibians, they require a moist environment to reproduce and survive, even though they can live on land.

Bryophytes commonly inhabit areas where water is readily available, such as swamps and the transitional zones between water and land, because they need water for reproduction.

25. (*d*) Statement I is correct, but statement II is incorrect.

The incorrect statement can be corrected as

In brown algae (Phaeophyceae), the zoospores are indeed pear-shaped and biflagellated, but the flagella are not equal in length. They are unequal, with one being longer than the other. Additionally, the flagella are typically attached laterally, not apically.

26. (*d*) Statements I, II, III and V are correct, while statement IV is incorrect and can be corrected as

Heterospory is characterised by the production of two types of spores, microspores and megaspores and is not necessarily due to a reduction in the number of spores within sporangia, but rather the differentiation of spores based on size and function.

27. (*c*) Both statement I and statement II are incorrect. They can be corrected as

In bryophytes, the dominant phase of the life cycle is the gametophyte, which is independent and photosynthetic. The sporophyte is dependent on the gametophyte and is not independent.

The sex organs (antheridia and archegonia) in bryophytes are multicellular structures. Antheridia produce multicellular sperm, and archegonia produce multicellular eggs.

28. (*d*) Statements I, II and V are correct. The incorrect statements can be corrected as

The microspores in gymnosperms like *Pinus* develop into the male gametophyte (pollen grains), but it is highly reduced, not enlarged. This male gametophyte is small and contained within the pollen grain.

Each microsporophyll (male cone scale) in *Pinus* typically bears multiple microsporangia, not just one. These microsporangia are sites where microspores (pollen grains) are produced.

29. (*c*) Ferns are vascular plants belonging to the group Pteridophyta. They are characterised by leaves called fronds, which are typically large and compound. The leaves of ferns are known as macrophylls as they have a complex vascular system and often show dichotomous or pinnate venation.

Salvinia is a genus of floating aquatic ferns belonging to the family–Salviniaceae. They are heterosporous, which means they produce two types of spores: microspores and megaspores.

30. (*b*) Both A and R are true and R is the correct explanation of A

Cycas is considered a living fossil because it has existed for hundreds of millions of years with little evolutionary change. Its current form is very similar to its ancient ancestors.

Cycas has a long fossil record dating back to the Mesozoic era. Despite its ancient origins, *Cycas* species are now found in limited areas, typically in tropical and subtropical regions.

31. (*b*) Mosses have an elaborate mechanism of spore dispersal, primarily through the structure of the capsule. The capsule has a specialised opening mechanism that facilitates efficient dispersal of spores with the help of peristome teeth.

32. (*c*) If the gametophyte (prothallus) becomes dependent on the sporophyte for nutrition, it could lead to the evolution of seed like structures, similar to gymnosperms, where the gametophyte is retained and nourished by the parent sporophyte.

33. (*c*) The predominant stage of the life cycle of a moss is the gametophyte which consists of two stages. The first stage is the protonema and the second stage is the leafy stage. The second stage develops from the secondary protonema as a lateral bud.

34. (*d*) A is true, but R is false. R can be corrected as

The phylogenetic classification system is a method of classifying organisms based on their evolutionary history. It does not solely depend on supporting fossil evidence. It primarily relies on multiple lines of evidence, including molecular data, embryological traits, etc.

35. (*b*) In bryophytes, the main plant body is haploid, i.e. gametophyte (n). Archegonium (n) and antheridium (n) produce egg cell and antherozoids, respectively *via* mitosis.

An antherozoid fuses with the egg to produce zygote. Zygotes do not undergo reduction division immediately. They produce a multicellular body called sporophyte. Some cells of the sporophyte undergo reduction division to produce haploid spores.

36. (*d*) Statement I is correct, but statement II is incorrect. The incorrect statement can be corrected as

At least a half of the total carbon dioxide fixation on earth is carried out by algae through photosynthesis. Being photosynthetic, they increase the level of dissolved oxygen in their immediate environment.

37. (*a*) The incorrect statement can be corrected as

Ectocarpus is a brown alga (Phaeophyceae).

The vegetative cells have a cellulosic wall usually covered on the outside by a gelatinous coating of algin.

38. (*b*) The overharvesting of red algae does not just affect the supply of commercial products. It can significantly disrupt marine ecosystem by removing a species that supports the food chain and habitat structure.

39. (*b*) Statement given in option (b) is correct. Rest statements are incorrect and these can be corrected as

They possess tap roots generally.

Gymnosperms include medium-sized trees or tall trees and shrubs

Their seeds are not enclosed by an ovary and thus, also not produce fruits.

40. (*c*) The gymnosperms are heterosporous, i.e. they produce haploid microspores and megaspore. The two kinds of spores are produced within sporangia that are borne on sporophylls which are arranged spirally along an axis to form cones. In *Cycas*, male cones and megasporophylls are borne on different trees, i.e. it is dioecious.

41. (*a*) Statement I is incorrect, but statement II is correct. The incorrect statement can be corrected as

In pteridophytes, the main plant is a sporophyte which is differentiated into true root, stem and leaves. These organs possess well-differentiated vascular tissues.

42. (*a*) *Chara* is a member of Chlorophyceae. The plant body or thallus of *Chara* is multicellular, macroscopic, filamentous and possesses pyrenoids as storage bodies and contain proteins. In Chara, the asexual reproduction takes place by secondary protonema, amorphous bulbils, amylum star and bulbils.

43. (*b*) Statements II, III and V are correct. The incorrect statements can be corrected as

Bryophytes include the various mosses and liverworts that are found commonly growing in moist, shaded areas in the hills.

Mosses are bryophytes, whereas ferns are pteridophytes.

44. (*b*) The presence of strobili allows pteridophytes to optimise their reproductive strategy by clustering sporangia, thereby increasing spore production and enhancing their ability to disperse spores efficiently. This adaptation plays a critical role in their reproductive success and survival in various environments.

45. (*b*) Bryophytes are called as amphibians of the plant kingdom because these plants can live in soil, but are dependent on water for sexual reproduction.

Specifically, water is essential for the movement of the antherozoids.

If the environment lacks water, but is suitable for the growth of the bryophytes. The male gametes would not be able to swim to the female gametes and this will prevent fertilisation. This will lead to the discontinuation of sporophyte.

46. (*d*) The plant body of brown algae is usually attached to the substratum by a holdfast and they also have stipe, and frond.
The holdfast helps them in withstanding strong ocean currents.

47. (*c*) The incorrect match pair can be corrected as
Equisetum is a pteridophyte. It has dominant sporophytic generation. Here, the gametophyte is a short - lived phase.

48. (*c*) In the heterosporous pteriodophytes, the female gametophyte remains attached to the parent sporophyte for varying periods. After fertilisation, the zygote develops into an embryo within the female gametophyte, while still being attached to the sporophyte. This retention of the female gametophyte and development of the embryo within it is considered a precursor of the seed habit in higher plants.

49. (*b*) *Gelidium* is a genus of red algae, and it typically reproduces *via* a complex life cycle involving non-motile gametes (oogamy), not anisogamy (where the gametes are different in size or form, but both are motile).

50. (*d*) A is true, but R is false. R can be corrected as
Microspores develop into male gametophytes and megaspores develop into female gametophytes.

Ch-4 Animal Kingdom

Topical Follow Thru

Test-1

1. (*b*) Ctenophores generally undergo external fertilisation. This process involves the release of eggs and sperm into the water, where fertilisation occurs externally.After fertilisation, ctenophores undergo indirect development. They typically have a larval stage known as a Cydippid larva, which undergo metamorphosis to transform into the adult form.

2. (*b*) Annelids, such as earthworms and leeches, are the first group in evolutionary terms to exhibit a true coelom. A true coelom is a body cavity that is completely lined with mesodermal tissue, providing a space for the development and suspension of internal organs.

3. (*b*) Metamerism refers to the segmentation of the body into a series of repetitive segments.
In Chordata, particularly in vertebrates, metamerism is evident in the segmented arrangement of muscles, vertebrae and nerves along the body axis.

4. (*a*) A is false, but R is true. A can be corrected as
Nematodes and rotifers are members of Aschelminthes. They are pseudocoelomate, meaning they have a body cavity that is not completely lined with mesodermal tissue. Instead, the mesoderm is present as scattered pouches in between ectoderm and endoderm.

5. (*c*) All the combinations are correct except one. In animals having an open circulatory system, blood (or haemolymph) is not confined to vessels, but is instead pumped into a haemocoel, where it directly bathes the organs. The blood is not circulated through a closed system of tubes.

6. (*d*) Based on given characteristics, the phylum is Ctenophora.
Ctenophores are radially symmetrical (like a wheel) and have two germ layers (ectoderm and endoderm) with a tissue-level organisation. They have the comb plates, which have rows of cilia for movement through the water.
They have a digestive system that combines extracellular digestion (outside cells) and intracellular digestion (within cells).
They only reproduce through sexual means.

7. (*c*) The given figures show radial and bilateral symmetry, respectively.
Pleurobrachia belongs to the phylum Ctenophora. It exhibits radial symmetry as an adult organism.
Nereis is a genus of polychaete worms belonging to the phylum Annelida. They exhibit bilateral symmetry.

8. (*a*) Statement I is incorrect, but statement II is correct. It can be corrected as
Liver flukes have an anterior triangular head with two lateral lobes, which are actually oral suckers used for attachment and feeding.

9. (*d*) Water transport system pathway is not a fundamental feature used for broad animal classification. It is specific to sponges and does not apply to most other animal groups. In contrast, the number of germ layers, the pattern of cellular organization and segmental repetition are fundamental features used in the classification for a wide range of animal phyla.

10. (*d*) The given diagrams are of Coelomate, Pseudocoelomate and Acoelomate and the phyla A, B and C in which these are likely to be found are Annelida, Aschelminthes and Platyhelminthes, respectively.
Animals possessing coelom are called coelomates, e.g. annelids, molluscs, arthropods, echinoderms, hemichordates and chordates. In some animals mesoderm is present in scattered pouches between ectoderm and mesoderm, known as pseudocoelomates, e.g. Aschelminthes. The animals in which the body cavity is absent are (called acoelomates e.g. Platyhelminthes.

11. (*c*) Scleroblasts are specialized cells in sponges that produce and secrete spicules, which forms the skeleton of the sponge. These spicules provide structural support and protection to the sponge.

12. (*d*) In Aschelminthes (nematodes), the excretory system consists of a pair of lateral excretory tubes that run along the length of the body. These tubes collect metabolic wastes from the body cavity and expel them through an excretory pore located near the anterior end of the organism. This system efficiently removes waste products from the body and helps in maintaining osmotic balance.

13. (*a*) The incorrect statement can be corrected as
Platyhelminthes are acoelomates, i.e. without coelom. Haemocoel is found in arthropods and mollusc.

14. (*b*) Sponges are multicelluar organism, yet they do not have respiratory organs because of the presence of highly porous body through which water flows. Gaseous exchange occurs through diffusion which allows oxygen to pass from water into sponge body.

15. (*b*) *Spongilla* is a freshwater sponge, found in various freshwater habitats. The other options (*Sycon*, *Euspongia* and *Pennatula*) are marine organisms and do not inhabit freshwater environments.

16. (*d*) In the given diagram, *A* is ectoderm, *B* is mesoglea and C is endoderm. This arrangement is found in diploblastic organisms like the coelenterates. In chordates, a true germinal layer called mesoderm is present in between the ectoderm and the endoderm and hence, they are triploblastic. Rest all the are statements are incorrect and can be corrected as
The given type of organisation is found in diploblastic animals like *Physalia, Adamsia*, etc., *Fasciola, hepatica* a platyhelminthic organism possesses triploblastic organisation.
B is mesoglea and is an undifferentiated layer that cannot differentiate into different cell types. Cells in ectoderm and endoderm can differentiate into other cell types of the body. They differentiate to form different tissues.

17. (*b*) Both statement I and statement II are correct.
In acoelomates there is no body cavity or coelom between the digestive tract and the outer body wall. Coelom is a fluid filled cavity that allows lubrication and prevents friction between the internal organs. They also allow movement in the organs and give them the necessary space to grow. But in acoelomates, the two tubes of the body are closely packed which limits movement.

18. (*a*) *Aurelia* is jelly fish while *Ctenoplana* is a member of phylum-Ctenophora. Both of these animals exhibits the property of bioluminescence (ability to produce light by a living system).

19. (*b*) Coelom or body cavity which is lined by mesoderm is a true coelom. Normally, it is a property of all bilaterally symmetrical organisms. However, echinoderms which are radially or bilaterally symmetrical possess a true coelom.

20. (*c*) Statements I and II are correct. Statements III and IV are incorrect and can be corrected as
Osculum acts as a large excretory pore. Water is drawn out of the body of sponges through the osculum.
The body is supported by a skeleton made up of spicules or spongin fibres.

21. (*c*) Both A and R are true, but R is not the correct explanation of A. A can be explained as
Cnidarians have tentacles armed with stinging cells called cnidocytes, which contain nematocysts.
As, the tentacles sense danger or a prey comes in contact, the nematocysts came out of the capsule and inject the toxin that paralyses or kills the prey or the predator.
These cnidocytes are also used for anchorage and defence.

22. (*d*) Statements III, IV and V are correct. Statements I and II are incorrect and can be corrected as
- Comb jellies, cnidarians and poriferans are all diploblastic organisms which show sexual mode of reproduction. However, comb jellies show only sexual mode, while Cnidaria and sponges show both asexual and sexual modes of reproduction.
- There is a single oral opening on hypostome in cnidarians.

23. (*b*) The incorrect statement can be corrected as
Flatworms have a single mouth and do not have an anus. Digestive tract is also absent since most of them are parasitic in nature.

24. (*a*) Muscular pharynx in aschelminthes like *Ancylostoma, Ascaris*, etc. are used to suck in food due to their rhythmic pumping action.

25. (*d*) *A* is *Ascaris* (Aschelminthes) while *B* is *Taenia* (Platyhelminthes). Both the organisms have internal fertilisation and both of them show parasitic feeding modes.
However, sexual dimorphism where males and females have distinct differences is observed in Aschelminthes, unlike platyhe lminthes.
Also, Platyhelminthes or flat worms are acoelomates while, Aschelminthes or roundworms are pseudocoelomates.

Test 2

1. (*a*) Statocysts are balancing organs present in arthropods. Insects belonging to this phylum uses statocyst to balance their movements.
Other options can be explained as
Antenna is a sensory organ that keeps them aware of their surrounding, while compound eyes are used to obtain several images of an object. Nematocysts are the stinging cells present in the cnidocytes of Cnidarians.

2. (*d*) All three organisms-leeches, cockroaches and scorpions-possess a ventral nerve cord. This nerve cord runs along the underside (ventral side) of the body and is responsible for transmitting nerve impulses and coordinating movement and sensory functions. They possess distinct segments or metameres.

3. (*b*) Malpighian tubules are specific to arthropods, not annelids. The annelids excrete waste through structures called nephridia, which filter waste products from the coelomic fluid.

4. (*b*) The members of phylum-Mollusca are usually dioecious and oviparous with indirect development (through larval stage).

Other options can be corrected as

- Hemichordata - have organ -system level of organisation.
- Arthropoda - body divided into head, throrax and abdomen; respiration takes place by gills, book gills, book lungs or tracheal system.
- Echinodermata - Radial symmetry in adult, usually external fertilisation.

5. (*b*) Hemichordates, include genera like *Saccoglossus* and *Balanoglossus*, have a stomochord in the collar region. This structure is considered to be similar to the notochord found in chordates, although it is not homologous.

The other statements can be correct as

The file-like rasping organ called radula is a characteristic feature of molluscs, not hemichordates.

Hemichordates do not have a chitinous exoskeleton. This characteristic is typical of arthropods.

Saccoglossus is a hemichordate, but *Antedon* is a crinoid, which belongs to the phylum Echinodermata.

6. (*b*) Incorrect statement can be corrected as

In phylum Mollusca, the body is divided into head, muscular foot and visceral hump. It lacks segmentation.

7. (*a*) The given figure is of *Pila*. Incorrect statements can be corrected as

- Body is covered by a calcareous shell and is unsegmented with a distinct head, muscular foot and visceral hump.
- They do not possess any water-vascular system.
- They are dioecious and oviparous with indirect development.

8. (*a*) The incorrect statement can be corrected as

Coelenterates (Cnidaria) have radial symmetry, meaning their body parts are arranged around a central axis, e.g., jellyfish and sea anemones.

Annelids, such as earthworms and leeches, have bilateral symmetry, meaning their body has a left and right side that are mirror images.

9. (*d*) Statement I is correct, but statement II is incorrect. The incorrect statement can be corrected as

Hemichordates have a rudimentary structure in the collar region called stomochord which is similar to notochord.

10. (*d*) *Saccoglossus* belongs to phylum-Hemichordata. Characters I and III are incorrect w.r.t the phylum and can be corrected as

Hemichordates are usually dioecious (separate sexes), undergo external fertilisation, and often have indirect development involving a larval stage. Their body is cylindrical and is composed of proboscis, collar and a trunk. They possess no segmentation.

11. (*a*) The largest phylum is Arthropoda and the second largest is mollusca. In both the phylum, animals are coelomates which means that they have a true coelom lined by mesoderm. Other options can be explained as

Metamerism is only observed in insects. The body of an arthropod is divided into head, thorax and abdomen, while that of mollusc is divided into head, muscular foot and viceral hump.

In Arthropoda, sensory organs are antennae, compound eyes, statocyst, etc., while Mollusca have sensory tentacles.

12. (*d*) Statement I is correct, but statement II is incorrect. Statement II can be corrected as

Radula is a file-like rasping organ which contains chitinous teeth. These are used for scraping and cutting the food following which it is passed into the oesophagus.

13. (*c*) Excretion in members of phylum- Echinodermata. For example, starfish takes place through water vascular system.

Remaining statements are incorrect and can be corrected as

Water filter system is the madreporite which is located on the aboral or dorsal surface.

Locomotion is conducted by tube feet. Muscular foot is the locomotory organ of the phylum Mollusca.

Fertilisation is external and takes place outside the body of the mother.

14. (*a*) The correct match is A-2, B-3, C-4, D-1.

- *Nereis* is an annelida and they have a closed circulation where blood is pumped into blood vessels.
- *Culex* belongs to phylum-Arthropoda and have segments or metameres in their body.
- *Aplysia* or sea-hare is a mollusc and they have feather-like gills in the mantle cavity.
- *Balanoglossus* is a hemichordate and they have gills for respiration.

15. (*d*) A is true, but R is false. R can be corrected as

Stomochord is a rudimentary structure placed in the collar region which is similar to notochord.

Hemichordates like *Balanoglossus* lacks true notochord therefore, they are not placed under the subphylum of chordates and are placed in a separate phylum.

Test 3

1. (*a*) *Chelone* (turtle) and *Testudo* (tortoise) belongs to the phylum-Reptilia. They have dry, cornified skin and their bodies are covered with epidermal scales. These scales protect them and prevents water loss.

2. (*d*) Protochordates possess a ventral muscular heart. Their circulatory systems are simpler.

3. (*c*) The class-Cyclostomata includes jawless fishes which are anadromous, meaning they migrate from the sea to freshwater rivers and streams to spawn. For example, sea lamprey.

4. (*d*) The incorrect statement and can be corrected as
Aves are able to maintain a constant body temperature. They are warm blooded (homoiothermous) animal.

5. (*c*) Both A and R are true, but R is not the correct explanation of A.
Both *Pteropus* and *Balaenoptera*, i.e. bat and whale, respectively belongs to class-Mammalia, because of the presence of milk producing glands, which provide nourishment to the young ones.
Showing parental care is the unique feature of class-Mammalia.

6. (*c*) Incorrect statement can be corrected as
Animals belonging to the phylum Chordata possess a notochord either during early embryonic life or throughout the life.
Humans belong to the phylum-Chordata.
In humans, notochord is present only in the embryonic stage, it is replaced by vertebral column in the adult form.

7. (*d*) Incorrect statement about amphibians can be corrected as
The class Reptilia have creeping or crawling mode of locomotion.

8. (*a*) Statement I is incorrect, but statement II is correct. Incorrect statement can be corrected as
Sexual dimorphism refers to differences in appearance between males and females of the same species. In cartilaginous fishes like sharks and sting rays, sexual dimorphism is present.

9. (*c*) The fish 'X' is *Myxine*, which belong to class Cyclostomata. These fishes are jawless. They have an elongated body bearing 6-15 pairs of gill slits for respiration. The cranium and vertebral column are cartilaginous. They posses closed circulatory system.
Other fishers can be identified as *Pterophyllum* and *Clarias* belongs to class-Osteichthyes and *Ichthyophis* is a limbless amphibian.

10. (*c*) X is notochord, which is replaced by a cartilaginous or bony vertebral column in adult of vertebrates. Whereas, Y is pharyngeal gill slits which only occur in embryonic stages of higher chordates and disappear before adult life.

11. (*b*) The correct match is A-2, B-3, C-1, D-4.
Torpedo is known for its electric organs.
Scoliodon is recognised as a dog fish.
Trygon is associated with a poison sting.
Pristis is also called saw fish.

12. (*b*) Members of Chondrichthyes differ from that of Osteichthyes, primarily in having placoid scale and gill slit without operculum.
Chondrichthyes have multiple gill slits (usually five to seven pairs) that are exposed and not covered by an operculum. This means the gills open directly to the water.

13. (*b*) The given figures P, Q, R and S are *Salamandra, Hippocampus Chelone* and *Ornithorhychus,* respectively. The *Ornithorhynchus* (platypus), is an exception of class Mammalia, because all the member of this class are viviparous, but platypus is oviparous. others statements can be corrected as
Hippocampus is an oviparous fish. The female sea horses deposit eggs into male sea horses's brood pouch and the eggs get fertilised in the pouch.
Salamandra belongs to class-Amphibia, while *Chelone* belong to class-Reptilia.

14. (*b*) Both statement I and statement II are correct.
Exocoetus (flying fish) belong to class–Osteichthyes.
These have air bladders under their skin, which help them to stay at their current water depth without expending energy in swimming.
Some members of class-Reptilia shed their skin for various reason. One of the prominent one is due to growth. The scales present on their body does not change in number but instead they just grow bigger in size. Because of which they cannot get fit into their old skin thus, shedding takes place.

15. (*a*) Statements I and II are correct regarding Osteichthyes where statements III and IV are incorrect and can be corrected as
Osteichthyes have bony endoskeleton therefore, they are also known as bony fishes. They include flying fish, *Hippocampus*, rohu, catla, magur, fighting fish and angel fish.

16. (*c*) *Ascidia* belongs to Urochordata while *Branchiostoma* belongs to Cephalochordata. Both of them do not posses a vertebral column.
Petromyzon and *Myxine* belongs to Cyclostomata and have a vertebral column made of cartilage.

17. (*d*) Statement III is incorrect and can be corrected as
In amphioxus, circulation is of closed type.
They show indirect development where the larvae undergo metamorphosis to convert into adult forms. Cilia beats in a synchronous manner to filter water while feeding. Protonephridia are the excretory organs.

18. (*a*) A is false, but R is true. A can be corrected as
Lampreys have a sucking circular mouth with teeth. The teeth helps them to cut through the scales of other fishes whom they parasitise. They lack jaws.

19. (*c*) In males of Chondrichthyes, pelvic fins bear claspers. These structures are involved in sperm transfer into the oviducts. Hence, in their absence sperms would not be transferred which would prevent the event of fertilisation in females.

20. (*d*) All the given characteristics belong to class-Chondrichthyes or cartilaginous fishes, e.g. *Pristis* (Saw fish), *Scoliodon* (Dog fish) and *Torpedo* (have electric organs), are Chondrichthyes.

21. (*d*) Statement I is correct, but statement II is incorrect. Statement II can be corrected as
Moist skin facilitates gas exchange in frogs when they are in water.
Tadpoles are the larval stages of frogs which have gills for respiration.
Bufo is an amphibian where alimentary canal, urinary and reproductive tracts open into a common chamber called cloaca which opens to the exterior.

22. (*c*) Statement III is incorrect regarding amphibians and reptiles. It can be corrected as
Fertilisation is external in amphibians like frogs. Internal fertilisation is observed in reptiles like snakes and lizzards.
Other options can be explained as
- *Ichthyophis* is a limbless amphibian and moves like a snake.
- External ear or pinnae are absent in both *Hemidactylus* (wall lizard) and *Hyla* (tree frog). They have tympanum.
- Three-chambered heart with two auricles and one ventricle is common for both amphibians and reptiles. Since, blood gets mixed, the efficiency of the circulatory system decreases which accounts for the poikilothermic nature or inability to maintain a constant internal temperature of the body.

23. (*d*) A is true, but R is false. R can be corrected as
Oil secretion from the epidermal sebaceous glands located at the base of the tail in birds help in keeping the feathers waterproof. This prevents wetting of the feather which keeps them light and aids in flying.

24. (*a*) The correct match is A-2, B-1, C-4, D-3.
Aptenodytes are penguins which belong to phylum–Aves. They have crops and gizzards for grinding the food.
Bangarus is krait which belongs to class-Reptilia. They are mostly terrestrial animals and their body is covered by dry and cornified skin, epidermal scales or scutes.
Platypus is an egg laying or oviparous mammal.
Rana is frog which belongs to amphibian class. They have a common opening for digestive, urinary and reproductive tract, called the cloaca.

25. (*d*) Statement I is correct, but statement II is incorrect. Statement II can be corrected as
In birds, the air sacs direct air flow to the lungs thus increasing the respiratory efficiency of the lungs for gas exchange during flight.
Hair in mammals provide insulation against cold and is hence an adaptation.

Chapter Break Thru

1. (*a*) *Chameleon* live on trees and bushes around the world. Some have prehensile tails that coil around the branches to maintain balance and help them climb.
They also show camouflage, i.e., the ability-they change their skin colour.

2. (*d*) A is true, but R is false. R can be corrected as
In annelids, both external and internal segmentation are present. Externally, the body is visibly divided into segments called metameres. Internally, this segmentation is reflected in structures such as septa, which divide the body cavity into segments.

3. (*c*) The correct match is A-2, B-1, C-4, D-3.
- Malpighian tubules are the excretory organs found in phylum-Arthropoda, e.g. *Laccifer*.
- Nephridia are the excretory organs in annelids. They help in osmoregulation, e.g. *Hirudinaria*, *Pheretima,* etc.
- Proboscis is the excretory organ in hemichordates, like *Balanoglossus*.
- Flame cells are excretory organs in Platyhelminthes or flat worms like *Fasciola* and *Taenia*.

4. (*d*) The given diagrams are of coelomates and acoelomate body organisation, respectively.
Loligo (squid), a mollusc possesses coelomate body organisation.
Ctenoplana, a ctenophore possesses acoelomate body organisation.

5. (*a*) The incorrect statement can be corrected as
Nereis is an aquatic annelid and dioecious, whereas earthworms and leeches are monoecious.

6. (*a*) Statement I is incorrect, but statement II is correct. The incorrect statement can be corrected as
Nematocytes (or poisonous capsules) are specialised cells found in cnidarians (such as jellyfish, corals, and sea anemones) used for capturing prey and defence. Poriferans (sponges) do not have nematocytes.

7. (*b*) Both statement I and statement II are correct.
Gorgonia (sea fan) is a member of phylum-Cnidaria. These animals have a central gastro-vascular cavity with single opening, mouth on hypostome.
Pinctada is a member of phylum-Mollusca.
These animals have very soft body. Thus, their body is covered with hard calcareous shell.
The soft and spongy layer of skin form a mantle over the viceral hump.

8. (*c*) The correct match is A-4, B-1, C-3, D-2.
Physalia is commonly called Portuguese man-of-war.
Adamsia is commonly known as the Sea anemone.
Meandrina is a genus of Brain coral.
Pennatula is commonly called Sea pen.

9. (*b*) Members of phylum-Aschelminthes (nematodes) possess a pseudocoelom, a type of body cavity that is partially lined by mesodermal tissue. In these organisms, the mesoderm appears as scattered pouches between the ectoderm and endoderm, providing a distinctive characteristic of their body structure. This pseudocoelom serves as a hydrostatic skeleton, aiding in movement and the distribution of nutrients, e.g.

Ascaris, Ancylostoma and *Wuchereria*, etc.

10. (*d*) In Porifera (sponges), the simplest type of canal system is the asconoid system. Here's how the water flows through this system: The water enters the sponge through small pores called ostia. It then flows into a large central cavity called the spongocoel. Finally, the water exits the sponge through a large opening called the osculum.

Thus, the correct sequence for water flow in the simplest canal system (asconoid type) is:

Ostia $\rightarrow$ Spongocoel $\rightarrow$ Osculum $\rightarrow$ Exterior

11. (*a*) Statement I is incorrect, but statement II is correct. The incorrect statement can be corrected as Classes Amphibia, Reptilia, Aves and Mammalia not Pisces, have two pairs of limbs and are thus grouped under Tetrapoda.

12. (*b*) Incorrect match pairs can be corrected as

Molluscs typically exhibit bilateral symmetry, not radial symmetry in adult. Bilateral symmetry means the body can be divided into two mirror-image halves along one plane.

13. (*c*) *Antedon*, commonly known as feather stars or crinoids, are echinoderms that are attached to the substratum by a stalk (usually in their juvenile stage) or by clinging to rocks or corals. They filter feed using their feathery arms.

14. (*a*) The correct match is given in A-2, B-4, C-1, D-3.

- *Ascidia* have sac-like body. They lac appendages.
- *Branchiostoma* belongs to the subphylum Cephalochordata. In them, notochord extends from head to tail and persists throughout their life.
- *Ophiura*, these are brittle stars, which belong to the phylum–Echinodermata.The larval form of these animals have bilateral symmetry where as the adult form exhibit radial symmetry.
- *Balanoglossus*, these are acorn worms, which belong to the phylum Hemichordata. These animals are dioecious, i.e. sexes are separate.

15. (*b*) Both statement I and statement II are correct.

Lancelets are indeed primitive vertebrates that resemble fish and belong to the subphylum Cephalochordata. They are jawless and have a fish-like appearance.

Lancelets do possess a notochord (a flexible rod that provides support), a tubular nerve cord (dorsal nerve cord) and pharyngeal gill slits throughout their entire life. These are defining characteristics of chordates, to which lancelets belong.

16. (*b*) The body of hemichordates is cylindrical comprising of proboscis, a collar and a long trunk. Echinoderms typically have a pentaradial symmetry as adults, with a central disc and radiating arms or structures.

17. (*b*) Nematodes are covered with a thick cuticle, but unlike the statement, they do undergo moulting (ecdysis). This is a crucial part of their growth process. The other statements are accurate descriptions of scyphozoans, flatworms, and ctenophores.

18. (*c*) Both A and R are true, but R is not the correct explanation of A.

The duck-billed platypus and anteater are classified due to their mammary glands (they produce milk for their young), which is a defining characteristic of mammals.

19. (*b*) In the life cycle of certain cnidarians, such as those in the class Hydrozoa (e.g., *Obelia*), there is an alternation of generations involving both polyp (P) and medusa (Q) forms.

Polyps are sessile (attached) and reproduce asexually. They produce medusae through a process called budding. In this process, new medusae bud off from the body of the polyp.

Medusae are free-swimming and reproduce sexually. They produce gametes (sperm and eggs).

When gametes from different medusae fuse during fertilization, they form a zygote. The zygote develops into a planula larva, which eventually settles down and transforms into a new polyp, thus completing the life cycle.

20. (*d*) *Carcharodon* belongs to Chondrichthyes. They have internal fertilisation whereas, *Exocoetus* belong to class-Osteichthyes and they have external fertilisation.

21. (*c*) Incorrect statement can be corrected as

Some annelids are monoecious (having both and female reproductive organs), e.g. earthworm and leeches, whereas many species are dioecious (having separate sexes), e.g. *Nereis*.

22. (*b*) *Taenia* (Tapeworm; B) do possesses hooks and suckers. These structures are adaptations that help them attach to their host. This adaptation is crucial for their parasitic lifestyle.

23. (*a*) *Labeo* (Rohu) is a type of freshwater fish commonly found in South Asia. It possesses four pairs of gills for respiration and has cycloid scales, which are typical of many teleost fish.

24. (*a*) Members of phyla-Mollusca, Urochordata (tunicates), Hemichordata and Arthropoda have open circulatory system.

While, annelids and chordates have closed circulatory system.

25. (*a*) Frogs do have eyelids. However, their upper eyelids are fused and immovable, while the lower eyelids are movable. This allows frogs to protect their eyes and keep them moist.

26. (*d*) A is true, but R is false. R can be corrected as

The exoskeleton in arthropods provides support and protection and serves as an attachment point for muscles, enabling efficient movement.

27. (*a*) Molluscs are soft-bodied animals with an unsegmented body featuring a distinct head, muscular foot, and visceral hump. In *Pila* (apple snail), the buccal cavity contains a radula, which is a rasping organ equipped with transverse rows of teeth.

28. (*d*) Statement I is correct, but statement II is incorrect, it can be corrected as

Bombyx (Silkworm) is an insect and has a segmented body with no calcareous shell.

Limulus (Horseshoe crab) also has a segmented body, though it has a hard exoskeleton, it is not entirely calcareous.

29. (*d*) A is false, but R is true. A can be corrected as

Coelom of Arthropoda is lined by mesodermal epithelium, but the coelomic cavity is greatly reduced.

30. (*a*) The insects that are known for their economic importance are,

Bombyx (Silkworm) used for silk production.

Laccifer (Lac Insect) used for shellac production.

Apis (Honey Bee) essential for pollination and honey production.

These insects are considered useful because they contribute to various industries.

Ch-5 Morphology of Flowering Plants

Topical Follow Thru

Test-1

1. (*c*) The tap root system is seen in dicot plants which include mustard, banyan and pea. The other plants, i.e., wheat, grass and *Monstera* are the monocot plants and possess the fibrous root system.

2. (*d*) The region of the root tip which possesses small-sized cells, with thin walls and dense protoplasm is the region of meristematic activity (C). These are located a few millimetres above the root cap.

3. (*a*) *Pistia* is an aquatic plant known as water lettuce. It has a characteristic structure where stems are modified into lateral branches with internodes. Each internode (space between nodes) on this lateral branch bears a rosette of leaves at the top and a tuft of roots at the bottom. This modification helps *Pistia* float on the water surface.

4. (*b*) The correct match is A-2, B-3, C-1, D-4.

Neem is an example of pinnately compound leaf.

Mustard is an example of alternate phyllotaxy.

Guava plant is an example of opposite phyllotaxy.

Silk cotton is an example of palmately compound leaf.

5. (*b*) Both A and R are true and R is the correct explanation of A.

Opuntia, commonly known as prickly pear cacti, have stems modified into phylloclades. These are flattened, green, photosynthetic stems that perform the functions of leaves.

These fleshy stems store water, enabling plant to survive in arid environments by providing a water reserve during dry conditions.

6. (*b*) Statements III and V are correct. Other statements are incorrect and can be corrected as

Monocotyledonous plants typically have a fibrous root system, not the tap root system.

In dicotyledonous plants, adventitious roots are not typically associated with forming a fibrous root system.

Wheat plants are monocotyledonous, not dicotyledonous and they have a fibrous root system.

7. (*d*) Statement I is correct, but statement II is incorrect. The incorrect statement can be corrected as

Maize and sugarcane are monocots and thus, they do not have tap roots. They have a fibrous root system, meaning their roots are numerous and relatively shallow. Stilt roots are not modifications of tap roots. Their primary function is to provide support, not to reach deeper into soil for water and nutrients.

8. (*a*) The correct match is A-4, B-1, C-2, D-3.

Pistia is an example of offset. It is the form of sub-aerial stem modification. Cucumber is an example of tendrils which is a form of aerial stem modification.

Citrus is an example of thorns which is a form of aerial stem modification.

Ginger is an example of rhizome which is a form of underground stem modification.

9. (*b*) Both A and R are true and R is the correct explanation of A.

Root cap protects the growing tips of the plant by secreting mucilage which allows smooth penetration through the soil layers. If root cap is not present, the root might not able to sustain the penetration pressure, resulting in permanent stoppage of its growth.

10. (*c*) Both A and R are true, but R is not the correct explanation of A.

Water hyacinth can spread rapidly because they propagate vegetatively using offset. Offset is a sub-aerial stem modification containing short internodes and each node bearing a rosette of leaves and a tuft of roots.

11. (*c*) Statements II and III are correct, but statements I and IV are in correct and can be corrected as

- Runners remain above the ground, e.g. grasses. Stolons are underground structures.
- Runners depend on mother plant and remain attached to the host plants for their energy requirements.

12. (*b*) The region of elongation is proximal to the meristematic region. Cells in the meristematic region show active division, and have thin walled cells with dense protoplasm. Region of elongation is responsible for the lengthwise growth or apical growth of plant roots.

13. (*d*) The given leaf is of silk cotton, which is a palmately compound leaf in which leaflets are attached at a common point.

The incorrect statements can be corrected as

The common axis bearing leaflets is called rachis in a pinnately compound leaf.

Incisions do not reach up to the midrib of lamina in simple leaves.

The given leaf represents palmately compound type of leaf, which is seen in silk cotton. Neem is pinnately compound leaf.

14. (*a*) Statement I is incorrect , but statement II is correct. Statement I can be corrected as

Australian *Acacia* has small leaves which are short-lived, yet the plant can photosynthesise. This is because in such plants, the petioles expand, become green and synthesise food.

15. (*a*) Statement I is incorrect, but statement II is correct. Statement I can be corrected as

Cutting down prop roots would affect the growth and stability of trees like banyan. This is because prop roots are adventitious roots that grow vertically downwards to support the branches of such trees. They are supportive structures.

Test 2

1. (*b*) Gulmohar is an example of a zygomorphic flower with imbricate aestivation. When a flower can be divided into two similar halves only in one particular vertical plane, the flower is called zygomorphic, e.g. pea, gulmohar, bean, etc. In imbricate aestivation, the margins overlap one another, but not in any particular direction, e.g. *Cassia* and gulmohar.

2. (*b*) In an inflorescence where flowers develop sequentially from base to tip, i.e. exhibit acropetal succession, the position of the youngest floral bud shall be distal.

3. (*d*) In bean and gulmohar, vexillary and imbricate aestivation are present, respectively.

Vexillary aestivation is characterised by one large petal (standard) overlapping two lateral petals (wings), which in turn overlap two smaller, lower petals (keel).

In imbricate aestivation, petals or sepals overlap each other in a non-specific manner, with at least one member completely outside and one completely inside.

4. (*b*) The edible portion of mango is the fleshy mesocarp. It is represented by part *C* in the given section.

5. (*d*) Statements II, IV and V are correct. Statements I and III are incorrect and can be corrected as

In epipetalous condition, cohesion occurs between the petals and the filament of the stamen.

The scutellum is a shield-shaped and large cotyledon of grasses.

6. (*d*) Statement I is correct, but statement II is incorrect. Incorrect statement can be corrected as

The asymmetrical flowers are found in *Canna*, where no plane can divide the flower into equal halves. Mustard shows actinomorphic flowers.

7. (*c*) Both statement I and statement II are incorrect. These can be corrected as

The margins touch one another without overlapping in valvate aestivation.

In mustard, adjacent petals lie close to each other and show valvate aestivation.

8. (*d*) A is true, but R is false. R can be corrected as

Maize is an albuminous seed in which endosperm is present.

The seeds in which the endosperm is completely absorbed by the seed itself are the ex-albuminous seeds, e.g. pea, gram and bean.

9. (*c*) In cymose, the young fruits are protected by flowers. The incorrect statements can be corrected as

Floral axis continues to grow in racemose inflorescence.

Flowers are borne laterally in acropetal succession in racemose inflorescence.

The transformation of a shoot tip into a flower is always solitary.

10. (*c*) In perigynous flower, the gynoecium is situated in the centre and other parts of flower are located on the rim of the thalamus almost at same level. Other statements are incorrect and can be corrected as

The thalamus is free from the wall of the ovary.

Gynoecium occupies the highest position in hypogynous flowers.

The ovary is half inferior.

11. (*d*) In *Calotropis*, valvate aestivation is observed.

Other options can be explained as

In *Cassia*, imbricate aestivation is observed, while in lady's fingers and cotton plant, twisted aestivation is observed.

12. (*b*) In *Argemone*, parietal placentation is observed. Parietal placentation is given in figure *C*, where the ovules develop on the inner wall of the ovary or on peripheral part.

13. (*a*) Statement I is incorrect, but statement II is correct.

The incorrect statement can be corrected as

The tegmen is typically thin and membranous, not thick and leathery.

In grains (e.g., wheat, rice), the pericarp (fruit wall) and the testa (seed coat) are indeed fused.

14. (*c*) The flower shown in the figure is epigynous. In this, the ovary is situated below the thalamus.

15. (*a*) The correct match is A-2, B-4, C-1, D-3.

Hibiscus is an example of plants with axile placentation, i.e., when placenta is axial and the ovules are attached to it in a multilocular ovary.

Pea is an example of plants with marginal placentation, i.e. when placenta forms a ridge along the ventral suture of the ovary and ovules are borne on this ridge forming two rows.

Dianthus is an example of plants with free central, i.e., when the ovules are borne on central axis and septa are absent.

Brassica is an example of plants with parietal placentation, i.e. when ovules develops on the inner wall of the ovary or on peripheral part.

16. (*c*) Both statement I and statement II are incorrect. These can be corrected as

In cymose inflorescence, the top flowers die faster than the bottom ones. Cymose shows basipetal succession, where older flowers are at the top while new flowers are at the bottom. Whereas, in racemose inflorescence, acropetal succession is observed, where new flowers are at the top, while older flowers are borne at the bottom.

The terminal bud develops a terminal flower in cymose inflorescence. In cymose type of inflorescence, the main axis terminates in a flower, hence is limited in growth.

17. (*c*) Statement III is incorrect and can be corrected as

Essential whorls of a flower has reproductive functions. The androecium and gynoecium are considered as the essential whorls of a flower and are involved in reproduction.

18. (*d*) Bracts are leaf-like structures present below an inflorescence. They protect the floral structures. When green, they contribute towards photosynthesis and when brightly coloured, they attract insects for pollination. However, they do not play any role in supporting the leaves or other foliage.

19. (*a*) 'A' is hypogynous flower where the gynoecium (the innermost whorl) occupies the highest position, while the other parts are situated below it. The ovary in such flowers is said to be superior, e.g., mustard.

Incorrect options can be corrected as

- 'B' and 'C' shows perigynous flowers. If gynoecium is situated in the centre and other parts of the flower are located on the rim of the thalamus almost at the same level, it is called perigynous. The ovary here is said to be half inferior, e.g., plum, rose, peach.
- 'D' is epigynous flower. The margin of thalamus grows upward enclosing the ovary completely and getting fused with it, the other parts of flower arise above the ovary. Hence, the ovary is said to be inferior, as in flowers of guava and cucumber.

20. (*b*) The gamosepalous flower have sepals that are fused together either completely or just at the base. *Hibiscus* is an example of gamosepalous flower. Other examples can be corrected as

Rosa and *Camellia* have polysepalous and polypetalous flowers. *Datura* have gamosepalous and gamopetalous flowers.

21. (*a*) The correct match is A-4, B-3, C-1, D-2.

- If the margins of sepals or petals completely overlap one another, but not in any particular direction, as in *Cassia* and gulmohar, the aestivation is called imbricate.
- If one margin of the appendage overlaps that of the next one and so on, as in china rose, lady's finger and cotton, it is called twisted aestivation.
- When sepals or petals in a whorl just touch one another at the margin, without overlapping, as in *Calotropis*, it is said to be valvate aestivation.
- In vexillary aestivation, there are five petals, the largest (standard) overlaps the two lateral petals (wings) which in turn, overlap the two smallest anterior petals (keel).

22. (*a*) A is false, but R is true. A can be corrected as

The bisexual flowers with staminode can undergo only cross pollination. This is because even though such bisexual flowers have both male and female parts, the stamens are sterile (staminode).

Such stamens cannot produce pollen grains and hence, they depend on pollens from other flowers borne on different plants.

23. (*c*) Both A and R are true, but R is not the correct explanation of A.

Pineapples are mostly propagated vegetatively since they are parthenocarpic. Parthenocarpic fruits are formed without fertilisation and are seedless. In the absence of seeds, they are propagated through their vegetative parts.

24. (*d*) Placentation is the arrangement of ovules in an ovary. Following fertilisation, ovules develop into seeds. Hence, the arrangement and number of ovules formed depend on the placentation observed in a flower.

Other options can be explained as

Inflorescence is the arrangement of flowers in the shoot axis, while aestivation is the arrangement of sepals or petals. Phyllotaxy is the arrangement of leaves.

25. (*a*) Statement II is incorrect and can be corrected as

Seeds of beans do not die at maturity. Peas and beans are non-endospermous, but they derive nourishment from the cotyledons which store food for them.

Test 3

1. (*c*) The correct floral formula of family-Fabaceae is

$$\% \; ⚥ \; K_{(5)} \; C_{1+2+(2)} \; A_{(9)+1} \; \underline{G}_1$$

Legume and pea belong to this family.

2. (*a*) The correct match is A-4, B-3, C-1, D-2.

Lupin (or *Lupinus*) is an ornamental plant whose trumpet-shaped flowers make it popular for summer flower.

Sesbania is a multipurpose fodder tree.

Sunhemp (*Crotalaria juncea*) is a fibrous legume.

Soyabean is an edible oil. It is mostly used for frying and baking.

3. (*c*) The floral diagram given in question is of family Gramineae. The cereals like rice and wheat belong to this family.

4. (*d*) The floral diagram represents the arrangement of ovules in an ovary, but not the position of gynoecium. Placentation can be seen in floral diagram, but not in floral formula.

Number of sepals and petals along with adhesion of stamen can be seen in both floral diagram as well as floral formula.

5. (*a*) The given plants belong to 4 families.

Hibiscus and cotton belong to the family-Malvaceae.

Bambusa and *Triticum* belongs to family-Gramineae.

Brassica belongs to family-Brassicaceae (Cruciferae).

Sunhemp belongs to family-Fabaceae.

6. (*c*) The correct match can be explained as

Chrysanthemum belongs to the family-Compositae and bears cypsela as its fruit. Cypsela is a simple, dry, single-seeded, indehiscent fruit.

7. (*a*) The correct floral formula of disc floret of sunflower is

$$\text{Br} \oplus ⚥ K_{(\text{Pappus})} \overset{\frown}{C_5 A_5} \bar{G}_{(2)}$$

The correct floral formula of ray floret of sunflower is

$$\text{Br} \% ♀ K_{(\text{pappus})} C_{(3\text{-}5)} A_0 \bar{G}_{(2)}$$

8. (*b*) Flowers of Brassicaceae are bisexual, ebracteate, actinomorphic (generally) flower with free sepals and petals, tetradynamous condition, bicarpellary, syncarpous, superior ovary with parietal placentation and their fruit is siliqua/silicula.

9. (*a*) The correct floral formula

$$\text{Br} \oplus ⚥ \text{Epi}_{3\text{-}9} K_{5 \text{ or } (5)} \overset{\frown}{C_5 A_\infty} \underline{G}_{(2\text{-}\infty)}$$

represents the mallow family, i.e. Malvaceae.

10. (*a*) The cotton plant belongs to the family-Malvaceae and the floral characters mentioned in question explain the same.

11. (d) In members of Brassicaceae, flowers are hypogynous with superior ovary.

12. (*d*) Features I and IV are correct with respect to members of Leguminosae, but features II and III are incorrect and can be corrected as

In members of Leguminosae, flowers have racemose inflorescence.

Their gynoecium is monocarpellary with superior ovary.

13. (*a*) The information conveyed through the given floral formula is $K_{(5)}$-Sepals 5, united (gamosepalous), C_5-Petals 5, free (polypetalous); $A_{(\infty)}$-Androecium infinite, fused; $\underline{G}_{(5)}$-Gynoecium pentacarpellary, syncarpous, superior ovary.

14. (*b*) Both statement I and statement II are correct. Perianth is a non-reproductive structure observed in members of family-Poaceae when the calyx and corolla are not differentiated.

15. (*c*) The given floral formula is of Brassicaceae family. Turnip, Radish, Cabbage, Broccoli are common examples of plants belonging to Brassicaceae or Cruciferae.

Other members along with their families are

- Sugarcane- Gramineae
- Marigold – Compositae
- Mallow - Malvaceae
- Tomato, Brinjal – Solanaceae

Chapter Break Thru

1. (c) In monocots, the fibrous roots are not differentiated into secondary roots.

2. (a) The absorption of water occurs from the root hair. Root hairs are present in the maturation zone.

3. (a) Statement I is incorrect, but statement II is correct. Statement I can be corrected as

Epicalyx is an additional whorl around the calyx of the flower. A flower without calyx and corolla is known as achlamydeous.

4. (a) Statement I is incorrect, but statement II is correct. The incorrect statement can be corrected as

The plumule and radicle are enclosed in sheaths called coleoptile and coleorhiza, respectively.

5. (a) The adventitious roots are found in grass, *Monstera* and banyan. Adventitious roots arise from parts of the plants other than radicle.

6. (c) Nodes are specific points on the stem where leaves, as well as branches and flowers, originate. This accurately describes the primary function of nodes. They are the regions where leaves are born.

7. (b) The incorrect statement can be corrected as

The stem of runners creeps over the ground and forms new niches, when older parts die or new parts are formed. It is seen in grasses and wild strawberries.

8. (b) Both statement I and statement II are correct.

In watermelon, stem tendrils are slender and spirally coiled, aiding the plant in climbing by providing support and attachment to other structures.

Respiratory roots, also known as pneumatophores, facilitate the exchange of gases, particularly by obtaining oxygen from the atmosphere, which is essential for plants growing in waterlogged or anaerobic conditions.

9. (a) The underground stems are found in potatoes, ginger, zaminkand, and *Colocasia*.

Potato stores nutrients in underground tubers, which are modified stems.

Ginger grows underground horizontally and is harvested as a rhizome.

Zaminkand like yams are underground tubers and are modified stems.

Colocasia has underground tubers (corms), which are modified stems.

10. (a) Mustard plants belongs to family–Brassicaceae or Cruciferae and show the features like presence of fused carpels, parietal placentation, actinomorphic flowers along with false septum in the ovary. On the other hand, the corresponding characters shown by pea are-monocarpellary ovary, marginal placentation, zygomorphic and hypogynous flowers. China rose shows twisted aestivation, axile placentation, monoadelphous stamens, hypogynous and zygomorphic flower. Pea and china rose belong to Fabaceae and Malvaceae, respectively and are zygomorphic and actinomorphic.

11. (a) Statement I is incorrect, but statement II is correct. Statement I can be corrected as

In dicotyledonous plants, leaves possess reticulate venation, while the arrangement of veins in a parallel fashion (side by side) is observed in monocotyledonous plants.

12. (b) The leaf is attached to the stem by the leaf base (*A*) and may bear two lateral small leaf-like structures called stipules (*B*). Petiole (*C*) provides the structural support to the leaf.

13. (a) The incorrect match pair can be corrected as

Pinnately compound leaves are observed in neem. *Alstonia* shows whorled phyllotaxy.

14. (b) Statements I and IV are correct. Other statements are incorrect and can be corrected as

Veins provide rigidity to the leaf blade or leaf lamina.

Buds are present in the axil of petiole of both simple and compound leaves, but not in the axil of leaflets of compound leaves.

15. (c) Hypogynous flowers show superior ovary, e.g. China rose.

Other incorrect options can be corrected as

The cucumber is epigynous, in which the ovary is inferior, not superior.

Ray florets of sunflowers are epigynous, not perigynous.

Rose is perigynous, not hypogynous.

16. (a) Statement IV is incorrect and can be corrected as

Leaves originate from the shoot apical meristem, not the root apical meristem.

17. (c) The correct match is A-3-i, B-2-iii, C-1-ii.

Hypogynous flower (*A*) contains superior ovary ($\underline{G}$) , e.g. mustard

Perigynous flower (*B*) possesses half inferior ovary (G-), e.g. rose

Epigynous flower (*C*) possesses inferior ovary ($\overline{G}$), e.g. guava.

18. (d) A is true, but R is false. R can be corrected as

Petiole is the part of the leaf that help to hold the blade to light. Long thin flexible petioles allow leaf blades to flutter in air. Hence, petiole helps in cooling the leaf.

19. (a) Vexillum is the standard petal of papilionaceous corolla.

20. (d) Statements II, IV and V are incorrect. These can be corrected as

In brinjal, the epipetalous stamen is found, whereas in lily, the epiphyllous stamen is found.

China rose possesses monoadelphous stamen.

Pea plant has a diadelphous androecium, i.e. all the stamens unite to form two bundles.

21. (c) Both statement I and statement II are incorrect. These can be corrected as

The female reproductive part consists of stigma, style and ovary. Stigma is the receptive organ for pollen grains and is located at the tip of the style.

22. (b) The correct match is A–3, B–1, C–2, D–4.

Fleshy cylindrical stem, i.e., a phylloclade is found in *Euphorbia.*

Flattened stem, i.e., a modified stem called phylloclade is found in *Opuntia*.

Stem thorns are found in *Citrus.*

Stem tendrils are found in cucumber.

23. (c) The correct match is B-2-iii. Figure *B* shows fibrous root system which arises from the base of the stem and includes monocotyledon ous plant such as wheat as its examples.

Figure *A* represents tap root system found in dicots such as mustard and shows presence of primary root along with its branches (secondary roots). Figure *C* represent adventitious roots found in *Monstera,* which arise from stem region.

24. (d) Statement I is correct, but statement II is incorrect. The incorrect statement can be corrected as

Both mango and coconut develop from monocarpellary superior ovary in which a single carpel occupies the highest position, while other floral parts are situated below it.

25. (b) The correct match is A-3, B-4, C-1, D-2.

Sweat pea belongs to the family of Fabaceae, *Hibiscus* belongs to Malvaceae, *Bambusa* belongs to Gramineae and *Helianthus* belongs to Compositae.

26. (b) *Indigofera* belongs to the family-Fabaceae.

27. (b) Statements III and IV are correct. Other incorrect statements can be corrected as

Castor is an endospermic seed.

Chilli possesses actinomorphic symmetry, while *Cassia* shows zygomorphic flowers.

28. (d) In the given question, *A* - Endosperm and *B* - Protein.

The endosperm of a monocot seed is surrounded by an aleurone layer, which is proteinaceous in nature.

29. (c) The floral formula provided belongs to the family-Fabaceae, which was previously known as Papilionoideae, a subfamily of the family-Leguminosae.

30. (b) Both A and R are true and R is the correct explanation of A.

Banana is a seedless fruit formed directly from the ovary without fertilisation.

31. (c) Both A and R are true, but R is not the correct explanation of A. It can be corrected as

The fleshy stem of *Opuntia* performs photosynthesis since they bear chlorophyll. *Opuntia* is a desert plant where the leaves are absent or reduced to minimise water loss by transpiration.

Hence, the stem containing chlorophyll photosynthesises and stores food.

32. (c) *Asparagus* is modified adventitious root that stores food. Incorrect statements can be corrected as

- Stilt roots of maize develop from parts other than the radicle. These roots are called adventitious roots.

• Sweet potato is a modified root specialised for storage. Potato is a modified stem.

• Banyan has underground roots developing from radicle, in addition to the adventitious prop roots.

33. (*a*) Statements I, II and IV are correct.
The incorrect statement can be corrected as
Ginger and turmeric develop from axillary buds.

34. (*d*) Banana has parallel venation, meaning the veins run parallel to one another on the lamina. They also have a fibrous root system where a tuft of equal sized roots emerge from the plant base. Such plants usually have a single cotyledon in them, i.e., monocotyledonous plants.

35. (*d*) Statement I is correct, but statement II is incorrect. Statement II can be corrected as
Whorled phyllotaxy is usually seen in plants with short internodes. If more than two leaves arise at a node and form a whorl, it is called whorled, as in *Alstonia*.

36. (*c*) The incorrect statement can be corrected as
Leaves are usually arranged in acropetal succession. In acropetal succession, older leaves are at the bottom, while the new leaves are formed at the top. In basipetal succession, older leaves are borne at the top, while the newly formed leaves occupy the bottom position.

37. (*a*) If gynoecium is situated in the centre and other parts of the flower are located on the rim of the thalamus almost at the same level, it is called perigynous. The ovary here is said to be half-inferior, e.g., plum, rose, peach.
Mustard, China rose and brinjal have hypogynous flowers with superior ovary. Guava, cucumber and ray florets of sunflower have epigynous flowers with inferior ovaries.

38. (*b*) In lily, sepals and petals are undifferentiated to form the perianth, individual units being called as tepals. They do not have distinct sepals and petals.

39. (*b*) Variation in the length of filaments is observed in mustard and *Salvia*. Syncarpous or fused carpels are present in mustard and tomato. Hypogynous flowers are present in mustard, China rose and brinjal. So, mustard is common to all of these characteristics. Mustard shows parietal placentation. From the given image, *Q* is parietal.

40. (*b*) Almond is a drupe. The entire pericarp which includes the epicarp, mesocarp and endocarp are inedible. The seeds are the edible part of almond.

41. (*c*) Both statement I and statement II are incorrect. These can be corrected as
Aleurone layer is present internal to the fused pericarp and seedcoat of monocots. This layers helps in utilisation of stored food by the developing embryo.

42. (*c*) Statement I is incorrect. It can be corrected as
Dicots can be albuminous or ex-albuminous. Example of albuminous seed is castor, while that of exalbuminous seeds are peas, beans and grams.

43. (*a*) The given placentation is axile. In axile placentation, the placenta is axial and the ovules are attached to it in a multilocular ovary. China rose, tomato and lemon show axile placentation. Mustard and *Argemone* shows parietal placentation. In peas, marginal placentation is observed. *Dianthus* and Primrose show free central, while sunflower and marigold show basal placentation.

44. (*d*) The given floral formula represents a plant family. In this, $\underline{G}$ represents that ovary is superior, while (2) means that there are two carpels which are united (syncarpous).
From the formula, it is understood that, flowers are actinomorphic, and five sepals are united that is gamosepalous.
Although, they show valvate aestivation, but it cannot be concluded from a floral formula. Aestivation can be concluded from a floral diagram, not floral formula.

45. (*d*) The given floral diagram is of Fabaceae family. *Sesbania, Trifolium* and *Indigofera* belong to Fabaceae family.
Asparagus, Colchicum, Aloe, Tulip and *Gloriosa* belongs to family-Liliaceae. Tobacco, Belladona, Ashwagandha belongs to Solanaceae family.

46. (*a*) Cabbage belongs to the family of Brassicaceae or Cruciferae. They show racemose inflorescence, do not have bracts (ebracteate) usually, have a superior ovary (hypogynous), its sepals and petals are free (polysepalous and polypetalous, respectively) and carpels are united (syncarpous).

47. (*b*) Bracteoles are secondary small bracts present between the leaf-like bracts and a flower. Bracteoles are commonly observed in plants belonging to the Malvaceae family, for example, *Hibiscus*.

48. (*a*) Lemongrass belongs to Poaceae family and can be used for deriving lemongrass oil which is an essential oil. Groundnut, soyabean and sunflower oil are cooking oil. Groundnut and soyabean belongs to Fabaceae family, while sunflower belongs to Compositae family.

49. (*c*) Polygamous is the condition of having male, female and bisexual flower on the same plant.

50. (*d*) Statement I is correct, but statement II is incorrect. Statement II can be corrected as
Fruits of *Helianthus* or sunflower are called cypsela. Siliqua are the fruits of plants belonging to the Brassicaceae family.

Ch-6 Anatomy of Flowering Plants

Topical Follow Thru

Test 1

1. (*d*) The cortex is the region found between the outermost layer, i.e. epidermis and the stele, which contains the vascular tissues. It primarily consists of parenchyma cells and aids in storage and transport of nutrients. The pericycle is the component of the stele, which is covered by endodermis. The pith refers to inner tissues located centrally. The vascular bundles are also within the stele, thus not defining the cortex region.

2. (*c*) *P* represents the axillary bud that is formed by some cells 'left behind' from shoot apical meristem during the formation of leaves and elongation of stem. It is present in the axils of leaves and are capable of forming a branch or a flower. *Q* represents the meristematic zone of shoot apical meristem which contains actively dividing cells.

3. (*d*) Plant tissue systems include the epidermal tissue system, which forms the outer protective layer; the fundamental tissue system, also known as the ground tissue system, which includes parenchyma, collenchyma and sclerenchyma; and the conducting tissue system, which consists of the vascular tissues, xylem and phloem. Connective tissue system is not a type of plant tissue system; it is a term used in animal biology.

4. (*d*) Statement I is correct, but statement II is incorrect. Incorrect statement can be corrected as The meristematic cells are usually small and thin walled with dense cytoplasm.

5. (*b*) Both A and R are true and R is the correct explanation of A. The cuticle is indeed a waxy layer found outside the shoot epidermis and is typically absent in roots. Its primary function is to prevent water loss, which is essential in aerial parts of the plant, but unnecessary in roots, which are generally adapted for water absorption rather than conservation.

6. (*b*) Image *A* shows bean-shaped stomata present in dicot plants, while image *B* shows dumb-bell shaped stomata found in monocot plants.

7. (*b*) The primary plant body is formed by primary meristems, which include the apical meristem and intercalary meristem. Intercalary meristems contribute to the elongation of plant organs, particularly in grasses. Cork cambium and interfascicular cambium are secondary meristems involved in the secondary growth of the plant. Intrafascicular cambium is also a secondary meristem that contributes to the formation of vascular tissue during secondary growth, not primary growth.

8. (*a*) The incorrect match pair can be corrected as
Parenchyma cells are involved in photosynthesis, storage and metabolic processes, but are not typically actively dividing. Collenchyma provides mechanical support, especially in young plants. Sclerenchyma includes sclereids, which are specialised for structural support. Meristem consists of undifferentiated, actively dividing cells responsible for plant growth.

9. (*b*) Collenchyma cells are living and are characterised by their uneven, angular wall thickening, which provides mechanical support to growing parts of plants. Epidermis is the outer protective layer. Sclerenchyma consists of dead cells with thick walls providing rigidity and xylem is a complex tissue involved in water and mineral transport.

10. (*d*) In a dicot stem, the vascular bundles are conjoint (xylem and phloem are present together) along the same radius and open (with a cambium layer between them), which allows for secondary growth. Dicot roots have radial vascular bundles, not conjoint. Monocot roots and monocot stems have closed vascular bundles (without cambium).

11. (*a*) The correct match is A-3, B-1, C-4, D-2.
    - Stomata are associated with the loss of water, as they are pores facilitating transpiration.
    - The cuticle helps preventing water loss due to its waxy, protective layer.
    - Guard cells regulate the opening of stomata, controlling gas exchange and water loss.
    - Subsidiary cells are modified epidermal cells that surround the stomata, assisting guard cells in their function.

12. (*c*) A vessel element is one of the cell components found in xylem. Vessel elements are typically found in flowering plants (e.g. *Mangifera indica*, *Triticum aestivum* and *Sorghum vulgare*), but are generally absent from most gymnosperms such as conifers, e.g. *Pinus sylvestris*.

13. (*c*) The epidermal tissue system includes structures like stomata (involved in exchange of gases and transpiration), root hairs (involved in absorption of water and minerals), subsidiary cells (surrounding guard cells of stomata) and trichomes (found in stem epidermis). The pith, however, is part of the ground tissue system and is located centrally in the stem and root, not within the epidermal tissue system.

14. (*c*) Bast fibres or phloem fibres are sclerenchymatous cells that are found in the secondary phloem, but are generally absent in the primary phloem.

15. (*c*) Statement given in option (c) is incorrect about tracheids. It can be corrected as
Thickening are of various types-annular, spiral, reticulate scalariform and pitted.

16. (*a*) Cells left behind from shoot apical meristem form axillary buds which are borne in the axil of leaves. These buds produce branches in a plant. Hence, apical meristem contributes towards the formation of branches.

17. (*b*) In tissue culture techniques, normally plant root and shoot tips are used to regenerate a disease free plant. This is because the root and shoot system is made up of meristematic tissues that have the ability to divide and increase in number. Also, infection in plants generally do not reach the meristematic regions, and hence, they are opted in tissue culture.

18. (*d*) A is true, but R is false. R can be corrected as
Petioles are made of collenchymatous tissue.
Collenchyma cells have walls that are thickened by cellulose, hemicellulose and pectin which make the wall thick. This provides mechanical support to the plant parts as well as flexibility which helps the petioles to bend without breaking.

19. (*c*) The pulp of mangoes is soft and usually made up of spongy parenchyma tissues. The pulp of pear is gritty in texture and is made up of sclerenchyma tissue.

20. (*b*) Statement I is incorrect and can be corrected as
Protoxylem lies towards the pith in stems. In stems, the protoxylem or the first formed xylem lies towards the centre or pith and this arrangement is called endarch. The metaxylem lies at the periphery.

21. (*d*) Sieve tubes at maturity lack nucleus and are controlled by the companion cells. Tracheids, which are a component of xylem also lack nucleus. Tracheids are dead cells just like vessels and fibres.
Companion cells and xylem parenchyma are living cells with an active protoplasm and nucleus.

22. (*c*) Both A and R are true, but R is not the correct explanation of A.
Epidermal surface of roots lack cuticle since roots are actively involved in water absorption. The waxy layer, if present in roots would prevent the absorption of water through root hairs.

23. (*b*) If chloroplasts are removed from the guard cells, food would not be synthesised here. However, the remaining part of the leaf, like the mesophyll still would be actively photosynthesising and manufacturing food. In the absence of proper solutes, water would not flow into the guard cells to make them turgid. This would interfere with the opening and closing of stomata.

24. (*a*) Dicot stems have open type of vascular bundles where xylem and phloem are separated by the presence of cambium between them. This cambium forms secondary xylem and secondary phloem, which in later stages, form wood and bark, respectively.

25. (*d*) Statement I is correct, but statement II is incorrect. Statement II can be corrected as
Ground tissues cannot divide. This is because ground tissues are made up of simple parenchyma that have lost the ability of division.

Test 2

1. (*c*) Epiblema → Cortex → Endodermis → Stele is the correct sequence of internal tissue organisation in a dicot root.
In a dicot root, the outermost layer is the epiblema, followed by the cortex. Inside the cortex, is the endodermis, which encloses the stele (vascular tissues including xylem and phloem). This sequence ensures proper structure and function for nutrient and water transport.

2. (*c*) Secondary growth involves the activity of the lateral or secondary meristems, namely the vascular cambium and cork cambium, leading to an increase in the thickness or girth of roots and shoots. This process is common in woody plants and contributes to the development of secondary tissues like secondary xylem and phloem.

3. (*b*) Both A and R are true and R is the correct explanation of A.
Lenticels, which allow gas exchange, form when the phellogen produces parenchymatous cells instead of cork cells, causing the epidermis to rupture and create these openings.

4. (*c*) The incorrect statement can be corrected as
Pericycle has two functions, i.e. formation of lateral roots along with the formation of vascular cambium.

5. (*c*) Statements I and IV are correct. Statements II, III and V are incorrect and can be corrected as
- Medullary rays are found in between the vascular bundle of dicot stems. They are absent in monocot stems and in roots.
- In a monocot stem, the hypodermis is sclerenchymatous.
- Monocot roots show radial (xylem and phloem side by side on different radii) and closed (absence of cambium) arrangement of vascular bundles.

6. (*b*) Monocot roots typically have polyarch xylem, meaning they possess multiple xylem strands, whereas dicot roots usually have fewer (diarch to hexarch). Reduced endodermis and underdeveloped pith are not distinctive features between monocot and dicot roots. Both monocot and dicot roots undergo primary growth.

7. (*b*) Secondary vascular tissues, i.e. secondary xylem and phloem are formed by the vascular cambium. Fascicular vascular cambium, interfascicular cambium and cork-cambium are examples of lateral meristems.

8. (*d*) In the given diagram of a dicot stem, the protoxylem is positioned towards the center (pith), indicating an endarch arrangement, which means the protoxylem develops from the inside out. The radial and closed vascular bundle is characteristic of monocot roots, not of dicot stem. The vascular bundle in dicot stem is conjoint and open.

9. (*d*) A is true, but R is false. R can be corrected as
In dicot stems, the casparian thickenings are absent. The endodermal cells contain dense, protoplasm, large nuclei and abundant starch grains. Because of this, the stem endodermis is called starch sheath.

10. (*b*) T.S. of wheat root, i.e. a monocot root, does not show presence of interfascicular cambium, i.e. closed vascular bundles. It is characterised by the presence of epidermis, cortex, endodermis (with casparian strips), pericycle, vascular bundles and pith. It has polyarch xylem bundles. Pith is large and well developed.

11. (*d*) In a transverse section of a dicot stem, the vascular bundles are conjoint and open, meaning they have both xylem and phloem together with a cambium layer in between, allowing for secondary growth. Monocot roots shows radial, closed vascular bundles. Monocot stems exhibit conjoint and closed vascular bundles. Dicot roots show presence of radial and open vascular bundles.

12. (*b*) Autumn wood, also known as latewood, typically has fewer and smaller xylary elements with thicker walls, contributing to denser and stronger wood. Springwood, or early wood, has vessels with wider cavities to facilitate rapid water transport. Heartwood provides mechanical support and sapwood is involved in the conduction of water and minerals.

13. (*d*) Statement I is correct, but statement II is incorrect. The incorrect statement can be corrected as
Bark formed early in the season is known as early or soft bark and bark formed later in the season is known as late or hard bark.

14. (*b*) Statement in option (b) is true. The incorrect statements can be corrected as
Stomata are present on both surfaces of the epidermis. Monocot leaves generally have parallel venation. Monocot leaves are common in grasses, not pulses. Pulses are dicot plants.

15. (*b*) Statements I, II and V are correct. Other statements are incorrect and can be corrected as
Pericycle is absent in the stems of monocots and hydrophytes.
The cortex is the zone that lies between the epidermis and the pericycle.

16. (*b*) Both statement I and statement II are correct. Epiblema is the outer epidermal surface in roots which extends to form unicellular root hairs that help in the absorption of water and minerals. Conjunctive tissue lies between xylem and phloem, and they store food since they are parenchymatous in nature.

17. (*c*) Both A and R are true, but R is not the correct explanation of A. Water can flow through plasmodesmata in root endodermis since the wall layer of endodermis is impregnated with suberin layer called casparian strips which are impervious to water.

18. (*a*) The tissue section being shown is that of monocot root. As compared to the dicot root which have fewer xylem bundles, there are usually more than six (polyarch) xylem bundles in the monocot root.
Incorrect statements can be corrected as
- Pitch is large and conspicuous.
- They do not show secondary growth due to absence of cambium.
- Vascular bundle is of closed type.

19. (*d*) The medullary rays which are present between the vascular bundles are parenchymatous in nature.

20. (*c*) The statement in option (c) is incorrect and can be corrected as
The given tissue sample is that of dicot stem. *A* is metaxylem and *B* is protoxylem. The given arrangement where protoxylem lies towards the centre (pith) and metaxylem is toward the periphery is called endarch.

21. (*a*) Statement I is incorrect, but statement II is correct. Statement I can be corrected as
Bundle sheath cells are present in both dicot and monocot leaves.
Bundle sheath cells are sclerenchymatous and are hence dead.

22. (*b*) Monocot stems have sclerenchymatous hypodermis, while dicot stems have collenchymatous hypodermis. Monocot stems have closed vascular bundle, while dicot stems have vascular bundles of open type. Both monocots and dicot stems have endarch xylem arrangement and conjoint vascular bundles.

23. (*b*) The lower or abaxial surface of a dorsiventral or dicot leaves bear the maximum number of stomata. Hence, they would transpire more and water loss from them would be highest in the lowest amount of time. This would turn cobalt chloride paper pink in the presence of moisture.

24. (*c*) In monocots like grasses, certain adaxial epidermal cells along the veins modify themselves into large, empty, colourless cells. These are called bulliform cells. When the bulliform cells in the leaves have absorbed water and are turgid, the leaf surface is exposed. When they are flaccid due to water stress, they make the leaves curl inwards to minimise water loss.

25. (*d*) Statement III is incorrect and can be corrected as
Half-moon shaped patches of sclerenchyma is unique to dicot stems.

Chapter Break Thru

1. (*b*) Xylem parenchyma, one of the elements of xylem, stores food and water materials in the form of starch or fat and other substances like tannins.
Xylem fibres, tracheid and vessels are dead elements of the xylem and do not store food and water materials.
Sclereids are a reduced form of sclerenchyma cells with highly thickened, lignified cellular walls and

do not store food and water materials.

2. (*b*) Parenchyma contain compactly arranged cells which are either closely packed or have large intercellular spaces.

3. (*c*) Phloem in gymnosperms lacks both sieve tube and companion cells. On the other hand, the phloem in angiosperms comprises of four elements named, sieve tube, companion cells, phloem parenchyma and phloem fibres.

4. (*c*) In dicot stems, vascular bundles are arranged in a ring, facilitating secondary growth. In dicot roots, vascular bundles are centrally located in a radial pattern. Monocot stems have scattered vascular bundles without a ring formation and monocot leaves feature parallel venation without ring-like vascular bundles.

5. (*d*) Increase in length of petiole results from the division of intercalary meristem. The petiole is the transition from the stem to the leaf blade.

6. (*b*) Collenchyma cells have cell walls rich in hemicellulose and pectin, which provide flexibility and mechanical support, especially in growing parts of plants. Sclerenchyma, in contrast, has thickened lignified walls. Xylem primarily contains lignin for water transport. Meristematic tissues are actively dividing cells with thin primary cell walls.

7. (*c*) Statements I, III and IV are correct. Only statement II is incorrect and can be corrected as
Intercalary meristem is a primary meristematic tissue, not a secondary meristematic tissue. It is found in monocots at the base of leaf blades and nodes.

8. (*d*) In dicotyledonous plant root, outermost layer is formed of unicellular hairs that are extensions of epidermal cells (III). The innermost layer of the cortex is known as endodermis (I). Phloem (IV) is present alternatively with the xylem. Lastly, metaxylem (II) found towards the pith.

9. (*a*) Statement I is incorrect, but statement II is correct. The incorrect statement can be corrected as
The epidermal tissue system forms the outermost covering of the whole plant body and comprises epidermal cells, stomata and the epidermal appendages- the trichomes and hairs.

10. (*b*) The incorrect statement can be corrected as
Albuminous cells are found in gymnosperms, in place of companion cells.

11. (*a*) The inner walls of guard cells are thick but not elastic; they are rigid to facilitate the opening and closing of the stomatal pore. In the stomatal apparatus, guard cells do possess chloroplasts and are typically surrounded by subsidiary cells. Stomata are crucial for gaseous exchange.

12. (*b*) Pericycle lies next to the endodermis, which are few layers of thick-walled parenchymatous cells. Initiation of lateral roots and vascular cambium during the secondary growth takes place in these cells.

13. (*d*) The diagram shows a primary dicot root structure, identifiable by the radial arrangement of xylem and phloem. The presence of the casparian strips found in the endodermis, further confirms that this is dicot root. Endarch xylem, where protoxylem is directed towards the center, is not characteristic of roots, but of stems.

14. (*c*) Statements II, III, IV and V are correct. Only statement I is incorrect and can be corrected as
The monocot stem has a sclerenchymatous hypodermis.
On the other hand, the dicot stem has collenchymatous cells in the hypodermis region.

15. (*b*) Both statement I and statement II are correct.
Root hairs are unicellular elongations of epidermal cells, while stem hairs or trichomes are typically multicellular. Trichomes can be branched or unbranched, soft or stiff and they help in preventing transpiration by reducing water loss.

16. (*c*) The incorrect statement can be corrected as
The tangential as well as radial walls of the endodermal cells have a deposition of water-impermeable, waxy material suberin in the form of casparian strips.

17. (*c*) Collenchymatous cells, characterised by their angular thickenings, are typically found in the hypodermis layer of the sunflower stem (i.e. a dicot stem). This layer is just beneath the epidermis and provides structural support.

18. (*b*) The incorrect statement can be corrected as
Epidermal cells are parenchymatous cells that are compactly arranged to form a continuous layer with cells containing a small amount of cytoplasm lining the cell wall and a large vacuole.

19. (*b*) Bulliform cells are found in grasses, large, empty and colourless, and they can absorb water, aiding in leaf folding during drought to minimise water loss. However, they are modifications of adaxial (upper) epidermal cells, not abaxial (lower) epidermal cells.

20. (*d*) A is true, but R is false. R can be corrected as
Dicot leaves are dorsiventral, meaning they have distinct upper (adaxial) and lower (abaxial) surfaces. However, typically the abaxial surface bears more stomata than the adaxial surface.

21. (*a*) In the given figure, of dicot leaf
A - Adaxial surface, *B* – Palisade cells, *C* – Spongy parenchyma cell, *D* – Abaxial surface.
The incorrect statements can be corrected as
B represents adaxially (upper surface) placed palisade parenchyma made up of elongated cells.
In a transverse section of a dicot leaf, the adaxial surface (*A*) is the upper surface. Below it, are the palisade

cells (*B*), which are closely packed and columnar. The spongy cells (*C*) are below the palisade cells and have a loose arrangement. The abaxial surface (*D*) is the lower surface of the leaf.

22. (*b*) Apical and intercalary meristems are referred to as primary meristems because they are present from the early stages of a plant's life and are responsible for the formation of the primary plant body, contributing to primary growth.

23. (*b*) Statements I and III are correct. Incorrect statements II and IV can be corrected as

- Heartwood is dark in colour, but in nature, it is very hard, durable and resistant to the attacks of microbes, organisms and insects.
- Heartwood does not conduct water, but it gives mechanical support to the stem.

24. (*a*) Statement I is incorrect, but statement II is correct. Statement I can be corrected as

Parenchymatous cells are usually present in cortex, pericycle, pith and medullary rays, in the primary stems and roots.

25. (*a*) In roots, the protoxylem, i.e. first formed primary xylem elements, lie towards periphery and metaxylem, i.e. later formed primary xylem, lie towards the centre. Such arrangement of primary xylem is called exarch.

26. (*d*) A is true, but R is false. R can be corrected as

Secondary growth is absent in monocot stems. However, monocot stems typically have closed vascular bundles, meaning they lack the vascular cambium necessary for the secondary growth.

27. (*d*) Statement I is correct, but statement II is incorrect. Incorrect statement can be corrected as

The conjoint vascular bundle, are either open or closed on the basis of presence or absence of cambium, respectively.

28. (*b*) The correct match is A-4, B-3, C-2, D-1.

- Cortex is the main zone lying between the epidermis and pericycle.
- Pericycle is present in between endodermis and stele. The pericycle cells may be parenchymatous or sclerenchymatous.
- Pith stores excretory substances such as tannins, phenols, etc.
- Medullary rays are helpful in the radial transport of food and water.

29. (*b*) Statements I, II and V are correct. Other statements are incorrect and can be corrected as

- Pericycle gives rise to lateral roots, not primary roots.
- Only the sieve tube elements and companion cells of phloem are connected by pit fields (forming plasmodesmatal connections), that is present between their common longitudinal walls.

30. (*d*) Open vascular bundle (with vascular cambium) is found in dicot stem, which is responsible for secondary growth. But, it is not surrounded by bundle sheath. This is the characteristic of monocot stems.

31. (*b*) The sieve elements are the primary food conducting tissue in plants. They are associated with companion cells because at maturity, they lack a prominent nucleus.

32. (*c*) Stomatal apparatus comprises of the stomatal pore, the guard cells and the specialised epidermal cells called subsidiary cells.

Epidermal cells form a part of the epidermal tissue system.

33. (*b*) Both statement I and statement II are correct.

Intrafascicular cambium is ontogenetically a primary meristem as it is present in plants from beginning and is embryonic in origin. Phellogen or cork cambium is a secondary meristem which causes secondary growth.

34. (*a*) The cell which is being observed is sclerenchymatous, a cell of simple tissue. Sclerenchyma cells are dead without a protoplasm and nucleus. They are elongated with a narrow lumen and are thickened due to the deposition of lignin.

35. (*a*) The incorrect statement can be corrected as

The given diagram shows radial arrangement of vascular bundles with exarch arrangement of xylem, which is seen in roots. In leaves and stems, conjoint arrangement is prevalent. In conjoint system, the xylem and phloem are jointly situated along the same radius of vascular bundles.

36. (*c*) The water impermeable layer is called casparian strips (suberised) which forces water and dissolved solutes to take the path of the cell's cytoplasm. Sugar loading into the sieve tubes for translocation is assisted by the companion cells which remain associated with the sieve elements.

37. (*a*) Statement III is correct with respect to pericycle. Other statements can be corrected as

- It is a multilayered structure. Endodermis is single layered and forms innermost to cortex.
- It comprises of both sclerenchymatous and parenchymatous cells.
- In dicots, it helps in the development of lateral roots.

38. (*b*) Cork cells, also known as phellem, are made of dead cells, whose walls are deposited with suberin. Suberin is a waxy material which makes the phellem impervious to water and gases.

39. (*b*) A monocot root can be distinguished from a dicot root by

- the presence of a polyarch (more than six) xylem bundles. In dicot root, there are usually two to four xylem and phloem bundles.
- There is an absence of lateral roots in monocots. Lateral roots are present only in dicots.
- Monocots have a large and well-developed pith, while root hairs are present in both monocot and dicot roots.

40. (*c*) The given tissue section is that of a monocot stem. P is hypodermis, which is made up of sclerenchyma and Q is ground tissue, which is made of parenchyma.

41. (*b*) The actively dividing meristematic cells are converted into permanent tissues with function of specialisation by the process of differentiation.

42. (*d*) A is true, but R is false. R can be corrected as

Jute fibres are phloem fibres made of dead sclerenchyma cells, whose walls are lignified. This makes them strong and thus, they are used commercially for making ropes, bags, etc.

43. (*d*) Statement I is correct, but statement II is incorrect. Statement II can be corrected as

Early formed phloem (protoxylem) has narrow sieve tubes, while metaphloem has bigger sieve tubes.

44. (*a*) Statement in option (a) is correct. Other statements are incorrect and can be corrected as

- Fibres or xylem fibres can be septate or aseptate.
- Vessels and tracheids are the primary water conducting tissues.
- Radial conduction of water is supported by ray parenchymatous cells of xylem.

45. (*a*) The correct match is A-4, B-2, C-1, D-3.

- Aerenchyma is a specialised parenchyma which contains air cavities that allow water plants to float in water by maintaining buoyancy.
- Collenchyma cells have depositions of cellulose, hemicellulose and pectin that causes thickening of the cell wall at corners.
- Sclerenchyma contains dead cells with lignified cell wall.
- Phloem parenchyma has pits through which plasmodesmata connects adjacent cells.

46. (*d*) The given tissue is that of a dicot stem. Out of all the four features, the presence of ring-like vascular bundles is typical for dicot stems. Starch sheath present in endodermis is also a distinct feature of dicot stems.

47. (*c*) The incorrect statement can be corrected as

Medullary rays serve as a link between the pith and cortex. They separate xylem and phloem bundles in dicot stems.

48. (*c*) In the given figure, *P* is adaxial epidermis, *Q* is palisade parenchyma, *R* is spongy parenchyma, *S* is bundle sheath cells. Palisade mesophyll cells have the highest density of chloroplast and undergo photosynthesis.

49. (*b*) In grasses, certain adaxial epidermal cells along the veins modify themselves into large, empty, colourless cells. These are called bulliform cells. When they are flaccid due to water stress, they make the leaves curl inwards to minimise water loss.

50. (*b*) Statements I and IV are incorrect and can be corrected as

Vascular bundles are surrounded by sclerenchymatous bundle sheath.

Phloem parenchyma is absent in monocot stems.

Ch-7 Structural Organisation in Animals

Topical Follow Thru

Test 1

1. (*b*) Cuboidal epithelium is commonly found in ducts of glands and tubular parts of nephrons in kidneys. Its main functions are secretion and absorption. The cuboidal epithelium is composed of a single layer of cube-like cells.

2. (*a*) The correct match is A– 4, B–1, C–2, D–3.

Squamous epithelium are found in the air sacs of lungs.

Ciliated epithelium are present in the inner surface of hollow organs such as Fallopian tube.

Compound epithelium are present in pharynx.

Glandular epithelium are specialised for secretion such as goblet cells.

3. (*b*) Both statement I and statement II are correct. In nearly all animal tissues, specialised junctions provide both structural and functional links between its individual cells. Tight junctions help to stop substances from leaking across a tissue. Whereas, gap junctions facilitate the cells to communicate with each other by connecting the cytoplasm of adjoining cells. It helps in rapid transfer of ions, small molecules and sometimes big molecules.

4. (*c*) Statements I, II and III are correct, while statements IV and V are incorrect. These can be corrected as

The cells of connective tissue secrete modified polysaccharides, which accumulate between cells and fibres and act as matrix.

Adipose tissue is a loose connective tissue.

5. (*b*) The neuroglial cell constitute the neural system along with neurons. They protect and support neurons. Neuroglia make up more than one half the volume of neural tissue in our body.

6. (*d*) The correct match is A- 4, B- 3, C- 2, D-1.

- Tendons attach skeletal muscles to bones.
- Ligaments connects bone to bone.

- Cartilage consists of chondrocytes which remain enclosed in small cavities within the matrix secreted by them.
- The bone cells are known as osteocytes.

7. (*d*) Statement I is correct, but statement II is incorrect. The incorrect statement can be corrected as
The cells of cardiac muscle tissue show striations.

8. (*a*) The given figure is of bone. The incorrect statement about bone can be corrected as
Bones have a hard and non-pliable ground substance rich in calcium salts and collagen fibres which give bone its strength.

9. (*b*) Both A and R true and R is the correct explanation of A.
The electrical signal swiftly travels along the plasma of neuron. The arrival of disturbance at neuron's ending may cause stimulation of adjacent neurons.

10. (*a*) Statement I is incorrect, but statement II is correct. Statement I can be corrected as
Adipose tissues are a type of loose connective tissue located beneath the skin. The cells of this tissue are specialised to store fats.

11. (*d*) White collagen fibres usually occur in bundles and provide strength and flexibility to tissues. Other options are incorrect and can be corrected as
Collagen fibres are generally shorter and the fibres are unbranched. On boiling, they form gelatine.

12. (*d*) Statement I is correct, but statement II is incorrect. The incorrect statement can be corrected as
A myofibril is present in the striated muscles. These are bundles of interconnected protein filaments of striated muscles.

13. (*c*) Both A and R are true, but R is not the correct explanation of A.
It can be explained as
A myelinated nerve fibre has constrictions at regular intervals called nodes of Ranvier, by jumping from node to node, the impulse can travel much more quickly. Thus, the presence of myelin sheath increases the velocity of conduction.

14. (*a*) Given figures are of glandular epithelium. They are mainly of two types : unicellular, consisting of isolated glandular cells (goblet cells of the alimentary canal) as shown in figure 'A' and multicellular, consisting of cluster of cells (salivary gland) as shown in figure 'B'.

15. (*b*) White adipose tissue acts as an insulator thus, reduces heat loss from the body.
Incorrect statements can be corrected as
Brown fat cannot substitute for food. However, it has a larger capacity for generating heat. Fibroblast synthesises fibres and matrix.
Collagen fibres are white and occur in bundles, they are unbranched and elastic.

16. (*d*) Statement I is correct, but statement II is incorrect. Statement II can be corrected as
Areolar tissue is a type of loose connective tissue in which cells and fibres are loosely arranged in a semi-fluid ground substance.

17. (*c*) Both A and R are true, but R is not the correct explanation of A.
Respiratory tract is made of smooth muscles since the smooth muscles functions on their own without voluntary control. This is required for continuous delivery of oxygen to the body.

18. (*a*) Neurons have the least regeneration power out of the given options. Therefore, neurons are least likely to be replaced by new cells.

19. (*d*) Ligaments connect bones together. If ligaments are cut or broken, then the bones will become unifixed and move freely at joints.

20. (*b*) Connective tissue is mesodermal in origin and possesses intercellular spaces.

21. (*b*) In the given figures,
A represents squamous epithelium,
B represents cuboidal epithelium,
C represents columnar epithelium,
D represents columnar cells bearing cilia (or ciliated epithelium).
It is the ciliated epithelium that is mainly present in the inner surface of hollow organs like bronchioles and fallopian tubes. Their functions is to move particles or mucus in a specific direction over the epithelium.

22. (*a*) In the given diagram of areolar tissue (a loose connective tissue), *A*-macrophage, *B*-fibroblast, *C*-collagen fibres and *D*-mast cell.
Fibroblasts (*B*) are the cells that produce and secrete fibres. Collagen fibres (*C*) are fibres of structural proteins that provide mechanical strength, elasticity and flexibility to the tissue.

23. (*d*) The figures *A* and *B* represent skeletal (striated) muscle tissue and smooth muscle tissue, respectively.
The incorrect statement w.r.t. the given muscle types can be corrected as
Skeletal muscles (A) are voluntary muscles, while smooth muscles (B) are involuntary muscles.

24. (*a*) Statements I, II and IV are correct. Statement III is incorrect and can be corrected as
In all the connective tissue except blood, the cells secrete modified polysaccharides, which accumulate between cells and fibres and act as matrix (ground substance).

25. (*d*) Statement I is correct, but statement II is incorrect. The incorrect statement can be corrected as
Tendons are examples of dense regular connective tissue. They attach skeletal muscles to bones.

Test 2

1. (*b*) In cockroaches, the 10th segment bears a pair of jointed filamentous structures called anal cerci. Other options can be corrected as
Anal styles or caudal styles are a pair of short, thread like structures present only in males. Gonapophysis is a structure present in genital pouch of male cockroaches.

2. (*d*) In cockroaches, the parts of the foregut in correct sequences are as follows.

Mouth → pharynx → oesophagus → crop → gizzard

The alimentary canal in cockroach has three regions, i.e. foregut, midgut and hindgut.

The foregut comprises of the mouth, which opens into a short tubular pharynx leading to a narrow tubular passage called oesophagus. This, in turn, opens into a sac-like structure called crop used for storing food. The crop is followed by gizzard or proventriculus, which help in grinding the food particles.

3. (*b*) The incorrect statement about respiratory system of cockroach can be corrected as

The first and third pairs of spiracles always remain open, while rest of the spiracles open only during inspiration.

4. (*c*) Both statement I and statement II are incorrect. They can be corrected as

Gizzard helps in grinding the food particles and gastric or hepatic caeca secrete digestive juices.

Malpighian tubules help in removal of excretory products from haemolymph.

5. (*a*) In frog, the duodenum receives bile from gall bladder and pancreatic juices from the pancreas through a common bile duct. Bile emulsifies fat and pancreatic juices digest carbohydrates and proteins.

6. (*c*) Both A and R are true, but R is not the correct explanation of A.

The female releases hundreds of egg in water and male discharges sperms over these eggs in order to fertilise them. Thus, in frog, fertilisation is external and takes place in water.

7. (*c*) Ostia are the apertures which allows oxygenated blood to enter the heart chambers of cockroach.

8. (*d*) The incorrect statement can be corrected as

In frogs, the blood is composed of plasma and blood cells. The blood cells are RBCs, WBCs and platelets. RBCs are nucleated and contain red coloured pigment namely haemoglobin.

9. (*b*) The correct match is A-2, B-1, C-4, D-3.

Male cockroach consist of a pair of testes, one lying on each lateral side in 4th-6th abdominal segments.

Female cockroach consist of two large ovaries, lying laterally in the 2nd- 6th segments.

A pair of spermatheca is present in the 6th -7th segments which opens into the genital chamber.

Mushroom shaped gland is present in the 6th-7th abdominal segments.

10. (*d*) Statements I, II and IV are correct. Statements III and V are incorrect. These can be corrected as

Each ovary of female cockroach is formed of a group of eight ovarian tubules or ovarioles.

The fertilised eggs of cockroach are encased in capsules called ootheca.

11. (*b*) Statements III and IV are incorrect and can be corrected as

Fertilisation is external and takes place in water in frog.

Development involves a larval stage, called as tadpole larva.

12. (*c*) The incorrect statement can be corrected as

In cockroach, nitrogenous wastes are absorbed by Malpighian tubules are converted into uric acid and excreted through hindgut afterwards.

13. (*b*) The compound eyes of cockroaches are situated at the dorsal surface of the head. Each eye consists of about 2000 hexagonal ommatidia. With the help of several ommatidia, a cockroach can receive several images of an object. This kind of vision is known as mosaic vision with more sensitivity, but less resolution.

14. (*b*) Both statement I and statement II are correct.

Heart is a muscular structure situated in the upper part of the body cavity. A triangular structure called sinus venous joins the right atrium. It receives blood through the major veins called vena cava. The chordae tendinae are strong, chord like tendons attached to the leaflets of the atrioventricular valve of the heart.

15. (*d*) Incorrect statement can be corrected as

Urea is formed from ammonia, which is released during deamination of excess amino acids in the liver.

16. (*c*) Both A and R are true, but R is not the correct explanation of A.

In frog, venous system has hepatic portal system. This system carries blood from the alimentary canal and its associated glands to the liver. It consist of a large hepatic portal vein that receives a number of tributaries from many organs.

17. (*d*) Statements I, II, III and V are incorrect and can be corrected as

- The head of cockroach lie anteriorly at right angle to the longitudinal body axis.
- Head region of cockroach is formed by the fusion of sixth segment.
- Anterior end of the cockroach head have biting and chewing type mouth parts.
- Hypopharynx lie within the cavity enclosed by the mouth part.

18. (*b*) Both A and R are true and R is the correct explanation of A.

Frogs are beneficial to mankind as they eat insects, which can damage food crops.

19. (*a*) Statement I is incorrect, but statement II is correct. Incorrect statement can be corrected as

Malpighian tubules are lined by glandular and ciliated cells.

20. (*b*) Statements I and IV are correct with respect to male cockroach. The incorrect statements can be corrected as

- The reproductive organ of female cockroach is present on 2nd and 6th abdominal segment, whereas in males, these are present on 4th and 6th abdominal segment.
- Spermatheca is a characteristic of female cockroach.

21. (*c*) In male frogs, yellowish ovoid testes are found attached to the upper part of kidneys by a peritoneum called mesorchium. It attaches the testes of frog to its kidney.

22. (*a*) The eyes of a frog are located behind the external nostrils on each side of the head. This placement allows the frog to see its surroundings effectively while keeping its body partially submerged in water.

23. (*c*) In the given figure of alimentary canal of cockroach.
I, II, III and IV represents mesenteron, salivary reservoir, crop and gizzard respectively. Gizzard (IV) has an outer layer of thick circular muscles and thick inner cuticle, forming six highly chitinous plate called teeth. These help in grinding the food.

24. (*a*) Statement I is incorrect, but statement II is correct.

- The incorrect statement can be corrected as
- Bile juice secreted by gall bladder emulsifies fat and the pancreatic juice digest carbohydrates and protein in frog.

25. (*c*) In the given figure of digestive system of frog, '*P*', '*Q*', '*R*' and '*S*' are lungs, intestine, ureter and cloaca repectively.

- The incorrect statement can be corrected as
- In female frogs, ureters and oviducts open separately into cloaca.

Chapter Break Thru

1. (*a*) The junction that performs cementing to keep neighbouring cells together is adhering junction. Other options can be corrected as
Tight junctions help to stop substances from leaking across a tissue. Gap junctions facilitate the cells to communicate with each other by connecting the cytoplasm of adjoining cells. Plasmodesmata are microscopic channels that traverse the cell walls of plant cells, facilitating the transport and communication between them.

2. (*d*) Incorrect statement can be corrected as
In dense irregular connective tissue, the collagen fibres are not arranged in parallel bundles. Instead, they are interwoven and arranged in multiple directions, providing strength and resistance to stress from various directions. The collagen fibres are present in rows between many parallel bundles of fibres in the dense regular connective tissue.

3. (*a*) Squamous epithelium is made of a single thin layer of flattened cells. They line the walls of blood vessel and air sacs of lungs and are involved in functions like forming a diffusion boundary.

4. (*a*) The bone cells (osteocytes) are present in the space called lacunae, whereas cartilage cells (chondrocytes) are enclosed in small cavities within the matrix secreted by them.

5. (*c*) Incorrect statement can be corrected as
Intercalated discs are not found in smooth muscles. These are found in cardiac muscles.

6. (*a*) Statement I is incorrect, but statement II is correct. Statement I can be corrected as
Fibrous cytoskeleton of microvilli help them in contraction and expansion, e.g. bicep muscles.

7. (*a*) The correct match is A–3, B–4, C–1, D–2.
Columnar epithelium is found in the lining of intestine and stomach.
The pseudostratified columnar epithelium is present in the trachea and large bronchi.
The cuboidal epithelium is present in the tubular parts of nephron in kidney.
Mammary gland, salivary glands, etc are exocrine glands.

8. (*b*) Statements I, II and IV are correct, while III and V are incorrect and can be corrected as

- Bones are strong due to the presence of hard and non-pliable ground substances, rich in calcium salts and collagen fibres.
- Biceps are voluntary and striated muscles.

9. (*b*) Both statement I and statement II are correct.

- The myelin sheath is a fatty layer that wraps around the axons of neurons, providing insulation and increasing the speed of electrical signal transmission.
- When a neuron is stimulated, it generates an action potential that quickly travels along its plasma membrane, transmitting the signal.

10. (*d*) Human heart is composed of all the four types of tissues, i.e. epithelial, connective, muscular and neural.

11. (*b*) Statements I, III and IV are correct. Statement II is incorrect. It can be corrected as
Gap junctions facilitate the cells to communicate with each other by connecting the cytoplasm of adjoining cells for rapid transfer of ions.

12. (*d*) The given structure represents labium (lower lip) of cockroach with labial palps.

13. (*b*) Both A and R are true and R is the correct explanation of A.
The thick layers of smooth muscles are responsible for the movement and mixing of food, ensuring it interacts effectively with digestive enzymes. This process is essential for digestion.

14. (*a*) Incorrect statement can be corrected as
Renal portal vein in frogs carries blood from the hind limbs and the posterior parts of the body to the kidneys, not from the lower part of the kidney.

15. (*b*) The incorrect match pair can be corrected as
Sweat glands are merocrine glands. Holocrine glands release substances by bursting cell membrane. Example-sebaceous glands.

16. (*d*) The incorrect statements can be corrected as
In frogs, developement is indirect. They undergo metamorphosis, starting as tadpoles (larval stage) and then transforming into adult frogs. Direct development means there is no

larval stage, which is not the case for frogs.

17. (*c*) The hindlimbs of frog ends in five digits and forelimbs ends in four digits. Rest statements are incorrect and can be corrected as

- Frogs are beneficial to humans because they consume insects and help safeguard crops.
- Frogs are ureotelic as they mainly live on land while the tadpoles are ammonotelic as they live in water and excrete ammonia as nitrogenous waste.
- It is the male frogs that have vocal sacs used to produce calls, especially during the breeding season. Female frogs generally do not have these vocal sacs.

18. (*c*) In the given diagram, *A*, *B*, *C* and *D* represent ovary, spermatheca, collaterial glands and genital chamber, respectively. Phallic gland is found in male reproductive system, not in female. It secretes the outer layer of spermatophore.

19. (*c*) The correct match is A-2, B-3, C-4, D-1.

- Cloaca is the common chamber receiving waste, reproductive and digestive materials before expulsion.
- Malpighian tubules are the excretory organs that remove nitrogenous wastes from the blood.
- Ventricle pumps blood to both lungs and the rest of the body.
- Spiracles are the openings on the body surface through which air enters and exits, facilitating respiration.

20. (*b*) The proximal convoluted tubule is lined by brush bordered cuboidal epithelium. Rest match pairs are incorrect. The incorrect match pairs can be corrected as

The salivary cells has glandular epithelium.

The moist surface of buccal cavity has non-keratinised compound epithelium.

Intestinal glands are exocrine glands.

21. (*b*) Statements III and V are incorrect. These can be corrected as

The nuclei of columnar epithelial cells are located at the base of the cell.

Exocrine glands secrete mucus, saliva, earwax, oil, milk, digestive enzymes and other cell products. Hormones are secreted by endocrine glands.

22. (*b*) Incorrect statement about compound epithelium can be corrected as

Compound epithelium provides complete protection to underlying tissues. It also covers the dry surface of the skin, moist surface of buccal cavity, pharynx, etc.

23. (*b*) In frogs, the medulla oblongata exits through the foramen magnum and extends into the spinal cord, which is protected by the vertebral column.

24. (*b*) Statements I and II are correct, while statements III and IV are incorrect and can be corrected as

- Network of trachea opens through 10 pairs of spiracles present on the lateral side of the body.
- Exchange of gases takes place at the tracheoles by diffusion.

25. (*d*) Statement I is correct, but statement II is incorrect. The incorrect statement can be corrected as

Smooth muscles are involuntary and operate without conscious control. They are found in organs such as the intestines and blood vessels. They are controlled by the autonomic nervous system.

26. (*c*) Diagram *A* depicts dense irregular connective tissue that has fibroblasts and many fibres (mostly collagen) and is present in the skin.

Diagram *B* depicts dense regular connective tissue where collagen fibres are present in rows between many parallel bundles of fibres, e.g. tendons and ligaments.

27. (*d*) Statement I is correct, but statement II is incorrect. The incorrect statement can be corrected as

Bone marrow, located in the cavities of certain bones, is responsible for producing blood cells. This includes red blood cells, white blood cells, and platelets, which are essential for oxygen transport, immune response, and blood clotting respectively.

28. (*d*) A is true, but R is false. R can be corrected as

Neuroglial cells do not protect or support the skeletal system. They are primarily involved in supporting and protecting neurons within the nervous system.

29. (*b*) The given figure is of smooth muscle cells. It is an involuntary muscle as its functioning cannot be directly controlled. It does not show striations and branching. These are found in the walls of internal organs such as blood vessels, stomach and intestine.

30. (*d*) An epithelium is a sheet or tube of firmly adherent cells with minimum (practically negligible) material and space between them.

31. (*b*) Both A and R are true and R is the correct explanation of A. Compound epithelium mostly contains two or more cell layers (multi-layered). This is important because the cell layers are exposed to the external environment and provide protection against chemical stresses and mechanical injuries and shocks, for example-the skin.

32. (*c*) Adhering junctions perform cementing to keep the cells together in a tissue. In their absence, the tissue system would lose its structural integrity.

33. (*a*) Adipose tissue are the fatty tissues of the body that store fats in them. Since fats have a density less than water, these type of tissues tend to float on the water surface.

34. (*b*) Both statement I and statement II are correct.

- Long bones like limb bones interact with skeletal muscles attached to them bring about movement.
- Biceps consist of straited muscles, which are closely attached to skeleton bone.

35. (*d*) Auto excitatory muscles are the cardiac muscles associated with heart. The intercalated discs provide mechanical and electrochemical connections between the adjacent muscle cells and allow cells and allow to contract as a unit.

36. (*d*) Statement I is incorrect, but statement II is correct. Statement I can be corrected as
Absorption structures in frogs and mammals are same which is intestinal villi and microvilli.

37. (*b*) Statement IV is correct with respect to cockroach. Rest statements are incorrect and can be corrected as
- Cockroaches have open type of circulatory system.
- Trachea is subdivided into tracheoles.
- Spiracles are present on the lateral side of the body.

38. (*b*) Both A and R are true and R is the correct explanation of A.
The head of a cockroach holds only a part of the nervous system, while the remaining is present in the ventral body surface. Hence, when we cut off the head, the cockroach lives for many days.

39. (*d*) The incorrect statement can be corrected as
In cockroaches, the nymphal stage has wing pads, however wings are present only in adult cockroaches.

40. (*c*) The presence of nictating membrane and webbed feets are the adaptation of a frog for survival in water. The nictitating membrane of a frog protects its eyes from water, while the webbed feet allows it to swim in water.

41. (*b*) The presence of features which allow us to distinguish between males and females of a species is called sexual dimorphism. Vocal sacs are structures present only in males. Other options can be explained as
- Copulatory pads are absent in females, but present in males.
- Cloaca and sensory papillae are present in both males and females.

42. (*b*) Areolar tissue is a loose connective tissue that supports internal organs of the body by providing a cushion effect.

43. (*a*) Fat bodies are yellowish structures located at the top of each kidney which stores fat and provide energy during breeding.

44. (*d*) *A* is mast cells, *B* is collagen fibres, *C* is fibroblasts, *D* is macrophages.
The incorrect statement w.r.t the given figure can be corrected as:
Macrophages play an important role in the immunity of the body.

45. (*a*) Statement I is incorrect, but statement II is correct. Statement I can be corrected as
Skeletal muscles exist in syncytium or multinucleated condition, while smooth muscles are uninucleated.

46. (*c*) Neuroglial cells support the neurons of the nervous system. They help in holding the neurons, proper functioning of synapses and support the neurons. They also bring nutrients and oxygen to them. However, impulse conduction occurs through axons of a neuron.

47. (*c*) Anal cerci are a pair of filamentous structures present in the 10th abdominal segment. They help in detecting vibrations in air and on the ground.

48. (*b*) Both A and R are true and R is the correct explanation of A.
Haemolymph in cockroaches are not involved in gaseous exchange process since they do not contain any respiratory pigment. Respiratory pigment like haemoglobin in humans are the oxygen carrying pigment proteins that help in gaseous exchange between the body cells and atmosphere. Cockroaches lack such respiratory pigments.

49. (*b*) The midbrain of frogs bear optic lobes that control vision in frogs. The hind brain contains medulla, while the forebrain contains olfactory lobes, cerebral hemisphere and diencephalon.

50. (*a*) Cockroaches excrete uric acid, which is less toxic than urea, excreted by frogs.

Ch-8 Cell : The Unit of Life

Topical Follow Thru

Test-1

1. (*b*) Rudolf Virchow (1885) first explained that cells divide and new cells are formed from pre-existing cells.
He modified cell theory and gave it a final shape.
The final theory says that all living organisms are composed of cells and products of cells and all cells arise from pre-existing cells.

2. (*b*) The incorrect match pair can be corrected as
WBCs (White Blood Cells) or leucocytes are amoeboid in shape. These are responsible for the production of immune response in our body.

3. (*b*) Nerve cells are usually very long and branched, as it helps in transmission of signals or electrical impulses over all parts of the body. On the other hand, columnar epithelial are long and narrow cells, their primary functions are secretion, excretion and absorption.

4. (*c*) Cell theory does not hold good because viruses do not have cellular organisation. Viruses are an exceptions to the cell theory as they are obligate parasites (subcellular in nature).
Paramecium, Rhizopus, are some examples which may or may not be exceptions to the theory.

5. (*a*) Cell differs greatly in size, shape and activities. For example, mycoplasma, the smallest cells are only 0.3 μm in length, while bacteria could be 3 to 5 μm. The largest isolated single cell is the egg of an ostrich. Among multicellular organisms, human red blood cells are about 7.0 μm in diameter.

6. (*d*) Statement I is correct, but statement II is incorrect. Incorrect statement can be corrected as
Animal cells contain a non-membrane bound organelles called centriole, which helps in cell division.

7. (*c*) Theodore Schwann, a British Zoologist, played a crucial role in the development of cell theory. While, examining plant cells, Schwann observed that, in addition to the plasma membrane, plant cells also had a rigid outer layer called the cell wall.

8. (*b*) Both A and R are true and R is the correct explanation of A.
Metabolically active cells are usually smaller due to higher nucleo-cytoplasmic ratio and higher surface volume ratio.
The former allow the nucleus to have better control on metabolic activities, while the latter help in quicker exchange of materials between the cell and its outside environment.

9. (*b*) The onion cell is a typical plant cell, has a distinct cell wall as its outer boundary and just within it is the cell membrane.

10. (*d*) Incorrect statement can be corrected as
Tissue system is absent in unicellular organisms.
These are made up of only one cell and tissue formation requires many cells. Instead, a single cell in a unicellular organism performs all the activities necessary for life, such as nutrition, reproduction and excretion.

11. (*c*) Statements I, IV and V are correct, while statements II and III are incorrect. These can be corrected as
The size of bacteria ranges from 3.0 – 5.0 μm.
Ribosomes are non-membrane bound organelles found in both eukaryotic and prokaryotic cells. Within the cell, ribosomes are found not only in the cytoplasm but also within the two organelles chloroplast in (plants) and mitochondria and on rough ER.

12. (*b*) Theodore Schwann, a British Zoologist, studied different types of animal cells and reported that cells had a thin outer layer which is today known as the 'plasma membrane'.

13. (*b*) Incorrect statement can be corrected as
In 1665, Robert Hooke was the first scientist who discovered the cells. He observed small tiny compartments like "honey comb" in a thin slice of cork. Living cells were first discovered by Antonie van Leeuwenhoek.

14. (*b*) Eukaryotic cells are distinguished from prokaryotic cells by their complex internal structure, which includes numerous membrane- bound organelles. These organelles are endoplasmic reticulum, Golgi complex, lysosomes, mitochondria, microbodies and vacuoles.

15. (*b*) The correct match is A–3, B–4, C–1, D–2.

- Schleiden and Schwann proposed cell theory. According to them, the body of all living beings is made up of cells.
- Rudolf Virchow proved that the cells divide and new cells are formed from the pre-existing cells division (*Omnis cellula-e-cellula*).
- Robert Brown (1831) discovered the nucleus in the pollen cells of the orchid root.
- Robert Hooke discovered the cell in 1665.

Test 2

1. (*c*) Bacteria consists of flagella, pili and fimbriae. Cilia are not found in bacteria.
Bacteria are prokaryotes whereas cilia are mostly found in eukaryotes.

2. (*d*) Mesosome do not help in locomotion. It helps in cell wall formation, DNA replication, secretion processes, respiration, etc.

3. (*a*) Statement I is incorrect, but statement II is correct. Incorrect statement can be corrected as
Pili and fimbriae are surface structures of the bacteria that do not play any role in motility.

4. (*a*) The correct match is A-2, B-3, C-4, D-1.
The four basic shapes of bacteria are given accordingly,
Bacillus - Rod-like, e.g. *Bacillus anthracis*.
Coccus - Spherical, e.g. *Streptococcus pneumoniae*.
Vibrio - Comma shaped, e.g. *Vibrio cholerae*.
Spirillum - Spiral, e.g. *Helicobacter pylori*.

5. (*b*) In prokaryotic cells, ribosomes are made up of two subunits, i.e. 50S and 30S unit which when present together form 70S unit.

6. (*d*) Incorrect match pair can be corrected as
All prokaryotes have a cell wall surrounding the cell membrane except in mycoplasma.

7. (*d*) Incorrect statement can be corrected as
Pili are elongated tubular structure made of a special protein whereas fimbriae are small bristle like fibres sprouting out of the cell.
Pili are involved in the mating process and fimbriae help in the attachment of bacteria to any surface.

8. (*c*) Many bacteria have small circular DNA outside the genomic DNA. These smaller DNA are called plasmid. The plasmid confers unique phenotypic characters to such bacteria, e.g. antibiotics resistance.

9. (*b*) Gas vacuoles are found in blue-green and purple and green photosynthetic bacteria.
It help in the storage of various substances including waste products, it also plays a major role in maintaining osmotic properties of the cell.

10. (*a*) Statement I is incorrect, but statement II is correct. Incorrect statement can be correct as
The glycocalyx layer when composed of loose sheath is known as slime layer.
The presence of amino acids along with polysaccharides is called capsule. It may be thick and tough.

11. (*c*) The bacteria which do not responds to Gram staining are Gram-negative bacteria. The other bacteria that take up stain are called Gram positive. Few examples of Gram negative bacteria includes *E. coli*, *Pseudomonas*, etc.

12. (*d*) Incorrect statement can be corrected as
The mesosome extensions are in the form of vesicles, tubules and lamellae.
Rest all the other statements are correct about mesosomes.

13. (*c*) Incorrect option can be corrected as
Prokaryotic cell lack a well developed nucleus and other organelles. Therefore, the single chromosome or circular DNA is basically naked, not enveloped by a nuclear membrane.

14. (*c*) Reserve material in prokaryotic cells are stored in the cytoplasm in the form of inclusion bodies. These are not bound by any membrane system and lie free in the cytoplasm. Phosphate granules, cyanophycean granules and glycogen granules are the examples of inclusion bodies.

15. (*a*) The cell envelope of prokaryotic cell consists of a tightly bound three layered structure, i.e. the outermost glycocalyx followed by the cell wall and then the plasma membrane.

Test 3

1. (*d*) Cell wall consists of lignin, hemicellulose, pectin and cellulose.
Plant cell wall is made up of cellulose hemicellulose, lignin and pectin. Fungal cell wall is made up of chitin.

2. (*d*) Incorrect statement can be corrected as
The endoplasmic reticulum is a network of cisternae, tubules and vesicles. Ribosomes are present on the outer surface of RER.

3. (*d*) Statement I is correct, but statement II is incorrect. Incorrect statement can be corrected as
Transitional vesicles are drop like structure associated with the convex forming face of the Golgi.

4. (*d*) Incorrect statement can be corrected as
Lysosomes are membrane bounded vesicular structures formed by the process of packaging in the Golgi apparatus.

5. (*d*) Statement I is correct, but statement II is incorrect. Incorrect statement can be corrected as
Most prokaryotes lack contractile vacuoles, while most protozoans have a contractile vacuole which periodically contracts and forces fluid and salts out of the cell, e.g. *Amoeba*.

6. (*c*) The centrosomes help in organising the spindle fibres and astral rays during cell division. It contains two centrioles which lie perpendicular to each other in which each has cartwheel like organisation. They are made up of nine evenly spaced peripheral fibrils of tubulin. The centriole contains hub that connects the tubules of peripheral triplets by radial spoke made up of proteins.

7. (*b*) Centrioles are involved in cell division and are present in animal cells, but are absent in plant cells.

8. (*b*) Both A and R are true and R is the correct explanation of A.
Mitochondria is a membrane-bound organelle which generate a large amount of cellular energy in the form of ATP (Adenosine Triphosphate). Therefore, they are called as the powerhouse of the cell.

9. (*a*) The biochemical investigation clearly revealed that the cell membranes possess protein and carbohydrate. The ratio of protein and lipid varies considerably in different cell types. In human beings, the membrane of the erythrocyte has approximately 52% protein and 40% lipids.

10. (*a*) Statement I is incorrect, but statement II is correct. Incorrect statement can be corrected as
Chloroplast synthesise food materials by photosynthesis. Besides photosynthesis, they can synthesise fatty acids and proteins.

11. (*c*) Statements I, II and III are correct regarding the cytoskeleton. Statements IV and V are incorrect. These can be corrected as
Cytoskeleton is not involve in protein synthesis or absorption of carbon dioxide. Rather, these are involved in maintaining cell shape and intracellular transport.
Eukaryotic cells possess a sub-microscopic complex supportive frame work of protein fibres and tubules. The cytoskeleton is formed of microtubules, microfilaments and intermediate filaments.
They are involved in functions such as mechanical support, motility and maintenance of the cell shape.

12. (*b*) Polar molecules, such as glucose, amino acids and ions cannot easily pass through the non-polar lipid bilayer because they are hydrophilic. These molecules require specific carrier protein to help them cross the membrane.

13. (*c*) Both A and R are true, but R is not the correct explanation of A.
As the polar molecules cannot pass through non-polar lipid bilayer, they require a carrier protein to facilitate transport.
A few ions or molecules are transported across the membrane against their concentration gradient, i.e., from lower to the higher concentration.
Such a transport is an energy dependent process, in which ATP is utilised and is called active transport.

14. (*a*) The number of mitochondria per cell is variable depending on the physiological activity of the cells.

15. (*c*) Both A and R are true, but R is not the correct explanation of A.

Ribosomes are the granular structures first observed under the electron microsope as dense particle by George Palade (1953).
They are made up of subunits, which when present together forms 70S in prokaryotic ribosomes and 80S in eukaryotic ribosomes. Here, S (Svedberg's unit) stands for the sedimentation co-efficient.

16. (*c*) Centromere is a primary constriction present on the chromosome where the chromatids are held together. Based on the position of the centromere, the chromosomes can be classified into four types
(i) Metacentric
(ii) Sub-metacentric
(iii) Acrocentric
(iv) Telocentric

17. (*a*) The nuclear envelope consist of two parallel membranes with a space in between. This space is called perinuclear space, which forms a barrier between the material present inside the nucleus and that of the cytoplasm.

18. (*d*) Statement I is correct, but statement II is incorrect. Incorrect statement can be corrected as
Peripheral proteins lie on the surface of the membrane while integral proteins are partially or totally buried in the membrane.

19. (*b*) Both chloroplast and mitochondria contain DNA is the correct statement. All other statements are incorrect and can be corrected as
The membrane bound matrix of chloroplasts is stroma and inside the stroma, thylakoids are present which form grana. These are not found in mitochondria.
The chloroplast are generally much larger than mitochondria.
The inner membrane of chloroplast is relatively less permeable.

20. (*c*) The eukaryotes include all the protists, plants, animals and fungi. In eukaryotic cells, there is an extensive compartmentalisation of cytoplasm through the presence of membrane bound organelles.

21. (*d*) The inner membrane forms a number of infoldings called the cristae.
Rest all are incorrect and can be corrected as
Outer membrane is responsible for exchange of metabolites and information between mitochondria and the cell.
The cristae is the number of infolding in inner membrane to increase the surface area.
The inner-fluid compartment is called matrix.

22. (*d*) SER and RER can be distinguished with their presence in fat and protein synthesising cells.
SER has a smooth membrane and synthesise cholesterol and lipids.
RER bears a large number of ribosomes on its cytoplasmic surface and provides a site for protein synthesis.

23. (*d*) A is true, but R is false. R can be corrected as
Mitochondria can synthesise some of their own proteins and divide by fission.

24. (*d*) Statements I, II and V are correct, whereas statements III and IV are incorrect and can be corrected as
Lysosomes are known as polymorphic cell organelle. It occurs in more than one form.
Tonoplast is selectively permeable as a result, the concentration of ions is relatively high in the vacuole as compared to the cytoplasm.

25. (*d*) Statement I is correct, but statement II is incorrect. Incorrect statement can be corrected as
The core of cilia is called axoneme which possess a number of microtubules running parallel to the long axis. These are present in arrangement of 9 + 2 array.

Chapter Break Thru

1. (*b*) The middle lamella is a layer mainly of calcium pectate which holds or glues the different neighbouring cells together. The cell wall and middle lamellae may be traversed by plasmodesmata which connect the cytoplasm of neighboring cells.

2. (*d*) Ribosome are the factories of protein synthesis, which remain associated with rough ER. Rough ER is called so due to the appearance of this organelle in electron micrographs. The roughness results from ribosomes, which are shredded on the membranes of the organelle. The major function of rough ER is to make proteins that are secreted by the cell.

3. (*b*) The organelle '*X*' in the given figure represents endoplasmic reticulum. It together with Golgi complex, lysosomes and vacuoles constitute the endomembrane system and remains in close association with the Golgi apparatus.
The ER often shows ribosomes attached to their outer surface and are actively involved in protein synthesis and secretion.

4. (*a*) Incorrect statement can be corrected as
Flip-flop movement is rarely found in lipid molecules, whereas it remains absent in protein molecules.

5. (*c*) The digestive enzymes present in the lysosomes comes under the categories of acid hydrolases. These are responsible for the digestion of all type of macromolecules, such as proteins, polysaccharides, etc.

6. (*c*) The cell wall of a young plant cell, the primary wall is capable of growth, which gradually diminishes as the cell matures and the secondary wall is formed on the inner (towards membrane) side of the cell.

7. (*c*) A special membranous structure is the mesosome which is formed by the extensions of plasma membrane into the cell. They help in cell wall formation, DNA replication and distribution to daughter cells.

8. (*a*) The correct match is A–2, B–4, C–3, D–1.
- Smooth endoplasmic reticulum is the site for synthesis of lipid.
- Mitochondria are the sites of aerobic respiration, which uses

oxygen to break down carbohydrates, fats and protein to produce ATP as energy of cell.

- Cristae are the partial partitions found in a mitochondria formed by infolding of the inner membrane.
- Rough ER is the site of protein synthesis.

9. (*c*) RER is easily observed in the cell. Other options are incorrect and can be corrected as

Secretory cell have both SER and RER.

Golgi apparatus is present in higher number in secretory cells.

Secretory granules are not found in nucleus.

10. (*b*) Statements I, III and IV are correct, but statements II and V are incorrect. These can be corrected as

Schleiden and Schwann together formulated the cell theory. This theory did not explain as to how new cells were formed.

The plasma membrane of prokaryotic cells is selectively permeable in nature and interacts with the outside world and this membrane is structurally similar to that of eukaryotes.

11. (*b*) In acrocentric chromosome, the centromere is present near the end of chromosomes. It forms a very short arm and a very long arm.

12. (*a*) The correct match is A–3, B–4, C–2, D–1.

- Chromatin refers to condensed structure of DNA.
- Cisternae is a flattened membrane vesicle found in ER and Golgi apparatus.
- Thylakoids are membrane bound compartments found in stroma.
- Centriole form the basal body of cilia or flagella.

13. (*b*) Both statement I and statement II are correct.

Golgi apparatus consist of many flat, disc-shaped sacs or cisternae of 0.5 μm to 1.0 μm diameter which are stacked parallel to each other. The Golgi cisternae are concentrically arranged near the nucleus with distinct convex *cis* or the forming face and concave *trans* or the maturing face.

14. (*c*) Golgi apparatus is the important site for the formation of glycoprotein and glycolipids. The contents synthesised by the endoplasmic reticulum are modified and packaged by the Golgi apparatus.

15. (*d*) Incorrect statement can be corrected as

Thylakoid is a membrane-bound compartment inside chloroplasts and cyanobacteria and is not present in the mitochondria. These are the site of the light-dependent reactions of photosynthesis. The inner compartment of mitochondria is called the matrix.

Rest other statements are correct.

16. (*b*) The correct match is A–3, B–4, C–1, D–2.

- Red Blood Cells (RBCs) are round and biconcave structure present in blood.
- The loose sheath structure of glycocalyx is called slime layer. Glycocalyx differ in composition and thickness among different bacteria.
- Golgi apparatus are responsible for packaging and import and export of materials.
- The movement of solvent molecules along concentration gradient by simple diffusion is called osmosis, e.g. water.

17. (*a*) Statement I is incorrect, but statement II is correct. Incorrect statement can be corrected as

The axoneme usually has nine pairs of doublets of radially arranged peripheral microtubules and a pair of centrally located microtubules, i.e. 9+2.

18. (*c*) Statement in option (c) is correct. Incorrect statements can be corrected as

Fluid mosaic model of cell membrane was proposed by Singer and Nicolson.

The lipid molecules in the plasma membrane are arranged in bilayer. Proteins are inserted into the lipid bilayer.

Na^+ and K^+ ions are transported against their concentration gradient across the cell membrane by active transport.

19. (*b*) The correct match is A–3, B–1, C–2, D–4.

- Acrocentric chromosome is one in which the centromere is situated very close to one end, i.e., centromere is sub terminal.
- Plasmodesmata connects the cytoplasm of two neighbouring cells.
- Telocentric chromosome is one in which the centromere is located at one end.
- The nuclear matrix or the nucleoplasm contains nucleolus and chromatin.

20. (*b*) Statements I, IV and V are correct, whereas statements II and III are incorrect. These can be corrected as

In plant cells, a secondary cell wall is formed internally to the primary wall.

Golgi apparatus is an important site for the formation of glycoproteins and glycolipids.

21. (*c*) Statement in options (a), (b) and (d) were the findings of Schwann, while statement in option (c) stands true for the finding of Schleiden, i.e. plant tissue consist of one or other types of cells.

22. (*a*) The fluidity of membranes in a plant in cold weather may be maintained by increasing the number of phospholipids with unsaturated hydrocarbon tails.

23. (*c*) Incorrect match-pair can be corrected as

Rough ER is involved in protein synthesis and secretion, whereas the synthesis of glycogen takes place in smooth ER, along with lipid production.

24. (*b*) Both statement I and statement II are correct.

The cell wall of young plant cell is the primary wall, which is capable of growth. It gradually diminishes as the cell matures and the secondary wall is formed on the inner (towards membrane) side of the cell.

25. (*b*) Mycoplasma are unique among prokaryotes. They lack a cell wall, making them resistant to antibiotic.

26. (*d*) Statement I is correct, but statement II is incorrect. Incorrect statement can be corrected as

Rough endoplasmic reticulum plays an important role in synthesising proteins. The smooth endoplasmic reticulum helps in the synthesis of lipids.

27. (*d*) Non-staining secondary constrictions at a constant location on some chromosomes create the appearance of a small fragment called a satellite. Secondary constrictions are narrow regions found at any point on a chromosome other than centromere.

28. (*c*) Both A and R are true, but R is not the correct explanation of A.

The axoneme usually has nine pairs of doublets of radially arranged peripheral microtubules and a pair of centrally located microtubules. Such an arrangement of axoneme is 9 +2 array. The central tubules are connected by bridges and connects to peripheral doublets by a radial spoke. Thus, there are nine radial spokes and two peripheral doublets connected by linkers.

29. (*b*) Chromatophores are membranous structures found in some photosynthetic bacteria, such as cyanobacteria. These structures contain pigments essential for photosynthesis.

30. (*a*) The correct match is A–2, B–1, C–4, D–3.

Pili are elongated tubular structures which are made up of tubulin protein. They are involved in bringing cells together (mating process).

Fimbriae are small bristles-like fibres, help in attachment of the cells to the surface.

Flagella is a rigid hollow cylindrical structure that has a role in the motility of bacteria.

Mesosomes are formed by the infolding of the plasma membrane, which helps in the replication of DNA.

31. (*a*) Statements I, III, IV and V are correct, while statement II is incorrect and can be corrected as

The endomembrane system is a group of membranes and organelles in eukaryotic cells that works together. It includes ER, Golgi complex, lysosomes and vacuoles.

32. (*d*) The correct match is A–2, B–4, C–1, D–3.

- Sheath is an extension of the cell wall that forms the limiting or covering membrane of flagellum.
- Mitochondrial matrix is made up of colloidal complex mainly formed of proteins.
- Axon has 11 fibrils, i.e. 9 + 2 arrangement.
- The two central single fibrils are connected by a double bridge of proteinaceous material.

33. (*b*) Prokaryotic cells do not have a well defined, membrane- bound nucleus. Instead, their genetic material is found in a region of the cell called the nucleoid.

34. (*b*) Reserve material in prokaryotic cells are stored in the cytoplasm in the form of inclusion bodies, e.g. phosphate granules cyanophycean granules and glycogen granules.

Other matches are incorrect and can be corrected as

In prokaryotes, ribosomes are of 70S type.

The cell wall is made up of peptidoglycan.

A plasmid is an extra cellular double-stranded (*ds*) circular DNA.

35. (*a*) *X* is representing the Kinetochore, a disc-shaped protein structure associated with duplicated chromatids in eukaryotic cells where the spindle fibres attach during cell division to pull sister chromatids apart.

36. (*d*) Statement I is correct, but statement II is incorrect. Incorrect statement can be corrected as

The centromere is the region of the chromosome, where sister chromatids are held together.

37. (*d*) In a lipid bilayer, lipids are free to move, but cannot leave the membrane. This feature of plasma membrane was explained by Singer and Nicolson in their quasi-fluid or fluid mosaic model of plasma membrane. The ability to move within the membrane is measured as its fluidity.

38. (*c*) Both statement I and statement II are incorrect. These can be corrected as

Eukaryotic cell do not contain mesosome. A specialised differentiated form of cell membrane called mesosome is the characterisitc of prokaryotes.

In eukaryotes, the cells genetic material, DNA is organised in chromosomes.

39. (*b*) Incorrect statement can be corrected as

The organised beating of cilia is produced by controlled sliding of outer doublet microtubules and is not controlled by fluxes of Ca^{2+} across the membrane.

40. (*d*) A is true, but R is false. R can be corrected as

The polar molecules cannot pass through the lipid bilayer as they are hydrophilic in nature. They require a carrier protein to facilitate their transport across the membrane.

41. (*b*) Cilia are small structures which work like oars causing the movement of either the cell or the surrounding fluid. Flagella are comparatively longer and responsible for cell movement.

42. (*c*) Microbodies are small, membrane- bound organelles that contain enzymes involved in various metabolic process. These are found in both plant and animal cells.

43. (*b*) In eukaryotic cells, ribosomes are 80S, and the two subunits are 60S and 40S.

44. (*a*) The cell envelope of prokaryotic cell consists of a tightly bound three layered structure, of which the outermost layer is glycocalyx followed by the cell wall and then the plasma membrane.

45. (*a*) Kinetochore is a disc- shaped protein structure. It is present in the centromere of the chromosome and attaches the chromosomes to the spindles of the microtubules.

46. (*c*) Microbodies are the eukaryotic cell organelles that are bound by a single membrane. These are absent in prokaryotic cells and are filled with different types of oxidative enzymes.

47. (*b*) Antonie van Leeuwenhoek first saw and described a live cell. Robert Brown later discovered the nucleus. Schleiden and Schwann gave the cell theory.

48. (*c*) Normal human RBCs have a biconcave shape, their diameter is about 7-8 μm and their thickness is about 2.5 μm.

49. (*b*) Carrier proteins are membrane transport proteins along with channel proteins that transport materials and information into the cell.

50. (*a*) A is false, but R is true, A can be corrected as

A telocentric chromosome have centromere at the very end of the chromosome. This gives the chromosome only one arm instead of two.

Ch-9 Biomolecules

Topical Follow Thru

Test 1

1. (*d*) During chemical analysis of cell constituents, proteins, nucleic acids, polysaccharides and lipids constitute acid insoluble fraction. In this, proteins, nucleic acids and polysaccharides are macromolecules and their molecular weights lie in the range of 10,000 Da and above, but lipids are not strictly macromolecules, since their molecular weights do not exceed 800 Da.

2. (*b*) Lecithin or phosphatidyl choline is the most abundant phospholipid in cell membrane. However, cephalin, phospatidylserine, phosphatidyl inositol are also present in cell membrane, but in less amount.

3. (*d*) Energy storage molecules are those molecules which store energy in the form of covalent bonds. Some molecules like glycogen (carbohydrate) and triglycerides (lipids) are synthesised by the cells and they are stored for the later release of energy.

4. (*b*) The incorrect statement about lipids can be corrected as

A fatty acid has a carboxyl group attached to an *R* group.

5. (*b*) Statements III, IV and V are correct. Statements I and II are incorrect and can be corrected as

Primary metabolites are biochemicals formed as intermediates and products of normal vital metabolic pathways of organisms.

The macromolecules of cytoplasm and cell organelles appear in acid insoluble pellet. The soluble part of cytosol and other cell parts appears in acid-soluble pellet.

6. (*c*) The incorrect match pair can be corrected as

Curcumin belongs to the group of curcuminoids, which are phenolic pigments responsible for the yellow colour of turmeric. The correct examples of alkaloids is morphine, codeine, etc.

7. (*c*) Alkaloids are secondary metabolites originally defined as pharmacologically active compounds. Terpenoids are derived from isoprene and can vary widely in structure and function.

8. (*a*) A is false, but R is true. A can be corrected as

Palmitic acid is saturated fatty acid. It is a fatty acid with 16 carbon chain and no double bond.

9. (*c*) Amino acids, e.g. arginine, lysine and histidine belong to basic amino acid category. The basic amino acid contains more than one amino group.

Other options can be explained as

Alanine, valine and glycine belong to neutral amino acid category.

Tyrosine, tryptophan and phenylalanine belong to aromatic amino acid category.

Glutamate and aspartate belong to acidic amino acid category.

10. (*c*) The cellular pool is the collection of thousands of biomolecules. It contains both organic and inorganic molecules. It is present in both aqueous phase and non-aqueous phase. Aqueous phase comprises of crystalloids and colloids dispersed in water. Non-aqueous phase comprises of chemicals deposited in cell membrane and cell wall.

11. (*a*) The correct match is A-4, B-3, C-1, D-2.

Average composition of cells are given below.

Proteins– 10-15%

Lipids –2%

Ions –1%

Nucleic acids –5-7%

12. (*b*) In the given diagram, the NH_2 group is protonated, since the amino acid behaves as a base and accepts proton in acidic conditions (in low pH).

13. (*b*) The incorrect statement can be corrected as

Acid soluble pool contains various organic as well as inorganic compounds that can be extracted by various separation techniques.

14. (*b*) Lipids form vesicles during the grinding of tissue. These vesicles are membrane-bound sacs that are insoluble in water and tend to separate along with the acid-insoluble pool and hence in the macromolecular fraction.

15. (*b*) The acid soluble pool contains compounds with molecular weights ranging from 18 to around 800 Da. These compounds include amino acids, nucleotides, simple sugar.

Test 2

1. (*b*) Starch shows blue colour in the presence of iodine because of its helical secondary structure which helps in holding iodine molecules.
2. (*d*) All of the given are the functions of proteins except option (d). The storage of genetic information is the role of nucleic acids, specifically DNA and RNA.
3. (*b*) The most abundant protein in the biosphere is RuBisCO. It plays an important role during the dark reaction of photosynthesis, by fixing CO_2 into a 3-carbon compound.
4. (*d*) Statement I is correct, but statement II is incorrect. Incorrect statement can be corrected as
   All biomacromolecules are polymers, e.g. lipids. Lipids are not polymers, since they lack a monomer repeating unit.
5. (*c*) Statements II and IV are correct.
   Incorrect statements can be corrected as
   Adult human haemoglobin is composed of two subunits of α type and two subunits of β-type.
   Haemoglobin is arranged into a manner in which these individual folded polypeptides or subunits are arranged with respect to each other and form quaternary structure.
6. (*b*) The correct match is A–1, B–4, C–3, D–2.
   - β- pleated sheet gives secondary structure of protein.
   - Tertiary structure gives 3-D view of a protein.
   - Glucosamine is a modified sugar.
   - RuBisCO is the most abundant enzyme in the whole biosphere.
7. (*c*) Both statement I and statement II are incorrect and can be corrected as
   Inulin is a polymer of fructose.
   Paper made from cotton fibre and plant pulp is cellulosic in nature.
8. (*b*) Statements I, II and V are correct, while statements III and IV are incorrect. The incorrect statements can be corrected as
   Monosaccharides are soluble in water, sparingly soluble in alcohol and insoluble in ether. They may exist in different isomeric forms.
   Starch is the storehouse of energy in plants.
9. (*c*) Under fasting, glycogen reserves of the body is broken down to increase the blood glucose levels. The monomeric glucose units in a glycogen molecule is released by breakdown or hydrolysis of glycosidic bond.
10. (*c*) Dietary protein serves several important functions. It provides the essential amino acids, which are not synthesised by our body. Hence, they have to be supplied through our diet.
11. (*b*) The correct match is A-3, B-1, C-2, D-4.
    - Linolenic acid is essential fatty acid as it belongs to PUFA (Poly Unsaturated Fatty Acid) category.
    - Cholesterol is steroid in nature. It is present in animal cell only.
    - Stearic acid is a saturated fatty acid.
    - Lecithin or phosphatidyl choline is a phospholipid.
12. (*c*) The glycosidic bond links multiple monosaccharides units to form polysaccharide.
    Peptide bond or amide bond links two amino acids. Both ether and ester bond are present in lipids.
13. (*b*) The given structure is of lecithin. It is a phospholipid and major component of the lipid bilayer of cell membranes.
14. (*c*) The incorrect statement can be corrected as
    In proteins, mostly right handed helices are observed. Left handed helices are rare in nature.
15. (*a*) Arachidonic acid has 20 carbon atoms (including the carboxyl carbon) and 4 double bonds.
    Linolenic acid has 18 carbon atoms with three double bonds.
    Palmitic acid has 16 carbons (including carboxyl carbon) and no double bond.
    Oleic acid has 18 carbon atoms with one double bond.
16. (*a*) A is false, but R is true. A can be corrected as
    Heat cannot degrade a protein at its primary structure.
    Heating does not alter the sequence of the amino acids since the peptide bonds linking the amino acid residues are not easily broken by heat.
17. (*c*) Both statement I and statement II are incorrect. These can be corrected as
    Iodine solution is typically yellowish brown in appearance. Only after reacting with starch, a blue-black coloured complex is formed.
    Starch upon hydrolysis, gives a negative iodine test. Upon hydrolysis, starch is broken into its monosaccharide units, which do not give a bluish-black colour on reaction with iodine.
18. (*d*) Ester bond is formed between a glycerol molecule and a phosphate group to form a phospholipid. The incorrect statements can be corrected as
    Phospholipids have a polar head group containing the phosphate molecule.
    Phospholipid tails form the core of membrane. The tail is made up of hydrophobic R-groups, which are shielded from the aqueous environment by forming the interior core of the membrane.
    The R-groups of a phospholipid are hydrophobic.
19. (*b*) Statements I and III are correct, whereas statements II and IV are incorrect. The incorrect statements can be corrected as
    Covalent bonds are found in primary, tertiary and quaternary structures of proteins.

Quaternary structures are stabilised by disulphide bridges, hydrogen bonds, ionic bonds and hydrophobic interactions.

20. (*c*) Heparin is a heteropolysaccharide found in granules of mast cells and is also produced by the liver. It is composed of repeating units of sulphated glucosamine and uronic acid and is linked together by α-1, 4-glycosidic bonds.

21. (*c*) Unsaturated fats contain double or triple bonds. This results in loose packing of the hydrocarbons around the bonds. As a result, they have a lower melting point and hence, remain liquid at room temperatures.

22. (*b*) Both A and R are true and R is the correct explanation of A Reducing sugar can act as a reducing agent and get oxidised in the process. However, polysaccharides like starch is a non-reducing sugar as it cannot reduce other substances. This is because their anomeric carbon is involved in glycosidic linkage.

23. (*c*) Both statement I and statement II are incorrect. These can be corrected as

Cysteine is essential for the tertiary and quaternary structure of proteins. Its residues form the disulphide bridges that stabilise the tertiary structure in proteins.

A dipeptide is stabilised by the formation of one peptide bond between two amino acids.

24. (*d*) *P* is the secondary structure of protein, precisely a helix. Here, the structure is stabilised by hydrogen bonding.

Q is the primary structure which contains amino acids linked by peptide bond, which is a type of covalent interaction.

25. (*d*) The correct match is A-3, B-4, C-1, D-2.

Glycogen is homopolysaccharides of glucose and acts as reserve food in animals, also called as animal starch.

Peptidoglycan is a heteropolysaccharide made up of repeating units of NAG (N-acetylglucosamine) and NAM (N-acetylmuramic Acid).

Sucrose is non-reducing sugar as it does not have free anomeric carbon.

Protein is a heteropolymer.

Test 3

1. (*c*) The enzymes isomerases include all enzymes catalysing inter-conversion of optical, geometric or positional isomers. Enzyme lyase catalyse removal of groups from substrates by mechanisms other than hydrolysis leaving double bonds. Transferases enzymes catalyse the transfer of group between substrates. Isozymes are enzyme that differ in amino acid sequence, but catalyse same chemical reaction.

2. (*b*) Both catabolic and anabolic pathways are coupled because catabolic reactions furnish the energy required for anabolism. Catabolic reaction transfers energy from complex molecules to ATP. Anabolic reactions transfer energy from ATP to complex molecules. Thus, the free energy released from one pathway is used to drive the other.

3. (*d*) Malonate is a competitive inhibitor of succinate dehydrogenase. The binding of succinate dehydrogenase to the substrate, succinate, is completely inhibited by malonate.

4. (*a*) Statement I is incorrect, but statement II is correct. Statement I can be corrected as

Hydrolases add water to break bonds like peptide, ester bonds, etc.

In condensation reaction, two molecules are linked or condensed with release of water and formation of bond between them. In hydrolysis, there is chemical incorporation of water to break bonds.

5. (*b*) The given reaction is catalysed by enzyme lyase. It acts by catalysing removal of group from substrate by mechanism other than hydrolysis leaving double bonds. The enzyme hydrolase catalyses hydrolysis action. Isomerase enzyme catalyses inter-conversion of optical, geometric or positional isomers. Transferase enzyme catalyses transfer of group.

6. (*c*) The graph (c) shows the correct effect of pH on the velocity of enzymatic reaction. This is because of the fact that every enzyme has an optimal pH where its action is maximum. Most enzymes show optimum activity in a pH range of about 6.0 to 7.5. A shift towards the alkaline or acid side rapidly decreases the enzyme activity and finally stops it altogether.

7. (*b*) Haem acts as the prosthetic group for enzymes catalases and peroxidases. Thus, haem acts as an important co-factor for enzymes catalase and peroxidase, but not carboxypeptidase.

Zn acts as an important metal co-factor of carboxypeptidase enzyme which forms coordinate bonds of carboxypeptidase enzyme, with the side chain of the enzyme active site and is required for enzyme action. Any enzymatic reaction slows down if the ambient temperature is lowered since the enzyme becomes inactive. Similarly, lowering substrate concentration lowers enzyme action.

8. (*b*) Both A and R are true and R is the correct explanation of A.

Change in pH above or below the optimum value, reduces the rate of enzyme action because change in pH brings about change in degree of ionisation of $—NH_2$, $—COOH$ and other ionisable groups of enzyme molecule.

9. (*b*) The structure of substrate gets transformed into the structure of product through formation of transition state structure.

10. (*c*) Both A and R are true, but R is not the correct explanation of A.
Coenzymes are organic compounds and their association with the apoenzyme is transient, usually occurring during the course of catalysis. The essential chemical components of many coenzymes are vitamins, as many of them are derived from vitamins. e.g., coenzyme Nicotinamide Adenine Dinucleotide (NAD) and NADP contain the vitamin niacin or nicotinamide.

11. (*a*) Malonate is the competitive inhibitor that competes with succinate for the active site of succinate dehydrogenase enzyme. Increasing substrate concentration, that is concentration of succinate, can reverse the inhibition of the enzyme.

12. (*b*) Allosteric modulation on feedback inhibition is an enzyme regulatory mechanism, where a product of a simple or chain reaction can function as temporary allosteric inhibitor, i.e. an inhibitor that combines with a regulatory or allosteric site (other than the active site) if its concentration crosses a threshold value. For example, excess of glucose-6-phosphate stops the activity of enzyme hexokinase that helps in its formation from glucose and ATP.

13. (*a*) Statements I, IV and V are correct. Statements II and III are incorrect and can be corrected as
The thermostable non-protein part is called cofactor. Thermostable substances are not readily destroyed or deactivated by heat.
An enzyme may have one to several active sites over it. Each active site is in the form of a crevice or deep pit.

14. (*a*) A is false, but R is true. A can be corrected as
When other conditions are constant, an increase in substrate concentration increase the rate of the enzyme-catalysed reaction, but when it is reached to a maximum (V_{max}), further increase in substrate concentration produces no additional effect.

This is because the enzyme molecules are fewer than the substrate molecules and there are no free enzyme molecules to bind with the additional substrate molecules.

15. (*b*) Incorrect statement can be corrected as
Enzymes are highly specific in order to effectively regulate biochemical reaction in the cell. Such specificity is the result of unique structures at the active site of the enzymes that allow them to bind to particular enzymes.

Chapter Test

1. (*a*) Adenine is a nitrogenous base. Adenosine and cytidine are nucleosides and guanylic acid is a nucleotide.

2. (*c*) Ribozymes are RNA molecules that can catalyse certain biochemical reactions, including RNA cleavage and modification, ligation, peptide bond formation, etc.

3. (*b*) Both statement I and statement II are correct.
Lipids are considered as macromolecules even though they are small in size. This is because lipids form vesicles from broken cell membranes during tissue grinding, which are water-insoluble and hence grouped with the macromolecular fraction.

4. (*c*) The given figure represents adenylic acid, a nucleotide. It is a monomer consisting of a phosphate group, a five-carbon sugar and a nitrogenous base (adenine). It forms polymeric chains of DNA alongwith other nucleotides.

5. (a) Statements III, IV and V are incorrect. These can be corrected as
An amino acids has four substituent groups occupying the four valency positions of carbon.
The chemical and physical properties of amino acids are essentially dependent on the amino, carboxyl and the *R* functional groups.

6. (*a*) A is false, but R is true. A can be corrected as
Secondary metabolites are not known to be involved in basic metabolic processes, but have significant ecological importance.

7. (*b*) The correct match is A-4, B-3, C-2, D-1.
Collagen is the intercellular ground substance. Receptors are proteins that receive stimulus. GLUT-4 is a glucose transporter protein. Insulin is hormone that regulates glucose.

8. (*c*) Nucleotide is the basic building block of nucleic acids (RNA and DNA). It consists of a sugar molecule attached to a phosphate group and a nitrogen containing base.

9. (*d*) The primary structure of a protein is the linear one dimensional sequence of amino acids that make up a polypeptide chain. The primary structure is usually written (while imagining it as a line) and is read from the N-terminus to the C-terminus.

10. (*c*) Enzymes isolated from organisms who normally live under extremely high temperatures, e.g., hot vents and sulphur springs are stable and retain their catalytic power even at high temperatures (upto 80 – 90°C).

11. (*c*) Activation energy is the minimum amount of extra energy needed by a reacting molecule to get converted into a product. When activation energy is low, more particles have enough energy to collide and react, resulting in a faster reaction.

12. (*a*) The correct match is A-1, B-2, C-4, D-3.
Glucosamine is a polysaccharide. Gums are polymeric secondary metabolites. Abrin is a toxin, while curcumin is a drug.

13. (*a*) The incorrect statement can be corrected as
The acid- insoluble pool consists of four types of organic compounds, i.e. proteins, nucleic acids, polysaccharide and lipids. All of these, except lipids, have molecular weight in the range of 10,000 Da and above. These group constitute biomacromolecules.

14. (*d*) The incorrect match pair can be corrected as
Glycine is a neutral amino acid. Amino acids such as tyrosine, phenylalanine, tryptophan are aromatic amino acids.

15. (*c*) Statements I, III and IV are correct, while statements II and V are incorrect. The incorrect statement can be corrected as
Hydrolysis of starch into glucose is an example of chemical reaction. Proteins are heteropolymers made of amino acids.

16. (*b*) Enzymes are biological catalysts made up of proteins and their functionality is highly dependent on temperature. Most enzymes are adapted to function optimally at 37°C. When the temperature rises above 40°C, they get denatured.

17. (*a*) Point B represents the transition state of substrate in an enzymatic reaction. It is an unstable structure that occur during all enzymatic reactions. These are transient structure and have the highest energy, existing between the substrate and the product.

18. (*c*) Both A and R are true, but R is not the correct explanation of A.
When the tissue is fully burnt, all the carbon compounds are oxidised to gaseous form (CO_2, water vapour) and are removed remaining part is called ash. This contains inorganic elements (e.g., Na, Mg, etc.).

19. (*a*) The correct order is II, IV, V, I, III.
The catalytic cycle of an enzyme action can be described in the following steps.

- The substrate binds to the active site of the enzyme.
- The enzyme alters its shape to fit more tightly around the substrate.
- Formation of enzyme-substrate complex.
- Formation of the the enzyme product complex.
- The enzyme releases the products and becomes ready for another catalytic cycle.

20. (*b*) The melting point of unsaturated fatty acids falls with the increase in number of double bonds which creates a link in molecular structure and prevents the tight packing of fatty acids. Therefore, fats having unsaturated fatty acids are generally liquids or oils even during winter.

21. (*d*) A number of enzymes require metal ions for their activity which form coordination bonds with side-chains at the active site and at the same time form one or more coordination bonds with the substrate.

22. (*c*) The incorrect statements can be corrected as
Glycerol is a polyhydroxy alcohol with trihydroxy propane structure. Lipids are composed of fatty acid chain linked by ester bond with polyhydroxy alcohol.
Glycerol is soluble in water, and is miscible in it.

23. (*b*) Both statement I and statement II are correct.
Both glycogen and starch are polysaccharides composed of glucose units that can be hydrolysed to release glucose for energy.

24. (*c*) Grinding the tissue in trichloroacetic acid helps to separate it into an acid-soluble pool and an acid insoluble fraction.

25. (*a*) Statement IV is incorrect. The incorrect statement can be corrected as
Cellulose is a polymeric polysaccharide consisting of only one type of monosaccharide, i.e. glucose.

26. (*c*) In the given case, sulphonamides act as competitive inhibitor due to its structural similarity to substrate (PABA) and carry out competitive inhibition. In this type of inhibition, V_{max} remains unchanged and K_m increases.

27. (*d*) The structures adopted by polypeptides can be divided into 4 levels of organisation, the primary, secondary, tertiary and quaternary structures.
The secondary structure pertains to the folding of parts of the polypeptide chains into regular structure, such as α-helices and β-pleated sheets.
β-pleated sheet involves two different regions of polypeptide chain lying side by side which are bound by hydrogen bonds.

28. (*c*) In peroxidase and catalase, which catalyse the breakdown of hydrogen peroxide to water and oxygen, haem is the prosthetic group and it is a part of the active site of the enzyme.

29. (*a*) In the given figure, *P* represents K_m, *Q* represents V_{max} and *R* represents $\frac{V_{max}}{2}$.

Enzyme activity is directly proportional to substrate concentration. With the increase in substrate concentration, the velocity of the enzymatic reaction rises at first. The reaction ultimately reaches a maximum velocity (V_{max}) which is not exceeded by any further rise in concentration of the substrate.

30. (*b*) An active site of an enzyme is a crevice or pocket into which the substrate fits. Through active site, an enzyme catalyse reactions at a high rate.

Ch-10 Cell Cycle and Cell Division

Topical Follow Thru

Test-1

1. (*c*) Interphase is the longest part of the cell cycle. In this phase the cell grow and duplicates its DNA. This phase include G_1, S, G_2 and M(Mitosis/meiosis).

2. (*a*) Incorrect match pair can be corrected as
The G_0-phase is a resting state where cells exit the cell cycle and do not prepare for DNA replication or cell division. It is not a phase between M and S instead, cells in G_0 are quiescent and can re-enter the cycle if needed, typically from the G_1-phase.

3. (*b*) The interphase is not termed as synthesis phase. S-phase or synthesis phase comes under interphase. This phase is termed as intermitosis or energy phase or preparatory phase.

4. (*b*) During the G_1-phase, the cell is metabolically active and grows by synthesising proteins and other macromolecules. However, DNA replication occurs in the S-phase, not the G_1-phase.

5. (*c*) The sequence of events including growth, DNA replication, and cell division.
The cell cycle encompasses the complete sequence of events a cell undergoes: growth (G_1-phase), DNA replication (S-phase), preparation for division (G_2-phase), and cell division (M phase).

6. (*c*) Both A and R are true, but R is not the correct explanation of A. It can be corrected as
During the G_1-phase, the amount of DNA or chromatin in the cell remains constant because DNA replication has not yet occurred. Cell size and the nucleus also grow during G_1. However, the increase in cell size and nuclear growth is not the reason for the constant DNA amount.

7. (*d*) The correct match is A-1, B-2, C-3, D-4.

- In G_1-phase, cell grows in size.
- In S-phase, DNA replication and chromosomes duplication occurs.
- In G_2-phase, cytoplasmic growth occurs i.e. proteins are synthesised in preparation for mitosis.
- In metaphase of M-phase, chromosomes are moved to spindle equator and get aligned along metaphase plate through spindle fibres.

8. (*d*) The G_0-phase is often referred to as the quiescent phase. The cell is metabolically active, but it is no longer proliferating. Cells in the G_0-phase exit the cell cycle and re-enter after receiving signals.

9. (*a*) Chromosomes are in their most extended form during the G_1-phase, allowing for active transcription and cell growth. In the S-phase, DNA replication occurs. The G_2-phase is preparatory for mitosis. During the M-phase, chromosomes are highly condensed to facilitate their segregation into daughter cells.

10. (*c*) In the given diagram *C* represents the G_2-phase which is the preparatory phase for mitosis or M-phase.
During the M-phase spindle fibres are formed that help separate and distribute the chromatids of chromosomes between 2 daughter cells. These spindle fibres are formed by the protein tubulin which is formed in the last phase of interphase which is G_2.

11. (*b*) A gamete with 10 chromosomes comes from a diploid organism, meaning the diploid number is 20. In the G_2-phase, the cell has already duplicated its DNA during the S-phase. Therefore, each chromosome now consists of two sister chromatids, but the chromosome count remains 20, as chromatids are counted as part of the same chromosome.

12. (*b*) During the G_2-phase, after DNA replication in the S-phase, each chromosome consists of two sister chromatids. This doubles the amount of DNA compared to a diploid cell in the G_1-phase, making it equivalent to the DNA content of a tetraploid cell.

13. (*d*) Mitosis is a process where a single cell divides to produce two genetically identical daughter cells, maintaining the same chromosome number as the parent cell. It involves a single nuclear division, not two, and does not include the pairing of homologous chromosomes, which occurs in meiosis.

14. (*a*) During prophase, chromosomes condense and become visible under a microscope, and the mitotic spindle begins to form, which includes the appearance of astral rays emanating from the centrosomes.

15. (*b*) The G_2-phase, occurring after DNA replication, is also a pre-mitotic phase where the cell prepares for mitosis. During G_2, the cell is metabolically active, and the amount of DNA is doubled compared to the G_1-phase, but not the number.

16. (*c*) Both A and R are true, but R is not the correct explanation of A. Mitosis ensures genetic similarity by producing identical daughter cells while keeping the chromosome number constant is crucial for species stability.

17. (*a*) During mitosis, DNA replication occurs once during the S-phase, followed by one round of nuclear division, resulting in two daughter cells with the same amount of DNA as the parent cell.

18. (*a*) Statement I is incorrect, but statement II is correct. Statement I can be corrected as
Golgi complex and endoplasmic reticulum become inconspicuous, i.e. it is not clearly visible. This is because these organelles undergo significant structural changes as the cell prepares for cell division.

19. (*d*) Spindle fibres are characteristic of eukaryotic cells. Spindle fibres are absent in prokaryotes.
The bacterial chromosome is attached to the plasma membrane during DNA synthesis and cell division. Thus, the plasma membrane acts as a substitute for the absence of spindle fibres in prokaryotes.

20. (*a*) If a cell has twice as much DNA as a normal functional cell it means that cell is preparing to divide. This is because when a cell divides, its DNA content doubles. This process is called DNA replication, which occurs in the S-phase of mitosis.

21. (*a*) This phase is the transition to metaphase from prophase
The diagram represents the metaphase of mitosis, where fibres attach to the kinetochores of chromosomes.
This stage follows prophase and precedes anaphase. Daughter chromosomes move to opposite poles during anaphase. Crossing over occurs in meiosis, not mitosis. Centrioles moving to opposite poles occur in prophase.

22. (*b*) Incorrect statement can be corrected as
The formation of a cell plate in plant cells starts in the center of the cell and graves outward to meet the existing lateral walls. The cell plate is a simple precursor that initiates the formation of a new cell wall.

23. (*c*) Anaphase - Separation of homologous chromosomes is incorrect match-pair which can be corrected as
In mitosis, anaphase involves the separation of sister chromatids, not homologous chromosomes, which separate during anaphase-I of meiosis.

24. (*a*) The complete disintegration of the nuclear envelope marks the start of the second phase of mitosis, hence the chromosomes are spread through the cytoplasm of the cell.

25. (*b*) If a gamete of flowering plants contains 20 chromosomes, the somatic cells will have 40 chromosomes (diploid).
During anaphase of mitosis, each chromosome splits into two sister chromatids, doubling the number of chromatids momentarily. Hence, there will be 80 chromatids (or chromosomes) during anaphase of mitosis.

Test 2

1. (*b*) Synapsis and formation of tetrads. During prophase-I of meiosis, homologous chromosomes pair up through synapsis and form tetrads, a unique feature not observed in mitosis.

2. (*a*) Anaphase-II begins with the simultaneous splitting of the centromere of each chromosome allowing them to move toward opposite poles of the cell by shortening of microtubules attached to kinetochores.

3. (*c*) Diakinesis is the final stage of meiotic prophase-I.
In diplotene stage the two homologous chromosomes do not separate completely, but remain attached together at one or more points as indicated by 'X' arrangement known as chiasmata. The displacement of chiasmata is termed as terminalisation of chiasmata, which is completed in diakinesis phase.

4. (*d*) A is true, but R is false. R can be corrected as
Nuclear division restore the original diploid chromosomal number in mitosis not in meiosis.
An individual organism consists of 46 chromosome. The number of chromosome is restored in the zygote because the zygote receive half of the chromosomes that is 23 chromosomes from each of the parents (both mother and father) and thus the number of chromosome remains constant as 46 in all organisms and does not increase from generation to generation.

5. (*c*) Incorrect statement can be corrected as
Meiosis involves DNA replication during the S-phase before meiosis-I begins. This replication ensures that each chromosome has two sister chromatids before being separated into different cells. Meiosis includes two successive cell division, producing four haploid cells and maintaining chromosome numbers across generations.

6. (*a*) Prophase-I, genetic variation. Crossing over occurs during prophase-I, where homologous chromosomes exchange genetic material, leading to genetic variation in the resulting gametes.

7. (*a*) The correct match is A-4, B-3, C-2, D-1.

- During zygotene phase, the homologous chromosomes start pairing together and this process of association is called synapsis. The complex formed by a pair of synapsed homologous chromosomes is called a bivalent or a tetrad.
- During pachytene stage, crossing over takes place between non-sister chromatids of the homologous chromosome.
- Chiasmata becomes visible during diplotene stage. Chiasmata is the point of contact between the two non-sister chromatids of homologous chromosome.
- Terminalisation of chiasmata gets completed during diakinesis phase where chromosomes gets freely distributed in the cytoplasm.

8. (*c*) Both statement I and statement II are incorrect. These can be corrected as
Meiosis occur in gonads and sporangia. It does not occur in bacteria or archaebacteria as their reproduction is via asexual processes.
The most common materials used for the study of meiosis are young anthers in floral buds and testis.

9. (*b*) Statements III, IV and V are correct. Incorrect statements are I and II. These can be corrected as
The repulsive force between the homologous chromosomes increases considerably at metaphase-I. Shorter chromosomes generally have fewer chiasmata than longer ones.

10. (*d*) A - Sexual, B - Meiosis. Organisms that reproduce exclusively through sexual reproduction undergo meiosis at some stage of their life cycle. Meiosis is a type of cell division that reduces the chromosome number by half, producing gametes (sperm and egg cells) necessary for sexual reproduction, ensuring genetic diversity in the offspring.

11. (*b*) During meiosis-I, homologous chromosomes segregate.
Meiosis-II resemble mitosis in which sister chromatids segregate from each other.

12. (*c*) Crossing over occurs during prophase-I of meiosis, where homologous chromosomes exchange segments of genetic material. This process creates new combinations of genes, contributing to genetic diversity in offspring. It does not occur between non-homologous chromosomes or sister chromatids.

13. (*a*) If $2n = 46$, during anaphase-I of meiosis, homologous chromosomes are separated and pulled to opposite poles of the cell. Although they are being separated, each pole will still have 46 chromosomes because the chromosomes are still duplicated and consist of two sister chromatids.

14. (*c*) The diagram shows a phase of meiosis, specifically anaphase-I, as indicated by the separation of homologous chromosomes. In this phase, homologous chromosomes are pulled apart to opposite poles of the cell, which is a key event distinguishing it from anaphase-II, where sister chromatids separate.

15. (*c*) In anaphase-II of meiosis actual haploidy in terms of DNA comes in, because in this stage sister chromatids of chromosome move towards opposite pole along with centromere.

16. (*b*) Meiosis is a reductional division. The diploid parent gametes are reduced to the haploid offspring. It involves the exchange of genes between homologous chromosome. The homologous chromosomes pair by cross over by a process known as synapsis and exchange the chromosomal segment which causes genetic recombination.
These variations in the offspring make organism more adaptable to the environment and these have a definite role in evolution.
Therefore, genetic recombinations are possible from generation to generation.

17. (*b*) Crossing over is the exchange of genetic material between two non-sister chromatids of homologous chromosomes. It occurs during the pachytene stage of meiotic prophase and leads to recombination.

18. (*a*) The stage being represented is anaphase-II of meiosis-II. Centromeres split during this stage and the chromatids reach opposite poles.

19. (*a*) Statement I is incorrect, but statement II is correct. Statement I can be corrected as
Tetrads are most distinctly observed in the pachytene stage.

20. (*c*) The quantity of DNA remains the same after meiosis I, since there is no DNA replication event in between. DNA replicates only during S phase of cell cycle.

21. (*b*) Both A and R are true and R is the correct explanation of A.
Crossing over normally occurs between non-sister chromatids of homologous chromosomes. This results in variation. However, when crossing over occurs between sister chromatids, there is no genetic variability. This is because sister chromatids are formed by replication of the same chromosome and are usually identical.

22. (*c*) Recombinase enzyme catalyzes the genetic exchange between the homologous chromosomes. New allelic combinations are observed due to recombination observed during pachytene stage, catalysed by recombinase enzyme.

23. (*a*) Kinetochores are protein discs where spindle fibres attach. Hence, when the spindle contracts to pull apart the chromatids, they help in their segregation process.

Any abnormality in kinetochore will result in hamper of its segregation during anaphase.

24. (*b*) Statements II and III are incorrect and can be corrected as

- DNA replication is restricted to the S-phase of interphase.
- Chromosomes start condensing after telophase-I, in the beginning of prophase-II.

25. (*a*) Statements II and III are correct. Statements I and IV are incorrect and can be corrected as

- Bead-like structure (chromatids) are present on condensed chromosomes.
- Centromere divides during meiosis.

Chapter Break Thru

1. (*b*) During G_1-phase the cell is metabolically active and continuously grows, but does not replicate its DNA. The synthesis of DNA takes place in S-phase.
Nuclear division occurs during karyokinesis.
Re-organisation of all cell components takes place in M-phase.

2. (*d*) Crossing over occurs at pachytene stage of prophase-I of meiosis. Rest other are significance of mitosis.

3. (*a*) During the S-phase, DNA replication begins in the nucleus, and the centriole duplicates in the cytoplasm.

4. (*a*) Some dividing cells exit the cell cycle and enter vegetative inactive stage, called quiescent stage (G_0). This process occurs at the end of M-phase and beginning of G_1-phase. Cells enter G_0 for varying amounts of time, and some cells enter the G_0-phase and stay there forever. This is because once they reach maturity, like nerve and heart cells they do not divide again, so they stay in the G_0-phase.

5. (*a*) During metaphase, chromosomes align at the cell's equatorial plate, ensuring each daughter cell will receive an identical set of chromosomes when the chromatids separate in the subsequent anaphase.

6. (*a*) Tetrads are never formed during mitosis. Therefore, the answer is 0. Tetrads are formed during zygotene stage of prophase-I of meiosis.

7. (*c*) Each mitotic division doubles the number of cells. To find the number of divisions needed to reach 256 cells, calculate (2^n = 256). Solving for n, we get $n = 8$ (number of divisions). Therefore, 8 mitotic divisions are required to produce 256 cells.

8. (*c*) Mitotic spindle are structure formed from microtubules in cytoplasm during cell division. Microtubules are made up of tubulin proteins. Spindle fibres move chromatids or chromosomes diametrically apart and gather then in two clusters at opposite ends (poles) of the cell.

9. (*a*) At the equatorial plate during metaphase-I of meiosis, there are bivalents. This stage is characterised by the alignment of homologous chromosome pairs (bivalents) at the cell's equatorial plane. Each bivalent consists of two homologous chromosomes, each made up of two sister chromatids. This arrangement ensures that homologous chromosomes are separated into different cells during the subsequent anaphase-I.

10. (*a*) The onion root tip is an ideal specimen for studying mitosis due to its rapid cell division and the clear visibility of different mitotic stages. The cells in this region frequently undergo mitosis, making it easier to observe and identify the various phases of cell division under a microscope.

11. (*a*) $2n \rightarrow 2n \rightarrow 2n \rightarrow 4n$.

In G_1, the number of DNA is $2n$. After DNA replication in the S phase, the cell has remain same i.e. $2n$ DNA in G_2 because newly formed DNA remain attached to the parental DNA at centromere. This $2n$ is maintained through metaphase. During anaphase, chromatids separate, briefly resulting in 4n until the cell divides, returning to 2n in each daughter cell.

12. (*d*) The genetic constitution of gametes is ultimately determined during anaphase-II of meiosis. In this stage, sister chromatids are separated and distributed to different gametes, ensuring each gamete recieves a distinct set of genetic information.

13. (*c*) During the leptotene stage of meiosis, the telomeres of all the chromosome gather close to the nuclear membrane and forms the shape of a bouquet.

14. (*d*) DNA replication is not depicted in the given diagram. The image shows homologous chromosomes with chiasmata indicating crossing over, where non-sister chromatids exchange genetic material. Terminalisation, the process where chiasmata move towards chromosome ends, is also shown. The absence of the DNA replication process, which occurs during the S-phase before meiosis, is the key missing element.

15. (*a*) A bivalent during meiosis-I consists of four chromatids and two centromeres. Each bivalent is formed by a pair of homologous chromosomes, each composed of two sister chromatids, held together by their centromeres.

16. (*b*) The enzyme recombinase is required at pachytene stage of meiosis, which aids in the recombination of genes between homologous chromosomes.

17. (*d*) The recombination nodule is the site on non-sister chromatids of homologous chromosomes where crossing over occurs. These nodules facilitate the exchange of genetic material during meiosis. A tetrad is the paired homologous chromosomes, a synapse is the pairing process, and chiasmata are the visible points where crossing over has occurred.

18. (*c*) This enzyme plays a crucial role in facilitating genetic recombination, increasing genetic diversity. It does not participate in the initial pairing of homologous chromosomes, separation of sister chromatids, or attachment of spindle fibers.

19. (*d*) The diagram depicts the formation of recombinant chromatids. Homologous chromosomes with segments exchanged between non-sister chromatids, indicating that crossing over has occurred, leading to the production of recombinant chromatids. This genetic recombination increases genetic variability in gametes.

20. (*c*) Interkinesis is a stage between meiosis-I and meiosis-II. During this phase, the cell undergoes a brief period of rest without DNA replication. It is distinct from interphase and does not occur between mitotic divisions.

21. (*b*) Nucleolus and nuclear membrane. During mitosis and meiosis, the nucleolus and nuclear membrane disassemble to facilitate chromosome segregation. The nuclear membrane dissolves, allowing spindle fibers to interact with chromosomes, while the nucleolus disassembles, ceasing ribosome production temporarily.

22. (*b*) Both A and R are true and R is the correct explanation of A.

The interphase is called the resting phase. It is the time during which the cell is preparing for division by undergoing both cell growth and DNA replication in an orderly manner.
However, there is no apparent activity related to division in this phase.

23. (*c*) The correct match is A-4, B-1, C-2, D-3.

- The S-phase stands for the synthesis phase which marks the replication phase of the cell cycle.
- During G_2-phase (Gap-2) of the cell cycle proteins are synthesised to prepare the cell for mitosis or meiosis.
- The G_0-stage is also referred to as resting or quiescent phase in the cell cycle. In this stage 'cells' are not actively dividing, which is why it is an inactive phase of the cell cycle.
- The G_1-phase (Gap-1) of the cell cycle is the metabolically active phase. During this phase, the cell prepares for DNA replication and subsequent division.

24. (*b*) During metaphase, chromosomes align at the cell's equatorial plate, making them highly condensed and visible. This alignment and condensation make it the easiest stage to count and study the chromosomes accurately under a microscope.

25. (*d*) Syncytium refers to a single cell containing multiple nuclei, formed when cells fail to undergo cytokinesis after karyokinesis. Cytokinesis is crucial for the separation of cytoplasm and the formation of individual daughter cells, distinct from syncytia formation.

26. (*b*) Both statement I and statement II are correct.

- Growth in multicellular animals occurs due to mitosis as the fertilised egg develops into an embryo, which finally forms an adult by repeated mitotic division.
- Mitosis also contributes in cell repairing as it replace old dead and worn out cells by the new cells.

27. (*c*) I, II and III are correct for meiosis result.

Meiosis results in the production of gametes, reduction in the number of chromosomes, and introduction of genetic variation. This process ensures genetic diversity and the formation of haploid cells necessary for sexual reproduction. Regeneration and vegetative reproduction are not outcomes of meiosis.

28. (*b*) After meiosis-I, the daughter cells are haploid and contain homologous chromosomes that have been separated. After meiosis-II, the daughter cells remain haploid, but they now contain sister chromatids that have been separated.

29. (*c*) During prophase-I, homologous chromosomes pair up in a process called synapsis, forming tetrads. Crossing over occurs between non-sister chromatids, leading to genetic recombination. This exchange of genetic material increases genetic diversity in the resulting gametes.

30. (*b*) Incorrect match pair can be corrected as

Sister chromatids are the chromatids of the same chromosomes that are separated by the centromere and contained same alleles at the same loci.

31. (*d*) Statement I is correct, but statement II is incorrect. Statement II can be corrected as

The cell remains metabolically active during interphase. Although interphase is the resting phase of the cell cycle, cells remain active and are preparing for division.

32. (*b*) One yeast cell divides into two daughter cells. Hence, $2^N = 64$, $N = 2^a \Rightarrow N = 6$

One Yeast cell has to endergo 6 divisions to form 64 yeast cells.

One division takes 90 minutes, thus 6 divisions take 90 x 6 = 540 minutes or 9 hrs.

33. (*a*) Statements II and IV are correct. Statements I and III are incorrect and can be corrected as

Cells in G_0 do not remain arrested permanently. If the damage in the cell is rectified it can re-enter cell cycle. If any cell damage is beyond repair, the cells can be programmed to destroy themselves.

All somatic cells or body cells do not undergo equational divisions. For example there are certain body cells like the nerve cells that do not divide at all.

34. (*c*) The stage being represented is the transition stage between prophase and metaphase.

- Metaphase is the best studied phase.
- Chromosomes are arranged along the equatorial plate during metaphase.
- Spindle fibres contract to pull the sister chromatids during anaphase.

35. (*a*) A is false, but R is true. A can be corrected as

Chromatid separation occurs in anaphase-II of meiosis-II and during anaphase of mitosis. During anaphase-I, the homologous chromosomes separate and are pulled to the opposite poles.

36. (*a*) The correct match is A-3, B-4, C-1, D-2.

- In late prophase stage of mitosis, nuclear membrane disintegrates completely. Nucleolus, Golgi, ER disappears.
- Telophase is the final stage of mitosis. Condensed and shortened chromosomes are decondensed back into loose entangled structures.
- During early prophase, chromosomes start to condense and shorten.
- During anaphase, the centromere of the chromosomes splits to separate the chromatids.

37. (*a*) Statement I is incorrect, but statement II is correct. Statement I can be corrected as

Karyokinesis and cytokinesis are independent events but karyokinesis precedes cytokinesis.

38. (*b*) Chiasma represents the points where genetic material is exchanged through the process of recombination. If there is no chiasma formation, there would be no exchange of genetic material between the homologous chromosomes, hence lesser recombination events would take place. This would lead to lesser variations in population.

Variations lead to evolution, and in the absence of the same, evolution would slow down.

39. (*d*) Synaptonemal complex is a protein scaffold that links the homologous chromosomes during synapsis, observed in zygotene of meiosis-I.

Mutation in synaptonemal complex prevents crossing over during prophase-I of meiosis-I.

40. (*c*) The correct match is A-3, B-1, C-4, D-2.

- Zygotene is a short lived stage of prophase-I and is characterised by the pairing of homologous chromosomes.
- Pachytene is the stage where crossing over takes place and genetic material is exchanged by the activity of recombinase enzyme.
- Diplotene stage can lasts for years in the oocytes of some vertebrates. It is characterized by dissolution of the synaptonemal complex.
- Diakinesis is the last stage of prophase-I of meiosis-I. It is the transition phase to metaphase.

41. (*d*) The stage being represented is metaphase-I of meiosis-I. Centromere splitting does not occur in the metaphase-I stage. Rather centromere splits in anaphase-II of meiosis-II and in mitotic anaphase.

42. (*c*) Both A and R are true, but R is not the correct explanation of A. Cell growth can disturb the nucleocytoplasmic ratio because when a cell grows in size, the cytoplasm volume increases however the size of the nucleus remains the same.

43. (*b*) Replication of DNA during the S-phase of cell cycle makes a cell irreversibly commit to division and completion of cell cycle.

44. (*c*) The homologous chromosomes in a tetrad are separated during anaphase-I of meiosis-I. If anaphase-I is deleted, the segregation would not occur, which could result in gain or loss of chromosomes.

45. (*b*) Both statement I and statement II are correct.

The leptonema stage is characterised by the bouquet formation. In this stage, the ends or the telomeres of all the chromosomes are arranged close to the nuclear envelope, thereby taking the shape of a bouquet.

46. (*d*) A tetrad consisting of four daughter cells are formed at the end of telophase-II of meiosis-II. Telophase of mitosis and meiosis-I results in formation of two daughter cells followed by cytokinesis. Interkinesis is the gap between meiosis-I and meiosis-II.

47. (*c*) Interkinesis is the stage between meiosis-I and meiosis-II. Meiosis-I produces two cells or a dyad towards its end, however meiosis-II produces a tetrad of cells.

48. (*a*) Exchange of genetic material occurs during crossing over of meiosis-I. During this process genes are exchanged between non-sister chromatids of homologous chromosomes.

49. (*b*) M-phase is the shortest phase of the cell cycle. G_2-phase takes longer than M-phase and in turn completes faster than S-phase. G_1-phase is the longest phase.

50. (*c*) A denotes G_0-phase, when a cell exits cell cycle. All the given options state a possible reason for the cell to exit cell cycle except for option (C). Presence of growth factors, do not prevent the cell from dividing, rather they act as signals that allow the cells to continue the cell cycle.

Ch-11 Photosynthesis in Higher Plants

Topical Follow Thru

Test-1

1. (*d*) Julius von Sachs discovered that photosynthesis produces glucose, demonstrating the role of chlorophyll in this process. Sachs' work laid the foundation for understanding the biochemical process of photosynthesis and glucose formation.

   Other options can be explained as

   Jan Ingenhousz showed that the sunlight is essential for the photosynthesis. TW Engelmann contributed in describing the first action spectrum of photosynthesis. Joseph Priestley explained the essentiality of air in the growth of green plants.

2. (*d*) Photosynthesis is restricted to only plants and some lower organisms. Rest statements are incorrect and can be corrected as

   The process of photosynthesis leads to plant weight gain. Raw materials used in photosynthesis are carbon dioxide and water. Products of photosynthesis are oxygen and organic substances.

3. (*c*) Statements II and III are incorrect. These can be corrected as
   Jan Ingenhousz placed his experimental setup once in the sunlight and once in the dark. He used aquatic plants for his experiment.

4. (*c*) Plants produce oxygen during photosynthesis.

   The experiment performed by Joseph Priestley shows that a candle remains lit and a mouse stays alive in the presence of a plant, indicating that the plant releases oxygen, which is necessary for both combustion and respiration. Without the plant, the candle is extinguished and the mouse dies due to the lack of oxygen.

5. (*d*) In the experiment by Engelmann, green alga *Cladophora* was grown in a suspension of aerobic bacteria. Bacteria would grow in the blue and red region, indicating the sites of oxygen evolution. If anaerobes were used, they would not grow at the oxygen evolution sites. Hence, the purpose of the experiment to detect the action spectrum would not be served.

6. (*c*) Statements I, III, IV and V are correct. Statement II is incorrect and can be corrected as
   In green plants, H_2O is the hydrogen donor and is oxidised to O_2.

7. (*d*) Statement I is correct, but statement II is incorrect. Incorrect statement can be corrected as
   Jan Ingenhousz found that aquatic plants released bubbles of oxygen only in the presence of sunlight.

8. (*c*) *X* (Carotenoids) are yellow, brown and orange pigments which prevent photo-oxidation of chlorophyll-*a* pigments.
   Y (Chlorophyll-*a*) is a bright or blue-green pigment. It is the main photosynthetic pigment responsible for trapping light. It is also called as reaction centre.

9. (*d*) A is true, but R is false. R can be corrected as

   The antenna molecules are located on outer side of the photosynthetic unit. They get excited and transfer energy to reaction center.

10. (*b*) At low light intensity, Chloroplasts position their flat surfaces parallel to the walls of mesophyll cells to maximise light absorption. At high light intensity, chloroplasts align their flat surfaces perpendicular to the walls to minimise exposure and prevent damage from excessive light. At moderate light intensity, they distribute randomly for optimal light capture. In the dark, chloroplasts are dispersed throughout the cytoplasm.

11. (*a*) Chlorophyll-*a* is the most abundant plant pigment globally, playing a crucial role in photosynthesis by capturing light energy and converting it into chemical energy. It is present in all the photosynthetic organisms, including plants, algae and cyanobacteria, making it the primary pigment essential for the process of photosynthesis.

12. (*a*) Paper chromatography is a simple and effective technique for separating photosynthetic pigments based on their solubility and affinity to the paper. This method allows for the clear separation and identification of different pigments, such as chlorophylls and carotenoids, by their distinct travel distances on the chromatography paper.

13. (*d*) The incorrect match pair can be corrected as
    Xanthophylls are pigments, which are commonly yellow in colour. They are a class of carotenoids which are pigments found in plants. They are typically yellow in color and play crucial role by protecting plant tissue from excessive light.

14. (*b*) The action spectrum indicates the overall photosynthesis rate at each light wavelength. The rate of photosynthesis can be studied by measuring the amount of oxygen evolved or the amount of CO_2 absorbed.

15. (*b*) The rate of photosynthesis in an action spectrum is typically measured by the amount of oxygen released. This method provides a direct indication of the photosynthetic activity because oxygen is a byproduct of the light-dependent reactions of photosynthesis.

By measuring the released O_2, scientists can determine the efficiency of photosynthesis at different wavelengths of light.

Test 2

1. (*a*) In chemiosmosis, there is a breakdown of proton gradient, not electron gradient. Proton gradient is important because it is the breakdown of this gradient that leads to the synthesis of ATP. The gradient is broken down due to the movement of protons across the membrane to the stroma through the transmembrane channel of the CF_0 of the ATP synthase. This provides enough energy to cause a conformational change in the CF_1 particle of the ATP synthase, which makes the enzyme synthesise several molecules of ATP. The reduction of $NADP^+$ to $NADPH + H^+$ involves NADP reductase enzyme present on the stroma side of membrane. It also requires electrons that come from the electron acceptor of PS-I along with protons.

2. (*d*) The incorrect match pair can be corrected as

Photosystem – Thylakoid membrane of chloroplast.

Photosystem-I (PS-I) is located on the outer surface and photosystem-II (PS-II) is located on the inner surface of thylakoid membrane.

3. (*b*) Both statement I and statement II are correct.

Photolytic activity refers to the splitting of water molecules into oxygen, protons and electrons, which occurs at the Oxygen-Evolving Complex (OEC) of Photosystem-II (PS-II). Electrons released during this process are passed through a series of electron carriers linked to the reaction center of PS-II.

The photochemical phase (light reaction) is a light-dependent process and occurs in the thylakoids of the grana region. This is located in the grana thylakoid of chloroplast and is responsible for trapping the light energy and also for the synthesis of ATP and NADPH.

4. (*d*) In non-cyclic photophosphorylation, the electrons move through the thylakoid membrane from PS-II to PS-I.

$NADP^+$ is then reduced to NADPH in the stroma of the chloroplast, where it is used in the Calvin cycle for carbon fixation.

The thylakoid lumen is the site of proton accumulation and the cytoplasm is not involved in this process.

5. (*b*) The correct match is A-2, B-1, C-4, D-3.

Photosystem-II is involved in photolysis of water.

Plastocyanin is a mobile copper containing electron carrier.

Pheophytin resembles chlorophyll in its structure, but lacks Mg.

Because of the peculiar shape, non-cyclic photophosphorylation (light reaction) and synthesis of assimilatory power (i.e. ATP and NADPH) it is called Z-scheme.

6. (*b*) The movement of electrons from PS-II to $NADP^+$ is *via* PS-I. It flows from a higher (+) to a lower (–) redox potential. Electrons from PS-II are transported uphill to the electron acceptor. Again they are transported downhill through electron carriers. Again from PS-I they are moved uphill to an electron acceptor. Later, these electrons are moved downhill to $NADP^+$. This process is represented by the Z-scheme, which illustrates the energy changes of electrons as they pass through the photosystems and the electron transport chain.

7. (*c*) Statements I and V are correct. The incorrect statements can be corrected as

C_3 cycle occurs in mesophyll cells and bundle sheath cells in case of C_3 and C_4 plants, respectively.

The first stable product of C_3 cycle is 3-phosphoglycerate.

The CO_2 acceptor is a 5-carbon molecule, ribulose-1, 5-bisphosphate.

8. (*c*) The incorrect statement can be corrected as

The enzyme RuBisCO, responsible for the primary fixation of CO_2 in the C_3 pathway, actually has a higher affinity for CO_2 than O_2. RuBisCO is the most abundant enzyme in the world and can interact with both CO_2 and O_2, catalysing the carboxylation and oxygenation reactions, respectively.

9. (*a*) Statement I is incorrect, but statement II is correct. statement I can be corrected as

$NADP^+$ is the final e^- acceptor of PS-I. During photosynthesis, PS-I capture photons and transfers electron to proteins and cofactors eventually reducing $NADP^+$ to NADPH. Thus $NADP^+$ is last electron acceptor of photophosphorylation.

10. (*c*) Statement III is correct about cyclic phosphorylation. In cyclic flow of electrons, PS-II is absent and water splitting or photolysis does not occur. Hence, there is no evolution of oxygen. Statements I, II and IV can be corrected as

Cyclic flow of electrons can occur only when light of wavelengths beyond 680 nm are available for excitation.

Only ATP is produced in the cyclic phosphorylation. This is because NADP reductase enzyme is absent in the stroma lamellae.

Cyclic phosphorylation is active only in stromal lamellae.

11. (*c*) Both A and R are true, but R is not the correct explanation of A.

Plastoquinone reduction maintains the concentration gradient since it removes a proton from the stroma while transporting an electron. When this molecule passes on its electron to the electron carrier on the inner side of the membrane, the proton is released into the inner side or the lumen side of the membrane. This creates a higher concentration of protons in the lumen than the stroma.

12. (*a*) The correct order is E-D-C-A-B.

Photolysis of water takes place on the inner side of the membrane, hence the protons that are produced by the splitting of water accumulate within the lumen of the thylakoids.

Electrons are transferred from PS-II to PS-I through number of carriers. One such carrier is plastoquinone which accepts hydrogen ions while transporting electron. When this molecule passes on its electron to the electron carrier on the inner side of the membrane, the proton is released into the inner side or the lumen side of the membrane.

The final acceptor is $NADP^+$ which is reduced by NADP reductase enzyme into NADPH + H^+.

This proton gradient is broken as the protons are transported by facilitated diffusion through the CF_0 channel of ATP synthase enzyme.

The breakdown of the gradient provides enough energy to cause a conformational change in the CF_1 particle of the ATP synthase, which makes the enzyme synthesise several molecules of energy packed ATP.

13. (*b*) In one turn of the cycle, 3 ATP molecules are consumed. For 1 glucose molecule, 6 turns of the cycle is needed. Hence for 6 glucose molecules, $6 \times 6 = 36$ turns of the cycle are needed. In one turn, 3 ATP is needed. So, for 36 turns,
$36 \times 3 = 108$ ATP molecules are needed.

14. (*c*) In C_3 pathway, 3-PGA to G3P conversion requires ATP hydrolysis. This is used in phosphorylating 3-PGA to form G3P. In the process, NADPH acts as the reducing agent and reduces 3-PGA, and in turn gets oxidised to $NADP^+$.

15. (*d*) The correct match is A-2, B-3, C-1, D-4.

- Carboxylation is the first step in C_3 pathway, where CO_2 is fixed to RuBP to form 3-PGA which is a three carbon compound.
- Sucrose synthesis occurs using triose phosphate as the substrate. Out of 12 molecules of glyceraldehyde-3-phosphate, two are used up in synthesis of sucrose, while the remaining 10 are used in regeneration of RuBP.
- In the reduction step, 3-PGA is reduced to form G3P. In this process, NADPH is oxidised to $NADP^+ + H^+$.
- Regeneration is the formation of ribulose-1, 5-bisphosphate, where one ATP molecule is hydrolysed.

Test 3

1. (*b*) Photorespiration involves the synthesis of two different compounds. During this process, ribulose-1,5-bisphosphate (RuBP) reacts with oxygen instead of carbon dioxide, leading to the formation of a two-carbon molecule called phosphoglycolate and a three-carbon molecule called 3-phosphoglycerate (3-PGA). Phosphoglycolate is then converted into glycolate, which is further processed in peroxisomes and mitochondria.

2. (*d*) The incorrect statement can be corrected as: The primary acceptor of CO_2 in C_4 pathway is Phosphoenol Pyruvate (PEP), a 3-carbon compound. It is fixed into oxaloacetic acid, which is a 4 carbon compound.

3. (*b*) The correct match is A-2, B-3, C-4, D-1.

- First product of CO_2 fixation in sugarcane (a C_4 plant) is a C_4 dicarboxylic acid known as Oxaloacetic Acid (OAA).
- In Kranz anatomy, the vascular bundles are surrounded by bundle sheath of large sized chlorenchymatous cells arranged like a wreath.
- Mesophyll cells are reduced in C_4 plants.
- Most of the highly productive crop plants belong to C_4 group.

4. (*b*) Both statement I and statement II are correct.

In C_4 cycle, bundle sheath cells contain RuBisCO, but not PEPCase, which is found in mesophyll cells. C_4 photosynthesis reduces photorespiration, a problem associated with RuBisCO in C_3 plants, enhancing photosynthetic efficiency.

5. (*d*) Photorespiration is considered a wasteful process because it does not produce ATP, NADPH or sugar, all of which are crucial for the plant's energy and growth. Instead, it consumes energy and releases fixed carbon dioxide without synthesising any useful products. However, the synthesis of oxygen is not relevant to why photorespiration is wasteful. Rather, oxygen is consumed during the C_2-pathway.

6. (*b*) Both A and R are true and R is the correct explanation of A.

In C_3 plants, photorespiration uses oxygen and releases carbon dioxide under light, which reduces their efficiency in comparison to C_4 plants. C_4 plants have greater productivity than C_3 plants because they have a mechanism to minimise photorespiration.

7. (*c*) In cold and foggy areas, the limiting factors for photosynthesis would be both light and temperature. Fog reduces the amount of sunlight reaching the plants limiting light availability, while low temperatures slow down the enzymatic reactions involved in photosynthesis.

8. (*b*) At higher light intensities, the rate of photosynthesis decreases primarily because of other factors becoming limiting, photo-oxidation of chlorophyll and saturation of the photosystem. Deactivation of antenna molecules and the destruction of carotenoids are not significant factors in this context.

9. (*b*) In the given graph, 'C' represents the plateau phase where the rate of photosynthesis no longer increases despite further increase in light intensity. This indicates that the photosynthetic machinery is fully saturated and working at maximum capacity.

10. (*c*) Plasmodesmata are the cytoplasmic connections that can be found between the bundle sheath and mesophyll cells. In its absence, sugar biosynthesis is affected since transport of C_4 acid to the bundle sheath would stop. It would also prevent regeneration of PEP, since this requires transport of C_3 acid back to the mesophyll cells. Oxaloacetic Acid or OAA formation occurs in mesophyll cells and require PEPcase enzyme and is not affected by plasmodesmata.

11. (*d*) Statement III is correct. Statements I, II and IV are incorrect and can be corrected as

    PEPCase is operational in mesophyll cells.

    Phosphoglycolate is not formed in the mesophyll cells of C_4 plants. Phosphoglycolate is a product formed in the process of plants undergoing photorespiration and thus, it is avoided due to the existence of Kranz anatomy in C_4 plants.

    Atmospheric CO_2 is fixed in mesophyll cells of C_4 plants. It is fixed as oxaloacetic acid by the PEPcase enzyme.

12. (*d*) Water stress in a plant can reduce the rate of photosynthesis directly or indirectly. It can result in guard cells to lose water and turn flaccid. This would close the stomatal aperture and decrease CO_2 availability. It will also decrease the surface area of the leaves, meaning reduction in the surface area of the lamina (due to wilting of plants), which would allow less amount of sunlight being incident on them. Hence, lesser sunlight would be available to drive light reaction.

    However, water stress affects chlorophyll synthesis indirectly by inhibiting its formation. This, in turn, affects photosynthetic rate.

13. (*b*) Both A and R are true and R is the correct explanation of A. Decarboxylation of malic acid in the bundle sheath cells of C_4 plants, increases the CO_2 concentration. This inhibits the oxygenase activity of RuBisCO, so that they can fix carbon into sugar.

14. (*b*) 3-PGA is first stable product in C_3 pathway, whereas 2-phosphoglycolate is formed in photorespiration. Step which is common to both the processes is the regeneration of RuBP which acts as substrate for both the processes. CO_2 is evolved in photorespiration, while it is fixed into 3-PGA in C_3 pathway. Reduction of 3-PGA into triose phosphate occurs in C_3 pathway. Synthesis of glycine and serine occurs in photorespiration.

15. (*b*) Both statement I and statement II are correct. Very high CO_2 levels can be toxic to the plants and hence, stomata closes. Due to closure of the stomata, water vapour also cannot escape which further lowers the transpiration rate.

Chapter Break Thru

1. (*c*) Accessory pigments, such as carotenoids and xanthophylls, absorb light and protect chlorophyll-*a* from photo-oxidation. Chlorophyll-*a* is the primary pigment involved in photosynthesis and its protection from oxidative damage ensures efficient light energy utilisation.

2. (*b*) The action spectrum indicates the evolution of oxygen gas. This experiment was conducted by Engelmann to develop the action spectrum of photosynthesis. The action spectrum coincides with the absorption spectrum of chlorophyll-*a* and *b*.

3. (*b*) The incorrect statement can be corrected as

    Chlorophyll-*b* is not present in all oxygenic photoautotrophs and occurs in green plants, green algae and Euglenophyceae.

    Chlorophyll-*b* is an accessory pigment that transfers light energy to chlorophyll-*a* and shows maximum absorption in the blue-red region.

4. (*b*) The incorrect statement about the absorption spectrum can be corrected as

    The height of the curve gives the relative absorbance at that wavelength.

    The absorption spectrum is a graph that shows the wavelengths of light absorbed by a substance, not the amount of product or response. The other statements correctly describe aspects of the absorption spectrum.

5. (*a*) PS-I is located in the outer thylakoid membrane of grana

(non-appressed membrane) and stroma lamellae of chloroplast. PS-II is located in the inner thylakoid membrane (appressed membrane) of the grana of chloroplast.

6. (*a*) Ferredoxin is a soluble protein which acts as an electron carrier and forms a constituent of PS-I. It passes electrons to NADP reductase complex which helps in reducing $NADP^+$ to NADPH.

7. (*c*) During cyclic photophosphorylation in photosynthesis, electrons from photosystem-I are excited by light energy and passed through an electron transport chain, generating a proton gradient across the thylakoid membrane. This gradient drives ATP synthase to produce ATP from ADP and inorganic phosphate. NADPH is not synthesised in cyclic photophosphorylation, as it occurs in stroma lamellae which lacks both PS-II and NADP reductase enzyme.

8. (*c*) The incorrect match pair can be corrected as

Plastocyanin-Mobile electron carrier

Plastocyanin is not a membrane-bound electron carrier; it is a mobile electron carrier that shuttles electrons between the cytochrome-b_6f complex and photosystem-I in the thylakoid lumen.

9. (*a*) Cytochrome-b_6f is functional in both cyclic and non-cyclic phosphorylation. In cyclic phosphorylation, electrons are cycled back to photosystem-I *via* cytochrome-b_6f, contributing to the proton gradient used for ATP synthesis. In non-cyclic phosphorylation, cytochrome-b_6f also transfers electrons from photosystem-II to photosystem-I. NADP reductase, plastoquinone and ferredoxin are only involved in non-cyclic phosphorylation (involving both PS-I and PS-II).

10. (*d*) In light reaction, plastoquinone facilitates the transfer of electrons from PS-II to cytochrome-b_6f complex. When sunlight falls on the reaction center (chlorophyll-*a*), it absorbs 680 nm wavelength of red light causing electrons to become excited and jump into an orbit farther from the atomic nucleus. These electrons are then picked by the electron acceptor which passes them to an electron transport system consisting of cytochrome.

11. (*b*) Melvin Calvin used radioactive ^{14}C in algal photosynthesis to trace the path of carbon during the dark reactions, leading to the discovery of the first CO_2 fixation product as PGA (Phosphoglyceric Acid). This discovery identified 3-Phosphoglyceric Acid (PGA) as the initial stable product in the Calvin cycle, which is the pathway for carbon fixation in C_3 plants.

12. (*b*) C_3-cycle proceeds in three stages, i.e. carboxylation, reduction (glycolytic reversal) and regeneration. Reduction is a series of reactions that leads to the formation of glucose (a carbohydrate).

The steps involve utilisation of 2 molecules of ATP for phosphorylation and two molecules of NADPH for reduction per CO_2 molecule fixed.

13. (*d*) Producing one molecule of triose phosphate (specifically, glyceraldehyde-3-phosphate, G3P) in the Calvin cycle involves 3 turns, and for every three CO_2 molecules fixed, a total of 9 ATP and 6 NADPH are used. Thus, 9 ATP are utilised in total for a single triose phosphate molecule.

14. (*b*) Statement in option (b) is correct. The incorrect statements can be corrected as

The diagram illustrates the Calvin cycle, which is the universal pathway for the production of glucose found in all photosynthetic plants, including C_3, C_4 and CAM plants. It was given by Melvin Calvin. This cycle involves the fixation of CO_2, reduction to form glyceraldehyde-3-phosphate and regeneration of ribulose-1, 5-bisphosphate, providing a common mechanism for carbon fixation in photosynthesis. Calvin cycle occurs in the mesophyll cells of C_3 plants and bundle sheath cells of C_4 plants.

15. (*b*) In the diagram, complex 'B' represents the cytochrome-b_6f complex, which pumps protons into the thylakoid lumen, creating a high electrochemical potential gradient necessary for ATP synthesis.

16. (*d*) Statement I is correct, but statement II is incorrect. The incorrect statement can be corrected as

The regeneration of a PEP molecule in the mesophyll cells requires the use of two ATP molecules to convert pyruvate back to PEP, ensuring the cycle can continue.

17. (*c*) C_4 plants differ from C_3 plants mainly due to the presence of RuBisCO in the bundle sheath cells of C_4 plants. In C_3 plants, RuBisCO is present in the mesophyll cells. In C_4 plants, mesophyll cells fix CO_2 to oxaloacetate and uses PEPCase enzyme instead of RuBisCO. Both C_3 and C_4 plants have the Calvin cycle and use RuBisCO enzyme for CO_2 fixation. The NADPH is used in the glucose formation for both C_3 and C_4 plants.

18. (*a*) The reaction responsible for the final fixation of CO_2 in C_4 plants is catalysed by RuBP carboxylase. In C_4 photosynthesis, after PEP carboxylase fixes CO_2 to form oxaloacetate (OAA) in mesophyll cells, OAA is converted to malate or aspartate and transported to bundle sheath cells. There, CO_2 is released and fixed by RuBP carboxylase (RuBisCO) in the Calvin cycle, generating 3-phosphoglycerate (PGA) and initiating carbohydrate synthesis. Thus, RuBP carboxylase facilitates the final fixation of CO_2 in C_4 plants.

19. (*c*) Plastocyanin, the electron carrier of light reaction is mobile. It transports electrons between cytochrome-b_6f complex and PS-I. It is a copper containing protein involved in electron transfer.

20. (*c*) The rate of photosynthesis is higher in intermittent light than in continuous light of the same duration. It does not increase the temperature which maintains conditions that favour biochemical reactions.

21. (*c*) A deficiency of water decreases the rate of photosynthesis due to the closure of stomata, wilting of leaves and the role of water as the source of electrons in photosynthetic reactions. The turgidity of leaves is maintained by sufficient water, not reduced by its deficiency.

22. (*a*) Incorrect match pair given in option (A) and can be corrected as

Cornelius van Niel stated that oxygen evolved by the green plants comes from H_2O. Other scientists, Ruben, Kamen et.al, proved that O_2 evolved during light reaction comes from water, not from CO_2.

23. (*a*) Statement I is incorrect, but statement II is correct. The incorrect statement can be corrected as

Joseph Priestley stated as a result of his experiment that the burning of candles or the respiration of mice produced foul air, which could be purified by plants.

24. (*d*) Statement I is correct, but statement II is incorrect. Incorrect statement can be corrected as

The electrons from PS-II are passed on by an electron acceptor which passes them to an ETS consisting of cytochromes.

25. (*d*) Statement in option (d) is incorrect and can be corrected as

In photosynthesis, ATP synthase facilitates the passive transport of protons from the thylakoid lumen to the stroma, not the other way around. This proton flow drives ATP synthesis by providing the necessary energy through a process called photophosphorylation, with the catalytic part protruding towards the stroma.

26. (*c*) Both A and R are true, but R is not the correct explanation of A.

According to the chemiosmotic hypothesis, protons indeed decrease in the stroma due to their accumulation in the thylakoid lumen, which creates a proton gradient. However, the decrease in stroma protons is directly due to their transport into the lumen, not just their accumulation in lumen.

27. (*d*) The correct match is A-2, B-3, C-4, D-1.

- Chlorophyll-*a* is involved in photo-conversion or the primary reaction of photosynthesis.
- In the C_3 pathway, the first product of CO_2 fixation is a C_3 acid, i.e. PGA.
- In the C_4 pathway, the first stable product is OAA.
- Mesophyll cells lack the RuBisCO enzyme in C_4 plants.

28. (*b*) Both A and R are true and R is the correct explanation of A.

A large production of CO_2 assimilated by photosynthesis is lost through photorespiration. Under certain circumstances, as much as 50% of the photosynthetic potential is lost in photorespiratory metabolism.

Thus, photorespiration may eventually reduce dry matter production and yield of the plant.

29. (*b*) In C_4 plants, the mesophyll cells fix CO_2 to produce oxaloacetic acid and subsequently malic acid or aspartic acid. These compounds are then transported to bundle-sheath cells for further processing. This initial fixation step helps to efficiently concentrate CO_2 around RuBisCO, minimising photorespiration. Phosphoglyceric acid and glucose are formed in mesophyll cells in C_3 plants.

30. (*c*) The incorrect statement can be corrected as

In C_4 plants, the initial fixation of CO_2 occurs in mesophyll cells. The primary acceptor of CO_2 is Phosphoenol Pyruvate (PEP). It combines with CO_2 in the presence of the enzyme PEP carboxylase to form the first stable product, i.e. Oxalocacetic Acid (OAA). C_3 plants lack the PEP carboxylase enzyme.

They possess the RuBisCO enzyme. This enzyme can work as both carboxylase (fixation of CO_2) and oxygenase (fixation of O_2). RuBisCO has a much greater affinity for CO_2 than for O_2 and the binding is competitive.

At higher temperatures, its affinity for CO_2 decreases and it works as an oxygenase. Therefore, at higher temperatures photosynthesis decreases in C_3 plants, while in C_4 plants, it increases.

31. (*a*) In purple and green sulphur bacteria, H_2S is the hydrogen donor and it reduces CO_2 to carbohydrate which is $CH_2O \cdot H_2S$ itself gets oxidised to sulphur or sulphate (SO_4^{2-}). There is no evolution of oxygen in this process.

32. (*c*) Aerobic bacteria would accumulate in the region where there is evolution of oxygen. The graph measures the action spectrum of photosynthesis, which is basically the oxygen production at different wavelength of light. Point A shows the maximum oxygen evolution, therefore bacterial density would be highest here. Point C denotes the point where oxygen evolution is almost zero, so bacterial density would be minimum here.

33. (*d*) A is true, but R is false. R can be corrected as
Light incident on smaller surface area, reduces photooxidative damage. Chloroplasts align themselves perpendicular to incident light under high light intensity. This makes the available surface area for light capture less, which prevents further photooxidation.

34. (*b*) The incorrect statement can be corrected as
Light reactions also require biological catalysts which are enzymes for formation of products. ATP synthase is needed for formation of ATP from ADP and Pi. NADP reductase catalyses the reduction of $NADP^+$ to NADPH.

35. (*d*) In the given graph, A is chlorophyll-*b*, B is carotenoids and C is chlorophyll-*a*. Chlorophyll-*a* is the reaction centre, while chlorophyll-*b* is associated with other accessory pigments to transfer energy to the reaction centre. This also protects the reaction centre from photooxidative damage. Carotenoids impart colour (yellow orange) to fruits and petals.

36. (*b*) Only statement IV is correct. Statements I, II and III can be corrected as

- Reaction centre is formed of only chlorophyll-*a*. Remaining pigments form the antennae complex of LHC or Light Harvesting Complex.
- Chlorophyll-*a* has an absorption maxima of 680 nm at photosystem-II, while in photosystem-I, it has an absorption peak at 700 nm.
- Pigment molecules in antennae are not proteinaceous in nature. They are rather bound to proteins in LHC.

37. (*b*) Without photolysis, there would be no supply of electrons to replace those lost by PS-II, which is essential for the electron transport chain and ATP production in photosynthesis.

38. (*a*) Statement I is incorrect, but statement II is correct. Statement I can be corrected as
PS-I is the final e^- acceptor in cyclic phosphorylation. In cyclic electron flow, electrons are transferred by plastocyanin back to the reaction centre at PS-I.

39. (*c*) Both A and R are true, but R is not the correct explanation of A. Cyclic electron flow cannot sustain photosynthesis because there is no production of NADPH. NADPH is required for reduction of PGA formed in C_3 cycle of dark phase into triose phosphate, which in turn gets converted to sugar. Hence, in the absence of NADPH, synthesis of sugar cannot take place in the biosynthetic phase.

40. (*c*) The hydrogen carrier associated with PS-II is plastoquinone. This molecule removes a proton from the stroma while transporting an electron. When this molecule passes on its electron to the electron carrier on the inner side of the membrane, the proton is released into the inner side or the lumen side of the membrane. This maintains the concentration gradient across the thylakoid membrane, which is broken down to release energy for ATP synthesis. Hence, if hydrogen carrier is replaced by electron carrier, normal electron transport would occur, but it would disrupt the proton gradient.

41. (*b*) The correct match is A-2, B-3, C-1, D-4.

- NADP reductase reduces $NADP^+$ to NADPH which is utilised in the C_3 pathway for sugar production.
- Cytochrome-b_6f acts as a proton pump and pumps protons across the thylakoid membrane into the lumen. This increases H^+ concentration in the lumen and makes it acidic.
- CF_0 is a transmembrane channel protein of ATP synthase enzyme that is involved in facilitated diffusion of protons from the lumen of thylakoid to the stroma. This type of transport without the involvement of energy down the concentration gradient is called passive transport.
- Plastocyanin is a mobile electron carrier protein which is associated with a single copper atom.

42. (*b*) Both statement I and statement II are correct.
Photolysis produces protons as well as oxygen which accumulate in the thylakoid lumen. The electrons released by photolysis, are needed to replace those removed from photosystem-I.

43. (*a*) Green algae would photosynthesise using the C_3 pathway. In this pathway, CO_2 is fixed into a three carbon compound, 3-phosphoglyceric Acid or PGA. PGA is the first stable product of C_3 cycle of sugar biosynthesis.
Since CO_2 is radio labelled and fixed into PGA, molecule of PGA will show radioactivity in given alga.

44. (*b*) Statements I, III, and IV are correct. Statements II and V are incorrect and can be corrected as
Oxaloacetic acid is a four carbon stable intermediate in C_4 pathway. OAA is formed by combining PEP with CO_2 catalysed by PEPCase enzyme.
At higher temperature, RuBisCO behaves as an oxygenase. At higher temperature, RuBisCO has greater affinity for oxygen than carbon dioxide, hence behaves as a oxygenase.

45. (*a*) For Calvin cycle to run continuously, RuBP has to be regenerated. This requires one ATP per cycle. In one turn of the Calvin cycle, one CO_2 gets fixed with RuBP to form two molecules of PGA. In one turn of the cycle, one RuBP is regenerated to continue the cycle.

46. (*c*) Both A and R are true, but R is not the correct explanation of A.

Peroxisomes play important role in C_3 plants because in such plants, photorespiration operates due to the oxygenase activity of RuBisCO. Glycolate formed in this wasteful process shuttles to peroxisomes, where it is converted to glycine.

47. (*c*) Oxaloacetic acid is the first stable product in C_4 pathway. It is formed by the action of PEPCase enzyme in mesophyll cells. OAA is converted to malic acid and transported to bundle sheath cells. In the bundle sheath cells, malic acid is decarboxylated to C_3 acid. The CO_2 released in the process enters into C_3 cycle operating there. Through C_3 pathway, glucose is synthesised. Hence, decarboxylation of C_4 acid is required for driving glucose production in bundle sheath cells of C_4 plants.

48. (*c*) Statement in option (c) is correct about photorespiration. Initial product of photorespiratory pathway is a two carbon compound, phosphoglycolate. Remaining statements can be corrected as

Sugarcane and maize plants are C_4 plants and due to the presence of Kranz anatomy, it is possible to eliminate photorespiration in them.

Even at higher temperatures, it is active in C_3 plants, but not in C_4 plants due to the presence of Kranz anatomy in C_4. At higher temperature, the oxygenase activity of RuBisCO is activated due to greater affinity for oxygen and hence this process takes place in C_3 plants.

There is no CO_2 fixation by photorespiration. Rather, CO_2 is released without formation of ATP or NADPH.

49. (*b*) Both statement I and statement II are correct.

Plants growing under the shades of trees of canopy layer in a dense forest receive very little sunlight, thus making light the limiting factor. At 10% of sunlight, chloroplasts saturation occurs and photosynthesis rate remains unaffected after that.

50. (*c*) Rice is a C_3 plant. At higher temperature, RuBisCO has greater affinity for oxygen and hence, behaves as oxygenase. This activates the photorespiration process resulting in evolution of CO_2 rather than formation of sugar. Also, higher temperature denatures enzymes since they are proteinaceous in nature. Dark reactions are completely controlled by enzymes and denaturation of the same will directly halt the C_3 pathway and formation of sugar.

Ch-12 Respiration in Plants

Topical Follow Thru

Test 1

1. (*c*) End product of anaerobic respiration in animals is lactic acid. Anaerobic respiration occurs in the absence of oxygen and is less efficient than aerobic respiration.

2. (*b*) Carbohydrates, particularly glucose, are the primary respiratory substrate in cellular respiration. They are readily oxidised to produce ATP, which provides energy for various cellular processes. While fats and proteins can also be used as respiratory substrates, carbohydrates are the most efficient and are preferentially utilised due to their faster metabolic conversion.

3. (*a*) Statement I is incorrect, but statement II is correct. Incorrect statement can be corrected as

ATP is utilised in two steps of glycolysis, first in conversion of glucose into glucose-6-phosphate and second in the conversion of fructose-6-phosphate into fructose-1, 6-bisphosphate. ATP is synthesised during the conversion of PEP to pyruvic acid through substrate level phosphorylation.

4. (*b*) Facultative anaerobes can switch between aerobic and anaerobic respiration based on oxygen availability, making them versatile in various environments. In contrast, obligate anaerobes can only perform anaerobic respiration and are often harmed or killed by the presence of oxygen. This fundamental difference allows facultative anaerobes to thrive in both oxygen-rich and oxygen-poor conditions.

5. (*b*) When a molecule of glucose undergoes fermentation, it produces a net gain of 2 ATP molecules. This occurs during glycolysis, where glucose is broken down into two molecules of pyruvate, generating 4 ATP molecules. However, since 2 ATP molecules are consumed during the initial steps of glycolysis, the net yield is 2 ATP. Fermentation allows glycolysis to continue by regenerating NAD^+ from NADH, enabling continuous ATP production in the absence of oxygen.

6. (*b*) During fermentation, which is an anaerobic process, NADH molecules generated during glycolysis donate their electrons to either acetaldehyde or pyruvate, depending on the type of fermentation (e.g. alcoholic fermentation or lactic acid fermentation). This donation regenerates NAD^+ from NADH, but no additional NADH molecules are produced as a result of the fermentation process itself. Thus, making total gain of NADH to zero.

7. (*b*) The correct match is A-4, B-3, C-2, D-1.
- Phosphorylation of glucose occurs in the presence of enzyme hexokinase.
- Aerobic catabolism of pyruvate in eukaryotes occurs inside mitochondria.
- Aerobic catabolism of pyruvate in prokaryotes occurs inside cytoplasm.
- Glucose 6-phosphate is converted into its isomer fructose-6-phosphate through the enzyme phosphoglucose isomerase.

8. (*b*) Plants do not have specialised respiratory organs because each cell can independently exchange gases directly with the environment through structures like stomata and lenticels. This decentralised system suffices due to the relatively lower energy demands of plants compared to animals and the widespread distribution of cells that facilitates efficient gas exchange.

9. (*b*) Both A and R are true and R is the correct explanation of A. Glycolysis results in a net gain of 2 ATP molecules per glucose molecule. Two ATP molecules are initially invested in the early steps of glycolysis (i.e., in formation of glucose-6-phosphate from glucose and fructose-1,6 bisphosphate from fructose-6-phosphate), while four ATP molecules are generated through substrate-level phosphorylation (during formation of BPGA to PGA and PEP to pyruvate), resulting in a net gain of 2 ATP molecules.

10. (*a*) Statements II and V are incorrect and can be corrected as
- Glycolysis is also called EMP pathway after the name of its discoverers, Embden, Meyerhof and Parnas.
- The electrons released in glycolysis are carried by 2 molecules of NADH.

11. (*b*) Option (b) correctly defines cellular respiration as the process by which cells oxidise complex compounds, primarily glucose, to release energy, which is used to form ATP. Stomata and lenticels help in gaseous exchange in plants. Cellular respiration is essential for energy production in cells.

12. (*b*) Alcoholic fermentation or anaerobic fermentation occurs in *S. cerevisiae* (yeast) in the case of absence of oxygen. The process of alcoholic fermentation occurs within the cytoplasm. Ethanol and CO_2 are released as by products.

13. (*b*) During glycolysis, the enzyme hexokinase catalyses the phosphorylation of glucose to form glucose-6-phosphate. This is the first step in glycolysis and is crucial for trapping glucose within the cell and preparing it for further breakdown. The other enzymes (phosphorylase, phosphoglucomutase and phosphoglucoisomerase) are involved in different metabolic processes and do not catalyse this specific reaction.

14. (*c*) Option (c) shows incorrect match. In anaerobic respiration, the final electron acceptor is typically not water. Anaerobic respiration involves the use of alternative electron acceptors such as nitrate, sulfate or carbon dioxide depending on the organism.

15. (*b*) In the given diagram, *A* – Lactic acid, *B* – Ethanol. Pyruvic acid is converted to lactic acid (*A*) through a process involving NADH, typically occurring under anaerobic conditions in muscle cells. Alternatively, pyruvic acid can be converted to ethanol (*B*) and CO_2 in yeast and some bacteria during fermentation. The conversion to ethanol also involves NADH, regenerating NAD^+ for glycolysis to continue.

16. (*d*) Statement III is correct. Other statements are incorrect and can be corrected as
- Fermentation does not yield much energy and it is very less as compared to aerobic or cellular respiration.
- During fermentation, one NAD^+ is regenerated from $NADH+H^+$.
- Anaerobic respiration results in the production of 2 ATP molecules.

17. (*b*) Option (b) shows the correct sequence of substrates in glycolysis. The correct complete sequence of glycolysis is as follows:
Glucose $\rightarrow$ G–6–P $\rightarrow$ DHAP $\rightarrow$ PGAL $\rightarrow$ BPGA $\rightarrow$ 3 –PGA $\rightarrow$ 2–PGA $\rightarrow$ PEP $\rightarrow$ Pyruvate

18. (*b*) Yeasts poison themselves to death when the concentration of alcohol reaches about 13 percent. So, the maximum concentration of alcohol in beverages that are naturally fermented is 13% only. Thus, to obtain alcoholic beverages of alcohol content greater than this concentration, we can use distillation.

19. (*d*) Statement I is correct, but statement II is incorrect. The incorrect statement can be corrected as

Plants, unlike animals have no specialised organs for gaseous exchange but they have openings like stomata and lenticels for this purpose.

20. (*b*) Both A and R are true and R is the correct explanation of A. Concentration of alcohol in naturally fermented beverages is less than 13% because more than 13% alcohol is toxic to the yeast which kills yeast and the process stops.

21. (*c*) During the conversion of 2–phosphoglycerate (2–PGA) to phosphoenolpyruvate (PEP), a water molecule is removed from the former substrate. This step is the only dehydration step of glycolysis.

22. (*c*) Lactic acid fermentation occurs when oxidative phosphorylation is not possible due to a lack of oxygen. In this, pyruvic acid is converted to lactic acid, and NAD^+, which is used in the glycolysis process, is regenerated. Muscle cramps are caused by an excessive buildup of lactic acid in the muscles.

23. (*a*) Conversion of BPGA (1, 3–bisphosphoglyceric acid) to 3-phosphoglyceric acid (PGA) in the presence of phosphoglycerate kinase, marks the "break even" point (i.e., 2 molecules of ATP consu med and 2 molecules synthesised) during glycolysis. The two ATPs that were consumed at the beginning of glycolysis have been regenerated here, in addition to two molecules of NADH, which can now be used to generate ATP through electron transport and oxidative phosphorylation.

24. (*d*) Statements I and IV are incorrect and can be corrected as In glycolysis, two redox equivalents are removed in the form of Hydrogen atoms from PGAL and transferred to a molecule of NAD^+ (not NADH).

Fermentation can take place in prokaryotes and in cellular eukaryotes.

25. (*b*) Both statement I and statement II are correct. In plants, glucose is derived from sucrose, the end product of photosynthesis, or from stored carbohydrates.
During oxidation within a cell, all the energy contained in respiratory substrates is not released free into the cell, or in a single step. It is released in series of slow step-wise reactions controlled by enzymes, and it is trapped as chemical energy in the form of ATP.

Test 2

1. (*d*) Pyruvate does not directly enter the Krebs' cycle. Instead, it is first converted into acetyl Co-A in the mitochondria, which then enters the Krebs' cycle.

2. (*b*) Within the mitochondrion, the proton gradient develops across the inner membrane. The electron transport chain, located in the inner membrane, pumps protons from the mitochondrial matrix into the intermembrane space (d), creating a high concentration of protons. This gradient drives ATP synthesis as protons flow back into the matrix through ATP synthase. The outer membrane (c) is permeable and does not maintain the gradient, and the matrix (a) is the innermost compartment where protons return to form ATP.

3. (*b*) The incorrect statement about Krebs' cycle can be corrected as The citric acid cycle or Krebs' cycle is a crucial step of cellular and aerobic respiration. It occurs in mitochondria and is involved only during aerobic respiration. Glycolysis is a common step in both aerobic and anaerobic respiration.

4. (*a*) During cellular respiration, the Electron Transport Chain (ETC) oxidises NADH and $FADH_2$, converting them back to NAD^+ and FAD releasing their stored energy to generate ATP.
The Krebs' cycle produces NADH and $FADH_2$. Glycolysis produces NADH and the link reaction produces NADH, but none of these processes oxidise them to regenerate NAD^+ and FAD.

5. (*d*) Reaction in option (d) does not occur in Krebs' cycle.
Conversion of 2-phosphoglycerate into phosphoenol pyruvate involves removal of water in the presence of enzyme enolase and is part of glycolytic pathway. This step does not occur in Krebs' cycle.

6. (*a*) Statement I is incorrect, but statement II is correct. Incorrect statement can be corrected as In oxidative decarboxylation (link reaction), pyruvic acid, Co-A and NAD^+ is converted into acetyl Co-A, CO_2 and NADH $+H^+$ in the presence of enzyme pyruvate dehydrogenase and Mg^{2+}.

7. (*b*) Here, A – Dicarboxylic acid, B – Tricarboxylic acid. In the Krebs' cycle, oxaloacetate (a dicarboxylic acid) condenses with acetyl Co-A to form citrate (a tricarboxylic acid), which is the first product of the cycle. This reaction is catalysed by the enzyme citrate synthase and is essential for the continuation of the cycle.

8. (*b*) In aerobic respiration, oxygen acts as the final electron acceptor in the electron transport chain. It combines with electrons and protons to form water, which is essential for the process of oxidative phosphorylation and ATP production.

9. (*c*) Both A and R are true, but R is not the correct explanation of A. Glycolysis indeed produces 8 ATP in aerobic respiration, considering the total ATP yield from substrate-level phosphorylation and subsequent oxidation of NADH in the ETC.

10. (*b*) In the Electron Transport Chain (ETC), a total of approximately 32-34 ATP molecules are produced per glucose molecule depending on the shuttle system.

This calculation typically includes 3 ATP molecules from each of the 10 NADH molecules (2 from glycolysis, 2 from link reaction and 6 from Krebs' cycle) (30 ATP) and 2 ATP molecules from each of the 2 $FADH_2$ (from Krebs' cycle) molecules (4 ATP), resulting in 34 ATP.

11. (*a*) Respiratory quotient varies due to different respiratory substrates used. When carbohydrates are used as substrate then the RQ will be 1. When fat and protein are used in respiration then RQ is less than 1.

12. (*b*) The correct match is A-2, B-1, C-4, D-3.

ETS, present in the inner mitochondrial membrane, consists of five molecular complexes and three sites for the transfer of protons across the membrane. Complex-I is NADH dehydrogenase, complex-II is succinate dehydrogenase, complex-III is cytochrome $-bc_1$ and complex-IV is cytochrome-*c* oxidase. Complex-V refers to the ATP synthase.

13. (*d*) Statements I and IV are correct. Incorrect statements II and III can be corrected as :

Glycerol would enter the respiratory pathway after being converted to PGAL.

All carbohydrates are usually first converted into glucose before they are used for respiration.

14. (*b*) The Respiratory Quotient (RQ) is a dimensionless number used in metabolic studies to assess the balance between the carbon dioxide produced and the oxygen consumed during the metabolic processes of respiration, indicating the predominant type of substrate being metabolised. It depends upon the type of respiratory substrate used during respiration.

15. (*d*) Statements I, II and V are correct. Incorrect statements are III and IV. These can be corrected as

- Some members of ETC also take part in proton transport along with electron transport.
- The common quinone and ubiquinone are mobile in the membranes of mitochondria.

16. (*a*) One molecule of glucose produces two molecules of pyruvate through glycolysis. One pyruvate is decarboxylated by pyruvate dehydrogenase to release one CO_2.

Thus, one molecule of glucose oxidation releases 2 CO_2 in the oxidative decarboxylation step. So, 3 molecules of glucose would produce $3 \times 2 = 6$ CO_2.

17. (*a*) The correct order of steps related to aerobic respiration is II-III-V-I-IV.

- Pyruvate is transported to the mitochondrial matrix, where it is oxidatively decarboxylated to form acetyl Co-A.
- The acetyl Co-A is condensed with oxaloacetic acid (OAA) to form citrate.
- Citrate is isomerised to form isocitrate. It is followed by two successive steps of decarboxylation, leading to the formation of α-ketoglutaric acid and then succinyl-Co-A.
- During the conversion of succinyl-Co-A to succinic acid a molecule of GTP is synthesised This is a substrate level phosphorylation.
- Succinate is converted to fumarate. Fumarase catalyses the conversion of fumarate to malate by addition of water.

18. (*a*) Statement I is incorrect, but statement II is correct. Statement I can be corrected as

24 ATP molecules can be generated from one glucose in the TCA cycle alone. In one round of TCA cycle, 3 NADH molecules, 1 $FADH_2$ and 1 ATP is formed. Every molecule of NADH is oxidised to form 3 ATP molecules, while one $FADH_2$ is oxidised to form 2 ATP molecules. So, a total of 12 ATP $(3\times 3)+(1\times 2)+1)$ are formed in one round of TCA cycle. Now, one molecule of glucose forms 2 pyruvate that enter TCA cycle. So, 24 (2×12) ATP molecules will be formed.

19. (*c*) Statement III is correct. Other statemets can be corrected as

- $FADH_2$ is part of TCA cycle and ETC.
- F_1 has the catalytic site for ATP synthesis.
- Electrons from NADH produced in the mitochondrial matrix during TCA, are oxidised by NADH dehydrogenase and transferred to ubiquinone.

20. (*d*) NADH dehydrogenase is complex I which oxidises NADH and transfers the electrons to the next complexes of ETC. Complex II is succinate dehydrogenase which transfers electrons to $FADH_2$ and serves as the second entry point of ETC.

21. (*a*) A is false, but R is true. A can be corrected as

Lysine and arginine are amino acids and need to be converted to pyruvic acid before entering the respiratory substrate.

22. (*d*) Decarboxylation of isocitrate and α-ketoglutarate reduces NAD^+ to NADH which is re-oxidised in the electron transport chain by NADH dehydrogenase. Conversion of succinate to fumarate generates $FADH_2$ which is also oxidised back in ETC.

23. (*c*) Pure proteins and fats due to their complex structure have to be broken down before they can be used as respiratory substrates. Hence, their break down is complex and takes more time to release energy by oxidising them.

24. (*d*) Fats, glycerol and acetyl Co-A can enter the respiratory pathway at different points. Fats would be converted to acetyl Co-A, and glycerol into PGAL before entering the respiratory pathway. Proteins cannot be used as the substrate since proteins need to be broken down first by proteases and later the amino acids have to be deaminated before they enter the pathway. Due to the absence of functional proteases, the first step in protein breakdown is halted, hence they cannot enter the respiratory pathway.

25. (*d*) The picture represents ATP synthase enzyme, (complex-V), where A is F_0 and B is F_1-particle. The incorrect statement can be corrected as

Protons flow through A down their concentration gradient. For each ATP produced, $4H^+$ passes through F_0 from the intermembrane space to the matrix down the electrochemical proton gradient.

Chapter Break Thru

1. (*c*) Phosphorylation is the first step of glycolysis. In this step, glucose is converted into glucose-6-phosphate by ATP in the presence of the enzyme hexokinase. This is an irreversible reaction and glucose gets trapped inside the cell after phosphorylation.

2. (*c*) Statement in option (c) is correct about anaerobic respiration.

Rest statements are incorrect and can be corrected as

Mitochondria are not required for anaerobic respiration.

It is found in fewer organisms, mostly in yeast, bacteria.

Pyruvate or its derivative is the ultimate acceptor of electrons and protons in anaerobic respiration.

3. (*c*) Glycolysis (I) and fermentation (III) both occur in the cytosol. Glycolysis, the process of breaking down glucose into pyruvate takes place entirely in the cytosol. Fermentation, which regenerates NAD^+ from NADH to allow glycolysis to continue under anaerobic conditions, also occurs in the cytosol. The citric acid cycle and electron transport system occur in the mitochondria.

4. (*c*) EMP pathway or glycolysis is the common pathway found in both aerobic and anaerobic respiration. It occurs in the cytoplasm of both prokaryotes and eukaryotes.

5. (*d*) The incorrect statement can be corrected as

The conversion of 1, 3-bisphosphoglycerate into 3-phosphoglycerate is the energy-yielding process in glycolysis. The conversion of 3-phosphoglycerate to 2-phosphoglycerate is not an energy-yielding step. ATP is not released during this event.

6. (*a*) Under insufficient aerobic conditions in muscle during rigorous exercise, pyruvic acid is converted to lactic acid. This process, known as lactic acid fermentation, allows glycolysis to continue by regenerating NAD^+ from NADH, even when oxygen is scarce.

The other option represent different metabolic fates of pyruvic acid: $CO_2 + H_2O$ is formed during complete aerobic respiration, acetyl Co-A + CO_2 is formed during the transition to the Krebs' cycle under aerobic conditions and ethanol + CO_2 is formed occurs in yeast and some bacteria during alcoholic fermentation.

7. (*c*) In glycolysis, the lysis or splitting step occurs when fructose 1,6-bisphosphate is cleaved into two three-carbon molecules: glyceraldehyde 3-phosphate and dihydroxyacetone phosphate (DHAP). This step is crucial for the continuation of the glycolytic pathway, allowing the subsequent steps to proceed and ultimately produce ATP.

8. (*d*) Option (d) shows the correct match. Tartaric acid (d) is an organic acid, and thus has a Respiratory Quotient (RQ) of more than one, indicating that it produces more CO_2 relative to the O_2 consumed. The RQ of other respiratory substrate can be corrected as

The RQ for starch (a) is typically around 1. Proteins (b) have an RQ of about 0.9, and palmitic acid (c), a fatty acid, has a RQ of about 0.7.

9. (*b*) Statement I is correct, but statements II, III and IV are incorrect and these can be corrected as

Pyruvate is first converted to acetyl Co-A, which then combines with OAA to form citrate.

Energy stored in NADH + H^+ and $FADH_2$ are released during ETC.

Substrate level phosphorylation occurs during conversion of succinyl Co-A to succinic acid only at single step.

10. (*b*) Cytochromes are proteins involved in the electron transport chain and are found in the cristae, the folds of the inner mitochondrial membrane. These structures increase the surface area for the electron transport chain, where cytochromes play a critical role in transferring electrons and facilitating the production of ATP.

11. (*d*) Oxidative phosphorylation does not take part in the Krebs' cycle. Instead, it occurs in the electron transport chain, where the energy from NADH and $FADH_2$, produced in the Krebs' cycle, is used to generate ATP. The Krebs' cycle includes substrate-level phosphorylation (a), where ATP is directly synthesised, acetylation (b) of oxaloacetate to form citrate, and oxidative decarboxylation (c) reactions that release CO_2.

12. (*c*) In Krebs' cycle, during hydration, enzyme fumarase adds a molecule of water to fumarate, forming another 4-carbon dicarboxylic acid called malate.

13. (*a*) In the given diagram of the Electron Transport Chain (ETC), the spaces A, B and C represents different mitochondrial compartments. 'A' is the intermembrane space where protons are pumped, 'B' is the inner mitochondrial membrane where the ETC complexes are located and 'C' is the matrix where the Krebs' cycle occurs and NADH is generated. This arrangement is essential for creating the proton gradient that drives ATP synthesis *via* ATP synthase.

14. (*d*) Succinate dehydrogenase is unique as it participates in both the TCA cycle and the Electron Transport System (ETS). In the TCA cycle, it catalyses the oxidation of succinate to fumarate, producing $FADH_2$. In the ETS, it functions as Complex-II, where $FADH_2$ donates electrons, which are then transferred through the chain to ultimately produce ATP. Pyruvate dehydrogenase links glycolysis to the TCA cycle. NADH reductase is involved in the ETS. Citrate synthase catalyses the first step of the TCA cycle.

15. (*a*) Oxygen plays a crucial role in the electron transport chain, where it accepts electrons at the end of the chain. This acceptance forms water and allows the electron transport chain to continue functioning, which is essential for the production of ATP through oxidative phosphorylation.

16. (*a*) In the electron transport chain, electrons are transferred through a specific sequence of cytochromes. They first pass from cytochrome-*b* to cytochrome-*c*, then to cytochrome-*a*, and finally to cytochrome-a_3. This orderly transfer facilitates the creation of a proton gradient across the inner mitochondrial membrane, ultimately driving ATP synthesis through oxidative phosphorylation.

17. (*c*) In a single turn of the Krebs' cycle, three molecules of NADH and one molecule of $FADH_2$ are produced. These high-energy electron carriers are generated through specific enzymatic reactions within the cycle. NADH and $FADH_2$ play critical roles in transferring electrons to the electron transport chain, where their energy is used to produce ATP through oxidative phosphorylation.

18. (*c*) Sucrose is converted into glucose and fructose by the enzyme, invertase, and these two monosaccharides readily enter the glycolytic pathway. Since these two monosaccharides can be phosphorylated directly by hexokinase.

19. (*d*) Carbohydrates, fats and proteins, all can be used as a respiratory substrate in cellular respiration. All of them first get converted to acetyl Co-A to enter into Krebs' cycle of aerobic cellular respiration. Thus, it is the common factor of respiration entering Krebs' cycle after breakdown of carbohydrates, fats and proteins.

20. (*b*) The correct sequence of RQ of various respiratory substrates is:
Carbohydrates > Proteins > Fats
The Respiratory Quotient (RQ) for carbohydrates is approximately, 1.0, for proteins around 0.9, and for fats, about 0.7. This sequence reflects the relative RQ values, indicating that carbohydrates have the highest RQ, followed by proteins and then fats have the lowest RQ. This order corresponds to the ratio of CO_2 produced to O_2 consumed during the metabolism of these macronutrients.

21. (*c*) The distance that gases must diffuse even in large, bulky plants is not great.

Plants do not have a specialised transportation system for oxygen because the distance that gases must diffuse, even in large, bulky plants, is relatively short. Each cell can efficiently exchange gases directly with the environment through stomata and lenticels. This diffusion is sufficient to meet their metabolic needs, making a specialised system unnecessary.

22. (*a*) Glycolysis is a pathway of cellular respiration that occurs in the cytosol and consists of two phases: the investment phase, where ATP is consumed to phosphorylate glucose and in the payoff phase, where ATP is produced along with pyruvate and NADH. This process allows cells to generate energy under both aerobic and anaerobic conditions.

23. (*c*) Both A and R are true, but R is not the correct explanation of A. The electron transport chain involves electrons passing through complexes-I to IV, which are coupled to complex-V (ATP synthase) for ATP production from ADP and inorganic phosphate. The number of ATP molecules synthesised depends on whether NADH or $FADH_2$ donates electrons.

24. (*d*) Statement I is correct, but statement II is incorrect. Incorrect statement can be corrected as Isocitrate is followed by two successive decarboxylation leading to formation of α-ketoglutaric acid and then succinyl Co-A.

25. (*a*) Statement in option (a) is incorrect with respect to the electron transport system and can be corrected as
Coenzyme-Q and cyt-*c* are mobile electron carriers. Co-Q receives the electrons from the complex-I and complex-II and passes them to the complex-III. Cyt-*c* operates between complex-III and IV.

26. (*b*) The incorrect match pair can be corrected as
Oxidative decarboxylation of pyruvate occurs in the mitochondrial matrix, not in the cytoplasm. During this process, pyruvate is converted into acetyl Co-A, producing NADH and CO_2.
Glycolysis occurs in the cytoplasm, while the TCA (Krebs') cycle occurs in the mitochondrial matrix. The ETC is located in the inner mitochondrial membrane.

27. (*b*) Germinating seeds exhibit the highest rate of respiration because they require a significant amount of energy for growth and development. During germination, metabolic activities increase to support cell division, nutrient mobilisation, and the establishment of the seedling, leading to a high demand for ATP production through respiration.

28. (*c*) The correct match is A-3, B-2, C-4, D-1.
- A respirometer is an instrument used for measuring the rate of respiration.
- RQ for a mixed diet (carbohydrates, proteins and fats) is about 0.85.
- The NADH synthesised in glycolysis is transferred into the mitochondria and undergoes oxidative phosphorylation.
- RQ is infinity in case of anaerobic respiration, where CO_2 is evolved, but O_2 is not consumed, e.g. alcoholic fermentation.

29. (*c*) Statements I, III and V are correct. Statements II and IV are incorrect. These can be corrected as
Gaseous exchange occurs between the cells and extracellular tissue fluid in animals, while in plants, it occurs between cells and inter-cellular spaces.
Amount of energy is produced large in an aerobic respiration. It produces around 18 times more energy compared to anaerobic respiraiton.

30. (*b*) Pyruvic acid (3C) is converted to an acetyl group (2C) through the process of oxidative decarboxylation, which occurs in the mitochondria. During this process, pyruvic acid is decarboxylated to form acetyl Co-A, releasing CO_2 and producing NADH. This step bridges glycolysis and the Krebs' cycle, facilitating the further breakdown of glucose for energy production.

31. (*b*) Plants do not require a respiratory organ since they do not present great demands for gas exchange. Loosely arranged parenchyma has air cavities while lenticels directly expose the living cells to the atmosphere.
However, in the absence of these two systems, plants would require a defined respiratory organ.
Conducting system in the form of xylem and phloem, as well as a waxy cuticle and stomatal pores are already present in a terrestrial plant species.

32. (*c*) Both statement I and statement II are incorrect. These can be corrected as
Facultative aerobes can survive in anoxic conditions. The normal respiratory pathway for facultative aerobes does not require oxygen.
Facultative aerobes are organisms that respire anaerobically (fermentation) under normal conditions, but can switch to aerobic respiration in the presence of oxygen.

33. (*b*) Isomers are compounds with the same molecular formula, but different structure.
Dihydroxyacetone phosphate (DHAP) and 3-phosphoglyceraldehyde (PGAL), 3-phosphoglyceric acid and 2-phosphoglyceric acid, Glucose and galactose are isomers of one another.

34. (*d*) Fumarate to malate conversion in TCA cycle is catalysed by fumarase which requires addition of water, hence it is a hydration reaction. The opposite phenomenon occurs during conversion of 2-phosphoglyceric acid to phosphorenol pyruvate in glycolysis. During this step of glycolysis, water is removed, hence dehydration reaction occurs.

35. (*d*) The energy yielding steps are conversion of BPGA to 3PGA and conversion of PEP to pyruvate. In each of these steps, two molecules each of ATP are produced. Hence, a total of four ATP molecules are generated in the energy yielding steps. The energy expending steps are conversion of glucose to glucose-6-phosphate and conversion of fructose-6-phosphate to fructose-1, 6-bisphosphate. Each of these steps consume one ATP molecule each. Hence, two ATP molecules are spent in the energy expending steps of glycolysis.

36. (*b*) Glycolysis generates NADH. This NADH acts as the reducing agent to reduce pyruvate into lactate. In the process, NADH is oxidised to NAD^+. Hence, glycolysis should precede anaerobic breakdown to yield lactate by the muscle cells.

37. (*c*) One molecule of glucose breaks down by glycolysis to give two molecules of pyruvate. Each molecule of pyruvate is converted to one molecule of CO_2 and one molecule of ethanol. Hence, one molecule of glucose would yield two molecules of ethanol by fermentation. To produce 8 molecules of ethanol, 4 molecules of glucose should be fermented.

38. (*d*) Statement I is incorrect, but statement II is correct. Statement I can be corrected as
GTP hydrolysis powers ATP synthesis in TCA cycle. During the conversion of succinyl Co-A to succinic acid, a molecule of GTP

is synthesised. This is a substrate level phosphorylation. In a coupled reaction, GTP is converted to GDP with the simultaneous synthesis of ATP from ADP.

39. (*a*) One turn of citric acid cycle yields 3 molecules of NADH, so 12 molecules would be generated in 4 turns. One glucose produces two pyruvate and each of the pyruvate enters the TCA cycle after being converted to acetyl Co-A. Hence, for each glucose, two turns of citric acid cycle operates, which generates 2 x 3 = 6 NADH. For generating 12 NADH, 2 glucose molecules should be used.

40. (*d*) A is true, but R is false. R can be corrected as
Succinate to fumarate conversion generates $FADH_2$. This $FADH_2$ generated is used in the ETS, where it donates its electrons to complex II or succinate dehydrogenase.

41. (*b*) Statement I is correct. Other statements can be corrected as
- Fe-S clusters are associated with both complex I and complex II.
- Ubiquinone is reduced by both $FADH_2$ and NADH.
- Cu ions act as cofactors for complex IV, which is cytochrome-*c* oxidase.

42. (*a*) Complex II is associated with $FADH_2$. Electrons from $FADH_2$ are transferred to Fe-S clusters which causes the reduction of Fe^{3+} to Fe^{2+}.

43. (*a*) A is false, but R is true. A can be corrected as
Intermembrane space has the lowest pH conditions. This is due to the fact that as electrons are transported through different complexes in ETS, some amount of energy is released which is used to pump protons from matrix to the intermembrane space. Thus, H^+ concentration rises in the intermembrane space which lowers the pH.

44. (*b*) Both statement I and statement II are correct.
As electrons are transported through different complexes, energy is used in pumping protons from the matrix to the intermembrane space.
Flow of H^+ ions or protons through F_0 channel of ATP synthase occurs down the electrochemical proton gradient, and is an energy independent passive process.

45. (*d*) In eukaryotes, 38 ATP molecules are generated by the process of aerobic respiration. However, two ATPs are consumed in transporting NADH from cytoplasm to mitochondria. Hence, a total of 36 ATP molecules are generated in eukaryotes.
Prokaryotes lack mitochondria and all the steps of aerobic respiration occurs in the cytoplasm itself. Hence, for prokaryotes 38 molecules are generated by aerobic respiration.

46. (*c*) Ubiquinol is the reduced form of ubiquinone. Ubiquinone is reduced by NADH and $FADH_2$ to form ubiquinol. Oxidation of ubiquinol to ubiquinone occurs by transfer of electrons to cytochrome- bc_1 or complex-III.

47. (*b*) Both A and R are true and R is the correct explanation of A.
NADH oxidation occurs slowly in fermentation than in aerobic respiration because in fermentation, ETS is lacking. In the absence of ETS, there is no electron acceptor which can quickly accept electrons from NADH and oxidise them back to NAD^+. Rather, in fermentation, the end product of glycolysis which is pyruvate, is used to oxidise NADH.

48. (*a*) The correct order is I-III-II-V-IV.
Proteins can also act as respiratory substrates.
- At first, the proteins are broken down into individual amino acids by protease enzyme.
- Amino acids are deaminated, which means removal of amino group in the form of ammonia.
- Amino acids are converted into pyruvate.
- Pyruvate undergoes oxidative decarboxylation to form acetyl Co-A.
- Acetyl Co-A condenses with OAA to form citrate, thereby completing the TCA cycle.

49. (*c*) Respiratory quotient or RQ would be greater than one when pyruvate is reduced to lactate by fermentation. In fermentation, since there is no evolution of oxygen, RQ is ∞.
Sucrose is a carbohydrate, so here the RQ is 1. For palmitic acid, which is a fatty acid, RQ would be 0.7 which is less than 1. Arginine is an amino acid, RQ would be about 0.9, which is also less than 1.

50. (*c*) Both statement I and statement II are incorrect. These can be corrected as
- Both NADH and $FADH_2$ take part in oxidative phosphorylation of ETS.
- Catalytic site of ATP synthase faces the mitochondrial matrix.

Ch-13 Plant Growth and Development

Toical Follow Thru

Test 1

1. (*c*) Plasticity refers to the phenomenon in which plants follows different pathways in response to environment or phases of life forming different kind of structures. Buttercup, larkspur, cotton and coriander show plasticity, whereas maize does not show plasticity.
2. (*d*) The correct match is A-2, B-4, C-3, D-1.
The continual elongation of roots is an example of arithmetic growth.
Geometric growth is characterised by gradual expansion in early phases and fast expansion in later stages. The example of geometric growth is early embryonic development.
The formation of meristems such as interfascicular cambium and cork cambium occur from fully differentiated parenchyma cells. This shows dedifferentiation.
Secondary phloem is formed by redifferentiation.
3. (*c*) Statements IV and V are incorrect and can be corrected as
The phase of maturation undergoes in the portion which is further away from the apex, i.e. more proximal to the phase of elongation. Every plant has an optimum temperature range which is best suited for its growth.
4. (*b*) The incorrect statement can be corrected as
Absolute growth rate is total growth per unit time which often shows initial rise followed by a decline.
5. (*a*) Statement I is incorrect, but statement II is correct. Statement I can be corrected as
Rate of respiration is quite high in elongation phase, but is usually lesser than that of cells in the formative phase.
6. (*c*) The correct match is A-2, B-4, C-1, D-3.
In meristematic phase, intercellular spaces are absent and if present, they are very small.
The development of tracheary elements is an example of differentiation.
Cells of maturation phase, attain their maximal size in terms of wall thickening.
Heterophylly in some plants such as cotton, buttercup, etc., is an example of plasticity.
7. (*c*) Both statement I and statement II are incorrect. These can be corrected as
Geometric growth occurs in microorganisms when they are provided with enough space and nutrition. Geometric growth is slow in the beginning when the cell number is small. Later, it progresses rapidly or exponentially.
8. (*c*) The cells proximal to meristematic zone represent the phase of elongation which shows characteristics like increased vacuolation, cell enlargement, etc.
9. (*b*) The correct sequence of the developmental process in a plant cell is
Cell division → elongation → differentiation → maturation.
The developmental process in a plant cell starts from cell division in which the divided cell grows and shows differentiation and gets matu ed.
10. (*d*) Statement I is correct, but statement II is incorrect. The incorrect statement can be corrected as
Growth is accompanied by metabolic processes (both anabolic and catabolic), that occur at the expense of energy.
11. (*c*) The cells present at root apex are rich in protoplasm, possess large conspicuous nuclei. Their cell walls are primary in nature, thin and cellulosic with abundant plasmodesmatal connections.
12. (*a*) The incorrect statement can be corrected as
Arithmetic growth follows mitotic cell division where only one daughter cell continues to divide while the other differentiates and matures.
13. (*c*) Both A and R are true, but R is not the correct explanation of A.
In most systems, the initial growth is slow (lag phase), and it increases rapidly thereafter – at an exponential rate (log or exponential phase). If we plot the graph of growth against time, we get a typical sigmoid or S-curve.
A sigmoid curve is a characteristic of living organism growing in a natural environment. It is typical for all cells, tissues and organs of a plant.
14. (*d*) The given diagram shows detection of zone of elongation by parallel line technique.
15. (*d*) Statement I is correct, but statement II is incorrect. Incorrect statement can be corrected as
Development in plants (i.e., both growth and differentiation) is under the control of intrinsic and extrinsic factors.
16. (*b*) Relative growth rate = (Growth in given time period/Measurement at start of time period × 100
$[(20-6)/6]\times 100 = 233.33\%$.
17. (*d*) Statement I is correct, but statement II is incorrect and can be corrected as
Growth is maximum in the phase of elongation. Increased vacuolation, cell enlargement and new cell wall deposition are the characteristics of the cells of this phase.
18. (*b*) The given figure shows geometric growth. In this, an idealised sigmoid (S) curve is obtained. It should be noted that this type of curve obtained as a result of geometric growth, is a characteristic of living organism growing in a natural environment.

19. (*c*) Relative growth (R. G.) is the growth of the given system per unit time expressed on a common basis, e.g., per unit initial parameter.
Leaf A : $10\,cm^2$ grows $5\,cm^2$ in an hour.
So, R. G. (A) $= \frac{5}{10} \times 100 = 50\%$
Leaf B : $25\,cm^2$ grows $5\,cm^2$ in an hour.
So, R. G. (B) $= \frac{5}{25} \times 100 = 20\%$
So, the relative growth of leaf A and leaf B are 50% and 20%, respectively.

20. (*c*) Statement IV is incorrect and can be corrected as.
The development in plant is flexible owing to its differentiation pattern that is open.

21. (*d*) The exponential growth can be expressed as
$W_1 = W_0 e^{rt}$
Where, W_1 = Final size (weight, height, number, etc.)
W_0 = initial size at the beginning of the period
r = growth rate
t = time of growth
e = base of natural logarithms.

22. (*d*) A tree showing seasonal activities show sigmoid or S-curve. In seasonal plants, in the spring season when leaves start growing, plants are said to be in the lag-phase, the summer season is known as an exponential phase as plant growth is maximum and in winter, show stationary or resting phase.

23. (*b*) Statements I, III and IV are correct. The incorrect statement can be corrected as
Growth in pollen tube is measured in terms of its length.

24. (*d*) The correct match is A-1, B-3, C-2. Apical meristems are present at terminal positions, e.g., root apical meristems and shoot apical meristem.
Intercalary meristem have localised growth.
Lateral meristem, also called as secondary growth, appears later in life.

25. (*b*) Tumors are the result of dedifferentiation. These are formed when a differentiated cell regains the capacity to divide and shows unrestained growth.
On the other hand, inter-fascicular cambium or vascular cambium is also the result of the dedifferentiation process only.

Test 2

1. (*d*) Ethylene shows triple response which does not include lateral growth of internodes. It includes swelling of nodes, elongation of internodes of stem and induction of horizontal growth of stem.

2. (*b*) The incorrect statement can be corrected as
Ethephon is used in aqueous form. It is the commercial product for providing ethylene. It is readily absorbed and transported within the plant and releases ethylene slowly.

3. (*d*) A is true, but R is false. R can be corrected as
All Gibberellic acid (GA) are acidic in nature and helps to delay senescence. Thus, the fruits can be left on the tree longer, so as to extend the market period.

4. (*d*) All statements are correct except statement I. The incorrect statement can be corrected as
Cytokinins promote the synthesis of chlorophyll.

5. (*c*) Both A and R are true, but R is not the correct explanation of A.
ABA is found to induce various types of responses in plants against stress conditions like the closure of the stomata during drought, seed domancy and also ensures germination of seed during favourable conditions. Therefore, ABA is called the stress hormone.

6. (*a*) Statement I is incorrect, but statement II is correct. Statement I can be corrected as
Under conditions of water stress, ABA inhibits the shoot growth and the overall growth in plants.

7. (*d*) A is true, but R is false. R can be corrected as
Ethephon induces femaleness in cucurbits. The increase in the number of female flowers results in a corresponding increase in the number of fruits. Hence, spraying of ethephon on cucurbits results in increase in number of fruits.

8. (*b*) The correct match is A-3, B-1, C-4, D-2.
• Natural auxin shows polar transport from stem apex to root apex.
• Ethylene enhances the respiration rate during ripening of the fruits. This rise in rate of respiration is called respiratory climactic.
• IBA (Indole Butyric acid) is used extensively in agricultural and horticultural practices.
• GA_3 is used to speed up the malting process in brewing industry.

9. (*d*) Statement I is correct, but statement II is incorrect. Incorrect statement can be corrected as
Ethylene is a gaseous plant hormone which promotes root growth and root hair formation, thus helping the plants to increase their absorption surface.

10. (*a*) Statement I is incorrect, but statement II is correct. Statement I can be corrected as
Cytokinins are synthesised in regions where rapid cell division occurs. For example, root apices, developing shoot buds, young fruits, etc.

11. (*d*) Among the given functions, promoting flowering in long day plants is antagonistic to function of ABA because it delays flowering.

12. (*d*) The incorrect match pair can be corrected as
Abscisic Acid (ABA) helps in induction of stomatal closure; while cytokinins promote growth of axillary bud by overcoming apical dominance.

13. (*c*) The incorrect statement can be corrected as
Kinetin is a modified form of adenine, a purine which was discovered from autoclaved herring sperm DNA.

14. (*c*) The incorrect statement can be corrected as

In long day and biennial plants, gibberellin promotes flowering, while in other plants, they inhibit it.

15. (*d*) A is true, but R is false. R can be corrected as
ABA promotes seed dormancy and inhibits germination. Action of ABA is counteracted by GA, which promotes seed germination at appropriate time. Thus, the bud dormancy is regulated by a balance between gibberellin and ABA.

16. (*d*) The incorrect match pair can be corrected as
Apical hook formation in dicot seedlings - Ethylene.

17. (*b*) Statements II and IV are incorrect. They can be corrected as
Not all the parts of plant show unlimited growth. The root apex and shoot apex having apical meristematic tissue show indefinite growth.
To increase sugar production in sugarcanes, they are sprayed with gibberellins (GA).

18. (*b*) If a person forgets to add cytokinin to the culture medium, then cell division, growth and differentiation will not occur properly and callus will not develop shoot buds. On the other hand, auxin is involved in the differentiation of roots. Their correct ratio is involved in organogenesis in the plant tissue culture.

19. (*b*) If a rotten fruit gets mixed with unripe fruits, then the ethylene produced from the rotten fruit will hasten the ripening of the unripe fruits. Ethylene enhances the respiration rate during ripening of fruits. This rise in the rate of respiration is called respiration climacteric.

20. (*a*) Statements II, IV and V are correct. The incorrect statements can be corrected as
Auxin induces rooting in a twig.
Ethylene accelerates abscission in flowers and fruits (thinning of cotton, cherry, walnut).

21. (*b*) The correct match is A-4, B-3, C-1, D-2, E-5.

- Coleoptile tip of canary grass showed presence of transmittable influence called auxin (experiment done by Darwin and Darwin).
- The volatile substance that was released from ripened oranges hastened the ripening of unripened bananas (experiment done by H H Cousins)
- Active substances released by fungal pathogen *Gibberella fujikuroi* causes bakanae disease in rice seedling which was later identified as gibberellic acid (experiment done by E. Kurosawa)
- Purification and chemical characterisation of three different kinds of inhibitors–inhibitor B, abscisin-II and dormin led to the discovery of ABA.
- Cytokinins were isolated from the yeast cells (experiments done by Skoog and coworkers).

22. (*b*) Both A and R are true and R is the correct explanation of A.
The relative ratio of cytokinin (Kinetin) to auxin (IAA) is very important in determining the nature of organogenesis in tissue culture. High level of kinetin results in shoot formation, while high concentration of auxin favours rooting.

23. (*d*) Statement I is correct, but statement II is incorrect. The incorrect statement can be corrected as :
Auxin can be bioassayed by Avena curvature assay. The α – amylase bioassay is used to bioassay hormone gibberellin.

24. (*b*) Auxin, GA and ABA are acidic in nature, but cytokinin is basic.

25. (*d*) Apples have lenticels on their skin, so they respire through them. They are wrapped in waxed paper after harvesting so as to prevent the respiration and over ripening of the apples.

Chapter Break Thru

1. (*c*) In pineapple plants, auxins and ethylene induce artificial flowering throughout the year to increase its yield.

2. (*d*) The incorrect statement about open form of growth can be corrected as
The meristematic cells have a thin primary cell wall.

3. (*b*) The correct match is A-4, B-1, C-2, D-3.

- Charles Darwin along with Francis Darwin first discovered auxin as a plant growth hormone synthesised in coleoptile tip of canary grass.
- Gibberellic acid was first discovered by E Kurosawa from the fungus *Gibberella fujikuroi* found on rice seedlings.
- Skoog and Miller discovered kinetin, a type of cytokinin found in coconut milk. It promotes cell division.
- Cousins confirmed the release of a volatile substance from ripened oranges and named it ethylene.

4. (*a*) Statement I is incorrect, but statement II is correct. The incorrect statement can be corrected as
Plants show indeterminate type of growth.
Plant growth is unique because plants retain the capacity for unlimited growth throughout their life.

5. (*a*) A is false, but R is true. A can be corrected as
The lateral meristems, vascular cambium and cork-cambium appear in the later phase of plant.

6. (*b*) Both statement I and statement II are correct.
Natural cytokinins are synthesised in regions where rapid cell division occurs, e.g. root apices, developing shoot buds, young fruits, etc. It helps to produce new leaves, chloroplasts in leaves, lateral shoot growth and adventitious shoot formation.

7. (*a*) A is false, but R is true. A can be corrected as
In waterlogged conditions, development of plants is poor and differentiation of tissues is retarded. This is because waterlogging inhibits root growth and root activity due to reduced availability of oxygen in soil air.

8. (*b*) Exponential or log phase cannot be sustained for longer period because the nutrients and space are limited and there is competition as well.

9. (*b*) Both statement I and statement II are correct.

Growth, at a cellular level, is principally a consequence of increase in the amount of protoplasm. Growth is, therefore, measured by a variety of parameters some of which are – increase in fresh weight, dry weight, length, area, volume and cell number. One single maize root apical meristem can give rise to more than 17,500 new cells per hour.

10. (*c*) Statements II, III and IV are incorrect and can be corrected as :

The lag phase in geometrical growth is represented by initial slower growth.

Exponential growth phase in geometrical growth is regarded as the 'grand phase of growth'.

The PGR ethylene belongs to category of both plant growth promoter and plant growth inhibitor. On the other hand, PGR abscisic acid belongs to the category of plant growth inhibitor.

11. (*c*) Phototropic movement is the result of uneven distribution of auxin (i.e., IAA, IBA etc.). In this way, curvature or bending takes place in plant stem, towards the source of light.

12. (*d*) The correct match is A-2, B- 4, C- 3, D- 1.

- The cell walls of the cells present in meristematic zone are primary in nature, thin and cellulosic with abundant plasmodesmatal connections.
- Increased vacuolation, cell enlargement and new cell wall deposition are the characteristics of the cells present in elongation phase.
- The cells of maturation zone, attain their maximal size in terms of wall thickening and protoplasmic modifications.
- Geometrical growth is observed when resources are limited.

13. (*c*) Dr. F Went isolated auxin from *Avena* coleoptile tip. His experiment demonstrated the polar movement of auxins.

14. (*b*) The growth of living system per unit time is called absolute growth rate. In the given figure, two leaves, A and B are drawn, that are of different sizes, but show absolute increase in area in the given time to give new area of A_1 and B_1. Both leaves A and B have increased their area by 5 cm^2 in a given time to produce A_1 and B_1 leaves. Thus, both of them possess AGR of 5 cm^2.

15. (*b*) Both statement I and statement II are correct. Water, oxygen and nutrients are very essential elements for growth. The plant cells grow in size by cell enlargement, which in turn, requires water.

16. (*b*) Presence of auxin causes apical dominance in plants and cytokinins are responsible for breaking of apical dominance.

17. (*b*) The living differentiated cells, that have lost the capacity to divide can regain the capacity of division under certain conditions. This phenomenon is termed as dedifferentiation. For example, formation of meristems – interfascicular cambium and cork cambium from fully differentiated parenchyma cells.

18. (*d*) Statements I, III and V are correct. Incorrect statements can be corrected as

2, 4–D is widely used to kill dicotyledonous weeds, but do not affect mature monocotyledonous plants.

There are a number of events in the life of a plant where more than one PGRs interact to affect that event, e.g. dormancy in seeds/buds, abscission, senescence, apical dominance, etc.

19. (*b*) The difference in shapes of leaves produced in air and those produced in water in buttercup represent the heterophyllous development due to environment. This phenomenon of heterophylly is an example of plasticity.

20. (*b*) The medium in tissue culture provides all the essential nutrients required for the growth and division of callus. Coconut milk contains cytokinins which help in the shooting process.

21. (*b*) Here, X represents GA_3 (gibberellins), while Y represents ethylene ($H_2C=CH_2$). GA_3 or gibberellic acid causes an increase in length of axis, e.g., increase the length of grapes stalks. Ethylene induces flowering in mango.

22. (*a*) The plants display an open style of growth because at the terminals of their roots and shoots, meristems-which are ultimately incharge of their limitless expansion-are present. In these constantly dividing cells, viruses cannot proliferate.

Due to the existence of "meristems" in their bodies, plants have the extraordinary capacity to grow continuously throughout their lives. Cells in meristems can divide and self-replicate.

As a result of the meristem cells' ongoing addition of new cells to the plant body, this type of growth is known as an "open form of growth."

23. (*c*) In dicotyledonous plants and gymnosperms, the lateral meristems, vascular cambium and cork-cambium appear later in life and are called secondary meristems. These are the meristems that cause the increase in the girth of the organs in which they are active. This is known as secondary growth of the plant.

24. (*d*) Statement I is correct, but statement II is incorrect. Incorrect statement can be corrected as

The constantly dividing cells, both at the root apex and the shoot apex, represent the meristematic phase of growth.

25. (*b*) Both A and R are true and R is the correct explanation of A.

Plants follow different pathways in response to environment or phases of life to form different kinds of structures.

This ability is called plasticity, e.g. heterophylly in cotton, coriander and larkspur. In such plants, the leaves of the juvenile plant are different in shape from those in mature plants.

26. (*d*) The given graph represents linear or arithmetic growth in which only one daughter cell continues to divide, while the other differentiates and matures. The arithmetic growth occurs when resources are unlimited.

27. (*c*) The correct match is A-2, B-3, C-4, D-1.

2, 4-dichlorophenoxy acetic acid (2, 4-D) is a synthetic auxin.

GA_3 is used for horticultural practices which helps to delay senescence.

Ethephon is the source of ethylene. In an aqueous solution, it is readily absorbed and transported with the plant.

ABA has a significant role in regulating seed dormancy.

28. (*b*) Both A and R are true and R is the correct explanation of A.

During differentiation, cells undergo few to major structural changes both in their cell walls and protoplasm. For example, to form a tracheary element, the cells would lose their protoplasm.

29. (*d*) The incorrect statement can be corrected as

Oxygen helps in releasing metabolic energy essential for growth activities.

30. (*b*) Both statement I and statement II are correct.

ABA and GA are antagonistic to each other. A higher concentration of ABA leads to seed dormancy and promotes senescence, whereas a higher concentration of GA promotes seed germination and delays senescence.

Ethylene and auxin have synergistic effect on flowering, e.g., in pineapple blossom.

Ch-14 Breathing and Exchange of Gases

Topical Follow Thru

Test 1

1. (*c*) Trachea is a straight tube expanding upto the mid-thoracic cavity, which divided at the level of fifth thoracic vertebra into a right and left primary bronchi. Each bronchi undergoes repeated divisions to form secondary and tertiary bronchi and bronchioles ending up in very thin terminal bronchioles.

2. (*d*) The possible cause for sudden death of a person after accident, when his brain, heart, stomach and kidney have not suffered from any injury is the puncture of the diaphragm. Inspiration is initiated with the contraction of diaphragm and if the diaphragm itself got punctured, the person will not be able to breathe and will die due to lack of oxygen.

3. (*b*) The correct sequence of steps in the order of their occurrence during expiration is

$V \rightarrow VI \rightarrow II \rightarrow III \rightarrow IV \rightarrow I$

Relaxation of the diaphragm and intercostal muscles returns the diaphragm and sternum to their normal positions and reduce the thoracic volume, and thereby the pulmonary volume. This leads to an increase in intra pulmonary presence to slightly above the atmospheric pressure causing the expulsion of air from the lungs i.e expiration.

4. (*b*) I and III are incorrect, II and IV are correct. Incorrect matches can be corrected as

Inspiratory capacity (IC) = Tidal Volume [IV]+ Inspiratory Reserve Volume

Residual Volume [RV] = Total Lung Capacity [TLC] - Vital Capacity [VC]

5. (*c*) Inspiration is initiated by the contraction of diaphragm which increases the volume of thoracic chamber in the antero- posterior axis. The contraction of external inter-costal muscles lifts up the ribs and sternum causing an increase in the volume of thoracic chamber in the dorso- ventral axis.

6. (*a*) Statement I is incorrect, but statement II is correct. Statement I can be corrected as

A small flap of tissue called the epiglottis protects the larynx. The epiglottis covers the larynx to prevent food and liquid from going into the lungs.

7. (*a*) The trachea, primary, secondary and tertiary bronchi and initial bronchioles are supported by incomplete cartilaginous rings to prevent collapsing in absence of air. Cartilaginous rings are incomplete because this permits the trachea to collapse slightly to allow food to pass down the oesophagus. They reinforce the lateral and anterior sides of the trachea for protecting and maintaining the airway.

8. (*c*) Breathing involves two stages- inspriation and expiration.

Expiration is the process through which areolar air is released out.

It is a passive process, in this both diaphragm and intercostal muscle relax. This returns the diaphragm and sternum to their normal positions and reduce the thoracic volume, causing the expulsion of the air from the lung.

9. (*a*) In earthworm and *Nereis,* cutaneous respiration is the sole method of respiration. Their skin is thin moist and vascular. Thus, the skin functions as respiratory surface.

10. (*b*) *B* represents trachea in the diagram. It allow passage of inspired and expired air into and out of the lung. Other labelled parts *A*, *C* and *D* can be identified as epiglottis, alveoli and diaphragm, respectively.

11. (*b*) The correct match is A-2, B-3, C-4, D-1.
Bronchial tree conducts air from trachea to the alveoli and continues to filter air through its mucous lining.
Larynx is the passage way for air. It prevents foreign objects from entering trachea and houses vocal cords. It is also called sound box.
Trachea is a flexible tube which connects larynx with tree. It divides into left and right primary bronchi.
Pharynx is the passage for air from nasal cavity to larynx and for food from mouth cavity to oesophagus.

12. (*c*) Both A and R are true, but R is not the correct explanation of A.
With the help of additional muscles in the abdomen the strength of inspiration and expiration can be increased.

13. (*d*) The nasal cavity acts as a sensory organ that can recognise many different smells as it has an olfactory odour.
Incorrect statements can be corrected as
- The nasal cavity is an air-filled, hollow, and large space that is present above the nose and in the middle of the face.
- The cavities are produced by the extinction of the two nostrils, which is divided by the nasal septum.
- The nasal cavity is found in the upper region of the pharynx.

14. (*c*) Both A and R are true, but R is not the correct explanation of A.
The terminal bronchiole does not possess the cartilaginous rings. Instead, they are supported by smooth muscle tissue, which surrounds each bronchiole.

15. (*b*) The correct match is A-4, B-1, C-2, D-3.
Tidal volume is approx. 500 mL. Inspiratory Reserve Volume averages 2500-3000 mL. Expiratory Reserve Volume average 1000 mL to 1100 mL. Residual Volume average 1100 mL to 1200 mL.

16. (*d*) The correct match is A-2, B-4, C-3, D-1.
The epiglottis is a flap of tissue located at the top of the larynx. It acts as a lid, closing over the larynx during swallowing to prevent food and liquids from entering the airway.
The trachea is commonly known as the 'windpipe' because it is the passage through which air moves in and out of the lungs.
The larynx, also known as the 'voice box,' is located at the top of the trachea.
Alveoli are tiny air sacs located at the end of the bronchioles in the lungs.

17. (*c*) The alveolar duct is part of the respiratory zone, where gaseous exchange occurs, and therefore it does not belong to the conducting part of the respiratory system.

18. (*a*) The correct match is A-3, B-2, C- 4, D-1.
The thoracic chamber is formed dorsally (posterior) by vertebral column, laterally by ribs . The sternum (breastbone) is located at the front of the chest, the diaphragm is a muscle located below the lungs and forms the lower boundary of the ventral cavity, so it corresponds to the ventral surface.

19. (*c*) The correct increasing order of their respiratory volumes is IV < III < I < II
Tidal Volume (TV) - ~500 mL
Residual Volume (RV) - ~1200 mL
Expiratory Capacity (EC) - ~1000-1500 mL
Inspiratory Capacity (IC) - ~3000-3500 mL

20. (*c*) Intrapleural pressure is the pressure within the pleural cavity, (the space between the lungs and the chest wall). It is typically negative relative to atmospheric pressure and helps to keep the lungs expanded and adhered to the chest wall. This negative pressure is crucial for preventing the collapse of the lungs.

21. (*c*) During inspiration, the external intercostal muscles contract, not relax. This contraction causes the ribcage to move upward and outward, increasing the thoracic volume. Relaxation of the external intercostal muscles occurs during expiration.

22. (*b*) Both A and R are true and R is the correct explanation of A.
During deep inspiration (or deep inhalation), the diaphragm contracts and moves downward, and the external intercostal muscles contract to lift the rib cage upward and outward. This contraction increases the volume of the thoracic cavity and decreases the pressure within it, allowing air to flow into the lungs.

23. (*c*) Incorrect statement can be corrected as
Exchange part of respiratory system i.e. alveoli and their ducts act as diffusion site for oxygen and carbon dioxide between blood and air.

24. (*d*) The correct sequence is II < IV < I < III.
Use of moist cuticle for gaseous exchange takes place in earthworm.
Tracheal system is present in insects to transport atmospheric air within body.
Gills are used by aquatic arthropods and molluscas.
Lungs are the vascularised bags used by terrestrial forms.

25. (*d*) Statement I is correct, but statement II is incorrect . The incorrect statement can be corrected as.
The rate of respiration affects how quickly air is moved in and out of the lungs, but the total volume of air that the lungs can hold (pulmonary volume) is determined by lung capacity, which remains relatively constant.

Test 2

1. (*c*) In the tissues, low pO_2, high pCO_2, high H^+ concentration and higher temperature are the favourable conditions for dissociation of oxygen from the oxyhaemoglobin.

2. (*c*) In asthma, bronchi swell and spasm of the smooth muscle takes place in the wall of smaller bronchi and bronchioles which obstruct the airways.

3. (*a*) The partial pressure of O_2 is lesser in systemic veins than in systemic arteries. The partial pressure of CO_2 is higher in tissues than in systemic arteries.

4. (*b*) Both A and R are true and R is the correct explanation of A.

RBCs contain a very high concentration of the enzyme carbonic anhydrase. This enzyme facilitates the following reaction in both directions.

$$CO_2 + H_2O \xrightleftharpoons{\text{Carbonic anhydrase}} H_2CO_3 \xrightleftharpoons{\text{Carbonic anhydrase}} HCO_3^- + H^+$$

5. (*b*) The correct match is A-2, B-1, C-4, D-3

pCO_2 in oxygenated blood is 40 mm Hg.

pCO_2 in atmospheric air is 0.3 mm Hg.

pO_2 in oxygenated blood and alveoli is 95 and 104 mm Hg, respectively.

6. (*b*) Given that,

100 mL of blood $= 15$ gm of haemoglobin

1 mL of blood

$= \frac{15}{100}$ gm of haemoglobin

135 mL of blood

$= \frac{15}{100} \times 135$ gm of haemoglobin

$\therefore$ 135 mL of blood will have 20.2 gm of haemoglobin

Also,

1 gm of haemoglobin carries $= 1.34$ mL of O_2

20.2 gm of haemoglobin will carry $= 1.34 \times 20.2 = 27$ mL of O_2.

Hence, 135 mL of blood will carry 27 mL of O_2.

7. (*d*) A chemosensitive area is situated adjacent to the rhythm centre which is highly sensitive to CO_2 and hydrogen ions. Increase in these substances can activate this centre, which in turn can signal the rhythm centre to make necessary adjustments in the respiratory process by which these substances can be eliminated.

8. (*c*) Increase in the CO_2 content of the blood decreases the pH of the blood. This decreases the affinity of O_2 with Hb. This is called Bohr effect and is closely related to the fact that deoxygenated Hb binds hydrogen ions more actively than does the Hb. This facilitates gaseous exchange because more O_2 released in the tissues where the amount of CO_2 is more due to metabolic activity. At the same time, more O_2 is taken up by the lungs or gills when the amount of CO_2 is low.

9. (*c*) In the given diagram of diffusion membrane A and B represents blood capillary and alveolar cavity. The oxygen concentration is low in blood capillary as compare to alveolar cavity.

10. (*a*) Statement I is incorrect, but statement II is correct. Statement I can be corrected as

Every 100 mL of oxygenated blood can deliver around 5 mL of O_2 to the tissues under normal physiological conditions.

11. (*a*) Statements I, III and V are correct, but statements II and IV are incorrect. These can be corrected as

About 7% of CO_2 is transported in a dissolved state through plasma, 23% as Carboaminohaemoglobin and 70% as bicarbonates.

Oxyhaemoglobin behaves as a strong acid. As the amount of oxyhaemoglobin formed in the lungs increases, more H^+ ions are released in the blood, thus increasing the acidity of blood. This is called Haldane effect.

12. (*c*) The incorrect statement can be corrected as

The partial pressure of O_2 and CO_2 in the systemic veins is not same as that in pulmonary vein. The partial pressure of oxygen and carbon dioxide in systemic vein is 40 mm Hg and 45 mm Hg, respectively and in pulmonary vein pO_2 and pCO_2 are 95 mm Hg and 40 mm Hg, respectively.

13. (*b*) Statements I, II and III are correct. While statements IV and V are incorrect and can be corrected as Occupational respiratory disorder is caused by inhalation of dust from the work place carrying particulate matter. The main organ affected is lung.

In asthma, there is spastic contraction of bronchiolar muscle during expiration.

14. (*b*) Basic rhythm of respiration is controlled by respiratory rhythm center present in the medulla region of the brain. Another centre in brain stem called pneumotaxic center that helps to coordinate the transition between inspiration and expiration is located in the pons region of brain stem.

15. (*c*) Cigarette smoking is the usual cause of emphysema. It is a chronic disorder in which alveolar walls are damaged due to which respiratory surface is decreased.

16. (*d*) Statement IV is correct while statements I, II and III are incorrect and can be corrected as

In tissues low pO_2, high CO_2, high H^+ concentration and high temperature favours dissociation of oxygen from the oxyhaemoglobin.

At the alveolar site where pCO_2 is low, carbonic acid (H_2CO_3) leads to the formation of CO_2 and H_2O in the presence of carbonic anhydrase.

Type II cells secrete surfactant to reduce surface tension and prevent alveolar collapse.

17. (*c*) Carbon monoxide has a much higher affinity for haemoglobin compared to oxygen. When CO binds to haemoglobin, it forms carboxyhaemoglobin, which significantly reduces haemoglobin's ability to bind and transport oxygen. This leads to impaired oxygen delivery to tissues

18. (*b*) The oxygen-haemoglobin dissociation curve illustrates the relationship betweeen the partial pressure of oxygen (pO_2) and the percentage of haemoglobin saturated with oxygen. A rightward shift in the curve indicates a decreased affinity of haemoglobin for oxygen, meaning that haemoglobin for oxygen, meaning that haemoglobin releases oxygen more readily.

19. (*b*) Both statement I and statement II are correct.
The primary function of systemic arteries is transporting oxygen-rich blood to organs and tissues.
Systemic arteries carry oxygenated blood from the left ventricle of the heart to the various tissues throughout the body with partial pressure of O_2 as 95mmHg and partial pressure of CO_2 as 40 mmHg.

20. (*b*) The correct match is A-2, B-1, C-3, D-4.
The chemosensitive area, located in the medulla oblongata, responds primarily to changes in the concentration of hydrogen ions.
The pneumotaxic center, located in the pons, helps to regulate the rate and pattern of breathing. It functions to inhibit inspiration, thereby reducing the duration of inspiration.
The rhythm center, located in the medulla oblongata, is responsible for generating the basic rhythm of breathing.
Role of oxygen is often considered less significant compared to the role of CO_2 and pH in controlling the rate and depth of breathing.

21. (*b*) Emphysema is characterised by the destruction of alveolar walls leading to increased lung compliance and difficulty in expiration. Alveolar walls are damaged due to decrease in surfactant.

22. (*b*) Both A and R are true and the R is the correct explanation of the A.
The rate of diffusion of gases across a membrane is influenced by several factors, including the thickness of the membrane and the solubility of the gases. According to Fick's law of diffusion, gases diffuse more readily if they are more soluble and if the membrane is thinner. CO_2 is more soluble in plasma than O_2, which contributes to its more efficient transport in the blood.

23. (*d*) Statement I is correct, while statements II , III and IV are incorrect and can be corrected as
The chloride shift occurs primarily in the tissues where CO_2 is produced and needs to be transported in the lungs.
The chloride shift is more pronounced in tissues with high pCO_2 levels where CO_2 is being converted into bicarbonate ions.

24. (*c*) Haemoglobin assists in the transport of CO_2 from the tissues to the lungs by binding CO_2 to form carbaminohemoglobin. This process helps carry CO_2 through the blood, where it is eventually released in the lungs and exhaled.

25. (*b*) Both statement I and statement II are correct. These can be explained as
The limit of exchange of gases between alveoli and pulmonary blood is diffusion capacity.
Oxygen content of the blood after leaving lungs is greater than that of the blood entering the lungs.

Chapter Break Thru

1. (*c*) Lungs do not collapse between breaths and some air always remains in the lungs, which can never be expelled. It is contributed by the negative intra pleural pressure which is lower than the atmospheric pressure that pulls the air outside to the lungs caused by elasticity of lungs, elasticity of chest wall and surface tension.

2. (*c*) Both A and R are true, but R is not the correct explanation of A.
Vital capacity is higher in people living at high altitude because the pressure of oxygen in the atmosphere is less, the body compensates by increasing ventilation. The topographical condition enables efficient lungs oxygen uptake, making the lungs work effectively by activating respiratory muscles and raising the heart rate and also there is improvement in the chest wall elasticity, resulting in higher level of the lungs function. Vital capacity is the amount of air, which one can inhale and exhale with maximum effort.

3. (*a*) Lungs are covered by a double layered pleura, with pleural fluid between them. It reduces friction on the lung- surface. The outer pleural membrane is in close contact with the thoracic lining whereas inner pleural membrane is in contact with the lung surface.

4. (*b*) Brain stem consist of 3 regions, i.e. midbrain, pons and medulla. Out of these three, medulla region of brain stem has respiratory rhythm center.

5. (*a*) Statement I is incorrect, but statement II is correct. Incorrect statement can be corrected as
The thoracic chamber is formed ventrally by sternum, lateraly by the ribs, dorsally by the vertebral column and on the lower side by the dome-shaped diaphragm.

6. (*b*) Larynx is entirely made up of cartilage. It is a cartilaginous box which helps in sound production and hence also known as sound box.

7. (*b*) The walls of trachea are non-collapsible due to the presence of incomplete rings of hyaline cartilage. The trachea, primary, secondary and tertiary bronchi, and initial bronchioles are supported by these incomplete cartilaginous sings.

8. (*c*) If the expiratory capacity is 1500 mL and tidal volume is 500 mL,
Then, the expiratory reserve volume will be
Expiratory Reserve Volume = Expiratory capacity – Tidal Volume
= 1500 mL – 500 mL = 1000 mL

9. (*c*) Both statement I and statement II are incorrect and can be corrected as
Exchange part is the site of actual diffusion of O_2 and CO_2 between blood and atmospheric air.
The anatomical set up of lungs in thorax is such that any change in the volume of the thoracic cavity will be reflected in the lung (pulmonary) cavity.

10. (*b*) Inspiration can occur if the pressure within the lungs is less than the atmospheric pressure, ie. there is a negative pressure in the lungs with respect to atmospheric pressure.

11. (*c*) The sequence of steps in the correct order of their occurrence during the process of inspiration is $V \rightarrow VI \rightarrow II \rightarrow I \rightarrow III \rightarrow IV$.

Inspiration is initiated by the contraction of diaphragm which increases the volume of thoracic chamber in the anterio-posterior axis. The contraction of external intercostal muscles lifts up the ribs and the sternum causing an increase in the volume of the thoracic chamber in the dorso-ventral axis. The overall increase in the thoracic volume causes a similar increase in pulmonary volume. This causes decrease in intra- pulmonary pressure which forces the air from outside to move into the lungs, i.e inspiration.

12. (*a*) The incorrect statement can be corrected as

Each terminal bronchiole gives rise to a number of very thin, irregular walled and vascularised bag-like structures called alveoli.

Rest other statements are correct.

13. (*d*) The incorrectly matched pair can be corrected as

Forceful expiration is an active process which occurs due to contraction of internal intercostal and abdominal muscles.

14. (*a*) Oxyhaemoglobin dissociates into oxygen and deoxyhaemoglobin when pO_2 is low in tissues. At high pO_2 in tissues and low pO_2 in blood oxyhaemoglobin will not dissociate into O_2 and haemoglobin and thus would not carry back CO_2 to lungs.

15. (*b*) The incorrect statement can be corrected as

Oxyhaemoglobin acts as strong acid. As more oxyhaemoglobin is formed, more H^+ ions are released, which increases the acidity of blood.

16. (*c*) The incorrectly matched pair can be corrected as

In deoxygenated blood, partial pressure of oxygen is 40 mmHg.

Rest of the options are correctly matched.

17. (*c*) Only statement I is correct regarding carbon dioxide transport. Statements II and III are incorrect and can be corrected as

The CO_2 dissolved in plasma forms carbonic acid in the presence of carbonic anhydrase. The concentration of carbonic acid remains constant due to the presence of sodium.

18. (*b*) Pneumotoxic center indirectly switch off inspiratory neurons, which shorten the duration of inspiration. When this region is more active, breathing rate is more rapid.

19. (*b*) The correct match is A-1, B-3, C-2, D-4

Total Lung Capacity includes FRC + TV + IRV

Expiratory capacity includes ERV + TV

Inspiratory Capacity includes IRV + TV

Vital Capacity includes ERV + TV + IRV.

20. (*d*) Carbon monoxide forms a stable compound with haemoglobin called carboxyhaemoglobin as the affinity of haemoglobin for carbon monoxide is 250 times greater than its affinity for oxygen.

This causes low supply of O_2 in cells leading to headache, nausea, dizzines, resulting in death too. Thus, the patient has been inhaling polluted air containing high content of carbon monoxide.

21. (*d*) If partial pressure of CO_2 rises to 100 mm Hg, then the person would die of oxygen deficiency because haemoglobin would not be able to load or unload the oxygen.

22. (*b*) The correct match is A–4, B–3, C–2, D–1.

The Bohr's effect describes haemoglobin's lower affinity for oxygen due to increase in the partial pressure of carbon dioxide. This lower affinity, in turn, enhances the dissociation of oxygen into tissues to meet the oxygen demand of the tissue.

Shift to left indicates the association of O_2 from Hb which occurs in the alveoli, it occurs when there is low H^+ concentration.

Shift to right indicates dissociation of oxygen from Hb in the body tissue. High H^+ concentration favours shift to right.

Myoglobin has more affinity for oxygen and shows hyperbolic curve.

23. (*d*) Statement I is correct, but statement II is incorrect and can be corrected as

About 20-25% of CO_2 is carried out by carbamino haemoglobin transported by RBCs whereas 70% of it carried as bicarbonate. About 7% of CO_2 is carried in a dissolved state through plasma.

24. (*c*) When the internal intercostal muscles contract and diaphragm relax, the ribs move downward and inward and diaphragm becomes dome- shaped, thus decreasing the volume of thoracic cavity and increasing the pressure inside as compared to the atmospheric pressure outside. This will cause the air to move out.

25. (*b*) In the given diagram, *A*, *B*, *C*, and *D* represent O_2 , CO_2, 40 mm Hg and 45 mm Hg respectively.

26. (*b*) The incorrect statement can be corrected as

Diffusion of gases take place across alveolar membrane. The membrane is very thin and richly supplied with blood capillaries.

27. (*a*) Statements II, III and V are correct. Statements I and IV are incorrect. Incorrect statements can be corrected as

Oxyhaemoglobin dissociates near tissues due to increase in acidity and decrease in pH. Arterial blood carries 48 mL carbon dioxide per 100 mL of blood.

28. (*b*) In emphysema, shortness of breath is caused by permanent damage to the small air sacs (alveoli) and small airways in lungs due to which respiratory surface is decreased.

29. (*c*) The correct matches are A–4, B–1, C–2, D–3.
In asthma, there is inflammation of bronchi and bronchioles. Silicosis is an occupational respiratory disorder. In emphysema, there is an abnormal distension of alveolar sac. Regular coughing is one of symptoms of bronchitis.

30. (*d*) Statement I is correct, but statement II is incorrect. It can be corrected as
Silicosis cannot be treated specifically. It is a type of chronic lungs disease, caused by the inhalation of large amounts of crystalline silica dust over many years.

31. (*b*) Statement I and II are correct.
During expiration, relaxation of diaphragm and the inter coastal muscles decreases the thoracic volume.
As a result, diaphragm comes back to its original position and become dome shaped. This leads to decrease in pulmonary volume and air is expelled out of the lungs.

32. (*c*) The incorrect statement can be corrected as
ERV + RV together constitute functional residual capacity which is volume of air that will remain in lungs of healthy individual after normal expiration.

33. (*b*) Both A and R are true and the R is the correct explanation for the A.
Increased pCO_2 rather than decreased pO_2 is the predominant factor driving increased breathing during intense activities can be explained by the sensitivity of central chemoreceptors to pH and pCO_2.

34. (*c*) Residual Volume (RV) cannot be measured directly with a spirometer as it represents the air remaining in the lungs after a maximal exhalation.

35. (*c*) A high pO_2 at the lungs (not at the tissue level) causes the curve to shift left, indicating increased haemoglobin affinity for oxygen. The right shift is associated with lower pO_2 or higher pCO_2 conditions, which help release oxygen in the tissues.

36. (*d*) Statement I is correct, but Statement II is incorrect. The incorrect statement can be corrected as
The Bohr effect is associated with a decrease in pH (acidosis), not an increase, which reduces haemoglobin's affinity for oxygen.

37. (*b*) External intercoastal muscles are located between the ribs and are responsible for elevating the ribs and expanding the thoracic cavity during inspiration. This action increases the volume of the thoracic cavity and allows air to flow into the lungs.
Diaphragm is a dome-shaped muscle located beneath the lungs. During inspiration, it contracts and moves downward, increasing the vertical dimension of the thoracic cavity and creating a negative pressure that draws air into the lungs.

38. (*a*) Statement I, II and IV are correct while statement III is incorrect. Incorrect statement can be corrected as
Silicosis is a type of pneumoconiosis caused by the inhalation of fine silica dust. It is primarily associated with occupations involving exposure to silica dust, such as mining.

39. (*a*) The nasal cavity warms, moistens, and filters the air before it travels to the lower respiratory tract.

40. (*a*) A is false, but R is true. A can be corrected as
The oxygen-haemoglobin dissociation curve shifts to the right in response to increased body temperature. This rightward shift indicates that haemoglobin has a decreased affinity for oxygen, which promotes oxygen release in the tissues.

41. (*a*) TLC is the sum of tidal volume, inspiratory reserve volume, expiratory reserve volume, and residual volume.

42. (*a*) Statements I, III and IV are correct while statement II is incorrect. The incorrect statement can be corrected as
According to Fick's law of diffusion, the rate of diffusion is inversely proportional to the thickness of the membrane. Therefore, diffusion is slower across thicker membranes.

43. (*c*) Statements I and IV are correct, while statements II and III are incorrect. The incorrect statements can be corrected as
The parietal pleura lines the thoracic cavity, while the visceral pleura adheres directly to the lung surface.
During normal respiration, the pleural cavity pressure is actually negative relative to atmospheric pressure. This negative pressure helps keep the lungs inflated and prevents collapsing.

44. (*b*) Both statement I and statement II are correct.
Peripheral chemoreceptors play a crucial role in detecting hypoxemia (low oxygen levels) and help regulate ventilation to maintain proper oxygenation of the blood. Central chemoreceptors, located in the medulla oblongata of the brainstem, primarily respond to changes in the pCO_2 levels in the cerebrospinal fluid. Since CO_2 can cross the blood-brain barrier and influence pH levels in the cerebrospinal fluid, these chemoreceptors are also sensitive to changes in pH.

45. (*b*) Contraction causes the diaphragm to move downward. As a result, the volume of the thoracic cavity increases. This expansion creates a negative pressure inside the lungs relative to atmospheric pressure, allowing air to flow into the lungs.

46. (*c*) Both A and R are true, but the R is not the correct explanation of A.
Amphibians possess highly vascularised skin. This vascularisation allows for efficient exchange of gases (oxygen and carbon dioxide) through the skin in a process called cutaneous respiration. This type of respiration is especially important in aquatic environments.

47. (*d*) The correct sequence for the transport of oxygen across blood is II $\rightarrow$ I $\rightarrow$ III $\rightarrow$ IV $\rightarrow$ V.
Oxygen moves from the alveoli, where its partial pressure is high, into the blood in the pulmonary capillaries, where its partial pressure is lower.

Once in the blood, oxygen binds to haemoglobin molecules.

The oxygen-bound haemoglobin carries oxygen through the bloodstream to the systemic circulation.

The oxygenated blood is pumped from the left side of the heart to the rest of the body.

In the systemic capillaries, where the partial pressure of oxygen is lower in the tissues compared to the blood, oxygen dissociates from haemoglobin and diffuses into the tissues.

48. (*b*) The incorrect match pair can be corrected as

The external intercostal muscles are involved in inspiration by elevating the ribs and expanding the thoracic cavity. These are not primarily involved in forced inspiration.

49. (*d*) Exchange of ions between RBC's and plasma at ling surface results is newerse chloride at shift to maintain pH. Chloride ions are pumped out and bicarbonate ions are taken inside which results in remonal of CO_2 from blood.

50. (*d*) Statement I is correct, but statement II is incorrect.

The incorrect statement can be corrected as

Total volume of air expired after normal inspiration is expiratory capacity which includes Tidal Volume (TV) and Expiratory Reserve Volume (ERV).

Ch-15 Body Fluids and Circulation

Topical Follow Thru

Test 1

1. (*c*) Eosinophils are the type of granulocytes that resist infections and are involved in allergic reactions.

2. (*a*) A is false, but R is true. A can be corrected as

A person with A^- blood can safely donate to a person with A^+ blood group as A^- individual lacks Rh antigens and antibody, thus there will be no cross reaction on mixing the blood of the A^- and A^+ individuals.

3. (*a*) Statements II and III are correct, while statements I, IV and V are incorrect and can be corrected as

• Rh antibodies develop in the blood plasma.

• Rh^- mother is given anti-Rh antibody after first pregnancy with Rh^+ child.

• Rh antibodies of the mother react with Rh antigens of the foetus during second pregnancy of Rh^- mother.

4. (*c*) The incorrect statement can be corrected as

Coagulating factors or clotting factors are present in the blood plasma in an inactive form.

5. (*b*) A person with dengue haemorrhagic fever has abnormally decreased levels of thrombocytes or platelets. This makes him/her susceptible to internal bleeding as the clotting process is affected by abnormally low platelets.

6. (*c*) Both statement I and statement II are incorrect. These can be corrected as

Spleen is regarded as the cemetery of RBCs. Erythrocytes live longer (120 days) than leucocytes of blood (12-20 days).

7. (*a*) The correct sequence is B-D-A-C-E

• At the injured site, both the damaged blood vessels and the platelets release certain clotting factors.

• By enzymatic cascade activation, thrombokinase is formed.

• Thrombokinase activates prothrombin into thrombin in the presence of calcium ions.

• Thrombin promotes conversion of soluble fibrinogen to insoluble fibrin.

• Fibrin forms a mesh where blood is trapped. This dark coloured structure formed is called a clot or coagulum.

8. (*d*) The correct match is A-4, B-3, C-2, D-1.

• About 60-65% of blood cells are neutrophils and hence, the most abundant WBCs.

• Basophils secrete heparin, serotonin, histamine, etc., all of which are involved in inflammatory reactions.

• Eosinophils resist infections and are associated with allergies. They constitute 2-3% of the total leucocytes.

• Monocytes along with neutrophils are phagocytic in nature and can engulf foreign pathogens.

9. (*d*) A is true, but R is false. R can be corrected as

Calcium ions are needed for the conversion of fibrinogen (soluble) to fibrin (insoluble).

10. (*c*) A person with B^- blood group can safely receive blood from O^- individuals as people with O^- blood group lack both antigens A and B, as well as Rh antigen. Hence, there is no chance of agglutination reaction between antigen and antibodies.

11. (*b*) Heparin is an anticoagulant, which is added to the blood collecting vials, to prevent blood from clotting in the tubes.

12. (*a*) Statement I is incorrect, but statement II is correct. The incorrect statement can be corrected as

Exchange of gases between blood and cells occur through the interstitial fluid.

13. (*c*) An antigen-antibody reaction will not occur when a person with type 'A' blood, is given type 'O' blood.

'A' blood group has antigen 'A' on RBCs and anti-B in the plasma. Since, there is no antigen on RBC in blood group 'O', so there is no antigen-antibody reaction.

14. (*c*) The type of WBCs which are abundantly present in the lymph are the lymphocytes.

15. (*c*) Statements III and V are correct. Statements I, II and IV are incorrect and can be corrected as

- Erythrocytes (RBCs) are enucleated and formed in the red bone marrow in the adult humans.
- Lymphocytes are agranulocytes that are responsible for immune response of the body. It is the platelets or thrombocytes which are produced from megakaryocytes.
- Blood group 'O' has anti-A and anti-B in the plasma.

16. (*d*) The correct match is A-2, B-1, C-4, D-3.

- Clotting factors are present in inactive form in blood plasma.
- Solutes (like Na^+, Mg^{2+}, etc.) present in plasma maintain the osmolarity of blood.
- Fibrinogen is involved in clotting and is present in soluble form in plasma.
- Globulins are involved in the immune system of the body.

17. (*b*) A healthy individual has 12-16 gms of haemoglobin in every 100 mL of blood. Haemoglobin is responsible for transporting oxygen in blood. Thus a decreased amount of haemoglobin would lower the oxygen carrying capacity of blood, and would in turn lead to lesser oxygen reaching the cells of the body. Oxygen is required for cellular respiration to generate energy. Hence the person feels easily tired by daily work.

18. (*d*) A is true, but R is false. R can be corrected as

Histamines released by basophils are associated with inflammation. Basophils secrete histamine, serotonin, heparin, etc., and are involved in inflammatory reactions. When ants bite, they release formic acid into the skin which can cause inflammation due to release of these chemicals.

19. (*a*) The safest option for this treatment would be serum. As serum has the same composition as plasma but lacks clotting factors and blood cells. Thus, serum would not clot when standing and would contain antibodies from the recovered person.

20. (*a*) The incorrect statement can be corrected as

Antibodies are found in both plasma and serum. Other statements can be explained as

Hormones are present in both plasma and serum.

Plasma is the liquid portion of blood. Plasma minus clotting factors is serum. Hence serum would not clot. Fibrinogens are involved in clotting hence they would be absent in serum.

21. (*a*) The correct match is A-2, B-3, C-1, D-4.

- A^- person has antigen A on surface of RBC and anti B antibody in plasma, however lacks Rh antigen.
- AB^+ person has antigen A and antigen B along with Rh antigen, but lacks antibodies.
- O^- person has anti A and anti B antibodies in plasma, however lacks antigen on RBC.
- O^+ person has anti A and anti B antibodies along with Rh antigen.

22. (*d*) If Rh^- mother is pregnant with Rh^+ child for first time, during her delivery of the first child, there is a possibility of exposure of the maternal blood to small amounts of the Rh+ve blood from the foetus. In such cases, the mother starts preparing antibodies against Rh antigen in her blood. During her second time being pregnant with Rh^+ child, the Rh antibodies from the mother (Rh-ve) can leak into the blood of the foetus (Rh+ve) and destroy the foetal RBCs. This could be fatal to the foetus or could cause severe anaemia and jaundice to the baby. This condition is called erythroblastosis foetalis.

23. (*b*) Both statement I and statement II are correct

Plasma plays an important role in initiating coagulation because most of the clotting factors present in plasma are in inactive form.

Platelet transfusion is required for people having abnormally low platelet count which causes clotting disorders.

24. (*c*) In the blood coagulation or clotting process, calcium ions are needed for conversion of inactive prothrombin into active thrombin. Calcium also plays a role in conversion of soluble fibrinogen into insoluble fibrin threads. However, calcium is not directly required for formation of thromboplastin and release of platelet factors.

25. (*c*) Interstitial fluid that leaks from the capillaries collects in the interstitial spaces but is drained into lymphatic ducts. In the absence of lymphatic vessels, the fluid would accumulate which would cause inflammation of the tissue. Diffusion of nutrients and oxygen would also be affected in the swollen tissue.

Test 2

1. (*b*) Tunica intima is the innermost layer of artery, made up of squamous epithelium that is in direct contact with blood.

2. (*c*) Both A and R are true, but R is not the correct explanation of A. A can be explained as

A person with less than 45 beats/minute requires a pacemaker implantation as the Sino Atrial Node (SAN) or the natural pacemaker, that initiates and maintains rhythmic contraction of the heart, is impaired in the given person.

3. (*c*) A is capillary and B is lymph vessel. Capillaries are formed by the fusion of arteries and veins and drain the blood into veins. Lymph vessels collect tissue fluid from the interstitial spaces and return them to circulation *via* veins.

4. (*b*) Statements I, III and V are correct. Statements II and IV are incorrect and can be corrected as

• Left atrium receives oxygenated blood, while the right atrium receives deoxygenated blood.

• Circulation in frogs is less efficient than birds. This is because frogs have incomplete double circulation where both oxygenated and deoxygenated blood gets mixed.

5. (*b*) Both statement I and statement II are correct. A thick-walled the inter-ventricular septum, separates the left and right ventricles that prevents mixing of blood. Damage to the interventricular septum can lower oxygen levels in blood. It ensures that blood flows properly through the heart.

6. (*c*) The correct match is A-2, B-1, C-3, D-4.

• Earthworms have a closed circulatory system where blood flows through closed network of blood vessels.

• Molluscs like snails have open circulatory system where blood is pumped into open spaces called the sinuses.

• Crocodiles though a reptile, have four-chambered heart with two atria and two ventricles.

• Frogs are amphibians and have a three-chambered heart with two atria and a single ventricle.

7. (*a*) Carotid arteries are the strongest blood vessels with thicker walls and muscular in nature. They consist of three distinct layers- tunica externa, tunica media and tunica intima, which are rigid, thick and highly muscular.

8. (*a*) The correct sequence is B-C-D-E-A.

• The action potential is generated at the sino atrial node (SAN), which initiates the heartbeat.

• The impulses next reach to the AV node located in the lower left corner of the right atrium close to the atrio-ventricular septum.

• From the AV node, the impulses are transmitted by the AV bundle reaching up to the interventricular septum.

• Next, the impulses are transmitted by the bundle of His.

• The Purkinje fibres finally conduct the impulses through the entire musculature of the heart.

9. (*b*) 20%. Cardiac output = Strokes volume × Heart rate.

During exercise, Cardiac output
= 5880 mL

Strokes volume = 70 mL

Therefore, 5880 = 70 × Heart rate

Heart rate = 5880/70= 84 beats/minute

Heart rate at rest = 70 beats/minute

Increase in heart rate
= (84-70)/70 × 100
=14/70 × 100 = 20%

10. (*b*) Both statement I and statement II are correct. Blood pressure is a measurement of the force that is used to pump blood through the arteries. There is usually a constant rate of blood pressure. The normal range of blood pressure in humans is 120/80 mm Hg. The two values denote the systolic and diastolic pressure, respectively.

11. (*d*) Aortic arch carries oxygenated blood from the left ventricle to all the parts of the body.

12. (*d*) Structure P is the liver. The hepatic portal vein carries blood from intestine to the liver before it is delivered to the systemic circulation.

13. (*b*) C is pulmonary vein that carries oxygenated blood from lungs to the left atria. D is aorta, the largest artery that pumps oxygenated blood to the body parts.

14. (*c*) During ventricular systole, the atrio-ventricular valves are shut closed to prevent back flow of blood into the atria. This results in production of the first heart sound, lub.

15. (*b*) A normal ECG has P-wave that represents atrial depolarisation, QRS complex represents ventricular depolarisation and T-wave that represents ventricular repolarisation.

16. (*b*) The correct sequence is B-A-C-E-D.

• The atria and ventricles are in relaxed state, blood from vena cava and pulmonary veins fill the heart chambers.

• The SAN generates action potential which stimulates both the atria to undergo a simultaneous contraction.

• Blood flow increases to the ventricles by 30 % due to atrial systole. The action potential is conducted to the ventricular side by the AV node and AV bundle from where the bundle of His transmits it through the entire ventricular musculature.

• As ventricles contract, the ventricular pressure increases causing the semilunar valves to open. Blood flows through the semilunar valves into the circulatory pathways. The AV valves are closed at this stage.

• As the ventricles relax, the ventricular pressure falls, causing the closure of semilunar valves which prevents the backflow of blood into the ventricles.

17. (*d*) Left atrium is exposed to more pressure than right atrium and thus have thicker walls than right atrium. Ventricles pump blood to either the lungs or the entire body, hence have thicker walls than atria. Also, the left ventricle pumps blood to the entire body compared to the right one which pumps blood to the lungs and hence, left ventricular walls are the thickest.

18. (*d*) Statements I, IV and V are correct, while statements II and III are incorrect and can be corrected as

• Contraction of the ventricles start shortly after Q-wave of QRS complex of an ECG.

• Counting the number of QRS complexes can give the heart rate.

19. (*c*) The septa separates the heart chambers and clearly demarcates the right and left side of the heart. This ensures, the right side of the heart deals with deoxygenated blood, while the left side of the heart deals with oxygenated blood, hence preventing mixing of the blood. This allows oxygen to be delivered quickly and efficiently to all the cells of the body for proper utilisation.

20. (*a*) Stimulation of adrenal medullary hormones and sympathetic branch of the autonomic nervous system, causes an increase in cardiac output and hence the heart rate.

21. (*d*) The correct match is A-2, B-1, C-3, D-4.

- The bundle of His originates from the AV bundle and divides into right and left bundles.
- AV node is located near the lower left corner of the right atrium close to the atrio-ventricular septum.
- Purkinje fibres spread along the ventricular musculature, conducting the action potential and thus bring about contraction of the ventricles.
- SAN is the natural pacemaker of the heart where action potential generates. It is responsible for initiation of heartbeat because of its autoexcitable nature.

22. (*b*) Medulla can control the cardiac functions through the autonomic nervous system. Initiation of the action potential occurs through the SAN located in the right atrium, which is autoexcitable in nature.

23. (*d*) Acute chest pain is often referred to as angina. This condition occurs due to reduced oxygen supply to the heart muscles. Often deposition of calcium, cholesterol, etc. can lead to narrowing of the arteries that can cause angina. However, sudden stoppage of heart is a different condition called cardiac arrest.

24. (*c*) Both A and R are true, but R is not the correct explanation of A. A can be explained as

A person with hypertension may be prescribed with medications for kidney damage as well, because persistent high blood pressure leads to heart diseases and also can damage vital organs of the body like kidneys and brain.

25. (*a*) The incorrect statement can be corrected as

Failure of enough blood to reach the heart is called myocardial ischemia. Atherosclerosis occurs due to the deposition of fat or cholesterol in the artery supplying blood to the musculature of heart.

Chapter Break Thru

1. (*c*) Platelets are formed from megakaryocytes which are special cells in the bone marrow.

2. (*a*) A is false, but R is true. A can be corrected as

O negative individual can donate blood to any one without compatibility test. O positive person lacks antigen A and B, however they contain Rh antigen. Thus, blood group matching is essential during blood transfusion.

3. (*b*) Correct components are B, C and E. Plasma without clotting factor forms serum. Haemoglobin is a component of the red blood cells.

4. (*b*) Basophils cause inflammatory reactions due to the secretion of histamine, heparin, etc. They are the least abundant WBCs (0.5-1%) and they are extremely short lived.

5. (*d*) Bicuspid valve regulates the flow of oxygenated blood from left atrium to left ventricle.

Aortic semilunar valve regulates the flow of oxygenated blood from left ventricle to the aorta. Tricuspid valve regulates flow of deoxygenated blood from right atrium to right ventricle, while pulmonary semilunar valve directs flow of deoxygenated blood from right ventricle to pulmonary artery.

6. (*c*) The type of circulation shown in the diagram is of a fish. Fishes have single circulation where deoxygenated blood is pumped by the heart to the gills. Thereafter, oxygenated blood from the gills is distributed to the rest of the body and deoxygenated blood from the body is drained back to the heart. In fishes, heart is two chambered with one atria and one ventricle.

7. (*a*) Statement I is incorrect, but statement II is correct. Statement I can be corrected as

An increase in ventricular pressure during ventricular systole forces open the semilunar valves.

8. (*b*) At the end of ventricular diastole, the fall in ventricular pressure opens the AV valves. If the valves do not open, blood drained by the veins into the atrium cannot flow into the ventricles. This would affect the volume of blood pumped by ventricles during systole and affect stroke volume and cardiac output. However, the generation of action potential takes place in the SAN, which will be unaffected.

9. (*b*) Only statement A is correct. While statements B, C and D can be corrected as

- The T-wave represents end of cardiac cycle.
- P-wave represents the excited state of atria.
- QRS represents ventricular depolarisation.

10. (*d*) Parasympathetic nerves of ANS cause a decrease in the rate of heart beat, speed of conduction of action potential and thereby the cardiac output.

11. (*d*) A is the SAN, B is AVN, C is bundle of His and D is left and right bundle branches. The SAN initiates the impulse for contraction of the atria during atrial systole. This increases the blood flow into the ventricles by 30 %. Thereafter, the impulses are conducted by the AVN, AV bundle and bundle of His to bring about contraction of the ventricles.

12. (*a*) A clot or coagulum is formed to stop bleeding from an injured surface. It contains damaged and worn out formed elements of blood like red blood cells, and platelets that activate the clotting process. The thin threads that form the meshwork are the fibrin proteins. However, a clot does not contain fibrinogen, which is present in soluble form in plasma. Thrombin converts fibrinogen to fibrin, to form the clot.

13. (*c*) Both statement I and statement II are incorrect. These can be corrected as

Lymph has the same mineral constituents like the plasma, however larger proteins are absent.

Lymphatic fluid runs in lymphatic vessels, but is returned to the main circulation by major veins.

14. (*a*) The correct match is A-4, B-1, C-2, D-3.

- B^- can receive blood from B^- person as well as O^-.
- O^- people do not have any antigens (A, B or Rh) and hence there is no chance of agglutination reactions. Thus O^- people can donate blood to all blood types.
- AB^- individuals can receive from all blood groups (A, B, AB, O) as they do not have anti A or anti B antibody. However, they lack Rh antigens, so they should receive blood from other negative blood groups, or else, it could lead to development of anti Rh antibodies in them, that can interfere with subsequent transfusions.
- Rh^- person can receive blood from Rh^+ person safely only once, as this would result in formation of anti Rh antibodies in them.

15. (*b*) Thrombokinase is formed by a series of linked enzymatic reactions (cascade process) involving a number of factors present in the plasma in an inactive state.

16. (*c*) As there are no closed blood vessels to circulate blood, the flow of blood cannot be regulated. Regulated blood flow is observed in closed circulatory system of chordates.

17. (*b*) If the resting heart rate is 70 beats/minute, then heart rate during exercise = 70 + 20/100 x 70

= 70 + 14 = 84 beats/ minute

Cardiac output = Stroke volume x Heart rate

Therefore, Stroke volume = Cardiac output/ Heart rate

= 6000/84 = 71.42 mL (~71 mL)

18. (*c*) Both A and R are true, but R is not the correct explanation of A.

It is advisable to avoid regular junk food particularly for middle aged people since fat and cholesterol can form plaques in the coronary arteries and restrict blood flow to the heart muscles.

19. (*c*) The left ventricles have thicker walls than right ventricles as they have to pump blood to larger distances to reach the entire body. Exchanging their walls, would make the left ventricular walls thinner. In order to pump blood, the left ventricles would exert a lot of pressure which would cause the thin walls to get damaged or even get ruptured.

20. (*d*) The separated layer at the top is the plasma that contains proteins, mineral salts, hormone, vitamins, inactive clotting factors, amino acids, etc. RBCs and WBCs are present in separate layers below the plasma.

21. (*c*) The recipient's serum should not contain the antibodies against the red blood corpuscles of the donor is correct statement. As donor's RBCs have a surface antigen, it should be ensured that recipient's serum should not contain antibodies against the antigen on red blood corpuscles of the donor. Otherwise, if transfusion is made between incompatible donor and recipient, agglutination reaction between antigens and antibodies will take place.

22. (*c*) A person who is suffering from allergic reaction will have elevated levels of eosinophils. 2-3% is the normal range of eosinophils in blood. All other types of WBCs would be elevated due to the bacterial infection.

23. (*d*) Statements I, IV and V are correct. Statements II and III can be corrected as

- The pulmonary circuit deals with both oxygenated and deoxygenated blood. The pulmonary artery carries deoxygenated blood from the right ventricle to the lungs for oxygenation, while the pulmonary veins carry oxygenated blood from the lungs to the left atria.
- Blood flow into the pulmonary artery is regulated by the pulmonary semilunar valves, to prevent back flow into the right ventricle.

24. (*c*) *A*– Pulmonary artery, *B* – Vena cava, *C* – Aorta, *D* – Pulmonary vein. Aorta is the largest artery and vena cava is the largest vein.

25. (*a*) The correct sequence is A-B-D-C-E.

- In systemic circulation, left ventricles contract and pump oxygenated blood into the aorta.
- The aorta divides into arteries which carry oxygenated blood into body cells.
- At the tissues, oxygen diffuses into the cells, while carbon dioxide diffuses out and blood becomes deoxygenated.
- The deoxygenated blood is carried by veins towards the heart.
- The deoxygenated blood is drained into the right atrium by the superior and inferior vena cava.

26. (*b*) Heart failure shows congestion of lungs as a main symptom. Heart failure is not the same as cardiac arrest, (when the heart stops beating) or a heart attack, (when the heart muscle is suddenly damaged by an inadequate blood supply).

27. (*c*) Both A and R are true, but R is not the correct explanation of A. A can be explained as

In contrast to veins, blood flows through the arteries with jerks, because the left ventricle of the heart pumps blood with a lot of force and this causes blood to flow with jerks in the arteries.

28. (*b*) The parasympathetic branch of the autonomic nervous system can decrease the speed of conduction of impulses, thereby reducing cardiac output and heart rate.

29. (*c*) Q wave is a part of QRS complex, where Q and S are small negative waves, while R is a positive wave.

30. (*a*) T-P segment represents the gap between two cardiac cycles where the heart muscles are electrically silent. It marks the gap before generation of the next action potential at the SAN.

31. (*d*) Oxygenated blood is carried by the arteries to the tissues. In the tissues, oxygen diffuses out of the capillaries to enter the body cells where it is utilised for cellular respiration. Thus, maximum oxygen is lost from capillaries surrounding the tissues. In the capillaries surrounding the alveoli, oxygen diffuses into the blood from the alveoli. The left auricle receives oxygenated blood by the pulmonary veins, which is next pumped to the left ventricles.

32. (*b*) The correct match is A-2, B-3, C- 4, D-1.

- B- lymphocytes are a type of agranulocytes that are involved in production of antibodies and immunity.
- Platelets are cell fragments produced from megakaryocytes that help in blood clotting.
- RBCs are the most abundantly found cells in blood that transport oxygen.
- Neutrophils occupy 60-65% of total WBCs in blood and are the most abundant WBCs involved in phagocytosis.

33. (*c*) Rh negative mother can develop antibodies against Rh antigen following the birth of her first Rh positive child. In case of second pregnancy with Rh positive child, the Rh antibodies from mother's blood can attack the foetus and destroy the foetal cells (erythroblatosis foetalis) and the child could die due to severe anaemia and jaundice. Hence, before her second pregnancy, she is administered with anti Rh antibodies.

34. (*c*) Eosinophils are involved in the inactivation of allergen complexes, antigen-antibody complexes and inflammatory substances. Their number rapidly increases due to infections and allergic reactions.

35. (*b*) Ant bite would cause inflammation. Basophils are the WBCs involved in inflammation by secreting chemicals like heparin, histamine, serotonin, etc. Whereas, fibrin is involved in blood clotting and would not be found in inflammatory reactions.

36. (*c*) Both A and R are true, but R is not the correct explanation of A. A can be explained as

Plasma of a person recovered from viral infection often contains antibodies that can be used for treating such infections.

37. (*a*) Statement I is incorrect, but statement II is correct. The incorrect statement can be corrected as

A person with B^- blood group can donate blood to B^+ individual. This is because B^- person contains antigen B just like B^+ person. Also B^- person does not contain Rh antigen that is present in B^+ individual. There is no chance of developing antibodies against Rh antigens in the donors blood, as he is the one donating, thus this transfusion is safe.

38. (*a*) Statement I is incorrect, but statement II is correct. Statement I can be corrected as

The factors responsible for Coronary Artery Disease (CAD) are hypercholesterolemia, smoking, hypertension, etc. Dysfunctioning of left ventricle causes heart failure.

39. (*c*) Both statement I and statement II are incorrect. These can be corrected as

Contraction of the arteries is facilitated by the tunica media layer made up of smooth muscles and elastic fibres. Tunica externa made of collagen fibres resists the force of blood in the arteries and protects them from damage.

40. (*c*) When we measure our pulse, we feel the pressure from the fingers due to pulse pressure. It is the difference between systolic and diastolic blood pressure.

A healthy pulse pressure is around 40 mm Hg, which is the force the heart generates when it contracts.

41. (*a*) The correct match is A-3, B-2, C-1, D-4.

- Albumin is a component of blood plasma that regulates osmotic balance.
- Adrenaline secreted by adrenal medulla, regulates cardiac output and heart rate.
- Calcium is an important clotting factor required during blood coagulation.
- Globulins are also plasma proteins involved in immune defence of the body.

42. (*b*) The correct match is A-2, B-3, C-1, D-4.

- P-wave represents action potential generated at SA node.
- QRS complex represent one pulse.
- T-wave marks the end of excitation of Purkinje fibres.
- In ECG, P-R interval correspond to time delay in AV node.

43. (*b*) In an ECG, counting the QRS complexes in a given time period gives the heart rate of a person.

In 30 minutes, 2100 QRS waves are seen. Therefore, in one minute, 2100/30 = 70 QRS complexes are seen. This gives the heart rate of a person which is 70 beats/minute.

44. (*c*) Statements I, III and V are correct, whereas statements II and IV are incorrect and can be corrected as

- Absence of valves can cause back flow of blood
- Mixing of blood is prevented by inter ventricular septum.

45. (*c*) The incorrect statement can be corrected as

The single ventricle in reptile heart pumps out mixed blood.

46. (*b*) Both statement I and statement II are correct. At the site of injury damaged blood vessels and platelets causes the release of certain factors that activate clotting. Thrombokinase is required for activating prothrombin to thrombin. Thus, a mutation in the gene for Thrombokinase can make it non-functional thereby failing the entire clotting system and the affected individual can bleed out.

47. (*c*) Both A and R are true, but R is not the correct explanation of A. Often lymph nodes in armpits are swollen in case of infections, as lymph contains immune cells like lymphocytes that are involved in eliciting immune responses against foreign pathogens.

48. (*b*) The walls of a vein are made up of three layers, the outer layer called tunica externa made up of collagen fibres, the middle tunica media made up of elastic fibres and smooth muscles and the inner most layer tunica intima made up of squamous endothelium.

Stratified epithelium does not form a part of the wall of the vein.

49. (*c*) Lub is the first heart sound produced by closure of the AV valves. During ventricular systole, a rise in ventricular pressure causes the tricuspid and bicuspid valves to close, thereby generating this sound.

50. (*a*) Statement I is incorrect, but statement II is correct. Statement I can be corrected as

Fear is often triggered by the sympathetic branch of the ANS, which causes an elevation in heart rate and cardiac output.

Ch-16 Excretory Products and their Elimination

Topical Follow Thru

Test 1

1. (*d*) Ammonia is the most toxic excretory product and is needed to be removed as soon as it is formed, whereas uric acid is least toxic and urea is relative lesser toxic than ammonia.

2. (*d*) Statement I is correct, but statement II is incorrect. It can be corrected as

Cortex extends deeper into the medullary pyramids to form renal columns.

3. (*b*) The correct order is B-D-E-C-A.

- Blood flows through the afferent arteriole and moves into the glomerulus.
- Blood is taken out of the glomerulus through the efferent arteriole.
- The efferent arteriole branches to form a fine network of capillaries the peritubular capillaries.
- A fine branch of the peritubular capillaries, form the U-shaped vasa recta running parallel to the Henle's loop.

4. (*c*) Both A and R are true, but R is not the correct explanation of A.

Majority of nephrons are confined to the cortical spaces of the kidneys as the PCT, DCT and Malpighian corpuscles are located in the cortex, while the loop of Henle extends only a little into the medulla.

5. (*c*) Both A and R are true, but R is not the correct explanation of A.

Reabsorption of molecules in the renal tubules require energy as most substances like glucose, amino acids and sodium ions undergo active transport with the involvement of energy of ATP.

6. (*d*) '*X*' represents vasa recta which is absent or highly reduced in cortical nephrons. Other statements can be corrected as

- Vasa recta arises from efferent arteriole rather than afferent arteriole.
- The NaCl is returned to the interstitiums by the ascending limb of vasa recta.
- Vasa recta is a network of arterioles, thus it contain oxygenated blood.

7. (*a*) Statement I is incorrect, but statement II is correct. Incorrect statement can be corrected as

Efferent arteriole forms numerous peritubular capillaries in the cortical region around the proximal and distal convoluted tubules of the nephrons.

8. (*d*) An increased acidic level of blood could be due to a defect in the secretion of hydrogen ions by the renal tubules. The PCT, DCT and collecting duct secretes ions like hydrogen and potassium which helps in regulating the pH and ion balance of blood. Failure to do so, would increase the concentration of these ions, that would make the blood more acidic.

9. (*a*) The correct match is A-3, B-4, C-2, D-1.

- PCT or Proximal Convoluted Tubule allows reabsorption of about 70-80% electrolytes, nutrients and water.
- Reabsorption is minimum in the ascending limb of Henle's loop. However this segment is majorly involved in maintaining the osmolarity of medullary interstitial fluid.
- Urine gets concentrated in the collecting duct due to reabsorption of huge amounts of water.
- DCT or Distal Convoluted Tubule is involved in conditional reabsorption of sodium and water, as well as bicarbonated (HCO^{3-}) ions.

10. (*d*) Statement I is correct, but statement II is incorrect. Incorrect statement can be corrected as

The JGA releases renin in response to a decrease in the glomerular filtration rate (GFR). When GFR drops, the JGA detects reduced sodium chloride levels and responds by secreting renin to help increase blood pressure and restore GFR.

11. (*c*) In the given diagram, *A*, *B*, *C* and *D* represents – Renal calyx, Renal pelvis, Ureter and Renal column respectively.

The collecting duct of several nephrons open into the large space called renal pelvis (*B*). From here, the urine is collected by the ureters and poured into the urinary bladder.

12. (*b*) *A* is the descending limb of Henle's loop. *B* is the ascending limb of Henle's loop. *C* is distal convoluted tubule and *D* is collecting duct. In collecting duct, the urine gets concentrated due to reabsorption of large volumes of water (hypertonic filtrate). The filtrate flowing through *A* is hypertonic as the descending limb is permeable to water, but almost impermeable to electrolyte, which concentrates the filtrate. The ascending limb is impermeable to water, but allows transport of electrolytes actively or passively. Therefore, as the concentrated filtrate (hypotonic) pass upward, it gets diluted due to the passage of electrolytes to the medullary fluid. The DCT thus contains hypotonic filtrate flowing through the ascending limb of loop of Henle.

13. (*d*) A is true, but R is false. R can be corrected as
The descending limb of the loop of Henle is actually permeable to water, but relatively impermeable to salts which leads to high concentration of filtrate. In contrast, the ascending limb is impermeable to water, but actively transports salts out of the filtrate.

14. (*c*) The correct match is A-4, B-3, C-1, D-2.
- The thick segment of the nephron (Loop of Henle) is lined with cuboidal epithelium.
- The thin segment of the descending limb of the nephron loop is lined with squamous epithelium, which is thinner and allows for efficient passive transport.
- The proximal convoluted tubule (PCT) is lined with cuboidal epithelial cells that have microvilli to increase surface area for absorption.
- Podocytes are specialised cells that form part of the visceral layer of Bowman's capsule, which wrap around the glomerular capillaries.

15. (*d*) Statements III, IV and V are correct. While statements I and II are incorrect and can be corrected as
- A person with GFR 125mL/min is not suffering from any abnormality. This is because about 90% of the filtrate is reabsorbed by the renal tubules, which would cause a final urine output of about 1.5 litres/day. In fact, GFR in a healthy individual is approximately 125 mL/min, i.e. 180 L per day.
- Tubular epithelium may or may not need energy for reabsorption since materials like glucose, amino acids, etc., are reabsorbed actively, whereas nitrogenous wastes are absorbed passively.

Test 2

1. (*a*) The transport of urea from the collecting tubule to the medullary interstitium, helps in increasing the solute concentration and osmolarity of the interstitium. This gradient established, allows easy passage of water from the collecting ducts to the interstitium, thus concentrating the filtrate (urine). It leads to formation of four times concentrated urine by collecting ducts, in comparison to the initial filtrate formed by the glomerulus.

2. (*a*) The correct order is B-C-A-E-D, that can be explained as
- An excessive loss of fluid activates the osmoreceptors of the body.
- The receptors stimulate the hypothalamus.
- Hypothalamus, in turn, stimulates the posterior pituitary to release Antidiuretic Hormone (ADH) or vasopressin.
- Vasopressin causes reabsorption of water from the latter parts of the kidney tubules.
- This lowers the urine output and prevents diuresis.

3. (*b*) The increase in osmolarity from 300 mOsmolL^{-1} in the cortex to 1200 mOsmolL^{-1} in inner medulla is due to a gradient established by sodium chloride (NaCl) and urea.

4. (*c*) Both A and R are true, but R is not the correct explanation of A.
Vasa recta located close to the Henle's loop, can disturb osmotic gradient, since the proximity between the two allows exchange of sodium chloride. The NaCl is transported by the ascending limb of Henle's loop which is exchanged with the descending limb of vasa recta. NaCl is returned to the interstitium by the ascending portion of vasa recta. This helps in establishing a gradient, which cause an increase in osmolarity in the inner medullary interstitium.

5. (*d*) If the blood pressure of a person increases, i.e., hypertension the Atrial Natriuretic Factor (ANF) causes vasodilation and lowers the secretion of renin and vasopressin. This lowers reabsorption of electrolytes and water, thereby decreasing blood pressure. Diuresis is a condition of high urine output, while hypoglycemia is low blood glucose levels. Hypotension is decrease in blood pressure.

6. (*c*) Diabetes mellitus is a disorder of the pancreas where insufficient insulin can increase the blood glucose levels. Thus, a person can excrete large amounts of glucose in his/her urine. Another characteristic of this disorder is the presence of ketone bodies in urine.

7. (*b*) The correct order is C-A-B-E-D. This can be explained as
- As urine fills up the urinary bladder, the bladder stretches to accommodate the urine which, in turn, activates the stretch receptors.
- The stretch receptors send sensory information to the Central Nervous System (CNS).
- The CNS sends motor impulses back to the urinary bladder.
- This causes simultaneous contraction of the smooth muscles of the bladder and relaxation of the urethral sphincter muscles.
- Finally, urine is eliminated through the urethra.

8. (*d*) Statement I is correct, but statement II is incorrect. Statement II can be corrected as
Stimulation of JG cells causes an increased secretion of aldosterone from the cortex. The JG cells on activation, secrete renin, which converts angiotensinogen to angiotensin-I. This further converts to angiotensin-II. The angiotensin-II

constricts blood vessels, thereby increasing blood pressure. It also causes secretion of aldosterone from the adrenal cortex, which causes reabsorption of sodium ions and water, thereby increasing blood pressure and GFR.

9. (*b*) The incorrect statement can be corrected as
Nitrogenous wastes are primarily excreted through urine. However, small amounts of nitrogenous wastes are also eliminated through sweat and saliva.

10. (*c*) Incorrect statement can be corrected as
Decreased ADH would result in less water reabsorption, leading to dilute urine ADH (antidiuretic hormone) increases the permeability of the collecting ducts to water, allowing more water to be reabsorbed, leading to the formation of concentrated urine.

11. (*b*) The dialysing fluid has the same composition as that of the blood plasma, except that it lacks nitrogenous wastes.
Hence, dialysing fluid has the same osmotic pressure as that of blood and is isotonic with respect to blood.

12. (*a*) The correct match is A-3, B-1, C-2, D-4.
- Uremia is the accumulation of urea in blood, which can lead to kidney failure.
- Ketonuria is the presence of ketone bodies in urine, which is a characteristic of diabetes mellitus.
- Glomerulonephritis is the inflammation of the glomeruli, and can be caused by certain infections in the kidney.
- Renal calculi are the kidney stones formed by crystallisation of salts like oxalates.

13. (*c*) Statements I, II and IV are correct. While statements III and V are incorrect. These can be corrected as
- After filtration, blood is treated with anti-heparin before it is released into the body, which helps in reversing the anti-coagulant effect of heparin.
- Nitrogenous wastes move through the membrane by the process of diffusion.

14. (*a*) Atrial Natriuretic Factor (ANF) is a vasodilator, that decreases blood pressure and GFR. It works antagonistically to renin- angiotensin mechanism. Other options can be corrected as ADH and angiotensin-II are powerful vasoconstrictors that can cause an increase in blood pressure and thus the Glomerular Filtration Rate (GFR). Aldosterone causes reabsorption of Na^+ and water from the distal parts of the tubule. This also leads to an increase in blood pressure and GFR.

15. (*b*) Due to the gradient established in the medullary interstitium, by NaCl and urea, water moves from segment *Y* (collecting duct) by the process of osmosis to the medullary interstitium. This concentrates the urine.

16. (*d*) Statement I is correct, but statement II is incorrect. The incorrect statement can be corrected as
ADH (Antidiuretic Hormone) primarily affects the collecting ducts and the distal convoluted tubule by enhancing water reabsorption. The ascending limb of the loop of Henle is impermeable to water.

17. (*d*) Statement I is correct, but statement II is incorrect. The incorrect statement can be corrected as
The filtrate flows in opposite directions in the two limbs of the loop of Henle, not in the same direction. The descending limb is permeable to water but impermeable to solutes, while the ascending limb is impermeable to water and actively transports ions out of the filtrate. This opposing flow creates the concentration gradient that allows for the production of concentrated urine.

18. (*b*) In haemodialysis, the semipermeable membrane is a crucial component that allows selective filtration. The primary function of this membrane is to allow small waste products (such as urea and excess electrolytes) to pass from the blood while retaining larger molecules like blood cells and proteins in the bloodstream.

19. (*b*) Incorrect statement can be corrected as
The contraction of the external urethral sphincter keeps the urethra closed, preventing the release of urine. Relaxation of the external urethral sphincter allows urine to flow from the bladder through the urethra and out of the body. This relaxation is usually a voluntary action controlled by the central nervous system.

20. (*b*) When blood glucose levels exceed the renal threshold (about 180 mg/dL), glucose enter into the urine because the proximal convoluted tubule (PCT) can no longer reabsorb all the glucose. This leads to the presence of glucose in the urine, a condition known as glucosuria.
The presence of glucose in the urine increases the osmolarity of the filtrate, which reduces water reabsorption, leading to increased urine output.

21. (*b*) The correct match is A-4, B-1, C-3, D-2.
- Aldosterone is a hormone produced by the adrenal glands that promotes sodium reabsorption in the kidneys, which in turn increases water retention and raises blood pressure.
- Antidiuretic hormone (ADH) acts on the kidneys to prevent diuresis (water loss), by promoting water reabsorption, particularly in the collecting ducts.
- Atrial natriuretic factor (ANF) causes vasodilation and reduces blood volume.
- Insulin is essential for glucose metabolism. The absence of insulin causes glycosuria (presence of glucose in urine).

22. (*a*) A is false, but R is true. A can be corrected as
While the kidneys play a major role in excreting metabolic waste through

urine, they are not the only organs involved in excretion. Other organs like the lungs (which excrete carbon dioxide), skin (which excretes sweat and other wastes), and liver (which detoxifies substances and excretes bile) also contribute to excretion.

23. (*c*) The incorrect statement can be corrected as
The pH of urine is generally slightly acidic, with a normal range of about 4.5 to 8.0. The typical pH is around 6.0, which is slightly acidic. Alkaline urine can occur under certain conditions depicting clinical abnormality.

24. (*c*) ANF causes the dilation of the afferent arterioles in the kidneys, which leads to an increase in blood flow to the glomerulus. This dilation increases the glomerular filtration rate (GFR), meaning more filtrate is produced in the nephron, leading to an increase in urine production.

25. (*a*) The ascending limb of the loop of Henle is impermeable to water but actively reabsorbs sodium and chloride ions. This active transport of ions into the medullary interstitium helps to create and maintain the high osmolarity of the medullary interstitial fluid, which is crucial for the countercurrent mechanism that concentrates urine.

Chapter Break Thru

1. (*c*) Aldosterone is released by the adrenal cortex upon activation by angiotensin-II. Aldosterone causes reabsorption of Na^+ and water from the distal parts of tubule. This leads to an increase in blood pressure and GFR.

2. (*a*) The correct sequence is C-A-D-B-E.
- Proteins undergo deamination to form ammonia in the liver.
- Ammonia is converted to urea in the liver.
- Blood containing urea is sent to the kidneys.
- Blood is filtered by the nephrons.
- Filtered blood returns to the circulation through the vena cava.

3. (*c*) Presence of glucose in urine is indicative of diabetes mellitus. In nephritis or glomerulonephritis, there is inflammation of the glomerulus, which can lower the GFR and thus, urine output. This condition leads to more fluid retention in the body. Other option can be explained as
Renal calculi or kidney stones occur due to crystallisation of oxalate salts in the kidneys.

4. (*b*) Uric acid requires very less amount of water for its removal. Thus, excretion in the form of uric acid is a water conserving method adopted by many birds. It is also excreted by reptiles, land snails and insects.

5. (*a*) A is false, but R is true. A can be corrected as
The efferent arteriole has a smaller diameter than the afferent arteriole. This causes blood to flow under pressure in the glomerulus and eventually gets filtered by the process of ultrafiltration.

6. (*d*) Presence of well-defined vasa recta proves that the nephrons in the tissue section are juxtamedullary nephrons, since vasa recta is small or highly reduced in cortical nephrons. In juxtamedullary nephrons, PCT, DCT and Malpighian tubules are confined to the cortex, while the loop of Henle extends deeper into the medulla. Vasa recta arises from fine branching of the peritubular capillaries and run parallel to the Henle's loop.

7. (*c*) Statements I, III and V are correct. While statemens II and IV are incorrect. These can be corrected as
- Conditional reabsorption of Na^+ and water takes place in the DCT.
- On average, around 25-30 gm of urea is excreted out of the body.

8. (*c*) Both statement I and statement II are incorrect. These can be corrected as
If blood becomes too much alkaline, PCT secretes ammonia into the filtrate. If H^+ secretion into the filtrate is increased, then it increases the pH of the blood, making it more alkaline.
The pH of the blood is maintained by the PCT, DCT and collecting ducts of the nephrons.

9. (*c*) Urea is transported to the medullary interstitium by the collecting tubules. This helps in maintaining the osmolarity and gradient in the medulla. Failure of returning urea to the medullary interstitium would disrupt this gradient and hence, water cannot pass out into the interstitium from the collecting tubules. Thus, urine will not be concentrated and will be diluted.

10. (*b*) Statements I, II and IV are correct. While statements III and V are incorrect and can be corrected as
Ascending limb of loop of Henle is also called diluting segment as it reabsorbs solutes.
Ascending limb of Henle's loop is impermeable to water.

11. (*d*) Antidiuretic hormone or vasopressin, prevents diuresis by reabsorption of water by the DCT and collecting tubules. It can also cause vasoconstriction of the blood vessels and increase blood pressure. Thus, a fall in the blood pressure would stimulate the neurohypophysis to release ADH that can increase blood pressure by causing vasoconstriction. Low osmolarity of blood means lower solute levels compared to fluid volume, which would not cause release of ADH. Similarly, increased fluid volume and High GFR will suppress ADH release from the posterior pituitary.

12. (*c*) Statements II, III and V are correct. While statements I and IV can be corrected as
- Micturition reflex is a voluntary signal of the central nervous system.
- Simultaneous contraction of the smooth muscles of the bladder and relaxation of the urethral sphincter is involved in micturition.

13. (*c*) The glomerular filtrate formed in the Malpighian corpuscles, has a composition similar to plasma, however it lacks proteins.

14. (*c*) Before pumping blood into the dialysing unit, it should be treated with anticoagulants like heparin. Heparin prevents clotting of blood, so that filtration can take place smoothly.

15. (*c*) Both A and R are true, but R is not the correct explanation of A. Complete absence of sweating can be toxic to the body cells, as sweat helps in removal of small amounts of nitrogenous wastes. In the complete absence of sweating, the concentration of these wastes would rise, which could be toxic to body cells.

16. (*c*) Structure *P* is Bowman's capsule. Slit pore and epithelial cells called podocytes are parts of the Bowman's capsule involved in filtration. Other option can be explained as
Endothelium makes up the glomerulus, while basement membrane lies between glomerulus and Bowman's capsule.

17. (*c*) Normally the ascending limb of Henle's loop is impermeable to water and permeable to electrolytes. This allows electrolytes to be transported to the interstitium, which dilutes the filtrate.
However, if the permeability is interchanged, i.e. the ascending limb is impermeable to electrolytes and permeable to water. This would cause water to move from the ascending limb to the interstitium, thus concentrating the filtrate and making it hypertonic. The same hypertonic and concentrated filtrate flows in the DCT and gets even more concentrated in the collecting tubules. Hence, a very concentrated urine would be formed.

18. (*d*) A is true, but R is false. R can be corrected as A person with diabetes insipidus suffers from deficiency of vasopressin or antidiuretic hormone.

19. (*b*) Reabsorption in DCT depends upon aldosterone and vasopressin. Under the influence of aldosterone, Na^+ is actively reabsorbed from the filtrate. Vasopressin helps in reabsorption of water.

20. (*b*) Statements I, II and IV are correct. Statements III and V are incorrect and can be corrected as
- NaCl levels in the interstitium is maintained by the ascending portion of vasa recta.
- Interstitial gradient is established by urea and NaCl flowing into the interstitium.

21. (*b*) Glomerulonephritis is the inflammation of the glomerular capillaries. An inflammation can block the filtration process, reducing the GFR and thereby retaining large volumes of fluid in the body. Uremia occurs if there is high percentage of urea in blood, due to the failure of kidneys. Renal calculi, also called kidney stones, occur due to crystallisation and deposition of salts in the kidneys.

22. (*d*) Statement I is correct, but statement II is incorrect. Statement II can be corrected as
A decrease in blood volume causes an increase in the osmolarity of blood.

23. (*b*) The correct match is A-3, B-1, C-2, D-4.
- Protonephridia or flame cells are the excretory organs of cephalochordates like amphioxus.
- Annelida like earthworms perform their excretory functions through nephridia.
- Insects like grasshopper, cockroach, etc., have Malpighian tubules as their excretory organs.
- Crustaceans like prawns have antennal glands or green glands as their excretory organs.

24. (*d*) In the given diagram,
A–Collecting duct, *B*–Distal Convoluted Tubule (DCT), *C*–Proximal Convoluted Tubule (PCT), *D*–Ascending limb of loop of Henle, *E*–Descending limb of loop of Henle.
- Reabsorption is maximum in PCT(C). Nearly all of the essential nutrients and 70-80 per cent of electrolytes and water are reabsorbed by this segment. Reabsorption is minimum in the ascending limb of loop of Henle (D).

25. (*b*) Both A and R are true and R is the correct explanation of A.
Terrestrial animals have to conserve water and hence excrete lesser toxic forms of nitrogenous wastes which requires minimum water for excretion. Hence, their excreta are in the form of pellet or paste, with very less amounts of water.

26. (*c*) Substances like glucose, amino acids and ions like Na^+ are transported actively in the renal tubules using the energy of ATP. However, nitrogenous wastes like NH_3, urea as well as water are transported passively without the use of energy in the form of ATP.

27. (*a*) Statement I is incorrect, but statement II is correct. Statement I can be corrected as
If blood becomes too acidic, HCO_3^- reabsorption is increased in the DCT. Presence of bicarbonate ions makes the blood alkaline, whereas their decreased concentration makes blood acidic.

28. (*a*) The correct order is B-C-D-A-E.
- The mechanism that counters ANF mechanism is the renin-angiotensin pathway. This pathway is activated in response to low blood pressure/GFR.
- A fall in GFR, activates the JG cells to release renin.
- Renin converts angiotensinogen to angiotensin-I.
- Angiotensin-I is further converted to angiotensin-II.
- Angiotensin II stimulates the adrenal cortex to secrete aldosterone. Aldosterone causes reabsorption of Na^+ and water from the distal parts of the tubule. This also leads to an increase in blood pressure and GFR.

29. (*c*) Liver maintains the level of amino acids in the blood. Amino acids are transported to the liver during digestion and most of the body's protein is synthesised here.

30. (*d*) ANF (Atrial Natriuretic Factor) inhibits reabsorption of sodium ions and water by DCT and collecting ducts. Reabsorption of sodium and water is facilitated by the hormones aldosterone (secreted by the adrenal cortex) and ADH (secreted by the posterior pituitary). However, ANF acts antagonistically to this mechanism.

31. (*d*) The afferent arteriole supplies blood to the glomerulus and is involved in regulating Glomerular Filtration Rate (GFR), while the efferent arteriole carries blood away from the glomerulus. Rest of the statements are incorrect and can be corrected as

The afferent arteriole controls the amount of blood entering the glomerulus and the efferent arteriole regulates the blood leaving the glomerulus, both affecting glomerular filtration rate (GFR) and overall blood pressure.

The afferent arteriole supplies blood to the glomerulus, and the efferent arteriole carries blood away from the glomerulus.

The diameter of the efferent arteriole is typically smaller than that of the afferent arteriole.

32. (*c*) Albumin is a large protein that is normally retained in the bloodstream and not filtered into the urine. The filtration barrier is designed to prevent the passage of large proteins and maintain their concentration in the blood. This selective filtration helps in maintaining protein levels in the blood and avoiding loss of essential proteins through urine.

33. (*d*) Statement I is correct, but statement II is incorrect. Statement II can be corrected as

Ammonotelism is not commonly observed in terrestrial animals because ammonia is highly toxic and requires a large amount of water to be safely excreted. Terrestrial animals typically use less toxic waste forms such as urea or uric acid, which are more suited to conserving water.

34. (*c*) Increased blood pressure in the glomerular capillaries increases the hydrostatic pressure within the glomerulus, which enhances the filtration of blood into the renal tubules. This would likely result in an increased GFR because higher blood pressure increases the pressure gradient driving filtration.

35. (*a*) The correct match is A-3, B-4, C-1, D-2.

- The vasa recta are long, straight capillaries that descend alongside the loop of Henle, forming a U-shaped structure in the medulla of the kidney.
- The renal artery carries oxygenated blood from the heart to the kidneys. The renal vein carries deoxygenated blood from the kidneys back to the heart.
- The glomerulus is a tuft of capillaries located within the Bowman's capsule of the nephron.

36. (*d*) Gills are crucial for respiration in aquatic animals, but they are not primarily involved in osmoregulation. They are mainly responsible for gaseous exchange, although they can play a secondary role in ion regulation.

37. (*c*) The Malpighian body, includes the Bowman's capsule and the glomerulus, is responsible for the initial filtration of blood to form the filtrate. Epithelium of bowman's capsule contain podocytes which are involved in ultrafiltration.

38. (*a*) Statements I and IV are correct. Statement I and II are incorrect. Incorrect statement can be corrected as

- The normal Glomerular Filtration Rate (GFR) for a healthy individual is approximately 125 mL/min, not per day. This rate represents the volume of filtrate formed per minute by the kidneys.
- While passive reabsorption of water occurs in parts of the nephron, such as the proximal convoluted tubule but it is associated with tubular reabsorption and not filtration.

39. (*c*) The glomerular capillaries have a unique structure that is essential for their function in filtration. They contain small pores called podocytes arranged in slits.

These pores allow the passage of water, ions, glucose, and other small solutes, but they restrict the passage of larger molecules like proteins.

40. (*d*) Statement I is correct, but statement II is incorrect. Incorrect statement can be corrected as Tubular secretion, particularly in the distal convoluted tubule and the collecting ducts, plays a role in maintaining the acid-base balance by secreting hydrogen ions (H^+) into the tubular fluid, which helps regulate the pH of the body fluids.

41. (*c*) The correct order is A-C-B-E-D.

- The outermost layer of the kidney, which surrounds the renal medulla and contains the renal corpuscles and convoluted tubules is cortex.
- Renal columns of Bertini are extensions of the renal cortex that run between the medullary pyramids, separating them.
- Medullary pyramids are located in the inner part of the kidney, these are cone-shaped structures within the renal medulla. The pyramids contain the collecting ducts and are responsible for the concentration of urine.

42. (*c*) The incorrect statement can be corrected as

Renin is released by JG cells in response to fall in GFR . It converts angiotensinogen into angiotensin I and further into angiotensin II, However the later is not formed in the liver but is produced in the bloodstream primarily in the lungs.

43. (*a*) The correct match is A-3, B-4 C-1, D-2.

- The average length of a human kidney is about 10-12 cm.
- The average width of the kidney is around 5-7 cm.
- The thickness of the kidney is typically around 2-3 cm.
- The average weight of a human kidney is between 120-170 gm.

44. (*b*) Statement I and II are correct. Statement III and IV are incorrect. The incorrect statement can be corrected as

- The juxtaglomerular cells are located at the junction of the distal convoluted tubule and afferent arteriole.
- The JGA does play a crucial role in regulating blood pressure, it

primarily does so by controlling the release of renin, not directly affecting the release of ADH.

45. (*b*) Both A and R are true and the R is the correct explanation of A.
The proximal convoluted tubule (PCT) plays a critical role in the reabsorption of water, ions, and nutrients. PCT is lined by simple cuboidal brush border epithelium which contain microvilli. The presence of microvilli on the lining of the PCT greatly enhances its surface area, which in turn increases the efficiency of reabsorption and causes 70-80 % reabsorption of electrolytes

46. (*b*) Both statement I and statement II are correct.
- Kidney stones are primarily composed of substances like calcium oxalate, calcium phosphate, uric acid, these are solid masses made of crystals that usually originate in the kidneys but can develop anywhere along the urinary tract.
- Glomerulonephritis is a group of diseases that injure the part of the kidney that filters blood, called the glomeruli. Glomerulonephritis can be caused by infections but it is also commonly linked to autoimmune diseases. In autoimmune conditions, the body's immune system mistakenly attacks its own tissues, including the glomeruli, leading to inflammation and damage.

47. (*c*) Both A and R are true, but R is not the correct explanation of A.
Tubular secretion is an important process in which excess hydrogen ions, potassium ions, creatinine, drugs, and other waste products are secreted from the blood into the tubular fluid. Tubular secretion occurs in both the proximal convoluted tubule (PCT), distal convoluted tubule (DCT), and the collecting duct. While significant secretion does occur in the DCT and collecting duct, the proximal convoluted tubule also plays a key role in tubular secretion.

48. (*b*) Renal cortex is the outer layer of the kidney, containing structures such as the Malpighian corpuscle (glomerulus and Bowman's capsule), Proximal Convoluted Tubules (PCT) and Distal Convoluted Tubules (DCT). Renal medulla is the inner region of the kidney, characterised by renal pyramids. It contains the collecting ducts (Duct of Bertini) and is involved in the final processing of urine.

49. (*c*) ADH is produced by the hypothalamus and released from the posterior pituitary gland. Its primary role in kidney function is to regulate water balance in the body by increasing the permeability of the collecting ducts and distal convoluted tubules in the kidneys. Deficiency of ADH causes diabetes insipidus.

50. (*b*) The long loops of Henle are essential for the countercurrent multiplication system, which generates a hyperosmotic (high solute concentration) environment in the medullary interstitium.
This osmotic gradient allows for the efficient reabsorption of water from the collecting ducts, which pass through this hyperosmotic medullary environment. Thus, urine becomes concentrated, and water is conserved.

Ch-17 Locomotion and Movement

Topical Follow Thru

Test 1

1. (*b*) G-actin or globular actin and meromyosin are monomeric proteins. Other options can be corrected as F-actin or filamentous actin is a polymer made up of monomeric G-actins. Tropomyosin is a complex protein made up of two filaments that run close to F-actin. Myosin is a polymeric protein made of monomeric myosin proteins called meromyosins.

2. (*c*) The release of neurotransmitter that is acetylcholine at the neuromuscular junction, causes the generation of action potential in the sarcolemma. This causes the release of calcium ions from the sarcoplasmic reticulum to the sarcoplasm. Thus, the highest calcium concentration would be in the sarcoplasm in the presence of acetylcholine.

3. (*d*) The structure labelled as *X* is the Z-line. During contraction of the muscle fibres, the Z-line is pulled inward due to the formation of cross bridge which causes shortening of the sarcomere.

4. (*c*) Both A and R are true, but R is not the correct explanation of A.
Troponin is a protein complex that plays a crucial role in muscle relaxation. In the resting state a subunit of troponin masks the active binding sites for myosin on the actin filaments.
This binding prevents the interaction between the myosin and actin filaments, thereby maintaining the muscle in a relaxed state. Troponin is distributed at regular intervals along the tropomyosin filament.

5. (*a*) The correct match is A-4, B-3, C-2, D-1.
- *Hydra* uses tentacles for capturing food and locomotion.
- Cilia are the fine hair like projections, that beat in a synchronous manner in the fallopian tube to facilitate the movement of the ovum.
- Protoplasmic streaming is used in amoeboid movements, by cytoskeletal elements like microfilaments.
- Flagella are the outgrowths of cell membrane that enables a spermatozoa to swim through the female tract to reach the ovum.

6. (*c*) Incorrect statement can be corrected as
Sarcoplasmic reticulum upon receiving the action potential releases Ca^{2+} ions into the sarcoplasm, around the thick and thin filaments.
Ca^{2+} binds with troponin - C and changes its shape.
It moves the troponin - tropomyosin complex away from the myosin binding sites on actin and thus, these sites get exposed.

7. (*b*) Both A and R are true and R is the correct explanation of A.
Locomotion involves a change in position. Bending down to pick up an object, involves muscular movements. However, the position remains unaltered. Hence, it cannot be classified as locomotion.

8. (*a*) The fascicles (structure *A*) or the muscle bundles are held together in place by a connective tissue layer made up of collagen called fascia. Hence, if collagen is degraded, the fascicles would fall apart due to loss of structural integrity. Actin and myosin are the proteins that make up the myofibrils. Troponin is a protein present on the F-actin filaments.

9. (*c*) The diagram represents contraction of muscle fibre by sliding filament model. During contraction, cross bridge formation is succeeded by pulling of the actin filaments towards the centre of A-band. The Z-line is pulled inward and the I-bands contract and get reduced in size. The H-zone formed by the region, not overlapped by thin filaments also disappears as the I-bands are pulled inward. However, the A-bands or anisotropic bands retain their length.

10. (*d*) Muscles appear red in colour due to a pigment called myoglobin, a oxygen - storing pigment. It receives oxygen from the RBCs and transport it to the mitochondria of muscle cells, where oxygen is used in cellular respiration to produce energy. Hence, red muscles are also known as aerobic muscles. It contains plenty of mitochondria and less number of sarcoplasmic reticulum.

11. (*a*) The correct match is A-2, B-3, C-4, D-1.

- The thick filaments in the 'A' band are held together in the middle of this band by a thin fibrous membrane called 'M' line. M-line is thus present at the centre of sarcomere which is the unit of contraction.
- The central part of thick filament, not overlapped by thin filaments is called the 'H' zone. It is visible during the resting state, however during contraction the H-zone is completely overlapped by the thin filaments and hence disappear.
- In the centre of each 'I' band is an elastic fibre called 'Z' line which bisects it. The thin filaments are firmly attached to the 'Z' line.
- During contraction, the Z line is pulled inward which pulls the I-band. However the A-band remains unaltered.

12. (*c*) If there is no release of neurotransmitter, action potential is not generated. Hence, there would be no spread of impulses through the sarcolemma and efflux of calcium into the sarcoplasm. ATP hydrolysis would also not occur.
Absence of the neurotransmitter would prevent the release of calcium ions from the sarcoplasmic reticulum to the sarcoplasm.

13. (*d*) In a resting state, the edges of thin filaments on either side of the thick filaments partially overlap the free ends of the thick filaments leaving the central part of the thick filaments. This central part of thick filament, not overlapped by thin filaments is called the 'H' zone. Hence, H-zone contains thick filaments only.

14. (*a*) White muscle fibres do not contain myoglobin, have a fast contraction rate and fatigue easily. They are required for high energy activities in a short course of time, since they fatigue easily. They posses more sarcoplasmic reticulum to facilitate faster release and re-uptake of calcium ions needed for contraction.

15. (*d*) Statement IV is correct.
Statements I, II and III are incorrect and can be corrected as

- Sarcoplasmic reticulum is higher in anaerobic muscles or white muscle fibres.
- Muscle with abundant myoglobin has more mitochondria. These are the red muscle fibres, which contain more amounts of myoglobin and can use more oxygen to generate ATP.
- Lactic acid accumulation is faster in white muscle fibres. White fibres undergo anaerobic respiration as they fatigue easily after short contraction phases.

Test 2

1. (*b*) Gout is inflammation of joints due to accumulation of uric acid crystals. High protein in the diet can lead to build up of high levels of uric acid, which can crystallise at the joints and tend to cause inflammation and pain. Hence, gout patients should consume a low protein diet.

2. (*a*) When someone is waving, there is wrist movement. The movement of the wrist is possible due to the gliding joint present at the carpals or the wrist bone.
Saddle joint is present between carpal and metacarpal of thumb.
Hinge joint is present in the knees and pivot joint allows movement of the neck.

3. (*b*) Both statement I and statement II are correct.
The U-shaped, hyoid bone is part of the skull. It is located at the base of buccal cavity and supports the tongue. Thus, it helps in swallowing and speaking.

4. (*c*) Both A and R are true, but R is not the correct explanation of A. A can be explained as
The intervertebral disc separates adjacent vertebra in the vertebral column, since they act as shock absorbers between the adjacent vertebrae in case of an impact.

5. (*d*) The lower jaw or the mandible is the only movable bone of the skull and moves while we speak. The rest (i.e. maxilla, zygomatic bone and hyoid) are immovable.

6. (*b*) In case of shoulder dislocation, the head of the humerus is shifted out of the socket called the glenoid cavity of scapula.

7. (*b*) Both A and R are true and R is the correct explanation of A.
With progressive age, functions of ovaries are slowed down, which decreases oestrogen production by the ovaries. Decreased oestrogen levels is associated with osteoporosis, where bones become weak and prone to fractures.

8. (*c*) Statements I, IV and V are correct while statements II and III are incorrect and can be corrected as
- At the sutures of the cranium, bones are attached together by dense fibrous connective tissue.
- Cartilaginous joints allow limited movement, to maintain the integrity of backbone.

9. (*d*) Statement I is correct, but statement II is incorrect. It can be corrected as
The ankle joint is a type of synovial joint, i.e. hinge joint
Three bones make up the ankle joint, which are the large tarsal bone, tibia and fibula of the leg.

10. (*c*) The odd statement regarding pelvic (hip) girdle can be corrected as-
Pectoral girdle provides articulation to the arm bones, whereas, pelvic girdle provides articulation to the bones of leg.

11. (*b*) *A*, *B* and *C* in the diagram represents cervical vertebra, thoracic vertebra and lumbar vertebra.
Thoracic vertebra (*B*) forms the articulation surface for the ribs.

12. (*a*) The correct match is A-3, B-4, C-2, D-1.
- Patella is a cup shaped bone that covers the knee ventrally.
- Radius and ulna make up the arm bone.
- Metacarpals are five small bones that form the palm.
- Pubic symphysis containing fibrous cartilage joins the two halves of pelvic girdle centrally.

13. (*a*) Only statement II is correct. Statements I, III and IV can be corrected as
- Each rib is a flat bone that connects dorsally to the vertebral column.
- Hyaline cartilage supports 8th, 9th and 10th rib to the sternum ventrally. The 8th, 9th and 10th pairs of ribs do not articulate directly with the sternum, but join the seventh rib with the help of hyaline cartilage. These are called false ribs.
- Floating ribs are connected dorsally and do not connect ventrally at all. Last 2 pairs (11th and 12th) of ribs are not connected ventrally and are therefore, called floating ribs.

14. (*a*) (i) is the pectoral girdle, (ii) is the pelvic girdle. The pectoral girdle contains the scapula and the clavicle. The ridge extending from the scapula is the acromion (P) which articulates with the clavicle. The cavity formed below the acromion is the glenoid cavity (R) where the head of the humerus articulates. The pelvic girdle consists of two coxal bones. Each coxal bone is formed by the fusion of three bones – ilium, ischium (S) and pubis. At the point of fusion of the above bones is a cavity called acetabulum (Q) to which the thigh bone articulates.

15. (*c*) Cartilaginous joint occurs between the vertebrae. However, the joint between atlas, the first vertebra and axis, the second vertebra is pivot joint which is a synovial joint that allows free movement.

16. (*b*) X is cartilage. It has slightly pliable matrix due to chondroitin salts. Other options can be corrected as
Calcium salts are components of the matrix of bones while collagen is a protein found in the matrix of both bones and cartilages.

17. (*d*) The lacrimal bone is a paired facial bone which supports the eye. It also supports the structure that facilitate tear secretion by the lacrimal or tear glands.

18. (*c*) Both A and R are true, but R is not the correct explanation of A. R can be corrected as
Fracture to the occipital condyle can cause immobilisation of head since occipital condyle provides the articulating surface for the skull with the atlas or first vertebrae. Thus, movement of the head is facilitated by this structure and a fracture can restrict the free movement and bring about immobilisation.

19. (*c*) Both statement I and statement II are incorrect. These can be corrected as
Each vertebra has a central hollow portion (neural canal) through which the spinal cord passes.
First vertebra is the atlas and it articulates with the occipital condyles.

20. (*c*) Ribs have two articulating surfaces. True ribs form the first seven pairs where they attach to the sternum ventrally by hyaline cartilage and dorsally to the thoracic vertebrae. False ribs (8th, 9th and 10th pair) do not articulate directly with the sternum but join the seventh rib with the help of hyaline cartilage. Last 2 pairs (11th and 12th) of ribs are not connected ventrally and are therefore, called floating ribs.
Hence, if hyaline cartilage is damaged, the ventral articulation of the first 10 pairs of ribs (true and false ribs) would be affected.

21. (*a*) 'A' is ball and socket joint, 'B' is hinge joint, 'C' is gliding joint and 'D' is saddle joint. A ball and socket joint is a type of synovial joint where a rounded bone (ball), moves within a depression of another bone (socket). This joint allows a wide range of movement and is found in the shoulders and hip of humans and other mammals.

22. (*b*) Both statement I and statement II are correct.
Ischium is one of the coxal bone or the hip bone that forms the pelvic girdle. Pelvic girdle consists of two coxal bones. Coxal is formed by

fusion of three bones ilium, ischium and pubis.

23. (*b*) Muscular dystrophy is a progressive degeneration of the muscles which is genetic. Hence, it can be passed on from affected person to his child.

24. (*d*) The elbows cannot be moved backwards due to the presence of hinge joint. The hinge joint allows only back and forth movement like hinges of doors. Other options can be explained as
Cartilaginous joints are present between two adjacent vertebra that allows very little movement. Fibrous joints are present in the skull that do not permit any movement. Pivot joint allows movement of head over the neck.

25. (*b*) Both statement I and statement II are correct.
Lumbar vertebrae are the vertebrae in abdominal region in humans. The lumbar vertebrae are the largest segments of the movable part of the vertebral column and can be distinguished by the absence of a foramen (hole) in the transverse process and by the absence of facets on the sides of the body. Lumbar vertebrae extend from the twelth thoracic vertebra down to the sacral vertebrae.

Chapter Break Thru

1. (*c*) The diagram represents muscle fibres maximally contracted. Inward movement of the Z-lines pulls the actin filaments inward and shortens the sarcomere.
The incorrect statements can be corrected as
- The change is associated with an increase in Ca^{2+} level in the sarcoplasm. Ca^{2+} is released from the sarcoplasmic reticulum to the sarcoplasm in response to the signal (neurotransmitter called acetylcholine) received at the neuromuscular junction.
- Energy is driven by ATP hydrolysis by the globular head of the meromyosin. The Heavy Meromyosin (HMM) is an ATPase and has ATP binding site. ATP hydrolysis, provides the energy for the myosin head to bind to the exposed active sites on actin to form a cross bridge.
- The H-zone which makes up the central portion of the thick filaments is overlapped during contraction.

2. (*b*) Both A and R are true and R is the correct explanation of A.
The red fibres contain more mitochondria than white fibres because the red fibres require more ATP as they contract for a longer time without muscular fatigue during aerobic respiration..

3. (*c*) Tetany characterised by wild muscular contraction occurs due to low calcium level in blood plasma.

4. (*d*) Statement I is correct, but statement II is incorrect. It can be corrected as
Bones at the elbow joint are protected from friction due to the synovial fluid present between them. The elbow joint is a hinge joint that allows movement in one direction.

5. (*c*) *A* is troponin, *B* is tropomyosin and *C* is F-actin. At resting state, when the muscles are relaxing, the troponin proteins masks the active binding sites for myosin on the actin filaments.
This prevents cross bridge formation and simultaneous contraction of muscles.

6. (*a*) The monomeric protein called meromyosin has two parts, the heavy meromyosin (HMM) and the light meromyosin (LMM). The HMM contains the head and short arm which forms the cross arm structure. The tail forms the LMM. So, tail is not a part of cross arm.

7. (*a*) The correct order is D-C-E-B-A.
- A motor impulse travels through the motor unit and reaches the neuromuscular junction.
- This causes release of neurotransmitter, acetylcholine at the neuromuscular junction.
- This is followed by generation of action potential at the sarcolemma of the muscle fibres.
- This stimulates the release of Ca^{2+} from the sarcoplasmic reticulum to the sarcoplasm.
- Ca^{2+} binds with a subunit of troponin on actin filaments and thereby remove the masking of active sites for myosin. Using ATP hydrolysis, the myosin head now binds to the exposed active sites on actin to form a cross bridge.

8. (*b*) The ankle joint is a type of hinge synovial joint that allows free movement in a particular direction only.

9. (*b*) Ball and socket joint and saddle joint allow movement in many direction. Ball and socket joint is present between humerus and pectoral girdle while saddle joint can be found between carpals and metacarpal of thumb.

10. (*b*) The correct match is A-1, B-4, C-2, D-3.
- Maxilla makes the upper jaw which is fixed or immovable.
- Temporal bone present above the ears, supports them.
- Hyoid bone present at the floor of buccal cavity, supports the tongue and thus helps in speaking.
- Stapes is an ear ossicle which is the smallest bone of the body.

11. (*c*) Visceral or smooth muscles are found in internal or visceral organs mostly. The activities of uterus, stomach wall and urinary bladder are not under voluntary control and are made up of smooth muscle. The diaphragm involved in respiration is however made up of skeletal or striated muscles.

12. (*b*) The labelled structure A is a muscle fibre or muscle cell. Statement (b) is incorrect about muscle fibre and can be corrected as
A muscle fibre contains sarcolemma enclosing the sarcoplasm that exists in syncytium or multi-nucleate condition.

13. (*a*) Only statement II is correct. Statements I, III and IV are incorrect and can be corrected as
- Elasticity of Z-line facilitates its movement during contraction.

• Changes in the I-band increase or decrease the length of sarcomere. Sarcomere is the portion between two successive Z-lines. A band retains their length during contraction.

• H-zone completely disappears when the fibres are under contraction. H-zone is the region of the thick filament not overlapped by the thin filaments, during relaxation. Under contraction, when the I-bands are pulled inward, the H-zone disappears as it is completely overlapped.

14. (*b*) Both statement I and statement II are correct.
The elbow joint is formed from three bones, namely humerus, radius and ulna. The elbow joint is a synovial joint where articulating surfaces enclose a fluid filled synovial cavity.

15. (*c*) The diagram shows cross bridge formation between actin and myosin filaments. Ca^{2+} binds to troponin and causes unmasking of the active site on actin where myosin head binds.

16. (*b*) Mitochondria undergoes cellular respiration to produce ATP. Since cardiac muscles are involuntarily involved in the beating of the heart, they require maximum energy. Hence, mitochondrial density would be highest in cardiac muscles, among the options given, i.e. nerve cell, skin cell and adipocytes.

17. (*a*) A is false, but R is true. A can be corrected as
In case of involuntary muscles, the muscle fibre always contracts with the maximum force and this force doesnot rise on increasing the strength of the stimulus. If the stimulus is of strength below the threshold, the muscle fibre does not contract at all.

18. (*c*) The number of bones present in a skeleton that runs along the middle longitudinal axis of the body is 80. The axial skeleton which forms the main axis and form four structures such as skull, vertebral column, sternum and ribs.

19. (*b*) Two forms of actin protein present in thin filaments are monomeric G-actin and polymeric F-actin.

20. (*a*) The rib cage is formed of thoracic vertebra, the sternum and ribs. There are 12 pairs of ribs, that is 24 bones, one sternum or breast bone and 12 thoracic vertebra. Thus, 37 (24 + 12 + 1) bones make up the rib cage.

21. (*b*) Sternum or breast bone is a flat bone that articulates with the true ribs. Coccyx and sacrum are vertebra which are formed by fusion of bones Coxal of the pelvic girdle is formed by the fusion of three bones – ilium, ischium and pubis.

22. (*d*) Statement I is correct, but statement II is incorrect. Statement II can be corrected as
Atlas provides the articulating surface for the two occipital condyles (dicondylic skill).

23. (*a*) The correct match is A-2, B-3, C-4, D-1.

• There are 7 cervical vertebrae in mammals.

• 7 pairs or 14 ribs form the true ribs that are dorsally connected to the vertebral column and ventrally to the sternum.

• Palm bones or the metacarpals are 5 in number in each hand.

• Wrist bone or the carpal is 8 in number in each hand.

24. (*b*) Statements I, III and IV are correct. While statements II and V are incorrect and can be corrected as

• Muscles of the bladder contain a single nucleus. Bladder is made of smooth muscles (involuntary muscles) that are uni- nucleated.

• All visceral muscles have unbranched appearance. They are spindle shaped and are unbranched.

25. (*d*) Statement I is correct, but statement II is incorrect. It can be corrected as
Coccyx located adjacent to sacral vertebrae, forms the last part of backbone.

26. (*c*) The correct match is A-4, B-3, C-1, D-2.

• Tetany is caused by wild contraction of the muscles due to low calcium levels in blood.

• Osteoporosis is an age related disorder affecting women more than men, since it is related to decreased oestrogen levels with age.

• Myasthenia gravis is an auto-immune disorder, where the neuromuscular junction is affected and thus involves damage of self cells by immune system of body.

• Muscular dystrophy is a genetic disorder where there is progressive deterioration of muscles.

27. (*b*) Both A and R are true and R is the correct explanation of A.
Repeated cycle of cross bridge formation and breakage continues till calcium ions are pumped back into the sarcoplasmic reticulum. This causes masking of the myosin binding sites on actin and the muscle fibres undergo relaxation.

28. (*d*) Pelvis is formed by three bones, the hip bone, the sacrum and the coccyx (tail bone).

29. (*c*) Both A and R are true, but R is not the correct explanation of A. It can be corrected as
Some WBCs of the blood have no definite shape and move like an *Amoeba*, as these cells often have to squeeze themselves out of thin blood vessels. Hence, they lack a definite shape and show amoeboid movement by protoplasmic projections.

30. (*c*) A is H-zone, B is I-band, C is A-band and X is Z-line. The phase shown in the diagram is that of relaxation. During relaxation,

• H-zone appears, since it is no longer overlapped by actin filaments. H-zone is overlapped and disappeared during contraction phase.

• The distance between Z-lines returns to its original length. The distance between two successive Z-lines shorten during contraction.

• I-bands return to their original position.

• A bands retain their original length.

31. (*a*) Statement I is incorrect, but statement II is correct. Statement I can be corrected as

All involuntary actions of human body are mediated by non-striated as well as striated muscles. Involuntary actions like movement of food through digestive tract, etc. are mediated by smooth muscles that do not show any striations (non-striated muscles).
However, the beating of the heart, which is involuntary, is regulated by cardiac muscles that have striations in them.

32. (*c*) Both A and R are correct, but R is not the correct explanation of A.
During contraction, the sarcomere shortens as the I band is pulled inward.
However, the A band remains unaltered. This is explained by the sliding filament theory which states that contraction of a muscle fibre takes place by the sliding of the thin filaments over the thick filaments.

33. (*a*) The correct match is A-3, B-1, C-4, D-2.
- Troponin is present at regular intervals on tropomyosin and binds to calcium when calcium levels rise in the sarcoplasm.
- HMM or Heavy Meromyosin contains the globular head and short arm which forms cross arm that projects outwards at regular distance and angle from each other from the surface of a polymerised myosin.
- Globular head of meromyosin, is an ATPase and has binding sites for ATP.
- G-actin or globular actin are monomeric proteins that make up the two F-actin filaments of each thin filament.

34. (*a*) Statement I is incorrect, but statement II is correct. Statement I can be corrected as
Fascia maintains the structural integrity of fascicles. Each organised skeletal muscle in our body is made of a number of muscle bundles or fascicles held together by a common collagenous connective tissue layer called fascia.

35. (*a*) Cross bridge is formed when the HMM or Heavy Meromyosin (consisting of head and short arm) binds to the active binding site on actin filaments. This process requires energy and ATP is hydrolysed by the globular ATPase head of meromyosin. This causes ADP and Pi to remain bound to the HMM. When the cross bridge breaks, ADP and Pi are released, while a new ATP is bound to the HMM.

36. (*b*) The correct order is II-I-III-V-IV
- ATP molecule binds to the globular head part of Heavy Meromyosin (HMM).
- This breaks the cross bridge formed between the HMM and actin.
- The process of cross bridge formation and breaking continues till all the calcium ions are pumped back to the sarcoplasmic reticulum, which causes masking of the actin filaments by troponin.
- The Z lines, at the centre of I bands return to their original position.
- The sarcomere, which was initially contracted, return to their original length and relax.

37. (*b*) Under resting conditions, troponin masks the active binding sites of myosin. This prevents the myosin head to bind actin and form cross bridge.
- Actin binding site is located on the globular head part of HMM.
- ATP binding sites are also present on the HMM.
- Calcium binds troponin that causes unmasking during contraction.

38. (*b*) Unstriated muscles are the smooth muscles involved in involuntary functions. Flow of blood through arteries and of urine through the urethra involves smooth muscles. Tongue and diaphragm contains skeletal muscles which are striated in their appearance.

39. (*b*) ATPase activity of the globular head of HMM, allows it to hydrolyse ATP and form ADP and Pi. This energy of ATP hydrolysis used to bind actin sites, thereby forming cross bridge and initiating contraction phase. Thus, in the absence of ATPase activity, contraction would not be initiated. The actin filaments and the I-bands would remain in relaxed state.

40. (*b*) Both A and R are correct and R is the correct explanation of A.
A chemical that inhibits muscle contraction can bind to the globular head of HMM. This is because the head has ATPase activity and hydrolyses ATP into ADP and Pi. The energy released is utilized in cross bridge formation.

41. (*d*) The correct match is A-3, B-4, C-2, D-1.
Zygomatic bone is a facial bone which is located the prominence of the cheek.
Parietal bone is a cranial bone which is greater portion of sides and roof of cranial cavity.
Vomer is a triangular facial bone that forms the inferior portion of nasal septum.
Occipital bone is a cranial bone which forms posterior part and most of the base of cranium. It possess foramen magnum in the inferior part through which medulla oblongata connects with spinal cord.

42. (*a*) Incorrect statement can be corrected as
In sponges, flagella of choanocyte cells maintain a regular current of water through the canal system.

43. (*b*) The term bicephalic refers to having two heads or two attachments. In the case of human ribs, these two attachments are found at the dorsal end, where they articulate with the vertebral column. One articulation is with the vertebral body and the other is with the transverse process of the vertebra. This double articulation gives the ribs their bicephalic nature.

44. (*b*) Both A and R are true and R is the correct explanation of A.
A muscle twitch is a single, contraction of a muscle fiber in response to a single nerve impulse.
Tetanus is a sustained muscle contraction caused by a rapid series of nerve impulse.
Tetanus occurs when the muscle is stimulated so rapidly, that it cannot

relax between contractions, leading to a sustained contraction.

45. (*c*) The sliding filament theory explains that muscle contraction occurs due to the interaction between actin (thin filaments) and myosin (thick filaments). When a muscle contracts, the myosin heads bind to the actin filaments and pull them towards the center of the sarcomere.

This sliding action shortens the sarcomere, resulting the overall contraction of the muscle.

46. (*c*) Synovial fluid is produced by the synovial membrane that lubricates the joint.

The stiffness of the synovial membrane with ageing renders it less able to produce the synovial fluid and thereby, causes stiffness of joints.

Its condition worsen immediately after awakening, prolonged resting or immobility.

47. (*b*) Both statement I and statement II are correct.

Gout is an inherited disorder of purine metabolism. In this, body forms excess amount of uric acid and crystals of sodium urate are deposited in the synovial joints.

Muscular dystrophy is a group genetic disorders characterised by damage and progressive skeletal muscle weakness overtime. It occurs due to lack of a protein called dystrophin, which is necessary for normal function of muscle.

48. (*b*) Incorrect statement can be corrected as

The human vertebral column actually consists of 33 vertebrae. These are divided into five regions: cervical (7 vertebrae), thoracic (12 vertebrae), lumbar (5 vertebrae), sacral (5 fused vertebrae) and coccygeal (4 fused vertebrae).

49. (*c*) Statements III, IV and V are incorrect. These can be corrected as

- Scapula is a large, flat and triangular bone that forms the posterior part of shoulder girdle, whereas clavicle is a long, narrow, S-shaped bone that forms the anterior part of shoulder girdle.
- Atlas supports the head and it consists of a complete ring of bone. Its upper surface possesses facets that articulates with the condyles of occipital bone.

Axis acts a pivot on which atlas turns to allow movement of head.

- Lumbar vertebrae are the largest and strongest vertebrae of human body. They are found in abdominal region and bear the weight of the trunk.

50. (*d*) In the given diagram, *A* represents troponin, *B*-tropomyosin and *C* is F-actin.

Incorrect option can be corrected as

Troponin found at regular intervals on tropomyosin (*B*).

It is responsible for keeping tropomyosin in place when muscle is relaxed.

Ch-18 Neural Control and Coordination

Topical Follow Thru

Test 1

1. (*b*) *Hydra* belongs to the phylum–Cnidaria. It possesses nerve cells (neurons) distributed throughout its body for coordinating various functions such as movement and response to stimuli. However, *Hydra* lacks a centralised brain or true nervous system like more complex animals. Instead of a brain, *Hydra* relies on a decentralised nerve net to carry out its basic nervous functions.

Other options can be explained as *Pheretima* (earthworm) and *Periplanata americana* (cockroach) possess brain along with a number of ganglia and neural tissues.

Scypha, a sponge, lacks any nervous system.

2. (*a*) If the terminal ends of an axon are in contact with the dendrites of four adjacent neurons, the nerve impulse has the potential to travel to all four neurons. The strength of the impulse received by each neuron might vary depending on factors like the distance from the axon terminal and the number of neurotransmitters released.

3. (*a*) Statements I and IV are correct regarding myelinated nerve fibre. The incorrect statements can be corrected as

Schwann cells produce myelin sheaths in the Peripheral Nervous System (PNS), not in the Central Nervous System (CNS). In the CNS, myelin sheaths are produced by oligodendrocytes.

Myelinated nerve fibres allow rapid conduction of nerve impulses. The myelin sheath insulates the axon, and the presence of nodes of Ranvier facilitates saltatory conduction, which significantly increases the speed of nerve impulse transmission.

4. (*b*) The correct match is A-4, B-1, C-8.

The structure responsible for maintaining the metabolic and synthetic activities of a neuron necessary for its survival and function is the cell body, i.e. 4 (soma or perikaryon). The cell body contains organelles such as the nucleus, Golgi apparatus, Endoplasmic Reticulum (ER) and Mitochondria, which carry out various metabolic processes and protein synthesis essential for the neuron's function and survival.

The structure that receives nerve impulses and passes them towards the cell body is the dendrite (1). They are specialised extensions of the neuron that receive signals from other neurons or sensory receptors and transmit them to the cell body.

The structure that contains vesicles of neurotransmitters is the synaptic knob, i.e. 8 (synaptic terminal). Synaptic knobs are located at the end of the axon and contain synaptic vesicles filled with neurotransmitters.

5. (*d*) Statement I is correct, but statement II is incorrect. The incorrect statement can be corrected as

The endocrine system primarily provides chemical integration through hormones, not neurotransmitters. Hormones are released into the bloodstream and regulate physiological processes in distant target cells, not neurotransmission between neurons.

6. (*b*) Dendrites receive synaptic inputs from other neurons through their synapses. The impulses or signals are transmitted along the dendrites towards the cell body (soma). This process allows the neuron to integrate incoming signals and respond appropriately.

The incorrect statements about dendrites can be corrected as

- They are branched cytoplasmic processes.
- Neurilemma surrounds the axons of the neurons.
- They are afferent processes.

7. (*b*) Afferent nerves, also known as sensory nerves, are responsible for carrying sensory information from the body to the Central Nervous System (CNS). This information includes signals from sensory receptors in the skin, muscles and organs, which are then processed by the brain and spinal cord to produce appropriate responses.

8. (*a*) The correct sequence is Threshold $\rightarrow$ depolarisation $\rightarrow$ repolarisation $\rightarrow$ hyperpolarisation.

- Threshold : The neuron reaches a critical threshold level of depolarisation due to incoming signals.
- Depolarisation : Voltage-gated sodium channels open, allowing sodium ions to rush into the neuron, causing a rapid depolarisation of the membrane potential.
- Repolarisation : Voltage-gated potassium channels open, allowing potassium ions to leave the neuron, which restores the membrane potential to its resting state.
- Hyperpolarisation : In some cases, the membrane potential briefly becomes more negative than the resting potential due to excessive potassium efflux.

9. (*c*) The sodium-potassium pump helps to maintain the electrochemical gradient necessary for various cellular processes, including nerve impulse transmission. For every cycle of the sodium-potassium pump,

- 3 Na^+ ions are pumped out of the cell.
- 2 K^+ ions are pumped into the cell.

This activity results in a higher concentration of Na^+ outside the cell and a higher concentration of K^+ inside the cell.

10. (*c*) Both A and R are true, but R is not the correct explanation of A.

Synaptic vesicles are small membrane-bound organelles found in the pre-synaptic neuron. They store neurotransmitters and release them into the synaptic cleft upon receiving an action potential.

The synaptic cleft is indeed a small gap between the pre-synaptic and post-synaptic neurons. Neurotransmitters released from synaptic vesicles diffuse across this gap and bind to specific receptors on the post-synaptic neuron, initiating or inhibiting a response in the post-synaptic neuron.

11. (*a*) Calcium ions (Ca^+), sodium ions (Na^+) and potassium ions (K^+) are all necessary for nerve conduction.

- Calcium ions play a role in neurotransmitter release at the synaptic terminal.
- Sodium ions are involved in the depolarisation phase of action potential propagation along the neuron.
- Potassium ions are involved in the repolarisation phase of action potential and in maintaining the resting membrane potential of neurons.

12. (*d*) Bipolar neurons are characterised by their unique structure, having one dendrite for receiving signals and one axon for transmitting signals. This distinguishes them from other types of neurons, such as multipolar neurons, which have multiple dendrites and one axon.

13. (*d*) The incorrect match pairs can be corrected as

- Resting membrane potential is typically around -70 mV.
- Depolarisation involves the opening of Na^+ gated channels, allowing sodium ions to enter the cell.
- Repolarisation involves the opening of K^+ gated channels, allowing potassium ions to exit the cell.

14. (*d*) A synaptic cleft is the small gap that separates the pre-synaptic neuron (sending neuron) from the post-synaptic neuron (receiving neuron). Neurotransmitters released from synaptic vesicles in the pre-synaptic neuron travel across this gap to bind to receptors on the post-synaptic neuron, thereby transmitting signals between neurons.

15. (*d*) The incorrect statement can be corrected as

While the neural system is known for its rapid coordination due to the speed of nerve impulses, it is not long-lived in the sense that its effects are generally immediate and transient. Long-term coordination and regulation are more characteristic of the endocrine system, which uses hormones that act over longer periods and have slower, but longer-lasting effects.

16. (*a*) The sensory neuron enters the spinal cord through the dorsal root of the spinal nerve. The ventral root is responsible for sending motor signals back out to muscles and organs. Depending on the point where the sensory neuron originates, it can enter the spinal cord through dorsal root.

17. (*b*) Unmyelinated nerve fibres are enclosed by a Schwann cell, but do not form a myelin sheath around the axon. It is sometimes referred to as an nerve fibre and it is found in the autonomic and somatic neural systems.

18. (*b*) The incorrect statement can be corrected as

In a chemical synapse, the membranes of the pre and post-synaptic neurons are separated by a fluid filled space called synaptic cleft. Chemicals called neurotrans mitter released from the pre-synaptic membrane which binds to specific receptors present on post-synaptic membrane.

Whereas at electrical synapses, the membrane of pre and post-synaptic neurons are in very close proximity. Thus, the impluse can flow directly from one neuron to other across these synapse.

19. (*b*) The incorrect statements can be corrected as

Parasympathetic nerve fibres are not contained in spinal nerves. They primarily travel through cranial nerves (such as the vagus nerve) and sacral nerves. Parasympathetic neurons originate in the brainstem (cranial nerves) and the sacral region of the spinal cord, not the thoracic and lumbar regions. In the parasympathetic nervous system, post-ganglionic fibres are usually shorter than those of sympathetic neurons. This is because parasympathetic ganglia are located closer to or within the target organs, resulting in shorter post-ganglionic fibres.

20. (*d*) Gated ion channels are present on the axonal membranes of neurons that regulate the transport of ions across the membrane. During the resting state of a neuron, the Na^+ ion channels are completely closed and hence, the axonal membrane is nearly impermeable to Na^+ ions. However, K^+ ion channels with high basal activation are present on the axonal membrane that help in maintaining negative membrane potential.

Therefore, when a neuron is in resting state, the axonal membrane is comparatively more permeable to K^+ ions and nearly impermeable to Na^+ ions.

21. (*d*) Statements I and II are correct. Incorrect statements are III and IV and these can be corrected as

When a nerve cell is stimulated, ion channels in the plasma membrane opens and Na^+ instantly diffuse down its concentration gradient into the cell. These cations over ride the negative charges in the intercellular fluid, so the inside of the membrane briefly become positive. This stage is called as depolarisation of the membrane.

22. (*b*) In the resting nerve fibre, higher concentration of sodium ions is found outside the cell, whereas inside the cell, potassium ions predominate. Due to this different concentration gradient, sodium ions tends to passively diffuse into the nerve fibre and potassium ions acquirer the tendency of diffusion out of the nerve fibre down their electrochemical gradients.

However, the membrane of a resting nerve fibre is more permeable to potassium than to sodium (selective permeability).

23. (*b*) Both A and R are true and R is the correct explanation of A.

The neuroglial cells are of three types, i.e. astrocytes, oligodendrocytes and microglia. Out of these, oligodendrocytes are the cells which form the myelin sheath around axon, thus are also called packing cells of the brain. The other cells like astrocytes are responsible for the separation of two neurons by providing insulation and microglia are phagocytic cells. Nearly 50% of all brain cells are neuroglia.

24. (*b*) Both statement I and statement II are correct.

The neural system of insects is considered better organised than other lower organisms due to the presence of brain, located in the head and the ganglia are a ventral chain of segmental bundles of neurons. These structures are connected to each other and to the body by primitive neural tissues.

The simplest nervous system is present in lower invertebrates. A true neuron or ganglion cells first appeared in coelenterates like *Hydra*.

25. (*d*) A nerve impulse is transmitted from one neuron to another with the help of chemicals called neurotransmitters that are released by the axon endings formed by the membrane of a pre-synaptic and post-synaptic neurons which may or may not be separated by synaptic cleft.

Test 2

1. (*c*) The hypothalamus is a crucial part of the brain that acts as the main control center for the Autonomic Nervous System (ANS). It regulates a variety of autonomic functions such as heart rate, blood pressure, body temperature and digestion. The hypothalamus integrates signals from the body and the brain and coordinates responses to maintain homeostasis.

The spinal cord, cerebellum and pons also play roles in the nervous system, but they do not primarily control the ANS.

2. (*a*) The thalamus is involved in relaying sensory information to the cerebral cortex. It does not directly regulate body temperature, hunger, or water balance. These functions are primarily controlled by other brain regions such as the hypothalamus (for temperature and hunger) and kidneys (for water balance).

3. (*d*) The correct match is A-2, B-4, C-3, D-1.

The dura mater is tough, outermost layer of the meninges that provides a strong, protective barrier for the brain.

The arachnoid mater is a delicate, spiderweb-like layer with projections (arachnoid trabeculae) that connects it to the pia mater.

The pia mater is the innermost layer that closely follows the contours of the brain and is rich in blood vessels, supplying oxygen and nutrients to the brain tissue.

The subdural space is a potential space located between the dura mater and the arachnoid mater, the two outermost layers of the meninges that surround and protect the brain and spinal cord.

4. (*d*) The olfactory lobe, also known as the olfactory bulb, is not a lobe of the cerebral hemisphere. It is involved in the sense of smell (olfaction). The olfactory bulb receives sensory input from olfactory receptor neurons in the nasal cavity and transmits this information to higher brain regions for processing.

5. (*b*) The visceral nervous system operates bidirectionally, with impulses traveling between the CNS (brain and spinal cord) and visceral organs (such as the heart, digestive organs and glands). This bidirectional communication allows for coordinated regulation of bodily functions.

6. (*d*) Ductless glands, also known as endocrine glands, secrete hormones directly into the bloodstream. These glands are under the control of the brain through the hypothalamus and pituitary gland, which regulate hormonal secretions and maintain homeostasis in the body.

7. (*b*) Both statement I and statement II are correct.

The limbic system is a complex structure formed from the inner parts of cerebral hemispheres and a group of associated deep structure. It is responsible for olfaction autonomic responses, regulation of sexual behaviour, expression of emotional reactions and motivation.

Pons consist of fibre tracts that interconnects different regions of brain.

8. (*d*) Incorrect match pair can be corrected as

The cerebellum is the posterior region of the brain. It is involved in the regulation of body posture. It helps maintain the balance of the body. Also, the cerebellum is the center for skill development.

Respiratory rate is not the function of the cerebellum, it is performed by medulla oblongata.

9. (*a*) The forebrain (or prosencephalon) is the rostral-most portion (towards front part) of the brain in vertebrates. During development, it separates into the diencephalon and the secondary prosencephalon, which includes the hypothalamus, the pre-optic area and the telencephalon.

10. (*c*) Subarachnoid space is located between the arachnoid mater and the pia mater. It is filled with CSF and is the main reservoir for it, containing the majority of the cerebrospinal fluid at any moment.

11. (*c*) Coordination of voluntary movements and fine motor skills are primarily managed by the cerebellum and motor cortex, not the brain stem (midbrain, pons and medulla oblongata).

The cerebellum is located at the back of brain underlying occipital and temporal lobes of cerebral cortex. It coordinates voluntary movements such as posture, balance, muscle activity and do not form part of brain stem.

12. (*c*) Statements I and IV are incorrect and can be corrected as

The corpora quadrigemina are actually located on the dorsal portion of the midbrain, not the ventral part. The corpora quadrigemina are four colliculi or lobes.

The cerebrum wraps around the thalamus, not the cerebellum, which is majority coordinating center for sensory and motor signal.

13. (*b*) The given figure is of human brain and *C* represents the medulla oblongata, which contains centres of respiration, cardiovascular reflexes and gastric secretion.

14. (*d*) Statement I is correct, but statement II is incorrect. Incorrect statement can be corrected as

The gray matter is located in the interior of the spinal cord and forms a horn like structure. White matter surrounds the gray matter and makes up the surrounding sections of spinal cord.

15. (*a*) A is false, but R is true. A can be corrected as

The layer of cells which covers the cerebral hemispheres is called cerebral cortex and is thrown into prominent folds. It is referred to as the gray matter due to its greyish appearance. Neuron cell bodies are concentrated here which give it the greyish appearance.

Chapter Break Thru

1. (*b*) Interneurons play a critical role in processing and integrating information within the CNS, particularly in the spinal cord, where they facilitate communication between sensory and motor neurons.

2. (*b*) The hippocampus is a brain structure that plays a crucial role in memory formation and recall. It helps in the conversion of short-term memories to long-term memories and is essential for learning and spatial navigation. Therefore, it functions as an index for recall of events and associated memories.

3. (*c*) The resting potential primarily occurs due to the different concentration of ions, especially sodium (Na^+) and potassium (K^+), across the cell membrane and the selective permeability of the membrane to these ions. The sodium-potassium pump helps to maintain these concentration gradients by actively transporting Na^+ out of the cell and K^+ into the cell.

4. (*c*) Electrical transmission between neurons occurs at electrical synapses, which are characterised by direct contact between the pre-synaptic and post-synaptic membranes. This contact is facilitated by structures called gap junctions, which allow ions and small molecules to pass directly from one neuron to the next, enabling rapid and synchronised electrical signaling.

5. (*c*) The (ii) match pair is incorrect and can be corrected as

Bipolar neuron have two processes - one axon and one dendrite. They are found in sensory organs like the retina of the eye (not specifically the cornea) and the olfactory epithelium (involved in smell).

6. (*d*) Autonomic nervous system, a type of peripheral nervous system transmits impulses from the CNS to the involuntary organs and smooth muscles of the body.

7. (*c*) The symptoms like tremor, halting speech and an irregular gait are indicative of dysfunction in motor control and coordination. These functions are primarily governed by the cerebellum of hind brain.

8. (*b*) The incorrect statement can be corrected as

Cerebrum consists of two cerebral hemispheres.

The cerebrum is the largest part of the brain and is located in the forebrain. It is responsible for higher cognitive functions such as thinking, perception and voluntary actions. The cerebellum is located at the back of the brain (hindbrain) below the cerebrum. It is primarily involved in coordination, balance, and motor control.

9. (*c*) Blocking Ca^{2+} channels prevents the influx of calcium ions into the pre-synaptic terminal. This blocks neurotransmitter release because calcium influx is necessary for synaptic vesicle fusion and neurotransmitter release.

Consequently, neurotransmitters are not available to bind to receptors on the post-synaptic neuron, leading to the inability of Na^+ channels to open and generate a post-synaptic potential.

10. (*c*) The parts labelled as 4, 5 and 6 represents the components of synaptic structure. They are : 4 - pre-synaptic membrane, 5- synaptic cleft and 6 - post-synaptic membrane.

11. (*b*) During the initiation of an action potential, sodium (Na^+) channels open, allowing Na^+ ions to rush into the axon. This influx of positive sodium ions causes the inside of the axon membrane to become more positively charged relative to the outside, reversing the membrane potential.

Potassium (K^+) ions play a role in repolarising the membrane later, but the initial depolarisation that triggers the action potential is primarily due to the influx of Na^+ ions.

12. (*a*) The part of the brain that controls intelligence and memory is the cerebrum (I) specifically the cerebral cortex. Within the cerebral cortex, different lobes and regions play key roles. Temporal lobe plays key role in memory and learning.

13. (*b*) Both statement I and statement II are correct.

The corpora quadrigemina, also known as the colliculi, which is located in the midbrain (mesencephalon) that plays a crucial role in processing both auditory and visual information.

The corpora quadrigemina are indeed located in the mesencephalon, which is the midbrain region of the brainstem.

14. (*c*) The glossopharyngeal (III) and trigeminal (IV) nerves are the mixed cranial nerves.

Trigeminal nerve (IV) is a mixed nerve. It has both sensory functions (providing sensation to the face) and motor functions (controlling muscles involved in mastication).

Hypoglossal nerve (II) is a motor nerve. It controls the muscles of the tongue.

Glossopharyngeal nerve (III) is a mixed nerve. It has sensory functions (sensing taste from the posterior region of the tongue and sensory information from the pharynx) and motor functions (innervating the stylopharyngeus muscle and aiding in the secretion of saliva).

Abducens nerve (VI) is a motor nerve. It controls the lateral rectus muscle, which is responsible for abducting the eye.

15. (*b*) The diencephalon is a region of the brain that is situated between the midbrain and the cerebral hemispheres. It plays a crucial role in many functions, including sensory and motor signal relay and regulation of consciousness and alertness. The diencephalon consists of three major parts named as epithalamus, thalamus, hypothalamus.

16. (*b*) The incorrect match pair can be corrected as

The limbic system is primarily involved in emotions, memory and arousal. It includes structures like the hippocampus, amygdala and hypothalamus, but it does not consist of fibrous tracts that control movement. Instead, it plays a crucial role in emotional responses and certain aspects of memory.

17. (*a*) Acetylcholine is a well-known neurotransmitter that is released from the synaptic vesicles at the axon endings of many neurons, particularly in the neuromuscular junction and within the central and peripheral nervous systems. It plays a critical role in transmitting nerve impulses across synapses.

18. (*c*) The dendrite (P) receives signal from neurotransmitter and transfers it across cell body (S). From cell body, signal travels to axon (Q) and reach synapse (R). Synaptic vesicles in synapse release neurotransmitter and impulse conduction is repeated across neuron.

19. (*d*) Statements I and III are correct. Statement II is incorrect and can be corrected as

Dopamine and acetylcholine are indeed neurotransmitters. But there are many others such as serotonin, nor-epinephrine and Gamma-Aminobutyric Acid (GABA). Neurotransmitters can be excitatory or inhibitory in nature.

20. (*d*) The incorrectly matched pair can be corrected as

Association areas are regions of the cerebral cortex, not the cerebellum, that integrate sensory information and higher cognitive functions such as memory, reasoning and language. The cerebellum is primarily involved in motor control and coordination, not higher cognitive functions.

21. (*d*) Statements I, III and V are correct. Rest statements are incorrect and can be corrected as

Efferent nerve fibres transmit motor impulses from the CNS to tissues (muscles or glands), enabling voluntary and involuntary actions.

The sympathetic and parasympathetic nervous systems are part of the autonomic nervous system, which controls involuntary actions like heart rate, digestion, and glandular secretion.

22. (*b*) Both A and R are true and R is the correct explanation of A.

In myelinated nerve fibers, the action potential (nerve impulse) does not travel as a continuous wave of depolarisation because the myelinated nerve fibres have nodes of Ranvier. These are the gaps in the myelin sheath that expose the axon membrane.

Transport pumps are concentrated at node of Ranvier. So, the nerve impluse does not travel a continuous wave of depolarisation. Instead, it jumps from one node of Ranvier to the next in a process called saltatory conduction.

23. (*b*) Both A and R are true and R is the correct explanation of A.

Nerve cells, or neurons, are typically amitotic, meaning they do not undergo cell division once fully formed in most parts of the nervous system. They do remain in interphase throughout their life cycle.

Neurons lack centrosomes, which are essential for organising microtubules during cell division in other types of cells. This absence contributes to their inability to divide.

24. (*a*) Statement I is incorrect, but statement II is correct. The incorrect statement can be corrected as

The thalamus relays sensory information related to reflexes, it's not the primary control center. It might indirectly influence these reflexes.

The medulla oblongata is the actual control center for many involuntary functions, including the reflexes mentioned.

25. (*c*) The correct match is A-4, B-3, C-1, D-2.

Purkinje cells are neurons with flask-shaped cell body (soma).

Nissl's granules are irregular fragments of endoplasmic reticulum attached to ribosomes.

Perikaryon is the cell body cyton of neuron.

Cytoplasm of neuron is called neuroplasm.

26. (*b*) The correct match is A-2, B-3, C-1, D-4.

- Amygdala is an almond-shaped structure in the limbic system associated with emotions like fear and aggression.
- Hippocampus is a part of the limbic system crucial for memory formation and consolidation.
- Thalamus acts as a relay center for sensory information and plays a role in integrating information from various parts of the body.
- Epithalamus is a smaller region above the thalamus, containing structures like the pineal body.

27. (*a*) The cardiac control center, which regulates heart rate and cardiac output, is primarily located in the medulla oblongata, not the pons.

28. (*d*) A is true, but R is false. R can be corrected as

- The neural system is better organised in insects. They possess a brain along with a number of ganglia and neural tissues.
- Vertebrates do have a more complex neural organisation compared to invertebrates. Their nervous system features a Central Nervous System (CNS) with a well-developed brain for integrating information and a peripheral nervous system for transmitting signals throughout the body. The brain allows for more sophisticated information processing, leading to complex behaviours.

29. (*b*) The correct match is A-3, B-2, C-4, D-1.

- Frontal lobe are associated with higher-order functions like planning, decision-making, and reasoning. While creativity can be a part of this, reasoning is a more central function.
- Occipital lobe contain the primary visual cortex, which is the primary area for processing visual information.
- Parietal lobe integrate sensory information from the body, including touch, pressure, and temperature.
- Temporal lobe plays a vital role in processing auditory information, language comprehension and memory.

30. (*d*) All the given statements are correct. They are discussed as follows

- The hypothalamus is responsible for regulating body temperature through mechanisms like sweating or shivering, and it also controls feelings of hunger and thirst.
- The limbic system includes structures in the brain involved in emotions, memory, and motivation, such as the amygdala and hippocampus.
- The hypothalamus and limbic system work together to regulate sexual behaviour, expression of emotional reactions and motivation.
- The hypothalamus secretes various hormones that control the pituitary gland and influence other bodily functions.
- The hypothalamus is positioned below the thalamus in the region of forebrain.

31. (*d*) A is true, but R is false. R can be corrected as

The resting membrane potential arises from three major factors: unequal distribution of ions in the ECF and cytosol, inability of most anions to leave the cell and electronic nature of the Na^+ / K^+ ATPase. In order to maintain this unequal distribution of ions, the neurons use chemical energy in the form of ATP.

32. (*b*) Broca's area also known as sensory speech or motor speech area, located into frontal lobe towards left side. It is associated with language area and also interprets translation of written words into speech. Damage or injury in Broca's area may result aphasia (inability to speak), auditory verbel disorder (word deafness) and affected read ability and understanding (word blindness).
Anosmia is medical term for loss of smell, which can happen when injury happens in the olfactory lobe.

33. (*d*) The incorrect match pairs can be corrected as
- Urinary bladder relaxes in sympathetic ANS, whereas constricts in parasympathetic ANS.
- Pupil dilates in sympathetic ANS, whereas constricts in parasympathetic ANS.
- Salivary gland inhibits secretion in sympathetic ANS, whereas stimulates secretion in parasympathetic ANS.

34. (*c*) Both statement I and statement II are incorrect. These can be corrected as
- Sensory functions senses certain changes (stimuli) both within body (interval environment) and outside body (external environment).
- Motor functions respond to stimuli by initiating muscular contractions or glandular secretions.

35. (*c*) The incorrect statement can be corrected as
A typical synapse consists of a bulbous expansion of a nerve terminal called a pre-synaptic knob, lying close to the membrane of a dendrite. The cytoplasm of the synaptic knob contains mitochondria, smooth endoplasmic reticulum, microfilaments and numerous synaptic vesicles.

36. (*b*) The incorrect statement can be corrected as
- In Annelida, nerves are of mixed type and CNS is made up of nerve ring and central nerve cord.
- Nervous system members of Platyhelminthes marks the beginning of a centralised nervous system encountered in higher animals.
- In hemichordates, nervous system is of primitive type resembling that of coelenterate and echinodermates, with both dorsal and ventral nerve cord.

37. (*d*) Cerebellum represented by *A* is second largest portion of the brain which lies posterior to medulla and pons and inferior to posterior portion of cerebrum.

38. (*d*) Statement I is correct, but statement II is incorrect. The incorrect statement can be corrected as
A wave of reversed polarity or depolarisation (action potential) moving down an axon is called a nerve impulse.

39. (*d*) A neuron have certain granular bodies called Nissl's granules found in the cell body and is made up of ribonucleic acid. They synthesis and release protein that are important for neuronal growth and regeneration of axons.

40. (*c*) The correct match is A-4, B-3, C-1, D-2.
- Gray matter is formed of cell bodies, non medullated nerve fibres, neuroglia, dendrites of association neurons and motor neurons. White matter is formed of medullated nerve fibres or myelinated axon of motor and sensory neurons, which appear white due to the presence of medullary sheath.
- There are 31 pairs of spinal nerves in the human body: Eight pairs of cervical nerves, twelve pairs of thoracic nerve, five pairs of lumbar nerves, five pair of sacral nerves and one pair of coccygeal.

41. (*a*) When faced with fear or perceived danger (such as watching a horror movie), the body activates the 'fight-or-flight' response. This response triggers physiological changes like increased heart rate and dry mouth to prepare the body for action. It is due to increased activity of the sympathetic nervous system.

42. (*c*) The correct match is A-2, B-1, C-4, D-3.
- Cerebrum is the part which is designated as the seat of intelligence and voluntary actions control.
- Cerebellum is the largest part of hind brain, controls smooth, coordinated movements, helps to maintain muscle tone, posture and balance.
- Pituitary gland is located inferior to the hypothalamus and is connected to the hypothalamus by a stalk.
- Hormonal secretion by the anterior pituitary is controlled by hypothalamus.
- Midbrain is a part of the CNS. It is small, but important structure that plays a crucial role in processing visual and auditory signals.

43. (*b*) Three regions are the primary divisions of the developing brain and form the basis for the development of the adult brain. These are as follows:
- Prosencephalon (forebrain) develops into the telencephalon and diencephalon.
- Mesencephalon (midbrain) remains as the midbrain.
- Rhombencephalon (hindbrain) develops into the metencephalon and myelencephalon.

44. (*b*) Both A and R are true and R is the correct explanation of A.
- Cholinergic neurons are those that release acetylcholine as their primary neurotransmitter. Both motor nerve fibers (somatic nervous system) and parasympathetic nerve fibers (autonomic nervous system) fall under this category. When stimulated, these neurons release acetylcholine into the synaptic cleft, which then binds to specific receptors on the target cells to produce a response.

45. (*b*) The two main neurotransmitters in vertebrate's nervous system are Acetylcholine (ACh) and nor-adrenaline, although other neurotransmitters also exist. Neurons releasing acetylcholine are described as cholinergic neurons and those releasing nor-adrenaline are described as adrenergic neurons.

46. (*b*) Myelinated nerve fibres are enclosed with Schwann cells, which form myelin sheath around the axon. This myelin sheath is discontinuous at some places of axon to form gaps. These gaps are called nodes of Ranvier.

47. (*c*) Nerve gas inhibits the neuromuscular activity by blocking the active sites of acetylcholinesterase enzyme and cause irreversible inhibition of cholinesterases, thus distorting its functions.

48. (*d*) Grey matter is the inner area of spinal cord and white matter surround it from outside. The location of white and grey matter is opposite to that in brain where grey matter forms the cortex around the inner white matter.

49. (*a*) The maintenance of the ionic gradients across the resting membrane is accomplished by active transport of ions.
One ATP is used to transfer Na^+ outside and K^+ inside by pump.

50. (*d*) Dendrites of efferent neurons are specialised to receive incoming signals from other neurons or sensory receptors, not to form receptors themselves. Receptors are typically located on sensory neurons or specialised cells in sensory organs.

Ch-19 Chemical Coordination and Integration

Topical Follow Thru

Test 1

1. (*d*) The hormones released from hypothalamus reach the pituitary gland through a portal circulatory system and regulate the functions of the anterior pituitary. These hormones are of two types-releasing hormone (e.g., GnRH) and inhibiting hormone (e.g. somatostatin).
On the other hand, gonadotrophins are released from the anterior pituitary (pars distalis), thus they do not require a portal circulation.

2. (*a*) A is false, but R is true. A can be corrected as
The posterior pituitary is stimulated under extreme dehydration. This is because the posterior pituitary secretes anti-diuretic hormone, which causes reabsorption of water from the distal tubules of the nephrons, thereby preventing diuresis.

3. (*d*) A is true, but R is false. R can be corrected as
Thyrocalcitonin increases calcium absorption by bones, thereby reducing blood calcium levels.

4. (*c*) The incorrect statement can be corrected as
Inhibiting hormones produced by hypothalamus are transported through portal circulation to the anterior pituitary or pars distalis.

5. (*b*) Disproportionate facial structure could mean acromegaly. This is caused by hypersecretion of growth hormone, which could happen if there is a tumour in the anterior pituitary.

6. (*b*) Reabsorption of calcium by renal tubules increases calcium levels in blood. Parathyroid hormone can also increase the blood calcium levels by demineralisation of bones, thus, high parathyroid hormone can increase calcium levels in blood.
Thyrocalcitonin works antagonist to parathyroid hormone, thus lowers blood calcium levels.

7. (*d*) Statement I is correct, but statement II is incorrect. The incorrect statement can be corrected as
Antibody production is related to humoral immunity provided by B-cells.

8. (*b*) Statements I, IV and V are correct, while statements II and III are incorrect and can be corrected as
Oxytocin secretion occurs during child birth process as well as during lactation, to stimulate milk ejection from mammary glands.
Pars intermedia of adenohypophysis, governs skin pigmentation as they secrete melanocyte stimulating hormone (MSH).

9. (*a*) One of the important symptoms of hypothyroidism in an adult woman is irregular menstruation and reduced metabolism. Thyroid hormones control basal metabolism, thus it can be concluded that thyroid hormone secretion is lowered in her body leading to hypothyroidism.

10. (*d*) The correct match is A-2, B-1, C-4, D-3.
- Melatonin from pineal gland regulates sleep wake cycle as well as body temperature.
- Oxytocin is secreted by posterior pituitary and stimulates uterine contraction during child birth. It is also secreted during lactation, post pregnancy to stimulate milk ejection from mammary glands.
- Thyroxine is secreted by the thyroid gland, and it maintains metabolism of the body. Apart from this, it also maintains erythropoiesis, or red blood cell formation.
- FSH or Follicle Stimulating Hormone, secreted by posterior pituitary, regulates the maturation of ovarian follicle leading to menstruation, when a girl reaches puberty.

11. (*c*) Prolactin (PRL) is secreted from pars distalis region of adenohypophysis, commonly called as anterior pituitary. It regulates the growth of the mammary glands and formation of milk in them.

12. (*c*) Statements I and II are incorrect and can be corrected as
- ADH mainly acts on the collecting tubule of kidney. It increases water reabsorption in this part.

• Sertoli cells are regualted by FSH secreted from the anterior pituitary gland.

13. (c) The correct match is A-1, B-5, C-2, D-3, E-4.

• Hypothalmic hormone gets transported to pituitary gland and act upon it.

• TSH (Thyroid Stimulating Hormone) acts on thyroid gland.

• ACTH (Adrenocorticotrophic Hormone) acts on adrenal glands.

• FSH (Follicle Stimulating Hormone) acts on male (testis) and female (ovary) gonads.

• MSH (Melanocyte Stimulating Hormone) acts on skin.

14. (*c*) Both statement I and statement II are incorrect. These can be corrected as

• Fall in blood Ca^{2+} levels will stimulate parathyroid gland to release parathyroid hormone.

• Thymus is a lobular structure located between lungs behind sternum on the ventral side of the immune system.

15. (*b*) Statement (b) is correct w.r.t. the given figure.

• In the given figure, *A*-Pineal gland, *B*-Hypothalamus, *C*-Pituitary and *D*-Thymus gland.

• Both pineal gland and thymus gland are involved in defence mechanism.

Other statements are incorrect and can be corrected as

• Hormones released by hypothalamus (B) go to pituitary (C) *via* portal connection or axonally.

• Some hormones that are released by hypothalamus (B) are stored in pituitary (C), e.g. oxytocin and vasopressin, released from hypothalamus, are stored in neurohypophysis (posterior pituitary).

• Thymus (D) secretes a peptide hormone called thymosin.

Test 2

1. (*d*) Glucagon increases blood glucose level by glycogenolysis and gluconeogenesis. Thus, it is a hyperglycemic hormone. Insulin stimulates glycogenesis and reduce blood glucose level, hence it is hypoglycemic hormone.

2. (*b*) Statements I, III and IV are correct whereas statements II and V are incorrect and can be corrected as Steroid hormones interact mostly with intercellular nuclear receptors. Secretions of Leydig cells regulates body hair growth. Leydig cells secretes androgens like testosterone which regulate body hair growth in both males and females.

3. (*b*) Both A and R are true and R is the correct explanation of A.

The secretion of bicarbonates by secretin, maintains an alkaline pH that is needed for enzyme action on food.

4. (*a*) The correct order is D-C-A-E-B.

• TSH is secreted by the anterior pituitary.

• TSH acts on thyroid glands and stimulates it to release thyroid hormones, T_3 and T_4.

• Thyroid hormones cross the cell membrane.

• Thyroid hormones interact with nuclear receptors to form hormone receptor complex.

• The hormone-receptor complex interacts with the genome to trigger physiological responses.

5. (*b*) Both statement I and statement II are correct.

All the hormones secreted by the GI tract, which includes gastrin, secretin, cholecystokinin (CCK) and gastric inhibitory peptide (GIP), are peptide hormones. CCK acts on both pancreas and gall bladder and stimulates the secretion of pancreatic enzymes and bile juice, respectively. Bile causes emulsification of fats which aids in their digestion.

6. (c) Epinephrine causes glycogenolysis which increases blood glucose. Cortisol stimulates gluconeogenesis that also increases blood glucose. Glucagon acts on the liver cells and stimulates glycogenolysis resulting in an increased blood sugar. Insulin causes glycogenesis that causes conversion of glucose to glycogen, hence decreases blood glucose. Hence, epinephrine, cortisol and glucagon produce the same effect on blood glucose.

7. (*a*) A is false, but R is true. A can be corrected as

Cortisol is administered to a patient after organ transplantation in order to suppress the immune system as it has anti-inflammatory activity.

On the other hand, adrenaline is rapidly secreted in body in response to stress of any kind or emergency (emergency hormone or hormone of flight).

8. (*d*) Statement I is correct, but statement II is incorrect and can be corrected as

Oestrogen is the primary hormone stimulating secondary sexual features in female.

9. (*b*) The incorrect statement can be corrected as

Cyclic AMP causes intracellular signal transduction.

Cyclic AMP is the second messenger operating in pathways where hormone interacts with membrane bound receptors.

10. (*d*) After a sugary snack, blood glucose levels increase. The body responds to this glucose spike by stimulating the β-cells of pancreas to secrete insulin. Insulin causes glycogenesis in liver and muscles, whereby excess glucose is converted to glycogen thereby decreasing the blood glucose levels. Insulin also stimulates uptake of glucose by liver and fat cells.

Gluconeogenesis increases blood glucose level and is stimulated by glucagon. Hence, it takes place under fasting conditions, and not after a sugary meal.

11. (*c*) Both A and R are true, but R is not the correct explanation of A.

Complete protein digestion in intestine, requires gastrin at the first step since gastrin acts on the gastric glands and stimulates the secretion of hydrochloric acid and pepsinogen. HCl is needed for activation of pepsinogen to pepsin that converts proteins into smaller peptides at the very first step of protein digestion.

12. (*b*) The correct match is A-2, B-3, C-1, D-4.

- Corpus luteum is the remnant of the Graafian follicle after ovulation and it secretes progesterone.
- Aldosterone secreted by the adrenal cortex is a mineralocorticoid which increases blood pressure by reabsorption of sodium ions and water from the renal tubules of kidney.
- Ovarian follicle secretes oestrogen, which helps in development of secondary sexual features in females.
- ANF or atrial natriuretic factor is secreted by the heart and causes dilation of blood vessels and decrease in blood pressure.

13. (*d*) Adrenal medulla is involved in generation of fight or flight response of the body and not in regulating electrolyte balance. Adrenal cortex secretes mineralocorticoids like aldosterone that regulate electrolyte balance by stimulating the reabsorption of Na^+ and water and excretion of K^+ and phosphate ions. Pituitary hormone like TSH acts on thyroid glands and ACTH from anterior pituitary acts on adrenal cortex. Thyroid hormones regulate salt water balance.

14. (*a*) Pituitary hormones and sex hormones are secreted by endocrine glands and transported through blood to their site of action. Pituitary hormone like LH, stimulates testes to secrete androgens which causes development of secondary sexual characteristic in males. Thus, both of them have the same cumulative effect on the body.
However, pituitary hormones are mostly peptides, proteins or polypeptides, while sex hormones are steroids in their chemical nature. Also, steroid hormones mostly interact with intracellular receptors, while pituitary hormones like FSH interact with membrane receptors.

15. (*d*) Statement I is correct, but statement II is incorrect. It can be corrected as
The glucose homeostasis in blood is maintained jointly by the two pancreatic hormones-insulin along with glucagon.

16. (*d*) A is true, but R is false. R can be corrected as
Insulin dependent diabetes mellitus is caused due to failure of β-cells to produce adequate amount of insulin.

17. (*b*) Progesterone is a female hormone secreted by corpus luteum. It supports pregnancy, it also acts on the mammary glands and stimulates the formation of alveoli (sac-like structures, which stores milk) and milk secretion.

18. (*c*) During stress, cortisol, aldosterone, vasopressin and glucagon are released, besides epinephrine and nor-epinephrine.

- Cortisol is the next most important hormone secreted during stress after epinephrine and nor-epinephrine.
- When an animal or human is exposed to any noxious potential stimuli, there is an increased secretion of ACTH and consequently, a rise in the circulating glucorticoid level.
- Glucagon helps to raise the blood glucose level required under the stress.
- Vasopressin and aldosterone helps in retention of water during stress.

19. (*b*) Both A and R are true and R is the correct explanation of A.
Hormones which interact with membrane-bound receptors normally do not enter the target cell, but generate secondary messengers to regulate further cellular events. E.g., peptide hormones like FSH and insulin.

20. (*d*) In the given figure, the mechanism of action of protein/polypeptide/peptide hormone can be seen. Here, A represents prolactin (a polypeptide hormone), B represents membrane-bound receptors and C represents example of secondary messenger (e.g. IP_3, Ca^{2+}, *c*AMP).

21. (*d*) Option (d) shows the correct match of gland with its hormone and function.
Other incorrect pairs can be corrected as

- Adrenal > Glucocorticoids > Gluconeogenesis, Lipolysis and Proteolysis
- Pancreas > Glucagon > Hyperglycemic hormone
- Cholecystokinin (CCK) > GI tract > Stimulation of gall bladder and pancreas for secretion of pancreatic enzymes and bile juice, respectively.

22. (*c*) The incorrect function of insulin can be corrected as
Insulin converts glucose into glycogen in the liver and muscles.

23. (*d*) The correct order of layers of adrenal cortex is

- Zona reticularis (II) → Zona fasciculata (III) → Zona glomerulosa (I).
- Zona reticularis is the inner layer of adrenal cortex.
- Zona fasciculata is its middle layer.
- Zona glomerulosa is its outer layer.

24. (*b*) Both statement I and statement II are correct.

- Inositol triphosphate (IP_3) is a secondary messenger and capable of driving a cascade of biochemical reactions and physiological changes in the target cell.
- Many non-endocrine tissues secrete hormones called growth factors, which are essential for the normal growth of tissues and their repairing/regeneration.

25. (*c*) A person's heartbeat increases at the time of interview. This can happen, when his sympathetic nervous system is activated leading to release of adrenaline and nor-adrenaline from adrenal medulla.

Chapter Break Thru

1. (*a*) The correct order is C-E-D-A-B

- GnRH is secreted by the hypothalamus and reaches the anterior pituitary by portal circulation.
- Pars distalis is stimulated by GnRH.

- Pars distalis releases LH or Luteinizing Hormone.
- LH stimulates interstitial cells to release androgens.
- Androgens cause development of male accessory structures like vas deferens.

2. (*a*) 'A' is parathyroid gland, while 'B' is thyroid gland. Follicular cells of thyroid gland secrete T_3 and T_4. Hormone secreted by parathyroid gland is parathyroid hormone that causes demineralisation of bones and increases blood calcium levels, hence it is hypercalcemic. Thyroid hormone thyrocalcitonin (TCT) decreases blood calcium levels by causing absorption of calcium by the bones.

3. (*d*) A is true, but R is false. R can be corrected as
Melatonin production increases in darkness. Melatonin which maintains circadian rhythm , also promotes sleep. It maintains sleep-wake cycle and is sensitive to light. Darkness stimulates melatonin secretion, which promotes sleep in a person.

4. (*b*) The correct match is A-2, B-3, C-4, D-1.
- Addison's disease is caused due to underproduction of hormones by the adrenal cortex that alters carbohydrate metabolism causing acute weakness and fatigue.
- Cretinism is caused due to hypothyroidism during pregnancy which causes the baby to have mental retardation and stunted growth.
- Grave's disease or exopthalmic goitre is a form of hyperthyroidism, characterised by enlargement of the thyroid gland, protrusion of the eyeballs, increased basal metabolic rate and weight loss.
- Diabetes insipidus is caused due to undersecretion of antidiuretic hormone or ADH from the posterior pituitary which causes excess water loss through urine or diuresis.

5. (*a*) Statement II is correct, while statements I, III and IV are incorrect and can be corrected as
- Hormones from the nuclei are transported by axons to pars nervosa.
- Somatostatin works antagonistic to growth hormone on body.
- Hypothalmic hormones may have a stimulating or inhibiting effect on other endocrine glands.

6. (*d*) Statement I is correct, but statement II is incorrect. Statement II can be corrected as
Thymosin causes differentiation of T-cells that promote cell mediated immunity.

7. (*c*) Parathyroid hormone secreted by parathyroid causes bone demineralisation, which increases blood calcium levels. In this way, bones are dissolved which make them fragile. Thyrocalcitonin secreted by thyroid gland increases absorption of calcium from blood and creates an opposite effect as that of parathyroid gland.

8. (*c*) Statements II, III and V are correct, but statements I and IV are incorrect and can be corrected as
- Adrenal medulla is the innermost region of adrenal gland. Zona reticularis is the innermost layer of adrenal cortex.
- Secretions of the adrenal glands are amino acid-derived or steroidal in nature.

9. (*c*) Thyroxine from thyroid glands stimulate red blood cell formation or erythropoiesis. Juxtaglomerular apparatus secrete erythropoietin that promotes erythropoiesis. Adrenal cortex secretes cortisol which also promotes RBC formation. Parathyroid is involved in calcium metabolism.

10. (*d*) Statement I is correct, but statement II is incorrect. Statement II can be corrected as
Oxytocin is produced by the hypothalamus and transported by its axon to the posterior lobe of pituitary gland.

11. (*c*) Incorrect statement can be corrected as
Gastrin maintains an acidic pH in the stomach. This is done by secretion of HCl by the gastric glands.

12. (*c*) A hormone which is bound at the cell surface interacts with membrane receptors and normally do not enter the cell. However, its effect or signal is relayed by second messengers generated intracellularly, like calcium (Ca^{2+}), cyclic AMP (*c*AMP) and IP_3.

13. (*d*) The correct match is A-2, B-3, C- 1, D-4.
T_3 or thyroid hormone is derivatives of iodothyronines. Cortisol produced by adrenal cortex is a steroid hormone. Adrenaline produced by adrenal medulla is an amino acid derivative. ANF or atrial natriuretic factor is a peptide hormone.

14. (*c*) The correct match pair can be explained as
Prolactin is secreted mostly after pregnancy and during breastfeeding, since it causes production of milk in the mammary glands.
The other incorrect pairs can be corrected as
Oestrogen is secreted maximally during puberty, as it results in development of secondary sexual features in women and maintains the menstrual cycle. Progesterone is secreted most during pregnancy as it is secreted by the corpus luteum and maintains the endometrium.
Oxytocin is secreted maximally during child birth as it stimulates uterine contraction.

15. (*a*) A is false, but R is true. A can be corrected as
Under fasting conditions, the blood glucose levels fall. The body deals with this condition by stimulating the pancreatic α-cells to secrete glucagon. Glucagon stimulates glycogenolysis or breakdown of glycogen to glucose, which increases blood glucose levels.

16. (*c*) Both A and R are true, but R is not the correct explanation of A.
Iodine is important for synthesis of thyroid hormones. If iodine levels are less, there would be undersecretion of thyroid hormones and hypothyroidism can be developed in pregnant women. This can cause mental retardation and stunted growth in the child, a condition known as cretinism.

17. (*a*) Anti-diuretic hormone secreted by the posterior pituitary stimulates resorption of water and electrolytes by the distal tubules and thereby reduces loss of water through urine (diuresis).
Thus, hyposecretion or under secretion of ADH can cause, diabetes insipidus, characterised by frequent urination and increased thirst. Hyposecretion can also cause lowering of blood pressure. Ketone body formation is associated with diabetes mellitus.

18. (*a*) Statement I is incorrect, but statement II is correct. Statement I can be corrected as
CCK is produced by the intestine and acts on the gall bladder and pancreas to release bile juice and pancreatic enzymes, respectively.

19. (*a*) Statement II is incorrect and can be corrected as
Piloerection in response to fear is triggered by the adrenal medulla.

20. (*c*) Epiphyseal plate is a type of cartilage that is present at the ends of long bones. It helps in the growth of the length of the bone. On reaching adolescence, this plate ossifies or closes. Thus, hypersecretion of growth hormone in adults does not cause further increase in height.

21. (*c*) Both A and R are true, but R is not the correct explanation of A.
Development of ulcers in stomach is related to hypersecretion of gastrin, because gastrin stimulates the gastric glands to secrete HCl.

22. (*c*) Only statement IV is correct. Statements I, II and III are incorrect and can be corrected as

- Growth in a person is controlled by pituitary and hypothalamus.
- Acromegaly and gigantism produces different effects on people. Gigantism occurs when there is increased GH secretion in a child, causing elongation of bones leading to very tall individuals. Acromegaly occurs in adulthood due to over secretion of GH that causes disfigurement, particularly of face.
- Dwarfism and somatostatin produce similar effect on body. Dwarfism is the condition where individuals are short statured with improper growth due to under secretion of GH. Somatostatin also inhibits the release of growth hormone from the pituitary.

23. (*b*) The correct order is B-D-A-E-C.

- GnRH is secreted by the hypothalamus.
- GnRH is released into portal circulation to reach the anterior pituitary.
- The anterior pituitary is stimulated to secrete gonadotrophins LH and FSH.
- LH acts on the Leydig cells to stimulate release of androgens.
- Androgens and FSH stimulate spermatogenesis which leads to sperm (i.e., male gamete) production.

24. (*a*) The correct match is A-3, B-1, C-2, D-4.

- Melatonin secreted by the pineal gland controls defence of the body and plays a role in immunity.
- Androgens secreted by testes and adrenal cortex controls secondary sexual features in males like a low pitched or deep voice.
- Oestrogen produced by the ovarian follicles controls secondary sexual features in women like a shrill or high pitched voice.
- MSH or Melanocyte Stimulating Hormone secreted by pars intermedia of the pituitary acts on melanocytes and regulate melanin or skin pigment formation.

25. (*b*) Both A and R are true and R is the correct explanation of A.
People with osteoporosis often show a decrease in bone mass density. Hence, giving them calcitonin can increase uptake of calcium from the blood and deposition in bones, hence slowing down their degradation.

26. (c) Lipolysis is the breakdown of stored fat to increase glucose in blood. Gluconeogenesis increases plasma glucose levels by formation of glucose.
Glycogenolysis is breakdown of glycogen into glucose. This process increases blood glucose levels.
Glycogenesis is conversion of glucose to glycogen in liver. This decreases blood glucose levels.
Hence under fasting, when blood glucose is less, lipolysis, glycogenolysis and gluconeogenesis is triggered.

27. (*b*) Thyroxine secretion depends on stimulation by the anterior pituitary hormone TSH or Thyroid Stimulating Hormone. It also depends on iodine, as iodine is needed for synthesis of thyroid hormones.
Hence, low iodine, would cause hyposecretion of thyroid hormones. Na^+ does not play a role in thyroxine secretion.

28. (*b*) Both statement I and statement II are correct.
Thymosin from thymus gland and melatonin from pineal gland, is associated with the defence of the body and immunity.

29. (*b*) Only statement I is correct statement II, III and IV can be corrected as

- Follicle Stimulating Hormone interacts with cell membrane as the receptors are membrane-bound receptors.
- FSH uses cyclic AMP or calcium ions for signal transmission.
- Androgens interact with intra cellular receptors.
- Hormones with membrane- bound receptors can be peptide or proteins, example FSH.

30. (*c*) Both A and R are true, but R is not the correct explanation of A.
Patients on insulin therapy, should never skip meals as insulin lowers blood glucose levels. If glucose falls beyond normal in blood, it can lead to hypoglycemia, and make the person faint. This could lead to fatalities. Hence, skipping meals is not advisable for such patients.

31. (*b*) Both A and R are correct and R is the correct explanation of A.
Adrenal glands are called 4 S glands as they control sugar metabolism, salt retention, sex hormone secretion and are source of energy.

32. (*b*) The incorrect statement w.r.t. the mechanism of hormonal action can be corrected as
Secondary messengers are involved in the case of mechanism of hormonal action of protein/peptide/ polypeptide hormones.
Iodothyronines and steroid hormone work due to interaction of hormone with intracellular receptors (mostly nuclear receptor).

33. (*c*) Both A and R are true, but R is not the correct explanation of A.
Pancreas is a composite gland as it acts as both exocrine and endocrine glands.

34. (*b*) Statements II, III and IV are correct. The incorrect statement can be corrected as
Addison's disease is caused due to hyposecretion of hormones from adrenal cortex.

35. (*a*) Pars distalis (A) or anterior pituitary of adenohypophysis secrete LH that regulates synthesis and secretion of androgens.
β-cells of islets of Langerhans secrete insulin (B) hormone that decrease blood sugar level.
Pars-distalis (C) (anterior pituitary) of adenohypophysis secretes ACTH (D), which stimulates the synthesis and secretion of glucocorticoids.

36. (*d*) Calcium plays a vital role in blood clotting (coagulation). Parathormone increases blood calcium to normal by drawing calcium from the bones into the plasma, by increasing calcium absorption in the digestion tract and by reducing loss of calcium in the urine. Deficiency of PTH will decrease level of Ca^{2+} in the blood, thus leading to delay in blood clotting.

37. (*b*) A person suffering injury to adrenal cortex will not be able to affect the secretion of adrenaline, as it is released by adrenal medulla. Other hormones are released by adrenal cortex only.

38. (*c*) Insulin hormone is secreted by the β-cells of 'islets of Langerhans' of pancreas. Deficiency of insulin hormone causes excess amount of glucose into blood called diabetes mellitus.

39. (*c*) Erythropoietin is a hormone that stimulates formation of RBCs in bone marrow. It is secreted by kidney. Erythropoietin is a glycoprotein hormone that is produced predominantly by specialised cells called interstitial cells in the kidney.

40. (*c*) Growth Hormone (GH) works properly with thyroxine secreted by thyroid. Thyroxine exerts a permissive effect upon the anabolic and metabolic effects of GH and increases pituitary synthesis of this protein hormone.

41. (*b*) The correct match is I-B, II-A, III-C.

- Zona glomerulosa is the outermost layer of adrenal cortex, responsible for producing mineralocorticoids such as aldosterone.
- Zona fasciculata is the middle layer of adrenal cortex, responsible for production and secretion of glucocorticoids such as aldosterone.
- Zona reticularis is the innermost layer of adrenal cortex, responsible for producing androgens.

42. (*b*) Statements II and III are correct. Other statements are incorrect and can be corrected as

- ADH (Anti-Diuretic Hormone), also known as vasopressin is released by hypothalamus and is transported to posterior pituitary (neurohypophysis) for its storage and release.
- Only follicular cells of thyroid cells are responsible for synthesis of two hormones called tetraiodothyronine or thyroxine (T_4) and triiodothyronine (T_3).

43. (*c*) Both statement I and statement II are incorrect and these can be corrected as

- The hormone important in the glucose metabolism is produced by pancreas.
- The neuroendocrine control centre of vertebrates consists of hypothalamus and pituitary gland.

44. (*b*) Option (b) shows the correct match pair out of the given ones. Other options can be corrected as

- TCT-hypocalcemic hormone (decreases Ca^{2+} level in blood).
- Glucagon-hyperglycemic hormone (increases levels of blood glucose).
- Insulin-hypoglycemic hormone (decreases levels of blood glucose).

45. (*c*) The given figure represents two parts of adrenal glands, i.e. adrenal cortex (A) and adrenal medulla (B). The option (c) is incorrect w.r.t. the given figure and can be corrected as
Aldosterone, i.e. released from adrenal cortex, acts mainly at the renal tubules and stimulates the reabsorption of Na^+ and water and excretion of K^+ and phosphate ions.

46. (*a*) Statement I is incorrect, but statement II is correct. The incorrect statement can be corrected as
Blood calcium level can be increased by the administration of PTH, not TCT.
TCT acts by increasing the bones Ca^{2+} level and decreasing bloods Ca^{2+} level.

47. (*d*) A is true, but R is false. R can be corrected as
When blood pressure is increased, ANF is secreted by atrial wall of our heart, which cause dilation of the blood vessels.

48. (*d*) Testosterone (most common androgen) is the hormone that acts on the central neural system and influences the male sexual behaviour (libido). The second hormone is oestrogen that regulates female sexual behaviour.

49. (*a*) Statement I is incorrect, but statement II is correct. The incorrect statement can be corrected as
Oestrogen is synthesised and secreted mainly by the growing ovarian follicles.

50. (*c*) Intense contraction in uterine wall during parturition is regulated by the action of posterior pituitary, which releases oxytocin. It stimulates the uterine muscle to dilate the cervix, move the baby down and out of the birth canal. Another name for posterior pituitary is neurohypophysis (Pars nervosa).

SPT1 Syllabus Part Thru 1

1. (*b*) Gemmae are small, asexual reproductive structures found in certain liverworts, particularly in the genus-*Marchantia* and other similar taxa. These gemmae are typically located in specialised cup-shaped structures called gemma cups. These cups are situated on the dorsal (upper) surface of the thallus, which is the flat, lobed, and often green structure that constitutes the main body of a liverwort.

2. (*b*) The nerve cord is a paired structure that runs along the ventral side of the cockroach's body. This nerve cord is a crucial component of the Cockroach's Central Nervous system (CNS) and is involved in coordinating various motor and reflexive functions. The ventral nerve cord consists of two parallel nerve trunks. These ganglia are clusters of nerve cells located at each segment of the cockroach's body.

3. (*d*) Statement I is correct, but statement II is incorrect. The incorrect statement can be corrected as
Triticum aestivum, whose common name is wheat, belongs to order-Poales and class-Monocotyledonae.

4. (*a*) The correct match is A-2, B-4, C-1, D-3.

5. (*a*) A is false, but R is true. A can be corrected as
Glandular epithelium plays a significant rule in secretion of mucus, saliva, milk, earwax and hormones. It is the compound epithelium that has a limited role in secretion and absorption.

6. (*d*) Statements II, IV and V are correct, while statements I and III are incorrect. These can be corrected as
   - Root cap is present below the region of meristematic activity. On the other hand, root hair arise from the epidermal cells present in the region of maturation.
   - Fibrous roots are seen in plants -like wheat (monocots), whereas tap root system is seen in mustard plant (dicots).

7. (*a*) The correct match is A-2, B-1, C-4, D-3.

8. (*c*) Both statement I and statement II are incorrect. These can be corrected as
   - The body of ctenophore bears eight external rows of ciliated comb plates.
   - Bioluminescence, which is the property of a living organism to emit light, is well-marked in ctenophores.

9. (*b*) Tracheids are elongated or tube like cells with thick and lignified walls and tapering ends. These are dead and without protoplasm.

10. (*b*) In sponges (Porifera), water enters through minutes pores (ostia) in the body wall into a central cavity, spongocoel, from where it goes out through the osculum.

11. (*b*) The incorrect statement can be corrected as
The radial conduction of water takes place by the ray parenchymatous cells and not by collenchymatous ones.

12. (*b*) The inner membrane is extensively folded into cristae, which increases its surface area. This increased surface area is crucial for housing the components of the electron transport chain, which are essential for ATP production.

13. (*b*) The correct match is A-3, B-4, C-2, D-1.

14. (*c*) *X* axis represents temperature, while *Y* axis represents enzyme activity. All enzymes function at an optimum temperature.
Their activity declines below or above this temperature range.

15. (*c*) Both statement I and statement II are incorrect. These can be corrected as
   - Cellulose is a polymeric polysaccharide (homopolymer) consisting of only one type of monosaccharides, i.e. glucose.
   - Inulin is a polymer of fructose.

16. (*c*) At anaphase-I, the homologous chromosomes separate, while sister chromatids remain associated at their centromere.

17. (*a*) Statements II, III and V are correct. Incorrect statements can be corrected as
   - The eukaryotic ribosomes are 80S, while the prokaryotic ribosomes are 70S.
   - A number of organised flattened membranous sacs called thylakoids are present in the stroma.

18. (*c*) Class-Phycomycetes or Zygomycetes is known for their sexual reproduction through the formation of zygosporangia.
This class includes bread mold (*Rhizopus stolonifer*), which are commonly found on stale bread and other decaying organic matter.
Other options can be explained as
Ascomycetes include yeast, *Aspergillus, Penicillium*, morels and truffels.
Basidiomycetes include mushroom, puffballs, rust and smut fungi.
Deuteromycetes include *Alternaria* and *Trichoderma*, etc.

19. (*d*) Rubber, cellulose and gums are polymeric substances. Morphine is an alkaloid, vinblastin is a drug and abrin is a toxin.

20. (*d*) A is true, but R is false. R can be corrected as
The walls of diatoms are embedded with silica and are indestructible.

21. (*b*) Statements III and IV are correct. Incorrect statements can be corrected as
- The male sex organ of bryophyte is called antheridium. They produce biflagellated antherozoids.
- The female sex organ called archegonium is flask shaped and produces a single egg.

22. (*c*) Both statement I and statement II are incorrect. They can be corrected as
- Palmitic acid has 16 carbons including carboxyl carbon.
- Arachidonic acid has 20 carbon atoms including the carboxyl carbon.

23. (*d*) The correct match is A-2, B-3, C-1, D-4.

24. (*c*) The Cruciferae family, also known as the Brassicaceae family, is characterised by the presence of siliqua or silicula fruits. These are typically short and broad dry fruits. Examples of economically significant crops in this family include *Iberis amara* and *Brassica campestris,* etc.

25. (*c*) Both statement I and statement II are incorrect. These can be corrected as
- In exarch, the protoxylem lies towards periphery and metaxylem lies towards the centre.
- In endarch, the protoxylem lies towards the centre and the metaxylem lies towards the periphery of the organ.

26. (*c*) The correct match is A-2, B-1, C-3, D-4.
- *Pinus* is a monoecious gymnosperm as in this, the male and female cones or strobili may be borne on the same tree.
- *Cycas* is a dioecious gymnosperm as in this, the male cones and megasporophylls are borne on different trees.
- Pteridophytes like *Salvinia* and *Selaginella* produce two kinds of spores, i.e. macro (large) and micro (small) spores, thus they are heterosporous.
- In majority of the pteridophytes, e.g. *Equisetum*, all the spores are of similar kinds. These are called homosporous.

27. (*c*) Both A and R are true, but R is not the correct explanation of A. A can be explained as
All enzymes are proteins, except ribozyme, but not all proteins are enzymes. Enzymes are made up of proteins. Only a few proteins, with the help of their active sites, have the ability to bind to the substrate in such a way that allows the reaction to take place efficiently. Some proteins are transport proteins, structural proteins and hormonal proteins.

28. (*b*) The incorrect statement can be corrected as
The stage between the two meiotic division is called interkinesis.

29. (*b*) The incorrect statement can be corrected as
Petunia, *Solanum* and *Datura* are placed in the family-Solanaceace. Families are characterised on the basis of both vegetative and reproductive features of plant species. *Felis* represents genus of cats and is placed in the family-Felidae.

30. (*b*) The correct match is A-4, B-1, C-2, D-3.

31. (*b*) The correct match is A-4, B-1, C-3, D-2.

32. (*d*) Martinus Beijerinck is credited with identifying the Tobacco Mosaic Virus (TMV) as the first virus to be described scientifically. He proposed that the disease was caused by a "contagious living fluid", a term he used to describe the infectious agent that could not be classified as a bacterium. This term highlighted the agent's ability to spread and cause disease despite being filtered through materials that would remove bacteria.

33. (*a*) A is false, but R is true. A can be corrected as
M-phase is also called as equational division, while G_2-phase is Gap 2 phase of mitosis, where proteins are synthesised in preparation for mitosis while cell growth continues.

34. (*a*) The correct match is A-2, B-1, C-4, D-3.
- Cuticle is a waxy thick layer found covering the epidermis. It is absent in roots. It prevents the water loss.
- Polyarch bundles (more than 6) can be found in monocot roots.
- Mesophyll tissue in leaves can be divided into palisade layer and spongy parenchyma.
- Sieve tube cells are living enucleated cells and their function is controlled by nucleated companion cells.

35. (*a*) A is false, but R is true. A can be corrected as
It is not *Pleurobrachia*, but *Obelia* that is dimorphic in nature and belongs to phylum-Cnidaria. *Pleurobrachia* belongs to phylum-Ctenophora.

36. (*c*) The intercalated discs present in cardiac muscles tissues, allows for synchronised contraction of cells.

37. (*b*) Both A and R are true and the R is the correct explanation of A.
The plasmodium stage of slime moulds is crucial for their movement and feeding, reflecting their *Amoeba*-like behavior. The plasmodium allows slime moulds to gather resources and later shift to a reproductive phase where spores are produced to continue the life cycle.

38. (*b*) Roots having fungal association in the form of mycorrhiza are seen in *Pinus*, while small specialised roots called coralloid roots associated with N_2-fixing cyanobacteria are seen in *Cycas*.

39. (*c*) The term "hub" typically refers to a central structure in the centriole, which is involved in microtubule organisation. However, the hub of the centriole is not lipid-based; it is composed of proteins and does not involve lipids.

The central part of the centriole is more accurately described as the central cylinder or the central hub composed of proteins.

40. (*c*) Both statement I and statement II are incorrect. These can be corrected as

- The midbrain of frog is characterised by a pair of optic lobes. Unpaired diencephalon is a part of forebrain.
- Hindbrain of frog consists of cerebellum and medulla oblongata.

41. (*c*) Both A and R are true, but R is not the correct explanation of A.

The leaves of gymnosperms such as in conifers are needle-like to reduce the surface area. Their thick cuticle and sunken stomata also help to reduce water loss as an adaptation to survive harsh conditions.

42. (*d*) Natural classification system proposed by Bentham and Hooker aims to group organisms based on their evolutionary relationships, shared ancestry, and genetic information, providing a more comprehensive understanding of their inter-relationship. Internal features such as anatomy, embryology, phytochemistry is also included in natural classification.

43. (*b*) The correct match is A-2, B-3, C-4, D-1.

- Vacuole is bound by a single membrane called tonoplast.
- Lysosomes are rich in almost all types of hydrolytic enzymes.
- Golgi apparatus is the important site of formation of glycoproteins and glycolipids.
- Plastids bear some specific pigments.

44. (*a*) Chlorophyceae are commonly called green algae. In members of this family, food is stored in the form of starch and cell wall is made up of cellulose. They are found in fresh water, brackish water and salt water.

Other options can be explained as

In Phaeophyceae, the food is stored in form of mannitol, laminarin and cell wall is composed of algin and cellulose. It is also found in fresh water (rare), brackish water, salt water.

Liverworts and mosses are bryophytes and their food is stored as starch. Their cell wall is made up of cellulose, hemicellulose and pectins. Bryophytes can be found in both terrestrial and aquatic regions. Thus, they are also called as 'amphibians of plant kingdom'.

45. (*c*) Male frogs often have larger and more developed vocal sacs during the breeding season. These vocal sacs are used to amplify their calls, which are crucial for attracting females and establishing territory. This feature is more pronounced in males as it directly relates to their mating behaviour. Male frog also shows presence of copulatory pad on the first digit of forelimbs.

46. (*b*) The given floral diagram is of Leguminosae or Fabaceae family. Its floral formula is % ⚥ K_5 $C_{1+2+(2)}$ $A_{(9)+1}$ $\underline{G}_1$. The flowers are pentamerous and hypogynous.

47. (*c*) Centrosome is an organelle usually containing two cylindrical structures called centrioles.

48. (*b*) Lysine is a basic amino acid and glutamic acid is an acidic amino acid.

49. (*d*) The epidermis originates from the protoderm, which is one of the three primary meristems (along with the ground meristem and procambium) responsible for primary growth in plants. The protoderm gives rise to the outermost layer of cells, the epidermis.

50. (*c*) Both statement I and statement II are incorrect. These can be corrected as

- Ribulose Bisphosphate Carboxylase- Oxygenase (RuBisCO) is the most abundant protein in whole of the biosphere.
- Collagen is the most abundant protein in the animal world.

51. (*a*) In dicot seeds, the cotyledons are the primary structures that store nutrients. They provide the necessary energy and nutrients to the developing embryo during germination until the seedling can start photosynthesis. Endosperm is completely used up in dicot seed. Micropyle provides entry to oxygen and water during seed germination and aleurone is protein rich layer formed by outer covering of endosperm.

52. (*a*) Statement I is incorrect, but statement II is correct. Incorrect statement can be corrected as

In plants such as bean, gram and pea, the endosperm is not present in mature seeds. These are called non-endospermous. In castor, endosperm is a food storing tissue and present in mature seed and thus, called endospermic seed.

53. (*c*) During non-competitive inhibition, there is no competition between the molecule for the active site of enzyme. Infact, inhibition occurs by the alteration of conformational structure of enzyme by a chemical. Inhibition is irreversible, since the effect of inhibitor cannot be reversed by increasing the substrate concentration and V_{max} gets lowered and K_m is unchanged.

54. (*b*) Palisade parenchyma is adaxially placed and is made up of elongated cells, which are arranged vertically and parallel to each other.

55. (*c*) The given diagram shows the transition to metaphase stage. During this stage, the nucleus disappears and the chromosomes appear in the cytoplasm of the cell.

56. (*c*) In a mature dicot stem, vascular bundles are typically arranged in a ring within the ground tissue. The xylem is located towards the centre of the stem, and the phloem is located towards the periphery (endarch condition). Between the xylem and phloem is the cambium layer, which is responsible for secondary growth.

57. (*d*) Given cell organelle is the chloroplast. *D* represents stroma which contains enzymes required for the synthesis of carbohydrates and proteins. It also contains small, double-stranded, circular DNA molecules and ribosomes.

58. (*a*) The correct sequence is II → V→ I → III → IV.

Proteins are synthesised by ribosomes attached to the rough ER. This is the initial step in the process. After synthesis, the newly formed proteins are packaged into transport vesicles that bud off from the rough ER. The transport vesicles then travel to and fuse with the Golgi apparatus, where they unload their contents. Within the Golgi apparatus, the protein undergoes further modifications, such as glycosylation, and is then packaged into new vesicles. Finally, the modified and packaged proteins are transported to their final destinations, which could be the plasma membrane for secretion or storage in secretory granules.

59. (*a*) Statements I, II and IV are correct. Statement III is incorrect and can be corrected as

Telophase is the final stage of mitosis where the nuclear envelope re-forms around each set of chromosomes, and the chromosomes begin to decondense. The formation of four genetically different daughter cells occurs during meiosis and not mitosis, since there is no exchange of genetic material.

60. (*b*) The correct statements are I, II and V. Statements III and IV are incorrect and can be corrected as

- Platyhelminthes have bilateral symmetry.
- Poriferans are acoelomates.

61. (*c*) Statements II, III and V are correct. Statements I and IV are incorrect and can be corrected as

- Phloem fibres are made up of sclerenchymatous cells.
- The first formed primary phloem consists of narrow sieve tubes and is called protophloem. Metaphloem is the later formed primary phloem.

62. (*b*) The incorrect statement can be corrected as

Prokaryotes like bacteria have a cell made up of peptidoglycan surrounding the cell membrane, except in mycoplasma.

63. (*a*) Cartilaginous fishes (e.g., sharks and rays) have exposed gill slits without an operculum. The operculum is a bony cover that protects the gill slits and it is absent in a cartilaginous fish. Bony fishes (e.g. rohu, catla) have an operculum that covers and protects their gill slits, which helps in the efficient movement of water over the gills.

64. (*d*) Statement I is correct, but statement II is incorrect . Incorrect statement can be corrected as

Extensive compartmentalisation is not seen in bacteria due to the presence of plasmids. Bacteria typically lack extensive internal compartmentalisation because they do not have membrane-bound organelles.

65. (*a*) The incorrect statement can be corrected as

A nucleotide has three chemically distinct components. One is a heterocyclic compound, second is a monosaccharide sugar and third is phosphoric acid or phosphate group.

66. (*a*) Tight junctions help to stop substances from leaking across a tissue.

67. (*a*) The correct sequence of events occurring during meiosis is as follows : I → IV → III → II. It can be explained as

Crossing over occurs resulting in the formation of recombination nodule (pachytene). This results in the formation of chiasmata, which terminalise later on. Reduction in the number of chromosomes occurs in telophase-I. Univalent chromosomes align at the equatorial plate in metaphase-II.

68. (*d*) A is true, but R is false. R can be corrected as

Dense connective tissue (e.g. tendons and ligaments) is specialised for strength and rigidity due to its high fibre content. It does not primarily function in cushioning or providing structural support to organs; instead, it is more about providing tensile strength.

Loose connective tissue is the one specialised for providing structural support and cushioning, not dense connective tissue.

69. (*d*) The correct match is A-3, B-4, C-2, D-1.

70. (*a*) Statement I is incorrect, but statement II is correct . Incorrect statement can be corrected as

In animal cells, cytokinesis is achieved through the formation of a cleavage furrow, not a cell plate. The cleavage furrow is a pinching in of the cell membrane that eventually divides the cell into two separate daughter cells.

Formation of cell plate occurs during cytokinesis in plant cells.

71. (*b*) The correct match is A-4, B-1, C-2, D-3.

72. (*a*) The correct match is A-2, B-1, C-3, D-4.

73. (*a*) A is false, but R is true. A can be corrected as

While some fungi do have motile gametes, this is not a characteristic of all fungi. Many fungi, particularly those in the Ascomycetes and Basidiomycetes, have non-motile gametes. Additionally, the presence of motile gametes is not a universal trait for the entire kingdom-Fungi. Plasmogamy is fusion between protoplasm of motile or non-motile gametes.

74. (*b*) An elaborate network of filamentous proteinaceous structures consisting of microtubules, microfilaments and intermediate filaments present in the cytoplasm are collectively referred to as the cytoskeleton.

75. (*b*) Both A and R are true, and the R is the correct explanation for A. Nephridia function by filtering the body fluids (haemolymph or coelomic fluid) to remove nitrogenous wastes, such as ammonia or urea, and help in maintaining osmotic balance. They are indeed excretory organs found in various invertebrates, such as annelids (e.g., earthworms) and some arthropods (e.g. certain types of crustaceans).

76. (*c*) The red algae (class-Rhodophyceae) usually reproduce vegetatively by fragmentation and brown algae (class-Phaeophyceae) reproduce asexually by biflagellated zoospores that are pear-shaped and have two unequal, laterally attached flagella.

77. (*a*) Statements I, II and IV are correct, while statements III and V are incorrect. These can be corrected as

- *Mucor* and *Rhizopus* belong to class-Phycomycetes.
- Rusts (*Puccinia* sp.) and smuts (*Ustilago* sp.) are parasites that belong to basidiomycetes, which grow in soil, on logs and tree stumps and in living plant bodies.

78. (*b*) The given representation is of mitochondria and statement (b) correctly relates with it. Oxysomes or F_0 - F_1 particles of ATP synthase complex, present over cristae, are involved in ATP release.

Other statements are incorrect and can be corrected as

The double membraned structure has intermembrane space, filled with matrix in between the two membranes. Cristae are modifications of inner layer.

Enzymes of Krebs' cycle are present in mitochondrial matrix, while those of ETS and oxidative phosphorylation are found in cristae.

Mitochondria are found mostly in actively metabolising cells and tissues.

79. (*b*) Statements III and IV are incorrect and can be corrected as

- *Pristis* (saw fish) and *Trygon* (sting ray) belong to class-Chondrichthyes.
- Air bladder, which regulates buoyancy, is present in Osteichthyes.

80. (*d*) Statement I is correct, but statement II is incorrect. It can be corrected as

In pteridophytes, the main plant body is indeed a sporophyte. It does not have two life cycles. Instead, it has an alternation of generations, including a dominant sporophyte and a thalloid, independent gametophytic generation.

81. (*a*) Statements I and II are incorrect and can be corrected as

- Frog has ten pairs of cranial nerves arising from the brain and 10 pairs of spinal nerves, arising from either side of spinal cord.
- Frogs have well developed male and female reproductive system.

82. (*b*) Amphibians have a heart with two atria and a single, partially divided ventricle. This arrangement allows for partial separation of oxygenated and deoxygenated blood, although some mixing still occurs.

Cartilaginous fish, such as sharks, have a heart with a single atrium and a single ventricle, which does not efficiently separate oxygenated and deoxygenated blood.

Crocodiles have a four-chambered heart with two atria and two ventricles, similar to birds and mammals. Most other reptiles have a three-chambered heart.

Birds have a four-chambered heart that allows efficient separation and flow of oxygenated and de-oxygenated blood.

83. (*d*) The incorrect statement can be corrected as

Tendons attach skeletal muscles to bone and ligaments attach one bone to another.

84. (*c*) The Gramineae family have raceme inflorescence. The flowers are small and not showy. The calyx is absent in grass flowers. The corolla is also absent.

85. (*c*) The incorrect statement can be corrected as

Reptilia are oviparous animals and development is direct.

86. (*d*) Statement I is correct, but statement II is incorrect. The incorrect statement can be corrected as

The extensions of plasma membranes exist in the form of vesicles, tubules and lamella. They help in cell wall formation and DNA replication, etc.

87. (*a*) The correct match is A-3, B-4, C-1, D-2.

88. (*b*) Recombinase enzymes are crucial for genetic recombination during meiosis. They facilitate the exchange of genetic material between homologous chromosomes by catalysing the formation of chiasmata, which are points where the homologous chromosomes cross over and exchange genetic material.

89. (*a*) Statement I is incorrect, but statement II is correct. The incorrect statement can be corrected as

The transition state is a crucial concept in chemical kinetics. It represents the highest energy point along the reaction pathway.
This state is an unstable, transient configuration of atoms where bonds are partially broken and new bonds are being formed. Reactants must overcome an energy barrier known as the activation energy to be converted into products.
The activation energy is the energy required to reach the transition state.

90. (*d*) Statements III and V are correct, while statement I, II and IV are incorrect. They can be corrected as.

- When stamens are attached to the perianth, the condition is epiphyllous as seen in flowers of lily.
- When stamens are attached to the petals, they are epipetalous, as seen in brinjal.
- Syncarpous refers to gynoecium where carpels are fused together, not free, as seen in mustard and tomato.

SPT2 Syllabus Part Thru 2

1. (*a*) It is the auxins that help in plant growth by cell elongation and not kinetin or cytokinins.
Cytokinin promotes cell division. They delay senescence by nutrient mobilisation. Cytokinins work opposite to auxin by inhibiting apical dominance. They also promote synthesis of chloroplast and thus indirectly regulating photosynthesis.

2. (*b*) The correct order is D-A-B-C-E.

- At the start of the cycle, oxaloacetate (4C) is condensed with acetyl Co-A (2C) to form citrate (6C).
- It is followed by two successive steps of decarboxylation, leading to the formation of α-ketoglutaric acid and then succinyl Co-A.
- During conversion of succinyl Co-A to succinic acid, a molecule of GTP is synthesised. This is a substrate level phosphorylation.
- Conversion of succinic acid to malic acid involves the reduction of FAD^+ to $FADH_2$.
- Malic acid is converted to oxaloacetic acid with reduction of NAD^+ to $NADH + H^+$.

3. (*c*) The incorrect statement can be corrected as
The S-wave is the second negative deflection on an ECG. The first negative deflection is the Q-wave.

4. (*d*) During ventricular diastole or relaxation of the ventricles, the ventricular pressure falls which causes the semilunar valves to close. The closure of the semilunar valves produces the second heart sound 'dub'.

5. (*c*) The diagram shows a membrane-bound receptor. Hormones like FSH interact with membrane-bound receptors and regulate cell's metabolism through second messengers like calcium or IP_3.
Nuclear receptors are located inside the cell and hormones like steroid hormones cross the cell membrane to reach such intracellular receptors.
Thus, in the given pathway, hormone will not cross the cell membrane as it interacts with membrane bound receptor.

6. (*d*) Cork cambium and interfascicular cambium are formed by dedifferentiation. Secondary xylem and secondary phloem are formed from redifferentiation of cambial cells.

7. (*c*) In the given figure,
A = Cell acclimatisation; B = Both daughter cells divide; C = Cells are metaboiically active.

- A is the lag phase in which cells acclimatise to new environment, hence initial growth is slow.
- B is the log phase of growth, wherein cells grow exponentially. Both progeny cells formed as a result of mitosis, retain their ability to divide and do so, thereby increasing in number.
- C is the stationary phase, where cells remain metabolically active, however the growth ceases.

8. (*a*) Macrophages are special types of WBCs associated with phagocytosis, and hence, their percentage in blood would increase in case of viral infections. Platelets are involved in blood clotting and would not increase during infection.
Eosinophils resist infection and hence would increase during a viral attack on the cells. Similarly lymphocytes which are involved in antibody production would increase during a viral infection.

9. (*a*) The correct order is B-A-C-E-D.

- At the site of injury, platelets and damaged tissue releases platelete and tissue factors respectively.
- This activates an enzyme cascade which involves linked enzymatic reactions.
- Next, there is formation of enzyme complex called thrombokinase.
- Thrombokinase converts prothrombin into active thrombin.

• Thrombin converts soluble fibrinogen into insoluble fibrin. Fibrin forms a network of thread that traps the formed elements of blood. The dark coloured scum formed at the site of injury which seals the wound and prevents leaking of blood, is called a clot or coagulum.

10. (*a*) Statement I is incorrect, but statement II is correct.

The incorrect statement can be corrected as

CO_2 saturation is reached at higher concentrations in C_3 plants.

11. (*d*) A is true, but R is false. R can be corrected as

Accessory pigments absorb the light energy and then transfer it to chlorophyll-*a*, thereby protecting it from photo-oxidation.

12. (*b*) The filtrate is isotonic with respect to blood, plasma only in PCT or proximal convoluted tubule. This is because, as the filtrate flows through the descending limb, of Henle's loop, it gets concentrated, while in the ascending limb, it becomes diluted. In the DCT, filtrate remains hypotonic.

13. (*a*) Thyrocalcitonin (TCT) decreases blood calcium level, while parathyroid hormone increases calcium levels by demineralisation of bones.

So, the increased absorption by intestine and reabsorption from kidneys increase the calcium levels in blood. Oversecretion of thyrocalcitonin decreases the calcium levels in blood.

14. (*a*) The correct order is B-E-C-A-D.

• NADH dehydrogenase oxidises NADH to NAD^+.

• Electrons are then transferred to ubiquinone. Ubiquinone also receives electron from $FADH_2$ and is reduced to ubiquinol.

• Ubiquinol is then oxidised with the transfer of electrons to cytochrome-*c* *via* cytochrome-bc_1 complex (complex III).

• Cytochrome-*c* is a small protein attached to the outer surface of the inner membrane and acts as a mobile carrier for transfer of electrons between complex III and IV.

• Oxygen is the final electron acceptor, which is reduced to form water.

15. (*d*) Statement I is correct, but statement II is incorrect. Statement II can be corrected as

In non-cyclic electron flow, the product of light reaction is ATP and NADPH. Non-cyclic electron flow is the *Z*-scheme, which operates with both the photosystems to produce NADPH and ATP.

Photosystem which is not coupled to water splitting is PS-I. It is found in stromal lamellae, where only PS I is found, and both PS-II and NADPH reductase is absent. This causes electrons to flow in a cyclic way back to PS-I.

16. (*a*) The correct order is C-D-A-B-E.

• PEP carboxylase in the mesophyll cells fixes CO_2 with PEP to form oxaloacetic acid (C_4 acid).

• Oxaloacetic acid is transported to the bundle sheath cells.

• Oxaloacetic acid is decarboxylated to form a C_3 acid.

• The CO_2 removed is fixed by C_3 or Calvin pathway to form glucose.

• The C_3 acid is transported back to mesophyll cells where it is converted back to PEP.

17. (*d*) In the given diagram, A, B, C and D represents PCT, descending limb of Henle's loop, ascending limb of Henle's loop and DCT, respectively. The filtrate in PCT is isotonic with respect to blood.

The descending limb is permeable to water and impermeable to electrolytes, and hence, it concentrates the filtrate. In the ascending limb, which is permeable to electrolyte, but impermeable to water, the filtrate gets diluted. Thus, diluted filtrate or hypotonic filtrate flows through the DCT.

18. (*a*) Statement I is incorrect, but statement II is correct. Statement I can be corrected as

Oxytocin is involved in milk ejection from the mammay gland, while oestrogens is involved in stimulation of growth and activities of female secondary sex organs, development of growing ovarian follicles and regulating female sexual behaviour.

19. (*b*) Statements I, II and IV are correct. While statements III and V are incorrect and can be corrected as

• Shoulder blade is a dorsally located bone of the pectoral girdle.

• Acetabulum cavity articulates with the longest bone of the body.

20. (*b*) The correct match is A-2, B-1, C-4, D-3.

• Rotifers excrete nitrogenous wastes through flame cells or protonephridia.

• Leeches and other annelids excrete nitrogenous wastes through nephridia.

• Insects like cockroaches excrete their wastes through malpighian tubules.

• Prawns and crustaceans excrete their wastes through antennal glands or green glands.

21. (*a*) Statements II and IV are correct. Statements I, III and V can be corrected as

• Glucose is the first molecule to enter the glycolytic pathway. Sucrose is converted to glucose and fructose by invertase in plants, which then enters into the glycolytic pathway.

• In one round of glycolysis, 4 ATP molecules are formed. 2 ATP molecules are formed when triose bisphosphate is converted to triose phosphate. Other 2 ATP molecules are formed when 2-phosphoenol pyruvate is converted to pyruvic acid.

• One of the glycolytic steps involves reduction of NAD^+ to $NADH + H^+$.

22. (*d*) A is true, but R is false. R can be corrected as
Auxin accumulates on the shaded side and promotes cell elongation.

23. (*d*) Statement I is correct, but statement II is incorrect. Statement II can be corrected as
Heterophylly is an adaptive strategy used by plants in response to environment.

24. (*b*) The correct match is A-4, B-1, C-2, D-3.
- Steroids secreted by adrenal cortex help in development of secondary sexual features during puberty.
- Hypoglycemia is caused by insulin, which lowers blood glucose level by glycogenesis. Glycogenesis is the conversion of glucose into glycogen.
- Cortisol is a glucocorticoid secreted by adrenal cortex which is anti-inflammatory in action.
- FSH or follicle stimulating hormone is secreted by anterior pituitary that causes spermatogenesis in the testes.

25. (*b*) The expiratory capacity can be calculated as
$\Rightarrow$ Tidal volume + Expiratory reserve volume
$\Rightarrow$ 500 mL + 1000 mL
$\Rightarrow$ 1500 mL

26. (*a*) The correct order of blood flow from the kidneys to the heart is A-E-D-B-C.
- Blood leaves the glomerulus through the efferent arterioles.
- Efferent arterioles branch to form peritubular capillaries.
- Blood flows through a branching network of the capillaries close to the Henle's loop in the vasa recta.
- Blood next flows through the renal venules.
- The renal venules fuse to form renal veins which leave the kidneys through the hilum. Blood is finally drained into the inferior vena cava of the heart.

27. (*d*) A is true, but R is false. R can be corrected as
Pure proteins or fats have to undergo a lots of steps for conversion into simpler molecules. This would require a lot of time and energy and hence, they are never preferred as respiratory substrates.

28. (*c*) 1 Calvin cycle, uses 3 ATP and 2 NADPH. To make one glucose molecule, 6 turns of the cycle is required, which will consume, 6×3 or 18 ATP and 6×2 or 12 NADPH. Now, for 3 glucose molecules, 6×3 or 18 turns of cycle would be needed which would consume, 18×3 or 54 ATP and 12×3 or 36 NADPH.

29. (*b*) Plastoquinone and plastocyanin are the H^+ acceptor and final electron acceptor of photosystem-II, respectively. Phaeophytin is the primary electron acceptor in PS-II.

30. (*c*) Statements II, III and V are correct, while statements I and IV are incorrect and can be corrected as
Lactic acid formation in muscles is dependent on pyruvate. The first step of glycolysis remains the same for both alcohol and lactic acid fermentation. Thus, pyruvate is formed, which is further converted to lactic acid and alcohol by action of enzymes pyruvate decarboxylase and alcohol dehydrogenase.
1 glucose molecule ferments to alcohol, to produce 2 ATP.

31. (*a*) The correct match is A-4, B-3, C-2, D-1.
- Muscular dystrophy is a genetic disorder with progressive degeneration of skeletal muscle.
- Tetany is wild uncontrolled muscular contraction, caused due to low calcium levels in plasma.
- Osteoporosis is age related disorder characterised by decreased bone mass and increased chances of fractures.
- Gout is caused due to accumulation of uric acid crystals at the joints. High protein diet can cause gout.

32. (*a*) The presence of a synaptic cleft, tells that it is a chemical synapse. *P* is the post-synaptic membrane, while *Q* is the pre-synaptic neuronal membrane. *R* is the receptor present on the post-synaptic neuron and *S* are the neurotransmitters released in response to a stimulus. Acetyl choline is a neurotransmitter.

33. (*a*) Statements I and IV are correct. Statements II and III can be corrected as
Potential at point B is maintained by efflux of three Na^+ ions and influx of two potassium ions.
Depolarisation travels from point A to point B.

34. (*b*) Both A and R are true and R is the correct explanation of A.
NAD^+ acts as the electron acceptor during decarboxylation of pyruvate into acetyl Co-A.
NAD^+ is reduced to NADH + H^+, while pyruvate is oxidised to acetyl Co-A during oxidative decarboxylation by pyruvate dehydrogenase enzyme.

35. (*b*) The correct match is A-3, B-1, C-4, D-2.
- Ubiquinol is reduced ubiquinone, which receives reducing equivalents *via* $FADH_2$ (complex II) that is generated during oxidation of succinate in the citric acid cycle.
- Complex IV refers to cytochrome-*c* oxidase complex containing cytochromes *a* and a_3, and two copper centres.
- Complex V is the ATP synthase enzyme that contains two components F_0 and F_1. F_0 is the integral membrane protein while F_1 is the peripheral membrane protein.
- The reduced ubiquinone (ubiquinol) is oxidised with the transfer of electrons to cytochrome-*c* *via* cytochrome-bc_1 complex (complex III).

36. (*c*) Englemann used aerobic bacteria, so that they can grow at regions of oxygen evolution by the photosynthetic algae. The regions of oxygen evolution is the action spectrum that coincides with absorption spectrum of chlorophyll-*a* and *b*. If anaerobes would be used, these bacteria won't grow at the points of oxygen evolution. They would rather concentrate where oxygen is absent. Hence, they cannot be used to identify action spectrum.

37. (*c*) Anoxygenic photosynthesis is where oxygen is not produced. Statements I, II and IV can be corrected as
- Light energy is converted to chemical energy.
- Energy in the form of ATP is produced.
- It is common in most prokaryotic systems like green and purple sulphur bacteria.

38. (*a*) The correct match is A -3, B-1, C-2, D-4
- Pons is a part of hind brain. It contains fibre tracts that interconnects all parts of the brain.
- Brain stem forms the connections between the brain and spinal cord. Three major regions that make up the brain stem are : mid brain, pons and medulla oblongata.
- The medulla contains centres which control respiration, cardiovascular reflexes and gastric secretions.
- Cerebellum, also part of hind brain controls, balances posture and coordination of the body.

39. (*c*) Both A and R are true, but R is not the correct explanation of A. K^+ permeability is crucial for re-excitation of axon at the end of a stimulus because the reversed polarity of the membrane is returned to normal by increasing potassium ion permeability at the end of an action potential.

40. (*b*) The correct order is B-D-C-E-A.
- Hypothalamus secretes GnRH.
- GnRH is released into portal circulation and reaches anterior pituitary.
- Anterior pituitary or pars distalis is stimulated to secrete two gonadotrophins, LH and FSH.
- LH acts on ovaries.
- Ovaries release ovum.

41. (*a*) Cyclic electron flow occurs in stromal lamella because it lacks PS-II as well as NADP reductase enzyme. The cyclic flow hence, results only in the synthesis of ATP, but not of $NADPH + H^+$. Cyclic photophosphorylation also occurs when only light of wavelengths beyond 680 nm are available for excitation. Photolysis or splitting of water is associated with PS-II.

42. (*c*) Both statement I and statement II are incorrect. These can be corrected as
One turn of the Krebs' cycle produces 12 molecules of ATP. In one turn of Krebs' cycle, 3 molecules of NADH and 1 molecule of $FADH_2$ is produced. 1 NADH yields 3 molecules of ATP, while 1 $FADH_2$ yields 2 molecules of ATP, thus a total of $(3 \times 3 = 9) + (1 \times 2 = 2)$ ATP molecules are produced in one turn. Additionally, during substrate level phosphorylation, 1 GTP hydrolysis is coupled to formation of 1 ATP molecule. Hence $9 + 2 + 1 = 12$ ATP molecules are produced in one turn of TCA cycle.

43. (*a*) In steps C (1, 3-phosphoglycerate $\rightarrow$ 3-phosphoglycerate) and D (2-phosphoenol pyruvate $\rightarrow$ Pyruvic acid), energy is generated by synthesis of ATP from ADP. In steps A (Glucose $\rightarrow$ Glucose-6- phosphate) and B (Fructose-6- phosphate $\rightarrow$ Fructose-1, -6-bisphosphate) energy is spent by ATP hydrolysis.

44. (*d*) Statement 'III' is correct whereas statements I, II and IV are incorrect and can be corrected as
Major part of cerebral cortex is associated with complex functions like memory. Major part of cortex is association area that has neither sensory nor motor function. Myelinated neurons of the inner parts of cerebrum gives the characteristic opaque coloration. Cortex contains cell bodies which give greyish color. Motivation drive in a person is controlled by the limbic system. The part around which cerebrum wraps is the thalamus which is a major coordinating centre for sensory and motor signalling.

45. (*d*) Statement I is correct, but statement II is incorrect. Statement II can be corrected as
In chemiosmosis, 4 protons are displaced for every ATP produced. Proton concentration is higher in the thylakoid lumen than the stroma, while it is higher in the intermembrane space of mitochondria. Thus, two opposite proton gradients are established for ATP synthesis in these two processes.

46. (*c*) At the tissues, oxygen is rapidly used by the cells.
Hence, the pO_2 is less, while pCO_2 is more. This favors formation of carbaminohaemoglobin, whereas the dissociation of carbaminohaemoglobin occurs at the alveoli. CO_2 in the tissues is converted into bicarbonate ions for transport, by the carbonic anhydrase enzyme. Also, at the tissue, oxyhaemoglobin dissociates.

47. (*d*) A is true, but R is false. R can be corrected as
The limbic system of the forebrain controls the emotional behaviour of a person under different situations. Whereas, the midbrain receives and

integrates visual, tactile and auditory inputs.

48. (*c*) Conditions B, C and D function in C_4 plants. Remaining statements can be corrected as

In C_4 plants, CO_2 concentration is increased in bundle sheath cells due to decarboxylation of C_4 acid.

The first stable product in C_4 pathway of C_4 plants is 4-C compound which is oxaloacetic acid.

49. (*a*) Statements I, II and V are correct. Statements III and IV are incorrect and can be corrected as

Sympathetic branch can increase the cardiac output during emergency. This leads to increase in heart rate and stroke volume.

Adrenaline exerts the same effect on heart as sympathetic branch. Both of these can increase the heart rate and cardiac output.

50. (*a*) The correct order is B-D-E-A-C.

- Due to suffocation, blood CO_2 levels and H^+ levels can increase.
- This activates the chemosensitive area of the brain.
- The chemosensitive area sends signal to the respiratory rhythm centre in medulla.
- The rhythm centre sends signal for contraction of diaphragm and intercostal muscles.
- This increases the rate of inspiration and expiration to eliminate excess CO_2.

51. (*b*) Both A and R are true and R is the correct explanation of A.

Photolysis is associated with PS-II. Splitting water molecule maintains a continuous supply of electrons to the PS-II reaction centre.

52. (*d*) In conversion of succinyl Co-A to succinic acid in the TCA cycle, there is substrate level phosphorylation, where GTP is synthesised from GDP. In a coupled reaction, GTP is converted to GDP with the simultaneous synthesis of ATP from ADP.

53. (*b*) Both A and R are true and R is the correct explanation of A.

The S-shaped curve is more realistic for an organism in the wild, or real world, because resources are not unlimited in real world. This affects the growth rate of an organism.

54. (*a*) A is false, but R is true. A can be corrected as

Aortic semilunar valves withstand the highest pressure out of all valves. This is because the left ventricles have to pump blood to the aorta with the highest pressure, so that oxygenated blood can reach to all parts of the body. Thus, the valve guarding the left ventricle and the aorta, which is the aortic semilunar valves, has to withstand the highest pressure.

55. (*a*) Statement I is incorrect, but statement II is correct. Statement I can be corrected as

SAN is responsible for initiation of action potential, whereas conduction of the impulses is mediated by the AV node to the ventricular musculature of the heart.

56. (*b*) Nodes of Ranvier are absent in neurons of somatic branch. Rest statements are incorrect and can be corrected as

Neurons of the somatic nervous system are unmyelinated. Hence, the Schwann cells do not secrete myelin sheath in such neurons.

Conduction of nerve impulses are slower than myelinated neurons of spinal nerves.

Most internal organs are innervated by neurons of the autonomic nervous system.

57. (*a*) The correct order is C-B-D-A-E.

- Relaxation of diaphragm and external intercostal muscles initiates the expiration process.
- This causes the diaphragm and sternum to return to their original position.
- The volume of thoracic cavity decreases in the dorso-ventral and antero-posterior axis.
- This causes an increase in intra-pulmonary pressure, or a positive pressure develops in the lungs compared to the outside atmospheric pressure.
- Thus, air is expelled from the lungs to the outside.

58. (*c*) The diagram represents contraction phase of muscle fibres.

Calcium ions are released into the sarcoplasm in response to action potential.

Calcium ions bind to a subunit of troponin which causes unmasking of myosin binding site on actin.

Energy for cross bridge formation is derived from ATP hydrolysis of the globular head of heavy meromyosin.

59. (*b*) Both statement I and statement II are correct. ATP hydrolysis generates ADP and inorganic phosphate. This Pi is added to glucose to form glucose-6-phosphate in the first step of glycolysis.

60. (*c*) Light can behave as a limiting factor in photosynthesis only when trees are grown in shade or in darker parts of the forest like the central or forest core.

61. (*c*) Both statement I and statement II are incorrect. These can be corrected as

Aerobic and anaerobic pathways of respiration occur simultaneously.

Functioning of cells require indirect use of energy from oxidation of substrates by formation of ATP followed by its hydrolysis when needed.

62. (*d*) The incorrect statement can be corrected as

Oxidation of $FADH_2$ generates ubiquinol which is the reduced form of ubiquinone.

63. (*a*) In the above image, *P* is alveoli, *Q* are the systemic veins, *R* is the systemic artery and *S* are the body tissues. The partial pressure of oxygen is higher in the alveoli, hence pO_2 is 104 mmHg. *Q* are the systemic veins carrying deoxygenated blood, hence pO_2 is

40 and pCO_2 is 45 mmHg. R is the systemic artery carrying oxygenated blood and hence pO_2 is 95 and pCO_2 is 40 mmHg. In the body cell(s), pO_2 is 40 mmHg and pCO_2 is 45 mmHg.

64. (*c*) Both A and R are correct, but R is not the correct explanation of A.
CO_2 diffuses at a much faster rate than O_2 through the diffusion membrane as the solubility of CO_2 is 20-25 times more than that of O_2.

65. (*c*) Both statement I and statement II are incorrect. These can be corrected as
- Pivot synovial joint is present between atlas and axis.
- Cartilaginous joints permit limited movement.

66. (*b*) The correct match is A-4, B-3, C-1, D-2.
- The inspiratory reserve volume is the additional volume of air, a person can inspire by a forcible inspiration. This averages 2500 mL to 3000 mL.
- Functional residual capacity is the volume of air that will remain in the lungs after a normal expiration. This includes ERV+RV
- Vital capacity is the maximum volume of air a person can breathe in after a forced expiration. This includes ERV, TV and IRV.
- Inspiratory capacity is total volume of air a person can inspire after a normal expiration. This includes Tidal Volume and Inspiratory Reserve Volume (TV+IRV). This averages 2500 to 3000 ml.

67. (*c*) Statements III, IV and V are correct while statements I and II are incorrect and can be corrected as
Piloerection (goosebumps) while watching a horror movie is induced by adrenal medullary hormone, adrenaline.
During fasting, liver cells undergo glycogenolysis, to maintain blood glucose. When blood glucose levels drop, glucagon acts on the liver cells to stimulate glycogenolysis or breakdown of glycogen into glucose, to increase its level in blood.

68. (*b*) The incorrect statement can be corrected as
Gibberellins and ethylene exhibit antagonistic effect on senescence. Gibberellins delay senescence, while ethylene promotes senescence.

69. (*a*) In both the pathways, NADH + H^+ acts as the reducing agent and reduces pyruvate. In turn, they get oxidised to form NAD^+.

70. (*a*) C_3 is the primary pathway for sugar biosynthesis in both C_3 and C_4 plants.
Other statements are incorrect and can be corrected as
- In C_4 plants, biosynthesis occurs in bundle sheath cells.
- RuBisCO behaves as carboxygenase in bundle sheath cells.
- Phosphoglycolate is formed in the mesophyll cells of C_3 plants.

71. (*a*) A is false, but R is true. A can be corrected as
If blood becomes too alkaline, PCT increases the secretion of ammonia into the filtrate.
This is because ammonia is alkaline in nature, thus secreting more ammonium ions into the filtrate would lower the pH of the blood and make it less alkaline. In the contrary, hydrogen ions make blood acidic, thus secreting more hydrogen ions, would reduce their concentration in blood, making blood even more alkaline.

72. (*d*) Statement I is correct, but statement II is incorrect. Incorrect statement can be corrected as
HMM contains the globular head and short arm of meromyosin.

73. (*c*) Both A and R are true, but R is not the correct explanation of A.
Menstruating women should include iodine in their diet, since iodine is needed for synthesis of thyroid hormones. Under secretion of thyroid hormones can cause irregular menstruation in women.

74. (*d*) The correct order is A-D-C-B-E.
- Influx of sodium ions reverses the polarity and generates action potential.
- Action potential reaches the axon terminals.
- This causes the synaptic vesicles to fuse with the plasma membrane and release the neurotransmitters at the synaptic cleft.
- The neurotransmitters bind to the receptors present on the post synaptic neuron membrane.
- This opens the ion channels allowing the action potential to be conducted in the post-synaptic neuron.

75. (*d*) The given graph represents arithmetic growth. Here, one of the daughter cell produced by mitosis divides. The other daughter cell differentiates and matures.

76. (*c*) Both A and R are true, but R is not the correct explanation of A.
C_4 plants show greater biomass productivity than C_3 plants, because C_4 plants have specialised bundle sheath cells where photorespiration is inhibited due to greater CO_2 concentration.

77. (*d*) Differentiated tissue used as explant in plant tissue culture, can be converted into undifferentiated mass i.e., callus, by dedifferentiation.

78. (*b*) Cortisol is a glucocorticoid which has anti-inflammatory properties and can suppress the immune system. After organ transplant, there are chances that body can cause immune reaction against the transplanted organ, hence the immune system is suppressed by administering cortisol.

79. (*a*) The graph represents percentage saturation of haemoglobin with oxygen. A shift in the curve to the right indicates dissociation of oxyhaemoglobin. The conditions which favor oxygen dissociation are low pH, and hence acidosis, low partial pressure of oxygen, high partial pressure of carbon dioxide, high temperature and high hydrogen ion concentration.

80. (*d*) A is true, but R is false. R can be corrected as
Ascending limb of Henle's loop is impermeable to water and permeable to electrolytes. This allows NaCl to be returned to the medullary interstitium, thereby maintaining concentration gradient and osmolarity of the interstitium.

81. (*a*) The given figure shows a sarcomere with different zones. *P* is the *Z*-line. *Q* is the A-band or anisotropic band. *R* is *I*-band or isotropic band and *S* is sarcomere extending between two successive *Z*-lines.

82. (*b*) I, II and III are useful for commercialisation and marketing of a plant or plant products.
Bolting is internode elongation just prior to flowering, which is induced by gibberellins. Chloroplast production is supported by cytokinins. Both of them are not directly related to a plant's commercialisation.

83. (*a*) P is plastoquinone which is a H^+ carrier. As it transfers electron, it releases the proton picked up from stroma into the lumen of thylakoid. Q is plastocyanin, which is the final acceptor of electrons in PS-II and transfers the electron to PS-I in non-cyclic photophosphorylation. This way, it reduces PS-I.

84. (*c*) The incorrect statements can be corrected as

- Auxin is applied to unorganised tissue to induce rooting in tissue culture. Kinetin, a cytokinin, induces shooting in tissue culture.
- Gibberellins are sprayed on sugarcane plants to increase stem length, which increases yield.
- Seed dormancy is an adaptive strategy induced by ABA to protect seeds.

85. (*b*) In public speaking, stage fright response causes a racing heart, sweating, etc. due to stimulation of the sympathetic branch of the autonomic nervous system.

86. (*c*) The incorrect statements can be corrected as

- Micturition reflex is under neural control.
- Stretch receptors send signal *via* sensory neurons to the CNS.
- Simultaneous contraction of bladder and relaxation of urethral sphincter eject urine.

87. (*d*) A is true, but R is false. R can be corrected as
Protons displaced from stroma to lumen, significantly reduces the pH of lumen.

88. (*a*) The experiment shows a coleoptile shoot tip in (*P*), while in (*Q*), shoot tip is cut. In the presence of coleoptile shoot tip, there is bending, while in its absence, there is no bending. Hence, it proves that coleoptile is the region where auxin is produced, as in its absence, there is no bending.

89. (*d*) The correct match is A-4, B -1, C-2, D-3.

- GA_3 is gibberellin which breaks seed dormancy and promote germination.
- IAA is Indole-3-acetic acid or auxin that promotes apical dominance.
- ABA or abscisic acid is a plant growth inhibitor that inhibits seed germination.
- Zeatin is cytokinin that works antagonistic to auxin in terms of apical dominance. Zeatin inhibits apical dominance.

90. (*a*) PGAL is 3-phospho-glyceraldehyde and is converted into 1, 3-bisphospho-glycerate or BPGA.

NSS1 NEET Stepping Stones 1

1. (*b*) Potato (*Solanum tuberosum*) and Brinjal (*Solanum melongena*) both belong to the genus *Solanum*, indicating that they have significant morphological similarities. The scientific name of other mentioned plants are as follows

- Cucumber–*Cucumis sativus*
- Wheat–*Triticum aestivum*
- Rice–*Oryza sativa*

2. (*d*) The correct match is A-3, B-4, C-2, D-1.

- Prions are misfolded protein and are causative agents of BSE.
- Bacteriophages affect bacteria usually contain *ds*DNA as genetic material.
- Lichen is a symbiont association between algae and fungi.
- Viroids are free RNA that affect plants causing potato spindle tuber disease.

3. (*d*) Statement I is correct, but statement II is incorrect.The incorrect statement can be corrected as

Methanogens are a type of archaebacteria that differ from other bacteria in having a different cell wall structure and this feature is responsible for their survival in extreme conditions.

4. (*a*) The given picture represents *Sphagnum*, which is a moss. It provides peat that has long been used as fuel and as packing material for the trans-shipment of living material because of their capacity to hold water.

5. (*c*) The correct match is A-3, B-2, C-1, D-4.

- Organisms such as sponges, coelenterates and flatworms do not have any specialised organ for respiration. They respire through general body surface.
- Earthworms respire through moist skin called cutaneous respiration.
- Insects have tracheal system for respiration.
- Arthropods living in water and molluscs respire through aquatic gills.

6. (*c*) The correct match is A-3, B-2, C-1, D-4.

- Afferent nerve fibres are sensory fibres that carry impulse from receptors such as skin to CNS.
- Efferent nerve fibres are motor nerves that carry impulse away from CNS to muscles.
- Autonomic nervous system is component of PNS that regulates heart rate, blood pressure, respiration.
- Myelinated nerve fibres are enveloped by Schwann cells which form myelin sheath around axon.

7. (*b*) Dinoflagellates are mostly marine and photosynthetic organisms. They are found in various colours due to the presence of different pigments in their cells.

8. (*c*) Brown algae (Phaeophyceae) are characterised by their large, complex multicellular bodies that include a holdfast for attachment, a stipe (stalk) and a leaf-like photosynthetic organ called a frond.

Options *A* and *B* are characteristics shared with other types of algae, while option *D* is incorrect as brown algae can exhibit isogamous, anisogamous or oogamous sexual reproduction. Therefore, option *C* correctly identifies a unique characteristic of brown algae.

9. (*a*) Animals that possess a body cavity lined by mesoderm are called coelomates. Animals with a body cavity not completely lined by mesoderm, but with scattered mesodermal pouches, are termed as pseudocoelomates. Animals that lack a body cavity altogether are acoelomates.

Option (a) accurately describes these distinctions based on the presence or absence of a mesoderm-lined body cavity.

10. (*b*) Ascomycetes produce asexual spores called conidia exogenously on the special mycelium called conidiophores. Upon germination, conidia produce mycelium.

11. (*c*) Both statement I and statement II are incorrect. These can be corrected as follows

- Podocytes create small spaces called filtration slits or slit pores that filter all the constituents of plasma except the proteins.
- On an average, 1100-1200 mL of blood is filtered by the kidney per minute, which constitute roughly 1/5th of the blood pumped out by each ventricle of the heart.

12. (*c*) The Golgi cisternae are concentrically arranged near the nucleus with distinct convex *cis* or the forming face and concave *trans* or the maturing face. The *cis* and *trans* faces of the organelle are entirely different, but interconnected.

13. (*c*) The correct match is A-1, B-2, C-3, D-4.

- Pyruvic acid a 3-carbon compound is final product of glycolysis.
- $NADH^+$ are coenzymes involved in redox reactions.
- Conversion of pyruvate to ethanol occurs in anaerobic cells such as yeast.
- Complete oxidation of pyruvate occurs in Krebs' cycle in mitochondria.

14. (*c*) The correct match is A-4, B-1, C-2, D-3.

- Cells responsible for growth of root are present in region of elongation.
- Root cap is a thimble like structure at the apex of root.

• Stem spreads out into branches and conduct water, minerals and photosynthates.

• Leaf lamina contains vein and veinlets and is the site of photosynthesis.

15. (*d*) *A-Aurelia*-Coelenterata *B-Euspongia*-Porifera, *C Pila*-Mollusca.

• *Aurelia* represents medusa stage of coelenterates which is umbrella shaped and produce polyp sexually.

• *Euspongia* or bath sponge belongs to Porifera with fibers made of spongin proteins.

• *Pila* or apple snail is a large freshwater, soft bodies and unsegmented snail belonging to Mollusca.

16. (*c*) The hypothalamus is part of the diencephalon, which is in the forebrain. It maintains homeostasis and along with limbic system it controls sexual behaviours, emotions and memory.

17. (*d*) Statement I is correct, but Statement II is incorrect. The incorrect statement can be corrected as

In dicotyledonous stems, cambium is present between phloem and xylem. These are called open vascular bundles and they possess the ability to form secondary xylem and phloem tissues.

18. (*b*) The correct match is A-4, B-3, C-2, D-1.

• Antigens are found on the surface of RBCs, while antibodies are present in blood plasma which help in detection of blood group.

• Individuals with blood group A have A antigen and blood group B have B antigen on surface of RBCs. O blood group does not carry any antigen, while AB carry both antigens (A and B) on RBCs surface.

19. (*d*) Reticulate venation is characterised by the formation of network by veinlets is the correct description of leaf venation. Other options are incorrect and can be corrected as

• Monocotyledonous plants exhibit parallel venation, not reticulate venation.

• Veins in dicotyledonous plants typically form a network of reticulate venation.

• Venation specifically refers to the arrangement of veins and veinlets within the lamina of a leaf.

20. (*b*) In monocot stems, e.g. in *Triticum aestivum* the vascular bundles are conjoint, i.e. they are closely spaced and arranged along a single radius.

21. (*c*) Cortisol and testosterone do not fall under the category of peptide, polypeptide, or protein hormones. These are steroid hormones.

22. (*d*) Vexillary aestivation, also known as papilionaceous aestivation, is characteristic of pea and bean flowers. In these flowers, the largest petal (standard) overlaps the two lateral petals (wings), which in turn overlap the two smallest anterior petals (keel).

23. (*b*) The given figure represents a conjoint open vascular bundle because the xylem and phloem are jointly situated along the same radius of vascular bundles. In this, *B* represents the cambium that is responsible for the secondary growth in plants.

24. (*c*) Both A and R are true, but R is not the correct explanation of A. Osteichthyes have streamlined bodies and cycloid or ctenoid scales to swim efficiently through water, protect themselves from predators, and maintain buoyancy. These adaptations help them survive and thrive in their aquatic habitats.

25. (*d*) Purkinje fibres conduct action potentials and are located in the ventricles, ensuring efficient contraction of the ventricular muscles.

26. (*b*) *A* represents guava, which has opposite phyllotaxy as seen in *Calotropis* and guava.

Picture *B* shows *Alstonia* which has a whorled phyllotaxy.

27. (*c*) The correct match is A-4, B-2, C-3, D-1.

• Aschelminthes are commonly called round worms their coelom is in the form of patches, hence called pseudocoelomate and they have complete alimentary canal.

• Annelida have metamerically segmented body; are commonly called ringworms and possess closed circulation and parapodia for locomotion.

• Body of arthropods is covered by chitinous exoskeleton. They have jointed appendages and possess open type of circulatory system.

• Mollusca have outer shell of $CaCO_3$ and their body is divided into head, foot and hump. Their mouth contains a file-like rasping organ for feeding called radula.

28. (*c*) Actinomorphic flowers can be divided into two equal radial halves in any plane passing through the centre, indicating radial symmetry.

Other options are incorrect and can be corrected as

The presence of bracts at the base of the pedicel defines whether a flower is bracteate or ebracteate. The number of floral appendages relates to the count of sepals, petals, stamens, and carpels, not necessarily to floral symmetry and the presence of both androecium and gynoecium indicates a bisexual flower.

29. (*a*) Statements I, II and III are correct, while statements IV and V are incorrect. The incorrect statements can be corrected as

• Bulliform cells are specialised epidermal cells found in grasses (monocot leaves), not in dicot leaves.

• The mesophyll contains chloroplasts and is primarily involved in photosynthesis, not structural support.

30. (*a*) In the given figure, A represents cervical vertebrae. The number of cervical vertebrae is seven in almost all mammals including human beings.

31. (*b*) Both statement I and statement II are correct.

• Calyx is the outermost whorl of flower and protects it in bud stage. It is also known as sepals may be united (gamosepalous) or free (polysepalous).

• Corolla are brightly coloured petals that vary greatly in plants, they may be tubular, bell-shaped, funnel shaped or wheel-shaped.

32. (*c*) The characteristics described in the question correspond to those found in sponges (phylum-Porifera). Sponges have a water transport or canal system where water enters through ostia, passes through a spongocoel and exits through an osculum. They possess choanocytes for feeding and reproduction occurs both sexually (formation of gametes) and asexually (fragmentation).

33. (*d*) The correct match is A-3, B-1, C-4, D-2.

• Thyroid gland produce hormone thyrocalcitonin which control calcium level in blood.

• Thymus is well developed in young children and is responsible for immunity.

• Adrenal medulla secretes catecholamines in response to stress.

• Ovary in female produces oestrogen and progesterone horomones.

34. (*b*) In temperate region, during winter season the cambium is less active and forms fewer xylary elements that have narrow vessels, this wood is called autumn wood.

35. (*a*) In marginal placentation, the placenta forms a ridge along the ventral suture of the ovary and the ovules are borne on the ridge forming two rows, as in pea.

36. (*d*) Option (d) represents the correct characteristic of phylum-Platyhelminthes. Other options are incorrect and can be corrected as

• Platyhelminthes are bilaterally symmetrical.

• Platyhelminthes do not have a closed circulatory system. Instead, diffusion is carried out for the transport of gases, nutrients, and wastes.

• Platyhelminthes possess specialised flame cells that help in osmoregulation and excretion.

37. (*d*) The correct match is A-2, B-3, C-1, D-4.

• Epiblema bears root hair and is outermost layer of root.

• Endodermis is innermost layer of cortex which contains casparian strips to block passage of water.

• Pericycle is parenchymatous layer that lies just inside endodermis.

• Pith is parenchymatous tissue which is cylindrical and soft and present in the central region of root.

38. (*c*) The external inter-costal muscles are essential for lifting the ribs and sternum during inspiration. This action increases the thoracic volume, reduce intra-pulmonary pressure below atmospheric pressure, and allows air to flow into the lungs. If these muscles were paralysed or unable to function properly, the chest would not expand adequately during inspiration. This would make it extremely difficult or impossible to inhale air into the lungs, potentially leading to respiratory arrest if not addressed timely.

39. (*d*) The correct match is A-1, B-2, C-4, D-3.

• Pressure gradient is difference between pressure in alveoli and atmosphere.

• Diffusion membrane is less than 1mm, thin membrane that allow exchange of gases.

• Partial pressure is the pressure exerted by a gas during exchange.

• Alveoli are thin, vascularised bag like structure that acts as site for gaseous exchange.

40. (*a*) In a floral formula, C represents corolla. Ashwagandha belongs to the family Solanaceae and has a corolla consisting of five, united petals exhibiting valvate aestivation.

41. (*b*) Both statement I and statement II are correct.

• TCA generates 3NADH, $1FADH_2$ and 1GTP or 1ATP during single cycle in mitochondria.

• ETS contains complex I-V on inner mitochondrial membrane to generate ATP by transfer of electrons.

42. (*b*) The correct match is A-3, B-4, C-1, D-2.

• Skeletal muscles are voluntary with alternate light and dark bands.

• Visceral muscles are found in internal organ like intestine and are involuntary and unbranched.

• Cardiac muscle are striated, involuntary muscles connected by intercalated disc.

• Myofibrils contain actin and myosin.

43. (*d*) The correct match is A-1, B-3, C-2, D-4.

• Plasticity is the response of plants towards environment as seen in Larkspur.

• Heterophylly is the difference in shape of leaves of plants such as cotton.

• Plant growth regulator are small, diverse chemicals of different nature that act as phytohormones.

• Inhibition of lateral buds by growing apical bud is apical dominance as seen under influence of auxin.

44. (*b*) Both A and R are true and R is the correct explanation of A. In polarised state, neurons have electrical difference across cell membrane due to presence of Na^+ and K^+ ions. Outer membrane has positive charge, while inner membrane have negative charge causing them to get excitable.

45. (*c*) Corpora quadrigemina is a part of midbrain that help in processing visual and auditory information.

46. (*a*) *A*-Carboxylation, *B*- Reduction, *C*- Regeneration.

• Calvin cycle mainly possesses three stages as follows- During carboxylation, CO_2 combines with ribulose-1, 5-bisphosphate. During reduction, carbohydrate is formed at the expense of the photochemically made ATP and NADPH and during regeneration, ribulose- 1, 5 -bisphosphate is formed again so that the cycle continues.

47. (*a*) Epithelial tissue has a free surface, which faces either a body fluid or the outside environment and thus provides a covering or a lining for some parts of the body.

48. (*b*) Both A and R are true and R is the correct explanation of A.

To perform chemical analysis of a living tissue, we can take any living tissue and grind it in trichloroacetic acid $[Cl_3CCOOH]$ using a mortar and a pestle, we obtain a thick slurry. After straining this, we get two fractions- one is called filtrate (acid-soluble pool) and the second, the retentate (acid-insoluble fraction).

49. (*a*) Gibberellins promote internode elongation before flowering and delay senesence in fruits. Other options are incorrect because gibberellins promote bolting in beet, delay senescence and increase the length of the stem.

50. (*a*) The skin of a frog is smooth and slippery due to the presence of mucus, which helps in maintaining a moist condition. This moisture is essential to prevent dehydration and also facilitates cutaneous respiration, involving the exchange of gases through the skin.

51. (*d*) Statement I is correct, but Statement II is incorrect and can be corrected as

The complete disintegration of the nuclear envelope occurs during prophase, not in metaphase.

In metaphase, the nuclear envelope is already dissolved, allowing the chromosomes to move freely within the cell.

52. (*b*) The correct match is A-4, B-3, C-2, D-1.

- Differentiation is the process by which cells.
- Dedifferentiation is process where cells once again regain their ability to divide.
- Redifferentiation is process by which dedifferentiated cell attains a particular function.
- Tumour is a mass of cell formed due to abnormal uncontrolled division.

53. (*b*) A zwitter ion is a dipolar ion with no overall electrical charge, but a zwitter ion molecule carries an equal number of positively and negatively charged functional group.

54. (*c*) Inclusion bodies in prokaryotic cells, such as phosphate granules, cyanophycean granules and glycogen granules, store reserve materials and lie freely in the cytoplasm. They are not bound by any membrane. Gas vacuoles are found in blue-green and purple and green photosynthetic bacteria, but are not involved in protein synthesis. Cyanophycean granules do not assist in motility, they are involved in storage.

55. (*d*) Only statement I represents the correct characteristic of C_4 plants as compared to C_3 plants. C_4 plants are adapted to dry tropical regions and exhibit Kranz anatomy, where bundle sheath cells form several layers around the vascular bundles and they have a high number of chloroplasts Other statements are incorrect and can be corrected as-

They tolerate higher temperatures, show a response to high light intensities, lack photorespiration and have greater productivity of biomass as compared to C_3 plants.

56. (*d*) A is true, but R is false. R can be corrected as

Cellulose is a polymeric polysaccharide consisting of only one type of monosaccharide namely, glucose.

57. (*a*) Animal cells undergo cytokinesis by forming a furrow in the plasma membrane, which deepens and divides the cytoplasm into two daughter cells. Plant cells, on the other hand, form a cell plate at the centre of the cell, which grows outward to separate the cytoplasm into two daughter cells.

58. (*c*) During phase B, DNA replication begins in the nucleus, and the centriole duplicates in the cytoplasm. Other options are incorrect and can be corrected as follows:

- The phase *E* represents the dividing phase of the cell cycle.
- In the 24-hour average duration of the cell cycle of a human cell, phase *D*, i.e. interphase, lasts for about 23 hours and the rest of one hour is designated for the division of the cell.
- During phase A, i.e. G_1-phase, the cell is metabolically active and continuously grows, but does not replicate its DNA.

59. (*b*) Statements II and III are correct, while statements I and IV are incorrect. Incorrect statements can be corrected as

- While the respiratory pathway does involve the breakdown of substrates for energy production, it also participates in synthesis processes, hence it is not exclusively catabolic.
- The respiratory pathway is considered amphibolic because it serves roles in both catabolism (breakdown) and anabolism (synthesis) of biomolecules.

60. (*b*) The bilayer arrangement of phospholipids, with polar heads facing the outer aqueous environment and hydrophobic tails protected inside, is crucial for maintaining selective permeability. This structure allows the membrane to control the entry and exit of different molecules while maintaining the hydrophobic interior, essential for membrane integrity and function.

61. (*d*) Statement I is correct, but statement II is incorrect. The ncorrect statement can be corrected as

The columnar epithelium is composed of a single layer of tall and slender cells. The cells are nucleated and the nuclei are located at the base.

62. (*c*) Incorrect statement can be corrected as

In the light reactions of photosynthesis, Photosystem-I (PS-I) and Photosystem-II (PS-II) have distinct reaction centres. The reaction centre in PS-II absorbs light at 680 nm and is referred to as P680. Conversely, the reaction centre in PS-I absorbs light at 700 nm and is called P700. Therefore, the reaction centre chlorophyll a in PS-I is P700.

63. (*a*) Statements I, II, III and IV are correct, while statement V is incorrect. Incorrect statement can be corrected as

Frogs undergo indirect development with a larval stage called tadpole this kind of development is called metamorphosis.

64. (*a*) The correct match is A-2, B-3, C-1, D-4.

- Interphase lasts for more than 95% duration of cell cycle.
- S-phase shows duplication of DNA. DNA becomes 4C from 2C.
- G_2 shows synthesis of proteins for mitosis.
- G_0 is quiescent stage where cells are active, but do not proliferate.

65. (*b*) The correct match is A-4, B-3, C-1, D-2.

- Vinblastin is an alkaloid drug used to treat breast cancer.
- Morphine, obtained from poppy is a potent analgesic.
- Ricin is a toxin naturally obtained from castor beans.
- Concanavalin-A is lectin obtain from jackbean.

66. (*b*) Squamous epithelium is a type of epithelial tissue characterised by flattened cells. It forms a diffusion boundary due to its thinness, allowing for rapid diffusion of substances across its surface. This type of epithelium is found in the lining of blood vessels (endothelium) and the air sacs of the lungs (alveoli).

67. (*c*) Option (c) represents the characteristic that distinguishes enzymes from inorganic catalysts. Enzymes catalyse reactions by lowering the activation energy. Other statements are incorrect and can be corrected as follows

- Enzymes are sensitive to high temperatures and functions optimally within a specific temperature range.
- Enzymes are primarily composed of proteins, not nucleic acids.
- Enzymes are sensitive to pH changes as pH affects their tertiary structure and the configuration of their active sites.

68. (*c*) The correct match is A-1, B-3, C-4, D-2.

- Chlorophyll-*a* is the reaction centre that contains blue-green colour pigment.
- Chlorophyll-*b* is an accessory pigment with yellow-green colour.
- Xanthophylls are yellow pigment and help protect chlorophyll-*a* from photo-oxidation.
- Carotenoids are yellow to yellow-orange colour hydrocarbons found in anti-oxidants.

69. (*b*) Statements I, III and IV are correct, while statement II and V are incorrect. The incorrect statements can be corrected as

- Oils have lower melting point and hence remain as oil in winter.
- Saturated fatty acids are without double bonds.

70. (*c*) *A*-Sapindales, *B*-Anacardiaceae. The correct pathway of taxonomic hierarchy of *Mangifera indica* is as follows

Angiospermae-Dicotyledonae-Sapindales-Anacardiaceae-*Mangifera indica*

71. (*c*) Statements II, III and IV are correct, while statement I is incorrect. It can be corrected as

The bones of the hand (forelimb) include the humerus, radius, ulna, carpals, metacarpals and phalanges. Tibia and fibula are the bones of hindlimbs.

72. (*a*) The correct match is A-3, B-4, C-1, D-2.

- RuBisCO is most abundant protein and has both oxygenase and carboxygenase activity.
- Cellulose is a polysaccharide, which is a polymer of glucose.
- Starch can hold I_2 molecule in its helical secondary structure.
- Prosthetic groups are tightly bound to apoenzyme.

73. (*b*) *A*-Fixation, *B*-Decarboxylation, *C*-Regeneration.

- In mesophyll cell, fixation of atmospheric CO_2 takes place.
- Decarboxylation of C_4 compound (OAA) to form 3-carbon acid occur in bundle sheath cell.
- CO_2 is utilised in Calvin cycle.
- Regeneration of C_3 acid into PEP occur in mesophyll cells.

74. (*a*) Statements I, II, III and V are correct. Statement IV is incorrect and can be corrected as

Cyanobacteria is a type of eubacteria or true bacteria. It is characterised by the presence of a rigid cell wall.

75. (*b*) Both statement I and statement II are correct.

• Myasthenia gravis is an autoimmune disorder where body's defence system attacks healthy cell and destroys it.

• Tetany is involuntary contraction of muscles leading to painful cramps caused due to low Ca^{2+} levels in blood.

76. (*b*) Incorrect statement can be corrected as

Collagen is not primarily an energy storage molecule, rather, it is a structural protein found abundantly in the animal world. It provides strength and support to tissues like skin, tendons, and bones.

77. (*c*) Statements I, II and III are correct, while statement IV is incorrect. Incorrect statement can be corrected as

Tryptophan is a aromatic amino acid due to its aromatic ring structure.

78. (*b*) The correct match is A-2, B-4, C-3, D-1.

• *Salvinia* is heterosporous pteriodophyte that produce two different type of spores.

• Carrageen is a seaweed polysaccharide obtained from red algae.

• *Cycas* is a gymnosperm that contain coralloid root showing N_2-fixing association with cyanobacteria..

• *Sequoia* or gaint redwood is a very large gymnosperm with thick woody stem.

79. (*a*) The correct match is A-3, B-4, C-2, D-1.

• Glycocalyx is outermost layer containing slime layer and capsule.

• Flagella are surface structures which provides motility to bacteria.

• Pili are composed of pilin proteins.

• Fimbrae are bristle-like structures that help in adhesion to host tissue.

80. (*a*) The correct match is A-3, B-4, C-2, D-1.

• PCT show active reabsorption of glucose, amino acid and 70-80% electrolyte.

• Henle's loop make urine more concentrated by maintaining osmolarity.

• DCT shows reabsorption of Na^+ and water and selective secretion of H^+ and K^+ ions.

• Collecting duct absorbs large amount of water to produce concentrated urine.

81. (*a*) Cell theory states that cells are the basic structural and functional units of all living organisms. This foundational principle was proposed by Matthias Schleiden and Theodore Schwann, who observed cells in plants and animals, respectively. However, some cells fall exception to cell theory. These include some bacteria, RBCs and sieve tubes.

82. (*c*) The correct match is A-1, B-3, C-4, D-2.

• Glomerulus is a tuft of capillaries inside bowman's capsule.

• Bowman's capsule is a cup-like structure enclosing glomerulus.

• DCT is highly coiled tube which opens into straight tube called collecting tube.

• Outermost layer of kidney is called renal capsule.

83. (*c*) Chemosynthetic autotrophic bacteria oxidise inorganic substances to produce ATP. They play a role in recycling nutrients, but do not have any role in the decomposition of organic matter.

84. (*c*) The correct match is A-3, B-2, C-4, D-1.

• Fibrinogens are inactive threads, activated into fibrin and are involved in clotting of blood.

• Globulins are antibody protein involved in cellular defense.

• Albumins are plasma protein that maintain osmotic balance in blood.

• Basophils are type of granulated WBCs, stained by basic dye and are involved in protecting body against pathogens. They secrete histamine and heparin.

85. (*c*) Features I and III are unique to prokaryotic cells compared to eukaryotic cells. Other features are not unique to prokaryotes. They can be explained as

• Prokaryotic cells do not have a well-defined nucleus.

• Prokaryotic cells lack a nuclear membrane.

86. (*c*) Myoglobin found in red fibres contain plenty of mitochondria that uses large amount of O_2 to produce ATP.

87. (*d*) Statement I is correct, but Statement II is incorrect. Statement II can be corrected as

Unlike bryophytes and pteridophytes, in gymnosperms, the male and female gametophytes do not have an independent free-living existence. They remain within the sporangia that is retained on the sporophytes.

88. (*c*) The correct match is A-3, B-2, C-4, D-1.

• ER has tubular network with ribosomes (RER) which produce protein and that without ribosome (SER) produce lipid.

• Golgi is involved in packaging of proteins and possess a *cis* and a *trans*-face.

• Lysosome contain digestive enzymes with acidic pH which are capable of digesting macromolecules like carbohydrates, proteins, lipids and nucleic acids.

• Vacuole is a membrane-bound organelle which store water and waste.

89. (*d*) The correct match is A-3, B-2, C-4, D-1.

• OAA is first product of C_4 cycle formed in bundle sheath cells.

- Bundle sheath cells form tightly packed layer around veins and vascular tissue.
- PEP accept CO_2 in mesophyll cell to form 4-carbon acid.
- C_4-pathway was discovered by Australian scientists Marshall Hatch and Charles Slack.

90. (*d*) Option (d) represents the correct description of given diagram.
The QRS complex represents the depolarisation of the ventricles, which initiates ventricular contraction.
Other features are incorrect and can be corrected as follows:

- P-wave represents the depolarisation of the atria, not the ventricles.
- QRS complex represents the depolarisation of the ventricles, not the repolarisation.
- T-wave represents the repolarisation of the ventricles, not the depolarisation of the atria.

NSS2 NEET Stepping Stones 2

1. (*d*) Intercalary meristem is primary meristem found in monocots such as bamboo and grasses which helps in elongation activity.

2. (*b*) The statements II, IV and V are not the effects of parathyroid hormone because

- Parathyroid hormone is a hypercalcemic hormone, *i.e.* it increases the blood calcium levels.
- It also increases the absorption of calcium from digested food.
- Glucocorticoids regulate carbohydrate

The statements I and III are associated with parathyroid hormone because parathyroid hormone stimulates the process of bone resorption.
Reabsorption of Ca^{2+} by renal tubules is also a function of PTH.

3. (*b*) Both statement I and statement II are correct.
Slime moulds are saprophytic protists. Their body moves along decaying twig and leaves engulfing organic material. Under suitable conditions, they form an aggregation called plasmodium, which may grow and spread over several feet.

4. (*b*) In most situations, ABA acts as an antagonist to GAs. For example, ABA promotes dormancy and inhibit germination of seed, while GA enhances germination.

5. (*b*) The correct match is A-4, B-3, C-2, D-1.
P-wave represents depolarisation of the atria.
QRS complex represents the depolarisation of the ventricles
T-wave represents the return of the ventricle from excited to normal state.
Stoke volume is important determinant of cardiac output.

6. (*c*) Quiescent centre is located centrally in the root apical mesistem. This region has comparatively inactive cells. These cells have a lower concentration of the proteins, DNA and RNA and these are maintained at a lower mitotic activity. It is responsible for providing the cells to the root apical meristem during the injury or the heavy growth period.

7. (*b*) *Lactobacillus* bacteria, is a heterotrophic bacteria, involved in the production of curd from milk.

8. (*d*) The correct match is A-2, B-1, C-4, D-3.
Erythrocytes (RBCs) are carrier of oxygen and help in gas transport.
Eosinophils resist infections and are also associated with allergic reaction.
Thrombocytes are also called platelets. They release substances, which are involved in the clotting of blood.
Contraction of heart muscle is called systole.

9. (*d*) Statement I is correct, but statement II is incorrect. The incorrect statement can be corrected as
Leaves of most of the dicotyledonous plants bear networks of veinlets in their lamina and constitute reticulate venation.

10. (*d*) Flavonoids and alkaloids are secondary metabolites and are not present in acid insoluble fraction.

11. (b) Both A and R are true and R is the correct explanation of A.
Jawless fishes like *Myxine* and *Petromyzon* are marine fishes belonging to class-Cyclostomata. During spawning they migrate to fresh water, since it reduces the chances of predation and ensure better survival of their offsprings.
The larvae after metamorphosis migrate back to the oceans.

12. (*b*) The statements I, III and V are correct. Statements II and IV are incorrect and can be corrected as
The companion cells are specialized parenchymatous, nucleated cells, which are closely associated with the sieve tube element (without nucleus) to control their activity.
Parenchyma are generally isodiametric, spherical, oval,round, polygonal or elongated in shape.

13. (c) The correct match is A-3, B-4, C-2, D-1.
Meandrina is commonly known as brain coral.

Wuchereria, commonly known as filarial worm, is a genus of parasitic roundworms responsible for causing lymphatic filariasis.

Cucumaria, commonly known as sea cucumber, belongs to phylum Echinodermata.

Hirudinaria, commonly known as the blood sucking leech, is a genus of leeches that parasitises large animals.

14. (*b*) Seed germination is very important phase in plant cycle, which establishes new generation of the plant. It is energy demanding process. Thus, in order to fulfill the demand, mitochondria count increases during seed germination.

15. (*c*) The correct match is A-2, B-1, C-4, D-3.

Psilotum belongs to class–Psilopsida is a primitive vascular plant known for its simple, dichotomously branching stems and lack of true leaves.

Selaginella belongs to class Lycopsida having scale like leaves and spore-producing structures called strobili.

Equisetum, commonly known as horsetail, belongs to class-Sphenopsida and is a genus of vascular plants characterised by its jointed stems and rough, silica-containing texture.

Adiantum, known as maidenhair fern, belongs to class–Pteropsida and is a genus of ferns with delicate, fan-shaped fronds.

16. (*a*) The given figure is of compound epithelium. It is made of more than one layer of cell. Its main function is to provide protection against chemical and mechanical stresses.

17. (*c*) Secondary cortex is also known as phelloderm. Other incorrect match pair can be corrected as

Cork cambium, also known as phellogen, develops in the cortex region of stem.

Cork is also known as phellem.

The spring wood is also known as early wood, while autumn wood is known as late wood.

18. (*d*) Chemiosmosis is crucial in both photosynthesis and cellular respiration. It relies on a membrane, proton pump, proton gradient and ATP synthase to convert proton gradient energy into ATP, essential for cellular functions.

19. (*d*) The correct match is A-3, B-1, C-4, D-2.

Sycon-belonging to the phylum-Porifera has body with pores and canals in walls.

Asterias - belonging to the phylum-Echinodermata contains water vascular system and shows radial symmetry.

Pleurobrachia-belonging to the phylum-Ctenophora has comb plates for locomotion

Bombyx-belonging to the phylum-Arthropoda has their exoskeleton made up of cuticle.

20. (*a*) Statement I is incorrect, but statement II is correct. The incorrect statement can be corrected as

The G_1-phase of the cell cycle is the interval between mitosis and initiation of DNA replication. It is not a check point.

21. (*c*) The incorrect statement can be corrected as

Biologists describe the protein structures at four levels, *i.e.* primary, secondary, tertiary and quaternary structure.

22. (*b*) The correct match is A-3, B-4, C-1, D-2.

Oxaloacetic acid - 4C compound

Phosphoglyceraldehyde - 3C compound

Isocitrate – 6C compound

α-ketoglutarate – 5C compound.

23. (*d*) Statement I is correct, but statement II is incorrect and can be corrected as

In female frogs, the ureters and oviduct open seperately in the cloaca.

24. (*d*) A is true, but R is false. R can be corrected as

Purine, i.e. adenine and guanine, have 9 membered ring structure, while pyrimidine, i.e. cytosine, thymine and uracil, have 6 membered ring structure.

25. (*d*) Statement I is correct, but statement II is incorrect. The incorrect statement can be corrected as

The atrio-ventricular node is located on the lower left corner of right atrium close to the atrio-ventricular septum.

26. (*b*) Both statement I and statement II are correct.

The primary CO_2 acceptor is a 3-carbon molecule, phosphoenol pyruvate (PEP) and is present in the mesophyll cells. Mesophyll cells of C_4 plants lack RuBisCO enzyme.

27. (*d*) Statement I is correct, but statement II is incorrect. The incorrect statement can be corrected as

Polyp is a sessile and cylindrical form, whereas medusa is free swimming and umbrella shaped.

28. (*c*) The enzyme that is membrane bound in Krebs' cycle is succinic dehydrogenase. It covert succinate to fumarate and also transfers electrons from succinate to quinones.

29. (*c*) The glomerular capillary blood pressure causes filteration of the blood through 3 layers, i.e. the endothelium of glomerular blood vessels, the epithelium of Bowman's capsule and a basement membrane between these two layers.

30. (*a*) The correct match is A-3, B-2, C-1.

The term 'virus' was given by Pasteur. WM Stanley showed that virus could be crystallised and crystals consist largely of proteins. MW Beijerinck demonstrated that the extract of the infected plants of tobacco could cause infection in healthy plant and called the fluid as *Contagium vivum fluidum*.

31. (*d*) Statement I is correct, but statement II is incorrect and can be corrected as
Thymus gland is a lobular structure which is located on the dorsal side of the heart and aorta.

32. (*c*) The left and right cerebral hemispheres are connected by a tract of nerve fibres called corpus callosum.

33. (*d*) The incorrect statement can be corrected as
In low concentration, ethylene stimulates root initiation and growth of lateral roots and root hair.
Ethylene is produced in plants from the amino acid methionine. It is synthesised in almost all plant parts.

34. (*a*) The correct match is A-3, B-4, C-2 and D-1.
Osteoporosis- Age related disorder caused due to decreased level of oestrogen.
Muscular dystrophy- Progressive degeneration of skeletal muscle.
Gout- It is caused due to accumulation of uric acid crystals.
Myasthenia gravis-Weakening and paralysis of skeletal muscle.

35. (*c*) Incorrect match pair can be corrected as– IAA (Indole Acetic Acid) is indole compound, while GA (Gibberellic acid) is terpene.

36. (*b*) The taxonomic categories showing hierarchial arrangement in ascending order are as follows
Mangifera → Anacardiaceae → Sapindales → Dicotyledonae → Angiospermae

37. (*d*) Hemichordates have a rudimentary structure in collar region called stomochord, which is similar to notochord.

38. (*c*) The correct match is A-3, B-1, C-2.
Tight junctions- Help to stop substances from leaking across a tissue.
Adhering junctions - Perform cementing to keep neighbouring cells together.
Gap junctions- Facilitate the cells to communicate with each other by connecting the cytoplasm of adjoining cells.

39. (*a*) The elongation phase is characterised by increased vacuolation, cell enlargement and new cell wall deposition, which contributes to the overall growth of the plant. In contrast, the maturation phase is associated with the cell reaching their maximal size and the meristematic phase involves active cell division.

40. (*c*) Both A and R are true, but R is not the correct explanation of A.
About 97% of O_2 is transported by RBCs in the blood. The remaining 3.0% of O_2 is carried in a dissolved state through the plasma. Therefore, haemoglobin cannot get saturated with oxygen more than 97% .

41. (*a*) The correct match is A-2, B-1, C-4, D-3.

- In the metacentric chromosome, the centromere is in the middle of the chromosomes.
- Acrocentric chromosome has a centromere close to the end of the chromosome.
- In the sub-metacentric chromosome, the centromere is slightly away from the middle of the chromosome.
- The telocentric chromosome has a terminal centromere.

42. (*c*) Gamosepalous calyx, imbricate aestivation and zygomorphic flowers are found in Leguminosae family.
Some plants belonging to this family are gram, soybean plant, ground nut, etc.

43. (*a*) Coelenterates, ctenophores and echinoderms (adult) exhibit radial symmetry. In this kind of body plan, any plane passing through the central axis of the body divides the organism into two identical halves.

44. (*b*) The correct match is A-2, B-3, C-4, D-1.
Rudolf Virchow in 1855 first explained that cells divide and new cells are formed from pre-existing cells, i.e. *Omnis cellula-e-cellula.*
Schwann proposed the hypothesis that the bodies of plants and animals are composed of cells and product of cells.
Antonie van Leeuwenhoek first saw and described a live cell.
Robert Brown discovered the nucleus.

45. (*c*) Incorrectly matched pair can be corected as
GLUT-4 is a protein which enables the transport of glucose into the cells.

46. (*a*) The correct match is A-3, B-2, C-1, D-4.
Cymose inflorescence shows arrangement of flower in basipetal manner.
Umbel is a flat topped cluster of stalked flowers.
Spike is the unbranched, elongated arrangement of sessile flowers.
In Racemose inflorescence, flower are arranged in acropetal manner.

47. (*d*) Statement I is correct, but Statement II is incorrect. Statement II can be corrected as
Crossing over, which occurs during prophase-I of meiosis, is not mediated by thrombokinase.
Thrombokinase is involved in the blood clotting process, not in genetic recombination. The process of crossing over is mediated by enzyme recombinase.

48. (*a*) Statement I is incorrect, but statement II is correct. It can be corrected as

NADP is universal hydrogen acceptor molecule, produced during aerobic respiration and also in anaerobic respiration and work as coenzyme in ATP generation.

49. (*c*) Incorrect match pair can be corrected as
Neurohypophysis (pars nervosa), also known as posterior pituitary, stores and releases two hormones called oxytocin and vasopressin. These hormones are actually synthesised by the hypothalamus and transported axonally to neurohypophysis.

50. (*b*) The correct match is A-2, B-1, C-3.
Cerebellum coordinates voluntary movements and balance.
Hypothalamus regulates body temperature, hunger and thirst.
Medulla oblongata controls voluntary functions like breathing and heartbeat.

51. (*b*) Both A and R are true, but R is not the correct explanation of A.
An increase in blood flow to the atria of the heart can cause the release of ANF. It causes vasodilation of blood vessels and therefore decreases blood pressure.

52. (*d*) The incorrect match pair can be corrected as
"Epipetalous" refers to a condition where the stamens are attached to the petals of the flower. The term "epipetalous" indicates that the stamens are inserted on the corolla (petals) rather than being separate from it, as seen in brinjal.

53. (*a*) Statement I is incorrect, but statement II is correct. The incorrect statement can be corrected as
Calotropis shows valvate aestivation as sepals or petals in a whorl just touch one another at the margin, without overlapping.

54. (*c*) The end of diakinesis is marked by the disappearance of the nucleolus and the breakdown of the nuclear envelop. It prepares the cell for the alignment of bivalent during metaphase.

55. (*d*) Statement I is correct, but statement II is incorrect. The incorrect statement can be corrected as
In 24 hour duration of cell cycle, cell division lasts for only about an hour.

56. (*c*) The correct match is A-2, B-3, C-4, D-1.
Mammals, many terrestrial amphibians and marine fishes like sharks mainly excrete urea and are ureotelic in nature.
Reptiles, birds, land snails and insects excrete nitrogenous wastes as uric acid in the form of pellet or paste.
Many bony fishes, aquatic amphibians and aquatic insects are ammonotelic in nature.
Water is reabsorbed in the proximal convulated tubule and Henle's loop

57. (*b*) The living differentiated cells that have lost the capacity to divide can regain the capacity of division under certain conditions. This phenomenon is termed as de-differentiation. For example, formation of meristems-interfascicular and cork cambium from fully differentiated parenchyma cells.

58. (*a*) The primary acceptor of CO_2 is phosphoenol pyruvic acid. Addition of CO_2 to any compound is called carboxylation.

59. (*a*) Statement I is incorrect, but statement II is correct. The incorrect statement can be corrected as
Impulse transmission across an electrical synapse is faster than chemical synapse.

60. (*b*) Protonema of moss and prothallus of fern, i.e. *Dryopteris* are gametophytic.

61. (*b*) The functional unit of the enzyme is known as holoenzyme, which is often made up of apoenzyme (the protein part) and a coenzyme (non-protein organic part) which is easily separable.
Holoenzyme (Active enzyme) → Apoenzyme (Protein part) + Coenzyme (Non-protein part)
The term prosthetic group is used when the non-protein moiety tightly binds (covalently) with the apoenzyme. The coenzyme can be separated by dialysis from the enzyme, while the prosthetic group cannot be seperated.

62. (*a*) In the figure, *A* represents the primary (1°) structure, *B* represents the secondary (2°) structure and *C* represents the tertiary (3°) structure of protein.

63. (*c*) Malpighian tubules present at the junction of midgut and hindgut helps in the removal of excretory products from haemolymph.

64. (*a*) Production of red blood cells primarily occurs in the red bone marrow located within certain bones of the sketetal system such as the ribs, sternum, pelvis and long bones. This function is not directly related to locomotion, but is essential for circulatory system.

65. (*b*) The correct match is A-4, B-1, C-3, D-2.
Chlorella and *Spirulina* are unicellular algae, rich in proteins and are used as food supplements by space travellers.
Ulothrix, belonging to class-Chlorophyceae have rigid cell wall made of an inner layer of cellulose and an outer layer of pectose.
Polysiphonia belongs to class-Rhodophyceae and its food is stored as floridean starch.
Fucus belong to Phaeophyceae and its and its food is stored as mannitol.

66. (*b*) P represents the anisotropic or 'A' band while Q represents the isotropic or I band.
A band gives dark appearance and hence, is also called dark band.
I band gives light appearance, hence is called light band.

67. (*a*) The correct match is A-4, B-1, C-2, D-3.

Chloroplast contain double-stranded circular DNA.

Amyloplasts store carbohydrates (starch), e.g. potato.

Active transport is an energy dependent process, in which ATP is utilised and known as active transport, e.g. Na^+ / K^+ pump.

Elaioplasts store fats and oil.

68. (*d*) Statements I, III and IV are correct, while statements II and V are incorrect. The incorrect statements can be corrected as

PCT aids in maintaining the pH and ionic balance of the body fluid by selective secretion of H^+, K^+ ions, ammonia and HCO_3^- into the filtrate.

Ascending portion of vasa recta returns NaCl to the interstitium.

69. (*b*) Apples are generally wrapped in waxed paper to prevent aerobic respiration by checking the entry of oxygen. This increases their self life.

70. (*a*) The correct match is A-2, B-3, C-4, D-1.

The residual volume is the volume of air remaining in the lungs even after a forcible expiration. It is about 1100 mL to 1200 mL.

Inspiratory reserve volume is the additional volume of air, a person can inspire. It is about 2500 to 3000 mL.

Expiratory reserve volume is the additional volume of air, a person can expire. It is about 1000 to 11000 mL.

Tidal volume is the volume of air inspired or expired during a normal respiration. It is about 500 mL.

71. (*b*) The chemosensitive area (also known as the chemoreceptor area) is part of the respiratory control system and is sensitive to changes in the concentration of hydrogen ions (pH) in the blood. This area helps regulate breathing by detecting changes in blood pH and adjusting respiratory rate accordingly.

72. (*d*) *Selaginella* and *Salvinia* represent evolution in seed habit as the female gametophytes in these plants are retained on the parent sporophytes for variable periods. The development of the zygotes into young embryos take place within the female gametophyte. This event is a precursor to the seed habit, considered an important step in evolution.

73. (*b*) The correct match is A-3, B-4, C-2, D-1.

- The thyroid gland is composed of follicles and stromal tissues.
- Deficiency of iodine in our diet result in hypothyroidism.
- Thymosins plays a major role in the differentiation of T-lymphocytes.
- The secretion of parathyroid hormone (PTH) is regulated by the circulating levels of calcium ion.

74. (*b*) Statements II and IV are incorrect and can be corrected as

A single U-shaped bone called hyoid is present at the base of the buccal cavity.

Below the acromion is a depression called glenoid cavity, which articulates with the head of humerus to form the shoulder joint.

Rest all the statements are correct.

75. (*c*) Monocot seeds are characterised by having a large central endosperm that serves as the main nutrient reserve for the developing embryo. The cotyledon (scutellum) is relatively small compared to the endosperm and assists in absorbing nutrients from it.

76. (*d*) The correct match is A-2, B-1, C-3.

Collateral vascular bundles are found in dicot stems with phloem located outside the xylem.

Bicollateral vascular bundles are found in monocot stems with phloem located both on the inside and outside of xylem.

Radial vascular bundles are found in roots with xylem and phloem arranged alternately around the central axis.

77. (*b*) In telophase-I, homologous chromosomes are separated into two daughter cells. The nuclear envelope reforms around each set of chromosomes, resulting in two haploid nuclei.

78. (*b*) Incorrect statement can be corrected as

In cockroaches and other insects, the heart is located along the dorsal (upper) side of the abdomen, not the mid-ventral line. The heart is a long, tubular structure that runs along the back and helps pump haemolymph through the haemocoel. It extends from the thorax to the abdomen and is involved in the circulation of haemolymph throughout the body.

79. (*c*) The incorrect statement can be corrected as

Only ATP is synthesised in cyclic flow of electrons during light reaction and not $NADPH + H^+$.

80. (*c*) Transferase enzyme catalyses a transfer of group, G (other than hydrogen) between a pair of substrates S and S′.

81. (*d*) Given diagram represent TS of bone. Bones have hard and non-pliable ground substance as it contain abundant of calcium salts and collagen fibres, which give bone its strength.

82. (*a*) Each coxal bone is formed by the fusion of three bones, i.e. ilium, ischium and pubis.

At the point of fusion of these bones, their is a cavity called the acetabulum to which the thigh bone articulates.

Other statements are incorrect.

Incorrect statement can be corrected as

- The shank region consists of tibia and fibula.
- Phalanges constitute 14 bones in a hindlimb.
- Patella is the largest among sesamoid bones.

83. (*c*) The correct match is A-3, B-1, C-2, D-4.

Secondary metabolites, also known as specialised metabolites, toxins,

secondary products, or natural products, are organic compounds produced by any life form. Some of the secondary metabolites are as follows
Lectins - Concanavalin -A
Terpenoids - Diterpenes
Drugs- Vinblastin, curcumin
Toxins- Abrin, ricin

84. (*c*) All the given description refers to the dicot root.
Dicot roots typically have two to four xylem and phloem patches as vascular tissue. Passage cells are found in the endodermis. Epidermal cells protrude in the form of unicellular root hairs.
Cambium ring of cells forms between phloem and xylem. There are 2 to 6 vascular bundles in the dicot root. Pith often does not exist in dicot root. Even if present, it is quite small.

85. (*c*) The incorrectly matched pair can be corrected as
The respiratory structure in scorpion is book lungs. Trachea is a respiratory organ of cockroach. Rest options are correctly matched pairs of given animals and their respiratory structures.

86. (*c*) Statement III is incorrect and can be corrected as
In echinoderms, removal of nitrogenous waste takes place through their body surface. Rest statements are correct.

87. (*b*) Both A and R are true and R is the correct explanation of A.
The conversion of glyceraldehyde-3-phosphate to 1, 3-bisphosphoglycerate is an oxidation reaction. This oxidation reaction occurs due to the use of NAD^+, an oxidising agent which gets converted to NADH by accepting a hydrogen molecule and this reaction is catalysed by the enzyme glyceraldehyde- 3 phosphate dehydrogenase.

88. (c) If, Cardiac output
= Stoke volume × Heart rate
Cardiac output = 4L or 4000 mL
- Blood volume in ventricles at the end of diastole = 100 mL
- Blood volume in venticles at the end of systole = 50 mL

Stoke volume = 100 – 50 = 50 mL
So,
4000 mL = 50 × Heart rate
Heart rate = 80 beats per minute.

89. (*d*) An enzyme increases the rate of reaction by bringing the reacting molecules into precise orientation with each other. It lowers the activation energy for a reaction, faster the rate. Thus, enzymes speed up reaction by lowering activation energy.

90.(*c*) 'The bundle of His' passes stimulus of contraction through Purkinje fibres. This happens as the impulse from the SA node, causes the atria to contract, pushing the blood through the open valves into the ventricles.
The electrical signal arrives at the AV node, which is located between the two atria.
From here, it travels through the bundle of His dividing into the left right bundle branches and through the Purkinje fibres.

NSS3 NEET Stepping Stones 3

1. (*b*) In anaphase-II of meiosis, sister chromatids move towards the opposite poles. It happens by shortening of microtubules attached to kinetochores.

2. (*d*) In *Triticum aestivum* (wheat), the primary root is short-lived and is replaced by a large number of roots. Wheat is a monocot plant where roots originate from the base of the stem and constitute the fibrous root system.

3. (*c*) Both statement I and statement II are incorrect. They can be corrected as
The chemical and physical properties of amino acids are essentially of the amino, carboxyl and R functional groups.
Gingelly oil have low melting point.

4. (*d*) Statements III and IV are incorrect. These can be corrected as
- Biological names are generally in Latin and written in italics. They are Latinised or derived from Latin, irrespective of their origin.
- The number of species that are known and described range between 1.7-1.8 million. This refers to biodiversity or the number and types of organisms present on earth.

5. (*d*) The correct match is A-3, B-4, C-1, D-2.
- Pharynx is a common passage for air and food.
- Vocal cord is located in the larynx which is cartilaginous box.
- Alveoli are irregular-walled and vascularised unit of respiratory system.
- Trachea divides at the level of 5th thoracic vertebra to form left and right primary bronchi.

6. (*a*) The basics of taxonomy like identification, naming and classification of organisms are universally evolved under international codes.

Based on the resemblances and distinct differences, each organism is identified and assigned a correct scientific/biological name comprising two words as per the binomial system of nomenclature.

7. (*d*) Statement I is correct, but statement II is incorrect. The incorrect statement can be corrected as

In animal cells, during the S-phase, DNA replication begins in the nucleus, and the centriole duplicates begins in the cytoplasm.

8. (*c*) Statements II and III are correct, while statements I, IV and V are incorrect. They can be corrected as

- A bud is present in the axils of petioles in both simple and compound leaves, but not in the axil of leaflets of the compound leaf.
- Leaf is a lateral outgrowth of stem developed exogenously at the node.
- The presence of nodes and internodes are the morphological features of stem and not leaves.

9. (*b*) The correct match is A-2, B-4, C-1, D-3.

- Plasma proteins, such as albumins help in osmotic balance.
- Erythrocytes or Red blood cells (RBC) are the most abundant of all the cells in blood.
- Basophils secrete histamine, serotonin, heparin, etc. and are involved inflammatory reactions.
- Eosinophils (2-3 per cent) resist infections and are associated with allergic reactions.

10. (*d*) Statement I is correct, but statement II is incorrect. The incorrect statement can be corrected as

Animal cells contain non-membrane bound organelle called centrosome which helps in cell division.

11. (*d*) The hypothalamic hormones that reach the pituitary gland through a portal circulatory system and regulate the functions of the anterior pituitary are GnRH and somatostatins.

Other options can be explained as Growth hormone and adrenocorticotrophic hormone are secreted by anterior pituitary, while oxytoxin and ADH are secreted by posterior pituitary.

12. (*c*) The fimbriae are small bristle like fibres sprouting out of the cell. These help bacteria to attach the rocks in streams and also to the host tissue.

13. (*a*) The correct match is A-4, B-3, C-2, D-1.

- *Sycon* belongs to phylum-Porifera. These animals have water canal system. The water enters into a central cavity through minute pores called ostia present in the body wall.
- *Ctenoplana* belongs to phylum-Ctenophora. Their body bears eight external rows of ciliated comb plates which help in locomotion.
- *Saccoglossus* belongs to phylum-Hemichordata. This phylum consists of a small group of worm-like marine animals. The body is cylindrical and is composed of a proboscis, a collar and a long trunk.
- *Dentalium* belongs to phylum-Mollusca. Its body is covered by a calcareous shell, which protects the soft and spongy body.

14. (*c*) The given figure shows thallus of *Laminaria*. Here, *X* is frond which is leaf-like photosynthetic organ in Phaeophyceae. The plant body is usually attached to the substratum by a holdfast (*Z*) and has a stalk called the stipe (*Y*).

Thus, among *X*, *Y* and *Z* the labelled part '*X*' represents the photosynthetic organ.

15. (*b*) During resting potential, the axonal membrane is comparatively more permeable to potassium ions (K^+) and nearly impermeable to sodium ions (Na^+). The ionic gradients across the resting membrane are maintained by the active transport of ions by the sodium-potassium pump, which transports 3 Na^+ outwards for every 2 K^+ into the cell.

16. (*b*) The correct match is A-4, B-3, C-2, D-1.

- Energy required for ATP synthesis in PS-II comes from proton gradient.
- During light reaction in photosynthesis, ATP, hydrogen and O_2 are formed.
- The dark reaction occurs through the Calvin cycle.
- PEP is primary CO_2 acceptor in C_4 plants.

17. (*c*) The correct match is A-2, B-3, C-4, D-1.

- Each rib is a thin flat bone connected dorsally to the vertebral column and ventrally to the sternum.
- Each vertebra has a central hollow portion (neural canal) through which the spinal cord passes.
- First vertebra is the atlas and it articulates with the occipital condyles.
- The spine of scapula is projected as a flat, expanded process called the acromion.

18. (*b*) The parts of seed, i.e. *A*, *B* and *C* are micropyle, hilum and seed coat, respectively. The hilum (*B*) is a scar on the seed coat through which the developing seeds are attached to the fruit.

19. (*b*) Features given in III, IV and V are the characteristic features of family-Leguminosae. Whereas, features I and II are not the characteristic features of family-Leguminosae and can be corrected as

The members of this family are herbs, shrubs and trees. Their leaves have reticulate venation.

20. (*b*) The correct match is A-3, B-4, C-1, D-2.

• Leaves originate from shoot apical meristems.

• The region of the stem where leaves are born are called nodes.

• In some leguminous plants, the leaf base may become swollen, which is called the pulvinus.

• In leaves, there is usually a middle prominent vein, which is known as the midrib.

21. (*d*) Phosphoglycolate is the end product of photorespiration. Photorespiration takes place in chloroplast, peroxisomes and mitochondria.

22. (*c*) Si (27.7%), Ca (3.6%) and Na (2.8%) are present in earth's crust in abundance compared to that of living tissue.

23. (*b*) Endoplasmic reticulum is tiny tubular structure scattered in the cytoplasm. It divides the intracellular space into two distinct compartments, i.e. luminal (inside ER) and extra luminal (cytoplasm) compartments.

24. (*a*) A is false, but R is true. A can be corrected as

When glomerular filtration rate increases, ANF is released by atrial wall. ANF dilates the blood vessels (vasodilation) to reduce the blood pressure which in turn reduces the GFR.

25. (*b*) The position of the mother axis with respect to the flower is represented by a dot on the top of the floral diagram. A floral diagram provides information about the number of parts of a flower, their arrangement and the relation they have with one another.

26. (*d*) The correct match is A-1, B-4, C-2, D-3.

• Melatonin helps in maintaining the normal rhythms of sleep-wake cycle.

• Excess secretion of growth hormone in adults especially in middle age can result in severe disfigurement (especially of the face) called acromegaly.

• ADH prevents diuresis, i.e. reduces water loss.

• ACTH secreted by anterior lobe of pituitary, also called pars distalis stimulates the synthesis and secretion of steroid hormones by adrenal cortex.

27. (*d*) The correct match is A-4, B-1, C-2, D-3.

• Disintegration of nuclear membrane occurs in prophase.

• Appearance of Golgi complex occurs in telophase.

• Division of centromere takes place in anaphase.

• Replication of DNA takes place in S-phase.

28. (*b*) The correct sequence of leucocytes in increasing order of their abundance is basophils (0.5-1%), eosinophils (2 -3%), monocytes (6-8%), lymphocytes (20-25%) and neutrophils (60-65%).

29. (*b*) The correct match is A-2, B-1, C-4, D-3.

• A sarcomere is the basic contractile unit of a myocyte.

• Light bands contain only actin filaments.

• Red muscle have oxygen carry pigment called myoglobin.

• White muscle fibers respire anaerobically which leads to accumulation of lactic acid.

30. (*d*) *Gonyaulax*, a red dinoflagellate, kills marine animals such as fishes by releasing toxin. It is mostly marine and photosynthetic and often causes red tides.

31. (*c*) Both A and R are true, but R is not the correct explanation of A.

Potato and brinjal are two different species, but both belong to the genus *Solanum* because they are closely related species.

Genus comprises a group of related species which has more characters in common in comparison to species of other genera.

32. (*c*) Both statement I and statement II are incorrect. These can be corrected as

The cerebrum wraps around a structure called thalamus, which is a major coordinating centre for sensory and motor signaling. The dorsal portion of the midbrain consists mainly of four round swellings (lobes) called corpora quadrigemina.

33. (*c*) The correct match is A-4, B-1, C-2, D-3.

• Several ribosomes may attach to a single *m*RNA and form a chain called polyribosome or polysome.

• Gas vacuoles are found in purple and green photosynthetic bacteria.

• A special membranous structure is the mesosome, which is formed by the extensions of plasma membrane into the cell.

• Loose glycocalyx sheath is called the slime layer.

34. (*d*) As we move higher, in the taxonomic hierarchy from species to kingdom, the number of common characteristics goes on decreasing. Lower the taxa, more are the characteristics that the members within the taxon share.

Thus, among order, family, class and genus, class will have the least similar characters and genus will have the highest similar character.

35. (*a*) The correct match is A-4, B-1, C-2, D-3.

- Wheat rust is caused by *Puccinia*.
- Most fungi are heterotrophic and absorb soluble organic matter from dead substrates and hence, are called saprophytes.
- Phycomycetes reproduce asexually by aplanospores (non-motile) or by zoospore (motile).
- Basidiomycetes grow in soil, on logs and tree stumps and in living plant bodies as parasites, e.g. rusts and smuts.

36. (*a*) The correct match is A-1, B-3, C-2, D-4.

- Male reproductive organs consists of a pair of yellowish ovoid testes, which are found adhered to the upper part of kidneys by a double fold of peritoneum called mesorchium.
- Vasa efferentia are 10-12 in number that arise from testes. They enter the kidneys on their side and open into Bidder's canal.
- Ureters in male frogs act as urinogenital tracts and open into the cloaca.
- A female frog can lay 2500 to 3000 ova or eggs at a time from the ovaries.

37. (*b*) The sudden elongation of the internode just before flowering in rosette plants is called bolting.

The PGR responsible for bolting is gibberellin.

38. (*b*) The incorrect statement can be corrected as

Cell growth results in disturbing the ratio between the nucleus and the cytoplasm. It therefore becomes essential for the cell to divide to restore the nucleo-cytoplasmic ratio.

39. (*d*) Statement I is correct, but statement II is incorrect. Incorrect statement can be corrected as

The long thin flexible petioles allow leaf blades to flutter in wind, thereby cooling the leaf and bringing fresh air to leaf surface.

40. (*b*) In mustard and *Argemone*, ovary is one-chambered, but it becomes two chambered due to the formation of the false septum. This type of placentation is called parietal placentation.

41. (*a*) Cardiac output is the amount of blood pumped by the heart in one minute. It is the product of strokes volume and heart rate.

Cardiac output = strokes volume × heart rate = 80 mL × 70 = 5600 mL.

42. (*c*) Statements I, II and IV are correct. Statements III and V are incorrect. These can be corrected as

- The non-polar tail of saturated hydrocarbons is protected from the aqueous environment.
- In human beings, the membrane of the erythrocyte has approximately 52 percent protein and 40 percent lipids.

43. (*a*) The correct match is A-2, B-3, C-4, D-1.

- Nephridia are the tubular excretory structures of earthworms and other annelids.
- Antennal glands or green glands perform the excretory function in crustaceans like prawns.
- Malpighian tubules are the excretory structures of most of the insects.
- Protonephridia or flame cells are the excretory structures in rotifers.

44. (*b*) Algae have cell wall, made of cellulose, galactans, mannans and minerals like calcium carbonate, while in other plants, it consists of cellulose, hemicellulose, pectins and proteins.

45. (*c*) The correct match is A-2, B-3, C-4, D-1.

- Higher temperature favours the formation of carbaminohamoglobin.
- Pneumotaxic center is located in pons. It moderates the respiratory rhythm center.
- Chemosensitive area is located adjacent to respiratory rhythm center.
- Low H^+ ion concentration favours the formation of oxyhaemoglobin.

46. (*d*) The DCTs of many nephrons open into a straight tube called collecting duct, many of which converge and open into the renal pelvis (*C*) through medullary pyramids in the calyces.

47. (*c*) The correct match is A-4, B-3, C-1, D-2.

- Many molecules can move briefly across the cell membrane without any requirement of energy and this is called passive transport.
- Movement of water by diffusion is called osmosis.
- A few ions or molecules are transported across the membrane against their concentration gradient. Such a transport is an energy-dependent process, in which ATP is utilised and is called active transport.
- An improve model of the structure of cell membrane was proposed by Singer and Nicolson (1972) widely accepted as the 'fluid mosaic model'

48. (*a*) The role-played by Luteinizing Hormones (LH) in males and females is secretion of androgens from Leydig cells, and ovulation, respectively. Anterior lobe of pituitary gland secretes LH..

49. (*d*) The correct match is A-4, B-1, C-2, D-3.

- In monocotyledons, one large and shield shaped cotyledon known as scutellum is present.
- In castor, the endosperm formed as a result of double fertilisation, is a food storing tissue and hence, they are called endospermic seeds.
- In coconut, the mesocarp is fibrous.
- When stamens are attached to the perianth, it is called epiphyllous; example-flowers of lily.

50. (*a*) Statements III, IV and V are correct, while statements I and II are incorrect. These can be corrected as

Salpa is a member of subphyla-Urochordata. In these, notochord is present only in larval tail. Whereas, in the members of subphyla-Vertebrata, notochord is replaced by cartilaginous or bony vertebral column.

Pristis in a cartilaginous fish which lack air bladder.

51. (*b*) The correct match is A-2, B-3, C-1, D-4.

- The association areas are responsible for complex functions like intersensory associations, memory and communication.
- Limbic system along with the hypothalamus, is involved in the regulation of sexual behaviour and expression of emotional reactions.
- Pons consists of fibre tracts that interconnect different regions of the brain.
- Brain stem forms the connections between the brain and spinal cord.

52. (*b*) In metaphase-I, homologous chromosomes line at the equatorial plate, whereas in metaphase-II sister chromatids line at the equatorial plate. Spindle fibres are attached to the kinetochores, and nucleolus and nuclear membrane disappear in both metaphase-I and II.

53. (*a*) The correct match is A-4, B-1, C-2, D-3.

- When carbohydrates are used as substrate and are completely oxidised, the RQ will be 1, because equal amounts of CO_2 and O_2 are evolved and consumed, respectively.
- When fats are used in respiration, the RQ is less than 1 (e.g. 0.7).
- When proteins are respiratory substrates, the ratio would be about 0.9.
- Organic acids have RQ greater than 1.

54. (*a*) Enzymes which catalyse biochemical reactions by joining of C-O, C-S, C-N, P-O bonds are ligases. Ligases are enzymes that are capable of catalysing the reaction of joining two large molecules by establishing a new chemical bond.

55. (*b*) The correct match is A-4, B-2, C-1, D-3.

- PCT is lined by simple cuboidal brush border epithelium which increases the surface area for reabsorption.
- Loop of Henle plays a significant role in the maintenance of high osmolarity of medullary interstitial fluid.
- DCT helps in sodium-potassium balance in blood.
- Large amounts of water could be reabsorbed from collecting duct to produce a concentrated urine.

56. (*c*) In dicot stems, a large number of rounded, parenchymatous cells with large intercellular spaces which occupy the central portion of the stem constitute the pith.

57. (*c*) The correct match is A-2, B-3, C-4, D-1.

- Multipolar neurons (with one axon and two or more dendrites) are found in the cerebral cortex.
- The gaps between two adjacent myelin sheaths are called nodes of Ranvier.
- Visceral nervous system is the part of the peripheral nervous system.
- The myelinated nerve fibres are enveloped with Schwann cells, which form a myelin sheath around the axon.

58. (*d*) Typically mitochondria is sausage-shaped or cylindrical having a diameter of 0.2-1.0 μm (average 0.5 μm) and length 1.0-4.1 μm. They have 70S ribosomes.

59. (*c*) Both statement I and statement II are incorrect and can be corrected as

- P-wave represents the electrical excitation of the atria, which leads to the contraction of both the atria.
- The end of the T-wave marks the end of systole.

60. (*b*) In adult women, irregular menstrual cycle can be due to hypothyroidism. Iodine is essential for the normal rate of hormone synthesis in the thyroid. Deficiency of iodine in our diet results in hypothyroidism.

61. (*d*) The correct match is A-2, B-4, C-1, D-3.

- Zeatin has cytokinin-like activities which is isolated from corn-kernels and coconut milk.
- Ethylene enhances the respiration rate during ripening of the fruits.
- ABA stimulates the closure of stomata and increases the tolerance of plants to various kinds of stresses.
- 2, 4-D is widely used to kill dicotyledonous weeds.

62. (*b*) Both statement I and statement II are correct.

Phloem fibres or bast fibres are made up of sclerenchymatous cells. These are generally absent in primary phloem, but are found in the secondary phloem. These are much elongated, branched and have needle-like apices. At maturity, these fibres lose their protoplasm and become dead.

63. (*c*) A person with glucose and ketone bodies in urine, has diabetes mellitus. In this disorder, blood glucose level is high due to absence or deficiency of insulin. Hence, one should consume low carbohydrate and sugar based diet to control blood glucose levels.

64. (*a*) The correct match is A-4, B-1, C-2, D-3.

- Lecithin is a phospholipid present in plasma membrane.
- Adenosine is a nucleoside formed by condensation of ribose sugar and adenine base.
- Peptidoglycan is a heteropolysaccharide. It has two monomeric units, i.e. NAM and NAG.
- Living state is a non-equilibrium state to be able to perform work.

65. (*c*) The correct match is A-2, B-3, C-4, D-1.

• Phosphorylation of glucose during glycolysis is catalysed by hexokinase.
• ETS is located in mitochondrial inner membrane.
• The end product of oxidative phosphorylation is ATP and H_2O.
• Cytochrome-*c* is an electron acceptor during ETS.

66. (*d*) The features gives in I and V are correct for dorsiventral leaves. Other incorrect features can corrected as
• Palisade parenchyma is made up of elongated cells, which are arranged vertically and parallel to each other. The spongy parenchyma are oval or round shaped and are loosely arranged below the palisade cells and extends to the lower epidermis.
• The size of the vascular bundles depend on the size of the veins. Thus, they are not equal in size.
• Bulliform cells are present in monocotyledonous leaves.

67. (*d*) The correct match is A-2, B-1, C-4, D-3.
• *Ichthyophis* is the scientific name of limbless amphibia.
• *Calotes* is the scientific name of garden lizard.
• *Aptenodytes* is the scientific name of penguin.
• *Balaenoptera* is the scientific name of blue whale.

68. (*d*) Archaebacteria survive in the gut of several ruminant animals such as cows and buffaloes because they have a different cell wall structure. This enables their survival in extreme conditions.

69. (*c*) Both statement I and statement II are incorrect and can be corrected as
• The function of our visceral organs is controlled by sympathetic and parasympathetic neural system.
• The axons transmit nerve impulses away from the cell body to a synapse or to a neuro-muscular junction.

70. (*a*) The correct match is A-4, B-1, C-2, D-3.
• Cambium possesses the ability to form secondary xylem and phloem tissues.
• Conjoint vascular bundles usually have the phloem located on the outer side of xylem.
• Epiblema is the outermost layer of root. Many of the cells of epiblema protrude in the form of unicellular root hairs.
• The parenchymatous cells which lie between the xylem and the phloem are called conjunctive tissue.

71. (*d*) Statements II and V are correct. Whereas, statements I, III and IV are incorrect and can be corrected as
• In the five kingdom classification of Whittaker, there is no mention of lichens and some acellular organisms like viruses, viroids and prions.
• Dmitri Ivanowsky (1892) recognised certain microbes as causal organism of the mosaic disease of tobacco.
• MW Beijerinck (1898) demonstrated that the extract of the infected plants of tobacco could cause infection in healthy plants.

72. (*a*) In *Cycas* and *Pinus*, the male and the female gametophytes do not have an independent free-living existence. They remain within the sporangia retained on the sporophytes.

73. (*a*) The correct match is A-3, B-1, C-4, D-2.
• Thymosins play a major role in the differentiation of T-lymphocytes, which provide cell-mediated immunity.
• The adrenal medulla secretes two hormones called adrenaline or epinephrine and nor-adrenaline or nor-epinephrine.
• Insulin acts on hepatocytes and adipocytes and enhance cellular glucose uptake.
• Corticoids which regulate the balance of water and minerals are called mineralocorticoids.

74. (*c*) Flowers of Mustard and *Datura* can be divided into two equal radial halves in any radial plane passing through the centre. This type of symmetry is said to be actinomorphic.
Pea, gulmohar, bean and *Cassia* are zygomorphic flower, while *Canna* is a symmetric flower.

75. (*a*) The given graph represents K_m, which is the concentration of substrate at which rate of reaction is half of the maximum value.
Rest of the statements are incorrect and can be corrected as
• Rate of enzyme catalysed reaction depends on concentration of substrate.
• K_m is the substrate concentration for which rate of reaction is half the maximum value.
• Enzymes react specifically with its substrate.

76. (*a*) Statement I is incorrect, but statement II is correct. Incorrect statement can be corrected as
The root hairs are unicellular elongations of the epidermal cells and help absorb water and minerals from the soil.

77. (*a*) The correct match is A-2, B-1, C-4, D-3.
• Malfunctioning of kidneys can lead to accumulation of urea in blood, a condition called uremia, which is highly harmful and may lead to kidney failure.
• In patients with kidney failure, urea can be removed by a process called haemodialysis.
• Renal calculi are stones or insoluble mass of crystallised salts (oxalates, etc.) formed within the kidney.

• Glomerulonephritis is inflammation of glomeruli of kidney.

78. (*b*) Statements II and IV are correct. Incorrect statements are I, III and V and these can be corrected as

• Joseph Priestley, in 1770, performed a series of experiments that revealed the essential role of air in the growth of green plants.

• TW Engelmann experimented on *Cladophora*.

• Part of the spectrum used in photosynthesis has a wavelength between 400-700 nm.

79. (*c*) Serine is neutral amino acid because it has one carboxyl and one amino groups. It is also called alcohol containing amino acid.

80. (*c*) Both A and R are true, but R is not true explanation of A.

Spraying juvenile conifers with GAs hasten the maturity period because it stimulates cell division and expansion in response to light or dark, thus leading to early flower production.

81. (*c*) The correct sequence of intermediate formation during glycolysis is V, II, I, III, IV.

Glucose-6-phosphate (6C) → Fructose-1, 6-bisphosphate (6C) → Glyceraldehyde-3-phosphate (3C) → 1, 3-bisphosphoglyceric acid (3C) → 2-phosphoglycerate (3C).

82. (*d*) The correct order of steps in M-phase is IV-I-III-II.

Centrosome which had undergone duplication during interphase, begins to move towards opposite poles of the cell (Late prophase).

Chromosomes are moved to spindle equator and get aligned along metaphase plate through spindle fibres to both poles (Metaphase). Chromatids separate and move to opposite poles (Anaphase). Nucleolus, Golgi complex and ER reform (in telophase).

83. (*b*) Erythroblastosis foetalis can be avoided by administering anti-Rh antibodies to the Rh-ve mother immediately after the delivery of the first child when mother is Rh negative and baby is Rh+ve. In the subsequent pregnancy, the Rh antibodies from the mother (Rh-ve) can leak into the blood of the foetus (Rh+ve) and destroy the foetal RBCs. This could be fatal to the foetus or could cause severe anaemia and jaundice to the baby. This condition is called erythroblastosis foetalis.

84. (*a*) In the given flowchart, A-Facial bones, B-Ribs, C-Ear ossicles. Axial skeleton contains 80 bones. Skull has two sets of bones, which includes cranial and facial bones. Each middle ear consists of three tiny bones-malleus, incus and stapes, collectively called ear ossicles. There are 12 pairs of ribs.

85. (*a*) Statements I, III and V are correct. Incorrect statements are II and IV. These can be corrected as

• Thymosin is responsible for differentiation of T lymphocytes.

• Leydig cells produce a group of hormones called androgens.

86. (*b*) The correct match is A-2, B-3, C-4, D-1.

• Ball and socket joint is present between humerus and pectoral girdle.

• Hinge joint is present in knee joint.

• Saddle joint occurs between carpal and metacarpal of thumb.

• Pivot joint occurs between atlas and axis.

87. (*c*) In the given figure of actin filament, 'Z' is troponin. Increase in Ca^{2+} level leads to the binding of calcium with a subunit of troponin on actin filaments which remove the masking of active sites for myosin.

88. (*a*) The correct match is A-3, B-4, C-1, D-2.

• Myasthenia gravis is an auto-immune disorder affecting neuromuscular junction leading to fatigue, weakening and paralysis of skeletal muscle.

• Muscular dystrophy is progressive degeneration of skeletal muscle mostly due to genetic disorder.

• Gout is an inflammation of joints due to accumulation of uric acid crystals.

• Tetany is rapid spasms (wild contractions) in muscle due to low Ca^{2+} in body fluid.

89.(*c*) Only statement IV is correct. Other incorrect statements can be corrected as

• Platyhelminthes have organ level of organisation.

• Poriferans have cellular level of organisation.

• All echinoderms have organ system level of organisation.

90. (*c*) The correct match is A-2, B-3, C-4, D-1.

• In leptotene stage, compaction of chromosomes take place.

• The synaptonemal complex is formed during zygotene.

• Recombination nodules is formed during pachytene.

• Terminalisation of chiasmata and separation of homologous chromosomes occur in diakinesis.

NSS4 NEET Stepping Stones 4

1. (*c*) The pigments of euglenoids are identical to those present in higher plants.

2. (*d*) Bronchi and bronchioles are supported by incomplete cartilaginous rings. This allows flexibility and helps in the movement of air through the respiratory tract.

3. (*a*) Statements I and V are correct. The other statements II, III and IV are incorrect and can be corrected as

- Meiosis-I is initiated after the S phase, not the G_2-phase, where the parental chromosomes have replicated to produce identical sister chromatids.
- Meiosis ensures the production of haploid, not diploid, phases in the life cycle of sexually reproducing organisms.
- Recombination occurs between non-sister chromatids of homologous chromosomes, not sister chromatids.

4. (*c*) During anaphase, chromatids begin their migration towards the two opposite poles. As each chromosome moves away from the equatorial plate, the centromere of each chromosome remains directed towards the pole and the arms of the chromosome trail behind.
Centromeres split and chromatids separate to move to opposite poles.

5. (*d*) Statement I is correct, but statement II is incorrect. The incorrect statement can be corrected as
Oxygen (O_2) and carbon dioxide (CO_2) are exchanged in the alveoli and tissues by simple diffusion, based on pressure/concentration gradients, not by active transport.

6. (*d*) The correct match is A- 3, B- 4, C- 2, D- 1.

7. (*d*) Statement I is correct, but statement II is incorrect. The incorrect statement can be corrected as Cyanobacteria can fix atmospheric nitrogen into compounds like nitrites and nitrate.

8. (*a*) In the given picture, A represents true ribs. These are the first seven pairs of ribs. Dorsally, they are attached to the thoracic vertebrae and ventrally connected to the sternum with the help of hyaline cartilage.
B represents false ribs. C represents floating ribs. D represents the sternum.

9. (*a*) Statements I, II, and IV are correct, while statements III and V are incorrect. The incorrect statements can be corrected as
Bacteria do not reproduce sexually by meiosis, instead they reproduce by adopting a primitive type of DNA transfer from one bacterium to the other. Bacteria reproduce by both sexual and asexual means.

10. (*c*) Both A and R are true, but R is not the correct explanation of A.
Autonomic neural system transmit impulses from the CNS to the involuntary organs and smooth muscles of the body. The autonomic neural system further divides into sympathetic neural system and parasympathetic neural system.

11. (*b*) Both statements I and II are correct.
Centrosome contain the cylindrical structures called centrioles in it. Both the centrioles in a centrosome lie perpendicular to each other.
Almost all plant cells have centrioles which are absent in almost all plant cells.

12. (*a*) Statement I is incorrect, but statement II is correct. The incorrect statement can be corrected as
Photosynthesis not only occurs in the green leaves, but also in other green parts of the plants, such as stem.

13. (*a*) The correct sequence for the process of respiration in humans is
$A \rightarrow B \rightarrow C \rightarrow D \rightarrow E$

(i) Breathing or pulmonary ventilation by which atmospheric air is drawn in and CO_2 rich alveolar air is released out.
(ii) Diffusion of gases (O_2 and CO_2) across alveolar membrane.
(iii) Transport of gases by the blood.
(iv) Diffusion of O_2 and CO_2 between blood and tissues.
(v) Utillisation of O_2 by the cells for catabolic reactions and resultant release of CO_2.

14. (*a*) Statement I is incorrect, but statement II is correct. Incorrect statement can be corrected as
Based on the chemical nature, hormones could be proteins, amino acids, steroids, etc.

15. (*c*) A and D describe the integral membrane proteins. Integral membrane proteins are embedded partially or totally within the lipid bilayer of cell membranes. They are typically hydrophobic in nature in order to interact with the hydrophobic tails of phospholipids. Peripheral proteins, on the other hand, are located on the surface of the membrane and are hydrophilic.

16. (*c*) Both A and R are correct, but R is not the correct explanation of A.
The bacterial cell envelope is characterised by three layers: glycocalyx, cell wall, and plasma membrane, which together function as a cohesive protective unit for the cell. Glycocalyx differs in composition and thickness among different bacteria. When it occurs as a loose sheath, it is called the slime layer.

17. (*d*) The animals 'A' and 'B' are *Balanoglossus* and *Hirudinaria,* respectively.
Balanoglossus belong to phylum Hemicordata.
They are marine animals with organ-system level of organisation. These animals have proboscis gland in order to facilitate excretion.

Hirudinaria belong to phylum-Annelida.

They exhibit organ-system level of organisation.

They have nephridia, which help in osmoregulation and excetion.

18. (*a*) Mesosomes in prokaryotic cells are specialised infoldings of the cell membrane. They play a crucial role in cellular respiration and if they are absent or removed, the efficiency of cellular respiration could be significantly affected. This would impact the cell's ability to generate ATP (Adenosine Triphosphate) through aerobic respiration.

19. (*b*) The correct match is A-3, B-2, C-1, D-4.

Dendrites are fine branches of cyton that transmit impulse towards the cyton.

Synaptic knob contains synaptic vesicles filled with neurotransmitters like acetylcholine.

Nodes of Ranvier are gaps between two adjacent myelin sheath.

Schwann cells form the myelin sheath, that wrap around the axon.

20. (*c*) Both A and R are true, but R is not the correct explanation of A.

A homopolymer is a polymer that consists of only one type of monomeric repeating unit. In the case of cellulose, it is composed entirely of glucose units.

21. (*d*) Integral proteins are partially or totally buried within the membrane. Other options are incorrect and can be corrected as follows:

- Cell membrane is mainly composed of lipids and proteins, not carbohydrates.
- Phospholipids have their polar heads facing outward towards the aqueous environment.
- Cholesterol is present in cell membrane.

22. (*a*) Statements I, II, and IV are correct. While statements III and V are incorrect and can be corrected as Cytotaxonomy which considers chromosome number and structure, is used to resolve classification confusion. Fossil evidence is not always available to support phylogenetic classification.

23. (*a*) The correct match is A-4, B-3, C-2, D-1.

Volvox shows oogamous reproduction with a large non-motile female gamete fusing with a small motile male gamete. *Ulothrix* produces similar sized gametes. *Fucus* is a brown algae producing algin. *Chlorella* has nutritional benefits.

24. (*b*) The genus–*Felis* includes domestic cats, while the genus *Panthera* includes larger cats like lions, tigers, and leopards. Both genera belong to the family–Felidae but differ in their species composition.

25. (*c*) The correct match is A-3, B-2, C-4, D-1.

26. (*d*) The correct match is A-1, B-3, C-4, D-2.

27. (*d*) Statement I is correct, but statement II is incorrect. The incorrect statement can be corrected as

The specific epithet in a scientific name starts with a small letter, not a capital letter.

28. (*d*) Statement I is correct, but statement II is incorrect. The incorrect statement can be corrected as

In gymnosperms, the male and female gametophytes do not have an independent free-living existence. They remain within the sporangia retained on the sporophytes.

29. (*b*) The incorrect statement can be corrected as

Tropomyosin runs close to the F actins throughout its length, not distributed at regular intervals.

30. (*a*) *Agaricus* (mushroom) is a member of class-Basidiomycetes in which vegetative reproduction occurs by fragmentation. Other statements are incorrect w.r.t. *Agaricus* and can be corrected as

- The mycelium is branched and septate.
- Asexual spores are generally not found in *Agaricus*.
- Sexual spores called basidiospores are exogenously produced on the basidium.

31. (*c*) In plants like grass, *Monstera* and the banyan tree, roots arise from parts of the plant other than the radicle and are called adventitious roots.

32. (*c*) SER is involved in detoxification, hence they are present densely in the liver cells of an alcoholic person.

33. (*d*) Mitosis is essential for cell growth, repair, and the replacement of cells. If mitosis fails to occur, tissues that rely on constant cell renewal, such as the epidermis, gut lining, and blood cells, will be unable to maintain their normal functions.

34. (*a*) The correct match is A-2, B-1, C-3, D-4.

35. (*d*) The correct sequence of animals is A-D-C-B.

Exocoetus (Flying fish) is a marine fish. *Bufo* (Toad) belongs to the class-Amphibia. *Chelone* (Turtle) belongs to the class-Reptilia *Corvus* (Crow) belongs to the class Aves.

36. (*b*) The absorption spectrum of chlorophyll-*a*, peaks in the blue and red regions, which corresponds to the wavelengths where maximum photosynthesis occurs. Other options are incorrect and can be corrected as follows

- The absorption spectrum of chlorophyll-*a* and the action spectrum of photosynthesis do not overlap across all wavelengths.
- There is overlapping between the absorption spectrum and the action spectrum, especially in the blue and red regions.
- Chlorophyll-*a* primarily absorbs light in the blue and red regions, not green.

37. (*b*) Spindle fibres attach to the kinetochores of chromosomes is the characteristic of metaphase. Others are incorrect statements which can be corrected as

- During metaphase, chromosomes are fully condensed and can be clearly observed under the microscope.

• Chromosomes moving to opposite poles of the cell occur during anaphase, not metaphase.
• Chromosomes are aligned along the metaphase plate at the centre of the cell and are not dispersed throughout the cytoplasm.

38. (*b*) Both A and R are correct and R is the correct explanation of A.
Flowers with bracts i.e. reduced leaf found at the base of pedicel are called bracteate and those without bracts, ebracteate.

39. (*d*) Epithelial tissues are defined by their structure and function. They have one free surface that faces either a body fluid or the outside environment. This allows them to perform functions such as protection, secretion, and absorption efficiently. The cells of epithelial tissues are closely connected at junctions, which helps maintain tissue integrity and function.

40. (*c*) Carbon fixation refers to the process where carbon dioxide is converted into organic compounds, which requires ATP and NADPH produced during light reactions.

41. (*d*) The correct match is A-1, B-2, C-3, D-4.
Leaf base is expanded into a sheath in monocot plants. Petiole is the stalk, which attaches leaf blade to stem. Pulvinus is the swollen structure present at the base of leaf petiole. Stipules are leaf like structures at leaf base.

42. (*a*) *Meandrina* or brain coral is a cnidarian. Its gastro-vascular cavity is characterised by the presence of a single opening, mouth and anus on the hypostome. Digestion is both extracellular and intracellular.

43. (*c*) Statements I, III, IV and V are correct, while statement II is incorrect. The incorrect statement can be corrected as
In lily, the stamens are fused with the tepals (whorls of the perianth), is known as epiphyllous.
Epipetalous stamens are attached to the petals, as in brinjal.

44. (*b*) Here, A-Thyroxine and B-LH, Thyroxine (thyroid hormone) plays an important role in the metabolism of carbohydrates, proteins and fats along with maintenance of water and electrolyte balance. LH induces ovulation of fully mature follicles and maintains the corpus luteum in female.

45. (*a*) Eosinophils represented by A (2-3 per cent of whole WBCs) resist infections and are also associated with allergic reactions. Monocytes represented by B (6-8 per cent of whole WBCs) are phagocytic cells which destroy foreign organisms entering the body.

46. (*b*) The racemose type of inflorescence is characterised by the main axis with continuous growth, with flowers borne laterally in acropetal succession. This means that the younger flowers are towards the apex, and the older ones are towards the base of the axis.

47. (*d*) Statement I is correct, but statement II is incorrect. The incorrect statement can be corrected as
Roundworms are bilaterally symmetrical animals. They do not exhibit radial symmetry.

48. (*a*) I, II, III and V are correct. Statement IV is incorrect and can be corrected as
Secondary metabolites are useful to human welfare. These are used as rubber, drugs, spices, scents and pigments. Some secondary metabolites have ecological importance also.

49. (*a*) Statements I, II, and III are correct, while IV and V are incorrect. These can be corrected as
• Echinoderms have an open circulatory system, not closed, and they do not have a heart.
• Echinoderms do not possess Malpighian tubules; they lacks an excretory system.

50. (*a*) Statements I, III, IV and V are correct, while statement II is incorrect. The incorrect statement can be corrected as
Not all connective tissues, secrete fibres of structural proteins called collagen or elastin, i.e. blood does not secrete these fibres.

51. (*b*) Unicellular or multicellular structures or outgrowths, known as trichomes, form a part of the epidermis. These trichomes are secretory in nature.

52. (*b*) Plum, rose and peach have perigynous gynoecium in which the gynoecium is situated in the centre and other parts of the flower are located on the rim of the thalamus almost at the same level. The ovary here is said to be half inferior.

53. (*c*) Both A and R are true, but R is not the correct explanation of A.
The brain of a frog is divided into forebrain, midbrain and hindbrain to perform different functions necessary for its survival. This division is similar to that seen in many vertebrates and allows for specialisation of brain regions to perform different functions.

54. (*b*) The correct match is A-3, B-1, C-2, D-4.

55. (*d*) The correct sequence is I $\rightarrow$ II $\rightarrow$ IV $\rightarrow$ III $\rightarrow$ V. The stages of prophase-I in meiosis occur in the following order
• Leptotene: Chromosomes become gradually visible.
• Zygotene: Chromosomes start pairing and form the synaptonemal complex.
• Pachytene: Recombination nodules appear and crossing over occurs.
• Diplotene: Synaptonemal complex dissolves and chiasmata form.
• Diakinesis: Chromosomes fully condense and the meiotic spindle assembles.

56. (*d*) The incorrect statement can be corrected as
Ethylene enhances fruit ripening and increases the respiratory rate during ripening, a condition known as respiratory climactic.

57. (*b*) Erythrocytes are devoid of a nucleus in most mammals and are biconcave in shape due to their composition, including haemoglobin, which gives them their characteristic red colour and shape.

58. (*a*) Dicotyledonous vascular bundles have cambium between phloem and xylem, enabling them to form secondary tissues like secondary xylem and phloem. In contrast, monocotyledonous vascular bundles lack cambium, preventing them from forming secondary tissues, and are referred to as closed vascular bundles.

59. (*a*) The correct match is A-2, B-1, C-3, D-4.

60. (*b*) Both A and R are true and R is the correct explanation of A.

Lipids are small molecular weight compounds, which are not strictly macromolecules even though they are found in the acid insoluble fraction of cellular components. They are present in cell membrane, which upon grinding (while doing analysis), form vesicles which are not soluble in water. Thus, they get separated along with acid insoluble pool in the macromolecular fraction.

61. (*b*) Statements II and IV are correct. Other features are incorrect and can be corrected as

- The outermost layer is epiblema, not endodermis.
- Endodermal cells have a deposition of water-impermeable suberin in the form of Casparian strips.
- The pith is small or inconspicuous.

62. (*b*) During glycolysis, sucrose is converted into glucose and fructose by the enzyme, invertase and these two monosaccharides readily enter the glycolytic pathway. Glucose and fructose are phosphorylated to give rise to glucose-6-phosphate by the activity of the enzyme hexokinase.

63. (*d*) I, II, III are correct, whereas IV and V are incorrect. These can be corrected as

- Lysine is a basic amino acid, not an aromatic amino acid.
- Glutamic acid is an acidic amino acid, not a basic amino acid.

64. (*a*) The correct match is A-2, B-3, C-1, D-4.

65. (*d*) Statement I is correct, but statement II is incorrect. The incorrect statement can be corrected as

The ascending limb actively transports electrolytes, but is impermeable to water, contributing to the dilution of the filtrate.

66. (*a*) In the given figure, *B* represents stroma. In stroma, enzymatic reactions synthesise sugar, which in turn forms starch.

Other labelling are

A-Stromal lamella,

C-Grana and

D-Starch granule.

67. (*c*) Statements I, III, IV and V are correct, while statement II is incorrect and can be corrected as

Blood group AB individuals can donate to AB recipients only.

68. (*c*) Competitive inhibitors are molecules that closely resemble the substrate of an enzyme. They bind reversibly to the active site of the enzyme, competing with the substrate for binding. Statements a, b and d are incorrect and can be corrected as

- Irreversible binding is a characteristic of irreversible inhibitors, not competitive inhibitors.
- Competitive inhibitors do not increase enzyme activity, instead they competitively inhibit it.
- Competitive inhibitors significantly reduce enzyme activity by interfering with substrate binding.

69. (*b*) Both statement I and statement II are correct.

The monocot stem has a sclerenchymatous hypodermis, a large number of scattered vascular bundles, each surrounded by a sclerenchymatous bundle sheath and a large conspicuous parenchymatous ground tissue. The phloem parenchyma is absent, and water containing cavities are present within the vascular bundles.

70. (*b*) Both A and R are true and R is the correct explanation of A.

Plant growth is unique because plants retain the capacity for unlimited growth thought out their life. This ability of the plant is due to presence of meristem at certain location in their body. The cells of such meristem have the capacity to divide and self-perpetuate.

71. (*a*) Thrombin is the enzyme that catalyses the conversion of fibrinogen (inactive soluble form) into fibrin (active insoluble form), which forms the meshwork of the blood clot.

72. (*c*) I, II, and IV are correct, while III is incorrect. It can be corrected as

Pancreatic juice in frogs contains digestive enzymes that act on carbohydrates, proteins, and fats, not just fats alone.

73. (*a*) RQ values can vary significantly depending on the organism's metabolic state and the type of substrates such as carbohydrates, fats, and proteins being oxidised. Other incorrect statements can be corrected as

- Proteins have an RQ of around 0.9, which is lower than carbohydrates (RQ $<$ 1).
- Using a single respiratory substrate does not always result in an RQ of 1; carbohydrates yield an RQ of 1, but fats and proteins yield different values.
- Fats have an RQ less than 1 (around 0.7), not 2 because they produce less CO_2 per unit of oxygen consumed.

74. (*b*) Elongation phase is characterised by increased vacuolation, where vacuoles within cells enlarge, cell enlargement occurs, and new cell wall deposition takes place.

75. (*a*) A represents vena cava that empties blood into the right atrium. B represents dorsal Aorta that carries blood from heart to tissues.

76. (*a*) Protonephridia or flame cells are the excretory structures in Platyhelminthes (Flatworms) and some other organisms like rotifers, some annelids, and cephalochordates (e.g., *Amphioxus*). These structures are primarily involved in ionic and fluid volume regulation, which is essential for osmoregulation in these organisms.

77. (*c*) The correct match is A-3, B-2, C-1, D-4.

Epidermis is the outer covering present on both surfaces of leaves with stomata abundant in the lower epidermis.

Mesophyll cells are parenchymatous and act as the site of photosynthesis.

Palisade parenchyma have elongated parallelly arranged cells.

Vascular tissues include xylem and phloem surrounded by bundle sheath.

78. (*c*) The correct match is A-4, B-1, C-2, D-3.

79. (*d*) A is true, but R is false. R can be corrected as

Subsidiary cells are specialised cells that are present near the guard cells. They do not directly regulate the stomatal aperture. Guard cells regulate the opening and closing of the stomatal aperture.

80. (*a*) The bacterial flagellum consists of three main parts: the filament, hook and basal body. Among these, the filament is the longest portion and extends from the cell surface to the outside, allowing the flagellum to function in movement.

81. (*c*) The given picture represents *Salvinia* which is a Heteroporous pteridophyte.

82. (*a*) Features A, B, and D are correct w.r.t. mycoplasma whereas features C and E are incorrect. The incorrect features can be corrected as follows Mycoplasma are the smallest known living cells and since they are pathogenic to animals and plants they are not autotrophic organisms.

83. (*a*) Statement I is incorrect, but statement II is correct. Incorrect statement can be corrected as

The remaining material after drying a living tissue sample is called dry weight, not 'wet weight.' The 'wet weight' refers to the initial weight of the living tissue before drying.

84. (*b*) The correct match is A-1, B-2, C-3, D-4.

Valvate: When sepals or petals in a whorl just touch one another at the margin, without overlapping, as in *Calotropis*.

Twisted: When one margin of the appendage overlaps that of the next one and so on as in china rose, lady finger and cotton.

Imbricate: When the margins of sepals or petals overlap one another but not in any particular direction as in *Cassia* and gulmohar.

Vexillary or papillionaceous:

When there are five petals, the largest (standard) overlaps the two lateral petals (wings), which in turn overlaps the two smallest anterior petals (keels).

85. (*a*) In the given figure, X represents the receptors on the post-synaptic neurons. The released neurotransmitters at the synapse bind to their specific receptors. This binding opens ion channels allowing the entry of ions which can generate a new potential (which may be either excitatory or inhibitory) in the post-synaptic neuron.

86. (*b*) Both statement I and statement II are correct.

In both lactic acid (yeast) and alcohol fermentation (bacteria) not much energy is released. Less than 7% of energy in glucose is released and not all of it is trapped as high energy bonds of ATP.

Facultative anaerobes respire aerobically under normal oxygen conditions. However, they can switch to fermentation under anoxic conditions.

87. (*a*) The incorrect statement can be corrected as proteins are heteropolymers, not homopolymers. A homopolymer consists of only one type of monomer repeating 'n' number of times, while proteins are made up of 20 different types of amino acids, making them heteropolymers.

88. (*b*) Only characteristics B and C are associated with skeletal muscles. Skeletal muscles are characterised by a striated appearance under the microscope and are closely associated with skeletal components of the body. They exist in syncitium or multi-nucleate condition.

Features A and B are incorrect and can be corrected as

- Skeletal muscles are under voluntary control and not involuntary.
- Skeletal muscles are not branched.

89. (*b*) Medullary rays consist of radially placed parenchymatous cells between vascular bundles.

90. (*a*) In the given picture of adrenal gland, *X* represent adrenal cortex. Underproduction of hormones by the adrenal cortex alters carbohydrate metabolism causing acute weakness and fatigue leading to a disease called Addison's disease.

The incorrect statement can be explained as

Adrenal medulla secretes catecholamines (adrenaline and noradrenaline).

Cortisol, a glucocorticoid secreted by adrenal cortex is a steroid, not a peptide hormone. It is involved in maintaining glucose levels in our body.

Androgenic steroids secreted by adrenal cortex play a role in the growth of mammary glands, pubic hair and facial hair during puberty in females.

NSS5 NEET Stepping Stones 5

1. (*a*) Stem tendrils which develop from axillary buds are slender and spirally coiled. They help plants to climb. These are found in cucumber, pumpkin, watermelon.

2. (*d*) The correct match is A–2, B–3, C–4, D–1.

3. (*b*) Underfunction of vasopressin results in a diminished ability of the kidney to conserve water leading to water loss and dehydration. This condition is known as diabetes insipidus.

4. (*a*) Cr-Jacob Disease (CJD) in humans is caused by an analogous variant of prions of bovine spongiform encephalopathy. Prions are agents consisting of abnormally folded protein.

5. (*c*) Both statement I and statement II are incorrect and can be corrected as Yeast can progress through the cell cycle in only about 90 minutes. In the 24 hour average duration of cell cycle of a human cell, cell division phase lasts for only about an hour.

6. (*a*) Sporophylls are distinct and compact in *Selaginella* and *Equisetum*. These structures are called strobili or cones.

7. (*b*) The correct match is A-3, B-4, C-1, D-2.
   - In fishes, the heart pumps out deoxygenated blood, which is oxygenated by the gills and supplied to the body parts from where deoxygenated blood is returned to the heart, called single circulation.
   - Amphibians and reptiles possess incomplete double circulation. The presence of single ventricle leads to mixing of oxygenated and deoxygenated blood.
   - Open circulatory system is present in arthropods and molluscs in which blood pumped by the heart passes through large vessels into open spaces or body cavities called sinuses.
   - Annelids and chordates have a closed circulatory system in which the blood pumped by the heart is always circulated through a closed network of blood vessels.

8. (*d*) Statements II, IV and V are correct. Incorrect statements can be corrected as
   - ICBN stands of International Code of Botanical Nomenclature.
   - Plant families-Convolvulaceae and Solanaceae are included in the order-Polymoniales mainly based on the floral characters.

9. (*a*) Ammonia produced by metabolism is converted into urea in the liver (*X*) of ureotelic animals and released into the blood (*Y*), which is filtered and excreted out by the kidneys.

10. (*c*) The correct match is A–2, B–3, C–4, D–1.

11. (*a*) Statements III and IV are correct and statements I, II and V are incorrect. Incorrect statements can be corrected as
    - Mycoplasma or PPLO are only 0.1-0.3 micrometer in length.
    - Bacteria are 3.0 - 5.0 micrometer in length.
    - Cells vary greatly in their shape and the shape of a cell may vary with the function they perform.

12. (*b*) The efferent arteriole emerging from the glomerulus forms a fine capillary network around the renal tubule called peritubular capillaries, which join to form renal vein.

13. (*c*) Both statement I and statement II are incorrect and can be corrected as *Rhizopus* is a fungus and it lacks, roots. In *Rhizophora*, many roots, come out of the ground and grow vertically upwards to get oxygen for respiration. Such roots are called pneumatophores.
    The cells present in region of meristematic activity are very small, thin walled with dense protoplasm.

14. (*b*) The correct match is A-4, B-3, C-1, D-2.
    - Tricuspid and bicuspid valves are located in atrio-ventricular septum.
    - Interatrial septum separates right and left atria.
    - Interventricular septum separates right and left ventricles.
    - Heart is protected by a double-walled membranous bag, pericardium, enclosing the pericardial fluid.

15. (*c*) In the given figure, the labelled part '*C*' is axillary bud. During the formation of leaves and elongation of a stem, some cells left behind from the shoot apical meristem, constitute the axillary buds. Such buds are present in the axils of leaves and are capable of forming branch or a flower.

16. (*a*) Statement I is incorrect, but statement II is correct. Statement I can be corrected as
    Enzymes generally function in a narrow range of optimum temperature and pH.

17. (*b*) The correct match is A–5, B–3, C–1, D–4, E–2.

18. (*b*) To produce one molecule of glucose ($C_6H_{12}O_6$), which consists of six carbon atoms, the Calvin cycle must turn six times. Each cycle fixes one carbon atom and it requires 3ATP molecules and 2 NADPH molecules.
    To make half of a molecule of glucose (3 carbon atoms), the cycles needs to run three times.
    ATP required
    $= 3 \text{ turns} \times 3 \text{ ATP} = 9\text{ATP}$
    NADPH required
    $= 3 \text{ turns} \times 2\text{NADPH}$
    $= 6\text{NADPH}$

19. (*c*) The correct match is A-1, B-3, C-4, D-2.
    Brain is covered by cranial meninges consisting of an outer layer called

duramater, middle layer called arachnoid and inner layer called piamater.

20. (*c*) The correct sequence is III, IV, I, II, V.
- The acetyl Co-A condenses with oxaloacetate (4C) to form citrate (6C).
- The oxidative decarboxylation of isocitrate to α-ketoglutarate (5C). CO_2 molecules release in this reaction.
- The oxidative decarboxylation of α-ketoglutarate (5C) produces succinyl Co-A (4C).
- The succinyl Co-A converts to succinate.
- The dehydrogenation of malate forming oxaloacetate.

21. (*a*) The correct match is A-3, B-4, C-1, D-2.
- The sequence of amino acids, i.e., the positional information in a protein such as the first amino acid, second one and so on is called the primary structure of a protein.
- Glucosamine is amino sugar.
- Haemoglobin has a quaternary structure of protein.
- Cellulose is homopolysaccharide.

22. (*a*) The three core molecules present in photosystem are chlorophyll, electron acceptor and electron donor
In the photosystems of plants, chlorophyll serves as the primary pigment. When chlorophyll absorbs light, it becomes excited and loses an electron, which is then transferred to an electron acceptor. To replenish the lost electron an electron donor is required.

23. (*c*) The correct match is III $\rightarrow$ I $\rightarrow$ IV $\rightarrow$ II.
First, the substrate binds to the active site of the enzyme, fitting into the active site $\rightarrow$ The binding of the substrate induces the enzyme to alter its shape, fitting more tightly around the substrate $\rightarrow$ The active site of the enzyme, now in close proximity of the substrate breaks the chemical bonds of the substrate and the new enzyme- product (EP) complex is formed. $\rightarrow$ The enzyme releases the products of the reaction and the free enzyme is ready to bind to another molecule of the substrate and run through the catalytic cycle once again.

24. (*c*) Both A and R are correct, but R is not the correct explanation of A.
Plant growth is unique because plants retain the capacity for unlimited growth throughout their life. This ability of the plants is due to the presence of meristems at certain locations in their body. The cells of such meristems have the capacity to divide and self-perpetuate.

25. (*d*) It represents oxygen dissociation curve. This given graph is useful in studying the effect of factors like pCO_2, H^+ concentration, etc. on binding of O_2 with haemoglobin.

26. (*a*) The correct match is A–4, B–3, C–1, D–2.

27. (*b*) 2,4-D (Auxin) widely used to kill dicotyledonous weeds, does not affect mature monocotyledonous plants. It is used to prepare weed free lawns by gardeners.

28. (*d*) Statement I is correct, but statement II is incorrect. Incorrect statement II can be corrected as
In eukaryotes, several ribosomes may attach to a single *m*RNA and form a chain called polysome or polyribosomes. Ribosomes of a polysome translate the messenger RNA into proteins.

29. (*a*) The correct order is A-C-B-E-D.
- GnRH is secreted by hypothalamus and released into portal circulation to reach the anterior pituitary.
- GnRH stimulates the pars distalis or anterior pituitary to secrete gonadotrophins, i.e. FSH and LH.
- FSH and LH are secreted by anterior pituitary and they act on ovaries.
- FSH causes the development of follicles in the ovaries.
- Increased LH secretion causes rupture of the mature Graafian follicle to release the ovum by the process of ovulation.

30. (*d*) A is true, but R is false. R can be corrected as
Conditional reabsorption of Na^+ and water takes place in the DCT, not in collecting duct.

31. (*d*) The correct match is A-2, B-3, C-4, D-1.

32. (*a*) Statements I, II and V are correct. Incorrect statements are III and IV. These can be corrected as
Protoxylem and the metaxylem are two type of primary xylem. In stems, there is endarch organisation with protoxylem towards the centre.

33. (*a*) A centre present in the pons region of the brain called pneumotaxic centre can moderate the functions of the respiratory rhythm centre. Neural signal from this centre of the pons can reduce the duration of inspiration to alter the respiratory rate.

34. (*b*) The incorrect statement can be corrected as
Biologically active protein has tertiary structure.

35. (*c*) The correct match is A-2, B-3, C-4, D-1.
- The metacentric chromosome has a centromere located in the middle forming two equal arms of the chromosome.
- The sub-metacentric chromosome has a centromere slightly away from the middle of the chromosome resulting into one shorter arm and one longer arm.
- The telocentric chromosome has a terminal centromere.
- In case of acrocentric chromosome, the centromere is situated close to its end forming one extremely short and one very long arm.

36. (*d*) Statement I is correct, but statement II is incorrect. The incorrect statement can be corrected as
Glucose and fructose are phosphorylated to give rise to glucose-6-phosphate by the activity of hexokinase.

37. (*b*) The correct match is A-2, B-3, C-4, D-1.

38. (*a*) Statements I, III and IV are correct and statements II and V are incorrect. These can be corrected as

- Palmitic acid has 16 carbons including carboxyl carbon.
- Simple lipid, glycerol is trihydroxy propane.

39. (*b*) The animal is *Salamandra*, it belongs to phylum-Chordata, subphylum-Vertebrata and class-Amphibia.

40. (*b*) During pachytene sub phase of prophase-I, the four chromatids of each bivalent chromosomes becomes distinct and clearly appears as tetrads. This stage is characterised by the appearance of recombination nodules, the sites at which crossing over occurs between non-sisters chromatids of the homologous chromosomes.

41. (*b*) The correct match is A-2, B-3, C-4, D-1.

42. (*a*) Myosin is a contractile protein that plays a crucial role in muscle contraction. It has an active site for ATPase, which allows it to hydrolyse ATP. This hydrolysis provides the energy needed for myosin to interact with actin.

43. (*c*) The correct match is A-2, B-3, C-4, D-1.

44. (*a*) Statement I is incorrect, but statement II is correct. Statement I can be corrected as
In catalase and peroxidase, haem is the prosthetic group and it is a part of the active site of the enzyme.

45. (*c*) The correct match is A-4, B-3, C-2, D-1.

- Steroids are synthesised in smooth endoplasmic reticulum.
- Phospholipids limit the permeability of cell membrane.
- Lysosomes contain hydrolytic enzymes.
- Packing of biomolecules for export takes place in Golgi bodies.

46. (*b*) The beginning of diplotene is recognised by the dissolution of the synaptonemal complex and the tendency of the recombined homologous chromosomes of the bivalents to separate from each other, except at the sites of crossovers. These X-shaped structures, are called chiasmata.

47. (*c*) Tunicates (urochordates) have notochord only in larval stage. It is present in the larval tail.

48. (*b*) Vinblastin and curcumin are secondary metabolites used as drugs. Secondary metabolites are the intermediates or product of metabolism. They are not vital for growth and survival of organisms but are essential for their interaction with the environment or produced in response to stress.

49. (*c*) Both A and R are true, but R is not the correct explanation of A.
At the tissue site where partial pressure of CO_2 is high due to catabolism, CO_2 diffuses into blood (RBCs and plasma) and forms HCO_3^- and H^+.

50. (*c*) The cell organelle '*X*' is leucoplast, which is classified under plastids. These are found in all plant cells and in euglenoids. They are double membranous, colourless plastids, having varied shapes and sizes with stored nutrients.

51. (*c*) Gonadotropin releasing hormone regulates the secretion of pituitary hormones, i.e. LH and FSH. LH directly induces the ovulation of fully matured Graafian follicles and maintains the corpus luteum, but the secretion of LH is regulated by GnRH. GnRH is secreted by hypothalamus.

52. (*b*) In the light-dependent reactions of photosynthesis, water plays a crucial role as a source of electrons. Water produces electrons through the process of photolysis.

53. (*a*) Statements I, II and IV are correct. Statements III and V can be corrected as

- At electrical synapses, the membranes of pre and post-synaptic neurons are in very close proximity.
- Electrical synapses are rare in our system.

54. (*b*) Increased vacuolation, cell enlargement and new cell wall deposition are the characteristics of the cells in phase of elongation. The cells proximal to the meristematic zone represent the phase of elongation.

55. (*a*) The correct match is A-3, B-4, C-2, D-1.

56. (*a*) In birds (*Corvus, Columba* and *Psittacula*), the digestive tract has additional chambers, the crop and gizzard.

57. (*c*) Both statement I and statement II are incorrect and can be corrected as
The P-wave represents the electrical excitation (or depolarisation) of the atria, which leads to the contraction of both the atria. The QRS complex represents the depolarisation of the ventricles, which initiates the ventricular contraction. The contraction starts shortly after Q and marks the beginning of the systole.

58. (*d*) In the given figure, *X* represents FAD, *Y* represents UQH_2 and *Z* represents Fe-S.

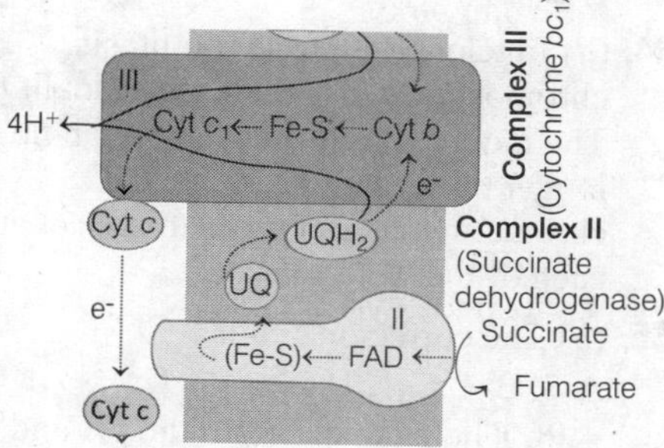

59. (*d*) The correct match is A-2, B-3, C-4, D-1.

- Asthma is a difficulty in breathing causing wheezing due to inflammation of bronchi and bronchioles.
- Emphysema is a chronic disorder in which alveolar walls are damaged due to which respiratory surface is decreased.
- Long exposure to dust can give rise to inflammation leading to fibrosis (proliferation of fibrous tissues) and thus causing serious lung damage.
- Occupational respiratory disorders can be prevented by wearing protective masks.

60. (*a*) Statements I, II and IV are correct, while statements III and V are incorrect they can be corrected as

- Ribozymes are nucleic acids with catalytic power.
- Enzymes lower the activation energy of reactions and greatly enhance the rate of the reactions.

61. (*d*) The given diagram is of *Salvinia* which produces two kinds of spores, macro (large) and micro (small) spores and thus, is known as heterosporous pteridophyte.

62. (*a*) The correct match is A-3, B-4, C-1, D-2.

- Vena cava drains deoxygenated blood from the different parts of body to the right atrium.
- Aorta arises from left ventricle and is guarded by semilunar valves.
- Tricuspid valves guards the opening present between right atrium and right ventricle.
- Pulmonary veins drain oxygenated blood into left atrium from the lungs.

63. (*b*) The correct match is A–3, B–4, C–2, D–1.

64. (*d*) In telophase phase of mitosis, chromosomes lose their individuality. The individual chromosomes can no longer be seen and each set of chromatin material tends to collect at each of the two poles.

65. (*b*) The correct match is A-3, B-4, C-1, D-2.

- PCT helps to maintain the pH and ionic balance of the body fluids by selective secretion of hydrogen ions and ammonia into the filtrate and by absorption of HCO_3^- from it.
- The cortex extends in between the medullary pyramids as renal columns called columns of Bertini.
- Epithelium (podocytes) of Bowman's capsule, endothelium of glomerular capillaries and the basement membrane form filtration membrane through which filtration of blood takes place and is known as glomerular filtration.
- Loop of Henle helps in the maintenance of high osmolarity of medullary interstitial fluid.

66. (*b*) Statements II and V are correct. Statements I, III and IV can be corrected as

- Meiosis occurs in only diploid cells.
- Meiosis-I has a long prophase, which is divided further into five phases.
- In metaphase-I, the bivalents arrange on the equatorial plate.

67. (*d*) Statement I is correct, but statement II is incorrect. The incorrect statement can be corrected as
The nerve impulse is conducted along the axon membrane in the form of a wave of depolarisation and repolarisation.

68. (*c*) Slime moulds, during unfavourable conditions, differentiates and forms fruiting bodies bearing spores at their tips. These spores possess true walls.

69. (*a*) The correct match is A-2, B-3, C-1, D-4.

70. (*b*) Statement (b) is correct, rest are incorrect. The incorrect statements can be corrected as
Persons with 'AB' group can receive blood from persons with AB as well as the other groups of blood. Person with blood group with A^- can receive blood from O^- donor. Nearly 80% humans are Rh^+.

71. (*d*) Statement I is correct, but statement II is incorrect. Statement II can be corrected as
Most of the photosynthesis takes place in the blue and red regions of the spectrum, but some photosynthesis also takes place at the other wavelengths of the visible spectrum.

72. (*c*) Both statement I and statement II are incorrect and these can be corrected as

- Partial pressure of CO_2 in oxygenated blood is 40 mm Hg.
- 20-25 percent of carbon dioxide is carried by haemoglobin as carbamino-haemoglobin.

73. (*d*) During the conversion of glyceraldehyde-3- phosphate to 1, 3-bisphosphoglyceric acid in glycolysis, NADH and H^+ are formed from NAD^+.

74. (*b*) The correct match is A-2, B-3, C-4, D-1.

- NADP contain the vitamin niacin as coenzyme.
- Ligases are enzymes which catalyse the biochemical reaction by linking together of two compounds.
- Malonate competitively inhibit the activity of enzyme succinic dehydrogenase.
- Lyases are the enzymes that catalyse the chemical reaction by removal of groups from substrates by mechanisms other than hydrolysis, leaving double bonds.

75. (*c*) Statement (c) is correct, rest are incorrect. Incorrect statements can be corrected as
Fibrous joint is present in the flat bones of skull. Pivot joint is present between atlas and axis. The cartilaginous joint between the adjacent vertebrae in the vertebral column permits limited movements.

76. (*d*) The correct match is A-1, B-3, C-2, D-4.
Algin obtained from brown algae and carrageen from red algae, are used commercially. *Chlorella*, a unicellular alga, rich in proteins, is used as food supplement, even by space travellers. *Porphyra* is a marine alga used as food.

77. (*c*) Statements I, IV and V are correct. Statements II and III are incorrect and can be corrected as

- In *Pinus*, roots have fungal association in the form of mycorrhiza.
- In gymnosperms, the male and the female gametophytes do not have an independent free-living existence unlike bryophytes and pteridophytes.

78. (*a*) The correct match is A-3, B-4, C-1, D-2.

- ADH facilitates water reabsorption from collecting duct and DCT, thereby preventing diuresis.
- A fall in GFR can activate the JG cells to release renin, which converts angiotensinogen in blood to

angiotensin-I and further to angiotensin-II.

- ANF can cause vasodilation and decreases the blood pressure.
- Angiotensin-II, being a powerful vasoconstrictor, increases the glomerular blood pressure and thereby GFR.

79. (*d*) Statement I is correct, but statement II is incorrect. The incorrect statement can be corrected as

Clot is formed by a series of linked enzymatic reactions (cascade process) involving a number of factors present in the plasma in an inactive state.

80. (*b*) The correct match is A-3, B-4, C-2, D-1.

- Moneran cell wall is non-cellulosic (polysaccharide and amino acid).
- The cell wall of plantae is cellulosic.
- Fungi have chitinous cell wall.
- Protists have cellular level of organisation.

81. (*d*) Statement (d) is incorrect. It can be corrected as

Gymnosperms lack vessels in their xylem. The presence of vessels is a characteristic feature of angiosperms.

82. (*d*) The correct match is A-4, B-1, C-2, D-3.

- *Ichthyophis* (limbless amphibia) is an amphibian in which fertilisation is external.
- *Calotes* (garden lizard) is a reptile. Its skin is covered by epidermal scale or scutes.
- *Balaenoptera* (blue whale) is a mammal. It is viviparous and development is direct.
- *Aptenodytes* (Penguin) is a bird. In birds, endoskeleton is fully ossified (bony) and the long bones are hollow with air cavities (pneumatic).

83. (*c*) The correct match is A–2, B–3, C–4, D–1.

- Antonie van Leeuwenhoek first saw and described a live cell.
- Robert Brown later discovered the nucleus.
- The model of the structure of cell membrane was proposed by Singer and Nicolson (1972), which was widely accepted as fluid mosaic model.
- Rudolf Virchow (1855) first explained that cells divide and new cells are formed from pre-existing cells, i.e. *Omnis cellula-e cellula*.

84. (*d*) Exopthalmic goitre is caused due to hypersecretion of thyroid hormones, while cretinism and myxedema are caused due to hyposecretion of thyroid hormones.

85. (*b*) Succinic acid, malic acid and oxaloacetic acid formed during TCA cycle have four carbon atoms.

86. (*c*) The correct match is A-2, B-4, C-3, D-1.

- The myelinated nerve fibres are enveloped with Schwann cells, which form a myelin sheath around the axon.
- Nissl's granules are present in cyton and dendrites.
- The gaps between two adjacent myelin sheaths are called nodes of Ranvier.
- Bipolar neurons possess one axon and one dendrite, e.g. in retina of the eye.

87. (*c*) Number of carbons in the primary CO_2 fixation product in C_3 and C_4 plants are 3 (PGA) and 4 (OAA), respectively.

88. (*c*) Statements I, II and IV are correct. Incorrect statement can be corrected as

A triangular structure called sinus venosus joins the right atrium. It receives blood through the major veins called vena cava.

89. (*d*) In hemichordates, body is unsegmented. They have a rudimentary structure in the collar region called stomochord, a structure similar to notochord. Fertilisation is external.

90. (*d*) The correct match is A-3, B-4, C-1, D-2.

- Ciliary movement occurs in most of our internal tubular organs, which are lined by ciliated epithelium.
- Flagellar movement helps in the swimming of spermatozoa.
- Cytoskeletal elements like microfilaments are involved in amoeboid movement.
- Peristalsis is an example of the muscular movement.

BIOLOGY-XIth

MIND MAP

MEDACE

Test 1

Syllabus
- What is Living?
- Biodiversity
- Need for Classification
- Taxonomy and Systematics
- Binomial Nomenclature

NCERT Old Page 03 to 08

For deeper insight, **Scan the QR Code**

Chapter 01

Characteristics of Living Organisms

- Life is a unique, complex organisation of molecules expressing itself through chemical reactions (metabolism) and reproduction.
- **Growth** Irreversible increase in mass or overall size of a tissue, an organism, or its parts.
  - Growth occurs when anabolism or synthetic processes exceed catabolism.
  - Growth is observed in both living and non-living beings, hence it cannot be taken as a defining property of living organisms.
- **Consciousness** Ability to sense their surroundings or environment and respond to these environmental stimuli which could be physical, chemical, or biological.
  - All organisms can sense and respond to environmental cues.
  - Human being is the only organism who is aware of himself, i.e. self-consciousness.
  - Consciousness, therefore, becomes the defining property of living organisms.
- **Reproduction** is the biological process; helps in the formation of new individuals from the parent of its own kind.
  - Types of reproduction - asexual and sexual.
  - There are some living organisms which do not reproduce at all, e.g., worker bees, mules, infertile human couples, etc.
  - Hence, reproduction cannot be an all-inclusive defining property of living organisms.
- **Metabolism** is the sum of all anabolic chemical reactions and catabolic chemical reactions.
  - Isolated metabolic reactions *in vitro* are not living things, but surely living reactions.
  - Metabolism is considered as defining feature of organism.
- **Cellular Organisation** Cell is made up of different biomolecules having specific organisation and performing different metabolic reactions.
  - Hence, cellular organisation of the body of an organism is the defining feature.
- **Homeostasis** is maintenance of a suitable and constant environment internally in an organism for the functioning of different body organs.

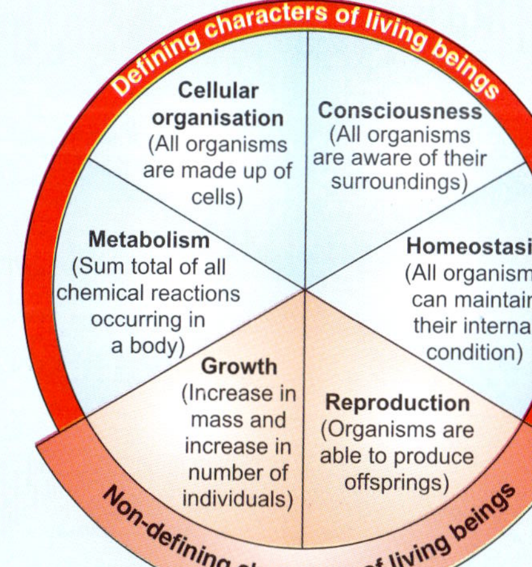

Taxonomy and Systematics

- **Biodiversity** Different types of animals, plants and microorganisms present on earth are considered as biodiversity of earth.
- **Classification** The method of placing organisms into groups (category) on the basis of similarities and dissimilarities in a systematic way.
- There are millions of plants and animals in the world.
- So as to standarise, facilitate their study and identification, certain criterias and principles were proposed.
- **Need of Classification**: It is necessary due to
  1. Convenience of study
  2. Knowledge of adaptation
  3. Knowledge of sequence of evolution
  4. Knowledge of phylogenetic relationships
  5. Discovery of new organisms
- **Taxonomy** It is the science of naming, describing and classifying organisms and includes all plants, animals and microorganisms of the world.
- **Systematics** ('*Systema*'-systematic arrangement of organisms) It is the study of biological diversity and the relationships among organisms.

Branches of Taxonomy

Various branches of taxonomy are as follows

Taxonomic fields	Basis
Classical (alpha) taxonomy	Includes the morphological characters of organisms.
Beta taxonomy	Includes anatomical characters along with physiological and genetic traits.
Gamma taxonomy	Deals with the phylogenetic relationships among organisms.
Morphotaxonomy	Morphological studies of organisms.
Artificial taxonomy	Habit and habitat of organisms.
Natural taxonomy	Natural similarity among organisms.
Chemotaxonomy	Presence or absence of chemicals in cells or tissues.
Cytotaxonomy	Cellular studies (chromosomal structure, number and behaviour).
Numerical or Phenetic taxonomy	Number of shared characters of various organisms.
Karyotaxonomy	Nuclear and chromosomal studies.
Experimental taxonomy	Experimental determination of genetic inter-relationships.
New systematics / Neotaxonomy (omega taxonomy)	Cytological, morphological, genetical, anatomical, paleontological and physiological characters.

Some important facts
- Accretion Growth by accumulation of material on the surface.
- In unicellular organisms, growth and reproduction are mutually inclusive or synonymous events.
- A person in coma or a brain-dead patient can neither be considered living nor non-living.
- All living organisms are self-replicating, evolving and self- regulating

Processes of Taxonomy

Four typical processes involved in taxonomy are as follows

1. **Characterisation** → Describing the morphology and other features of an organism.
2. **Identification** → Correct description of an organism.
3. **Nomenclature** → Assigning proper name to an organism.
4. **Classification** → Grouping the organism in convenient categories based on its characters.

Nomenclature

Names of the organism can be :
1. **Scientific / Technical Name**
   Same across the world for one particular organism, e.g. *Mangifera indica*.
2. **Vernacular / Common Name**
   Names vary from place to place, e.g. Mango is also known as Aam in hindi.

Systems of Nomenclature

1. **Binomial System of Classification**
   Scientific name of organism with two parts containing genus and species, e.g. *Panthera tigris* (tiger).
2. **Trinomial System of Classification**
   Scientific name of organism with three parts containing genus, species and subspecies, e.g. *Panthera tigris tigris* (Bengal tiger).
3. **Polynomial System of Classification**
   Name consists of many words. e.g., *Caryophyllum saxatilis folis gramineus umbellatus corymbia.*

Rules of Nomenclature

1. **Rules of Binomial Nomenclature**
   - Scientific name is either of Latin origin or Latinised if derived from any other language.
   - First letter of generic name is capitalised, while first letter of specific epithet is written in small letter.
   - Both the words in the name must be underlined (when handwritten) or Italicised (when printed).
   - Author's name is followed after the specific epithet and written in abbreviated form, e.g. *Mimosa pudica* Linn.
   - If species name contains two or more words, a hyphen is put between these words, e.g. *Hibiscus rosa-sinesis.*
   - If a scientific name contains same generic name and specific epithet, it is called a **tautonym**. e.g. *Gorilla gorilla* (not valid for plants).
2. **Rule of priority** says that in case of two or more existing names for an organism, the oldest one is recognised as the valid name and others are called synonyms.

Codes of Nomenclature

- Biologists give names to the organisms, based on the agreed principles and criteria.
- These names are acceptable all over the world.
- To accomplish this, five codes have been established.
  - **ICBN** International Code of Botanical Nomenclature
  - **ICZN** International Code of Zoological Nomenclature
  - **ICNB** International Code of Nomenclature of Bacteria
  - **ICVN** International Code of Viral Nomenclature
  - **ICNCP** International Code of Nomenclature for Cultivated Plants

Syllabus

- Concept of Species
- Taxonomical Hierarchy

NCERT New Page 06 to 08

For deeper insight, **Scan the QR Code**

Taxonomic Categories

- **Taxon** refers to a group of similar, genetically related individuals having certain characters distinct from those of other group.
- Arrangement of taxonomic categories in a descending order during the classification of an organism is called **taxonomic hierarchy** (Linnean hierarchy).
- Each step represents a rank or category, where the category is a part of overall taxonomic arrangement.
- Higher taxonomic category- Fewer number of common characters.
- With few characteristics in common, tracing the relationships to other taxa of the same level becomes tedious.
- All insects possess three pairs of jointed legs and so can be given a common rank or category at some level, i.e. class-Insecta.
- Mammals represent animals with hair on the skin, external ears, mammary glands, etc., so at some level, these can be placed in the same category, i.e. class-Mammalia.
- But dogs, mammals, animals are all taxa, but of different hierarchical categories like species, class and kingdom, respectively.
- **Clade (Monophyletic taxon)** A taxon that includes a common ancestral point.

Species

- Lowest and the basic category of classification.
- It is a group of individuals with similar morphological, anatomical, biochemical, and cytological characters.
- **Biological Species Concept** Individual of species can naturally interbreed and produce fertile offsprings; Given by **Ernst Mayr.**

Genus

- A group of related species.
- Members of genus have comparatively less characters in common in comparison to individual species of that genera.
- Example, Potato (*Solanum tuberosum*) and brinjal (*Solanum melongena*) belong to same genus-*Solanum.*
- Genus-*Panthera* include lion, leopard and tiger with several common features, though species are different.

Family

- A group of related genera with less similarities among the members as compared to genus and species.
- This taxon is characterised on the basis of both vegetative and reproductive features of plants.
- Example, Family-Solanaceae includes four related genera-*Solanum*, *Petunia*, *Datura* and *Atropa*.
- Family-Felidae includes genera-*Panthera* and *Felis* (cat).

Order

- A group of related families which exhibit only few similar characters.
- The number of similar characters are less in number as compared to different genera included in a family.
- Example, Order-Polymoniales has plant families like Convolvulaceae and Solanaceae.
- In animals, order-Carnivora includes families like Felidae (cat) and Canidae (dog).

Class

- It is a group of related orders.
- Example, Plant orders like Sapindales (mango) and Polymoniales are included in class-Dicotyledonae and plant orders like Asparagales and Poales are included in class-Monocotyledonae.
- In animals, order-Primata (man, monkey) and Carnivora (cat, dog) are included in class - Mammalia.

Phylum/Division

- A group of related classes.
- The category 'phylum' is used in Animalia, while 'division' is used in Plantae.
- The phylum-Chordata of animals contains the following classes: Mammalia (mammals), Aves (birds), Reptilia (reptiles), Amphibia (amphibians) Chondrichthyes and Osteichthyes (fishes).
- In case of plants, classes with few similar characters like dicots and monocots constitute division-Angiospermae.

Kingdom

- It is the highest category in hierarchy with related phyla or divisions.
- Kingdom-Animalia includes all animals belonging to different phyla from Porifera to Chordata.
- Kingdom-Plantae includes all plants of various divisions, i.e., Algae, Bryophyta, Pteridophyta, Gymnospermae and Angiospermae.
- **Note** - Higher taxonomic categories, i.e., from order to kingdom, are identified based on the aggregate characters.

Categories and Corresponding Suffix

Category	Suffix
Division	— phyta (plants)
Class	— phyceae or -opsida or -ae (plants)
Order	— ales (plants)
Family	— aceae (plants), -idae (animals)

Some Organisms with their Taxonomic Categories

Common Name	Man	Housefly	Mango	Wheat
Biological Name	*Homo sapiens*	*Musca domestica*	*Mangifera indica*	*Triticum aestivum*
Genus	*Homo*	*Musca*	*Mangifera*	*Triticum*
Family	Hominidae	Muscidae	Anacardiaceae	Poaceae
Order	Primata	Diptera	Sapindales	Poales
Class	Mammalia	Insecta	Dicotyledonae	Monocotyledonae
Phylum/ Division	Chordata	Arthropoda	Angiospermae	Angiospermae

Taxonomic Categories

Types of Species

- **Morpho species** divided on the basis of morphological characters only.
- **Taxonomic species** having definite binomial name.
- **Sibling species** morphologically similar species which do not interbreed.
- **Allopatric species** belonging to distinct geographical areas.
- **Sympatric species** belonging to overlapping geographical areas.
- **Parapatric species** sharing a very narrow overlapping zone.
- **Polytypic species** having two or more sub-species.
- **Allochronic** belonging to different time period.
- **Synchronic** belonging to same time period.

Test 1

Syllabus
- Five Kingdom Classification
- Salient Features and Classification of Monera

NCERT Page 10 to 14

For deeper insight, **Scan the QR Code**

Earlier Classification

- Earliest classification given by **Aristotle.**
- Classified plants into **herbs, shrubs** and **trees**.
- Classified animals into **anaima** (having no RBCs) and **enaima** (having RBCs).
- Two kingdom (Linnaeus): Plantae and Animalia.
- Three kingdom (Haeckel): Plantae, Animalia and Protista.
- Four kingdom (Copeland): Plantae, Animalia, Protista and Monera.

Classification

- Arrangement of organisms into groups (taxa) based on their distinctive characteristics reflecting their similarities and dissimilarities.

Six Kingdom Classification

- **Carl Woese** gave 3 domains (Archaea, Bacteria and Eukarya). He suggested a separate kingdom for Archaebacteria.
- It separates prokaryotes (Monera) into two groups such as Eubacteria (now Bacteria) and Archaebacteria (now Archaea).

Characters	Five kingdoms				
	Monera	Protista	Fungi	Plantae	Animalia
Cell type	Prokaryotic	Eukaryotic	Eukaryotic	Eukaryotic	Eukaryotic
Cell wall	Non-cellulosic (polysaccharide + amino acid)	Present in some	Present with chitin	Present (Cellulose)	Absent
Nuclear membrane	Absent	Present	Present	Present	Present
Body organisation	Cellular	Cellular	Multicellular/ loose tissue	Tissue/ Organ	Tissue/ Organ/ Organ system
Mode of nutrition	Autotrophic (chemosynthetic and photosynthetic) and Heterotrophic (saprophytic/parasitic)	Autotrophic (photosynthetic) and heterotrophic	Heterotrophic (saprophytic/parasitic)	Autotrophic (photosynthetic)	Heterotrophic (holozoic/ saprophytic, etc.)

Five Kingdom Classification

- **Robert H Whittaker** proposed a five kingdom classification system to place all organisms properly.
- 5 kingdoms- Monera, Protista, Fungi, Plantae and Animalia.
- The main criteria for classification- cell structure, body organisation, mode of nutrition, reproduction and phylogenetic relationships.

Kingdom-Monera

Comprises of most primitive and simplest organisms.

Characteristics
- Unicellular organisms.
- Cell wall is made up of peptidoglycan.
- Cellulose is absent.
- Naked DNA lies in the cytoplasm (nucleoid).
- Nutrition is autotrophic, saprophytic, parasitic and symbiotic.
- Generally follows asexual mode of reproduction.
- Sexual reproduction present, but gametes are absent.
- Kingdom-Monera includes Archaebacteria, Eubacteria (Cyanobacteria and Mycoplasma).

Bacteria

- **Archaebacteria** (primitive bacteria)
  - **Methanogens** (methane producing bacteria) e.g. *Methanothrix*
  - **Halophiles** (salty/marine bacteria) e.g. *Halococcus*
  - **Thermoacidophiles** (present in acidic sulphur springs) e.g. *Sulfolobus*
- **Eubacteria** (true bacteria)
  - **On the basis of staining behaviour**
    - **Gram-positive bacteria** e.g. *Clostridium*
    - **Gram-negative bacteria** e.g. *Rhizobium*
  - **On the basis of structure**
    - **Coccus** (rounded) — Non-motile
    - **Bacillus** (rod-like) — Motile
    - **Spirillum** (spiral) — Motile
    - **Vibrio** (comma-like) — Motile
  - **On the basis of nutrition**
    - **Autotrophic**
      - Photosynthetic bacteria
      - Chemosynthetic bacteria (Purple and sulphur bacteria)
    - **Heterotrophic**
      - Saprophytic
      - Symbiotic
      - Parasitic

Archaebacteria

- Most primitive prokaryotes. Absence of peptidoglycan in their cell wall.
- Cell membrane possesses monolayer of branched chain lipids.

Eubacteria

- They are true bacteria, lacking a well-organised nucleus, membrane bound cell organelles.
- Characterised by peptidoglycan wall, a compacted but naked DNA with attached mesosome.
- Reproduce asexually as well as sexually.
- Asexual reproduction is by fission, budding and spore formation.
- Sexual reproduction is by transformation, conjugation and transduction.

Inclusion body, Ribosomes, Plasma membrane, Plasmid, Fimbriae, Mesosome, Flagella, Capsule, Cytoplasm, Nuclear area (nucleoid), Peptidoglycan cell wall

A typical bacterial cell

Cyanobacteria (Blue-green algae)

- Gram-negative, photosynthetic prokaryotes.
- May be unicellular, colonial or filamentous.
- A specific structure, heterocyst has the ability to fix atmospheric nitrogen, e.g. *Nostoc* and *Anabaena*.

Mycoplasma (Mollicutes)

- Simplest and smallest free-living prokaryotes.
- They lack cell wall, aerobes or facultative anaerobes.
- They are also known as **PPLO** (Pleuro Pneumonia-Like Organisms.)

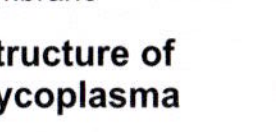

Structure of Mycoplasma

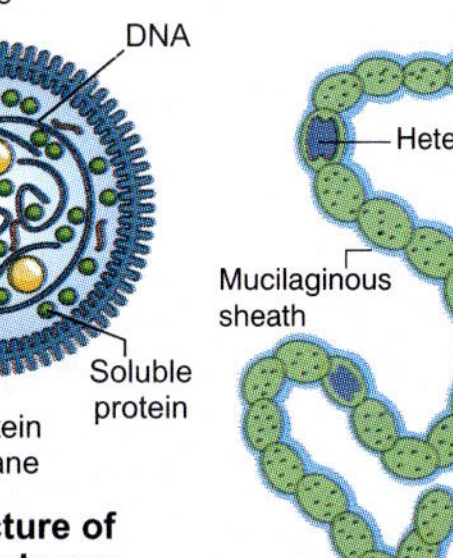

Cyanobacteria

Test 2

Syllabus

- Salient Features and Classification of Protista and Fungi into Major Groups

NCERT Page 14 to 19

For deeper insight, **Scan the QR Code**

Kingdom-Protista

- Unicellular, eukaryotes that can be solitary and colonial.
- They are surrounded by a cell membrane which may be covered by the pellicle, shell or cellulosic wall and have membrane-bound organelles.
- Locomotion is brought about by the pseudopodia, flagella and cilia.
- Nutrition may be photosynthetic, holozoic, parasitic and mixotrophic.
- Reproduction by asexual and sexual methods.

Chrysophytes

- Includes **diatoms** and **golden algae** (desmids).
- Microscopic and floats passively in water currents.
- Most of them are photosynthetic.
- Cell wall has silica and thus indestructible.
- Body look likes soap box.
- Form diatomaceous earth.
- Are chief producers in the oceans.

Dinoflagellates

- Mostly marine and photosynthetic.
- Appear in various colours depending on main pigments present in their walls.
- Biflagellated One lies longitudinally and other transversely.
- Cell wall has stiff cellulosic plates on the outer surface.
- Responsible for red tides, e.g. *Gonyaulax*
- Toxins released by organisms may kill other marine animals (fishes).

Protozoans

- Heterotrophs and live as predators or parasites, primitive relatives of animals.
- There are four major groups of protozoans
  - **Amoeboid Protozoans** Live in freshwater, sea water or moist soil; move and capture their prey using pseudopodia, e.g. *Amoeba*; marine forms have silica shells; some forms like *Entamoeba* are parasites.
  - **Flagellated Protozoans** Free-living or parasitic and have flagella; parasitic forms; causes diseases like sleeping sickness, e.g. *Trypanosoma*.
  - **Ciliated Protozoans** Aquatic, actively moving organisms (having cilia); have cavity (gullet); e.g. *Paramoecium*.
  - **Sporozoans** Possess infectious spore-like stage in their life cycle; most notorious is *Plasmodium* (malarial parasite).

Euglenoids

- These are freshwater forms, found in stagnant water.
- Photosynthetic in the presence of sunlight and predators in the absence of sunlight (mixotrophic).
- Photosynthetic pigment is identical to plants.
- Biflagellated, with one short and one long flagella.
- Cell wall is absent, but proteinaceous pellicle is present, e.g. *Euglena*.

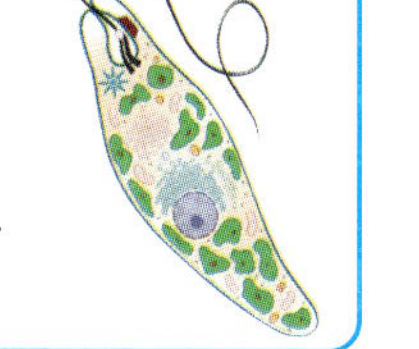

Slime Moulds

- These are saprophytic protists.
- Body moves along decaying twigs and leaves engulfing organic material.
- Under favourable conditions, form plasmodium and under unfavourable conditions, plasmodium differentiates and forms fruiting bodies.
- Spores have true walls; resistant to adverse conditions and dispersed by air currents.

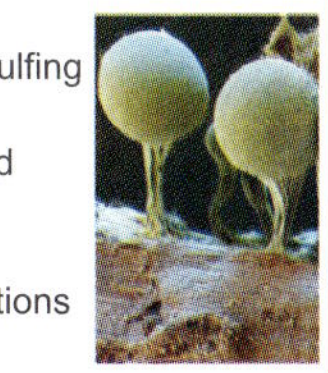

Kingdom-Fungi

- Fungi are heterotrophic and show a great diversity in morphology and habitat.
- Fungi are cosmopolitan and grow in warm and humid environment.
- Yeasts are unicellular. Other fungi are filamentous, consisting of hyphae and mycelium (network of hyphae).
- **Coenocytic Hyphae** Continuous tubes filled with multinucleated cytoplasm; others have septae or cross walls in their hyphae.
- **Cell Walls** Chitin and polysaccharides.
- **Symbionts** In association with algae as lichens and with roots of higher plants as mycorrhiza.
- **Saprophytic Fungi** Absorb soluble organic matter from dead substrates.
- **Parasitic Fungi** Obtain food from host.

Parameters	Phycomycetes	Ascomycetes (Sac fungi)	Basidiomycetes (Club fungi)	Deuteromycetes (Imperfect fungi)
Habitat	Aquatic habitat and on decaying wood or as obligate parasites on plant.	Coprophilous, saprophytic decomposers or parasitic.	Grow in soil, on logs and tree stumps or as parasites, e.g. rust and smuts.	Saprophytes, parasites and some of them are decomposers and help in mineral recycling.
Mycelium	Aseptate and coenocytic.	Branched and septate.	Branched and septate	Branched and septate
Asexual Reproduction	By endogenously produced zoospores (motile) or aplanospores (non-motile).	Conidia (asexual spores) produced exogenously.	Generally not found, but vegetatively by fragmentation.	Conidia (asexual spores)
Sexual Reproduction	Zygospore is formed by the fusion of two gametes.	Ascospores produced in asci, which is turn are arranged in fruiting bodies called ascocarp.	Sex organs are absent. Sexual spores are basidiospores formed on basidium inside basidiocarps.	Absent
Examples	*Mucor*, *Rhizopus* (bread mould) and *Albugo* (the parasitic fungi on mustard). 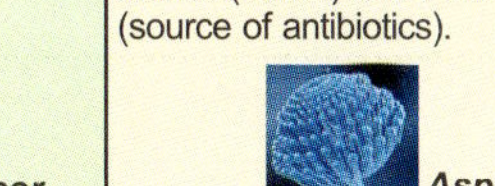 ***Mucor***	*Aspergillus*, *Claviceps*, *Neurospora* (used in biochemical and genetic work), morels and truffles (edible) and *Penicillium* (source of antibiotics).  ***Aspergillus***	*Agaricus*, *Ustilago* (smut fungi), *Puccinia* (rust fungi), bracket fungi and puffballs.  ***Agaricus***	*Alternaria*, *Colletotrichum* and *Trichoderma*  ***Alternaria***

Reproduction in Fungi

- Reproduction in fungi is vegetative, asexual and sexual.
- In some fungi, the various sexual spores are produced in distinct structures called fruiting bodies.
- The sexual cycle involves the following three steps
  - -Plasmogamy
  - -Karyogamy
  - -Meiosis in zygote resulting in haploid spores
- In Ascomycetes and Basidiomycetes, an intervening **dikaryotic stage** ($n + n$, i.e. two nuclei per cell) occurs. This condition is called **dikaryon** and the phase is called **dikaryophase** of fungus.

Test 3

Syllabus
- Lichens
- Viruses and Viroids

NCERT Page 19 to 21

For deeper insight, **Scan the QR Code**

* Kingdom–Plantae

- Includes all multicellular eukaryotic chlorophyll containing organisms called plants, contain cellulosic cell wall.
- Some are partially heterotrophic such as insectivorous plants like bladderwort and Venus flytrap or parasites as *Cuscuta*.
- Reproduce both asexually and sexually.
- Life cycle has two distinct phases; diploid sporophytic and haploid gametophytic, phenomenon called **alternation of generation**.

* Kingdom–Animalia

- Includes heterotrophic eukaryotic organisms called animals.
- These are multicellular and lack cell walls.
- Mode of nutrition is holozoic.
- Store food as glycogen or fat.
- Are capable of locomotion.
- Higher forms show elaborate sensory and neuromotor mechanism.
- Sexual reproduction by fusion of male and female gametes followed by embryological developments.
- Includes vertebrates and invertebrates.

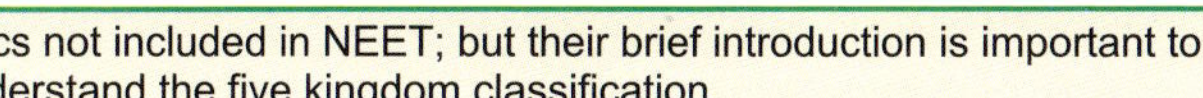

* Topics not included in NEET; but their brief introduction is important to understand the five kingdom classification.

Viruses, Viroids, Prions and Lichens

- In RH Whittaker's system, there is no mention of lichens and acellular organisms (viruses, viroids and prions).

Viruses

- Viruses are non-cellular organisms that are characterised by having an inert crystalline structure outside the living cell.
- Viruses contain either RNA or DNA.
- Bacteriophages (bacterial-infecting viruses) usually have *ds*DNA, viruses that infect plants generally have *ss*RNA. Animal infecting viruses have either *ss*RNA or *ds*RNA or *ds*DNA as genetic material.
- Protein coat is called **capsid** which is made up of **capsomeres**, which protect the nucleic acid.
- Virus was recognised by **DJ Ivanowsky**; named by **MW Beijerinck**.
- Viruses causes diseases in animals as well as plants. They cause mumps, small pox, herpes and influenza in animals.

Viroids

- Discovered by **TO Diener**.
- Was found to be **free RNA**, devoid of protein coat, hence named viroid.
- Cause **potato spindle tuber** disease.

Prions

- They are abnormally folded proteins; similar in size to viruses; cause **Bovine Spongiform Encephalopathy** (BSE) commonly called **mad cow disease** in cattle and its analogous variant **Cr Jacob Disease** (CJD) humans.

Lichens

- Symbiotic association between algae and fungi.
- The algal component is **phycobiont** (autotrophic) and fungal component is **mycobiont** (heterotrophic).
- Lichens are good pollution indicators; they do not grow in polluted areas.

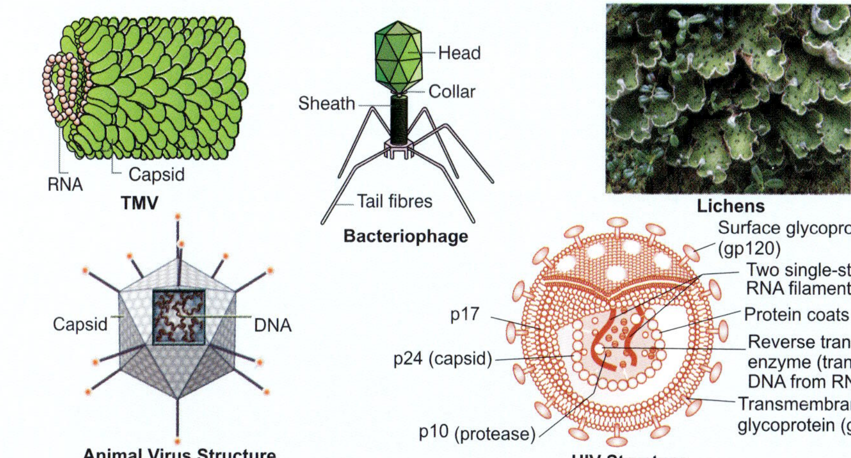

Syllabus

- Biological Systems of Classification and Classification of Plants
- Salient Features of Algae

NCERT Page 23 to 28

For deeper insight, **Scan the QR Code**

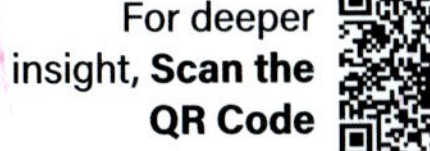

Biological Systems of Classification

- A scientific method that involves grouping organisms into a hierarchical series of groups and sub-groups based on their similarities and differences.
- Main three types of systems of classification have been recognised.

Artificial Classification

- Used only gross superficial morphological characters like habit, colour, number and shapes of leaves, etc.
- Based mainly on vegetative characters or on the androecium structure (system given by **Linnaeus**).

Limitations

- Separated closely related species as they were based on a few characteristics; gave equal weightage to vegetative and sexual characters.
- This is not acceptable because vegetative characters are more easily affected by environment.

Natural System of Classification

- Based on natural affinities among organisms and consider both external and internal features, like ultra-structure, anatomy, embryology and phytochemistry.
- Such a classification for flowering plants was given by **George Bentham** and **Joseph Dalton Hooker**

Phylogenetic Classification

- Based on evolutionary relationship between the various organisms.
- This assumes that organisms belonging to the same taxa have a common ancestor.
- Given by **Engler** and **Prantl**.

Branches of Taxonomy

- Characterisation, identification, classification and nomenclature are the processes that are basic to taxonomy.
- Based on characteristics, all living organisms can be classified into different taxa. This process of classification is taxonomy.
- External (morphology) and internal structure (anatomy), the cytological information like chromosome structure, number and behaviour (cytotaxonomy), development process, ecological information of organisms along with chemical constituents of their cells (chemotaxonomy) are essential and form the basis of modern taxonomic studies.

Classification of Plants

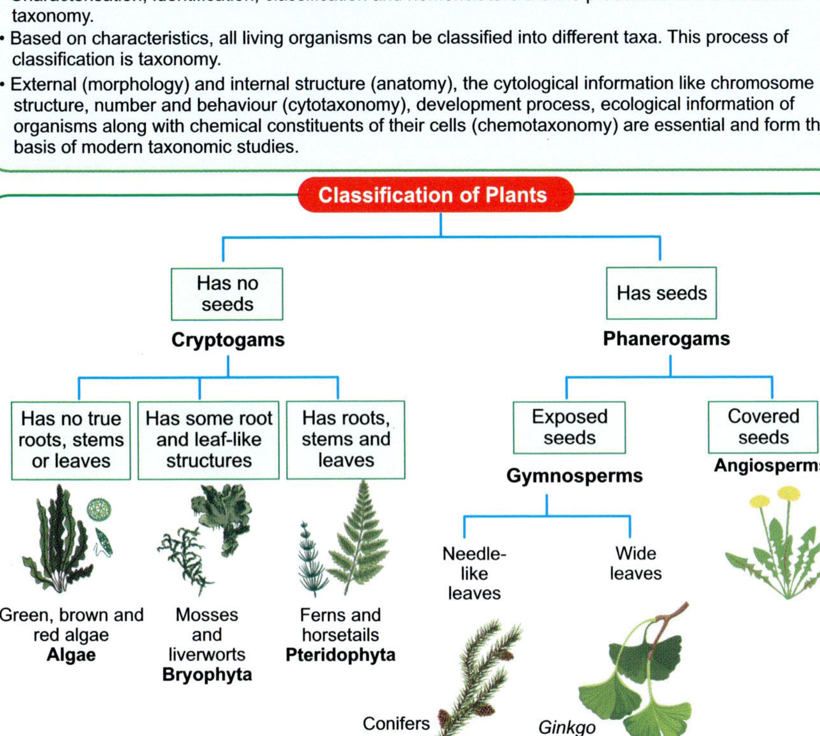

Algae

- Simplest plants with thallus-like body and no vascular tissues.
- Body may be unicellular, colonial, filamentous or parenchymatous.
- Mostly aquatic, but also found in terrestrial habitats like tree trunks, wet rocks, moist soil, etc.
- Reproduction occurs by vegetative method (fragmentation), asexual spores (zoospores) and sexual methods (isogamy/anisogamy/oogamy).
- **Economic and Ecological Importance** CO_2 fixation, producers in aquatic food chain, food (*Porphyra*), production of algin (brown algae), carrageen (red algae) and agar (*Gelidium* and *Gracilaria*), algal bloom, protein source and space food (*Chlorella* and *Spirulina*).
- Occurs in association with fungi (lichen) and animals (e.g. on sloth bear).
- **Three Main Classes** Chlorophyceae, Phaeophyceae and Rhodophyceae.

General Features of Three Main Classes of Algae

Features	Chlorophyceae	Phaeophyceae	Rhodophyceae
Common name	Green algae	Brown algae	Red algae
Plant body	Unicellular, colonial or filamentous	Simple branched, filamentous form to profusely branched forms	Multicellular, complex
Habitat	Freshwater, brackish water, salt water	Freshwater (rare), brackish water, salt water	Freshwater (some), brackish water, salt water (most)
Pigments	Chlorophyll-*a*, *b*	Chlorophyll-*a*, *c*, fucoxanthin	Chlorophyll-*a*, *d*, phycoerythrin
Stored food	Starch	Mannitol, laminarin	Floridean starch
Cell wall	Cellulose	Cellulose and algin	Cellulose, pectin and polysulphate esters
Flagella	2-8, equal, apical	2, unequal, lateral	Absent
Examples	*Chlamydomonas, Volvox, Spirogyra*	*Fucus, Ectocarpus, Sargassum*	*Polysiphonia, Porphyra, Gracilaria*
Other features	Presence of pyrenoid, different shapes of chloroplast.	Presence of holdfast, stipe and frond, fucosan vesicles (in some), pyriform gametes.	Complex post-fertilisation event in sexual reproduction.
	Flagellum, Vacuole, Cytoplasm, Pigment spot, Cell wall, Nucleus, Pyrenoid; ***Chlamydomonas***	Frond, Stipe, Holdfast; ***Laminaria***	Main axis, Branches; ***Polysiphonia***

Test 2

Syllabus
- Salient Features of Bryophytes, Pteridophytes and Gymnosperms

NCERT Page 28 to 33

For deeper insight, **Scan the QR Code**

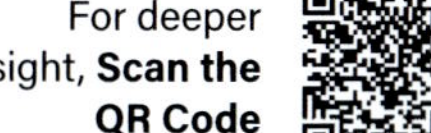

Bryophytes

- 'Amphibians of plant kingdom.'
- Plants with thalloid body lacking true root, stem and leaves and are attached to substrate by rhizoids.
- Possess no vascular tissues, but have conducting tissues called **hydroids** and **leptoids**.
- Follow haplo-diplontic life cycle with a dominant free-living haploid gametophyte and short diploid sporophyte (foot, seta and capsule).
- Reproduction occurs by vegetative means (fragmentation, tubers, gemmae, buds) and sexual methods.
- Sex organs are multicellular and jacketed. Antheridium (male sex organ) produces biflagellated antherozoids. Archegonium (female sex organ) is flask-shaped and produces a single egg.
- **Economic and Ecological Importance** Food for animals, production of peat (fuel), prevention of soil erosion.
- **Two Main Classes** Liverworts and mosses.

Riccia

Mosses (Bryopsida)

Two stages of gametophyte

1. **Protonema** which develops directly from spore and is a green, creeping and frequently filamentous.
2. **Leafy stage** developing directly from secondary protonema as lateral bud having upright, slender axes with spirally arranged leaves.

- Vegetative reproduction is by fragmentation and budding.
- Sexual organs are placed at apex of leafy shoots.
- Sporophyte is more developed than liverworts, e.g. *Funaria*.

Sporophyte, Capsule, Seta, Leaves, Gametophyte, Main axis, Rhizoids

***Funaria* (cord moss)**

Antheridial branch, Branches, Archegonial branch

***Sphagnum* (bog moss)**

Gymnosperms

- Group of seed-bearing plants with an ovules on an open sporophyll, which are not modified into flower-like structure (non-flowering plants).
- Includes oldest (*Pinus longaeva*) and largest (*Sequoia*) living trees known.
- Sporophyte is woody and evergreen, shrubs with no herbaceous member.
- Stem-unbranched (*Cycas*)/branched (*Pinus*); Root-tap root; leaves-simple/compound.
- Leaves possess adaptive features likes needle-like leaves, thick cuticle and sunken stomata.
- Vascular tissues contains xylem and phloem generally without vessels (Exception: in *Gnetum*, *Ephedra* and *Welwitschia,* true vessels are present).
- Soft wood is formed in gymnosperms due to secondary growth without vessels.
- They are heterosporous with microspores (♂) and megaspores (♀) which are produced in microsporangia and megasporangia, respectively borne on the sporophylls.
- Microsporophylls and megasporophylls are arranged spirally on axis to form male and female cones, respectively.
- **Importance** Food, timber, paper, medicines, evolutionary significance (*Gingko* as living fossil plant).
- **Four Main Classes** Cycadopsida (*Cycas*), Ginkgopsida (*Ginkgo*), Coniferopsida (*Pinus*) and Gnetopsida (*Gnetum*).

Cycas

Pinus

Liverworts (Hepaticopsida)

- Thalloid gametophyte.
- Asexual reproduction occurs by fragmentation or gemmae. Gemmae are asexual buds on receptacles called **gemma cup** and become detached from parent to form new individual.
- Sexual organs are placed on same (homothallic) or different thalli (heterothallic).
- Sporophyte is simple and differentiated into foot, seta and capsule.
- Simplest and most primitive sporophyte in bryophytes is found in *Riccia*.
- Spores produced within the capsule germinate to form free-living gametophytes, e.g. *Marchantia*.

Archegoniophore, Gemma cup, Rhizoids

Female thallus of *Marchantia*

Antheridiophore, Gemma cup, Rhizoids

Male thallus of *Marchantia*

Pteridophytes

- Seedless vascular plants that have main sporophytic plant body and inconspicuous gametophyte.
- Main plant body is a sporophyte differentiated into true root, stem and leaves.
- Possess well-differentiated vascular tissues (lacking vessels, sieve tubes and companion cells).
- Sporophytes bears sporangia which bear spores, which on germination give rise to a thalloid, free-living gametophyte called **prothallus**.
- Prothallus bears male and female sex organs called **antheridia** and **archegonia**, respectively.
- Male gamete is transferred to archegonium (*via* water) for fertilisation and form zygote to produce a sporophyte.
- Intermediate between bryophytes and higher vascular plants.
- **Economic and Ecological Importance** Food (*Marsilea*), scouring, soil-binders, ornamental use, N_2- fixation (*Azolla*) and medicinal purpose (*Equisetum*), etc.
- **Major Classes** Psilopsida (*Psilotum*), Lycopsida (*Selaginella*), Sphenopsida (*Equisetum*) and Pteropsida (*Pteris*).

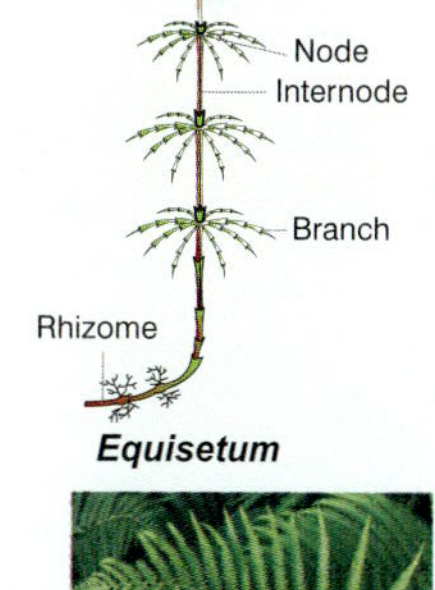

Equisetum

Fern

Test 1

Syllabus
- Salient Features and Classification of Animals-Non-chordates (Porifera to Aschelminthes)

NCERT Page 37 to 43

For deeper insight, **Scan the QR Code**

Classification of Kingdom-Animalia

Kingdom-Animalia is broadly classified based on common fundamental features as

Kingdom	Levels of Organisation	Symmetry	Body Cavity or Coelom (body cavity lined by mesoderm)	Phylum	
Animalia (Multicellular)	Cellular level		(Acoelomata)	Porifera	Diploblastic
	Tissue/Organ/ Organ system	Radial (Any plane passing through central axis divides the organism into two equal halves)	(Acoelomata)	Coelenterata (Cnidaria)	Diploblastic
				Ctenophora	Diploblastic
		Bilateral (Only one plane passing through organisms divides it in equal halves)	Acoelomate (without coelom)	Platyhelminthes	Triploblastic
			Pseudocoelomate (False coelom, i.e. mesoderm is present as scattered pouches)	Aschelminthes	Triploblastic
			Coelomate (with true coelom, i.e. body cavity lined by mesoderm)	Annelida	Triploblastic
				Arthropoda	Triploblastic
				Mollusca	Triploblastic
				*Echinodermata	Triploblastic
				Hemichordata	Triploblastic
				Chordata	Triploblastic

* Echinodermata shows radial or bilateral symmetry depending on the stage.
- Other basis of classification include presence of notochord, segmentation and arrangement of embryonic layers (diploblastic /triploblastic).

Phylum-Coelenterata (Cnidaria)

- Mostly marine; freshwater (*Hydra*), sessile or free-swimming.
- Coral form; diploblastic.
- Cnidoblasts or cnidocytes (containing nematocysts): anchorage, defence and for capture of prey.
- Gastrovascular cavity with hypostome.
- Digestion : intracellular and extracellular.
- External fertilisation; indirect / direct development.
- Polymorphism; metagenesis (alternation of generation by both forms in certain cnidarians, e.g. *Obelia*).

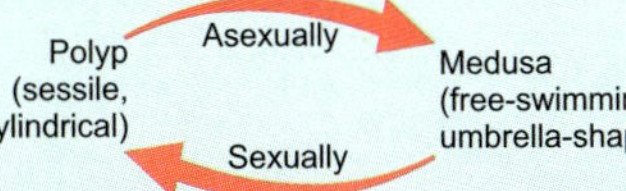

- e.g., *Physalia*, *Adamsia*, *Pennatula*.

Phylum-Platyhelminthes (Flatworms)

- Free-living or endoparasitic mostly.
- Dorso-ventrally flattened; hooks and suckers present in parasitic forms.
- Incomplete digestive system (mostly); extracellular digestion.
- Some absorb nutrients by body surface.
- Flame cells for excretion and osmoregulation.
- Internal fertilisation; indirect development .
- Regeneration (asexual reproduction) hermaphrodite (separate sexes).
- e.g. *Taenia*, *Fasciola* and *Planaria* (high regeneration).

Phylum-Porifera (Sponges)

- Mostly marine; freshwater (*Spongilla*).
- Water canal system: Ostia, spongocoel (lined by choanocytes or collar cells), osculum.
- Intracellular digestion.
- Endoskeleton supported by spicules or spongin fibres.
- Hermaphrodites; reproduce asexually by fragmentation and sexually by gamete formation.
- Internal fertilisation; indirect development.
- e.g., *Sycon* (Scypha), *Euspongia* (Bath sponge).

Phylum-Ctenophora (Sea Walnuts)

- Exclusively marine; diploblastic organisms.
- 8 external rows of ciliated comb plates; bioluminescence.
- Digestion: intracellular and extracellular.
- Sexually reproducing animals; sexes are not separate.
- External fertilisation; indirect development.
- e.g. *Pleurobrachia* and *Ctenoplana*.

Phylum-Aschelminthes (Roundworms)

- Free-living, aquatic, terrestrial or parasitic.
- Often worm shaped, elongated.
- Complete digestive system with well-developed muscular pharynx; extracellular digestion.
- Renette cells for excretory function.
- Dioecious organism with distinct sexual dimorphism; female is generally longer than males; the posterior end of male is curved.
- Internal fertilisation; direct/indirect development .
- e.g. *Ascaris*, *Wuchereria*, *Ancylostoma*.

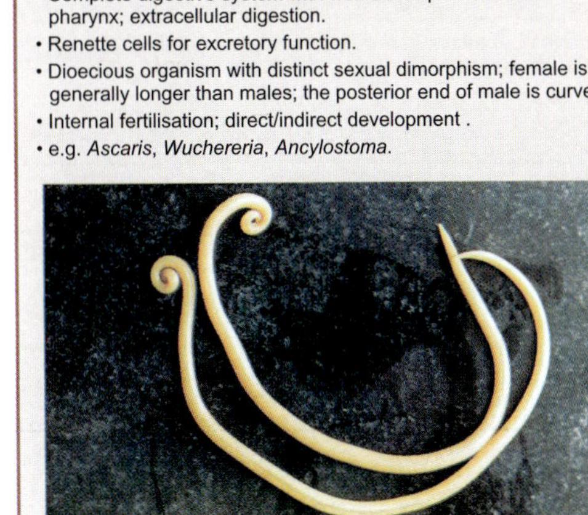

Test 2

Syllabus

- Salient Features and Classification of Animals (Annelida to Hemichordata)

NCERT Page 43 to 45

For deeper insight, **Scan the QR Code**

Parameters	Annelida (Segmented worms)	Arthropoda (Joint appendages) Largest phylum	Mollusca (Soft bodied) Second largest phylum	Echinodermata (Spiny skinned)	Hemichordata (Half chordates)
Habitat	Aquatic (marine and freshwater) or terrestrial	Aquatic and terrestrial	Terrestrial and aquatic	Exclusively marine	Marine (worm like)
Body structure and segmentation	Distinct segments-metameres/annuli	Head, thorax, abdomen; segmented	Head, muscular foot, visceral hump; not segmented	Star-like; not segmented	Proboscis, collar, trunk; not segmented
Locomotory structure	Longitudinal and circular muscles; parapodia/lateral appendages in *Nereis* (swimming)	Jointed appendages	Muscular foot	Water vascular system with tube feet	No locomotory structure
Exoskeleton	No exoskeleton	Chitinous/cuticle	Calcareous shell	No exoskeleton	No exoskeleton
Digestive system and digestion	Complete; extracellular digestion	Complete, extracellular	Complete; extracellular or intracellular	Complete; intracellular or extracellular	Complete; both intracellular and extracellular
Respiratory system	Absent; exchange of gases by diffusion through body wall and gills	Present; gills, book gills, tracheal system, book lungs	Present; feather-like gills in mantle cavity	Present; water vascular system	Present; gills
Circulatory system	Closed	Open; presence of haemocoel	Open	Open	Open
Excretory system or organ	Nephridia	Malpighian tubules or green glands	Gills	Absent	Proboscis gland
Nervous system	Paired ganglia connected by lateral nerves to a double ventral nerve cord	Paired ganglia with double ventral nerve cord	Paired ganglia	Nerve ring + Radial nerve	Nerve plexus
Monoecious/ Dioecious	Monoecious– Earthworm, leech Dioecious–*Nereis* (aquatic form)	Mostly dioecious	Usually dioecious	Dioecious	Dioecious
Fertilisation	External / internal	Usually internal	External/internal	Usually external	External
Development	Direct/indirect	Direct/Indirect	Indirect	Indirect with free-swimming larva	Indirect
Unique features and examples	Body segmentation like rings; e.g. *Nereis, Pheretima, Hirudinaria*	Presence of sensory organs (antenna, eyes) and statocysts or balancing organs; e.g. *Apis, Anopheles, Locusta, Limulus*	Mouth with file-like rasping organ, radula (for feeding); e.g. *Pila, Loligo, Octopus*	Adult forms are radially symmetrical but larvae are bilaterally symmetrical; e.g. *Asterias, Echinus, Ophiura*	Presence of rudimentary stomochord; e.g. *Balanoglossus, Saccoglossus*

Test 3

Syllabus
- Salient Features and Classification of Animals-Chordates (upto classes level)

NCERT Page 45 to 51

For deeper insight, **Scan the QR Code**

Sub-phylum- Cephalochordata
- Exclusively marine.
- Notochord extends from head to tail region throughout their life.
- e.g. *Branchiostoma* (Amphioxus or Lancelet).

Phylum-Chordata
- Presence of notochord, paired pharyngeal gill slits and a dorsal hollow nerve cord.
- The central nervous system is hollow, dorsal and single.
- The heart is ventral.
- These are triploblastic, bilaterally symmetrical and coelomate with organ-system level of organisation.
- Have a closed circulatory system.
- Presence of post-anal part (tail).

Sub-phylum-Vertebrata
- Possess notochord during the embryonic period.
- The notochord is replaced by a cartilaginous or bony vertebral column in adults.
- All vertebrates are chordates, but not all chordates are vertebrates.
- A ventral muscular heart with two, three, or four chambers; kidneys for excretion and osmoregulation; and paired appendages (fins or limbs).

Agnatha
- Jaws are missing.
- Paired fins are almost always missing.

Class-Cyclostomata
- Bearing 6-15 pairs of gill slits for respiration.
- Ectoparasite; have a sucking and circular mouth.
- Their body is devoid of scales and paired fins.
- Cranium and vertebral column are cartilaginous.
- Marine, but migrate for spawning to freshwater, then die.
- e.g. *Petromyzon* (lamprey) and *Myxine* (hagfish).

Sub-phylum-Urochordata or Tunicates
- Exclusively marine.
- Notochord found only in larval tail.
- Filter feeders.
- e.g. *Ascidia, Salpa, Doliolum*.

Class - Chondrichthyes
- Marine; streamlined body with cartilaginous endoskeleton.
- Cold-blooded (poikilothermous)
- Ventral mouth and teeth are modified placoid scales.
- Gill slits without operculum, tough skin (placoid scales).
- Two-chambered heart.
- Persistent notochord throughout life.
- Swim constantly to avoid sinking (no air bladder).
- Sexes are separate, internal fertilisation and viviparous (mostly).
- In males, pelvic fins bear claspers.
- e.g., *Scoliodon* (Dog fish), *Pristis* (Saw fish), *Carcharodon* (Great white shark), *Trygon* (Sting ray).

Gnathostomata
- Jawed vertebrates.
- Having true jaws and paired limbs.
- 2 Super classes-**Pisces** (aquatic; bearing fins) and **Tetrapoda** (terrestrial; bearing limbs).

Class-Osteichthyes
- Both marine and freshwater fishes with bony endoskeleton and streamlined body.
- Terminal mouth.
- Four pairs of gill slits with operculum; cycloid/ctenoid scales.
- Two-chambered heart; cold-blooded.
- Presence of air bladder for regulating buoyancy.
- Sexes are separate; external fertilisation; oviparous and direct development.
- e.g., Marine – *Exocoetus* (Flying fish), *Hippocampus* (Seahorse); Freshwater – *Labeo* (Rohu), *Catla* (Katla), *Clarias* (Magur); Aquarium – *Betta* (Fighting fish), *Pterophyllum* (Angel fish).

Class-Amphibia
- Both aquatic and terrestrial habitats.
- Two pairs of limbs; head and trunk.
- Moist skin without scales; eyelids and tympanum; cloaca present
- Respiration: by gills, lungs and moist skin.
- Heart : 3 chambered (two auricles and one ventricle); poikilothermous organisms.
- External fertilisation; oviparous; indirect development
- e.g., *Bufo, Rana, Salamandra*.

Class-Aves
- Possess beak and forelimbs (wings); feathers (insulator)
- Dry skin without glands, except oil glands at base of tail.
- Bony endoskeleton.
- Digestive tract: additional chambers (crop and gizzard).
- 4 chambered heart; endothermic; warm blooded.
- Respiration through lungs.
- Separate sexes; internal fertilisation; oviparous and direct development.
- e.g., *Corvus, Columba, Pavo, Neophron*.

Class-Reptilia
- Mostly terrestrial; creeping and crawling.
- Epidermal and cornified scales.
- Tympanum represents ear; two pairs of limbs (if present).
- 3 chambered heart (Exception: Crocodiles with 4 chambered); poikilotherms.
- Internal fertilisation, oviparous; direct development.
- e.g. *Chelone, Chameleon, Alligator*.

Class-Mammalia
- Present in variety of habitats.
- Mammary gland present two-pairs of limbs.
- Skin covered with hair; presence of pinnae and different types of teeth.
- Four-chambered heart; homeotherms.
- Respiration through lungs.
- Internal fertilisation; viviparous (Exception-Platypus).
- e.g., *Macropus, Pteropus, Camelus*.

Test 1

Syllabus

- Morphology and Modification; Different Parts of Flowering Plants (Roots, Stems and Leaves).

NCERT Old Page 65 to 71

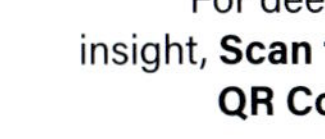

For deeper insight, **Scan the QR Code**

Chapter 05

The Root

- Underground, non-green parts of the plant.
- Lacks nodes, leaves and buds.
- Elongation of radicle forms primary root.
- Primary root bears lateral roots of several orders that are referred to as secondary and tertiary roots.

Types of Root

Main root

Laterals

Tap root (e.g., in dicots such as mustard).

Fibrous root (e.g., in monocots, such as wheat).

Adventitious roots (originate from parts other than radicle, e.g., *Monstera*).

Regions of Root

Root hairs

Region of maturation (possesses root hairs)

Region of elongation (responsible for growth of root in length)

Region of meristematic activity (actively dividing cells)

Root cap (protects root apex)

Stem and Its Modifications

- Ascending part of plant axis bearing nodes and internodes.
- Contains flowers, leaves, etc.
- Develops from plumule of embryo of germinating seed.
- Bears bud which may be terminal or axillary.

Stem Modifications

Modifications	Types
Underground stems	• Rhizome (Ginger, Turmeric) • Bulb (Onion, Garlic) • Corm (*Colocasia*, *Crocus*) • Tuber (Potato)
Subaerial stems	• Runner (Lawn grass) • Sucker (*Chrysanthemum*, Mint) • Stolon (Jasmine, *Colocasia*) • Offset (*Pistia*, *Eichhornia*)
Aerial stems	• Stem tendrils (*Cucurbita*, Grapevine) • Thorns (modified axillary bud; *Bougainvillea*) • Phylloclade (*Euphorbia*) • Bulbil (Lily)

Root Modifications

- Roots in some plants change their structure to perform different functions other than absorption of water and minerals such as food storage, support and respiration.

Storage of Food

- Tap root — Carrot, Turnip.
- Adventitious root — Sweet potato.

Prop Root

- Arises from branches to support them.
- e.g. Banyan.

Stilt Root

- Supporting root coming out from lower nodes.
- e.g. Maize, Sugarcane.

Pneumatophore

- Root growing vertically upward for oxygen in plants of swampy area.
- e.g. *Rhizophora*.

Functions of Roots

- Absorption of water and minerals from soil.
- Provide anchorage to plant parts.
- Storage of reserve food materials.
- Synthesis of Plant Growth Regulators (PGRs).

Leaf

- A lateral, generally flat structure; develops at node and bears a bud in its axil.
- Arise from shoot apical meristem and arranged in acropetal order.

Parts of leaf

Types of Leaves

Simple (e.g. Peepal tree)

Pinnately compound (e.g. Neem)

Palmately compound (e.g. Silk cotton)

Phyllotaxy

Arrangement of leaves around the stem; three main types of leaf arrangement are:

1. **Alternate** A single leaf originates at each node and leaves are arranged in an alternate fashion, e.g. mustard, China rose, sunflower, etc.
2. **Opposite** Two leaves arise at each node and they lie opposite each other, e.g. guava, *Calotropis*, etc.
3. **Whorled** More than two leaves arise at each node and form a whorl. This type of arrangement is found in *Alstonia*.

Alternate (e.g. China rose, Mustard, Sunflower)

Opposite (e.g. *Calotropis*, Guava)

Whorled (e.g. *Alstonia*)

Leaf Venation

Specific arrangement of veins in a leaf.

Types of Venation in Leaf

1. Reticulate Venation

- In this venation, main vein divides into few veinlets. These veinlets are irregularly distributed and form a network or reticulum in the lamina.
- It is the characteristic feature of dicotyledonous plants, e.g. peepal, mango, etc.

2. Parallel Venation

- It is the arrangement of veins in parallel fashion.
- This type of venation is the characteristic feature of monocotyledons, e.g. rice, wheat, banana, etc.

Reticulate (network of veins; in dicots)

Parallel (in monocots)

Modifications of Leaves

When other structures of the plant cannot develop and perform a particular function, the leaves can be modified to perform their functions. These functions can include the storage of food, protection of the plant and support to the plant.

These modifications are as follows

- Phyllode (Australian *Acacia*).
- Leaf spines (*Opuntia*).
- Tendrils of leaf (*Lathyrus aphaca*).
- Leaflet hooks (*Bignonia* sp.).
- Insectivorous leaves (Venus flytrap).

Test 2

Syllabus
- Inflorescence-Cymose and Racemose
- Flower, Fruit and Seed

NCERT Old Page 71 to 77

For deeper insight, **Scan the QR Code**

Chapter 05

Flower

- Reproductive unit in angiosperms.
- Generally, flower has four whorls : Calyx, corolla, androecium, and gynoecium.

Androecium (Unit-Stamen)
- It represents the male reproductive organ.
- When stamens are attached to the petals, they are **epipetalous**, e.g. brinjal.
- When stamens are attached to the perianth, the condition is called **epiphyllous**, e.g. lily.
- The stamens may be united into one bunch or one bundle, i.e. **monoadelphous,** e.g. China rose, may be grouped into two bundles, i.e. **diadelphous,** e.g. pea or into more than two bundles, i.e. **polyadelphous,** e.g. *Citrus*.

Anther, Filament, Stigma, Style, Ovary, Pedicel

Calyx
- It is made up of units called **sepals**.
- It provides protection to the flower in the bud stage.
- A bract-like structure found externally to the sepals constitutes the epicalyx. Sepals can be free from each other, i.e. **polysepalous** or fused with each other, i.e. **gamosepalous**.

Gynoecium (Unit-Pistil/Carpel)
- It is a female reproductive part of the flower.
- When more than one carpel is present, they may be free and called **apocarpous**, e.g. lotus and rose.
- When carpels are fused together, the gynoecium is called **syncarpous**, e.g. brinjal, tomato,

Corolla
- It is composed of petals and lies inner to calyx.
- It may also be **gamopetalous** (petals united), e.g. elder berry or **polypetalous** (petals free), e.g. rose.

Placentation

- It is the arrangement of ovules within the ovary.

Types of Placentation	Descriptions with Examples	Diagrams
Marginal	There is a single placenta which develops along the junction of two fused margins, e.g. pea.	
Axile	Multicarpellary, syncarpous gynoecium inward growth of carpel's margin forms a multicarpellary condition. Placenta arises from central axis bearing ovules in a multilocular ovary; e.g. *Solanum,* China rose, lemon.	
Parietal	Ovules bearing placenta grow inward to form false septa and thus ovary becomes bilocular; e.g. mustard and trilocular; e.g. *Cucurbita*.	
Free central	The ovary is unilocular and ovules are borne on the central-axis and not connected to the ovary wall by septum. e.g. *Dianthus,* primrose.	
Basal	The ovary is unilocular and the single ovule is borne at the base of the ovary attached by a single placenta; e.g. sunflower, wheat.	

Types of Flower

- Based on the presence of **sex organs**
  - **Unisexual** (both androecium and gynoecium)
  - **Bisexual** (only androecium or only gynoecium)
- A flower may be trimerous, tetramerous or pentamerous when the **floral appendages** are in multiples of 3, 4 or 5, respectively.
- On the basis of **floral symmetry**, there are following three conditions in flowers:

Actinomorphic (e.g. Mustard, *Datura*) **Zygomorphic** (e.g. Pea, Gulmohar) **Asymmetric** (e.g. *Canna*)

Inflorescence

Arrangement of flowers on floral axis (peduncle).

Racemose
- Unlimited growth of main axis.
- Flowers borne acropetally, e.g. mustard.

Cymose
- Limited growth of main axis.
- Flowers borne basipetally, e.g. *Solanum*.

Aestivation

The mode of arrangement of sepals or petals in floral bud with respect to the other members of the same whorl. It is of following types:

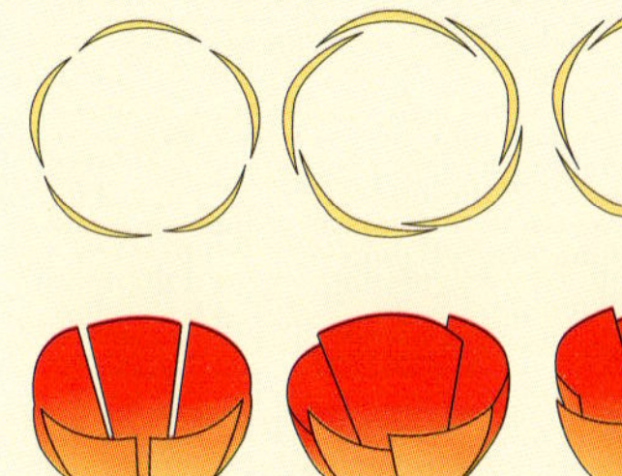

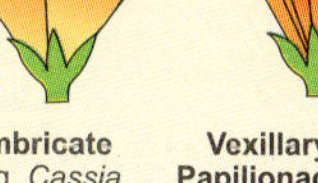

Valvate e.g. *Calotropis*

Twisted e.g. China rose, lady's finger and cotton

Imbricate e.g. *Cassia* and gulmohar

Vexillary or Papilionaceous e.g. pea and bean flowers

Types of Flower Based on Position of Ovary

- **Hypogynous Flower (Superior ovary):** The gynoecium occupies the highest position, while the other parts are situated below it.
- **Perigynous Flower (Half inferior ovary):** If gynoecium is situated in the centre and other parts of the flower are located on the rim of the thalamus, almost at the same level.
- **Epigynous Flowers (Inferior):** The margin of thalamus grows upward enclosing the ovary completely and getting fused with it, the other parts of flower arise above the ovary.

Hypogynous superior ovary (e.g. mustard)

Perigynous half inferior ovary (e.g. rose)

Epigynous inferior ovary (e.g. ray florets of sunflower)

Fruit

- Fruit is the ripened or mature ovary.
- Composed of fruit wall, pericarp and seeds.
- Mesocarp is fibrous in coconut, while fleshy edible in mango.

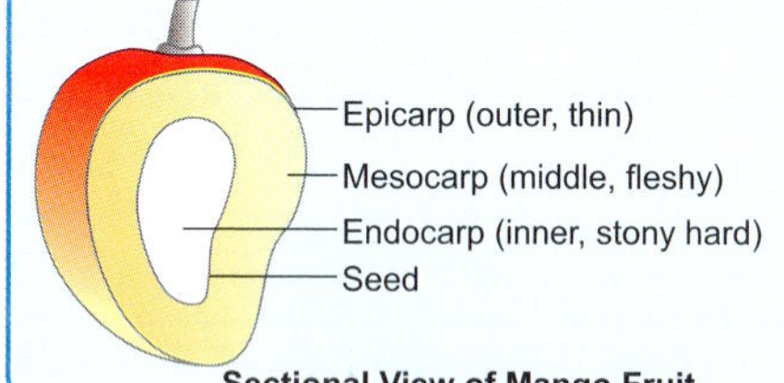

Sectional View of Mango Fruit

Seed

- Seed coat has two layers - outer testa and inner tegmen.

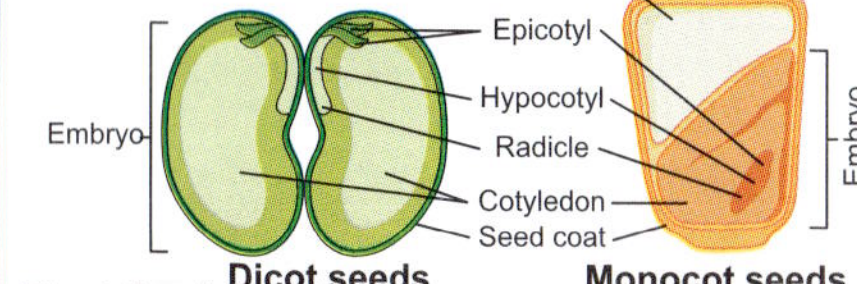

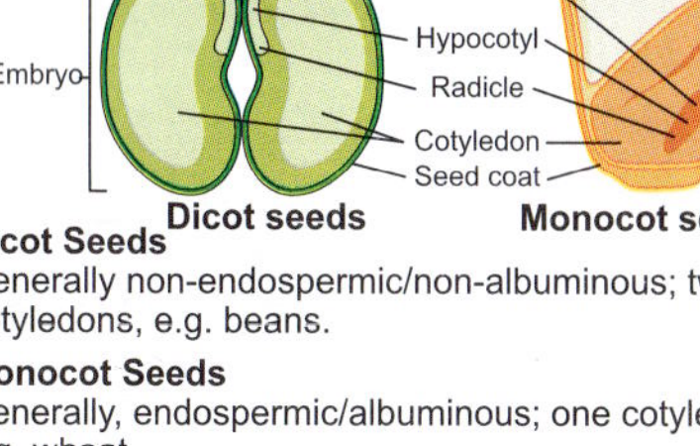

Dicot seeds **Monocot seeds**

Dicot Seeds
Generally non-endospermic/non-albuminous; two cotyledons, e.g. beans.

Monocot Seeds
Generally, endospermic/albuminous; one cotyledons e.g. wheat.

Test 3

Syllabus

- Families : Malvaceae, Cruciferae, Compositae, Gramineae, Leguminosae

NCERT Old Page 78 to 79

For deeper insight, **Scan the QR Code**

Chapter 05

Characteristics	Leguminosae (Pea family)	Gramineae (Grass family)	Compositae (Asteraceae)	Cruciferae (Brassicaceae)	Malvaceae (Mallow family)
Habit	Trees, shrubs and rarely herbs.	Annual, biennial or perennials, herbs, shrubs.	Mostly annual, rarely biennial herbs, shrubs, sometimes tree.	Annual or perennial herbs.	Annual, biennial, herbs, shrubs and trees.
Inflorescence	Racemose	Spike of spikelets or panicles of spikelets, short axis rachilla, glumes at base of the rachilla; series of florets are present above glumes.	Head/capitulum-terminal or axillary, flat peduncle, surrounded by involucre.	Corymbose raceme or corymb	Solitary terminal or axillary cymose or raceme.
Flower	Bracteate or ebracteate, bisexual, zygomorphic, pentamerous, complete.	Bracteate and bracteolate, bisexual or rarely unisexual (*Zea mays*) sessile, zygomorphic incomplete, hypogynous.	Bracteate or ebracteate, hermaphrodite or unisexual, complete or incomplete, actinomorphic or zygomorphic, epigynous, pentamerous.	Ebracteate, Bisexual, actinomorphic (may be zygomorphic), hypogynous, tetramerous.	Bracteate, bracteolate, bisexual, actinomorphic, complete, pentamerous, hypogynous.
Calyx	Five sepals, gamosepalous imbricate/valvate aestivation.	They consist of perianth which is represented by membranous scales	Absent or hairy pappus or scaly, persistant, normally present in the form of pappus (2 or 3).	Four sepals, polysepalous in two whorls, imbricate aestivation.	Five sepals, free or united at base, valvate aestivation.
Corolla	Five petals, polypetalous, vexillary aestivation		Five petals, gamopetalous, tubular, valvate aestivation.	Four, polypetalous cruciform and reduced in some plants.	Five petals, polypetalous
Androecium	Ten stamens, diadelphous, anther dithecous, introrse.	Usually, stamens are 3 (rarely 6), polyandrous, filament long, anther dithecous, versatile, linear, extrorse.	Five stamens, syngenesious, dithecous, basifixed, introrse.	Six stamens; polyandrous tetradynamous (2+4), dithecous, introrse.	Numerous stamens, monoadelphous, epipetalous, monothecous, extrose anthers reniform.
Gynoecium	Monocarpellary, ovary superior unilocular with many ovules, marginal placentation.	Monocarpellary with superior ovary, unilocular with single ovule, style short or absent, stigma two and feathery, basal placentation.	Bicarpellary, syncarpous, inferior ovary, unilocular, single ovule in each locule, style single, stigma bifid, basal placentation.	Bicarpellary, syncarpous, superior ovary, unilocular with parietal placentation.	A compound pistil of one to many carpel (multicarpellary), syncarpous, ovary superior, axile placentation.
Fruit	Legume	Caryopsis	Cypsela	Siliqua or silicula	Capsule or schizocarp
Seed	One to many and non-endospermic	Endospermic	Non-endospermic.	Small, non-endospermic.	Seed with curved embryo and scanty endosperm.
Floral formulae	Br % ⚥ $K_{(5)}\ C_{1+2+(2)}\widehat{A_{(9)+1}}\ \underline{G}_1$	Br % ⚥ $P_{2(lodicules)}\ A_{3-6}\ \underline{G}_1$	**Ray florets** Br % ♀ $K_{Pappus}\ C_{(3-5)}\ A_0\ \overline{G}_{(2)}$ **Disc florets** Br ⊕ ⚥ $K_{Pappus}\ \widehat{C_{(5)}A_{(5)}}\ \overline{G}_{(2)}$	Ebr ⊕ ⚥ $K_{2+2}\ C_4\ A_{2+4}\ \underline{G}_{(2)}$	Br ⊕ ⚥ $Epi_{3-9}\ K_{5\ or\ (5)}\ \widehat{C_5 A_{(\infty)}}\ \underline{G}_{(2-\infty)}$
Floral diagrams			Ray floret Disc floret		

Symbols: Br – Bracteate, EBr – Ebracteate, ⊕ – Actinomorphic, % – Zygomorphic, ⚥ – Bisexual, ♀ – Female, ♂ – Male, K – Calyx, C – Corolla, P – Perianth, A – Androecium, G – Gynoecium, $\underline{G}$ – Superior ovary, $\overline{G}$ – Inferior ovary, G- Semi-inferior ovary, ( ) – Fused, $\widehat{CA}$ – Epipetalous.

Test 1

Syllabus

- Plant Tissues

NCERT Old Page 84 to 90

For deeper insight, **Scan the QR Code**

Chapter 06

Types of Meristematic Tissues or Meristem

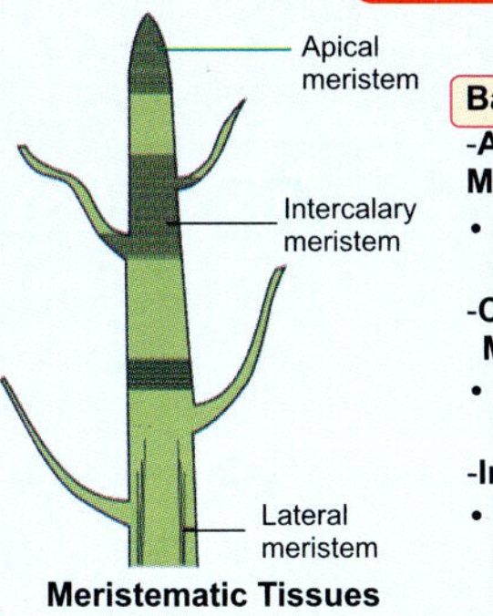

Meristematic Tissues

Based on Location

- **Apical or Terminal Meristem**
  - Located on the tips of roots and stem.
- **Cambium or Lateral Meristem**
  - Located under the bark.
- **Intercalary Meristem**
  - Located in the leaves and internodes.

Based on Origin

- **Promeristem**
  - It originates from embryo.
- **Primary Meristem**
  - It originates from promeristem.
- **Secondary Meristem**
  - It originates from permanent tissues.

Based on Function

- **Protoderm**
  - Protects from mechanical shocks.
- **Procambium**
  - Gives rise to the xylem and phloem.
- **Ground Meristem**
  - Forms the cortex, pericycle and pith.

Tissue System

Epidermal Tissue

- **Cuticle** (waxy thick layer)
- **Epidermis** (outermost layer; protection)
- **Epidermal Appendages**
  - **Epidermal hairs** (roots; absorbs water and minerals; unicellular).
  - **Trichomes** (stems; prevent water loss; usually multicellular).
- **Stomata** (transpiration and gaseous exchange)

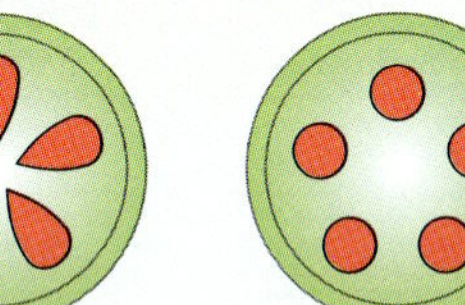

Bean-Shaped Stomata (Dicots) Dumb-bell-Shaped Guard cell (Monocots)

Ground Tissue

- Hypodermis
- Cortex
- Endodermis
- Pericycle
- Medullary rays and pith

Vascular Tissue

Xylem

- Tracheid
- Vessels
- Xylem parenchyma
- Xylem fibres

Phloem

- Sieve
- Companion cells
- Phloem parenchyma
- Phloem fibres

Simple Permanent Tissue

Features	Parenchyma	Collenchyma	Sclerenchyma
Cell shape	Isodiametric, oval, polygonal cell	Circular, oval or polyhedral	Variable in shape; in form of fibres and sclereids
Cell wall	Thin cellulosic cell wall	Uneven thickening on their cell wall.	Lignified secondary cell
Cytoplasm	Abundant	Present	Absent
Nucleus	Present (Living tissue)	Present (Living tissue)	Absent (Dead tissue)
Vacuoles	Large vacuole	Vacuolated	Absent
Occurrence	Basic packing tissue; all soft part of plant; pith, cortex, medullary rays	Dicot stems (hypodermis), petiole and young stem	Monocot stems (hypodermis), seed, pulp of fruits, fruit wall of nuts
Intercellular spaces	Present	Absent	Absent
Functions	Food storage, photosynthesis	Provide tensile strength	Protection from stress and strain
Diagrammatical representation			

Complex Permanent Tissue

Xylem	Phloem
Conducts water and minerals.	Conducts organic solutes or food materials.
Conduction is mostly unidirectional, i.e. from roots to apical parts of the plant.	Conduction may be bidirectional, i.e. from leaves to storage organs and growing parts or from storage organs to growing parts of plants.
Conducting channels are tracheids and vessels.	Conducting channels are sieve tubes.

Arrangement of Xylem

Types of arrangement indicating direction of radial differentiation of the primary xylem.

Exarch (centripetal)

- Protoxylem towards periphery and metaxylem towards centre in roots.

Endarch (centrifugal)

- Protoxylem lies towards the centre and metaxylem towards the periphery of organ in stem.

Mesarch

- The direction of differentiation of xylem is both centrifugal and centripetal; found in ferns.

Metaxylem
Protoxylem

Types of Vascular Bundles

Radial Bundles (Xylem and phloem occur on different radii)

Xylem
Phloem

Conjoint Bundles (Xylem and phloem are situated at the same radius of vascular bundle)

Collateral Bundles

Phloem
Vascular cambium
Xylem
Open with cambium
Closed without cambium

Bicollateral Bundles

Xylem
Phloem
Cambium
Phloem

Concentric Bundles (One vascular element completely surrounds the other)

Amphicribral

Amphivasal

Phloem
Xylem

Test 2

Syllabus

- Anatomy of Different Parts of Flowering Plants (Roots, Stems and Leaves)

NCERT Old Page 90 to 98

For deeper insight, **Scan the QR Code**

Anatomy of Dicot and Monocot Roots

Dicot Root

- Cortex comparatively narrower.
- Endoderm is less thickened with more prominent Casparian strips.
- 2-5 xylem and phloem bundles.
- Pith is small or inconspicuous or absent.
- Secondary growth takes place with the help of vascular cambium and cork cambium.
- Conjunctive tissue-parenchymatous.

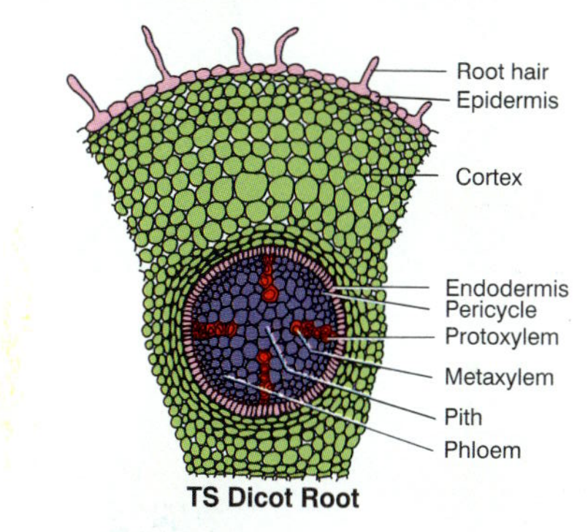

TS Dicot Root

Monocot Root

- Cortex wide
- Endodermis with highly thickened Casparian strips (only visible in young roots).
- Xylem and phloem are more than 6 (polyarch).
- Pith is well-developed and large.
- Secondary growth is absent due to the absence of cambium.
- Conjunctive tissue-sclerenchymatous.

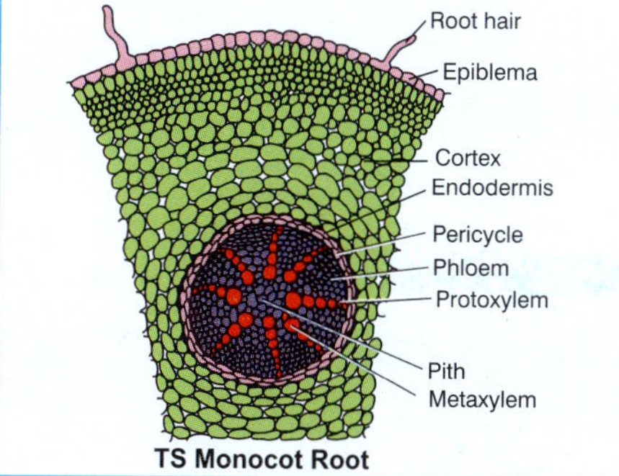

TS Monocot Root

Anatomy of Dicot and Monocot Stems

Epidermal hair
Epidermis
Hypodermis
Parenchyma
Endodermis
Pericycle
Vascular bundle
Medullary rays
Pith

TS Dicot Stem

Dicot Stem

- Hypodermis is collenchymatous.
- Vascular bundles almost uniform size and wedge-shaped and are arranged in a ring.
- Vascular bundles are open.
- Presence of secondary growth (presence of cambium).
- Pith is well-developed; presence of endodermis and pericycle.

Epidermis
Hypodermis
Vascular bundles
Ground tissue

TS Monocot Stem

Monocot Stem

- Hypodermis is sclerenchymatous.
- Vascular bundles are numerous and of different sizes with oval-shape and scattered throughout the ground tissues.
- Vascular bundles are closed.
- Absence of secondary growth (no cambium).
- Pith is not well-developed or absent; absence of endodermis and pericycle.

Anatomy of Dorsiventral (Dicot) and Isobilateral (Monocot) Leaf

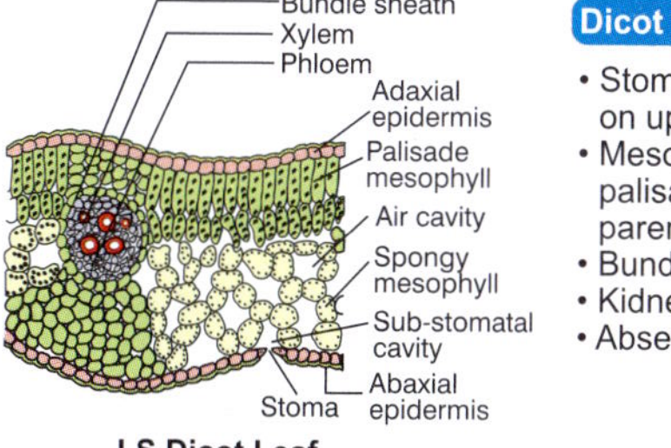

LS Dicot Leaf

Dicot Leaf

- Stomata absent or less abundant on upper side.
- Mesophyll differentiated into palisade parenchyma and spongy parenchyma.
- Bundle sheath is single- layered.
- Kidney-shaped guard cells.
- Absence of bulliform cells.

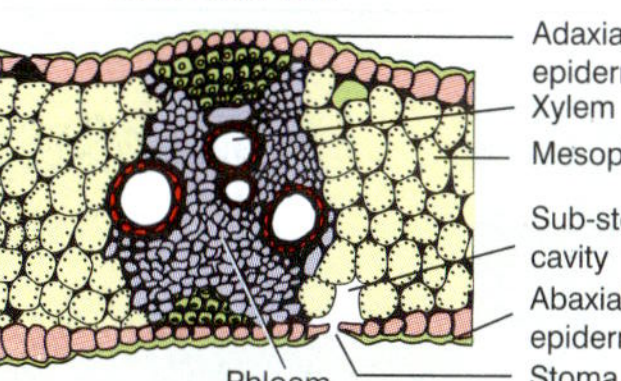

LS Monocot Leaf

Monocot Leaf

- Stomata equally distributed on both sides.
- Undifferentiated mesophyll.
- One or two layered bundle sheath.
- Dumb-bell shaped guard cells.
- Presence of bulliform cells

Secondary Growth in Dicot Stems

- Results in increase in girth (diameter) in plants.
- Vascular cambium and cork cambium are involved in secondary growth.

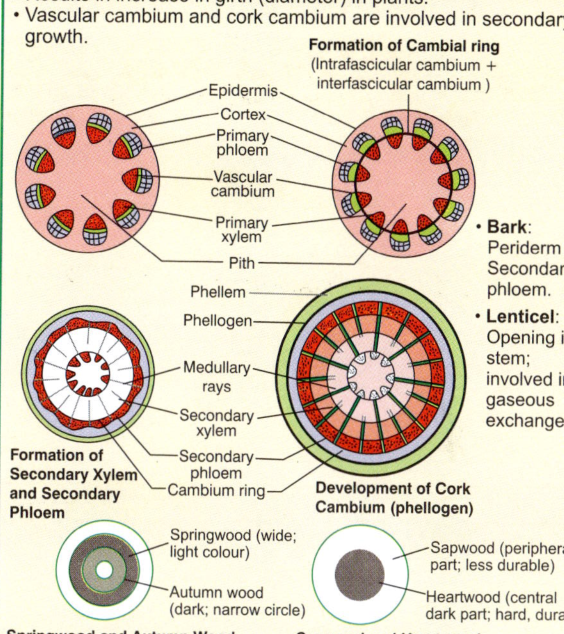

- **Bark**: Periderm + Secondary phloem.
- **Lenticel**: Opening in stem; involved in gaseous exchange.

Secondary Growth in Dicot Roots

- Occurs with activity of secondary meristems (vascular cambium) produced in stele and cortex.
- Increases girth of dicot roots.

Epiblema
Cortex
Endodermis
Primary phloem
Pericycle
Protoxylem
Cambium
Metaxylem (primary xylem)
Epiblema
Cork
Rays
Epidermis
Cortex
Secondary phloem
Phellogen
Primary xylem
Cambium
Secondary xylem
Primary phloem (gets crushed)

Test 1

Syllabus
- Animal Tissues (Epithelium, Connective, Neural and Muscle Tissue)

NCERT Old Page 100 to 106

For deeper insight, **Scan the QR Code**

Epithelium Tissues

Simple Epithelium Single layer of cells
- **Squamous Epithelium** (Flattened cells)
  - Found in the walls of blood vessels and lung alveoli.
  - **Functions** Forms a diffusion boundary.

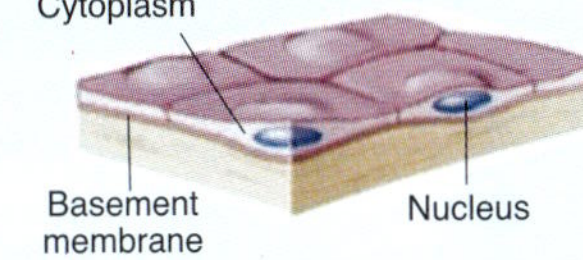

- **Cuboidal Epithelium** (Cube-like cells)
  - Found in ducts of glands and tubular parts of nephrons in kidneys.
  - **Functions** Secretion and absorption.

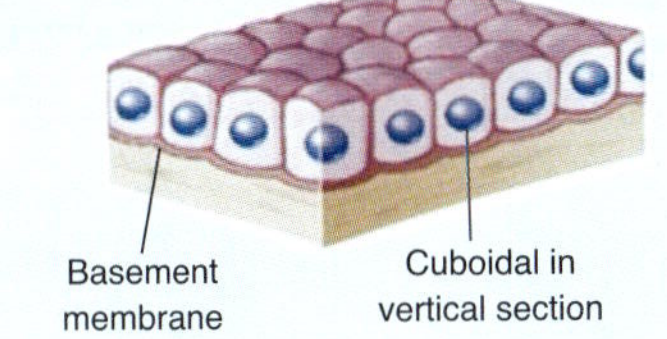

- **Columnar Epithelium** (Tall and slender cells)
  - Found in the lining of stomach and intestine.
  - **Functions** Secretion and absorption.

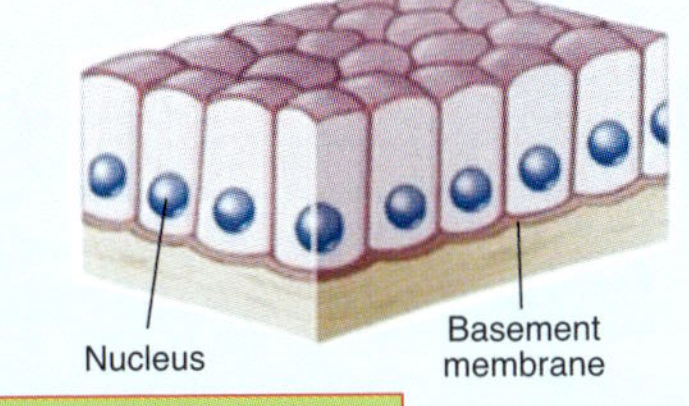

Compound Epithelium
- More than one layer of cells; limited role in secretion and absorption.
- **Functions** Protect against chemical and mechanical stresses.

Cell Junctions Provides structural and functional links between adjacent cells.

Three types of cell junctions are as follows
- **Tight Junctions** Help to stop substances from leaking across a tissue.
- **Adhering Junctions** Perform cementing to keep neighbouring cells together.
- **Gap Junctions** Facilitate communication between adjoining cells by connecting the cytoplasm for rapid transfer of ions and molecules.

Modification of Columnar or Cuboidal Cells
- **Ciliated Epithelium** Present in inner surface of hollow organs like bronchioles and Fallopian tubes.
  - **Functions** To move particles or mucus in a specific direction.
- **Glandular Epithelium**:
  - **Unicellular** (e.g. Goblet cells of the alimentary canal).
  - **Multicellular** (e.g. Salivary glands)

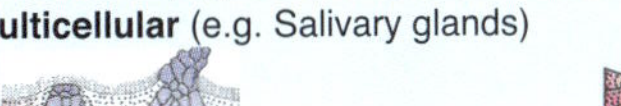
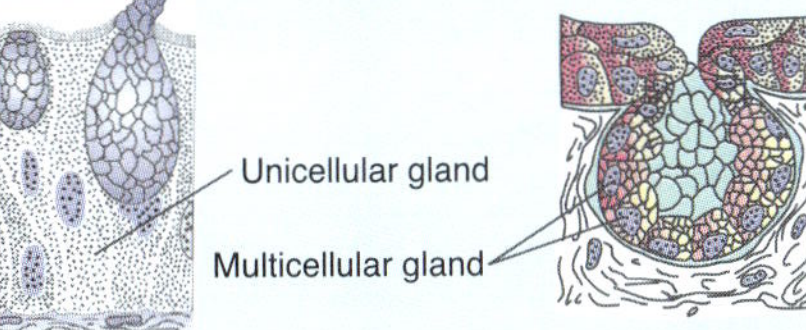
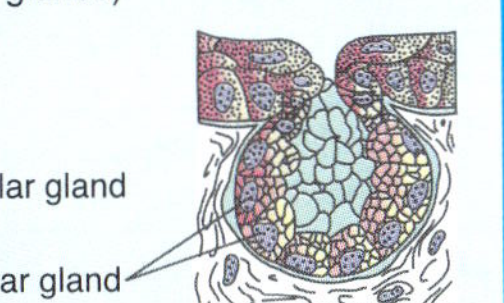

- Glands are 2 types (Based on mode of pouring their secretion): Exocrine glands and endocrine glands (Ductless).

Neural Tissue

- Made up of neurons (Unit of neural system).
- Responsible for control and coordination of the body.
- Neurons are excitable cells and carry impulses.
- Neurons are protected and supported by neuroglial cells.
- Neuroglia make up more than half the volume of neural tissue.

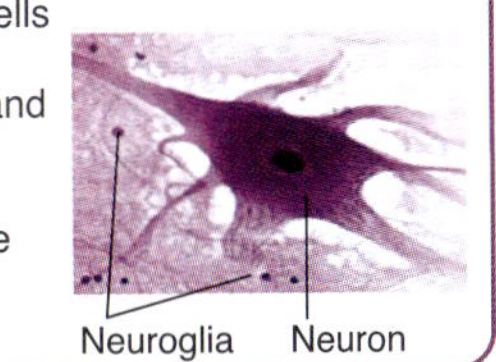

Muscle Tissues

Striated (Skeletal)	Non-striated (Smooth)	Cardiac
Present in the limbs, body walls, tongue, pharynx, etc.	Present in the oesophagus, urino-genital tract, iris of eye, arrector pili muscles of hair, etc.	Present in the wall of the heart, pulmonary veins and superior vena cava.
Cylindrical	Spindle-shaped	Cylindrical
Fibres unbranched	Fibres unbranched	Fibres branched
Multinucleated	Uninucleated	Uninucleated
Light and dark bands present.	Light and dark bands absent	Faint light and dark bands present
Blood supply is abundant	Blood supply is scanty	Blood supply is abundant.
Very rapid contraction	Slow contraction	Rapid contraction
They get fatigued soon	They do not get fatigued	They never get fatigued
Voluntary	Involuntary	Involuntary

Connective Tissues

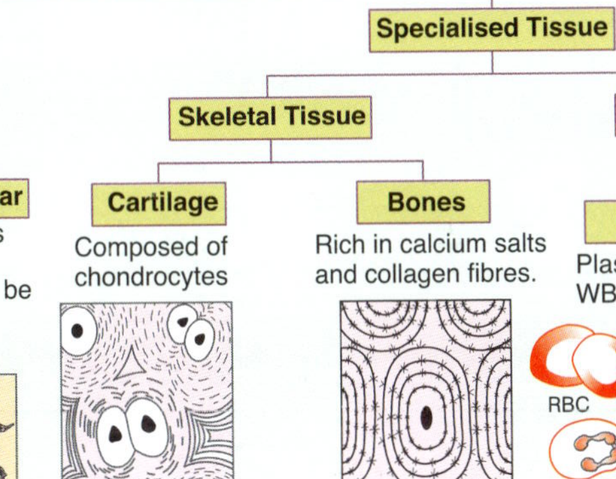

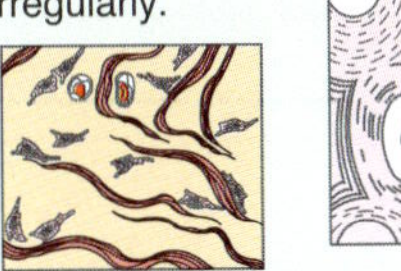

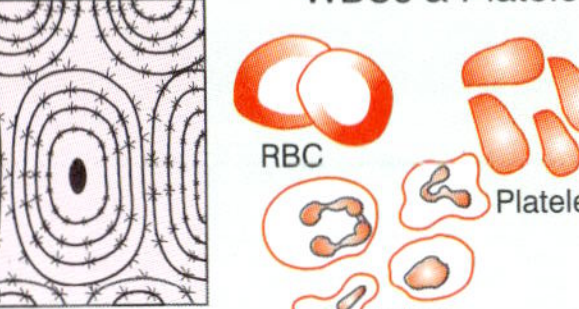
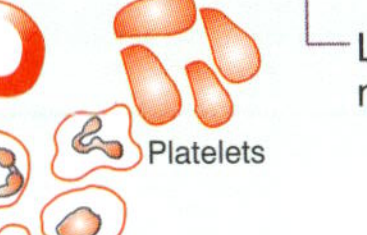

Test 2

Syllabus

- Morphology, Anatomy and Functions of Different Systems (Digestive, Circulatory, Respiratory, Nervous and Reproductive) of Frog and Cockroach

NCERT Old Page 111 to 120

For deeper insight, **Scan the QR Code**

Chapter 07

Frog: *Rana tigrina* (Amphibia, Chordata)

- Sexual dimorphism (vocal sacs and copulatory pads only in males).
- **Body** Head (mouth, external nostrils, bulged eyes, tympanum) and trunk (forelimbs, hindlimbs, webbed feet).

Digestive System

Heart, Gall bladder, Lung, Fat bodies, Kidney, Ureter, Urinary bladder, Cloaca, Oesophagus, Liver (Secretes bile), Stomach, Intestine, Rectum, Cloacal aperture

Alimentary Canal of Frog

Respiratory, Excretory, Circulatory, Nervous and Sensory System

Respiratory System
- On land-buccal cavity, skin, lungs (Pulmonary).
- On water-skin (Cutaneous).
- During hibernation and aestivation - skin.

Excretory System
- Ureotelic animal; system consists of a pair of kidney, ureters, cloaca and urinary bladder.

Circulatory System
- Closed type; 3-chambered myogenic heart (2 atria +1 ventricle); RBCs-nucleated
- Two portal systems - Hepatic and renal.

Nervous System
- 3 divisions - Central (Brain and spinal cord), Peripheral (Cranial and spinal nerves) and Autonomous (Sympathetic and parasympathetic).

Sensory System
- Touch (Sensory papillae) • Taste (Taste buds) • Smell (Nasal epithelium) • Vision (Eye)
- Hearing (Tympanum with internal ears).

Reproductive System

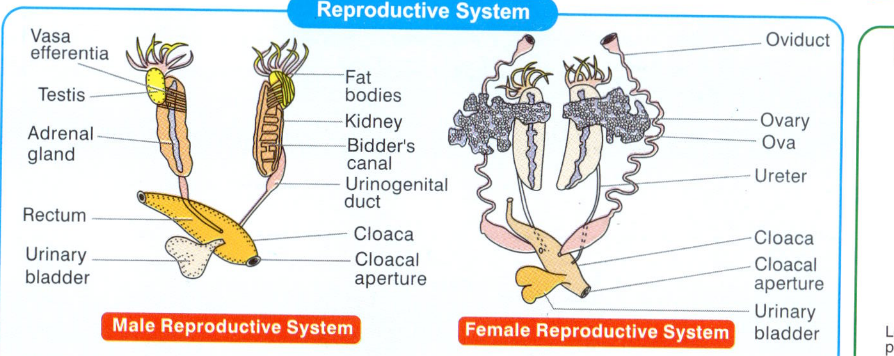

Male Reproductive System **Female Reproductive System**

Life Cycle
- A mature female can lay 2500 to 3000 ova (eggs) at a time.
- Fertilisation is external and takes place in water. Development involves a larval stage called tadpole.

Cockroach : *Periplaneta americana* (Arthropoda)

- Body covered by chitinous exoskeleton.
- Body is segmented with three distinct regions-head, thorax and abdomen.
- Hardened plates in each segment is called sclerites.
- Presence of arthrodial membrane joining terga, sterna and pleura.

Filiform antenna Thread-like, tactile, olfactory and thermal receptor.

Forewings or tegmina Mesothoracic, used for protection

Hindwings Transparent, membranous, used for flying.

Anal cercus Present on the 10th segment of both sexes

Compound eyes

Head Small, triangular, hypognathous condition
Mouth consists of labrum, a pair of mandible, a pair of maxillae, labium and hypopharynx.

Prothoracic leg

Prothorax, Mesothorax, Metathorax — **Thorax** Prothorax possess largest terga (Pronotum),

Abdomen Contains 10 segments, (7th sternum in female is boat-shaped.)

Mesothoracic leg

Metathoracic leg

Anal style (Caudal style): Unjointed, thread-like structure present on the 9th sternum of male; absent in female.

Morphology of Cockroach

Respiratory, Excretory, Circulatory, Digestive and Nervous System

Respiratory System Network of trachea which opens through 10 pairs of spiracles.

Excretion and Osmoregulation By Malpighian tubules; uricotelic.

Circulatory System Open type; contractile heart; blood (Haemolymph) flows freely in blood cavity (Haemocoel); lacks respiratory pigment.

Nervous System
- Consists of series of fused, segmentally arranged ganglia.
- Brain represented by supra-oesophageal ganglion.
- Each eye consists of 2000 hexagonal ommatidia.

Digestive System

Salivary gland, Salivary reservoir, Oesophagus, Pharynx, Crop, Gizzard, Hepatic caeca, Mesenteron or midgut, Malpighian tubules, Ileum, Colon, Rectum

Alimentary Canal of Cockroach

Reproductive System

Male Reproductive System

Testis (4th - 6th segment), Phallic gland, Small tubules, Long tubules, Seminal vesicle (Store sperms), Vas deferens, Ejaculatory duct, Right phallomere, Ventral phallomere, Anal cercus, Caudal style, Pseudopenis, Titillator, Left phallomere

Female Reproductive System

Spermatheca, Gonapophyses, Ovary (with ovarian tubules), Oviduct, Common oviduct or vagina, Collaterial gland, Genital chamber, Vestibulum, Genital pouch

Life Cycle Female produces 9-10 oothecae; fertilised eggs encased in capsules called **oothecae** (contains 14-16 eggs on an average); development is paurometabolous (incomplete metamorphism); Nymph grows by moulting about 13 times to reach adult form.

Test 1

Syllabus • Cell Theory and Cell as the Basic Unit of Life

NCERT Page 87 to 89

For deeper insight, **Scan the QR Code**

Chapter 08

Cell

- Structural and functional unit of all living organisms.
- **Cytology** The branch of biology which deals with the study of cells, their formation and structure.
- Unicellular organisms like *Amoeba*, *Paramoecium*, bacteria, yeast, etc. are capable of
  - independent existence and
  - performing the essential functions of life.

An overview of cell

- Each cell contains a dense, membrane-bound organelle known as the **nucleus** (DNA).
- The cellular volume is occupied by cytoplasm, a viscous, semi-fluid substance.
- Cytoplasm, a semi-fluid medium, fills the intracellular space and is the primary site of many cellular activities in plant and animal cells.
- Based on cellular structure, there are two types of cells
  - Prokaryotic cells
  - Eukaryotic cells

Prokaryotic *v/s* Eukaryotic Cells

Characteristics	Prokaryotic	Eukaryotic
Size of cell	Typically 0.2-2 μm in diameter	Typically 10-100 μm in diameter
Nucleus	No nuclear membrane or nucleoli (nucleoid)	True nucleus consisting of nuclear membrane and nucleoli
Membrane-enclosed organelles	Absent	Present; involves lysosomes, Golgi complex, ER, mitochondria, chloroplasts and microbodies
Ribosomes	Present in cytoplasm	Present in cytoplasm, mitochondria, chloroplasts and on ER
Chromosome (DNA) arrangement	Single circular chromosome; lacks histones	Multiple linear chromosomes with histones

Cell Discovery : Time Line

1665 **Robert Hooke**, an English botanist, **discovered cell** in cork slice; the term 'cell' was derived from Latin word (*cella*-a little room). He explained his observations in a book, namely, *Micrographia*. He found the rigid cell walls of dead cells.

Antonie van Leeuwenhoek, also known as the father of Microbiology. He observed **free-living cells** in pond water. **1674**

1831 **Robert Brown**, Scottish botanist, **discovered** the **nucleus**.

Purkinje coined the term '**protoplasm**' (The cytoplasm and nucleus of a cell) for the fluid substance of the cell. **1839**

1838 & 1839 The **cell theory** was proposed by **Matthias Schleiden** and **Theodore Schwann**.

Theodore Schwann, a British Zoologist, was first to observe cells, have a thin outer layer which is known as **plasma membrane**.

The **cell theory** was also **further** explained by **Rudolf Virchow** by suggesting that all cells arise from pre-existing cell. This concept of cell arising from pre-existing cell was stated by Virchow as "***Omnis cellula-e-cellula***". **1855**

1940 **Vladimir Zworykin** invented the **electron microscope** which enabled us to see the complex structure of the cell.

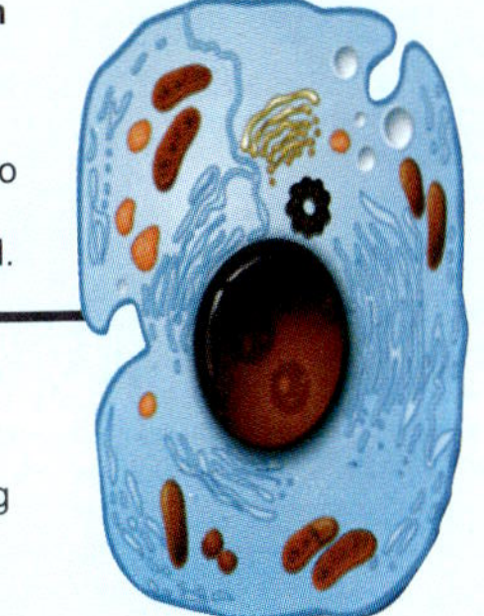

Shape and size of cell

Cell Size

- There are a few examples that help us to observe the varying range of size of the cells.
- The smallest cell available in the environment is of Mycoplasma with a size range of 0.1-0.3 μm.
- The bacterial cell range is 3-5 μm.
- The viruses are smaller in size (0.02-0.2 μm).
- Unicellular eukaryotes have a size of 10-100 μm.
- The largest unicellular cell of the plant kingdom is of a green alga, *Acetabularia,* which is upto 10 cm in length.
- Nerve cells are some of the longest cells.
- Among multicellular organisms, human red blood cells are about 7.0 μm in diameter.
- The largest isolated single cell of the animal kingdom is the egg of an ostrich.
- The surface area to volume ratio of the cell is inversely related to the size of the cell.
- Hence, the smaller cells having high surface area to volume ratio are metabolically more active than larger cells with low surface area to volume ratio.

Cell Shape

- The cells vary in their shapes as they are disc-like polygonal, columnar, cuboid, amoeboid, thread-like or irregular.
- The shape of a cell is related to its position such as flat in surface cells, polygonal in the cortex and functions such as nerve cells that are branched and long in structure to conduct impulses and sperms, the male reproductive cells that have tails for motility.

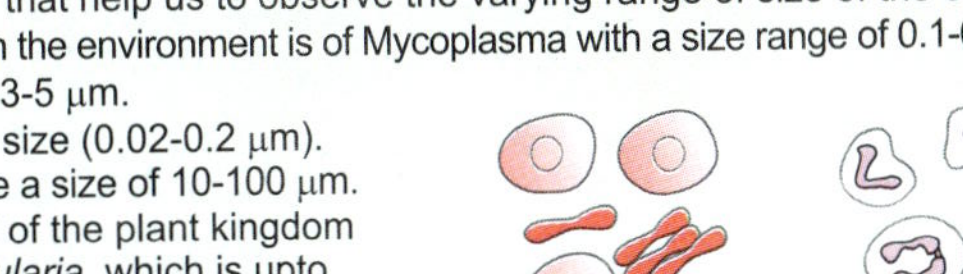

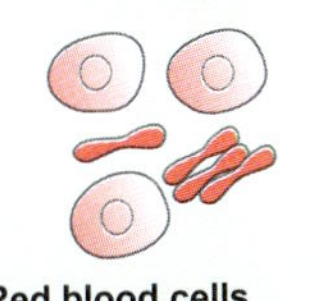

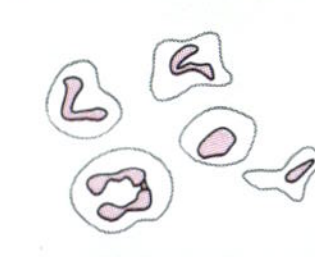

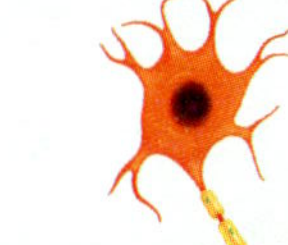

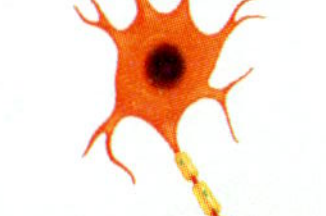

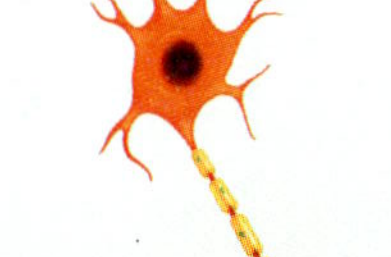

Red blood cells (round and biconcave)

White blood cells (amoeboid)

Columnar epithelial cells (long and narrow)

Nerve cell (branched and long)

A tracheid (elongated)

Mesophyll cells (round and oval)

Cell Theory

Cell theory is one of the unifying theories in biology and one that is universally accepted by all biologists. The theory states that

- All living organisms are made up of one or more cells.
- All cells arise from other pre-existing cells.

Expanded version of the cell theory also includes

- All cells are essentially the same in chemical composition and metabolic activities
- The functions of an organism as a whole is the outcome of the activities and interaction of the constituent cells.
- Cells carry genetic material passed onto daughter cells during cellular division.

Exceptions to Cell Theory

- Viruses do not possess a cellular machinery, even though they are considered as organisms.
- The prokaryotic cells lack nuclear membrane around their genetic material.
- RBCs and sieve tubes lack nucleus and major cell organelles, still these survive for considerable time.
- Certain fungi and algae are made up of undivided mass of protoplasm in which numerous nuclei lie scattered, e.g. *Rhizopus* (Fungus) and *Vaucheria* (Alga).

Test 2

Syllabus
- Structure of a Prokaryotic Cell

NCERT Page 89 to 91

For deeper insight, **Scan the QR Code**

Chapter 08

Prokaryotic Cell

General Features

- Lacks membrane-bound cell organelles.
- Represented by bacteria, blue-green algae, mycoplasma or PPLO.
- Generally smaller and multiply more rapidly than eukaryotic cells.
- In addition to **genomic DNA**, many bacteria have small circular DNA outside the genomic DNA called **plasmids** (resistance to antibiotics).
- Genetic material is generally naked, with no nucleus.
- Plasmid DNA is used to monitor bacterial transformation with foreign DNA.
- All prokaryotes have a cell wall surrounding the cell membrane (**except** Mycoplasma).
- Cell walls serve as a protective barrier and contribute to the structural integrity of the organism.
- The composition of prokaryotic cell walls differs significantly between the domains-Bacteria and Archaea.
- In some bacteria, a **capsule** may be present outside the cell wall.
- **Cell Shapes** Spherical (coccus), rod-shaped (bacillus), spiral (spirillum) and comma-shaped (vibrio).
- Bacterial cells, as a representative example of prokaryotes, exhibit a variety in structures and shapes.

Prokaryotic cells have a unique set of characteristics

- Lack of nuclear membrane and organelles such as mitochondria, Golgi bodies, chloroplasts, and lysosomes.
- Presence of a **single chromosome without histone proteins**.
- Plasma membrane functions analogous to mitochondrial membranes in carrying respiratory enzymes.
- Reproduction primarily through asexual mode like binary fission and, with conjugation as a form of sexual reproduction.
- **Nucleoid** region containing DNA and RNA.
- **Ribosomes** for protein synthesis.
- **Cytosol** housing a cytoskeleton for cellular organisation.
- Unique structure called **inclusion bodies** are found.

Cell Envelope and its Modifications

- Most prokaryotic cells have cell envelope, which is tightly bound three layered structure.
- The outermost **glycocalyx** is followed by **cell wall** and then the **plasma membrane.**
- **Glycocalyx** may be a loose sheath called **slime layer** or thick and tough called the **capsule**.
- The **cell wall** prevents bacteria from bursting or collapsing.
- Extension of **plasma membrane** into the cell in the form of vesicles, tubules and lamellae are **mesosomes**.
- Mesosomes help in cell wall formation, DNA replication, distribution of daughter cells, respiration, secretion process and increase the surface area of plasma membrane.
- In cyanobacteria, chromatophores contain pigments.
- Each layer of the cell envelope performs distinct function; they act together as a single protective unit.
- The plasma membrane is selectively permeable in nature and interacts with the outside world; structurally similar to that of eukaryotes.
- Bacteria may be motile or non-motile. If motile, they have **flagella** which is composed of three parts- **filament, hook** and **basal body**.
- **Pili** and **fimbriae** do not play role in motility.
- Bacteria, on the basis of the differences in the cell envelope, can be Gram-positive or Gram-negative. They can be distinguished based on Gram staining technique (Christian Gram).
- Gram-positive bacteria are characterised by thick (multilayered) peptidoglycan, but lack an outer membrane.
- Gram-negative bacteria are characterised by thin (single-layered) peptidoglycan, but possess an outer membrane.

Structure of Typical Bacterial Cell

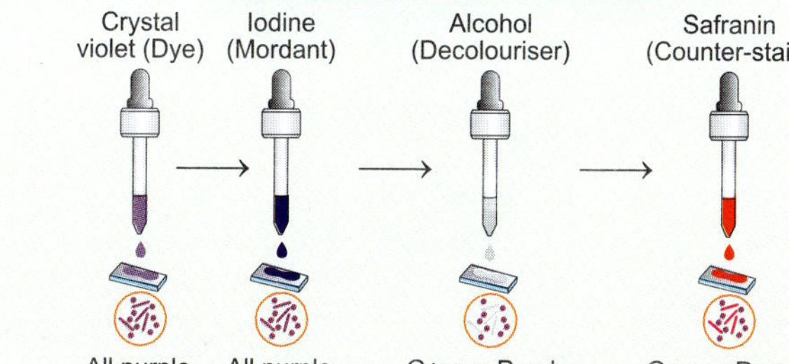

Ribosomes and Inclusion Bodies

- **Ribosomes** are 70S, has subunits 50S and 30S. Several ribosomes may attach to a single *m*RNA and form a chain called **polyribosome** or **polysome**.
- Ribosomes are associated with plasma membrane; made up of *r*RNA and protein.
- The ribosomes of a polysome translate the *m*RNA into proteins.

Inclusion Bodies

- Stored reserve material; bacteria contain inclusion bodies in the form of metachromatic granules, e.g. phosphate granules, cyanophycean granules and glycogen granules.
- Gas vacuoles are non-membrane bound small, hollow cylindrical structure (provides buoyancy) found in blue-green algae, purple and green photosynthetic bacteria.

Gram-Staining : Procedure

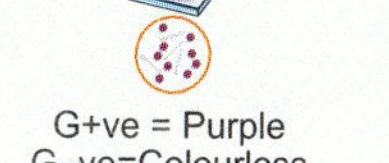

Test 3

Syllabus
- Structure of Eukaryotic Cells
- Cell Organelles and Special Structures Related to Cell

NCERT Page 91 to 102

For deeper insight, **Scan the QR Code**

Cytoskeleton

- The cytoskeletal fibres include **microtubules, intermediate filaments** and **microfilaments**.
- Microtubules are hollow cylindrical structures built from tubulin protein.
- Microtubules perform functions like intracellular transport of materials, cellular motility, chromosomal movement and so on.

Endoplasmic Reticulum

- Membrane-bound channels seen in the form of network of delicate strands and vesicles in cytoplasm.
- It is of two types, i.e. **smooth ER** (with no ribosomes) and **rough ER** (with ribosomes).
- RER is involved in protein synthesis and secretion.
- SER is the major site for lipid synthesis.

Nucleus
RER
Ribosome
SER

Ribosomes

- Made up of RNA and proteins.
- Granules-like non-membranous cell organelles found in both prokaryotes and eukaryotes.
- They synthesise proteins.
- Ribosomes are of two types, i.e., 70S in prokaryotes and 80S in eukaryotes.
- Each of them has two subunits, one larger and one smaller.

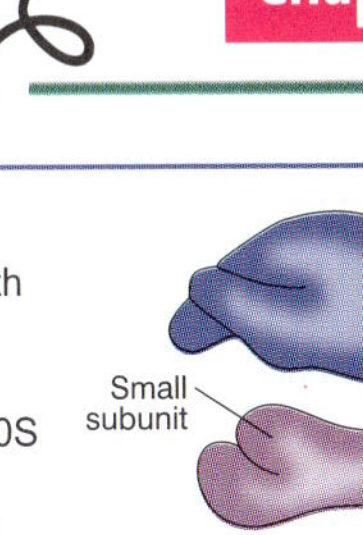

Microbodies

- Membrane-bound minute vesicles present in both plant and animal cells containing various enzymes.
- e.g. **peroxisomes** & **glyoxysomes**.

Nucleus

- Possesses a double membrane with pores and its outer nuclear membrane.
- Interphase nucleus has highly extended and elaborate nucleoprotein fibres called chromatin, nuclear matrix and nucleoli.
- Controls the hereditary characters of an organism.
- **Chromosomes** are condensed form of DNA associated with protein.
- Chromosomes can be classified as **metacentric, sub metacentric, acrocentric** and **telocentric** depending on the location of centromere.

Nucleoplasm (nuclear matrix)
Nuclear pore
Nuclear membrane
Nucleolus (site of RNA synthesis)

Plastids

- These are double membrane-bound structures and semi-autonomous organelles found in plants.
- Based on pigments, they are of three types
  (a) **Chromoplasts** (carotenoids)
  (b) **Leucoplasts** (colourless)
  (c) **Chloroplasts** (chlorophylls)

Lysosomes

Also known as **suicidal bags of the cell**; single membrane-bound structures, containing hydrolytic enzymes in them.

Cell Wall

- Present in plant (cellulose, hemicellulose, pectins and proteins) and fungal cells (chitin) in eukaryotes. It consists of three layers

Middle lamella (calcium pectate), **primary cell wall, secondary cell wall**

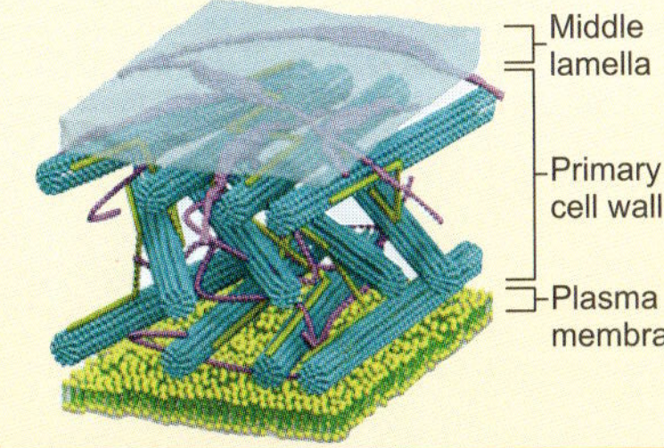
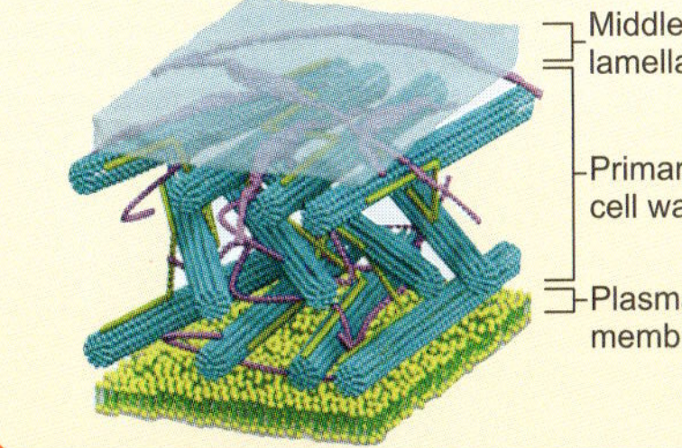
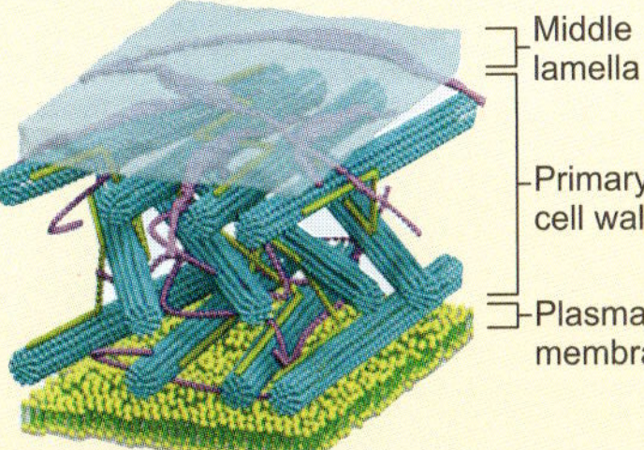

Cilia and Flagella

- These are hair-like outgrowths of the cell membrane with the 9 + 2 pattern organisation.
- **Cilia** are small structures that cause the movement of either the cell or the surrounding fluid.
- **Flagella** are comparatively longer and are responsible for cell movement.

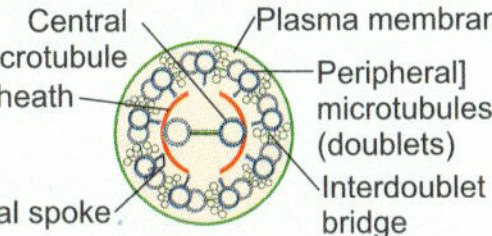

Cell Membrane

- The membrane is a fluid mosaic of phospholipids (arranged in bilayer) and proteins (integral and peripheral).
- Model of structure given by **Singer** and **Nicolson-Fluid mosaic model**.
- It allows only selected substances into the cell, maintains cell shape, plays role in cell-cell recognition, and controls and regulates reaction sequences.

Peripheral protein
Phospholipid bilayer
Integral protein
Cholesterol

Centrosome and Centriole

- Centrosome contains two cylindrical, rod-shaped structures known as centrioles.
- Centrioles are oriented at right angles to each other.
- Centrioles form the basal body of cilia or flagella and spindle fibres that give rise to spindle apparatus during cell division in animal cells.

Golgi Apparatus

- Discovered by **Camillo Golgi.**
- Composed of flattened vesicles in stacks (cisternae) which receive protein from ER.
- Golgi packages materials, to be delivered either to the intracellular targets or secreted outside the cell.
- It is involved in the formation of lysosomes vesicles, glycoproteins and glycolipids.

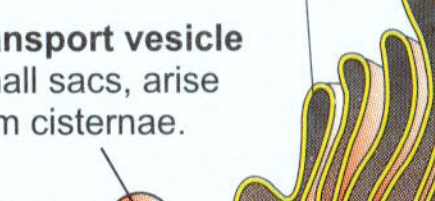
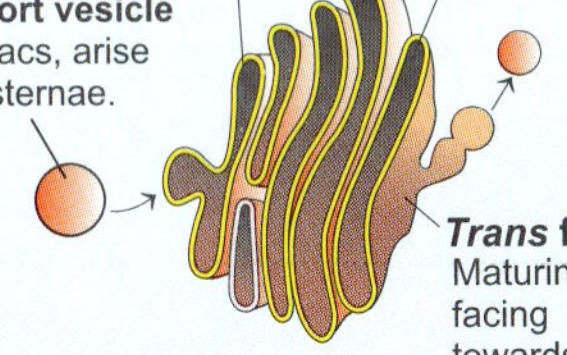

Mitochondria

- Double membrane-bound structure with the outer membrane and the inner membrane having specific enzymes.
- It is the site of aerobic respiration. So, they are termed as '**powerhouse of the cell**'.
- The inner membrane is folded into projections called **cristae**, which contain numerous tiny particles called **oxysomes** or **F_1-particles.**

Vacuoles

- Single membrane (tonoplast) bound structures found in the cytoplasm.
- It contains water, sap, excretory products, and other products that are not useful for the cell.
- Presence of **contractile vacuole** in *Amoeba* (osmoregulation) and **food vacuole** in many protists (for engulfing food).

Test 1

Syllabus
- Chemical Constituents of Living Cells
- Biomolecules

NCERT Page 104 to 109

For deeper insight, **Scan the QR Code**

Chapter 09

Biomolecules

All the carbon compounds that we get from living tissues can be called '**biomolecules**'. However, living organisms have also got inorganic elements and compounds in them.

Chemical Composition of Living Tissues

- Living tissue + Trichloroacetic acid → Grinding → Thick slurry → Filter through cloth

Filtrate (Acid-soluble pool) → Biomicromolecules (Molecular weight < 1000 Da)
- **Amino acids**
- **Sugars**
- **Nucleotides**

Retentate (Acid-insoluble pool) → Biomacromolecules (Molecular weight > 10,000 Da)
- ***Lipids**
- **Proteins**
- **Nucleic acids**
- **Polysaccharides**

*Lipids are not strictly biomacromolecules (molecular weight does not exceed 800 Da).

Metabolites

Primary Metabolites	Secondary Metabolites
Identifiable functions	Not involved in primary metabolism
Roles in physiological processes	No direct function in growth and development
e.g. sugars, amino acids, lipids, etc.	Human welfare: rubber, drugs, spices and pigments; Ecological importance-flavonoids, antibiotics, etc.

Some Important Secondary Metabolites

Pigments	Carotenoids, anthocyanins, etc.
Alkaloids	Morphine, codeine, etc.
Terpenoids	Monoterpenes, diterpenes, etc.
Essential oils	Lemon grass oil, etc.
Toxins	Abrin, ricin
Lectins	Concanavalin-A
Drugs	Vinblastin, curcumin, etc.
Polymeric substances	Rubber, gums, cellulose.

Amino Acids

- Organic compounds containing an amino group and an acidic group as substituents on same carbon, i.e., α-carbon, (α-amino acids).
- Substituted methane; four substituent groups occupying four valency positions.
- Chemical and physical properties of amino acids are essentially of amino, carboxyl and *R*-functional groups.
- 20 types of amino acids are used for protein synthesis.

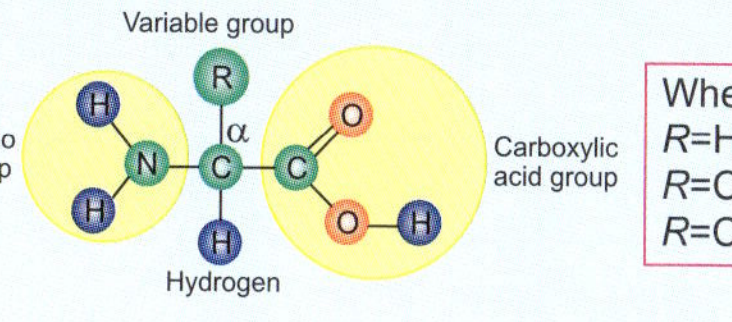

When,
R=H → Glycine
R=CH_3 → Alanine
R=CH_2–OH → Serine

Zwitter Ion

In neutral solution, the amino acid molecule exists as a dipolar **Zwitter ion** (containing both positive and negative ionic group).

$$H_3\overset{+}{N}-\underset{}{\overset{R}{\overset{|}{CH}}}-COOH \rightleftharpoons H_3\overset{+}{N}-\overset{R}{\overset{|}{CH}}-COO^- \rightleftharpoons H_2N-\overset{R}{\overset{|}{CH}}-COO^-$$

(At acidic pH) (Zwitter ionic form) (At alkaline pH)

- As alpha-carbon atom is asymmetric, therefore, all other naturally occurring alpha-amino acids are optically active, except glycine.
- These exist both in 'D' (right-sided) and 'L' (left-sided) forms. L- configuration is the most naturally occurring amino acid.
- L-amino acids are represented by writing the-NH_2 group on the left-hand side.
- Based on the type of side chain, amino acids can be
  - **Aromatic** (e.g. tryptophan, phenylalanine, tyrosine)
  - **Acidic** (e.g. aspartic acid, glutamic acid)
  - **Basic** (e.g. arginine, lysine)
  - **Neutral** (e.g. valine)
- Based on their essentiality in the body
  - **Essential** e.g. lysine, leucine, isoleucine, tryptophan, etc.
  - **Non-essential** e.g. glycine, alanine, serine, proline.

Characteristic Features of Amino Acids

- Amino acids are generally colourless, crystalline solids.
- These are water-soluble and have high boiling and melting point.
- These behave like salts rather than simple amines or carboxylic acids. This behaviour is due to the presence of both basic (amino group) and acidic (carboxyl group) groups in the same molecule.

Elemental Analysis of Living Tissues

- Elemental analysis gives elemental composition of living tissues in the form of hydrogen, oxygen, chlorine, carbon, etc.
- Living tissue — weigh → Wet weight; — dry and weigh (All water evaporates) → Dry weight
- Dried living tissue — Burn (All carbon compounds oxidise to CO, and water vapour) → '**Ash**' (contains only inorganic elements)
- C, H, O, N and S are more in any living organisms than in earth's crust.
- Si, Ca and Na are present in earth's crust in abundance compared to that of living tissue.
- Oxygen is the most abundant element in living organism.
- Analytical technique gives an idea about the molecular formula and the probable structure of the compound.
- Water is the most abundant chemical in living organisms.

Comparison of Elements Present in Non-living and Living Matter*

Elements	% Weight of (Earth's Crust)	% Weight of (Human Body)
Hydrogen (H)	0.14	0.5
Carbon (C)	0.03	18.5
Oxygen (O)	46.6	65.0
Nitrogen (N)	Very little	3.3
Sulphur (S)	0.03	0.3
Sodium (Na)	2.8	0.2
Calcium (Ca)	3.6	1.5
Magnesium (Mg)	2.1	0.1
Silicon (Si)	27.7	Negligible

Test 2

Syllabus
- Structure and Function of Proteins, Carbohydrates and Lipids

NCERT Page 106, 109 to 112

For deeper insight, **Scan the QR Code**

Chapter 09

Carbohydrates

- Carbohydrates contains a group of naturally occurring carbonyl compounds (aldehydes or ketones) and several hydroxyl groups.
- They are represented by $(CH_2O)_n$.

Types of Carbohydrates

Reducing Sugar (with free aldehyde or keto group)
- **Monosaccharides** (one sugar molecule)
  - Triose
  - Tetrose
  - Pentose
  - Hexose
  - Heptose
- **Oligosaccharides** (2-9 monosaccharides)
  - Disaccharide (Sucrose, maltose, lactose)
  - Raffinose

Non-Reducing Sugar (do not have free aldehyde or keto group)
- **Polysaccharide** (10 or more sugar molecules)
  - **Homopolysaccharide** (Starch, glycogen)
  - **Heteropolysaccharide** (Heparin)

Polysaccharides

Long chain polymers of monosaccharides (sugars) bound with glycosidic bonds.

(i) **Starch** (polymer of glucose; occurs in 2 forms-amylose (linear) and amylopectin (branched); forms helical secondary structure; can hold I_2 to give blue-black colour; storage polysaccharide in plants).

(ii) **Cellulose** (homopolymer of glucose; no complex helices).

(iii) **Glycogen** (branched homopolymer; storage polysaccharide in animals).

(iv) **Inulin** (polymer of fructose).

(v) **Chitin** (homopolymer of N-acetyl glucosamine; exoskeleton of arthropods).

CH_2OH, O, OH, HO, OH, OH

$C_6H_{12}O_6$ (Glucose)

$HOCH_2$, O, OH, OH, OH

$C_5H_{10}O_5$ (Ribose)

Importance of Carbohydrates
- Forms a large portion of our food.
- Honey as an instant source of energy.
- Starch and glycogen as storage molecules in plants and animals, respectively.
- Cell wall of plants and bacteria is made from cellulose and peptidoglycan, respectively. They provide various raw materials for many important industries like paper, textiles, lacquers and breweries.

Proteins

- Heteropolymers of amino acids and are polypeptides linked by peptide bond.

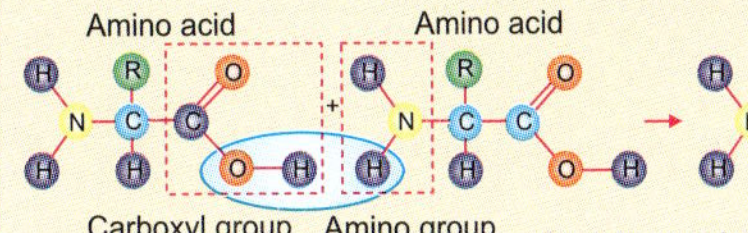

Protein synthesis

- **Functions** As intercellular ground substance (collagen), as enzyme (trypsin), as hormone (insulin), to fight infections (antibodies), as sensory receptors, and to enable glucose transport in cell (GLUT-4).
- Most abundant protein in animal world is collagen, while most abundant protein in the biosphere is RuBisCO.

Structure of Proteins

Primary Structure of Protein
- Linear sequence of amino acids.
- Protein is imagined as a line; left end-first (N-terminal) amino acid; right end-last (C-terminal) amino acid.

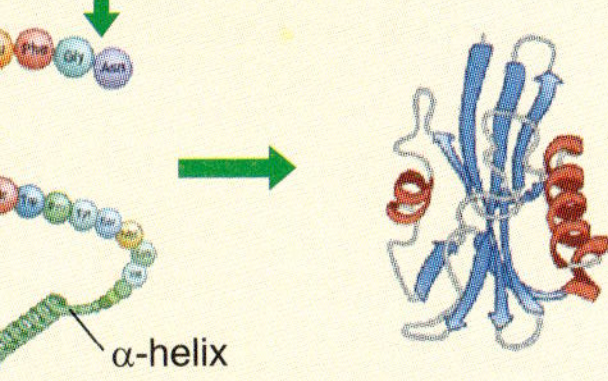

Secondary Structure of Protein
- Folding of polypeptide chains, e.g. keratin.

Tertiary Structure of Protein
- 3-D ball like structure, e.g. myoglobin.

Quarternary Structure of Protein
- e.g. haemoglobin (2α and 2β subunits)

Types of Proteins
- **Simple**
  - Fibrous (Collagen, Elastin, Keratin)
  - Globular (RuBisCO, Albumin, Globulin, Histone protein)
- **Conjugated** (Nucleoproteins, Glycoproteins, Lipoproteins)
- **Derived**
  - Primary (Fibrin, Fibrinogen)
  - Secondary (Proteoses, Peptones Polypeptides)

Denaturation of Proteins
- Proteins can lose their biological activity. Various changes in the surroundings of a protein such as pH, temperature, presence of salts or certain chemical agents can disrupt the complex 3-D structure of the proteins.
- Due to physical and chemical changes, the H-bonds are disturbed.
- During the denaturation of proteins, the secondary and tertiary structures get destroyed and only the primary structure is retained.

Lipids

- Generally not soluble in water.
- They could be simple fatty acids; carboxyl group attached to an *R* group forms fatty acids; *R* can be ethyl $(-C_2H_5)$, or methyl (CH_3) or higher number of $-CH_2$ groups (1 carbon to 19 carbons).

e.g. (i) Palmitic acid has 16 carbons (including carboxyl carbon) and no double bond.

(ii) Arachidonic acid contains 20 carbon atoms (which includes the carboxyl carbon) and 4 double bonds.

(iii) Linolenic acid (18 carbon atoms with 3 double bonds)

(iv) Oleic acid (18 carbon atoms with 1 double bond)

- **Fatty Acids** (insoluble long chain hydrocarbons with one carboxyl group).
- Saturated fatty acids (do not possess double bond), e.g., palmitic acid
- Unsaturated fatty acids (possess one or more double bonds), e.g., arachidonic acid; MUFA and PUFA.

Classification of Lipids
- **Simple**
  - **Fats and Oils** (ester of higher fatty acids with glycerol). Fatty acid + Glycerol (Trihydroxy propane)→ Simple lipids
  - **Waxes** (ester of higher fatty acids with alcohol), e.g. bee wax.
- **Compound**
  - **Phospholipids** (2 fatty acid attached to glycerol; found in cell membrane; e.g. lecithin).
  - **Glycolipids** (fatty acid, alcohol sphingosine and sugar).
- **Derived**
  - **Sterols** (alcohol steroids) e.g. cholesterol.

$CH_3—(CH_2)_{14}—COOH$

Fatty acid (Palmitic acid)

$CH_2—OH$
|
$CH—OH$
|
$CH_2—OH$

Glycerol

Test 3

Syllabus
- Structure and Function of Nucleic Acids
- Enzymes-Types, Properties, Enzyme Action, Classification and Nomenclature of Enzymes

NCERT Page 111 to 118

For deeper insight, **Scan the QR Code**

Chapter 09

Nucleic Acids

- Heteropolymers of nucleotides that consists of a monosaccharide (sugar), phosphate group and nitrogenous base.
- Can be DNA (with 2-deoxyribose sugar) or RNA (with ribose sugar).
- Pairing of nitrogenous bases in nucleic acids:
A = T (DNA)/ U (RNA); G ≡ C

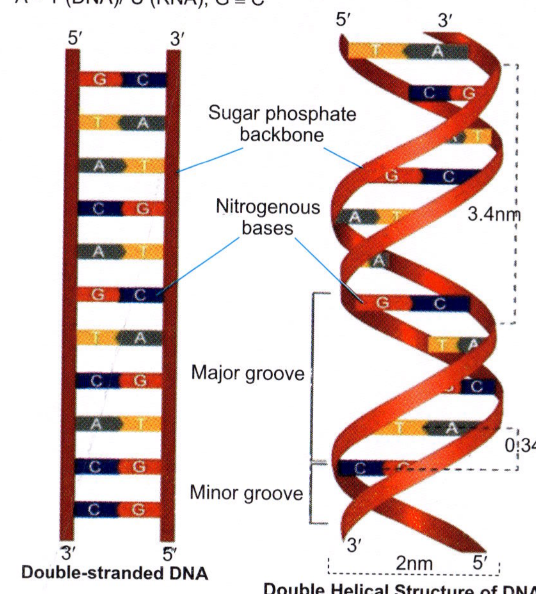

Double-stranded DNA

Double Helical Structure of DNA

Structural Components of Nucleic Acids

- **Nucleoside** Nitrogenous base + Sugar (e.g. adenosine, guanosine).
- **Nucleotide** Nitrogenous base + Sugar + Phosphate group (e.g. adenylic acid, guanylic acid, thymidylic acid).
- **Sugars** Sweet and water-soluble carbohydrates and are formed of C, H and O in the ratio of 1 : 2 : 1.

Phosphate

Base

Sugar

Deoxyribose Nucleotide

- **Nitrogenous Bases:** Carbon compounds with heterocyclic rings.

Purines
- **Adenine** (A)
- **Guanine** (G)

Pyrimidine
- **Cytosine** (C)
- **Thymine** (T; DNA)
- **Uracil** (U; RNA)

Enzyme

- Biocatalyst influencing speed of biochemical reactions without taking part in it.
- Almost all enzymes are proteins (e.g. ribozyme is a RNA molecule).

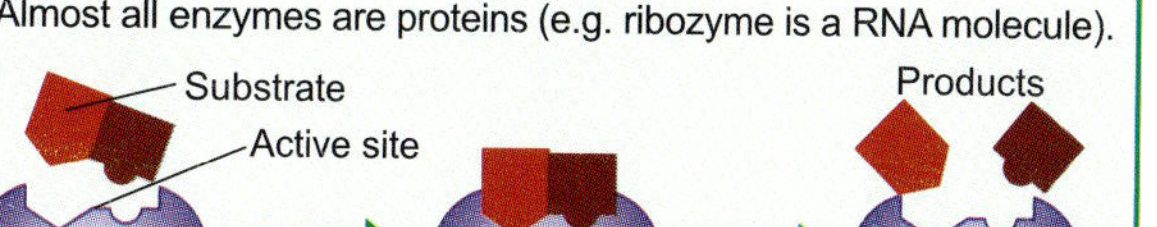

Lock and Key Model of Enzyme

- It gets damaged at high temperature (**exception**-enzymes isolated from thermophiles).
- Lowers the activation energy of reactions.

Coenzyme
Substrate

Apoenzyme (protein portion; inactive) + **Cofactor** (non-protein portion; activator) → **Holoenzyme** (whole enzyme; active)

Structure of an Active Enzyme

- **Cofactors** may be **Prosthetic groups** [organic; tightly bound to apoenzyme, e.g. haem group], **co-enzymes** [organic; transient association with apoenzyme, e.g. vitamins], **metal ions** [Zn^{2+} in carboxypeptidase].

Enzymes and Activation Energy

- It is the minimum amount of energy required to initiate a chemical reaction.
- Transition state: high-energy unstable state.
- If 'P' is at lower energy level than 'S' - Reaction is exothermic.
- If 'S' is at lower energy level than 'P' - Reaction is endothermic.

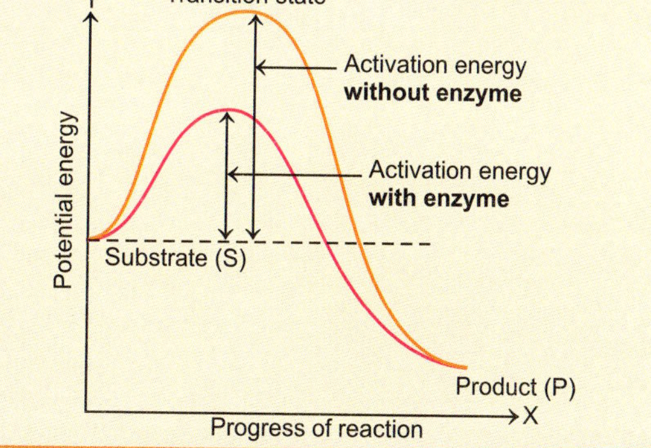

Classification and Nomenclature of Enzymes

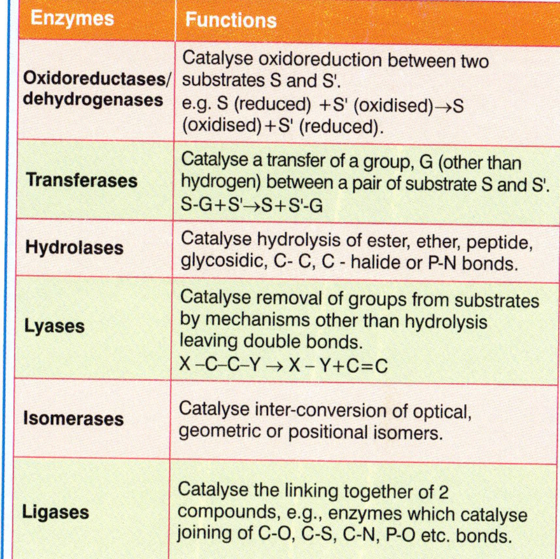

Enzymes	Functions
Oxidoreductases/ dehydrogenases	Catalyse oxidoreduction between two substrates S and S'. e.g. S (reduced) + S' (oxidised) → S (oxidised) + S' (reduced).
Transferases	Catalyse a transfer of a group, G (other than hydrogen) between a pair of substrate S and S'. S-G+S' → S+S'-G
Hydrolases	Catalyse hydrolysis of ester, ether, peptide, glycosidic, C- C, C - halide or P-N bonds.
Lyases	Catalyse removal of groups from substrates by mechanisms other than hydrolysis leaving double bonds. X –C–C–Y → X – Y+C=C
Isomerases	Catalyse inter-conversion of optical, geometric or positional isomers.
Ligases	Catalyse the linking together of 2 compounds, e.g., enzymes which catalyse joining of C-O, C-S, C-N, P-O etc. bonds.

Types of Enzyme Inhibition

(a) **Competitive Inhibition** (e.g. inhibition of succinic dehydrogenase by malonate) Inhibitor binds at active site; enzyme action declines; K_m Increases, V_{max} unaffected.

(b) **Non-competitive Inhibition** Inhibitor binds at sites other than active sites; K_m unaffected, V_{max} decreases.

(c) **Allosteric Modulation (Feedback inhibition)** Inhibitor binds to enzyme at specific site other than active site, but change the structure of active site to affect substrate binding.

Factors Affecting Enzymatic Action

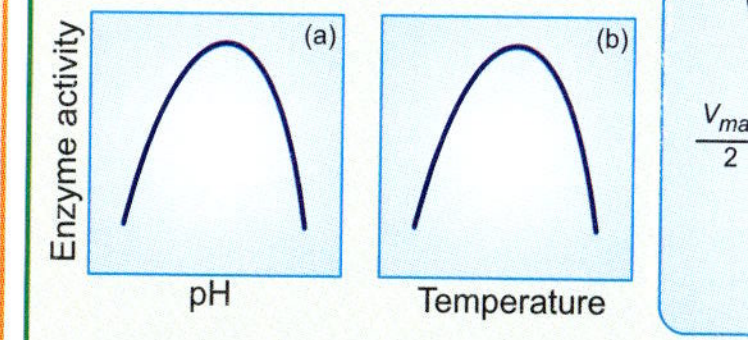

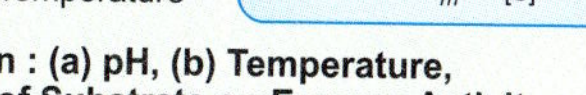

Effect of Change in : (a) pH, (b) Temperature, (c) Concentration of Substrate on Enzyme Activity

Test 1

Syllabus
- Cell Division: Cell Cycle
- Mitosis
- Significance of Mitosis

NCERT Page 120 to 125

For deeper insight, **Scan the QR Code**

Cell Cycle: Overview

- It is sequence of events by which a cell duplicates its genome, synthesises the other constituents of the cell and eventually divides into two daughter cells.
- Cell growth results in disturbing the ratio between the nucleus and cytoplasm. It therefore becomes essential for the cell to divide to restore the nucleo-cytoplasmic ratio.
- Cell growth (in terms of cytoplasmic increase) is a continuous process.
- Duration of cell cycle can vary from organism to organism and also from cell type to cell type.
- e.g., yeast's cell cycle duration -90 minutes, human's cell cycle duration - 24 hours [but cell division proper (M-phase) lasts for only about an hour].

Phases of Cell Cycle

- **Interphase**: Time during which cell prepares for division by undergoing both cell growth and DNA replication.
  - **G_1-phase** (Gap 1)
  - **S-phase** (Synthetic)
  - **G_2-phase** (Gap 2)
- **M-phase**: (Mitotic phase) Period of actual division

Generation Time The period between two cell divisions in a cell.

M-phase (1 hr); Karyokinesis; Prophase; Metaphase; Anaphase; Telophase; Cytokinesis; G_0-phase; Cell in G_0-phase; Cell repeating cell cycle; **G_2-phase** RNA and protein synthesis (4 hrs); **S-phase** DNA duplicates; replication of chromosomes (8 hrs); **G_1-phase** protein synthesis; growth of nucleus (11 hrs); Interphase

Cell Cycle in Humans (24 hrs)

Interphase

$G_1 \rightarrow$ Interval between mitosis and initiation of DNA replication.
- Cell is metabolically active and continuously grows, but does not replicate its DNA.
- Most of the cell organelles duplicate.

$G_0 \rightarrow$ Some cells do not divide further, exit G_1 phase to enter an inactive stage called **quiescent stage** (G_0) of the cell cycle. Cells in this stage remain **metabolically active**, but no longer proliferate unless called on to do so, depending on the requirement of the organism, e.g. heart cells.

$S \rightarrow$ This phase marks the phase of DNA replication and chromosome duplication.
- Amount of DNA per cell doubles, but there is no increase in initial chromosome number.
- In animal cells, **centriole duplicates** in cytoplasm.
- DNA replication begins in nucleus.

$G_2 \rightarrow$ Proteins are synthesised in preparation for mitosis, while cell growth continues.

G_2-checkpoint controlled by completion of DNA replication, DNA damage/ mutation, cell size, etc.

Metaphase checkpoint controlled by spindle fibre or microtubule attachment to chromosomes.

M; G_2; G_1; S DNA Synthesis; G_0

G_1-checkpoint controlled by cell size, growth factors and cell environment, etc.

Cell Cycle Checkpoints

Mitosis (Equational Division)

Results in two diploid daughter cells with identical genetic composition.

Karyokinesis (Nuclear Division)

Prophase
- Chromosomal material **condenses**; centriole moves towards opposite poles; ER, nuclear membrane, Golgi complex **disappears**.

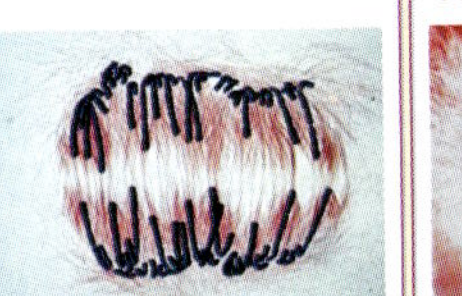

Metaphase
- **Condensation** of chromosomal material **completes**.
- Chromosomes get arranged at **metaphase plate**.

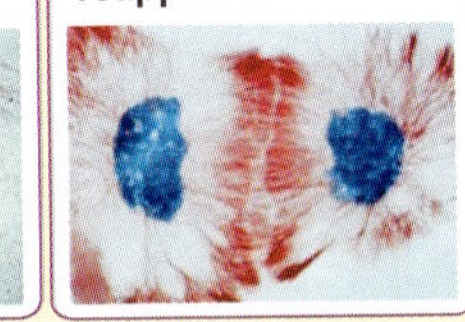

Anaphase
- **Splitting** of chromosome into two sister chromatids and they starts to move towards opposite poles.

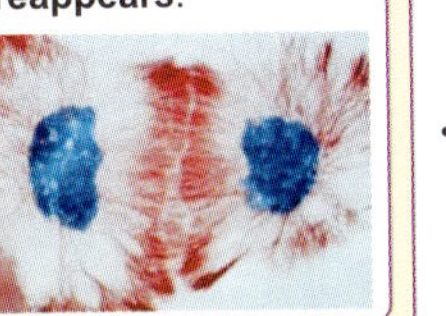

Telophase
- Chromosomes loses its identity as discrete unit.
- Nuclear membrane, nucleolus, ER and Golgi complex **reappears**.

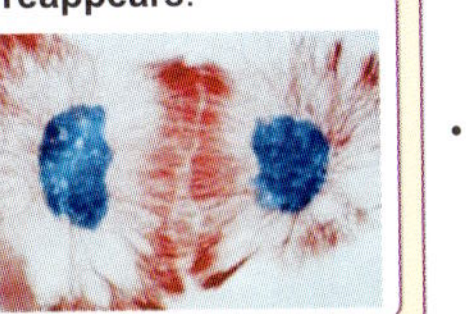

Cytokinesis (Cytoplasmic Division)

- It is division of cytoplasm at the end of which cell division gets completed.
- In **animal cells**, it is achieved by the appearance of a **furrow** in the plasma membrane.
- In **plant cells**, cytokinesis is achieved by wall formation, which starts in the centre of the cell and grows outward to meet the existing lateral wall.
- The formation of new cell wall begins with the formation of a simple precursor, called the **cell plate** that represents the middle lamella between the wall of two adjacent cells.
- When karyokinesis is not followed by cytokinesis, a multinucleate condition arises leading to formation of **syncytium**, e.g. liquid endosperm in coconut.

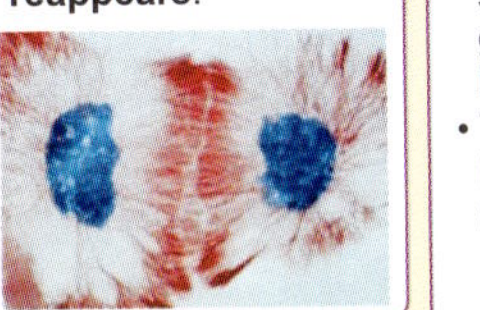
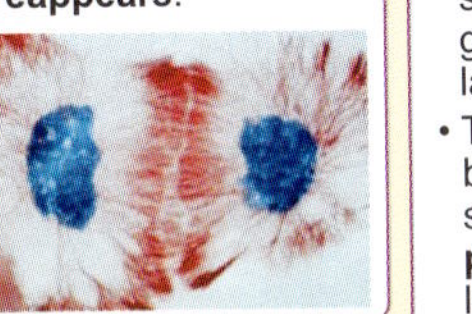
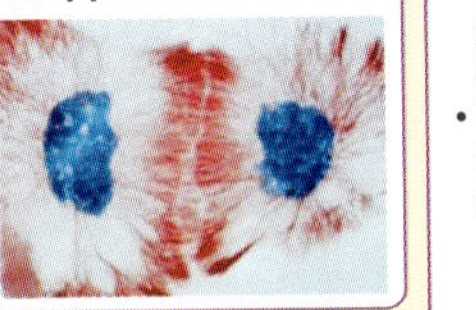

In Animal Cell: By Deepening of **Cell Furrow**.

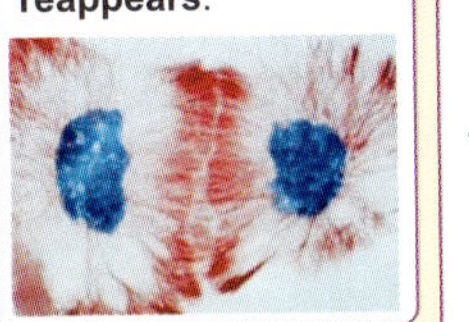
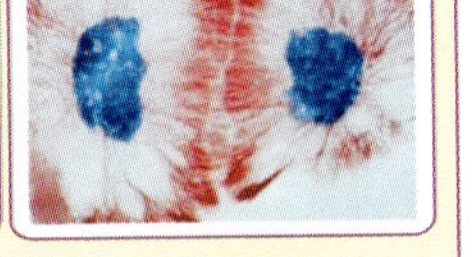

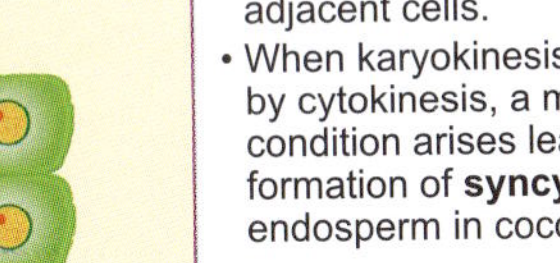
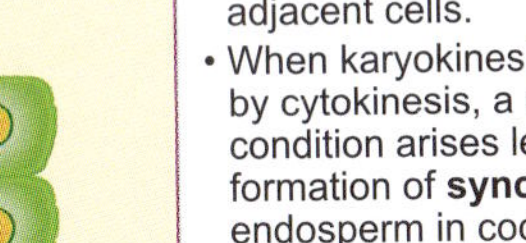

In Plant Cell: By Formation of **Cell Plate**.

Cytokinesis

Significance of Mitosis

- Mitosis usually results in identical genetic complement in daughter cells.
- Growth of multicellular organisms.
- Cell repair.
- Restoration of nucleo-cytoplasmic ratio.
- Mitotic division in apical and lateral meristem results in continuous growth of plants throughout their life.
- In some lower plants and in some social insects, haploid cells also divide by mitosis.

Test 2

Syllabus
- Meiosis
- Significance of Meiosis

NCERT Page 125 to 128

For deeper insight, **Scan the QR Code**

Chapter 10

Meiosis

- Specialised kind of cell division that reduces the chromosome number by half; results in the production of haploid daughter cells.
- Meiosis ensures the production of haploid phase in the life cycle of sexually reproducing organisms, whereas fertilisation restores the diploid phase.
- Meiosis involves two sequential cycles of nuclear division, i.e. meiosis-I and meiosis-II, but only single cycle of DNA replication. Meiosis-I is initiated after parental chromosomes have replicated.
- Four haploid cells are formed at the end of meiosis-II.

Significance of Meiosis

- Responsible for the formation of sex cells or gametes that are responsible for sexual reproduction.
- Activates the genetic information for the development of sex cells and deactivates the sporophytic information.
- Maintains the constant number of chromosomes by halving the same. This is important because the chromosome number doubles after fertilisation.
- Independent assortment of maternal and paternal chromosomes takes place; chromosomes and the traits controlled by them are reshuffled.
- Genetic mutation occurs due to irregularities in cell division by meiosis. The mutations that are beneficial are carried on by natural selection.
- Crossing over produces a new combination of traits and variations that are favourable for survival.

Meiosis-I (Reductional Phase)

Prophase I
- Typically **longer** and more complex when compared to prophase of mitosis.

Metaphase I
- Bivalent chromosomes **align** on the **equatorial plate** (metaphasic plate).
- Microtubules from the opposite poles of the spindle attach to the kinetochore of homologous chromosomes.

Anaphase I
- **Homologous chromosomes separate**, while **sister chromatids** remain **associated** at their centromere.

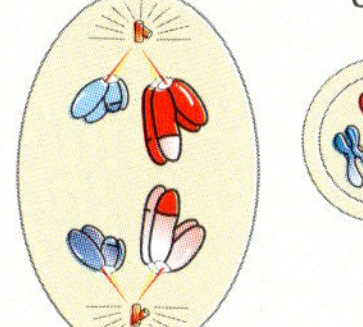

Telophase I
- The nuclear membrane and nucleolus **reappear**.
- **Cytokinesis** follows and this leads to formation of haploid **dyad** of cells.

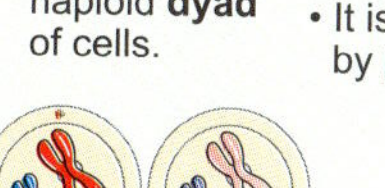

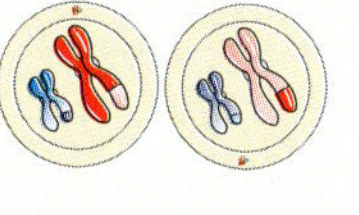

Interkinesis
- It is the stage **between two meiotic divisions**.
- It is generally short-lived.
- **No DNA replication.**
- It is followed by prophase II.

Leptotene
- Chromosomes become gradually visible under the light microscope.
- The **compaction** of chromosomes continues throughout leptotene.

Zygotene
- Homologous chromosomes pair by process called **synapsis**.
- Synapsis is accompanied by formation of complex structure called **synaptonemal complex**.
- The complex formed by a pair of synapsed homologous chromosomes is called **bivalent** or a **tetrad.**
- Leptotene and zygotene are relatively short-lived compared to the pachytene.

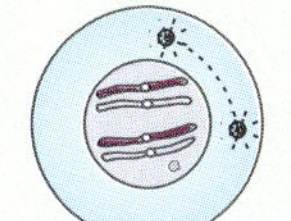

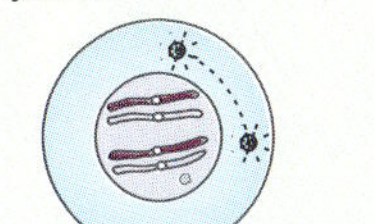

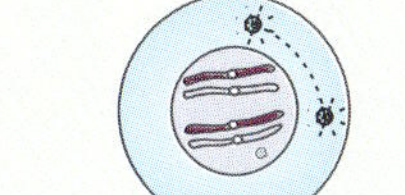

Pachytene
- Four chromatids of each bivalent become distinct and **clearly appears as tetrads**; characterised by appearance of **recombination nodule**, the sites at which crossing over occurs between non-sister chromatids of the homologous chromosomes.
- **Crossing over** is exchange of genetic material between two homologous chromosomes. It is an enzyme-mediated process, enzyme involved is called **recombinase**.
- Crossing over leads to recombination of genetic material which is completed by the end of pachytene leaving chromosomes linked at the sites of crossing over.

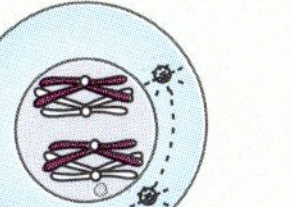

Diplotene
- Beginning of diplotene is recognised by the **dissolution of synaptonemal complex** and tendency of the recombined homologous chromosomes of the bivalents to separate from each other, except at the site of cross overs.
- This **X-shaped structures** (site of crossing over) are called **chiasmata**.
- In oocytes of some vertebrates, diplotene can last for months or years (dictyotene).

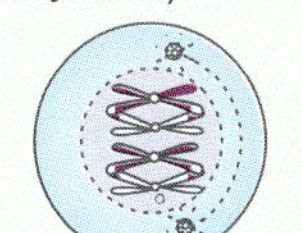

Diakinesis
- This is marked by **terminalisation of chiasmata.**
- Chromosomes are fully condensed and meiotic spindle is assembled to **prepare the homologous chromosomes for separation**. By the end of diakinesis, the nucleolus disappears and nuclear envelope also breaks down.
- Diakinesis represents transition to metaphase.

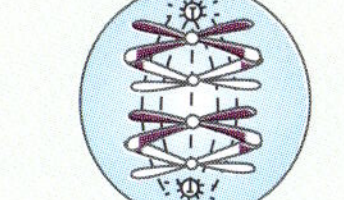

Meiosis-II (Equational Phase)

Prophase II
- Initiated immediately after cytokinesis.
- Nuclear membrane disappears by the end of prophase II.
- Chromosomes again become **compact**.

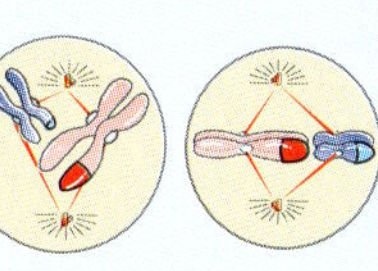

Metaphase II
- Chromosomes **align at the equator**.
- Microtubules from opposite poles of the spindle get attached to the kinetochore of sister chromatids.

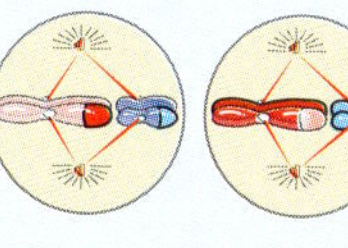

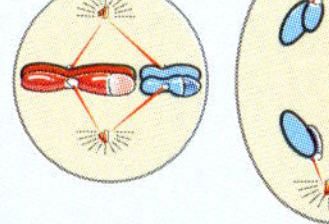

Anaphase II
- **Splitting of centromere** allowing chromosomes to move towards opposite poles of the cell by shortening of microtubules attached to the kinetochores.

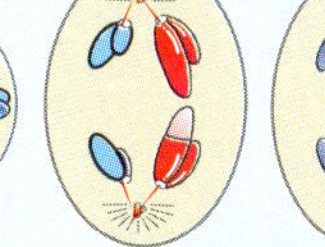

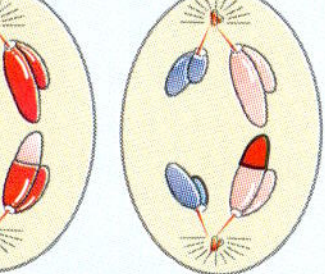

Telophase II
- Karyokinesis of meiosis ends with telophase II.
- Two groups of chromosomes once again get enclosed by a nuclear envelope.
- **Cytokinesis** follows; resulting in the formation of haploid **tetrad** of cells.

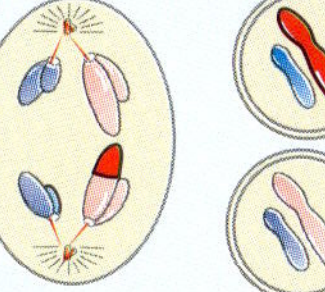

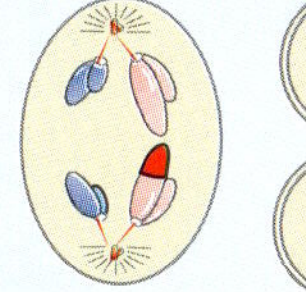

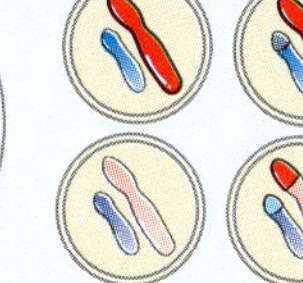

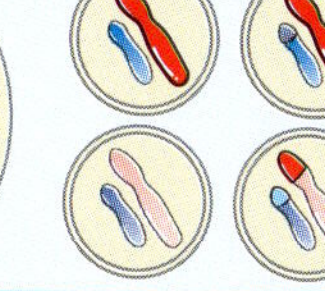

Test 1

Syllabus
- Photosynthesis as a Means of Autotrophic Nutrition
- Site of Photosynthesis
- Pigments Involved in Photosynthesis

NCERT Page 133 to 138

For deeper insight, **Scan the QR Code**

Photosynthesis

- It is a physico-chemical process by which green plants use light energy to synthesise organic compounds.
- Photosynthesis is important for two reasons
  - It is the primary source of food for all living organisms.
  - It is the only process responsible for the release of oxygen into the atmosphere by green plants.

$$6\ CO_2 + 12H_2O \xrightarrow{\text{Light}} C_6H_{12}O_6 + 6H_2O + 6O_2$$

- Experiment for starch formation on variegated leaf or a leaf that was partially covered with black paper, and exposed to light showed that photosynthesis occurred only in green part of leaves in the presence of light.
- Experiment where a part of leaf is enclosed in a test-tube with some KOH soaked cotton (which absorbs CO_2), while the other half is exposed to air followed by set-up kept in light, proved that CO_2 is needed for photosynthesis.

Early Experiments

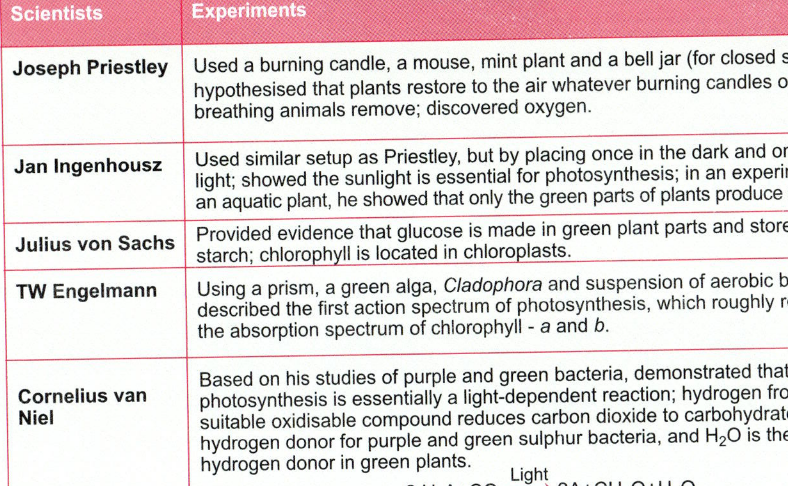

Scientists	Experiments
Joseph Priestley	Used a burning candle, a mouse, mint plant and a bell jar (for closed space); hypothesised that plants restore to the air whatever burning candles or breathing animals remove; discovered oxygen.
Jan Ingenhousz	Used similar setup as Priestley, but by placing once in the dark and once in the light; showed the sunlight is essential for photosynthesis; in an experiment with an aquatic plant, he showed that only the green parts of plants produce oxygen.
Julius von Sachs	Provided evidence that glucose is made in green plant parts and stored as starch; chlorophyll is located in chloroplasts.
TW Engelmann	Using a prism, a green alga, *Cladophora* and suspension of aerobic bacteria, described the first action spectrum of photosynthesis, which roughly resembled the absorption spectrum of chlorophyll - *a* and *b*.
Cornelius van Niel	Based on his studies of purple and green bacteria, demonstrated that photosynthesis is essentially a light-dependent reaction; hydrogen from a suitable oxidisable compound reduces carbon dioxide to carbohydrates; H_2S is hydrogen donor for purple and green sulphur bacteria, and H_2O is the hydrogen donor in green plants. $2\ H_2A + CO_2 \xrightarrow{\text{Light}} 2A + CH_2O + H_2O$

Site of Photosynthesis

- Photosynthesis takes place in green parts of the plants, mainly in the mesophyll cells of the leaves, which have large number of chloroplasts.
- Usually, the chloroplasts align themselves along the walls of mesophyll cells to get optimum quantity of the incident light, e.g.
  - **Low light intensity** Chloroplasts align parallel to the walls of mesophyll cells.
  - **Higher light intensity** Chloroplasts align perpendicular to the walls to mesophyll cells.
- There is a clear division labour within the chloroplast.
- The membrane system **(thylakoid membrane)** is responsible for trapping light energy during the photochemical phase (light reaction) and also for the synthesis of ATP and NADPH. The pigments are distributed in the membrane system.
- **Stroma** has enzymes for the reduction of carbon dioxide into carbohydrates and formation of starch (dark reaction or biosynthetic phase).

Stroma lamella (connects grana)
Thylakoid (site of light reaction)
Stroma (site of dark reaction)
Granum (stacks of thylakoid)
Inner membrane
Inter-membrane space
Outer membrane

A Diagrammatic Representation of Chloroplast

Pigments Involved in Photosynthesis

- Leaf-pigments of any green plant can be separated through paper chromatography.
- There are four pigments: chlorophyll-*a*, chlorophyll-*b*, carotene and xanthophyll (carotenoids).
  - **Chlorophyll-*a*** Bright green or bluish green.
  - **Chlorophyll-*b*** Yellowish green.
  - **Xanthophyll** Yellow.
  - **Carotene** Yellow-orange or reddish.
- These pigments have the ability to absorb light at specific wavelengths.
- **Accessory Pigments** Chlorophyll-*b*, carotenoids (carotenes and xanthophylls).

Pigments	Light Absorbed
Chlorophyll-*a* and *b*	Maximun absorbance in blue (400-500 nm) and red (650-680 nm) region.
Carotenoids	400-500 nm; maximum absorbance in blue-green (450 nm) region.

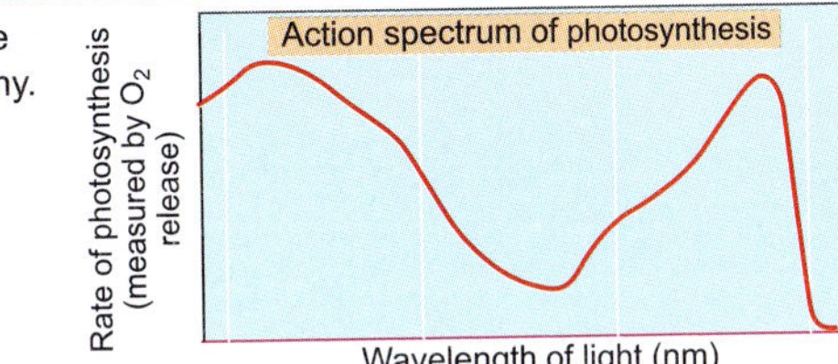

- Relative rates of photosynthesis at different wavelengths of light.
- Maximum photosynthesis in blue-violet and red part of visible light spectrum.

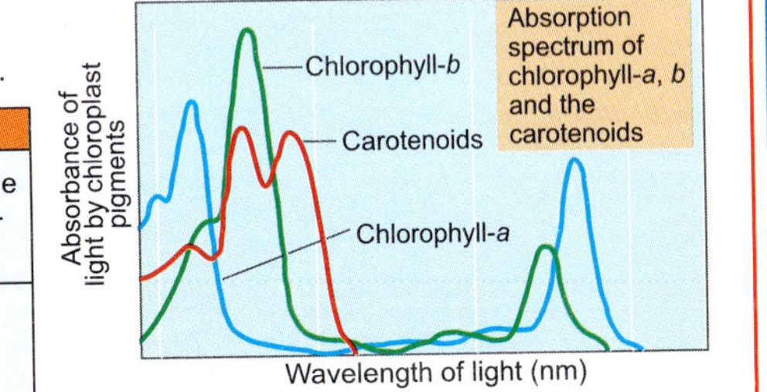

- Amount of different wavelengths of light absorbed by photosynthetic pigments.

Red Drop and The Emerson Enhancement Effect

- Lights of wavelength beyond 700nm proves to be useless for photosynthesis. This results in a huge drop of inefficiency leading to **red drop effect**.
- **Emerson** described the phenomenon where the rate of photosynthesis increases, when low levels of red light (around 680 nm) and far red light (around 700 nm) are combined, and there is greater enhancement of photosynthetic rate.

Test 2

Syllabus
- Photochemical and Biosynthetic Phases of Photosynthesis
- Cyclic and Non-cyclic Phosphorylation
- Chemiosmotic Hypothesis

NCERT Page 138 to 145

For deeper insight, **Scan the QR Code**

Light Harvesting Complex

- Light reaction or the photochemical phase includes:
  - Light absorption;
  - Water splitting;
  - Oxygen release;
  - ATP and NADPH formation
- Several protein complexes are involved in the process.
- The pigments are organised into two photosystems.
  - PS-I (with absorption maxima at 700 nm) and PS-II (with absorption maxima at 680 nm).
- Each photosystem has a **reaction centre** (chlorophyll-*a*) and **antennae** (other pigments except chlorophyll-*a*).

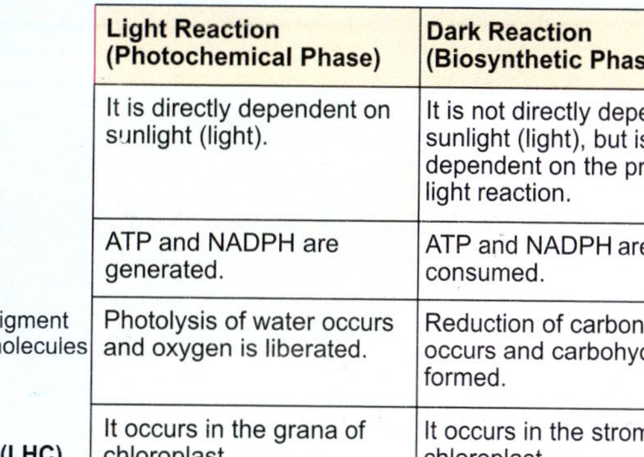

Light Harvesting Complex (LHC)

Light Reaction (Photochemical Phase)	Dark Reaction (Biosynthetic Phase)
It is directly dependent on sunlight (light).	It is not directly dependent on sunlight (light), but is dependent on the products of light reaction.
ATP and NADPH are generated.	ATP and NADPH are consumed.
Photolysis of water occurs and oxygen is liberated.	Reduction of carbon dioxide occurs and carbohydrate is formed.
It occurs in the grana of chloroplast.	It occurs in the stroma of chloroplast.

Dark Reaction

- Involves carbon reduction and fixation cycle (Calvin/C_3 cycle)

- Primary acceptor of CO_2-**RuBP**
- First stable product-**PGA** (C_3 acid).

3x CO_2
3xRuBP
1 Carboxylation (Fixation of carbon by carboxylation of RuBP)
6x3–PGA
6ATP → 6ADP +6Pi
6x1, 3-BPG
6NADPH → 6NADP⁺
2 Reduction (Reduction of fixed carbon to begin the synthesis of triose phosphate)
6xG3P
1xG3P
Glucose and other sugars
5xG3P
3 Regeneration (Synthesis of starting compound, RuBP)
3ATP → 3ADP+3Pi

Overall Reaction for 6 turns : $6RuBP+6CO_2+18ATP+12NADPH+H^+ \rightarrow 6RuBP + C_6H_{12}O_6 + 18ADP + 18Pi + 12NADP^+$

Light Reaction

Non-cyclic Phosphorylation

Reduction / Oxidation
Sun, 2 photon, Reaction centre, P 680, Antenna molecule, H_2O, 2e⁻, 1/2 O_2, $2H^+$
Primary acceptor, e⁻, PQ, 2e⁻, Cytochrome complex, ADP +Pi → ATP, 2e⁻, PC
Sun, Primary acceptor, P 700, Reaction centre, Antenna molecule, Fd, NADP +2e⁻, 2NADPH, 2 photon

- Both PS-I and PS-II
- Photolysis of water
- Oxygen formation
- ATP synthesis occurs
- NADPH synthesis occurs
- Z - shape (Z - scheme)

Cyclic Phosphorylation

Reduction / Oxidation
Sun, 2 photon, Reaction centre, P 700, Antenna molecule, Primary acceptor, e⁻, Fd, 2e⁻, ADP+Pi → ATP, PQ, Cytochrome complex, 2e⁻, PC, ADP+Pi → ATP

- Only PS-I
- No photolysis of water
- No oxygen formation
- ATP synthesis occurs
- No NADPH synthesis
- Cyclic process

Chemiosmotic Hypothesis

- ATP synthesis is linked to development of a proton gradient across a membrane.
- Proton accumulation is towards the inside of the membrane (lumen).

The steps includes
- **Proton Gradient** Protons are pumped through special channels in the membrane from the inner to the outer compartment, creating a proton gradient.
- **Proton Diffusion** Protons diffuse down the gradient through a transport protein called **ATP synthase**.
- **ATP Synthesis** Use energy from the oxidation of organic compounds or light to synthesise ATP.

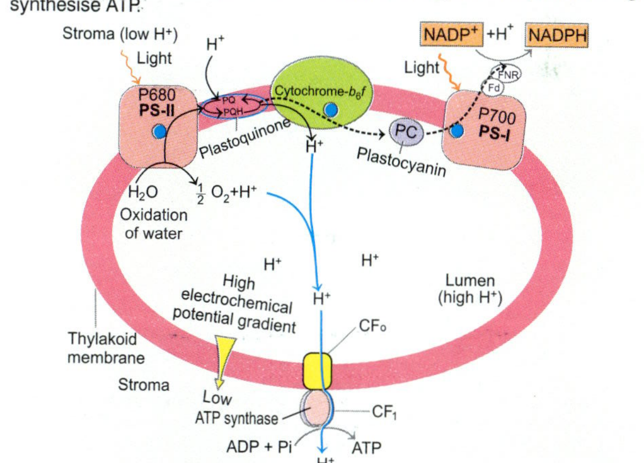

Splitting of Water

- **PS-II** continuously supplies electrons which becomes available by splitting of water.
- Water splitting complex is associated with PS-II, which itself is physically located on inner side of membrane of thylakoid.
- Water splits into H, [O] and electrons.

  $2H_2O \longrightarrow 4H^+ + O_2 + 4e^-$
- This creates oxygen, one of the net products of photosynthesis.

Test 3

Syllabus

- C_4-Pathway
- Photorespiration
- Factors Affecting Photosynthesis

NCERT Page 145 to 150

For deeper insight, **Scan the QR Code**

Chapter 11

C_4-pathway (Hatch-Slack Cycle)

- Seen in plants adapted to dry tropical regions, e.g. maize and *Sorghum*.
- Plant with C_4-pathway shows presence of special type of leaf anatomy, ability to tolerate higher temperatures, show response to high light intensities; lack photorespiration and have greater biomass productivity.
- In C_4 plants, leaves show Kranz anatomy, i.e. the particularly large cells around the vascular bundles, which may form several layers or 'wreath-like' arrangement and are called **bundle sheath cells**.
- Bundle sheath cells have a large number of chloroplasts, thick walls impervious to gaseous exchange and no intercellular spaces.
- This cyclic pathway is **Hatch** and **Slack pathway**.
- It is partly completed in mesophyll and partly in bundle sheath cell.
- C_4 plants with **Kranz anatomy** are more efficient than C_3 plants.

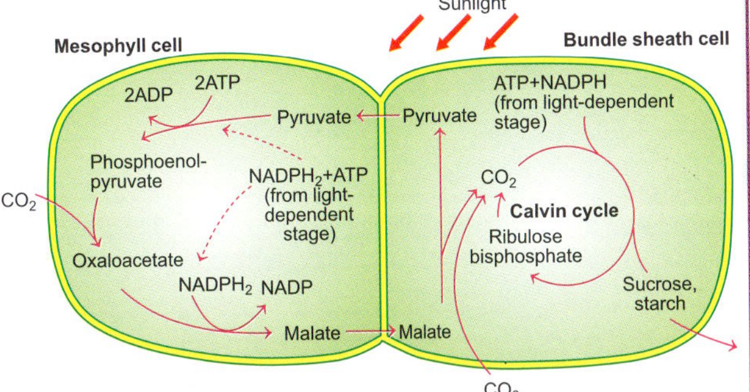

An Outline of the Photosynthetic Metabolism in C_4 Plants

Mesophyll Cell	Bundle Sheath Cells	
• Primary CO_2, acceptor is a 3-C compound PEP. • Enzyme for this fixation is PEPCase. • Lacks RuBisCO • First carbon compound formed is OAA, which forms malic acid or aspartic acid and transported to bundle sheath cells.	• Malic acid/Aspartic acid CO_2 → Enters Calvin cycle, a pathway common to all plants. • Rich in RuBisCO, but lack PEPCase.	3-Carbon molecule → Transported to mesophyll and converted to PEP

Photorespiration

- **RuBisCO** is the most abundant enzyme in the world.
- It has an active site that can bind to both CO_2 and O_2, thus binding is competitive.
- Relative concentration of O_2 and CO_2 determines which of the two will bind to the enzyme.
- RuBisCO has a much greater affinity for CO_2.
- In C_3 plants, some O_2 does bind to RuBisCO and hence, CO_2 fixation is decreased, as seen in the following reaction

$$RuBP + O_2 \xrightarrow{RuBisCO} \text{3-PGA (3C)} + \text{2-phosphoglycolate (2C)}$$

- In photorespiration, there is neither synthesis of sugars, nor of ATP.
- It results in release of CO_2 with utilisation of ATP.
- In this process, the first stable product is a 2C compound. Thus, this process is also called **C_2-pathway**.
- The biological function of photorespiration is not known yet.
- In C_4 plants, photorespiration does not occur. They have mechanism to increase the concentration of CO_2 at the enzyme site. This ensures that the RuBisCO functions as a carboxylase minimising the oxygenase activity.

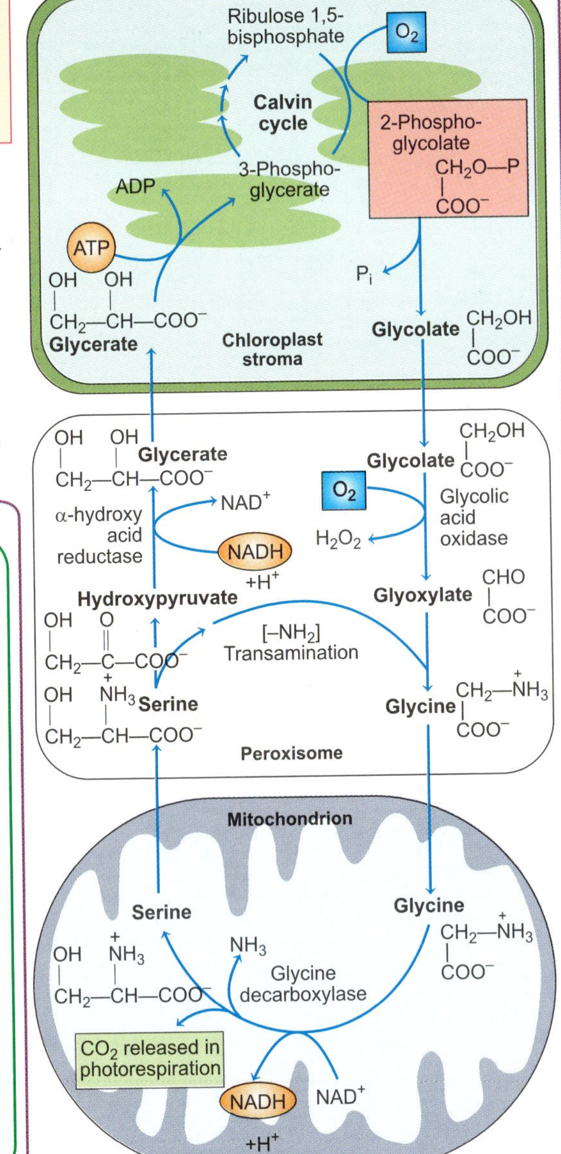

Factors affecting Photosynthesis

- Photosynthesis is under the influence of both internal and external factors.
  - **Internal Factors** Number, size, age and orientation of leaves, mesophyll cells and chloroplasts, internal CO_2 concentration and the amount of chlorophyll.
  - **External Factors** Availability of sunlight, temperature, CO_2 concentration and water.
- **Light** Saturation occurs at 10% of the full sunlight.
  - Linear relationship between incident light and CO_2, fixation rates at low light intensities.
- **CO_2 Concentration** Major limiting factor.
  - Current CO_2 availability is limiting only to C_3 plants.
- **Temperature** Dark reactions being enzymatic are temperature controlled. Light reactions are also temperature sensitive.
  - C_3 plants show lower temperature optimum.
- **Water** Water stress causes the stomata to close, hence reducing CO_2 availability.
- **Blackman's Law of Limiting Factor** When chemical process is affected by more than one factor; rate will be determined by the factor, which is nearest to its minimal value.

  It is the factor which directly affects the process, if its quantity is changed.

Test 1

Syllabus
- Gaseous Exchange
- Cellular Respiration-Glycolysis, Fermentation (Anaerobic Respiration)

NCERT Page 153 to 158

For deeper insight, **Scan the QR Code**

Chapter 12

Fermentation (Anaerobic Respiration)

- Occurs in **cytosol**.
- Conversion of pyruvate to alcohol and organic acids in the absence of oxygen.
- **Alcoholic Fermentation (By Yeast):** Incomplete oxidation of glucose is achieved under anaerobic conditions to produce CO_2 and ethanol; involves enzymes **pyruvate decarboxylase** and **alcohol dehydrogenase**.
- **Lactic Acid Fermentation:** In **bacteria** and **muscle cells;** pyruvate is reduced to lactic acid by **lactate dehydrogenase**.
- In humans, lactic acid is formed in muscles during prolonged starvation or exercise. These muscle cells respire anaerobically during this period.
- Less than **7%** of the energy in glucose is released.
- Hazardous as either acid or alcohol is produced.
- Yeasts poison themselves to death when concentration of alcohol reaches about **13%**.
- It **regenerates NAD^+** so that glycolysis can proceed. Other types of fermentation are - **butyric acid fermentation** (end product is butyric acid) and **acetic acid fermentation** (end product is acetic acid).The former is common in *Clostridium butyricum* and the latter is common in bacteria.

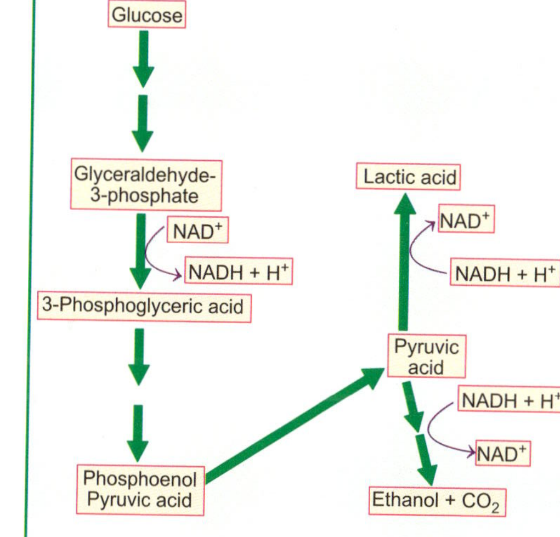

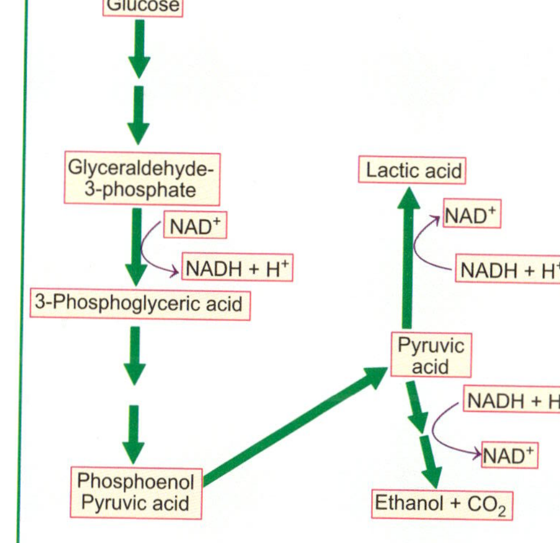

Applications of Fermentation

This process is used in various industries to produce a variety of substances. Some of its important applications are
- In the production of antibiotics, vitamins, dairy products and alcohol, etc.
- It is also used for tanning of leather, retting of fibres and in curing of tea and coffee.
- In processing of food beverages and production of organic solvents.

Respiration

- Liberation of energy from food by chemical breakdown.
- **Gaseous exchange** occurs between environment and organisms through body surface or special respiratory organs. It does not involve any chemical reaction.
- **Cellular respiration** is the chemical breakdown of food substrate mediated by several enzymes to release energy stored in chemical bonds.
- **Types of Cellular Respiration**

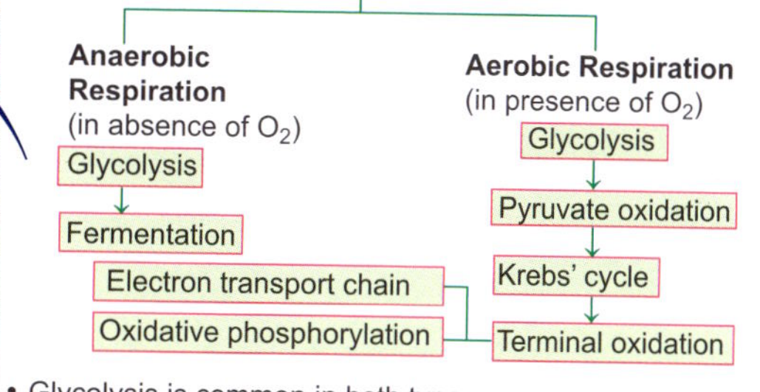

- Glycolysis is common in both types.
- Overall reaction for cellular respiration is

$$C_6H_{12}O_6 + 6O_2 \rightarrow 6CO_2 + 6H_2O + \text{Energy (in form of ATPs)}$$

Fate of Pyruvic Acid

There are three major ways in which cells handle pyruvic acid

Carbohydrates → Glucose → Pyruvic acid

- Absence of O_2 → Alcoholic fermentation: $C_2H_5OH + CO_2$ + Energy (in yeast)
- Absence of O_2 → Lactic acid fermentation: $C_3H_6O_3$ + Energy (in our muscle cells)
- Presence of O_2 → Aerobic respiration: $CO_2 + H_2O$ + Energy (in mitochondria)

Net Result of Glycolysis

Overall Reaction:

$$\text{Glucose} + 2NAD^+ + 2ADP + 2Pi \longrightarrow 2\text{ Pyruvate} + 2NADH + 2H^+ + 2ATP + 2H_2O$$

- Thus, the total or net gain of ATP in glycolysis process is (4 ATP produced-2 ATP consumed) +6 ATP from NADH = 8 ATP molecules per 1 glucose molecule.

Glycolysis or EMP Pathway

- It is an oxidative process, in which one molecule of glucose is converted into two molecules of pyruvic acid.
- The complete process is a series of ten enzyme-mediated reactions, releasing energy in the form of ATP and NADH.
- It occurs in the **cytosol or cytoplasm** of all living organisms.
- Known as **EMP pathway**; named after three scientists **(Embden-Meyerhof-Parnas)** who discovered it.

Preparatory (energy consuming) phase

1. Glucose (6C) — **Hexokinase** (ATP → ADP)
2. Glucose-6-phosphate (6C) — **Phosphoglucoisomerase**
3. Fructose-6-phosphate (6C) — **Phosphofructokinase** (ATP → ADP)
4. Fructose-1,6-bisphosphate (6C) — **Aldolase**
5. Triose phosphate (3C) (glyceraldehyde-3-phosphate) ⇌ **Isomerase** ⇌ Triose phosphate (3C) (Dihydroxy acetone phosphate)

Pay-off (energy producing) phase

Glyceraldehyde 3-phosphate dehydrogenase (NAD^+ → NADH+H^+)

6. 2 x Triose bisphosphate (3C) (1, 3-bisphosphoglyceric acid) — **Phosphoglycerokinase** (Substrate level phosphorylation) (ADP → ATP)
7. 2 x Triose phosphate (3C) (3- phosphoglyceric acid) — **Phosphoglyceromutase**
8. 2 × 2-phosphoglycerate (3C) — **Enolase** (H_2O)
9. 2 × 2-phosphoenolpyruvate (3C) — **Pyruvate kinase** (Substrate level phosphorylation) (ADP → ATP)
10. 2 × Pyruvic acid (3C)

Net output→2 Pyruvate+2ATP+2NADH (+2H$^+$) or 2 Pyruvate +8 ATP

Test 2

Syllabus

- Aerobic Respiration (TCA Cycle and Electron Transport System)
- Energy Relations-Number of ATP Molecules Generated
- Amphibolic Pathway's
- Respiratory Quotient

NCERT Page 158 to 164

For deeper insight, **Scan the QR Code**

Pyruvate Oxidation/ Oxidative Decarboxylation

- Occurs in **mitochondria**.
- It involves conversion of glycolysis product, pyruvate into acetyl Co-A that enters next step, i.e., Krebs' cycle. It is also called **link reaction** as it links glycolysis with Krebs' cycle.

$$\text{Pyruvate} + \text{Co-A} \xrightarrow[\substack{Mg^{2+} \\ NAD^+ \to NADH+H^+}]{\text{Pyruvate dehydrogenase complex}} \text{Acetyl Co-A} + CO_2 \text{ (enters Krebs' cycle)}$$

- It requires the participation of several coenzymes, including NAD^+, thiamine pyrophosphate, lipoic acid and coenzyme-A.

Krebs' Cycle

- Occurs in **mitochondrial matrix**.
- There are three steps in the cycle where NAD^+ is reduced to $NADH^+$ and one step where FAD^+ is reduced to $FADH_2$.
- ATP is formed from GTP in a coupled reaction.
- **Products of TCA cycle** → 3NADH + 1$FADH_2$ + 1ATP + 2CO_2
- TCA cycle is an **amphibolic pathway.**
- All enzymes of TCA cycle are located in the mitochondrial matrix, **except** succinate dehydrogenase, i.e. located in inner membrane in eukaryotes.

Pyruvic acid + Co-A → (NAD^+ → $NADH+H^+$) → Acetyl Co-A, H_2O

CITRIC ACID CYCLE (2 turns per glucose)

1. Oxaloacetate + Acetyl Co-A → Citrate (Citrate synthase; Co-A–SH released)
2. Citrate → *Cis* Aconitate (Aconitase; H_2O)
3. *Cis* Aconitate → Isocitrate (Aconitase; H_2O)
4. Isocitrate → Oxalosuccinate (Isocitrate dehydrogenase; NAD^+ → NADH + H^+)
5. Oxalosuccinate → α-ketoglutarate (Isocitrate dehydrogenase; CO_2)
6. α-ketoglutarate → Succinyl-Co-A (α-ketoglutarate dehydrogenase; NAD^+ + Co-A - SH → NADH + H^+ + CO_2)
7. Succinyl-Co-A → Succinate (Succinate thiokinase; GDP → GTP, Co-A-SH)
8. Succinate → Fumarate (Succinate dehydrogenase; FAD^+ → $FADH_2$)
9. Fumarate → Malate (Fumarase; H_2O)
10. Malate → Oxaloacetate (Malate dehydrogenase; NAD^+ → NADH + H^+)

The overall equation of Krebs' cycle is as follows

$$[\text{Pyruvic acid} + 4NAD^+ + FAD^+ + 2H_2O + ADP + Pi \xrightarrow[\text{matrix}]{\text{Mitochondrial}} 3CO_2 + 4NADH + 4H^+ + FADH_2 + ATP] \times 2$$

Electron Transport Chain (ETC) and Oxidative Phosphorylation

- Occurs in the **inner mitochondrial membrane**.
- Inner membrane has five complexes (enzymes), of which **first four constitute ETC** and the last, **fifth one** is associated with **oxidative phosphorylation**.

  Complex I : NADH - Coenzyme-Q reductase / NADH dehydrogenase (FMN, Fe-S)
  Complex II : Succinate - Coenzyme-Q reductase/succinate dehydrogenase (Fe-S, UQ)
  Complex III : Coenzyme-Q - Cytochrome-*c* reductase / cytochrome-*bc* complex (Fe-S, UQ)
  Complex IV : Cytochrome-*c* oxidase (cytochrome-a_1, cytochrome-a_3 and two copper centres).
  Complex V : ATP synthase (F_0 - F_1 particle)
- ATP synthase consists of two major components-F_0 and F_1.
- The $\mathbf{F_1}$ head piece is a peripheral membrane protein complex and contains the site for synthesis of ATP from ADP and inorganic phosphate.
- $\mathbf{F_0}$ is an integral membrane protein complex that forms the channel through which protons cross the inner membrane.

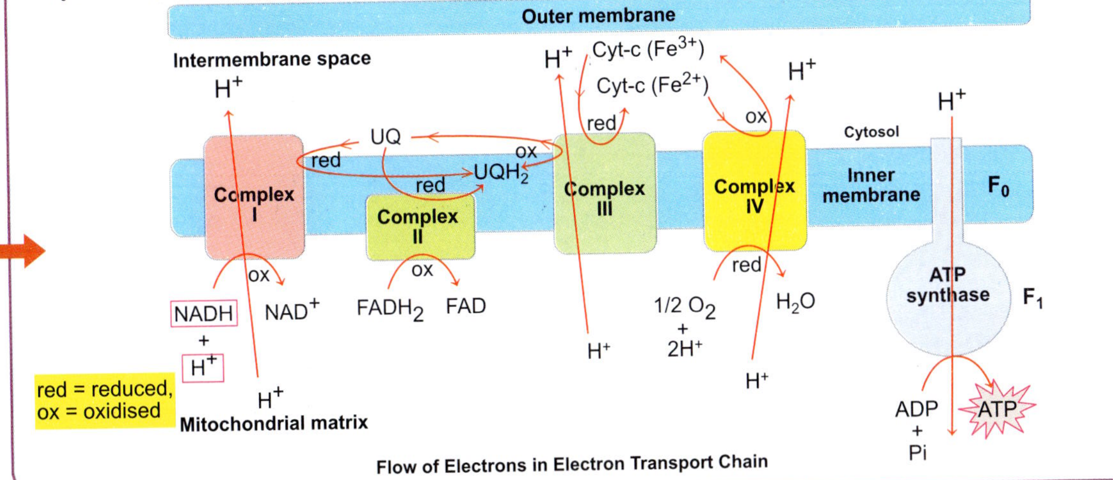

Flow of Electrons in Electron Transport Chain

Respiratory Balance Sheet

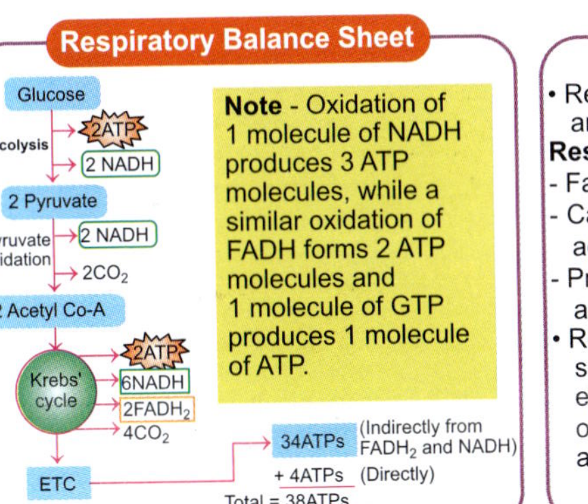

Note - Oxidation of 1 molecule of NADH produces 3 ATP molecules, while a similar oxidation of FADH forms 2 ATP molecules and 1 molecule of GTP produces 1 molecule of ATP.

Amphibolic Pathway

- Respiratory pathway involves both anabolism and catabolism.

Respiratory Substrate

- Fats→Fatty acid→Acetyl Co-A
- Carbohydrate→Glucose→Pyruvic acid→Acetyl Co-A
- Proteins→Amino acid→Pyruvic acid→Acetyl Co-A

- Respiration process contains some important intermediates, e.g., acetyl Co-A; succinyl Co-A; oxaloacetic acid; α-ketoglutaric acid.

Respiratory Quotient (RQ)

- Ratio of volume of CO_2 produced to the volume of oxygen consumed.

$$RQ = \frac{\text{Volume of } CO_2 \text{ produced}}{\text{Volume of } O_2 \text{ consumed}}$$

- RQ can be unity, more than one, less than one, zero and infinity.
- **RQ for different respiratory substrates**
  - Proteins =0.9
  - Fats ⇒ < 1 (e.g. tripalmitin = 0.7)
  - Organic acids ⇒ > 1
  - Carbohydrates = 1
  - Anaerobic respiration = ∞

Test 1

Syllabus

- Seed Germination
- Phases of Growth and Plant Growth Rate
- Conditions of Growth
- Differentiation, Dedifferentiation and Redifferentiation
- Sequence of Developmental Process in a Plant Cell

NCERT Page 166 to 174

For deeper insight, **Scan the QR Code**

Growth

- **Growth *Vs* Development**
  - Growth is defined as an irreversible increase in size of an organ or its parts, even of an individual cell.
  - Development is the sum of two processes- growth and differentiation.
- **Plant growth generally is indeterminate.**
  - It means that plant growth continues throughout life.
- Two types of growth based on sequence
  (i) **Primary Growth** Elongation of plant along their axis (due to the division of root and shoot apex).
  (ii) **Secondary Growth** Growth in diameter due to the activity of cambium.
- **Growth is measurable.**
  - At cellular level, measured as increase in amount of protoplasm.
  - Growth can be in term of increase in cell number and increase in size.
- **Phases of Growth**
  - **Meristematic Phase** Constant division of cells in shoot and roots.
  - **Elongation Phase** Cell enlargement, increased vacuole formation and new cell wall deposition.
  - **Maturation Phase** Protoplasm and cell wall thickening has attained maximum growth.

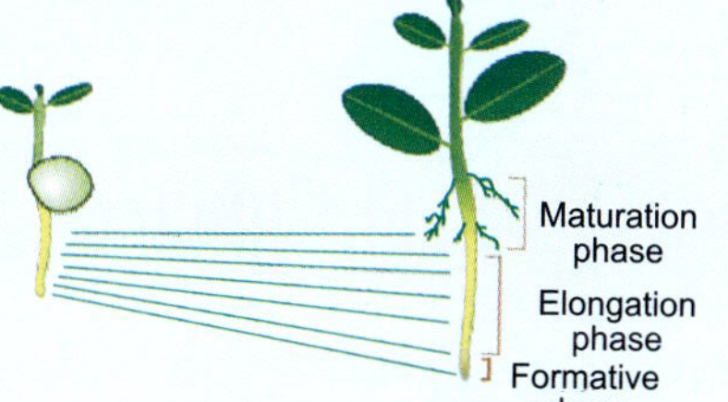

Seed Germination

- Process by which a dormant embryo becomes active, grows out of the seed coat and develops into a seedling.
- Important favourable environmental conditions for seed germination is- moisture, air, suitable temperature and proper light.
- **Types of Seed Germination**
  - **Hypogeal** Epicotyl grows first and cotyledons remain underground; e.g., rice, wheat, maize, pea etc.
  - **Epigeal** Hypocotyl grows first, pushing up the cotyledons to the soil surface; e.g. cotton, castor, tamarind, onion, etc.

Growth Rates

- Increase in growth per unit time.
- It can be arithmetic or geometrical.

Arithmetic

- The rate of growth is constant and increase in growth occurs in arithmetic progression.

$1 \xrightarrow{+1} 2 \xrightarrow{+1} 3 \xrightarrow{+1} 4 \xrightarrow{+1} 5 \xrightarrow{+1} 6$

- Found in root and shoot elongation.
- $L_t = L_o + rt$

Length after time

= Length at beginning + Growth rate × Time

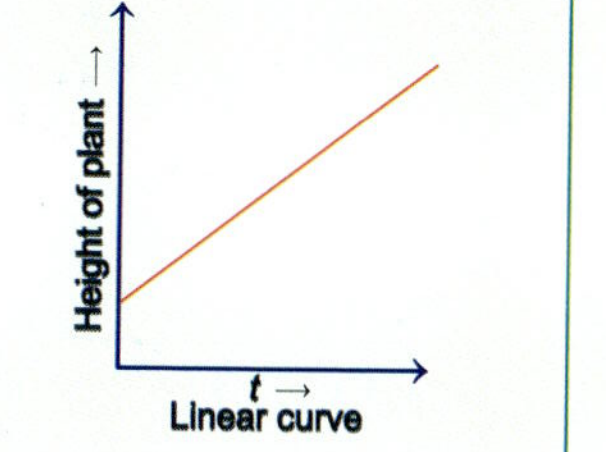

- Availability of unlimited nutrient supply.
- Following one mitotic cell division, only one daughter cell continues to divide, while the other differentiates and matures.

Geometric

- Here, the initial growth is slow, but increases rapidly thereafter. Here, exponential growth occurs.

$1 \xrightarrow{x2} 2 \xrightarrow{x2} 4 \xrightarrow{x2} 8 \xrightarrow{x2} 16 \xrightarrow{x2} 32$

- Common in unicellular organisms growing under nutrient rich medium.
- $W_1 = W_0\, e^{rt}$

Final size

= Initial size × Base of natural logarithms (Growth rate × Time)

Size of organ — Lag — Exponential (log) — Stationary — t — S-shaped (sigmoid) curve

- Availability of limited nutrient supply
- Here, both the progeny cells following mitotic cell division retain the ability to divide and continue to do so.

Growth Measurment of Living System

(i) Measurement and comparison of total growth per unit time is called **Absolute Growth Rate (AGR).**

(ii) The growth of given system per unit time expressed on a common basis, e.g., per unit initial parameter, is called **Relative Growth Rate (RGR).**

Let us understand it from the following example

A[1] 10 cm² — A 5 cm²

AGR=(10-5)cm²=5cm²
RGR=(10-5)/5×100=100%

B[1] 55 cm² — B 50 cm²

AGR=(55-50)cm²=5cm²
RGR=(55-50)/50×100=10%

Development in Plants

- Development is a term that includes all changes that an organism goes through during its life cycle from germination of the seed to senescence.
- Sequence of development in higher plants is as follows

Meristematic cell → (Cell Division; Plasmatic growth) → New cell → (Expansion) → Enlarged cell → (Differentiation) → Differentiated cell → (Maturation) → Mature cell → (Senescence) → Death

- **Plasticity** Ability of a plant to follow different pathways and produce different structures in response to environment, e.g. heterophylly.
- **Heterophylly** Phenomenon of appearance of different forms of leaves on the same plant, e.g. butter cup (due to different environment) and larkspur (difference in shapes of juveline and mature leaves).

Conditions of Growth

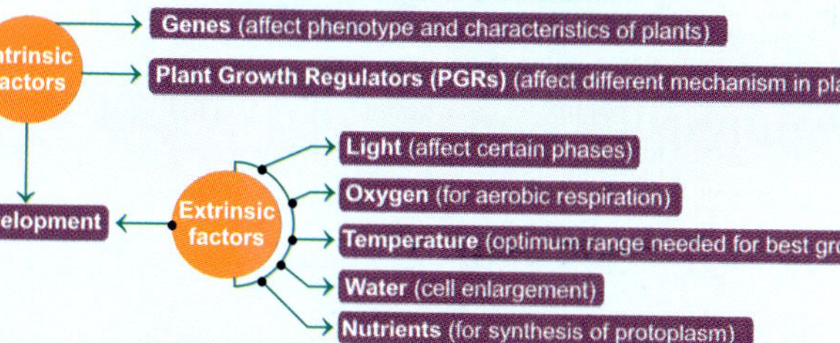

Differentiation, Dedifferentiation and Redifferentiation

Differentiation
The cells derived from root and shoot apical meristems and cambium differentiate and mature to perform specific functions. This act leading to maturation is termed differentiation, e.g. formation of tracheary element.

Dedifferentiation
Living differentiated cells that have lost the capacity to divide can regain capacity of division under certain conditions. This phenomenon is dedifferentiation, e.g. formation of interfascicular and cork-cambium from parenchyma cells.

Redifferentiation
Dedifferentiated meristems are able to divide and produce cells that once again lose capacity to divide but mature to perform specific functions, i.e. get redifferentiated.
e.g. secondary xylem, secondary cortex, cork, etc.

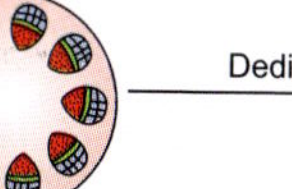

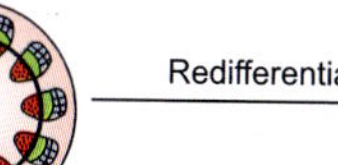

Process of Dedifferentiation and Redifferentiation (Shown in a Plant Tissue)

Test 2

Syllabus

- Plant Growth Regulators (Auxin, Gibberellins, Cytokinin, Ethylene and ABA).

NCERT Page 175 to 178

For deeper insight, **Scan the QR Code**

Plant Growth Regulators

Broadly divided into two groups based on their functions in a living plant body.

PGRs

Plant Growth Promoter
- Involved in Growth promoting activities like-
- Cell division
- Cell enlargement
- Pattern formation
- Tropic growth
- Flowering
- Fruiting and seed formation

1. **Auxin** (indole compounds; IAA).
2. **Gibberellins** (GA, terpenes)
3. **Cytokinin** (adenine derivatives): (N-furfurylamino purine or kinetin)

Plant Growth Inhibitor
- Involved in Growth inhibiting activities like-
- Response to wounds.
- Stresses of biotic and abiotic origin.
- Dormancy and abscission.

e.g., **Abscisic acid** (derivatives of carotenoids).

*The gaseous PGR, **ethylene**, could fit either of the groups, but it is largely an inhibitor of growth activities.

Auxin

- **Charles Darwin** and his son **Francis Darwin** studied phototropism in canary grass.
- **FW Went** isolated auxin from tips of coleoptiles of oat seedlings.
- First isolated from human urine.
- Produced by growing apices of stems and roots.
- **IAA** and **IBA** isolated from plants.
- **NAA**, **2,4-D** are synthetic.

Indole-3-Acetic Acid (IAA)

Physiological Effects
- **Initiates rooting** in stem cuttings.
- Promotes **flowering in pineapples**.
- **Helps prevent fruit and leaf drop at early stages**, but promotes abscission of older mature leaves and fruits.
- Promotes **apical dominance**
- Induces **parthenocarpy** in tomatoes.
- 2,4-D kills dicot weeds; used to prepare **weed-free lawns**; do not kill monocotyledons.
- Auxin controls **xylem differentiation** and helps in **cell division.**

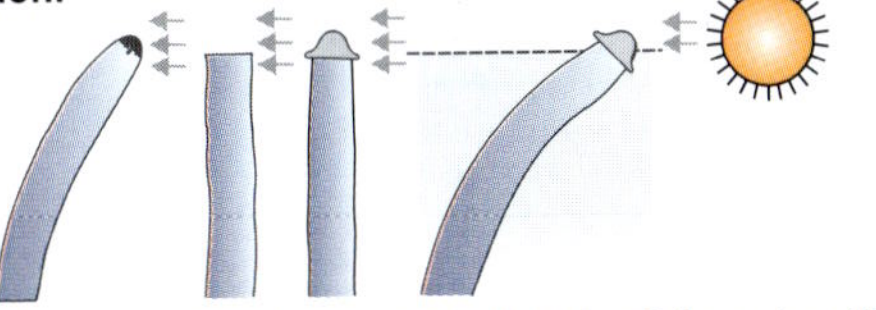

Experiment used to demonstrate that tip of the coleoptile is the source of auxin. (Arrows indicate direction of light).

Gibberellins (GA)

- Bakanae (foolish seedling) disease in rice was caused by fungal pathogen, *G. fujikuroi*. **Kurosawa** helped understand it.
- Later, the chemical gibberellic acid was identified.
- GA_1 was discovered first and remains intensively studied form.
- All GAs are acidic.

Physiological Effects
- Increase length of grapes stalk.
- Cause fruits like apples to elongate and improve shape.
- They delay senescence.
- Used to speed up malting process in brewing industry.
- Increase length of stem and yield by 20 tonnes per hectare in sugarcane.
- Spraying juvenile conifers with GAs hastens maturity period.
- Promote bolting (internodal elongation) in beet, cabbages and many plants with rosette habit.

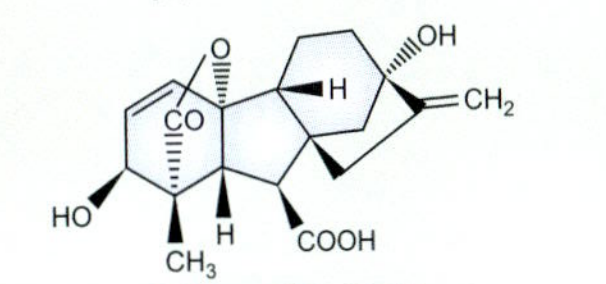

Gibberellin (GA)

Ethylene

- Discovered by **HH Cousins** (1910) from ripened oranges that hastened ripening of stored unripened bananas.
- Synthesised in large amounts by tissues undergoing senescence and ripening fruits.

Physiological Effects
- Horizontal growth of seedlings, swelling of axis and **apical hook formation** in dicot seedlings.
- **Promotes senescence** and abscission in leaves and flowers.
- Effective in **fruit ripening**, by increasing rate of respiration; called **respiratory climactic**.
- **Breaks** seed and bud dormancy.
- **Initiates germination** in peanut seeds, sprouting of potato tubers.
- Promotes rapid internode/**petiole elongation** in deep water rice plants.
- Promotes root growth and **root hair formation**.
- Initiates flowering and helps in **synchronising fruit-set in pineapples**.
- Induces **flowering in mango**.
- **Ethephon** is source of ethylene. It hastens fruit ripening in tomatoes and apples and accelerates abscission in flowers and fruits.
- Promotes **female flowers in cucumbers**, increasing yield.

Ethylene

Cytokinin

- **Skoog** and **Miller** crystallised cytokinesis promoting active substance, kinetin, a modified form of adenine from autoclaved herring sperm DNA.
- **Kinetin** does not occur naturally in plants.
- **Zeatin**, the naturally occurring cytokinin was isolated from corn-kernels and coconut milk.
- Synthesised in regions of rapid cell-division like root apices, developing shoot buds, young fruits etc.

Physiological Effects
- Helps produce new leaves, chloroplasts in leaves, lateral shoot growth and adventitious shoot formation.
- Overcomes apical dominance.
- Promotes nutrient mobilisation.
- Helps delay leaf senescence.

Zeatin

Abscisic Acid (ABA)

- In 1960s, different groups of scientists discovered growth inhibitors and named them as inhibitor-b, abscisin II and dormin. Later, they were found to be chemically identical and named as abscisic acid.

Physiological Effects
- Regulates **abscission and dormancy.**
- **Inhibits seed germination**.
- Stimulates **closure of stomata.**
- Plays important role in seed development, maturation and dormancy.
- By **inducing dormancy**, ABA helps seeds to withstand desiccation and other factors unfavourable for growth.
- In most situations, ABA acts as an **antagonist to GAs**.

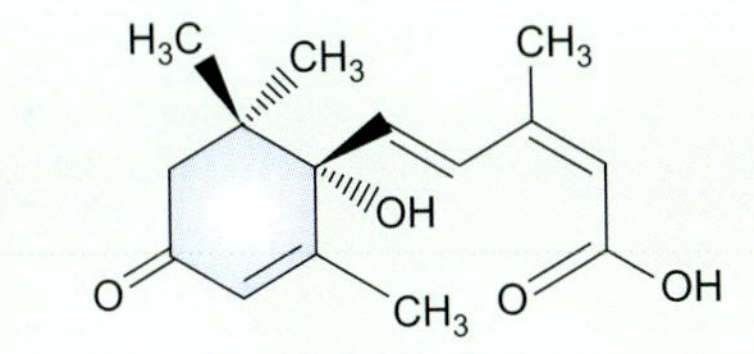

Abscisic Acid (ABA)

Test 1

Syllabus
- Respiratory Organs in Animals
- Respiratory System in Humans
- Mechanism of Breathing
- Respiratory Volumes

NCERT Page 183 to 187

For deeper insight, **Scan the QR Code**

Breathing *v/s* Respiration

Breathing is a physical process that involves inhalation and exhalation. On the other hand, respiration is a biochemical process that takes places at the cellular level.

Respiratory Organs in Animals

(i) Sponges, coelenterates, flatworms — Simple diffusion over body surface.
(ii) Earthworm — Moist skin or cuticle
(iii) Insects — Tracheal system
(iv) Aquatic arthropods and molluscs — Gills
(v) Terrestrial forms — Lungs

Respiratory Tract in Humans

A pair of external nostrils
↓↑
Nasal chamber through nasal passage
↓↑
Nasopharynx
↓↑
Oropharynx
↓↑
Laryngopharynx
↓↑
Glottis (Larynx - '**Sound box**')
↓↑
Trachea (Windpipe)
↓↑
Bronchi
↓↑
Bronchioles
↓↑
Alveolar ducts
↓↑
Atria
↓↑
Alveolar sac
↓↑
Alveoli

Pharynx (Nasopharynx, Oropharynx, Laryngopharynx)

Lungs (covered by double layered pleura)

Conducting part

Exchange/ Respiratory part

- **Functions of Conducting Part**
  - Humidification of air,
  - Transport of air,
  - Traps dust present in inhaled air,
  - Bring air to body temperature,
- **Function of Exchange/Respiratory Part**
  - Exchange of gases

Human Respiratory System

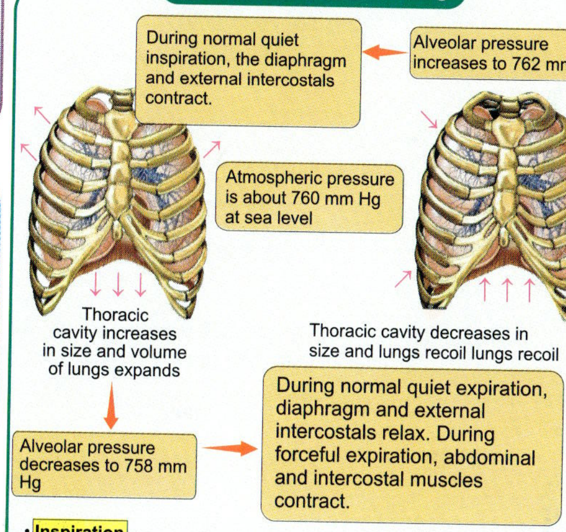

Respiratory Volumes and Capacities

Lung Volumes

Lung Capacities

6000 mL
5000 mL
4000 mL
3000 mL
(500 mL)
2000 mL
1000 mL

IRV (2500-3000 mL)

TV

ERV (1000-1100 mL)

RV (1100-1200 mL)

Inhalation

Exhalation

VC (IRV+TV+ERV) (3500-4500 mL)

IC (TV+IRV) (3000-3500 mL)

FRC (ERV+RV) (2500 mL)

TLC (VC+RV) (5800-6000 mL)

- The lung capacities and volumes can be measured by using a device called **spirometer**, except RV, FRC and TLC.
- **Dead Space** Gas volume that does not undergo gas exchange.

Steps Involved in Respiration

The steps involved in the process of respiration are
- Pulmonary ventilation or breathing that involves drawing of atmospheric air in and expelling of carbon dioxide rich air from alveoli.
- Diffusion of gases, both O_2 and CO_2, across the alveolar membrane.
- Transport of gases *via* blood.
- Diffusion of gases between the blood and the tissues.
- Utilisation of O_2, by the cells for catabolic reactions and resultant release of CO_2, i.e., cellular respiration.

Mechanism of Breathing

During normal quiet inspiration, the diaphragm and external intercostals contract.

Alveolar pressure increases to 762 mmHg

Atmospheric pressure is about 760 mm Hg at sea level

Thoracic cavity increases in size and volume of lungs expands

Thoracic cavity decreases in size and lungs recoil lungs recoil

Alveolar pressure decreases to 758 mm Hg

During normal quiet expiration, diaphragm and external intercostals relax. During forceful expiration, abdominal and intercostal muscles contract.

- **Inspiration**
  Characterised by following features
  - Diaphragm contracted
  - Volume of thorax increased
  - Ribs and sternum raised by contraction of inter-coastal muscles.
  - Air enters into the lungs.
- **Expiration**
  Characterised by following features
  - Diaphragm relaxed and arched upward
  - Volume of thorax decreased
  - Ribs and sternum returned to original position after relaxation of inter costal muscles
  - Air expelled from lung
- On an average, a healthy human breathe 12-16 times/ minute.

Important Facts

- Lungs are the only organs that can float on water.
- Humans can live even without one lung.
- Study of lung disease is called **pulmonology**.
- Left lung of humans is slightly smaller than right lung.

Test 2

Syllabus
- Exchange of Gases
- Transport of Gases and Regulation of Respiration
- Disorders-Asthma, Emphysema, Occupational Respiratory Disorders

NCERT Page 187 to 191

For deeper insight, **Scan the QR Code**

Exchange of Gases

- Occurs at alveoli of lungs and tissue cells simultaneously due to differential partial pressure of CO_2 and O_2 from region of higher partial pressure to lower partial pressure.

Diffusion of O_2
pO_2 in alveolar air = 104 mm Hg
pO_2 in venous blood = 40 mm Hg
O_2 diffuses from alveoli to venous blood.

Diffusion of CO_2
pCO_2 in venous blood = 45 mm Hg
pCO_2 in alveolar air = 40 mm Hg
CO_2 diffuses from venous blood to alveoli.

- Solubility of CO_2 is 20-25 times higher than that of O_2.

Gaseous Exchange at Tissue Level

116 32 pO_2 pCO_2 (6) Exhaled air
Inhaled air (1) 159 0.3 pO_2 pCO_2
Alveolar epithelial cells; Alveolar spaces; CO_2; O_2
(2) 104 40 pO_2 pCO_2
Blood entering alveolar capillaries; Alveolar capillaries
40 45 pO_2 pCO_2 (5)
Pulmonary arteries and systemic veins; Pulmonary veins and systemic arteries (3) 95 40 pO_2 pCO_2
Heart
<40 <45 pO_2 pCO_2 (4) Body tissue; CO_2; O_2; Systemic capillaries

Respiratory Gas	Atmospheric Air	Alveoli	Blood (Deoxygenated)	Blood (Oxygenated)	Tissues
O_2	159	104	40	95	40
CO_2	0.3	40	45	40	45

Partial Pressures (in mm Hg) of Oxygen and Carbon Dioxide at Different Parts Involved in Diffusion in Comparison to those in Atmosphere

Gaseous Exchange at Alveoli Level

- Primary sites of exchange of gases.
- Exchange of gases occur between blood and tissues by simple diffusion.
- Based on pressure/concentration gradient.
- Respiratory membrane is formed by : thin squamous epithelium of the alveoli, endothelium of alveolar capillaries, basement substance (Composed of a thin basement membrane supporting the squamous epithelium and the basement membrane surrounding the single layer endothelial cells of capillaries) between them.

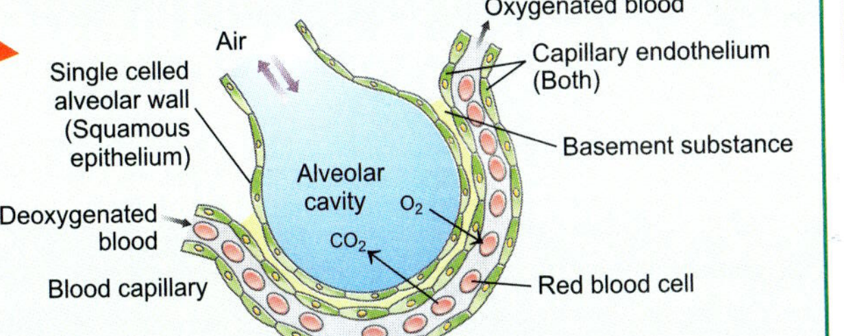

Diagrammatic Section of an Alveolus with a Pulmonary Capillary

Regulation of Respiration

- Respiratory rhythm centre in medulla of brain is primarily responsible for this regulation.
- Pneumotaxic centre in pons region moderates the function of respiratory rhythm centre.
- Chemosensitive area adjacent to rhythm centre is highly sensitive to CO2 and H+ ions.
- Chemoreceptors associated with aortic arch and carotid artery also can recognise changes in CO2 and H+ concentration and send necessary signals to the rhythm centre for remedial actions.

Disorders of Respiratory System

Name of Disorders	Descriptions
Asphyxia	Suffocation due to lack of oxygen and retention of carbon dioxide.
Asthma	Difficulty in breathing that causes wheezing due to inflammation of bronchi and bronchioles.
Bronchitis	Inflammation of the bronchi caused due to irritants such as smoke, air pollution or infection.
Dyspnea	Distressed breathing or breathing with difficulty.
Emphysema	Irreversible distension of the alveolar walls ; respiratory surface decreases; cigarette smoking is a major cause.
Occupational lung disease	Inflammation and fibrosis of lungs due to long exposure to dust, chemicals; also called 'diseases of industrial workers'.

Transport of Gases

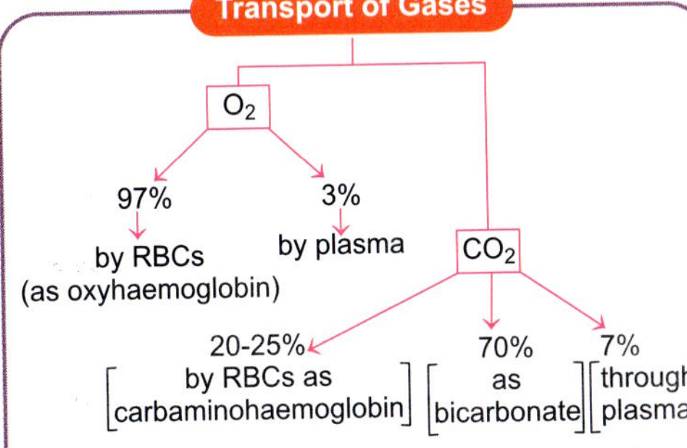

Transport of O_2
- O_2 binds with haemoglobin to form oxyhaemoglobin.
- Each haemoglobin can bind to maximum of four O_2 molecules.

Oxygen Dissociation Curve
- A sigmoid curve showing relationship between % of saturation of haemoglobin with O_2 in blood and pO_2 in the blood.
- Increase in H^+ concentration, CO_2, temperature decreases the affinity of haemoglobin for oxygen.
- Every 100 mL of oxygenated blood can deliver around 5 mL of O_2 to the tissues under normal physiological conditions.

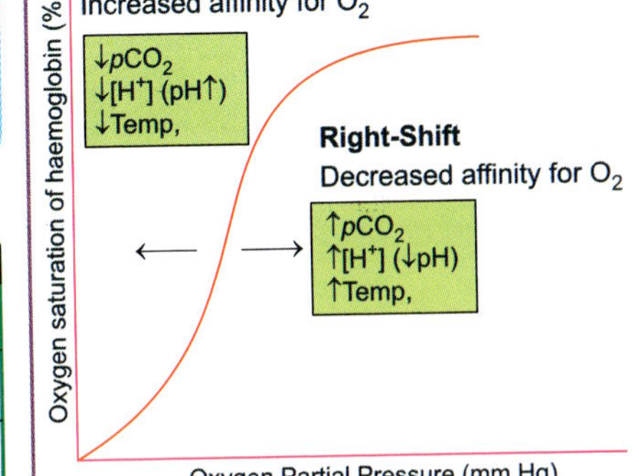

Oxygen Dissociation Curve

Transport of CO_2
- Most of the CO_2 is transported as HCO_3^- with the help of enzyme **carbonic anhydrase**.
- In the tissues, where pCO_2 is high, it gets associated with blood, while in the alveoli, where pCO_2 is low, it gets removed from blood.

Test 1

Syllabus
- Composition of Blood
- Blood Groups
- Coagulation of Blood
- Composition of Lymph and its Function

NCERT Page 193 to 197

For deeper insight, **Scan the QR Code**

Blood

- A fluid connective tissue which is mesodermal in origin.
- Contains two main components; the fluid part is the plasma and the solid part is the corpuscles.
- **Functions of Blood**
  - Transport of nutrients, metabolic wastes and hormones.
  - Regulation of body temperature.
  - Helps in protection against diseases.
  - Clotting of blood at the site of injury.
  - Maintenance of pH.

Blood Groups

- Grouping of blood: On the basis of antigens and Rh factors.
- ABO blood grouping discovered by **Landsteiner**.
- ABO blood grouping is based on the presence or absence of antigen A and/or antigen B on the surface of RBCs.
- **Agglutination** (coagulation) **of Blood** – Transfusion of mismatched blood group leads to coagulation of blood cells which is fatal for an individual.
- **Universal donor**- O^- group
- **Universal recipient** – AB^+ group

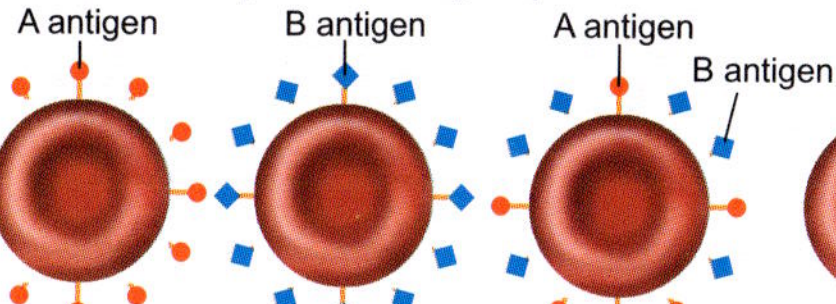

Coagulation of Blood

Injured tissue → Releases → Thromboplastin → Ca^{2+} proteins

Blood platelets → Disintegrate and release → Platelet factor-3 (platelet thromboplastin) → Ca^{2+} proteins

Step I Prothrombinase → Inactivates heparin and catalyses

Step II Prothrombin $\xrightarrow{Ca^{2+}}$ Thrombin

Step III Fibrinogen $\xrightarrow{Ca^{2+}}$ Fibrin

(Fibrin + Blood cells) → Clot

Role of Thrombocytes in Blood Coagulation

Lymphocytes

- Constitutes 20-25% of the total leucocytes.
- Lymphocytes are of two types, i.e. B-lymphocytes and T-lymphocytes.

Monocytes

6-8% of the total leucocytes are monocytes; phagocytic cells.

Agranulocytes

Red Blood Cells

- RBCs are enucleated.
- RBCs are the carrier of oxygen in the blood.
- RBCs of camel consist of nucleus.
- *Amphiuma* has the largest RBC of about 62 mm (approx).
- Musk deer has the smallest RBC of about 2.5 mm (approx).

White Blood Cells

- WBCs are nucleated.
- Leucocytes/WBCs defend the body against infection.
- They stimulates the production of progesterone hormone.

Granulocytes

Eosinophils

Eosinophils constitute 2-3% of the total leucocytes; involved in allergic reactions.

Basophils

Constitute only 0.5-1% of total leucocytes; secrete histamine, heparin and serotonin, etc.

Neutrophils

These cells make up 60-65% of the total leucocytes; phagocytic cells.

Components of Blood

Blood vessel

Blood Plasma

It is a crystallo-colloidal mixture; contains factors for blood clotting

Platelets

- These cells are produced in red bone marrow from megakaryocyte.
- They prevent and stop bleeding.

Rh-Grouping

- Rh-antigen is a protein discovered in **Rhesus monkeys**.
- It is also present on the surface of RBCs of human beings.
- Rh-positive individuals – About 80% of human individuals have Rh-positive blood group.
- Rh-negative individuals – About 20% of human individuals have Rh-negative blood group.
- If Rh-positive blood is transfused into an Rh-negative individual, specific anti-Rh antibodies are formed in the blood of the recipient.

Lymphatic System

- It is a complex system of fluid drainage and transport, immune response and disease resistance.
- **Lymphoid organs** The organs which secrete lymph are called lymphoid organs. Besides the lymph nodes, tonsils, thymus glands, Peyer's patches, liver and spleen are the other lymphoid organs that secrete lymph.

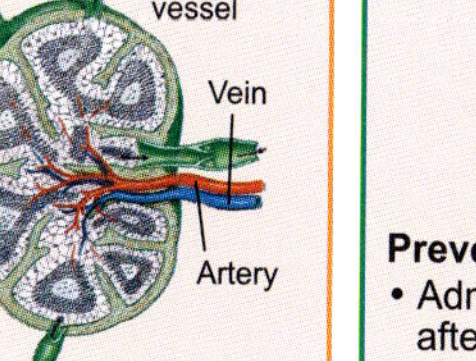

Rh Incompatibility

Mother (Rh-ve) → ← **Foetus** (Rh+ve)

↓

1st baby normal, as during pregnancy, no mixing of blood takes place due to separation by placenta

↓

During delivery, there are chances of mixing of blood

↓

Rh-ve mother makes antibodies against Rh antigen

↓

Antibodies cross placenta in subsequent pregnancy

↓

Severe anaemia and jaundice in baby

↓

Erythroblastosis foetalis

Prevention
- Administering anti-Rh antibodies to the mother immediately after 1st delivery, can save 2nd baby.

Test 2

Syllabus
- Human Circulatory System-Structure of Human Heart and Blood Vessels
- Cardiac Cycle and Cardiac Output
- ECG
- Double Circulation
- Regulation of Cardiac Activity
- Disorders-Hypertension, CAD, Angina Pectoris, Heart Failure

NCERT Page 197 to 203

For deeper insight, **Scan the QR Code**

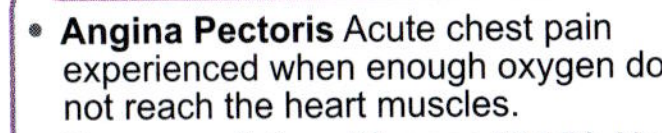

Chapter 15

Internal View of Heart

- **Aorta** (Receives oxygenated blood from left ventricle and send it to the various body parts)
- **Superior vena cava** (Receives deoxygenated blood from upper part of body and sends it to right atrium)
- **Right pulmonary artery**
- **Right pulmonary vein**
- **Right atrium** (Receives deoxygenated blood from vena cava)
- **Tricuspid valve**
- **Right ventricle** (Receives deoxygenated blood from right atrium and sends it to the lungs)
- **Inferior vena cava** (Receives deoxygenated blood from lower parts of body and sends it to right atrium)
- **Aorta**
- **Papillary muscle** (Provide stability for chordae)
- **Pulmonary semilunar valve**
- **Left pulmonary artery** (Receives deoxygenated blood from right ventricle and send it to lungs)
- **Aortic semilunar valves**
- **Left pulmonary veins** (Receives oxygenated blood from lungs and send it to left atrium)
- **Left atrium** (Receives oxygenated blood from the lungs through pulmonary veins)
- **Bicuspid (mitral) valve**
- **Chordae tendinae**
- **Left ventricle** (Receives oxygenated blood from left atrium and sends it to body parts, except lungs.)
- **Inter ventricular septum**

Layers of blood vessels: Tunica externa (outermost), Tunica media (middle) and Tunica intima (innermost).

Location of Heart Valves

Location of Heart Valves
Pulmonary valve An entrance to pulmonary artery
Aortic valve An entrance to aorta
Bicuspid valve Between left atrium and left ventricle
Tricuspid valve Between right atrium and right ventricle

Heart valves

Fibrous connective tissue

Venous System

- Veins combines to form venous system
- Brings blood back to heart from different body parts.
- Carries deoxygenated blood except, pulmonary vein.

Arterial System

- All arteries combine to form arterial system; carry blood from heart to different body parts.
- All arteries carry oxygenated or pure blood, except pulmonary artery that carries impure or deoxygenated blood.

Coronary Circulation

- Blood flow to and from the cardiac musculature.
- Coronary arteries supply oxygenated blood to the heart muscle.
- Cardiac veins then drain away the blood after it has been deoxygenated.

Heartbeat

- Each heartbeat has two phases, i.e., systole and diastole.
- Heart of healthy adult beats 72 times per minute.

Cardiac Cycle

- It involves heartbeat or one cycle of contraction and relaxation of cardiac muscles.
- It is of 0.8 second.

Electrical Conduction in the Heart

SA node (pacemaker)
AV node
1 SA node depolarises
2 Electrical activity goes rapidly to AV node via internodal pathways
3 Depolarisation spreads more slowly across atria. Conduction slows through AV node.
4 Depolarisation moves rapidly through ventricular conducting system to the apex of the heart.
5 Depolarisation wave spreads upward from the apex.

Double Circulation

- The human circulatory system is a double circulatory system. It has two separate circuits and blood passes through the heart twice.
- It include two types of circulations
  - (i) **Systemic Circulation** This circuit involves the circulation of oxygenated blood between heart and body organs.
  - (ii) **Pulmonary Circulation** This circuit involves the circulation of deoxygenated blood between heart and lungs.

ECG and Description of Waves

- ECG is a graphic record of the electric current produced by the excitation of cardiac muscles.
- A normal ECG is composed of
  - (i) **P-wave** depolarisation of atria.
  - (ii) **QRS- complex** depolarisation of ventricle.
  - (iv) **T-wave** repolarisation of ventricles; its end marks end of systole.

P Q R S T

Hepatic Portal System

- It is a venous system that returns blood from digestive tract and spleen to liver.
- This system, thus comprises of hepatic portal vein and its tributaries.

Heart → Abdominal aorta → Proper hepatic artery → Liver; Hepatic portal vein → Liver → Hepatic veins → Inferior vena cava → Heart

Disorders of Circulatory System

- **Angina Pectoris** Acute chest pain experienced when enough oxygen does not reach the heart muscles.
- **Coronary Artery Disease (CAD)** Also called **atherosclerosis**; vessels deposited with deposits of calcium, fat, cholesterol and fibrous tissue; narrowing of lumen of arteries, affects blood supply.
- **Hypertension** (High blood pressure) Blood pressure more than the normal (120/80); leads to heart disease and also affects brain and kidney.
- **Heart Failure** Heart not pumping blood effectively to meet body's needs.
- **Cardiac Arrest** Complete stoppage of the heartbeat.

Test 1

Syllabus
- Mode of Excretion-Ammonotelism, Ureotelism, Uricotelism
- Human Excretory System: Structure and Function
- Urine Formation
- Role of Other Organs in Excretion

NCERT Page 205 to 210

For deeper insight, **Scan the QR Code**

Chapter 16

Human Excretory System

- In human, the excretory system consists of
  (i) The **kidneys**, which secrete urine.
  (ii) The **ureters**, to carry the urine from the kidney to the bladder.
  (iii) The **urinary bladder**, which acts as a reservoir.
  (iv) The **urethra**, for discharge of urine from the bladder.

Human Excretory System: Structure

Inferior vena cava
Pelvis
Medulla
Cortex
Adrenal gland
Renal artery
Renal vein
Kidney
Dorsal aorta
Ureter
Urinary bladder
Urethra

Excretion

- Elimination of metabolic wastes like ammonia, urea, uric acid, etc. from the tissues.
- Ammonia is the most harmful, while uric acid is the least harmful excretory product and need large and little amount of water for excretion, respectively.

Mode of Excretion
(On the Basis of Types of Excretory End Products)

Ammonotelism
- Excretion of ammonia.
- Bony fishes, aquatic amphibians and aquatic insects.

Ureotelism
- Excretion of urea.
- Mammals, many terrestrial amphibians and marine fishes.

Uricotelism
- Excretion of uric acid.
- Snails, reptiles, birds and insects.

Excretory Structures in Animal Kingdom
- Protonephridia (flame cells) - Flatworms
- Nephridia - Annelida
- Malpighian tubule - Insects
- Antennal or green glands - Crustaceans

Kidney

- 1 pair, bean shaped, reddish brown.
- Between T_{12}-L_3 vertebra, close to dorsal inner wall of abdominal cavity.
- Have stretch receptors; guarded by sphincters.

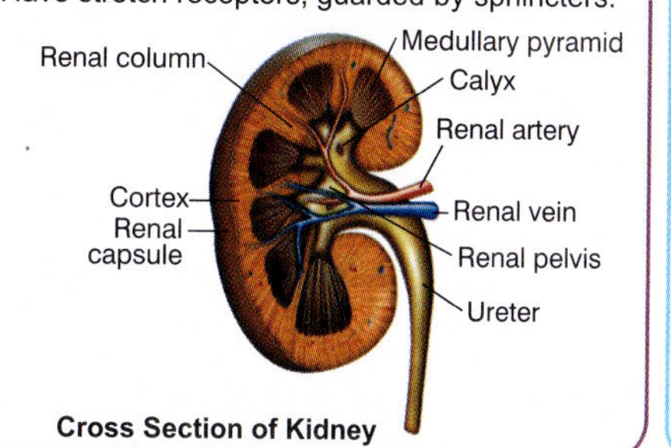

Cross Section of Kidney

Nephron

- Structural and functional unit of the kidneys.
- Each kidney contains millions of nephron.

Distal tubule
Proximal tubule
Bowman's capsule
Glomerulus
collecting duct
Arterioles
Branch of renal vein
Branch of renal artery
Loop of Henle
Capillaries
Ascending limb
Descending limb

An individual nephron and its blood supply

Podocytes
Mesangial cells
Efferent arteriole
Distal tubule
Renal sympathetic nerve fibre
Juxtaglomerular cells
Afferent arteriole
Smooth muscle cells
Macula densa

The Juxtamedullary Apparatus

Types of Nephron

Juxtamedullary
(Mainly lie in inner cortex, 15% of total nephron)

Cortical
(Mainly lie in renal cortex; 85% of total nephron; highly reduced vasa recta)

Roles of Other Organs in Excretion

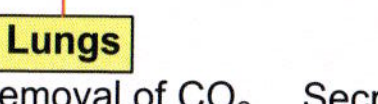

Lungs
Removal of CO_2 (200 mL/ min or 18 L / day) and water.

Liver
Secretes bilirubin, biliverdin, cholesterol, degraded steroid hormones, vitamins and drugs which pass through digestive tract.

Skin

Sweat glands
Eliminate small amount of urea, NaCl and lactic acid, etc. through sweat.

Sebaceous glands
Eliminate sterols, hydrocarbons and waxes through sebum.

Saliva
Elimination of small amount of nitrogenous wastes.

Steps of Urine Formation

Glomerular Filtration : Water, nutrients and wastes are filtered from

Tubular Reabsorption: In the Proximal Convoluted Tubule (PCT), most water and nutrients are reabsorbed into the blood.

Tubular Secretion In the Distal Convoluted Tubule (DCT) additional wastes are actively secreted into the tubule from the blood.

Concentration In the collecting duct, additional water may leave the blood, creating urine that is more concentrated than the blood.

Glomerular Filtration Rate (GFR)
The amount of filtrate formed by kidney per minute is GFR.
In healthy individual, it is about 125 mL/min, i.e. 180L

Test 2

Syllabus
- Osmoregulation; Mechanism of Concentration of the Filtrate
- Regulation of Kidney Function-Renin-Angiotensin, ANF, ADH and Diabetes Insipidus
- Disorders- Uremia, Renal Failure, Renal Calculi, Nephritis; Dialysis and Artificial Kidney

NCERT Page 210 to 214

For deeper insight, **Scan the QR Code**

Chapter 16

Mechanism of Concentration of the Filtrate

- It is the **mechanism of urine concentration**. The flow of filtrate in the limbs of Henle's loop and the flow of blood in the two limbs of vasa recta is in opposite direction, thus forming a counter-current.
- It maintains the gradient of increasing osmolarity of medullary interstitium. This gradient is mainly caused by **NaCl** and **urea**. There occurs reabsorption of ions and water in long loop of juxta-medullary nephron and recycling of salts and urea in vasa recta.

Glomerular (Bowman's capsule); Glomerulus; Afferent arteriole; Efferent arteriole; Proximal convoluted tubule; Distal convoluted tubule; Collecting duct; Interstitial fluid in renal medulla; Osmotic gradient (300, 400, 600, 800, 1000, 1200); Loop of Henle; Papillary duct; Concentrated urine; Urea

1. Symporters in thick assending limb cause bulid up of Na^+ and Cl^- in the renal medulla
2. Counter-current flow through loop of Henle establishes an osmotic gradient
3. Principal cells in collecting duct reabsorb more water when ADH is present
4. Urea recycling causes build up of urea in the renal medulla

Key: H_2O; Na^+Cl^-; Blood flow; Presence of Na^+-K^+-$2Cl^-$ symporters; Flow of tubular fluid

Interstitial fluid in renal cortex; Descending; Ascending; Vasa recta

Regulation of Kidney Function

- **Control by ADH** (Anti-Diuretic Hormone) **(e.g. Vasopressin)**

Decrease in body fluid volume → Activation of osmoreceptors → Stimulation of hypothalamus → Release of ADH (from posterior pituitary gland) → Facilitates water reabsorption from DCT → Prevents diuresis

Increase in body fluid volume → Switch off the osmoreceptors → Signal to hypothalamus → Suppress the ADH release → Reduce water reabsorption → Excessive loss of water from body

- **Control by ANF** (Atrial Natriuretic Factor)

Increase in blood flow to atria of heart releases ANF. → Causes vasodilation and thus decreases blood pressure. → ANF acts as a check on renin-angiotensin mechanism.

- **Control by Renin Angiotensin Aldosterone System** (RAAS)

Fall in GFR —Renin (JG cells)→ Angiotensinogen → Angiotensin-I → Angiotensin-II —Acts on→ Adrenal cortex → Increase glomerular blood pressure and also secretes → Aldosterone → Reabsorption of Na^+ and water from DCT

* **Diabetes Insipidus** It is a rare disorder that causes the body to make too much urine due to low production or improper usage of

Characteristics and Composition of Urine

- An adult human excretes on an average **1 to 1.5 L of urine per day**.
- On an average, **25-30 gm of urea** is excreted out per day.
- Light yellow; pH-6.
- Produced urine is nearly 4 times concentrated than initial filtrate.
- **Diabetes Mellitus** Indicated by Glycosuria (presence of glucose in urine), ketonuria (presence of

Disorders of Excretory System

- **Uremia** Accumulation of urea in blood due to kidney malfunction.
- **Renal Calculi** Formation of insoluble mass of crystallised salts (oxalates or phosphates of calcium). They are removed through surgery (nephrolithotomy) or broken by laser.
- **Glomerulonephritis** Inflammation of glomeruli of kidney. It occurs due to congenital kidney defect or by an allergic reaction to the toxins of bacteria such as *Streptococcus*.
- **Renal Failure** It is the partial or total inability of kidneys to carry

Artificial Kidney

- Artificial kidney called **haemodialyser,** is a machine used to filtre blood of damaged kidney. This is called **haemodialysis.**

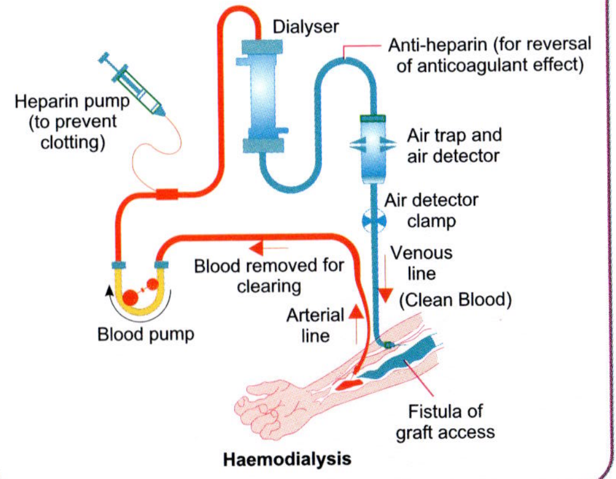

Haemodialysis

Kidney Transplantation

- Done in case of total failure of kidney.
- Kidney transplantation is classified as cadaveric (deceased donor) or living donor kidney transplant.
- Living donor kidney transplants are further classified as genetically related (blood related) or unrelated transplants.
- In this process, both the damaged kidneys of patients are removed by surgery and a functional kidney from a healthy donor preferably from close relative is taken and transplanted in the patient's body.
- Recipient has to take some immunosuppressents to suppress immune system. Recipient and donor, both can survive on one kidney.

Micturition

- The expulsion of urine from the urinary bladder.
- A reflex process, but can be controlled voluntarily upto some extent in grown up children and adults.
- The **CNS** (Central Nervous System) sends the signal which cause the stretching of urinary bladder when it gets filled with urine.
- In response, the stretch receptors on the walls of the bladder sends signals to the CNS.
- CNS passes on motor message to initiate the contraction of smooth muscles of bladder and simultaneous relaxation of the urethral

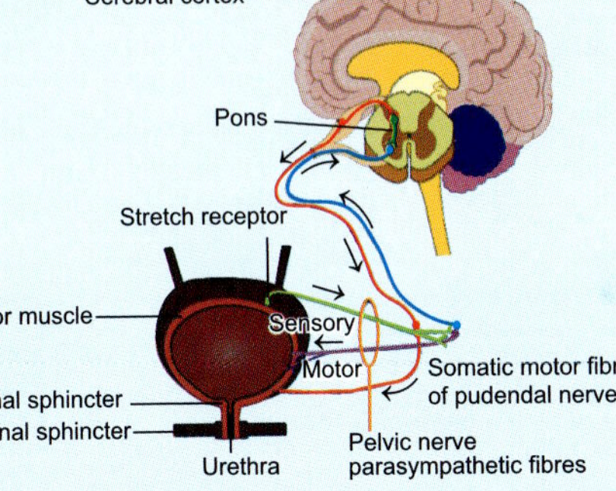

Syllabus

- Types of Movement- Ciliary, Muscular, Flagellar
- Skeletal Muscles-Contractile Protein and Muscle Contraction

NCERT Page 217 to 223

For deeper insight, **Scan the QR Code**

Movement and Locomotion

- **Locomotion** Voluntary movements resulting in change in place/location.
- All locomotions are movements, but all movements are not locomotion.
- *Paramoecium* - Cilia helps in movement of food through cytopharynx and in locomotion as well.
- *Hydra* -Tentacles are used for capturing of prey and also for locomotion.

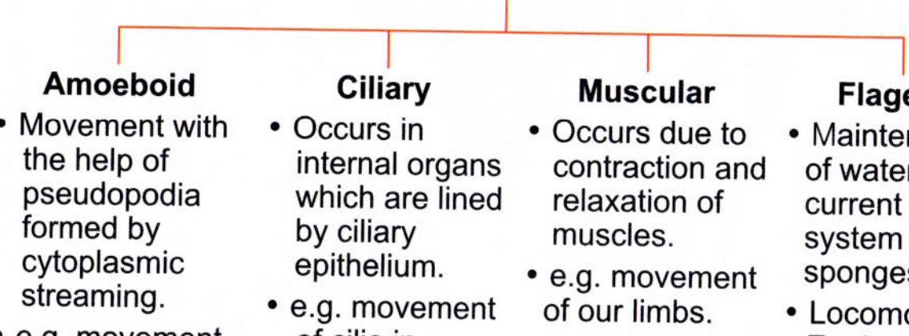

Types of Movements

Amoeboid
- Movement with the help of pseudopodia formed by cytoplasmic streaming.
- e.g. movement of leucocytes, macrophages.

Ciliary
- Occurs in internal organs which are lined by ciliary epithelium.
- e.g. movement of cilia in trachea.

Muscular
- Occurs due to contraction and relaxation of muscles.
- e.g. movement of our limbs.

Flagellar
- Maintenance of water current in canal system of sponges.
- Locomotion in *Euglena*, swimming of spermatozoa

Muscles

- Originate from the embryonic mesoderm; made up of muscle fibres.
- 600 muscles in human body contributing about 40% of the total body weight.
- Characteristics of muscles: contractability, excitability, conductivity.
- Based on the location, there are three types of muscles: skeletal, smooth and cardiac muscles.

Types of Muscle Fibres

Red Muscle Fibres	White Muscle Fibres
Thinner fibres.	Thicker fibres.
Dark red in colour due to the accumulation of more myoglobin.	White or pale yellow in colour due to less or no accumulation of myoglobin.
More mitochondria.	Less mitochondria.
Carry out aerobic contraction.	Carry out anaerobic contraction.
Found in muscles required to undergo prolonged contraction, e.g. extensor muscle on back of human body.	Found in muscles that contract faster, e.g. muscles of the eyeball.

Skeletal Muscles

- Muscles attached to skeletal, components.
- Striated, multi-nucleate
- Voluntary

Skeletal muscle
Tendon
Bone
Muscle fibres
Transverse (T) tubule
Myofibrils
Sarcoplasmic reticulum
Sarcolemma (plasma membrane)
Mitochondrion
Sacromere
Actin myofilament
Myosin myofilament

Organisation of Skeletal Muscle

Z-line
Thin filament
Thick filament
M-line
Thin filament
Z-line
(Elastic fibre bisecting I-band)
Sarcomere
(Functional unit of contraction; portion between two successive Z-line)
Zone of overlap
H-zone
Zone of overlap
I-band (Light band; actin proteins)
A-band (Dark band; myosin proteins)
I-band (Light band)

Detailed Structure of Myofibril

Structure of Actin and Myosin Filament

- **Actin**
  Made up of 2 'F' actins helically wound to each other.
  Two filaments of tropomyosin protein also run close to 'F' actins throughout its length.
  A complex protein troponin is distributed at regular intervals on tropomyosin.

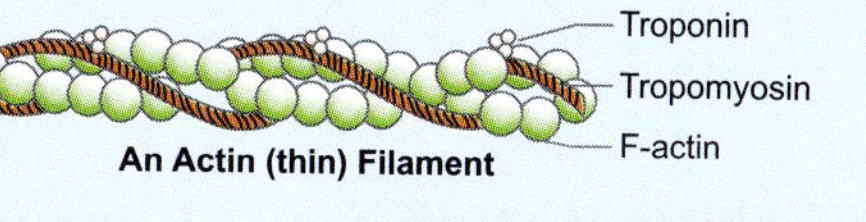

An Actin (thin) Filament

- **Myosin**
  - Polymer of meromyosin.
  - Each meromyosin has two components - a globular head (heavy meromyosin) with short arm and a tail (light meromyosin).
  - Head with its short arm is called **cross arm.**

Actin binding sites
ATP binding sites
Head
Cross arm

Myosin monomere

Mechanism of Muscle Contraction

- Contraction of muscle fibre takes place by sliding of actin and myosin (Sliding filament theory).

Actin filament
P ADP
Myosin filament
(Cocking of myosin head)
Cross bridge
Myosin head
(Formation of cross bridge)
P ADP
Sliding / rotation
ATP
(Breaking of cross bridge)

The Contraction Cycle

- **Sliding Filament Theory**
  - Impulse arrives at neuromuscular junction.
  - It stimulates the sarcoplasmic reticulum to release calcium ions.
  - The calcium attaches to the troponin which removes tropomyosin from the myosin binding site on actin.
  - The myosin and actin form cross bridge.
  - The ATPase present on the myosin head converts the ATP to ADP, Pi and energy.
  - The myosin head binds the actin sliding over each other which allows the muscle to shorten.
  - The stimulation stops and the calcium ions are removed.
  - The muscle returns back to the normal position.

H-zone
I-band
A-band
Relaxed
Z-line
Z-line
Z-line
Contracting (Sarcomere shortens, I-band reduced, length of A band retained)
Maximally contracted
Two sarcomeres

Test 2

Syllabus
- Skeletal System and its Function
- Joints
- Disorders of Muscular and Skeletal System-Myasthenia Gravis, Muscular Dystrophy, Tetany, Arthritis, Osteoporosis, Gout

NCERT Page 224 to 227

For deeper insight, **Scan the QR Code**

Human Skeletal System

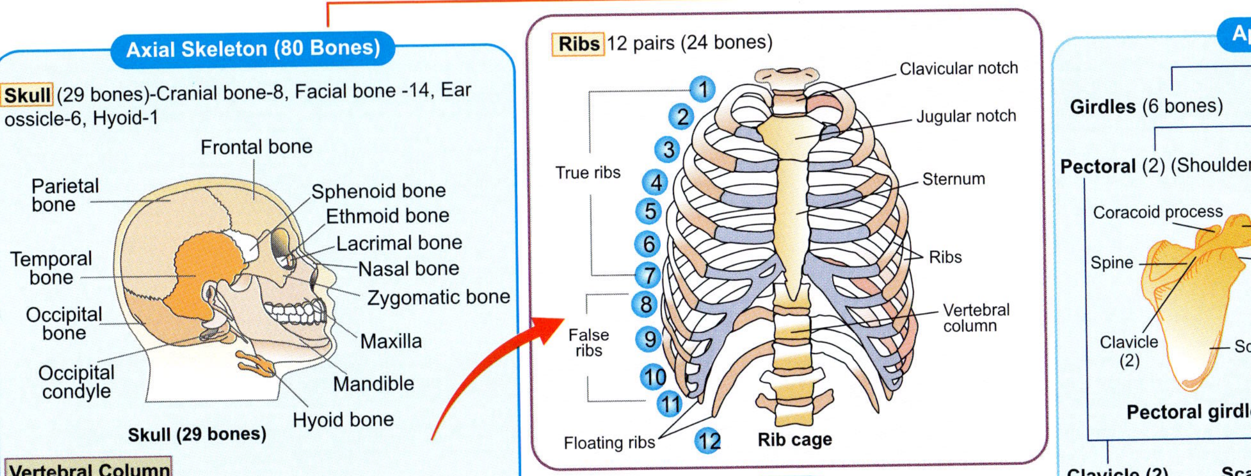

Axial Skeleton (80 Bones)

Skull (29 bones)-Cranial bone-8, Facial bone -14, Ear ossicle-6, Hyoid-1

Vertebral Column
- 26 serially arranged units called **vertebrae**.

Cervical region (7) (curved anteriorly)
Thoracic region (12) (curved posteriorly)
Lumbar region (5) (curved anteriorly)
Sacral (1-fused) and coccygeal region (1-fused) (curved posteriorly)

First cervical vertebra (atlas)
Second cervical vertebra (axis)
Seventh cervical vertebra
First thoracic vertebra
Intervertebral disk
Twelveth thoracic vertebra
First lumbar vertebra
Inter vertebral foramina
Transverse process
Spinous process
Sacral promontory
Fifth lumbar vertebra
Sacrum
Coccyx

Vertebral Column (26 bones)

Sternum (1) Flat dagger-shaped bone; provides a surface to attach muscle and helps in respiratory mechanism.

Ribs 12 pairs (24 bones)

Joints

Structure where two bones articulate; acts as fulcrum

Types of joints

- **Fibrous Joints** (Do not allow movement) → e.g. shown by flat skull bones
- **Cartilaginous Joints** (Allow very slight movement) → e.g. joints between the bones of skull
- **Synovial Joints** (Freely movable) → e.g. joint between adjacent vertebrae
  - **Ball and Socket Joints** e.g. between humerus and pectoral girdle, between femur and pelvic girdle.
  - **Hinge Joints** e.g. knee joint, elbow joint.
  - **Pivot Joints** e.g. atlas and axis
  - **Gliding Joints** e.g. between carpals
  - **Saddle Joints** e.g. between carpals and metacarpals of thumb

Appendicular Skeleton (126 Bones)

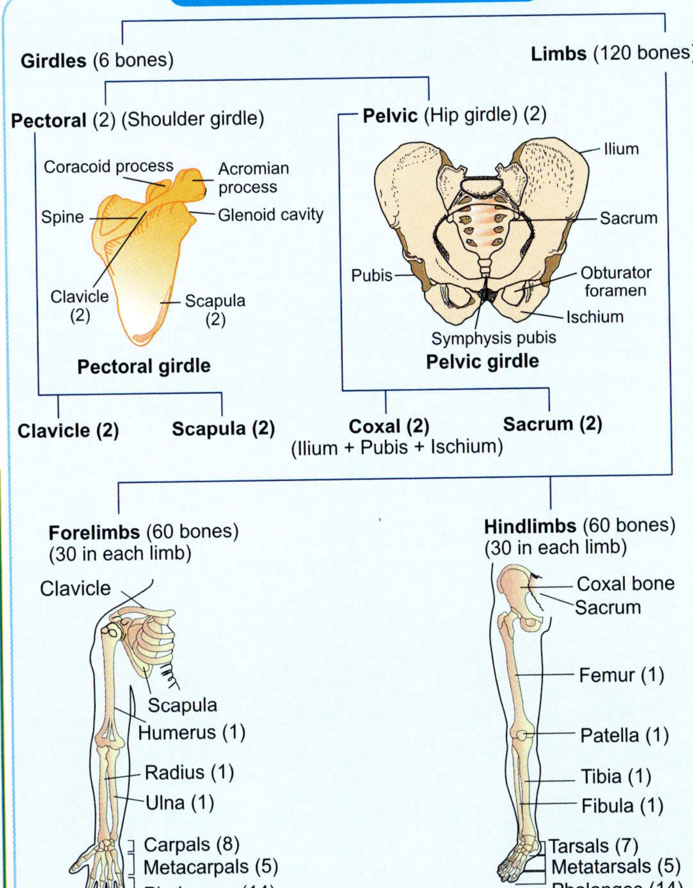

Girdles (6 bones)
- **Pectoral** (2) (Shoulder girdle): **Clavicle (2)**, **Scapula (2)**
- **Pelvic** (Hip girdle) (2): **Coxal (2)** (Ilium + Pubis + Ischium), **Sacrum (2)**

Limbs (120 bones)
- **Forelimbs** (60 bones) (30 in each limb): Clavicle, Scapula, Humerus (1), Radius (1), Ulna (1), Carpals (8), Metacarpals (5), Phalanges (14)
- **Hindlimbs** (60 bones) (30 in each limb): Coxal bone, Sacrum, Femur (1), Patella (1), Tibia (1), Fibula (1), Tarsals (7), Metatarsals (5), Phalanges (14)

Disorders of Muscular and Skeletal System

- **Myasthenia Gravis** Auto-immune disorder affecting neuromuscular Junction
- **Muscular Dystrophy** Progressive degeneration of skeletal muscle mostly due to genetic disorder.
- **Tetany** Rapid spasms in muscle due to low Ca^{++} in body fluid.
- **Arthritis** Inflammation of joints.
- **Osteoporosis** Age-related disorder; characterised by decreased bone mass.
- **Gout** Inflammation of joints due to accumulation of uric acid crystals.

Test 1

Syllabus	• Nervous System in Humans • Neurons and Nerves • Generation and Conduction of Nerve Impulse	• Peripheral and Visceral Nervous System	NCERT Page 230 to 235

For deeper insight, **Scan the QR Code**

Chapter 18

Coordination

- It is the process through which two or more organs interact and complement the functions of one another.
- In human body, the neural system and the endocrine system jointly coordinate and integrate all the activities of the organs.

Neural System in Some Organisms

- ***Hydra*** Composed of network of neurons.
- **Insects** Organised neural system where brain is present along with ganglia and neural tissues.
- **Vertebrates** Well-developed neural system.

Human Neural System

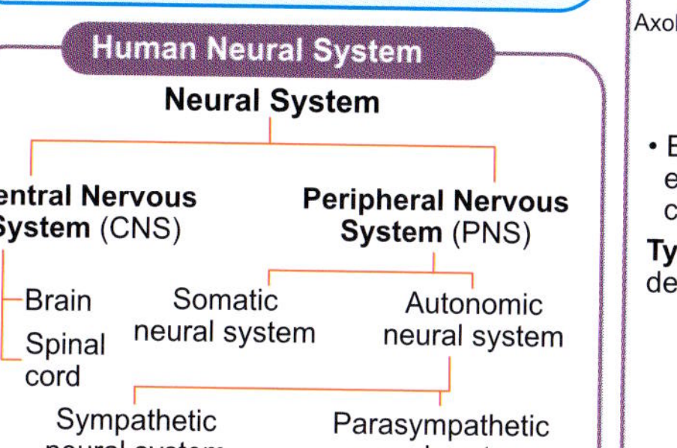

Nerve Fibres of PNS

- **Afferent fibres** (Transmit impulses from tissues/organs to the CNS)
- **Efferent fibres** (Transmit impulses from the CNS to concerned tissues/organs)

Types of Axon

Medullated/ Myelinated Axons	Non-medullated/Non-Myelinated Axons
Medullary or myelin sheath is present.	Medullary or myelin sheath is absent.
Nodes of Ranvier and internodes are present.	Nodes and internodes are absent.
These occur in white matter of brain and spinal cord in cranial and spinal nerves.	These occur in grey matter of brain and spinal cord and in autonomous and somatic nervous systems.
Impulse conduction is faster.	Impulse conduction is slower.

Neuron

- Structural and functional unit of neural system.
- A group of neurons forms a **nerve**.

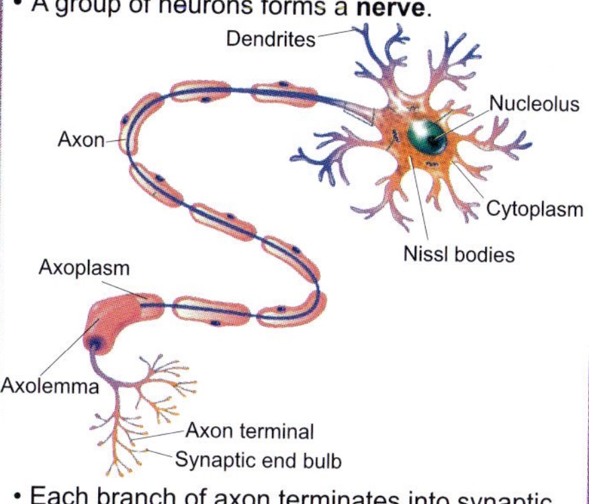

- Each branch of axon terminates into synaptic end which possess synaptic vesicles containing chemicals called **neurotransmitters.**

Types of Neuron Based on number of axon and dendrites

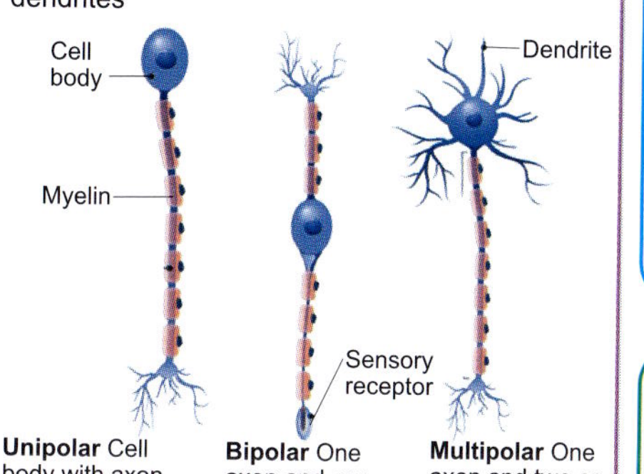

- **Unipolar** Cell body with axon only; found usually in the embryonic stage.
- **Bipolar** One axon and one dendrite; found in retina of eye.
- **Multipolar** One axon and two or more dendrites; found in cerebral cortex.

Transmission of Impulse

- A nerve impulse is transmitted from one neuron to another through synapses.
- There are two types of synapses:
  1. **Electrical Synapse** Here, the membranes of pre and post-synaptic neurons are in very close proximity; quick transmission.
  2. **Chemical Synapse** Here, the membrane of pre and post-synaptic neuron are separated by fluid filled space called **synaptic cleft**. Neurotransmitters are involved here.

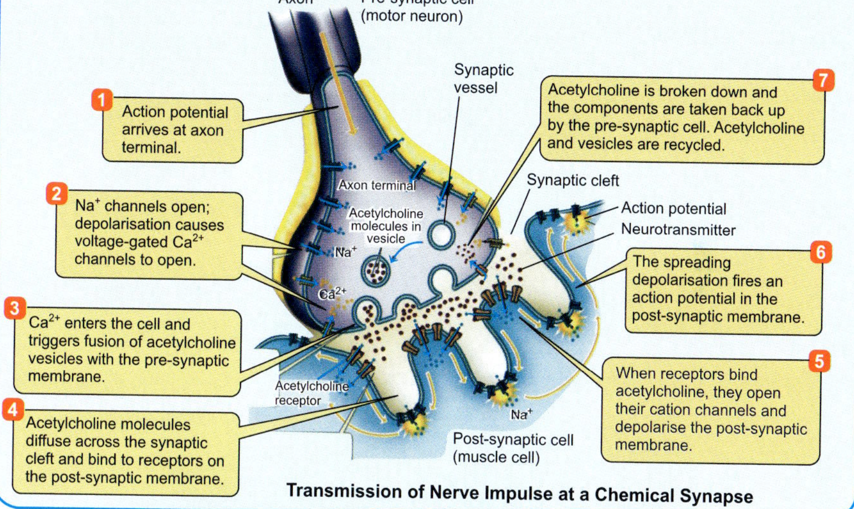

Transmission of Nerve Impulse at a Chemical Synapse

Generation and Conduction of Nerve Impulse

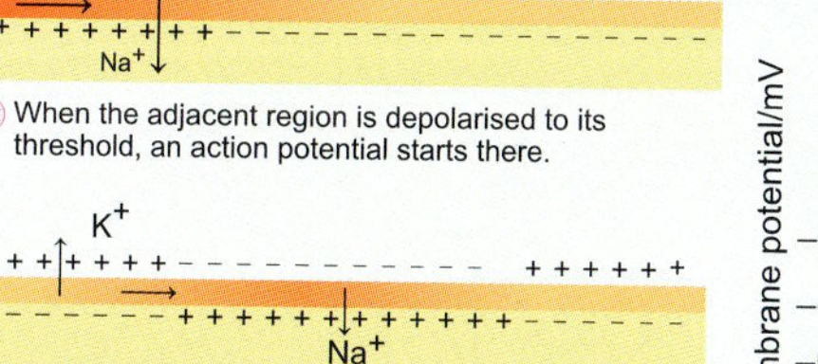

1. At the start, the membrane is completely polarised.
2. When an action potential is initiated, a region of the membrane depolarised. As a result, the adjacent regions become depolarised.
3. When the adjacent region is depolarised to its threshold, an action potential starts there.
4. Repolarisation occurs due to the outward flow of K^+ ions. The depolarisation spreads forward, triggering and action potential.

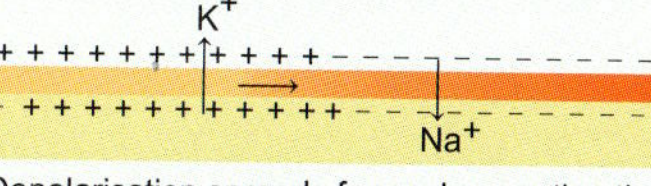

5. Depolarisation spreads forward, repeating the process.

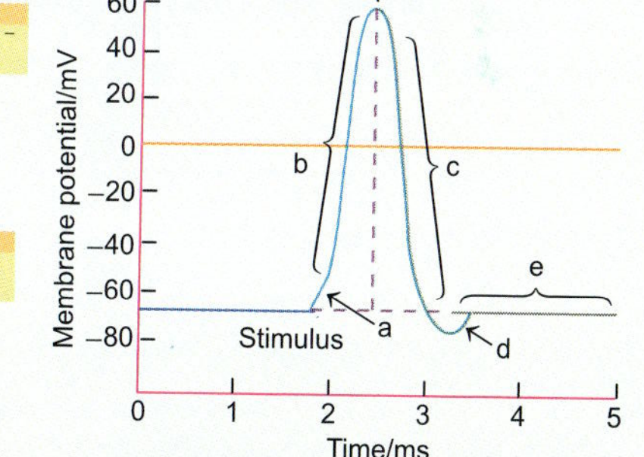

(a) Threshold, (b) Depolarisation, (c) Repolarisation, (d) Hyperpolarisation, (e) Resting membrane potential (f) Spike potential

A Nerve Conduction Graph

Test 2

Syllabus

- Central Nervous System (Brain-Forebrain, Midbrain, Hindbrain and Spinal Cord)

NCERT Page 235 to 236

For deeper insight, **Scan the QR Code**

Chapter 18

Central Nervous System

- Acts as command and control system of the body.
- Consists of brain and spinal cord.

Protective coverings – Skull, Meninges

Features	Outer	Middle	Inner
Name of meninges	Duramater	Arachnoid	Piamater
In contact with	Skull	—	Brain

- **Major Divisions of Brain**

Divisions	Major Parts
Forebrain	Cerebrum, thalamus, hypothalamus
Midbrain	Corpora quadrigemina
Hindbrain	Pons, medulla, cerebellum

- **Cerebrospinal Fluid (CSF)**: Colourless, slightly alkaline fluid similar to the plasma; absorbs shock or jerk to protect brain and spinal cord.

Spinal Cord

- Located in the mid thoracic region.
- Continuous with the medulla oblongata through foramen magnum of the skull.
- It lies inside the neural canal of vertebral column.

Gray matter; White matter; Posterior (dorsal) horn; Lateral horn; Anterior (ventral) horn; Posterior (dorsal) columns; Lateral columns; Anterior columns

TS Spinal Cord

Functions of Spinal Cord

- The spinal cord conducts impulses to and from the brain.
- The dorsal funiculus has ascending nerve tract for conducting sensory impulses towards the brain.
- Lateral and ventral funiculi conduct motor impulses from the brain to spinal cord.
- It controls most of the reflex activities.

Brain and Its Components

- Brain is central information processing organ of the body.

Forebrain

Cerebrum

- Major part of brain
- Cleft divides it longitudinally into right and left **cerebral hemispheres**, connected by **corpus callosum.**

Thalamus

- Major coordinating centre for sensory and motor signalling.

Hypothalamus

- Lies at base of thalamus.
- Has various centres for controlling body temperature, urge for eating and drinking.
- Secretes hormones.

Pineal gland; Corpus callosum; Frontal lobe; Parietal lobe; Limbic lobe; Occipital lobe; Temporal lobe

Pituitary gland

- Controls the release of most hormones.

Sagittal Section of Human Brain

Midbrain

Cerebral Aqueduct

- Canal passes through midbrain.

Corpora Quadrigemina

- Located between thalamus/hypothalamus and pons.
- 4 lobes on dorsal side between forebrain and pons.
- Integrates visual, tactile and auditory inputs.

Hindbrain

Pons

- Fibrous tract that connects different regions of the brain.

Cerebellum

- Convoluted surface to accommodate more neurons.
- Integrates information received from semicircular canal and auditory system.

Medulla Oblongata

- Connects brain to spinal cord.
- Has centres for controlling respiration, cardiovascular reflexes and gastric secretions.

Regions in Cerebral Hemisphere	Appearance	Composition
Outer cortex Inner cortex	Grey White	Concentrated cell bodies Myelinated nerve fibres

Cerebral Cortex

- **Sensory areas** (Integration of sensory information)
- **Motor areas** (Consists the skeletal muscle)
- **Association areas** (Neither sensory nor motor)
  - Functions
    - Inter-sensory associations (Multisensory integration)
    - Memory (Episodic memory formed)
    - Communication (Speaking and writing)

Basic Functions of Brain

Controls the voluntary movements	Controls hunger, thirst
Balance of body	Circadian rhythms
Functioning of vital organs (kidneys, lungs, heart)	Human behaviour
Thermoregulation	Activities of endocrine glands

Limbic System/Limbic Lobe

The medial border of temporal lobe; loop of cortical structures surrounding the corpus callosum and thalamus.

- **Parts included** Inner part of cerebral hemisphere, hippocampus (sea-horse-shaped; converts short term memory to long term memory) amygdala (almond-shaped; associated with the normal emotions) and hypothalamus
- **Functions** Involved in expression of emotional reactions e.g., excitement , pleasure, rage, fear; motivation, regulation of sexual behaviour, autonomic responses and olfaction.

Test 1

Syllabus

- Endocrine Glands And Hormones; Human Endocrine System-Hypothalamus, Pituitary, Pineal, Thyroid and Parathyroid Gland
- Disorders Related to Hypo and Hyperactivity of Hormones -Dwarfism, Gigantism, Acromegaly, Diabetes insipidus

NCERT Page 239 to 243

For deeper insight, **Scan the QR Code**

Chapter 19

Endocrine Glands and Hormones

Endocrine Glands
- Ductless glands.
- Secretions - Hormones
- Neural System+Endocrine System → Jointly regulate the physiological functions in the body.
- Invertebrates - Very simple endocrine system.
- Vertebrates - Large number of hormones.

Hormones
- Released into blood and transported to target organ.
- Non-nutrient chemicals
- Act as intercellular messengers
- Produced in trace amounts.
- Have low molecular weight.
- Excess or deficiency leads to disorders.

Hypothalamus

- Major link between nervous and endocrine systems.
- It is the basal part of diencephalon.
- Neurosecretory cells (nuclei) of hypothalamus secrete the following types of hormones
  - **Releasing Hormone** Stimulates secretions of pituitary hormones, e.g. GnRH
  - **Inhibiting Hormone** Inhibits secretions of pituitary hormones, e.g. Somatostatins
  - **Oxytocin and Vasopressin** Transported axonally and stored in pituitary.

Thymus Gland

- Located on dorsal side of heart and aorta.
- Secretes peptide hormones, thymosin which play role in differentiation of T-lymphocytes (helps in cell-mediated immunity).
- Thymosin also produce antibodies for humoral immunity.

Interlobular septum — Medulla — Thymic corpuscle — Capsule — Cortex — Lymph duct — Vein — Artery

Figure Showing Thymus Gland

Parathyroid Gland

- Located on the back side of thyroid gland. Each lobe of thyroid gland has its one pair.
- Secretes peptide hormone called **Parathyroid Hormone (PTH),** which regulates calcium levels in blood (hypercalcemic hormone).

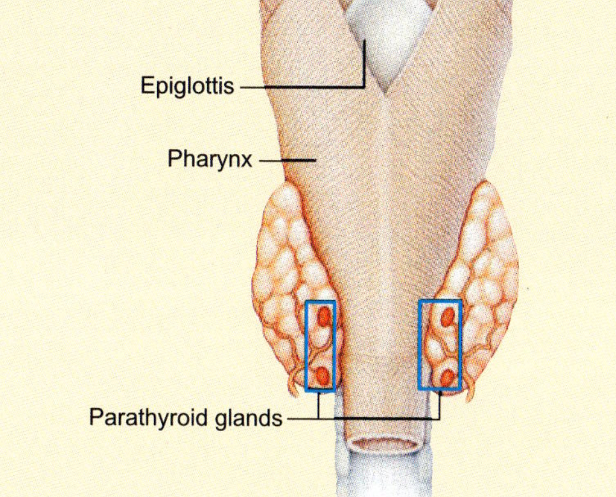

Figure Showing Location of Parathyroid Gland

Thyroid Gland

- It has two lobes on either side of trachea inter-connected by isthmus (connective tissue).
- Follicular cells synthesise **tetraiodothyronine** or **thyroxine (T_4)** and **tri-iodothyronine (T_3)**.
- **Hypothyroidism** Enlargement of thyroid gland.
- May lead to mental retardation and stunted growth **(Cretinism),** deaf mutism in baby during pregnancy.
- **Hyperthyroidism** Affects body physiology due to high synthesis of thyroid gland.
- **Exophthalmic Goitre** Form of hyperthyroidism with enlargement of thyroid gland; BMR increases.

Thyroid cartilage (Adam's apple) — Blood vessel — Thyroid gland — Trachea (windpipe)

(Largest endocrine gland)

Figure Showing Location of Thyroid Hormone

Pituitary Gland

- Located in a body cavity called **sella tursica**.
- Attached to hypothalamus by a stalk.

Pituitary Gland
- **Adenohypophysis** (Anterior lobe)
  - **Pars distalis**
    - **Growth Hormone** (GH)
    - **Prolactin** (PRL)
    - **Thyroid Stimulating Hormone** (TSH)
    - **Adrenocorticotropic Hormone** (ACTH)
    - **Luteinizing Hormone** (LH)
    - **Follicle Stimulating Hormone** (FSH)
  - **Pars intermedia**
- **Neurohypophysis** (Posterior lobe) Do not release any hormone but stores and releases the given hormones
  - **Oxytocin**
  - **Vasopressin** (ADH)

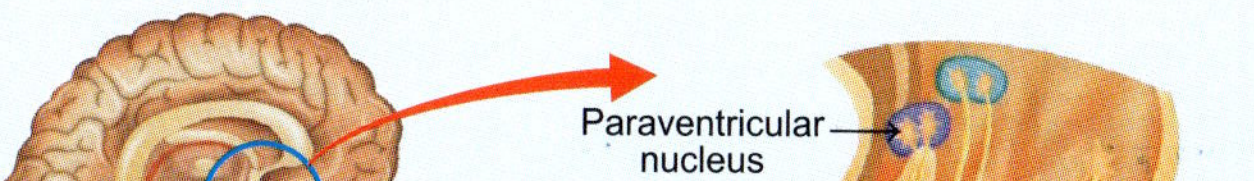

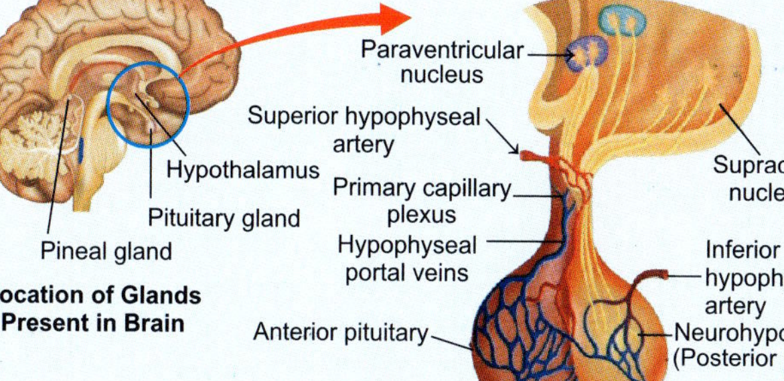

Location of Glands Present in Brain

Location of Pituitary Gland in Brain

Disorders

Diseases	Causes	Symptoms
Dwarfism	Hyposecretion of GH	Stunted growth
Gigantism	Hypersecretion of GH	Abnormal growth of the body
Acromegaly	Hypersecretion of GH	Severe disfigurement, especially of face
Diabetes insipidus	Hyposecretion of ADH	Diminished ability of the kidney to conserve water leading to water loss and dehydration

Pineal Gland

- Located on dorsal side of forebrain.
- Smallest endocrine gland.
- Secretes melatonin for regulation of 24 hrs rhythm, sleep-wake cycle, menstrual cycle, pigmentation.

Test 2

Syllabus

- Adrenal Gland
- Pancreas
- Gonads

- Mechanism of Hormone Action
- Roles of Hormones as Messengers and Regulators
- Hypo and Hyperactivity Disorders-Diabetes Mellitus, Addison's Disease

NCERT Page 243 to 249

For deeper insight, **Scan the QR Code**

Chapter 19

Adrenal Gland

- Located at upper side of each kidney.
- It has two parts: Adrenal medulla (centrally located) and adrenal cortex (peripheral).
  Adrenal medulla secretes adrenaline (epinephrine) and nor-adrenaline (nor-epinephrine).
  Adrenal cortex secretes androgenic steroids, glucocorticoids (e.g. cortisol) and mineralocorticoids (e.g. aldosterone).

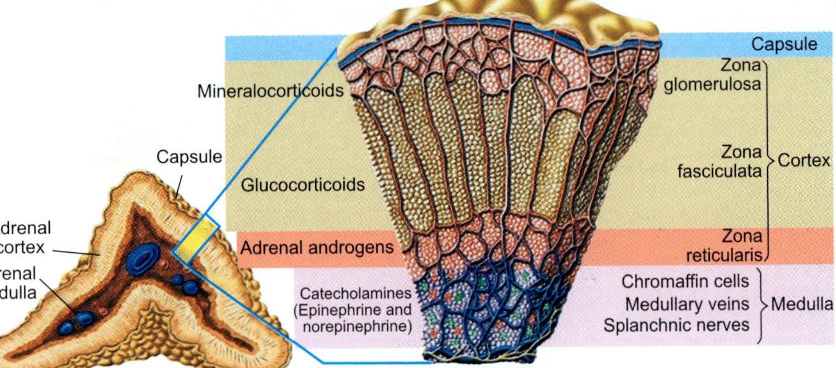

Transverse Section **Microscopic Section**

Addison's Disease-Caused due to underproduction of cortisol and aldosterone (adrenal cortex hormone)

Pancreas

- A dual/composite gland, i.e. exocrine and endocrine functions.
- It contains about 1-2 millions of islets of Langerhans which has glucagon secreting α-**cells** and insulin secreting β-**cells**.
- **Glucagon** hyperglycemic hormone stimulates gluconeogenesis; increases blood sugar level.
- **Insulin** hypoglycemic hormone stimulates glycogenesis; decreased blood sugar level.

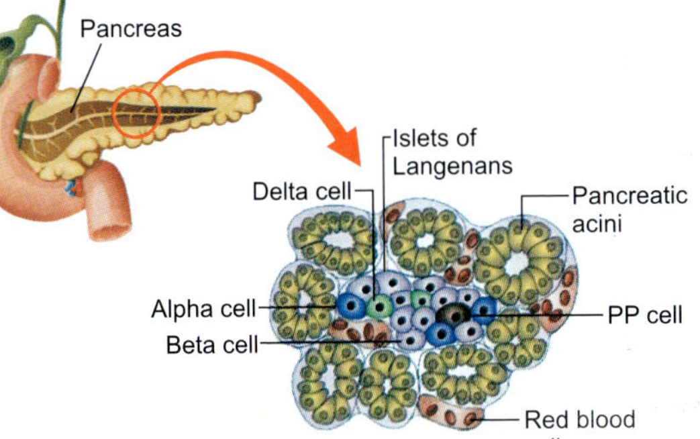

Internal Structure of Pancreas

Diabetes Mellitus Caused due to prolonged hyperglycemia as a result of hyposecretion of insulin.

Ovary (Female Gonad)

- A pair of ovaries (in females) in abdomen produces one ovum per menstrual cycle.
- Composed of ovarian follicles and stromal tissues.
- Ovarian follicles produce **oestrogen** (steroid hormone) which helps in stimulation of growth of female secondary sex organs, female behaviour, mammary glands development.

Testis (Male Gonad)

- A pair of testis present in the scrotal sac in males.
- Composed of seminiferous tubules and interstitial cells.
- Leydig (interstitial) cells produce **androgens** (mainly **testosterone**).

Steroid Hormone Action

1. Steroid hormone diffuses across the membrane and reach the nucleus.
2. It binds to the intracellular hormone receptor to form hormone-receptor complex.
3. The complex binds to the transcription factor which further binds to the DNA.
4. The particular gene gets activated and transcribed.
5. Its transcription leads to the synthesis of a specific protein that influences the metabolism of target cell.

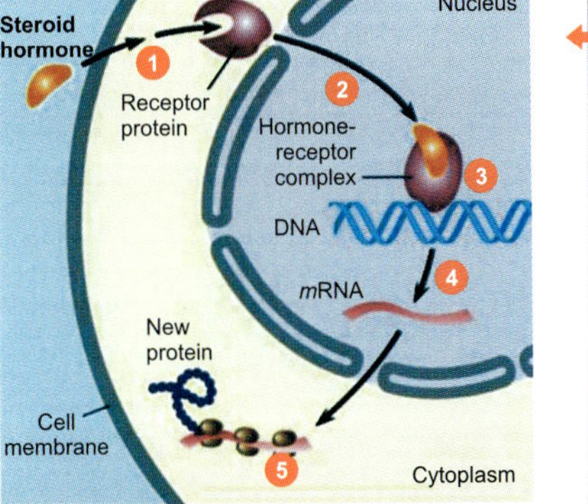

Hormones of Heart, Kidney And Gastrointestinal Tract

- **Heart (Atrial wall)** Releases ANF (reduce blood pressure by dilating blood vessels).
- **Kidney (JG cells)** Releases erythropoietin (erythropoiesis)
- **Gastro-Intestinal Tract (GIT)** Releases GIP/Gastric Inhibitory Peptide (inhibits gastric secretion), Gastrin (acts on gastric glands and stimulates secretion of HCl and pepsinogen), Cholecystokinin or CCK (acts on exocrine part of pancreas and gall bladder to stimulate secretion of pancreatic enzymes and bile juice), and secretin (acts on exocrine part of pancreas and stimulates secretion of water and bicarbonates).
- **Non-endocrine Tissue** Releases growth factors (essential for normal growth, repair and regeneration of tissue).

Mechanism of Hormone Action

- Hormones bind to the specific receptors (hormone receptors) to produce their specific effects on target cells/tissues.
- These receptors are of two types
  (a) **Membrane-bound extracellular receptors** (present on cell membrane of the target cells)
  (b) **Intracellular receptors** (present inside the target cells)
- **Water soluble hormones** (peptide hormone) require membrane-bound receptors and generate secondary messenger, e.g., insulin, glucagon, pituitary hormones, hypothalamic hormones, etc.
- **Lipid soluble hormone** (steroid hormone) being hydrophobic can pass through cell membrane easily, e.g. cortisol, testosterone, estradiol and progesterone.

Peptide Hormone Action

1. Hormone (first or primary messenger) binds with hormone receptor present on outer surface of plasma membrane.
2. Hormone-receptor complex is formed.
3. This complex activates adenylate cyclase enzyme.
4. Adenylate cyclase catalyses the conversion of ATP into cyclic AMP (cAMP).
5. cAMP (secondary messenger) activates appropriate enzyme and accelerate the biochemical reactions in the target cell.

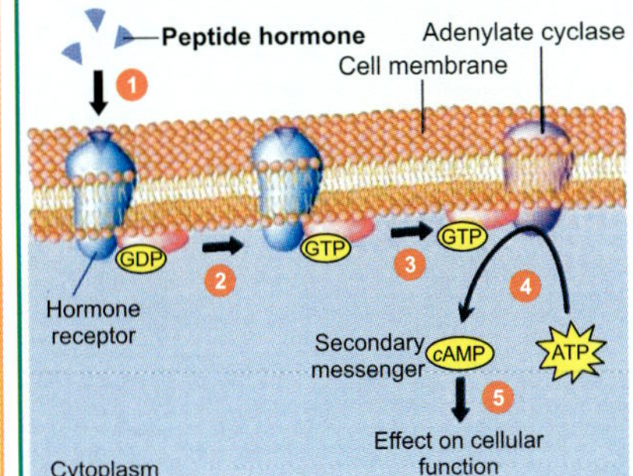

OMR SHEET

ROLL No.

1	1	1	1	1	1	1	1	1	1
2	2	2	2	2	2	2	2	2	2
3	3	3	3	3	3	3	3	3	3
4	4	4	4	4	4	4	4	4	4
5	5	5	5	5	5	5	5	5	5
6	6	6	6	6	6	6	6	6	6
7	7	7	7	7	7	7	7	7	7
8	8	8	8	8	8	8	8	8	8
9	9	9	9	9	9	9	9	9	9
0	0	0	0	0	0	0	0	0	0

TEST BOOKLET No.

1	1	1	1	1	1	1
2	2	2	2	2	2	2
3	3	3	3	3	3	3
4	4	4	4	4	4	4
5	5	5	5	5	5	5
6	6	6	6	6	6	6
7	7	7	7	7	7	7
8	8	8	8	8	8	8
9	9	9	9	9	9	9
0	0	0	0	0	0	0

TEST BOOKLET Code

Q No.	Response				Q No.	Response			
001	a	b	c	d	051	a	b	c	d
002	a	b	c	d	052	a	b	c	d
003	a	b	c	d	053	a	b	c	d
004	a	b	c	d	054	a	b	c	d
005	a	b	c	d	055	a	b	c	d
006	a	b	c	d	056	a	b	c	d
007	a	b	c	d	057	a	b	c	d
008	a	b	c	d	058	a	b	c	d
009	a	b	c	d	059	a	b	c	d
010	a	b	c	d	060	a	b	c	d
011	a	b	c	d	061	a	b	c	d
012	a	b	c	d	062	a	b	c	d
013	a	b	c	d	063	a	b	c	d
014	a	b	c	d	064	a	b	c	d
015	a	b	c	d	065	a	b	c	d
016	a	b	c	d	066	a	b	c	d
017	a	b	c	d	067	a	b	c	d
018	a	b	c	d	068	a	b	c	d
019	a	b	c	d	069	a	b	c	d
020	a	b	c	d	070	a	b	c	d
021	a	b	c	d	071	a	b	c	d
022	a	b	c	d	072	a	b	c	d
023	a	b	c	d	073	a	b	c	d
024	a	b	c	d	074	a	b	c	d
025	a	b	c	d	075	a	b	c	d
026	a	b	c	d	076	a	b	c	d
027	a	b	c	d	077	a	b	c	d
028	a	b	c	d	078	a	b	c	d
029	a	b	c	d	079	a	b	c	d
030	a	b	c	d	080	a	b	c	d
031	a	b	c	d	081	a	b	c	d
032	a	b	c	d	082	a	b	c	d
033	a	b	c	d	083	a	b	c	d
034	a	b	c	d	084	a	b	c	d
035	a	b	c	d	085	a	b	c	d
036	a	b	c	d	086	a	b	c	d
037	a	b	c	d	087	a	b	c	d
038	a	b	c	d	088	a	b	c	d
039	a	b	c	d	089	a	b	c	d
040	a	b	c	d	090	a	b	c	d
041	a	b	c	d	091	a	b	c	d
042	a	b	c	d	092	a	b	c	d
043	a	b	c	d	093	a	b	c	d
044	a	b	c	d	094	a	b	c	d
045	a	b	c	d	095	a	b	c	d
046	a	b	c	d	096	a	b	c	d
047	a	b	c	d	097	a	b	c	d
048	a	b	c	d	098	a	b	c	d
049	a	b	c	d	099	a	b	c	d
050	a	b	c	d	100	a	b	c	d

DECLARATION BY THE CANDIDATE

I declare that particulars and signature on this OMR Answer sheet are mine and are Name as in Attendance Sheet. I fruther declare that particulars filled in and Signature as well as the circles darkened on this ORIGINALCOPY is same as in OFFICE COPY.

Signature with time (in running handwriting)

CANDIDATE's NAME (in running handwriting)

MOTHER's NAME (in running handwriting)

FATHER's NAME (in running handwriting)

CANDIDATE LEFT HAND IMPRESSION

SIGNATURE OF INVIGILATOR'S WITH TIME

1

2

MEDACE

OMR SHEET

ROLL No.

1	1	1	1	1	1	1	1	1	1
2	2	2	2	2	2	2	2	2	2
3	3	3	3	3	3	3	3	3	3
4	4	4	4	4	4	4	4	4	4
5	5	5	5	5	5	5	5	5	5
6	6	6	6	6	6	6	6	6	6
7	7	7	7	7	7	7	7	7	7
8	8	8	8	8	8	8	8	8	8
9	9	9	9	9	9	9	9	9	9
0	0	0	0	0	0	0	0	0	0

TEST BOOKLET No.

1	1	1	1	1	1	1
2	2	2	2	2	2	2
3	3	3	3	3	3	3
4	4	4	4	4	4	4
5	5	5	5	5	5	5
6	6	6	6	6	6	6
7	7	7	7	7	7	7
8	8	8	8	8	8	8
9	9	9	9	9	9	9
0	0	0	0	0	0	0

TEST BOOKLET Code

Q No.	Response				Q No.	Response			
001	a	b	c	d	051	a	b	c	d
002	a	b	c	d	052	a	b	c	d
003	a	b	c	d	053	a	b	c	d
004	a	b	c	d	054	a	b	c	d
005	a	b	c	d	055	a	b	c	d
006	a	b	c	d	056	a	b	c	d
007	a	b	c	d	057	a	b	c	d
008	a	b	c	d	058	a	b	c	d
009	a	b	c	d	059	a	b	c	d
010	a	b	c	d	060	a	b	c	d
011	a	b	c	d	061	a	b	c	d
012	a	b	c	d	062	a	b	c	d
013	a	b	c	d	063	a	b	c	d
014	a	b	c	d	064	a	b	c	d
015	a	b	c	d	065	a	b	c	d
016	a	b	c	d	066	a	b	c	d
017	a	b	c	d	067	a	b	c	d
018	a	b	c	d	068	a	b	c	d
019	a	b	c	d	069	a	b	c	d
020	a	b	c	d	070	a	b	c	d
021	a	b	c	d	071	a	b	c	d
022	a	b	c	d	072	a	b	c	d
023	a	b	c	d	073	a	b	c	d
024	a	b	c	d	074	a	b	c	d
025	a	b	c	d	075	a	b	c	d
026	a	b	c	d	076	a	b	c	d
027	a	b	c	d	077	a	b	c	d
028	a	b	c	d	078	a	b	c	d
029	a	b	c	d	079	a	b	c	d
030	a	b	c	d	080	a	b	c	d
031	a	b	c	d	081	a	b	c	d
032	a	b	c	d	082	a	b	c	d
033	a	b	c	d	083	a	b	c	d
034	a	b	c	d	084	a	b	c	d
035	a	b	c	d	085	a	b	c	d
036	a	b	c	d	086	a	b	c	d
037	a	b	c	d	087	a	b	c	d
038	a	b	c	d	088	a	b	c	d
039	a	b	c	d	089	a	b	c	d
040	a	b	c	d	090	a	b	c	d
041	a	b	c	d	091	a	b	c	d
042	a	b	c	d	092	a	b	c	d
043	a	b	c	d	093	a	b	c	d
044	a	b	c	d	094	a	b	c	d
045	a	b	c	d	095	a	b	c	d
046	a	b	c	d	096	a	b	c	d
047	a	b	c	d	097	a	b	c	d
048	a	b	c	d	098	a	b	c	d
049	a	b	c	d	099	a	b	c	d
050	a	b	c	d	100	a	b	c	d

DECLARATION BY THE CANDIDATE

I declare that particulars and signature on this OMR Answer sheet are mine and are Name as in Attendance Sheet. I fruther declare that particulars filled in and Signature as well as the circles darkened on this ORIGINALCOPY is same as in OFFICE COPY.

Signature with time (in running handwriting)

CANDIDATE's NAME (in running handwriting)

MOTHER's NAME (in running handwriting)

FATHER's NAME (in running handwriting)

CANDIDATE LEFT HAND IMPRESSION

SIGNATURE OF INVIGILATOR'S WITH TIME

1

2

MEDACE

OMR SHEET

ROLL No.

1	1	1	1	1	1	1	1	1	1
2	2	2	2	2	2	2	2	2	2
3	3	3	3	3	3	3	3	3	3
4	4	4	4	4	4	4	4	4	4
5	5	5	5	5	5	5	5	5	5
6	6	6	6	6	6	6	6	6	6
7	7	7	7	7	7	7	7	7	7
8	8	8	8	8	8	8	8	8	8
9	9	9	9	9	9	9	9	9	9
0	0	0	0	0	0	0	0	0	0

TEST BOOKLET No.

1	1	1	1	1	1	1
2	2	2	2	2	2	2
3	3	3	3	3	3	3
4	4	4	4	4	4	4
5	5	5	5	5	5	5
6	6	6	6	6	6	6
7	7	7	7	7	7	7
8	8	8	8	8	8	8
9	9	9	9	9	9	9
0	0	0	0	0	0	0

TEST BOOKLET Code

Q No.	Response				Q No.	Response			
001	a	b	c	d	051	a	b	c	d
002	a	b	c	d	052	a	b	c	d
003	a	b	c	d	053	a	b	c	d
004	a	b	c	d	054	a	b	c	d
005	a	b	c	d	055	a	b	c	d
006	a	b	c	d	056	a	b	c	d
007	a	b	c	d	057	a	b	c	d
008	a	b	c	d	058	a	b	c	d
009	a	b	c	d	059	a	b	c	d
010	a	b	c	d	060	a	b	c	d
011	a	b	c	d	061	a	b	c	d
012	a	b	c	d	062	a	b	c	d
013	a	b	c	d	063	a	b	c	d
014	a	b	c	d	064	a	b	c	d
015	a	b	c	d	065	a	b	c	d
016	a	b	c	d	066	a	b	c	d
017	a	b	c	d	067	a	b	c	d
018	a	b	c	d	068	a	b	c	d
019	a	b	c	d	069	a	b	c	d
020	a	b	c	d	070	a	b	c	d
021	a	b	c	d	071	a	b	c	d
022	a	b	c	d	072	a	b	c	d
023	a	b	c	d	073	a	b	c	d
024	a	b	c	d	074	a	b	c	d
025	a	b	c	d	075	a	b	c	d
026	a	b	c	d	076	a	b	c	d
027	a	b	c	d	077	a	b	c	d
028	a	b	c	d	078	a	b	c	d
029	a	b	c	d	079	a	b	c	d
030	a	b	c	d	080	a	b	c	d
031	a	b	c	d	081	a	b	c	d
032	a	b	c	d	082	a	b	c	d
033	a	b	c	d	083	a	b	c	d
034	a	b	c	d	084	a	b	c	d
035	a	b	c	d	085	a	b	c	d
036	a	b	c	d	086	a	b	c	d
037	a	b	c	d	087	a	b	c	d
038	a	b	c	d	088	a	b	c	d
039	a	b	c	d	089	a	b	c	d
040	a	b	c	d	090	a	b	c	d
041	a	b	c	d	091	a	b	c	d
042	a	b	c	d	092	a	b	c	d
043	a	b	c	d	093	a	b	c	d
044	a	b	c	d	094	a	b	c	d
045	a	b	c	d	095	a	b	c	d
046	a	b	c	d	096	a	b	c	d
047	a	b	c	d	097	a	b	c	d
048	a	b	c	d	098	a	b	c	d
049	a	b	c	d	099	a	b	c	d
050	a	b	c	d	100	a	b	c	d

DECLARATION BY THE CANDIDATE

I declare that particulars and signature on this OMR Answer sheet are mine and are Name as in Attendance Sheet. I fruther declare that particulars filled in and Signature as well as the circles darkened on this ORIGINALCOPY is same as in OFFICE COPY.

Signature with time (in running handwriting)

CANDIDATE's NAME (in running handwriting)

MOTHER's NAME (in running handwriting)

FATHER's NAME (in running handwriting)

CANDIDATE LEFT HAND IMPRESSION

SIGNATURE OF INVIGILATOR'S WITH TIME

1

2

MED ACE

OMR SHEET

ROLL No.

1	1	1	1	1	1	1	1	1	1
2	2	2	2	2	2	2	2	2	2
3	3	3	3	3	3	3	3	3	3
4	4	4	4	4	4	4	4	4	4
5	5	5	5	5	5	5	5	5	5
6	6	6	6	6	6	6	6	6	6
7	7	7	7	7	7	7	7	7	7
8	8	8	8	8	8	8	8	8	8
9	9	9	9	9	9	9	9	9	9
0	0	0	0	0	0	0	0	0	0

TEST BOOKLET No.

1	1	1	1	1	1	1
2	2	2	2	2	2	2
3	3	3	3	3	3	3
4	4	4	4	4	4	4
5	5	5	5	5	5	5
6	6	6	6	6	6	6
7	7	7	7	7	7	7
8	8	8	8	8	8	8
9	9	9	9	9	9	9
0	0	0	0	0	0	0

TEST BOOKLET Code

Q No.	Response				Q No.	Response			
001	a	b	c	d	051	a	b	c	d
002	a	b	c	d	052	a	b	c	d
003	a	b	c	d	053	a	b	c	d
004	a	b	c	d	054	a	b	c	d
005	a	b	c	d	055	a	b	c	d
006	a	b	c	d	056	a	b	c	d
007	a	b	c	d	057	a	b	c	d
008	a	b	c	d	058	a	b	c	d
009	a	b	c	d	059	a	b	c	d
010	a	b	c	d	060	a	b	c	d
011	a	b	c	d	061	a	b	c	d
012	a	b	c	d	062	a	b	c	d
013	a	b	c	d	063	a	b	c	d
014	a	b	c	d	064	a	b	c	d
015	a	b	c	d	065	a	b	c	d
016	a	b	c	d	066	a	b	c	d
017	a	b	c	d	067	a	b	c	d
018	a	b	c	d	068	a	b	c	d
019	a	b	c	d	069	a	b	c	d
020	a	b	c	d	070	a	b	c	d
021	a	b	c	d	071	a	b	c	d
022	a	b	c	d	072	a	b	c	d
023	a	b	c	d	073	a	b	c	d
024	a	b	c	d	074	a	b	c	d
025	a	b	c	d	075	a	b	c	d
026	a	b	c	d	076	a	b	c	d
027	a	b	c	d	077	a	b	c	d
028	a	b	c	d	078	a	b	c	d
029	a	b	c	d	079	a	b	c	d
030	a	b	c	d	080	a	b	c	d
031	a	b	c	d	081	a	b	c	d
032	a	b	c	d	082	a	b	c	d
033	a	b	c	d	083	a	b	c	d
034	a	b	c	d	084	a	b	c	d
035	a	b	c	d	085	a	b	c	d
036	a	b	c	d	086	a	b	c	d
037	a	b	c	d	087	a	b	c	d
038	a	b	c	d	088	a	b	c	d
039	a	b	c	d	089	a	b	c	d
040	a	b	c	d	090	a	b	c	d
041	a	b	c	d	091	a	b	c	d
042	a	b	c	d	092	a	b	c	d
043	a	b	c	d	093	a	b	c	d
044	a	b	c	d	094	a	b	c	d
045	a	b	c	d	095	a	b	c	d
046	a	b	c	d	096	a	b	c	d
047	a	b	c	d	097	a	b	c	d
048	a	b	c	d	098	a	b	c	d
049	a	b	c	d	099	a	b	c	d
050	a	b	c	d	100	a	b	c	d

DECLARATION BY THE CANDIDATE

I declare that particulars and signature on this OMR Answer sheet are mine and are Name as in Attendance Sheet. I fruther declare that particulars filled in and Signature as well as the circles darkened on this ORIGINALCOPY is same as in OFFICE COPY.

Signature with time (in running handwriting)

CANDIDATE's NAME (in running handwriting)

MOTHER's NAME (in running handwriting)

FATHER's NAME (in running handwriting)

CANDIDATE LEFT HAND IMPRESSION

SIGNATURE OF INVIGILATOR'S WITH TIME

1

2

OMR SHEET

ROLL No.

1	1	1	1	1	1	1	1	1	1
2	2	2	2	2	2	2	2	2	2
3	3	3	3	3	3	3	3	3	3
4	4	4	4	4	4	4	4	4	4
5	5	5	5	5	5	5	5	5	5
6	6	6	6	6	6	6	6	6	6
7	7	7	7	7	7	7	7	7	7
8	8	8	8	8	8	8	8	8	8
9	9	9	9	9	9	9	9	9	9
0	0	0	0	0	0	0	0	0	0

TEST BOOKLET No.

1	1	1	1	1	1	1
2	2	2	2	2	2	2
3	3	3	3	3	3	3
4	4	4	4	4	4	4
5	5	5	5	5	5	5
6	6	6	6	6	6	6
7	7	7	7	7	7	7
8	8	8	8	8	8	8
9	9	9	9	9	9	9
0	0	0	0	0	0	0

TEST BOOKLET Code

Q No.	Response				Q No.	Response			
001	a	b	c	d	051	a	b	c	d
002	a	b	c	d	052	a	b	c	d
003	a	b	c	d	053	a	b	c	d
004	a	b	c	d	054	a	b	c	d
005	a	b	c	d	055	a	b	c	d
006	a	b	c	d	056	a	b	c	d
007	a	b	c	d	057	a	b	c	d
008	a	b	c	d	058	a	b	c	d
009	a	b	c	d	059	a	b	c	d
010	a	b	c	d	060	a	b	c	d
011	a	b	c	d	061	a	b	c	d
012	a	b	c	d	062	a	b	c	d
013	a	b	c	d	063	a	b	c	d
014	a	b	c	d	064	a	b	c	d
015	a	b	c	d	065	a	b	c	d
016	a	b	c	d	066	a	b	c	d
017	a	b	c	d	067	a	b	c	d
018	a	b	c	d	068	a	b	c	d
019	a	b	c	d	069	a	b	c	d
020	a	b	c	d	070	a	b	c	d
021	a	b	c	d	071	a	b	c	d
022	a	b	c	d	072	a	b	c	d
023	a	b	c	d	073	a	b	c	d
024	a	b	c	d	074	a	b	c	d
025	a	b	c	d	075	a	b	c	d
026	a	b	c	d	076	a	b	c	d
027	a	b	c	d	077	a	b	c	d
028	a	b	c	d	078	a	b	c	d
029	a	b	c	d	079	a	b	c	d
030	a	b	c	d	080	a	b	c	d
031	a	b	c	d	081	a	b	c	d
032	a	b	c	d	082	a	b	c	d
033	a	b	c	d	083	a	b	c	d
034	a	b	c	d	084	a	b	c	d
035	a	b	c	d	085	a	b	c	d
036	a	b	c	d	086	a	b	c	d
037	a	b	c	d	087	a	b	c	d
038	a	b	c	d	088	a	b	c	d
039	a	b	c	d	089	a	b	c	d
040	a	b	c	d	090	a	b	c	d
041	a	b	c	d	091	a	b	c	d
042	a	b	c	d	092	a	b	c	d
043	a	b	c	d	093	a	b	c	d
044	a	b	c	d	094	a	b	c	d
045	a	b	c	d	095	a	b	c	d
046	a	b	c	d	096	a	b	c	d
047	a	b	c	d	097	a	b	c	d
048	a	b	c	d	098	a	b	c	d
049	a	b	c	d	099	a	b	c	d
050	a	b	c	d	100	a	b	c	d

DECLARATION BY THE CANDIDATE

I declare that particulars and signature on this OMR Answer sheet are mine and are Name as in Attendance Sheet. I fruther declare that particulars filled in and Signature as well as the circles darkened on this ORIGINALCOPY is same as in OFFICE COPY.

Signature with time (in running handwriting)

CANDIDATE's NAME (in running handwriting)

MOTHER's NAME (in running handwriting)

FATHER's NAME (in running handwriting)

CANDIDATE LEFT HAND IMPRESSION

SIGNATURE OF INVIGILATOR'S WITH TIME

1

2

MED ACE

OMR SHEET

ROLL No.

1	1	1	1	1	1	1	1	1	1
2	2	2	2	2	2	2	2	2	2
3	3	3	3	3	3	3	3	3	3
4	4	4	4	4	4	4	4	4	4
5	5	5	5	5	5	5	5	5	5
6	6	6	6	6	6	6	6	6	6
7	7	7	7	7	7	7	7	7	7
8	8	8	8	8	8	8	8	8	8
9	9	9	9	9	9	9	9	9	9
0	0	0	0	0	0	0	0	0	0

TEST BOOKLET No.

1	1	1	1	1	1	1
2	2	2	2	2	2	2
3	3	3	3	3	3	3
4	4	4	4	4	4	4
5	5	5	5	5	5	5
6	6	6	6	6	6	6
7	7	7	7	7	7	7
8	8	8	8	8	8	8
9	9	9	9	9	9	9
0	0	0	0	0	0	0

TEST BOOKLET Code

Q No.	Response				Q No.	Response			
001	a	b	c	d	051	a	b	c	d
002	a	b	c	d	052	a	b	c	d
003	a	b	c	d	053	a	b	c	d
004	a	b	c	d	054	a	b	c	d
005	a	b	c	d	055	a	b	c	d
006	a	b	c	d	056	a	b	c	d
007	a	b	c	d	057	a	b	c	d
008	a	b	c	d	058	a	b	c	d
009	a	b	c	d	059	a	b	c	d
010	a	b	c	d	060	a	b	c	d
011	a	b	c	d	061	a	b	c	d
012	a	b	c	d	062	a	b	c	d
013	a	b	c	d	063	a	b	c	d
014	a	b	c	d	064	a	b	c	d
015	a	b	c	d	065	a	b	c	d
016	a	b	c	d	066	a	b	c	d
017	a	b	c	d	067	a	b	c	d
018	a	b	c	d	068	a	b	c	d
019	a	b	c	d	069	a	b	c	d
020	a	b	c	d	070	a	b	c	d
021	a	b	c	d	071	a	b	c	d
022	a	b	c	d	072	a	b	c	d
023	a	b	c	d	073	a	b	c	d
024	a	b	c	d	074	a	b	c	d
025	a	b	c	d	075	a	b	c	d
026	a	b	c	d	076	a	b	c	d
027	a	b	c	d	077	a	b	c	d
028	a	b	c	d	078	a	b	c	d
029	a	b	c	d	079	a	b	c	d
030	a	b	c	d	080	a	b	c	d
031	a	b	c	d	081	a	b	c	d
032	a	b	c	d	082	a	b	c	d
033	a	b	c	d	083	a	b	c	d
034	a	b	c	d	084	a	b	c	d
035	a	b	c	d	085	a	b	c	d
036	a	b	c	d	086	a	b	c	d
037	a	b	c	d	087	a	b	c	d
038	a	b	c	d	088	a	b	c	d
039	a	b	c	d	089	a	b	c	d
040	a	b	c	d	090	a	b	c	d
041	a	b	c	d	091	a	b	c	d
042	a	b	c	d	092	a	b	c	d
043	a	b	c	d	093	a	b	c	d
044	a	b	c	d	094	a	b	c	d
045	a	b	c	d	095	a	b	c	d
046	a	b	c	d	096	a	b	c	d
047	a	b	c	d	097	a	b	c	d
048	a	b	c	d	098	a	b	c	d
049	a	b	c	d	099	a	b	c	d
050	a	b	c	d	100	a	b	c	d

DECLARATION BY THE CANDIDATE

I declare that particulars and signature on this OMR Answer sheet are mine and are Name as in Attendance Sheet. I fruther declare that particulars filled in and Signature as well as the circles darkened on this ORIGINALCOPY is same as in OFFICE COPY.

Signature with time (in running handwriting)

CANDIDATE's NAME (in running handwriting)

MOTHER's NAME (in running handwriting)

FATHER's NAME (in running handwriting)

CANDIDATE LEFT HAND IMPRESSION

SIGNATURE OF INVIGILATOR'S WITH TIME

1

2

OMR SHEET

ROLL No.

1	1	1	1	1	1	1	1	1	1
2	2	2	2	2	2	2	2	2	2
3	3	3	3	3	3	3	3	3	3
4	4	4	4	4	4	4	4	4	4
5	5	5	5	5	5	5	5	5	5
6	6	6	6	6	6	6	6	6	6
7	7	7	7	7	7	7	7	7	7
8	8	8	8	8	8	8	8	8	8
9	9	9	9	9	9	9	9	9	9
0	0	0	0	0	0	0	0	0	0

TEST BOOKLET No.

1	1	1	1	1	1	1
2	2	2	2	2	2	2
3	3	3	3	3	3	3
4	4	4	4	4	4	4
5	5	5	5	5	5	5
6	6	6	6	6	6	6
7	7	7	7	7	7	7
8	8	8	8	8	8	8
9	9	9	9	9	9	9
0	0	0	0	0	0	0

TEST BOOKLET Code

Q No.	Response				Q No.	Response			
001	a	b	c	d	051	a	b	c	d
002	a	b	c	d	052	a	b	c	d
003	a	b	c	d	053	a	b	c	d
004	a	b	c	d	054	a	b	c	d
005	a	b	c	d	055	a	b	c	d
006	a	b	c	d	056	a	b	c	d
007	a	b	c	d	057	a	b	c	d
008	a	b	c	d	058	a	b	c	d
009	a	b	c	d	059	a	b	c	d
010	a	b	c	d	060	a	b	c	d
011	a	b	c	d	061	a	b	c	d
012	a	b	c	d	062	a	b	c	d
013	a	b	c	d	063	a	b	c	d
014	a	b	c	d	064	a	b	c	d
015	a	b	c	d	065	a	b	c	d
016	a	b	c	d	066	a	b	c	d
017	a	b	c	d	067	a	b	c	d
018	a	b	c	d	068	a	b	c	d
019	a	b	c	d	069	a	b	c	d
020	a	b	c	d	070	a	b	c	d
021	a	b	c	d	071	a	b	c	d
022	a	b	c	d	072	a	b	c	d
023	a	b	c	d	073	a	b	c	d
024	a	b	c	d	074	a	b	c	d
025	a	b	c	d	075	a	b	c	d
026	a	b	c	d	076	a	b	c	d
027	a	b	c	d	077	a	b	c	d
028	a	b	c	d	078	a	b	c	d
029	a	b	c	d	079	a	b	c	d
030	a	b	c	d	080	a	b	c	d
031	a	b	c	d	081	a	b	c	d
032	a	b	c	d	082	a	b	c	d
033	a	b	c	d	083	a	b	c	d
034	a	b	c	d	084	a	b	c	d
035	a	b	c	d	085	a	b	c	d
036	a	b	c	d	086	a	b	c	d
037	a	b	c	d	087	a	b	c	d
038	a	b	c	d	088	a	b	c	d
039	a	b	c	d	089	a	b	c	d
040	a	b	c	d	090	a	b	c	d
041	a	b	c	d	091	a	b	c	d
042	a	b	c	d	092	a	b	c	d
043	a	b	c	d	093	a	b	c	d
044	a	b	c	d	094	a	b	c	d
045	a	b	c	d	095	a	b	c	d
046	a	b	c	d	096	a	b	c	d
047	a	b	c	d	097	a	b	c	d
048	a	b	c	d	098	a	b	c	d
049	a	b	c	d	099	a	b	c	d
050	a	b	c	d	100	a	b	c	d

DECLARATION BY THE CANDIDATE

I declare that particulars and signature on this OMR Answer sheet are mine and are Name as in Attendance Sheet. I fruther declare that particulars filled in and Signature as well as the circles darkened on this ORIGINALCOPY is same as in OFFICE COPY.

Signature with time (in running handwriting)

CANDIDATE's NAME (in running handwriting)

MOTHER's NAME (in running handwriting)

FATHER's NAME (in running handwriting)

CANDIDATE LEFT HAND IMPRESSION

SIGNATURE OF INVIGILATOR'S WITH TIME

1

2

OMR SHEET

ROLL No.

1 1 1 1 1 1 1 1 1 1
2 2 2 2 2 2 2 2 2 2
3 3 3 3 3 3 3 3 3 3
4 4 4 4 4 4 4 4 4 4
5 5 5 5 5 5 5 5 5 5
6 6 6 6 6 6 6 6 6 6
7 7 7 7 7 7 7 7 7 7
8 8 8 8 8 8 8 8 8 8
9 9 9 9 9 9 9 9 9 9
0 0 0 0 0 0 0 0 0 0

TEST BOOKLET No.

1 1 1 1 1 1 1
2 2 2 2 2 2 2
3 3 3 3 3 3 3
4 4 4 4 4 4 4
5 5 5 5 5 5 5
6 6 6 6 6 6 6
7 7 7 7 7 7 7
8 8 8 8 8 8 8
9 9 9 9 9 9 9
0 0 0 0 0 0 0

TEST BOOKLET Code

Q No.	Response				Q No.	Response			
001	a	b	c	d	051	a	b	c	d
002	a	b	c	d	052	a	b	c	d
003	a	b	c	d	053	a	b	c	d
004	a	b	c	d	054	a	b	c	d
005	a	b	c	d	055	a	b	c	d
006	a	b	c	d	056	a	b	c	d
007	a	b	c	d	057	a	b	c	d
008	a	b	c	d	058	a	b	c	d
009	a	b	c	d	059	a	b	c	d
010	a	b	c	d	060	a	b	c	d
011	a	b	c	d	061	a	b	c	d
012	a	b	c	d	062	a	b	c	d
013	a	b	c	d	063	a	b	c	d
014	a	b	c	d	064	a	b	c	d
015	a	b	c	d	065	a	b	c	d
016	a	b	c	d	066	a	b	c	d
017	a	b	c	d	067	a	b	c	d
018	a	b	c	d	068	a	b	c	d
019	a	b	c	d	069	a	b	c	d
020	a	b	c	d	070	a	b	c	d
021	a	b	c	d	071	a	b	c	d
022	a	b	c	d	072	a	b	c	d
023	a	b	c	d	073	a	b	c	d
024	a	b	c	d	074	a	b	c	d
025	a	b	c	d	075	a	b	c	d
026	a	b	c	d	076	a	b	c	d
027	a	b	c	d	077	a	b	c	d
028	a	b	c	d	078	a	b	c	d
029	a	b	c	d	079	a	b	c	d
030	a	b	c	d	080	a	b	c	d
031	a	b	c	d	081	a	b	c	d
032	a	b	c	d	082	a	b	c	d
033	a	b	c	d	083	a	b	c	d
034	a	b	c	d	084	a	b	c	d
035	a	b	c	d	085	a	b	c	d
036	a	b	c	d	086	a	b	c	d
037	a	b	c	d	087	a	b	c	d
038	a	b	c	d	088	a	b	c	d
039	a	b	c	d	089	a	b	c	d
040	a	b	c	d	090	a	b	c	d
041	a	b	c	d	091	a	b	c	d
042	a	b	c	d	092	a	b	c	d
043	a	b	c	d	093	a	b	c	d
044	a	b	c	d	094	a	b	c	d
045	a	b	c	d	095	a	b	c	d
046	a	b	c	d	096	a	b	c	d
047	a	b	c	d	097	a	b	c	d
048	a	b	c	d	098	a	b	c	d
049	a	b	c	d	099	a	b	c	d
050	a	b	c	d	100	a	b	c	d

DECLARATION BY THE CANDIDATE

I declare that particulars and signature on this OMR Answer sheet are mine and are Name as in Attendance Sheet. I fruther declare that particulars filled in and Signature as well as the circles darkened on this ORIGINALCOPY is same as in OFFICE COPY.

Signature with time (in running handwriting)

CANDIDATE's NAME (in running handwriting)

MOTHER's NAME (in running handwriting)

FATHER's NAME (in running handwriting)

CANDIDATE LEFT HAND IMPRESSION

SIGNATURE OF INVIGILATOR'S WITH TIME

1

2

MEDACE

OMR SHEET

ROLL No.

1	1	1	1	1	1	1	1	1	1
2	2	2	2	2	2	2	2	2	2
3	3	3	3	3	3	3	3	3	3
4	4	4	4	4	4	4	4	4	4
5	5	5	5	5	5	5	5	5	5
6	6	6	6	6	6	6	6	6	6
7	7	7	7	7	7	7	7	7	7
8	8	8	8	8	8	8	8	8	8
9	9	9	9	9	9	9	9	9	9
0	0	0	0	0	0	0	0	0	0

TEST BOOKLET No.

1	1	1	1	1	1	1
2	2	2	2	2	2	2
3	3	3	3	3	3	3
4	4	4	4	4	4	4
5	5	5	5	5	5	5
6	6	6	6	6	6	6
7	7	7	7	7	7	7
8	8	8	8	8	8	8
9	9	9	9	9	9	9
0	0	0	0	0	0	0

TEST BOOKLET Code

Q No.	Response				Q No.	Response			
001	a	b	c	d	051	a	b	c	d
002	a	b	c	d	052	a	b	c	d
003	a	b	c	d	053	a	b	c	d
004	a	b	c	d	054	a	b	c	d
005	a	b	c	d	055	a	b	c	d
006	a	b	c	d	056	a	b	c	d
007	a	b	c	d	057	a	b	c	d
008	a	b	c	d	058	a	b	c	d
009	a	b	c	d	059	a	b	c	d
010	a	b	c	d	060	a	b	c	d
011	a	b	c	d	061	a	b	c	d
012	a	b	c	d	062	a	b	c	d
013	a	b	c	d	063	a	b	c	d
014	a	b	c	d	064	a	b	c	d
015	a	b	c	d	065	a	b	c	d
016	a	b	c	d	066	a	b	c	d
017	a	b	c	d	067	a	b	c	d
018	a	b	c	d	068	a	b	c	d
019	a	b	c	d	069	a	b	c	d
020	a	b	c	d	070	a	b	c	d
021	a	b	c	d	071	a	b	c	d
022	a	b	c	d	072	a	b	c	d
023	a	b	c	d	073	a	b	c	d
024	a	b	c	d	074	a	b	c	d
025	a	b	c	d	075	a	b	c	d
026	a	b	c	d	076	a	b	c	d
027	a	b	c	d	077	a	b	c	d
028	a	b	c	d	078	a	b	c	d
029	a	b	c	d	079	a	b	c	d
030	a	b	c	d	080	a	b	c	d
031	a	b	c	d	081	a	b	c	d
032	a	b	c	d	082	a	b	c	d
033	a	b	c	d	083	a	b	c	d
034	a	b	c	d	084	a	b	c	d
035	a	b	c	d	085	a	b	c	d
036	a	b	c	d	086	a	b	c	d
037	a	b	c	d	087	a	b	c	d
038	a	b	c	d	088	a	b	c	d
039	a	b	c	d	089	a	b	c	d
040	a	b	c	d	090	a	b	c	d
041	a	b	c	d	091	a	b	c	d
042	a	b	c	d	092	a	b	c	d
043	a	b	c	d	093	a	b	c	d
044	a	b	c	d	094	a	b	c	d
045	a	b	c	d	095	a	b	c	d
046	a	b	c	d	096	a	b	c	d
047	a	b	c	d	097	a	b	c	d
048	a	b	c	d	098	a	b	c	d
049	a	b	c	d	099	a	b	c	d
050	a	b	c	d	100	a	b	c	d

DECLARATION BY THE CANDIDATE

I declare that particulars and signature on this OMR Answer sheet are mine and are Name as in Attendance Sheet. I fruther declare that particulars filled in and Signature as well as the circles darkened on this ORIGINALCOPY is same as in OFFICE COPY.

Signature with time (in running handwriting)

CANDIDATE's NAME (in running handwriting)

MOTHER's NAME (in running handwriting)

FATHER's NAME (in running handwriting)

CANDIDATE LEFT HAND IMPRESSION

SIGNATURE OF INVIGILATOR'S WITH TIME

1

2

OMR SHEET

ROLL No.

1	1	1	1	1	1	1	1	1	1
2	2	2	2	2	2	2	2	2	2
3	3	3	3	3	3	3	3	3	3
4	4	4	4	4	4	4	4	4	4
5	5	5	5	5	5	5	5	5	5
6	6	6	6	6	6	6	6	6	6
7	7	7	7	7	7	7	7	7	7
8	8	8	8	8	8	8	8	8	8
9	9	9	9	9	9	9	9	9	9
0	0	0	0	0	0	0	0	0	0

TEST BOOKLET No.

1	1	1	1	1	1	1
2	2	2	2	2	2	2
3	3	3	3	3	3	3
4	4	4	4	4	4	4
5	5	5	5	5	5	5
6	6	6	6	6	6	6
7	7	7	7	7	7	7
8	8	8	8	8	8	8
9	9	9	9	9	9	9
0	0	0	0	0	0	0

TEST BOOKLET Code

DECLARATION BY THE CANDIDATE

I declare that particulars and signature on this OMR Answer sheet are mine and are Name as in Attendance Sheet. I fruther declare that particulars filled in and Signature as well as the circles darkened on this ORIGINALCOPY is same as in OFFICE COPY.

Signature with time (in running handwriting)

CANDIDATE's NAME (in running handwriting)

Q No.	Response				Q No.	Response			
001	a	b	c	d	051	a	b	c	d
002	a	b	c	d	052	a	b	c	d
003	a	b	c	d	053	a	b	c	d
004	a	b	c	d	054	a	b	c	d
005	a	b	c	d	055	a	b	c	d
006	a	b	c	d	056	a	b	c	d
007	a	b	c	d	057	a	b	c	d
008	a	b	c	d	058	a	b	c	d
009	a	b	c	d	059	a	b	c	d
010	a	b	c	d	060	a	b	c	d
011	a	b	c	d	061	a	b	c	d
012	a	b	c	d	062	a	b	c	d
013	a	b	c	d	063	a	b	c	d
014	a	b	c	d	064	a	b	c	d
015	a	b	c	d	065	a	b	c	d
016	a	b	c	d	066	a	b	c	d
017	a	b	c	d	067	a	b	c	d
018	a	b	c	d	068	a	b	c	d
019	a	b	c	d	069	a	b	c	d
020	a	b	c	d	070	a	b	c	d
021	a	b	c	d	071	a	b	c	d
022	a	b	c	d	072	a	b	c	d
023	a	b	c	d	073	a	b	c	d
024	a	b	c	d	074	a	b	c	d
025	a	b	c	d	075	a	b	c	d
026	a	b	c	d	076	a	b	c	d
027	a	b	c	d	077	a	b	c	d
028	a	b	c	d	078	a	b	c	d
029	a	b	c	d	079	a	b	c	d
030	a	b	c	d	080	a	b	c	d
031	a	b	c	d	081	a	b	c	d
032	a	b	c	d	082	a	b	c	d
033	a	b	c	d	083	a	b	c	d
034	a	b	c	d	084	a	b	c	d
035	a	b	c	d	085	a	b	c	d
036	a	b	c	d	086	a	b	c	d
037	a	b	c	d	087	a	b	c	d
038	a	b	c	d	088	a	b	c	d
039	a	b	c	d	089	a	b	c	d
040	a	b	c	d	090	a	b	c	d
041	a	b	c	d	091	a	b	c	d
042	a	b	c	d	092	a	b	c	d
043	a	b	c	d	093	a	b	c	d
044	a	b	c	d	094	a	b	c	d
045	a	b	c	d	095	a	b	c	d
046	a	b	c	d	096	a	b	c	d
047	a	b	c	d	097	a	b	c	d
048	a	b	c	d	098	a	b	c	d
049	a	b	c	d	099	a	b	c	d
050	a	b	c	d	100	a	b	c	d

MOTHER's NAME (in running handwriting)

FATHER's NAME (in running handwriting)

CANDIDATE LEFT HAND IMPRESSION

SIGNATURE OF INVIGILATOR'S WITH TIME

1

2

MEDACE

OMR SHEET

ROLL No.

1	1	1	1	1	1	1	1	1	1
2	2	2	2	2	2	2	2	2	2
3	3	3	3	3	3	3	3	3	3
4	4	4	4	4	4	4	4	4	4
5	5	5	5	5	5	5	5	5	5
6	6	6	6	6	6	6	6	6	6
7	7	7	7	7	7	7	7	7	7
8	8	8	8	8	8	8	8	8	8
9	9	9	9	9	9	9	9	9	9
0	0	0	0	0	0	0	0	0	0

TEST BOOKLET No.

1	1	1	1	1	1	1
2	2	2	2	2	2	2
3	3	3	3	3	3	3
4	4	4	4	4	4	4
5	5	5	5	5	5	5
6	6	6	6	6	6	6
7	7	7	7	7	7	7
8	8	8	8	8	8	8
9	9	9	9	9	9	9
0	0	0	0	0	0	0

TEST BOOKLET Code

Q No.	Response				Q No.	Response			
001	a	b	c	d	051	a	b	c	d
002	a	b	c	d	052	a	b	c	d
003	a	b	c	d	053	a	b	c	d
004	a	b	c	d	054	a	b	c	d
005	a	b	c	d	055	a	b	c	d
006	a	b	c	d	056	a	b	c	d
007	a	b	c	d	057	a	b	c	d
008	a	b	c	d	058	a	b	c	d
009	a	b	c	d	059	a	b	c	d
010	a	b	c	d	060	a	b	c	d
011	a	b	c	d	061	a	b	c	d
012	a	b	c	d	062	a	b	c	d
013	a	b	c	d	063	a	b	c	d
014	a	b	c	d	064	a	b	c	d
015	a	b	c	d	065	a	b	c	d
016	a	b	c	d	066	a	b	c	d
017	a	b	c	d	067	a	b	c	d
018	a	b	c	d	068	a	b	c	d
019	a	b	c	d	069	a	b	c	d
020	a	b	c	d	070	a	b	c	d
021	a	b	c	d	071	a	b	c	d
022	a	b	c	d	072	a	b	c	d
023	a	b	c	d	073	a	b	c	d
024	a	b	c	d	074	a	b	c	d
025	a	b	c	d	075	a	b	c	d
026	a	b	c	d	076	a	b	c	d
027	a	b	c	d	077	a	b	c	d
028	a	b	c	d	078	a	b	c	d
029	a	b	c	d	079	a	b	c	d
030	a	b	c	d	080	a	b	c	d
031	a	b	c	d	081	a	b	c	d
032	a	b	c	d	082	a	b	c	d
033	a	b	c	d	083	a	b	c	d
034	a	b	c	d	084	a	b	c	d
035	a	b	c	d	085	a	b	c	d
036	a	b	c	d	086	a	b	c	d
037	a	b	c	d	087	a	b	c	d
038	a	b	c	d	088	a	b	c	d
039	a	b	c	d	089	a	b	c	d
040	a	b	c	d	090	a	b	c	d
041	a	b	c	d	091	a	b	c	d
042	a	b	c	d	092	a	b	c	d
043	a	b	c	d	093	a	b	c	d
044	a	b	c	d	094	a	b	c	d
045	a	b	c	d	095	a	b	c	d
046	a	b	c	d	096	a	b	c	d
047	a	b	c	d	097	a	b	c	d
048	a	b	c	d	098	a	b	c	d
049	a	b	c	d	099	a	b	c	d
050	a	b	c	d	100	a	b	c	d

DECLARATION BY THE CANDIDATE

I declare that particulars and signature on this OMR Answer sheet are mine and are Name as in Attendance Sheet. I fruther declare that particulars filled in and Signature as well as the circles darkened on this ORIGINALCOPY is same as in OFFICE COPY.

Signature with time (in running handwriting)

CANDIDATE's NAME (in running handwriting)

MOTHER's NAME (in running handwriting)

FATHER's NAME (in running handwriting)

CANDIDATE LEFT HAND IMPRESSION

SIGNATURE OF INVIGILATOR'S WITH TIME

1

2

MEDACE

OMR SHEET

ROLL No.

1	1	1	1	1	1	1	1	1	1
2	2	2	2	2	2	2	2	2	2
3	3	3	3	3	3	3	3	3	3
4	4	4	4	4	4	4	4	4	4
5	5	5	5	5	5	5	5	5	5
6	6	6	6	6	6	6	6	6	6
7	7	7	7	7	7	7	7	7	7
8	8	8	8	8	8	8	8	8	8
9	9	9	9	9	9	9	9	9	9
0	0	0	0	0	0	0	0	0	0

TEST BOOKLET No.

1	1	1	1	1	1	1
2	2	2	2	2	2	2
3	3	3	3	3	3	3
4	4	4	4	4	4	4
5	5	5	5	5	5	5
6	6	6	6	6	6	6
7	7	7	7	7	7	7
8	8	8	8	8	8	8
9	9	9	9	9	9	9
0	0	0	0	0	0	0

TEST BOOKLET Code

Q No.	Response			
001	a	b	c	d
002	a	b	c	d
003	a	b	c	d
004	a	b	c	d
005	a	b	c	d
006	a	b	c	d
007	a	b	c	d
008	a	b	c	d
009	a	b	c	d
010	a	b	c	d
011	a	b	c	d
012	a	b	c	d
013	a	b	c	d
014	a	b	c	d
015	a	b	c	d
016	a	b	c	d
017	a	b	c	d
018	a	b	c	d
019	a	b	c	d
020	a	b	c	d
021	a	b	c	d
022	a	b	c	d
023	a	b	c	d
024	a	b	c	d
025	a	b	c	d
026	a	b	c	d
027	a	b	c	d
028	a	b	c	d
029	a	b	c	d
030	a	b	c	d
031	a	b	c	d
032	a	b	c	d
033	a	b	c	d
034	a	b	c	d
035	a	b	c	d
036	a	b	c	d
037	a	b	c	d
038	a	b	c	d
039	a	b	c	d
040	a	b	c	d
041	a	b	c	d
042	a	b	c	d
043	a	b	c	d
044	a	b	c	d
045	a	b	c	d
046	a	b	c	d
047	a	b	c	d
048	a	b	c	d
049	a	b	c	d
050	a	b	c	d

Q No.	Response			
051	a	b	c	d
052	a	b	c	d
053	a	b	c	d
054	a	b	c	d
055	a	b	c	d
056	a	b	c	d
057	a	b	c	d
058	a	b	c	d
059	a	b	c	d
060	a	b	c	d
061	a	b	c	d
062	a	b	c	d
063	a	b	c	d
064	a	b	c	d
065	a	b	c	d
066	a	b	c	d
067	a	b	c	d
068	a	b	c	d
069	a	b	c	d
070	a	b	c	d
071	a	b	c	d
072	a	b	c	d
073	a	b	c	d
074	a	b	c	d
075	a	b	c	d
076	a	b	c	d
077	a	b	c	d
078	a	b	c	d
079	a	b	c	d
080	a	b	c	d
081	a	b	c	d
082	a	b	c	d
083	a	b	c	d
084	a	b	c	d
085	a	b	c	d
086	a	b	c	d
087	a	b	c	d
088	a	b	c	d
089	a	b	c	d
090	a	b	c	d
091	a	b	c	d
092	a	b	c	d
093	a	b	c	d
094	a	b	c	d
095	a	b	c	d
096	a	b	c	d
097	a	b	c	d
098	a	b	c	d
099	a	b	c	d
100	a	b	c	d

DECLARATION BY THE CANDIDATE

I declare that particulars and signature on this OMR Answer sheet are mine and are Name as in Attendance Sheet. I fruther declare that particulars filled in and Signature as well as the circles darkened on this ORIGINALCOPY is same as in OFFICE COPY.

Signature with time (in running handwriting)

CANDIDATE's NAME (in running handwriting)

MOTHER's NAME (in running handwriting)

FATHER's NAME (in running handwriting)

CANDIDATE LEFT HAND IMPRESSION

SIGNATURE OF INVIGILATOR'S WITH TIME

1

2

OMR SHEET

ROLL No.

1	1	1	1	1	1	1	1	1	1
2	2	2	2	2	2	2	2	2	2
3	3	3	3	3	3	3	3	3	3
4	4	4	4	4	4	4	4	4	4
5	5	5	5	5	5	5	5	5	5
6	6	6	6	6	6	6	6	6	6
7	7	7	7	7	7	7	7	7	7
8	8	8	8	8	8	8	8	8	8
9	9	9	9	9	9	9	9	9	9
0	0	0	0	0	0	0	0	0	0

TEST BOOKLET No.

1	1	1	1	1	1	1
2	2	2	2	2	2	2
3	3	3	3	3	3	3
4	4	4	4	4	4	4
5	5	5	5	5	5	5
6	6	6	6	6	6	6
7	7	7	7	7	7	7
8	8	8	8	8	8	8
9	9	9	9	9	9	9
0	0	0	0	0	0	0

TEST BOOKLET Code

Q No.	Response				Q No.	Response			
001	a	b	c	d	051	a	b	c	d
002	a	b	c	d	052	a	b	c	d
003	a	b	c	d	053	a	b	c	d
004	a	b	c	d	054	a	b	c	d
005	a	b	c	d	055	a	b	c	d
006	a	b	c	d	056	a	b	c	d
007	a	b	c	d	057	a	b	c	d
008	a	b	c	d	058	a	b	c	d
009	a	b	c	d	059	a	b	c	d
010	a	b	c	d	060	a	b	c	d
011	a	b	c	d	061	a	b	c	d
012	a	b	c	d	062	a	b	c	d
013	a	b	c	d	063	a	b	c	d
014	a	b	c	d	064	a	b	c	d
015	a	b	c	d	065	a	b	c	d
016	a	b	c	d	066	a	b	c	d
017	a	b	c	d	067	a	b	c	d
018	a	b	c	d	068	a	b	c	d
019	a	b	c	d	069	a	b	c	d
020	a	b	c	d	070	a	b	c	d
021	a	b	c	d	071	a	b	c	d
022	a	b	c	d	072	a	b	c	d
023	a	b	c	d	073	a	b	c	d
024	a	b	c	d	074	a	b	c	d
025	a	b	c	d	075	a	b	c	d
026	a	b	c	d	076	a	b	c	d
027	a	b	c	d	077	a	b	c	d
028	a	b	c	d	078	a	b	c	d
029	a	b	c	d	079	a	b	c	d
030	a	b	c	d	080	a	b	c	d
031	a	b	c	d	081	a	b	c	d
032	a	b	c	d	082	a	b	c	d
033	a	b	c	d	083	a	b	c	d
034	a	b	c	d	084	a	b	c	d
035	a	b	c	d	085	a	b	c	d
036	a	b	c	d	086	a	b	c	d
037	a	b	c	d	087	a	b	c	d
038	a	b	c	d	088	a	b	c	d
039	a	b	c	d	089	a	b	c	d
040	a	b	c	d	090	a	b	c	d
041	a	b	c	d	091	a	b	c	d
042	a	b	c	d	092	a	b	c	d
043	a	b	c	d	093	a	b	c	d
044	a	b	c	d	094	a	b	c	d
045	a	b	c	d	095	a	b	c	d
046	a	b	c	d	096	a	b	c	d
047	a	b	c	d	097	a	b	c	d
048	a	b	c	d	098	a	b	c	d
049	a	b	c	d	099	a	b	c	d
050	a	b	c	d	100	a	b	c	d

DECLARATION BY THE CANDIDATE

I declare that particulars and signature on this OMR Answer sheet are mine and are Name as in Attendance Sheet. I fruther declare that particulars filled in and Signature as well as the circles darkened on this ORIGINALCOPY is same as in OFFICE COPY.

Signature with time (in running handwriting)

CANDIDATE's NAME (in running handwriting)

MOTHER's NAME (in running handwriting)

FATHER's NAME (in running handwriting)

CANDIDATE LEFT HAND IMPRESSION

SIGNATURE OF INVIGILATOR'S WITH TIME

1

2

OMR SHEET

ROLL No.

1	1	1	1	1	1	1	1	1	1
2	2	2	2	2	2	2	2	2	2
3	3	3	3	3	3	3	3	3	3
4	4	4	4	4	4	4	4	4	4
5	5	5	5	5	5	5	5	5	5
6	6	6	6	6	6	6	6	6	6
7	7	7	7	7	7	7	7	7	7
8	8	8	8	8	8	8	8	8	8
9	9	9	9	9	9	9	9	9	9
0	0	0	0	0	0	0	0	0	0

TEST BOOKLET No.

1	1	1	1	1	1	1
2	2	2	2	2	2	2
3	3	3	3	3	3	3
4	4	4	4	4	4	4
5	5	5	5	5	5	5
6	6	6	6	6	6	6
7	7	7	7	7	7	7
8	8	8	8	8	8	8
9	9	9	9	9	9	9
0	0	0	0	0	0	0

TEST BOOKLET Code

Q No.	Response				Q No.	Response			
001	a	b	c	d	051	a	b	c	d
002	a	b	c	d	052	a	b	c	d
003	a	b	c	d	053	a	b	c	d
004	a	b	c	d	054	a	b	c	d
005	a	b	c	d	055	a	b	c	d
006	a	b	c	d	056	a	b	c	d
007	a	b	c	d	057	a	b	c	d
008	a	b	c	d	058	a	b	c	d
009	a	b	c	d	059	a	b	c	d
010	a	b	c	d	060	a	b	c	d
011	a	b	c	d	061	a	b	c	d
012	a	b	c	d	062	a	b	c	d
013	a	b	c	d	063	a	b	c	d
014	a	b	c	d	064	a	b	c	d
015	a	b	c	d	065	a	b	c	d
016	a	b	c	d	066	a	b	c	d
017	a	b	c	d	067	a	b	c	d
018	a	b	c	d	068	a	b	c	d
019	a	b	c	d	069	a	b	c	d
020	a	b	c	d	070	a	b	c	d
021	a	b	c	d	071	a	b	c	d
022	a	b	c	d	072	a	b	c	d
023	a	b	c	d	073	a	b	c	d
024	a	b	c	d	074	a	b	c	d
025	a	b	c	d	075	a	b	c	d
026	a	b	c	d	076	a	b	c	d
027	a	b	c	d	077	a	b	c	d
028	a	b	c	d	078	a	b	c	d
029	a	b	c	d	079	a	b	c	d
030	a	b	c	d	080	a	b	c	d
031	a	b	c	d	081	a	b	c	d
032	a	b	c	d	082	a	b	c	d
033	a	b	c	d	083	a	b	c	d
034	a	b	c	d	084	a	b	c	d
035	a	b	c	d	085	a	b	c	d
036	a	b	c	d	086	a	b	c	d
037	a	b	c	d	087	a	b	c	d
038	a	b	c	d	088	a	b	c	d
039	a	b	c	d	089	a	b	c	d
040	a	b	c	d	090	a	b	c	d
041	a	b	c	d	091	a	b	c	d
042	a	b	c	d	092	a	b	c	d
043	a	b	c	d	093	a	b	c	d
044	a	b	c	d	094	a	b	c	d
045	a	b	c	d	095	a	b	c	d
046	a	b	c	d	096	a	b	c	d
047	a	b	c	d	097	a	b	c	d
048	a	b	c	d	098	a	b	c	d
049	a	b	c	d	099	a	b	c	d
050	a	b	c	d	100	a	b	c	d

DECLARATION BY THE CANDIDATE

I declare that particulars and signature on this OMR Answer sheet are mine and are Name as in Attendance Sheet. I fruther declare that particulars filled in and Signature as well as the circles darkened on this ORIGINALCOPY is same as in OFFICE COPY.

Signature with time (in running handwriting)

CANDIDATE's NAME (in running handwriting)

MOTHER's NAME (in running handwriting)

FATHER's NAME (in running handwriting)

CANDIDATE LEFT HAND IMPRESSION

SIGNATURE OF INVIGILATOR'S WITH TIME

1

2

MED+ACE

OMR SHEET

ROLL No.

1	1	1	1	1	1	1	1	1	1
2	2	2	2	2	2	2	2	2	2
3	3	3	3	3	3	3	3	3	3
4	4	4	4	4	4	4	4	4	4
5	5	5	5	5	5	5	5	5	5
6	6	6	6	6	6	6	6	6	6
7	7	7	7	7	7	7	7	7	7
8	8	8	8	8	8	8	8	8	8
9	9	9	9	9	9	9	9	9	9
0	0	0	0	0	0	0	0	0	0

TEST BOOKLET No.

1	1	1	1	1	1	1
2	2	2	2	2	2	2
3	3	3	3	3	3	3
4	4	4	4	4	4	4
5	5	5	5	5	5	5
6	6	6	6	6	6	6
7	7	7	7	7	7	7
8	8	8	8	8	8	8
9	9	9	9	9	9	9
0	0	0	0	0	0	0

TEST BOOKLET Code

Q No.	Response				Q No.	Response			
001	a	b	c	d	051	a	b	c	d
002	a	b	c	d	052	a	b	c	d
003	a	b	c	d	053	a	b	c	d
004	a	b	c	d	054	a	b	c	d
005	a	b	c	d	055	a	b	c	d
006	a	b	c	d	056	a	b	c	d
007	a	b	c	d	057	a	b	c	d
008	a	b	c	d	058	a	b	c	d
009	a	b	c	d	059	a	b	c	d
010	a	b	c	d	060	a	b	c	d
011	a	b	c	d	061	a	b	c	d
012	a	b	c	d	062	a	b	c	d
013	a	b	c	d	063	a	b	c	d
014	a	b	c	d	064	a	b	c	d
015	a	b	c	d	065	a	b	c	d
016	a	b	c	d	066	a	b	c	d
017	a	b	c	d	067	a	b	c	d
018	a	b	c	d	068	a	b	c	d
019	a	b	c	d	069	a	b	c	d
020	a	b	c	d	070	a	b	c	d
021	a	b	c	d	071	a	b	c	d
022	a	b	c	d	072	a	b	c	d
023	a	b	c	d	073	a	b	c	d
024	a	b	c	d	074	a	b	c	d
025	a	b	c	d	075	a	b	c	d
026	a	b	c	d	076	a	b	c	d
027	a	b	c	d	077	a	b	c	d
028	a	b	c	d	078	a	b	c	d
029	a	b	c	d	079	a	b	c	d
030	a	b	c	d	080	a	b	c	d
031	a	b	c	d	081	a	b	c	d
032	a	b	c	d	082	a	b	c	d
033	a	b	c	d	083	a	b	c	d
034	a	b	c	d	084	a	b	c	d
035	a	b	c	d	085	a	b	c	d
036	a	b	c	d	086	a	b	c	d
037	a	b	c	d	087	a	b	c	d
038	a	b	c	d	088	a	b	c	d
039	a	b	c	d	089	a	b	c	d
040	a	b	c	d	090	a	b	c	d
041	a	b	c	d	091	a	b	c	d
042	a	b	c	d	092	a	b	c	d
043	a	b	c	d	093	a	b	c	d
044	a	b	c	d	094	a	b	c	d
045	a	b	c	d	095	a	b	c	d
046	a	b	c	d	096	a	b	c	d
047	a	b	c	d	097	a	b	c	d
048	a	b	c	d	098	a	b	c	d
049	a	b	c	d	099	a	b	c	d
050	a	b	c	d	100	a	b	c	d

DECLARATION BY THE CANDIDATE

I declare that particulars and signature on this OMR Answer sheet are mine and are Name as in Attendance Sheet. I fruther declare that particulars filled in and Signature as well as the circles darkened on this ORIGINALCOPY is same as in OFFICE COPY.

Signature with time (in running handwriting)

CANDIDATE's NAME (in running handwriting)

MOTHER's NAME (in running handwriting)

FATHER's NAME (in running handwriting)

CANDIDATE LEFT HAND IMPRESSION

SIGNATURE OF INVIGILATOR'S WITH TIME

1

2

OMR SHEET

ROLL No.

1	1	1	1	1	1	1	1	1	1
2	2	2	2	2	2	2	2	2	2
3	3	3	3	3	3	3	3	3	3
4	4	4	4	4	4	4	4	4	4
5	5	5	5	5	5	5	5	5	5
6	6	6	6	6	6	6	6	6	6
7	7	7	7	7	7	7	7	7	7
8	8	8	8	8	8	8	8	8	8
9	9	9	9	9	9	9	9	9	9
0	0	0	0	0	0	0	0	0	0

TEST BOOKLET No.

1	1	1	1	1	1	1
2	2	2	2	2	2	2
3	3	3	3	3	3	3
4	4	4	4	4	4	4
5	5	5	5	5	5	5
6	6	6	6	6	6	6
7	7	7	7	7	7	7
8	8	8	8	8	8	8
9	9	9	9	9	9	9
0	0	0	0	0	0	0

TEST BOOKLET Code

Q No.	Response				Q No.	Response			
001	a	b	c	d	051	a	b	c	d
002	a	b	c	d	052	a	b	c	d
003	a	b	c	d	053	a	b	c	d
004	a	b	c	d	054	a	b	c	d
005	a	b	c	d	055	a	b	c	d
006	a	b	c	d	056	a	b	c	d
007	a	b	c	d	057	a	b	c	d
008	a	b	c	d	058	a	b	c	d
009	a	b	c	d	059	a	b	c	d
010	a	b	c	d	060	a	b	c	d
011	a	b	c	d	061	a	b	c	d
012	a	b	c	d	062	a	b	c	d
013	a	b	c	d	063	a	b	c	d
014	a	b	c	d	064	a	b	c	d
015	a	b	c	d	065	a	b	c	d
016	a	b	c	d	066	a	b	c	d
017	a	b	c	d	067	a	b	c	d
018	a	b	c	d	068	a	b	c	d
019	a	b	c	d	069	a	b	c	d
020	a	b	c	d	070	a	b	c	d
021	a	b	c	d	071	a	b	c	d
022	a	b	c	d	072	a	b	c	d
023	a	b	c	d	073	a	b	c	d
024	a	b	c	d	074	a	b	c	d
025	a	b	c	d	075	a	b	c	d
026	a	b	c	d	076	a	b	c	d
027	a	b	c	d	077	a	b	c	d
028	a	b	c	d	078	a	b	c	d
029	a	b	c	d	079	a	b	c	d
030	a	b	c	d	080	a	b	c	d
031	a	b	c	d	081	a	b	c	d
032	a	b	c	d	082	a	b	c	d
033	a	b	c	d	083	a	b	c	d
034	a	b	c	d	084	a	b	c	d
035	a	b	c	d	085	a	b	c	d
036	a	b	c	d	086	a	b	c	d
037	a	b	c	d	087	a	b	c	d
038	a	b	c	d	088	a	b	c	d
039	a	b	c	d	089	a	b	c	d
040	a	b	c	d	090	a	b	c	d
041	a	b	c	d	091	a	b	c	d
042	a	b	c	d	092	a	b	c	d
043	a	b	c	d	093	a	b	c	d
044	a	b	c	d	094	a	b	c	d
045	a	b	c	d	095	a	b	c	d
046	a	b	c	d	096	a	b	c	d
047	a	b	c	d	097	a	b	c	d
048	a	b	c	d	098	a	b	c	d
049	a	b	c	d	099	a	b	c	d
050	a	b	c	d	100	a	b	c	d

DECLARATION BY THE CANDIDATE

I declare that particulars and signature on this OMR Answer sheet are mine and are Name as in Attendance Sheet. I fruther declare that particulars filled in and Signature as well as the circles darkened on this ORIGINALCOPY is same as in OFFICE COPY.

Signature with time (in running handwriting)

CANDIDATE's NAME (in running handwriting)

MOTHER's NAME (in running handwriting)

FATHER's NAME (in running handwriting)

CANDIDATE LEFT HAND IMPRESSION

SIGNATURE OF INVIGILATOR'S WITH TIME

1

2

OMR SHEET

ROLL No.

1	1	1	1	1	1	1	1	1	1
2	2	2	2	2	2	2	2	2	2
3	3	3	3	3	3	3	3	3	3
4	4	4	4	4	4	4	4	4	4
5	5	5	5	5	5	5	5	5	5
6	6	6	6	6	6	6	6	6	6
7	7	7	7	7	7	7	7	7	7
8	8	8	8	8	8	8	8	8	8
9	9	9	9	9	9	9	9	9	9
0	0	0	0	0	0	0	0	0	0

TEST BOOKLET No.

1	1	1	1	1	1	1
2	2	2	2	2	2	2
3	3	3	3	3	3	3
4	4	4	4	4	4	4
5	5	5	5	5	5	5
6	6	6	6	6	6	6
7	7	7	7	7	7	7
8	8	8	8	8	8	8
9	9	9	9	9	9	9
0	0	0	0	0	0	0

TEST BOOKLET Code

Q No.	Response	Q No.	Response
001	ⓐ ⓑ ⓒ ⓓ	051	ⓐ ⓑ ⓒ ⓓ
002	ⓐ ⓑ ⓒ ⓓ	052	ⓐ ⓑ ⓒ ⓓ
003	ⓐ ⓑ ⓒ ⓓ	053	ⓐ ⓑ ⓒ ⓓ
004	ⓐ ⓑ ⓒ ⓓ	054	ⓐ ⓑ ⓒ ⓓ
005	ⓐ ⓑ ⓒ ⓓ	055	ⓐ ⓑ ⓒ ⓓ
006	ⓐ ⓑ ⓒ ⓓ	056	ⓐ ⓑ ⓒ ⓓ
007	ⓐ ⓑ ⓒ ⓓ	057	ⓐ ⓑ ⓒ ⓓ
008	ⓐ ⓑ ⓒ ⓓ	058	ⓐ ⓑ ⓒ ⓓ
009	ⓐ ⓑ ⓒ ⓓ	059	ⓐ ⓑ ⓒ ⓓ
010	ⓐ ⓑ ⓒ ⓓ	060	ⓐ ⓑ ⓒ ⓓ
011	ⓐ ⓑ ⓒ ⓓ	061	ⓐ ⓑ ⓒ ⓓ
012	ⓐ ⓑ ⓒ ⓓ	062	ⓐ ⓑ ⓒ ⓓ
013	ⓐ ⓑ ⓒ ⓓ	063	ⓐ ⓑ ⓒ ⓓ
014	ⓐ ⓑ ⓒ ⓓ	064	ⓐ ⓑ ⓒ ⓓ
015	ⓐ ⓑ ⓒ ⓓ	065	ⓐ ⓑ ⓒ ⓓ
016	ⓐ ⓑ ⓒ ⓓ	066	ⓐ ⓑ ⓒ ⓓ
017	ⓐ ⓑ ⓒ ⓓ	067	ⓐ ⓑ ⓒ ⓓ
018	ⓐ ⓑ ⓒ ⓓ	068	ⓐ ⓑ ⓒ ⓓ
019	ⓐ ⓑ ⓒ ⓓ	069	ⓐ ⓑ ⓒ ⓓ
020	ⓐ ⓑ ⓒ ⓓ	070	ⓐ ⓑ ⓒ ⓓ
021	ⓐ ⓑ ⓒ ⓓ	071	ⓐ ⓑ ⓒ ⓓ
022	ⓐ ⓑ ⓒ ⓓ	072	ⓐ ⓑ ⓒ ⓓ
023	ⓐ ⓑ ⓒ ⓓ	073	ⓐ ⓑ ⓒ ⓓ
024	ⓐ ⓑ ⓒ ⓓ	074	ⓐ ⓑ ⓒ ⓓ
025	ⓐ ⓑ ⓒ ⓓ	075	ⓐ ⓑ ⓒ ⓓ
026	ⓐ ⓑ ⓒ ⓓ	076	ⓐ ⓑ ⓒ ⓓ
027	ⓐ ⓑ ⓒ ⓓ	077	ⓐ ⓑ ⓒ ⓓ
028	ⓐ ⓑ ⓒ ⓓ	078	ⓐ ⓑ ⓒ ⓓ
029	ⓐ ⓑ ⓒ ⓓ	079	ⓐ ⓑ ⓒ ⓓ
030	ⓐ ⓑ ⓒ ⓓ	080	ⓐ ⓑ ⓒ ⓓ
031	ⓐ ⓑ ⓒ ⓓ	081	ⓐ ⓑ ⓒ ⓓ
032	ⓐ ⓑ ⓒ ⓓ	082	ⓐ ⓑ ⓒ ⓓ
033	ⓐ ⓑ ⓒ ⓓ	083	ⓐ ⓑ ⓒ ⓓ
034	ⓐ ⓑ ⓒ ⓓ	084	ⓐ ⓑ ⓒ ⓓ
035	ⓐ ⓑ ⓒ ⓓ	085	ⓐ ⓑ ⓒ ⓓ
036	ⓐ ⓑ ⓒ ⓓ	086	ⓐ ⓑ ⓒ ⓓ
037	ⓐ ⓑ ⓒ ⓓ	087	ⓐ ⓑ ⓒ ⓓ
038	ⓐ ⓑ ⓒ ⓓ	088	ⓐ ⓑ ⓒ ⓓ
039	ⓐ ⓑ ⓒ ⓓ	089	ⓐ ⓑ ⓒ ⓓ
040	ⓐ ⓑ ⓒ ⓓ	090	ⓐ ⓑ ⓒ ⓓ
041	ⓐ ⓑ ⓒ ⓓ	091	ⓐ ⓑ ⓒ ⓓ
042	ⓐ ⓑ ⓒ ⓓ	092	ⓐ ⓑ ⓒ ⓓ
043	ⓐ ⓑ ⓒ ⓓ	093	ⓐ ⓑ ⓒ ⓓ
044	ⓐ ⓑ ⓒ ⓓ	094	ⓐ ⓑ ⓒ ⓓ
045	ⓐ ⓑ ⓒ ⓓ	095	ⓐ ⓑ ⓒ ⓓ
046	ⓐ ⓑ ⓒ ⓓ	096	ⓐ ⓑ ⓒ ⓓ
047	ⓐ ⓑ ⓒ ⓓ	097	ⓐ ⓑ ⓒ ⓓ
048	ⓐ ⓑ ⓒ ⓓ	098	ⓐ ⓑ ⓒ ⓓ
049	ⓐ ⓑ ⓒ ⓓ	099	ⓐ ⓑ ⓒ ⓓ
050	ⓐ ⓑ ⓒ ⓓ	100	ⓐ ⓑ ⓒ ⓓ

DECLARATION BY THE CANDIDATE

I declare that particulars and signature on this OMR Answer sheet are mine and are Name as in Attendance Sheet. I fruther declare that particulars filled in and Signature as well as the circles darkened on this ORIGINALCOPY is same as in OFFICE COPY.

Signature with time (in running handwriting)

CANDIDATE's NAME (in running handwriting)

MOTHER's NAME (in running handwriting)

FATHER's NAME (in running handwriting)

CANDIDATE LEFT HAND IMPRESSION

SIGNATURE OF INVIGILATOR'S WITH TIME

1

2

OMR SHEET

ROLL No.

1	1	1	1	1	1	1	1	1	1
2	2	2	2	2	2	2	2	2	2
3	3	3	3	3	3	3	3	3	3
4	4	4	4	4	4	4	4	4	4
5	5	5	5	5	5	5	5	5	5
6	6	6	6	6	6	6	6	6	6
7	7	7	7	7	7	7	7	7	7
8	8	8	8	8	8	8	8	8	8
9	9	9	9	9	9	9	9	9	9
0	0	0	0	0	0	0	0	0	0

TEST BOOKLET No.

1	1	1	1	1	1	1
2	2	2	2	2	2	2
3	3	3	3	3	3	3
4	4	4	4	4	4	4
5	5	5	5	5	5	5
6	6	6	6	6	6	6
7	7	7	7	7	7	7
8	8	8	8	8	8	8
9	9	9	9	9	9	9
0	0	0	0	0	0	0

TEST BOOKLET Code

Q No.	Response				Q No.	Response			
001	a	b	c	d	051	a	b	c	d
002	a	b	c	d	052	a	b	c	d
003	a	b	c	d	053	a	b	c	d
004	a	b	c	d	054	a	b	c	d
005	a	b	c	d	055	a	b	c	d
006	a	b	c	d	056	a	b	c	d
007	a	b	c	d	057	a	b	c	d
008	a	b	c	d	058	a	b	c	d
009	a	b	c	d	059	a	b	c	d
010	a	b	c	d	060	a	b	c	d
011	a	b	c	d	061	a	b	c	d
012	a	b	c	d	062	a	b	c	d
013	a	b	c	d	063	a	b	c	d
014	a	b	c	d	064	a	b	c	d
015	a	b	c	d	065	a	b	c	d
016	a	b	c	d	066	a	b	c	d
017	a	b	c	d	067	a	b	c	d
018	a	b	c	d	068	a	b	c	d
019	a	b	c	d	069	a	b	c	d
020	a	b	c	d	070	a	b	c	d
021	a	b	c	d	071	a	b	c	d
022	a	b	c	d	072	a	b	c	d
023	a	b	c	d	073	a	b	c	d
024	a	b	c	d	074	a	b	c	d
025	a	b	c	d	075	a	b	c	d
026	a	b	c	d	076	a	b	c	d
027	a	b	c	d	077	a	b	c	d
028	a	b	c	d	078	a	b	c	d
029	a	b	c	d	079	a	b	c	d
030	a	b	c	d	080	a	b	c	d
031	a	b	c	d	081	a	b	c	d
032	a	b	c	d	082	a	b	c	d
033	a	b	c	d	083	a	b	c	d
034	a	b	c	d	084	a	b	c	d
035	a	b	c	d	085	a	b	c	d
036	a	b	c	d	086	a	b	c	d
037	a	b	c	d	087	a	b	c	d
038	a	b	c	d	088	a	b	c	d
039	a	b	c	d	089	a	b	c	d
040	a	b	c	d	090	a	b	c	d
041	a	b	c	d	091	a	b	c	d
042	a	b	c	d	092	a	b	c	d
043	a	b	c	d	093	a	b	c	d
044	a	b	c	d	094	a	b	c	d
045	a	b	c	d	095	a	b	c	d
046	a	b	c	d	096	a	b	c	d
047	a	b	c	d	097	a	b	c	d
048	a	b	c	d	098	a	b	c	d
049	a	b	c	d	099	a	b	c	d
050	a	b	c	d	100	a	b	c	d

DECLARATION BY THE CANDIDATE

I declare that particulars and signature on this OMR Answer sheet are mine and are Name as in Attendance Sheet. I fruther declare that particulars filled in and Signature as well as the circles darkened on this ORIGINALCOPY is same as in OFFICE COPY.

Signature with time (in running handwriting)

CANDIDATE's NAME (in running handwriting)

MOTHER's NAME (in running handwriting)

FATHER's NAME (in running handwriting)

CANDIDATE LEFT HAND IMPRESSION

SIGNATURE OF INVIGILATOR'S WITH TIME

1

2

OMR SHEET

ROLL No.

1	1	1	1	1	1	1	1	1	1
2	2	2	2	2	2	2	2	2	2
3	3	3	3	3	3	3	3	3	3
4	4	4	4	4	4	4	4	4	4
5	5	5	5	5	5	5	5	5	5
6	6	6	6	6	6	6	6	6	6
7	7	7	7	7	7	7	7	7	7
8	8	8	8	8	8	8	8	8	8
9	9	9	9	9	9	9	9	9	9
0	0	0	0	0	0	0	0	0	0

TEST BOOKLET No.

1	1	1	1	1	1	1
2	2	2	2	2	2	2
3	3	3	3	3	3	3
4	4	4	4	4	4	4
5	5	5	5	5	5	5
6	6	6	6	6	6	6
7	7	7	7	7	7	7
8	8	8	8	8	8	8
9	9	9	9	9	9	9
0	0	0	0	0	0	0

TEST BOOKLET Code

Q No.	Response	Q No.	Response
001	a b c d	051	a b c d
002	a b c d	052	a b c d
003	a b c d	053	a b c d
004	a b c d	054	a b c d
005	a b c d	055	a b c d
006	a b c d	056	a b c d
007	a b c d	057	a b c d
008	a b c d	058	a b c d
009	a b c d	059	a b c d
010	a b c d	060	a b c d
011	a b c d	061	a b c d
012	a b c d	062	a b c d
013	a b c d	063	a b c d
014	a b c d	064	a b c d
015	a b c d	065	a b c d
016	a b c d	066	a b c d
017	a b c d	067	a b c d
018	a b c d	068	a b c d
019	a b c d	069	a b c d
020	a b c d	070	a b c d
021	a b c d	071	a b c d
022	a b c d	072	a b c d
023	a b c d	073	a b c d
024	a b c d	074	a b c d
025	a b c d	075	a b c d
026	a b c d	076	a b c d
027	a b c d	077	a b c d
028	a b c d	078	a b c d
029	a b c d	079	a b c d
030	a b c d	080	a b c d
031	a b c d	081	a b c d
032	a b c d	082	a b c d
033	a b c d	083	a b c d
034	a b c d	084	a b c d
035	a b c d	085	a b c d
036	a b c d	086	a b c d
037	a b c d	087	a b c d
038	a b c d	088	a b c d
039	a b c d	089	a b c d
040	a b c d	090	a b c d
041	a b c d	091	a b c d
042	a b c d	092	a b c d
043	a b c d	093	a b c d
044	a b c d	094	a b c d
045	a b c d	095	a b c d
046	a b c d	096	a b c d
047	a b c d	097	a b c d
048	a b c d	098	a b c d
049	a b c d	099	a b c d
050	a b c d	100	a b c d

DECLARATION BY THE CANDIDATE

I declare that particulars and signature on this OMR Answer sheet are mine and are Name as in Attendance Sheet. I fruther declare that particulars filled in and Signature as well as the circles darkened on this ORIGINALCOPY is same as in OFFICE COPY.

Signature with time (in running handwriting)

CANDIDATE's NAME (in running handwriting)

MOTHER's NAME (in running handwriting)

FATHER's NAME (in running handwriting)

CANDIDATE LEFT HAND IMPRESSION

SIGNATURE OF INVIGILATOR'S WITH TIME

1

2

OMR SHEET

ROLL No.

1	1	1	1	1	1	1	1	1	1
2	2	2	2	2	2	2	2	2	2
3	3	3	3	3	3	3	3	3	3
4	4	4	4	4	4	4	4	4	4
5	5	5	5	5	5	5	5	5	5
6	6	6	6	6	6	6	6	6	6
7	7	7	7	7	7	7	7	7	7
8	8	8	8	8	8	8	8	8	8
9	9	9	9	9	9	9	9	9	9
0	0	0	0	0	0	0	0	0	0

TEST BOOKLET No.

1	1	1	1	1	1	1
2	2	2	2	2	2	2
3	3	3	3	3	3	3
4	4	4	4	4	4	4
5	5	5	5	5	5	5
6	6	6	6	6	6	6
7	7	7	7	7	7	7
8	8	8	8	8	8	8
9	9	9	9	9	9	9
0	0	0	0	0	0	0

TEST BOOKLET Code

Q No.	Response				Q No.	Response			
001	a	b	c	d	051	a	b	c	d
002	a	b	c	d	052	a	b	c	d
003	a	b	c	d	053	a	b	c	d
004	a	b	c	d	054	a	b	c	d
005	a	b	c	d	055	a	b	c	d
006	a	b	c	d	056	a	b	c	d
007	a	b	c	d	057	a	b	c	d
008	a	b	c	d	058	a	b	c	d
009	a	b	c	d	059	a	b	c	d
010	a	b	c	d	060	a	b	c	d
011	a	b	c	d	061	a	b	c	d
012	a	b	c	d	062	a	b	c	d
013	a	b	c	d	063	a	b	c	d
014	a	b	c	d	064	a	b	c	d
015	a	b	c	d	065	a	b	c	d
016	a	b	c	d	066	a	b	c	d
017	a	b	c	d	067	a	b	c	d
018	a	b	c	d	068	a	b	c	d
019	a	b	c	d	069	a	b	c	d
020	a	b	c	d	070	a	b	c	d
021	a	b	c	d	071	a	b	c	d
022	a	b	c	d	072	a	b	c	d
023	a	b	c	d	073	a	b	c	d
024	a	b	c	d	074	a	b	c	d
025	a	b	c	d	075	a	b	c	d
026	a	b	c	d	076	a	b	c	d
027	a	b	c	d	077	a	b	c	d
028	a	b	c	d	078	a	b	c	d
029	a	b	c	d	079	a	b	c	d
030	a	b	c	d	080	a	b	c	d
031	a	b	c	d	081	a	b	c	d
032	a	b	c	d	082	a	b	c	d
033	a	b	c	d	083	a	b	c	d
034	a	b	c	d	084	a	b	c	d
035	a	b	c	d	085	a	b	c	d
036	a	b	c	d	086	a	b	c	d
037	a	b	c	d	087	a	b	c	d
038	a	b	c	d	088	a	b	c	d
039	a	b	c	d	089	a	b	c	d
040	a	b	c	d	090	a	b	c	d
041	a	b	c	d	091	a	b	c	d
042	a	b	c	d	092	a	b	c	d
043	a	b	c	d	093	a	b	c	d
044	a	b	c	d	094	a	b	c	d
045	a	b	c	d	095	a	b	c	d
046	a	b	c	d	096	a	b	c	d
047	a	b	c	d	097	a	b	c	d
048	a	b	c	d	098	a	b	c	d
049	a	b	c	d	099	a	b	c	d
050	a	b	c	d	100	a	b	c	d

DECLARATION BY THE CANDIDATE

I declare that particulars and signature on this OMR Answer sheet are mine and are Name as in Attendance Sheet. I fruther declare that particulars filled in and Signature as well as the circles darkened on this ORIGINALCOPY is same as in OFFICE COPY.

Signature with time (in running handwriting)

CANDIDATE's NAME (in running handwriting)

MOTHER's NAME (in running handwriting)

FATHER's NAME (in running handwriting)

CANDIDATE LEFT HAND IMPRESSION

SIGNATURE OF INVIGILATOR'S WITH TIME

1

2

MEDACE

OMR SHEET

ROLL No.

1	1	1	1	1	1	1	1	1	1
2	2	2	2	2	2	2	2	2	2
3	3	3	3	3	3	3	3	3	3
4	4	4	4	4	4	4	4	4	4
5	5	5	5	5	5	5	5	5	5
6	6	6	6	6	6	6	6	6	6
7	7	7	7	7	7	7	7	7	7
8	8	8	8	8	8	8	8	8	8
9	9	9	9	9	9	9	9	9	9
0	0	0	0	0	0	0	0	0	0

TEST BOOKLET No.

1	1	1	1	1	1	1
2	2	2	2	2	2	2
3	3	3	3	3	3	3
4	4	4	4	4	4	4
5	5	5	5	5	5	5
6	6	6	6	6	6	6
7	7	7	7	7	7	7
8	8	8	8	8	8	8
9	9	9	9	9	9	9
0	0	0	0	0	0	0

TEST BOOKLET Code

Q No.	Response				Q No.	Response			
001	a	b	c	d	051	a	b	c	d
002	a	b	c	d	052	a	b	c	d
003	a	b	c	d	053	a	b	c	d
004	a	b	c	d	054	a	b	c	d
005	a	b	c	d	055	a	b	c	d
006	a	b	c	d	056	a	b	c	d
007	a	b	c	d	057	a	b	c	d
008	a	b	c	d	058	a	b	c	d
009	a	b	c	d	059	a	b	c	d
010	a	b	c	d	060	a	b	c	d
011	a	b	c	d	061	a	b	c	d
012	a	b	c	d	062	a	b	c	d
013	a	b	c	d	063	a	b	c	d
014	a	b	c	d	064	a	b	c	d
015	a	b	c	d	065	a	b	c	d
016	a	b	c	d	066	a	b	c	d
017	a	b	c	d	067	a	b	c	d
018	a	b	c	d	068	a	b	c	d
019	a	b	c	d	069	a	b	c	d
020	a	b	c	d	070	a	b	c	d
021	a	b	c	d	071	a	b	c	d
022	a	b	c	d	072	a	b	c	d
023	a	b	c	d	073	a	b	c	d
024	a	b	c	d	074	a	b	c	d
025	a	b	c	d	075	a	b	c	d
026	a	b	c	d	076	a	b	c	d
027	a	b	c	d	077	a	b	c	d
028	a	b	c	d	078	a	b	c	d
029	a	b	c	d	079	a	b	c	d
030	a	b	c	d	080	a	b	c	d
031	a	b	c	d	081	a	b	c	d
032	a	b	c	d	082	a	b	c	d
033	a	b	c	d	083	a	b	c	d
034	a	b	c	d	084	a	b	c	d
035	a	b	c	d	085	a	b	c	d
036	a	b	c	d	086	a	b	c	d
037	a	b	c	d	087	a	b	c	d
038	a	b	c	d	088	a	b	c	d
039	a	b	c	d	089	a	b	c	d
040	a	b	c	d	090	a	b	c	d
041	a	b	c	d	091	a	b	c	d
042	a	b	c	d	092	a	b	c	d
043	a	b	c	d	093	a	b	c	d
044	a	b	c	d	094	a	b	c	d
045	a	b	c	d	095	a	b	c	d
046	a	b	c	d	096	a	b	c	d
047	a	b	c	d	097	a	b	c	d
048	a	b	c	d	098	a	b	c	d
049	a	b	c	d	099	a	b	c	d
050	a	b	c	d	100	a	b	c	d

DECLARATION BY THE CANDIDATE

I declare that particulars and signature on this OMR Answer sheet are mine and are Name as in Attendance Sheet. I fruther declare that particulars filled in and Signature as well as the circles darkened on this ORIGINALCOPY is same as in OFFICE COPY.

Signature with time (in running handwriting)

CANDIDATE's NAME (in running handwriting)

MOTHER's NAME (in running handwriting)

FATHER's NAME (in running handwriting)

CANDIDATE LEFT HAND IMPRESSION

SIGNATURE OF INVIGILATOR'S WITH TIME

1

2